0711:

EPIC

EPIC:

BRITAIN'S HEROIC MUSE
1790–1910

HERBERT F. TUCKER

OXFORD
UNIVERSITY PRESS

OXFORD
UNIVERSITY PRESS

Great Clarendon Street, Oxford OX2 6DP

Oxford University Press is a department of the University of Oxford.
It furthers the University's objective of excellence in research, scholarship,
and education by publishing worldwide in

Oxford New York

Auckland Cape Town Dar es Salaam Hong Kong Karachi
Kuala Lumpur Madrid Melbourne Mexico City Nairobi
New Delhi Shanghai Taipei Toronto

With offices in

Argentina Austria Brazil Chile Czech Republic France Greece
Guatemala Hungary Italy Japan Poland Portugal Singapore
South Korea Switzerland Thailand Turkey Ukraine Vietnam

Oxford is a registered trade mark of Oxford University Press
in the UK and in certain other countries

Published in the United States
by Oxford University Press Inc., New York

British Library Cataloguing in Publication Data

Data available

Library of Congress Cataloging in Publication Data

Data available

Typeset by SPI Publisher Services, Pondicherry, India
Printed in Great Britain
on acid-free paper by
Biddles Ltd., King's Lynn, Norfolk

ISBN 978–0–19–923298–7

1 3 5 7 9 10 8 6 4 2

for Zora and Chloe
who grew up with it
but so much faster

Acknowledgments

Ten years to read, ten years to write: Coleridge's formula for the epic labor he never accomplished has proven a little too close for comfort. Two decades' accumulated obligation spreads so wide, and has seeped so far down, as to place an honest inclusiveness beyond the reach of these public thanks. So I must pare my list of creditors to the really conspicuous ones, trusting one more time to the kind understanding of many colleagues, students, and friends whom I don't name here but haven't forgotten either. We both know who you are.

When this project was launched it looked much smaller, and cuter. I undertook it between 1986 and 1988 at the University of Virginia during research leave provided by the Center for Advanced Studies (now renamed for my late colleague Edgar Shannon). My institutional home since that far-off beginning, UVa has arranged sabbatical release more than once in support of my research; the staff at Alderman Library have been generous with their collections and sedulous to fetch from other archives the obscurer tomes and pamphlets I kept asking for. The project mutated from a cloud of notions into a manuscript during an essential year's fellowship, funded by the American Council of Learned Societies, at the National Humanities Center in 2000–01. There in the Research Triangle a library staff unflagging in resourcefulness and cheer obtained the books I needed, the administrators shaped an environment that let me find range and footing, and a set of lively-minded colleagues provided responses to chapters-in-progress that instilled confidence. On two occasions visiting faculty appointments in London, at Regent's College and then with the study-abroad program of New York University, gave access to the holdings of the British Library in its storied former home and then its sparkling new one. I send thanks there and, for sundry courtesies, to the Beinecke Library at Yale, the New York Public Library, and the Sawyer Library at Williams College.

For their initial indulgence and now their permissions to republish, I also thank the editors of several journals and books in which trial versions of the arguments in this book first saw daylight. Two Tennyson essays explored at greater length the discussion that frames Chapter 10, one appearing in *ELH* (1991) and the other in a special *Victorian Poetry* issue (1992) edited by Gerhard Joseph. Three essays date from 1993, when my colleague Alison Booth included in her collection *Famous Last Words* a reading of *Aurora Leigh* that forms the conclusion to Chapter 9, when my argument about *The Ring and the Book* in Chapter 10 got formulated in a contribution to the late Lloyd Davis's *Virginal Sexuality and Textuality,* and when a portion of Chapter 11 on Swinburne's *Tristram* debuted in *Influence and Resistance in Nineteenth-Century English Poetry*, edited by Kim Blank and the late Margot Louis. *Victorian Poetry* included parts of Chapters 9 and 11 in special issues on Spasmodism (2004) and on Morris (1996), which were edited respectively by Charles LaPorte and Jason Rudy, and by Florence Boos. From its quaint research base of graphite on filecards the project has radiated into digital venues: the Southey portions of three early chapters were culled for an essay in *Romanticism on the 'Net* 32–33 (2003–04); and that electronic journal's maiden reticulation across the full nineteenth century as *Romanticism and Victorianism on the 'Net* 47 (2007) includes my discussion of Doughty's *The Dawn in Britain* from Chapter 12.

For this last publication opportunity, as for my first inkling that *The Dawn in Britain* so much as existed—and, well beyond that, for a steady current of encouragement across years of friendly conversation outdone only by the exemplary challenge that his own work upholds—I remain indebted to what has been my happiest of windfalls in a lucky career, the nonpareil collegiality of Jerry McGann.

Students at Virginia have kept me company with remarkably little complaint on long marches through tracts of Romantic and Victorian verse narrative that nobody should hazard solo. In class not only did these brave readers put questions obliging me to figure out what I thought and meant; but often their response to what we read, by diverting my argument from the channel I had paved for it, in effect diversified that argument into a new pattern. Conference audiences in New Orleans, San Diego, Morgantown, Bloomington, and London, Ontario, have heard me out and engaged me afterwards with tonic rejoinders. I am grateful for the hospitality extended to an invited lecturer by the English departments at Hamilton College and Tel Aviv University, as for their patient listening and encouraging response. Each performance on the academical-minstrel circuit has improved the odds of my writing about remote matters so as to be understandingly attended to.

The final lap of my long course has been sweetened by the welcome accorded this project at Oxford University Press, where I especially thank Andrew McNeillie and Tom Chandler. The former generously took the book in; the latter expertly took it apart for tighter reassembly.

The Turner canvas reproduced on the dust jacket travels with an anecdote— I draw it from Raymond Lister's 1989 book *British Romantic Painting*—that is worth rehearsing here if only for its miniature refraction of the pageantry of loftiness and inertia, daring and catastrophe, that will gild, even as it litters, the chapters ahead. When that many-minded woman of culture Elizabeth Rigby (Lady Eastlake) viewed the overwhelming canvas, she turned to the painter with a game hunch: "*The End of the World*, Mr. Turner?" "No, ma'am," he is said to have replied: "*Hannibal Crossing the Alps.*" Like his theme, ours here is not the cosmic but the human tale. All the same, do mind the elephants.

H. F. T.

Charlottesville
July 2007

Contents

A Note on Parenthetical References in the Text

Throughout these chapters, a punctuated numeral in parentheses refers to the pertinent passage as it occurs in the edition I worked from. (Editions are specified in the Bibliography of Poems Cited, 602–26.) For thrift's sake these references vary without warning as the enumerations in my sources vary. Thus (3.17) may in a given instance indicate Book 3, line 17; or Canto 3, stanza 17; or Part 3, page 17; and so on. By preference I use line numbers where these are available, but often they are not. Opportunistic and arbitrary as this method confessedly is, it should at least lead inquirers to the passage they are looking for.

I

The Very Idea:

Epic in the Head

In *The Critic as Artist* (1890) Oscar Wilde has his proxy Gilbert list among the topics canvassed by the self-conscious Greeks of Alexandria "the artistic value of the epic form in an age so modern as theirs."[1] Looking back two millennia to the good old days when modernity was really new, Wilde is kidding as usual; and as usual he means what he says. For his contemporaries the mind of classical Greece was more than a laughing matter; to them it mirrored the mind of nineteenth-century Britain as surely as Gilbert's dialogue with Ernest mirrors the mind of Oscar Wilde to us. Wilde's joke partook of an uncanny logic that, disclosing the familiar within the foreign, had pervaded reflection on the "value of the epic form" for a hundred years. Around 1890 epic in Britain happened to be entering the one fallow period within what this book will show was a continuously fertile Romantic and Victorian history; but it was not only towards the end of the long nineteenth century that the genre fell under

---

[1] *Literary Criticism of Oscar Wilde*, ed. Stanley Weintraub (Lincoln: University of Nebraska Press, 1968) 210. Wilde is right about the Alexandrians, whose development of the idyll form as a modern compromise with old epic influenced Victorian poetry strongly. See H. M. McLuhan, "Tennyson and the Romantic Epic," in *Critical Essays on the Poetry of Tennyson*, ed. John Killham (London: Routledge and Kegan Paul, 1960) 86–95; Robert Pattison, *Tennyson and Tradition* (Cambridge, Mass.: Harvard University Press, 1979) 15–39; Richard Jenkyns, *The Victorians and Ancient Greece* (Cambridge, Mass.: Harvard University Press, 1980) 21–38. John Kevin Newman, *The Classical Epic Tradition* (Madison: University of Wisconsin Press, 1986), maintains that Alexandrian modes of coping with epic persist through Chaucer and Milton into 19th-cent. fiction and 20th-cent. film. On the Victorian tendency to regard the ancient Greeks as cultural contemporaries see Frank Turner, *The Greek Heritage in Victorian Britain* (New Haven and London: Yale University Press, 1981); Linda Dowling, *Hellenism and Homosexuality in Victorian Oxford* (Ithaca and London: Cornell University Press, 1994). About ancient Rome an *a fortiori* case might simply instance Matthew Arnold's 1857 lecture "On the Modern Element in Literature," which cites next to no post-classical authors and finds its paragon of modernity in Virgil.

suspicion of anachronism. Such suspicion has shadowed epic as long as it has been modern: if not since Wilde's Alexandria, then certainly since the decades flanking 1700 when John Dryden and Alexander Pope elaborated "Augustan" poetry within a London neoclassically renovated. For these authors, as for their Renaissance forerunners and their successors into our time, the exemplary career of that premier Augustan poet and direct Alexandrian heir Virgil established the composition of an epic as the last rite of passage to full poetic majority, the summative test of art. This was a test that, during the twelve decades covered by this book, more major British poets than not approached with fear and trembling.[2] The trepidation that accompanied a poet's approach to epic, and that even where it is not corroborated in a preface or surviving letter always leaves a trace somewhere in the resulting poem, came only half from self-doubt. The other half came from doubts that were entertained on every hand about the genre itself.

From 1858, close to the midpoint of our story, the Laureate-in-Chief speaks for all his tribe: "I wish that you would disabuse your own minds and those of others, as far as you can, that I am about an Epic of King Arthur. I should be crazed to attempt such a thing in the heart of the 19th Century."[3] Alfred Tennyson's gruff deprecation is not about King Arthur, or chivalry, or antiquity of subject as such. In fact the legendary matter of Arthur formed the substance of a book comprising four *Idylls of the King* that he would publish the next year; and he would do so fully confident that, whatever else he had made his new book into, it was not an epic. Instead, Tennyson's apprehensiveness was "about an Epic," whether hazarded on this theme or any other. That way madness lay, he knew; yet he also knew it was a way his contemporaries suspected he was tempted to try. And they were right: within another decade the leading Victorian bard's *furor poeticus* would drive his Arthurian poem into epic territory after all, by the feat of generic conversion that frames our Chapter 10 below. If the gambler's malaria of hope and prudence, denial and recklessness, thus afflicted an author basking in every honor his era could bestow, we may safely regard Tennyson's generic hand-washing as the symptom of a contagion that none might escape.

---

[2] In Robert Burns, George Crabbe, Gerard Manley Hopkins, and the two Rossettis, we may number on the fingers of one hand those who declined the challenge—bearing in mind that, while many failings converged to block Coleridge's long-meditated epic, lack of interest was not among them.

[3] Letter of 11 Dec. 1858 to Ticknor and Fields, his publisher in America: *The Letters of Alfred Lord Tennyson*, ed. Cecil Y. Lang and Edgar F. Shannon, Jr. (Cambridge, Mass.: Harvard University Press, 1981–90) 2: 212.

Nor even now are we who apply the stethoscope of literary history to "the heart of the 19th Century" immune to the stress that made Tennyson's murmur. We bring to the very idea of epic a rash of doubts that are not only similar to those presented in the nineteenth century but continuous with them, for reasons rooted in the modernity that our moment shares with that not so very bygone time.[4] Like the Romantics and Victorians we want to belong to the sort of unified community that once embraced epic as its own; and yet that is not what we want at all. We endorse, and we discredit, the thought that our lives acquire meaning through participation in a large, whole, and absorbing history, whose collective dimension has an importance that as modern individuals we both covet and mistrust. Stirred even to applause by the epic poet's mission to symbolize "the accepted unconscious metaphysic of his age" (so one circumspect analyst called it at the close of the period this book covers), as regards our own age we harbor an acute reluctance to subscribe to anything of the kind.[5] For all of us, in the twenty-first century as in the nineteenth, the prospect of writing an epic poem devoted to such a mission—in truth, even the prospect of faithfully *reading* one—savors of a dare; embarked upon, it has about it the feeling of a stunt; and the result, whatever other qualities it may claim, cannot well avoid being regarded as a freak. So a book that goes on at such length as the one I have written, pursuing a redundantly confessed literary anachronism "in an age so modern," owes its reader an apology.

Mine, of course, has been underway for three paragraphs now. By diagnosing the ambivalence that epic prompted in Romantic and Victorian minds as a syndrome in which we still participate, I mean to purchase interest in the genre. Our suspicion about epic's modern irrelevance should itself prompt suspicion, or at least curiosity, about the mix of respect and

[4] The argument of this chapter converges with those of two recent books that came to my notice after I had composed it. For Robert Crawford, *The Modern Poet: Poetry, Academia, and Knowledge since the 1750s* (Oxford: Oxford University Press, 2001), the modernity of poetry after the Enlightenment inheres in its being both scholarly and wild, "at once ancient and *à la mode*" (p. 20). Similarly, Simon Dentith in *Epic and Empire in Nineteenth-Century Britain* (Cambridge: Cambridge University Press, 2006) investigates "various reworkings of a problematic" that hinges on "the interdependence, which is to say the incompatibility, of modernity with epic," whereby "consciousness of the archaism of epic entails a concomitant consciousness of the modernity of the present era" (3–4, 13).

[5] Lascelles Abercrombie, *The Epic* (London: Secker, 1914) 39. In *Imagination and Power: A Study of Poetry on Public Themes* (London: Chatto and Windus, 1971), Thomas R. Edwards discusses the "complicated self-awareness" that epic induces. "It associates us gratifyingly with past greatness, with heroes who are *our* heroes; yet it also reminds us soberingly that it all *is* past, that we are less than our heritage. It allows us an imaginative association with greatness even as it makes us recognize that we are ordinary men—and it allows us some comfort in this rueful understanding" (11).

aversion that keeps the genre in pious modern quarantine as a literary
irrelevance. The long conspiracy to make the ongoing appeal of epic look
like a sideshow attraction, safely off the common reader's beaten path,
operates with maximum force where that reader has been schooled in our
standard literary history. Such a scholar imbibes a lesson that comes in
several versions, not always compatible with each other but invariably
militating against the project of this book. The splendor of epic, so the
lesson runs, is a glory that *was*.[6] For the severe purist it vanished millennia
ago when literacy broke up the world of oral narrative; but on most
accounts epic has enjoyed one or more visitations of second wind in literary
and eventually print dispensations: Virgil's Rome, Dante's Italy and then
Tasso's, the England of Spenser and, at the end of the line, Milton.
Occasionally advocates have petitioned for a post-Miltonic stay of execu-
tion into the eighteenth or early nineteenth century.[7] In the end, though,
literary history must have its victim. At whatever point the historian fixes,
thereupon the date of epic prolixity was out, the curfew tolled the knell, and
the genre gave up the ghost—either as a natural casualty of great old age or
as a sacrifice exacted to consecrate the birth of that modern consciousness
from whose vantage literary history is perennially put together.

　　This latter explanation of the death of epic takes most compact, memorable
(and for now probably inexpugnable) shape in triumphalist accounts of the
history of the novel. These accounts depict prose fiction as the genre in which
modernity stands forth over epic's dead body.[8] Like the axioms of modern

---

　　[6] Thus Robert Scholes and Robert Kellogg in their classic *The Nature of Narrative* (New York: Oxford
University Press, 1966) hand their readers the sobering news up front: "The epic poem is as dead as the
dinosaur" (11). A generation later for J. B. Hainsworth in *The Idea of Epic* (Berkeley: University of
California Press, 1991), that "the genre died" (viii) is a fact to be explained and not a proposition to be
tested. This commonplace forms a springboard for much livelier discussion in Frederick T. Griffiths and
Stanley J. Rabinowitz, *Novel Epics: Gogol, Dostoevsky, and National Narrative* (Evanston: Northwestern
University Press, 1990). Conceding that epic is "long dead, indeed recurrently dead," these authors
propose that the genre "maintains its preeminence as the victim of choice for the dominant literary form,"
through the "millennial parasitism whereby it thrives through the nostalgia and condescension of its
various replacements until they are themselves replaced" (12, 15).
　　[7] See R. D. Havens, *The Influence of Milton on English Poetry* (Cambridge, Mass.: Harvard
University Press, 1922): "The epic may...be said to have been moribund throughout the second
quarter of the nineteenth century and to have died soon after. It has never revived" (313).
The coincidence of publication date between Havens's study, and *Ulysses* and *The Waste Land*,
opens onto the modernist developments I proceed to discuss.
　　[8] The *locus classicus* for such an account is Ian Watt, *The Rise of the Novel: Studies in Defoe, Richardson,
and Fielding* (Berkeley: University of California Press, 1957). See also, *inter alia*, Thomas E. Maresca,
Epic to Novel (Columbus: Ohio State University Press, 1974); Paul Hunter, *Before Novels: The Cultural
Contexts of Eighteenth-Century English Fiction* (New York: Norton, 1990) 338–51. *Per contra*, Martin
Mueller (*The Iliad*, London: Allen and Unwin, 1984, 192) crisply remarks that the two "critical facts

history from which the depiction borrows much of its formidable power (the rise of the middle class and of empirical science, the supplanting of feudalism by markets and monarchy by democracy), this account of generic supersession is equally amenable to explanatory models of lineal handoff and of revolutionary overthrow. Standard literary history's relative indifference as to causes suggests that *how* the change occurred matters less to the historian than the founding presumption *that* it occurred. As a practical matter the two models often coexist, for example in E. M. W. Tillyard's definitive generic histories of major narrative in English, where *The English Epic and Its Background* yields with the years—the 1700s, to be specific, when he tells us "the epic impulse left poetry for the novel"—to *The Epic Strain in the English Novel.*[9]

It is among the virtues of Tillyard's work to wield frankly the judgments about literary value that, often more covertly but in all cases necessarily, underpin work along this line of literary-historical argument. Evaluative judgments are required to police the scene as soon as it is conceded—as on overwhelming evidence it must be conceded—that works of conspicuously epic shape and aspiration have continued to appear, on a nearly annual basis, years after whatever generic expiration date the gazette of literary history has announced. Explaining this teeming evidence away obliges the historian to turn critic, round up the intruding senile delinquents and convict them of failing to observe the clearly posted criteria, or—by a less contestable, more candidly authoritarian indictment—of lacking the epic genre's authentic character or spirit, which *ex hypothesi* has passed away beyond human recovery. In any case the capital verdict against epic is a foregone conclusion dialectically entailed on generic traditionalism by the privilege it accords, wittingly or not, to the inviolable uniqueness of the modern.

From this dialectical entailment, and the act of critical judgment that it may flourish or harbor but cannot dispense with, has sprung a revivalist movement that also deserves our notice here. This movement subscribes to a heterodox exceptionalism maintaining that, under circumstances sufficiently

for an understanding of the life of the *Iliad* in the nineteenth century" are the epic's "opposition to the bourgeois novel" and "the boys' school as the template for the cult of the heroic." The best contemporary study, David Quint's *Epic and Empire: Politics and Generic Form from Virgil to Milton* (Princeton: Princeton University Press, 1993), embraces the standard account axiomatically: when "the fortunes of a martial aristocracy ... waned in the seventeenth century, the classically modeled epic poem gave way to the 'modern' romance and the novel" (360). Already at the turn of the 19th cent. the supersession of epic by novel was an undisputed fact to John Millar in *An Historical View of the English Government* (London: Mawman, 1803) 4: 326–34.

⁹ Tillyard, *The English Epic and its Background* (London: Chatto and Windus, 1954) 14, again 109, 147, 528–31; and *The Epic Strain in the English Novel* (London: Chatto and Windus, 1958).

extraordinary, epic can make a comeback after all. No matter when it died—which it certainly did do, the revivalist holds, way back somewhere in an inhospitable past—it was born again in the second quarter of the twentieth century. In its broadest and strongest form the argument privileges the century of modernism over the half-millennium of modernity: it pursues, that is, a corollary of twentieth-century modernism's self-definition as the unprecedented maker-new of all things, including the literary genres and media. The Great War having eviscerated and flattened European civilization, a generic reconfiguration took place, the hard-line exceptionalist affirms, such that James Joyce's *Ulysses* made richer sense as an epic than as a novel, or that Ezra Pound's ambition for the *Cantos* became not eccentric to its culture but chorically representative.[10] Alternatively, the rise of new media—cinema in particular—fostered a change in the relations among producers and consumers of major narrative that made epic possible once more in the twentieth century, on radically changed terms of page and screen.[11]

When it is formulated at full strength, this heterodox revision of epic traditionalism effects a drastic historical severance. It awards to the revived genre a contemporary inclusiveness across the culture, like Dante's or Homer's once upon a time; but such breadth of reference comes at the forfeit (a steep one for literary history) of longitudinal continuity down the centuries. Reluctance to pay this forfeit may explain the appeal of a weaker variant of exceptionalism, which rests content to champion not an entire avant-garde but a single resuscitated work. This or that major poem, it is argued, turns out miraculously to make the grade, winning out in spite of adverse odds—and indeed in the face of the criterion of cultural centrality on which stronger accounts, be they traditionalist or modernist, insist. Traveling light, and requiring little more than the toolkit of evaluative critique, this gambit is historically adaptable in a way that the strong-modernist heterodoxy is not. With its help critics can airlift William Wordsworth's *The Prelude*, say, or Elizabeth Barrett Browning's *Aurora Leigh* over the frontier without

---

[10] See Hugh Kenner, *The Pound Era* (Berkeley: University of California Press, 1971); Paul Fussell, *The Great War and Modern Memory* (New York: Oxford University Press, 1975); Mary Ellis Gibson, *Epic Reinvented: Ezra Pound and the Victorians* (Ithaca: Cornell University Press, 1995); Vincent Sherry, *The Great War and the Language of Modernism* (New York: Oxford University Press, 2003). A vigorous antirevivalist case waiving the verse/prose distinction is mounted for literature from across the Atlantic by John P. McWilliams, Jr., in *The American Epic: Transforming a Genre, 1770–1860* (Cambridge: Cambridge University Press, 1989).

[11] See Derek Elley, *The Epic Film: Myth and History* (London: Routledge, 1984). Quint builds the coda to his book (*Epic and Empire*, 361–68) on a reading of Eisenstein's *Aleksandr Nevsky*.

confronting the intellectual structure that keeps the embargo in force. Like other modes of literary history by special indulgence, this one serves to confirm business as usual: it leaves intact the arrangement that entombs epic beneath the cornerstone of the modern.

With friends like these, the would-be historian of epic during the long nineteenth century needs no enemies. While I too hope to gain here an audience for some disregarded poems, and to boost the prestige of several others better known, my book cherishes a wider ambition, which is to cast doubt on the prevailing structure of understanding that is sustained alike by traditionalist and exceptionalist narratives of modern epic history. There can be no dispute that the ancient grounds of epic have shifted, dramatically and more than once, since the seventeenth century; or that what happened to the genre in the 1920s displayed a violence of formal invention proportionate to the violence of the war that modernist writing had to respond to. That the novel departed from the epic transformatively is a thesis in literary history that nobody will deny. Yet these propositions by themselves cannot tell the whole truth even about the matters they ostensibly treat. How novels emerged from older modes of epic and assumed by the nineteenth century the distinctive shapes they did—domestic, Gothic, *Bildungsroman*, adventure, and the rest—is a story we do not firmly know until we know what changes were concurrently undergone by the surviving tradition of epic itself.[12] What radical changes the first modernists visited on epic can be only notionally apprehended, and at best coarsely appreciated, without reference to the genre's continuous tradition during the preceding century, of which the modernists themselves were aware even if those who study them are not.[13] To correct an astigmatizing ignorance about the occluded tradition of epic poetry during the genre's retroactively

[12] To take an extreme example that, treating a different national literature, should be minimally controversial here: how German Romantic narrative fed from epic into prose-fictional forms is a question that Alan Menhennet's *The Romantic Movement* (London: Croom Helm, 1981) can neither answer nor indeed pose, since the author on one hand uses "epic" as a synonym for "narrative" and on the other devotes two full chapters to "Epic Writing" with exclusive concentration on novels, *novelle*, and *Märchen* in prose. Or consider, more subtly and closer to home, Jeffrey M. Perl's assumption in *The Tradition of Return: The Implicit History of Modern Literature* (Princeton: Princeton University Press, 1984) 145, that Joyce's *Ulysses* "marks but the climax of what Hegel dubbed the 'bourgeois epic,'" a long tradition in which, "since the Renaissance, the novel has sought to define itself in relation to the epic." The assumption is richly justified, yet the finer points of definition in the novel's generic development cannot but elude a literary history to which concurrently developing self-definition on the part of epic poetry, in and shortly before Joyce's lifetime, remains a dead letter.

[13] This book, quite long enough already, concludes at the point where a reappraisal of modernist epic might begin. I sketch out terms for such a reappraisal in "Doughty's *The Dawn in Britain* and the Modernist Eclipse of the Victorian," *RaVoN* 1 (2007), which incorporates a portion of Ch. 12 below.

(and ideologically) darkened ages is the larger purpose of this book. It will have succeeded if it muffles the lonesome territorial *Eureka!* that the Byronist, Browningite, and Hardyan seem doomed to repeat—rightly, since they have indeed in each case found a modern epic; but tragicomically too, since they seem never to hear each other's cries or suspect that the woods may be full of game. Above all, this book will have succeeded if it puts a hitch into our customary recitation of some literary-historical myths that are, if too handy to lose altogether, also too smooth to be true.

These like other myth-strength stories are things that no quantity of disconfirming evidence is likely to dislodge. Only an alternative story can hope to do that, so such a story is what this book provides. The present chapter is anomalous in moving along a plane of theory rather than narrative: after this mildly polemical introductory apology will come a second section on generic definition and then a third sketching the epic idea in its neoclassical and Enlightenment developments from Milton's death to our *terminus a quo* 1790. The rest of the chapters form a stepwise chronicle of the British epic poem from 1790 to 1910, pretty closely observed throughout and in each chapter loosely thematized according to the gust of the zeitgeist as a given decade's epic output shows it blowing. Focus nearly always falls on whatever poem the chronicle has before it; focal distance contracts or relaxes, and treatment is lengthened or curtailed, in ratio to the interest the poem at hand may claim. Perhaps three dozen poems receive extended discussion, with tacit or footnoted acknowledgment of the often quite substantial body of criticism that most of them have individually attracted.

In general I rejoice to concur with the verdict of my predecessors concerning the extraordinary degree of achieved complexity that the main Romantic and Victorian epics exhibit—their literary merit, to reclaim a term that I may have seemed to disparage above, but that will be found indispensable by anyone who sets out to read period epics, as I have done, by the gross. A great many poems get merely glancing mention, though this will stretch to paragraph length where an epic even of indifferent quality acquires interest from, and feeds into, a chapter's theme. Quite often my commentary on a poem is the first of which I am aware; I hope it will not be the last, and hope that now and then what I have said about an obscure text will motivate further reading and commentary. To this end a bibliographical appendix lists the primary epic materials comprehensively, by first edition (usually rare) and, where one is known to me, by internet address (whereby access to obscure poetic texts has grown apace since I took up this project).

No such comprehensiveness is claimed for the coverage the book achieves. Where I have learned of a poem's existence and managed to locate it, my reading has nearly always found a place however brief in the chronicle below; but the experience of composing these chapters has made nothing more clear than that some hitherto overlooked poem will become known to me the month this book goes to press.

I trust all the same that, when such a poem does turn up, the chapter it would have belonged to will offer it a good home. The bibliography and index will guide readers to local quarry; but the book is conceived and written by the chapter, and it is at this level of organization that I expect it to prove most useful. Where the interest in epic ran particularly high—interest measurable sheerly in the quantity of titles produced, more engagingly in the quality of imaginative synthesis that, at a given juncture, circumstance enabled and talent seized—then the chapter runs particularly long. Even the biggest chapter, though, is meant to offer like the rest a single and intelligible view of the years it represents. Whether this purpose holds is for others to decide, but the intention itself will be evident in a couple of ways. The span of years surveyed varies with the topic rather than the calendar, with results ranging from a half-decade (Chs. 3 and 5) to a quarter-century (Ch. 11). And within a given chapter the chronological sequence is subordinated to the exposition of argument; I have not scrupled to poach across my own period boundaries where a throwback or anticipation seems illustrative.

The chapter arguments themselves are seldom if ever arrestingly new; they conform more often than not to the received political and social history of the long nineteenth century. They are honestly come by, nonetheless, grown from the seed of close reading, or rather the macropoetic equivalent of close reading that the genre demands, and that seeks its data in story template and narratorial armature instead of scansion and imagery. A reader fully aware that parliamentary reform was in the 1830s air may still find it refreshing to discover that poets followed suit during that decade by isolating and dramatically expanding the grand-consult topos they derived from classical epic practice (Ch. 7). Likewise the highway joining epic to empire turns out to have been paved most typically, as the century waned, by a curatorial or anthological mode of getting it all narratively together (Ch. 11). Findings like these should possess some interest for the scholar framing a period hypothesis that draws on quite different literary genres, and there may be matter here to repay the attention of nonliterary historians as well.

I have tried to keep the account lively, especially when managing sequences of poems that few readers will recognize. This has meant eschewing all but the most skeletal plot summary, and striking a balance between brisk survey of secondary or tertiary epics and a more leisurely consideration of works of the first magnitude.[14] Wherever a conjunction of dates suggests it, I have also tried to constellate major works with each other and looked for productive synergy. While otherwise the juncture of 1805 has no special privilege, the completion around then of epic poems by Wordsworth, Robert Southey, Mary Tighe, Walter Scott, and William Blake reveals patterns that our generally author-centered criticism of these poems has tended to overlook (Ch. 3). Again, the appearance shortly before 1870 of epics by Tennyson, Robert Browning, George Eliot, and William Morris, coinciding not just with each other but with the second major crest of British electoral legislation, invites an attempt to connect the history of major poetry more particularly than usual to the history of the nation (Ch. 10). The attempt I have made can surely be bettered; my apologetic plea here is simply that disciplinary protocols have discouraged the very framing of questions that could advance matters, especially given the categorical erasure of the epic genre from our working picture of the nineteenth century.

Restoring this occluded picture does not ultimately call for theoretical arguments, *explications de texte*, or even the thick description of epic texts concurrently produced. All these have their part to play; yet where literary-historical myth blocks the path, with myth's combined advantages of inertia and resilience, all that can clear it off is the patient, elementary exercise of a counter-narrative. We need to tell a different story, one that organizes phases into episodes and then connects the episodes in series to a history that matters. Above and beyond acquaintance with a shelf of nineteenth-century epics, that is, we need to take account of nineteenth-century epic itself, as an historical continuum correlative with other continua, inside literature and out, that link the premises of the Enlightenment to those of modernism. The long account of these matters that is offered in this book should have a value beyond the sum of its parts. Yet, as only a few are likely to make the whole trek with me, I am eager to equip those who can hike just a chapter or two with some sense of the larger itinerary. For their sake here follows an executive summary of the entire

[14] Plot summaries for a number of the poems this book treats are given in Adam Roberts, *Romantic and Victorian Long Poems: A Guide* (Aldershot: Ashgate, 1999).

narrative—not a who's-who, but an overview, as it were from the strato-spheric standpoint of those choral spirits in Thomas Hardy's *The Dynasts* who, it will be suggested at the close of the book, are actually stand-ins for the epic reader anyhow.

Into the climate of expectant generic incubation that prevailed in the 1780s, and to which this chapter will return in conclusion, the shock of the French Revolution introduced a newly experimental frame of mind. Poetic tinkerers went about reinventing epic more or less from scratch, and their jury-rigged machinery plundered spare parts from classical, romance, and ballad sources, less in imitation of revered models than in order to investigate at heroic scale the nature and limits of the *genre humain* as it had been lately called into revolutionary question (Ch. 2). By century's end the seamy side of humanity had been turned out for all to behold, through the hijacking of the Revolution across war-torn Europe and also the oppressive reaction Continental events provoked at home; the epic field in Britain was divided between militantly patriotic propagandists on one hand, and on the other hand chastened former radicals refining narrative explorations of how a mistaken cause might be revisited and made good (Ch. 3). A sadder but wiser phase of Romanticism next found epoists abandoning this fundamen-tally Enlightenment-driven model of diagnosis and correction, in favor of darker encounters with the mysteries of guilt and atonement, endurance and forgiveness—characteristics held before the public mind by the continued stress of war. Under the unrivaled influence of Scott, sheer story resumed its old sway, and the sharing of a tale now became less a way of solving a problem than of treating a chronic condition (Ch. 4). With the coming of peace the strained national compact of Britain relaxed at last, on one hand into lighter modes that coaxed epic into a commodified style of literary experience, on the other hand into a fractioning along ethnic and class lines of the public interest for which epic spoke (Ch. 5). As Byron succeeded Scott on the poetic throne, his annihilation of existing heroic ideals and radical redefinition of the will-to-narrate drove epic into a bankruptcy from which nothing could redeem it short of apocalypse; the field was accordingly dominated during the later 1820s by eschatological themes and the evangelical certitudes that went with them (Ch. 6).

From the Romantic edge of doom epic pulled back circa 1830, around the inaugurally Victorian hour of national reform, and rescued out of the mode of totalitarian judgment the genre's forensic and deliberative capacity, coupled with a marked new interest in dramatic modes friendly to exchange and debate

(Ch. 7). This identification of the national interest with diversity-management thereupon fanned epic outwards, with the 1840s, into an apparently postnationalist outsourcing of Britishness; this development both reflected the geographic expansion of empire and subjoined to it a bid for the *translatio imperii* from Roman, Greek, and more racily Aryan origins into the keeping of a Britain now imagining its dynasty in collective terms larger than the national (Ch. 8). The expansionist impulse splashed into the 1850s as epic spasmody, a buffo recrudescent Romanticism whose star flamed out for good in the most entertaining of Victorian culture wars but whose influence remained to fertilize the most abidingly original anglophone poetry of the mid-century (Ch. 9). To this textural poetics of style succeeded in the next decade a structural poetics of myth. Fed by new discourses of culturalist comparatism that arose with empire's steady traffic, the mythological epic of the 1860s witnessed some of the Victorians' profoundest literary inquiry into the terms and costs of group allegiance (Ch. 10). This structural rigor abated across the last third of the century: as comparatism declined into collecting, the global portrait gallery or anthology of eras became a characteristic epic form, underwritten by a finally imperialist ideal of civilized progress. Broad yet slack, such provincially complacent metropolitanism met its generic rebuke in a dissenting minority tradition of epic narratives in tragic mode (Ch. 11). The genre's slumber at the very *fin-de-siècle* gave way at last to an Edwardian efflorescence: around 1905 several major works returned, as if preconcertedly, to themes deriving from British history and resumed, as if presciently, the unfinished business of national assessment within a now ominous context of world-historical struggle (Ch. 12).

So runs, in breathless and faceless summary, the long proof of nineteenth-century epic that fills the chapters ahead. It is a sketch whose internal variation I hope will suggest how adaptable the genre turned out to be, and how responsive it remained to contemporary concerns as they arose and changed with the decades. Only more searching acquaintance with individual works can bear out a further general proposition about all this generic variety: that the combination of the nineteenth-century epic poem's esteem value (confessedly superlative) with its market value (ordinarily minimal, though with spectacular exceptions) freed poets to take creative risks with narrative that their novelist and historian contemporaries in prose could seldom afford.[15] The poets were

[15] Franco Moretti, *Modern Epic: The World-System from Goethe to Garcia Marquez*, tr. Quintin Hoare (London and New York: Verso, 1996), reverses Bakhtin's valuation of the respective flexibilities of the major modern narrative genres: "the polyphonic form of the modern West is

moreover impelled to such liberties, by the complex of ambition and doubt that, as we saw at starting, was indissolubly attached to epic's very idea. Both in themselves and in their chosen generic vehicle, the epoists of the nineteenth century had something to prove.

Modern thinking about the epic genre exhibits remarkable stability, not because it is in some final way correct but because it is modern: the problem it perennially addresses is not the essence of epic but the accidence of modernity. The working definition of epic that critics in our time take for granted—even the least theoretical of us can reluctantly produce it if we have to—reposes on fundamentals that would have won approval at once from their counterparts two centuries ago. At the point where our survey starts, the era of the French Revolution, there had lately occurred a deep shift in epic's theoretical premises, one that the last section of this chapter will rehearse as the replacement of a formal by a cultural criterion for epic unity. The orientation towards the genre that resulted from this shift consistently subtended the many poems the rest of the book takes up; nor has any rival orientation arisen to challenge it seriously in the hundred years since the eve of World War I, where our survey concludes.[16] It is tempting to ascribe a record so signally unanimous, when it occurs in a field like literary theory that thrives on contention, to forces other than consciously intellectual. Our unanimity as theorists of epic savors of codependency with the unanimity that, we all agree, is constitutive of epic itself.

For it is the very idea of epic to tell a sponsoring culture its own story, from a vantage whose privilege transpires through the successful articulation of a collective identity that links origins to destinies by way of heroic values in imagined action. *Consensus* furnishes the currency of an epic system where rendition of the generally acknowledged merges through explanation of the generally understood into prescription of the generally regulative—which then feeds back into the system to start the self-reinforcing cycle of facts, truths, and norms all over again. To narrate the tale of the tribe is at once to

not the novel, but if anything precisely the epic, which specializes in the heterogeneous space of the world-system, and must learn to provide a stage for its many different voices" (56).

[16] Donald M. Foerster, *The Fortunes of Epic Poetry: A Study in English and American Criticism 1750–1950* (n.p.: Catholic University of America Press, 1962), discerns little change across the 19th cent. in "the prevalent view as to the attributes of a truly great poem," which "was not pronouncedly different from what it had been in the time of Pope" (192). Since the span covered by Foerster's study, the stolid aplomb with which C. M. Bowra opens *From Virgil to Milton* (London: Macmillan, 1967) has yet to be seriously disturbed: "In the disputable and usually futile task of classifying the forms of poetry there is no great quarrel about the epic" (1).

receive an order, to describe an order, and to issue an order, in a powerful gyrostabilized loop that, if we may judge from the recent history of epic theory, sheds a portion of steadying influence on all who move within its orbit.

The clearest sign of this exponential consensus inhabiting epic theory is that it furnishes the enduring reference point from which leading disputes in epic studies during the past two centuries are to be grasped. As debate over the unity of Homer raged across the nineteenth century between single-source unitarians and text-shredding, palimpsest-decoding analysts, both sides gravitated alike to theses rooted in a shared postulate of cultural coherence. The ideas of order in archaic and in classical Greece that were invoked, respectively, by the unitarian and the analyst differed from each other greatly; but it was to those ideas of order, to the explanatory power of Aegean or Athenian society's imputed wholeness, that either party in the Homeric dispute appealed when clinching its case.[17] A century later, in renewed pursuit of unsolved Homeric questions, and in the teeth of resistance from diehard *littérateurs*, an ethnographically bolstered generation of epic oralists introduced performative ideas about medium and venue that changed much in epic studies.[18] Yet these ideas left untouched, if they did not indeed strengthen, basic assumptions about the group mentality whose systematic intelligibility let the *Odyssey*, *Beowulf*, or *Chanson de Roland* speak. As the twentieth century grew older these assumptions would escort into the canon further oral-epic congeners from Africa, native America, and other cultural sites formerly invisible from the scholarly mainstream. Such canon-diversification has been facilitated in our time by the way controversy *about* epic interpretation has tended to migrate *inside* epic interpretation: the tensed density of mixed message we have learned to read in Virgil or Milton, H.D. or Derek Walcott, has substituted a complex for a simple unity as the expected point of epic reference.[19] Still, a unity it remains, the expression of a cultural system conflicted but not transcended; and on major poetry that treats imperial metropole or island outpost we continue to train, under conditions of globalization, species of the holistic thinking that has long attached to the epic idea.

---

[17] Witness, on either side of the Homeric question—as of our period of study here—F. A. Wolf, *Prolegomena ad Homerum* (1795) and Andrew Lang, *Homer and His Age* (1906).

[18] Albert B. Lord, *The Singer of Tales* (Cambridge, Mass.: Harvard University Press, 1960) both summarizes and further contributes to this phase of epic studies. Its chief figure, Milman Parry, is discussed in Dentith, *Epic and Empire*, 196–98.

[19] A development ably discussed in Joseph Farrell's review of Quint's *Epic and Empire* and of Susanne Wofford's *The Choice of Achilles: The Ideology of Figure in the Epic* (Stanford: Stanford University Press, 1992): *Bryn Mawr Classical Review* 4 (1993) 481–89.

That idea, as these reflections will suggest, is rather a neutral enabler of debate than a partaker; its taproot plunges well beneath the weather. We may confirm this neutrality in another register by considering the twentieth-century theorists of genre who remain most influential within studies of narrative. Not long after our *terminus ad quem* Gyorgy Lukács and Mikhail Bakhtin produced monumentally synthetic studies of the novel, whose leverage relied on the unwobbling fulcrum of the same generic idea that concerns us here.[20] Each of these theorists stakes his modernity, and that of the great novels he admires, on the *fait accompli* of a generic coup: the deposition of both epic and that inviolable societal unison which the idea of epic presupposes. The subtlety Lukács and Bakhtin evince as theorists and readers of fiction quite deserts them whenever they look back, now with regret and now with relief, on the tumbled monolith that was epic. Such blindness is a price forthrightly paid down for their insight into novels, and it need detain us no longer than to observe that a great deal of what Lukács and Bakhtin say about the prose fiction of the nineteenth century will also find exemplification among the period's verse epics.

The point to stress at present is that these leading modern epiphobes start from the same premise that during the next generation served such distinguished epiphile successors in narrative theory as Erich Auerbach and Northrop Frye.[21] Auerbach in *Mimesis* works details of story technique up into cultural history, on the strength of a conviction that the complex forms of

[20] Lukács, *The Theory of the Novel: A Historical-Philosophical Essay on the Forms of Great Epic Literature* (1920), tr. Anna Bostock (Cambridge, Mass.: MIT Press, 1971); Bakhtin, *The Dialogic Imagination*, tr. Caryl Emerson and Michael Holquist (Austin: University of Texas Press, 1981), esp. ch. 1 ("Epic and Novel," 1941). Admittedly Lukács breaches his own generic firewall when, on the final page of *The Theory* he glimpses Tolstoy glimpsing "the form of the renewed epic" (152). By 1936 he would apply "epic" as a term of Marxist honor to describe the extremity of the Russian novelist's "pre-revolutionary" critique of an emergent capitalization of human relations: see "Tolstoy and the Development of Realism," in *Studies in European Realism*, tr. Edith Bone (London: Hillway, 1950) 148–78. On this last point and its historical circumstances see Galin Tihanov, *The Master and the Slave: Lukács, Bakhtin, and the Ideas of Their Time* (Oxford: Clarendon Press, 2000) 114–22; with equivalent and salutary "astonishment" Tihanov notes both Lukács's failure to show historically how it happened that the novel broke loose from the epic (120) and Bakhtin's programmatic insistence on the utter change which that break, whenever it took place, produced *ipso facto* clear across the genres (146). As Masaki Mori curtly remarks in *Epic Grandeur: Toward a Comparative Poetics of the Epic* (Albany: State University of New York Press, 1997), the works that Bakhtin is prepared to call epics "essentially belong to the sphere of anthropology. Bakhtin's argument would exclude all the major epic works in the West" (35). See also Griffiths and Rabinowitz, *Novel Epics*, 18–28; Dentith, *Epic and Empire*, 114–18.

[21] Auerbach, *Mimesis: The Representation of Reality in Western Literature* (1946), tr. Willard R. Trask (Princeton: Princeton University Press, 1953); Frye, *Fearful Symmetry: A Study of William Blake* (Princeton: Princeton University Press, 1947) and *Anatomy of Criticism: Four Essays* (Princeton: Princeton University Press, 1957).

major narrative coincide, in Flaubert as in Homer, with the complex forms of a rich social whole. Frye, primarily concerned in *Anatomy of Criticism* to place the epic system within a literary system larger still, nevertheless rests his running reference to extra-literary contexts on a conviction which is basically identical with Auerbach's—and Bakhtin's and Lukács's too. The epiphobe, seeing the continence of epic from outside, is struck by the exclusiveness on which its defining cultural fusion depends; the epiphile, reading instead from within, is struck by how inclusive the system is, and of how many different constituents. Like the rest of the contestants just enumerated, both parties agree to disagree, poising a difference comparatively superficial upon bedrock assumptions about epic's culturally consensual regimen that everybody has been making for a long time.

From this basis in cultural consensus flow most of the generic criteria that determine whether a given work gets discussed in this book.[22] First among these criteria is, to put it flatly, *length*; to put it roundly, *scope*. No mere count of lines or pages can decide when an epic scope has been attained or even— since in this matter it is sometimes right to take the wish for the deed— whole-mindedly aspired to. Length and scope do vouch for each other, though, once we cross a threshold where the reader is identifiably addressed as the member of a collectivity that knows itself as such in historical time. That is because the textual embodiment of such knowledge takes time; and the measure of time in print is in the first instance a matter of massed, bound volume. "A Poem, in Twelve Books" does not just log a bibliographic inventory but makes a clear promise of large and general reference. Such promise balloons out as the numbers go up—in the chapters ahead consideration of poems in 24, 28, 30, and 48 books awaits the persevering reader— and even when the numbers go down to 9 or 7 or 4, and nomenclature retrenches from book to canto, the practice of quantitative enumeration

---

[22] The ground I tread in this section, smooth already with many footprints, is recently, and very systematically, measured out in Hermann Fischer, *Romantic Verse Narrative: The History of a Genre*, 1964, tr. Sue Bollans (Cambridge: Cambridge University Press, 1991) 15–24. I have no quarrel with Fischer's flexibly cautious weighing of epic's generic properties; given what has been said already here, it would be a surprise if I did. But I can give no quarter to Fischer's refusal to make room in the epic genre for *The Prelude* ("subjective, biographical") and *Don Juan* (Byron is not "representative of his age"), or to his categorical denial that "an epic set in an individualistic, capitalist society" is so much as imaginable. Thus, in literary studies at least, *facile est communia proprie dicere*, while the devil is in the details of particular analysis and judgment: *hic labor, hoc opus est*.

per se sustains a qualitative expectation, which to this day our colloquial honorific "great" and its synonyms may illustrate.[23]

The promise of epic scale is also made literally visible along linear and spatial dimensions; that the poetic line should be long and the page full was a serious matter, and not just to visually oriented epoists like Blake and Morris. Still more commonly poets aspired to analogous effects in soundspace: while the genre's license for magniloquence carried no security against its explosion in incompetent hands, a skilled epic verse maker could, even within relatively small compass, build up an orotundity that adequated scope to ambition on faith. The specimen or approval epics that dot our early chapters earn credit in proportion as they render for the duration, albeit at episodic rather than full scale, a world whose intended auditorium hums with the communal significance, on an at least implicitly world-historical stage, of the persons and action they sing. This intention accredits, if not the fragment poem as such, then the epicizing subset of that Romantic genre for which John Keats's *Hyperion* stands in vocal splendor as nonpareil exemplar.[24]

A further means of epic aggrandizement, perhaps the most telling of all, was genre-absorption. That it takes all kinds to make an epic is a commonplace.[25] But the commonplace has critical work to do when we come to assess the rival claims of the epic and the romance, or the epic and the novel, as Romantic and Victorian poets respectively had frequent occasion to do. These genres were the major predators at the top of the literary food chain, and in Scott, Eliot, and

---

[23] For Roberts, *Long Poems*, length is an epic criterion especially applicable to poetry from the 19th cent., for reasons to do with the inflationary debasement attending the sublime and the historical sense (3, 10–14); G. Headley, "The Early Nineteenth-Century Epic: The Harvey Thesis Examined," *Journal of European Studies* 21 (1991), doubts "that length as such can be a defining characteristic" (201).

[24] Among our poets here Landor and Tennyson tie for second place in doing what Emile Deschamps said in 1828 that Alfred de Vigny had done in the *Kurzepos* genre: "Il a su être grand sans être long": quoted in William Calin, *A Muse for Heroes: Nine Centuries of the Epic in France* (Toronto and Buffalo: University of Toronto Press, 1983) 319. On the generic dialectic of fragmentation with totality see Balachandra Rajan, *The Form of the Unfinished: English Poetics from Spenser to Pound* (Princeton: Princeton University Press, 1985); also Thomas McFarland, *Romanticism and the Forms of Ruin: Wordsworth, Coleridge, and Modalities of Fragmentation* (Princeton: Princeton University Press, 1981); Marjorie Levinson, *The Romantic Fragment Poem: A Critique of a Form* (Chapel Hill: University of North Carolina Press, 1986); Ann Janowitz, *England's Ruins: Poetic Purpose and the National Landscape* (Oxford: Blackwell, 1990).

[25] As Joseph Trapp put the matter in his Latin *Lectures on Poetry* (1711–1719, tr. 1742), the "Epic Poem . . . comprehends within its Sphere all the other Kinds of Poetry whatever": quoted in William Keach, "Poetry, after 1740," in *The Cambridge History of Literary Criticism*, vol. 4, ed. H. B. Nisbet and Claude Rawson (Cambridge: Cambridge University Press, 1997) 119. The topos is still vivid towards the end of our period for Andrew Lang in *Homer and the Epic* (London: Longmans, 1893): "The epic is thus the sum of all poetry—tragedy, comedy, lyric, dirge, idyll, are all blended in its great furnace into one glorious metal, and one colossal group"—into which group he goes on to recruit the "romance" and "tale" into the bargain (7).

Hardy (to look no further) we find them grappling or repelling each other in a contest that our received literary history has often been too quick to call in favor of the modern challenger. Even where an upstart contender for generic supremacy did not engrossingly concern a given poet, the older genre still had to eat in order to live; and the meal that epic made of pastoral, georgic, ode, ballad, soliloquy, epigram, oratory, epistle, *et cetera* was a standing narratological demonstration of its definitive roominess—a generic amplitude from which poetry's shuffling preference today for the nondescript "long poem" seems a regrettable declension into one thin dimension.

Mention of a few limiting cases omitted from the following pages may frame this issue of size most efficiently. Neither Samuel Taylor Coleridge's "Rime of the Ancyent Marinere" (1798) at the opening phase of our story is included, nor Wilde's "Ballad of Reading Gaol" (1898) at the end. This is not because their balladry as such counts against them, but because each poet's quite different adaptation of the ballad tradition for a modern purpose dilutes that tradition's collectivity, for the sake of an individualized psychology that is traumatically agonized by a personal rhythm pitting obscure guilt against imperfect atonement. (An argument that lobbied harder than I can do on behalf of these works' collective spokesmanship would, of course, be making my generic point the other way round.) When we turn to Christina Rossetti's "Goblin Market" (1862) the juvenile clip of the verse is more nearly an *ipso facto* disqualifier, but again the real problem lies with how extensive an audience interpellation the poem performs. Rossetti's radiant parable expands within a horizon not civic and multiple but domestic and familial: a limiting circumstance that the overtly epicizing manner and content of several standout similes in the poem underscore, in effect, by contrast. "The Wreck of the *Deutschland*" by Gerard Manley Hopkins requires a closer call, since here the lineation is nothing if not rangy, and since the two narrative episodes of the poem, by what might be called sprung diegesis, amplify in respectively metaphysical and national directions the given topic of church/state enmity. If this ode were Blake's and dated 1795, it might have found room in the chapter following this one; but Hopkins wrote it in 1875, by which point the imperial culture that epic had to bespeak or denounce asked of an ocean-going tale the wider scope of a collectivity differently conceived. For an English epic of that late date Hopkins's greater lyric was just too short-sighted along the dimensions that counted.[26]

---

[26] The poems I thus exclude have indeed been read, like Eliot's *The Waste Land* at the end of our period, as epics. See, e.g., Karl Kroeber, "'The Rime of the Ancient Mariner' as Stylized Epic," *Transactions of the Wisconsin Society of Sciences, Arts, and Letters* 46 (1957) 179–89; Dorothy Mermin, "Heroic Sisterhood in 'Goblin Market,'" *Victorian Poetry* 21 (1983) 107–18.

A criterion easier to apply but harder to defend in principle is that of *verse*. Even the most obvious defense, the overwhelming respect that nineteenth-century literary culture paid to the ennobling power of meter and rhyme, is not airtight: François de Fénelon's *Télémaque* and James Macpherson's Ossian productions were in prose, yet they were regularly invoked as epic poems well before our story begins. So, at our balance point between Romantic and Victorian dispensations, was Thomas Carlyle's *French Revolution*, and by a most prosy reader at that, John Stuart Mill.[27] Also, of course, that ingratiating but not illegitimate pretender to the epic throne, the nineteenth-century novel, which as late as 1853 Matthew Arnold affected to call "the domestic epic."[28] Although each of Scott's two earliest verse romances plays an important part in our story, and his prosody therein cast an influence both long and wide, merely to demur at his switch into prose with *Waverley* savors of pedantry. Bypassing the series of novels which that epochal book inaugurated is admittedly like getting off on a mere technicality. Just that is what we do below, nonetheless, even as place is found along the way for brief notice of a number of inferior novels that happened to be written in verse. The historical novel and the extended prose history are genuine and challenging highlands of epic territory whose nineteenth-century summits we sight at times but do not attempt.[29] The focus here remains the epic poem in verse, if for no better reason than sheer expediency in setting limits to a study that few readers will wish longer than it already is.

Better reasons than usage and expediency do exist, all the same, for the choice of verse, whether our choice now or the poets' choice once upon a time; and they are reasons that lead back to the very idea of epic consensus. Prose of such lucidity as Thomas Babington Macaulay's in the *History of England* or Eliot's in an indisputably historical novel like *Romola* (or a less obviously historical one like the epic-flexing *Middlemarch*) possessed clear advantages when it came to transporting the reader across years of change. Historical otherness was made familiar through prose's trick of effacing itself in the interests of thick realist rendition. Yet this very facility was in another point of view an impediment to the performance of certain collateral duties of the

---

[27] Mill's review of Carlyle, from the *London and Westminster Review* 27 (July 1837) 17–53, is reprinted in Mill's *Essays on French History and Historians*, ed. John M. Robson and John C. Cairns (Toronto and London: University of Toronto Press, 1985).

[28] Arnold, Preface to *Poems* (1853): *The Complete Poems*, 2nd edn. Kenneth and Miriam Allott (London: Longman, 1979) 658.

[29] I take greater liberties of this kind in ch. 14 of the Victorian volume (ed. Kate Flint) in the forthcoming *Cambridge History of English Literature*.

historical imagination. The closer the verbal medium came to annihilating the years that separated 1860 from 1660, or 1490 (or 1830), the more it falsified what remained a crucial dimension of historical understanding: respect for the resistance posed by the medium of time itself. The value of distance, of regard for the alienating intransigence of the temporal span-between, might be more faithfully represented by the alienness of poetic verse than by companionable prose.

This was so, first, by reason of obvious artifice. A discourse strongly marked as such by rhyme or meter might render with incomparable force a given deed or scene, but its very facility in the punctual rendition of an *act* hampered its rendition of a sustained *action*. Verse stood in the way of a reader's immersion in the totalizing illusion a plotted narrative wove; and by virtue of this blockage it could also stand for the hard labor of reconstruction on which historical time-travel, however effortless it seems, must always actually ride. A second-order corollary of this effect, incidentally, helps restore the tarnished use-and-wont defense submitted above: because to nineteenth-century minds verse inevitably appeared an elder mode for written narrative, the mere choice of verse did something to place readers in a kind of running touch with the anteriority they read about. The pseudo-antiquity of verse blocked certain well-trodden paths of access to historical alterity, then, but it opened up other paths that were quite different from those maintained by the workaday prose norm. (In this respect verse functioned rather like the speculative quaintness of diction to which, during philology's early nineteenth-century reign over the sciences, most poetry was in practice more hospitable than most prose.[30])

What went for historical otherness also went for cultural otherness: at a time when spectra of development running from savagery to civilization ruled all but a few European minds, the processes of world-historical recuperation and of global cultural encounter seemed like versions of each other. Epic's cognate associations with the old and with the primitive helped nineteenth-century

---

[30] Taken together Dennis Taylor's twinned studies, *Hardy's Metres and Victorian Prosody* (Oxford: Clarendon Press, 1988) and *Hardy's Literary Language and Victorian Philology* (Oxford: Clarendon Press, 1993), splendidly illuminate in retrospect a century-long linkage between prosodic and lexical considerations. Hardy's practice sums and epitomizes "the peculiar nature of nineteenth-century historicism, which is a sort of hiatus between the synchronic standardizing of the Augustan age and the synchronic modernism of the twentieth century" (*Language*, 82). From Landor to Doughty, the lexical tradition of 19th-cent. British epic is in its main tendency rather archaeological than neologistic: it revives rather than innovates. See Manfred Görlach, *English in Nineteenth-Century England: An Introduction* (Cambridge: Cambridge University Press, 1999) 24, on the 19th-cent. decline in major authors' influence on the shaping of English.

lays do the essential work of rendering perceptible—now bringing up close, now setting far off—the complex wholeness of the cultural materials they handled. This is not the place for circumstantial illustration of verse's advantages over mainstream prose in flexibility of focus and agility of pace; nor, alas, can the following chapters often pause for such illustration as the best Romantic and Victorian epoists' genius in this aspect of the art deserves. A polemical claim must suffice: these advantages of verse narrative exist, they were known to exist during the long nineteenth century by poets and readers both, and they made verse an experimentally fertile medium of exchange that, by foregrounding the artifice of representation, brought out with maximum clarity the forms of societal consensus that it was epic's business to represent.[31]

Why represent these social forms, however, in the form of a *narrative*? More to the present purpose, why omit from this book long poems in verse that frame urgently shared societal concern in some form other than a story, as do Percy Bysshe Shelley's *Queen Mab* (1813), Robert Montgomery's *The Omnipresence of the Deity* (1828), Barrett Browning's *Casa Guidi Windows* (1851), James Thomson's *The City of Dreadful Night* (1874)? Again an antiquarian explanation is at hand, and again it will take us only so far. Elder and primitive cultures, for as long as they have been cultures, have done their remembering and teaching in narrative; if folkways are the building blocks of conscious community, folk tales are the blueprint and archive for their assembly and retrieval. Even synchronic systems of social organization like law and kinship, one might add, draw heavily on story forms like precedent and genealogy. But then with these honorary recruits to narrative understanding come other forms of knowing that are harder to subdue to the narrative yoke, and that have become more conspicuous with the advance of scientific modernity. To look no further than the eighteenth century: the Enlightenment not only regrounded social and political thought in a discourse of contract and right rather than tradition and custom, and organized its essential general knowledge in taxonomic displays granting privilege to the tabular synopsis of reason, but furthermore rewarded authors who devised literary forms that corresponded with these developments. We shall turn in the next section of this chapter to consider narrative exemplars of changing eighteenth-century ideas about epic, but it must be conceded first that the major poems in which the period housed its

---

[31] In contrast to this claim a bracing, hostile account of the "tranquillizing" properties of epic verse near the start of our period is found in A. D. Harvey, *English Poetry in a Changing Society* (New York: St Martin's Press, 1980) 140–41.

collective wisdom repeatedly assumed other than chiefly narrative forms. From Alexander Pope in *An Essay on Man* (1711) and James Thomson in *The Seasons* (1730) to William Cowper in *The Task* (1785), eighteenth-century poets joined their prose contemporaries in preferring essay, survey, dialogue, and other discursive modes that laid a topic out for dissection rather than recounting. In an age that effectively invented social science, these rather than narrative were the modes deemed likeliest to promote understanding.

As surety for the bond between epic and story, then, our antiquarian rationale appears no worse than its counterpart respecting verse, but not much better. A much better rationale does await us, though, around the next bend in literary history after the Enlightenment. For with the turn of the nineteenth century the normatively taxonomic matchup between factual knowledge and the synchronic categories of reason declined. Or rather, as the new century would have us put it, they *evolved*, into a resurgent narrativity that was, all told, the most robust feature of Romantic and Victorian intellectual life.[32] Understanding during the nineteenth century still appealed to structure as it had done during the eighteenth, but its work was not complete until structure was apprehended as the result and temporary instantiation of an ongoing process; *relation*, that molecule of knowledge, meant not only tallying but telling. In this sense the proliferation of nineteenth-century titles featuring *Origin* and *Development* in the prose corresponded to the many genre subtitles that await us in pages ahead. "An Epic Poem, in Six Cantos" carried a clear implication that the order of those cantos would follow the sequence of a plot. Narrative became the definitive form for collective self-understanding just as it became the default form for understanding in general; it became, in a sense that defines nineteenth-century modernity, the saturated form of generalization as such.[33]

---

[32] This historical advent of the narrative norm gives Peter Brooks his point of departure in *Reading for the Plot: Design and Intention in Narrative* (Cambridge, Mass.: Harvard University Press, 1984) xi–xii. The phenomenon is remarked around mid-century by George L. Craik, whose *Compendious History of English Literature, and of the English Language, from the Norman Conquest* (New York: Scribner, 1864), associates with the influence of Scott upon nineteenth-century literature "the great preponderance in it of the element of narrative" (2: 503, 557).

[33] That the tack my argument takes here seems uncontroversial now is due to the resurgence of historicism in literary studies during the latter 20th cent. It is well to remember, if only for literary history's sake, that a still worthy book like Karl Kroeber's *Romantic Narrative Art* (Madison: University of Wisconsin Press, 1960) could immerse itself in our topic and declare that the "growing historical consciousness" of the age of Gibbon actually "worked against the creation of authentic epic," since "the historical method is antagonistic to the epical method" (87).

This last large claim hinges on the post-Enlightenment valorization of history, the triumph of time as the fundamental category in which modern experience was apprehended. With the nineteenth century became the modality of being: to exist was to be under development or in decline, on the make or on the mend, but at all events in process. In natural and social sciences change watered, and eroded, all things; and in order to explain how matters stood in a cliff face, on a tangled bank, or within the human family it was not just interesting but necessary to know how matters had come to pass. This entailed knowing how they would come to pass away, as well; and the plangent elegiac appreciation of transiency that attended the historicization of modern experience served not only to accompany nineteenth-century intellectual endeavor but, paradoxically, to spur its further advance. From nebula to tissue, from testament to syllable, one had to learn that nothing had always been or would forever be. But that meant one might aspire to find the law of the change, integrate its differential into a compensatory permanence by writing its code.

Romantic and Victorian epic aspired to be a writing of this kind, performed in the currency of a narrative that was typically paid out in two denominations. One was the sheer telling of a plot, usually one that was sticky with the consensual cohesiveness that defines the genre. Such a plot called forth normative virtues from the protagonists, as they rose to the test of hardships that set at risk the welfare, and so highlighted the values, of the society they upheld. The other denomination was the story of this telling, which subsumed the present narrative within a chain of transmission. This it did either explicitly, by various means of legendary attribution, or else by implication, through conventions that claimed for the narrative a place in the tradition of epic writing.

Since the plot of a nineteenth-century epic nearly always came from far away in place or time or both, its sheer telling abetted an effect we just saw verse obtaining by other means: it set the reader in an alienated and relativized position with regard to the action. The *longue durée* of epic scope let patriarchal Canaan or medieval France emerge by sedimentation of details, folkways, choices taken and reasons given, as a place unto itself: a site that decidedly was not Georgian or Victorian Britain in the process of democratic or industrial reconstruction. From an outsider position gradually built up over protracted narrative time, readers grasped the more distinctly the consensual cohesiveness of a world to which their not belonging helped convince them the characters inside it did belong. And it was to the modern anomie that came with this conviction of excludedness that epic's outside story was ordained to minister.[34] Fighting history with history, the meta-plot of epic resettled the reader into compensatory neighborhood with the estranged realities of the story. It did so by figuring that story as one episode, whole and closed, within a story much larger: the enveloping history of a continuous culture whose defining condition, be it providentially guided or ecologically emergent, was developmental and open.[35] The following chapters will show that this outside story of the

[34] On this epic-defining cultural crisis our best guide remains Hans W. Frei's magisterial *The Eclipse of Biblical Narrative: A Study in Eighteenth and Nineteenth Century Hermeneutics* (New Haven and London: Yale University Press, 1974). Frei's argument as it pertains here runs, in brutally curt outline, as follows. By the end of the 18th cent. modernity's profound shift from textual authority towards empirical verification had invalidated Calvin's supposition "that interpretive thought can and need only comprehend the meaning that is, or emerges from, the cumulative sequence and its teleological pattern, *because the interpreter himself is part of that real sequence*" (36, emphasis mine). At this historical crisis Herder sought in the idea of culture a profoundly influential compensation for the interpreter's eviction from his former biblical home. The postulation "of a universal and distinctively human phenomenon—that of cultural spirit," in one stroke both localized the interpreter within "a specific historical location, that of the present" (191–92) and, by grasping the present as a moment within cultural history—effectively a new *real sequence*—offered "a modern substitute for the unitary meaning of the Bible that had been provided in earlier days by figural interpretation" (199). It remained for Strauss in the 19th cent. to draw a corollary with important epic consequences: for modern biblical interpretation "the meaning of the representation is the consciousness doing the representing," because "myths refer not to specific events but to general cultural conditions and kinds of group consciousness" (239).

   Within the secular scripture of poetry, then, specific and coherent "kinds of group consciousness" like those deposited within the textual strata comprising biblical history became the cornerstones of culture, and furnished the building blocks from which to construct that renewable literary kind, the modern epic. With a view to English literary history, where the novel had developed sooner than in Germany, and in a pluralist direction, Stephen Prickett proposes important adjustments to Frei in "Poetics and Narrative: Biblical Criticism and the Nineteenth-Century Novel" in *The Critical Spirit and the Will to Believe: Essays in Nineteenth-Century Literature and Religion*, ed. David Jasper and T. R. Wright (Basingstoke and London: Macmillan, 1989) 1–22; also in *Origins of Narrative: The Romantic Appropriation of the Bible* (Cambridge: Cambridge University Press, 1996). As Thomas A. Vogler concludes from a study of major Romantic exemplars, "The epic leads up to the anticipation of a future state; we are not now in that state, but we can share in the anticipation of it generated by the epic poem. It is when an epic can no longer achieve this effect that it becomes an historical document rather than a contemporary poem": *Preludes to Vision: The Epic Venture in Blake, Wordsworth, Keats, and Hart Crane* (Berkeley: University of California Press, 1971) 198.

[35] Hegel, characteristically, looked beyond the epic nationalism of his generation to a like figure of world-historical comprehensiveness. "The rounding-off and the finished shape of the epic lies not only in the particular content of the specific action but just as much in the entirety of the world-view, the objective realization of which the epic undertakes to describe; and the unity of the epic is in fact only perfect when there is brought before us in all their entirety not only the particular action as a closed whole in itself but also, in the course of the action, the total world within the entire circumference of which it moves": *Aesthetics: Lectures on Fine Art*, tr. T. M. Knox (Oxford: Clarendon Press, 1975) 2: 1090. It is not clear whether the spheric "entire circumference" in this passage has a fourth or temporal dimension, but for Hegel it certainly ought to. For a history of holism that, extending further back than its title would suggest, is laced with a salutary skepticism about the idea's special hold on the rootless or "inorganic" intellect, see Martin Jay, *Marxism and Totality: The Adventures of a Concept from Lukacs to Habermas* (Berkeley & Los Angeles: University of California Press, 1984).

telling came in different sizes—confessional, national, classed, raced, civiliza-
tional, humanitarian—which varied with a given poet's ambition and agenda,
and (not least) with the climate of inflation or retrenchment that prevailed in a
given decade. A constant aim, however, was to embrace the cultural moment
of the inner story, remote in time or place as it might be, as located on a
continuum that led to the cultural moment of the metropolitan nineteenth
century. Epic poetry could thereby recoup as accrued gains the losses of
belonging and of meaning that modernity extorted, but that literature might
give back.[36]

In compassing this aim the poets were assisted by an ever ready analogy
between the longing for a place within the narrative of culture and the
ambition for a niche within the tradition of epic.[37] Dissembling this ambition
under cover of modesty and spurning the tradition in the name of outdoing
it were two aspects of the same complex of ambivalent homage, which
notoriously flourished during the Romantic genre revolt and lived to a hale
old age among the blander, or cagier, Victorians and Edwardians. The thirst
for full epic recognition that we have remarked as nearly universal among the
long century's poets finds persistent, particular attestation in their recourse to
the genre's more accidental but by the same token patently conspicuous
conventions. The invocation, the simile, the descent from heaven or into
hell are not criteria for epic but its tokens, secondary characteristics that, for

[36] On this question—of a recuperable continuity—my account of epic's modern condition
signally differs from the admirable account Simon Dentith furnishes in *Epic and Empire*. Recognizing
much the same codependency between modernity's conceptions of itself and of its epic antecedents,
entailing the same constitutive dialectic of distance and participation, we valorize quite different
modes of literary response. Dentith regularly scouts *continuity* (22, 67, 91), which he treats as nearly
synonymous with *identity* and regards as tinged by Burkean conservatism, nationalism, and racialism;
for him the key term is *equivalence of experience* (44, 97, 159, etc.), an effect variously contrived by
pastiche or by the formal or thematic transfer of modern and antique elements into each other's
matrix. To this synchronic figure for literary relation I have preferred the diachrony of self-repairing
tradition, which at the level of generic convention, as of verbal allusion, rests on the postulate of a
continuum. This construct or "outside story" is the chamber that shapes the echoes literary history
hears, which resemble the original they reverberate yet never pretend to equivalence. The postulate
of continuity is in itself neither conservative nor radical, but rather the condition of possibility for any
such valuation of the change that it narrates.
[37] Quint, *Epic and Empire*, discerns within the elder epics "a literary tradition whose very
continuity seems to constitute another second-order master narrative, a kind of second nature"
(15). Brian Wilkie, *Romantic Poets and Epic Tradition* (Madison and Milwaukee: University of
Wisconsin Press, 1965) 7–19, defines the genre rather by the epoist's acknowledged intention to
join a tradition than by the resulting epic's conventional properties, which in any event the greatest
works often radically and sometimes explicitly transform. See also Hainsworth, *Idea of Epic*, 146–47,
on the dialectic of "innovation" and "filiation" within the epic tradition.

genre as for sex, serve purposes of advertisement. What has been said thus far will prepare us to receive these technical, secondary generic characteristics as expressing epic's primary investment in the recuperatively coherentist program of modern culture. Bold-faced or latent, mutant or rote, the epic conventions that litter the nineteenth-century landscape were not fossils but proofs attesting the bard's membership in a guild and the reader's stake in a heritage.

The poet who invoked the Muse was calling up, and upon, a tradition, so as to summon a readership predisposed to conceive the entire epic transaction in collectively affiliative terms. Obviously this is the game when, at the end of the day, we find Noyes practicing invocation as convocation, jointly calling on "England" and "America" to form an anglophone commonwealth and back each other up in the world by backing the shared tale of Drake's navigation and imperial dream (Ch. 12). But the same work may be done much more quietly: even the inward summons to the Holy Spirit, as we discover it here and there in earlier chapters after the epic manner of Milton, turns out to intend an auditory that is at least a congregation wide, and that sometimes, like Milton's, extends to all humankind. Likewise Browning, making a muse of his late wife at the threshold of *The Ring and the Book* (Ch. 10), presses lyric intimacy into a service at once archetypally mythic—the virgin mother whom Western love espouses—and historically punctual—the early-modern elective affinities of free marital consent, which are very much at issue in the poem. At the same time Morris, exposing a gambit as long as the century, frankly puts the reader on the receiving end of his unprepossessing invocation to *The Earthly Paradise*: a languid "Apology" that lounges into Victorian parlors so as to sign armchair travelers up for the tour of their cultural lives.

The Muse performs, for the outside story of the telling, much the same service that is performed in-house by those venerable domestics known as epic "machinery." This neoclassical term for gods, angels, and sprites comes to startling life with our next chapter, where it figures the generic technology that galvanized the genre during the 1790s; and portions of that weird energy persist in the tradition all the way from Blake to Hardy. The superhuman agents that strafe and stalk major verse narrative during the nineteenth century represent one of epic's great open questions: the definition of the human when, grown heroic, humanity learns the hard way where its limits are and how far it may prove possible to budge them. Especially during Victorian years the commanding interest taken by science in this question of human definition, and the permeation of ordinary life by an industrial machinery, production, and regimen, laid a premium on epic's longstanding imaginative acquaintance with occult, purposeful force. R. H. Horne's eponymous hero in *Orion* allegorizes gigantic industry to the Carlylean tune of the steam hammer (Ch. 8); with much more subtlety, and pessimism to match, a generation later Tennyson vests the agency behind his *Idylls of the King* in a post-angelic machinery as swift and indifferent as the telegraph: namely, the circuitry of public opinion, epic's secret sharer in the decentered culture of a democratiz-ing, technological age (Ch. 10).

One major component in the collectivized Act of the age was perforce martial. Warfare and, just as important, alternative expressions of a warrior ethos left a characteristic impress on nineteenth-century epic. For years on end at the start of our period the British nation stood at war with a brand-new France that was simultaneously in chaos and on the march. The multiform French revolution included a mass mobilization whose penetration of civilian life was without precedent, and to which Britain responded in kind with a mass mobilization of its own. This nation-forging effort had a literary arm that generated propaganda, some of it in the form of heroic poetry converting the prestige of Homeric–Virgilian strife epic to current patriotic ends. The poetry also tended, however, to reflect more pervasively than did the elder tradition dimensions of experience that the current war's invasion of the civilian mind opened to new epic representation. Poets discovered in the unprecedented quality of modern nationalism a charter, and in romance modes *inter alia* the narrative means, to carry the strife epic into fresh domestic territory. The accomplishment of this mission released an unintended consequence: the inertially pacific, largely feminine perspectives that poets encountered on taking epic home introduced into the national story, whether on purpose or not, an abidingly subversive energy that conditioned the course of the genre for as much of the foreseeable future as this book looks back on.[38]

In the main, albeit with a few remarkably sanguinary exceptions, nineteenth-century epic found its militant legacy somewhat embarrassing. The genre took refuge in the deflected strife of war games, which were again richly sanctioned by episodes from Homer, Virgil, and their Renaissance continu-ators. The athleticism of the hunt and the joust, racing and swimming, and in final if privileged reduction the bardic poetry slam, all helped divert

---

[38] For an overview of the terms on which Victorian poets came to the duties of national imagination, see Matthew Reynolds, *The Realms of Verse 1830–1870: English Poetry in a Time of Nation-Building* (Oxford and New York: Oxford University Press, 2001) 19–43, 203–17.

the genre's old blood lust in the direction of *paideia*: culture, that is, in the
nineteenth century's favorite sense of the term as schooling. Most Romantic
and Victorian epoists thought of themselves as public educators. Whether
Muse-instructed teachers of brilliance or grinding pedants—our chapters
showcase both possibilities in plenty, and sometimes in the same poet—they
came forward consciously with lessons to impart. Their texts presuppose in
the reader the same appetite for improvement that drew contemporary
audiences into the sanctuary and lyceum, venues their epic tours had a
way of visiting, too, on slightest pretext. Oratory and strife came together in
another venue that enjoyed ancient sanction, the high moot or consult. At
nodal crises in political representation like 1790, 1830, and 1870, the great
games of parliamentary legislation and legal trial attracted especially keen
attention in epic's designedly civic theater (Chs. 2, 7, 10). But forensic
assemblies of this kind remained in favor across the century, out of motives
ranging from Thomas Moore's mischief (Ch. 5) and Thomas Hardy's irony
(Ch. 12) to the no-nonsense, irony-proof totalitarianism of the apocalyptic
epics that ruled the 1820s (Ch. 6).

Among secondary conventions of the genre the extended simile remains the
easiest for epic-readers to spot, as it was the easiest for epic-writers to produce.
Indeed, on the often bad eminence of 1850s spasmodism, the choice of epic
occasionally seems a mere platform for the ignition of similes that spangle the
page without advancing any larger design (Ch. 9). For the most part, however,
the trope was engaged in the central cultural mission of the genre: as they had
done since the *Iliad*, epic similes in the nineteenth century looked up from the
tale's business to look around at its constituency, implying by networks of
analogical correspondence the horizon within which the plot was to signify,
and the breadth of interests on which it claimed to touch.[39] This work of
exemplary linkage spanning wide reaches of experience was geography of a
kind, and it became particularly important when, with the expansion of trade
to imperial proportions, the progress of science was diversifying the known
world, and was prompting urgent meditation on what a worldly knowledge of
culture and especially of nature portended.[40] Simile's work thus adjoined

[39] See Stephen A. Nimis, *Narrative Semiotics in the Epic Tradition: The Simile* (Bloomington
and Indianapolis: Indiana University Press, 1987), on simile's suturing function—which the
assumption that epic died with Milton prevents his pursuing into later centuries.

[40] Epic geography is treated in Moretti, *Modern Epic*, 47–56; Dentith, *Epic and Empire*, 115–26.
See E. S. Dallas, *Poetics: An Essay on Poetry* (London: Smith, Elder, 1852): simile constitutes
"a continual assertion, a living witness, that in epic poesy the mind is looking below the surface of
things" (212). This affirmation belongs with Dallas's thesis that epic constitutes a narrative kind
of science, since "to tell truth is to show cause" and "a narrative, in giving facts, can and does give

machinery's as just discussed; it also verged on another epic device, the catalogue or inventory. This device was more honored in the breach than in the nineteenth-century observance, although the period's grossly obese generic hulks had to batten on it incessantly. In capable hands, and in conjunction with the national exhibition, the museum, the department store—all of which, matured during our period of study, generated catalogues of their own—the epic list or roster shouldered directly the labor of collateral coverage that simile discharged in a more glancing way. Both put the *encyclo-* into the modern *paideia* that fell to epic as the genre that, in theory, knew it all.

Still, as we have seen, epic's essential way of knowing is narrative; and the synchronic extension of reference that the simile and catalogue offer are ultimately supplements to the diachronic, diegetic carriage that makes an epic go. Every generic convention briefly taken up here—along with others we have passed over, like ekphrasis, proem, or hierogamy—had the same crucial outside job to do, beyond the specific uses to which nineteenth-century poets adapted it. This was the job of earning legitimacy within the genre, affiliating the modern text with a venerable line of precursors, and by that liaison affirming continuity between modernity and its cultural ancestry. One last convention that picked up this allusive relation, and doubled it back for extra stiffness, was the fractal device of the embedded prophecy or flashback. This narrative device operates at a perpendicular to the devices of simile and catalogue we just considered. Like predecessors since Aeneas, the Romantic or Victorian hero who shapes forth a future by making out a past must go up or down, rather than out or around, in order to find it. The vertical passage to inferno or empyrean, cave or summit, complements the horizontally mapped geography of epic comprehensiveness; that is because such a passage presents the wholeness of culture not in encyclopedic containment but in the one stream of historic time. The hero's consultation of the sage or sybil, or indeed of the empowered book, halts the plot in order to declare how that plot inhabits and resumes the great cultural story. Much as, for psychoanalysis, a dream-within-a-dream can expose a true wish which the framing dream has disguised, so a given epic's nested narrative implant hatches a much larger plot, which is the one it shares with its congeners. It incubates what we are calling the genre's very idea: the privileged configuration that subsists between the conduct of a narrated action and the definitive patterns of the culture that it bespeaks, that nurtured it, and with whose further survival its own is bound up. This very idea of epic was there to ground the genre, right across the long nineteenth century, because it had been installed during the long eighteenth.[41] It remains now to show in broad outline how that happened: how the culturalist platform undergirding Romantic and Victorian epic came to be set in place.

Say, Muse, what cause first moved . . . ? Calliope may oblige when pestered in this strain; try it on Clio, though, and she will look off and change the subject. In a sense the historian of any advanced phase of modernity is the chronicler and analyst of a double reaction: not just the reaction belated moderns had to the novelties of their moment, but their reaction to the way previous moderns had reacted to the once equally shocking novelties of theirs. Neoclassical and Enlightenment reactions to the new radiance, or glare, that our names for them commemorate subsided successively into habits of mind which their heirs had to learn from, or else break from. One such legacy was the concept of the modern itself, in the differential relation with antiquity into which the mentalities we call the Renaissance and the Reformation had cast it. Another was the concept of literature as a secular locus of humane value that, lying open to talent rather than under authority, remained perennially subject to debate. Both these modern legacies came together in a quarrel of ancients with moderns that, in the broadest sense, was a condition spanning the seventeenth and eighteenth centuries.[42]

From this chronic condition a distinct historical outline begins to emerge when we survey the thinking about epic poetry to which the genre's

[41] I rejoice to concur with Tilottama Rajan, "Theories of Genre," in *Cambridge History of Literary Criticism*, vol. 5, ed. Marshall Brown (Cambridge: Cambridge University Press, 2000) 226: "Instituting a hermeneutics of genre, romanticism replaces earlier pragmatic or formalist approaches with a *phenomenological* approach to genres as expressing sometimes conflicted states of (cultural) consciousness. Genres are seen not in terms of effects or structural features, but as sites of negotiation." Detailed examination of the epic genre in Britain will suggest, however, that there the change from formal to cultural consciousness was not an effect of romanticism but one of its inaugurating conditions. The topic is summarily frisked in my chapter on "Epic" in *A Companion to Victorian Poetry*, ed. Richard Cronin, Alison Chapman, and Antony Harrison (Oxford: Blackwell, 2002) 25–41.

[42] Foerster, *Fortunes*, 8–10, derives from the Ancients/Moderns *Querelle* the rise of an historical sense among the English Augustans and an accompanying shift in aesthetic criteria; his earlier *Homer in English Criticism: The Historical Approach in the Eighteenth Century* (New Haven: Yale University Press, 1947), pursues the question at book length. Frank E. Manuel, *The Eighteenth Century Confronts the Gods* (Cambridge, Mass.: Harvard University Press, 1959) 10–20, draws out the pertinence of the ancients/moderns quarrel to the cultivation of new ideas about primitive society and mythological thinking.

unbroken prestige across the era kept spurring literary minds. Within a year of John Milton's death in 1674—that putative expiration-date for epic which it is an ambition of this book to prorogue—there appeared in Paris not only the classic statement of Neoclassicism, *L'Art Poétique* by Nicolas Boileau-Despréaux, but two major restatements of principles drawn from Aristotle's *Poetics*, a founding text held in highest regard since its dissemination by Italian commentators a century before. Thomas Rymer's translation of René Rapin's *Reflections on Aristotle's Poetics* (1674) put into English hands that same year a treatise centered on the genre of tragedy. More influential for our purposes was the *Traité du Poème Epique* that René Le Bossu published in 1675. While not translated for another twenty years, it appeared at a time when one would have been hard pressed to find an English reader interested in its topic who could not at least work out the argument in the original. John Dryden for one by 1679 was casually alluding to "Bossu, the best of modern critics" in one of his prefaces, and he repeated the compliment often until his death in 1700.[43] Half a century after publication, when Pope equipped his *Odyssey* translation (1726) with "A General View of the Epic Poem," it was expressly and exclusively "Extracted from Bossu."[44]

A few of Pope's extracts will suggest that what made Le Bossu's recension of Aristotelian thought so memorable was its systematic development of the idea of singularity. "The Epic Poets were oblig'd to unite in one single Idea, in one and the same Person, and in an Action which appear'd singular, all that look'd like it in different persons, and in various actions." Because success lay in "proposing one single Idea, and collecting all things so well together, as to be present to our minds all at once; therefore the Poets have reduc'd all to one single action, under one and the same design, and in a body whose members and parts should be homogeneous" (4). One can scarcely miss the point; nor can one help speculating that a theory so monist spoke to concerns that, while differently felt in the France of Louis XIV and in England from Charles II to Queen Anne, defined an era in which new philosophy, sectarian divisiveness, and socio-political experiment fed a strong appetite among the reading classes

[43] Preface to *Troilus and Cressida,* in *Selected Criticism,* ed. James Kinsley and George Parfitt (Oxford: Clarendon Press, 1970) 165. See also Dryden's *Discourse Concerning the Original and Progress of Satire* (1693, 227–28), and his preface to *Fables, Ancient and Modern* (1700, 288).

[44] *The Poems of Alexander Pope,* ed. John Butt, Maynard Mack et al., vol. 9 (London: Methuen, 1967) 3. For Le Bossu's text in first English translation, see *Le Bossu and Voltaire on the Epic,* ed. Stuart Curran (Gainesville: Scholars, 1970), which provides a lively brief introduction.

for stability, clarity, and rule. Le Bossu actually introduces his insistence on unity by explaining that what had "oblig'd" the ancient masters to cleave to it was the risk of attention-dispersal that lurked within polytheism even in their day. Thomas Hobbes had translated Homer within a few years of the *Traité*, and there is something nearly Hobbesian about Le Bossu's injunction to train the shaping form of heroic poetry like a social organism. Enumerating a series of "qualifications in the Epic Action," he begins, "the first is its *Unity*, the second its *Integrity*," whence he derives corresponding principles for narrative structure: "The first is, to make use of no Episode but what arises from the very platform and foundation of the Action, and is as it were a natural member of the body. The second is, exactly to Unite these Episodes and these Members with one another" (11).

Le Bossu's "one single Idea" grounded a methodizing formalism that was, for its time, thoroughly modern; and the association it freshly created between the epic genre and the imperative to formal unity outlived by many decades its season *à la mode*. At the same time, what was most modern about the streamlined system of Le Bossu—reducing to rules for executive procedure what was formerly learned by the slow imitation of examples—also expressed the insecurity with which around the turn of the eighteenth century Neoclassicism possessed its traditions. With the new century the inconvenience of such a rigid armor as Le Bossu's exposed it to attack and, what was more damaging, circumvention. John Dennis mounted early (1701, 1704) defenses of English spontaneous genius against French regulation, reaching back to Milton in particular for support. Joseph Addison, who in one famous sequence of *Spectator* papers (1711–12) expressed his admiration for Milton almost in spite of the duly cited rules, in another unsettlingly invoked Le Bossu's precepts one by one to show how the old vernacular ballad "Chevy Chase" met the criteria for an heroic poem. In "A RECEIT to make an EPICK POEM" (1713) Pope with his Scriblerian cohort mocked the prescriptive nature of a mere "Knowledge of Mechanick Rules, which contribute to the Structure of different sorts of Poetry, as the Receits of good Houswives do to the making Puddings."[45]

Furthermore, Pope equipped his first and best Homeric translation, the *Iliad* of 1715, with a quite different apparatus from the formalist preface that his

---

[45] *The Guardian,* 10 June 1713: rpt. in *The Prose Works of Alexander Pope* (Oxford: Blackwell, 1936) 1: 115–20. Epic recipe, that nearly palindromic critical subgenre, persisted across the 19th cent.: see Ch. 9, n. 35 and to Ch. 10, n. 80.

Odyssey received a decade later.[46] Pope's own *Iliad* preface was a Longinian encomium on Homer's unmatchable fire of invention, and it was notably silent on matters of structure or technique; to it, moreover, he appended a subcontracted "Essay on the Life, Writings, and Learning of Homer" providing contextual information of historical and cultural kinds that portended the shape of things to come in eighteenth-century thinking about the epic genre.[47] Before proceeding to these later developments, we should note that the cloven apparatus to Pope's *Iliad*—one part warmly engaged appreciation, one part cool scholarly background—reflected neatly a larger, unresolved Augustan contest between modern and ancient perspectives on literary value. For at just this time Paris was witnessing a fresh outbreak of hostilities in the perennial *Querelle*, as dueling Homeric translations produced by the *ancienne* Dacier and the *moderne* La Motte drew down a storm of pamphleteering and salon oratory. By 1717 this skirmish had come to truce again, but on new grounds: the two camps undertook to tolerate one another in a spirit of historical relativism.[48] While this French entente was no more intellectually stable than the front-matter to Pope's *Iliad* was theoretically self-consistent, each early-century standoff represents something momentous, the recognition of which had meant nothing to Le Bossu: the validity of historically and culturally specific premises for grasping the effects of a great epic poem.

Within the next ten years Voltaire would publish—in English, betokening his approval of the state of theoretical deregulation across the Channel—an *Essay on Epick Poetry* (1727) urging that poets and critics alike consult the genius of the nation and age that a work represents; and an anonymously published *Collection of Old Ballads* (1723–25) would defend its selection of contents on the basis of historical rather than literary interest. The respect both

---

[46] H. T. Swedenberg, Jr., *The Theory of the Epic in England 1650–1800* (Berkeley and Los Angeles: University of California Press, 1944) 70, considers Pope "one of the freest agents among the English critics" of his time, who were in the main still fixated on the neoclassic system of rules.

[47] *The Poems of Alexander Pope*, ed. John Butt, Maynard Mack et al., vol. 7 (London: Methuen, 1967). The "Essay" on Homeric contexts was contributed by Pope's friend Thomas Parnell. A linchpin between the two essays may be found in the following passage, though it is only an aside, from Pope's (14): "When we read *Homer*, we ought to reflect that we are reading the most ancient Author in the Heathen World; and those who consider him in this Light, will double their Pleasure in the Perusal of him. Let them think they are growing acquainted with Nations and People that are now no more; that they are stepping almost three thousand Years back into the remotest Antiquity, and entertaining themselves with a clear and surprizing Vision of Things no where else to be found, the only true mirror of that ancient World."

[48] See the discussion of the 1716 *Querelle* and its unstable resolution in Douglas Lane Patey, "Ancients and Moderns," in *The Cambridge History of Literary Criticism*, vol. 4, ed. H. B. Nisbet and Claude Rawson (Cambridge: Cambridge University Press, 1997) 52–71.

these works paid to contextual particularity, however, remained such as to reinforce the divide over which the ongoing *Querelle* had been suspended: the tastes and manners recorded in the classics of antiquity versus those prevailing in the modern world. The persistence of such a divide is puzzling, if only because it consorts so ill with that unity which all parties concurred in regarding as epic's special merit. Le Bossu's prestige alone, we feel, should have sufficed to prompt Pope or Voltaire not only to associate the accidents of Homer's poems, but to identify Homer's unique fiery essence, with what Pope's preface had acknowledged was "a clear and surprizing Vision of Things no where else to be found" save in the genius of his ancient time and place. Yet no one had gone so far as to attempt a merger between ancient and modern spheres by adducing the acknowledged cultural and historical foreignness of antiquity as crucial to the superlative excellence of its poetry. Giambattista Vico stood ready to do so in unregarded Naples, but what might have been the epochal impact of his *Scienza Nuova* (1725, especially book 3, "Discovery of the True Homer") had no reception, among English authors at least, until the next century. And by that time the decisive step had been made, so irreversibly and influentially that it surprises us in retrospect that it should have taken so long as it did.

The causeway linking formal to cultural bases for epic unity was crossed first by an obscure Scottish foot. Literary-historical interest in Thomas Blackwell of Aberdeen confines itself to his *Enquiry into the Life and Writings of Homer*, yet this 1735 book in effect resolved the ancients/moderns quarrel by inventing the sociology of literature. Representing Homer as the creature of his cultural moment, Blackwell undertook to show in detail "the Influence that publick *Manners* have upon Writing," with reference to "the *different Periods* or Steps, naturally succeeding in the *Progression of Manners.*"[49] This progressive framework of long social change let Blackwell not only concede the discrepancy of ancient with modern values but exult in that discrepancy as the very basis of his present delight in the old epics: "The *Marvellous* and *Wonderful* is the Nerve of the Epic Strain: But what marvellous Things happen in a well-ordered State?" (27). From an embrace of radical difference between primitive and civilized stages of culture springs Blackwell's appreciation in Homer of "Metaphor of the boldest, daring, and most natural kind" (41–42). What he at bottom

---

[49] *An Enquiry into the Life and Writings of Homer*, 2nd edn. (1736; rpt. Hildesheim and New York: Georg Olms, 1976) 71, 77. Blackwell collaborated on another book, *Letters Concerning Mythology* (1757), which reiterates the social-contextualist principles of the *Enquiry*.

appreciates *is* that radical difference, and it emboldens him to sketch out a phased cultural history in which at a later time and place "Virgil's Poem was to be read by a People deeply disciplin'd . . . into publick Virtue" (339), while the *Odyssey*, looking backward, reveals even in Homer an awareness of the ruder "Manners of the Times preceding his own" (263–64). In sum, the distinction of Homer's works proceeds from a convergence of climatic, linguistic, religious, socio-economic, and political advantages so maximally conducive to poetic excellence as to have produced that excellence. The unity of Homer's rude and fermenting culture, manifest on all sides and brought into burning focus by the circumstances of live performance, explains the unity of his epic effect, "that *just Measure of Probability and Wonder* which runs thro' the greatest part of his Works" (121).

Le Bossu had derived epic's unity of effect from a moral idea illustrated in coherent action; Blackwell derived it, sixty years since, from morality in a sharply different sense, the *mores* suffusing a coherent culture. This latter coherence—so new a concept that for us even to name it *culture* flirts with anachronism—was perceptible to Blackwell at all because of its extreme remoteness from the modernity he knew; and this meant that his was a Homer that could only be admired from afar.[50] The "*Marvellous* and *Wonderful*" on which Blackwell repeatedly lays stress as properties of the *Iliad* and *Odyssey* derive, substantially and organically, from the long distance separating their premises from his. Although he does not draw the inference, his book unmistakably implies that the sociological reading proposed there is by nature an alienated reading. Tasting the highest of literary enjoyments apparently obliges us to abandon our own home values for the sake of a wild stranger's. Or if this is impossible—*since* this is impossible—the widespread modern delight in so alienated an experience proves that those home values of ours are at some level broken, riven by a deep contradiction that, in an Enlightened era, ought to prompt a correspondingly deep concern.

While what Blackwell implied about Homer's prestige failed at first to penetrate the modern mind, developments soon arose in the parallel field of biblical scholarship that could not be ignored. Arguments like Blackwell's were publicly advanced about the Old Testament by the prominent divines William Warburton (*The Divine Legation of Moses Demonstrated*, 1738–41) and

---

[50] On the idea of *culture* in its emergence from, and recombination with, the idea of *civilization* during the century before 1850 see George W. Stocking, Jr., *Victorian Anthropology* (New York: Free Press, 1987) 17–44.

Robert Lowth (*Lectures on the Sacred Poetry of the Hebrews*, Latin 1753, English 1787). Both authors were bishops in the Church of England and had the strongest motives for maintaining the authoritative unity of scripture. Each proposed to do so, remarkably, by reading the Bible as literature that in its very inspiration was expressive of the historical and cultural circumstances surrounding its composition. Those circumstances being as primitive as Homer's were for Blackwell, the bishops emphasized the highly metaphoric character of expression across the Law and the Prophets, in order to save the sacred text's truthfulness for an age whose modern sciences included the same newly sophisticated textual analytics and hermeneutics that the *Legation* and the *Lectures* themselves put into practice.[51] The splitting off of literal from metaphorical meanings—a talent on which the Enlightenment mind plumed itself—was at the same time a symptom of modern malaise, which the ancient strength of biblically unitary metaphor exposed to the eye of faith for the puny thing it was. Christian readers of earnest intellect stood at mid-century beside those first looking into Blackwell's Homer: at a crossroads posing a dilemma of allegiances, whose origins were literary and textual but whose consequences placed a world view at risk.

For this sore the church had salves, compounded to offer the Christian a guaranteed place within the historical structure of biblical events—a category rapidly expanding to embrace the composition and reception of scripture as historical events in their own right. Figural typology not only made sense of patriarchal deeds and the metaphors arising from them in the Mosaic text; the kind of sense typology made was historical. The same thought, therefore, that read Adam as a type of Christ, and found the Exodus fulfilled in the Redeemer's deliverance of humankind from sin, included within its all-enveloping narrative project the reader's historical moment as well. Likewise the notion of progressive revelation, while it had escaped the cathedral sanctuary and fallen into unruly hands like the seventeenth-century Commonwealth sectarians' and contemporary Methodists', irrigated modern conviction with the living waters of a tradition continuously inspired. While the traditional biblical narrative was destined for eclipse (in Hans Frei's crucial phrase), this eclipse was neither total nor

---

[51] For parallels between Blackwell's Homer and Lowth's Bible see Rolf P. Lessenich, *Aspects of English Preromanticism* (Köln: Böhlau, 1989) 144–57; Scott Harshbarger, "Robert Lowth's *Sacred Hebrew Poetry* and the Oral Dimension of Romantic Rhetoric," in *Rhetorical Traditions and British Romantic Literature*, ed. Don H. Bialostosky and Lawrence D. Needham (Bloomington and Indianapolis: Indiana University Press, 1995) 199–214.

permanent; furthermore, like other eclipses it involved the conjunction of bodies almost identically shaped. What darkened the face of biblical narrative in the eighteenth century was the transit of its isomorphic secular twin, progressivism—alias the march of intellect, alias cultural evolution, alias the Whig interpretation of history, alias Western Civ: the plan with a thousand faces. This secular mega-narrative could eclipse the biblical one in the eighteenth century only on condition of its meeting the need its predecessor had met. It had to secure the future by supplying a flexible framework that held contemporary experience in meaningful relationship with a past that was essentially different from the present yet still recognizable by it. The new secular body of thought did this, banging the drum loudly, by placing the difference between antiquity and modernity under the aegis of amelioration. All the while, albeit less insistently, it cherished the recognition of antiquity by modernity as a reliquary potency, strong to summon back for imaginative consultation elder cultural virtues otherwise forfeit to the triumph of change.

Among the thousand Janus faces of the dialectical progress narrative, the avatar claiming our attention is none other than this chapter's protagonist, the very idea of epic. The principle that "civilization" denoted both a system of institutions now in process and the vast episodic story behind that system was germinally present already in Blackwell, whom we saw stationing Homeric culture between a shaggier archaism in the background and the Roman urbanity that lay ahead. The history that Blackwell thus set into archaic and classical motion was a history that included himself and his waningly Neoclassical moment too. That his generation could be profoundly moved by Homer meant that some portion of the age to which Homer had originally spoken remained a moving ingredient within their modernity.

When in 1767 another British man of letters, Robert Wood, resumed Blackwell's theme, he ascribed to the *Iliad* "those feelings, which are common to every age and country" and then in the next breath, with no evident sense of contradiction, underscored the distinct "character of the times" Homer addressed, and "the circumstances, which belonged to his period of society."[52] For Wood this last term "society" names a continuum

---

[52] Robert Wood, *An Essay on the Original Genius and Writings of Homer* (prefixed 1767 to *A Comparative View of the Antient and Present State of the Troade*; published separately 1769) xii–xiii. The difference between Blackwell's tentativeness and Wood's confidence in advancing much the same line of thought reflects a generational change in the cultural landscape whose chief watershed was the Ossian phenomenon.

whose temporal dimension is constitutive, and of which we all inhabit one "period" or another. Bearing in mind Homer's "early stage in the progress of manners" frees us, Wood affirms, from the old absurdity of allegoresis (298–301). But it does so, we should add, only by substituting for it something very much like an allegory of modernity: the staged, progressive pageant of the secular *figura* whose name is historical development.

By the time Wood went to press with his *Essay* on Homer, its confident formulations were asserting what few doubted any longer. The cultural relativism that had emerged from the Paris *Querelle* had made antiquity and modernity safe for each other, and in turn that relativism had been saved from its own anomic energy by the steadying compass of progressivism. For this the later eighteenth century had to thank not so much the obscure Blackwell as the current of ideas on which his book had bobbed up early, and which soon swept to prominence such French luminaries as the Baron de Montesquieu (*Spirit of the Laws*, 1748) and Jean-Jacques Rousseau (*Discourse on Inequality*, 1755), and in Germany J. J. Winckelmann (*History of Ancient Art*, 1764), J. G. Herder (*Essay on the Origin of Language*, 1772), and the learned J. G. Eichhorn on the Old Testament (1780) and F. A. Wolf on Homer (1795). By different channels all these sources of new thought about revered origins flowed into an enlightened historiography whose shapeliness of plot line reasserted something like the old epic criterion of formal unity, which justified modernity twice over: it served both as the clear pedigree to which modern historians could confidently look back, and as the mark of written finish whereby the histories they composed could claim a culminating vantage that transcended what they surveyed.[53]

Along with the broadening of cultural inquiry from literature into laws, artifacts, and folkways that these names imply there came, in Britain, a momentous recovery of modernity's *other* other, the nonclassical (Gothic) and vernacular Middle Ages. The year 1762 marked a watershed in this movement of recovery, comparable to that of 1674 from which we began. Again a pair of churchmen took the lead, with Richard Hurd's *Letters on Chivalry and Romance* and Thomas Percy's *Reliques of Ancient English Poetry*.

---

[53] On the convergence between epic and historiography by the close of the eighteenth century, epitomized in Gibbon, see Martin Aske, *Keats and Hellenism: An Essay* (Cambridge: Cambridge University Press, 1985) 75–84, and Ian Haywood, *The Making of History: A Study of the Literary Forgeries of James Macpherson and Thomas Chatterton* (London and Toronto: Associated University Presses, 1986) 42–57. As early as 1752 James Moor of Glasgow in "An Essay on Historical Composition" (published 1759) made out an Aristotelian case for history as a species of epic writing.

Each strikes us as a work of enthusiasm more (or less) than properly episcopal, until we recall how bishops were peers of the realm, and how integral to the national constitution the established church remained at this juncture.[54] The former publication was a lover's apology invoking the beauties of medieval romance to excuse what appeared as blemishes only when romance was held to a classic standard that had never suited it to begin with, and in which the enraptured author did not really believe. The latter was an edition that, in sharp distinction from the blunt historicism of the anonymous 1725 *Old Ballads* we glanced at above, solicited the reader's delight in home-grown balladry as an aesthetic experience fully worthy on its own terms.[55]

And then, also in 1762, there was Ossian. A multiplex publishing event, a national controversy, an international craze: to a literary world primed for primitivism, James Macpherson's prose transmission of the edited or coordinated or supplemented or invented fragments of ancient Gaelic verse in his possession brings into focus most of the issues that have exercised us here. Inverting (and then some) the ratio found in Percy's *Reliques* between a compiling translator's fidelity to the text and a collaborative copyeditor's poetic improvement of it, Macpherson approached editing as one of the fine arts.[56] In *Fragments of Ancient Poetry* (1760), then *Fingal: An Ancient Epic Poem, in Six Books* (1762), and then for good measure *Temora: An Ancient Epic Poem, in Eight Books* (1763) he (re)constructed a primitive world whose notable self-consistency may be plotted handily on the axes of cultural synchrony and diachrony introduced above. Little beyond warfare and poetry claims the attention of Macpherson's ancient clansmen, who tend to be warriors, bards,

---

[54] Gerald Newman, *The Rise of English Nationalism: A Cultural History 1740–1830* (New York: St. Martin's, 1987), depicts Hurd's medievalism, along with much else in the Gothic revival, as a polemical work of "anti-French literary nationalism" (109). Percy's nationalism is spoken for in the title of his anthology.

[55] This is not to say that Percy was anything but a liberal practitioner of expurgation, emendation, and supplementation to meet a modern taste. Walter Scott's fastidious retention in *Minstrelsy of the Scottish Border* (1802) of old words and phrases as "barbarisms, which stamp upon the tales their age and their nation" (1: cxxviii) was the hallmark of a later editorial generation that worked, nevertheless, fundamentally in the pioneering antiquarian spirit of Percy.

[56] Even Macpherson's prose had a prosody resonant with late-breaking ideas about primitive epic style: see Jeremy M. Downes, *Recursive Desire: Rereading Epic Tradition* (Tuscaloosa and London: University of Alabama Press, 1997), on the Ossianic "binary pattern of recursion and completion" (132). As Howard Weinbrot points out in discussing mid-century British philo-semitism, the parallel periodicity of Ossianic prose reflected that to which Lowth had called attention in Hebrew verse: *Britannia's Issue: The Rise of British Literature from Dryden to Ossian* (Cambridge: Cambridge University Press, 1993) 456.

or better yet warrior-bards, of a uniformly high-minded integrity whose social analogue is a structure in which chieftains conduct themselves as first among equals. So conversably egalitarian a society, engaged in folk practices so simple and so few, make up the picture—the diagram, really—of a most homogeneous culture.[57]

To this textbookish faux ethnography, due in some measure no doubt to his old Aberdeen instructor Blackwell, Macpherson adds an unexpected, indeed inspired supplement. He pours over the tribal life of his poems a shared strain of feeling whose timbre is not at all the naïve and direct passion of the ancients. It is instead a sentimentally compounded strain, in which the prominent note is a yearning after the glory days that are, while not yet gone in Ossian's time, felt even by the heroes to be already on the wane. This sentimental supplement to the primitive was Macpherson's most brilliant innovation, and its diachronic invitation to the historical fancy was the key to his poems' enormous popularity.[58] For us here it also illuminates, as by gaslight, the eighteenth-century thinking about epic that the Ossian books summed up by performing it. The flow of poetic feeling tapped into the emotional undercurrent that in all permutations of the ancients/moderns debate had allied contemporary with antique experience, and then ran with it—ran home, that is, to the hearth of sensibility at which circa 1760 the European reader was learning to keep warm against a variety of chilling modern developments. Because Fingal, Cuthullin, and Ossian were in their tender hearts and plangent accents Men of Feeling of quite contemporary stamp, the reader's road back to cultural basics—viable in Homer but manifestly rocky—here was paved along a slope of benevolent intention and appealing regret.

Nor was this all. There was more to Macpherson's strategy than mere resemblance between heroes and readers; there was a cunning reciprocation. That note of melancholy in which a hero nobly rued the incipient demise of his way of life symmetrically requited (and so evoked) the condition of the modern reader, who was bent on reimagining a vanished past that swam in and

---

[57] Fiona J. Stafford, *The Sublime Savage: A Study of James Macpherson and the Poems of Ossian* (Edinburgh: Edinburgh University Press, 1988) 178, regards Ossianic culture as effectually democratic in the image of personal relations it held up to 18th-cent. readers. Macpherson's investment in national homogenization is discussed by Leith Davis in *Acts of Union: Scotland and the Literary Negotiation of the British Nation, 1707–1830* (Stanford: Stanford University Press, 1998) 77–88.

[58] Nobody was better placed to grasp this key, or wield it himself, than Walter Scott, who in an 1805 review drily ascribed to Macpherson's Fingal "all the strength and bravery of Achilles, with the courtesy, sentiment, and high-breeding of Sir Charles Grandison": *Edinburgh Review* 6 (July 1805) 446.

out of focus like the ubiquitous mist effects that the poems' descriptive passages spread over glen and crag. The Ossianic hero's reluctance to disappear into a scrap of scenery, or balladry, offered a perfect match with the sentimental reader's conviction that from such a scrap it remained possible, even at this late date, for the genius of modernity to extrapolate whole a vanished way of life.[59] Reader met hero in the gloaming, on an emotional ground that at once lamented the alienation, and affirmed the retrieval, of precisely the connect-edness between present and past which it had by Macpherson's day become the very idea of epic to declare. The bond between them was a union of culturally kindred spirits, which is incidentally what the proliferation of ghosts in *Fingal* was all about.[60]

That this is the theory of epic which the Ossian poems put into practice is matter not just for conjecture but of prominent contemporary attestation. Even as Macpherson was confecting his transcripts, his countryman and intellectual crony Hugh Blair was with comparable industry equipping the operation with full theoretical cover. He had an essay on Ossian in draft form as early as 1759; after a couple of years' lecturing and anonymous publication on the question, he went into print with *A Critical Dissertation on the Poems of Ossian* in 1763 and rapidly incorporated remarks on the new sequel *Temora* into his second edition; and then after 1765 Blair's remarks accompanied each edition of the epics Macpherson sold. This inside story or party line on Ossian joined at the hip the century's formalist and culturalist approaches to epic unity. Fifty years earlier Pope's *Iliad* had sequestered critical response from scholarly background; to coordinate the two in a medium of fervent praise was Blair's purpose exactly. Originating in "the first ages of society" (49) and bearing "all the marks of greatest antiquity" (68), which would not be complete without stigmata of transmission through a guild of Druidic bards (61), the epic poetry of Ossian is at the same time—and *for these very reasons*—a

[59] See Katie Trumpener, *Bardic Nationalism: The Romantic Novel and the British Empire* (Princeton: Princeton University Press, 1997) 71–76. The true subject in the Ossian poems "is not epic heroism but the vicissitudes of oral tradition" (75).

[60] As Quint remarks, "The ancient heroic characters described in the poems become hard to distinguish from the ghosts—often those characters' very own ghosts—whom the bard invokes at the beginning of his songs as the traditional epic poet might call on his muse"; the way "Ossian already experiences the belatedness of his romantic readers" forecasts how, within the pan-European nationalist revival of medieval epics in the next century, "the bards seem to lament the passing of the very heroic ages they describe" (*Epic and Empire*, 346–47, 360). Downes, *Recursive Desire*, 139–41, correlating Macpherson's ubiquitous ghosts with the brief, discrete *nekuia* of book 11 from the *Odyssey*, measures thereby the declension of the Ossian poems towards an epic poetics of fragmen-tation and discontinuous "futility."

paragon of generic correctness: "Examined even according to Aristotle's rules, it will be found to have all the essential requisites of a true and regular epic; and to have several of them in so high a degree, as at first view to raise our astonishment on finding Ossian's composition so agreeable to rules of which he was entirely ignorant" (73); "Unity is indeed observed with greater exactness in Fingal, than in almost any other epic composition" (75).

Commentary here is superfluous on the coincidence Blair found so amazing between the criteria for epic that had arisen in his lifetime and the properties of the bestseller to which his *Dissertation* was hitched. "Aristotle's rules," as Blair goes on to enumerate them, are unmistakably those of Le Bossu.[61] But of course between our seventeenth- and eighteenth-century critical lawgivers there subsists a crucial difference that defines an epoch: the formal unity Blair eulogizes is a function of that primitive cultural unity which alone will suffice to explain how Ossian for very ignorance could not help imparting a Homer-like unity to his poetry.[62] Somewhat more surprising is the explicitness with which Blair praises the result in terms derived from contemporary fashions in literary taste: "The two great charac-teristics of Ossian's poetry are, tenderness and sublimity" (71). Epic's traffic with the sublime is a long story, of course, one that crests with Milton (and Edmund Burke's readings of Milton in his 1757 *Philosophical Enquiry* into the topic) and that will be seen to have many a nineteenth-century sequel.

---

[61] As if to corroborate our thesis here, in Blair's celebrated 1783 *Lectures on Rhetoric and Belles Lettres* he goes out of his way during lecture 42, "Epic Poetry," to denigrate Le Bossu's formulaic approach to unity as "one of the most frigid, and absurd ideas, that ever entered into the mind of a Critic": rpt. ed. Harold F. Harding (Carbondale and Edwardsville: Southern Illinois University Press, 1965) 2: 407. Out of his way, because Blair's way is Le Bossu's after all: before long he is bestowing his highest praise on the "regular Epic," in which circumstances "are all made to conspire for the accomplishment of one end"; "the unity must lie in the subject itself; and arise from all the parts combining into one whole" (2: 413).

[62] Within fifty years Blair's primitivist assertion would enjoy the authority of a commonplace, affirmed in one neat stroke, and by the two most prominent epoists of the first Romantic generation at that, when Scott's 1824 *Britannica* article on "Romance" cited the introduction Robert Southey had given his 1817 edition of Malory: "In similar stages of civilisation, or states of society, the fictions of different people will bear a corresponding resemblance, notwithstanding the difference of time and scene." *Essays on Chivalry, Romance, and the Drama* (1834; rpt. Freeport: Books for Libraries, 1972) 174. By mid-cent., Turner observes in *The Greek Heritage*, 145, defenders like Gladstone and William Mure routinely "confused the issue of the unity of Homeric authorship with that of the historical reality of the epic narrative." By the end of our period of study the explanatory power of cultural unity (in this case its lack) was wielded quite automatically when W. Macneile Dixon, *English Epic and Heroic Poetry* (London: Dent 1912) 47, diagnosed *Beowulf* as a case of formally arrested development, a text "frozen" in structural imperfection "because at no stage in their history were the people from whom it sprang welded into political unity."

But the property in Blair's Macpherson that demands our attention here is that of "tenderness," which Blair also calls "the moral or sentimental sublime" of "virtuous and noble sentiment . . . a generous valour, void of cruelty" and brimming with "sensibility." Blair's summation of the total effect comes pat on its later eighteenth-century cue: "the heroic mixed with the elegiac strain; admiration tempered with pity" (127). There in a phrase lies the Ossianic formula. Heroic greatness anticipatorily mourns its own passage from the world of deeds into that of *legend*, which is to say, the realm of the to-be-read, where future readers will pity, even as they admire, the heroism that came once to pass.[63]

Macpherson's formula made the Ossian poems the signal epic achievement of their century, one might almost say the single such achievement. Ideas about epic poetry, rather than epic poems, have preoccupied this introductory chapter, not for want of exemplars but simply because during the eighteenth century the theory rather than the practice of epic was where the genre lived. The standard epic poem of the day was an exercise in epic theory by other means. Worst was the straight-up epos that, from Richard Blackmore's *Prince Arthur* (1695) to Richard Glover's *Athenaid* (1787), spent its force in merely executing a pattern laid down by Le Bossu.[64] Now as at all times genuine epic expression had to find, as Macpherson unerringly did, a poetic form adequate to the cultural tensions that energized the age, which in the eighteenth century meant engaging the debate of modernity with antiquity. Yet this task was one to which the obelisks of heroic unity that the polite public thought it wanted—even poems garnering wide esteem, like Glover's *Leonidas* (1737)

[63] Crawford, *The Modern Poet*, 67, provides a salutary reminder that in Macpherson this complex of feeling arose "from a war threatening a civilization" (that of the Highlands in the wake of 1745), and remarks that the situation recurred within the postwar modernism of Eliot and Pound. All three figures merit appraisal in the light of what Franklin P. Court, *Institutionalizing English Literature: The Culture and Politics of Literary Study 1750–1900* (Stanford: Stanford University Press, 1992) 38, says about Blair's project of "constructing a mythic vision of the past from texts and authors that promote ethnocentric political convictions."

[64] See Peter Hägin, *The Epic Hero and the Decline of Heroic Poetry* (Bern: Francke, 1964): "The choric character of the epic was to be expressed in a concrete choric action involving multitudes of people under the leadership of a great hero who represented not himself but the moral, spiritual and political beliefs of the poet's own age" (31; see also 52–55). This formula, which as Hägin shows is suited to a depressingly high proportion of 18th-cent. epics, could do no more than reproduce the ancients/moderns standoff, until Macpherson discovered in historicist nostalgia an effect capable of forging the culturalist link concurrently envisioned in theory. Arguably this effect let the Ossian poems span the divide between martial and sentimental values to which Laura Runge ascribes a decline in heroic writing after mid-century: *Gender and Language in British Literary Criticism 1660–1790* (Cambridge, Cambridge University Press, 1997) 182–85.

and William Willkie's *Epigoniad* (1757)—proved quite unequal. In contrast the mock heroics of Dryden and Pope, part encomium part travesty, did express the definitive contradiction of the age, which also emerged under different permutation in the epic-patterned novels of Henry Fielding. In widely disparate iterations of the same Augustan program, *The Rape of the Lock* (1712) and *Joseph Andrews* (1742) held ancient paradigms and modern realities up for mutual critique.[65] Within these ironic, allusive forms it was modernity that carried the day; and while it formed part of Augustan satire's inner charity to make the defeat of epic feel like a noble immolation, the outcome resembled generic suicide too nearly to sustain a tradition that needed more than salt and rue to live on. Before an earnest affirmation could be wrested from the Augustans' arch duplicity, epic wholeness and heroic value had to migrate from chiefly formal and moral neoclassic grounds to the cultural grounds on which *Fingal* and *Temora* reposed. Once that migration had occurred, for better or worse the disappearance of traditional values appeared in the register not of a loss (the Augustan sting) but of a sacrifice (the Ossianic melancholy) making all good in the end.

The relaxation of standards that accompanied epic's new culturalist rationale formed part of a relaxation in generic criteria across the board. The Ossian books were poetic prose; though Christopher Smart wrote no epic, at just Macpherson's moment he set about psalming the cosmos in prosaic verse (*Jubilate Agno*, 1759–63). Herder, who made a new gospel of *das Volk* out of the antidogmatic observations of Blackwell and Wood (and, better late than never, Vico), swiftly drew from culturalism the corollary that genres were mere epiphenomena into which the genius of a people might indifferently fall: a position also congruent with Bishop Lowth's on the genre-fluid poetics of the Hebrew Bible.[66] To this speculative strong-mindedness was added, in the same year as Herder's *Origin of Language*, a genre-busting *Essay on the Arts Commonly Called Imitative* (1772) by the orientalist scholar William Jones. Among the first intellectual

[65] Weinbrot, *Britannia's Issue*, 303–7, puts his substantial learning about the Homeric debate to work overthrowing Pope's alleged Augustan poise and claiming *The Rape of the Lock*—in keeping with the entire thesis of his important if lopsided book—as a hands-down rout for the forces of the modern.

[66] Ian Balfour, *The Rhetoric of Romantic Prophecy* (Stanford: Stanford University Press, 2002), affirms the epic-spiritedness of Herder's Hebraism: it "expresses not a longing for a theocratic regime but rather a desire for a unified public whose one language can be translated, almost insensibly, from God to the prophets to the people" (114). Balfour also underscores, in the hermeneutic writings of Hurd, "his repeated claims for the totalized and systematic character of Biblical prophecy" (86).

fruits of British imperial ambition, Jones's pathbreaking studies of poetry from India, Persia, and Arabia made genre distinctions seem otiose and—worse, perhaps, to an Enlightened judgment—parochial, beside a welling lyrical expressivity that his research challenged Western minds to situate within a greatly expanded cosmopolitan horizon of communicable human culture.

High-profile anticipations such as these should be borne in mind as we approach the period of British Romanticism proper, to which the common ascription of a meltdown in the literary genres is on several overlapping counts mistaken. First, as we have just seen, at the level of literary theory not only were the horses gone and the stall doors swinging, but the more adventurous pre-Romantic thinkers had already set about demolishing the barn. Second, at the level of literary practice such Romantic experiments as indubitably did take place in genre-bending relied implicitly for their effectiveness on the continued presence of genre distinctions that were, if not especially articulate (and those surrounding epic were not), still rigid enough to be bent.[67] Third, the robustness of such distinctions right across the nineteenth century shows that the ichor of genre is, like the ethereal substance of Milton's warring angels, a plasma that bleeds to heal: at the end of our day we find that Noyes's *Drake: An English Epic* (1906), Owen Meredith's *King Poppy: A Fantasia* (1892), and Hardy's *The Dynasts: An Epic-Drama* (1910) are still in different ways staking, evading, or qualifying claims that presuppose the intelligibility of the genres their subtitles name. What the universal solvency proclaimed by Herder, Jones, and others did in its time effectually propose was that hereafter genre should function within the literary system as an heuristic. Not an enforceable rule but a performable role, epic was now to be negotiated among poets within the tradition, and between poets and readers in the marketplace of literary ideas.

Especially under the new culturalist dispensation, everyone involved had an interest in seeing that epic's stock in the market should remain, if not constant, then high. Setting a standard for reference up and down the genres, epic

---

[67] A point resoundingly affirmed in Stuart Curran's preface to *Poetic Form and British Romanticism* (New York and Oxford: Oxford University Press, 1986) 5, and clinched in the chapters that come after it. His chapter on epic arises to a memorable formulation of much that the present chapter has been propounding: "What makes the epic so fascinating a genre is precisely that there are so few examples, that the rules are so arbitrary and so arbitrarily insisted on by readers long after they have shed their cultural relevance, and that, against that critical expectation, the only great successes come from bending or openly breaking those rules so as to reform the cultural link" (174).

secured transactions among its constituent kinds—say, when choral ode meets
forensic address in an important cluster of eighteenth-century texts—and it
served as a senior, if typically dormant, partner when a genre like travelogue
raised its sights from a landscape to a people—as happens in Byron across
the gamut (Ch. 5) or in such intermittently ethnographic works as Thulia
Henderson's *Olga* (Ch. 9) or Alfred Domett's *Ranolf and Amohia* (Ch. 11).[68]
Even when not partnership but hostile takeover was in prospect, the place
that the metrical romance or world-historical novel coveted was the place that
epic held; and the attitude of the prospective usurper tended to betray
an ambivalence lefthandedly decorous, because supportive of the generic
hierarchy within which it meant to trade up.

To appreciate ambivalence on this order is a standing challenge for the
critical engagement with primary texts on which literary history chiefly
depends, and to which this book seeks to contribute in practice. In due
decorum, however, we should exit this theoretical chapter by summoning
two amiable, loosely argued works of theory from our liminal decade the
1780s and glimpsing how ambivalently they regard epic's place in the hier-
archy of genres. Each title is squarely planted on a genre; furthermore, by
assuming the form of a genre conspicuously differing from the standard essay,
each keeps genre at the front of the reader's mind. Each argument both
advocates the relaxation of standards and mixture of strains, and yet remains
jealous to preserve a degree of generic dignity at the top of the scale. Clara
Reeve's *The Progress of Romance* (1785) moves quickly into dialogue format and
stays there, while her mouthpiece Euphrasia patiently wears down the straw
man Hortensius' resistance to admitting romance upon an equal footing with
epic. She bases her argument for equality on grounds of comparable antiquity,
content, and contemporary reception: "They spring from the same root,—
they describe the same actions and circumstances,—they produce the same
effects, and they are continually mistaken for each other."[69] Euphrasia's mantra
"A Romance, is nothing but an Epic in prose" (1 : 51, also 1 : 13, 1 : 86) implies a
reciprocal formula—an epic is nothing but a romance in verse—that offers us,

---

[68] On para-epical anthem genres, and the concomitant prehistory of British national mobilization
before the French Revolution, see Weinbrot, *Britannia's Issue*, and Suvir Kaul, *Poems of Nation,
Anthems of Empire: English Verse in the Long Eighteenth Century* (Charlottesville and London: University
of Virginia Press, 2000). The latter's census of texts shows how, even under conditions of national
consciousness that ought to have inspired an epic treatment, the century's preferred poetic mode was
discursive or scenic rather than narrative.

[69] Clara Reeve, *The Progress of Romance* (1785; rpt. New York: Facsimile Text Society, 1930) 1: 16.

in passing, a gauge for the change that Scott would effect early in the next century when he made precisely that implied formula stick. But the fact that Reeve left this reciprocal formula undeclared, whether she dreamt of it or not, shows which way the theoretic wind blew circa 1780: strongly in epic's favor, through the front door and out the parlor window.

Evidently the same generic prejudice gave William Hayley his title in 1782 for *An Essay on Epic Poetry*, since in substance the work was actually an essay on the generally uncertain state of things poetical in the last quarter of the eighteenth century. Taking the form of five hortatory epistles addressed to the poet William Mason—in Popean heroic couplets, thus public, and thus manifesto-like in their exhortations—Hayley's book is half verse, half opinionated endnotes in chatty prose, and wholly representative of the confused sense of opportunity that prevailed in literary Britain at the time of its publication.[70] It is obvious that talking about epic, or purporting to, offers Hayley a way of capturing attention in order to talk about the many generations of poets for whom epic has been, as it remains for him, the king of kinds; and about the many genres, including the modern novel, that hold from epic's court the literary status of crown dependencies. Epistles 1 and 4 say nothing about heroic poetry, the epistles in between give a potted history of the genre from Homer to Pope, and in epistle 5 Hayley advises Mason to seek epic subjects in British history, Gothic lore, and the mythology of India (prophetic on all three counts, we shall find), while also eschewing supernatural machinery (to what little avail Chapter 2 will show). The impression overwhelmingly left by Hayley's arbitrary topic-hopping is that, while the bad news is that nothing is doing in poetical Britain just now, the good news is that anything goes. Today is the first day of the rest of the genre.

The disdain Hayley feels for the clipping of eagle pinions to critical specifications finds its match in Euphrasia's final, leveling concession from *The Progress of Romance* that the real criterion, for romance and epic alike, is neither form nor content nor genealogy but "genius" (2: 71). The joint call that Hayley and Reeve issued for the liberation of spontaneous ingenuity echoed a decade later among the freemasonry of epic engineers who await us in the chapter ahead, and who proved epic's resources anew once the

---

[70] See the facsimile edition by M. Celeste Williamson (Gainesville: Scholars, 1968). Joseph Wittreich, Jr., develops the importance of Hayley's *Essay* to all the principal first-generation Romantics in "Domes of Mental Pleasure: Blake's Epics and Hayley's Epic Theory," *Studies in Philology* 69 (1972) 101–29.

debacle of revolutionary France had made the tin innocence of Hayley's rhetoric seem at once prelusive and obsolete. Deregulated "genius" should be not anarchic, Reeve maintained, but rather the unconsciously methodical exhalation of a culture suffusing a whole people and time. Such was the genius suffusing her time, at least; on that point Reeve was as positive as Hayley. To the late taunt of Hortensius (retiring beaten and licking his wounds), "According to your account, Epic poets are as plentiful as mushrooms," Euphrasia has a ready reply: "Not so neither—they are rare, but not so scarce as is generally believed" (2: 69). Epic remains special, that is, but not inaccessible; within the compass of our place and moment, but not so common as to obviate the exceptional literary diligence that may train it up, once found, into the genuine produce of our climate.

By the 1780s literary minds in Britain had put behind them the grousing of crinkly Neoclassicism about epic's supersession by an inhospitable modernity. They had learned to believe that the sort of cultural work epic had always done remained to be done afresh under transitional circumstances that were not *ipso facto* different from the transitional circumstances that had prevailed in Virgil's time, and Homer's, and Moses'. The British reading classes were prepared to associate epic's cultural work with the advancing strength of a prosperous nation, to associate the national advance with the progress of civilization, and to receive with acclaim any complex narrative of elevated bearing that might enshrine these associations in a form suitable for transmission to posterity. They were—as Matthew Arnold would say at the midpoint of the long century on which we now embark, in a poem called "The Scholar-Gipsy" that expressly looked back to Milton's time and resumed in its title the dialectic of modern progress that has furnished our theme—waiting for the spark from heaven to fall.

It fell quite soon, but not from heaven exactly. It came with a whiff of smoke on the wind from Paris around the middle of 1789.

2

On Calliope's Jalopy:

Epic Rebuilt 1790–1800

In the last decade of the eighteenth century, all of a sudden and it seems on every hand, a motley crew of British poets cranked up Calliope's rattletrap again. Small wonder that the vehicle emitted much steam and noise on starting, or that its fitful lurches proved wayward and short. Not only was the engine seized up with rust, but parts were hard to find and harder to mate with each other; besides, while everybody knew more or less what it was supposed to do, almost nobody had hands-on experience of how the whole contraption worked. After long disuse—punctuated as we saw in Chapter 1 by largely curatorial description of epic's proper ends in theory, illustrated by dutiful poems that read like theory by other means—the genre began reinventing itself. The order of the day was earnest fiddling, on the part of a freemasonry of poet-tinkers enjoying the mood of optimism that quickens any first whack at a big thing worth doing, whether or not the thing is done particularly well.[1] William Gifford's mock-epic *Baviad* was off the block as early as 1791 to tar and feather new poets who to his implacably conservative eye did the thing particularly badly. But in its reactionary belligerence such satire was also off the mark: work so cheerfully self-depreciatory as that of the earliest Romantic epoists was inoculated in advance against it.

Before the decade was out the best practitioners would be proving the resources of epic with much generic address, coupling romance to history

---

[1] A broader backdrop against which to view the epicizing activity of the decade is given in Paul Keen, *The Crisis of Literature in the 1790s: Print Culture and the Public Sphere* (Cambridge: Cambridge University Press, 1999). The *de facto* motto that 1790s authors hoisted on banners of literary disinterestedness—"What was good for literature was good for the nation" (85)—was readily reversible, as the next decade would show.

and torquing narrative against visionary modes in order to outline a national
mission for convulsively troubled times.[2] But of this culture-wars weaponry
the epicizing poets astir around 1790 remained innocent, or nearly. The
gadgets they brought forth remain comparatively speaking toys of culture,
wound up by their contrivers rather to go than to go anywhere special.
What else explains a curio like Ann Holmes's *An Epic Poem on Adam and Eve*
(1800), bound in a slim booklet that had room left over for "Two Ladies in
Disguise, a Short Pastoral; also The Soliloquy of a Young Lady; together
with a Poem, an Elegy, and A Vindication of Fate in Marriage: to which is
added Rules for Polite Behaviour"? Holmes's sweep in twenty-eight
printed pages from primal epic to modern etiquette is, on balance, fetching;
and yet in this amateur sampler we find in epitome the improvisatory spirit
that was concurrently galvanizing the experiments of William Blake
and Walter Savage Landor. Lively extemporization, in combination with
ill-dissembled vagueness as to what modern ends the reinvented genre
might serve, virtually ensured a naïve and hobbyistic foregrounding of
its means. The cobbled-up early-Romantic epic evinces a curiosity about
its own mechanics that, once we relax the guard of haughty generic
expectation, still at two centuries' remove can cast an infectious charm.

Where does epic come from? What are its goals? Above all, what keeps it
moving? In the 1790s these linked questions of transmission were paramount,
to judge from the omnipresence of what the eighteenth century continued
to call, with excellent cause, *epic machinery*. At a time when the groggy genre
was thawing out from neoclassical hibernation, it was of utmost moment
that it should produce, not just outward and visible bibliographic identity
papers—numbered books if not numbered lines, and beefy ranks of heroic
pentameter—but their inward and narrative counterparts as well: the extended

---

[2] The interplay between epic and romance as templates for the plotting of history furnishes a
leading argument of David Quint's important *Epic and Empire: Politics and Generic Form from Virgil to
Milton* (Princeton: Princeton University Press, 1993), which shows how the winners' narrative of epic
and the losers' narrative of romance have been respectively subjugating and sapping one an other since
the age of Augustus. That was when Virgil entailed the contest of romance with epic on all his heirs
in the practice of a genre that, as Philip Hardie postulates, "strives for totality and completion, yet is at
the same time driven obsessively to repetition and reworking": *The Epic Successors of Virgil: A Study in
the Dynamics of a Tradition* (Cambridge: Cambridge University Press, 1993) 1. See also Robert Scholes
and Robert Kellogg, *The Nature of Narrative* (New York: Oxford University Press, 1966), on the
Aeneid as "a synthetic epic, which is to say a romance in epic's clothing" (70). As relations between
epic and romance will punctuate this chapter, a scholarly caveat is in order from Stuart Curran, *Poetic
Form and British Romanticism* (New York and Oxford: Oxford University Press, 1986): the old English
metrical romances, as opposed to ballads, did not make their appearance in modern redaction until
the first years of the nineteenth century (129, 158).

invocation or simile, say, or the catalogue or consult, together with what these aggrandizing conventions stood for: human capacity tasked to the limit, and at that limit an engagement with beings of more than human scope. These last figures especially greased the wheels of epic circa 1790, performing the medial and remedial work of machinery in a double sense that involves both *means* and *meanings*. In diegetic terms, the spirits and giants and demons and allegories that pervade our inaugural Romantic-era epics are means to an end, helping the poet get things stirring with a cold jump-start or keep things lively with a fresh kick in the plot. At the same time, in exegetic terms the dominance of supernatural machinery assists the rehabilitation of epic by securing the genre's significance or—to put the matter less precisely, and thus more truly—its meaningfulness. In its gawky extremity the exact meaning of a 1790s epic might be clear, or it might not; the frequent tread of superhuman agents along its borders left no doubt that it did mean something, though, and something of high import. Machinery extras proved essential because they were badges of generic affiliation that no reader would disregard.

Consider first a few epical by-blows laid on the doorstep of the decade this chapter studies. Richard Hole gave *Arthur; or, The Northern Enchantment* (1789) not only the subtitle *A Poetical Romance in Seven Books*, but also a cast of wizards and genii that, while they may have emerged from Bishop Percy's *Reliques*, Paul Henri Mallet's *Northern Antiquities*, and other Ossianized lairs in the folkloric high country, functionally affirmed his poem's kinship with the leafier romance epics of Ariosto and Spenser.[3] A quite differently Gothic tale in verse appeared the same year from a serving-woman named Elizabeth Hands who somehow obtained subscriptions for her book from the likes of Edmund Burke, Charles Fox, and Joseph Banks. Perhaps the appeal of *The Death of Amnon: A Poem* lay in the fusion of an epic manner suited to the Old Testament (2 Samuel furnishes the matter) with the psychological interiority of a modern novel of feeling. This fusion appears in the systematic subordination of affairs of state to family matters: David and Absalom are major players but scarcely royals in any but a

---

[3] John Hoole, translator of Tasso (1764) and Ariosto (1783), had fortified his preface to the former by citing Bishop Hurd's then recent defense of "Gothic machines" against the ancient pagan ones: rpt. in *The Works of the English Poets, from Chaucer to Cowper*, vol. 21 (London: Chalmers, 1810) 391. Richard Hole's briefer Nordic excursion "The Tomb of Gunnar" (also 1789) was decorated, like his epicizing *Arthur*, "with the familiar images and diction of the sanguinary sublime" of standard eighteenth-century issue: Arthur Wawn, *The Vikings and the Victorians: Inventing the Old North in Nineteenth-Century Britain* (Cambridge: D. S. Brewer, 2000) 251; see also Rolf P. Lessenich, *Aspects of English Preromanticism* (Köln: Böhlau, 1989) 176.

celebrity sense; and the central events are covert incest, private betrayal, and personal revenge. Generic fusion also appears in Hands's principal flirtation with epic machinery, in a pivotal passage detailing Amnon's crippling guilt at having raped his sister Tamar.[4] Are the abstractions enlisted here allegorical machines, or the working vocabulary of an enlightened psychology?

> But he that dares pervert this giv'n blessing,
> To ruin and destroy their innocence,
> Shall feel pursuing vengeance, nor escape
> Her rod uplifted, nor avert the stroke.
> Conviction's sword shall pierce him, and remorse
> With all the tortures of the mind assail,
> Till he a victim falls to grim despair;
> Except repentance timely to his aid
> Come with her tears, to sooth, to mitigate;
> While her attendant hope extends a ray,
> To point where mercy spreads her healing wings.

> (3.18)

As each entrant in Hands's parade of motives strikes its emblematic attitude in place along the vengeance-to-mercy spectrum, it is tempting to impose the capital letters that might have been expected in 1789 but that Hands pointedly did without. Hers was to be a psychodrama of human passion and conscience in a practically secular world; yet, all the same, her text remains stalked by the Spenserian ghost of Grim Despair. Evidently to make a modern heart beat after biblical transplantation required prosthesis: narrative pacemakers, we might call the figures in this passage, encouraging the story towards epic amplitude as surely as the author's decision did to conduct her narration in blank verse.

Our liminal year 1789 witnessed another epicizing of Bible narrative in Elizabeth Smith's *Israel: A Poem in Four Books*, a revision of her 1787 *The Brethren: Paraphrased from Part of the History of Israel and His Family, in Holy Writ*. Here we find the poet installing what emerges all told as the '90s machinery of choice, the plummet-and-hoist of a Miltonic pulley of angels. Smith exploits the ample opportunities for dream-messaging made available by the Joseph

---

[4] These genre formations evidently express social pressures impinging on the rendition of such a theme by a woman poet, which Hands spiritedly addressed elsewhere in the volume that contained *The Death of Amnon*: see Joel Haefner, "The Romantic Scene(s) of Writing," in *Re-Visioning Romanticism: British Women Writers, 1776–1837*, ed. Haefner and Carol Shiner Wilson (Philadelphia: University of Pennsylvania Press, 1994) 265–67.

saga, and admits a single cameo appearance from the pit by the ghost of Abel, but these come as sideshows to the poem's main epic drivers, the winged descents from heaven that Gabriel tirelessly executes.[5] Richard Cumberland's *Calvary; Or the Death of Christ* (1792), manifestly a sequel to *Paradise Regained,* complemented the angel-free narrative of Milton's brief epic by reaching back further to *Paradise Lost* for its machinery of contending angelic intercessors. In *Emanuel; or, Paradise Regained: An Epic Poem* (1797) the comparably industrious but less accomplished James Ogden—author back in 1762 of *The British Lion Rous'd,* nine verse books touting naval victory in the just-concluded Seven Years' War—plodded on fecklessly for nine books more, this time in the footsteps of a great poem he had no business rewriting. Ogden did come up with one noteworthy invention, and typically for the decade it was a mechanical widget: his Satan not only fails as Milton's did to tempt Jesus, but incidentally runs into trouble from a faction of "plebeian" demons—we may as well call them the party machine, such being the democratic indignities even in Hell these days—to whom he is bureaucratically accountable (8.135–36). Erasmus Darwin's *sui generis* yet decidedly epicizing hybrid *The Botanic Garden* (1791) summoned back, for further erotic mischief, the miniature Rosicrucian machinery that had served at the beginning of the century in *The Rape of the Lock,* when Pope took quaint cover there in elemental faerie from the still-singeing radiance of Milton. By systematically incorporating so conspicuous a convention as epic machinery—seraphical, gnomish, or in between—all these poems placed themselves within a tradition that had fallen on hard times but in which they meant to claim a place, and whose devices they meant to run, it often seems, just to see what might happen.

A second poem called *Israel* appeared in two volumes at mid-decade from "Serena" (pseudonym of Sara Leigh Pike), and its subtitle *A Juvenile Poem*—disclaiming but not hiding an epic hope—is emblematic of the genre's adolescent appeal at this period. In nine cantos centered on Joseph and then sixteen on Moses, Pike sends in and then out of Egypt a nation of Israel whose providential fortunes portend Britain's at her present crisis (Introduction, 1.8, 2.16). Pike like Elizabeth Smith calls on Gabriel and other seraphic messengers *passim*; and like James Ogden she enlists, only to drop almost immediately,

---

[5] While Thomas M. Greene's classic *The Descent from Heaven: A Study in Epic Continuity* (New Haven: Yale University Press, 1963) touches on none of the epics discussed here, numerous examples from this chapter and the next attest the excellent health of the descent topos well into the Romantic era.

some Satanic troublemakers as backup for Pharaoh's slapstick wise men (2.5.37). But when narrative push comes to shove and inspiration rather than ornament is at stake, she bypasses mechanical expedients in favor of the invisible, virtually immediate agency of divine power within human breasts. God extends his own Holy Spirit to cheer Joseph up in jail (1.2), and twice expressly dispatches the same "sacred spirit" to fly "Forth from the heav'n of heav'ns" and touch Moses' soul into prophetic action (2.4.34, 2.7.57). At one early point Reuben, providentially moved "by latent springs" (1.1.20), intercedes with his brothers to spare captive Joseph's life. If those "springs" suggest the operation of a gland, not a watch, this is because Pike has already made it clear that hers is a poem in which organic feeling supervenes on mechanical contrivance.

Such a Sensibility-era synchromesh of artifice with feeling had been modeled already, albeit under the weight of a crushingly unpropitious didacticism, in a pair of evangelist epics from 1789: Joseph Swain's *Redemption: A Poem in Five Books* (eight books in the second edition, 1797) and William Gilbank's *The Day of Pentecost, or Man Restored: A Poem in Twelve Books*. The former need detain us no longer than to note that, despite Swain's prefatory disclaimer of candidacy for "EPIC BAYS" and renunciation of "the imaginary world of machinery" (xiii), his repudiation of "smiling fiction" comes in the course of an invocation to the Muse (1.4), and that his Noah can hardly spare a weather eye for the gathering Deluge, so rapt is he with its typological application: "So ride the saints secure in Christ their ark" (5.176).[6] Gilbank's poem is more interesting because more forthright in its dogmatic purpose yet also more concerned to contrive a narrative form viably suited to that purpose. A most blunt preface lays out the stainless thesis: "The principal Object of the following Work is to give a clear and comprehensive View of the Theory of our most holy Religion" (5). To this thesis, as to a mast, the poet then lashes his narrative against the tempting vagrancy of "seemingly unconnected and unmeaning incidents" (7). He does this right away by endowing his main event, the Pentecostal gift of tongues to the Apostles, with an essentially literary and exegetical bonus: "Before their open'd eyes in order fair | And long succession the bright Annals lay," such that at a typological glance "Their comprehension scann'd

---

[6] For an argument that the Protestant tradition of figural interpretation could work radicalizing effects in biblical epic see Terence Hoagwood's preface to Smith's *Brethren* (Delmar: Scholars' Facsimiles, 1991), which draws out that poem's attunement through the Joseph saga to contemporary issues like grain shortage and political liberty.

the height, the depth, | The length, the breadth, of God's unequall'd love" (2.175–82).

The rest is (sacred) history, ten full books of it. Yet by prophylactically arming his protagonists with a synopsis of the history they inhabit—total comprehension of which, we must suppose, exactly equals his own "clear and comprehensive View" of Christian doctrine—the poet has so forestalled plot with "Theory" as to render any descent of Christian machinery super-fluous, be it dove's or flame's. An epic Luddite, Gilbank whelms narrative's intermediacy by the pre-emptive infusion of truth, in which the rest of the poem can only furnish steady drill. One nice device at the very start forecasts this poem's determination to turn itself off for the reader's higher benefit. Having no more than embarked on an account of the Fall and Redemption, Gilbank remembers that he has forgotten something:

> Long had mankind
> His ignominious tyranny endur'd;
> When to fulfill——
> > But how may I presume
> To tell of truth restor'd, of bliss to man
> Regain'd; and not to my adventurous song
> Thy aid invoke, all animating Spirit,
> Essential Effluence of Deity?

(1.52–58)

Rehearsing an allusive mini-Pentecost of his own, the poet finds fulfillment not where Milton did, in the mediations of "adventurous song" as epic story, but in its obliteration by a lyric animus directly transfused. In this soberest of poems, there remains something antic about the creakily staged spontaneity that wheels an invocation in from the wings.

The whole set-up breathes a '90s spirit, such as we also find when Sara Pike's heroic couplets in *Israel* break out now and then into tetrameter quatrains, or when her earnest absorption in imagining narrative realities lets down the drawbridge of epic hauteur. "I'm Joseph!" exclaims her hero to his long-lost brothers (1.6.76); the very deity dispenses with ceremony in declaring, "For I am GOD, and there's no god but me" (2.10.82). At such intervals, as when Moses spends several lines chasing the elusively squiggly serpent that his rod keeps turning into, we can correlate this poem's childlike appeal with its curiosity about the limits of the genre it has pulled out of the attic. Pike's reluctance to send an angel on a god's errand, along with her Gilbank-like replacement of conventional epic invocation with a direct supplication to the Lord at the head of the poem (1.1), captures a decade's curiosity about the scope and powers, not just of the epic but of the poetic imagination.[7]

This Romantic curiosity was, famously, bound up with timely questions about the scope and powers of human action as such, questions that the presence of epic machinery highlighted without resolving.[8] Opening out celestial or chthonic backgrounds that far exceed the local action of the plot, the superhuman element in one obvious sense ennobles human agents; but in another sense it dwarfs them, by driving the plot over their unwitting heads and through their passive wills. It is the latter fate that, in Hole's *Arthur*, awaits the puppet protagonists Arthur and Imogen. In repelling the Saxon and Dane invaders these ostensible heroes are actually no more than playthings of a destiny worked out in advance, and by magic, in the struggle waged against the Weird Sisters and Urda by Merlin, whose commerce with a more than human world makes him the poem's hero in all but name.[9] Stranger effects arose in two contemporary epics based on recent events. In *The Conquest of Quebec: An Epic Poem in Eight Books* (1790) Henry Murphy, cleaving at a stroke through the diplomatic and strategic tangles of the late campaign in Canada, endowed his parliamentary hero Pitt with divine inspiration and rewarded his slain martial hero Wolfe with a film-strip

---

[7] Marilyn Butler, *Romantics, Rebels and Reactionaries: English Literature and its Background 1760–1830* (Oxford: Oxford University Press, 1981), forcefully arguing that the 1790s were in sum a conservative decade that cracked down on literary innovation, makes exception for forms of "the antique" that enjoyed—like the antique form of epic—a presumptive "ideological neutrality" (37–38).

[8] This point is present by implication in the enormously influential Regius lectures that Hugh Blair delivered at the University of Edinburgh and published in 1783. The great Ossian apologist knows that in "Epic Poetry" (lecture 42) machinery is strictly speaking unnecessary: Macpherson himself dispensed with it. Still, Blair allows that machinery has its uses in a genre whose purpose "is to extend our ideas of human perfection" and "where admiration and lofty ideas are supposed to reign": *Lectures on Rhetoric and Belles Lettres*, rpt. ed. Harold F. Harding (Carbondale and Edwardsville: Southern Illinois University Press, 1965) 2: 411, 424. Brian Wilkie, *Romantic Poets and Epic Tradition* (Madison and Milwaukee: University of Wisconsin Press, 1965), finds at stake in "all the seemingly superficial critical discussion of 'machinery' " an underlying sense "that human life is enacted in a setting of mystery, that somehow life derives urgency and poignancy from the darkness or vastness which surrounds and impinges on it" (9).

[9] This plotted rendezvous with destiny joins forces with what James D. Merriman points to, in the one searching assessment that Hole's poem has received, as a distinctly epic pattern of Virgilian conventions and Miltonic echoes: *The Flower of Kings: A Study of the Arthurian Legend in England between 1485 and 1835* (Lawrence: University Press of Kansas, 1973) 107–12. The poem is also appreciatively noted in Margaret Omberg, *Scandinavian Themes in English Poetry, 1760–1800* (Uppsala: Studia Anglistica Upsaliensia, 1976) 105 *et passim*.

forecast of Britain's future, projected in heaven, and in person, by Almighty God. Before grappling with Milton, that toiler James Ogden in a former epic *The Revolution: An Epic Poem, in Twelve Books* (1790) dignified the modern birth of his nation in 1688 with good and wicked angels who respectively speed and impede what both parties more or less clearly discern as a foregone conclusion, Britain's promotion under William of Orange to the vanguard of a Europe destined "to expel what remained of the Feudal System" (xiii). William's heroism is reduced, by repeated forecasts of the coming eighteenth century (books 2 and 11), to gratefully expectant passivity before the zeitgeist. This strategy rapidly and ironically redounded upon the unhappily titled poem itself, which while glancing here and there at "this Revolution in France" regarded it as no more important than 1790 news items like Russo-Turkish affairs or Britain's dispute with Spain over Gibraltar. Within a couple of years, of course, it had become unthinkable to publish as *The Revolution* a work of any kind on any topic but France. No wonder Ogden retreated to stabler biblical ground in *Emanuel* before the decade was out: his heroic prototype had incurred with exceptional haste the obsolescence that lay in wait for many another epic vehicle that would hitch its shiny wagon to the star of current events.

Such was the fate that ambushed a more circumspect poet of the day, James Brown, DD. In the preface to *Britain Preserved: A Poem: In Seven Books* (1800), Brown winds back the decade to explain with what bad luck he had in 1789 brought his *felix culpa* loyalist narrative of the American Revolution (indolent Britain's salutary wake-up call, which in rousing Pitt saved all) up to its *terminus ad quem*—only to realize during the early nineties, while on the verge of print, that events across the Channel "might seem to have turned the very Title into an absurdity, if not a satire" (xxii). Gingerly scouting the term "epic," Brown nevertheless devotes most of the preface to defending the propriety, while conceding the novelty, of accommodating "modern names, manners, characters, and actions, to the higher species of Poetry" (x), a species whose distinctive "stile and manner" as Brown describes them, together with the telltale phrase "unity of design" (xx), unmistakably mark it as the heroic poem. Nor will the severer differentia of grand style and built unity suffice, Brown has found, to get his show on the road: that work calls for heavy machinery. Thus, to make national politics live on the page (4.15–24), and to pull off the delicate trick of celebrating an ostensibly losing side, Brown has vanquished his own "strong aversion to allegory" (xiii) and foregrounded such figures as Luxury and Corruption, who loom large in books 1 and 2 as Satan's favorite instruments for the toppling of empires past their prime.

To these allegories the poet adds his own undisguised favorite, the democratic crowd-pleaser Morogogue (i.e. Captain of Fools)—alias in his several avatars Jack Straw, Wat Tyler, Jack Cade and others from centuries past, and resurgent in 1770s London in the riotous person of General Gordon. Less a conceptual allegory than a recurrent disorder within the life cycle of states, in this poem of firm political orthodoxy Morogogue anticipates the sort of visionary historical function that Blake was elaborating for radical purposes at just the same time. And, again like Blake, and such brothers in '90s radicalism as will greet us in Landor and Robert Southey, Brown displays a lively sense of analogy between "unity of design" in the smooth operation of an epic and in the principles of government. Britain's nadir in the American conflict proceeds

> by blank defect
> Of one great guiding mind, fit to combine
> The jarring wheels, and to one end direct
> The various movements of the vast machine.
>
> (5.248–51)

Fittingly this defect is supplied by a statesman whose patron is none other than the god of poetry: "A PITT, with all APOLLO's youthful fire," arises to slay "the Python, PARTY" (6.706–09) and ushers in an age when the exportation to Cathay, Africa, South America, and even France of a free British order— disciplined by rigorous speech and press censorship (7.129)—will foreshadow the millennium, under a deity higher than Apollo far.

This wheezing finale betrays Brown's trouble, characteristic for his era, in getting the available spare parts of allegory and history, paganism and Christianity, to engage with each other and with current events. Over the long haul of the long nineteenth century, traditional epic machinery proved better suited to the treatment of traditional epic material, where the enchantment of historical distance let an enlarged human heroism more nearly hold its own. It was the commerce of history with transcendence that lay at the heart of Cumberland's sacred theme in *Calvary*, where the angelic reciprocations of epic enginery let him finesse the potential sacrilege of depicting Jesus Christ as either too merely human a hero, or too clearly (and too soon) something much more than that. Just this dilemma of heroic definition exercises Cumberland's Judas Iscariot, who like the Satan of *Paradise*

Regained seems half a reader of the poem he is in, and betrays Jesus out of an insatiable need to know whether he is the Christ, and thus to what order of epic being he belongs: man or, as it were, machine (3.162–70). The special case of Judas throws into relief a tendency from which he constitutes an interesting partial exception: the tendency of epic machinery to render human agency instrumental, indeed to *automate* it. In the hands of poor authors—and they will be always with us in the pages ahead—this tendency was chiefly an unplanned consequence of invoking supernatural powers to quicken a stalled narrative, or merely to get from one episode to the next. But its persistence among skilled authors who had other choices at their disposal suggests that in the pre-emption of agency by epic machinery they were probing, by inherited ancient means, vividly modern questions about human freedom, in its relation to what the eighteenth century had identified as *inter alia* the laws of society, the mechanical operation of the spirit, and the biological drives.

It was this last set of constraints that the epic animus of Darwin's *Botanic Garden* pointedly addressed, defining the human condition not from the top down but from the bottom up. In part 1, *The Economy of Vegetation*, his exuberant machines of salamander, gnome, nymph, and sylph figure respectively the astronomical, geological, hydrological, and meteorological determinants of biological life. Part 2, *The Loves of the Plants* (written first in 1789), then offers an interpretation of this life that is cast exclusively in terms of sexual reproduction. The poem's bipartite, four-cantos-apiece structure follows the ingenious polymorphism of vegetable love—the botanical apparatus of sexual reproduction—across Carolus Linnaeus' exhaustive and amazing tabulation, in books that Darwin had just translated from Latin into English, of its efflorescent permutation. The mischief behind Darwin's poker-faced scientific innocence in retailing such matters lay in the way he flushed out the human imagination from its hiding place in Enlightened objectivity. Each birds-and-bees coupling is knowingly troped in *Homo sapiens* terms as a more or less decorous orgy of trysting beaux and belles, the extended conceits gathered into a vast bouquet of similes.

Were these similes epic similes? Were Darwin's vehicular mechanics an epic machinery? No, inasmuch as they amplified no continuous narrative (the poem has none).[10] Yes, inasmuch as Darwin, by proffering an account both elemental and comprehensive of life's great *sine qua non*, was implicating

[10] Alan Liu, *Wordsworth: The Sense of History* (Stanford: Stanford University Press 1989), reads the epic similes that Wordsworth "embedded within description" a few years later in *The Prelude* as "signs of a repressed narrative" and components of "a preemptive strategy" impeding the thrust towards

humanity fully within what his grandson Charles with admirable family loyalty would call the *mechanism* of sexual and natural selection. From our distant literary-historical endzone of 1910 the literary historian and quondam mock-epoist W. J. Courthope looked back across Darwin's long century to find in *The Botanic Garden* a work of strict science whose poet "employed his imagination, analytically, for the discovery of principles adequate to explain the mechanical forces of Nature."[11] Mechanical forces, indeed: where mechanism was all, it behoved the hot-rodding, radically scientific imagination to strip the generic pageant-wagon down for action to a chassis of machinery and nothing but.

Thus Erasmus Darwin, like his classic original Lucretius, told no extended epic story but instead honored the Enlightenment by reciting the order of things, the *Rerum Natura*. Reciprocal principles of random sampling and associative juxtaposition let the poet recruit into his catalogical text a congeries of matters, histories, manufactures, and institutions as old as humanity and as diverse as the planet. At the same time, though, he could implicitly claim to be telling the story behind all stories. After all, what was the point of salience on which Darwin focused—without a blush, indeed with something like a pornographer's exuberance in variation—but the same episodic climax towards which the *Odyssey* and most of its romance-plotted successors in epic and fiction have always built, and without which there would of course be no stories to tell or hearers to care?[12] In its impudence of execution, from the lightly slumbering wit of couplet rhyme right up to the sumptuous finery of *beaux-arts* illustrated elegance, *The Botanic Garden* was at once acclaimed, and from reactionary quarters just as correctly decried, as the subversive work of a revolutionary sympathizer. Yet in the reductiveness of its biological imperative the poem underscored constraints on human agency

allegorical meaning (580, 128). That Darwin dismissed such meaning out of hand does not mean that his brash charivari did not teach the soberest, and subtlest, of Romantics a poetic trick or two to play with natural history.

[11] W. J. Courthope, *A History of English Poetry*, vol. 6 (London: Macmillan 1910) 35. The pervasion of Darwin's biological thinking by mechanical models is discussed by Maureen McNeil, "The Scientific Muse: The Poetry of Erasmus Darwin," in *Languages of Nature: Critical Essays on Science and Literature*, ed. L. J. Jordanova (London: Free Association, 1986) 164–203. Despite an unsteady grasp of *machinery* in its specifically poetic sense—due perhaps to the attention Darwin pays to industrial machines in *The Botanic Garden*—the linkage McNeil finds among "the pathetic fallacy, personification, and machinery" (200) remains suggestive.

[12] Jon Mee, *Dangerous Enthusiasm: William Blake and the Culture of Radicalism in the 1790s* (Oxford: Clarendon, 1992) 145–56, places Darwin in the context of Richard Payne Knight's scandalously speculative 1786 *Discourse on the Worship of Priapus*, and Blake's illuminated art of comic strip tease in the context of both.

no less binding than those that contemporary epics of a more conventional sort, and a more conservative program, were mechanically imposing from above by *deus ex machina* means.[13]

The naughty narrative abeyance of Darwin carried to an extreme one feature that each of these early Romantic epics also manifests: the practice of departing from the main plot into a visionary mode from which that main plot is comprehended anew and at large. In Hole's *Arthur* the mode is Spenserian dream, when the entranced Merlin receives from an allegorically decorated "Genius of the Isle" assurances of Prince Arthur's future glory, and thereby of Britain's. In *The Thymbriad* (1794), a capable seven-book blank-versification of Xenophon's *Cyropædia*, Sophia Burrell pauses midway in the textbook exhibition of Cyrus' ideal heroism to dally, romance-fashion, with a poetic hermit who has renounced status and fame at court, embraces pacificism and science, and sounds, in fact, a bit like Erasmus Darwin: "by Nature charm'd | I court the Muses, to record *her* praise" (4.84). Burrell's will to show what, against steep odds, "a female pen" might do in martial mode made her adhere closely to neoclassical epic convention. Yet her confession that in grappling with warfare "I find myself beguil'd | Far in a labyrinth" (6.129) chimes uncannily with the romance detour into anti-war sentiment that she planted at the epic center.[14] Likewise Ann Yearsley in *Brutus: A Fragment* (leadoff poem from her 1796 *The Rural Lyre*) sends the Troy- and Italy-emigrant Brutus, his wayfaring and military conquests dispatched in under five hundred lines, off at the end into the woods of romance, there to mate with a conveniently shipwrecked Trojan lass who will mother his British dynasty. Their union is no less plausible than those Yearsley effects at the ideological level between the allegory of Liberty and the counter-revolutionary imperative to "order" and "union" (178–88); or at the level of genre between epic accomplishment (history as done deal) and romance potentiality (Britain's future as the stuff of desire, a wonder in the making).[15]

---

[13] Richard Cronin, *The Politics of Romantic Poetry: In Search of the Pure Commonwealth* (Houndmills: Macmillan, 2000) 29–47, assesses what we might call first-generation social Darwinism: the libertine materialism of *The Botanic Garden* unwittingly anticipates an order of industrial mechanization whose human toll the poet's own machinery excuses him from imagining.

[14] Adeline Johns-Putra, "Gendering Telemachus: Anna Seward and the Epic Rewriting of Fénelon's *Télémaque*," in *Approaches to the Anglo and American Female Epic, 1620–1982*, ed. Bernard Schweizer (Aldershot: Ashgate, 2006) 85–97, a little unfairly brandishes Burrell's conformism (*Telemachus*, 1794) as foil to the softer Sensibility traits of Seward's freely translated fragment from 1779. Seward's *Louisa, a Poetical Novel* (1784) marked out early a new generic pressure from which the' 90s epic in its main tendency swerved away, but to which our story in these chapters will have regular reference.

[15] On these definitive binaries see Donna Landry, *The Muses of Resistance: Laboring-Class Women's Poetry in Britain, 1739–1796* (Cambridge: Cambridge University Press, 1990) 175.

The poet's own epic accomplishment in *Brutus* bespeaks that of the decade, regarded as a generic forge: Yearsley's preface "offers this humble specimen as a spark, from whence she wishes a body of fire may arise in the imagination of some more able Poet" (p. 1). In abler poets' hands and in worse, during the 1790s epic kept flickering in and out of life as constituent literary modes were struck sparkishly together or just dully lumped. The *Lumpenepos* we have met already in the likes of Swain and Gilbank. Cumberland attempts something more interesting in *Calvary*, where with the conclusion of the action in book 6 the poetic mode alters entirely and from a sermonic exegesis of the last words of Christ the poet ascends to two final books that mingle, like the last two of *Paradise Lost*, prophetic overview with theological gloss. Murphy attempts the same at the death of General Wolfe in *The Conquest of Quebec*, though the shortness of elapsed time gives his hero little to look forward to but, bathetically, the promised reign of the sitting King George III. None of these gear-shifts in narrative mode is executed deftly; they all remain *mechanical* in a pejorative as well as a descriptive sense. Still, the common endeavor they represent serves notice that epic survived the eighteenth century as a structure not monolithic, *pace* its theorists, but composite. In practice it disclosed a dynamic of interior differentiation that even relatively inexpert poets were alert to, and that the best poets of the rising generation would within a few years be exploiting under the crystallizing pressure exerted on the national imagination by events in France and reactions at home.

William Blake was the first among these poets in every respect save that which a public can pay—since as an epoist he had no public to speak of. His *French Revolution* (1791) was the earliest British application of epic's cultural-political resources to the most ostentatiously eligible of current events, the Revolution that we have seen overtaking James Ogden's poem and then James Brown's. In the same exploratory spirit Blake returned for years afterward to the drawing board, producing on almost an annual basis model prototypes in the form of radically experimental epyllia: *Visions of the Daughters of Albion* and *America a Prophecy* in 1793, *Europe a Prophecy* and *The [First] Book of Urizen* in 1794, and in 1795 *The Song of Los*, *The Book of Los*, and *The Book of Ahania*. Blake undertook these Lambeth prophecies or pocket epics as sample episodes of an as-yet inchoate larger design that was not so much promised as it was heuristically postulated, in token of the vastness of canvas that the artist's vision implied from the very beginning. That larger vision saw the light of publication only in later decades with *Milton* (1804–08?) and *Jerusalem*

(1804–20?), works of much wider scope that later chapters will consider alongside others contemporary with their completion. Still, in tracing here Blake's progress from the trial epyllion to that manuscript epic-in-perpetual-progress *Vala* (1797–1807?), it is essential that we bear the larger project in mind, as did the poet himself.

So marked, indeed, is the epic ambition of Blake, and so lovingly studied by twentieth-century scholarship, that we risk overlooking the peculiarity, and thus the significance, of its existing at all. For what this painter–engraver had to show in images, the British visual arts lay open, and at a high point of their development, in history painting foremost among other media. For what he had to say in words, he might and did turn ringingly to manifestos, lyrics, epigrams, and other literary forms that demanded minimal narrative investment. Blake had a redemptive vision of wrathful prophecy, which his *Songs* and *The Marriage of Heaven and Hell* expressed in forms of an unsurpassed meditative depth and polemical impact. Yet clearly these were not enough; his was a vision that needed *telling* as well as showing. (To leave unrecounted an indignation such as fueled Blake's unstoppable output was, "A Poison Tree" warns, to risk embroilment in a worsening plot: "I told it not, my wrath did grow.") Blake's compulsion not just to portray or declare but to *narrate* arose, we should suppose, because narrative as such—the personal and collective histories we inherit and transmit—formed part of his vision's substance. He was a history painter with radical ideas, about history and depiction alike, that demanded illustration in a written temporality. Spelling out his vision entailed imagining the scene of storytelling again and again, interrogating the processes of narrative in a critical dialectic for which the rich if jumbled resources of epic during the 1790s offered the widest field to radical art.

Murphy's *Quebec* had gone back a generation for its theme but had trouble maintaining a viable epic distance. Blake went back in *The French Revolution* to the day before yesterday, and yet as a piece of reportage the poem feels reverse-telescopically remote, projecting its newsreel footage against long tracking shots of panoramic scope that encourage a *sub specie aeternitatis* regard. The promissory subtitle, *A Poem in Seven Books*—false in its promise, since "Book the First" is all Blake wrote—feeds this same sense that what we see is much less than what by implication we should be getting. Against a set of shifting scenic backdrops that render France emphatically a *land*, this version of the epic parliament (the conventional episode, that is, which gets the early books of the *Iliad* and *Paradise Lost* going) is a sequence of freestanding arias that induce impressive tremors but educe no reply. None of the orating French nobles listens to his peers; as a result the poem bypasses the traditional debaters' exchange of views in favor of a contest among visions.[16]

We might attribute this odd, energetic stasis to novice ineptitude, were it not that a contest among visions remained central to the epic writing that this novice was expertly to pursue for the next three decades. The inertia of the *ancien régime*, whereby in line 1 "The dead brood over Europe," has not dissipated by the final page, where "The enormous dead, lift up their pale fires" (302); what light Blake's lurid sequence of speeches does emit, however, has arisen from just such acts of imagination as generate these very personifications of the burden of the past. There are giants working in the earth of France as it labors to bring forth the human. Revolutionary emancipation of the "Hands, head, bosom, and parts of love" (185) calls for freshly humanized representation of both the body politic as it might be and the body under political regimentation as it is, its millennial subjection made perceptible by art:

> The saw, and the hammer, the chisel, the pencil, the pen, and the instruments
> Of heavenly song sound in the wilds once forbidden, to teach the laborious plowman
> And shepherd.
>
> (231–32)

Pastoral shepherd and georgic plowman can work free of the oppressions of unconscious custom once an epic vision draws those oppressions forth, subsuming their blinkered genres and casting them, with the plots that sustain them, out into the open for all to see.

It is this conviction about the epic publication of truth that fuels Blake's else puzzling mania during the 1790s for the articulation of one no-win scenario after another. In *Visions of the Daughters of Albion* we find much oratory but scant dialogue, and precious little that can be called dialectic in any sense that portends progress out of sexual impasse. In *America* liberation is a *fait accompli*, in *Europe* a fat chance, and in both prophecies the living behave in so dazed a way

---

[16] P. H. Butter finds in this first Blakean lay's "eloquent expression of contrary visions" the seed of the illuminated epics to come: "Blake's *The French Revolution*," *Yearbook of English Studies* 19 (1989) 19. In larger view, Blake's perspectivism early and late may be understood as a mechanism for coping with the dilemma that, according to E. M. W. Tillyard, made British epic impossible after the French Revolution, since "once you let it in you became a partisan and had no chance of being the steady and settled voice of a large body of men. Or, if you tried to be reasonable, you risked being tame or at least unwarmed by the proper epic fire": *The English Epic and its Background* (London: Chatto & Windus 1954) 529.

that the most vital prospect is that of arousing the dead: "The Grave shrieks with delight... | Her bosom swells with wild desire" (*Song of Los*, plate 7). Nowadays the dead are the ones who, not unlike the dry bones of the epic genre, preserve the "desires of ancient times" (*America*, plate 15) yet who by the same token tie desire up, engrossing energies that might be better invested in living. These observations are descriptions, not complaints—on my part, and also on the part of the poet-prophet, whose trial epics systematically stymie narrative in order to activate perspective instead.[17] Blake focused his lays of the '90s not on history but on historiography as he conceived it: the juxtapositive study of history's constructed and competing versions. Because historiography makes history in a double sense—shaping the record of the past, also clarifying the inherited dynamic whose present momentum preludes the future—its work was prophetic of any epic work of larger scope. That is why Blake wrote so many of these minor prophecies, and why they internally consist of visions at loggerheads with each other, or else encumbered by technical difficulties that rivet attention on the faulty machinery of their transmission. The case of "the stern Bard" who smashes his harp to pieces, "asham'd of his own song" (*America*, plate 2), paradigmatically literalizes what keeps happening by other means in these poems where energy is spent to the point of exhaustion but nothing proceeds.

We shall see how characteristic of the decade this narrative deadlock of Blake's was when, in chapters ahead, we take up the longer-plotted and more fully moralized epics he engraved after 1800. In the meantime we can see how radical a break with eighteenth-century modes was effected by that 1790s spirit of which Blake was but the freest exponent, if we compare his noisy patterns of self-interference with such a narrative modesty as governs Mary Scott's 1788 *Messiah: A Poem, in Two Parts*. Here was the life of Christ, conveyed in suitably heroic couplets, yet with as little attention as possible

---

[17] The point is elaborated by Joseph A. Wittreich, Jr., in " 'Sublime Allegory': Blake's Epic Manifesto and the Milton Tradition," *Blake Studies* 4 (1972): the way to make epic poems "convert upward into a mythology rather than downward in history" is by "ignoring their narrative and concentrating on their vision," and thus discarding "the Aristotelian notion of imitative action" in favor of "the unity of design" (22, 30–31). Robert Essick, *William Blake and the Language of Adam* (Oxford: Clarendon, 1989) 121, likewise distinguishing historical from universal frames of reference, finds Blake chiastically intercrossing the two by simile and personification, so as ultimately to break the distinction down. See also Ronald L. Grimes, "Time and Space in Blake's Major Prophecies," in *Blake's Sublime Allegory: Essays on* The Four Zoas, Milton, Jerusalem, ed. Stuart Curran and Joseph A. Wittreich (Madison: University of Wisconsin Press, 1973): "vision is none other than the breaking down of strict chronological and causal sequences," so that "each event is a 'miracle' in the sense that its cause is not immediately evident" (64).

to the biographical ministry of Jesus. Scott takes much interest in prophetic anticipations of her Messiah, and in his preparative years in childhood, at baptism, and in the wilderness (part 1); then part 2 leaps to Gethsemane, Calvary, the Resurrection, and the Gentile conversions that launched the history of the church. What fills the space between is neither parable nor miracle, but Christian doctrine, expounded in a discursive mode lying outside narrative altogether: the mode that, as we saw, Gilbank actually privileged one year later in *The Day of Pentecost*, but had the generic tact to frame out typologically into narrative.

When an early note of Mary Scott's cites "Mr. *Hayley*'s animated exhortation to Mr. *Mason* to write a national Epic Poem" (from the verse tractatus of 1785 that we glimpsed in Chapter 1), she means to disclaim either arms or the man as themes to which her muse is suited, in observance of a gender decorum that many a woman epoist would follow. Curiously, though, in eliding the life of the man of sorrows Scott lays claim to a daunting master-narrative of Christian history past and future, one that empowers her to turn prophetess and "enfold" Hayley's mere nationalism in an international ecumenism that is yet to be (2.18, 412–23). Blake taught resistance to bigotry and warfare as earnestly as Mary Scott and William Gilbank did. But for Blake narrative was not the alternative to teaching that it was for them, nor was it in vast historical outline the doctrinal lesson taught. Instead, it was the very means of instruction, and it involved among other things unlearning nearly everything that an account like theirs had presupposed.

Blake sent epic narrative not off to the sidelines but out on strike. And the epic point of his tirelessly replayed work stoppage was, ultimately, human re-creation. Matters had come to the sorry pass of the 1790s—oppression, revolution, terror, reaction, oppression renewed—through the perceptual lockdown and channeling that were wrought by a set of pervasive cultural narratives pivoting on domination and submission, crime and sacrifice. These narratives, prominent in traditional epic "Bibles or sacred codes," on one hand were long since dead, being congealed "forms of worship" that had once been "poetic tales" (*Marriage*, plates 4 and 11); on the other hand they were stories that refused to die, showing a resilient capacity to co-opt dissent by absorption into their ancient, mythic, categorical strength. Blake's steady aim was to reclaim alliance with the one power that was older still than these old stories, and stronger because it had made them to begin with: the creative imagination. His epically calisthenic work of the '90s compassed this aim by deliberate wreckage, throwing the switch of narrative transmission only to contrive interruption of its circuitry, through the juxtaposition of equivalent generic components that were internally consistent with themselves but incompatible with each other. "Unity is the cloke of Folly," Blake grumbled in his late glossa "On Homer's Poetry" (1820); and "Those who will have Unity exclusively in Homer come out with a Moral like a sting in the tail" (*Writings*, ed. Bentley, p. 668). The alternative he had worked out twenty years earlier was to implant a sting in the tale, to moralize the narrative act as such. The failures of dialogue, wrenchings of scenic perspective, and explosions of normal plotting in his 1790s lays bespeak an epic program of cultural sabotage.

Narrative conducted according to this program might render "the historical fact in its poetical vigour," in a way that a conventional account's "dull round of probabilities and possibilities" never could (*Descriptive Catalogue*, 1809: "Number V. The Ancient Britons"). If, as Blake went on to say, "the history of all times and places is nothing else but improbabilities and impossibilities," then the way to alert minds to "miracle or prodigy" was to break the round of customary association. Discontinuous, porous, mutually infiltrating story lines might keep faith, furthermore, with the eldest traditions of epic as advanced scholarship in Blake's day was learning to read them. Wolf's 1795 *Prolegomena ad Homerum* was deploying the tools of critical philology to unstitch the *Iliad* into patchworked scraps of bardic song.[18] Blake's *Los* and *Ahania*, published that same year, were attempting something of the same kind in reverse. When Blake's marginalia to Bishop Watson's 1797 *Apology for the Bible* adduced the *Iliad* and "the acts of Moses," along with "the *Edda* of Iceland the Songs of Fingal the accounts of North American Savages (as they are calld)," as works fabricated "by Inspiration" (*Writings*, ed. Bentley, pp. 1413–15), he had been to school with the bishops of a generation before—Robert Lowth, Richard Hurd, Thomas Percy (see Ch. 1)—whose respective analytic recoveries of scripture, chivalric romance, and national balladry had been conducted not in spite of the strangeness of those texts but on account of it.[19]

---

[18] Paul Fry detects a drop in Homeric prestige consequent on Wolf's work. "The fact is, Homer simply was not mentioned or thought about as often as he was before the 1790s": "Classical Standards in the Period," in *The Cambridge History of Literary Criticism*, vol. 5, ed. Marshall Brown (Cambridge: Cambridge University Press, 2000) 19. The evidence of epics from this decade suggests that discouragement of the ideal of an original Homer's unsurpassable genius gave fresh heart to the ingenious, the literary engineers of whom Blake was *primus inter pares*.

[19] Thus Ian Balfour, *The Rhetoric of Romantic Prophecy* (Stanford: Stanford University Press, 2002), calls *prophetic*—in a sense of that term plainly derived from the eighteenth-century episcopacy (Hurd revising Warburton)—a manifestly Blakean "resistance to narrative, a resistance to inscribing the prophetic performative into a narrative that would resolve all difficulties into a coherent story"

Blake's recuperative program is carried out with greatest clarity in *The [First] Book of Urizen* and at greatest length in his doomed, unengraved *fin-de-siècle* masterpiece *Vala, or, The Death and Judgement of the Ancient Man; A Dream of Nine Nights*—alias after 1804 *The Four Zoas*—two works the instability of whose very titles reflects their narrative procedures. *Urizen* was Blake's first extended exercise in redrafting the book of Genesis, a venture doubly subversive. Not only does his Jehovah figure (Urizen) in the name of creation wreak havoc within an order of life that preexists his meddling fiat; the very imagination of such a preexisting order invalidates his claim to an absolute authority grounded in absolute originality. To impute motives like anxiety and attributes like cunning, or for that matter courage, to a *soi-disant* [First] Cause is to subvert its claim to serene primacy. Blake spoils Urizen's creation myth, conforming it instead to a Virgilian (thus epically belated, romance-tinged) pattern of exile, wandering, and compensatory foundation. Urizen remains indisputably heroic, in his own book and Blake's *Book* too, although in the latter he must share the palm with the more emotionally complex and further romance-estranged heroism of Los, sorrowing pity connoisseur and exasperated engineer for damage-control ("Truth has bounds. Error none": *Book of Los*, plate 4); and with the terminally belated sentimental heroism of Orc, the man of feeling reduced to an enraged Gothic neuron firing at random into the dark. That none of these protagonists comes to good has much to do with the fact that none proves to be the proactive originator he fancies himself. The reactive posture of each is made plain both by the generic antecedents he unwittingly mimics and by the ragged but continuous plot line in which he is obliviously, often wilfully, stuck. Everybody does hard labor under the burden of the past, or rather of his own seriously flawed version of the past as self-sculpted, form-fitting history. The frantic, defensive maintenance of this identity fiction becomes for each protagonist an end in itself, which blocks access not just to others' presence but to free participation in the present as such.

To call Blake's strategy of exposure in *Urizen* mock-epic is to see that he shares with those mockers Pope and Swift at the start of the century a certain irony-grounding stake in the truth: the fixed, real account of things that poets know but that heroes, dunce-like, don't. It is to suspect, therefore,

(105). See also James Rieger, " 'The Hem of Their Garments': The Bard's Song in *Milton*," in Curran and Wittreich, *Essays*, 278, on the way "a narrative sequence that runs counterclockwise, as it were, to that of the fable itself" bears out Lowth's ideas about prophecy; and Mee, *Dangerous Enthusiasm*, 23–25, on the fine-weave prosodic reproduction of such resistance in a syntactic parallelism like that which Lowth had analyzed in Hebrew verse.

that the comparative clarity of this epic lay was obtained on premises inconsistent with its deeper visionary radicalism. With all such inconsistency Blake in *Vala* made as total a break as can well be imagined. This massive work in nine Nights, which the poet could not bring himself to publish and which several thorough scholars declare (without pejoration) cannot strictly speaking be *read* at all, unfurls at epic length the interference patterns typical of Blake's minor prophetic epyllia.[20] The entire plot is neither entire nor a plot. Rather, it is a tissue of competing visions cast as narratives of origin, within which the accounts of catastrophe advanced by Tharmas, Urizen, Urthona, and others, together with the blame they shed and the plans they imply, display not only the usual built-in Blakean mutual discrepancy but a new narratological wrinkle: now the rival stories have become aware of one another and strive for mastery through tactics of mutual nesting, infiltration, outflanking, and parody. The plot, as we say, thickens. What results is a dense narrative ecology that seems to have mastered Blake himself (two completely different seventh Nights survive in manuscript) and that left all prospect of an emergent master narrative far behind. The old epic invocation *Say first, O Muse, what cause* is a command that defies execution here. Despite a general acknowledgment of the fallenness of the present and a universal thirst for redemption, there is no knowing where to begin the work of repair, because there is no ground for agreement as to when or even whence the fall began.[21] There are only stories—quest, strife, foundation, intrigue, played out at levels concurrently marital, national, and cosmic— subgenres to which the traditionally hospitable warehouse of epic has been crowbarred open, in *Vala*, for no end of plunder and stash.

Where there is only fiction, only invention, the security of judgment is precluded. Not that the poem is without plenty of critique or that any of the squabbling Zoas hesitates to point an accusatory finger; but Blake's principled

---

[20] The incoherentist case is made forcefully by Donald Ault, "Re-Visioning *The Four Zoas*," in *Unnam'd Forms: Blake and Textuality*, ed. Nelson Hilton and Thomas A. Vogler (Berkeley: University of California Press, 1986) 105–39, and exhaustively in his *Narrative Unbound: Re-Visioning Blake's* The Four Zoas (Barrytown: Station Hill, 1987). See also Kathryn S. Freeman, *Blake's Nostos: Fragmentation and Nondualism in* The Four Zoas (Albany: SUNY Press, 1997).

[21] As Fred Dotort observes in *The Dialectic of Vision: A Contrary Reading of William Blake's* Jerusalem (Barrytown: Station Hill Arts, 1998), the harder you look at *Vala*, "the more difficult it becomes to find any event that does not depend on the preexistence of another event . . . in a never-resolving cycle" (35). George Anthony Rosso, Jr., *Blake's Prophetic Workshop: A Study of* The Four Zoas (Lewisburg: Associated University Presses, 1993), interprets such cycling as readerly drill: the design "to pit the prophetic and rationalist versions of Creation on a collision course, and to keep *repeating* the collisions, night after night"—the latter version locking into form what the former opens as fluent myth—obliges the reader (again repeatedly) to take a stand (63, 135).

abdication of narrative mastery meant loosening the normative controls that had figured so largely in the eighteenth century's standard valorization of epic, as a form maximizing both matter and the order to which that matter is judicially subdued within a plot. Nevertheless, it is towards Judgment that the mob scene of *Vala* wholly surges. The poem ends, in Night the Ninth, with the first of the great genre-busting scenes of apocalypse that are the glories of Blakean epic. That revisionary Judgment is a judgment on narrative: not a verdict against storytelling, but a moratorium on totalizing vistas of the kind whose fictive comprehensiveness all the foregoing bicker and smoke have shown to be bankruptingly dear.[22]

> Urizen said, I have Erred & my Error remains with me
> What Chain encompasses in what Lock is the river of light confind
> That issues forth in the morning by measure & the evening by carefulness
> Where shall we take our stand to view the infinite & unbounded
> Or where are human feet for Lo our eyes are in the heavens

(9.21–25)

The last two wonderful lines not only highlight Urizen's delusional, dictatorial *métier*—monopoly on an alleged unwobbling objectivity—but also quiz their own residually complacent rhetoric. By swift yet graded declension, our archetypal control freak's concession to the flow of the unforeseen emerges as his rhetorical questions dissolve into genuine ones, and thence into declarative epiphany. Even every Blakean's favorite perspectivist metaphor of the standpoint gets swept off its feet, to go the apocalyptic way of all tropes. "Where are human feet?" is a real not a rhetorical query; and merely to pose it brings on a renewal of vision, an infinite unbinding of "view" beyond stance or advantage.

Yet not beyond measure.[23] The fourteener line that Blake embraced as a sign of epic vernacularity (the folk ballad's four-by-three joined in a flexible seven-beat unit) offers a breathtaking juncture when the mid-line apostrophe

---

[22] On Blake's vista-juggling see Morton D. Paley, *The Apocalyptic Sublime* (New Haven and London: Yale University Press, 1986) 121, 171. As Grimes puts it, "Urizen does not seek a new perspective; he seeks to be outside of perspective" (80)—an impossible dilemma on which in the next passage we see Blake's favorite fall guy tripping up in the very effort to get out of it. According to Andrew M. Cooper, *Doubt and Identity in Romantic Poetry* (New Haven and London: Yale University Press, 1988), the Zoas rehearse Blake's own frustration with the ineluctable inadequacy of formal embodiment as such (55–56).

[23] See the appreciation of metrical tradition and renewal in William Kumbier, "Blake's Epic Meter," *Studies in Romanticism* 17 (1978) 163–92. He finds in the '90s lays an inventory of "concise poetic formulations of crucial moments in his myth, which function much like epic formulae," which Blake joins, as Homer did his metrical epithets, into the longer lines of the major prophecies

"for Lo" hands Urizen's curiosity about grounding premises over to sudden, delighted revelation. Where are human feet? Listen up: they're right here, in a pulsation of verse that restores the full presence from which we unaccountably prefer to turn aside, like Blake's addled heroes, and tell each other stories about how terrifically we lost it once upon a time. The late resolution of Urizen's sight neither presupposes nor entails absolution from his past. He erred, and his error "remains with him"; he would not be Urizen without it, for it remains that through which he sees. He cannot let it go, but he can now for once let it be. Leaving the story of his story alone lets this most isolated of the Zoas reclaim human fellowship, offering "my Error" in exchange for "our eyes."

This humanizing moment furnishes occasion to remark that difficult clarification of Blake's which links his epic work of the 1790s most closely to his contemporaries': namely, the role that his machinery of "Visionary Forms Dramatic" plays in the delineation of the human condition and imagination of a human prospect.[24] The Zoas, Emanations, Spectres and company are both more than human and less. Like the gods of Homeric epic, they can represent historical forces, ethical ideals, bodily and psychic drives. We have encountered these options already in the machinery fabricated by epoists contemporary with Blake; what is extraordinary about Blake in this regard is that he treats them evenhandedly, as if outer and inner compulsions possessing macro sweep and micro intimacy are all one, constraints whose demands must be reckoned with yet by the same token must be challenged. Sometimes indeed Blake's giant forms play all these parts at once; and yet, however they are read, they never cease behaving (again as with Homer's pantheon) like men and women laboring under difficulties and in pursuit of purposes that are defined by their relations with each other. The higher naïveté in which the reading of Blake offers constant training on one hand keeps faith with the *Aha!*

(169–70). See also, on the vernacular politics of Blake's chosen measures, David Punter, "Blake: Social Relations of Poetic Form," *Literature and History*, 8 (1982) 182–205; David Fuller, *Blake's Heroic Argument* (London: Croom Helm, 1988) 90–92.

[24] In a letter of 25 April 1803 to Thomas Butts, Blake announces his having composed an "immense number of verses on One Grand Theme Similar to Homers Iliad or Miltons Paradise Lost the Persons & Machinery intirely new to the Inhabitants of Earth (some of the Persons Excepted)" (*Writings*, ed. Bentley, 1572). The parenthetic retraction is funny, and revealing too: persons come and persons go—in Blake's epics they certainly do—but when it comes to patent machinery this son of the 1790s yields to nobody. Stewart Crehan, *Blake in Context* (Dublin: Gill and Macmillan, 1984), correlates the attenuation of "machinery" in the classical sense with that of the "god-hero-people division" it traditionally underwrote (292): a Romantic-era development resisted, for that very reason, by many an angel and demon from the reactionary epics these chapters discuss.

spirit of an inventive decade, while on the other hand pursuing curiosity (about, *inter alia*, what machinery and other epic means may mean) to ethical depths of which his contemporaries in the genre seldom suspected the existence.

The allegorical promiscuity of personages who can mean so many things on so many levels is simultaneously oppressive and liberating.[25] The same overdetermination that can crush and fatigue interpretation can also set it free, just as inversely Blake's revolutionary insistence that the human condition is man-made can either give the mind wings or shackle it more firmly than ever within the designer manacles itself has forged. There are no proper men or women in the 1790s prophecies (except Albion and Jerusalem, both well out of the way and under apocalyptic wraps) because Blake's constant aim is to discern the human condition as one of unrealized possibility; because, in other words, there are no proper men or women in the world. Not any more. Or not yet. With his obstreperous homemade machinery Blake meant to educe the human: if he could but wake the dead, he just might succeed in alerting the living, now or in decades ahead, to what precious opportunities lay before them.[26]

At about the time Blake went into training for *Vala*, a book-length epic was conceived, written, and elegantly published by the one contemporary who matched him in stamina and output, the future poet laureate Robert Southey. Southey will be with us as often as any epoist these chapters treat. He was a writer of talent, who has been eclipsed in our literary histories by writers of genius. But his talent, while no match for the immense ambition that impelled it, more than suffices to distinguish him from Hole, Murphy, Cumberland and all the tertiary fry who teemed in the Romantic period's heroic shoals. Had Southey not been good, he would never have drawn out Byron's satirical best in *The Vision of Judgment*, which is where most readers

[25] Geoffrey Hartman's insight into matters Blakean is to be valued the more because it proceeds from puzzled antipathy: "These decomposing and recomposing gods, these expanding and contracting metamorphs, display recognizable human emotions on a sublime stage that leaves nothing to the imagination because it is the imagination." " 'Was It for This? . . .': Wordsworth and the Birth of the Gods," in *Romantic Revolutions: Criticism and Theory*, ed. Kenneth R. Johnston et al. (Bloomington and Indianapolis: Indiana University Press, 1990) 16.

[26] Norman Wacker's comment that in *Jerusalem* "The resurrection of the slumbering Albion is also an attempt to resurrect the sublimated figure of the human embedded in the impersonality of classical discourse"—of classical epic in particular—underscores the continuity between Blake's '90s epyllia and the major illuminated epics of the decades ahead: "Epic and the Modern Long Poem: Virgil, Blake, and Pound," *Comparative Literature* 42 (1990) 134.

today meet him. Nor would Byron have bestowed on him such pains in the dedication to his own contrary epic *Don Juan*: Southey made an especially choice epic foil because he had committed himself so fully to the genre in younger years, and because he had by 1815 so evidently bent a once radical and experimental spirit to the service of established power.[27]

It took nerve to compose at 18, in the year 1793, an English epic that glorified Joan of Arc and the French resistance she marshaled against invaders from England.[28] It took more than that to see the poem through the press when the aftermath of the Terror in Paris had induced Britain to dig in against France for what would turn out to be two embattled decades. While an extensively revised second edition of 1798 mollified the original with stylistic blandishments and an infusion of neutral antiquarian notes, underneath it all the political bravado at the core of Southey's conception survived intact. This may be why in 1837 the old laureate, not content to apologize for *Joan of Arc: An Epic Poem* as a very lengthy youthful indiscretion, set about reforming it altogether, currying diction, tone, and plot to favor the Tory mood of young Queen Victoria's coronation. Yet the censurable version Southey had published at 21 escaped in its day both censorship and, for the most part, censure. Rather it was happy in its supporters, two of whom rank as epic aspirants in their own right: Joseph Cottle, who published the poem in Bristol in 1796, and Samuel Taylor Coleridge, who contributed the first, philosophically adventurous half of book 2. The poem was warmly enough received to speed Southey on a career that would compass no less than four more ventures in the epic kind—*Thalaba the Destroyer* (1801), *Madoc* (1805), *The Curse of Kehama* (1810), and *Roderick, the Last of the Goths* (1814)—before he returned to make *Joan* safe for posterity.

If the first *Joan* enjoyed a charmed life in a hostile world, in this it resembled its heroine. Indeed, it resembled all Southey's typical protagonists.

---

[27] On the depth of Byron's self-disgusted identification with Southey see Jerome J. McGann, "Byron, Mobility, and the Poetics of Historical Ventriloquism," *Romanticism Past and Present* 9 (1985) 67–82.

[28] Political nerve, yes; but behind that, sheer chutzpah. "Is it possible that a person of classical education can have so slight an opinion of (perhaps) the most arduous effort of human invention, as to suffer the fervour and confidence of youth to hurry him in such a manner through a design which may fix the reputation of a whole life?" John Aiken, unsigned review of *Joan* in *Monthly Review* n.s. 19 (1796) 361–68. The generic lability of the '90s emerges from comparison of *Joan* with Charlotte Smith's "The Emigrants," also from 1793 and on a French/English theme whose epic potential the poet expressly declines in order to foster sympathetic sensibility as such. On Smith's elected position "*outside* English history" see Jacqueline M. Labbe, "The Exiled Self: Images of War in Charlotte Smith's 'The Emigrants,'" in *Romantic Wars: Studies in Culture and Conflict, 1793–1822*, ed. Philip Shaw (Aldershot: Ashgate, 2000) 51.

The immaculate chastity of purpose that characterizes a Southey hero (and that captivated his sometime disciple Shelley and his lifelong fan Cardinal Newman) is best grasped as proceeding from the evidently congenital disconnect in the poet's mind between episodic series and epic meaning. As readers since Coleridge have observed, Southey's diegetic propulsion is seldom distracted by the synchronizing energies of pattern, whereby foreshadowing and recollection fold a story line on itself, for example, or structural parallels reinforce or complicate a theme. (Only in *Kehama* would he indulge such measures of extravagance-control, and then only under the most stuffily orientalist protest: see Ch. 4.) For reasons partly involving the exceptionally spare variant of Enlightenment deism that ruled his youth, Southey lacked the storyteller's birthright faith in the magnetism of plot. Fascinated though he was by myth and national legend, his remained the abstracted fascination of a student who was content to know that people believed in certain empowered tales—and that *peoples* did too, the world over—but who was not about to join them. One obvious result of this detachment was Southey's deliberate exploitation, in successive epics, of belief systems native to Arabia, Mesoamerica, India, and, albeit more gingerly, Catholic Europe—an exploitation foreshadowed in epic similes that appear in *Joan* at 6.97, 6.127, and 8.348 respectively.[29] A subtler result at work within these vicarious national epics was a narrative infidelity sundering sequence from consequence. Deeply ingrained skepticism about the self-evidence of proximate causality made Southey the most sheerly linear of major nineteenth-century epoists. His plotting would degenerate to chronicling had he not run through each epic an all-purpose drive shaft to which every event in the narrative sequence is geared. Each

[29] These anticipations are specifically noted by Richard Cronin, "*Gebir* and Jacobin Poetry," in his *1798: The Year of the* Lyrical Ballads (Houndmills: Macmillan, 1998) 113. The dream of an encyclopedical-epical inventory lasted Southey into his thirties. He crowed to William Taylor in 1805, heady with *Madoc*, "You will see my Hippogryff touch at Hindostan, fly back to Scandinavia, and then carry me among the fire-worshippers of Istakhar": quoted by Herbert G. Wright, "Southey's Relations with Finland and Scandinavia," *Modern Language Review* 27 (1932) 149. Three years later Southey itemized for Anna Seward his plans to cover "the Runic, the Keltic, the Greek, the Jewish, the Roman Catholick, and the Japanese": *New Letters,* ed. Kenneth Curry (New York: Columbia University Press, 1965) 2: 476. Most of the scheme went unrealized, yet it seems significant that the cultural geographies Southey did write up into epic confirm more or less Linda Ray Pratt's hypothesis, in *Imperial Eyes* (New York and London: Routledge, 1992), "that Romanticism originated in the contact zones of America [*Madoc*, also *Paraguay*], North Africa [bounded by Arabian *Thalaba* and Spanish *Roderick*], and the South Seas [*Kehama*, or close]" (138, interpolations mine). This impulse eventually came home in the auto-colonizing work Southey did for English readers when he edited anthologies like *Specimens of the Later English Poets* (1807), and *Select Works of the British Poets from Chaucer to Jonson* (1831).

incident in a Southey epic is connected to a perspicuous ultimate cause whose advancement is identical with virtue and whose hindrance is the sole business of the wicked.

Thus the two most committed epic poets of the first Romantic generation, each dubious about the coherence of cultural master narratives, took the 1790s epic revival in opposite directions. Blake's one-man workshop turned out a series of epyllia that cut, shuffled, and redealt the elements of the genre in varieties of self-subverting narrative. Southey in contrast, though with an equivalent brashness, set about hatching plots of the largest kind he could imagine. Where Blake, embarrassingly rich in the peripheral vision of collateral meanings, spent the decade breaking narrative up into its components and out into its options, Southey's lesser but expedient gift was long-range tunnel vision. His fifteen-years' gestation of *Madoc*, the epic project for which he himself cherished highest regard, was punctuated by the short work he made of both *Joan* and *Thalaba*, each dispatched in a matter of months once the problem of inconsequence was solved by hitching the narrative to the all-purpose through-line of an indomitable, otherworldly will. The result of this solution, which characterizes equivalently Southey's large output in belletristic scholarship and in nonfiction prose narrative, remained appreciable across the nineteenth century.[30]

Meanwhile, where *Thalaba* is the more remarkable performance, *Joan* is the more instructive in its emergence from the conventions of elder epic into improvised 1790s novelty. Southey strutted his conversancy with the tradition in a cocky preface to the first edition, and also in the poem, which sports invocations, allegorical machinery, prophetic visions, consults, battles, heroic similes and didactic asides. All these conventions are rendered with a cordial buoyancy calculated to fill Hayley's prescription, a decade earlier, that epic in an Age of Feeling should be warm as well as lofty (Ch. 1).[31] To this end Southey chose a protagonist whose femininity opened his poem to the softer

---

[30] As an admiring Edward Dowden observed late in the day, "History as written by Southey is narrative rendered spiritual by moral ardour": *Southey* (1888; rpt. New York: AMS Press, 1968) 196.

[31] Of Hayley's verse *Essay on Epic Poetry* (1782) Southey judged that "A greater effect was produced upon the rising generation of scholars, by the Notes to his Essay on Epic Poetry, than by any other contemporary work, the Relics of Ancient Poetry alone excepted": *Quarterly Review* 31 (1825) 283. Rising scholars, and also rising poets: Hayley had advocated the feminizing of epic (*Joan*), preached down epic machinery (*Madoc, Roderick*), and recommended topics drawn from the mythology of India (*Kehama*). Wilkie, *Romantic Poets*, 41, remarks that Southey, uniquely among major Romantic epoists, concerned himself less with his generic exemplars' practice than with "the legalisms of epic *theory*."

emotions, and who entered on her sterner epic duties as more a catalyst than a reagent. Joan's statecraft is in essence a summons, the sharing of a contagious belief; and her soldiership on the battlefield conducts a physical demonstration, by the breastplate of faith and sword of righteousness, that pure moral force can't be beat.[32]

We may briefly highlight *Joan*'s inventiveness by seeing how an epic of the same year, George Skene's *Donald Bane: An Heroic Poem in Three Books* (1796), carved much of the same late-century matter up into more conventional portions. This poem figures the contrast between its eponymous hero and a decadent Robert the Bruce as a Highland/Lowland binary, whose familiar gender-marking promotes the coded virtues of epic into patriarchal triumph over the feminized, pacific and sentimental values of lyric and romance. This plot burden rests on the shoulders of Donald's son, aptly named Macdonald, who takes one giant stride per book toward full ideological majority. Beginning the poem under torturous confinement at the hands of his father's evil viceroy, he emerges from this domestic hell through the intervention of Flora, an ingenue agemate who, for a limited time only, engrosses the derring-do to herself. But such gender-bending, doomed here to very short half-life, earns Flora instant death by shipwreck at the start of book 2, which fast becomes a bloodbath of single-combat episodes in which the hesitant noncombatant Macdonald joins, fatefully, at book's end for the sake of his kingly sire. Carnage and ruin rule the day in book 3, for which Skene doubly apologizes, first in a poetic proem to the book, and then by plot means: the ghost of slain Malcolm having appeared to Donald Bane with news of Flora's death and exhorted him to lay down arms and make peace, Donald heroically spurns this advice in favor of lots more clannish *aristeia* leading to his eventual death. Once Macdonald has been reconciled to the Bruce by saving him from a wild boar attack, this extraordinarily sanguinary poem ends in the manner of Ossian, with the son chanting the exploits of the father in just such verse, we suppose, as we have been reading.

Skene's aggressively traditional epic all but commands attention to the fusion it effects between the march of its incidents and the defense of its values. Southey's *Joan of Arc*, too, bristles with rectitude and has a fitting tale

---

[32] Looking back at *Joan* over the enraptured young Shelley's shoulder, William Keach in *Arbitrary Power: Romanticism, Language, Politics* (Princeton and Oxford: Princeton University Press, 2004) 111–13, recasts Southey's vesting of moral autonomy in his prophetess heroine as a variant of the Romantic challenge of giving voice to the mind's own authority (which Shelley would explicate in canto 7 of *The Revolt of Islam*).

to tell; yet what is most remarkable about *Joan* is the failure to convert moral force into anything like the consequential narrative design of *Donald Bane*. Southey proffers as generic credentials the epic conventions we enumerated above—again the parallel with his heroine's self-recited résumé before the prince at Orleans is striking—but the poet takes little interest in how these might be integrated into a compelling narrative argument. His major set piece is the ninth and penultimate book, in which the story defers to the "Vision of the Maid," where Joan in effect dreams the meaning of her poem. Ever since the prophecies of the *Odyssey* and *Aeneid*, epic shifts of register like this one have made otherworldly disclosures feed back into the main narrative line; even a native visionary like Southey's favorite Spenser, when pausing to dilate on a medially stationed bower or temple, makes that dilation tell on the narrative in complex ways. But book 9 of *Joan* is a jumble of allegorical cameos—Despair and Expectation appear, but so does Henry of England, the whole being chaperoned by the complaisant figure of Joan's just-dead boyfriend Theodore—which eschews connection either to the foregoing plot (book 10 will resume that from book 8 without a hitch) or to what the generic tradition would particularly solicit at such a juncture, the historical pertinence binding this plot to the time of the poet and his readers. This defection could hardly be more deliberate: when at one point Theodore expressly offers Joan an epic chance to stake a claim on the future and "read the book of Fate" (9.785), she declines point-blank and he praises her for it, departing into yet another allegorical display of the timeless choices leading to social bliss or dole. Not for nothing did a scrupulous prefatory acknowledgment of Coleridge's allegorical contribution to book 2 single out as Southey's own the exclusively *moral* allegories.

Joan's choice not to know the story in book 9 is the same choice Southey makes throughout the poem. Time and again he bypasses opportunities to amplify the significance of an episode, even where these opportunities stare us in the face. Book 4 takes Joan to "St. Catherine's sacred fane" (4.54), where the martyr's gruesome torture as depicted in an altar piece offers a standing invitation to forecast the immolation awaiting Joan herself, an event that lies beyond the scope of Southey's ten books but that every reader's knowledge must link inescapably to his theme. But never mind: "Her eye averting from the storied woe, | The delegated damsel knelt" (4.116–17): the invitation seems deliberately turned down, and by the poet as well as Joan. When a later heroic simile envisions another altar, this one flaming in Mexico with human sacrifice (6.95–113: a refugee, perhaps, from the Aztec scenery already contemplated for *Madoc*), the poet again does nothing to activate its potential for a narrative foreshadowing of Joan's "storied woe." Joan herself, meanwhile, does foresee her end—more than once "on her memory flash'd the flaming pile" (4.373)—but Southey carefully restricts her knowledge to that inward eye which is the bliss of solitude. He cloisters the passion of martyrdom away from action in the world and sequesters meaning in spots of time, oases of consciousness.[33]

The effect of this division of epic labor is a curious moral neutrality within the action itself, curious in what is undisguisedly the work of a '90s leftist crusader, yet arguably instrumental in winning it a favorable reception at a hard time. The English knights come off as political opponents to a France with which we are meant to sympathize. But they do not come off as villains: they do nothing especially wrong, because deeds themselves here are morally indifferent. The abstraction of the poem's moral sphere from its field of action left morality available for appropriation in ways that might reverse the spin ostensibly imparted by the plot. Joan's medieval French nationalism had little to do with her independently inspired virtue, which thus became internationally fungible for imaginative use by contemporary British nationalists, girding as they were for a new invasion that threatened to wash back across the Channel the other way.[34]

In *Joan of Arc*, then, Southey found his way to a cloven form that at one and the same time glowed with ethical fervor and had nothing to prove. The valorous proof of epic rapidly worked loose from the concatenation of incident, to be captured instead in a moral reserve fund that, while it supported the story as a whole—Joan the "delegated Maid" must mobilize France by inspiration alone—and remained available at need to explain this

---

[33] These considerations support Cronin's contention that in writing *Joan* Southey approached epic as a generically subordinate aberration within the right course of human culture, "a vicious interruption of that pastoral happiness which it is the highest human ambition to achieve" (*Politics*, 68). See likewise Curran, *Poetic Form*, 168. On the other side of the question stands a contemporary reader who found the omission of Joan's martyrdom unforgivable; Thomas De Quincey, epicure of plangency, reckoned the heroine's true grandeur commensurate only with "the ransom which she, a solitary girl, paid in her own person for the national deliverance": *Collected Writings*, ed. David Masson (Edinburgh: Black, 1890) 5 :241. If at this stage the personal and the national were at all mutually fungible for Southey, it was in the currency of ideas, not deeds. Only in *Roderick* would the two spheres for deliverance converge, and then with problematic results (Ch. 4).

[34] Compare Southey's remark in a 1793 letter to G. C. Bedford: "Some critic (is it not Addison?) observes that an Epic poem ought to be national—with all due deference the nationality is of much the same use as a tolling bell or a storm of thunder and lightning upon the stage—a trick to catch the vulgar" (*New Letters*, 1: 238). This in a letter written on Bastille Day.

change of heart or that feat of arms, nevertheless wielded no force in the story's unfolding probability. The liability that such an inconsequent form brought with it has been permanently established by literary history's verdict against Southey's epics. Yet in Southey's day it also brought manifest advantages. Political neutrality was a prudent posture for a rising writer of the unsettled 1790s to adopt, and it bore moreover at least a superficial resemblance to the nonpartisan generosity with which the *Iliad* surveyed Trojan and Greek alike: the Homeric single combat between the disenchanted Frenchman Conrade and the disappointed Englishman Talbot in Southey's book 10 not only is fought without national animus but also is narrated that way.

Still more important for the career ahead of Southey was the attractive, if over the long haul fatal, epic facility that the *Joan of Arc* model promised him—and, through him, a brigade of imitators in decades to come. Where there was a superintendent will, there was a way to transform any reasonably sequential chronicle of nations into the stuff of epic: the narrative equivalent of providential oversight and direction, typically transmitted through a delegated hero, might make any serial record, and *a fortiori* a biblical one, eligible for epic honors. Poets had but to do their homework and hitch their narrative wagon to a star, or rather to the spheric machinery of transcendence. The traditions of allegory that Southey had picked up from the eighteenth century served him well in the task of epic evaluation to which he was called by the events of the 1790s. Along with young contemporaries of greater gifts like Blake, or like Landor, to whom we turn next, Southey assayed epic by counterpoising plots against meanings, diegetic against visionary modes. Admittedly the allegorical machinery to which he first turned his hand proved junk, a deadweight drag on the motor of narrative. He had the good sense to see this, though, and threw it out, detaching "The Vision of the Maid of Orleans" for publication as the entirely separable poem it was, and omitting it from the second and subsequent editions.

Even as *Joan of Arc* showed up his failure to integrate larger, allegory-worthy meanings into a narrative structure, it showed him the way to implant meaning in a superhero who could become the imaginative equivalent of an allegory, a machine in himself. Southey's engineering feat of the 1790s was to transform the lightning rod of the early Romantic sublime into a power source that drove plots, not from within by inherent probability, but from above by supernatural prompting. This prototype as Southey developed it for the nineteenth century sprang directly from eighteenth-century exemplars like Glover's *Leonidas*, where the hero served as choragus to a massive national ensemble. But, where the older choral identity inhered in a fabric of belief seamlessly continuous with that of the poet's own age, Southey split this fabric into a proto-ethnographic grasp of culturally specific detail on one hand, and on the other hand the morally transcendent position of the Romantic sublime. Consequently the epic poet's new freedom to plunder the globe for its fables came at the cost of enslaving the epic protagonist to a robotic program of strenuous, solitary virtue.

The full development of this model in *Thalaba*, just across the turn of the century, was made possible by the waning decade's last important epic experiment, the young Walter Savage Landor's anonymously published *Gebir: A Poem in Seven Books* (1798). Landor drew his plot from the longish prose *History of Charoba, Queen of Aegypt* that Clara Reeve had appended to her *Progress of Romance* in 1785 (see Ch. 1). While *Gebir* keeps a chivalrous republican's faith with this incipiently feminist source—it is witchcraft that finally lays low the giant king, and the strongest of the characters is a free-thinking nymph who likes to wrestle—the change in focus from Charoba to Gebir, and from history to poem, reflects Landor's severely masculine plan to see how much astringent classicizing such romance stuff would bear.[35] What reputation the poem retains is due to the stylistic consequences of this plan: arresting vignette descriptions of scene and action, struck off in clean fresh lines of blank verse whose marble chastity seems about a century out of synch with its moment. The less happy narrative experimentation that went with these local effects was timely nevertheless. Typical of epic endeavor in the 1790s, the plot of *Gebir* is made awkward by what looks to the eye of literary history like a young British Jacobin poet's unrepentant belatedness within that rightward-veering decade.[36]

[35] Alan Richardson finds Landor initially "less bent on feminizing epic than on masculinizing romance," though when he recast the poem in 1803 the turn of Napoleonic events since 1798 had persuaded him to disown epic's Virgilian linkage to empire and "shift the poem's generic balance decisively in favor of its romance elements": "Epic Ambivalence: Imperial Politics and Romantic Deflection in Williams's *Peru* and Landor's *Gebir*," in *Romanticism, Race, and Imperial Culture, 1780–1834*, ed. Richardson and Sonia Hofkosh (Bloomington and Indianapolis: Indiana University Press, 1996) 274, 277. See also Herbert Lindenberger, *On Wordsworth's* Prelude (Princeton: Princeton University Press, 1963) 117. Interplay between the two genres at this time is discussed in more general terms by Curran, *Poetic Form*, and by Marlon Ross, "Romancing the Nation-State: The Poetics of Romantic Nationalism," in *Macropolitics of Nineteenth-Century Literature: Nationalism, Exoticism, Imperialism*, ed. Jonathan Arac and Harriet Ritvo (Philadelphia: University of Pennsylvania Press, 1991) 56–85.
[36] Pierre Vitoux, "*Gebir* as an Heroic Poem," *Wordsworth Circle* 7 (1976), correlates the poem's contest between epic and pastoral genres with its playing against traditional military heroism "a humanitarian and liberal inspiration" (53–54). See also Wilkie, *Romantic Poets*, 49–58; Simon

Landor took the same eager chisel to his story that he took to his poetic line; and the resulting narrative, while here and there it handsomely exemplifies verse's privilege to tell a great deal in a small space, is also disconcertingly liable to velocity changes and jump-cuts of a Blakean abruptness, without a discernible Blakean rationale. "Compendious and exclusive": so ran Landor's own account in later years of the *Gebir* style, an account as self-illustrative as it was accurate.[37] Some opening lines from the poem will give a good idea what he was talking about. Here is Landor announcing his argument and launching its execution in one compact stroke:

> how, incens'd
> By meditating on primeval wrongs,
> He blew his battle-horn, at which uprose
> Whole nations: how, ten thousand, mightiest men,
> He call'd aloud; and soon Charoba saw
> His dark helm hover o'er the land of Nile.
>   What should the damsel do? should royal knees
> Bend suppliant? or defenceless hands engage
> Men of gigantic force, gigantic arms?
>
> (1.16–24)

These lines provide our introduction to Charoba, and practically the first news we have, for that matter, of Gebir himself. Such a plunge *in medissimas res* not only deserts the oral roots of epic but strips its written leaves as well; and we shall not see its telegraphic like again before Browning's *Sordello* (Ch. 7), that ill-fated experiment of Landor's literary executor-to-be; and then not again until Landor's only literary soul-mate for sheer orneriness confronts us in the Edwardian epoist Charles M. Doughty (Ch. 12). The

---

Bainbridge, *Napoleon and English Romanticism* (Cambridge: Cambridge University Press, 1995) 30–49. For a bracing, counterintuitive reading of this generic relation, see Cronin, *Politics*, 127, who poises his argument against the overall account of the Romantic war epic given by Curran, *Poetic Form*, 168. Butler, *Romantics,* observes that the pastoral, like its obverse the Gothic, had a special claim to epic favor in an era whose primitivism tended "to reject the ephemeral in favour of the essential" (16).

[37] Letter of 1850 to John Forster, in the latter's *Walter Savage Landor: A Biography* (London: Chapman and Hall, 1869) 46. Likening the result of this "dazzling experiment" (75) to "motion-picture speed for an audience familiar with other narratives" (6), Robert Pinsky in *Landor's Poetry* (Chicago and London: University of Chicago Press, 1968) opens a literary-historical reel whose fast-forward unwinding might take us to Hardy's cinematic practice in *The Dynasts* (Ch. 12). For Karl Kroeber, in contrast, the problem with *Gebir* is that it keeps subsiding into still shots arresting narrative and forfeiting "the dynamism of the full Romantic style": "Trends in Minor Romantic Narrative Poetry," in *Some British Romantics: A Collection of Essays,* ed. James V. Logan, John E. Jordan, and Northrop Frye (Columbus: Ohio State University Press, 1966) 281.

reader who suspects the medium here of being something other than English may be comforted to know that parts of the poem were first drafted in Latin verse, and that within a few years Landor would turn the whole into Latin as *Gebirus* (1803).[38]

Plot summary is of little use where a narrative is presented at so nearly summary a speed to begin with. Suffice it that into seven short books Landor packs military maneuvers, the clash of kingdoms, the building of a new city on the ruins of an old, an underworld descent to consult prophetic ancestry, the performance of national rites and black arts, and a skyborne Mediterranean travelogue that fast-forwards to the European convulsions of the present, with a promise at the end of "Captivity led captive, War o'erthrown" (6.299). Self-evidently more than a poem of modest dimensions can manage, this superflux of epical matters in effect forces a question about generic proprieties, assaying the respective capacities of heroic and romance plot modes.[39] Landor in later years liked to counterbalance the "classick" and "romantick," more often than not ambushing his overt adherence to the former with sudden declarations of Clara Reeve-like allegiance to the latter as richer in possibility or better fitted to modern needs. Something of the kind happens in *Gebir* as well, which balances a European king with an African queen, contrasts one brother bent on regime-founding with another devoted to pastoral retreat—and so innocent of dynastic ambition as to confess on his honeymoon that he "Had never thought of progeny" (6.190)—and celebrates a wedding in each of its final books. Or rather fails to celebrate, since the poem ends with Gebir's convulsive death by poisoning: the assassination of a still young king who has lived by epic values forms the denouement of a supervenient (nec)romantic counterplot.

This self-denying epic finale puts into retrospective question the values for which Gebir has stood, chief among them the values of dynastic retrospective

---

[38] R. H. Super, *Walter Savage Landor* (New York: New York University Press, 1954) 522. Jonathan Wordsworth, introducing the facsimile *Gebir* (Oxford and New York: Woodstock, 1993), observes that the poet "writes English as if he could hear the Latin case-endings."

[39] Having long since settled on "heroic idyl" as his generic label of choice for *Gebir,* and for its fragmentary congeners *The Phocaeans* and *Crysaor* (1802), in a very late imaginary conversation (1853) Landor has Archdeacon Hare tell him, apropos the first of these, "The most disappointed of its readers would be the reader who expected to find an epic in it. To the *epic* not only its certain spirit, but its certain form, is requisite": *Complete Works,* ed. T. Earle Welby (London: Chapman and Hall, 1927–36) 6: 28. Fifty years before, however, to conjure as much as the genre's "certain spirit" was no mean feat, and Landor had shown it could be done. Douglas Bush showers *Crysaor* with praise in *Mythology and the Romantic Tradition in English Poetry* (1937; rpt. Cambridge, Mass.: Harvard University Press, 1969) 238–39.

and prospective duty as such. Dynastic obligation and ambition figure largely
in the poem, as in the Virgilian tradition to which it belongs. But they come to
nought here, in part because Landor's republicanism found them politically
abhorrent, in part because his imagination, for all the abundant historicism
of his later writings, recoiled at the very temporality of dynasticism. Power
was an intoxicant whose obsession with antecedence and posterity bred
political tyranny, even as perceptually it tainted the living moment, in
much the way the young king's poisoned wedding garment taints him.
(This narrative politics also governs Landor's thousand-line heroic text of
1802, *The Phocaeans*, whose inchmeal narrative advance, relieved by moments
of descriptive finesse, achieves an unflinching pathos peculiarly suited to
his Virgilian thematic of evacuation, exile, and endurance.) When Gebir at
the middle of the poem goes down like Aeneas to the dead he finds his
forebears appallingly alien, strange beyond reclamation, a far and enfeebled
cry from the obliging shades of Virgil: "Cold, speechless, palsied, not the
soothing voice | Of friendship . . . | Beyond man's home condition they!"
(3.175–78).

   In light of the poet's earlier confession that we don't really pay calls on the
dead any more—"never may I trespass o'er the stream | Of jealous Acheron"
(3.7–8)—we may see that the departed of *Gebir* sound weak and foreign
because they are in truth practically inaccessible, and in just the way that
the ceaselessly receding past itself is inaccessible: "can any, with outstripping
voice, | The parting Sun's gigantic strides recall?" (3.17–18). This is a gener-
ically damaging concession, at least if epic is conceived on Gebir's terms of
obedient converse with predecessors who, once upon a time, from their own
historical actuality willed our present. It is less so if history becomes recuper-
able on the invitational terms of imaginary conversation (to borrow a phrase
Landor went on to make his own), where the present hosts the past rather than
vice versa. To see how much Landor's nerveless underworld resembles
Homer's, and to recognize in the prevalent sunlit clarity of *Gebir* the narrative
manner for which in Landor's lifetime the verse of Homer was most consist-
ently praised, is to glimpse how in killing off his hero Landor shook off a
moribund generic fealty. He saved epic for modernity by restoring it to a fresh
encounter with the contemporaneity that to him classicism, as against neo-
classical decadence or muddy vernacularity, represented.[40] For this restorative

---

[40] For John Holloway, *Widening Horizons in English Verse* (Evanston: Northwestern University
Press, 1967), *Gebir* is not "a classical poem" because its chief sources were so "deeply impregnated
with orientalism" of a radical cast: Beckford's 1786 *Vathek* furnished its hell, Volney's 1791 *Ruins* its

purpose—which *mutatis mutandis* was Blake's purpose too—neither epic nor romance conventions were in themselves adequate. But a poet who had taken their measure might, by playing them off against each other, engender something new. James Ogden at the head of the decade had stood against the miscegenation of literary kinds:

> Begin the song, a shepherd's rustic lays
> Suit not this theme, though pitch'd to choicest reeds,
> Fame's trumpet best records heroic deeds.
>
> (*The Revolution*, 1.1–3)

For Ogden the way to aggrandize the Glorious Revolution was to press it back generically and stylistically into a mold much older than its centurion events. Landor ran his cross-grained, cross-bred epic quite the other way, escorting antiquity into the arms of the present. In doing so he made one of the most interesting generic investments of the decade, and the dividend it paid was that frontal incisiveness of description whose style has been crisp these two hundred years.

Among the first to register this effect was Southey, who gave *Gebir* an adoring review in 1798 and, to judge from the reform of his own epic manners, took Landor's point about freeing heroism from ancestor-worship, and thereby epic from a neoclassic grip. Southey's magnum-opus-in-prospect *Madoc*, to which the following chapter will return, began shedding the poetical habits of diction and syntax that had held *Joan of Arc* up, and back, on eighteenth-century stilts. In *Thalaba* we see him undertake a reclamation like Landor's of the continuous epic present, but by opposite stylistic means. It was to Southey that Landor later confessed how in striving for narrative condensation in *Gebir* he had "boiled away" too much; Southey seems to have reacted to the poem by writing one of his own that incessantly boiled over.[41] *Thalaba*'s manner of

architecture (39–40). But Landor's classicism had less to do with the origins of his material, or its accrued meanings, than with the fresh shape art gave it. So a splendid conceit at the end of book 6 would suggest, where "Time,—Time himself throws off his motly garb | Figur'd with monstrous men and monstrous gods, | And in pure vesture enters their pure fanes, | A proud partaker of their festivals" (6.301–04). On sources and analogues see also Stanley Williams, "The Story of Gebir," *PMLA* 36 (1924) 615–31.

[41] Landor's comment is reported by George Saintsbury in ch. 9 of the *Cambridge History of English Literature*, vol. 13, ed. W. A. Ward (Cambridge: Cambridge University Press, 1917) 210. Years afterwards Landor observed, in his 1849 tribute "To the Author of *Festus* on the Classick and Romantick," that "my friend | The genial Southey" stood among the classics and yet in his writing was "often too indulgent, too profuse" (ll. 88–91): *Complete Works*, 14: 166. Southey's classicism,

proceeding is an extravagant advance, from one flashpoint crisis to the next, that engrosses the page-turning reader in intensities of instant gratification. Southey's raid on the orient led like Landor's through exotic wonders and antagonistic necromancy to the immolation of the foredoomed hero, but *Thalaba* answered *Gebir*'s severity with programmatic excess. The calculated heedlessness of the poem owed something, too, to the other influence its preface adduces besides Landor—the genial recreation Southey routinely took during these years with his friend Humphrey Davy's "bag of nitrous oxide."[42] The gassy hilarity of this most conspicuous of Southey's contributions to High Romanticism takes effect notably at the level of style, in the unrhymed, purposely unenjambed, irregularly metered iambics that he gathered into short, untaxing strophes as if to counter the experimental astringency of Landor. Southey does all he can here to facilitate the reader's uptake, through a medium that is elaborately casual, of an episodic narrative that is unrelentingly amazing.[43]

Casual amazement: one form or another of this tension governed British attitudes across the nineteenth century toward an Orient that fascinated them equally by its hierarchical rigidity and also by its indulged deviancy; the Quran, as it were, and also the *Arabian Nights*. This same tension defines many formal aspects of *Thalaba the Destroyer* as well. On one hand the poem is so flagrantly improvised that the initial preface (dated 1800) found it advisable to discount "the *improvisatore* tune" as a thing unworthy. Yet what else may be expected of a work composed at the rapid clip in which the preface of 1837 takes retrospective pride, and which indeed was instrumental to the effect of precipitancy that the poem communicates to this day? The variable blank strophe—an ostentatious innovation circa 1800, and in retrospect an oasis along the route to free verse later in the century—in delivering its one image per line delivered too a virtual declaration of form's subordinate transparency to all-enthralling vision.[44] That vision is one of primitive exoticism, focused

wrote Landor, consisted in a power well beyond Coleridge's or Wordsworth's to "grasp great subjects, and completely master them": quoted in *Robert Southey: The Critical Heritage*, ed. Lionel Madden (London and Boston: Routledge, 1972) 425.

[42] In a letter of 5 Sept. 1799 Southey confided to William Taylor, "I can conceive this gas to be the atmosphere of Mohammed's Paradise" (*New Letters* 1: 129).

[43] Southey's early subtitle *A Rhythmical Romance* declared this intention, perhaps a little too openly—though half a century later, in the hour of spasmody, it would have hit the height of literary fashion: William St. Clair, *The Reading Nation in the Romantic Period* (Cambridge: Cambridge University Press, 2004) 211.

[44] William Taylor's unsigned review of *Thalaba*, being the work of a friend, seems to speak for Southey in ascribing to the style "a plasticity and variety of which epic poetry offers no other example" and

and magnified by a verse counterpart of the cadenced prose with which, a generation earlier, the Ossian books had spellbound the public with their own, comparably primitivist vision. Macpherson's heir Walter Scott would follow Southey in nothing else, but he was nevertheless to study the epic effectiveness of this prosodic relaxation and turn it in new directions before the new decade was out.

Rapt by a purpose that exacts total subordination of poetry's technical means to its narrative ends, *Thalaba* occupies much the same position as does Thalaba himself. Book 1 wastes no time binding the boy to an unbreakable vow of vengeance, and with its fulfillment in book 12 poem and hero expire on the same self-dealt stroke. In *Joan of Arc* Southey's reluctance to imagine Joan's end precluded so neat a fit of protagonist to plot; still, *Thalaba*'s totalitarian logic is simply that of *Joan* taken to its extreme. The poem pursues Thalaba's quest and nothing but; by the same token, Thalaba *is* his mission. Inscribing a pattern that has descended in our time to the likes of James Bond and Rambo, Thalaba's character embodies pure agency, whereby antecedents and affections fall away to expose a naked will that, being stripped of properties, is not in any meaningful sense his own. Asked where he is going, he truly answers that he doesn't know: "My purpose is to hold | Straight on" (8.18.246–47). Asked his name in the final book by a man whom his revenge quest has fortuitously benefited and whom he has just told to get out of the way and "Return to life," Thalaba can only pronounce "the name of God" and leap into an abyss (12.16.254, 12.17.259). Asked by "the all-beholding Prophet" himself what it is that he finally wants, he can only tell the truth: "One only earthly wish have I,—to work | Thy will" (12.31.470, 12.32.79–80). This is the ecstasy of agency, and in whatever relation it may stand to Islamic teachings, it crowns an orientalist fantasy of utter submission that has proved mightily handy to the poet whose will the hero works. Contemporary university students will quickly recognize in the hero-mounted instantaneous narrative forwardness of *Thalaba* a forerunner of the video-games perspective they have grown up with. Although the poem does not offer, as Blake's mature epics do, a customizable interactive narrative technology, all the same it sustains a sense

declaring, "The author calls it a metrical romance; he might have called it a lyrical one; for the story is told, as in an ode, by implication; not directly, as in an epopoeia. It is a gallery of successive pictures": *Critical Review*, 2nd series, 39 (1803) 369–79. Half a century later E. S. Dallas in his *Poetics: An Essay on Poetry* (London: Smith, Elder, 1852) would call the bluff of Southey's "arabesque" and illustrate its "plain sense" prosody by relineating the opening stanza effortlessly in standard blank verse (187–88)—a point made again in Courthope, *A History of English Poetry*, 6: 224. See the discussion of Southey's stanza and genre as they affected his most brilliant disciple in David Duff, *Romance and Revolution: Shelley and the Politics of a Genre* (Cambridge: Cambridge University Press, 1994).

that some other sequence of events might as well have occurred as the one we are given. The arbitrariness attaching to what does happen to happen points us back, again, to the narrative omnipotence—for it is that, rather than omniscience—whose creature Thalaba is.

Where singleness is virtue, the villainous are almost by definition the poem's double agents. Bearers of irony and dabblers in wit, they make it their job to tempt the hero with dubieties that he, in defeating, puts out of mind and beyond the pale. The poem's first sophisticate, an Old Man who anticipates Tennyson's Merlin with his fondness for discussing philosophy in public places—"the weeds | Of Falsehood root in the aged pile of Truth"; "Son, what thou say'st is true, and it is false" (4.9.183)—proves none other than Lobaba the Domdaniel sorcerer, bent behind the smokescreen of his paradoxes on filching Thalaba's ring of power. The creepiest monster of them all, Zohak by name, grows snakes from his shoulders that feed on his brain until he strangles them, "of himself / Co-sentient and inseparable parts" (5.28.351–52): so much for Romantic self-consciousness. In the poem's longest unbroken strophe (and block of iambic pentameter), its subtlest mage Mohareb twits the hero with his merely agential status: "Thou, Thalaba, hast chosen ill thy part, | If choice it may be called, where will was not, | Nor searching doubt" (9.14.182–84). But all this equivocation is wasted breath: *if* is a word that evaporates from the working vocabulary of a hero who knows but one condition. "The Talisman is Faith" (5.43.519), Thalaba learns at the thetic climax of his mid-poem descent to the underworld; and faith rules doubt clean out.

Nor is this all in *Thalaba* that faith rules out, for Thalaban faith is a condition of simplicity costing not less than everything. To speak of a learning curve on the hero's part distorts the daunting uniformity of the work's effect, but if there is any gain in heroic knowledge here it is a deepening confidence, on the part of "the delegated youth" (4.1.3), echoing a favorite epithet from *Joan*), that "Destiny | Hath marked me from mankind!" (7.12.128–29, also 7.29.370–71). Mark that *from*: the plot relentlessly shows that "the chosen Arab's" (6.4.29) being elected *among* mankind entails his being isolated *against* mankind too. Paradises pall, pleasures crumble, associates betray, and drop-dead beauties keep doing just that. For a fleeting interval late in the poem "the Arabian's heart | Yearn'd after human intercourse" (10.8.88–89), the possibility of which flickers up in a girl he meets who, bred among magical simulacra, seems just his type. But the reader knows what is coming: her sudden murder terminally underscores the rules of the poem, which are that Thalaba may consummate his mission only by crossing a one-way Dantesque threshold into the Domdaniel cavern, "All earthly thoughts, all human hopes | And passions now put off" (12.11.151–52)—*all* passions, including the one he started with, "revenge, | The last rebellious feeling" (11.28.346–47).

By this point even the crudest accidents of psychological motive (and thus of character) are sublimated into essence, into the operation of a plot that has been looped all along in gyres of self-fulfilling prophecy. Thalaba's mission after all is vengeance for the death of his father Hodeirah, whom as the poem begins Okba has murdered in order to avert the prophesied destruction of his race by Hodeirah's—which is to say, by the very thing the murder incites, Thalaba's itinerary of vengeance. This perfectly closed circuit of cause and effect, firmly traced out by books 1 and 2, is then indelibly inked by all the books that follow. The tenth book, spins off an epicycle for good measure: Okba produces an astrological decree requiring the death of either Thalaba or Laila (his new best girl and Okba's daughter); Thalaba prepares to go under the knife, but then Laila, intervening, receives the fatal wound instead. This is what passes for irony in the *Thalaba* plot, which not only disables all merely intermediate causation, but leaves characters, Thalaba most of all, helplessly alone in a world so charged with fatality as to render human initiative irrelevant.

Southey designated this poem a "romance" and not an epic, but that was in the same 1800 preface in which he said he was not improvising, so perhaps he should not be believed on this point either.[45] *Thalaba*'s claim to a place in the history of nineteenth-century epic rests on the manic fusion, the hell-bent coherentism, of its overdriven narrative. Here is a work in which the clichés of daemonical Romanticism actually come true: alienated autonomy in the world-concentering hero, and sheer unbeholden creativity in the extemporizing poet, are in *Thalaba* not elements of some subtilizing dialectic with Wordsworthian nature or Shelleyan political culture. They are the whole story, a story whose welded wholeness promotes them with dismaying self-consistency. To the extent that a deracinated individualism occupied the throne of the Romantic ideology, *Thalaba* was its epic.[46] That the poem shed

---

[45] Richard Hoffpauir, "The Thematic Structure of Southey's Epic Poetry," *Wordsworth Circle* 6 (1975) 241–42 summarizes Southey's tergiversation as to the genre of his poems. See also Wilkie, 36, 234.

[46] Wilkie, *Romantic Poets*, 29, approaches Southeyan epic in terms of a definitive Romantic "paradox": "extreme individualism in combination with extreme group-consciousness." For Dean A. Miller, *The Epic Hero* (Baltimore and London: Johns Hopkins University Press, 2000), "the romantic recovery of the powerful individual" after the failure of revolutionary rationalism at the turn of Napoleon's century posed "a serious and specifically modern problem" opening resurgent ideas of the archaic hero to takeover by the first stirrings of a fascism to come (20).

an influence for years appears in various writings by Byron, Moore, and especially Shelley that exhibit more or less of epic ambition (see Ch. 5); and its energetic single-mindedness is still to be felt in the epics of biblical apocalypse that came into vogue during the 1820s (see Ch. 6). *Robinson Crusoe, Caleb Williams,* and *Frankenstein* were by contrast temporizing fables of sociability, which is what the bourgeois-domestic clauses of their generic contract as novels obliged them to be. With *Joan of Arc* we watch over a Romanticism in incubation, within an evidently epic shell. With *Thalaba* we see Southey early, unerringly, riding the spiritual updraft of the age: an Icarus no doubt, an epic simpleton if you like, but unignorable by virtue of the very strength that his simplistic abandon unleashed. No work of its period makes it plainer that the emergent modern individualist was also an isolato beyond the reach of reason and deprecation, a profoundly dangerous man. Epic heroism bionically hard-wired with epic machinery: *The Destroyer.*

The claim of *Thalaba* to epic standing finds another basis in the larger oeuvre of which it eventually formed part. The long poems Southey went on to write carried out a comparative-culturalist logic at which eighteenth-century thinking about the epic genre had arrived: the coherence of a narrative's design stood for the governing design—and thereby the colonially governable tendency—of the culture the narrative represented.[47] Thus, as coming chapters will show, *The Curse of Kehama* redid the essential quest plot of *Thalaba* in a lavishly proliferant mode befitting Hindu polytheism rather than the desert monotheism of Arabian Islam; *Madoc* (also, years later, the 1825 idyll *A Tale of Paraguay*) juxtaposed Native American with European colonial cultures, in narratives endorsing the supersession of the former by the latter; and *Roderick* performed a similar narrative arbitration between ailing and flourishing branches of European civilization. A panorama of epics: Southey's grand plan was in itself epic, as we say; and in saying so we acknowledge a collusion of the muse with the museum that wielded an increasing authority in Britain during his lifetime.[48] The ideal of epic comprehensiveness now

---

[47] According to Javed Majeed, *Ungoverned Imaginings: James Mill's* The History of British India *and Orientalism* (Oxford: Clarendon Press, 1992), Southey followed the founding example of William Jones in presenting "his mythological poems as self-contained wholes which were faithful to their originals" (52). This "rhetoric of authenticity and fidelity" succeeded, we may add, because it was also an epic rhetoric of holism. Imputing consistency to an alien culture, through the postulate of a ruling passion, gave colonizers the key to its tranquil governance.

[48] Nigel Leask, " 'Wandering through Eblis': Absorption and Containment in Romantic Exoticism," in *Romanticism and Colonialism: Writing and Empire, 1780–1830,* ed. Tim Fulford and Peter J. Kitson (Cambridge: Cambridge University Press, 1998) 165–88, offers a strongly theorized model for reading Southey's exotic epics as declensions from the former encyclopedic ideal of the

summoned panoptical omniscience to prove itself exhaustively; the epic catalogue learned from the archival one how much there was to know, and the epic poet was increasingly obliged to certify his vision by some recognized evidentiary canon.

Symptomatic of this collusion was the quantity of notes that Southey appended to *Thalaba* and its successors, in a development that became so hard and fast a convention of the Romantic epic that by the 1830s he returned to the once lightly annotated *Joan*, did his homework on fifteenth-century France, and decked it out like the rest. Southey did not invent this convention: right across the eighteenth century, new long poems had come into the world wrapped in apparatus appropriate to learned editions of classics. This dressing-up of newborns to look like elders had, and has, something funny about it, as Pope well knew in tricking forth his *Dunciad*; but by the second half of the century William Willkie or Richard Glover could with utmost sobriety introduce his new epic as if it were a dignified version of itself. What Southey was the first author to do with this mildly Ossianic tradition of bibliographic self-legitimation was drive a wedge into the discursive crack between the voice of epic poetry and that of editorial prose. The authority of validation that is *ipso facto* vested in commentary becomes, in Southey's notes to *Thalaba*, cognitive superiority to the imaginative content of the poem, which the notes expressly denigrate as childish nonsense, laughable superstition.[49]

Inoculating *Thalaba* against itself, he purchases immunity from the infection of Arabia and its unbridled fancifulness—or, when he sees his way, the infection of Spain, or France, or (that Arabia at the heart of the Continent)

---

genre into a disorientingly panoramic mode held in unsteady check by Humboldtian scientific expertise. As a result, for Southey unlike his cannier successors Byron and Moore, "Technical innovation and formal poetic experimentation . . . compromise the Anglocentric and imperialist discourse in whose service the poems are enrolled" (183).

[49] See Clare A. Simmons, " 'Useful and Wasteful Both': Southey's *Thalaba the Destroyer* and the Function of Annotation in the Romantic Oriental Poem," *Genre* 27 (1994) 83–104. C. H. Herford's late-Victorian assessment of Southey in *The Age of Wordsworth* (1897; rpt. Freeport, N.Y.: Books for Libraries, 1971) states a tension to which his better twentieth-century critics have returned: "He was too 'enlightened' to penetrate into the inner genius of the faiths whose picturesque beauty he admired" (208). See also Ernest Bernhardt-Kabisch, *Robert Southey* (Boston: Twayne, 1977) 84, who finds the mythological poet "caught between the Enlightenment's latitudinarian interests and its residual ethnocentrism or new positivist arrogance" (p. 84); Mark Storey, *Robert Southey: A Life* (Oxford and New York: Oxford University Press, 1997): "Southey was clearly seduced by the very material that half of him found repellent" (120). Marilyn Butler limns *Thalaba* with less ambivalence as the work of a Volneyan Enlightenment hardliner: "Shelley and the Empire in the East," in *Shelley: Poet and Legislator of the World*, ed. Betty T. Bennett and Stuart Curran (Baltimore and London: Johns Hopkins University Press, 1996) 162–64.

credulous Catholic Rome. The rationalist skepticism that, as we noted above, palsied Southey's faith in narrative's merely customary probabilities here comes out into the open as the occasionally indignant, but always imperturbable, confidence of a man who knows better than to believe such stuff as his own poetic dreams are made on.[50] The last note to book 8 as much as concedes that its plot details are of no consequence, waives probable explanation, and flaunts the poem's genuine objective: "What could not a Domdanielite perform? The narration would have interrupted the flow of the main story." With telling candor Southey affirms here what the verse fluency and narrative overdetermination of *Thalaba* have already amply suggested. Byplay is nothing, forward motion all; let "the flow of the main story" go on, and damn the expense. The irony, dubiety, and sophistication that might have retarded narrative flow have made their way into the notes instead, there to demarcate an urbane Western perspective that, precisely by reason of its vigilant orientalism, runs no risk of going oriental.

This most single-minded of poems thus forms only one side of a double-minded text; yet the total text, the book that is *Thalaba the Destroyer*, is not quite the schizophrenic production it may seem. For the relation of poem to notes is a temporal relation, one that implies an historical progression from childishness to maturity, from primitive to cultured stages, that in orientalist and other aspects was to be nineteenth-century Britain's favorite story about itself: *La Légende des Siècles* in Victor Hugo's epic slogan (1859–83), *The Ascent of Man* in Mathilde Blind's (1888; see Ch. 11). The unstoppable momentum of Thalaba's reckless quest is not finally checked by Southey's ruthless notes. Rather, it takes them over, fusing with "the flow of the main story" the westward course of empire (*translatio imperii* in a sense that epic never forgot), the spread of enlightenment, and the universal currency of instrumental reason. These were chief determinants of what is the main story indeed, the one looming behind our literary history in this book, the modern tribal tale of which *Thalaba* and its globe-trotting, century-spanning, annotated successors were exponents. Their internal totalities, so rote in extravagance and indeed so much like each other under the costumes and paint, could of course do no more than mock the sundry complexities of the ill-understood cultures of

---

[50] "Metaphysics had become an anathema to Southey, and here it is seen that the evil sorcerers in the poem are no other than the metaphysicians of the School of Locke": Imdad Husein, *English Romantic Poetry and Oriental Influences* (Lahore: Nadeem, 1994) 36. By the same token, however, Southey found deeply appealing what he understood to be Islam's essential combination of "antitrinitarian nonconformity" with "austere and submissive fatalism": Daniel E. White, *Early Romanticism and Religious Dissent* (Cambridge: Cambridge University Press, 2006) 169.

which Southey and his successors aimed to render account. But the mirror they held up to the early nineteenth century was prophetic.

Occidental self-confidence does for our paradigmatic annotative epoist what the talisman that is faith does for his hero. Southey rings himself round with a magic charm whose spell he ceaselessly, contemptuously murmurs from the first page of notes forward. "A waste of ornament and labor characterizes all the works of the Orientalists," "conveying no idea whatever," "absurd," "worthless"; "They have lost their metaphorical rubbish in passing through the filter of a French translation" (note to 1.13). Passing through the occidental filter of French reason and subjected to English prosodic measure, the matter of Araby passes the redemptive test of time and runs the gauntlet of historical progress. So too may fallen "Bagdad" be saved from itself and restored to former glory, "when the enlightened arm | Of Europe conquers to redeem the East!" (5.6). The homology here between Europe's arm and Thalaba's poises their parallel conquests on a dizzying edge where redeeming the oriental past looks very much like destroying it in the name of its future, which is going to be nothing if not the Western present.

From its appearance in 1801 *Thalaba* spurred ambitious nineteenth-century verse narrative on an impetuous course that successors could follow only if they tamed and harnessed it first.[51] They would always have to check its precipitancy—monitor, curb, and correct it—because it represented a force that epic could neither quite coexist nor quite dispense with. On one hand the purely negative energy that Southey's tale unleashed was culturally unsustainable and thus, for a genre radically invested like epic in the continuity of culture, suicidal. On the other hand the entire text comprising tale and annotation essentialized an unstable compound, on which epics would feed for a hundred years, between the forward thrust of a coherent linear plot and the enginery of that progressive ideology which was, hands down, the century's preferred form of continuity.

[51] Foremost among these successors may be ranked the poet who has served this chapter as Southey's mighty opposite, William Blake: see Curran, *Poetic Form*, 135, for remarks about the influence of *Thalaba* "on climactic acts of self-annihilation in *Milton* and *Jerusalem*."

3

Under Correction:

Epic Conscripted 1800–1805

We saw in the previous chapter how new poets of the 1790s assembled Romantic epic with a little romance here, a little epic there, and plenty of steam from the revolutionary bellows. At the turn of the century Robert Southey in *Thalaba the Destroyer* had taken matters to an extreme that would have stunned even liberal thinkers about the genre like William Hayley and Clara Reeve (Ch. 1) only two decades before. By its nature, however, such extremity was unsustainable: if the genre was not to burn out, it would need to cool down. And that is what it did. Southey's publisher, his agemate Joseph Cottle, marked the new decade with an epic of his own composing that can have stunned no one. *Alfred, An Epic Poem, in Twenty-Four Books* (1800) was both generically unimpeachable and quite dead. It was in fact just the sort of production that, although in curiously short supply during the swing decade of the nineties, we should expect to find an embattled era modeling on the marmoreal eighteenth-century heroic ideals it knew best, especially once poetry's temporarily neglected state duties were resumed. For with the start of the nineteenth century the ideological ups and downs of culture skirmish gave place to war indeed, as far as the eye could see: war on a more than European map unrolling from Gibraltar to Moscow, and from the Baltic to the Nile; and war on a calendar extending into all the future that an heroically configured past could help a United Kingdom imagine. Now was a time for epic, even in minds not especially devoted to the arts of poetry.[1]

Given the convergence of patriotic with antiquarian interests circa 1800, and of enlightenment with inspirationalist premises, we should be surprised

---

[1] Southey observed to John Rickman in a letter of October 1800, "My Joan of Arc has revived the epomania that Boileau cured the French of 120 years ago." Quoted in A. D. Harvey, "The English

had a deep-background history poem like Cottle's *Alfred* failed to appear, or like the two poems, obligingly titled *Britannia*, that flanked it by a few years on either side. The first of these, *Britannia: A Poem* (1797), went back behind Alfred the Great to Britain's dark third century under the Roman yoke, which Samuel Hull Wilcocke rendered epical for a thousand lines or so by inviting readers to take the insurrection of Carausius and Cassibelan (uncle to Shakespeare's Cymbeline) as an earnest of what might be in store should another Continental empire now cross the Channel. Joint invocation of the Spanish Armada two hundred years ago and of the French landing in Ireland just the other week (lines 12–47) insistently mythologizes a national pattern—or, rather, it nationalizes a mythic pattern. For, while Ossian is very much on Wilcocke's mind, the purpose that drives this epyllion is to recruit Macpherson's quaint border patrol of 1760 and impress it into the practical service of supporting a collective unity suddenly and intransigently nationalist. Just which Celtic *gens* the ancient Britons may belong to is of no more moment than which particular Ossianic meaning or melancholy may attach to the failure of their rebellion. Within the myth of British freedom marshaled by Wilcocke's poem, a Britain under occupation can have no history to speak of. The usable past begins only when Carausius negotiates the launching of a first British fleet: because the *classis Britannica* means the beginning of the end of colonial subjugation—because, that is, the future has ratified it—that event can furnish national history with the sort of epic background that anxious readers were starting to think it had better have.[2]

Within a few years, the very explicitly subtitled *Britannia: A National Epic Poem in Twenty Books* (1801) pushed the point of collective origin back further yet. John Ogilvie rushed in all the way to where Pope had feared to tread, through the loophole of legend that whispered of Britain's ancient

---

Epic in the Romantic Period," *Philological Quarterly* 55 (1976) 244. The epic explosion catalogued in Harvey's article receives further inventory and refinement in *English Poetry in a Changing Society* (New York: St. Martin's Press, 1980); also in John Schellenberger, "More Early Nineteenth-Century Epics," *Notes and Queries* 30 (1983) 213–14; Roger Simpson, "Epics in the Romantic Era," *Notes and Queries* 33 (1986) 160–61; G. Headley, "The Early Nineteenth-Century Epic: The Harvey Thesis Examined," *Journal of European Studies* 21 (1991) 201–8.

[2] While Oxford librarians had known about *Beowulf* for over a hundred years as an antiquarian curiosity, properly literary reception of the ur-English epic commences during the period treated in this chapter. Sharon Turner's *History of the Anglo-Saxons* (1799–1805) called the manuscript "the most interesting relic of the Anglo-Saxon poetry which time has suffered us to receive" (2: 294); and his terms "relic" and "us" imply a cultural structure of lineal inheritance with whose linguistic and ethnic roots the early century's thinking about epic was much entwined.

settlement by Trojan refugees under Brutus.[3] Ogilvie assigned as heavy a workload to epic machinery as any poet of the 1790s had done. Satan's noisy demons put heart into a fell gang of isle-usurping giants; and a single Guardian Spirit of Britain, reporting directly to God, steadies the victorious course of Brutus and pours much favor on the local allies he finds among a tribe of pure-worshiping aboriginal protestants-in-waiting. A fifty-page prefatory "Critical Dissertation on Epic Machinery" defends the poet's reliance on this motley angelic crew. Full of the polemical spirit we found two chapters ago in his schoolmates James Macpherson and Hugh Blair, this essay adduces every reason except the likeliest one: without supernatural reinforcements Ogilvie's wisp of a myth had too little fiber to sustain anything approaching the twenty books he had in mind.[4]

By 1800, though, as the instance of Wilcocke portends, a properly "national epic poem" needed a firmer basis in received history than Ogilvie could pretend to; and to this need such an Alfrediad as Cottle's was ideally suited to minister. Indeed such an Alfrediad as Cottle's did appear, one year after Cottle's, when the poet laureate Henry James Pye issued his own six-book *Alfred*, complete with a preface backdating the poem's composition by a decade so as to seize the high ground from that (unmentioned) Bristol upstart who had dared to scoop him. Pye's stiff-coupleted poem owed its slender interest to the contemporary applications he found for a set of stagey actions and prophecies parade-drilled to honor the nine-hundredth anniversary of the good king's death.[5] Saxon Alfred and Hanoverian George embodied, Pye could tell, the same national constitution, the one that had always preserved free Britons from imprudent gambles on democracy (3.236), and that prospered the more securely when it enjoyed the reinforcement of willing Celts: centuries ago it was the Scottish troops who made the difference in ridding the island of Danes,

[3] In his last years Pope worked without issue at a blank-verse epic on Brutus, planned at four-book scale. The theme received fragmentary treatment by Ann Yearsley (Ch. 2) half a decade before Ogilvie published *Britannia*.

[4] An Aberdeen pupil of Thomas Blackwell's like Macpherson (see Ch. 1), Ogilvie had in 1777 published *Rona: A Poem in Seven Books*, an epic of the Hebrides, and then in 1787 and 1789 two books of the unfinished *The Fane of the Druids: A Poem*. See Rolf P. Lessenich, *Aspects of English Preromanticism* (Köln: Böhlau, 1989) 265–70.

[5] Pye's one previous epicizing venture was *Naucratia; or Naval Dominion: A Poem* (1798), at eighty pages short in its time for the genre and in conception a mere chronicle scudding past the reviewing stand. Pye's *Alfred* and Cottle's are compared, in forking relation to Southey, in Lynda Pratt, "Patriot Poetics and the Romantic National Epic: Placing and Displacing Southey's *Joan of Arc*," in *Placing and Displacing Romanticism*, ed. Peter J. Kitson (Aldershot: Ashgate, 2001) 95–101.

and for Pye in the wake of invasion scares it was the contemporary act of Union with Ireland (also 1801). So firm is the confidence Pye's Alfred places in learning and the arts as pillars of national order that his own chief bard's rapt vision builds to a forecast of welfare whose crowning achievement will be nothing less than this very confection of the Laureate's—plucked "from the epic wire" (6.618), and yet anything but literary news.

Younger by a long and historically-challenged generation than Pye and Ogilvie, Cottle did better than this, thanks to a more resilient sense of the tension between old and new modalities. His *Alfred* gave the British reader a human history that was expressly divested of "machinery, battles, classical allusions, and supernatural agency" and was composed instead according to modern "principles of poetic pleasure" (Preface, ii). But because these same principles required an imaginative expanse unlicensed by "the sober dialogue of the moderns" (theirs being the gray domain of prose), Cottle sought his theme in the ancient struggle between Saxon and Dane, implicitly representing by it the tension between boldness and polish that a modern epic should sustain. Viking savagery and English civilization find their respective voices in the opening two books, terrific and mellifluous in that order, which is the order whereby supervention means gentle subjugation. The vindicating trial of the modern is writ large in a structural symmetry that brings Alfred's fortunes down to a twelfth-book nadir, whence he steadily rises for twelve books more.

The royal hero earns his victory, moreover, less by the discredited means of arms, although books 17–18 give plenty of earnest play to what the poet has decried as "the mere reciprocation of slaughter" (1804 Preface, 22), than by acts of impersonation that Cottle arranges symmetrically around the epic midpoint. Dwelling incognito at first among his people—burning the neatherds' cakes but soon endeared by this legendary common touch—Alfred climbs back into power by infiltrating the Danish camp as a feckless harper, in a virtuoso lyrical masquerade that enables a key intelligence coup. The exercise not of arms, then, but of a trained sympathetic penetration distinguishes the hero with a modern future; so does his act of kingly pardon near the end of the poem, effecting bloodless Danish conquests on English soil through Christian conversion. At every turn Alfred confronts his adversaries as if they were his antecedents—figures, so to speak, in a history he can read—and he overcomes them by the preemptive right of supersession. Although the guardian angel who visits Alfred at the close violates Cottle's prefatory ban on epic machinery, the angel's diplomatic immunity is evidently due to the purely ideological nature of his mission. He neither intervenes in the action nor mounts the usual dazzling, detailed forecast of greatest hits from Britain's future. Instead he celebrates the realization, in King Alfred, of a powerful political idea: the union of kingship's ancient mystique with an emergent cult of personality, through the modern charisma of merit.

This was not quite the Napoleonic *carrière ouverte aux talents*, but it is intriguing to find Cottle idealizing autocracy as meritocracy in a poem whose invasion scenario simultaneously spoke to embattled Britain's fears lest the armies of the French Republic become the berserkers of today. The liberal worthiness and modern personality he bestowed on Alfred struck a temperate balance between Cottle's abiding 1790s freethought and the steadying patriotism that he, like his associates Southey and S. T. Coleridge, and their associate William Wordsworth, found increasingly congenial by the turn of the century.[6] The figure of King Alfred soon focused a similar moderation within yet a third Alfredian epic, the Reverend Joseph Sympson's *Science Revived, or The Vision of Alfred: A Poem in Eight Books* (1802). All eight books of Sympson's didactic couplets console a despondent Alfred with a prophecy of the march of mind from his Dark Ages into the enlightened and prosperous present that (no less consolingly to its anxious denizen the reader) portends even better things to come. Displaying a confidence at which clergymen-authors later in the century might only marvel, the poet ascribes all earthly good to Liberty and her sister Science, who from the Palace of Genius neatly declaims, "My sister breathes the spirit, I suggest | Th' immortal plan, and Britons act the rest" (8.201). Arguably it was the patriotic corner on progress that made palatable this Cumberland cleric's moral technology. "Knowledge alone can render mortals good" (8.205)—and Britons alone can render knowledge up and make good on it. Most significant for our purposes is Sympson's choice to give his lesson the form of a *narrative*, wherein the history of ideas dovetails with that of the nation. Again Alfred grounds a progressive tradition of art and science that runs from Crusade and Reformation to Glorious Revolution and Enlightenment, and whose momentum into the future secures Liberty and Science against all falling now and hereafter. The

---

[6] Duncan Wu's note on "Cottle's *Alfred*: Another Coleridge-Inspired Epic," *Charles Lamb Bulletin* 73 (1991) 19–22, while it fails to establish the case implied in its title, confirms Cottle's association with chief epoists of his generation by collecting disparaging remarks about *Alfred* from Wordsworth, Southey, and others.

evident charge to readers is that they make sure not to let King Alfred's side down when the going gets tough.

Sympson devoted just a first book to Alfred's circumstances, Cottle just a last book to Alfred's vision. But this difference merely underscores their shared investment in the plotted dream of national progress that, housing the contradictions of their own position, likewise showed them how to do the work that with the new century British epic claimed as its own: to imagine an ever-divisible public into unity in the face of crisis. Story and vision, as we saw and heard amid the industrious revolutionary epicry of Chapter 2, were often at odds. Now, under the aegis of improvement, the two not only got along better but finally became complementary media susceptible of mutual translation. The preponderance of this progressivist unification may explain why the earliest epics of the nineteenth century remained entirely nonprogressive from an artistic point of view. Addressed though they were to their moment, they would have been at home formally in the middle of the previous century. This feature, which manifestly let the poets complete them and facilitated their contemporary assimilation, throws into retrospective relief the extraordinary formal brio with which epoists a decade before had staged their jagged contests between history and romance.

Heroic torsos and samples continued to appear in the new century as in the old, but with motives that were if not simpler then blunter, and are harder to participate now at two centuries' remove. The poets offered not proofs of epic but epics on approval, avowed experiments on the public taste. In this commercial spirit "a sort of subjoined advertisement" is what sad candor obliged John Thelwall to call his "Specimens of *The Hope of Albion; or, Edwin of Northumbria: An Epic Poem*" (1801). Thelwall's performance is noteworthy for its rehearsal on seventh-century grounds of a political persecution not unlike that which he says has kept him from making any more headway with, *inter alia*, his pre-Norman (indeed pre-Alfredian) epic of Saxon democracy. Thelwall, who was to serve as Wordsworth's model for the Solitary in *The Excursion* (Ch. 4), was already at this time among the best-known of England's retreated radicals.[7] It is tempting to ascribe the

---

[7] On Thelwall's political and literary relations at the time see Damian Walford Davies, *Presences That Disturb: Models of Romantic Identity in the Literature and Culture of the 1790s* (Cardiff: University of Wales Press, 2002) 193–240. Susan Matthews, "*Jerusalem* and Nationalism," in *Beyond Romanticism: New Approaches to Texts and Contexts 1780–1832*, ed. Stephen Copley and John Whale

failure of his project to its ideological whipsawing on the generically urgent question of patriotism, endorsed first as "sublimest rage" (1.26) but soon reproved as "national pride that steels | The obdurate heart, presumptuous" (2.334–36). In any case, when the voice of the people spoke bluntly in the marketplace and nobody subscribed for the sequel, none was published.

A similar fate awaited the trial balloon of an obscurer poet, John Lowe, Jr, of Manchester. Lowe's 1803 book of *Poems* showcased an "Episode" from an "Epic Poem," whose undigested pageantry of heaven, conspectus of the creation, and concluding apostrophe to the chemical elements (shades of Erasmus Darwin!) evinced salesmanship but evidently did not garner patronage—and can show us, by contrasting example, how much power of invention had gone into the difficult but more forcefully concentrated trial epics of Blake and Landor a few years before. Thelwall came back before the public in 1805 with *The Trident of Albion: An Epic Effusion*, a generically curious knock-off that was half an oratory handbook in prose, half a verse compound of invocation with rapt pageantry of Britain's naval might from Celtic Carausius to the rapidly ubiquitous national martyr Lord Nelson. That an "effusion" of a few hundred lines might entitle itself to epic honors— provided it inculcated with unflagging stridency a quintessence of pure patriotism "Unanimous, | From rank to rank" (209–10)—marks one extreme of poetry's impressment at the national hour of need.

As the existence of these abortively marketed epyllia suggests, the new century was growing accustomed to epic's services. Readers were learning to regard the reactivated genre as a significant player in the public sphere where, since the Revolution in France, a newly self-conscious civic discourse was fashioning the national identity in whose name it would increasingly behove a state to act.[8] That the name thus invoked was most often royal does not mean that in championing Carausius, Edwin, Alfred, or Richard these Romantic-era poets were principally defending monarchy as such. The

(London and New York: Routledge, 1992), briefly assesses the tonal expression of Thelwall's situation in *The Hope of Albion* (90).

[8] A parallel development took place in the related genre of the encyclopedia, whose tilt in nationalist and historicist directions, already perceptible in the second edition of the *Encyclopædia Britannica* (1777), became unmistakable when to the Enlightenment compendium of knowledge the new century added "biography, history, religion, law, political economy, geography"—topics that "could not be easily separated from national politics": Richard Yeo, *Encyclopædic Visions: Scientific Dictionaries and Enlightenment Culture* (Cambridge: Cambridge University Press, 2001) 176–78, 243.

epic subject circa 1800 was, rather, a national sovereignty that had not in the general mind come free yet from its older regalia into the abstracter currency in which advanced political thought could trade. And the intermediate status of the developing national idea was hospitable, because it was analogous, to the condition of the mainstream epic poem in reluctant emergence from the chaperonage of chivalric or neoclassical models. Tasso, Camoens, and especially Spenser, all in their High Renaissance day codependent cultural supporters of a dynastic political dispensation, remained conspicuously available for imitation in spite of Milton's towering counterexample—while, for more conservative imitators, to spite Milton and what he stood for was part of the point.

The breadth of ideological opportunity that opened out for the enlisted epic under these circumstances may be suggested by two accidentally convergent works that appeared in 1801. *Richard the First: A Poem, in Eighteen Books* by Sir James Bland Burges mounts a modern campaign for the principles of loyalty and order, conducted under cover of the famous Crusade of its twelfth-century hero. The poet's reactionary agenda emerges beyond doubt in book 12, where insurgency back in England precipitates a debate, squarely stacked towards a foregone conclusion, on the relative merits of anarchic democracy and monarchic rule. In fact the whole poem is constructed on two-sided (and lop-sided) conflicts of this kind: Richard faces off against Saladin as do Christianity against Islam, angels against demons, and selflessness against greed. In keeping with this rigid binarism, and in partial disclosure of the modern pertinence vitalizing his poem, Burges devotes as much attention to the debating hall and the courtroom as to the battlefield. Richard spends the long middle third of the poem at trial in Europe on regrettably trumped-up charges, and much of the narrative of knightly exploit arises there in flashback mode during the course of his defense: a diegetic epitome, incidentally, of Burges's summoning up the past as evidence clinching a present polemic.

Near the middle of this epic middle occurs the king's account of the celebrated siege of Acre on the Syrian coast, which a combined French and English force had wrested in 1190 from Muslim control. The inconvenience of first-person battle narrative, an inadvisable choice under the best of epic circumstances, is aggravated here by Burges's chosen format of Spenserian stanzas; but the episode has a crucial role to play, all the same, in an epic dedicated to national unity. For it was again at Acre, in 1799, that English forces had prevailed against an entrenched enemy, this time the French under the all but invincible Napoleon. Through the eye that epic regularly opens at mid-course to prophetic types and shadows, Burges meant to show his reader an inspiring medieval parallel worthy of future imitation. It must have surprised him in the year of publication to find someone looking back the other way, in the unlikely person of Hannah Cowley (better known as the lyrical Anna Matilda of Della Cruscan fame), to affirm that events of epic importance were unfolding in his own lifetime. In identifying her *Siege of Acre* as *An Epic Poem in Six Books* (1801), Cowley defied at least two expectations that Burges and those who thought like him endorsed. Here was an epic in heroic couplets written by a mere woman, and it was based besides on nothing hoarier than yesterday's news.[9]

This instant epic, as fresh as Blake's *French Revolution* a decade before, drew on the classical precedent of Lucan's *Pharsalia* in fixing on current events ("When actions real, *living* men arise," 6.119), and also in eschewing the traditional Muse of "FICTION" for the sake of "Celestial truth! I seize the theme from thee!" (1.3). Within the poem, in fact, the personage most fixated on classical precedent is Cowley's Napoleon, a diligent student of his models in the Egyptian campaigns of Alexander and Antony. Obsession with personal grandeur on this antique scale is, it seems, the part of a villain; for Cowley the real hero is collective, the "ENGLISH TARS" (1.5) who inspire the poem's choral sources of "National Gratitude" (6.124). Still and all, an epic gratitude requires the magnifying lens of precedent; so, halfway through the poem, when the modern English fleet breasts the horizon it comes to succor not just the troops but off in the near distance Lebanon, Carmel, Nazareth: the sacred goals, that is, of the Crusaders in days gone by. The plainest sign of this aggrandizing intention is Cowley's title, which military history went on to keep as a name only for the actions of 1190, but by which she had at the time good reason to hope an epic luster might be added to the actions of six hundred years later.

Like other early female epoists on their generic best behavior, Cowley cleaves to a topic unexceptionably martial and patriotic. Yet she breaks with tradition by diffusing heroism across the armed forces and declining to concentrate the national mission in a chosen individual—as the effusive

[9] Cowley's poem alone—not to mention those that Henry Murphy and James Brown had based during the previous decade on quite recent events (Ch. 2)—suffices to contradict the sweeping claim in Marilyn Gaull's otherwise useful *English Romanticism: The Human Context* (New York and London: Norton, 1988) that "this revolutionary age generated no contemporary epics except comic ones such as Byron's or mythic ones such as Blake's" (285).

Thelwall would do for Nelson in 1805, and likewise the admiral-worshiping Reverend William Hamilton Drummond in 1807 (*The Battle of Trafalgar, An Heroic Poem*). It may have taken a woman among poets to grasp at once an emerging military reality that the later Napoleonic campaigns would soon establish for all to see: weaponry and strategy, and behind them deep changes involving the unprecedented civilian mobilization of an entire nation for war, vested new importance in a dramatic expansion of *esprit de corps*, to which a poetry of cooperative, diffusive heroism might better minister than the older heroic game of single-winner-take-all.

It was in a cooperative spirit that another woman poet, Mary Tighe, turned to an altogether different side of the epic tradition with *Psyche, or the Legend of Love*, a poem in six Spenserian cantos printed privately in 1805 and then published to some acclaim in 1811. Not martial chronicle but marital allegory, *Psyche* marks a significant relay point in the modern transmission of the faithful-loves topos from the grounds of chivalric epic to those of domestic fiction.[10] The heroine Psyche is in the first instance imagined as a real woman. She has a family, nasty sisters included, whose acknowledged claims on her bring trouble; she has a dark and sexy lover-husband and, in the background, a powerful and hard-to-please mother-in-law; she has, above all, a body whose sensations Tighe renders with intriguing finesse. Part of the finesse arises from Psyche's being a real woman but something else besides: an allegorical representation of the soul as it matures into love through encounters with such personifications as Vanity, Credulity, Suspicion, and the finer-tuned perils of escapist Chastity and selfish Indifference.[11] This allegorical license releases Tighe's female protagonist into a more adventurous life than was made available to heroines in the prose fiction of the day, a bonus that promotes this generically transitional work, scarcely but discernibly, to epical rank. Psyche enters the poem miserable and alone in a wilderness of "untrodden forests" (1.4); the plot, after a quick

[10] John M. Anderson reads *Psyche* in consistently epic terms that are inflected, no less consistently, by the poet's independent feminine take on such matters as the Muse, similes drawn from nature, and saccharine domestic closure: "Mary Tighe, *Psyche*," in *A Companion to Romanticism*, ed. Duncan Wu (Oxford: Blackwell, 1998) 199–203.

[11] Uses to which Tighe and her contemporaries put Spenserian allegory are discussed by Greg Kucich in *Keats, Shelley, and Romantic Spenserianism* (University Park: Pennsylvania State University Press, 1991) 97–103. James Chandler, *England in 1819: The Politics of Literary Culture and the Case of Romantic Historicism* (Chicago and London: University of Chicago Press, 1998) 402–8, shrewdly notes that Tighe's self-conscious allegoresis made *Psyche* in effect a Psychology text for the soul's self-study, thus opening the myth to appropriation in Keats's 1819 ode.

flashback, consists of her quest to undo an error that she acknowledges, with dignity, as her own fault. Choosing her domestic destiny rather than passively accepting it, Psyche does not just find her place but actively quests for it.[12] In the allegorical process she gets plenty of support, of course, but then so do Cowley's troops in *The Siege of Acre*. Among the virtues that both of these very different female epoists celebrate are those that make cooperation work: knowing when to call for help, knowing good help from bad when it comes, and combining inner resources with those that enlist the kindness of strangers.[13]

Which is to say that *Psyche* knew a good deal about the sort of thing that an expanding readership were learning to appreciate in another rapidly adolescent genre of Tighe's day, the domestic novel. The fact that prose fictions effecting *Bildung* through relationship were called by the same name that many contemporary readers would have found for *Psyche*—romance—reminds us how much overlap obtained among genres adjacent to epic, and it suggests how much negotiating room between genres remained available even when the international political standoff had hardened to belligerence. The flexible genre that lent its name to Romanticism may have received that honor because it made especially fast alliance with other kinds that were deciding what to become; and this cooperativeness probably had something to do with its inherent hospitality to accounts of becoming as such. On its sterner, epic-fortified flank romance promised to bestow unity on what might else be merely miscellaneous wandering, especially given Tighe's conspicuous *in medias res* opening: "Much wearied with her long and dreary way . . ." (1.1). Epic helped this premise achieve the unity of a developmental sequence, where an initial condition of dislocation or disguise unfolds into a spatio-temporal itinerary, and adventure means advance. The capaciousness of epicizing romance in this regard is striking when we consider that it hosted *Thalaba* as well as *Psyche*. The interdependent ethos and corrective plot of the latter contrast sharply with the former's relentless exacerbation, where the hero never misplaces a confidence because he never trusts a soul. If in large outline the literary future lay with Tighe's allegorical *Bildungsroman* prototype, via Jane Austen and Charlotte Brontë, it is no less true that the hyperbolic

---

[12] See Adeline Johns-Putra, *Heroes and Housewives: Women's Epic Poetry and Domestic Ideology in the Romantic Age (1770–1835)* (Bern: Peter Lang, 2001) 188–91.

[13] On the way Tighe's poetics of reciprocity claims a Spenserian license in mythographic revisionism and even syntactic reversibility, see Harriet Kramer Linkin, "Recuperating Romanticism in Mary Tighe's *Psyche*," in *Romanticism and Women Poets: Opening the Doors of Reception*, ed. Linkin and Stephen C. Behrendt (Lexington: University Press of Kentucky, 1999) 151–57.

incorrigibility of heroic virtue in *Thalaba* epitomizes a feature that persisted in epicizing works, especially works of lesser rank, across the long century this book studies. The unrelaxing ethical self-identity that rules a poem like Murphy's *Conquest of Quebec* from Chapter 2, or Burges's *Richard* here, will put starch in plenty of congeners in chapters ahead.

Our history now arrives, however, at a cluster of major epics all of which repudiate this very feature. All of them moreover have their protagonists repudiate it—responsibly if, like Psyche, belatedly—as a huge mistake whose diagnosis and rectification furnishes the central interest of the plot. Blake's *Milton: A Poem in Two Books* (1804), Wordsworth's *The Prelude, or, Growth of a Poet's Mind: An Autobiographical Poem* (published 1850 under this posthumous title but fully drafted by 1805), and Southey's *Madoc* (1805) all hinge on a correction-of-course: the deliberate emendation of a once engrossing and empowering worldview that has proven to be a half truth and thus, on epic's holistic terms, a dangerous illusion.[14] These poets arrived by independent routes at much the same new idea about how a narrative pivoting on second thoughts and a change of mind might fulfill epic's comprehensive purposes. By a further, fractal implication, the revisionary plots the poets mounted were also revisionist with respect to their prior endeavors in the genre.[15] In this latter regard, from the standpoint our chapter has reached all three of these major statements from radicalized 1790s poets, for all their originality of conception and performance, con- form in some degree to the different zeitgeist that 1800 blew in. They were not nationalist works of standard cast, to be sure; yet the way they girded for epic unity—corrective and collective at once—expressed an ambition that overlapped with the militant nationalism now occupying Britain's cultural

[14] If a footnote can throw up its hands this may be the place—correction and revision being thematically at issue here—to concede the vexed difficulty of dating any of Blake's major prophecies by any instrument so mundane as a calendar year, or by any distinction so unsustainable as that between composition and publication. In his exhaustive *Blake and the Idea of the Book* (Princeton: Princeton University Press, 1993), Joseph Viscomi unscrews the doors from the jambs and broadly dates *Vala* 1797–1807, *Milton* 1804–18, *Jerusalem* 1818–27, with further allowance for much overlapping commerce among them. By such an account the places these three works find in three chapters of the present book are at least not indefensible. In treating *Milton* as a work formed *c.*1805, I follow the lead of scholars readier than Viscomi to accommodate conventional ideas of authorship, who generally set the dates of substantial completion early.

[15] Editorial questions of absorbing interest arise because both *The Prelude* (1799, 1805, 1850, to look no closer) and *Milton* (see previous note) survive in markedly different versions. These questions will not engage us here, except as we note the consistency between the poems' history of textual revision and their internally revisionist thematic. As for Southey, once he had at last finished *Madoc* he left it alone: his revisionary monument remained the epic of visionary heroism *Joan of Arc* (1796, 1798, 1837).

center.[16] Inasmuch as something of the kind might also be said of *Psyche*, as that poem remakes Venus from a bad rival into a good mother and builds within the gentler canons of romance towards a cooperative ethos of belonging, Tighe's long poem makes a fourth within the revisionary company of 1805. Nor is that all, for our *Wunderjahr* recruited yet a fifth member in Walter Scott's *The Lay of the Last Minstrel*. Taking up first the three narratives of heroic self-correction that engrossed Scott's more strenuous contemporaries will let us appreciate, at chapter's end, the peculiarly quizzical generosity with which he subjected a version of that definitively Romantic plot to historicist understanding, within a verse format whose instant popularity opened new channels for long verse narrative in the years ahead.

Milton and *The Prelude* have each attracted enough cogent interpretation to permit here a joint reading that highlights shared properties illustrative of their moment in the history of epic. One property to mention at starting is the *de facto* private circulation of each poem among a tiny circle of the poet's acquaintance. That Wordsworth would not, and Blake could not, find a broader readership for his first finished epic reflects the exception each work took to the conventions of a genre that in most hands, as we have seen, was busy rehearsing generic business as usual within the arena prepared for it in Britain's national discourse. Opening lines set the tone by breaking sharply with the epic tradition they revise. Blake invokes the Muses from a Helicon in "my Brain" and an Aganippe "descending down the Nerves of my right arm" (1.5–7). Wordsworth hails in the "gentle breeze" an inspiration that, "half-conscious of the joy it brings" (1.1–3), is already a semi-angelic messenger, a new epic machine more brazenly under the patent of nature than even Darwin's had been a decade before.[17] The large action of both epics remains true to these revisionist beginnings. Milton in Blake's poem is most a hero when he forswears classically heroic victory over his adversaries, turns annihilating force against his own destructive selfhood, and, free at last "from the silly Greek & Latin slaves of the Sword" (Preface), invests the virtues of strife in arts of peace. Book 1 of *The Prelude* catalogues eligible epic

---

[16] In the long view, all three poets promoted early nineteenth-century British nationalism in its progressive aspect. Like other Low Church adherents of an "anti-aristocratic social philosophy," they pursued the old goal of equality but did so under patriotic cover: see Gerald Newman, *The Rise of English Nationalism: A Cultural History 1740–1830* (New York: St. Martin's, 1987) 241.

[17] See Brian Wilkie, *Romantic Poets and Epic Tradition* (Madison and Milwaukee: University of Wisconsin Press, 1965) 80, on Wordsworth's machinery.

themes of the ordinary kind (157–224)—several of which Wordsworth's successors would in fact treat within the decade.[18] Yet these he discards, backing almost imperceptibly into the unprepossessing territory of personal memoir, like a shy suitor who has come calling for Calliope and falls for her mother instead. Moreover, and in accordance with the generic redefinition here implied, the epic crisis that arrives many books later in *The Prelude* hinges on the memoirist's climactic renunciation of political action in the world. Wordsworth forswears traditional epic greatness the same way Blake's Milton does, by a fraught process of disaffiliation from the acknowledged virtues he has vested in a closely cathected double (the Satanic Robespierre: 10.535–66), whose expurgation from the text marks the emergence of a corrected Romantic ideal.[19]

Each poet's disavowal of existing norms was also, to be sure, a radical recovery of those norms. *Milton* celebrates as its victory an abolition of the very distinction between victors and losers, and *The Prelude* renounces activism only to pursue a cultural politics of transformation that will be more oblique but deeper-rooted.[20] Both poets' exercise of a loyal opposition from within the tradition was continuous with that tradition as received from Homer and transmitted by Virgil. All the same, with these

[18] Among these unwitting gleaners in Wordsworth's epic field we treat in Chapter 4 Holford's *Wallace*, Walker's *Gustavus Vasa*, and Drummond's *Odin*. Kenneth R. Johnston, *Wordsworth and The Recluse* (New Haven and London: Yale University Press, 1984), observes strong family resemblance, not only among the poet's rejected themes, but between them and the eventual theme of *The Prelude* (94, 128). See also Wilkie, *Romantic Poets*, 66–70.

[19] See Brooke Hopkins, "Representing Robespierre," in *History and Myth: Essays on English Romantic Literature*, ed. Stephen C. Behrendt (Detroit: Wayne State University Press, 1990): for Wordsworth "Robespierre's murder appeared to mean that the satanic part of himself had been murdered as well"—a terrorist coup rendered inevitably problematic by the persistence of the very "kind of power" in which victim and assassin alike dealt (123, 126). In Blake's poem a similar logic informs the climactic confrontation between Milton and his finally recognized double Satan. Ronald Paulson, *Representations of Revolution (1789–1820)* (New Haven and London: Yale University Press, 1983), sees how the two epics draw alike on a Burkean pattern of "internalization," wherein political revolution models the very process by which it is rejected in favor of transformations personal and cultural in nature (251, 272–75).

[20] It was never, in Wordsworth's mind at least, a question of recantation but rather of singing more effectually. See Zera Fink, "Wordsworth and the English Republican Tradition," *Journal of English and Germanic Philology* 47 (1948) 107–26. On publication of *The Prelude*, Macaulay wrote in his journal for 28 July 1850, "The poem is in the last degree Jacobinical, indeed Socialist": quoted in Stephen Gill, *Wordsworth and the Victorians* (Oxford: Clarendon Press, 1998) 29. Marilyn Butler, *Romantics, Rebels and Reactionaries: English Literature and its Background 1760–1830* (Oxford: Oxford University Press, 1981) 66–67, grounds *The Prelude*'s claim to be "a national epic" in the balance it expressly strikes between "the social, secular ideology sustaining the Revolution" and "the ideology of the conservative powers," including "the emotional appeal of traditional religion," that was resurgent in Britain during the period of its composition.

first fully achieved Romantic epics we encounter a quantum shift. Blake's and Wordsworth's reinterpretations of central generic norms were so fundamental as to have made the poems legible in their day as epics only to contemporaries who brought to them enough conversancy with the epic past to open their minds to what the genre might look like in the future. This meant Coleridge, of course, for *The Prelude*, which expressly addresses him throughout; for *Milton*, problematically but here irresistibly, it meant that same William Hayley whose patronizing stance towards epic in 1782 (as we met it in Chapter 1) and towards Blake himself (as it provokingly emerged in literal poetic patronage two decades later) were kindred forms of the same false friendship.

Such readers, fit though very few, would also have observed another quite traditional feature of these highly original works: citationally coded into each of them is a declaration of its summative place in the poet's work to date. The scholarship on classical, medieval, and neoclassical epic that accumulated during the eighteenth century had made much of the place an heroic poem held in a poet's progress from the lesser into the greater genres. Systematically if idiosyncratically, Blake and Wordsworth declared their majority by recapitulating within the text of *Milton* and *The Prelude* this career development from wind sprint into the full afflatus of *longue haleine*.[21] They made a version of their own most ambitious earlier writing a part—an essential part, but only a part—of the new epic whole, which correctively judged the mode of that earlier writing by putting it in its place. In such self-allusive maneuvers the poet took personally, by intimate professional example, the revisionist ethos that informed his larger, course-correcting plot.

Readers may rue Blake's choice to premise the reparative odyssey of his hero Milton on the lengthy audition of "A Bard's prophetic Song" that feels like something out of the murky depths of *Vala, or The Four Zoas*.[22] But the thwarted narrative tangle of the Bard's song affects Milton as it does precisely because of the way it is told; its intricate narrative frustration here

---

[21] On epic's role in the ubiquitous poet's progress see Johnston, *Wordsworth and* The Recluse, 11–12. Stuart Peterfreund, "*The Prelude*: Wordsworth's Metamorphic Epic," *Genre* 14 (1981) 441–72, illustrates the recapitulative principle extensively in Wordsworth, also remarking its presence in Blake and Keats. Alan Liu, *Wordsworth: The Sense of History* (Stanford: Stanford University Press, 1989), finds the poet recapitulating the genres, including epic, in order to free himself of the entanglement with historical determination that is specific to each (223, 361).

[22] Thomas A. Vogler observes that, in the shrill "Bardity" of the Bard's Song, Blake offers "a parody of his own style": "Re: Naming MIL/TON," in *Unnam'd Forms: Blake and Textuality*, ed. Vogler and Nelson Hilton (Berkeley: University of California Press, 1986) 152.

functions deliberately to provoke. "Mine is the fault!" mutters Los (8.19), "I am the Author of this Sin!" proclaims Leutha (11.35); and all the while the conjunctions "For" and "But" and "So," when we press them for the explanatory help they seem to offer, instead trade places in a mazy dance of etiological cross- and counter-ascription. With insoluble exasperations of this kind the reader of Blake's 1790s epyllia is already acquainted (Ch. 2). What *Milton: A Poem* goes on to recount is how such things are reacted to by a reader of genius, an Eternal intelligence in fact with a gift for indignation, whom the text names John Milton. Here is a reader capable of taking charge, which is to say of taking blame and taking action too. As the sheer pileup of blame narratives within the Bard's song bankrupts accountability, it precipitates in the Eternal mind of Milton a new understanding that the corrective fix must be now or never. Responsibility and opportunity exist in the present if anywhere; and a thoroughly fresh interpretation of that sublimely initiatory guilt-trip *Paradise Lost*, channeled through the rapt person of William Blake in his own back yard, becomes a recreative act worthy of a new form. That form turns out to be prismatic, polymorphously complex, yet free at last of the story-jamming impedimenta dragged across the Bard's song by all those doomed attempts to straighten out the past. The new form for narrative that Blake found in *Milton* is so fully given to the present moment (the one that Satan's Watch Fiends cannot find) as to extemporize a space *ex tempore*, out of time altogether. Blake's epic-inhibiting 1790s suspicion that continuous plots were oppressive master narratives in disguise gave way here to a plot about the abdication of mastery, period.[23]

Wordsworth, with comparable daring, frames the glad preamble of *Prelude* 1.1–54—after the fact and thus to the reader's surprise—as a quotation from his own younger self. The passage thus framed stands at once as a rebuke to the unpurged anxiety he proceeds to confess and as a challenge to his maturer understanding of what spontaneous natural joy means as a cultural force in his disenchanted day. Wordsworth's casual opening thus performs the work of epic invocation, posing a question to which the whole poem will narrate a reply, within the elaborate interchange of

---

[23] Or as Andrew Cooper puts it in *Doubt and Identity in Romantic Poetry* (New Haven and London: Yale University Press, 1988), "*Milton* progressively uses up its various narrative styles," calling every subgenre it invokes into question until "*Milton* the poem self-annihilates just like Milton the character" (59). Serial acts of expurgation spelled out in narrative time mount, not to the cluttered gridlock of *Vala*, but to an instantaneous exhaustion that zeroes out Blake's mythological account and presents the world anew (72–73)—an emendation structurally comparable to the chastened Wordsworth's at the start of *Prelude* 11.

sensory stimulus with reflective response for which this opening sets the pattern.[24] We now know how often the stimulant passages ("spots of time," 11.257) came straight from the poet's notebooks of the 1790s and thus how Wordsworth, like Blake, was both a rhapsode at work stitching epic out of unconnected episodes formerly drafted and a critic recognizing the inadequacy of such episodes unless they could be fitted into a larger fabric. In Wordsworth's case the sinuous unifying thread was a commentary that made connected sense out of unreprocessed sensation. The text grew epical in the course of giving significant direction to the fraught anecdotes that primary memory had generated: first through tentative, subtly changing interpretation of the discrete spots of time themselves, and secondarily through their arrangement as intervals within an evolving life story.

All long poems are made out of shorter ones, and as the venerable genre of genres epic had long embedded and assimilated heterogeneous constituents in its broader design. *Milton* and *The Prelude*, however, not only incorporated such constituents but metabolized them, making the supersession of first drafts by second thoughts their very theme. Wordsworth expressly presents the spots of time as food by which the mind is "nourished and invisibly repaired": he repairs to them a confessedly broken man, and they "lift" him up "when fallen" (11.264–67). Although Blake scorned the notion that the Muses were daughters of Memory, and condemned the appearance of evasive abstraction in Wordsworth's mnemonic imagination, what *The Prelude* calls "repair" and "renovation" (11.259) bears comparison with what *Milton* presents under the sign of "The Reprobate who never cease to Believe" (plate 25). Reprobation as reproof, or scolding, is what the Bard's stormy tale has been all about, to no good end beyond that of moving Milton to go and do otherwise. But the term also names a re-probation, a fresh inquest into what took place during a prior trial of faith, so as not to debunk it but to recover its authentic power. Never to "cease to Believe" is an active rather than static condition, and for both Blake and Wordsworth

[24] Generously conceived, this interchange is the great and consistent theme of Wordsworth's poetry. Its most generous critical conception to date occurs in Liu's remarkable book, which grounds the Wordsworthian experience of "sense" in a narrativizing structure of anticipatory retrospect. Johnston, *Wordsworth and* The Recluse, 88, epitomizes the structure thus: "Once upon a time I am living happily ever after." It was the plotted design of *The Prelude* to bring this deep structure—history in the pre-emptive making—to consciousness at book length. David Bromwich, *A Choice of Inheritance: Self and Community from Edmund Burke to Robert Frost* (Cambridge, Mass., and London: Harvard University Press, 1989) correlates this epic project to the newly elective quality that history assumed in the revolutionary era: "then for the first time, a general defense of history can take on an air of heroic defiance" (56).

circa 1805 it exacted the re-proof of epic by perseverance in a continuing origination.

"How shall I trace the history, where seek | The origin of what I then have felt?" (2.365–66) asks Wordsworth, dangling inquiry over the enjambed line in order to recollect in bemused tranquility what he already knows: that, since each thought traced faithfully backwards "Hath no beginning" (2.236), the imagination has no choice but to start over. Blake's plate 3 contrives a matching prosodic stunt, amid his usual epic fourteeners, with the hypermetrical gnomic motto "All things begin & end in Albions ancient Druid rocky shore," where the enjambed extra foot "-ky shore" hangs in a cloud over pictured Stonehenge, to make game of where art begins or ends along a margin (key, shore) of multimedia text. Again, since an epic poem was classically a duodecimal entity, Blake first engraved "in 12 Books" on his title plate; but then, having contrived to contract the whole affair of *Milton* into just two books, he didn't scruple to rub out the place-holding digit "1" and so install a late change of mind bibliographically at the top of his reader's experience. The second chance is where one starts from.

Never-ceasing faith in the ever-present identity of origins and ends is not a disposition conducive to extended narrative, but these poems bet that the risk and renewal of such a faith can be. Blake and Wordsworth had both known despondency during the years before they wrote these first full epics, and the political determinants of that despondency gave them reason to deem their experience typical of the generation to which they belonged and wished to speak. They wished to speak, moreover, in terms that would consist with the revolutionary principles for which the political hopes of their generation had suffered and nearly died.[25] Hence the fundamentally *corrective* character of the plot actions they embraced. Milton belatedly sees that an unpurged aspect of his Satan's ruling passion, pride, has without his realizing it tainted *Paradise Lost* with self-righteousness clear up to heaven. Seeing also (as Satan never could) that late is never too late, he plunges to eternal death in order to wash off the not-human from what he has made.

---

[25] On the governing role this purpose held for Wordsworth and Coleridge alike, see Johnston, *Wordsworth and* The Recluse, xv, 64. At the end of the *Prelude* narrative, "There was nothing left to do but make Imagination the full antagonist of the Revolution, not because they were so different, but because, in his experience and the experience of the best minds of his generation, they had seemed so promisingly similar" (174).

Wordsworth's mood is less operatic but similar in structure: led by the best of intentions to misconstrue the best of upbringings (nature's), he gives his heart to a revolutionary ideal that sours and spoils. Bereft of political identity, despairing of moral questions and deserted by creative joy, the poet recovers all these things again, through a self-recognition that eludes explanation—as does the self-recognition of Blake's Milton, at once lost and saved in the untheorizable, yet still narratable, pulsation of an artery. The resistance of the Wordsworthian redemptive moment to appropriation by religion, philosophy, psychology, morality, or politics is both expressed and compensated by *The Prelude*'s widening threefold plot structure: Cambridge, then home (books 3–4); London, then home again to the Lakes (books 7–8); France, then home again at last to England (books 9–10). The spots of time lie embedded "in our existence" (11.257), not open to our understanding.[26] Like them, the plotted epiphanies of conversion and return in the poet's life demand recording as urgently as they defy translation into any medium beyond the epic song. Their record in that song confers a critical dividend: the now-conscious recapture of what Wordsworth unwittingly lost, in the first place, because ignorance was the bliss in which he had possessed it.

To hell and back: a harrowing trip, and the source of many an epic souvenir; yet it may lie just around the corner. That both poems retrace this Virgilian, Dantesque, Miltonic trajectory more than once is a cardinal feature of their revisionary design. Wordsworth in retrospect grasps his unhappiness at Cambridge and disgusted horror at London as having rehearsed his agony of political identity in France. He grasps too at a chastened hope on which we shall see *The Excursion* built in Chapter 4: the hope that multiple survival has graven into his poem a pattern with future instructive potential. Blake from the twelfth plate until the end of *Milton* underscores by narrative refraction his motif of heroic descent—down from heaven, through inter-dimensional earthly geography and history centered on Blake himself, and on thence into the abyss of selfhood. Each sequentially told confrontation Milton undergoes—with Urizen, a pretty easy mark; then with Wm Blake the engraver, willing to help out if an excitable butterfingers;

[26] The logical disconnect between traumatic event and overflowing emotion that Johnston, *Wordsworth and* The Recluse, 69, remarks in the two-part *Prelude* of 1798–99 was largely respected in the epic expansions of 1805 and 1850, where the intercalated discourse is apter to muse on mystery than to decode it.

then with that colony or gaggle of persons Ololon; then with Satan himself, the very demon in Milton's own looking-glass—makes a vivid history.[27] But these incidents are at the same time concurrent versions of one action prophetically apprehended. What was refractory in the Bard's song is in the narrative proper prismatically splayed, as by Zoa spectrography, into mutually focusing corrective lenses.[28]

Thus both epics render the many-sided emendation of a single flaw that has meanwhile produced a whole lot of unintended consequences. The differential repetition of the poet-hero's central deed generalizes this deed chorically to cover a multitude of sinners, as it strengthens by mythic complication an affiliation to the epic convention of underworld descent. The two poems adapt other conventions to like effect, for example those of the epic metropolis and the dynastic wedding. Blake beholds in Satan "A ruind Man: a ruind building of God not made with hands," whose decadence then brings forth in the text what it has brought forth in the history of civilization—"stupendous ruins | Arches & pyramids & porches" (38.16–22)—which Blake's giant forms labor in turn to reconceive as the Bride who is the human city Jerusalem, Albion's partner of spousal desire.[29] Wordsworth on his urban tour regards London as a city insane and maddening, at once sign and cause of mankind's fall; in its stead he seeks foundation in the "One great society" of "the noble living and the noble dead" (10.968–69), a society consecrated by the hierogamy of imagination and world under the rainbow sign of a natural piety kinder than Virgil's, truer than Milton's, more honest than both.[30]

---

[27] For W. J. T. Mitchell, "Blake's Radical Comedy: Dramatic Structure as Meaning in *Milton*," in *Blake's Sublime Allegory: Essays on* The Four Zoas, Milton, Jerusalem, ed. Stuart Curran and Joseph A. Wittreich, Jr. (Madison: University of Wisconsin Press, 1973) 306, Ololon's plurality is that of an epic chorus showing, in counterpoise to Milton's death-bound solo heroism, how "to live and hope": "a vision of all the Lord's people becoming prophets." With infectious irreverence Andrew Elfenbein, *Romantic Genius: The Prehistory of a Homosexual Role* (New York: Columbia University Press, 1999), highlights the polymorphous, transsexual goofiness of Ololon, whose performance of an "omnigendered Blakean ridiculous" rescues the sublime "narcissistic pseudo-genius" of male individualism from itself (170, 159).

[28] See Albert J. Rivero, "Typology, History, and Blake's *Milton*," *Journal of English and Germanic Philology*, 81 (1982): "*Milton* portrays not so much an action as a visionary moment within which that action is apprehended" in Blake's version of typological overlay (45).

[29] Fred Whitehead proposes reading Blake's civics as a restitution of the primal sociological fall that took place when the great cities arose *c.*4000 BCE. "William Blake and Radical Tradition," in Norman Rudich, *Weapons of Criticism: Marxism in America and the Literary Tradition* (Palo Alto: Ramparts Press, 1976) 193–94.

[30] Abbie Findlay Potts, *Wordsworth's* Prelude: *A Study of Its Literary Form* (Ithaca: Cornell University Press, 1953), concludes from her exhaustive review of the poet's working manuscripts

It is a commonplace that Romantic epic poems take the poetic self as their focus. *Milton* and *The Prelude* certainly do so, but we misunderstand them if we take this self-centeredness as indicating a radically subjective orientation that somehow swept into hegemonic power with the new century, just as we misunderstand the literary history of the period if we suppose lyric to have been its leading genre.[31] In fact the continuing prestige of epic among the Romantic poets ran almost directly counter to any such drastic shift within the generic hierarchy or its subtending philosophical or social premises; another half century would need to elapse before the Spasmodist poets indeed overhauled epic in the image of a colossal lyric (Ch. 9). So the presence of Blake within *Milton*, and even of Wordsworth within an admittedly autobiographical epic, calls for other sorts of explanation that are consistent with the poets' ambition to speak not for themselves but, through themselves, for their country. They realized this ambition by coming forward as *exemplary* figures: imaginative creations, that is, regularly obtruded as such on the reader's attention. Blake in several graphic and written plates (notably 21 and 29) makes a literal spectacle of himself, stands out within the fiction *as* a fiction and not apart from it. Wordsworth's famous self-interruption during the Simplon narrative of book 6, where the imagination rises up to block "the eye and progress of my song" (6.526), is only the most conspicuous of many apostrophes and asides within *The Prelude*, which keep before our minds the work of writing that has gone into the work we read.[32]

Two richly interactive and partially opposed effects follow from this self-obtrusive practice. The first is healthy skepticism on the reader's part, without the postulation of which Blake certainly, and Wordsworth probably, could

and eighteenth-century models that the epic-making social dimension of vision in *The Prelude* is due to the deliberate embrace of a "pre-Christian myth" of "primal Man guarded by vestal Nature" (362). On the edifying interplay of ruin with metropole in Wordsworth's democratic-humanist imagination, see Johnston, *Wordsworth and* The Recluse, xxiii.

[31] Indispensable correctives to this still widespread supposition of lyric predominance are found in Marilyn Butler, *Romantics*; and in Stuart Curran, *Poetic Form and British Romanticism* (New York and Oxford: Oxford University Press, 1986). We are likelier to get at the truth about generic relations by asking how at this turbulent epoch the generic amplitude of the epic, or the novel, fostered change within the lyric constituency it incubated. On this theme in our two poets see Herbert Lindenberger, *On Wordsworth's* Prelude (Princeton: Princeton University Press, 1963) 102–16; Peter A. Taylor, "Providence and the Moment in Blake's *Milton*," *Blake Studies* 4 (1971) 43–60; James Chandler, *Wordsworth's Second Nature: A Study of the Poetry and Politics* (Chicago and London: University of Chicago Press, 1984) 206; Liu, *Wordsworth*, 51, 214, 428.

[32] Lindenberger, *On Wordsworth's* Prelude, 9–14, appreciates the generic significance of what these passages dramatize: the poet's struggle with questions of spokesmanship.

never have pursued a connected narrative so far. Both poets solicit a resistant reader, because both poets know—have indeed thrown an unflattering spotlight on, via the humiliation of their own idealism—the capacity of an ambitiously inclusive plot to ensnare the best of minds. A second solicitation, equally strong, accompanies this first one: that the reader in resisting the work should also collaborate in forwarding it. Hence the dialogism noted by every reader of Wordsworth, the alternation between bursts of narrative or descriptive power and stretches of patient rumination, either one of which left to itself would blunt readerly response. Hence too the elaborated tactics of Blake's illuminated plates, where the block of color and the wall of words defend against each other's seductive hegemony. These forms of dynamic interplay, exemplifying the extroverted incorporation of the poet as historical individual into the action of his epic, mean that the poem is itself a living sequel of that action, and therefore that the action is—"Not in a mystical and idle sense," as Wordsworth insisted, "But in the words of reason deeply weighed" (2.234–35)—not yet concluded. The reader's interval of appreciatively imaginative engagement with the text qualitatively adjoins the interval of creative criticism in which the poet wrote it.

Since epics first were *written*, say since Virgil treated his Aeneas to an underground prophecy of the generosity of his patron and the reign of his emperor, major instances of the genre have reached a hand through time to catch the far-off interest of their absent reader's present. The complex recompense that literary epic has always sought for the primal loss of orality emerges in the Romantic poet's contriving to make epic both a record of events and eventful in its own right—and "eventful" in the etymological sense of that term: still forthcoming, imperfect, consequential because prelusive. Blake's "Finis" on plate 43 of *Milton* balances, by design, an infinitive one-liner that contests it: "To go forth to the Great Harvest & Vintage of the Nations." Likewise the last verse paragraph of *The Prelude* addresses, through Coleridge, the eventual reader whom Wordsworth intends to go forth to:

> we may be
> United helpers forward of a day
> Of firmer trust, joint labourers in the work—
> Should Providence such grace to us vouchsafe—
> Of their redemption, surely yet to come.
>
> (13.437–41)

Inviting readers to become "joint labourers in the work," the foundational Romantic epic pursues by modern means the old generic aim of communal recruitment into the project of provident trust that is culture. Wordsworth and Blake thus set a pattern in which we shall see the century's most experimental, tentative, and conscientious epoists working distinct variations. Shelley and Browning, Byron and Hardy too, were able to finish their epics only by leaving them, in the infinitive and invocatory sense pioneered here, undone.

Southey, in contrast, and much like his hero Prince Madoc, got things done. Comparison to the master poets just named reveals Southey as the perennial journeyman he was, especially in the long-meditated work of 1805 that was to have been his masterpiece but never measured up. Southey seems to have been disappointed by *Madoc*, as for different reasons the reader will be whose appetite for postcolonialist critique has been whetted by learning that the plot involves pre-Columbian Welsh emigration to Central America, which region was astir with nationalism in the early nineteenth century, and distinctly an object of Britain's commercially interested eye.[33] *Madoc* is too ethnocentrically complacent to make for comfortable reading now, yet it is also a little too fair-minded to reward really eager ideological assault. Besides, for all its surface adventurism the poem is too bland, like its unexceptional blank verse, to take us far into the heart of any but a bureaucratically gray darkness.[34] *Madoc*, in short, is an *Aeneid* for the Romantic period, a budding poet laureate's official portrait of a blameless captain wandering between two worlds, founding a makeshift regime, and dutifully patrolling there an order as humanely maintained as the nature of the case will permit. Here are Virgil's probity, Virgil's compassionate piety (compassion-fatigue included), even some of Virgil's openness to internal

[33] Robert Aguirre, *Informal Empire: Mexico and Central America in Victorian Culture* (Minneapolis: University of Minnesota Press, 2005) dates from the turn-of-the-century expeditions by Alexander von Humboldt "the British quest for and representation of pre-Columbian antiquity," in which *Madoc* was an early entrant. For a longer and more conventional historical perspective on Anglo-Mesoamerican relations see Elie Halévy, *The Liberal Awakening* (1923), tr. E. I. Watkin (New York: Barnes and Noble, 1961) 165–87.

[34] The subtlest ideological assessment the poem has received centers on its mediation of imperial themes via Welsh–English cultural politics: Caroline Franklin, "The Welsh American Dream: Iolo Morganwg, Robert Southey and the Madoc Legend," in *English Romanticism and the Celtic World*, ed. Gerald Carruthers and Alan Rawes (Cambridge: Cambridge University Press, 2003) 69–84.

subversion of the party line.[35] Absent Virgil's depth of feeling, however, and his brilliance of articulation, the poem remains something of the chore it must have become for Southey—supremely task-oriented poet though he was—as he put it aside and took it up again over the course of fifteen years.

Gestating his most properly epic work at the same time as Blake and Wordsworth, Southey settled like them on a plot that valorized the second chance. The poem comes in two unequal parts: "Madoc in Wales" runs to eighteen chapter-like books, "Madoc in Aztlan" to twenty-seven; and these proportionable multiples of nine attest a designed imbalance that tilts interest toward the later, westerly course of empire. Both theaters of action are cursed by military strife and diplomatic infighting, which it is Madoc's lot to escape in Wales and his job to eliminate in Mexico, once he has become, as all this poet's protagonists must, an underdog outsider. Moreover, Southey has Madoc make the twelfth-century trip to the New World twice, each time espousing on a different order of magnitude the cause of the oppressed Hoamen community against imperial Aztec armies. (Note in passing the similarity of this succor-punch plot to Ogilvie's in *Britannia*: the ripening of local assistance into fixed dominion would prove a familiar sequence during Britain's imperial century.) Madoc's double exposure to Wales and Mexico works a change in him, but it is only the strictly limited kind of change of which in Chapter 2 we found Southey epics capable: confirmatory intensification of the *status quo ante*. That is, Madoc becomes surer than ever that the Welsh scene has no place for him, and then on his return across the Atlantic confirms a suspicion, which he has nursed all along, that the only way to coexist with the Aztecs is to control and ultimately overthrow them. Where Wordsworth's correction-of-course in *The Prelude* meant turning homeward, and Blake's in *Milton* meant perpetual wholesale reformation, Southey's meant escalation of what, being right to begin with, had only to become even righter.

Like Blake and Wordsworth, Southey supplemented the revisionism of this epic action with a recitation of his own past practice in the genre. Remembering the weirdly cloven text of *Thalaba*, we might say that the task

---

[35] Southey's original preface to *Joan of Arc* had blandly affirmed, "There are few readers who do not prefer Turnus to Aeneas.... What avails a man's piety to the gods, if, in all his dealings with men, he prove himself a villain?" (*Poetical Works* 1: 16). Parallels with the *Aeneid* are discussed by Kenneth Curry in "Southey's *Madoc*: The Manuscript of 1794," *Philological Quarterly* 22 (1943) 347–69.

UNDER CORRECTION: 1800-1805

he set himself in *Madoc* was to integrate the antithetical strengths of that text's poetry and of its notes, by combining in one person two apparently inimical forms of excellence: infallible heroic drive and imperturbable modern knowledge. Although more temperate than Southey's earlier epics, this poem that climaxes in a literal volcanic eruption seethes throughout with an energy that nothing on two continents can quite contain. King David of Wales, the hero's brother, fevers incessantly into unfocused ambition; and he has a transatlantic opposite number in the hyperkinetic warrior Tlalala (not Thalaba, but close), whom the prospect of cultural disenfranchisement drives to suicide on the poem's last page. The presence of these foil characters suggests that Madoc is meant to be different—a statesman, a liberal centrist— yet under the incumbent weight of the duties that define him there courses the wild antinomian will of a natural Southey alien, born to run. The entire plot turns, after all, on this prince's dangerous superfluity at home; and, even in the new land he reshapes to fit his own image of justice, he remains at bottom an exile, an outsider belonging to Thalaba's breed and Joan's. None of the serial crises with which he must cope affects Madoc as wretchedly as the image of his own will that greets him in the daily monotony of racing nowhere on the open sea, at "The centre of that drear circumference, | Progressive, yet no change!" where "speed was toiling in infinity" (1.4.751–54). When Southeyan drive slips the yoke of work it turns into the nightmare of purposelessness, disclosing in "the dreary vacancy of heaven" (1.4.795) an existential void that the formidable industry of the poet, as of all his epic protagonists, seems by turns to fill and to flee.

Yet the fugitive who thus runs on empty is at the same time Southey's most fully fledged version of the epic hero as enlightened man of reason in a disenchanted world. No supernatural machinery here, no wonders beyond the explanatory reach of science.[36] One way to frame the streamlined modern fit between rational protagonist and knowable cosmos is to observe that Madoc himself could have composed the notes to *Madoc*, which are more copious than *Thalaba*'s but much better-behaved to strangers: rather than vaunt and sneer, they respectfully ballast the poem on its linear,

---

[36] Lady Anne Hamilton's *The Epics of the Ton; or, The Glories of the Great World: A Poem, in Two Books* (1807), a celebrity scandal sheet in mock-heroic couplets, includes Southey among its satiric targets. Book 2 ("The Male Book") gets underway by making fun of the "exordium of Madoc" (2.14), and observes near the close that "It is but of late years that an Epic, without machinery, could be expected to be tolerated" (2.1333).

historically diligent way. The aplomb of modern western superiority was vouchsafed by the poet in this work to his hero, who not only prevails easily over hosts of Amerindians through European know-how (tempered weaponry, superior tactics) but also reveals an insight into the dynamics of cultural difference that is worthy of a modern ethnographer.[37] When an Aztec chief supposes the new European arrival to be "more than man," Madoc decides not to "undeceive him" but to "let it work," qualifying his omissive white lie with a home truth: "Our knowledge is our power" (1.6.1313). What this means is soon glossed by Cynetha, an old blind Welshman who sees it all: "First prove your power; | Be in the battle terrible, but spare | The fallen"; neutralizing numerical odds by this machiavellian exhibition of mercy, "Ye shall be | As gods among them" (1.7.1428–29). Neither Madoc nor Southey flinches at the Miltonic thunder of this last allusion—temptation and fall are, apparently, routine costs of doing colonial business—and before long a peace is firmed up by disclaimers of conquest, the allowance of free rein to local folkways, and above all Cynetha's inspired insinuation that in praising his God to the Aztecs he is merely stating the deep truth that underpins their mythology already: "I do but waken up a living sense | That sleeps within ye!" (1.8.1738–39). So it is that the power of the textual annotator infiltrates the epic action and becomes a political force to conjure with.

Alas, two can play this game. It turns out that, among those Aztec folkways Madoc has sworn to leave intact, there sleep oppositional forces that the other side can conjure with as well. While he is away in Wales a revanchist priest stirs up popular resistance around the ancient Snake-God cult ("Before these things I was," 2.3.451), and when the noble but politic King Yuhidthiton concedes that "we must keep the path our fathers kept" (2.5.723), Madoc finds his comparatist bluff called and has to fall back on main force. Foreclosing all dissent "with authority | From Heaven, to give the law, and to enforce | Obedience" (2.8.1374–76), Madoc orders the Hoamen tribe baptized en masse and thereby "made | Partakers" (2.9.1490–91) of that same worship which was earlier asserted to be theirs by unconstrained intuition. The enjambments just quoted will suggest with what grim zest Southey narrates this change in the colonial weather, which opens the season on enough espionage, stratagem, and slaughter to fill out the poem's

---

[37] Jean Raimond, *Robert Southey* (Paris: Didier, 1968) is Gallically blunt: in *Madoc* the supernatural seems that way only to the natives (241).

long remainder. It seems that Cynetha had it wrong, that Madoc's attempt to play the diplomat—the same part that Southey's friend Cottle had lately written for his King Alfred to play in winning the hearts and minds of savage Danes—was now a tactical blunder, and must be scrapped for harsher measures.

It is tempting to read in this episode an allegory of epic's recent turn away from the critical and experimental mode of the 1790s to don the breastplate of versified *raison d'état*, and within that turn to read Southey's defection from a vanguard into an establishment poetry where he might err no longer and shine instead with the Laureate Pye. That is what Byron saw when he looked back at Southey's career, and what he saw is now etched indelibly into literary history. If only for that reason, we should try to counterbalance Byron's lapsarian view with some stress on the continuity between this moment in *Madoc* and the way Southey had gone about epic from the first. For it was his peculiar contribution to the Romantic literature of self-correction that blossomed around 1805 to treat conversion as a matter of turning up the volume. Having dallied with clemency, power now must show its hand plainly. That meant ideology must come clean too; and the way Southey exulted in the purge should be familiar to us from the profiles of Thalaba and indeed of Joan.[38]

From this moment forward in the action of *Madoc* not just the Aztec cult but also the rites of twelfth-century Catholics (including, retroactively, the Welsh bardic ceremonies) are to be regarded as human instruments, wielded with specific leverage and point by knowable interests. All that mumbo-jumbo is so much epical-political machinery, and Southey's epic wants nothing to do with it. "Pure was the faith of Madoc" (1.13.2624)—so puritan, in the refinement of its antithetical energy, that outward religion at its touch must crumble into cultural accidentals. The labor of demystification crowns *Madoc* with its narrative climax in the penultimate book, portentously titled "The Close of the Century." Just as the embattled native priesthood dig in at the Aztec *fin de siècle* for an ultimate contest against the European usurper, their indigenous last stand is preempted when a volcano

[38] Tim Fulford, "Romanticism and Colonialism: Races, Places, Peoples, 1800–1830," in *Romanticism and Colonialism: Writing and Empire, 1780–1830*, ed. Fulford and Peter J. Kitson (Cambridge: Cambridge University Press, 1998) 36, finds figured in *Madoc* as in Southey's flanking epics a "disturbing similarity between Britain and the peoples of its empire." He quotes from the *Eclectic Review* a contemporary complaint about *Madoc*'s "deification of a marauder, possibly as savage as the Indians themselves."

drowns the holy city in lava. If it is nature that trumps civilization here, it is a nature whose ironic sense of timing allies it with a modern anomie, deeply shared by the poet, that can regard nothing as sacred.[39]

What all this ruthless ideological defoliation leaves behind is an *ad hoc* heroism compounded half of pity and half of righteousness, and spared from coming to grips with its contradictions only by the state of emergency that runs it ragged. Madoc, the permanent alien who sees through everything but his own frenetic purposefulness, sees things through to the bittersweet end of being "left sole Lord" (2.27.5280). As the Aztecs become emigrants in their turn and take their household gods away ("No Priest must dwell among us," says Madoc's cathartic decree at 2.27.5142), the sole remaining Lord is a universal-solvent deistic abstraction; the sole remaining comfort is the emaciated nobility that Madoc and Yuhidthiton hail in each other's disenchanted, faintly Homeric adieux.[40] This epic leaves its hero, the conqueror of little and founder of nothing, spearheading disaster relief; and in this aftermath he ends where he began. Early in the poem, just before Madoc narrates his American travels, the "chief of Bards" (1.2.329) sings to the Welsh court the exploits of their ancestral hero Owen. It is an oral epic of national "triumph," which Southey hurries past for the sake of Madoc's telling reaction. Exultant at first, he is then swallowed up in "oppressive memory" of "the fate of all his gallant house" and weeps for "days that were no more" (1.2.357–64). That this lachrymose Aeneas ends

[39] From *Joan of Arc* forward, this manner of Southey's consistently drew fire from the faithful. An unsigned 1815 review of *Roderick* in the *Christian Observer* acutely remarked, in all the poet's epic endnotes, "the different style of thinking and feeling which they appear to shew in the poet and the commentator.... There is something hard, something sarcastic, something scoffing.... 'the knowing style.'" See also the review of *Kehama* in the *Monthly Mirror* (1811): both are excerpted in *Robert Southey: The Critical Heritage*, ed. Lionel Madden (London and Boston: Routledge, 1972) 189 and 134. It fell to the bellwether of early Victorian orthodoxy, John Keble, to defend what was probably close to the then Laureate's own view of the matter. Keble devoted a portion of his Latin lectures at Oxford to reclaiming Southey's practice "by reason of the implied, underlying comparison which the reader's mind spontaneously institutes for itself. While we read, we reflect, that is to say, how one affected and influenced, in this or that manner, by these erroneous beliefs, would develop when once brought to a knowledge of sound and pure religious truth." *Keble's Lectures on Poetry 1832–1841,* tr. Edward Kershaw Francis (Oxford: Clarendon, 1912), 2: 314.

[40] Once colonial *Realpolitik* has wrung the Pantisocratic idealism out of Southey's American venture *Madoc* becomes, as Richard Hoffpauir says, "the bleakest and most uncompromising of his epic moral visions": "The Thematic Structure of Southey's Epic Poetry: Part II," *Wordsworth Circle* 7 (1976) 109. Anna Seward—herself the translator years before of Fénelon's moralized Homer—saw something of the same kind, and grasped its Homeric affiliations, in the figure of "Yuhidthiton, conquered and wandering into exile. He seems to me, in some sort, the Hector of this epic": letter of 15 August 1809 to Southey, in *Letters* (Edinburgh: Constable, 1811) 6: 359.

as a gutted Achilles, succoring the Priam of the Aztecs but unaffected by any felt share in his doom, suggests that Southey's largest project of epic integration could not help reproducing what *Joan* and *Thalaba* had also displayed but had been less chastened by: a radical cleavage between actuating value and consequential action—a split that matters here because so many of his epic successors would exhibit it too.[41]

When the one epicizing poet of his generation who was to outdo Southey in contemporary renown came on the scene in 1805, he too probed the dissociation of motives from deeds, but with a lightness of touch that permanently affected the options for epic writing in the century ahead. "Ancient Metrical Romance" was the classification Scott gave to *The Lay of the Last Minstrel: A Poem* in his introduction, which by disclaiming "combined and regular narrative" disclaimed epic. These gestures deserve no more belief than do Southey's calling *Thalaba* a romance and disdaining for *Madoc* "the degraded title of Epic" (Preface). But in retrospect, and fortified by the remarks Scott later appended on his adaptation of ballad meter, we can recover a sense of how closely the *Lay* skirted epic borders. This would have been instantly apparent to readers whose sharp memory of the Ossian controversy was kept fresh by editions of balladry, themselves controversial, spanning the same years our last two chapters have covered, from revised versions of Percy's *Reliques* to Joseph Ritson's *Ancient Songs* (1790) and subsequent collections to Scott's own *Minstrelsy of the Scottish Border* (1802–3), which would reach a third edition by 1806. George Ellis's thorough scholarship in *Specimens of Early English Metrical Romances*, published the same year as *The Lay*, set Scott's chosen genre on a continuum running from *trouveur* balladry through "something like an epic fable" in the "ruder hands" of the Normans to the Italian refinement of "a new and splendid species of epic poetry."[42] Among contemporary poets Wordsworth

---

[41] In the long view this schism, with its accompanying melancholy, is a generic entailment from Virgil, one that seems to have descended with special purity to Southey via Spenser and Milton. A. D. Nuttall, *Openings: Narrative Beginnings from the Epic to the Novel* (Oxford: Clarendon, 1992), calls it "the special masochism of canonical epic" (86); it also seems close to what Elizabeth J. Bellamy means in attributing neurosis categorically to the "epic subject" because "the libidinal impulses of romance have been left *unrepresented* within the manifest narrative of epic ideology": *Translations of Power: Narcissism and the Unconscious in Epic History* (Ithaca and London: Cornell University Press, 1992) 32.

[42] Ellis, *Specimens of Early English Metrical Romances, Chiefly Written during the Early Part of the Fourteenth Century* (1805; 2nd edn. London: Longman, 1811) 1: 28. Leith Davis, *Acts of Union: Scotland and the Literary Negotiation of the British Nation, 1707–1830* (Stanford: Stanford University

and Coleridge had adapted these forms with epoch-marking originality in *Lyrical Ballads* (1798) and the unpublished but circulating "Christabel," and Southey's "metrical ballads" were cited by Scott as precedents for his own original work. To weigh with these instances the debt owed to the ballad stanza by Blake's epic fourteeners is to appreciate the many-sided adjacency of balladry to epic for the first Romantic generation.

Among this company Scott the poet was uniquely close to the means of balladry's dissemination—primarily through the compromises involved in editing collections for print, secondarily through the conditions of oral performance which the old writings evoked. His major contribution to Romantic epic writing, accordingly, was to insist on the performance values, even the entertainment values, which that writing had as yet only glancingly acknowledged.[43] It was the hypothesis of the previous chapter that epic during the 1790s should have been fun to write; yet not many of that decade's products were (at least designedly) much fun to read. So it is too with the top-of-the-century epics considered here thus far: the Bard's song in Milton is a declamation, not a show; Wordsworth's confessions and exhortations to his "Friend" and stand-in auditor Coleridge are famously, uniformly earnest; the sobriety quotient in Southey's epics if anything goes up as his overblown episodes plummet towards bathos. That the muse of epic might be amusing—a seemingly unavoidable inference from the acknowledged roots of the genre in live performance—was a condition that the first Romantic epics in their hunger for dignity had suppressed. Scott's *Lay* flushed that suppressed condition out into the open, matching it with an open, easily readable verse derivative of popular balladry and smacking too, for good measure in the odd tail-rhyme, of Chaucer's

---

Press, 1998), situates the *Minstrelsy* in relation to Macpherson and Percy, finding in Scott's work "if not an epic of Scotland, then at least a series of sketches that would suggest epic possibilities" (153).

[43] When Scott's long historico-ethnographical preface to the *Minstrelsy* finally comes to discuss the poetry, he instinctively moves, not towards the usual high ground of primitive statecraft or religion, but towards entertainment values: the minstrel harper's songs were "probably the sole resources against *ennui*, during the short intervals of repose from military adventure" (1.cix). Harvey assesses the literary result of this orientation: "What Scott achieved with *The Lay of the Last Minstrel* was the combination of the bulk—and the room for development of plot—of the epic, with the dash, readability, and fervour of the ballads" (*English Poetry*, 99). Marlon B. Ross, "Scott's Chivalric Pose: The Function of Metrical Romance in the Romantic Period," *Genre* 19 (1986) 272–79, approaches the entertainment quotient of the poems as a strategic distraction from contemporary realities, notably the new and class-finessing market conditions that enabled their success.

clowning in *Sir Thopas*.[44] Scott's reward for this indiscretion marks a watershed in literary history: by the time of his death in 1832 sales of *The Lay* had crested the extraordinary figure of forty thousand copies. A few poems that dwelt in the suburbs of epic had, admittedly, kept in touch with this aspect of the genre: there was mischief in Darwin's *Botanic Garden*, and in *Psyche* Tighe could blush into much gentler mirth. It is not accidental that Scott's poem, like these, has to do on both of its narrative levels with quanta of flirtation and courtship for which sterner epic paradigms showed faint tolerance.

The narrative levels themselves, however, were *The Lay*'s chief means of foregrounding narrative as performance, on its shuttle between the substance and the telling of the Last Minstrel's tale. Scholarship honoring this first investigation of what Scott would make his lifelong theme—the means and limits of historical continuity between present and past—has gone to work on both the old (immediately post-Stuart) frame of the poem and the older (imminently Elizabethan) world picture therein contained; but these elements will not bear much scrutiny. Neither the central-casting Minstrel nor the Duchess who favors his entertainment is memorably drawn; and it is plain from the kindly intercalations of the Duchess and her ladies that even they do not value the story he offers them much more highly than the dispassionate modern reader can. Yet all this scarcely matters. The secret of the poem's success lay elsewhere: in the means of its transmission, in the ingenious modulation of new-old verse and in the presentation of the narrative frame as itself a text in motion, i.e., a narrative possessing independent value.[45] The speed with which these same means were adopted by contemporary poets suggests as much; so does their recurrence as fixtures of long verse narrative across the nineteenth century.

---

[44] The best approach to the verse as such remains Donald Davie's practical application of a Jakobsonian "poetry of grammar" in "The Poetry of Sir Walter Scott," *Proceedings of the British Academy* 47 (1961) 61–75. Thomas Crawford extends Davie's remarks to consider effects of cumulative augmentation as a "ballad epic" technique in "Scott as a Poet," *Etudes Anglaises* 24 (1971) 478–91; and in *Scott* (Edinburgh: Scottish Academic Press, 1982) 36–37, 44–45.

[45] The interest lies, not in evocation of any given time, but in the interwoven "contrast and interpenetration of *times*" (Crawford, *Scott*, 44). As Robert Crawford puts it in *Devolving English Literature* (Oxford: Clarendon Press, 1992), Scott's frame technique here as later in the *Waverley* novels "lends an elegiac, distancing tinge to the adventure, a scholarly wordiness which at once fully explains and consciously distances the action" (117). The same effect is reinforced at a further remove by the numerous antiquarian notes accompanying the 1805 and later editions: detailed consideration of Scott's "poetry of scholarship" occurs in J. H. Alexander, The Lay of the Last Minstrel: *Three Essays* (Salzburg: Universität Salzburg, 1978) 176–96.

The enduring technical appeal that Scott's innovations held for authors, and the aesthetic spell they cast on readers, cannot have been due for long to the novelty they possessed on first appearance. Scott himself was the first to find the vein played out when he turned from *Rokeby* in 1813 to what prose might offer in *Waverley* the next year. What the narrative devices of *The Lay of the Last Minstrel* had actually done, and kept promising to do for later, less agile imitators, was tap and manage vast reserves of Romantic-era anxiety over time: modernity's irreversible usurpation of an increasingly marginalized tradition; the pastness of the past, and what that implied about both the transiency of the present and the dubious authenticity of any recapture of so fugitive a stuff as history.[46] These temporal themes early-Romantic epoists had tended to omit—whether in innocence or in conscious and active suppression is a nice question, given the inherent antiquity of the form they chose to work in. Landor and Wordsworth are apparent exceptions; yet in *Gebir* the inertia of the past means the end of epic, while Wordsworth's temporal meditations however complex take place almost exclusively on the field of a single lifespan (in *The Excursion*, we shall find, as well as *The Prelude*). For Cumberland, Blake, Southey, and the rest, the relation of past to present remained serenely unproblematic. Not so, however, for Scott or, to judge from the enthusiasm *The Lay* excited, for the reading public either. History was a problem, not just a resource. With unobtrusive genius Scott both acknowledged the problem and proposed to solve it through the continuity-therapy that a sympathetic writer and reader might conspire to effect.

This solution saturates the narrative at both levels, and is especially evident in the relation between them: the Bard and Duchess transact so well because they meet each other's wants. "While thus he pour'd the lengthen'd tale" (2.34), she sips at his story as he drains her wine, with a mutual refreshment showing how the past and the present can host one

---

[46] Jane Millgate, *Walter Scott: The Making of the Novelist* (Edinburgh: Edinburgh University Press, 1984), correlates Scott's "uneasiness" as a poetic creator with the erection of protectively binding frames that induce an effect "curiously double, drawing the reader into the world of the poem even while continually reminding him of its fictionality" (18). What James Buzard, "Translation and Tourism: Scott's *Waverley* and the Rendering of Culture," *Yale Journal of Criticism* 8 (1995) 45 *declares about Waverley* already had pertinence to *The Lay*: like "Scotland itself" in the early 19th cent., it "tests the limits of readers' and tourists' willingness to overlook the evidence of phoniness." For Dino Franco Felluga, *The Perversity of Poetry* (Albany: State University of New York Press, 2005), the split-level appeal of Scott's nostalgia depends on our understanding, "even on the level of his works' diegesis, that medievalism is always already in the process of being superseded" (52–53).

another after all, and, when conditions are right, achieve a conviviality in excess of the actual quality of the fare. Reciprocal entertainment: a tale of bygone but knowable days in a diction quaint but not too old may find a home in ears attuned by sympathy. Furthermore, the nineteenth-century reader's reception of the framing tale of the tale's recovery operates, by suasive sleight of hand, as an *a fortiori* attestation of the internal tale's probability.

> It is the secret sympathy,
> The silver link, the silken tie,
> Which heart to heart, and mind to mind
> In body and in soul can bind.
>
> (5.13)

Thus the Minstrel, aside to his hearers, also stakes Scott's claim to a poetics of "True love" that tropes, in the currency of sentimentalism, a pervasive historicist desire.[47]

Such time-travel bromides were strong medicine once, and the fact that we swallow them reluctantly nowadays attests the success with which Scott sponsored their distribution two hundred years ago. To his credit Scott also acknowledged, from the very first, that at the basis of his trade lay those mind-altering substances ink and paper. For with great candor he planted at the core of *The Lay of the Last Minstrel* a technology of enchantment that took, as his poem did, the form of a book brought back from afar by a man named Scott: Michael Scott, in this instance, a dead wizard and Holy Land pilgrim from the thirteenth century who swims up into living Tudor memory through what an 1830 note merrily calls "a poetical anachronism." It is the gambit of *The Lay* to establish a relationship between the anachronizing poetry that annuls centuries and the magical power of "words" (2.13, 2.14) wrought into the wizard's "Book of Might" (2.19).[48] The "glamour" or "gramarye" of this Book, its binding *grammar*, takes the form of spells that enchant the mind with "delusion" (3.9, 3.11), spells moreover that must be not only studied but recited in order to take effect. In other words magic,

[47] Nancy Goslee demonstrates that Scott's invocation of "cultural nostalgia" to foster a politically conciliatory, interpersonal "emotional intensity" persisted into his last romance epic: " 'Letters in the Irish Tongue': Interpreting Ireland in Scott's 'Rokeby,' " in *Scott and his Influence,* ed. J. H. Alexander and David Hewitt (Aberdeen: Association for Scottish Literary Studies, 1983) 48.
[48] Felluga, *Perversity of Poetry,* 64–66, works out this relationship between the two Scotts' books as governed by the inexorable if fuzzy logic whereby well-seasoned half-belief in heroic romance reproves the vulgarity of whole-hog Gothic credulity.

like the Minstrel's lay, is a doubly *performative* language art, which makes things happen in the world by virtue of its entertainment in the mind through vocal performance. The poetic language describing the Book's agency twinkles with wordplay: to pore over it awhile is to "read a spell," folksily speaking; "might" as power blends with "might" as the auxiliary verb that entertains possibilities.

And then there is Gilpin Horner, the legendary figure on whom (Walter) Scott's aristocratic patroness ordered him to write her a ballad. This folk grotesque whose theft and return of the magic Book form a major strand of plot is so consistently called the "Goblin-Page" that we nearly miss the double-entendre of his nemesis in the final canto: "Resistless flash'd the levin-brand, | And fill'd the hall with smouldering smoke, | As on the elvish page it broke" (6.25). This act, whereby ancient magic reclasps its own and the eldritch page we read about vanishes for good, figures the act of inscriptive violence whereby orality yields to literacy in the apparition of the "page" mechanically "branded," the enchanting (and copyright-protected) page we read. An early reviewer hailed in Scott's supernatural book and page an epic "machinery" employed to "very happy effect," and so it was.[49] To recall Wordsworth's searching cultural inquest into the reading of books (*Prelude,* book 5), or Blake's obsessive recurrence to their inscription and material production as weaponry for "mental fight" (*Milton,* Preface), is to appreciate at once the contemporary resonance of Scott's chosen machinery and, thanks to the sureness of touch that made him Wizard of the North, his unique success in actually working the machinery of print culture to so swift and broad a result. That result is figured by the poem's final canto as nothing short of revelatory, in the full *Dies Irae* sense: the fiery consumption of the written page, "shrivelling like a parched scroll" (6.31) within a revocalized manifestation of full presence on altogether modern terms.[50]

---

[49] *Literary Journal* (March 1805), rpt. in *Scott: The Critical Heritage*, ed. John O. Hayden (New York: Barnes and Noble, 1970) 27. Richard Cronin, *The Politics of Romantic Poetry: In Search of the Pure Commonwealth* (Houndmills: Macmillan, 2000) 98, underscores "the negligible role in the poem's plot" that is played by the Book of Might; Scott's machinery is there to mobilize the poem's other plot, we may conclude, the connection between present and past that we call history. Nearly at the end of our period a throwaway remark of Gilbert Murray's crowns the 19th-cent. migration from oral to literate premises for epic that Scott had begun. In archaic Greece, Murray proposes, consulting the Muses meant neither more nor less than reading a traditional book like Michael Scott's: see *The Rise of the Greek Epic* (Oxford: Clarendon Press, 1907) 94–95.

[50] See Nancy M. Goslee, *Scott the Rhymer* (Lexington: University Press of Kentucky, 1988) 39–40. Scott's evocation of apocalyptic imagery suggests the urgency of his project as analyzed by Ross: "to repress the threat of print by representing the *reading* experience of his own poems as a *listening* experience" ("Scott's Chivalric Prose," 285).

A brand-new magic supervenes irreversibly upon an ancient one. Southey and Tighe with their sorceries malign or benevolent, Blake and Wordsworth with their Druids bloodthirsty or chaste, all implied as much in their dawn-of-the-century epics. But a performative redefinition of magic was the very condition of possibility for Scott's oeuvre, just as to assess the good and evil of an historicist supervention on the antique charm remained its challenge. The Book within the book turns inside out the illusionism of toll-free travel along the confluent streams of voice and history—not to debunk it, but to see how it works. It works by imagination as regards a story's internal continuity with itself, and by sympathy as regards the story's reception in the world. The Minstrel frankly makes things up as he goes along on "the full tide of song": "Each blank, in faithless memory void, | The poet's glowing thought supplied" (Introduction). And the muse who overcomes these voids of memory is, in a development that will permanently divert the course of epic into new channels, the fictively surrogated but in truth anonymous reader facing the page from the other side of the mass transaction that published poetry here momentously became.

The sympathetic reader's demicroyant acceptance of the story ("In pity half, and half sincere": 4.35) knits it into the world's fabric—even as that acceptance, having become part of the larger story, forms a fresh knot in the expanding design. "All mourn the Minstrel's harp unstrung, | Their name unknown, their praise unsung" (5.2), admonishes Scott's bard, all the while implying the culturalist epic tenet that is its converse: great poems presuppose great audiences, and readers acclaiming a narrative memorialize themselves thereby to posterity. *The Lay of the Last Minstrel* forwarded that burden expressly, betting the credibility of its own plot on the favorable reception that it indeed received, from a readership eager to be known to the future as shareholders in its version of who they were. As the latest Wizard of the North settled on modern terms into his namesake's medieval role, his pastiche *Lay* showed why no minstrel should ever be accounted the last.[51]

---

[51] A point nicely illustrated, with reference to the final lines' installation of the Minstrel at a border confluence, by Susan Oliver, *Scott, Byron and the Poetics of Cultural Encounter* (Houndmills: Palgrave, 2005) 81–82.

4

In Expiation:

Epic Atonement 1805–1815

It would take a few years, and the maturation of Scott's epic vision in *Marmion* (1808), before a class of poets in training caught the trick of *The Lay of the Last Minstrel* and turned its narrative innovation into a national pastime.[1] Meanwhile by any quantitative measure an older, neoclassical epic model prevailed, in a succession of works that shouldered the burden of nation-formation in time of war. Of the poems we next consider, only the last two are planted in British soil and based on events in British history; but they all ponder in translucent analogy the weighty questions of Britain's internal constitution and place in the world. "My Muse, expand thy wing, | And bid a nation listen while I sing" (1.10), exhorted George Woodley at the launch of *Britain's Bulwarks; or, The British Seaman: A Poem, in Eight Books* (1811), with every confidence that the readers of Britain should prove as patriotically attentive to duty as her tars. Woodley's plot takes the form of a supposed voyage, in books titled "The Outfit," "The Blockade," "The Action," and so on, by a fighting vessel christened *The British Oak*, which vanquishes Frenchmen in the Indies, weathers a Florida hurricane, and is rewarded at last (book 8, "The Return") with news of a well-earned peace. Smooth sailing is ensured to the couplet narrative by the government-issue

[1] Epomania, a nonce coinage by none other than Robert Southey in an 1800 letter, was fast becoming one of the stock jokes the literary world liked to tell about itself. When William Godwin (under the pseudonym Edward Baldwin) envisioned *The Pantheon* in 1806, he wrote that "Calliope, the Epic Muse, was represented bearing books in her hands" (172)—presumably lots of them. In 1808 the *Edinburgh Review* observed, "A correspondent wrote us lately an account of a tea-drinking in the west of England, at which there assisted no fewer than six epic poets—a host of Parnassian strength, certainly equal to six-and-thirty ordinary bards" (11: 362): quoted in R. D. Havens, *The Influence of Milton on English Poetry* (Cambridge, Mass.: Harvard University Press, 1922) 276.

quality of its incidents and persons, and also by a chauvinist progressivism that equates steady improvements in shipbuilding and navigation with Britannia's unquestioned fitness to rule much more than the waves. The same self-taught author's more hurriedly prepared epic from the next year, *Portugal Delivered, A Poem, in Five Books*, requites naval with military glory in a celebration of Wellington's recent Peninsular victories. Here an introductory invocation of Homer's power and equations of Portugal with Ilion, Lisbon with Troy, and Tagus with Scamander (1.5–6) give Woodley's canvas all the generic stretch he needs for what is little more than a versified chronicle of maneuvers in which "men who dare be free" put to flight "The slaves of guilt" (5.114).

A subtler poet who had earlier played the same strong naval suit, William Lisle Bowles, did the usual rite of circumspection at what he falsely called "a time so unfavourable to long poems" (Introduction) and subtitled *The Spirit of Discovery by Sea: A Descriptive and Historical Poem* (1804, second edition 1809). But it is clear from the way he summoned his harp to "a louder and a loftier strain" (1.1), and invoked the shade of Camoens and the spirit of the Thames, that he like Woodley had epic on the brain. Bowles's prefatory analysis of the poem tells how much trouble he had unifying its parts; the arrangement he hit on was after all the standard one for the time, a progress plot that rendered his subtitle nearly redundant: "descriptive" meant "historical," because seeing was organized by narration. The nautical archetype Noah is visited atop Mt. Ararat by an angelic vision whose panorama—a topos that ran strong from Virgil to Milton, and had just been memorably adapted by Bowles's contemporary Wordsworth at the end of the unpublished *Prelude*—transfers command immediately from the visual to the historical sense. Genealogy links all the sailors the poem surveys back to their parent Noah, whose ancestral dominion is diversified across the globe over time. The art of navigation evolves through ever bolder craft from Phoenicia to Portugal to contemporary Britain, which resumes and maximizes the Noachite dominion in an apotheosis of commerce rendering conquest obsolete (1.172, 5 *passim*) and crowning man "The sovereign of the globe!" (2.190).[2] Such soft-core nationalism reminds us that there was

[2] By invoking Camoens and expressly correlating Britain's current with Portugal's former dominion of the seas, Bowles allied his poem with William Julius Mickle's popular 1776 translation of *The Lusiads*. Mickle's apparatus promoted "the Epic Poem of Commerce" by insisting on the historical importance of "events which gave birth to the present commercial system of the world" (xxxiv); "The Fall of Troy is nothing to this" (297).

more than one way to prevail during the decade that was Nelson's as well as Napoleon's. Lauding as the key to international betterment what were in effect the naval means of British domination, Bowles was one of the first poets to practice nationalism without preaching it. He would not be the last.

Other contemporaries preferred working by national analogy. James Montgomery's *The Wanderer of Switzerland* (1806) really did concern legitimately Swiss sorrows brought on by the French occupation of 1798–1803, but that event fastened as it did on the British political imagination because what had befallen one small country protected by natural barriers from its aggressive neighbor might befall another. A lifelong epoist whom we shall meet again, and whose versecraft and sales both rose consistently above the humdrum generic average, Montgomery debuts here trumpeting "To the Public" that "an heroic subject is celebrated in a lyric measure," namely a quatrain stanza the ballad tune of which is *heimlich* to an English ear, and the cue for which he may have heard in Scott's *Lay* the year before.[3] Montgomery's minoritizing choice to treat a small nation in a morselized format raises interesting questions about what might be called epic confederation. We need not grant him the insight that Napoleon's invasion of Switzerland actually fostered the consolidation of the cantons into national unity, to find in his choice of vernacular stanza verse a poet's curiosity about how the relentless imagination of invasion might be fostering something of the kind in the country where his "heroic subject" would be read. The confederation idea may also have underlain Joel Barlow's decision to publish as *The Columbiad* in 1807 an enlarged edition of one of the few American epics that had any impact in nineteenth-century Britain; and Thomas Campbell's highly popular idyll *Gertrude of Wyoming* (1809), while not by any stretch an epic, nevertheless showed a Pennsylvania outpost swept by world history at the time of the American Revolution.[4] *E pluribus unum* was a motto with the widest resonance during these years for states established as well as new: even the oldest were inventing themselves under revolutionary pressure during the heyday of a nationalism that took reactionary forms as readily as experimental ones.

★

[3] Hermann Fischer, *Romantic Verse Narrative: The History of a Genre*, 1964, tr. Sue Bollans (Cambridge: Cambridge University Press, 1991) 133, credits Montgomery jointly with Scott for developing *c.*1804 an heroic tetrameter form out of the ballad stanza.

[4] *The Vision of Columbus: A Poem in Nine Books*, which Barlow had published in 1787, forms a conspicuous watermark in the history of nationalist epic. It may have influenced Southey's work on Joan and the *Vision of the Maid of Orleans* that he extracted from it.

Because the United Kingdom (so called only since the 1801 Act of Union incorporated Northern Ireland) was in reactionary formation during the dubious times this chapter treats, it was natural that a poetic kind renowned for the integration of heterogeneous parts should draw topics from the most sacred of anthologies, that Book of books the Bible. John Stewart published a *Resurrection* in 1808 that followed up on Cumberland's *Calvary* and Ogden's *Emanuel* from the 1790s; its gospel and apocalypse narratives were perfunctorily rehearsed pretexts for the exposition and application of doctrine in which, here as with the Bible epics surveyed in Chapter 2, the Christian poet's interest chiefly lay. The eclipse of biblical narrative that transpired across the nineteenth century took shape at this early juncture, it seems, out of a nervous clerical diffidence in the sacred tale's capacity to carry meaning unsupported by regular and officious commentary.[5] (The warring nation's story, rather than the church militant's, now enjoyed implicit trust of the sort that typological reading had formerly bestowed on scripture.) A partial exception to this doctrinal rule is found among the remains left behind in 1806 by Southey's young *protégé* Henry Kirke White. *The Christiad: A Divine Poem* had enough ambition to pick up the gospel tale right where *Paradise Regained* had left off, and enough narrative imagination to fill that spare tale out in a spirit of invention not unlike Milton's. While the one completed book takes a promising interest in the political falling-out between a humiliated Satan and the demonic backbenchers he must report to, the dutifully imitative Miltonism of the verse suffices to explain why White, and no doubt other poetizing clerics lost to literary history, went no further.

It was with Old Testament narrative that the new decade did its heaviest political lifting. We have seen how Bowles's epicizing paean exploited in Noah the universalizing power of Genesis, as Milton had done before him in *Paradise Lost*. When it came to the building and maintenance of a people, though, more eligible models were to be found in Exodus and the

---

[5] Here I borrow from Hans Frei's *The Eclipse of Biblical Narrative: A Study in Eighteenth and Nineteenth Century Hermeneutics* (New Haven and London: Yale University Press, 1974) not only the title phrase but the context of "biblical theology" that he adduces as a halfway house frequented by inquirers benighted between the old hermeneutic dispensation and the new (173–74). Something approaching post-typological panic underlay the need, most urgently felt among clerical epoists, to make up for those points in which the unassisted Bible seemed *c.*1800 to fall short of what a satisfactory world-historical testament should be. The epic supplement might be continuity across uniformitarian historical time, corroboration by realistic detail, doctrinal explicitness, or some combination thereof; turn-of-the-century verse narratives from the Bible furnish helps of all these kinds.

chronicles of the Hebrew judges and kings. This ancient national history had in addition inspired a respectable seventeenth-century tradition reaching back through Dryden's *Absalom and Achitophel* and Abraham Cowley's *Davideis* to the biblicized culture wars of the Interregnum, when the fight for England had been waged in part by rival interpretations of scripture history. By 1807 it was too late for *bona fide* British Israelitism (*pace* Blake); yet that year witnessed three epics cut from the same cloth, weaving the warp of contemporary conditions against the woof of the Bible: William Sotheby's *Saul: A Poem in Two Parts*, Charles Hoyle's *Exodus: An Epic Poem in Thirteen Books*, and a joint effort by two veterans of the genre (Richard Cumberland and James Bland Burges) who reenlisted as such on the title page, *The Exodiad: A Poem. By the Authors of Calvary and Richard the First.*

In a veritably providential division of labor, the first of these Exodus epics finished up exactly where the second began, with a complacent view from Sinai's shore of a regiment of drowned Egyptians; in other respects, however, the two works diverge too sharply in intent, and sheer skill, to make any preconcerted conspiracy likely. Hoyle, chaplain to the Duke of Marlborough, proffers his epic as if it were a credential for patronage, submitted as evidence of politely learned fitness for that post. His Egyptian plagues are almost too genteel to offend, and his demons are such myopically incompetent supporters of Pharaoh that Hoyle seems not to have minded the strangeness of having them do their (unavailing) damnedest to *prevent* what by rights should have been a demons' night on the town, the massacre of a nation's first-born.

Cumberland and Burges aimed higher with *The Exodiad*, and struck a harder blow in favor of the authoritative order on which they believed Britain's welfare depended. Their prefatory claim to have produced the first joint epic meant forgetting the Southey/Coleridge *Joan* of 1796, which these staunch conservatives were probably only too happy to do. Beyond question the later work was the better joined, boasting a unison of manner that expressed in style the authors' theme of the subordination of individuals to a common purpose. More daring was their adapting to this conservative end the same studiously intricate blank verse in which Milton the republican had written an epic of individual freedom. In these and other ways *The Exodiad* ably executed its mission of illustrating the current situation of the British people by reference to an analogue that had the force of an archetype. Only now and then is the analogical hand conspicuously tipped, as when the Israelites, looking back across a Red Sea that might as well be a British Channel, relish their memory of a tyrannical Napoleon-Pharaoh made petty in the satire of hindsight: "I will pursue, he cried, I will o'ertake" (1.7.117). Again, when a report of "fifty thousand fighting men" (2.103.871) from one of the twelve tribes alone invites the extrapolating reader to place the census of Israelite men, women, and children at well over a million, the poem has been seduced, by the massive new European realities that it aspires to address covertly, into exceeding what its old epic devices can actually cope with.

In narrative design the poem is chillingly deft. Eschewing the fleshpots of Egypt that seduced Hoyle and numerous future epoists, Cumberland and Burges presuppose the Exodus itself as a *fait accompli*. The poem thus plunges into the desert and *in medias res publicas,* so as to represent crises in the governance of a state that (like Britain) has outlived the glorious euphoria of its launching, and must now amid difficulties find the way towards consummating its promise. That way lies in popular submission to a virtuous elite unafraid to wield "the armed hand | Of strong authority" (2.299.794). At war the Israelites prevail against the Amalekites in book 2 and the Moabites in book 8 through superior organization in the hierarchy of command and tighter cohesion on the field; and exactly these arts, transposed to politics, are the instruments of their peace. Domestic security demands unanimity, and that in turn demands surveillance of such dissenters as may prate about "liberty of mind" (4.193.273) or doubt the spiritual election of Moses and his cabinet. Chief among these seditious epic villains is Korah, a Hebrew Thersites who suffers regular humiliation at the hands of that straight-arrow judge-apparent Joshua, and who opines with at least some appearance of justice, on hearing Moses' campaign biography, "His whole life is a fable" (1.51.1004). This fascinating supposition marks Korah as a first, politically motivated exponent of the Higher Criticism of scripture; but his *in situ* experiment in doubt swiftly proves to have been playing with fire. It is not long before the resentful apostate sells his soul to the demon god Chemos, devotes his own children to human sacrifice, and falls at last through the yawning ground into hell's fiery depths. "Mark that man," Jethro warns a listening populace, "And purge your congregation from his stain" (3.161.803).

Such purgative scapegoating had lately been brought to new refinement across Europe by statist forces of every stripe. Revolutionary and reactionary regimes alike found the practice especially useful, irrespective of the yield in actual traitors, as a way of training the public to look after itself and toe the line. Self-government by collective inquisition and purge focused the national mind in ways of which Cumberland and Burges evidently approved. Furthermore, it activated national self-consciousness in ways that the *Exodiad* narrators manifestly found more reliable than others— more so than, to choose a pointed example made keen on their analogical grindstone, the sharing of power among popularly elected representatives. Books 4–6 concern the grassroots nomination by each of the twelve tribes of a delegate to the squadron of spies that is dispatched to reconnoiter the promised land. This power-sharing ward policy vexes Joshua to distraction, and even Moses is about as apologetic in ordering its implementation as a leader can well be who is acting on direct orders from God.

These leaders' elitist anxiety expresses that of the *Exodiad* authors, who worked the biblical episode for all it was worth in demonstrating the perils of democracy, and then in effect crushed it out of political mind beneath the heel of *raison d'état*, in the form of Korah's *de facto* execution in book 6 and the necessity of mustering to war in book 7. The authors' alarm over the issue was well grounded, nevertheless, and it would persist into the poetry of their most thoughtful successors. The consent of the governed was to be increasingly recognized as a *sine qua non* of the modern state; how to reinforce that consent, without at the same time enfranchising constituencies to assert their independence, remained an ideological sore spot that elicited a variety of treatments in epic form. Within a generation *The Exodiad*'s resort to overwhelming theocratic force would be available only to the eschatological epic (Ch. 6), an emergent subgenre in which the mass mobilization of countless souls under divine authority continued to express a proto-fascist political content, lurid but genuine, well into the Victorian period.

Sotheby's *Saul* is in every way less purposive and adroitly turned than *The Exodiad*, and yet the very infirmity of the work earns honorable mention in the history of its genre. Sotheby seems to signal as much in naming after the infirm King Saul an epic that cannot keep for long from celebrating the triumphal narrative of the wholesomer King David who displaced him, and whose exploits, after crowning the first four-book part of *Saul*, quite dominate part 2. In fact the poem's most interesting effects lie in the interplay between David's generically commonplace rising action and the tragic action that centers on Saul's stepwise decline into madness, loss of authority, descent to the subterranean Witch of Endor, and sure-fire fall upon his own sword after a losing battle. While the flawed king's psychopathology is imagined with scarcely more sympathy than Korah's in *The Exodiad*, Sotheby nevertheless showed some boldness, given the mood of British militancy and the precarious mental health of George III, in seating his epic madman not on the national sidelines but on the throne.

He showed boldness of a different, Romantic kind in conceiving a hero whose blessing was also a curse, whose privileged relation to the ordinance of heaven was genuine and at the same time radically corrupt. In a telling episode from the penultimate book, David in exile feigns madness as a strategic disguise that he can and does throw off with a clear (and instantly answered) summons to Jehovah for rescue. Saul's madness is by contrast the real thing: it remains his crooked yet authentic pathway to the reality of the Lord, which is for Sotheby as for other biblical epoists the reality whose register is national history. Saul's is "a mind distraught," the invocation declares, "With guilt-avenging horror," because "Saul rebellious, disobey'd | Jehovah" (1.1.9–10, 37–38). This burden of the past, carried forward into the future as *guilt*, was in germ a conception of the first importance for the next phase in the development of nineteenth-century epic. Although Sotheby forsook it for the pleasanter task of cheering blameless David on, the twist he gave to national history through a guilty Saul remained for better poets to probe, and to nurse, in the years just ahead.

Another minor poet and epic recidivist, Joseph Cottle, pointed the way toward such developments the next year in *The Fall of Cambria* (1808). This largely conventional narrative of Edward I's thirteenth-century annexation of Wales to England posed with new forthrightness a question that had tugged at the sleeve of Cottle's confrere Southey while writing *Madoc* (Ch. 3). What place should modern heroic poetry reserve for a narrative other than the one inscribed by history's victors? Southey's latest epic had imagined several options: an exit into silence beyond the pale (Yuhidthiton's emigration), the pyrrhic glory of a terminal episode within the master narrative (Tlalala's suicide), or anonymous assimilation into that narrative (the Hoamen tribe)—this last option being further ironized, though Southey downplays the irony, by the historical failure of the Madoc regime to leave any American trace. The question of alternative histories got collateral reinforcement in 1808 with the publication of English selections, translated by Henry Boyd and the persistent William Hayley, from the most impressively sympathetic treatment any Western epic had accorded native America, Ercilla's sixteenth-century monument to the Andean resistance

Araucana—to which theme Maria Williams had turned for her *Peru* (1786) and Bowles would return in a few years with *The Missionary*.

Cottle's contribution was to bring the issues that these overseas narratives raised back to British soil, with an epic pitting not Saxon against Dane, as in his earlier *Alfred*, but future Briton against future Briton: the stuff, that is, of civil war. This choice of subject meant pitting two narrative discourses against each other as well. Cottle's title named the first of these, a victims' tragic history of decline and fall at the hands of Norman *force majeure* and latter-day forwardness. But this was a discourse predicated on the other, right-side-out victors' epic—it might have been called *The Conquest of Wales*—which was constantly presupposed by the plot of British and world history that Cottle understood and had indeed dramatized in his own national-unity epic just a few years previously. The conflict between these two histories generates the poem's one interesting experiment on the conventions of its genre: to dismiss supernatural agents and see "how far lyrical pieces may counteract the disadvantage of these omissions, and become a rational and effective substitute for them" (Preface v). The purpose of this lyric machinery, so to call it, beyond welcoming the host of bards Cottle wanted to invite into his epic text, is to enlist the reader's "sympathy" (xxv) with the doomed cause of Wales.

Although Cottle never says so, we may safely infer from what he does say, and from the drearier deployments practiced by his epic contemporaries, that machinery of the traditional supernatural sort had it come into play would have exerted an opposite effect. By this point in the development of the epic genre, that is, the only overarching choral narrative that supernatural agency might imaginably support was the victorious narrative of providential national progress. To put the matter with only slight hyperbole: by this point the progress narrative in effect *was* that supernatural agency. A dozen years' habituation to modern war had prepared British poets and their readers to lend credence most freely to a story in which the operation of a transpersonal, transhistorical power found for their country a starring role.

Cottle's prefatory adjectives "rational and effective" give the game away: Edward I must win because rational effectiveness must. The compensatory recourse to sympathy for the Welsh victims in their fall is thus from the first a function of the advancing modernity that is to victimize them. The lyrical machinery is run off the national-historical drive shaft. Cottle's rational and effective provision of an index of all the "lyrical pieces" for readers' convenience makes the same point in the form of a displaced cultural necrology.

So do a couple of aftermath episodes from the final books. In book 21, having won the poem's big battle, Edward receives the surviving bard Lhyrarch with high praise for poets—but only as alchemists of passion, and expressly not as historical chroniclers. Two books later Lhyrarch, quick on the uptake, has devised a song equating poetry with a liberty that abides above the fray, appertaining not to politics but to the maintenance of a fastness within the self (23.702–10). This independently elaborated Romantic ideology, corresponding as it does to Wordsworth's position in the final books of *The Prelude* and, with a twist, throughout *The Excursion*, corresponds in the first instance to Cottle's ostensibly noncommittal position as a modern Briton: heir to both sides, and answerable to both histories, that have been long since absorbed into a national narrative transcending each.

Lhyrarch is another Last Minstrel, and the well-intentioned if well-insulated sympathy poetics that Cottle advances through this figure suggests that he had read Scott's *Lay* and been intrigued by that poem's unrealized potential for a more thoroughly national, more fully epic resolution. So had Scott, to judge from his next bestseller *Marmion: A Tale of Flodden Field*. This poem of 1808 was an epic transaction that brilliantly infused into the entertaining sophistication of the *Lay* a tone and an ethos addressing the national trouble that contemporary epics of a more turgid sort had begun churning up. Instructed perhaps by *Madoc*, which he read more than once, Scott showed in *Marmion* how heroes' guilt and victims' history might conspire to support a narrative economy of loss and gain; and he suggested how a reader's speculative investment in such a narrative economy might redound to the national interest. He did so by correlating the breaking and keeping of faith, at several structural levels, with the maintenance of continuity between past and present on which personal identity and British history alike depended; and by infusing into the narrated flow of heroic psychology the epochal theme of historical change which *The Lay of the Last Minstrel* had been content merely to stage.[6]

---

[6] C. I. Rothery, "Scott's Narrative Poetry and the Classical Form of the Historical Novel," in *Scott and his Influence*, ed. J. H. Alexander and David Hewitt (Aberdeen: Association for Scottish Literary Studies, 1983) 67, discriminates the antiquarianism of *The Lay*, which "does not dramatise the way that the old became new," from the properly historicist rendition of "collision between clan society and centralised royal authority" in *The Lady of the Lake*—a rendition already in place, we may add, with *Marmion*. The poems' inquiry into historical change as a matter of enforced and radical discontinuity, not naturalized evolution, anticipates the thematics of conversion and guilt in *Ivanhoe* as analyzed in Michael Ragussis, *Figures of Conversion: "The Jewish Question" and English National Identity* (Durham and London: Duke University Press, 1995) 93–95, 125–26.

Plot matters more to *Marmion* than it did to *The Lay*. That is no very strong claim, but it does suggest a shift in the generic center of gravity, especially when taken in conjunction with Scott's later observation that romance most resembles epic in those works "where each part of the narrative bears a due proportion to the others, and the whole draws gradually towards a final and satisfactory conclusion."[7] Every admirer of the poem is struck by the way all circumstances converge on the catastrophic battle of Flodden to give cantos 5 and 6 their ringing epic timbre. Setting a pattern that Scott's novels would retrace with surer mastery, in their advance from duel to warfare his characters are gradually, irresistibly swept up by the course of a grand public history in whose dynamic their personal motives and intrigues are retrospectively seen to have been implicated all along. It is nevertheless the swirl of the eddy rather than the force of the current that primarily engages Scott in *Marmion*, a poem that has less forthright than meander, and that in jump-cutting among episodes can seem to have a subplot too many.

But this same abundance of collateral intrigue emphasizes what interested Scott more than any plot, and that was plottedness itself. Nobody in *Marmion* is innocent of a history that is crisscrossed by human directives, which furthermore, to darken the contrast, manifest an extraordinarily high degree of apostasy and betrayal. Even the ingenue figures are used goods: when De Wilton finally throws off his Palmer's garb the melodrama of revelation is immediately upstaged by how wasted this "second Cain" (6.7.209) looks to Lady Clara, who herself we have lately learned is not just "a perjured nun" now but years ago had a material (forger's) hand in effecting De Wilton's betrayal (5.23.660). Such in this somber tale is the checkered career of the more or less virtuous, whom on their due repent- ance Scott reserves for a more or less happy ending. Clara and De Wilton are good, we infer, in proportion to their marginal position within a national drama that markedly tends to corrupt insiders who are higher up. Marmion himself, at narrative dead center, shares with Sotheby's Saul the distinction of being a powerfully ambiguous, not to say villainous, eponym. Our protagonist is a knight who once seduced one lover and bound her over for execution, and is now closing in on an heiress whose suitor he has fraudulently betrayed and meant to kill. Still higher up, at the sociopolitical apex of the tale, we meet in Scotland's King James a rash philanderer and

---

[7] "Romance," *Encyclopaedia Britannica*, 1824: in *Essays on Chivalry, Romance, and the Drama* (1834; rpt. Freeport: Books for Libraries, 1972) 137. For germane remarks on the same topic see the (ghost-written) introduction to the first edition of *The Bridal of Triermain* (1813).

vindictive politician whom the poem holds responsible for provoking the battle that will maim his kingdom's independence forever.[8] Both these spotted characters are also glamorous leaders and brave warriors, to be sure, and by death on the battlefield both pay for their sins in epic's time-honored sterling currency. By the same token, though, it is the calculus of atonement that measures what their deaths mean, together with the national catastrophe of which they are part.

Scott's choice to build his most important poem on such morally broken ground is unprecedented in the epic writing we have surveyed to this point. It should be understood with a view to the fault-line of intermediacy and compromise that seams every aspect of *Marmion*, and that the poem renders as the scar of a national history. King James and Marmion are mercurial men whose political impulsiveness and moral flexibility are the attributes of an early-modern cultural instability. Neither of them knows just what to believe. The "awful summons" (5.25.735) at Edinburgh that enjoins James to avoid battle fails in its appeal, but that appeal is accurately pitched to the king's notoriously "superstitious temper" (Scott's note, 76). Superstitious half-belief is indeed the temper of the times, and it is more fully explored in canto 3 when Marmion, overhearing a ghost-story about a local spirit that can be compelled to tell fortunes, determines against his own better judgment on a midnight consultation. The interview comes to nothing, and as usual Scott has a rational explanation for what Marmion has seen . . . or believes he has seen . . . or would like to believe . . . for the abiding interest of this episode, as it spills over into canto 4, is the conflict it highlights within a man of this world who cannot relinquish his need for contact with the next. Belief in the world to come is almost a thing of the past, but not quite. If Marmion cannot share in the piety of the good Abbess who ducks in and out of the plot, neither does he enjoy the fancy-free disenchantment of his squire Fitz-Eustace, who from the vantage of a younger generation finds his master's "fond credulity," "stirr'd by an idle tale," the thing in the episode to "wonder" at (3.30.588, 580, 576). Marmion, characteristically, wonders at his wonder too, enough to tell Fitz-Eustace to keep his mouth shut lest people find out "that I could credit such a tale" (3.28.548).[9]

---

[8] The poem's abundant references to sin, guilt, and remorse, with the conspicuous mystery of concealment that both enwraps and expresses them, are itemized by J. H. Alexander in *Marmion: Studies in Interpretation and Composition* (Salzburg: Universität Salzburg, 1982) 43–52.

[9] The morally checkered character of the hero and the plot's traffic with the supernatural are phenomena that correlate at a point where the historical slopes of change in morality and in

This plaited betwixt-and-betweenness makes Marmion the man of the hour, as Byron, the man of the hour to come, rapidly discerned: "Now forging scrolls, now foremost in the fight, | Not quite a Felon, yet but half a Knight | . . . | A mighty mixture of the great and base" (*English Bards and Scotch Reviewers*, 1808; 167–70). Marmion emerges an archetypal denizen of that perennial border-time where the epic imagination of Scott learned to dwell.[10] The ambivalent intermediacy Scott imputed to Marmion makes the English knight an instinctive diplomat from the first, as on arrival in Scotland he fences for negotiating advantage with Sir Hugh the Heron and—having endured and duly, insincerely, praised an epic harper for what strikes him privately as a "barbarous lay" (1.13.208)—successfully angles for the reconnaissance help he needs in order to spy on the mustering enemy. Here as in his later jockeying with the poet David Lindesay and with King James, Marmion alternately obeys the canons of hospitable honor and puts them to tactical use: sometimes they are mere means of compassing an objective, while at other times they sting him to the chivalric quick.

This compromised relation to the values one lives by marks a quite new species of heroism, whose epic potential Scott had flirted with in *The Lay of the Last Minstrel* and here took firmly in hand.[11] He made it the substance of what filled the place of epic invocation in *Marmion*, his prefatory verse

metaphysics intersect. This may be why Francis Jeffrey, writing in the *Edinburgh Review* (April 1808), lodged adjacent charges against "the extreme and monstrous improbability of almost all the incidents" and against Marmion's being "not only a villain, but a mean and sordid villain": rpt. in *Scott: The Critical Heritage*, ed. John O. Hayden (New York: Barnes and Noble, 1970) 39–40. Alexander, *Two Studies in Romantic Reviewing: The Reviewing of Walter Scott's Poetry* (Salzburg: Universität Salzburg, 1976) 2: 367, reports the villainous hero "almost universally condemned" by the poem's first reviewers.

[10] Scott had bivouacked along that frontier first in the notes to his 1802 ballad edition *Minstrelsy of the Scottish Border*. Now ironically superior to Scott's materials, and now plangently elegiac—and thus much richer in tonality than Southey's self-annotation in *Thalaba* the year before—these notes, like those that accompanied *The Lay of the Last Minstrel*, are nowhere more conflicted than when the supernatural is at issue. Nancy Goslee, "*Marmion* and the Metaphor of Forgery," *Scottish Literary Journal* 7 (1980) 85–95, finds in this conflict a parallel with Scott's ambivalence about mixing fiction with history. See also Clare A. Simmons's astute remark that, despite the 1513 date of Flodden, Marmion's cloven consciousness marks him as "still medieval, or perhaps more properly, a medievalist": "Medievalism and the Romantic Poet-Editor in Scott's *Marmion*," *Poetica* 39 (1993) 100.

[11] We should antedate to *Marmion* Scott's epoch-making contribution to historiographic art: the attribution of cloven class interests or, equivalently, overlapping period mentalities to a major character who remains only imperfectly aware of them as such. Although the phenomenon recurs in the poetry all the way to *Harold the Dauntless* (where in auto-parodic mode Scott decks his Nordic berserkers out in chivalric trappings), the honor of its inauguration is typically reserved by criticism for *Waverley*—and thus, of course, for the novel: see, e.g., David Brown, *Walter Scott and the Historical Imagination* (London: Routledge and Kegan Paul, 1979) 20.

epistles to friends. In one sense the easeful candor of these familiar addresses, which constitute nearly one-fourth of the entire text, counterpoises the burden of dark suspicion that prevails in the narrative. Yet what they are candid about is typically some aspect of the same divided state of mind that stamps Scott's sixteenth-century protagonist an early modern. Against an autumnal or wintry background these introductions survey a shrunken ground across which conceded cultural and political losses cast lengthy shadows, even as Scott strives to uphold in compensation an imaginative faith that can flourish even on doubtful premises, in "tradition's dubious light | That hovers 'twixt the day and night" (5.125). Again and again these latter-day invocations summon not the Muse but the power to entertain (and to get half lost in) fictions of extravagance that Scott and his cronies can neither directly credit nor willingly do without. "Few have read romance so well" (1.250) as these conspiratorially addressed gentlemen, whose praiseworthy reading entails expertise in the willing suspension of disbelief. Scott's correspondents, and by clear extension his well-reading audience, constitute an *ad hoc* faith community held together by the willing reception of reported improbabilities that work the more strongly for being unconstrained by classic rules (3), for being embedded in vernacular tradition (6), and above all for being to everybody's stricter judgment, as to Marmion's stricter judgment concerning the ghost story, incredible.[12]

The conversational crisis lyrics with which Scott armed *Marmion* earn their place in an epic texture by openly confiding what the odes Cottle wrote and indexed for *The Fall of Cambria* could not afford to hint: modern heroism is a believable option only on the latter-day terms of optional belief. Only by imparting this confidence to his reader can Scott impart an epic momentum to modern poetry. That is why each of his addresses to a stand-in reader invokes the question of epic, and why several pose it at length. Scott teasingly refrained from calling *Marmion* an epic: "Any historical

---

[12] Scott thus now incorporates into his featured story the sophistication that he confided in *The Lay* to his frame—and in the *Minstrelsy* to his apparatus: his lengthy editorial introduction to that anthology, for example, or the essay "On the Fairies of Popular Superstition" that he appended to its second volume. The interplay in *Marmion* of story and epistolary proemata is discussed by J. D. McClatchy, "The Ravages of Time: The Function of the *Marmion* Epistles," *Studies in Scottish Literature* 9 (1972) 256–63; and by Kathryn Sutherland, "Defining the Self in the Poetry of Scott and Wordsworth," in Alexander and Hewitt, *Scott and his Influence*, 51–62. See esp. Stuart Curran's remark in *Poetic Form and British Romanticism* (New York and Oxford: Oxford University Press, 1986) 139, on "the extent to which Scott deliberately accentuates and exploits the antiromantic," which always accompanies romance "within an almost marsupial envelopment."

narrative," averred his preface to the first edition, "far more an attempt at epic composition, exceeded his plan of a romantic tale."[13] Southey and others had framed such disclaimers so often that they may be accounted by this point a convention of the genre; it fell to Scott to electrify this convention by making the diffidence it expresses a consistently thematized ethos within the plot. The poet's and reader's half-belief in epic is enacted repeatedly by characters experiencing something very much like it—enacted and also enlisted, since, as both the cantos and the introductions demonstrate, to acknowledge an illusion as such is not to annul its power.

Fitz-Eustace's repeated comparison of some actual incident to what he has read in "a huge romantic tome" (4.4.88), likening Clara for example to "some love-lorn Fay" or "in Romance, some spell-bound Queen" (6.3.96, 97), simultaneously incites and forbids us to see her that way. Reading thus in a mode of continual citation, we find ourselves recreating, albeit on terms wholly literary and elective, a transcriptive simulacrum of the ancient scene of epic recitation.[14] Readers' belief in the epic turns on the characters' belief, in the epic—hinges upon it while also switching it on. The kind of homogeneity between diegesis and exegesis, tale and meaning, that *The Lay of the Last Minstrel* commemorated as obtaining once upon a time among traditional bard, inherited theme, and collective audience, lives again on Scott's "spell-bound" page, which through the iterability of print expands the sense of audience to national proportions. Now in *Marmion* "the secret sympathy" pervading the earlier poem, "Which heart to heart, and mind to mind, | In body and in soul can bind" (*Lay* 5.13), involves a shared guilty awareness of the inarticulate compromises modernity makes whether affirming or disavowing its faith in persons, customs, or national ideals.

Marmion's belief-entertaining circuitry rapidly involved readers who numbered in the tens of thousands. It also, crucially, involved a quantum

---

[13] Karl Kroeber, *Romantic Narrative Art* (Madison: University of Wisconsin Press, 1960) 169, speaks with notable crispness for a long line of critics before and since who follow Scott in denying the name of epic to his long poems. The intrepid if bewildered assignments of genre that contemporary readers ventured to make are surveyed by Alexander, *Reviewing*, 43–58.

[14] Hence, in part, the undercurrent of irreality arising from "the general fluxile nature of experience" conveyed by both the epistles and the cantos (Alexander, *Studies in Interpretation*, 80). For John Pikoulis, "Scott and 'Marmion': The Discovery of Identity," *Modern Language Review* 66 (1971) 738, the poem's "sense of things lost, or nearly grasped, receding into the past to leave a world strained by their promise and their memory" defines it as a romance rather than an epic; my argument in the present chapter hinges on Scott's definitively epic success in identifying just this strain with the emergent complex of modern nationalism.

of bad faith. The willing suspension of disbelief cannot will away the consciousness of that suspension; in fact, for those who "read romance so well" as Scott would have them do, it should not even try. A modern credulity that models itself on Marmion's is originally flawed and knows it. Marmion certainly knows it, and in the critical form of guilty conscience:

> Yet conquest by that meanness won
> He almost loath'd to think upon,
> Led him, at times, to hate the cause,
> Which made him burst through honour's laws.

> (5.28.829–32)

The key words here are "almost" and "at times," which suspend Marmion's judgment on himself in a manner analogous to the suspension of disbelief that sent him out after midnight in canto 3 to scare up a soothsayer. Both these suspensions foster a diffuse narrative suspense: instead of the clarity of old faith and the dictates of honor bright, a haze of decadent or inchoate valuation spreads across the poetic scene the menace of an obligation acknowledged but undischarged—*and therefore perpetually pending*. The burden of incumbency is what precipitates the plot into epic action and significance. After the passage just quoted we see Marmion bent only on battle, evincing a grand national loyalty that may atone for the "meanness" of his disloyalty in personal relations.

Guilt of Marmion's brooding modern kind differs from Homeric shame, which is incurred or removed punctually and in the presence of witnesses.[15] Guilt subsists in prolongation, biding its time, building history forward from the past into the future, and structuring the narrative meaning of history from the inside out, so that deeds in the world become the expressions of an inward motive often obscure even to the doer. Scott apologized in his 1830 preface for linking "the nature of Marmion's guilt" to forgery, "the crime of a commercial, rather than a proud and warlike age"; but this like Scott's other disclaimers is not to be taken at face value. It is, rather, like the coy "poetical anachronism" of Michael Scott's wizard longevity in *The Lay*, a sure sign that authorial magic is afoot. The forward anachronism of his knight's "commercial" forgery suits to a T the early modern crossroads at which Scott placed *Marmion*, even as it complements the fashion in which this best-selling epic counterfeit reaches backward to put the touch on

---

[15] See E. R. Dodds, *The Greeks and the Irrational* (Berkeley: University of California Press, 1951).

balladry. For the whole poem is a piece of bad faith that challenges the reader to make it good by endorsing its truth, on grounds simultaneously moral and historic.

Marmion not only depicts the guilty way we believe now but also tells how we got that way, at a representative juncture when we traded communal wholeness, dearly but correctly, for the compromised terms of modern nationhood.[16] Here the representative juncture happens to be Flodden Field in 1513, where the crippling of Scotland was a step toward the prosperity enjoyed by a consolidated Great Britain three centuries later—but, by that token, a limping step whose traumatic site made itself a permanent part of the body politic, beyond the intermittency of its conscious commemoration. Scott's subsequent poetry and fiction show that any of a dozen historical crises might have served equally well to make this point about national memory, which the arbitrariness and anachronistic seasoning of his first choice do not invalidate but secure.[17] Modernity is a chronically recurrent condition, one that sustains itself by running back to an origin it discernibly yet incompletely differs from.

Harboring the incompleteness of that difference as guilt—accepted because shared, and carried forward because perennially unpaid—is the work of national history as Scott momentously defined it for the nineteenth century. And he taught the world how to do this work in the novel only after undertaking it first in epic poetry, the literary genre with which

---

[16] At Flodden the combination of Scottish shame with English glory engenders in Scott a representatively British guilt, which canto 6 delegates to Marmion, an Englishman fighting on Scotland's losing side. Understanding the poem this way helps explain matters that puzzle Iain Crichton Smith, "Poetry in Scott's Narrative Verse," in *Sir Walter Scott: The Long-Forgotten Melody*, ed. Alan Bold (London: Vision, 1983): "how superficial and yet curiously involved the plots" of the poem are, and also why the "apparently unscrupulous climber" Marmion should suddenly have an access of guilt (116, 123). That this access of national guilt accompanied Britain's awareness of an imperial destiny may be inferred from the negative nineteenth-century instance of the (guilt-free, pre-imperial) United States, as analyzed in Martin Green's important studies *The Great American Adventure* (Boston: Beacon, 1984) 3–19, and *The Adventurous Male: Chapters in the History of the White Male Mind* (University Park: Pennsylvania State University Press, 1993) 17–30. Green analyzes Scott's fiction as a serial foundation epic in *Dreams of Adventure, Deeds of Empire* (New York: Basic Books, 1979) 104–28.

[17] Coleridge was quick to see in the Waverley novels a common weave that ran deep enough into the fabric of modernity to ensure their enduring appeal: "the contest between the loyalists and their opponents can never be *obsolete*, for it is the contest between the two great moving principles of social humanity; religious adherence to the past and the ancient, the desire and the admiration of permanence, on the one hand; and the passion for increase of knowledge, for truth, as the offspring of reason—in short, the mighty instincts of *progression* and *free agency*, on the other." Letter of 8 April 1820 to Thomas Allsop, quoted in T. M. Raysor, *Coleridge's Miscellaneous Criticism* (Cambridge, Mass.: Harvard University Press, 1936) 341–42.

national history was most firmly associated in his lifetime.[18] When J. C. Shairp, writing on "The Homeric Spirit in Walter Scott" (1882), descried in *Marmion*'s last canto "the full pinion of epic poetry," and Thomas Hardy a long generation later called *Marmion* "the most Homeric poem in the English language," both Victorians were attesting the brilliance (necessarily un-Homeric) with which Scott had forged a nationally credible equivalent out of precisely the reluctant skepticism that made the old epic wholeness a modern impossibility.[19] The assembly and engagement of troops in cantos 4–6 are indeed wonderfully handled; Scott owes his massed and crowded effects less to selection and enumeration, though, than to the quantity of participatory identification built up during the preceding cantos in the reader.

The peculiar currency of guilt in *Marmion* does not so much conscript readers as enlist them: they willingly throw their weight behind a contest each side of which is struggling for a constituent modern value. " 'Here, by this Cross,' he gently said, | 'You well may view the scene' " (6.23.691–92): thus Marmion ushers Clara to an elevation that "Did all the field command" (6.22.680) and on which Scott bestows enough attention to warrant our understanding it symbolically. It matters that our stand-in should occupy

---

[18] Nancy Goslee, *Scott the Rhymer* (Lexington: University Press of Kentucky, 1988), associates the wandering motion of romance with the poet's reluctance to yield as he must to "the continuum of historical development," which in its inexorability constitutes romance's epic nemesis or "apocalyptic" limit (208). In his historical retrospect the poet apprehends the difference between romance dilation and epic historicity as "a delay on the threshold of major, progressive change" (16). This critical formulation illuminates in a new way Hazlitt's witty epithet for Scott in *The Spirit of the Age* as "prophesier of things past." For Scott imputes this quantum of retrospectively glimpsed "delay" to his characters; but he does so *in reverse*, in the form of an anxious guilt of incompletion that feels, as it were, forwards—the direction in which our history is actually lived. In Joseph Valente's terms from " 'Upon the Braes': History and Hermeneutics in *Waverley*," *Studies in Romanticism* 24 (1986) 270, Scott "conveys, in a visceral manner, a sense of history as a submarine force depositing consequences that can only be seized upon retrospectively," that "can never be observed," but that remains "essential to the differential operation of meaning." When this invisibly haunted, anxiogenic condition precipitates "longing for some intervening transcendent power" (Goslee, *Scott the Rhymer*, 61), an epic circuit is closed "that virtually creates a power with a kind of communal imagination." Alexander Welsh's name for this fundamentally epic power of civic morality is "the tyranny of the superego" at work within a newly inaugurated culture of "public opinion": *The Hero of the Waverley Novels, With New Essays on Scott* (1968; Princeton: Princeton University Press, 1992) 17, 117. See also Pikoulis, "Scott and 'Marmion,' " 740–44.

[19] Shairp, *Aspects of Poetry* (Oxford: Clarendon Press, 1881) 338; Hardy, quoted in Harold Orel, "Hardy and the Epic Tradition," *English Literature in Transition* 9 (1966) 187–89. The comparison of Scott to Homer is a favorite commonplace in Victorian writing about either poet, for reasons that impinge on epic's association with historical events: see Herbert Grierson, "The Man and the Poet" (1940), in *Sir Walter Scott Lectures 1940–1948*, ed. W. L. Renwick (Edinburgh: Edinburgh University Press, 1950) 17.

high English ground along the border river Tweed; it matters more that she should be an English lady, a noncombatant doubly above the fray; it matters most that she should be divided in her loyalties, since the English forces include both her tormentor Marmion and her lover De Wilton.[20] If "by this Cross" love triumphs over fear, the victorious epic referent is not Christian doctrine but a crux in the national history. Putting the reader in Clara's place, Scott evolves a new sense of British history as a progress narrative painstakingly aware of, and responsible for, the pains that progress takes.

"O what a tangled web we weave, | When first we practice to deceive!" (6.17.532–33). *Marmion* exempted none of its principals from deceiving each other; it moreover represented collective self-deception as the condition, guiltily half-discerned, of modern nationhood; and it made that condition the basis for an enormous popularity. Readers evidently responded to Scott's seductive entanglement more fully than most writers knew how to do in the romance-styled imitations that poured from British presses during the following years. That goes for the foremost of Scott imitators, Walter Scott himself. In *The Lady of the Lake* (1810) and *Rokeby* (1813) he untwined for separate consideration historical factors that the epic web of *Marmion* had woven together: in the former, the conflict between waning and emerging cultural formations, represented in figures who are nearly allegories of those formations; in the latter, the narrative burden of guilt as it fastens on, and bends inward into personhood, figures enmeshed in the density of national events, the latter now further complicated by New World buccaneering. Scott's decline hereafter through perfunctory self-imitation in *The Bridal of Triermain* (1813) and *The Lord of the Isles* (1815) towards the outright parody of *Harold the Dauntless: A Poem, in Six Cantos* (1817) confirms that by mid-decade he had designated Byron his heir in metrical romance and was saving himself for prose fiction. Having by his own successes created a newly robust market for the long poem, Scott was to some degree jostled out of it by all the poets eagerly rushing in.

An orderly account of epic poetry during the years after *Marmion* is made difficult by the sheer volume of new work, and also by the generic relaxation that Scott's success tended to diffuse among aspiring practitioners.

---

[20] In all these ways, and consistently with Scott's invariant "need to establish a locus of observation," Clara stands in for the reader: Jane Millgate, *Walter Scott: The Making of the Novelist* (Edinburgh: Edinburgh University Press, 1984) 25.

Neoclassical ideas receded before a chivalric revival that promoted the more permissive traditions of romance epic as it descended via Spenser from the Continent—this at a time when current events on the Continent were engrossing the attention of the British public as seldom before, and when the identity and welfare of a nation long at war were more explicitly affiliated than ever with civil society and domestic life. "Fierce warres and faithfull loues" were now again the epic themes: while an individual work ordinarily emphasized one of these over the other, Scott's example created an expectation that the genre would effect some correlation between the two. Poetry sales and war efforts alike declared that the national interest lay in a balance of conquest with courtliness, adventure with home values, men's stories with women's.[21]

That balance was often distinctly lopsided. On the distaff side yarnspinners of both sexes produced poems centering on a medieval lady whose rank confers a power that her gender sharply constrains. The most fractious of these heroines boils over in the virtually Achillean wrath of *Margaret of Anjou* (1816) by Margaret Holford (later Hodson), to which we shall return; hers is a limiting case that, like Southey's Joan of Arc twenty years earlier, defines what the typical poetic heroine of the period is not. She is not an extremist in the exercise of physical or moral athleticism, but instead a firmly contextualized player within usually dynastic high-life scenarios of courtship and intrigue that she has not created and must do her epic work within. In Francis Hodgson's *Lady Jane Grey: A Tale, in Two Books* (1809) and Sotheby's *Constance de Castile: A Poem, in Ten Cantos* (1810) the figure of the heroine wields the social power of feminine favor and, more impressively, exhibits the moral power of feminine endurance (unto martyrdom, in the first case) of a naughty world whose dominion she contests by immaculate counterexample. In Mary Russell Mitford's *Blanch* (1813) she also dies a saintly death, but has more fun along the way. Wrongly hounded from court, Princess Blanch traverses Spain in peasant disguise and then cross-dressed, passing in and out of convent and caliphate to be finally arraigned as co-respondent in the adultery trial of the mad queen. We have not met such

---

[21] A quite different factor in the breadth and longevity of literary influence wielded by Scott's verse narratives is adduced by William St. Clair, *The Reading Nation in the Romantic Period* (Cambridge: Cambridge University Press, 2004) 419: where the novels of Scott qualified for extended protection under the copyright laws of 1842, the poems were older and did not; as a result, publishers continued bringing out cheap editions and school editions throughout the Victorian period.

epic mobility in a heroine since Tighe's *Psyche* (Ch. 3); but Mitford regards Blanch through the looking-glass of history rather than allegory, and of history as denominated by the highly explicit title of the book in which the poem appeared: *Narrative Poems on the Female Character, in the Various Relations of Human Life*. However improbable Blanch's troubles and adventures, what gets her into them each time (cantos 1 and 2) is an assignment all too probable, a babysitting job.

That the "various relations of human life" are the stuff of history would become so dear a theme to apologists for prose fiction (and to historians, from Macaulay forward, who borrowed novelists' techniques) that it is important to reclaim here its concurrent bearing on verse narrative after Scott. Historically and culturally overdetermined heroines who were neither amazons nor allegories could matter in epicizing poetry once *Marmion* had made historical and cultural overdetermination heroic. If heroism was virtue in densely imagined context, then the conspicuously contextualized situation of women suited them well to perform as protagonists. Conversely, the limited but authentic nineteenth-century exercise of a woman's right to choose (her husband) made the deliberating heroine a central figure in works as diverse as Hodgson's chivalric sketch *Sir Edgar* (1810) and William Herbert's book-length skaldic *Helga: A Poem, In Seven Cantos* (1815). Each of these works hinges on how a woman takes her pick of suitors who represent more or less stereotypical masculine norms, which in turn represent rival cultural or national formations. This same principle of female discrimination among representative candidates migrates from the narrative center to the frame with *The Queen's Wake: A Legendary Poem* (1815) by James Hogg. This poem made Hogg's reputation by amplifying canto 6 from *The Lay of the Last Minstrel* into a battle of the bards, fifteen of whom vie for a prize that is awarded at length by Mary Queen of Scots to a certain Ettrick shepherd.

A similar contest had structured an anonymous work in six cantos entitled *The Crusaders, or The Minstrels of Acre* (1808). Published too early to register the force of *Marmion*, this poem about poetry in history took over from Scott's *Last Minstrel* the tetrameter rhymes and the framing format of bardic performance that Hogg and, in a slightly later phase, Thomas Moore would shortly be exploiting to better effect. Given the patriot valence that we found in Chapter 3 clinging at this time to the name of Acre, it is a curious twist here to have English and French minstrels sharing the stage after the battle, just as English and French knights have shared its victor honors. Such a mix of international harmony with national interest proved, however, unstable. As if alert but averse to its own internal ideological conflict, *The Crusaders* goes on a permanent detour into typologized biblical prophecy and global apocalyptics that leave current events far behind. Yet when the mouthpiece for this vision, a Lake District natural-pietist who is King Richard's favorite poet, winds up with a prayer for all Crusaders, "And chiefly for my brethren dear, | Sons of our Northern Isles" (6.31), the jarringly undiplomatic resumption of patriotism as usual illustrates what ecumenical perils awaited the Christian epoist at the Napoleonic hour.

In ways that are obvious, each of these epicizing romance narratives trivialized Scott's achievement. There remains a sense, though, in which they exposed to plainest view that elevation of the trivial, or valorization of the historically contingent, which formed Scott's special contribution to the general descendental movement within Romanticism. Intrinsic to this contribution was the entertainment value of the romance mode, one regularly observed sign of which was the common versification Scott's epigones adopted. Stanzaic, common-metered, or at the height of dignity tetrameter-coupleted, these free-form poems had learned that whatever lesson they aspired to teach had better be delivered with a reader-friendly fluency, and with a care to keep things both comfortable and lively. It was only a matter of time before such amenities attracted long poetic narrative to subjects set in the present. This *terminus ad quem* was approximated in Mitford's five-canto narrative of the late-breaking H. M. S. *Bounty* story in *Christina, the Maid of the South Seas* (1811). It was attained outright in *The Veils; or the Triumph of Constancy* (1815): a *jeu d'esprit* elaborated with Popean–Darwinian sylphic machinery by Eleanor Porden, who would return to the lists some years later with a learned chivalric epic but wrote here about what trials and rewards a teenaged young lady might decorously know. In the process Porden brought out for a fresh airing the para-genre of the verse novel, withdrawn since its Sensibility debut a long generation ago.[22]

Smoothing the grade up Parnassus was also an informing design of the several contemporary romance epics that followed *Marmion* along more typically masculine paths out of cloister and bower into battle. Among

---

[22] Porden's poem showed sufficient *esprit* to earn her election at 16 to the Institut de France: Francis Spufford, *I May Be Some Time: Ice and the English Imagination* (New York: St. Martin's Press, 1997) 52. Stephen C. Behrendt finds that even in *The Veils* Porden "aspires to the broad sweep of the epic," albeit "uneasily": "The Gap That Is Not a Gap," in *Romanticism and Women Poets: Opening the Doors of Reception*, ed. Behrendt and Harriet Kramer Linkin (Lexington: University Press of Kentucky, 1999) 40.

these thematically unimpeachable strife epics most were more sternly con-
ceived than versified: only Richard Wharton's *Roncesvalles: A Poem, in Five
Cantos* (1812) and William Walker's specimen epic *Gustavus Vasa* (1813)
stuck with heroic couplets; only Thomas Northmore's severely Miltonic-
republican *Washington, or Liberty Restored. A Poem, in Ten Books* (1809) and
Southey's *Roderick, The Last of the Goths* (1814) embraced blank verse. Bertie
Ambrosse in *Opoleyta* (1815) switches from tetrameter couplets into pen-
tameter reverb when underscoring a moral or—often the same thing—
comparing his "Tale of Ind" to matters western and contemporary. It says
much about the ascendancy of Scott that when John Wilson Croker set
about composing, in *The Battles of Talavera* (1809), an instant-epic tribute to
that year's British victory over Napoleon, he did so in an *ad hoc* ballad-based
stanza that Hannah Cowley would not have dreamed of using for just the
same purpose a scant decade before (Ch. 3).

   As the war years dragged on, Britons felt on one hand less threatened by
imminent invasion and on the other increasingly fatigued by the strain of
two decades' resistance. There accordingly arose a patriotism of lighter
gauge, and an epic manner to go with it. One hardly knows what to call
the work that Thomas Dibdin called in 1813 *A Metrical History of England; or,
Recollections in Rhyme, of Some of the Most Prominent Features in our National
Chronology, from the Landing of Julius Caesar, to the Commencement of the
Regency, in 1812*. The impresario author's calling it that much will at least
give some idea of its scope, and a soupçon, too, of its flagrant waywardness.
Formal division into twelve parts stakes as usual an epic claim, and that the
two volumes break where the Wars of the Roses produce the Tudor
ascendancy betokens a serious endeavor to split off, and in the process
derive, modern Britain from its ancient and medieval antecedents. Dibdin
furthermore accompanies the poetic narrative in each part with literary
extracts in verse and—tellingly, once he hits the Glorious Revolution of
1688—in prose, so fleshing out the *res gestae* chronicle he intends as "not
unuseful to Children" with a cultural amplitude worthy of the age of Scott.
Still, keeping those youngsters amused, and their book-buying parents into
the bargain, is manifestly Dibdin's first consideration. His prosody is all over
the place, finding a dozen rhymes for "Eliza" in part 8, and juxtaposing in
part 3 a dignified treatment of King Alfred in strait-laced heroic couplets
with an account of the Norman Conquest that unaccountably takes form as
a parody of Gray's Elegy. This jaunty Regency anticipation of *1066 and All
That* looks ahead in the short run to internationalized mock-epic aspects of

Moore and Byron that await us in the next chapter, and at longer range to the spiritualized solemnities of world-historical conspectus that Chapter 11 will consider. These comparisons draw out, in turn, what is unique to the moment Dibdin's performance lights up: a nationalism secure enough to make fun of itself; the *paideia* function of a robust epic genre that supports, and survives, some pretty ragged doggerelizing.

Where contemporary patriotism gravitated towards vernacular forms evocative of the Middle Ages, poems with medieval settings or vernacular forms were *ipso facto* staking a significant patriotic claim—the more obviously when, with Sotheby's *Constance*, Mitford's *Blanch*, and Wharton's *Roncesvalles*, they set their action on the Iberian peninsula where Wellington's troops had lately slugged it out with Napoleon's. It was understood *a fortiori* that a poem like J. W. Cunningham's *De Rancé* (1815) tracing the ruinous corruption and final redemption of a seventeenth-century Frenchman, in stout tetrameters, must subserve a morality fundamentally patriotic. The teenaged epoist Walker dodged such competition by heading for sixteenth-century Scandinavia with *Gustavus Vasa*, but before long he hearkened back to the present in order to invoke "eternal freedom" and draw the parallel to contemporary struggles of liberation, "Since Spain is now, what Sweden was before" (3.83.35). John Doddridge Humphreys drops everything in the middle of *Prince Malcolm: In Five Cantos* (1813) to wish, a bit disconcertingly, that he were singing of Wellington and Napoleon instead of Malcolm and Macbeth. J. H. Merivale apologizes halfway through *Orlando in Roncesvalles* (1814) for animadversions against Napoleon—but then, as he points out, the well-established hospitality of *ottava rima* to digression practically invited a patriotic poet to put some English on his imported stanza. The male poet anonymously impersonated by Margaret Holford in *Wallace; or, the Fight of Falkirk* (1809) protests how much "*native* attachment" underlies his publication of an evidently Scott-inspired "metrical romance," ties off his dedication with two Spenserian stanzas lauding George III, showcases his invocation with liberally varied prosody, and settles into loyal tetrameter for the duration of the tale. Herbert's tetrameter couplets in *Helga* can feel like a runic imitation that connects his old Norse lore—he had translated *Select Icelandic Poetry* in 1806 and would retain scholarly prestige well into the century—to forgotten but stirring roots of the Anglo-Saxon stock. (Sharon Turner's multi-volume *History of the Anglo-Saxons* had been fully issued in 1805.) In all these works the exotic improbability of romance dressed itself for epic nationalism by meeting a widespread expectation that tales of military adventure should more or less explicitly allegorize current events.

If any romance epic of this period might seem exempt from suspicion of harboring national allegory, it would be Southey's *The Curse of Kehama* (1810). In fact no such exemption obtains: that all-purpose Satanic scourge Bonaparte emerges even here as quarry for an allegorical interpretation of the poem to which *obiter dicta* by Southey himself let slip the leash.[23] Be that as it may, on its own coruscating, ear-splitting terms *The Curse of Kehama* is a work whose literal diegesis escapes all bounds of probability. Manifestly the poet conceived it in the same spirit of exhilaration that engendered *Thalaba the Destroyer:* the prevalent creative high of the 1790s, that is, licked into articulate shape by the brave instance of Landor, to whom *The Curse of Kehama* was dedicated. Yet the proliferant psychedelia of *Kehama* make *Thalaba* look like a decorous idyll. Southey took care to establish that he had begun his Indian epic a decade before publication, or in other words at the time of *Thalaba*; and he ascribed to the mere matter in hand—what he regarded with carefully advertised contempt as the hyperbole-beggaring extravagance of Hindu mythology, "the most monstrous in its fables and the most fatal in its effects" (1810 preface)—his correspondingly superlative ambition "to combine the utmost richness of versification with the greatest freedom" (1838 preface). The student of developments in Romantic verse narrative will impute an additional motive: the spread and clang of *Kehama*'s seething strophes suggest an attempt on Southey's part to overtake at any cost a set of epic developments that *Thalaba* had helped sponsor but that had, since Scott, outflanked him.[24]

[23] Proceeding on Marilyn Butler's hint (72) from "Byron and the Empire of the East," in *Byron: Augustan and Romantic*, ed. Andrew Rutherford (New York: St. Martin's Press, 1990), Simon Bainbridge makes as strong a case for allegorizing *Kehama* as the evidence can possibly bear: *Napoleon and English Romanticism* (Cambridge: Cambridge University Press, 1995) 119–25. While Bainbridge's circumstantial recovery of "the poem's historical force" ignores the poem's gale-strength *rhetorical* force—and sheer improbability of incident—the all but compulsory ritual invocation of Napoleon in the several contemporaneous epics just cited seems, admittedly, improbable too. Southey very likely was a Bonarticipant like the rest. For Balachandra Rajan, *Under Western Eyes: India from Milton to Macaulay* (Durham and London: Duke University Press, 1999), Kehama is "a more monstrous Napoleon, threatening not merely Europe but also the cosmos," with an ambition that is irrelevant to Hindu religion but "does say something in passing about the methods and motives of empire builders" (148, 151).

[24] Rajan, *Under Western Eyes*, 154, finds Southey embarrassed by a half-consciousness of ideological belatedness: "Southey's commitment to an imperial discourse, underlined in the prose and in the two prefaces, is impeded by his involvement in a literary discourse of world humanism not yet adjusted to the imperial claim. The poem, as a result, is overdetermined by its loyalties."

The plot is notoriously unbelievable in its episodes and inconsequent in their relation. If that sounds like critical aspersion, it is; and yet the historian of taste, subjoining that any poem adored by both Percy Bysshe Shelley and John Henry Newman must have gotten something right, could do worse than propose the massive improbability of the work as a secret of its success.[25] Ingredient in the poem's lavish stimulus to imagination and ostentatious moral probity was the believe-it-or-not challenge it posed to the readerly exercise of a credulity that was so far out there as to feel heroic, transgressive, exposed. Rhyme was the new accessory Southey bestowed in *The Curse of Kehama* on the unbound stanzaic scheme he had debuted in *Thalaba*, and arguably one purpose for this formal upgrade was to meet a decade's rising tide of competition in poetic romance.[26] Moreover, in default of plot's sequential correlation the story is held together by a sort of narrative equivalent for rhyme. The extravagant incidents of *Kehama* rhyme with each other, conformed into patterns of parallel and contrast that brace up an aesthetic coherence quite independent of the absurdity of its constituent elements.

Not once but twice does the insatiable tyrant Kehama daily sacrifice one hallowed steed for a hundred days in a row (books 8 and 12), as if to spend the poem's way out of plot-inflation by striking off more and more of the same fantastic currency. Our peasant hero Ladurlad plunges not twice but thrice, deeper each time, on successive rescue missions into a river (3), then into a submarine city (15), and at last into the Padalon or divine Underworld itself (22).[27] At the beginning of the twenty-fourth and final book Southey

---

[25] Critical scholarship on Shelley long ago established the indebtedness to *Kehama* of his orientalizing plots, among them *The Revolt of Islam* (see Ch. 5). As for Newman, witness the essay he wrote as a young man on "Poetry, with Reference to Aristotle's Poetics" (1829): "Southey is admirable. Other writers are content to conduct their heroes to temporal happiness;—Southey refuses present comfort to his Ladurlad, Thalaba, and Roderick, but carries them on through suffering to another world": *Essays Critical and Historical* (London: Longmans, Green, 1872) 16. The elder Catholic convert remained true to his old literary affection: "Thalaba has ever been to my feelings the most sublime of English Poems—I don't know Spenser—I mean morally sublime. And his poems generally end, not with a marriage, but with death and future glory. . . . They are epics, not a string of sonnets or epigrams. . . . I read Kehama and got it well nigh by heart." Letter of 22 March 1850 to J. M. Capes, quoted in *Robert Southey: The Critical Heritage*, ed. Lionel Madden (London and Boston: Routledge, 1972) 422. And *Kehama* has its admirers in our time: witness Kenneth Hopkins, *English Poetry: A Short History* (Philadelphia and New York: Lippincott, 1962) 309: "a very fine poem indeed."

[26] Southey wrote to Scott himself in a letter of 30 July 1809, "The rhymes are as irregular as your own, but in a different key": *The Life and Correspondence of Robert Southey*, ed. Charles Cuthbert Southey (London: Longman, 1849) 3: 247.

[27] Javed Majeed, *Ungoverned Imaginings: James Mill's* The History of British India *and Orientalism* (Oxford: Clarendon Press, 1992) 49–50, offers some interpretive cover with an astute suggestion that in the eastern epics' imagery of depth (also of echoes) Southey was sowing the text with

literalizes the supervention of spatial pattern on temporal narrative—miraculously privy, we might be pardoned for supposing, to Blake criticism from the twentieth century—by having Kehama appear simultaneously at all eight Gates of Hell, "on every side, | In the same indivisible point of time" (24.2). And then, to cap a list of symmetries that might be much lengthened but to little purpose, the curse Kehama has pronounced on Ladurlad in book 2 redounds on his own head, where it figures at once as the ultimate crown of his power and as the terminal self-administration of an impossible, inevitable, and above all else ineffable suicide.

This titular curse, conjoining eternal invulnerability with eternal discomfort, strongly approximates the condition of total immunity reached by Thalaba at the end of his quest. Apprehending this likeness, we might then grasp all Southey's lateral equilibration and buttressing as an attempt to cope with what happens when such a condition is an initial narrative donnée. His epic Achilles has no heel, so his story has no traction; forward motion being stymied, nothing significant can *eventuate* because anything can *happen*. All that remains is wonder, or a masque of wonders taken for signs that, because they cannot signify in the usual way of narrative buildup and denouement, fold back on themselves like Southey's redundantly rhymed stanzas. *Thalaba* hyped sheer incident to a point at which heroic agency dissolved in action-packed deediness; *Kehama*'s elephantine spectacularization of the scenic bankrupts the bedazzled imagination, which does not so much conceive scenes as it receives an incessant, and to that extent unsustainable, rush of grandeur.[28]

The hyperaestheticization of this anomalous gong of an epic at last discloses, beyond Napoleonic or other allegory, its significance as a British national poem produced in a decade of nationalism under the influence of Scott. However fantastically estranged its mode of representation, Southey's

---

figures for his own scholarly delving and retrieval. One might also thus interpret the poet's complementary fascination with the paralysis of the living and reanimation of the dead (73, 78).

[28] This rush was what readers of *Thalaba* had either loved or hated. Contrast an unsigned review from the *Monthly Magazine* (1802)—"Whatever loss of interest this poem may sustain, as a whole, by an apparent driftlessness of the events and characters, is compensated for by the busy variety, the picturesque imagery, and striking originality of the parts"—with Francis Jeffrey's contemporaneous volley at the Lakers in the first number of the *Edinburgh Review*: "It is needless to speak of the fatigue that is produced by this unceasing summons to admiration, or of the compassion which is excited by the spectacle of these eternal strivings and distortions. Those authors appear to forget, that a whole poem cannot be made up of striking passages" (quoted in *Critical Heritage*, 67, 69–70).

theme here was India. And to Britain around the turn of the nineteeth century India was no neutral zone, but the major proving ground of empire. As the exploits of empire came palpably to shape a British identity in ceaseless transition, it no longer sufficed to approach the template colony India as a hopeless congeries incapable of self-government, and therefore in need of benign intercession from without. The maturing imperial imagination found it necessary to regard India (always with loftily colonial detachment) as a unitary *whole*. Regarded thus, the vast Indian entity became governable after all, because it became imaginable—if imaginable only *en masse* as a brilliant array of highly generalized, repetitious, symmetrically disposed effects. To this dual imperial need *The Curse of Kehama* ministered twice over: in its copious notes, which yield no ground to those of *Thalaba* in their degree of orientalist contempt, and also in its narrative system of redundant internal correspondences. That the latter added up to nothing proved the progressive rightness of the attitudes expressed in the former—which was thus immunized, Kehama-like, against critique. In this ulterior logic of subjugation by enlightenment, as in ways more ostentatiously superficial, the poem is too nearly a swollen reprise of *Thalaba* to detain us longer here. But it does show how, at the heart of Britain's most epically active era, the stakes of ethnocentric imagining had become perceptibly higher, and sharper at the point.

Among the many poems of heroic contest that this chapter inventories, even neoclassicizing holdouts hearkened to the romance note that persistently rippled the epic harp of patriot days. This is especially so when one considers the way romance elements mitigate epic strife and cue the dynastic and martial ethos of the genre to ulterior purposes mollified by family or social history. Wharton in *Roncesvalles* drew on "the characters and machinery of Romance" while duly aiming "to reduce the luxuriance of Italian Fable within some rule and limit" (vi). But to prove epic by curbing romance was, of course, to remain dependent on romance as the seductive generic other, an other that is here consistently gendered female and often manifested by means of sex. Thus the *prima donna* in Wharton's "machinery of Romance" is Urganda, an African demoness melding Virgil's Juno and Harpy in one implacable airborne person; the major poem-extending delay is due to Orlando's unknightly rape of Angelica and theft of her magic ring in Cathay (books 3–4); and the great anticipatory consolation for the tragic losses at Roncesvalles is the embowered sexual congress of Ruggiero with the maiden knight Bradamante, from whose loins will spring the House of Brunswick to fill "the majestick throne of Albion" (11.301). As the mention of even these few events will indicate, there is substantial curvature in Wharton's dynastic-epic line; and it confesses the sway of romance over epic at this phase in generic history.

The telltale sign in Ambrosse's *Opoleyta* that the guilty Muslim hero Abdullah is redeemable—setting him apart at a stroke from Marmion implicitly and Napoleon expressly—is the tear he sheds ("virtue's harbinger," 3.75–76) when unmanned by the innocence of a fair Hindu captive (2.37). In other, more sternly blood-and-iron epics, romance rounds the picture in a way that is strictly superfluous but that, we thereby see, the extenuating conventions of the moment solicited. Merivale begins his *Orlando* poem with the premonitions of the hero's wife Aldabelle, a cameo figure who returns only to end the poem by mourning her widowhood. Both Holford's *Wallace* and Herbert's *Helga* conclude with a scene in which a good wife beholds her doomed hero's body and promptly dies herself. Such superventions of the connubial on the militaristic evince some unease with the triumphalism that has attended the tragic heroism of those bravehearts Roland and Wallace under other literary-historical dispensations, and point us back to moral and narrative problematics in Scott, where subaltern history reverberates like a persistent accusatory echo.

The history of a subaltern's subaltern—a slave—receives frontal treatment in at least one epicizing poem from the period, *Yuli; the African: A Poem in Six Cantos* (1810). This anonymously published antislavery narrative advertises its enlightenment in its form: heroic couplets equally serviceable for storytelling and for didactic morality. Granted that the author, who seems unsure where Angola and Ethiopia precisely are (3.41), can be disconcertingly unaware that the sublime vocabulary of *rapture* and *transport* requires careful handling in a tale about the slave trade (3.54, 4.72). Still, the poem signals the availability of epic form in the new century both to represent victims' history and to evoke correlations between that history and the master narrative with which the genre remained primarily associated. In the same year, and by way of admonition rather than protest—slavery was swept from British shores in 1807—James Montgomery also turned to heroic couplets, if not quite to the heroic poem, with the four-part *The West Indies*. This abolitionist tale of the slave trade hangs its generic head in shame at the national complicity in human traffic (2.203: "Britannia shared the glory and the guilt"), praising Southey's *Madoc* in the same breath with Spenser's and Milton's epics, yet for its own part conscientiously forswearing the "loftier numbers" of conquest epic in order "to sing, in melancholy strains, | Of Charib martyrdoms and negro chains" (1.127–28).

These hard-hitting works on New World slavery contrast sharply with another 1810 poem in heroic couplets, *The Voyage of Columbus* by Samuel Rogers, a poet so little anonymous that he would eventually be offered the laureateship. Rogers's coy performance in twelve terse cantos with plump apparatus is a sort of readers'-digest epic, outlining by samples the kind of heroic narrative that a dozen uncondensed books might have amounted to. Barlow's unfurled *Columbiad* of three years before having been just such a work, Rogers made his mark instead by means of the packaging with which he outfitted the revised text of 1812. This version presents the poem as translated remains of an "Original in the Castilian language," allegedly contemporary with Columbus himself but "evidently of an after-time" (163). The putative manuscript of this translated original includes a tetrameter postscript to the effect that Cortez and Pizarro once sought it out for study—whether as a conquistador's manual or as a spur to penitence (such as might befit its monastic repository), Rogers omits to say. All this fancy footwork, in a manner learned from Southey and Scott—and studied by Byron and Moore, who respectively dedicated to Rogers *The Giaour* and *Lalla Rookh* (Ch. 5)—seems designed to refract the moral duplicity of conquest. Cantos 11 and 12 of *The Voyage of Columbus* forecast the enslavement of the native Americans and destruction of their civilization, but then swallow up regret in an angel's visionary promise of brotherhood and peace.[29]

A like oscillation practically provides Bowles's *The Missionary: A Poem* (1813) with its structuring principle. The title character is a priest in the Andes who sets aside pacifism in the final canto to give his blessing to the indigenous armed resistance against Spain; and the poem's central figure, Lautaro, a converted Indian, holds back on Christian principles from the great, decisive battle only to rush in at the last in defense of his father (7.221–37). The plot of filial rescue represents here, as it did in Skene's *Donald Bane* two decades before (Ch. 2), the reinstatement of epic in

---

[29] Nigel Leask, *British Romantic Writers and the East: Anxieties of Empire* (Cambridge: Cambridge University Press, 1992) 30–32, lays out Rogers's ambivalence and considers its effect on the Oriental tales of Byron. In the matter of textual apparatus Rogers's debt to Scott is apparent to W. J. Courthope in his *History of English Poetry* (London: Macmillan, 1895–1910) 6: 99.

paradigmatically patrilinear form.[30] Yet the intervening years have made a difference. When Bowles's Lautaro digs in at the end, with his Spanish bride Indiana and their mixed-race child, to endure the inevitable conquest of Chile, the generic hybridity of the poem fitly connotes both the compromised texture of national history and the ambivalence with which Bowles (unlike Skene) approached it. "Let the guilty blush, | The white man," said the epigraph to *Yuli*: blush, and then act to remove the moral stain within. Rogers and Bowles were blushing, all right, nor were they whitewashing colonialism. But they were far from sharing *Yuli*'s confidence about what was to be done. Colonial conquest had occurred, it had often been brutally wrong, and its legacy persisted within the present: this, they thought, was the cargo that contemporary epic had to declare, letting the duties fall where they might.

Evidently Britain's own triumph in the struggle with France—increasingly likely when *The Missionary* first appeared, a *fait accompli* by the second edition of 1815—was hospitable to reservations about the cost and effect of victory; and romance modes offered ampler hospitality to narrative enactment of those reservations than strife-epic did. The best bow to the arts of peace that Northmore's republican rigor could manage in *Washington* (1809) was an awkward special dispensation, after the victory at Yorktown, that absented Mammon from Hell awhile to abide among men and forward liberty through the improvement of world commerce (book 10). Not that strife-epic as such knew no such reserve—witness the end of the *Iliad* (indeed, of *Madoc*) or Blake's deliberate correction of the victory ethos in *Milton*—but that, at this juncture, the dues of the softened heart were payable in the wages of romance. Did a softened heart mean a slackened nerve, a lapse from Scott's tough, guilty love into the stock liberality of a rote, unquestioning sympathy? There is often something suspect about such a change in the weather, and literary history is lucky when its suspicions are anticipated in a whistle-blowingly contrarian work like our next exhibit.

Of its kind and for its time Margaret Holford's *Margaret of Anjou* is a better than average read, with its urgently pointed irregular stanzas and surprisingly

[30] On Bowles's ethos of " 'benevolent' paternalism" see Tim Fulford, "Romanticism and Colonialism: Races, Places, Peoples, 1800–1830," in *Romanticism and Colonialism: Writing and Empire, 1780–1830*, ed. Fulford and Peter J. Kitson (Cambridge: Cambridge University Press, 1998) 35.

direct diction, its feminist edge, its disguise plotting and bracingly unapolo-
getic demonstration of machiavellian atheism in a heroine from the fifteenth
century. Of special interest here is how, by these same means, Holford's
1816 poem performs a lucid reading of the career that epic had run during
the ten years or so before its publication. Bent on clarification in its every
aspect, this poem that disguises a noblewoman as a rustic leech (canto 3), a
nobleman as a monk (canto 6), and a king as a hermit (canto 7), *à la* Scott,
unmasks them all in the interests of unmasking the epic essence of romance
itself when stripped of padding and evasion. Canto 6 invokes an escapist
muse of "Fancy" and "dream," but only so as to escape it, in turn, through
the increasingly revelatory action of this ten-book poem's second half.
Here Margaret's son Prince Edward, formerly a "sweet, yet blighted rose,
which lay | Helpless and prone" while she defended him with a spear
(3.25), finds his manhood, marries a suitably strong woman, and sees that
"the world | Cries out for action! War again" (9.7). This last phrase speaks
the ambition of the poem too. In his maturing belligerence the prince but
shows himself worthy of his mother, a dynast "concenter'd, and austere"
(1.52) from beginning to end, "the English Pallas" (10.7) who, scorning
feudal values for classical, prizes patriotism over mere "private love" (4.64),
never quails at black magic (7.18) or priestcraft (10.23), and indeed holds the
mystique of metaphysical origins in a contempt at which Marmion would
blench: "In time of need | *Whence* helps arise I little heed" (7.8).

Strategist and deal-maker, even at times (so a contemporary reviewer
opined) "a dæmon in human form": all these and more Queen Margaret is.[31]
What she is *not* is a man; and for that reason she may not, alas, quite become
a hero within the genre for whose traditional values she strives so hard.
Indeed, the impossibility of her becoming a hero may be regarded as this
fierce epic's exasperating *donnée*. While her thirst for "A high, a wonderful
career" may be in itself "a path sublime" (10.23), it also demarcates a
collision course with the historical limitations that her sex imposes—or, to
refine the point, the limitations that epic imposes when it submits imagin-
ation to the facts of gender history. In 1813 Eliza Francis's *The Rival Roses, or
Wars of York and Lancaster*, a metrical romance in the manner of Scott, had
strapped falchion and helm on the same historical Margaret and sent her

[31] *New Monthly Magazine* 5 (1816) 444: quoted and discussed in John M. Anderson's unpub-
lished doctoral dissertation, *Beyond Calliope: Epics by Women Poets of the Romantic Period* (Boston
College, 1993) 178.

forth to do battle in sudden pentameter (canto 6)—with dubious documentary warrant, and with the ultimate aim of heaping opprobrium on so
brawlingly masculine a fomentress of civil war (2.142). Francis's work,
however, had represented the standard sort of decorum-enforcement that
Holford's second epic—the one she dedicated to her mother and affixed
only her maiden name to—angrily eschews. Obliged to sit out the Battle of
Tewkesbury, and confronted at last with the assassinated corpse of Edward,
the son she has raised up in her own soul's image, Queen Margaret like
Aldabelle and Helga, and like the wife of Wallace in Holford's own earlier
epic romance of 1809, gives up the ghost. But unlike those romance
bystanders, she does not go quietly. Nor does she even die, exactly, since
as Holford knew the historical Margaret had some years yet to live after
the moment when the poem concludes. Margaret's literary end is stranger
than death: she apoplectically explodes, cursing everything in sight, a female
Thalaba sprung at last from the world's ramparts, lost in an epic space
outside the wrap with which romance in the Scott tradition dresses as
inevitable the history that hurts.

Rage on the order of Holford's atheistic Margaret, if it does not become a
metaphysic in itself, at least prompts reflection on the desirability of one.
Such reflection was conducted in yet another set of contemporary works,
from this richest of epic decades, that revived the genre's traditionally
twinned concerns with cosmology and theodicy. Appeal to the law of the
cosmos—the order of things, how it really is—had always been a baseline of
epic's claims to historical truth and encyclopedic knowledge; and there had
always been active commerce between these claims and a temperamental
disposition to affirm that the ordinance of reality was fundamentally just.
Early nineteenth-century epoists' adoption of guilt as an heroic entailment
put the genre under interesting pressure, however, by introducing a moral
imbalance that did not fit neatly into the interlocking congruences of action
and value on which the fundamental idea of epic unanimity reposed. Once
it was clear that on the level of heroic moral psychology all would not
be made right within Marmion, Margaret of Anjou, and their successors,
the genre felt new obligation to justify the ways of culture and history with
reference to some higher realm, whose rectitude transcended the protagonist's failure to attain it.

The apotheosis of outrage in *Margaret of Anjou* offers one sort of testimony to
this obligation. Another appears in the briskness with which a complementary

pair of contemporary epical projects shook it off: Hogg's euphoric *The Pilgrims of the Sun* (1815) and Thomas Love Peacock's grim unpublished fragment *Ahrimanes* (drafted 1814). In the former we encounter what Shelley's contemporary *Queen Mab* might have become had it taken a narrative form, and had Shelley been capable like Hogg of regional or national affections.[32] Hogg's affections of this kind transpire charmingly to ballast a most volatile plot: an angel squires a fresh-minded Scots lass across the universe on an out-of-body trip that expands all her horizons, converts her to a vaguely deistical nature-worship, and prepares her to become his bride happily ever after on an Ettrick sheep farm. Peacock's poem, as begun in two Spenserian cantos and then sketched in divergent prose drafts, is also imaginable *mutatis mutandis* as the work of his friend Shelley, to whom he would soon be lending assistance with *The Revolt of Islam* (Ch. 5). *Ahrimanes* traces the erotic and political career of a young Persian, inconstant to begin with and soon corrupted by power, across a plot whose shocking randomness demonstrates the cloven Zoroastrian truth of things, which is that Necessity long ago set the benevolent god Oromaze and the vindictive god Ahrimanes at permanent loggerheads over the fate of the world. While the survival of both a utopian and a pessimistic draft conclusion gives this Manichean cosmogony an apt textual enactment, Peacock's working title shows him girding for the worst, just in case.[33]

In effect Hogg's and Peacock's mischievous gnostic sketches bid good riddance to theodicy as such, since a cosmic outlook so self-evidently good as the one or bad as the other needed no justification. At the time, of course, these dismissals shared a sniper's agenda of affronting the mainstream Christian theodicies they sent up: Panglossian natural theology for Hogg, and for Peacock the seamier side of Calvinism's distant, inscrutably arbitrary God. These epicizing troublemakers were joined in a few years by a third, Sir William Drummond, the first half of whose *Odin: A Poem; in Eight Books*

---

[32] Courthope makes the connection between Hogg's poem and Shelley's (6: 416). Hogg's planetary-tourism plot also superficially resembles that of the hoaxing "New Epic" (1812), allegedly by Rosa Matilda (pseud. for Charlotte Dacre), whose mock-review with extracts is attributed to Byron by David V. Erdman, "Byron's Mock Review of Rosa Matilda's Epic on the Prince Regent—A New Attribution," *Keats–Shelley Journal* 19 (1970) 101–17.

[33] Each possibility, utopian and dystopian, found epic play in Shelley's *Revolt of Islam*. On the genetic relation between that poem and Peacock's, see Kenneth Neill Cameron, "Shelley and *Ahrimanes*," *Modern Language Quarterly* 3 (1942) 287–95; also Carlos Baker, *Shelley's Major Poetry: The Fabric of a Vision* (Princeton: Princeton University Press, 1948) 64–72; Ross Woodman, *The Apocalyptic Vision in the Poetry of Shelley* (Toronto: University of Toronto Press, 1964) 92–98.

and Two Parts (1817, never completed) propounded a neat narrative argument in religious relativism. Here the epic theme was one that Wordsworth had vetted alongside others in *Prelude* 1.185–89: the migration northward from Asia of Mithridates' son Pharnaces. This emigrant prince, having been defeated by Caesar's legions, goes on in turn to conquer Scandinavia by passing himself off as Odin incarnate and dynastically heading a new hybrid people, whom he names "Goths" (4.162), and whose eventual destruction of Caesar's heirs the poem places beyond prophetic doubt.[34] To the single-minded, far-sighted Pharnaces the impersonation of deity is a political device. *Rome vaut bien la messe*: that is, the distant prospect of vengeance on Rome justifies abandoning the enlightened Mithraism of his fathers and embracing the local savagery of Nordic human sacrifice. Indeed, the analogy of barbaric sacrifice to the Christian eucharist slumbers within the text as a subversive corollary of Drummond's comparatist, superstition-debunking practice of identifying deities across cultures, such that Siva, Ahriman, Moloch, and Dionysus, for example, are all one with the Norse Loke (3.111–13). Like the aggressive euhemerism whereby his plot grows a god from a man—or, for that matter, like the allegorical intepretation of scripture as an esoteric astronomical code in his freethinking mythological study 1811 *Oedipus Judaicus*—Drummond's humanism consistently relativized faith-based values. It thereby nudged epic toward an ethical openness that was worthy of Holford's *Margaret*—"I ask not what is evil, or what good" (1.46), avers his exiled hero—and that other epoists of the years after Waterloo would embrace more frankly still.

Meanwhile, on the orthodox side of this opening moral divide, during these years biblical epic remained active, and at its best responsive to shifts that Scott had inaugurated in the premises of taste. We have seen how in Sotheby's *Saul* this most stable subgenre contributed its mite to *Marmion*'s nationalist-narrative bargain with sin and atonement; in time it also took something away for uses of its own. Hitherto Romantic religious epic had made little of the sinner's inward drama of expiation. Despite the central

---

[34] Andrew Wawn, *The Vikings and the Victorians: Inventing the Old North in Nineteenth-Century Britain* (Cambridge: D. S. Brewer, 2000), identifies this revenge pattern as standard within the Odin narrative that descended from Gray, Percy, Gibbon, and Mallet in the eighteenth century (206). The pattern continues to inform Southey's late Scandinavian venture "The Race of Odin" (1827).

place redemption held in Christian dogma, epoists had tended either to make narrative subserve doctrinal exposition, or else to trust the ethic of moral transformation to speak for itself through the externals of plot. The latter choice had been Cumberland's in *Calvary*, which was largely content to rehearse the events of Holy Week, the harrowing of Hell, and the Ascension. When his adoring ephebe Charlotte Dixon ventured to fill in and finish Cumberland's 1790s job in 1814, she reversed his emphases, in keeping with the new century's evident distrust of unchaperoned narration. *The Mount of Olives, or the Resurrection and Ascension: A Poem, in Continuation of Calvary* is an unfinished work that has trouble getting off the ground, but off the ground is certainly where it wants to be. Delineating the meaning of events rather than the events themselves is this author's forte, and her devoting two hundred lines of book 1 to the risen Christ's exposition of his life's typological meaning proves it exhaustively. What Christ does not do is say what the labor of redemption *felt* like; yet in the years after *Marmion* it is a little surprising that Dixon should not have moved at all in this psychological direction. Between Cumberland's diegetic and Dixon's exegetic modes a cultural space had opened up by 1810 for the rendition of religious experience as such, and other religious epoists were readier than she to explore it.

One of them was James Montgomery, a devout Moravian Brother whose penchant for theologized natural history would emerge in some of the more interesting epic works of the 1820s (Ch. 6). As early as 1813, when he came on the scene with *The World before the Flood: A Poem, in Ten Cantos*, he designed as the centerpiece of his Genesis-based tale a sort of reliquary textual implant: a paean to the Creation that has within the tale become something of a patriarchal golden oldie, composed by Jubal long ago, and well beloved even by so hardened a criminal scoffer as Cain. The tale itself, however, concerns a more modern protagonist, the minstrel named Javan who can perform the old hymn to perfection but who, for all the early world as if he belonged in *Marmion*, is too hip to believe in it. Raised in a pacifist valley enclave headed by the good Enoch, Javan has been seduced since then by the glamour of cities whose warmongering and decadence plainly show us that their antediluvian days are numbered. He is eventually reclaimed into the fold, marries his old sweetheart, and lives piously ever after—thanks to a last-canto exertion of God's overwhelming force that confounds the human armies, spares the simple valley, and lifts the rapt Enoch directly to Heaven.

This miraculous climax is the narrative analogue of the ethic of redemption that would make Montgomery a darling of evangelical missionaries well into the century. But redemption, we should emphasize, can rehabilitate Javan only because he is fallen to begin with. A Scott hero in patriarch's clothing, Javan is the modern possessor of a divided mind, the chosen simplification of which entails a return from urban to pastoral allegiances that Montgomery frankly hinges on nothing short of an act of God. This radical providentialist vantage, in one sense, marked *The World before the Flood* as work a decade ahead of its time. In another sense, the poem implicitly framed a critique of the chief thrust of contemporary epic writing.[35] Through his Javan's career Montgomery recognized, only to subsume it wholesale into a vaster explanatory narrative of *ecclesia* rather than *res publica*, the validity of the secular association that Romantic epoists were forging between national continuity and a burden of obligations still potent because still unfulfilled.

We can see the same maneuver performed at greater length in the last of Cottle's epics, *Messiah: A Poem, in Twenty-Eight Books* (1815). The title is pure typology, since Messiah nowhere plays a human part: the first half of the narrative arrives at the Exodus from Egypt, prime type of redemption; the second half at the death of David, received into heaven in book 28 as redemption's privileged prophet, with a forecast of what the New Testament will bring. Messiah, the superintendent guide of his chosen people, operates as the agency of history itself—which is, Cottle explained in a preface, what the poem is really all about: "The Agency of MESSIAH, through the whole of these events, gives, it is presumed, an *unity* to the action, which no other subject, thus extended, could possess" (v). By now Cottle was no novice in the matter of epic unity; and there is admirable consistency in his progress from the unification of England in *Alfred* under a good and diligent king, to the unification of Britain as forwarded by the puissant if amoral King Edward in *The Fall of Cambria*, to the potential unification of mankind that is envisioned here through Messiah's invisible sway, over and above the figural destiny of Israel under Moses and David. *Messiah*'s last twelve books indeed constitute a Davidic epic, a national poem that might have been. But Cottle purposely subsumes this possibility within a larger, typological vision the meaning of which is redemptive—and

---

[35] On such terms we may recoup for sharper insight Curran's complaint that "Montgomery does in fact break free from the grip of biblical and Miltonic scriptures, but his poem cannot truly sustain either epic purpose or pressure" (*Poetic Form*, 166).

the condition for which is, very explicitly, the failure of unassisted human agency whether individual or collective. Alfred had embodied a young man's heroic dream, Edward his subsequent disillusion; the redemptive promise of *Messiah* effected a synthesis extending the reach of epic beyond the boundaries of the nation and the limits of the human. Like Montgomery, Cottle invoked a framework transcending Scott's domain of a nationally focused world-history; yet the basis of fallen heroism that both these religious poets worked from was one that Scott had arguably redefined for their moment on secular terms.

The three major poets of the first Romantic generation who revisited epic at about this time were roughly Cottle's agemates. Like him, they returned to epic as men chastened—by their own advancing years, by what the embattled nineteenth century had made of the promise of the 1790s, and also by the new cultural channels cut by a genre in spate. While this chastening took a distinct and characteristic form with each poet, it will be instructive first to consider certain similarities linking Southey's *Roderick, the Last of the Goths: A Tragic Poem* (1814), Wordsworth's *The Excursion: Being a Portion of The Recluse, a Poem* (also 1814), and Blake's *Jerusalem: The Emanation of the Giant Albion* (engraved 1820, largely completed by mid-decade); and also to compare these epics with those their authors had completed a decade before. The new works share a thematic of guilt, forgiveness, and endurance that is notably absent from *Madoc, Milton,* and *The Prelude*: works that were not defective for this absence, but that the later epics let us see had been organized by a different ethos implying a simpler narrative model. Circa 1805 the model had been problem-solving, which was the practical legacy each poet brought into the new century from the social and generic engineering to which the 1790s had been attuned. The return of Prince Madoc to Aztlan, of Milton to the realm of Generation, and of Wordsworth to England, had in each instance been undertaken in order to correct an error for which the hero was responsible and which he could successfully rectify, by taking appropriate reparative action in a world that might with due effort be understood and improved.

By 1815 or so, if we may judge by the final efforts of the era's three leading epic poets, this narrative model no longer availed to describe the world, to define heroism, or to declare any relation between the two that an action of national significance might illustrate. Now a more complex moral calculus arose—subtler, softer, yet no less binding for that—to account for human deeds individually and collectively performed, and especially to shape the history that those deeds amounted to. As error yields to sin in these later epics, regret to remorse, correction to expiation and redemption, the ideal of perfectibility recedes, and with it the prestige of origins and the allure of solutions. Redemption, indeed, loses much of its customary climactic force. Instead it becomes a way of life, a mode of narrative acceptance that enlarges the capacity to encounter a sorrowful past faithfully, without apology or distortion. While changes in the master publications of poets so mature and strong-minded are scarcely explained by reference to the changes that Scott and his romance-epic imitators had wrought during the intervening years, these surely played a part. If nothing else, the nationalization of guilt and the affiliation of patriotism with continuity had achieved since 1805 a literary salience that any epic aspiring to the genre's fullness of encyclopedic assimilation must engage with.

So the matter evidently presented itself to Southey. But, because his penchant for transcendental simplification did not consort with the half-tones of moral compromise, when he rose to the new call with *Roderick* what he produced was a cloven melodrama. It is as if the poem Southey recognized he ought to write, and the poem he had it in him to write, coexisted here without consulting each other. On one hand Roderick, unlike any previous Southey protagonist, is a deeply guilty being, who never doubts that the loss of his crown and name has been permanently merited by a dark crime from his past. The plot laboriously reveals what this crime was— adulterous sexual assault—but the real interest of the poem lies in how the crime is to be expiated.[36] The means of atonement is to be Roderick's mission of leading a national resistance movement that will free Spain from Moorish tyranny, and that will incidentally enable his incognito reconciliation with all whom he has wronged. Like Joan and Madoc, Thalaba and Ladurlad, Roderick is a long-odds champion of the oppressed; but here for once a Southey hero staggers under burdens confessedly of his own making.

Thus far into moral complexity Southey advanced to meet the spirit of the age, and no farther. For his way of handling a hero's guilt was, characteristically, to drive it to extremity and leave it there. The remorseful

---

[36] Edward Meachen, "History and Transcendence in Robert Southey's Epic Poems," *Studies in English Literature* 19 (1979), proposes that "Man's first crime, according to Southey, was a sexual act. . . . Every epic portrays a rape scene and in every case the sexual crime leads to death" (602). If so, then in *Roderick* the poet was confronting directly a generic trauma his earlier epics had occluded.

penitence of Roderick swiftly becomes a luxuriantly ascetic narrative med-
ium equivalent to Madoc's repressive "self-controul" (*Roderick* 17.4484) or
Thalaba's all-destroying talisman ("the heart is dead," 19.4987), to Kehama's
curse or Joan's charisma (in battle the hero is made invulnerable by "the
shield of Heaven," 25.7117). No virtuous Thalaba leavens the moral lump of
Southey's Muslims now.[37] Rather, the narrative places them in a uniformly
polarized moral glare so as to clarify its program, which is that Roderick's
soul should, "in redeeming this lost land, work out | Redemption for herself"
(4.989). The entire plot is scrupulously contrived to make these two
redemptions, of self and of land, dovetail. At the epic midpoint, in disguise
and in the "commanding majesty" of his priestly "delegated power"
(12.3146, 3199)—again that favorite epithet, the one yoke sized to all
Southey heroes—Roderick receives from a massed convention of "People
and Prince" their unison "vow for Spain | And for the Lord of Hosts"
(12.3195–96). In the final book his identity is discovered and celebrated by
patriotic troops exultantly driving the craven Moors before them with a
battlecry motto that might well be the poem's: "Roderick and Victory! |
Roderick and Vengeance!" (25.7006–7).[38]

Thus Southey's Spanish plot explicated with unusual fullness an argu-
ment, the national vindication of a private crime, which epic writers in
Britain since Scott had drawn upon but had mainly been content to imply.
By laying the matter out in so formulaic and frictionless a way Southey ran,
as he seems partly to have recognized, the risk of trivializing the very guilt
that made it go. This may be why he literally made Roderick go, spiriting
him off the battlefield of his triumph to pursue, the last page tells us, further
penance in a distant hermitage—a narrative (ir)resolution, consistent with
Scott's epic poetics of guilt, that Bertie Ambrosse adopted at just the same
time for his compromised Muslim patriot Abdullah in *Opoleyta* (4.104–7).
This resolution confirms Roderick's Joan-like status as a political catalyst
rather than a reagent. It also confirms the enabling paradox that, if you are

---

[37] The poet's orientalism soured with the years from supercilious indulgence into toxic
vituperation. Long ago Byron Porter Smith, *Islam in English Literature* (Beirut: American Press,
1939) decried in Southey's 1808 edition of *The Chronicle of the Cid* "the nadir of opinion
concerning Muhammad in English literature" (156).

[38] See Philip Connell, *Romanticism, Economics and the Question of "Culture"* (Oxford: Oxford
University Press, 2001) 264, on the way Southey's "bibliophilic antiquarian historiography" thus
gravitated towards "a single consciousness embedded within a particular historical milieu."

a Romantic hero, you can expiate your guilt and have it too. Duplicitous moral accountancy did not come easily to Southey's straight-ahead imagination, but he did see that it was entailed on him by the thematics of epic guilt. It produced in the last five books the poem's most interesting feature: the co-presence of two parallel yet incompatible ethics—vengeance and forgiveness—two conceptions of the claim lodged by past injustice against future reparation, and thus two narratives about the significance of history.

Moral bifurcation sets in with the figure of Count Julian, a renegado who has conformed to Islam for reasons of state and who will return to the Christian church before the end. But with the appearance of this confessionally compromised figure (whom Landor had elevated to tragic stature in a closet drama of 1812), the poem's expiatory design splits down the forking paths of punishment and of mercy, values each of which Southey felt obliged to air in the poem although he could not begin to resolve them. Book 21 in particular is a handsomely composed interlude in which Roderick, Julian, and his daughter Florinda (Roderick wronged her, but she loves him still) discuss guilt, forgiveness, and moral freedom in an inconclusive dialogue that Wordsworth should have admired, especially for the way it opens out at last, with nearly Homeric aplomb, onto a description of the encamped armies by moonlight:

> The silver cloud diffusing slowly passed,
> And now, into its airy elements
> Resolved, is gone; while through the azure depth
> Alone in heaven the glorious Moon pursues
> Her course appointed, with indifferent beams
> Shining upon the silent hills around,
> And the dark tents of that unholy host,
> Who, all unconscious of impending fate,
> Take their last slumber there.

(21.5734–42)

Here is as achieved a piece of writing as Southey's vast epic output offers, a disclosure in style of the stoicism that was essentially his. Also essential to this poet, however, was a restless drive for narrative results, which impelled him in the next books to contrive sharply discordant enactments of the ethical positions that book 21 so delicately balanced. One plot line leads from betrayal to ambush to full annihilation under the "Roderick and Vengeance!" slogan, inspired by the stricken Julian's legacy: "Vengeance! in that good word doth Julian make | His testament" (24.6437–38).[39] And yet this brazen ethic cedes place to its golden opposite not three pages later, as the same stricken Julian grants Roderick's request for full pardon, and his aggrieved, ecstatic daughter follows suit. That both Julian and Florinda no sooner declare their forgiveness than they perish on the spot is more here than a melodramatic effect; it suggests why Southey had to give mercy itself such short shrift and treat it as a purely private matter. For he apprehended forgiveness as a narrative dead end. If forgiveness did not lie outside history altogether, still it lacked anything like the worldly future that the vindictive side of penitent expiation conspicuously possessed. We may conclude that Roderick's going on to fight and survive a last battle as "the Avenger" (25.6658, 6999) is of a piece with his going off to repent in a hermitage. Epic heroism as Southey finally conceived it required his hero to remain, for the life of the story, unforgiven.[40]

In Blake's *Jerusalem*, by contrast, forgiveness is the whole story. It is at once a suffusive ethic, an earnest aesthetic challenge, and the condition of narrative possibility for comprehensive history itself. Time and again, just as we turn to a new plate of hopelessly idiosyncratic mytho–psycho–political syncretism and unpardonably demanding analogical cross-reference to what feels like the same speech or scene twice-remembered from halfway across the poem—just then is when Blake hands us a lucid reminder that forgiveness is all of divinity that we can hope to know, and that the only way to know it is by practice.[41] The frantic scene before us snaps into focus as the spitting image of our fallen impatience with it, whether it be Albion and Vala guiltily witholding forgiveness from themselves and thus from others, or Los and Jerusalem striving to embrace the otherness, and the manifest imperfection, of their specters and children as independent creations for

---

[39] As Mark Storey puts it in *Robert Southey: A Life* (Oxford University Press, 1997), "For all the Christian colouring, Roderick is a later manifestation of Thalaba the Destroyer" (231).

[40] Although Southey's epic imagination had no room for it—save as a pastoral phase to be transcended—his prose would increasingly articulate a bourgeois-individualist alternative to epic absolutism, what Connell calls "the morally ennobling practice of aesthetic cultivation in a private environment of domestic independence" (272–73). The path between *Roderick* and *A Tale of Paraguay* (Ch. 6) arguably leads in this direction.

[41] Kroeber, "Delivering *Jerusalem*," in *Blake's Sublime Allegory: Essays on* The Four Zoas, Milton, Jerusalem, ed. Stuart Curran and Joseph A. Wittreich, Jr. (Madison: University of Wisconsin Press, 1973) 352–53, correlates the *repetitious* quality of citation here (as against Blake's earlier *allusiveness*) with the literalist eschewal of metaphor in *Jerusalem*, and associates both features with the oral epic tradition. Curran, *Poetic Form*, 177, calling *Jerusalem* "outspokenly antiheroic," says that the figure of Jesus "represents the solution to a world doomed to traditional epic repetition."

whom they acknowledge responsibility, and with whom they have work to do. Reading well or ill, Blake's giant forms are there before us. They wrestle as we must to redeem comprehension from understanding—to save the big picture from the merely clear one—and they assure us that to keep reading this hard and incorrigible text is to participate in its collaboratively heroizing ethos.

We can become part of this solution only by confessing that we are part of the problem. This is more radically the case in *Jerusalem* than in Blake's earlier epics.[42] There mercy and self-annihilation were also cardinal virtues, to be sure; yet a problem like the poet's epic error in *Milton* arose in order to be fixed and then moved beyond. In *Jerusalem* there is no beyond, no *hors-texte*, no sublation of antithetical forces into a narrative of progress such as subtends Scott's epic historiography or, we may see from a Blakean vantage, such as governs Southey's foreclosing of mercy from the vindictive national vision of judgment in *Roderick*. In *Jerusalem* the forgiveness that is everything is, in the final analysis, the only thing that really is; and the length of the poem is due to the heaped-plate plenary indulgence it extends to those failures of mercy which constitute the bulk of the action. The poem's iterations go nowhere but back into itself, in a principled, headlong process of recycling that morally renovates the tactical and political self-interruptedness of narrative in *Vala* and the minor epics of the 1790s. In those works a welter of mutually interfering causal determinants valorized the present moment, the creative crux of artistic and political opportunity. In contrast, the patience-trying rehearsals of *Jerusalem* tirelessly correlate the present moment with the whole-ness of time—a correlation that Jerusalem herself amazingly performs by dilating a moment into millennia at 48.30–37. Each moment potentially epitomizes the totality of history, because without vital reference to history no moment can become really present in the first place. The form of this abstract-sounding yet entirely concrete relationship between now and always is forgiveness. It presents us with the present—fore-gives it us, and us it—on condition that we accept the fullness of time which is the mercy of eternity.

This holistic, eminently epic condition is non-negotiable and self-enforcing, perpetually open and nearly impossible to meet sustainedly. That is the burden of Blake's narrative form: a back-feeding involute, in which a set of mutually perforating stories establish that the ultimate consequence of

---

[42] Stewart Crehan, *Blake in Context* (Dublin: Gill and Macmillan 1984) 318, emphasizes the centrality of guilt and forgiveness in *Jerusalem*.

failing to grasp the whole pattern is nothing more, or less, than needing to try again. The proximate consequences are many, among them neurosis, vindictive co-dependency, family dysfunction, national crisis, and the dismal record of several thousand years' so-called civilization. While the whole story remains the story of the whole, it is these evasions of totality that engross the poem and furnish its spaces. It is one thing to confide in beautiful invocation that "Within your bosoms I reside, and you reside in me" (4.19): a confidence whose ambiguous attribution (who speaks this line to whom?) performs the reciprocity it affirms among bard, reader, and attentively dictating savior-muse. It is something else again to share residence with a bosom companion you despise and fear as the embodiment of your own all-too-familiar worst impulses; "It is easier to forgive an Enemy than to forgive a Friend" (91.1).

Just this is the difficult condition of Los when we meet him at the forge with his live-in Spectre in plate 6. If we think of this odd-couple domestic scenario as a deliberately deflationary sequel to the reparative heroic–satanic anagnorisis of *Milton*, we appreciate the alternative heroism of Los's decision, not just to correct the Spectre, but to take him into the business and put "Pride & Self-righteousness" (8.30) to work. The plot-launching event in *Milton*, we recall from Chapter 3, was the great poet's thunderstruck repudiation of his own Eternal perch on an atonement-secured platform of renunciative "Moral Virtue."[43] From the vantage of *Jerusalem*, however, it looks as though the satisfactory arrangement that obtains at the finale of the earlier epic harbors a viral strain of the same can-do spiritual engineering that brought on trouble in the first place. The sublime Puritan's residual hankering after the satisfaction of debts affiliates *Milton* with the very state of affairs his purgative odyssey was supposed to correct.[44] This is why, where Blake's Milton stripped for action by forswearing his spectral selfhood, Los in *Jerusalem* collaborates with his instead. That is to say, Los forgives himself—something that righteous Milton never quite thought he had to do—and he proves it, not by repairing his wrongs but by absorbing them apprentice-like into the intimate and minute particulars of his art.[45] Before

---

[43] Florence Sandler outlines theological issues in "The Iconoclastic Enterprise: Blake's Critique of 'Milton's Religion,'" *Blake Studies* 5 (1972) 13–57.

[44] For William Richey, *Blake's Altering Aesthetic* (Columbia and London: University of Missouri Press, 1996) 99, *Jerusalem* purges off those remnants of the classical agon that had clung to *Milton*.

[45] I concur here shorthandedly with a case made at greater length by James Ferguson, "Prefaces to *Jerusalem*," in *Interpreting Blake*, ed. Michael Phillips (Cambridge: Cambridge University Press, 1978) 171: "Los must learn to reserve his wrath only for himself in the form of his Spectre . . . It is

Los can *forge*, in the always doubled sense that term possesses for Blake, he must *forgive*. The strokes of his hammer undertake not to *forget*, by dint of obliteration, but to re-member, by a process of increasingly distinct articulation. We constantly encounter vivid poetic analogues to this articulative process in Blake's recourse to the linguistic root cellar—"English, the rough basement, | Los built the stubborn structure of the Language" (40.58–59)— and in the surprisingly declarative, untroped, simile-shy literalness with which, in this final epic modality of his, Blake strives to get things straight.

The great obstacle to getting things straight is the perversity of a conscience that is at once eager to detect guilt and unable to bear it. *Jerusalem* calls this perverse complex "strong & mighty Shame," and shows how its "brazen fetters" (10.34) shackle the epic imagination by shutting down narrative alternatives to anything but shame's reproduction "for ever & ever without end" (10.50). This stalled singularity is the Spectre's particular nightmare, but it oppresses plenty of other figures in the poem. Albion especially is covered with "Sin and Shame" (18.13), from which he avers that he "can never return" (22.15); "I have erred! I am ashamed! and will never return more" (23.16). "What have I said? What have I done?" (24.1): Albion keeps alleging unverified causes that remain obscure—to him and us—for a very good reason. He and his progeny keep covering them up, shifting an imputed blame to Jerusalem and stigmatizing her in self-perpetuating moral self-projection: "Cast! Cast her into the Potters field" (18.32). Whereas guilt must be dwelt upon and lived through in redemptive time—worked over, as Los does with his Spectre—Albion and company will not give shame the time it takes to grow into guilt. Shame remains eternally present, burningly unredeemable, alleviated only by desperate and increasingly wasteful measures of denial and surrogation.[46] And, by prophetic paradox, this exhausting fixation on the shameful present blinds Albion to the presence of the present: he might as well be asleep, which is how the plot repeatedly represents him. *Jerusalem* is littered with the trashy effects of Albion's inability to regard, never mind recycle, the past. He stays so busy putting all that

a constant theme of *Jerusalem* that the only way to deal with others is in pity"—the redemptive affect into which Los at length hammers out his impressive surplus of wrath. On anger-management in the person of Albion, see Andrew M. Stauffer, *Anger, Revolution, and Romanticism* (Cambridge: Cambridge University Press, 2005) 80–84.

[46] As Kroeber puts it, "Filled with shame, a man lacks the power of self-forgiveness, from which forgiveness of others arises" ("Delivering *Jerusalem*," 357).

behind him, in order to move on, that he never does move on or (it amounts to the same thing) see what lies all around him and before.

The narrative devastation that comes of this benighted refuse-management policy has made the poem notorious. Yet Blake's thesis falls less on the plot than on the policy that wastes it, and on what the garble of the plot reveals about the severe incapacitation of the historical sense under a regime of shame that would rather go to epic lengths than find itself for a moment in the wrong. This is the hypocritical regime against which Los struggles as a figure for the historical poet who will have "kept the Divine Vision in time of trouble" (95.20), maintaining that the past is "Permanent, & not lost not lost nor vanishd," "every little act, | Word, work. & wish, that has existed, all remaining still" (13.60–61). In the sculptured halls of Los "All things acted on Earth are seen," and "every pathetic story possible to happen from hate or /Wayward Love & every sorrow and distress is carved" (16.63–64). If this inventory has something fetchingly pathetic about it, something vulnerably fallible, that very fallibility is part of the story. For Los's antidote to the amnesiac conspiracy woven by the Daughters of Albion is precisely, heroically, to bring his own secrets out into the open: "to forgetfulness | They wooe Los continually to subdue his strength: he continually | Shews them his Spectre: sending him abroad" (17.9–11). With rough but affirmative action Los thus publishes, if not the whole truth (something the poem never displays anyhow), then at least nothing but the truth. He practices history's enabling precondition, candor, with the clear implication that claiming to have nothing to be ashamed of—as it shocked Blake to find Rousseau claiming in his *Confessions* (52)—may be the greatest shame of all. Forgive them, for they know not what they may, once they are forgiven, at last afford to know.[47]

Jerusalem herself would agree but put the matter a little differently, lamenting that a bizarre rash of family calumnies has disturbed, what it cannot take away, her sensible homebody manners "Where we live, forgetting error, not pondering on evil" (20.7). Here speaks an easygoing practical innocence that, while not yet the stuff of epic, is nevertheless close enough to

[47] Stuart Curran, "The Structures of *Jerusalem*," in *Blake's Sublime Allegory*, sees that in *Jerusalem* "Blake's epic purpose is not reformation, but conversion" (345), an "heroic enlargement of comprehension" that necessitates a para-narrative sort of progress keyed to "the slowly maturing consolidation of error by which Los defines the logic of man's fallen state" (341). Jeanne Moskal relates this final epic effect of Blake's four-part poem to the harmonized synopsis of the Gospels, as opposed to the diachronic typology of reform that governs *Milton: Blake, Ethics, and Forgiveness* (Tuscaloosa and London: University of Alabama Press, 1994) 170–74.

Blake's ethos of forgiveness to merit further elucidation. It rapidly gets it. For Jerusalem is talking here with Vala, who is the poem's maven of righteous indignation and who nurses a distinctly different notion from Jerusalem's about what "forgetting error" means. Since Vala's idea of a miserable time is obsessively to "number moments over and over; | Stringing them on their remembrance as on a thread of sorrow" (20.17–18), her sole recourse throughout the poem is violent repression—"seek not to revive the Dead!" (80.31)—repression of a Freudian sort that eventually becomes Sadean too, and at Jerusalem's expense. Still Jerusalem rejoins, in the tone of firm mildness that she more than anyone shares with Blake's Jesus, "What is Sin but a little | Error & fault that is soon forgiven; but mercy is not a Sin | Nor pity nor love nor kind forgiveness" (20.23–25). With the change from *forgetting* to *forgiving* Blake brings his heroine up to epic strength, and prepares her later reproach to Albion in the throes of his shame: "Why wilt thou number," she asks, "every little fibre of my Soul" (22.20)? Jerusalem's abstention from self-justification is striking, as is her dialectically forceful echo of Los's guardianship of "every little act." Where shame elicits blinding denial, and makes of history not a door of perception but a punishment (thus Vala, 20) or even a weapon (thus the Spectre of Los, 33), nothing short of forgiveness will let the past come true.

As with the personal past, so with national history. In Blake's vast analogy the woman Jerusalem is also a city, the giant man Albion also an island people; "States" at once are frames of mind (which individuals forgivably pass in and out of), are variable results of Blake's technical page production, and are equally variable, eminently reform-worthy modes of political organization (25.13, 49.65–75). In our own day national commissions of truth and reconciliation make it easier for our contemporaries than it was for Blake's to grasp what the forgiving vision of *Jerusalem* might portend as a matter of practical politics. That neither reparation nor healing can take place without memory; that memory itself is baffled, especially in the face of wholesale atrocity, until amnesty creates a space for it—these ideas, whose time we say has come, had come already to Blake in the era of Napoleon and Wellington. Indeed, Blake seems to have regarded British nationalism itself as such a merciful space: at once a halfway house on the way to the multicultural internationalism that rays out from *Jerusalem* like a utopian corona, and a house whose need to be put in order, as a locally discrete collectivity, had a claim on the forgiven imagination. The dazzling syncretism of the poem's allusiveness to twenty years of European war and two hundred of global colonialism leaves no doubt that Blake placed Albion in a worldwide system that not only defined Britain's options but stood to be directly affected by how those options were exercised. The address "To the Jews" (27) that prefaces chapter 2—for that matter the corresponding chapter prefaces Blake's addresses to the Public, the Deists, and the Christians in his chapters 1, 3, and 4—evince awareness that to tell the Britons their story in the epoch of Waterloo was to advise a world-historically chosen people. At the same time, the responsibilities that a politics of forgiveness brought into clear focus started at home; or, in a familiar line from *Milton* that Blake quoted with new resonance in *Jerusalem* twice, "All things Begin & End in Albions Ancient Druid Rocky Shore" (27, 32.15). "I go forth to Create | States," announces an anonymous "voice from the Furnaces" (35.15–17); yet this voice itself goes forth from a state, which is, inescapably, Regency England.

Nationalism is not only the epic badge of *Jerusalem* but also its hedge against the ever-present risk of the "Abstract objecting power, that Negatives every thing" (10.10). Once spectral abstraction takes the form of spectatorial detachment, "pitying & weeping, as at a trajic scene" (41.29) where the suffering is somebody else's, proxy sympathies crowd out the living relatedness of convinced participation, whereby we not only become what we behold but become aware of our beholdenness, our being weighed in the balance. "Are not Religion & Politics the Same Thing? Brotherhood is Religion" (57.10): the line redefines *fraternité*, which had guillotined its losses in the 1790s, in terms of an ongoing recovery of fellowship among persons sharing the inheritance of a tradition. It is because Blake appropriated membership in the British church and nation as models for beholden inclusiveness that his chapters 2 and 3 were so hard on the practices of surrogate sacrifice that the British church and nation in his day swore by. Unlike "the Perpetual Mutual Sacrifice in Great Eternity" (61.23), the doctrine of vicarious atonement defeated its own purpose: "It is Moral Severity, & destroys Mercy in its Victim" (39.26).[48] As for the secular pieties

---

[48] In Blake's revisionist Christianity, incarnation and eucharist converge on the point of sacrifice, where a confusion of literal with figurative meanings has let dogmatic idolatry usurp the one thing needful, the believer's free gift of self. According to Blake's 1809 *Descriptive Catalogue* ("Number V. The Ancient Britons"), this confusion is an old story: those archetypes of priestcraft the Druids went wrong when they "began to turn allegoric and mental signification into corporeal command, whereby human sacrifice would have depopulated the earth." Jerome Christensen's trenchant remarks in *Lord Byron's Strength: Romantic Writing and Commercial Society* (Baltimore and London: Johns Hopkins University Press, 1993) xxi–xxii, on the resistance to sacrificialism in Romantic literature leave Blake oddly unmentioned.

of the emergent nation-state, they depressed mental and prolonged corpor-
eal warfare by beating the plowshares back into swords: "They forg'd the
sword on Cheviot, the chariot of war & the battle-ax" (65.14). In specifying
the Border hill of Cheviot as a united kingdom's anvil, Blake may have been
glancing at the way Scott had hammered guilt into patriotism. Marmion
and his successors were epic forms bound over to the idol of militancy,
Vala-style, gambling the national future on an expiation whose shriftless
privacy made it a dangerously absurd abstraction.

From the early 1790s forward Blake had never been above dallying with
absurdity. But the absurdities of *Jerusalem* are due to the extremity of its
concrete literality, its suspicious concern over how much a rhetorical figure
like metaphor suppresses.[49] "He siez'd the bars of condens'd thoughts,
to forge them" (9.4): like Los in this line, Blake expresses relationship by
juxtapositive condensation, aligning and welding his personal assailants in
Felpham with the world's philosophers; England with Israel; Norse with
Druidic with Semitic mythologies, in a (con)fusion that, however absurd or
brilliant its local eccentricities, inculcates a powerful sense of the interlock of
elements within systems, and the impingement of systems upon each other.
Above all, he constantly returns *Jerusalem* to the proof of the minute
particular: several astonishing plates in the last third of the poem approach
the status of sheer census or inventory. Plates like 71 and 72 seem at once the
oldest kind of writing in the text (think of the tabular *Iliad* catalogues that
even Homer handles like fragile antiques) and the most up-to-date (Walt
Whitman, on the line from Manhattan). Their wall of words is uncannily
prescient of modern official monumentation, even as they tenderly defend
local forms of ungeneralized, stubbornly specific lore, which the advance of
the monumentally modern was in Blake's lifetime annihilating left and
right.[50] In a wonderfully refreshing aside, he concludes these feats of ac-
countancy by muttering that the anguished labors of the sons of Los would

---

[49] Blake's final epic practice revises the Pauline opposition between letter and spirit, via tropes
of bodily ingestion that are rooted, Ian Balfour points out, in the older prophetic tradition of
Jeremiah and Ezekiel. The figure of "the prophet literally eating the words of God" bears too on a
eucharistic mode of quotation that for Blake involves "the prophetic sacrifice of one to another
and of one's own words to those of another": *The Rhetoric of Romantic Prophecy* (Stanford: Stanford
University Press, 2002) 160–61.

[50] On the textual architecture of Blake's word-wall pagination see Vincent Arthur De Luca,
Words of Eternity: Blake and the Poetics of the Sublime (Princeton: Princeton University Press, 1991)
89–94.

be "Long to tell" (73.9). A mock! Tongue long in cheek, the epoist in effect begs our pardon for not getting it all down, not even in a hundred plates and many pictures worth a thousand words apiece. We grant that pardon in the comic relief of understanding that the forms of totality that constitute our knowledge are as numerous, variable, and endless as the minute particulars they comprise.

Tout pardonner, c'est tout comprendre. If that is true, and for Blake by the time he was finished with epic it was true, then so is this corollary: the ampler the forgiveness, the wider the comprehension of the everything to which every thing, "every little act," belongs. As encyclopedia yields to gospel in the great final plates of the poem, the comprehension to which *Jerusalem* aspires stands revealed as neither subjective nor objective but relational, its epic grammar less nominative or accusative than *dative*. It is the dative, the case of the gift and the sake, that heads each chapter ("To the Public" and so forth), as it utterly dominates the sublime final dialogue between Albion and Jesus on plate 96. The dative preposition/prefix *for* rings there in nearly every line. It puts up front the leading motive of Blake's most lavish offering, presented to a readership whom contemporary disregard obliged him to imagine as the distantly indirect objects of an importunately providential love. The poem including history holds time up for understanding, and renders it free to whoever knows that the present entails the totality, that the gift entails the forgiveness, and that these two entailments are one.

While the one epic that Wordsworth gave the public in his lifetime was no bestseller, it met steadily with just the kind of *succès d'estime* that eluded Blake. And for the admiration it garnered well into the Victorian period *The Excursion* has suffered ever since, plummeting in direct proportion to the boost Blake's epics received from twentieth-century readers eager to cry up what the nineteenth century could least abide. By remaining largely unread in our day, *The Excursion* has kept its (not unmerited) reputation as a sort of lay sermon combining the ruminative dullness of dutiful orthodoxy with a certain prickly-spirited density of rhetorical demand.[51] The chief casualty of this neglect has been appreciation of the daemonic wildness of imagination

---

[51] For a lively bill of the accumulated grievances against *The Excursion*, answered by a fresh set of reasons for reading the poem anyway, see Richard Gravil, *Wordsworth's Bardic Vocation, 1787–1842* (Houndmills: Palgrave, 2003) 203–24.

from which both these reader-deterrent features ultimately spring. At the heart of the poem lies an apocalyptically volatile, dauntingly alien energy, which most of the heavier solemnities are there to counteract: the homage to natural beauty, the snug local communitarianism, the stolid credal commitments to church, state, and the national history that entwines them. To recognize in this ballast the matter of our genre is to approach *The Excursion* as an epic at odds with and even in spite of itself, a transcendental vision broken to mundane harness for its own good.[52]

In a preface Wordsworth concedes that, within the immense plan of his philosophic masterpiece-in-prospect *The Recluse,* we have before us in *The Excursion* the portion that is "designed to refer more to passing events, and to an existing state of things"—to the sphere, that is, of history-like narrative action.[53] The preface concludes with a magnificent heroic proem, which Wordsworth first composed around 1798 at the start of his epic labor towards *The Prelude,* and which while not actually an invocation sounds a great deal like one. At least it is not an invocation that invokes any power other than the autonomous bliss of solitude that furnishes its irrepressible theme:

> Of Truth, of Grandeur, Beauty, Love, and Hope,
> And melancholy Fear subdued by Faith;
> Of blessèd consolations in distress;

[52] This conflict underlies Geoffrey Hartman's seminal account of the poet (and, to a degree, his animus against *The Excursion*) in *Wordsworth's Poetry 1787–1814* (New Haven and London: Yale University Press, 1964). Frances Ferguson, *Wordsworth: Language as Counter-Spirit* (New Haven and London: Yale University Press, 1977), analyzes in *The Excursion* a "spell" of "self-purification" by means of a "system of internal checks and balances" (197)—the same tension that makes the poem a failure in the estimation of an earlier critic like Kroeber, who appreciates Wordsworth's transcendental faith in "the private reality of poetic vision" but finds it squandered in unaccountable yarnspinning (*Romantic Narrative Art,* 110–11). Brian Wilkie, in contrast, calls *The Excursion* "discursive rather than narrative": *Romantic Poets and Epic Tradition* (Madison and Milwaukee: University of Wisconsin Press, 1965) 77. Better guidance comes from Kenneth R. Johnston's exemplary *Wordsworth and* The Recluse (New Haven and London: Yale University Press, 1984), on the poet's epic evolution "to a tertiary compromise between acts of the mind and their necessary containment and conservation in the social, educational, and religious institutions of human civilization" (15); also Jean-Pierre Mileur, *The Critical Romance: The Critic as Reader, Writer, Hero* (Madison: University of Wisconsin Press, 1990) 48–49, 68–70. For specific bearings of this root conflict on the poet's social vision see Michael H. Friedman, *The Making of a Tory Humanist: William Wordsworth and the Idea of Community* (New York: Columbia University Press, 1979).

[53] A letter to Sir George Beaumont of 3 June 1805 describes Wordsworth's disappointment with the finished *Prelude* and looks ahead to "the task of my life" as "a narrative poem of the Epic kind": *The Early Letters of William and Dorothy Wordsworth,* ed. Ernest de Selincourt (Oxford: Clarendon Press, 1935) 497. Jonathan Wordsworth, "That Wordsworth 'Epic,'" *Wordsworth Circle* 11 (1980) 34–35, offers cautionary remarks on interpreting this letter.

> Of moral strength, and intellectual Power;
> Of joy in widest commonalty spread;
> Of the individual Mind that keeps her own
> Inviolate retirement, subject there
> To Conscience only, and the law supreme
> Of that Intelligence which governs all—
> I sing.
>
> (14–23)

The way this series of topics builds to "the individual Mind," then gets stuck there in ministries of diplomatic qualification, lets us know where the action is, even should we somehow not have guessed it from Wordsworth's earlier poetry. Still, since the rumor mill so routinely besmirches *The Excursion* for traducing the high standard of solitary meditative strength, it may be well to cite a few passages from the poem that uphold this antinomian standard as explicitly as any the poet ever wrote. Item: the Solitary's cloudscaped vision of a "wilderness of building" whose unpeopled architecture is "the revealed abode | Of Spirits in beatitude" whom he prays he may instantly die and join (2.830–77). Item: the Wanderer's assertion that at the zenith of contemplation "the scale | Of time and conscious nature disappear, | Lost in unsearchable eternity" (3.110–12), and his lament that meanwhile at lesser altitudes "the endowment of immortal power | Is matched unequally with custom, time, | And domineering faculties of sense" (4.205–07). Item: the Wanderer's interrupting his tale of poor Margaret, the most pathetically affecting of the poem's many stories, to let the Poet know how

> not seldom, in my walks,
> A momentary trance comes over me;
> And to myself I seem to muse on One
> By sorrow laid asleep; or borne away,
> A human being destined to awake
> To human life, or something very near
> To human life.
>
> (1.783–89)

The eerie serenity of this Olympian inquest into something speculatively called "human," coming in the middle of what has felt so much like a human-interest feature story, clinches what our other items will have suggested already. Wordsworth's resounding talk about the individual mind's inviolate retirement is no idle boast, or idle threat, but the candid disclosure of a force his poem constantly reckons with. This force, moreover, is indifferent if not hostile to time, nature, custom, sense—to the appurtenances of narrative, in short, and thus to the worldly orientation of the epic genre.[54]

Wordsworth thus broods an epic intention that would strike us as self-contradictory to the point of paralysis, were it not the expression of a paradox to which we were accustomed long ago, by the capitalist order of things and by the Romanticism that expressed it—and expressed it nowhere more influentially than in the writings of Wordsworth himself. This paradox is the modern paradox of an individualist culture: the unlikely yet manifest viability of a monadic community that comprises, and somehow coordinates, persons who regard themselves and each other, not in an obvious and idle sense but as a matter of bedrock conviction, as free and uniquely self-actualizing beings.[55] Southey had expressed this emergent individualist ethos more or less heedlessly; Scott had cannily exploited it. But only Blake and Wordsworth apprehended it as *the* problem of their moment and wrote epics frontally devoted to its articulation. Moreover, only Wordsworth did so in full public view, and only in *The Excursion*.

We now habitually, and rightly, approach *The Prelude*'s rival generic allegiances to autobiography and to epic as representing a modern dilemma whereby the self splinters off from collectivity.[56] The fact remains, however,

[54] Ferguson, *Counter-Spirit*, 201, and Sharon M. Setzer, "Wordsworth's Wanderer, the Epitaph, and the Uncanny," *Genre* 24 (1991) 361–79, stress the Wanderer's status as an otherworldly ascetic or a ghost, and in either case marginally human at best. Alison Hickey, *Impure Conceits: Rhetoric and Ideology in Wordsworth's* Excursion (Stanford: Stanford University Press, 1997), shows how such a characterization helps advance the poet's second epic from questions of individual to those of "collective autobiography: how can we write ourselves as a community, a nation, an empire?" (149). She furthermore shows how paradoxically the social bonds of the poem spring from the uncanny power of "moments of suspended reference," where "the feeling has been disengaged from its particular referents and attenuated to a silent brooding on blankness" (83–84).

[55] Celeste Langan correlates the poem's programmatic and conflicted liberalism with its conversion of political forces (the Solitary) into economic, spiritual, and aesthetic ones (respectively the Wanderer, Pastor, and narrating poet): see *Romantic Vagrancy: Wordsworth and the Simulation of Freedom* (Cambridge: Cambridge University Press, 1995) 225–29. On the social text of the poem see also David Simpson, *Wordsworth's Historical Imagination: The Poetry of Displacement* (New York: Methuen, 1987) 185–212.

[56] See Curran, "Wordsworth and the Forms of Poetry," in *The Age of William Wordsworth*, ed. Kenneth R. Johnston and Gene W. Ruoff (New Brunswick and London: Rutgers University Press, 1987) 129–32, on the "composite" mixture of genres in Wordsworth's epics—in which category he, unlike most critics, includes not just *The Prelude* but *The Excursion* too. Annabel Patterson, "Wordsworth's Georgic: Genre and Structure in *The Excursion*," *Wordsworth Circle* 9 (1978) 149, analyzes the latter as a species of georgic, poised "to mediate between Wordsworthian epic and pastoral"; this case of generic special pleading becomes a persuasive norm within Kevis Goodman's subtle reading of *The Excursion* in *Georgic Modernity and British Romanticism: Poetry and the Mediation of History* (Cambridge: Cambridge University Press, 2004) 106–43. On the assignment of genre see also Judson Stanley Lyon, *The Excursion: A Study* (New Haven: Yale University Press, 1950) 134–38; Roydon Salick, "*The Excursion* as Epic," *Literary Half-Yearly* 32 (1991) 86–110.

that Wordsworth's fullest negotiation of the epic impasse posed by an
increasingly individualist culture comes in *The Excursion*—read whole,
that is, not as overt doctrine but as the experiment in distributed narrative
that it is. The terms grounding this negotiation are suggested in the poem's
one very long endnote, which incorporates Wordsworth's first "Essay upon
Epitaphs."[57] This note contains the arresting, pregnant avowal that "the
social affections could not have unfolded themselves uncountenanced by
the faith that Man is an immortal being." On this view society—which, as
distinct from politics, supplies Wordsworth's steady theme in *The Excur-
sion*—sustains itself against the corrosive awareness of death by relying
on "an intimation or assurance within us, that some part of our nature is
imperishable."[58] While assurance here arises primarily from "communica-
tions with our internal Being," the very term "communications" suggests
that this grounding "assurance" is not an inviolably private intuition but
rather a socially mediated belief. Indeed, it is one of the chief functions of
society to declare and reinforce this belief through a system of institutions
that includes established religion, tombstone inscriptions, and, to judge
from *The Excursion*, the frequent spontaneous sharing of life stories among
friends, guests, or even casual acquaintances.[59]

---

[57] The peculiarity of this note, as against the practice of Southey or Scott, may have elicited
Hazlitt's malicious recommendation that all the "narrative and description" be given "in plain
prose as notes at the end," so as to free the verse of this "scholastic romance" for its main task of
"general reasoning": *Examiner* review of 1814, in *Complete Works*, ed. P. P. Howe (London and
Toronto: Dent, 1930) 4: 112–13.

[58] Compare a letter Wordsworth wrote to the infidel Landor on 21 January 1824, attributing all
religion—that is, culture essentialized—to the universal thirst for immortality, and all abiding
literary interest to that which "turns upon infinity . . . where limits vanish": *The Letters of William
and Dorothy Wordsworth: The Later Years*, ed. Ernest de Selincourt (Oxford: Clarendon Press, 1939)
134–35. This vanishing limit on which society is uncannily founded, Mark Canuel contends in
Religion, Toleration, and British Writing, 1790–1830 (Cambridge: Cambridge University Press, 2002),
found an exact institutional analogue in Wordsworth's conception of the nondoctrinal absorbency
of the Church. "Rather than eliminating dissent, the national church absorbs, encloses, and directs
it," by so treating "disagreement as a kind of agreement" that the Solitary appears at last to have
been already renovated, already a participant in the community that he had apparently resisted";
"both structure and state of mind dissolve in landscape and atmosphere" (163, 171–72).

[59] As this list may suggest, the interplay of oral with scribal forms of communication in
Wordsworth's talkily written poem is extremely subtle. Epitaph counterpoises anecdote as
excursus does excursion, always to the final advantage, in this *published* epic (as against the
somehow imaginatively pre-literate because withheld *Prelude*), of the literary. Wordsworth's
practice confirms the insight of Jeremy M. Downes that "the written epic (in part because it is
written)" gravitates with the durability of its medium "toward a poetry of survival rather than of
death," the latter being the high road to heroic glory in oral epic: *Recursive Desire: Rereading Epic
Tradition* (Tuscaloosa and London: University of Alabama Press, 1997) 111.

That such storytelling conduced to the upkeep of society will go without saying here, although it should be noted in passing that Wordsworth based another long poem on just this theme at just this time. The excellent if decidedly para-heroic *White Doe of Rylstone; or, The Fate of the Nortons: A Poem* (1815, written 1809), set in Tudor times and in seven cantos of variable tetrameter, remains the most important verse imitation of Scott before Byron's, and in formal terms the most accomplished bar none. Eschewing alike the jauntiness of *The Lay* and the guiltiness of *Marmion*, Wordsworth here invested Scott's form with his own signature dialectics of recuperation, and in the process he made the poem's loss-and-gain plot and post-balladic status into figures for each other. Lady Emily's youthful prospects are dead, and so are the old ballads; but in each case a decomposition into legend nourishes community: "dead,—/ Dead—but to live again on earth, | A second and yet nobler birth" (7.1843–45).[60] *The Excursion* rehearsed this motif generously; at the same time, in its epic capacity it inquired more deeply than *The White Doe* could into the dependence of communities upon stories, especially stories that by dwelling on painful events tender to the listener a large helping of hurt.

Where is the good, *The Excursion* wants to know, of such collectively imparted pain? When the Wanderer pauses in Margaret's tale to ask, "Why should we thus . . . disturb | The calm of nature with our restless thoughts?" (1.599–604), the determination with which the Poet "begged of the old Man that, for my sake, | He would resume his story" (1.624–25) also provokes the question why its resumption should be for *his* sake, which is to say the sake of his readers.[61] The ultimate answer to this question is that

---

[60] See Curran, *Poetic Form*, 140–42. St. Clair, *The Reading Nation*, 160, reports that Wordsworth wrote *The White Doe* at the urging of his publisher Longman, with an eye to the expanding market for verse romance. Small wonder, then, that Wordsworth was keen to contrast with Scott's architecture of climactic "termination or catastrophe" his own practice of educing "moral and spiritual" success from his characters' "external and substantial" failure: quoted in Lane Cooper, *Experiments in Education* (Ithaca: Cornell University Press, 1943) 59. On genre in this poem see Willard Spiegelman, *Wordsworth's Heroes* (Berkeley and Los Angeles: University of California Press, 1985) 166–89.

[61] "The strangeness of *The Excursion*," as Ferguson puts it, "is that it is the Reader's rather than the Poet's poem" (*Counter-Spirit*, 205). Tilottama Rajan ascribes this effect to the poem's "shift from mimesis to discourse": "The Other Reading: Transactional Epic in Milton, Blake, and Wordsworth," in *Milton, the Metaphysicals, and Romanticism*, ed. Lisa Low and Anthony John Harding (Cambridge: Cambridge University Press, 1994) 42–44. Johnston, *Wordsworth and* The Recluse, 6, identifies as "the true plot of the first *Recluse* poems"—that is, of the vast epic program dating from 1797 within which both *The Prelude* and *The Excursion* were parts—"the effort of an external narrator to respond adequately to a tale he's been told and now retells." Writer and reader thus double each other, by "Wordsworth's characteristic trope of generalization in *The*

the restlessness of thought aroused and nourished by pathetic tales constitutes that blessed assurance on which the "Epitaphs" essay paradoxically premises the social affections: the imperishable autonomy of the active soul. This answer is reached by an argument sufficiently subtle to serve as *The Excursion*'s epic rationale, spreading across nine books to compass and assess the transmission and keeping of the nearly two dozen short stories they contain.[62] The stories themselves resolutely turn aside from standard epic topics: unlike the "days of yore," "these our unimaginative days" hold no place for bards (2.1, 2.24), save in the prostitution downtown of the "Hired minstrel of voluptuous blandishment" (6.355) or uptown of "the heaven-born poet" who glorifies war (7.363). In lieu of such traditions Wordsworth proposes, to the indignation of Francis Jeffrey in an essay that has become as well known as the poem (*Edinburgh Review*, November 1814), life narratives of common folk that are deliberately unassuming—indeed, before long ostentatiously so.[63] "Ah who (and with such rapture as befits | The hallowed theme) will rise and celebrate | The good man's purposes and deeds," asks the Pastor, recasting the affinities of epic and romance so as to see they will be "spread o'er field, | Hamlet, and town" (7.374–83)? The self-nominating Wordsworthian *ahem* that one hears behind this rhetorical invitation is unmistakable, yet it is also unmistakably enlivened by a dramatic ambivalence about just what kinds of story—and thus what ideals of human goodness—actually befit such hallowing rapture.

It is an ambivalence expressly dramatized within the poem. The raconteur Pastor has stipulated, in advance of his narrative summons to the local

---

Recluse: story-telling to achieve a sense of logical force by rhetorical multiplication" (220). In other words, *The Excursion* practices an Ovidian or Chaucerian "*decentralization of imagination*" (286, 297), a kind of epic whose second great expositor in the nineteenth century awaits us in William Morris (Ch. 10). Norman Vance, *The Victorians and Ancient Rome* (Oxford: Blackwell, 1997) 168, remarks Wordsworth's debt to Ovid. On Wordsworth's "decentered and indirect" narrative argument see also Esther Schor, *Bearing the Dead: The British Culture of Mourning from the Enlightenment to Victoria* (Princeton: Princeton University Press, 1994) 183–86.

[62] For an account of "argument" in the poem that is as rhetoric-dialectical as mine is epic-narratological, see George Myerson, *The Argumentative Imagination: Wordsworth, Dryden, Religious Dialogues* (Manchester and New York: Manchester University Press, 1992), esp. 22–23. Sally Bushell, *Re-Reading* The Excursion: *Narrative, Response, and the Wordsworthian Dramatic Voice* (Aldershot: Ashgate, 2002) regards narrative itself as an "active 'currency' of exchange and recompense" (137), and she distinguishes the Wanderer's illustrative *exempla* from the Pastor's more collective and apparently passive attempt in the stories of books 6 and 7 "to *perform* (communally) the central intentions of the text" (195).

[63] It is in this evenhandedly ethnographic spirit that the Wanderer commends ancient Greek myths to the Solitary at 4.718–62 and 4.847–87. See Alex Zwerdling, "Wordsworth and Greek Myth," *University of Toronto Quarterly* 33 (1964) 341–54.

dead, that he will confine himself to stories evoking "love, esteem, | And admiration" (6.648–49); not long before this, however, the Solitary has championed "tragic" themes, "the dread strife | Of poor humanity's afflicted will | Struggling in vain with ruthless destiny" (6.555–57). One sign of the subtlety of *The Excursion* is how hard it is to assign most of its tales to either the Solitary's side or the Pastor's. This is because Wordsworth wagered the poem on a rooted conviction that the idyllic and the tragic were one, that the best narrative might be simultaneously an exemplary and a cautionary tale. The story that British field, hamlet, and town all needed most to hear circa 1815 was that of persons bearing up under breakdown, living through the losses brought on by wrong or hardship, finding the internal resources to endure—or, if ultimately missing these, still maintaining through a life's conduct the one thing needful: a bracing consciousness of the discrepancy between what the heart requires and what the world provides. *Disappointment* forms the mainspring of Wordworthian narrative, because it at once attests the immortalizing surplus of a desire unmet by this life, and invests that surplus in the fund of society, where it yields the human interest of community-bonding sympathy. This is the plan that lines the Wanderer's deep pockets of sympathetic reserve: "He could *afford* to suffer | With those whom he saw suffer" (1.370–71). "Earth to despise," the Wanderer allows—*contemptus mundi*—is child's play beside the challenge "to converse with heaven," by which he means, in effect and perhaps disconcertingly, neither more nor less than to dwell on earth, "to frame | Conceptions equal to the soul's desires" and then emphatically "to *keep* | Heights which the soul is competent to gain" (4.128–37).[64]

This challenge being frankly "impossible," the slippage between the framing soul's conception and its soaring desire constitutes a fortunate shortfall. Forfeited contentment comes back, through the mediations of disappointment, sorrow, and endurance, as the cardinal Wordsworthian virtue of *hope*:

---

[64] The "gaining" and "keeping" of "heights" in this metaphor derived from generalship, as no survivor of Napoleonic Europe needed reminding. The prevalence of military imagery throughout *The Excursion* illustrates Wordsworth's conviction that, as he told John Scott on 11 June 1816, "martial qualities are the natural efflorescence of a healthy state of society," and that "tendencies to degradation in our national chivalry may be counteracted by the existence of those capabilities for war in time of peace." Earlier he had complained to Coleridge of Charles Lamb's failure to appreciate *The White Doe of Rylstone* for its narrated "victories in the world of spirit" (19 April 1808). *Letters of William and Dorothy Wordsworth: The Middle Years*, ed. de Selincourt (Oxford: Clarendon Press, 1937) 2: 748 and 1: 198.

                                    power abides
              In man's celestial spirit; virtue thus
              Sets forth and magnifies herself; thus feeds
              A calm, a beautiful, and silent fire,
              From the encumbrances of mortal life,
              From error, disappointment—nay, from guilt;
              And sometimes, so relenting justice wills,
              From palpable oppressions of despair.

                                    (4.1070–77)

Such are the terms in which *The Excursion* works an original variation on the debited or "encumbered" narrative economy that this chapter has traced from Scott. The balance carried forward as guilt in *Marmion* or *Roderick*, and as a mindful forgiveness in *Jerusalem*, appears in *The Excursion* as hope instead. This is why in the above passage the last word goes not to "guilt"—which ominously if only momentarily claims it—but rather to the more renewable energy of "despair," which participates in the drive of its defining opposite hope, which aims in turn not to cancel the past in atonement, but to open out the future in disenchanted, genuine expectation. The culture-forging fire-in-the-belly of guilt seems not to have been imaginatively accessible to Wordsworth, who privately confessed to a scandalized Henry Crabb Robinson that he had no need of a personal redeemer, and whom fellow epoist James Montgomery in a discerning review chastised for merely posing as a Christian.[65] The great, blinkered strength that was Wordsworth's in middle age had little use for the narrative vectors of wrong ("error" was mine, saith *The Prelude*) or of remorse and repentance. The poet who had written "Guilt and Sorrow" in the 1790s now found guilt a thin vein; but sorrow, in its permanence, shared the nature of infinity.

   It was the business of *The Excursion* to link, if not transform, that fund of boundless sorrow to a hope capable of sustaining not only individual lives but the life of community, we might even say culture itself in Wordsworth's matured vision of it.[66] The first half of the poem blazoned its purpose as

---

[65] The remark to Crabb Robinson dates from 1812 and is quoted in M. H. Abrams, *Natural Supernaturalism: Tradition and Revolution in Romantic Literature* (New York: Norton, 1973) 120. Montgomery lodged his charge in the *Eclectic Review*, 2nd ser. 3 (January 1815) 13–39. Another affronted reviewer was John Wilson, who reprinted his pseudonymous remarks on *The Excursion* in *Recreations of Christopher North* (1842; new edn. Edinburgh: Blackwood, 1864) 2: 58.

[66] What Kurt Fosso, "Community and Mourning in Wordsworth's *The Ruined Cottage*, 1797–1798," *Studies in Philology* 92 (1995), says of "The Ruined Cottage" (book 1) proves true of the entire poem it belongs to: community is "centered on the underlying inefficacy and interminability

"Despondency Corrected," which is the title to book 4 and the theme of the entire plot surrounding the Solitary in the preceding books as well.[67] The dour Solitary is a post-revolutionary Man of Feeling and most particularly a connoisseur of hope, a disposition which he is far from sentimentalizing or taking for granted. The poem has no more chilling moment than his hard-earned warning to those whose confident happiness lulls them into living "without the aid of hope"; for when reverses inevitably come, then "slighted Hope *will* be avenged; and, when | Ye need her favours, ye shall find her not" (3.457–60). To stave off "fear—doubt—and agony," he advises, it is necessary to *practice* hope, not as an obstinate abstraction (which it becomes for Margaret in her ruined cottage) but as a daily imaginative calisthenic. In this the Solitary's experience of the French Revolution gives him the advantage of his chronicler the Poet, who remains prone to believe—did the sanguine poet of *The Prelude* not share this belief?—in the efficacy of such generalized cheer drill as swells the Wanderer's oratory in books 3 and 4. The Solitary will none of it: genuine despondency is not to be forestalled in the abstract or "corrected" like a faulty proof. Hope's best exercise resides elsewhere, in the sympathetically apprehended fear and doubt and agony of other lives—better yet, perhaps, in grappling with these grand affects' meaner daily shadows, anxiety and annoyance.

It is to these, therefore, that the second half of *The Excursion* opens its books, culling from humble lives an array of anecdotal simples whose dreariness quotient is manifestly part of their medicinal value. "The food of hope | Is meditated action" (9.20–21): suggestively mingling the joint human needs to plan ahead and to look back, this deceptively terse apothegm states the effect of

of mourning" (335). This mode of permanence served the instinctively Pelagian Wordsworth much as the narrative impetus of guilt served Scott and Byron, in a common structural configuration setting the three of them apart from Southey on one hand, Blake on the other.

[67] As the sheer duration of this apparent repair job may suggest, by the time he wrote *The Excursion* Wordsworth no longer regarded despondency-correction as a reparative task on the order of *The Prelude*: it was instead therapy for a chronic way of life. For discussion of this difference in historiographic terms see two *Wordsworth Circle* essays by Barbara T. Gates: "Wordsworth's Lessons from the Past" 7 (1976) 133–41 draws out the moral-exemplary orientation of *The Prelude*; "Providential History and *The Excursion*" 9 (1978) 178–81 follows the poet's second, faith-based epic from the grounds of instrumental reason into "realistic hope" enabled by "stoical acceptance." Jeffrey Baker, "Casualties of the Revolution: Wordsworth and his 'Solitary' Self," *Yearbook of English Studies* 19 (1989), sets the poet of *The Excursion* into ongoing therapeutic dialogue with his "rejected self" the Solitary in order, not to purge the *Doppelgänger*, but to hold it "at bay" (104). William Howard makes out a compatible case for the poet's detachment from the Poet, whom he creates to be a mildly unreliable narrator: "Narrative Irony in *The Excursion*," *Studies in Romanticism* 24 (1985) 511–30.

the odd congeries of vignette narratives occupying books 5–8, testimonies of the dead related in a graveyard, contestedly received by the Pastor's several listeners, brief in exposition but long on psychic endurance—and long, too, on the social theory that we have seen Wordsworth attaches in the "Essay on Epitaphs" to such endurance.[68] For "meditated action" both sums up the past and summons up "the sweet air of futurity" (9.25). Wordsworth correlates the moral force of what these narrative books' classically epic consultation of the dead has disclosed with a forward momentum that, before the last book is over, will generate a call for British renovation through a system of state-sponsored schools.

Needless to say, a model for this system exists in *The Excursion* itself, which while stressing the didactic aspect of its genre has squarely embraced narrative as its primary mode of instruction.[69] Spontaneous yet coordinated, an empowering discipline for the modern liberal subject, Wordsworth's plan for public education takes after his poem. "We will teach them how," Wordsworth had crowed to Coleridge in the upbeat cultural workers' program that concludes *The Prelude* of 1805. Maybe, *The Excursion* now says, but we need some normal-schooling first; before teaching them how, we had better learn how to teach. Epic *paideia* has little to do with punctual correction for the Wordsworth of 1814, a lot to do with reiterative, cumulative training in the habits and expectations that toughen independ-ence: regular exposure to how much there is to bear, evidence that people

---

[68] Johnston, *Wordsworth and* The Recluse, 292, frames a telling comparison with *Jerusalem*: "Blake's mythos tells us that achieving the extraordinary is not impossible, whereas Wordsworth's graveyard stories insist repeatedly that maintaining the ordinary is not easy." Albert Wlecke, *Wordsworth and the Sublime* (Berkeley and Los Angeles: University of California Press, 1973) 114–17, correlates hope in *The Excursion* with a contingency-transcending temporality suggestive of the "Epitaphs" essay.

[69] Paul Hamilton recapitulates a long-standing verdict—it dates from the damage-controlling notice that Lamb placed in the *Quarterly Review* (October 1814)—against the diegetic disappoint-ments of *The Excursion*: "the larger plot within which incidents are placed can seem to be nothing more than the provisional character of incident—the failure of each tragic narrative to become *the* authoritative pronouncement of the poem": *Wordsworth* (Brighton: Harvester, 1986) 144. Hickey, agreeing that the poem "repeatedly frustrates any expectations we might have entertained of narrative progression," directs us instead to the ingredient power of its anecdotal contexture (which, we may add, affiliates this epic with the *Canterbury Tales* and *Metamorphoses*). It is *The Excursion*'s collected-stories format, with its "ideal of loosely and arbitrarily sequenced transitions" (222) that bridges "the apparent gap between its ambiguous social vision and its dramatization of epistemological uncertainty" (16–18). Julie Ellison, " 'Nice Arts' and 'Potent Enginery': The Gendered Economy of Wordsworth's Fancy," *Centennial Review* 33 (1989) 456–64, discusses the capriciously nuanced transitional logic of *The Excursion*'s final books.

regularly contrive to bear it, and reassurance that the common stamina of the world both requires and sanctions hopes that are more than worldly.[70]

What makes the Solitary vulnerable to despondency when we first meet him is that his solitude lacks focus and depth. Despite his epithet he enjoys a social life as active as anyone's in the poem, what with helping the needy, showing up at funerals, and attending to the young; his house is practically a hobby shop of diversions (2.660–70). But all this activity indicates what is wrong. The Solitary is busy avoiding something, still tracing the pattern he cut when, in grief over the death of his young family, he tried to lose himself in France as a fellow traveler, and again in America as an emigrant tourist. These shallow experiments in ideological direction and national allegiance are presented—in sharp contrast to the genuinely *political* heartbreak from which *The Prelude* arose—as the stopgap measures of an *emotional* refugee. The Solitary's idealism and skepticism alike are cognate modes of self-avoidance, that is, of failure to confront sincerely the circumstances of a life that, he suspects, "Is fashioned like an ill-constructed tale" (5.432) and will not hold up under scrutiny.

The Solitary's problem is not too much solitude, then, but too little, and too little fathomed. His is a representative case that, magnified by an epic lens, diagnoses a crisis of national dimensions. For in Wordsworth's analysis the accelerating advance of modern individualism—he expressly brought commerce, colonialism, science, industrialization, and more into the epic mix circa 1815—had outstripped the ability of a culture under stress to produce confident individuals. This condition admitted of no quick remedy, and it is far from clear that the Solitary at the end of the poem is free from what ailed him at the beginning. But then the modern condition demanded not a cure but long-term care, of a homeopathic kind that, administered one-on-one by means of personal narrative, fought solitariness with more solitariness. The therapy for nervous self-regard turned out to be self-reliance, which was grounded ultimately in a benign version of the same intensity of individuation that it combatted. It was towards self-culture, after all, that the educational program of *The Excursion* sought to

---

[70] William H. Galperin's searching *Revision and Authority in Wordsworth: The Interpretation of a Career* (Philadelphia: University of Pennsylvania Press, 1989) fortifies against the temptation to read the poet's second epic as flatly retracting the ethos of self-correction in the first. The revision is more radically authoritative than that: "unlike 'growth' in *The Prelude*, progress is not progress in *The Excursion*, but a series of doublings or repetitions" (45). Compare Bushell on the principle of multiplication through versioned re-telling (*Re-reading* The Excursion, 59, 117); and recall the difference in tactics between Blake's *Milton* and *Jerusalem*.

turn the attention, and the power, of the state: epic individualism wrought out into the theory of a feasible cultural practice.[71] As for the Church: spirits as diverse as Montgomery, Jeffrey, and John Keats saw right away how untroubled was the afterthought that let Wordsworth clothe his culture-subtending immortalism in Anglican vestments. *The Excursion* assumed position as one of an individualist century's major epics because it was, no less than *The Prelude*, an epic of the egotistical sublime.

[71] A remark the poet made to Thomas Poole in a letter of 13 March 1815 puts Bell's monitorial system of pupil instruction on the same continuum with the print technology that enables modern literature, and most pointedly such a late-stage secondary epic as *The Excursion*: "Next to the Art of Printing it is the noblest invention for the improvement of the human species" (quoted in Lyon, *The Excursion*, 57). For Bushell, *Re-reading* The Excursion, 235–36, Wordsworth's epic intention of enlarging to national dimension in the Poet the clerisy function that the Pastor performs on a local scale conjures "an almost anthropological anxiety," for which the education scheme imperfectly compensates. See also Alan Richardson, *Literature, Education, and Romanticism: Reading as Social Practice, 1780–1832* (Cambridge: Cambridge University Press, 1994) 263–66; Connell, *Romanticism, Economics*, 163–80.

5

In Style:

Epic Plush 1815–1820

The general quality of epic innovation may have dipped a notch after 1815; but the decline was not steep, and it opened onto a fertile plateau that attracted several cultivators of brilliance. Southey and Wordsworth had maintained the strength of the genre at a juncture when victory at Waterloo and the terms of long-awaited peace in Europe boosted a British national pride that would be issuing a varied peacetime summons to the epic muse for the duration of the century. These very incitements, of course, had their down side: Britain's emergent supremacy required new cultural forms from a new generation of poets, who as a group did not share the sense of national identification that two decades of revolution and war had impressed on their elders. Those elders, whether compliant or exasperated with the nation-state, had all been compelled by events to define themselves in relation to it; their heirs, having lived through the formative crises of revolution and wartime only in part, and mainly as children, were not shaped by them in the same ways. Under conditions of postwar decompression, British inter-ests hitherto bound together began unraveling. Younger imaginations awoke to difference and dissension within the national compact, and they freely embraced special interests or eccentric perspectives.[1] Not only that, but with youth's ruthless insight into the ardors and follies of an older

---

[1] "Wordsworth would say that one has to have experienced the Revolution. Keats says that one cannot have. This is not only the difference between two generations but between the egotistical sublime and negative capability": Ronald Paulson, *Representations of Revolution (1789–1820)* (New Haven and London: Yale University Press, 1983) 285. For other valuations of this generational shift see Marilyn Butler, *Romantics, Rebels and Reactionaries: English Literature and its Background 1760–1830* (Oxford: Oxford University Press, 1981) 88; A. D. Harvey, *English Poetry in a Changing Society* (New York: St Martin's Press, 1980) 3–5; Peter Graham, "A 'Polished Horde':

generation, some new poets attached their own authenticity to a noncom-
mittal stance not readily compatible with the prevailing characteristics of
heroism. To these considerations a swiftly changing literary economy added
a motive of its own: the historical novel, into which Scott now began
pouring his trend-setting genius, presented a clear alternative to the genre
of verse epic that young authors of national ambition would have embraced
a few years before as a matter of course.[2]

At the head of this new generation stood Lord Byron, whose near omission
from our long Chapter 4 was both tactically expedient and strategically
justified. The midsize oriental tales that he published to great acclaim and at
a better-than-annual clip between 1813 and 1816 made him Scott's obvious
heir in the poetry market. It is nearly as obvious—witness a title like *The
Giaour: A Fragment of a Turkish Tale*—that the fast-moving wares Byron carried
to market were not epics. The disqualification is a matter not of size but of
fundamental narrative conception. Byron's major difference from Scott,
whose example had taught him much about prosody, imagery and intrigue,
narrative continuity and montage, lay in the refusal to correlate heroic with
collective interests. Byron's glamorous Giaour and Corsair made their indel-
ible mark precisely by shrouding the guilty past against all exposure and by
declining either to repent or to acknowledge any institution or power that
might dispense remission. They thus heightened the intensity of the present
moment—always Byron's strong suit—by cutting themselves off from just the
kind of antecedent affiliation and future development that Scott and Words-
worth, and in a different register Blake, were concurrently making essential to
the Romantic epic.[3] "The wound that time can never heal" (*Giaour* 921) is
kept that way by "impenitent Remorse" (*Corsair* 2.331), an agenbite of inwit

The Great World in *Don Juan*," *Bulletin of Research in the Humanities* 86 (1983) 255–68. Beneath and
behind these literary schismatics lay Britain's greatly delayed postwar leap into class-consciousness:
see Harold Perkin, *The Origins of Modern English Society 1780–1880* (London: Routledge, 1969) 209.

[2] Graham McMaster, *Scott and Society* (Cambridge: Cambridge University Press, 1981) 49–50,
highlights the transition to a postwar literary economy that Richard Cronin, *The Politics of Romantic
Poetry: In Search of the Pure Commonwealth* (Houndmills: Macmillan, 2000), puts in a nutshell: "after
Waterloo, Scott's fame was so quickly eclipsed by Byron's" because *Childe Harold* was "the first
post-war poem" (103).

[3] The "unprotected" quality that defines the Byronic hero may be derived by subtraction from the
model of *Marmion*, or indeed of Scott's long-range model *Paradise Lost*. The force of his guilt stands out
as a permanent condition because it goes unrecruited (and so unrecuperated) by a national mission: see
Jerome J. McGann, *Don Juan in Context* (Chicago and London: University of Chicago Press, 1975)
26–31. See also Butler, *Romantics, Rebels and Reactionaries*, 118: the Byronic hero's rebellion is "drained
of ideological content, to a degree actually remarkable in the literature of the period."

that defines the Byronic hero by constituting a black hole in narrative. "Woe without name, or hope, or end" (*Giaour* 276) possesses a privative moral sublimity all its own, but it cannot wear the epic patent. Even when we concede that "omniscience" is a canard or tautological mirage, the epic genre still cannot tolerate the cognitive deficit that arises when, to take a late scene from *Lara* that expressly breaks with its prototype late in the *Odyssey*, the exposure of a mysterious hero's scars means nothing to anybody: "But all unknown his glory or his guilt" (2.546), and that is that.

At every opportunity the orientalizing Byron replaces the historically representative, collectively foundational gesture by the charismatic *beau geste*. Even when Lara finds himself leading, somehow, a popular uprising, the poet pointedly asks, "What cared he for the freedom of the crowd?" (2.252). It seems generically emblematic that the last act of Byron's last tale of this period, *The Siege of Corinth: A Poem*, should be the deliberately counter-epical, scantily motivated, and (by the very source his preface cites) historically controverted blowing up of a city. The poet may have been driven to such an extremity of explicitness by the tide of imitators that soon arose about him, as it had done about Scott a few years before. Robert Etty's *The Cossack: A Poem in Three Cantos* (1815), for example, heads east into the Caucasian cradle of the West, and manages in short compass to flash a lot of saber, as his Cossacks assail Calmuck Tartars on one hand and Turks on the other. But all this derring-do, as in the Byronic tales that Etty's variable tetrameters imitate, is background to the essential and unwavering romance between chivalrous Kouteskoff and his spotless mountain girl Zamasta: a myth of national concern, in other words, is precisely what Kouteskoff's swashbuckling Cossack detachment is detached from. What is true of such Byronic tales is *a fortiori* true of the declamatory travelogue in *Childe Harold's Pilgrimage* (1812–18), a work whose wild popularity was due to its way of subordinating opinion, description, and momentum to the advancement of a central self without evident motive, bearing, or goal.[4] Here again was a venue where epic need not apply.

---

[4] McGann, *Fiery Dust: Byron's Poetic Development* (Chicago and London: University of Chicago Press, 1968), makes this freedom from "ethical consistency" the very condition of Byron's self-mythologization (65, 286–87). While *The Giaour* imitates oral tradition in its improvisatory character, it does so only "as a means of self-dramatization (which is approximately the reverse of the purpose of a true oral poet)" (148). *A fortiori*, the eastern tales carry no brief of any kind for "colonialism or imperialism, which is rather criticized *tout court* from the moral standpoint of aristocratic classical republicanism": Nigel Leask, *British Romantic Writers and the East: Anxieties of Empire* (Cambridge: Cambridge University Press, 1992) 27.

That central self of Byron's did have a great epic poem in it, with which this chapter will conclude. But his earlier experiments will serve us best here as cyclonic systems indicating a drop in national atmospheric pressure to which other epoists of the time were also soon responding. Those who refused to respond did so at their peril. James Bland Burges's *The Dragon Knight: A Poem, in Twelve Cantos* (1818) was a no-nonsense couplet epic crammed with chivalric exploits in unlikely Maeonian Asia Minor; it was also as unreadable as any poem this book discusses, and one hopes that Burges in churning it out had the wit to yearn, if not for his late friend Cumberland, then for the sense of national mission that had inspired their collaboration years before on the distinctly superior *Exodiad* (Ch. 4). Foremost in national mission, and in that alone, was the vast and hasty contribution made by John Gwilliam to the instant-epic tradition we met in recent chapters with Hannah Cowley's *Siege of Acre* and John Croker's *Talavera*. Gwilliam offered six hundred pages of ballad quatrains on the Hundred Days before Waterloo entitled *The Imperial Captive; or, The Unexampled Career of the Ex-Emperor, Napoleon, from the Period of his Quitting Elba to that of his Surrender to the English Nation, Circumstantially Developed* (1817). Such a title leaves the commentator little to do but stress the last two words as premonitory of this chronicular epic's strictly stepwise pace, point to the ballad-quatrain format as suited to hymning a national triumph but hardly to narrating it—and mention a couple of less predictable elements in that triumph: Gwilliam's habit of blurting out, in spite of himself, that Napoleon had transcended the rules of morality, not just broken them; and his interesting prophecy that France and England after long strife would now become allies.

The supersession of conquest by alliance was also highly attractive to more talented poets who brought to the straight strife epic a longer historical vision and reach. The pains lavished on research by James Mann or David Carey, whichever it was who wrote the anonymous *Macbeth: A Poem, in Six Cantos* (1817), and by the future church historian Henry Hart Milman in *Samor, Lord of the Bright City: An Heroic Poem* (1818), seem so much scholarly security paid down for the release of an imagination that in actuality caught fire from unattested fanciful traditions. This shared feature suggests that under the emergent postwar dispensation national mythology held more integrative promise than national history did. Both works were blank-verse invasion epics of a kind that recent years had made familiar; but where

Cottle's Alfred or Southey's Roderick had stood on historical ground against the Danes or Moors, exemplifying a history that might recur at any minute in the form of Napoleon's Frenchmen, here Macbeth and Samor were presented at legend's length, grappling through their military adversaries with foes less palpable and difficulties more ideological.

One of these difficulties arose from the visibility that identity groups often reclaim once the solidarity of protracted warfare is no longer in force. The *Macbeth* authors went out of their way in canto 3, having lauded Britain's present naval might, to single out Scotland's special distinction in scholarship and industry—a gratuitous subnationalist reflex that the Scots-repel-Danes plot does not entail and that might well have been suppressed in right-thinking North Britons just a few years earlier. So it had been in the 1809 *Philemon, or, The Progress of Virtue: A Poem*, where with a Scot's "national feeling" William Laurence Brown had delineated "the national characters of the southern, and northern divisions of our Island" (preface, ix), only to enlist his hero, for all the world like Scott's Waverley, on the Hanoverian side at Culloden in the tenth and final book. Contrast with this cooperativeness the way two oversized, epicizing celebrations of 1816 bearing Edinburgh imprints—Henry Davidson's *Waterloo: A Poem* and David Home Buchan's *The Battle of Waterloo: A Poem*—made the victory that Britain and her allies had won under an Irish general an occasion for setting Scottish valor above all the rest. Under the cover of history Mann or Carey flexed much the same subnationalist muscle in *Macbeth*, both because it was newly admissible and because they meant to recapture it within a rationale more permanent than wars and treaties, a rationale indeed as old as the hills. For their capably written blank verse abounded in scenic description, often recalling Wordsworth's similarly intended imagery in *The Excursion*, to demonstrate that England and Scotland were one *land*, an island polity coherent and defensible. The tranquil beauty of nature in such postwar poetry, even when the terrain was chiefly used for troop maneuvers, was thus making a new kind of peacetime point.

In *Samor*, likewise, the theme of warfare between Celtic Britons and encroaching Saxons exposes ethnic fault lines to which in book 4 an earthquake, no less, raises portentous objection, and which the Saxon devastation of the British hero's city Gloucester makes him swear to score in blood ("Be thou my bride, | Oh Britain!" 5.481–82). Weaning Samor from vengeance—keeping the poem safe, that is, for the nineteenth century—requires such strong measures as an apostrophe to the shade of

Nelson as avatar of the happy union awaiting Briton and Saxon "strength |
And valour blent" (4.389–90, first edition); and then, atop Mt. Snowdon
(*pace* Wordsworth), Merlin's visionary pageant leading from Arthur through
William the Conqueror and William of Orange to the Tree of Empire and
River of Freedom, "eloquent | In harmony of discord" (8.490–91). Such
historical progress visions were a well-established convention of epic nation-
alism; this one, however, sandwiches its actual history between a primal
legend and a utopian allegory, in token that its binding force of nationalism
is to be apprehended less as fact than as myth.[5] By patriotic sublimation Samor
himself becomes nearly an allegory of *esprit de corps*, and through his inspir-
ation in the final books Milman transcends pedestrian single-combat narrative
to achieve the kind of at-large mobilization of contending masses in which
epics of the 1820s were to find a mounting fascination.

At the height of such war mobilization, we saw in Chapter 4, epic poets
sought in the Bible fortifying narratives of chosen national purpose. The
sudden relaxation of that purpose finds striking illustration in the compara-
tive fewness of biblical epics appearing in the first years of peace. The six
"canticles" of Charles Smith's *The Mosiad, or Israel Delivered* (1815) condense
exactly the same narrative matter that had occupied Cumberland and
Burges in *The Exodiad*, but that 1808 poem's emphasis on disciplined
solidarity yields here to an emancipatory poetics ("FREEDOM my theme,
and LIBERTY my muse!" 1.6), which the dedication page cants towards
denominational factionalism: "To the Great and Respectable Body of
Dissenters in England." Religious dissent dared speak its name in a relaxed
postwar climate less vigilant to root out sedition—under cover, too, of a
Bible myth that might be told to diverse effect by diverse parties. Again, it
was to the mythic portion of the biblical fusion of legend with history that
J. F. Pennie turned in an 1817 blank-verse Davideid in eleven books, *The
Royal Minstrel; or, The Witcheries of Endor: An Epic Poem*. The national
anxiety brooded, fledged, and tamed in Sotheby's *Saul* ten years before is
here dismissed in favor of entertainment: Pennie cleaves to the most
romantically legendary aspects of his story, dispatching David towards battle
and kingship with bucolic if not pacifist reluctance, and thereafter embroil-
ing his begrudgingly enthroned hero in amours at the drop of an eyelash.

---

[5] A point appreciatively developed by Beverly Taylor and Elisabeth Brewer in *The Return of
King Arthur: British and American Arthurian Literature since 1800* (Totowa: Barnes and Noble, 1983)
42–44.

A newly centrifugal swirl in the national air made it less easy than it had been, only yesterday, to forge an epic unity. When Byron derided Milman as an "ox of verse, who ploughs for every line," an "artificial hard | Labourer" (*Don Juan* 11.58), he was right: *Samor* and *Macbeth* were toilsome poems, through which we can see the strain that the national epic was starting to show. It had become harder since Waterloo—the name occurs with ominous, moral-pointing suddenness in the last line of *Macbeth*—to rally into unity a Britain no longer menaced from without. Lesser epoists saw the need to try but shirked Milman's quantum of effort, treating similarly epic junctures of history in a high style but declining to link the affairs of their principals to an animating national idea, and thereby declining generically from epic towards romance. The title of Mary Linwood's *The Anglo-Cambrian: A Poem in Four Cantos* (1818) is an epithet for her protagonist, an English prince who loves a Welsh princess at the time when his father's armies are overrunning her father's realm. The hyphen in the title, a first in our generic history, is eloquent in its ambiguous simultaneous evocation of ethnic fission and national fusion. While this poem and Cottle's *Fall of Cambria*, published a decade before it, are set at the same historical crisis and repose on the same general promise—Britain's greatness will spring from the union of peoples—for Linwood this promise remains mere background to a tale of personal affection and feud. If anything the eventual death of Princess Emma symbolizes the death of old Wales without issue, and thus the cancellation of the promise; but then it is difficult to credit that the symbolic intention with which Linwood framed the poem ever really informed her imagination of its episodes.

This depoliticized state of affairs persists, albeit with a negative twist, in a kindred work of the same year, W. E. Meredith's *Llewelyn ap Jorwerth: A Poem, in Five Cantos*. Ostentatiously Welsh in its title and its Gaelic-name-dropping Spenserians, this poem of the thirteenth century nevertheless takes but a wavering interest in national politics. True, Meredith depicts Llewelyn's marriage with the daughter of England's Henry III as an Anglo-Cambrian union gone bad. But it is disparity of age and sensibility, nothing rooted in ethnicity or statecraft, that drives young Queen Ellinor into the arms of a knightly seducer and finally off an ocean clifftop (5.34). This spectacular finale owes more to Sappho than to Gray's Bard half a century before, and probably more still to the interiorized mystique that Byron's oriental nursery had just been grafting onto *Marmion* stock. Meredith shows his true colors when the tale shunts stout King Llewelyn aside to lavish two full cantos on the introversive sorrows of a wayfaring Norman palmer—the knightly seducer's father, as it turns out, but no matter. Description engrosses narrative action as this glamorous stranger's fantasies of vengeance crowd out, *Hamlet*-like, the deed itself: the figure who catches and holds Meredith's eye is the Romantic pilgrim who has left Wales furthest behind, has done the crusader tour to Kedron and Calvary, has even "washed in Jordan's flood, | But this dark gloomy soul would not be clean" (5.14).

Here and in James Bird's *The Vale of Slaughden: A Poem, in Five Cantos* (1819), written like Linwood's poem in heroic couplets, we watch a generic manner working loose from the matter, and the duties, for which it had been impressed by political circumstances since the turn of the century. Bird recurs to the days that engrossed us in Chapter 3, when King Alfred more than once repelled the Danes, but now this material functions as an epic implant within an essentially romance structure of expectation. The king's wars are little more than an alternative stage of action withdrawing a Devon prince for a couple of cantos from the real story: how he is shipwrecked near the cottage of a poor and virtuous family who nurse him back to health, how the maiden of the house wastes away during his wartime absence, how on his return from the wars she confesses her passion and dies in his arms. The next year Bryan Waller Procter (pseud. "Barry Cornwall") in *Marcian Colonna: An Italian Tale* reversed Bird's generic proportions, to much the same result. The eponymous aristocrat and his beloved go into exile from Rome to escape the duty their dynastic status imposes, only to resign themselves to it when family keeps intruding on their hideaways and even their dreams. We know already how dull epic writing could prove at times in the early nineteenth century, but in the works we are now considering it is actually treated as such by the very poets who wrote under its protection. Where twenty years before what had engrossed Landor was how to strike a new epic line in *Gebir* through romance materials (Ch 2), now for Linwood and Meredith, Bird and Procter, the line of novelty ran the other way. Epic might hold down the narrative fort, but it was romance that breathed freshness.

Further down this path of development stands prose fiction, to which a half-sibling resemblance appears in a work portending the Regency resumption of that interrupted eighteenth-century genre the verse novel: *Emilia of Lindinau; or, The Field of Leipsic: A Poem, in Four Cantos* (1815). The split title got Mary Arnald Houghton's priorities straight, since the business of the poem is to marry its heroine to her childhood sweetheart (who happens to

be off resisting Napoleon on the German side), after overcoming the
objections of her father (who happens to be doing the same), through the
intervention of a high-minded outlaw chief (whose band happen to get
involved skirmishing with a French platoon). Warfare, treated with apolo-
getic delicacy (2.2.67), serves as backdrop to Houghton's family romance;
and in canto 4 the battlefield outside Leipzig figures primarily as a reunion
site. Still, in the end even this nascent novella bespeaks the embattled
circumstances of a composition history overtaken by the shocks of war.
For the harper at Emilia's wedding feast catches instant visionary fire, ups
the tetrameter tempo from iambic to anapestic, and foresees Napoleon's
return, the Hundred Days, Waterloo, and, with admittedly improbable
clairvoyance from his Prussian vantage, the future glory of a Pax Britannica
(4.17.197). The national summons to which Houghton explains in a foot-
note she had to respond would not sound again for ninety years in so
commanding a way; its last-minute epic impressment here illustrates by
way of contrast the sudden deflation of national claims that would coincide
with its year of publication, and that grounds this chapter of our story.

What most clearly expresses all these narratives' late-Regency indecision
about heroic conventions and values is not the arbitrary way romantic
privacy and epic obligation stack up against each other, but the way they
stay mutually disconnected. It is as if these works possessed the ingredients
of the *Waverley* novel but, lacking the pattern, forgot to knit the internal
correspondence between personal and political realities that made Scott's
fiction in the fullest sense historical. Houghton's Lindinau is only superfi-
cially a German castle, or indeed one inhabited in the nineteenth century.
Meredith's medieval Wales is a melodrama set peopled by Regency types.
Linwood and Bird, for all their ostensible interest in British history, might as
well have located their stories in the Grecian isles of ancient Hellenistic
romance, or among the South American valleys to which Southey turned,
starting in 1814, for the post-epic poem of private life and faith that he
would publish in 1825 as *A Tale of Paraguay*.

Straight epic looks like rigor mortis in Burges; *Macbeth* and *Samor* strain to
keep faith at once with their genre and with its changed national context;
while poems that bent as far as Linwood's towards romance bid fair to
elude even E. M. W. Tillyard's capacious, indispensable adjective *epicizing*.[6]

---

[6] E. M. W. Tillyard, *The English Epic and its Background* (London: Chatto and Windus, 1954).

The most interesting and characteristic productions of these years, however, owed their success to bending farther still, in feats of Romantic involution that focused epic poetry on itself with a kind of experimental, troubleshooting curiosity for which the urgencies of the nation had afforded little room since the 1790s. Back then, as we saw in Chapter 2, the challenge of jump-starting modern epic had prompted a squad of tinkers to try new things with machinery and plot structure; these efforts underlay, and were in numerous respects recapitulated within, such recent masterpieces as *The Excursion* and *Jerusalem*. Now the focus of curiosity fell on texture rather than structure, on conveying the gloss and feel of the genre rather than sustaining a strong narrative throughline. Epic had been up and running long enough in modern guise to have established a stylistic register, which it was time for the most inquisitive younger poets to explore and expand. We have just seen how the established style of heroic couplets came to a minor poet like James Bird already semi-detached from the old heroic content, and how he pretty unreflectively applied it to a new one. Abler contemporaries plied their craft more thoroughly, adapting it all the way down into the niceties of form. They thematized Britain's peace dividend—the national opportunity for self-recreation—by involving protagonists who were poets in plots that were allegories of creativity. And they put their mouth where their money was by elaborating, as the inertia of high generic prestige had made it difficult to imagine doing since the turn of the century, new options for epic style.

Peter Bayley's *Idwal, and Other Portions of a Poem* (1817) was less an epic than a public offer to write one: a specimen epic, in fact, of the sort that John Lowe and John Thelwall had produced earlier in the century and that we shall see shortly brought to tantalizingly consummate imperfection by John Keats a year or two later. The prospective subject is, yet again, the medieval English invasion of Wales; but Bayley showed himself a man of the hour by presenting for approval a poet who is reckoned interesting because, like the specimen poem itself, he is still in training and far from ready for prime time at the *eisteddfod*. All that we learn about Idwal's youth, love of nature, reclusive habits, and rich fancy mark his as a poetic sensibility of standard Romantic issue—he even possesses a Wordsworthian "free excursive mind" (700)—yet it says something that, at a time when *The Prelude* was still in the drawer, the development of this among all possible figures should have struck Bayley as the smart way to come before a Regency public. The awful death that awaits Idwal, thrown from a crag in punishment for overhearing a political conspiracy—for getting even just that close, we may infer, to political concerns of a traditionally epic sort—suggests that Bayley had at least a moderately distant take on the sentimental-Sapphic aspect of his indulged young bard's formative years.

A reader willing to credit Bayley with some ironic resilience on this score may take further interest in the separate episode called "The Hostages" that he bound in the same covers with *Idwal*. Here a villainous Sicilian mage named Zolfino clouds men's minds with a multimedia cinema device that blends together color, animation, sounds, and odors. Since in the pre-cinematic nineteenth century the technology fittest to render such a combination was poetry itself—a claim that Hardy's *Dynasts* will richly substantiate at the end of our long day in Chapter 12—this synaesthesia machine of Bayley's links his curiosity with Keats's and Shelley's as to what the powers and limits of poetry might be. Meanwhile Shelley's friend Peacock, whom we met briefly in Chapter 4, published in the romance narrative of *Rhododaphne, or The Thessalian Spell* (1818) another oddly exhilarated budget of bad news about the malignancy of an oral magic very like poetry's. Here a sexually predatory nymph keeps coming between a swain and his unwell beloved, wielding the polymorphous power that lives in the lips many times over: in drink, in kisses, in seductive speech, and of course in song. While this power is trumped in the final canto by heavenly ("Uranian") Love, it is no last-canto rescue that the poem makes memorable, but the inventive, amoral persistence of pagan Rhododaphne's poetic wiles in the meantime.[7]

Assaying a feminine poetry's strength in weakness, and tendering a rosier report on that timely subject, were the principal concerns of Matilda Betham in *The Lay of Marie: A Poem* (1816). Here the poet in a medieval pinch is no less a minstrel than Marie de France, a woman of beauty and talent whose mixed birth bars her from being quite a lady, but whose ambiguous situation in late Norman times fits her to go between the French and English courts as an envoy without portfolio. Marie moves through the world, in fact, as its unacknowledged diplomat; and the way she uses the public *éclat* of performance to further a benign personal agenda takes part, like the career of Bayley's Idwal, in the Romantic assertion of poetic autonomy. In the wake of Madame de Staël's 1807 novel *Corinne* but well in advance of Letitia Landon's *Improvisatrice* (1824), Betham's Marie is an extemporizer. Unlike these sisters in the art,

---

[7] Peacock's romance gets a brief, appreciative treatment, with reference to Hunt and Keats, in Karl Kroeber's "Trends in Minor Romantic Narrative Poetry," in *Some British Romantics: A Collection of Essays*, ed. James V. Logan, John E. Jordan, and Northrop Frye (Columbus: Ohio State University Press, 1966) 282–86.

though, Marie makes things happen by using poetry's power to influence the influential. Her long central performance is a hybrid of free inspiration with preconcerted technique that the poem follows in detail from tuneup to cadenza. The innocent ulterior motive is to make an ancient Arthurian legend play out, under thin fictional disguise and in the presence of its mighty perpetrator, a complex political intrigue of which Marie and her family have been victims (2.44). The happy result is to awaken by sympathy the viceregal Baron's better nature, and move him to rebuke hidden guilt and reward neglected merit (2.17–18).

Thus poetry makes policy: before all is said Marie's four-canto recital has averted a war and restored her to her missing husband, their child, and with them a domestic bliss that admittedly looks a lot like the end of her stage career. In the meantime, however, Betham has made an original, epical contribution to the unrelievedly lyrical Sensibility tradition of the melancholy chanteuse, by endowing melancholy with historical causes that imagination can engage and affect in a practical way. Works of the second rank though they be, *Idwal* and *Marie* let us see how at this time it had become second nature to make poetry stand proxy for culture. The assumption of an epic manner borrowed from Scott served notice, even here, that to assay poetry's rights and powers was to do something very much like it for the evolving social formation that it was the poet's highest calling to articulate.[8] This was a calling that would reverberate far into a century repeatedly attracted to the topos of the poet as hero. Major narrative statements by both Brownings, Philip James Bailey's *Festus* (1839 *et seq.*) and its many imitators in mid-century spasmody and beyond, evince the stamina of the topos and will show us in chapters ahead what a range of celebratory and critical valuation it disclosed. Nowhere is the compound of both motives—celebration and critique together—present in higher concentration than in the epic writings of Keats, Shelley, and Byron with which this chapter will close. By looking first at a pair of their associates, and how lucidly their design to epicize without angst bespoke the temper of the time, we may better appreciate what was at stake when the greatest Romantics of the second generation put that temper to epic trial.

★

[8] Jonathan Wordsworth, citing Coleridge's flattering hope that Betham might become a national poetess, points out that her most ambitious poem centers on "the first great woman poet of the English language": *The Bright Work Grows: Women Writers of the Romantic Age* (Poole: Woodstock Books, 1997) 208.

Ulterior motives for poetry are the whole *raison d'être* of Thomas Moore's runaway bestseller *Lalla Rookh: An Oriental Romance* (1817). The most deliberately ingratiating long poem in English since *The Lay of the Last Minstrel*, Moore's entertainment like Scott's owed its popularity much less to the inherent interest of its constituent verse and framing prose narratives than to the sparkle and warmth of their conjunction, wherein a sequence of poetic tales endear a masquerading minstrel-prince to his susceptible, true-hearted bride. These tales dally with epic only to put it down, for in *Lalla Rookh* epic is not an imperative but an option. It is moreover an option systematically if merrily declined, with a firmness of purpose that makes Moore's oriental romance quite continuous with those his friend and model Byron had just been publishing.[9] The prevailing tone is set in the first paragraphs, where we meet the great chamberlain Fadladeen, a stock comic blowhard claiming authority in all matters "from the mixture of a conserve of rose-leaves to the composition of an epic poem," of whom "all the cooks and poets of Delhi stood in awe" (4). These telltale Scriblerian conjunctions reduce epic to an acquired taste: not a staple cultural feat but a cultured person's accomplishment, in a quite modern sense of that term on which our ingenu hero the young prince Feramorz swiftly capitalizes.[10]

With four bardic performances Feramorz woos Lalla Rookh incognito and in full public view. Half these performances are mistily charming wisdom-fables of loving faith, the other half epic material broken to a romance yoke and interpolated with airy prose. "The Fire-Worshippers," for example, transposes to Persia an ethnic-resistance plot hatched from Moore's Irish nationalism and artistically bred up out of Southey and Scott, in Byronized tetrameters that provide an apt rendition of private passion but collapse under fire into evasive grotesquerie: "The sword hangs, clogg'd with massacre"; "What ruin glares! what carnage swims!" (122). The verse cares no more for warfare than the plot does for the fire-worshippers' political rebellion—or than the royal pretender to the lyre seems to care for his impending duties as heir apparent to the throne of what is, after all,

---

[9] An anonymous writer in *The British Review* 10 (1817) 30–54, having expected an epic, was disappointed to find nothing but ornament and imagery. On elements of collaboration and competition bearing on *Lalla Rookh* see Jeffrey W. Vail, *The Literary Relationship of Lord Byron and Thomas Moore* (Baltimore and London: Johns Hopkins University Press, 2001) 104 ff.

[10] Feramorz's accomplishment thus figured that of his poet. As the wit and lyricist Moore sought "to accommodate himself to the taste of the public" at a time when "the fashion of the day was for narrative," he had to rely "on the secondary qualities of elaborate finish, profusion of ornament, and variety of interest": Stephen Gwynn, *Thomas Moore* (London: Macmillan, 1905) 86.

only "the Lesser Bucharia." What really matters is that our prince be charming; and some familiarity with the awful things epics wots of is one of the charms he should not be without.

Moore's implication that political energies lead, in practice, practically nowhere is unfolded with keener zest in the heroic-coupleted "Veiled Prophet of Khorassan," where Azim and Zelica lose each other, and ultimately their lives, after the ideological manipulator Mokanna has seduced their idealism under the motto "Freedom to the World" (8). Tragedy yesterday but a farce today, Mokanna's 1790s-sounding program of liberation from false consciousness, "That whole dark pile of human mockeries" (10), appears in this poem of 1817 as merely a device to neutralize partisan commitment by coopting revolutionary thinking.[11] As the young principals' strenuous efforts at self-deprogramming come to nought, the narrative builds to a nihilistic climax that has Azim stab Zelica dead while she is dressed in the discredited prophet's veil. That veil is, in effect, the rhetoric of freedom itself, a livery easy to adopt but dangerous to wear and hard to shed. If the plot strongly proposes the wisdom of never donning it in the first place, this is a wisdom well tempered to the historical moment of *Lalla Rookh* and its new generation of blasé postwar readers. The veiled prophet Mokanna exploits epic commitment only as an instrument for ends other than epic; so does the bard-impersonating prince Feramorz, who knows like Betham's Marie how heart-softening stories can make things happen; so does the critic Fedladeen, who consistently pontificates by reserving judgment. And so, behind them all, does the unacknowledged legislator Moore, laying down a new law of the diversified ideological portfolio: Entertain beliefs the way you should entertain strangers; keep your heart open, but keep your options open too. The potentially epic poetry that *Lalla Rookh* embeds, steps back from, and sizes up is an *à la carte* item after all. It is an experience to be chosen, or not, from a narrative sampler; one strongly flavored item among others on a bill of literary fare.[12]

---

[11] In this Moore's Mokanna descends from Lobaba, the equivocating villain-in-chief of Southey's *Thalaba* (Ch. 2): see Vail, *Literary Relationship*, 126–30.

[12] Francis Jeffrey caught, or was caught by, this aspect of Moore's poem in an *Edinburgh Review* piece from February 1823: "Poetry, in his hands, becomes a kind of cosmetic art: it is the poetry of the toilette." Witting suspension of disbelief typified reviews of *Lalla Rookh*: Javed Majeed, *Ungoverned Imaginings: James Mill's* The History of British India *and Orientalism* (Oxford: Clarendon 1992) 102–4, traces a pattern whereby critics first detect Moore's ruses and then succumb to them anyhow.

As the still-common Romantic practice of listing subscribers can remind us, epic patronage was at least as old as Virgil, and it is unlikely that epic *patronizing*—a certain condescension to the genre itself—was much younger. It fell to Scott, as we saw in Chapter 3, to make the patronizing of epic itself a theme for ambitious verse narrative in *The Lay of the Last Minstrel*, and in poetry it was Moore who took the next stride in the same direction.[13] To a greater degree even than Byron, Moore at the dawn of literary mass-marketing forecast a comfortable noon over which not the subscribing patron but the paying customer would reign, and he catered to the rising consumerism of the century in a form calculated to attract. Hogg and Wordsworth had lately ventured into multiple narrative (Ch. 4); but beside Moore's aggressive pitch *The Queen's Wake* was a grab bag and *The Excursion* a secular lectionary. Neither work glimpsed such sales as Scott and Moore basked in—indeed, almost no book-length nineteenth-century poem would do so, despite steadily rising literacy and falling prices—and the cultural elitist in Wordsworth was fully capable of taking an avant-garde pride in that fact. Across the century a conviction would persist that the more evidently a book-length poem epicized, the more it should flaunt its disregard for the sort of public that a mere market for books could convene—the more, in other words, it should behave like something other than a novel.

Yet the advertising of disregard was advertising no less, a way of announcing one's niche to a readership of the like-minded. The economy of preferences to which literary customers were habituating themselves during the Regency years could not but take its toll on even the austerest epoist. The strait-laced poet fulfilling old conventions to the letter and the experimentalist hazarding new devices disallowed by the prose-fiction traffic were alike conspicuous for scouting fiction; and they became more conspicuous with each passing year after *Waverley*, Waterloo, and *Lalla Rookh*. Moreover, the terms of probability that made for narrative coherence were increasingly affected by the newly optative mode of peacetime consumption whereby an embattled people were fanning out into a spectrum of tasters or market aesthetes. No matter where or when an epic was set, its action was to be increasingly governed by the deliberations of characters, like the denizens of

---

[13] Hogg's 1816 *Mador of the Moor*, written in unimproving imitation of *The Lady of the Lake*, shows how tired the old Scott mode had by this time become—as no one knew better than Scott himself.

novels, whose birthright was what made Bayley's Idwal and Moore's Lalla modern: the liberal power to mull, compare, and choose.

The option on epic that Moore discounted in *Lalla Rookh* assumed an answerable narrative form but not, as regards its versification, an answerable style. Although the four parts of the poem varied from each other, all uniformly hewed to stock lines of style that the preceding decade had made current. It followed from Moore's modality of display, however, and from the larger liberalization of literary custom in which it participated, that epic was ripe for an aesthetic reformation that went all the way from large-motor narrative coordination down to the fingertip delicacies of phrasing. As epic became available as not just a literary kind but a kind of experience, an imaginative environment that the choosy poetry browser might pick out to inhabit for a while, the feel and sound of that experience became generic features detachable for testing and reformulation. Leigh Hunt grasped this opportunity in *The Story of Rimini: A Poem* (1816), calling for "the revival of what appears to me a proper English versification" conducted in "a freer spirit" and joined to "a free and idiomatic cast of language" calculated to touch the natural feelings. While comparable demands for stylistic liberation had accompanied epics as diverse as Southey's *Thalaba* and Blake's *Jerusalem* (not to mention the brief for blank verse that Milton had prefixed to *Paradise Lost*), Hunt's reform was especially important because it was an inside job. It occurred within one of the principal epic forms, the heroic couplet, opened here to moderately frequent enjambment and feminine rhyme, and above all released from its classic two-line clasp into units running, rococo-fashion, to as many lines as the descriptive and narrative matter might want.[14] Hunt's reform also took place within an idyllic genre manifestly parasitic on epic: his poem was a hundred-page epyllion in four cantos bred from two dozen lines out of Dante's *Inferno*, under the tempering influence of Boccaccio's commentary. He expanded on his austere original—chosen, one supposes, precisely on account of its austerity—by digressing with frank hedonism into Alexandrian ekphrasis, medievalized pageantry, and a lexical freshening that might rub color back into the cheeks of a standard English grown

---

[14] What Rodney Stenning Edgecombe, *Leigh Hunt and the Poetry of Fancy* (Cranbury: Associated University Presses, 1994) 41, calls Hunt's "spirit of continuousness" also plays over his closer encounters with epic when translating passages from the *Iliad*: see Louis Landré, *Leigh Hunt* (Paris: Belles-Lettres, 1936) 2: 237—38, for comparisons to Pope's couplet translation in point of enjambed speed and flow.

wan with propriety since the Restoration.[15] The cream of the entire experiment was the correspondence Hunt contrived between these narrative indulgences and his marked and subversive slackening of the Florentine's severe moral pitch.

Soliciting a sympathetic fresh hearing for the celebrated sinners Paolo and Francesca, Hunt fleshes out their *Story* and makes it a point to dally with the senses. The plot of course offered rich pretext for such dalliance, and the poem extends itself through lush circumstantial descriptiveness into a *de facto* demonstration of the liberal's doctrine of extenuating circumstances, tested here on one of the naughtiest misbehaviors in literature. If the charming principals thus escape blame, they must nevertheless pay their way out of trouble with a certain insipidity. The strongest-drawn character is the one who passes in Hunt's tolerant climate for a villain: it is Giovanni, brother and husband, whose sternness shapes what action there is, and whose unbendingly constabulary, epic manner—"A sort of fierce demand on your respect" (3.119)—stands in for the formal style of neoclassical heroic copulation that Hunt's versification did all it could to limber up. As if for our ease of comparison, this older manner persisted in another *Inferno* spinoff that appeared shortly after Hunt's in 1820: *Pia Della Pietra: A Tale*, by the same William Herbert whose rather scholarly Nordic epic *Helga* we noticed in Chapter 4. The scrupulously closed couplets of this latter Dantesque epyllion bespeak in style an *askesis* that is matched by the way Herbert shears the narrative of any descriptive ornament that might distract from his overriding ethos of self-denial. Whether by intention or coincidence, *Pia Della Pietra* reads like a puritanical riposte to *A Story of Rimini*, one that throws into strong relief what was remarkable about Hunt's practice in its time and remains significant for our history now.

For what Hunt did in *The Story of Rimini* was transform canonically epic material into a commodified stuff, through the cultivation of a manner newly customized to suit both a rising generation and a rising metro-commercial class who had less use for epic greatness than any before them, and knew it. Thirsty ambition, tragic sacrifice, the subsumption of personal wishes in collective

<hr>

[15] Richard M. Turley, *The Politics of Language in Romantic Literature* (Houndmills: Palgrave, 2002) 70–75, relates Hunt's experimentation to philological concerns that bear with equal force on the culturalist-epic theory of Herder *et al.* (see Ch. 1) and on the linguistically charged "Cockney" epithet hurled by Hunt's critics. Alison Milbank, *Dante and the Victorians* (Manchester and New York: Manchester University Press, 1998) 22–23, conceding the poem's animus against "the artificial moral fixity of Dante, as Hunt reads him," nevertheless enters a welcome caveat against comparable critical fixity: in reviving the "materiality of language," *Rimini* affirmed a principle fundamentally Dantesque.

glory had gone out, and very quickly too, with Napoleon and the British resistance he had inspired.[16] The battlefield gave ground to the villa garden, its suburbanity translucently apparent through Hunt's Italian dress as in Moore's Persian robes, as readers relaxed into literary delights that should be neither too explicitly ardent nor too undisguisedly mimetic of their own bourgeois daili-ness.[17] At the end of this line lay the verse novel proper, represented for us already by two works of 1815, Houghton's *Emilia* and Eleanor Porden's *The Veils* (Ch. 4), and now once again by Harriet Downing's 1816 *Mary; or Female Friendship: A Poem in Twelve Books* of tidy-coupleted sentiment such as one imagines Jane Austen's Mary Bennet reading with approval. This tale of kind constancy rewarded sprouts the usual feminine disclaimers of any genre-bending ambition to render "warlike Knight | Seizing fair Lady" on "some magic steed" (1.7)—crabby Pegasus himself advising the poet, in fact, to invoke "some quiet nag, or donkey" (6.80)—and it features as masculine accoutre-ments an eligible vicar who in hours of leisure "cloth'd old *Homer* in new dress again" (5.60) and a domestically inert Earl who, in tandem with Giovanni of Rimini, "could not feel | In aught an int'rest, save the commonweal" (5.53).

Downing and Hunt alike veered away from epic strife, then, yet they at the same time reenlisted aspects of the genre as instruments for elevating the tone of the ordinary. Critics defending an older generic dispensation acidly pointed out that the result was that modern species of vulgarity which manifests itself in the wish to have left vulgar things behind: that will to gentility which expresses the anxious imbalance fed by an arriving class's paradoxically elitist egalitarianism.[18] To "Cockney," the unerring word

[16] See Philip Shaw, "Leigh Hunt and the Aesthetics of Post-War Liberalism," in his collection *Romantic Wars: Studies in Culture and Conflict* (Aldershot: Ashgate, 2000) 196–97.

[17] As Kroeber, *Romantic Narrative Art* (Madison: University of Wisconsin Press, 1960) 125, reminds us, under cover of middle-class respectability Hunt was conducting a celebration of "pleasure in liberated passion" that links his agenda to those of Byron, Shelley, and Keats. On *Rimini* and the reputation the Regency suburb acquired as a moral frontier zone see Elizabeth Jones, "Suburb Sinners: Sex and Disease in the Cockney School," in *Leigh Hunt: Life, Poetics, Politics*, ed. Nicholas Roe (London and New York: Routledge, 2003) 87–91.

[18] For Greg Kucich, the epicizing social aim of Hunt's tactics was "to reimagine from within the iron centre of despotism, prejudice, and self-interest a new liberated social order governed by art, beauty and sociability": "Hunt, Keats and the Aesthetics of Excess," in *Leigh Hunt*, ed. Roe, 128–29. Cronin shows how Hunt's aim entailed, in the name of a provocative new criterion of "taste," susceptibility to "the indecorous demand for attention made by the small" and impatience with the "subordination of part to whole, and of the less to the more important that secures the economy of classical narrative" (*Politics*, 184–86). For Michael J. Sider, however, just these decorous subordinations persist from Hunt's adopted romance model to compromise his radicalism: *The Dialogic Keats: Time and History in the Major Poems* (Washington: Catholic University of America Press, 1998) 52–58, 65. See also Ayumi Mizukoshi, *Keats, Hunt, and the Aesthetics of Pleasure* (Houndmills: Palgrave, 2001) 26.

such critics found for Hunt, we now prefer the neutrally alien "Biedermeier," which has the advantage of placing the phenomena it describes within a European cultural context. But the reviewers' original nasty epithet did point to the urban and commercial heart of the matter. The newly consumerist form of international relations in postwar Britain may be seen from not just *Examiner* Hunt's Italian experiment in customer satisfaction but the Persian import business run by Moore the Irishman too—exhibits to which we may as well add the aristocrat enterprise of Byron's *Don Juan*, beginning as it does with a Mediterranean adultery like Hunt's and bringing the grand European tour back through London to cry its wares in England after all.

Literary history's favorite matriculant in the "Cockney" school remains, of course, the brilliant planet that swam into Leigh Hunt's ken in 1816, John Keats. Another reason to note Hunt's mild manifesto and easy Regency way with the couplet is that *The Story of Rimini* inspired a young poet of genius to work through its manner (apprenticed with *Endymion* and *Isabella*, a master with *Lamia* and beyond) into greatness. In a friendly 1817 sonnet "On *The Story of Rimini*" Keats placed Hunt's poem "where the little rivers run" and looked through it to "a region of his own, | A bower for his spirit" whose un-Huntlike images of fallen seed and leaf anticipate the graver burden of the *Hyperion* poems to come. Those poems would keep faith with a vocation deeper-laid than his acquaintance with Hunt: since student days Keats had believed, as he later wrote to his old schoolmaster, "that epic was of all the king, | Round, vast, and spanning all like Saturn's ring" ("To Charles Cowden Clarke," 1816, 66–67). Though Keats never came close to finishing an epic, the genre is what all his best work was written towards; and he rose higher than any longer-lived contemporary to the textural challenge that was especially posed by epic during his active years, which coincide with this chapter's span: the challenge of sustaining an epic voice not just credible in tonal amplitude, but compelling. That was the task of the moment, and Keats accomplished it. But he wanted more: he wanted to articulate a great tale of this life, within a medium accommodating the play of speculative intellect along the vectors of desire. If to want this was to want the moon—Endymion's syndrome—it is consoling to think that in reaching after architectonic structure, and grasping stylistic poise instead, Keats through the happy magic of synecdoche got—Endymion's reward—all the grandeur he had really ever wanted.

This thought, however, will console only those readers who are consoled by *Endymion: A Poetic Romance* (1818), and who are therefore liable to miss what was most personal in the irremediably stately sorrow of Keats's first *Hyperion* fragment (1820) and the glory-bitten asperity of his second (written 1819, published 1856). Qualities of tone and movement are all that these pieces give us to go on, each being an extraordinarily capable arrival at a situation from which a narrative might ensue. That none does in fact ensue has vexed some commentators into futile extrapolation, others into reading the fragments as works satisfactory in themselves and needing no completion. We do better to sustain a dialectical understanding that an awareness of their poverty is what makes these texts rich. The gigantic torsos Keats did produce ripple with yearning for the motion and wholeness of the epic action he didn't produce. Meanwhile, devotion to beauty forbade him to compass the greater life he sought, until he had first proven by extended example how it should sound and feel. *Hyperion: A Fragment* and *The Fall of Hyperion: A Dream* made beautiful a creative frustration whose unattainable object was in large part generic. Where most of the poems we have just been considering turned deliberately aside from epic, whether in resignation or relief, these essays in greatness by Keats though incomplete kept in steady view the heroic standing they must behold or cease to be.[19]

Hyperion balances on the verge of epic by rendering its characters nearly but never quite human, and by maintaining as its narrative tense the pause between an enervating past and a future that brims with portents yet seems inimical to plans that might actively cope with them. Keats's epic, like those Shelley and Wordsworth had published shortly before, premises a disabling loss as the given condition of the culture for which modern epic ambition presumes to speak. But the Romantic problem of psychopolitical *disappointment* addressed by those earlier poems is far too compromised an affect to have part in the primal, essentialized experience of loss that Keats undertakes to render. The Titan protagonists of *Hyperion* have been thrown, pent, and dazed to the point where they cannot say—nor does the poem ever say—just who or what has hit them. It remains abundantly clear, all the same, from their sculpturesque arrest that these former wielders of divine will have tasted limitation for the first time, and that their victimage has awakened a range of emotions hitherto unknown:

---

[19] Marjorie Levinson offers two distinct, astringent readings of the fractional ratio between the *Hyperion* poems: *The Romantic Fragment Poem: A Critique of a Form* (Chapel Hill: University of North Carolina Press, 1986) 173–87; and *Keats's Life of Allegory: The Origins of a Style* (Oxford: Blackwell, 1988) 191–226. See also Jeremy M. Downes, *Recursive Desire: Rereading Epic Tradition* (Tuscaloosa and London: University of Alabama Press, 1997) 147–205.

Hyperion's anger, Thea's pity, and subtler developments like Saturn's magnificently rendered apathy in the opening lines of book 1.

The Titans are what Blake would have called giant forms humanizing, and Keats by all the resources of his first epic style—slowness of tempo, density of music, dilation of attention span—invites the reader to reciprocate the heroic ordeal and become a human form titanizing. At our best Keats encourages us to expand in fancy and meet his groping protagonists halfway. Byron praised Keats for contriving here "to talk about the gods of late, | Much as they might have been supposed to speak" (*Don Juan* 11.476–77), a candid tribute that is the more generous in view of Byron's active dislike of most of the Keats he read, and that is couched precisely in the terms of epic mannerism that were most alive at this Regency interval. To what Byron observed it is important only to add that Keats's gods felt so believable because they were so hard at work contriving to speak, from sudden and unprecedented experience, about what was in effect their unwilling declension to the human condition.

That condition for Keats is overwhelmingly one of victimage, or submission before superior force. Politically valenced albeit ambiguously so, this condition of preemptive circumstantiality is stamped onto the Titans' whereabouts and written into their tentative, all but soliloquizing exchanges.[20] It is a condition chiefly evident in the passivity of all they do or contemplate doing, and its primary linguistic marker is that abundance of past passive participles which distinguishes Keats's mature style:

> As when, upon a tranced summer-night,
> Those green-rob'd senators of mighty woods,
> Tall oaks, branch-charmed by the earnest stars,
> Dream, and so dream all night without a stir . . .
>
> (1.72–75)

> . . . many more, the brawniest in assault,
> Were pent in regions of laborious breath;

---

[20] On the engagements with politics and history that feed, and partly thwart, the epic ambition of *Hyperion* see J. Philip Eggers, "Memory in Mankind: Keats's Historical Imagination," *PMLA* 86 (1971) 990–98; June Q. Koch, "Politics in Keats's Poetry," *Journal of English and Germanic Philology* 71 (1972) 491–501; and, among other contributions to the dedicated issue of *Studies in Romanticism* 25 (1986), Morris Dickstein's "Keats and Politics" (175–81), David Bromwich's "Keats's Radicalism" (197–210), and Alan J. Bewell's "The Political Implications of Keats's Classicist Aesthetics" (220–29). Daniel P. Watkins, *Keats's Poetry and the Politics of the Imagination* (Brighton: Harvester, 1986), reads the action of *Hyperion* as a "privatization" of "the once collective spirit of the Titans" (95–97). The Druidic allegory outlined by Christine Gallant, *Keats and Romantic Celticism* (Houndmills: Palgrave, 2005) 67–82 and 126–33, while it is unconvincing in political specificity, draws out the extent to which Keats's return to epic elements entailed a return to Ossian.

> Dungeon'd in opaque element, to keep
> Their clenched teeth still clench'd, and all their limbs
> Lock'd up like veins of metal, crampt and screw'd.

(2.22-25)

If to be epic is to be human, the mark of humanity here is a prescriptive belatedness, a having-been-done-by that shows affinities on one hand with the epic tale's claim to have spoken in advance for the audience who receive it, and on the other hand with this modern poet's frustrated career ambition to frame such a tale in inhospitable times.

Keats thus uncannily sustains an epic effect without being able to produce an epic cause.[21] Indeed, *Hyperion* would lose the name of action altogether were its past-participial fixation not countervailed by an orientation towards the future—obtruded a little awkwardly, and due less to the poem's situational logic than to what seems sheer human need. Keats wrote set speeches for Coelus in book 1 and Oceanus in book 2 that open the poem's fatalism to progressivist interpretation, proclaiming an unfolding genealogy of beauty and might whose meaning is betterment and whose purpose is benign. This somewhat deliberate cheer (as Yeats would call it in "Ego Dominus Tuus") remains a vision of the inevitable no less fatalistic than what has come before—a recurrent pattern in the nineteenth-century history of collective self-medication, with which many a lesser epic from the heyday of Victorian empire will inure us by Chapter 11 (over Yeats's gallant protest in *Oisin*). The garnered prospect of ripening gain as Keats imagines it in later portions of *Hyperion* inspires no more will to act than did the heavier emotions brought on his Titans in the opening lines by the contemplation of irreversible disaster.

And yet deliberate cheer is still, at least, cheer: the change of perspective prompts a mood swing that adds admiration, love, and hope to the Titans' new emotions and thus approximates them more fully to humanity. It is this expanded range of feeling that, in the fresh-departure palinode of book 3, Apollo finds "Pour into the wide hollows of my brain, | And deify me."

---

[21] Keats's premium on epic effects of monumentality shows a strong period affinity with his mentor Hazlitt's reader-centered or consumer poetics in *Lectures on the English Poets* (1818). Judy Little, *Keats as a Narrative Poet: A Test of Invention* (Lincoln: University of Nebraska Press, 1975) 128-37, correlates these affective values with the emphasis in *Hyperion* on tableaux stationed for contemplation rather than on episodic action; Sider interprets the stance of the Titans as figuring an antiqued, ambivalently superseded Bakhtinian "epic chronotope" (*The Dialogic Keats*, 115-24). Andrew Bennett, *Keats, Narrative and Audience* (Cambridge: Cambridge University Press, 1994) 152-54, shows how the "comprehensive doctoring" that is *The Fall* flushes into the open "the question of response" that the objectivity of *Hyperion* harbors.

It is otherwise with Keats's nascent Olympian, however, than with his afflicted Titans. The anguished commotion of responsive affects comes to Apollo along with a welter of stimuli: "Names, deeds, grey legends, dire events, rebellions | Majesties, sovran voices, agonies, | Creations and destroyings" (3.114–20)—a veritable if ill-sorted catalogue of plot materials for an epic poem, an *Universalwissenschaft* without syllabus or index.[22] With this jumble of objective correlatives Keats scribbled a promissory note to ante up for the higher-stakes game he meant to play if he could. The "Knowledge enormous" that "makes a god" of Apollo is the gift of Mnemosyne and the curse of the Muses her children: whether it makes a god of its possessor, or is only to die for, is the equivocation on which Keats left the poem, hoping to refocus its issues and try again.

The brilliant revision we know as *The Fall of Hyperion* got no closer, in fact, to forwarding an epic action. Instead this sequel redoubled the already marked introductoriness of its predecessor, introducing it in turn by subjecting it to preliminary interrogation. "That full draught is parent of my theme" (*Fall* 1.46)—the draft manuscript of *Hyperion*, that is, regarded by its poetic offspring with an oedipal ambivalence that zeroes in on what it might mean, and what it might cost, for a fragmentary "draught" to have been "full." The inquisitorial spotlight that Keats throws here on *Hyperion* explores particularly the one respect in which it did compass an epic grandeur: the extraordinary spaciousness of its style. *The Fall*, in a no less extraordinary act of self-critical allegoresis, literally revisits that style by stepping inside and writing it up. Keats now projects the achieved *Hyperion* amplitude as the space of a vast man-dwarfing cathedral, lofty yet hollow, which art has constructed as an interiorized simulacrum of the same exterior world from which it offers sanctuary.[23]

---

[22] See Nicholas Roe, *John Keats and the Culture of Dissent* (Oxford: Clarendon Press, 1997) 44. Jeffrey N. Cox, *Poetry and Politics in the Cockney School: Keats, Shelley, Hunt and their Circle* (Cambridge: Cambridge University Press, 1998), proposes that with the Cockney-pastoral manner that opens the fragmentary book 3 Keats re-created *Hyperion* "not as a failed epic about a war in heaven but as a completed epyllion" whose moderation of demand was consistent with the neoteric and Alexandrian ideals that the Hunt circle embraced (157, 164–65).

[23] For analysis of the verse architecture in which this space is rendered see William Reid Manierre, "Versification and Imagery in *The Fall of Hyperion*," *Texas Studies in Literature and Language* 3 (1961) 266–70. In the sequence of Keats's "halted epics" Geoffrey Hartman finds him "by poetic justice, compelled to enter his own fiction in a form that seems to be him but is increasingly empty," pumped out under pressure of sublimity: *The Fate of Reading and Other Essays* (Chicago and London: University of Chicago Press, 1975) 68–69; Levinson's hypothesis about the stylistically staged *faux* consciousness of *Hyperion* 3 suggests how that text was already rehearsing what *The Fall* went on to perform otherwise (*Allegory*, 203–4).

Such a self-sustaining structure invites inquiry into its function; and this is the question duly and mercilessly put to the dreaming poet by the temple's one denizen, the titanic catechist Moneta, whose "globed" and "hollow brain" (1.245, 276) in one sense miniaturizes, in another literalizes, the epic rotunda in which he finds her. This empty spaciousness is what you have accomplished, but why? To what earthly good, she asks, does your poetic magniloquence minister? By way of answer Keats stammers out that the true poet is "a sage; | A humanist, physician to all men" (1.189–90): a therapist dispensing such comfort, we may surmise, as the beautiful *Hyperion* was full of, in the large quietude of its manner and the stoic aplomb of its progressivist purchase on mutability. Moneta's answer to this answer is both surprising and apt. She requires the poet to reoccupy his earlier poetic draft, not as a profane tourist in Elgin-marbled contemplation of spatial form but as a candidate submitting to the epic test of time that is narrative.[24] The summons Keats hears now is, in proof of his poethood as defined by the induction to *The Fall*, to "tell thy dream" (1.12). He is to try on his own pulses the comfort he has alleged his art provides, and to do so under conditions of heightened perception enabling (and obliging) him "To see as a God sees, and take the depth | Of things as nimbly as the outward eye | Can size and shape pervade" (1.304–06). Moneta offers Keats, if he can sustain it, the part he had sketched out in *Hyperion* for Apollo.[25]

This kinesthetic enlargement of empathetic witness sounds nice, in a Moore or Hunt kind of way; but, in bitterly explicit chastisement of the Regency mode Keats had grown up in, it proves little short of torture.

[24] In an interpretation harmonic with the one offered here, Ralph Pite proposes that rereading Dante in the summer of 1819 reminded Keats of "his self-implication (in and by the act of writing) which [*Hyperion*] had sought to disregard": *The Circle of Our Vision: Dante's Presence in English Romantic Poetry* (Oxford: Clarendon Press, 1994) 120. For Nancy Goslee, *Uriel's Eye: Miltonic Stationing and Statuary in Blake, Keats, and Shelley* (University: University of Alabama Press, 1985), the sculpturesque forms of the Titans represent the Romantic–Hellenist dream "of an immortal, saving art," which *The Fall* subjects to critique as "a false vision of wholeness" (122–31). The staying power of that false vision, and of its linkage in Keats's mind to the "abstract" idea of epic, forms a leading theme of the unsparing inquest by John Jones, *John Keats's Dream of Truth* (London: Chatto and Windus, 1969) 69–104; Dorothy Van Ghent evaluates it more neutrally in *Keats: The Myth of the Hero*, ed. Jeffrey C. Robinson (Princeton: Princeton University Press, 1983) 199–207. For Martin Aske, *Keats and Hellenism: An Essay* (Cambridge: Cambridge University Press, 1985), the pallid monumentality of *Hyperion* resumes in allegoric recessional both the history of epic and, *contra* Voltaire and Gibbon, "the 'pastness' of the past" (75); see also Bruce Haley, *Living Forms: Romantics and the Monumental Figure* (Albany: State University of New York Press, 2003) 245–52.
[25] This is roughly the part allotted to the poet-figure in Wordsworth's *Excursion*, which Keats greatly admired and which modeled not only characteristic imagery for *Hyperion* but also *The Fall*'s prescription of narrative as shock therapy for imagistic paralysis. See Sperry, *Keats the Poet* (Princeton: Princeton University Press, 1973) 165–79; Thomas A. Reed, "Keats and the Gregarious Advance of Intellect in *Hyperion*," *ELH* 55 (1988) 213–19.

As the scene of the fallen Titans unfolds before him, this time not narrated by Moneta but screened on her retina with minimal voiceover, the poet's new perceptual endowment exposes him to untold agonies of sensory and moral endurance.[26] It is as if to take Apollo's Olympian part is to take the part of the abjected Titans too, and in a mode not just of notional pity but of excruciating sympathy. Reframed by *The Fall* and replayed in what seems still slower motion than the tempo *molto largo* of the original, the extended inaction of *Hyperion* becomes an heroic trial of suffering in which passionate commiseration, or immiserated compassion, engrosses the role of plot. Bodily witness becomes participant martyrdom: "Without stay or prop, | But my own weak mortality, I bore | The load of this eternal quietude" (1.388–90).[27] The "Knowledge enormous" of deeds and events that initiated Apollo into godhood cedes priority now to an "enormous ken" (1.303)—the power to know the truth inside and out, a voluminous cognitive capacity that is independent of, and apparently void of, specific propositional knowledge.[28] This enormity of ken is visited on a merely human figure whose humanity it distends, and whose standing as "a sage, | A humanist" depends on what he can stand. How much he can take in will depend, for this empath at the top of his form and at the limit of his endurance, on how much he can take. Imaginative altruism invests humanity with a kind of heroic outreach that was inaccessible to the self-absorbed or compensatorily theorizing Titans of *Hyperion* but now becomes legible

[26] Untold—ostentatiously so—in *Hyperion* 3, where Apollo's introduction to a new world of "agonies, | Creations and destroyings" never decides whether for a god the knowledge of such things comes with the territory or must be experientially undergone. For analysis of this impasse see Helen E. Haworth, "The Titans, Apollo, and the Fortunate Fall in Keats's Poetry," *Studies in English Literature* 10 (1970) 637–49; Stuart A. Ende, *Keats and the Sublime* (New Haven and London: Yale University Press, 1976) 112; for explanation by way of mythic archetypes see Van Ghent, *Myth of the Hero*, 187–93, and Tilottama Rajan, *Dark Interpreter: The Discourse of Romanticism* (Ithaca and London: Cornell University Press, 1980) 156–62. At all events *The Fall* leaves no doubt—despite Moneta's anaesthesiological white lie at 1.247–48—that "the modern poet's burden is the pain of consciousness," which "finds knowledge only in suffering": John Barnard, *John Keats* (Cambridge: Cambridge University Press, 1987) 129, 137. Biomedical contexts for this burden are adduced by Hermione de Almeida, *Romantic Medicine and John Keats* (New York: Oxford University Press, 1991) 303–11.

[27] Irene H. Chayes, "Dreamer, Poet, and Poem in *The Fall of Hyperion*," *Philological Quarterly* 46 (1967) 510–13 considers the remarkable frieze-frame effect Keats contrived here in revising, by suspension (yet not suspense), the Saturn–Thea interview from book 1 of *Hyperion*.

[28] Keats's open, or empty, signature of unconcludedness is a matter on which criticism still tries conclusions, e.g. Butler, *Romantics, Rebels and Revolutionaries*, 154; Susan Wolfson *The Questioning Presence: Wordsworth, Keats, and the Interrogative Mode in Romantic Poetry* (Ithaca and London: Cornell University Press, 1986) 344–61; Levinson, *Allegory*; and Cronin, *Politics*, 190: Keats "sought to inscribe his own name in the book of literature by the production of poems that betrayed the cultural disabilities that disqualified him from inclusion within it."

by degrees in Moneta's face, as fellow-feeling for human pain informs her ministry of sorrow.

The higher stakes of negative capability for which Keats came at last to play entailed a Romantic intensification of self-knowledge after all. As the criterion for epic became not completeness of understanding but openness of nerve, the strategy became not to get finished but to stay quick.[29] To this end, better a living fragment than a generic automaton cut to measure and forced into procrustean shape, and better a style feeling its way than one that, prematurely arrived, had no plot to develop and so nowhere to go. Accordingly Keats devised for *The Fall*, chiefly out of Cary's translation of Dante (completed 1812), a spare pentameter style that set off by disenchanting contrast *Hyperion*'s Miltonic orotundity; the later version embedded the earlier one, that is, within an alien medium that militated against readerly absorption in its consolatory splendors.[30] The brusque conversion of a sanctuary space to a trial room in Keats's new proem figured the altered status of answerable style in his sharpening epic vision. By 1820, which was already the beginning of the sick man's end, Keats lacked the time, the learning, and perhaps the narrative address to get it all panoptically together. But he had learned, the hard way, that there was nowhere to hide—an epic conviction that challenges comparison with the best of his contemporaries'. He had independently, credibly evolved a total form of knowing, like Blake's poetics of universal forgiveness and Wordsworth's of long-suffering perseverance, that

[29] As Leslie Brisman reads the incorporation of *Hyperion* into *The Fall,* "Moneta gives the poet the opportunity to see, in the story of the titans, the story of himself"; as Keats renounces his pagan faith in natural renewal and "chooses for his subject a myth of the failure to begin anew," he so directs "the funeral of myth" as to make of that last rite, for one last time, a typically Keatsian "point of incipience": *Romantic Origins* (Ithaca and London: Cornell University Press, 1978) 98–102. From an expressly postmodern platform Carol L. Bernstein pauses, with Saturn and Apollo, over a discourse that "proclaims his subjectivity at the same time that it makes it other than himself," precipitating an "awareness of oneself experiencing" that serves to "halt narrative": "Subjectivity as Critique and the Critique of Subjectivity in Keats's *Hyperion*," in *After the Future: Postmodern Times and Places,* ed. Gary Shapiro (Albany, State University of New York Press, 1990) 50, 46. To convert that very haltedness to narrative—extending Brisman's "point of incipience" into a story line—was the epicizing coup Keats attempted in *The Fall.* Only thus, Charles J. Rzepka points out, might an other-directed yet self-conscious poetry responsibly *bear witness* and *stand by*: *The Self as Mind: Vision and Identity in Wordsworth, Coleridge, and Keats* (Cambridge, Mass.: Harvard University Press, 1986) 227–37.

[30] Paul D. Sheats, "Stylistic Discipline in *The Fall of Hyperion*," *Keats–Shelley Journal* 17 (1968), analyzes the "anatomical and painful" askesis whereby in Keats's final body of verse "His vulnerability is his strength" (81, 88). For Dickstein, however, in *Keats and his Poetry: A Study in Development* (Chicago and London: University of Chicago Press, 1971), "the epic grandeur of the earlier poem is maimed and softened without being transformed" (262). On the persistence of Miltonic echoes in both poems see Jonathan Bate, "Keats's Two *Hyperion*s and the Problem of Milton," in *Romantic Revisions,* ed. Robert Brinkley and Keith Hanley (Cambridge: Cambridge University Press, 1992) 321–38. The discussion is at once technical and exhilarating in M. R. Ridley, *Keats's Craftsmanship: A Study in Poetic Development* (Oxford: Clarendon Press, 1933) 57–95 and 266–80.

might accommodate whatever historical and political syntheses the years to
come, had there been for him years to come, would afford.[31]

Keats's most poetically gifted peer never knew what it was to wait for
historical and political syntheses to jell into a theme worthy of publication.
These came to Shelley with the air he breathed, and it is impossible to
imagine his undertaking any poem longer than a song that was not centrally
inspired by his "passion for reforming the world" (Preface to *Prometheus
Unbound*, 1819), and for the rhetoric and ideas that might effect such reform.
Radical political analysis, advanced philosophical speculation, an inter-
national outlook, and a utopianism that not only hungered after liberty and
equality but imagined their realization in concrete, compelling detail: Shel-
ley possessed these qualifications in precocious abundance and exercised
them for the better part of a decade. The question with which he had to
grapple was what imaginative shape to give his reforming idealism. The
frontal, scarcely veiled didacticism of *Queen Mab: A Philosophical Poem* (1813)
had been a reasonable place to start. Deep down, however, the mode of
Queen Mab belonged to the previous century; and, besides, Shelley had only
to look about him after the passage of a few years to see that the mode was not
working.[32] Early in the period this chapter covers, he grasped that a world
not about to be reasoned into utopia might nevertheless be led towards its
ethical possibility by imaginative means more oblique in their operation.

Yes, but which means? By 1819 Shelley had settled on dramatic and lyric
forms that dispensed with narrative mediation, presenting plot and argument
alike in the immediacy of what we would call real time, and leaving ample
scope for the kinds of choral and ecstatic rhapsody at which he excelled and on
whose wings he aspired to take readers with him.[33] He had decided, that is,

[31] There has been ample speculation about where a healthy and resolute Keats might have
taken the resumed epic narrative. For sharply divergent samples see Edward B. Hungerford, *Shores
of Darkness* (1941; rpt. Cleveland: Meridian, 1963) 137–41; Pierre Vitoux, "Keats's Epic Design in
Hyperion," *Studies in Romanticism* 14 (1975) 165–83.

[32] Yet *Queen Mab*'s standing as a 19th-cent. epic is vigorously championed by Stuart Curran,
Poetic Form and British Romanticism (New York and Oxford: Oxford University Press, 1986) 172–73.

[33] Although Lukács never discusses Shelley, the way he disallows epic utopianism *tout court*
offers inadvertent commentary on this poet's generic experiments, as indeed on those of several
later 19th-cent. congeners: "Any attempt at a properly utopian epic must fail because it is bound,
subjectively or objectively, to transcend the empirical and spill over into the lyrical or dramatic;
and such overlapping can never be fruitful for the epic"; "the great epic is a form bound to the
historical moment, and any attempt to depict the utopian as existent can only end in destroying
the form." *The Theory of the Novel: A Historic-Philosophical Essay on the Forms of Great Epic Literature*,
tr. Anna Bostock (1915; Cambridge, Mass.: MIT Press, 1971) 46, 152.

against epic. But he did so only after giving it a long trial run, in the twelve-canto narrative that had conveyed his "first serious appeal to the Public" in *Laon and Cythna; or The Revolution of the Golden City* (1817, suppressed and revised as *The Revolt of Islam*, 1818). The patent deficiencies of this work make it hard to doubt the wisdom of Shelley's deserting it for modes more congenial.[34] Yet his initial working subtitle for it was right too: *A Vision of the Nineteenth Century*. Shelley's epic reveals a strong, consistent understanding of what the genre had meant in his lifetime—in other words, since the climacteric of the French Revolution—and of what cultural work might be performed by an epic transposition of that revolution into a venue that was less properly oriental, despite the new title, than allegorically analytic.[35]

In equal measure idealistic and ideological, *The Revolt of Islam* attests from beginning to end an unshaken faith in the power of eloquence to mold and change minds.[36] Time and again a reported episode, a song, even a slogan shouted in season is all it takes to turn the tide of oppression or rebellion, revive or check a movement of opinions or of troops. In this obviously

[34] Commending this decision, Curran in *Shelley's Annus Mirabilis: The Maturing of an Epic Vision* (San Marino: Huntington Library, 1975) 29–32, ascribes the failures of *The Revolt* to its aesthetically passive conformity with a Southeyan epic tradition from which the poet dissented politically and intellectually; so does Cronin, *Shelley's Poetic Thoughts* (New York: St. Martin's Press, 1981) 131. For David Duff, *Romance and Revolution: Shelley and the Politics of a Genre* (Cambridge: Cambridge University Press, 1994), who regards that tradition as one of "revolutionary romance" (162), this conformity exhibits the virtue of fidelity to radical precedent. On the question of genre see also Brian Wilkie, *Romantic Poets and Epic Tradition* (Madison and Milwaukee: University of Wisconsin Press, 1965) 117–25; Gerald McNiece, *Shelley and the Revolutionary Idea* (Cambridge, Mass.: Harvard University Press, 1969) 215–17; Desmond King-Hele, *Shelley: His Thought and Work* (3rd edn. Cranbury: Associated University Presses, 1984) 84.

[35] The choice of a borderland where Greeks faced off against Ottomans at "the unstable fringe of a decidedly old-fashioned empire" resumed Scott's epic formula but superficially, since Shelley represented his antagonists as nearly ahistorical archetypes for liberation and reaction: Jack Donovan, "The Storyteller," in *The Cambridge Companion to Shelley*, ed. Timothy Morton (Cambridge: Cambridge University Press, 2006) 93. As Carlos Baker pointed out long ago in *Shelley's Major Poetry: The Fabric of a Vision* (Princeton: Princeton University Press, 1948), the focus of Shelley's epic is not specific but cosmic, spanning "the world from the English Channel to Antarctica, from China to Egypt, and from Persia to Pandemonium"(77).

[36] On the poem's ideological warfare and rhetorical armory see Wilkie, *Romantic Poets*, 139–41; McNiece, *Shelley and the Revolutionary Idea*, 202, 206–10; on eloquence as politicized magic see Duff, *Romance and Revolution*, 156–57. William A. Ulmer, *Shelleyan Eros: The Rhetoric of Romantic Love* (Princeton: Princeton University Press, 1990) 65–73, investigates the elitism that invests public eloquence with compulsory power; Gary Kelly, "From Avant-Garde to Vanguardism: The Shelleys' Romantic Feminism in *Laon and Cythna* and *Frankenstein*," in *Shelley: Poet and Legislator of the World*, ed. Betty T. Bennett and Stuart Curran (Baltimore and London: Johns Hopkins University Press, 1996), emphasizes the "postrevolutionary ambivalences" attending Shelley's feminism and nonviolence (79–82). For Stuart Peterfreund, *Shelley among Others: The Play of the Intertext and the Idea of Language* (Johns Hopkins University Press, 2002) 142–67, the plot hinges on the protagonists' endeavor to materialize and so defamiliarize the morally neutral power of language to create and also deceive.

hyper-historical work of fantasy cities and visionary landscapes, the contest between insurgency and reaction is archetypal, cyclical, and even at its most specific no more than (in Shelley's own description) "the *beau ideal*, as it were, of the French Revolution."[37] It is also, with pointed reference to the activist present, not yet over. On both sides of what Shelley clearly regards as an ongoing struggle the real armory consists not of weapons but of ideas. The category of ideas, moreover, includes narratives: the poem keeps an epic faith by showing how political disputes reduce to contending histories. Laon, who recites the last eleven cantos, begins his tale by conceding dismissively that "I heard, as all have heard, the various story | Of human life" (2.3.685, 2.9.739)—i.e. the party line maintained by "Feeble historians" and time-serving "chroniclers" (2.3.687–89)—but tells how he went on to learn hope among the (presumably Greek) ruins, where "monuments of less ungentle creeds | Tell their own tale" (2.11.761). Not preach their own sermon in stone, but tell their own tale: Shelley's faith in the narrative carriage of ideology underwrites his early embrace of epic as a mode he expressly calls in the preface "narrative, not didactic."

Just such a self-told tale is *The Revolt of Islam*, the narrative of a failed revolution whose leaders once slain join the immortal cadre of an ideological rebel alliance inspiring all those who will follow. The later cantos repeatedly pit, against the establishment narratives furnished by King and Priest (e.g. 12.12–13), revolutionary accounts that typically emerge in supervenient flashback (e.g. 12.24–32) to contradict the despotism of prevailing appearances.[38] That more often than not the overlords have won

[37] Letter of 13 October 1817 to an unnamed publisher, in *Letters of Percy Bysshe Shelley*, ed. Roger Ingpen (London: Pitman, 1909), 2: 559. The effectiveness that persuasive rhetoric enjoys within the plot of *The Revolt* is a utopian projection rather than an imitation, in Byron's epic spirit, of things as they are. Nigel Wood finds Shelley saying as much in his preface, where the re-establishment of Continental tyranny on the ruins of revolution means that history itself is anarchic not rational, and therefore that "the aesthetic or artistic could no longer be safely mimetic" in its project of rendering truth: "Introduction" to *Don Juan* (Buckingham: Open University Press, 1993) 20; see also Wilkie, *Romantic Poets*, 134; Duff, *Romance and Revolution*, 160–61. For Harold Orel, in contrast, the option to idealize the Revolution was a privilege Shelley's generation enjoyed because they were born too late to have experienced it: "Shelley's *The Revolt of Islam*: The Last Great Poem of the English Enlightenment?", *Studies on Voltaire and the Eighteenth Century* 89 (1972) 1188. On either interpretation, this swerve from accidental to essential representation affiliates Shelley with his Enlightenment and early Greek-revival forebears as described by Butler, *Romantics, Rebels and Revolutionaries*, 16–20, 127–31.

[38] Donovan, "Storyteller," 96, identifies these moments of narrative supplement with Shelley's "establishing a mental continuum that binds the present to past"—a signal epic function, which in an earlier essay Donovan associates with Virgilian dialectics of amnesia and anagnorisis: " 'Lethean Joy': Memory and Recognition in *Laon and Cythna*," in *Evaluating Shelley*, ed. Timothy Clark and Jerrold E. Hogle (Edinburgh: Edinburgh University Press, 1996) 134–38.

counts for less, within a utopian calculus, than that the underdogs are getting their hearing now, in this poem, whose stanzaic build undergirds the analogy between it and the chambered "Temple of the Spirit" in which its story is framed.[39] Given the extreme (indeed implausible) lability of the people, swayed by voice after voice and swaying from cause to cause, the public sphere remains wide open to fresh persuasion, of which *The Revolt* addresses its reader as both an object and a recruitable agent. Shelley's epic story about the politics of prevalent stories means that it is never too late for either side's story to prevail, and therefore that despair is, like triumph, always premature.

"When the last hope of trampled France had failed," runs the first line of this post-Waterloo poem, "From visions of despair I rose" (1.1.129). By rehearsing the cycle of failure and revival here begun *The Revolt* undertook, as surely as Wordsworth had done with more complexity in *The Excursion*, to forestall despondency by training the imagination on disappointment and its survival. Thus Cythna's despondency is corrected when, at a turning point in the plot, she understands that "we live in our own world, and mine was made | From glorious fantasies of hope departed" (7.30.3091–92): hope's exit is imagination's cue to enter the stage of world history and begin the work of epic renewal. Shelley read *The Excursion* often and with admiration, and arguably owed to it the conception, voiced more than once in his preface, that following "the reverses of hope in the progress of French liberty," "gloom and misanthropy have become the characteristics of the age in which we live, the solace of a disappointment that unconsciously finds relief only in the wilful exaggeration of its own despair. . . . I am aware, methinks, of a slow, gradual, silent change. In that belief I have composed the following Poem."[40]

Grasping the Romantic premise that epic narrative was a political tool, Shelley held further that the aptest tool for moving the mass mind must be the most thoroughly epic, that is, the most coherently unified. Indeed, his optimism reposed in part on the superior inclusiveness of a popular egali-tarianism: the left would win out because it brought everyone together on

---

[39] See Douglas Thorpe, "Shelley's Golden Verbal City," *Journal of English and Germanic Philology* 86 (1987) 215–27; also P. M. S. Dawson, *The Unacknowledged Legislator: Shelley and Politics* (Oxford: Oxford University Press, 1980) 74.

[40] The constitutive insecurity of such a prospect leaves the poem as open to interpretive apprehension as is the future it faces: for a reading that stresses ambivalence in *The Revolt* see Michael O'Neill, "A More Hazardous Exercise: Shelley's Revolutionary Imaginings," *Yearbook of English Studies* 19 (1989) 261–64.

common ground, against which a right wing that divided in the short term
to conquer could not ultimately stand. Shelley's villains are exclusionist
sectarians who withdraw from the collective good into hierarchies of
privilege. The feminism of *The Revolt*—where a nonviolent woman warrior
makes free love, bears babies, forms study groups, harangues multitudes—is
only the most noteworthy aspect of an emancipation that forms at once the
goal of radical struggle and its grounding means. The passion of Laon and
Cythna for politics is of a piece with their passion for each other; their
unsettlingly incestuous likeness is a figure for the recognition of self in other
on which Shelley's theories of society and of art were based alike.[41] Enthu-
siastic, explicit sex finds a place in this epic (right at the canto 6 midpoint),
much as erotic derivatives like visionary excitement and rapt debate do: all
conspire together as political activities that, by defying oppressive custom,
loosen its icy grip. Even vegetarianism, that toe-stubbing plank in the
ideological platform of Shelley's teenage opus *Queen Mab*, here helps
articulate an integrative ecopolitics of union and continuity. *The Revolt*
regards humanity as continuous with its natural context and animal
origins (hymned in the elaborate lyric after 5.51) and makes it a point to
go beyond the human into the bestial world, foregrounding with red tooth
and claw the grappling snake and eagle of canto 1, and giving a memorable,
silent but still gently Homeric role to the rebels' faithful horse (6.26,
6.43–45).[42]

---

[41] The openness of the literal sibling incest in *Laon and Cythna* was of course a major motive behind
publisher Charles Ollier's withdrawal of his name. Shelley's radically epic challenge to rooted cultural
constraint is discussed at length in Donovan, "*Laon and Cythna*: Nature, Custom, Desire," *Keats–
Shelley Review* 2 (1987) 49–90, and briefly in Duff, *Romance and Revolution*, 189–90. For Samuel
Lyndon Gladden in *Shelley's Textual Seductions: Plotting Utopia in the Erotic and Political Works* (New
York and London: Routledge, 2002) 235–42, the play and pleasure of the text rehearse a sexual
politics of shifting reciprocity, while Tedi Chichester Bonca, *Shelley's Mirrors of Love: Narcissism,
Sacrifice, and Sorority* (Albany: State University of New York Press, 1999), goes so far as to read the
entire plot as an "elaborate exercise in imaginative transsexualism" (107–19). Cronin stakes out a
ground on which all these readings may consort: *The Revolt* corrected its 1790s congeners by insisting
that "revolutionary principles are not upheld in opposition to the claims of love, rather each is an
aspect of the other" (*Shelley*, 102). And Hogle, *Shelley's Process: Radical Transference and the Development
of His Major Works* (New York: Oxford University Press, 1988) 101–2, seizes the analytic ground of
Shelley's revolutionary confidence in erotic "interreflection": the sibling love of the heroes represents
the "embodiment of a process that will survive their oppressors because it is the forgotten basis of
oppression," i.e. pre-hierarchical transference itself. William Keach responds to Hogle's provocation
by citing the revisionary epic heroism of Southey's *Joan of Arc*: see *Arbitrary Power: Romanticism,
Language, Politics* (Princeton and Oxford: Princeton University Press, 2004) 111–21.

[42] On this aspect of Shelley's epic encyclopedism see Timothy Morton, *Shelley and the Revolution in
Taste: The Body and the Natural World* (Cambridge: Cambridge University Press, 1994) 110–16.

A unifying force within the poem more pervasive still, and more representative of the epic poetics of its moment, is Shelley's dazzling descriptive manner. John Stuart Mill, having tried hard to love Shelley and failed, pronounced the poet defective in "the consecutiveness of thought necessary for a long poem."[43] This will never do; yet even those who adore Shelley's precipitancy must concede its liability to blind the eye of narrative and stymie momentum, a liability aggravated here by the choice to write in Spenserian stanzas for their "brilliancy and magnificence of sound" (Preface). The plan "to enlist the harmony of metrical language, the ethereal combinations of the fancy, the rapid and subtle transitions of human passion," betrays all too frankly (and forecasts in the very launch of adjectives just quoted) a visionary impatience with the ordinary interests of story. But the feel of Shelleyan narrative—the drive and gleam and weave and blur that any extended passage from *The Revolt* will impart—forms a distinctive yet characteristic exhibit in the Regency gallery of epic textures, even as it resonates with the poem's other features of integrative design.[44] As frustration and hope chase one another across the cantos, the passing episodes come to seem merely mutually reminiscent and lapse into an inconsequence that never elicits the metanarrative sort of justification that, say, Blake's staged inconsequence does. The style of *The Revolt*, however, manages with wonderful exuberance to hold the poem at that Shelleyan point,

[43] John Stuart Mill, "The Two Kinds of Poetry," *Monthly Repository* (1833), rpt. in *Autobiography and Literary Essays*, ed. John M. Robson and Jack Stillinger, vol. 1 of *Collected Works* (Toronto and Buffalo: University of Toronto Press, 1981) 359. A case for the poem's architectonic soundness, and its allegorical and symbolic integrity, is patiently set forth by Richard S. Haswell, "Shelley's *The Revolt of Islam*: 'The Connexion of Its Parts,'" *Keats–Shelley Journal* 25 (1976) 81–102; see also the structural outline in Curran, *Annus Mirabilis*, 28. Thorpe carries this initiative further into the realm of the classic foundation epic, positing an "internalization of architecture, such that the authentic city turns out to be a poem," which amid the ruins of history "still remains, and not just as a reminder, but as an active instrument of reformation" (217). Instrumental activism—a sort of hope drill for Regency liberals—drives the entire plot's repeating mechanism as analyzed by Michael Scrivener, *Radical Shelley: The Philosophical Anarchism and Utopian Thought of Percy Bysshe Shelley* (Princeton: Princeton University Press, 1982) 124–27. Kucich, *Keats, Shelley, and Romantic Spenserianism* (University Park: Pennsylvania State University Press, 1991) 272–80, elucidates plot parallels between *The Revolt* and book 1 of *The Faerie Queene*, and also the skewing of these parallels that results from Shelley's didactic ambivalence.

[44] In this sense the note of textural appreciation that tempered John Gibson Lockhart's 1819 review of the poem in *Blackwood's* was less anomalous than it was prescient of a shift in criticism from partisan to aesthetic terms, or from overt to covert ideological response: see Kim Wheatley, *Shelley and His Readers: Beyond Paranoid Politics* (Columbia and London: University of Missouri Press, 1999) 51–57. This shift is anticipated in the second half of the poem, where incantation supervenes on rhetoric as the prime verbal persuader: see Anya Taylor, *Magic and English Romanticism* (Athens: University of Georgia Press, 1979) 193–200.

equivalently aesthetic and political, where music and moonlight and feeling are one, and all things flow to all.[45]

An adroit, swift, often gymnastically reflexive syntax of elaborate return ministers to this effect; at least as important is the fertility of the poem's epic similes. Astral, tempestuous, geological, botanical analogies diversify the action—again, admittedly, to the point of distraction—in a cumulative registration of the oneness of the world, amounting to an eminently epic argument that those who champion human unity have the cosmos on their side.[46] These hidden persuaders, the figures of poetic rather than forensic rhetoric ("narrative, not didactic"), bear Shelley's message farther into the mind than do the declamations and incidents they adorn. Presumably it was his own comparison between the different modalities of rhetoric his epic combined that decided him to abandon the genre. He may have been returning to it at the end: *The Triumph of Life* shows him assaying, like Keats, a Dantesque visionary narrative of unfathomed promise, which had he lived might have led nineteenth-century epic down roads it never effectually took. Meanwhile in the dramatic form of *Prometheus Unbound* he made, on essentially the same ideological impetus as had motivated *The Revolt of Islam*, a masterpiece that manages ritual severity and rhapsodic sublimity at once. Meanwhile, and with all its faults, Shelley's one proper epic remains a demonstration that a strong political will and an epic ambition could still coexist, during those warily wised-up years when the liberalism of a Hunt or Moore or Keats had gone, as far as their verse narratives were concerned, into pretty leafy cover.

Testimony such as Shelley's remains the more desirable when we consider how flamboyantly the one great epic poem of the Regency era paraded its commitment, if not to nothing at all, then to nothing very much. This was *Don Juan*, the spoiler's *pièce de résistance*; a scoffer's manual, apostate's bible, and rake's progressive supper in one; the broken dandy's guide from High Romantic *Sturm und Drang* into the comforts, and challenges, of a

---

[45] Reacting in a letter of 11 Dec. 1817 to William Godwin's reaction to the poem, Shelley with self-analytic acumen separated out the imaginative gifts that converge at best in his epic fusions of multeity and unity: "to apprehend minute & remote distinctions of feeling whether relative to external nature, or the living beings which surround us, & to communicate the conceptions which result from considering either the moral or the material universe as a whole": *Letters*, 1: 577. See the fine appreciation by G. Wilson Knight in *The Starlit Dome: Studies in the Poetry of Vision* (Oxford: Oxford University Press, 1941) 188–89.

[46] This forms the affirmative side of the poet's steady Lucretianism, atheism forming the negative: see Paul Turner, "Shelley and Lucretius," *Review of English Studies* n.s. 10 (1959) 269–82.

Biedermeier middle age. It is the one indispensable poem of its moment— an extended one, appearing in four installments between 1819 and 1824—and it is as certainly an epic poem as Byron's earlier productions are not. Mock-epic it is too, of course: there is no work in the entire tradition that on one hand more persistently derides traditional generic conventions or on the other hand more pointedly quizzes current realities for wanting the very virtues that the tradition once enforced. From the opening "I want a hero" (1.1) and "Hail Muse! et cetera" (3.1) to the late "Begin, | *Paulo majora*" (12.193–94) and "But now I will begin my poem" (12.425) and the very late "knights and dames I sing, | Such as the times may furnish" (15.193–94) *Don Juan* sports generically self-conscious flippancies, which not even Byron's enormous verve as an entertainer could keep from wearing thin were the poem nothing more than an entertainment on the order of *Lalla Rookh*. But it was much more. In practice these passages and dozens like them flash out real fire because in them Byron's steely wit struck against something that was not wit: an heroic purpose, hard as flint, to summon the English public to its senses by a reclamation of English that renewed in epic idiolect the common tongue.[47]

"I now mean to be serious" (13.1): this richly performative canto-opener characteristically means what it says by outflanking—fooling its way around—the serious liability of clichés to say what everybody says but nobody in particular means. *Difficile est communia proprie dicere*, quoth the poem's epigraph from Horace: It's hard to phrase commonplaces your own way.[48] Byron did it by beating the plowshare of complacency that has furrowed the literary culture this chapter surveys back into a sword, and burnishing the shield of culturally protectionist irony into a mirror that showed contemporary Britons what they were, and he with them. He reflected back an image—now brilliant, now gaudily grotesque—of what they sounded and felt and thought like. This was something his defamiliarizing years of exile disposed him to do, and at the same time something his

[47] A hundred years after the fact it was apparent to a scholar otherwise skeptical about modern epic's viability, W. Macneile Dixon in *English Epic and Heroic Poetry* (London: Dent 1912), that *Don Juan* was "an epic in the modern manner, probably the only manner in which the taste of latter days would willingly accept it" (303). McGann gives good prefatory reasons for regarding the question of the poem's epic status "a pseudo-problem" (*Context*, xii–xiii, 1–4). Frederick L. Beaty, *Byron the Satirist* (DeKalb: Northern Illinois University Press, 1985) 138–46, makes the case for accepting the hybrid generic label of "Epic Satire" that the poet himself proposes at 14.99.

[48] Our deepest and longest gloss on this epigraph, after *Don Juan* itself, is Jerome Christensen's reading of it in *Lord Byron's Strength: Romantic Writing and Commercial Society* (Baltimore and London: Johns Hopkins University Press, 1993) xxiv–xxv, 214–57, 325–28.

unique celebrity positioned him to do, since as the prototype matinée idol he himself had been an object of public image-projection on a mass scale for years.[49] Whether we now hold cheap the easy post-Waterloo penchant for self-mockery, or whether we embrace it as a harmless and wholesome postwar recreation, a slacker's profile so defined the era that no poem of culturally comprehensive ambition could afford not to be, in substantial part, mock-epic.[50]

It was failure to meet this condition, we might say, that doomed to brilliant minority the efforts of Byron's greatest peers, who, although they could not but recognize the challenge of the age, also could not in practice rise to it as he did. Keats's relentlessly ascetic self-inquisition in *The Fall of Hyperion* may be seen as an attempt to find steady work for the critical spirit that adjoined Regency knowingness, but the attempt gave out; one of the most intriguing questions his curtailed career raises is whether Keats would in time have contrived an epic manner (both *The Fall* and *Lamia* hint at one) whose critically leavened high seriousness was capable of earnest grasping. Shelley did in a sense contrive such a manner in *The Revolt of Islam*, inasmuch as the fluent succession of scenes and profusion of images made relative and tentative any one prospect; still, no one will deny that his poem faces up poorly to the incredulous smile it keeps eliciting unawares. This was the smile that Byron preempted in *Don Juan*, even as he coopted mock-epic's critique of the weightier solemnities, with the aim of sustaining— over the years, over an absurdist abyss—a vantage that was epic not in spite of its constituent irony but on account of it. The same allergy to affirmation that had formerly unfitted the oriental tales for epic had now become, half a

---

[49] See Karen McGuire, "Byron Superstar: The Poet in Neverland," in *Contemporary Studies on Lord Byron*, ed. William D. Brewer (Lewiston, NY: Mellen, 2001) 141–59. On the role of reconstructed slang in Byron's conversable simulacrum of orality, see Bernard Beatty, *Byron's Don Juan* (London and Sydney: Croom Helm, 1985) 43–47. For Bennett, *Romantic Poets and the Culture of Posterity* (Cambridge: Cambridge University Press, 1999), Byron's unique celebrity let him subject the Romantic vanguard's fiction of deferred recognition—the ideological consolation we find at the heart of Shelley's *Revolt of Islam*—to radical if ambivalent critique: "any attempt to shore up meaning against the ruins of time is subject to the catachresis of others' citation, or more generally to the scandal of the unpredictability and arbitrariness of reading itself" (196). Byron's repertoire of genre-specific styles, McGann suggests, was devised in recognition of this modern scandal (*Context*, 76–86).

[50] George M. Ridenour, *The Style of Don Juan* (1960; rpt. New Haven: Archon, 1969) 69–73, shows the poem repeatedly establishing its postwar status in a literal, diegetic sense: the narrative does not build towards epic strife but recedes from it—not least in the anticlimactic, glamour-aversive siege of Ismail (cantos 7–8). What the narrative receded into, by a default typical of the period this chapter has studied, was *style*. Thus for Wilkie, 225, Byron's heroism in *Don Juan* is "one specific *style* of action rather than the *substance* of a code of values."

decade later, a malaise widely enough shared within the reading public to constitute a peculiarly modern sort of common denominator. If Marmion's dark secret had inspired the Byronic hero of the oriental tales, *Don Juan* in effect published the dark secret of *Marmion* itself.[51]

Erecting on such a peculiarly modern basis "an epic as much in the spirit of our day as the Iliad was in Homer's" demanded measures no less peculiarly modern, including the invalidation of many of the traditional ones.[52] "My poem's epic, and is meant to be | Divided"—and the double-take whereby this enjambed disclosure equivocates being with meaning, and purpose with execution, warns us how much faith, and how little, to vest in the double-negative claim that caps its stanza: "So that my name of Epic's no misnomer." We do eventually get, just as the first canto has contracted to supply them, "Love, and War, a heavy gale at sea," all circumstantially rendered with rare, unsparing frankness. If the poet reneges on his promise of "new mythological machinery, | And very handsome supernatural scenery," these shortfalls turn out to be part of the cost of doing business under the new management of a spanking new realism. The principle that, in every respect but historical literality, "this story's actually true" compensates the loss of the supernatural with "A panoramic view of Hell" on earth—situated, unmistakably, in shipwreck and warfare, but also and more subtly to be found, like Byron's true but evanescent Heaven, in the exigent and always social orbit of human relations (1.200–02).

Likewise, epic's reputation for mapping the world and epitomizing its history is one that Byron may be suspected of struggling to live up to or, with the maturation of his runaway picaro, grow into; but this expectation *Don Juan* in practice faithfully disappoints, with a view to overhauling it.

---

[51] "A Cambrian Colloquy on the Decline and Fall of Poetry" in *Fraser's Magazine* for December 1834, attributed to Joseph Downes, looks back two decades to the way Byron put paid first to "the mock-chivalry school,—the ballad-epic," and then (presumably via *Don Juan*) to his own "head-quarters of pirates, murderers, and moping gentlemen" (651). Michael G. Cooke, *The Blind Man Traces the Circle: On the Patterns and Philosophy of Byron's Poetry* (Princeton: Princeton University Press, 1969), declares "the whole of *Don Juan* a multiform statement of obligatory irresolution ... but not without the most inveterate probing of reputed paths to resolution" (132), paced out with the design "to put us through the actual experience of objective disorganization and incongruity" (147).

[52] Quoted from Thomas Medwin's *Journal of the Conversations of Lord Byron* (London: Colburn, 1824) 164. On the same occasion the poet went nimbly on: "Poor Juan shall be guillotined in the French Revolution! What do you think of my plot? It shall have twenty-four books too, the legitimate number. Episodes it has, and will have, out of number; and my spirits, good or bad, must serve for the machinery. If that be not an epic, if it be not strictly according to Aristotle, I don't know what an epic poem means" (166).

True, the action acquires a more than Virgilian range with Juan's migration from Spain throughout the Mediterranean to Russia and England, in carriage and on shipboard, across the gender line and back again, downscale to slavery and foot-soldiering, upscale to the favors of amorous sultana, empress-tsar, and duchess. Yet the more epical the theater of action, in siege or shipwreck or *belle assemblée*, the less investment the writing evinces in such effects of accumulation and symbolic enlargement as were routine within the genre, even in the rote performances of Byron's dedicatee Southey, the epoist he loved to hate. The best-told stories in *Don Juan* come from the first half and antedate its flirtation with becoming a grand post-Napoleonic conspectus of the crowding of European history towards the watershed of 1790 or so, when the Revolution was in infancy and the poet was too. This momentarily plausible project disappeared from Byron's agenda as his poem matured in the novelistic direction from which Pushkin was to take his cue in *Evgeny Onegin*: the later cantos' most memorable scenes take place at table or in chambers (boudoirs wherever possible); in private or domestic space, not the halls and fields of epic.

The gravitation of *Don Juan* towards intimate dyadic exchange, and within such exchange towards its essence in erotic intimacy, enforces a truth about which Byron rejoices to concur with that earlier sexual reductionist Erasmus Darwin (Ch. 2). The more exotically our outward-bound tale shifts locale, the more what really counts turns out to be the same homely, arousing, unruly, indispensable thing: "that great Cause of war, or peace, or what | You please (it causes all the things which be)" (9.57).[53] Within this poem so enamored of "Fact!" as such, narrative pride of place goes to the facts of life, promoted out of the romance repertoire into an epic prominence. What makes the *Don Juan* world go round is love, or something that passes for love, or that must go by that name pending a better one.

---

[53] Beatty's running remarks on sexual narratology suggest how peculiar an epic feature the seduction/reduction of *Don Juan* is. A seduction scene forms "the culmination of each section in the poem which, once clearly attained or unattained, involves a break in time" (32). Because "sexual life is inherently repetitive" and "the old game will in time seem a new one" (94)—remaining, i.e., the same old game all the while—"the major episodes of *Don Juan*... are, as it were, renewed immediately from the same starting point" after each seduction has blanked the former narrative out, a process that "cannot in itself reach any terminus" (124). Thus the privilege Byron accords to human life's fundamental fact makes his poem a foundation epic without dynastic issue—but by the same token, as Peter J. Manning shows in examining this same sexual-narrative complex, the focus of a perpetual renewal, as "the poem advances by negating the obsessions to which it returns, and then moving on, again and again": "*Don Juan* and Byron's Imperceptiveness to the English Word" (1979), rpt. in *Reading Romantics: Text and Context* (New York: Oxford University Press, 1990) 136.

And the intimacy thus thematized in the plot represents, in turn, the richest and freshest intimacy in the poem, which is the way raconteur and reader cozy up to each other. The deeply original story of *Don Juan* is the one for which the escapades of Byron's eponymous naïf serve as both a pretext and, within the poem's episodic drift, an exemplification of digressiveness writ large. This story is the one lying right on the surface: the strife and quest of the poem's telling; the rally of joke, confession, and teasing that performs not deeds but attitudes.[54] This story involves not indicative reference to what once was but interpellative conference right now, through a process not merely private either but shared, flexible, and under constant negotiation between two minds: the *chaise-longue* poet's, enthroned in the open air; and the reader's whom he flatters into attendance and convinces of the present reality of fellowship both with him and with a company of the like-minded, variably convened in modern literature's unchartered, inviolable space.[55]

According to the culturalist theory of epic in place when Byron was born (Ch. 1), the genre involved its audience by purporting to rehearse a story from the past that remained their story now. Scott and Moore erected this premise into a structural principle, with narratives so centered on the site of performance as in effect to invoke the reading (and purchasing) public as their muse. With *Don Juan* the performative principle completed its Regency migration from structure to texture. Here the involvement-by-flirtation never stops, the momentum never subsides into shape; or rather the working sense of shape is patterned not on architecture but on dance, Byron leading all right but going nowhere unless we follow—which is to say, unless like a worthy partner we anticipate, collaborate, correct, and recover along with him. If these be truisms of all communication, they were never so nakedly (shockingly) exposed as in Byron's epic, which again is epic in proportion as it puts to proof, within a genuine sense of national crisis, the communicative resources of English in the early nineteenth century, and as it stages those

[54] On the homology of digression with episode see McGann, *Context*, 100–07. Charles Eric Reeves, "Continual Seduction: The Reading of *Don Juan*," *Studies in Romanticism* 17 (1978) 453–63, posits as the poem's main principle of coherence the now seductive, now antagonistic affair between poet and reader—a complicitous process analyzed further by William H. Galperin in *The Return of the Visible in British Romanticism* (Baltimore and London: Johns Hopkins University Press, 1993) 275–78. On seduction both within the text and by it see Moyra Haslett, *Byron's* Don Juan *and the Don Juan Legend* (Oxford: Clarendon Press, 1997).
[55] Jane Stabler, *Byron, Poetics and History* (Cambridge: Cambridge University Press, 2002), connects Byron's "digressive contingency" with the dialectical "experience of contemporaneousness and historical difference" that it engenders in the reader (9).

resources at maximum visibility. To recognize the figure we conspiratorially tread with the poet as an act of love is to surprise the poem in its most consistently affirmative aspect.

The proving ground, dance floor, and negotiating table of *Don Juan* is the *ottava rima* stanza. Writing in rhyme-rich Italian, robust Ariosto and devout Tasso had between them spread out a spectrum of tonal possibilities, which the comparative poverty of rhyme in English reined back in, with a deliberate and salutary awkwardness.[56] Finding three pairs of like endings, stanza after challenged stanza in a work of any length, became enough of a stunt to attract notice and usually raise a laugh, which the concluding couplet might then pivot on and clinch. This was the point of the thoroughly mock-epic *Prospectus and Specimen of an Intended National Work* that John Hookham Frere published in 1817, under the name of the Brothers Whistlecraft, on preposterous Arthurian premises and with a satirical eye to "Madoc and Marmion" (1.8) as well as to the reams of pompous, hasty, or abortive epic verse that had littered the Romantic landscape. Enchanted by the liberties Frere took within the *ottava rima* form, and tickled to find *in* the market such a satire *on* the market, Byron took measures to retrace the steps of "Whistlecraft" through mock-epic's ordeal-by-laughter into the real thing.[57] He made of the stanza's very arbitrariness and implausibility a figure for modern civilization and its discontents, for the ambivalence with which thinking persons—a poet and a reader, say—might agree to regard the cultural fashions that have fashioned them, constraining the

---

[56] Hugh Blair, *Lectures on Rhetoric and Belles-Lettres* (1783; ed. and rpt. in 2 vols., Harold F. Harding, Carbondale and Edwardsville: Southern Illinois University Press, 1965), was reacting to the *Orlando Furioso* before Byron was born in terms that anticipate reactions to *Don Juan* ever since his death: Ariosto "despised all regularity of plan," yet "there is so much epic matter in the Orlando Furioso," and "it unites all sorts of poetry." Ariosto "is always master of his subject; seems to play himself with it; and leave us sometimes at a loss to know whether he be serious or in jest" (2: 199).

[57] Against a generic purism like John Lauber's in *"Don Juan* as Anti-Epic," *Studies in English Literature* 8 (1968) 607–19, the poem's enterprising graft of satire onto epic has become a regular theme in criticism. See Ridenour, *Style*, 14–18; Alvin B. Kernan, *The Plot of Satire* (New Haven: Yale University Press, 1965); Arthur David Kahn, "Byron's *Single Difference* with Homer and Virgil: The Redefinition of the Epic in *Don Juan*," *Arcadia* 5 (1970) 143–62; Donald H. Reiman, *"Don Juan* in Epic Context," *Studies in Romanticism* 16 (1977) 587–94. Frederick Garber, "Irony and Organicism: Origin and Textuality," *Essays in Literature* 10:2 (1983) 282 argues that the encyclopedic quality of Byron's irony makes the poem "a meta-discourse, a global discourse," and finally, in terms congenial to epic, "an encompassing text." Manning's summary is apt: "The comprehensiveness of *Don Juan* and the much debated question of its status as epic are subjects that can be reformulated in terms of the inclusiveness of the response it figures but does not restrict"— except in acknowledging the restrictions imposed by the repertory of cultural roles that may be in play at any moment (*"Don Juan* and Byron's Imperceptiveness," 140).

modern heart and mind but also providing, within measure, the means to set them free.[58]

At just the time when Scott, Austen and other novelists were paving the high road of bourgeois realism, Byron pointed verse narrative away from illusionistic, representational structure toward self-conscious, presentational texture; and his index was the subversively exposed contingency of rhyme. No reader can be so indefatigably heroic as to ride each stanza with the poet, scouting the second *a* and *b* rhymes as they rise, then guessing at the third, and surfing the couplet as it breaks to start the process afresh. But every reader does some of this, at some level of awareness, some of the time: if Byron's showy duple and treble rhymes don't turn the trick, then his explicit references to rhyming must, as indeed may any of his numberless auto-referential glances at genre, at narrativity, at the mounting census of stanzas themselves. "The coast—I think it was the coast that I | Was just describing—yes, it was the coast" (2.1441–42): no matter how properly the ensuing rhymes with "I" and "coast" behave themselves, the damage to referentiality is already deftly done, through the proleptically tripled iteration of those two words in these two unobtrusively musical lines—as well, of course, as through an ostentatious extroversion of the ordinarily secreted scene of composition, the mysterious place that poems come from.[59]

"But to my subject—let me see—what was it? | Oh—the third canto and the pretty pair" (3.645–46): pivoting here from a gratuitous slap at "turncoat" Southey to the idyll of Juan and Haidée, Byron's fit of absent-mindedness seems to license a belief that we are assisting at the birth of the poem, on the hallowed ground-zero of spontaneous creativity from which even a storytelling commitment to "subject" constitutes a kind of fallen digression. But this belief too proves to be a piece of Romantic claptrap. Byron invalidated the spontaneity license in advance, we see, by laying down the law of two foregoing rhymes apiece for "was it" and "pair," which occur in the fifth

---

[58] An improvisation within fixed limits, the form of the stanza rehearses what Kroeber names as Byron's overall achievement during the five-year evolution of the poem: supple narrative rendition of "his consciousnesss of the individual's double role—that of a free agent and that of a creature conditioned by the shifting pressures of his society" (*Romantic Narrative Art*, 165). Andrew Franta reads *Don Juan* as a consistent appeal to the former role against the latter, as a false consciousness grown peculiarly insidious under the regime of public opinion: *Romanticism and the Rise of the Mass Public* (Cambridge: Cambridge University Press, 2007) 48–53. See also Keach, 46–67 *et passim*.

[59] Frederick Garber, *Self, Text, and Romantic Irony: The Example of Byron* (Princeton: Princeton University Press, 1988) 202–8, reads the opening of *Don Juan* as a debut performance of its thematics of origination.

and sixth lines of their stanza yet must have come first in the order of composition and thus preconcerted the set-up of lines 1–4. The illusion that we are eavesdropping on a great improviser (thus 15.20) is punctured by a stanza thus formally provisioned, and so is the yet more seductive illusion that we have caught him at a rare lapse into wool-gathering.[60] The residually nostalgic orality of *The Lay of the Last Minstrel* or *Lay of Marie* is preemptively proscribed because literally pre-scribed; the exigent formal fixity of the stanza has been calling the tune all along, and right before our eyes. Byron's epic tactics of reader-involvement have allured us into the modern recognition that we find ourselves in print.

So we can take a turn with Lord Byron—if we decline, then we can hardly read his poem—but he will not let us forget for long that the jazz we spin to is a record however lively, and the record of a premeditated composition at that. Collaboration with this epic exacts renunciation of the bardolatrous indulgence in synthetic *viva voce* that most Romantic epics offered readers in compensation for the alienating damages of modernity and the opportunistic anonymity of publication. Byron's stanza rushed him into print and kept him there, in the thick of a media glut whose debasement of language threatened to blunt the very instruments that might diagnose and check it. "I will war at least in words," runs the poet's evolving motto, "with all who war | With thought" (9.185–86). His choice of weapon for this one-man stand is modern English, a field of force whose gravitation draws *Don Juan* inexorably in its latest cantos to modern England—which has been the poem's foregone venue all along (as the stinging dedicatory challenge to a sitting Laureate has disclosed), in a *bona fide* if unexpected rewrite of the early century's nationalist charter for epic poetry.[61]

---

[60] On Byron's interest in the *improvisatore* tradition see McGann, *Fiery Dust*, 279–82; also Edwin Morgan, "Voice, Tone, and Transition in *Don Juan*," in *Byron: Wrath and Rhyme*, ed. Alan Bold (London: Vision, 1983) 63–64. Zachary Leader, *Revision and Romantic Authorship* (Oxford: Clarendon Press, 1996) 78–120, draws out the provisional character of Byron's rewritings, in principle and practice. Reiman, "*Don Juan*," 588–91, finds in the poem's kaleidoscopic foregroundedness a modern resumption of the mode of naïve or primary epic, poised like Homer's in retrospect across the passing of an order (here, that of the Lockean Enlightenment); see also Kahn, "Byron's *Single Difference*," 159–62, for discussion of this rearguard aspect of the poem.

[61] According to Graham, *Don Juan and Regency England* (Charlottesville and London: University of Virginia Press, 1990), Byron's epic "is always about England—and never more so than when at its most exotic," and his English "the language of a seafaring commercial culture, one prone to import things—but also an island culture, one that transforms and domesticates them" (4–5). "In his own way," says Wilkie, "Byron was trying to be doctrinal to a nation" (*Romantic Poets*, 211).

The declaration of word war just quoted comes on the heels of two cantos subjecting martial glory to ruthless scrutiny, on precisely the grounds that modern war, while fed with real flesh and blood, is won or lost on paper, in irrelevant strategics beforehand and then afterwards in impertinent, glory-mongering reportage and swollen gazettes of the dead. Society in peacetime is likewise a paper edifice upheld by newspapers, receipts, letters, dispatches, pulp epics, tinder reviews, in short by *cant*, the poem's first rhyme word and its most pronounced antagonist. As the discursive bribery greasing the wheels of society, cant has its uses, not least for a brand of comic satire whose ironic techniques of doublespeak it so closely resembles.[62] Cant rises into an epic theme, however, once it is seen to pollute the public sphere by clouding the issues and obscuring the general discernment; when it circulates so generally that, whether actually believed or not, habitual usage makes it functionally equivalent to the truth. *Don Juan* is the epic for an age of bullshit.

More than once Byron's war in words between love and cant, authenticity and simulation, comes to focus in a favorite rhyme—*passion* with *fashion*—which he handles so as to stress not opposition between the terms but their disturbing continuity with each another. The point is one that pierces to the essence of Byronism: "Thus to their extreme verge the passions brought | Dash into poetry, which is but passion, | Or at least was so ere it grew a fashion" (4.846–48). The literary-historical truism that firebrands of poetry, such as were flourished by Childe Harold or the Corsair, smolder out in conventionality is shadowed by a more troubling suggestion: passion as we know it grows not old but outmoded, because, popularized by such poetry as Byron's, it has obeyed the mode from the start. In the England of *Don Juan* this eventuality is particularly likely, since with the advance of polite society what everybody is supposed to think has usurped directness of feeling altogether, and on Juan's arrival there "He found himself extremely in the fashion, | Which serves our thinking people for a passion" (11.263–64). Should a British lady take Juan up as "a *grande passion*," moreover, "Nine times in ten 'tis but caprice or fashion, | Coquetry" (12.611–12). Why a French *grande passion* here, and not the perfectly eligible English "grand passion"? Byron is fond of macaronic translingualism—Spanish, Greek, Russian, Latin, Italian all play cameo roles here or there in his rhymes—and here the practice flushes out, with a little help from the Frenchy words

---

[62] Garber, "Irony and Organism," 271–90, draws out the duplicitous texture, and suggests the political stakes, of this resemblance between Byron's weapon and his target.

caprice and *coquetry* on either side, the fact that English *fashion* is a foreign derivative even in terms of sheer etymology.[63]

Pronounce the stanza in question? You can't unless you cant. To try speaking the lines aloud without traducing French, or English, or the rhyme, is to execute in paradigm the circuitry that marks *Don Juan* as a tertiary epic both flaunting and discounting its pseudo-chattiness. That circuitry runs from the stanza read on the page through the inner ear of a virtual (which is to say, an impossible) orality and thence into the unvoiced provocation of thought, whose domain proves to be print after all, the medium in which Byron circa 1820 found a culture of automatism and fashionable sham prolif- erating as never before. The problem is already with us in the poem's very first stanza, especially in our time when a reader is so much likelier to speak Spanish than when Byron published it. To make the *b* rhyme work, we have to read "Juan" on its first appearance to chime with "new one" and "true one," or in other words to perform an aurally-policed reconstruction of an alphabetically- driven phonetic mispronunciation of our hero's, and poem's, name. *Difficile est*, indeed. "Were things but only called by their right name" (14.815)!

They never are, alas, not even in *Don Juan*. In order to rectify the tongue the poet must write his own calling in a nomenclature no sooner trusted than gone wrong. "Ne'er doubt | This: when I speak, I don't hint, I speak out" (11.703-4). Can there be a more dubious moment in the entire poem than this precariously enjambed impersonation of prophetic forthspeaking? How speak out, when in the words immediately preceding "every scribe in some slight turn of diction | Will hint allusions never meant"? Byron's way of speaking out lay through that slight scribal "turn of diction," which twisted a perverted language against itself and diverted verse into allusion, aside, and backtalk. His epic part was to ventriloquize in the always slightly tinny echo chamber of his stanza the voices of old tradition and new argot, supine accommodation and, yes, bluff plain-dealing too, in an accent not their own but near enough to prompt doubt whether they should ever be anyone's again. "It is the sublime of *that there* sort of writing," he crowed after the unstoppable tide of stanzas was aflow in 1819; "it may be bawdy but is it not good English? It may be profligate but is it not *life*, is it not *the thing*?"[64] A vandal patriot in exile, Byron alienated English from

---

[63] On Byron's polyglossia see Manning, *Byron and His Fictions* (Detroit: Wayne State University Press, 1978) 238-40.

[64] Letter of 26 October 1819 to Douglas Kinnaird, in *Letters and Journals*, ed. Marchand 6 (1976) 232.

itself, made a medium of exchange into a medium of art, in order that it might be seen and not believed. Rearranging the language from within, dislocating and redisplaying it on the foreign framework of the *ottava rima*, he fought jargon with slang, cant with graffiti, and the mechanization of discourse with the semi-automatic extemporization of those serendipitous, secret-sharer rhymes.

6

To the Ending Doom:

Epic Apocalypse 1820–1830

The inside job Lord Byron did on the operating system that supported Don Juan's story was an epic job, all right, but a drastic one that held far-reaching consequences for its genre. Byron's scandalous persistence in it unto death, gauntlet flung down and scabbard discarded, cost him whole sectors of the genteel following he had attracted a decade before. At the same time and by the same token, it earned him a second massive readership among the working classes and the international avant-garde.[1] If this crowning effort of the most epically active period in English literature was not quite a prolegomenon to all future epics, for decades its abashing example continued to daunt any poet for whom an enlarged comprehension of the human prospect included even a modest quantum of skeptical diffidence or bemused resignation. Nor were such queasy side-effects of modernity rarer after the Regency than before: the slow fissuring of the national polity in the years between Peterloo and the First Reform Bill overlay, and to minds anxiously attuned bespoke, profound tremors within the cultural (and biblical) bedrock, such as would be coolly expounded at decade's end in Charles Lyell's epochal *Principles of Geology*. Attitudinizing in the void, Byron's pyrotechnically anti-heroic monologue of an epic told on readers as it did precisely because it acknowledged,

---

[1] See the figures, tables, and discussion in William St. Clair, "The Impact of Byron's Writings: An Evaluative Approach," in *Byron: Augustan and Romantic*, ed. Andrew Rutherford (New York: St. Martin's Press, 1990) 1–25; an extended context for these is established in his remarkable book *The Reading Nation in the Romantic Period* (Cambridge: Cambridge University Press, 2004). See also Keith Walker *Byron's Readers : A Study of Attitudes towards Byron, 1812–1832* (Salzburg: Universität Salzburg, 1979).

installment by increasingly explicit installment, a cultural malaise that was widely shared.[2]

What was imitable in the Byronic effect showed itself soon across a range of Ovidian epyllia by more or less free-spirited contemporaries for whom to epicize after Byron was to pose in the metaphysical nude. These works included George Croly's steamy *The Angel of the World: An Arabian Tale* (1820) and knowing *May Fair: In Four Cantos* (1827); Moore's liberal-hearted *The Loves of the Angels: A Poem* (1823); and, most originally, Letitia Landon's *The Improvisatrice* (1824) and *The Troubadour* (1825), where nihilism and sentiment vie at tempting the reader into the wrongs that the narrative, such as it is, complains of. Hogg's *Queen Hynde: A Poem, in Six Books* (1825), while its badinage was as ham-fisted as Byron's was deft, remains an "epic song" (5.351) noteworthy for the way it grafted reader-flirtatiousness onto the stalk of narrative, along with nervously jokey citation of the heroic tradition (including Ossian and at least a smattering of Gaelic). Hogg had cultivated this hybrid with an epic mind as early as 1817, then broke the business off after a couple of books. By the time he resumed his manuscript in 1824, *Don Juan* had so reconfigured the literary field that Hogg found it impossible to proceed to any tune besides the knowingly "uncouth Harp" (6.361) of outright mock-heroics. That subgenre offered the only way now for even a man of the literary demi-monde like Hogg to make his earnestly meant patriotic fantasy of a sixth-century Highlands Camelot tell; and he embodied its burly "elemental energies" (1.54) in the poem's best and most joco-serious invention, the arch royal-impersonator Lady Wene.[3] Beyond ephemeral 1820s contemporaries like these, the mention of such diverse and distinguished apostles as Pushkin and Heine abroad, and in years to come the Brownings and Clough and Hardy at home, will suggest what reaches of space, time, and creative temperament *Don Juan*

---

[2] George M. Ridenour's considered response in *The Style of* Don Juan (1960; rpt. New Haven: Archon, 1969) articulates what appears to have been the tenor of thoughtful literary response to Byron's epic c.1820: "a beautiful, exciting, touching, and rather terrifying vision of a personal and cultural dead end" (xiii).

[3] Hogg's letter of 10 July 1824 to Southey fairly recapitulates the tone of the hasty endeavor it records: "I have no news but that I am just sending the last sheets of an *Epic Poem* to press!" Quoted in Suzanne Gilbert and Douglas S. Mack's edition of *Queen Hynde* (Edinburgh: Edinburgh University Press, 1998) 221. The editors' introduction documents sources, aims, and reception *in extenso*, giving particular attention to parallels with Scott and Byron. The most ambitious critical engagement with the poem as a national epic is Elaine D. Petrie's in "*Queen Hynde* and the Black Bull of Norroway," in *Papers Given at the Second James Hogg Society Conference*, ed. Gillian Hughes (Aberdeen: Association for Scottish Literary Studies, 1988) 128–43.

laid under its spell—laid, that is to say, under an obligation to admit irony into the epic chorus, give it teeth as well as voice, and so tell a more exactingly self-conscious tale than their poet precursors or novelist peers.

To this significant long-range influence we must in contrast enumerate a short-term effect that was downright contraceptive. There appeared as many epical English poems in the three years before the first cantos of *Don Juan* was published as there did in the ten years after it, and Byron, were laid to rest in 1824. (If we exclude the new subgenre of apocalypse towards which this chapter is headed, the ratio becomes much steeper.) All of a sudden, nobody wanted to be associated with the heroic name of a kind of poetry that for twenty years had been pouring from British presses. The reader who keeps track of such things will find more of the present chapter's poems than not subtitled merely "A Poem," while exactly one, and a pretty nondescript exemplar at that, calls itself "An Epic Poem." More than Lord Byron was involved in this generic retrenchment, of course. Chapter 5 speculated that, wartime having exaggerated the Romantic production of strife epics, during the aftermath of 1815 some abatement of demand was to be expected. Given the traditional slowness of epic germination, it makes sense that this abatement should have become most perceptible some time after 1820. It also bears reemphasis that the prodigious, still fully contemporary example of Scott diverted towards prose fiction some portion of what epic aspiration did remain. All these points conceded, in the long backward view it looks very much as though the Attic salt Byron sowed in the furrows of major verse narrative between 1819 and 1824 poisoned the territory for years.[4]

As has been said of a still greater epic summa, *Paradise Lost*, Byron's masterpiece seemed to have exhausted the genre, by confiscating the options in narrative verse for rendition of a representative modern consciousness. The bad Lord's ceaseless sniping at all pretenders to the epic throne was discouraging enough, but a stronger generic deterrent lay in the daunting example of his own madcap occupancy. The vividly personal influence he shed across Europe, and across the nineteenth century, suggests how in its own time and place the force of *Don Juan* must have astonished— struck dumb—those poets who could best appreciate how fundamentally it

---

[4] It poisoned the very well itself had drawn from, "Whistlecraft" Frere's 1817 adaptation of Pulci's quattocento mock-epicry in the *Morgante Maggiore*. By the 1840s Frere was explaining that *Don Juan* had put further installments of his own poem out of the question: see Anne Barton, *Byron:* Don Juan (Cambridge: Cambridge University Press, 1992) 23.

rewrote the rules of the art. When news broke of Byron's epochal death, and for decades thereafter, a stream of elegists, assailants, and assorted poseurs went after his celebrity crown in sundry ways. But epic's way was not among them, something that the aggressive spoofing of young T. B. Macaulay's 1824 "Prophetic Account of a Grand National Epic Poem, to Be Entitled 'The Wellingtoniad,' and to Be Published A.D. 2824" aimed to establish.[5] With very few exceptions, the heroic poems which did appear in Britain during the early 1820s came from poets who were in one way or another removed from the literary mainstream. At a time when the world's most conspicuous author had made the arterial routes impassable by the usual agents (male poets at the top of their powers), marginal access to high-minded forms of national spokesmanship remained possible only for poets of lower profile: an aged man, a child, a woman.

Of this circumstance the aged man of the group, at least, was well aware. Richard Payne Knight was born in 1751, had made a name in arts and letters during the 1790s, and would die in Byron's year 1824. He was an old enough literary hand to know that *Alfred: A Romance in Rhyme* (1823) treated an overdone subject in an overworn style, the closed heroic couplet. But he was also too old to care and did not mind saying so. His preface craves indulgence for upholding a purer taste than today's epicizing whippersnappers and the "apish multitude" who applaud their unwholesome wares can remember, or gratify (xxv); the poetic narrative pauses to scold "noisy nonsense" for counterfeiting "The true sublime of genuine genius" (3.51). All that is worst about the age is epitomized in the (Byron-associated) figure of Napoleon, whose villainies preoccupy fully half of Knight's preface and the last ten pages of his visionary twelfth-book peroration. These accessories bring out more strongly than anything in Cottle, Pye, or Sympson the imminent-invasion allegory implied by their Alfred epics (Ch. 3), but which in 1823 come years too late, of course, to arouse more than a memory of alarm. Knight's coyly epic-disclaiming "romance" recalls congeners of a decade before even in its more more up-to-date features: the unusual authority that the plot gives

---

[5] *Knight's Quarterly Magazine* for November 1824. Samuel C. Chew, *Byron in England: His Fame and After-Fame* (1924; rpt. New York: Russell and Russell, 1965), remains a lively guide to the broken, crowded ground the Byron phenomenon left behind. See also Jay A. Ward, *The Critical Reputation of Byron's Don Juan in Britain* (Salzburg: Universität Salzburg, 1979). Good recent guides to this unique *Nachleben* are Andrew Elfenbein, *Byron and the Victorians* (Cambridge: Cambridge University Press, 1995), and Dino Felluga, *The Perversity of Poetry: Romantic Ideology and the Popular Male Poet of Genius* (Albany: State University of New York Press, 2005).

its unusually prominent women (cross-dressed now and then); and the Swedenborgian machinery of "Emanations" whose principal task is to enforce the laws of history by blunting innovation and supporting "The general unity of order's reign" (2.44). Insulated as in a time capsule from the winds of change, Knight's *Alfred* matters to literary history as evidence that only so stiff-necked a throwback could survive the inhospitable climate that had set in since the period to which the poem belonged in everything but publication date.

What callous defiance accomplished at 70, callow ignorance might do at 14. Elizabeth Barrett Barrett would become one of the canniest Victorian epoists, in part because the amazingly early start given her career in the privately published two-book *Battle of Marathon: A Poem* (1820) got so much undefended naïveté out of her system so fast.[6] The 14-year-old author sustained her timely exercise in Greek nationalism as a creditable imitation of Homer's most Popean manner, that eighteenth-century style whose unreconstructed timbre must have rung most true to the proud father who funded the private printing of its fifty copies. A plucky preface established further epic credentials, apologizing for the use of machinery that Glover had found superfluous when handling a like topic in *Leonidas* almost a century before, but finding warrant in Homer and Virgil nonetheless. One suspects a covert analogy between Barrett's long poetic odds and those that Athens beats in the story ("one little city rising undaunted, and daring her innumerable enemies," crows the preface), and suspicion strengthens as the narrative opens on Aristides' rebuffing the imputation that he is a mere boy not to be listened to. Rejoining in the accents of Southey's youthful Joan that he is directly, divinely inspired—the same claim Aurora Leigh will lodge forty years later, albeit through the lusher and thornier hedge awaiting us in Chapter 9—Aristides inspires instantaneous conviction in his elders and acquires enough civic authority to be waxing indignant before long that a Persian herald should dare "T' insult experienced age, t' insult a Greek!'" (1.207).

The implied equation here between growing up and standing tall in the boots of nationalism likewise rules the tight coil of five cantos that Sibella Elizabeth Hatfield published at 25 as *The Wanderer of Scandinavia, or Sweden*

---

[6] This poem in two books has a way of growing on its admirers, literally. Simon Avery and Rebecca Stott, in *Elizabeth Barrett Browning* (London: Longman, 2003) 45, describe *The Battle of Marathon* as a four-book epic, while Margaret Reynolds, taking the epicizing wish for the deed in her edition of *Aurora Leigh* (New York: Norton, 1996), logs *The Battle* in at a hefty twelve (558).

Delivered (1826), Britain's fullest treatment of the matter of Gustavus Vasa that Wordsworth had floated as an epic option in lines 1.211–12 of the unpublished *Prelude* (Ch. 3) and William Walker briefly exercised in 1813 (Ch. 4). Hatfield fortifies her two-volume "lay" (5.103) against the romance divagation portended in its title, as also in its Scott-inspired tetrameters, by the unerring affective discipline of a hero whose patriotic passion may mature but "wanders never" (2.94). The Gothic romance of an exile's escape in canto 1, and then the domestic romance of puppy love in canto 2, ripen across two more cantos of Scandinavian travelogue into a love of country that sublimates the lesser loves of person and landscape. These psychic preliminaries established, a final canto nearly as long as all the first four together explodes, with considerable structural address, into an epic of national liberation. Reduced by his associates' treason and theft to toiling in Dalecarlia's mines alongside the Dane-oppressed peasantry, Gustavus finds his true political base there, deep in the womb of the land. He raises up from scratch an army whose victories lead across seven subtitled "Contests" and the ritual space of four seasons, through single combat and pitched battles involving battalions and fleets, until his coronation signals a resurgent nation's protestant freedom from priest-ridden imperial occupation. The price such triumph exacts is incessant recruitment to patriotic ends of the hero's every feeling—for his sweetheart, old friends and retainers, and last of all the high-minded mother who, having schooled her son in nationalist self-denial, returns to liberated Sweden only to swoon dead in his arms (5.162, 311).

"My heart must now my country's be │...│ My country I am wholly thine!" (3.171): here speaks, in Gustavus, an eighteenth-century man of feeling bound and determined by the hoop of a Napoleonic-era iron crown. The radical, and historically unfashionable, simplification of motive and affect performed by Hatfield's poem spreads out at greater narrative length the same conscription of emotion that was mandated in Elizabeth Barrett's violent brace of episodes. There the fantastic zeal with which matrons vie in offering their babies up to war (1.746), and the derisive attribution of the Persians' defeat to their effeminacy (2.987), could hardly have sprung from a more filially masculine teenage imagination. But *The Battle of Marathon* discloses a representative and not just a biographical interest when we find something like its falsetto toughness in contemporaneous work—not just by the inexperienced Hatfield, but by one of the most seasoned and capable women poets of the Romantic era.

Joanna Baillie's *Metrical Legends of Exalted Characters* (1821) showcased, with "William Wallace" and "Christopher Columbus," mid-length epyllia that, in contrast to Baillie's confidently accomplished dramatic work of twenty years before in *A Series of Plays* (1798), cleave with a beginner's fastidiousness to the straitened path of stepwise narration. Equally single-minded in his march to greatness, each of Baillie's heroes whether inspired or balked evinces an impatience to get on with it that should perhaps be imputed to the poet. "For the fierce tumult in his breast | To speedy, dreadful action press'd" ("Wallace" 22.292–93): to recall the richly inward purposes to which Scott's *Marmion*, and then in its wake the tales of Byron, put such "fierce tumult" is to appreciate how thoroughly *Metrical Legends* surrenders, Gustavus-like, to the one destiny of plot. Each Baillie hero is also dutifully soldered into a collectivity whose "thrilling sympathy" ("Wallace" 39.507) or "grand choral burst" ("Columbus" 27.524) supersedes all lesser human bonds; each is correspondingly frustrated by the villainy of merely personal motives that seduce others but to which real heroism is deaf. This morality Baillie underscores by having Columbus transgress it in just one particular. Her paragon's collusion in the *Realpolitik* of New World slavery, litmus test that this issue was for the anglophone liberal mind circa 1820, constitutes a defection from his own heroic truth: "For who may stern ambition serve, and still | His nobler nature trust?" (34.635–36).

Who indeed? Hatfield's Gustavus, Barrett's Aristides, that's who; and behind them the stick-figure heroic paragons of neoclassical epic at its least creative. But who else? Such a question might have furnished with its point of moral origin an epic action of some subtlety, and so it arguably would have done in one of Baillie's dramas from 1798. That by 1821 she should have found it necessary to shrink the ambit of her own imagining to so narrow and high a course of legendary fidelity says much about the shift in literary culture with which this chapter must cope. "Stern ambition" and "nobler nature" having been set at loggerheads by *Don Juan*, even a well-established poet's ambition to write epic now had to scramble in self-justification. Versions of Scott's "Breathes there the man . . ." topos from *Marmion* begin the legend of Wallace (1.2) and frame that of Columbus (1.1, 62.997), in an apologetic progression that snatches at patriotism, then creaturely piety, then assurances—inviting scorn in the wake of *The Excursion*—to the effect that such conventionally heroic examples matter because they prove the immortality of the soul. The sequence of Baillie's scavenger hunt for an heroic rationale leads, ominously, towards the eschatological motive that would dominate new epic during the decade ahead.

Thus Joanna Baillie, exemplifying at 60 a generic second childhood as strictly regimented as the epic's first Romantic youth in the 1790s had been effusively inventive, stands comparison with the actual child Elizabeth Barrett. To be sure, Barrett's aspiration to an epic virtue would over the years vanish but not perish; having disobeyed among other bans the one her father placed on reading *Don Juan,* she would form the project of emulating that men's poem on women's terms, and would carry it off too. But the undisguised innocence of her maiden effort and Hatfield's—recouped as it were in the chastened "legend lay" of a Baillie who not only knew her epic predecessors (Holford on Wallace, Barlow and Rogers on Columbus turn up in her notes) but also understood how the vandal Byron had just shredded the rules—shows what Payne Knight's septuagenarian truculence also showed: how wide a quietness reigned circa 1820 at the cultural center epic had used to frequent.

Another point for surveying the altered scene presents itself in Eleanor Porden, who was ten years Barrett's senior, which is to say at the turn of the decade still a quite young woman. This fiancée of the arctic explorer John Franklin had published in her teens a young lady's verse novel we glanced at in Chapter 4, and she came again before the public in 1822 at sixteen-book gauge with *Coeur de Lion; or The Third Crusade: A Poem.* Here was a full-dress couplet epic of major ambition, exhibiting over a hundred pages of notes, a long and intelligent prefatory discourse on the Crusades, and a broad political outlook to match.[7] Although a much better poem than Burges's on the same topic from the turn of the century, Porden's was still a poem of the same stripe as his, deeply rooted in patriotism from its dedicatory ode to George IV through its adoringly maintained idealization of Richard I. In a new and welcome twist, Porden represents her hero as the English monarch who during the Christian Middle Ages had most embodied a cosmopolitan European spirit.

Coeur de Lion looks better still beside the preposterous *Waterloo: A Poem in Two Parts* that Harriet Cope published in the same year, advertising it as her "warlike offspring" even "if it be not entitled to the appellation of a regular epic poem" (i). The dizzily repetitive rhyme scheme of *abaaab* sixains was a choice that *Don Juan* alone, had the warlike author but glimpsed into a

---

[7] Adeline Johns-Putra, *Heroes and Housewives: Women's Epic Poetry and Domestic Ideology in the Romantic Age, 1770–1835* (Bern: Peter Lang, 2001), traces the extent of Porden's research (49) but overemphasizes the conservatism of her ideology (79–82).

work so *risqué*, should have made unthinkable in a serious narrative at this time. Cope's fawning silver-fork epic spends on the martyrdom of the Bourbons as many awkward stanzas as on the battle itself, which, redressing that royal indignity, reduces in effect to anachronistic single combat bleached in the glare of aristocratic patriotism. The very hyperbole into which Cope is repeatedly betrayed when handling events her readers could easily verify or disconfirm, often from living memory, does at least give some foretaste of the extreme straits to which epic at this juncture was driven. Straitening came more naturally, and with a better grace, to Mary Anne Cursham's anonymously published *Martin Luther: A Poem* (1825), which invokes "Truth" as its muse in part 1, marches its heroic couplets along a lineal genealogy of truth-tellers from Socrates to Luther, and cleaves single-file in parts 2 and 3 to a one-way route through what amounts to a Protestant saint's life diversified by not a single vernacular (folksy, bodily) incident.

Porden, like Cope and Cursham in only this regard—wherein all three women, and young Elizabeth Barrett too, anticipate the apocalypticists to whom we presently turn—makes it her epic task to generalize historical incident in the direction of universal moral absolutism. Richard's foes are not really the Saracens, whom he and the poem treat respectfully, but instead the machinery of "hellish Genii" to whose goadings the Saracens are exposed through the misfortune of lacking the true faith. Porden takes lively interest in episodes of exchange and coexistence between Islamic and Christian cultures: vows of peace are sworn at the Holy Sepulcher in the last book; and when Richard has the torched city of Ascalon rebuilt in book 9, "gothic masses" and lighter "Ionian" mingle eclectically with "playful arabesque." Still, the murderous if unruffled ethnocentrism of the whole is ultimately secured by the good king's straight line to the one God (no machinery needed here), and by the one God's ordinance of a straight line of plotted triumph. As the fiend Moozallil confides to his fellows in an access of demonic candor, "RICHARD must triumph, and ye know he must" (6.850); at the close there is nothing for the final line to say of Richard but that "His task was ended, and his GOD approved" (16.1093). Thus in Porden's epic Barrett's youthful inspirationism embraced Knight's old-fashioned panoramic nationalism to engender a work that was well done, yet that by 1822 a reader of Moore and Byron should have been surprised to see done at all.

★

A more usual course for epicizing tales on secular themes during the genre-blasted 1820s was discreet withdrawal. Epic stepped back from the limelight into a territorial penumbra, typically retrenching the action to fit its own reduced circumstances. Plots often had to do with a remnant and marginalized people's aspiration for mere survival, on whatever compromised terms remained available in the aftermath of decimating conflict. Take for example *Elgiva, or the Monks: An Historical Poem* (1824) by Elizabeth Ham. As a close reading of the title may suggest, Ham's eighth-century England is big enough either for the free-spirited Anglo-Saxon heroine Elgiva, or for Saint Dunstan and his punitive monastic regime, but not for both. A sympathetic, nature-loving pagan culture is on the way out, a militantly regimented Christianity on the way in; and as befits such a tug of sympathies against realities, where history's gain is romance's loss and vice versa, Ham contrives for her four cantos a decent imitation of the tetrameter verseways of Walter Scott. Suborned, tortured, and finally martyred to the progress of faith, dauntless Elgiva dies with a curse on her lips that will haunt the sadistic (and Byronic) figure of the triumphant monk all his life. Indeed, in the very long run this Saxon maiden's denunciation of Rome will be vindicated by the Protestant England that is to come; but this is a prospect dimmed by the pathos to which Ham's narrative chiefly aspires.[8]

Felicia Hemans, the most characteristic poet of the decade, wrote no epic. Nevertheless, she made headway towards her trademark idylls of patriotic domesticity through two epicizing narratives; and these poems work more adroitly the thematics of retreat that we have seen in *Elgiva*. In each of the three heroic-couplet cantos of Hemans's *The Abencerrage* (1819), the Moorish protagonist Hamet wears a smaller political hat and occupies a more distinctly marginal position. Scion of the oppressed (and slant-eponymous) Aben-Zurrah clan during the final 1492 phase of the long Castilian reconquest of Spain, Hamet starts out as an insurgent partisan under Moorish rule; but then he becomes by turns a renegade warrior on the Christian side and, once the Moors are ousted, a bandit leader in the hills outside Granada. We see him first in arms within the Alhambra itself, then on the battlefield in a scene of literal aftermath, and at last permanently sidelined from the political process, caught up in a personal vendetta that, in a scene straight out of

---

[8] For Johns-Putra *Elgiva* typifies the premium placed by female epoists on "martyrdom and moral courage rather than physical and military bravery" (*Heroes and Housewives*, 144). The expiring heroine's prophetic word, we might add, brings out martyrdom's root sense of *witness* and so links the martyr epic to the epics of apocalypse that were contemporary with it.

Moore's "Fire-Worshippers" from *Lalla Rookh*, takes the life of his beloved Zayda, a prototype for Hemans's many self-sacrificing heroines to come.[9]

The change of venue from a vibrant to an empty Alhambra, and thence to the mere natural cavern that serves as sacrificial "temple" in canto 3, marks an epic-evasive trajectory that Hemans pursued further in *The Forest Sanctuary* (1825), a poem that holes up from heroism by traveling to the wilds of sixteenth-century North America. Here another Iberian exile, this one a functionally Protestant refugee from the Inquisition, tells his son the story of their transatlantic flight into the liberty of solitude. The earliest thing the nameless father can remember is the epic tone of martial balladry, "the old tuneful names of Spain's heroic race" (1.12). But the effect of beholding the *auto-da-fé* martyrdom of family and friends—described at pageant length in the poem's adapted Spenserians—is strictly limited to making first a Protestant convert of him and then a fugitive.[10] The point of the story he tells is to impart to his son a heritage of spiritual freedom which clearly, if oddly, entails freedom from interpersonal responsibility and thus *a fortiori* from political guilt.

In this Wordsworthian settlement of scores with world history Hemans's emigrant Spaniard resembles her outlawed Hamet in his claim that "A grief like mine might expiate all the past" (*Abencerrage* 3.478). Zayda's chiming deprecation "Oh! be his guilt forgotten in his woes" (*Abencerrage* 3.555) might well serve as motto to the highly successful poetic career that awaited Hemans shortly after the publication of these narrative poems. Their message is a far cry from both the Byronic refusal of expiation and the conversion of

[9] Gary Kelly, "Gender and Memory in Post-Revolutionary Women's Writing," in *Memory and Memorials, 1789–1914*, ed. Matthew Campbell, Jacqueline M. Labbe, and Sally Shuttleworth (London and New York: Routledge, 2000), finds Hemans looking in this work through "death, the figure for ultimate impasse," towards natural and cultural modes of commemoration reflecting her bardic self-conception as "repository and reproducer of national identity" (129–30). On the place of exile in Hemans, and of Hemans in a tradition of exilic writing that includes Scott, Southey, and Byron, see Nanora Sweet, "Gender and Modernity in *The Abencerrage*: Hemans, Rushdie, and 'The Moor's Last Sigh,' " in *Felicia Hemans: Reimagining Poetry in the Nineteenth Century* ed. Sweet and Julie Melnyk (Houndmills: Palgrave, 2001) 181–95.

[10] Anthony John Harding, "Felicia Hemans and the Effacement of Woman," in *Romantic Women Writers*, ed. Paula R. Feldman and Theresa M. Kelley (Hanover and London: University Press of New England, 1995) 145–46, observes a gender role-reversal where the female martyrs in Spain exhibit courage and the male narrator in America becomes a nurturer. On this theme see also Marlon B. Ross, *The Contours of Masculine Desire: Romanticism and the Rise of Women's Poetry* (New York: Oxford University Press, 1989) 294; and, with reference to Hemans' evacuation of native Americans as well as women from her *Sanctuary*, Nancy M. Goslee, "Hemans's 'Red Indians': Reading Stereotypes," in *Romanticism, Race, and Imperial Culture, 1780–1834*, ed. Alan Richardson and Sonia Hofkosh (Bloomington and Indianapolis: Indiana University Press, 1996) 242–44.

guilt into political capital in the verse narratives of Scott. The epic summons
to choral belonging and collective action has lost its former draw: it dwindles
right before our eyes across the three cantos of *The Abencerrage*, and it is
bespoken from the first in *The Forest Sanctuary* by a solo aria strictly elegiac in
kind.[11] The moral power of the politically stranded muse, in what Hemans
justifiably thought one of her best poems, inhabits a citadel of the sidelined
spirit. There echo usurps voice and all that remains of communal immediacy
is the Spanish Protestant's unmediated communing with his Bible and his
memories.

    We shall discover how loudly the 1820s project of reactivating epic's
suspended moral authority and collective force would call for apocalyptic
measures. Absent such measures, Hemans's narratives default to a condition
of sympathetic resignation, which we found among Elizabeth Ham's Saxons,
and which also at this juncture nurtured a brief efflorescence of the metrical
tale en route to becoming the full-blown verse novel.[12] An 1819 example
greets us in *Dunrie: A Poem* by Harriet Ewing. The motif of retreat dominates
this four-canto family saga, set in Languedoc during a lull in the late French
wars, near a tranquil convent whose name, La Paix, possesses an allegorical
force that the poet underlines by regular reference to spheres of war and
conquest. Those spheres—Ewing works in mention of Siberia and India
(3.144), with one especially villainous Arab (canto 4)—while they subsist
outside the plot, nevertheless furnish its motor power, as a brace of long-
absent fathers return to lay abrupt demands on their sheltered families that
lead, no less abruptly, to a happy ending. The blessing these traveled fathers
bestow on the first motions of their children's hearts corresponds, at some
level, to the way the poet encases her domestic tale in unchanging octosyl-
labic couplets, a verse measure much stricter than was normal during the
Regency heyday of Moore and Byron, Hunt and Keats. Indeed, the poem's
strongest taste of things to come lies in its insistent morality of control through

[11] John M. Anderson, "The Triumph of Voice in Felicia Hemans's *The Forest Sanctuary*," in
Sweet and Melnyk, *Felicia Hemans*, 56, discusses the role of choral motifs in "destabilizing
alternative approaches to established epic." Hemans' interest here in a redefinition of heroism is
further suggested by her publishing the lyric "Casabianca" in the second edition (1829) of *The
Forest Sanctuary: With Other Poems*.

[12] A way station just beyond our epic pale appears in *Ellen Fitzarthur: A Metrical Tale, in Five
Cantos* (1820) by Caroline Bowles—no relation to W. L. Bowles of this and earlier chapters, but in
later years Southey's second wife. Here a plot of shipwrecked love recalling James Bird's in *The
Vale of Slaughden*, from the year before, swerves clean away from the civic concerns that Ch. 5
found Bird imperfectly dodging. Extracts are given by Virginia Blain in *Caroline Bowles Southey:
The Making of a Woman Writer* (Aldershot: Ashgate, 1998) 37–42.

self-denial, which furnishes inspiration to the eponymous tutor Dunrie, an emigrant Briton who has learned unflagging Christian stoicism the hard way. "Peace may still | Wait on the subjugated will" (4.186): this distillation of Dunrie's pastoral counsel within the family circle, even as it articulates a national understanding of what it took to defeat Napoleon, forecasts the zeal with which 1820s apocalypticists were about to celebrate the species-wide subjugation of the will as an epic theme whose time had come.

Another verse novel or romance of this period, Catherine Luby's *The Spirit of the Lakes; or Mucruss Abbey: A Poem in Three Cantos* (1822), works out a kindred theme about the abeyance or futility of the will, in the comparative formal elevation of heroic couplets, and in a plot of nearly geometrical symmetry. Gentle Desmond, returning in hermit's garb at the end of life to the ruined abbey at Killarney, tells how his innocent courtship of Adela was frustrated years ago when Count Montaldo in wicked lust abducted her and ordered him killed. It turns out that Desmond is not the only one to have escaped and returned to the scene of the crime. A madwoman who haunts the place singing Irish melodies of lost love *à la* Tom Moore—"the spirit of the lakes," in titular fact—is none other than Adela; and before long Montaldo too comes back, not so badly racked by guilt but that, happening on the finally reunited elders at the ruins, he repeats the crime by stabbing his innocent rival all over again. Yet now, just as before, he trespasses in vain, since Desmond has already died of shock and joy in the arms of his beloved. And now, just as before, Montaldo pursues Adela in vain, the two leaping to their death this time from the Killarney cliffs by moonlight. Luby's schematic exercise in repetition-compulsion drives a last nail into the coffin of the first Romantics' belief in the second chance, as we found that belief confessed in Chapter 3 and retracted in Chapter 4. Her plot's ruinous fixation on the past, along with the dramatic ironies and melodramatic disclosures it anchors, models in little the consummate vantage to which the apocalyptic epics of the decade concurrently repaired. All were in strategic retreat from the true Byronic threat of the moment, which was not villainous glamour but corrosive mockery—which, alas, this poem fatally invites.

Meanwhile the paradigm of strategic retreat had also fastened on a stalwart pair of older epic imaginations, Southey and Bowles. The former began writing *A Tale of Paraguay* (1825) in 1814, having just whisked the hero of his *Roderick* off the political battlefield and into a hermitage for private expiation without term. His Paraguay, too, is an asylum, subsisting all but outside history and virtually without tears. Southey's America, like

Hemans's in *The Forest Sanctuary* and quite unlike his own in *Madoc* twenty years before, is a land that catastrophe has purged of contingency. His Native American principals are the sole couple to have survived a plague that wiped out their tribe; and they have deliberately set cultural superstructures aside to raise a new family in natural piety.[13] So clear is the isolated faith of these Paraguayans that, when they make contact with conquistadors and a Jesuit mission, they can take Christianity right in stride. All things have been pure to the pure Southey hero since Joan and Thalaba, but never with the blandly amiable self-sufficiency that distinguishes this rusticated, conflict-finessing spirituality as a birth of the 1820s.

As for Bowles, whose 1815 South American poem *The Missionary* had plunged into the issues of conquest and resistance that Southey's *Paraguay* sidesteps, his work of the new decade performed more clearly even than Hemans's the transfer of epic energies from secular into spiritual keeping. *The Grave of the Last Saxon; or, The Legend of the Curfew* (1822) expressly took up in blank verse "a subject of national history" (Preface), the submission of England's native population to the Norman yoke just after the Battle of Hastings. This "patriot theme" (Introduction 60) presumably was too hot to handle when war was actually in progress against a nineteenth-century French conqueror, by whom the ancient insult to England might at any moment be repeated. Like Scott in *Marmion* (Ch. 4) or Mann and Carey in *Macbeth* (Ch. 5), Bowles revisits the site of a once-deep national dissension, in order to stress that the trauma of Hastings is one that long time has finally healed. But not obliterated: on the contrary, the healing power of the centuries since 1066 is for Bowles one with Britons' matching power to remember the burdens under which William the Conqueror anciently made them groan. The blessings of virtuous memory become plainer by contrast with Bowles's William, who figures as a sore winner made anxious by a guilt whose obverse is the patient commemoration of Saxon Harold's grave by his affectionate siblings and widow. William's imposition of the hated curfew tolls, to the ear of epic, the knell of a tyranny whose days must

---

[13] Philip Connell, *Romanticism, Economics and the Question of "Culture"* (Oxford: Oxford University Press, 2001), suggests that in Southey's matured view just such isolation was the proper nursery of social virtue. He quotes Southey's 1829 *Sir Thomas More, or, Colloquies on the Progress and Prospects of Society* on "the morally ennobling practice of aesthetic cultivation in a private environment of domestic independence" (272). Ernest Bernhardt-Kabisch, *Robert Southey* (Boston: Twayne, 1977), concludes that the poet's was always an imagination prone to deluge (82–83); it seems right, then, that he should have sat as Laureate during the heyday of Noachite epic.

be numbered among a people who will stay undefeated so long as they do not forget.

This creditable twist on Scott's secular historicism came back, ratcheted up to a new pitch, in Bowles's final epic endeavor *St. John in Patmos: A Poem* (1832). Aftermath and conquest again set the scene, but its removal from England to the Holy Land and from Harold's fall to that of the Temple at Jerusalem introduce a visionary overlay that makes of a national history a worldwide revelation. Indeed, it is this transformation—from historical occurrences to recurrent archetypes—that constitutes the poem's main action and inspires its strange marriage of spirituality to epic machinery, whereby the aged disciple John in island exile receives seraphic wire reports of the Roman sack of Jerusalem and then dreams these events into the prophetic matter of the Book of Revelation. The overthrow of Jerusalem portends that of Rome, which in turn portends that of empire as such, when it is regarded under the anagogic aspect of eternity. The fifth and final part of the poem leaps nineteen centuries ahead to draw a moral for the latest of empires, namely the one in which Bowles resides. If Britannia is to avoid the fate of her predecessors, she must espouse the worldview of eternity as her own, transcend merely national identity, and emerge as a spiritualized imperial *ecclesia* to Christianize the globe (5.180–215).

Something momentous had changed between Bowles's epical poems of 1822 and 1832, and not just in the sexagenarian poet. Memory's visionary project in *St. John*—complete with cinematic projection—differs sharply from the low-grade recollection valorized in *The Last Saxon*, not to mention the merely expository flashbacks Southey used to bring his *Last of the Goths* up to speed, or the antiquarian byplay of Scott's *Last Minstrel*.[14] Last Things, no longer what they used to be, were now of the first moment. Furthermore, they now resided not in the past but, in imaginative impact if not diegetic fact, in the future.[15] These differences, correlative with the difference between a

[14] To think ahead a few years to Mary Shelley's *The Last Man* (1826) is also to recall the specter of species-extinction that had stalked the imagination of Keats as he worked on the *Hyperion* poems, where by the end Moneta, vestal of a vanished race, stands as Last Titan: see Hermione de Almeida's discussion of Keats and natural history, "Prophetic Extinction and the Misbegotten Dream in Keats," in *The Persistence of Poetry: Bicentennial Essays on Keats*, ed. Robert M. Ryan and Ronald A. Sharp (Amherst: University of Massachusetts Press, 1998) 165–82.

[15] The mounting popularity of futurist prose narrative in Britain is tabulated in I. F. Clarke's annotated bibliography *The Tale of the Future, from the Beginning to the Present Day* (1972; 3rd edn. London: Library Association, 1978).

dwindled custodial nationalism and an as yet inchoate but vigorously insurgent transnationalism, marks out the principal development of epic in Britain during the Georgian twenties.[16] To grasp it is to be ready to understand what can otherwise seem merely bizarre: the rash of immoderate, overween- ing, fiercely pious epics that from 1820 or so rehearsed versions of the end of the world that were either directly biblical or inspired by a Bible-based typology.

So abrupt and widespread a craving for apocalypse must have had nu- merous causes, most of them related to epochal developments within the Church of England. The ecclesiastical left witnessed a resurgence in evan- gelical and methodistical fervor impatient of temporal remedies, while a long-prepared loosening of the church–state bond that the vigilance of the war decades had kept in good repair called forth from the authoritarian right in the 1820s an armory of apologetics increasingly militant in character.[17] In the cultural formation that resulted, three factors seem particularly salient for the student of totalizing poetic form: inclusiveness, sublimity, earnest- ness. A poem that took up its stand at the end of things cultural or cosmic was by definition summative and thus met handsomely the epic criterion of comprehensiveness: it looked back across the generations and, by imagina- tive implication when not in literal fact, across the nations, since the kind of cataclysm to which it gravitated included every zone and people. Such a poem was uniquely situated to appreciate the beauty of the long, provi- dential view and to enjoy a share in its narrative power, as God's plan for history came to perfection and time drew to its close.[18]

---

[16] Hedva Ben-Israel, *English Historians on the French Revolution* (Cambridge: Cambridge Uni- versity Press, 1968), remarks on the historiographic deficit in continuous national narrative at this time (115–16). For Katie Trumpener, *Bardic Nationalism: The Romantic Novel and the British Empire* (Princeton: Princeton University Press, 1997) 12, "cultural nationalism often appears in the 1810s and 1820s as reactive or reactionary," because superseded as an instrument of radical analysis by the emergent category of class.

[17] The influential headmaster-to-be Thomas Arnold, for example, was possessed during the later 1820s by the "idea not of an alliance or union, but of the absolute identity of the Church with the State": A. P. Stanley, *The Life and Correspondence of Thomas Arnold, D.D.*, 6th edn. (London: Fellowes, 1846) 39, 173. The apologetic masterpiece of the decade was Coleridge's *On the Constitution of the Church and State, According to the Idea of Each: With Aids Toward a Right Judgment on the Late Catholic Bill* (London: Hurst, Chance, 1830).

[18] See John Wolffe, *The Protestant Crusade in Great Britain, 1829–1860* (Oxford: Oxford Uni- versity Press, 1991), on the 1820s rise of "a sharp dualism, viewing the world as under God's judgement and heading for imminent catastrophe," where Romantic yearning met Enlightenment system "in an attempt to make sense of the action of God in history in the face of the disorder of contemporary events" (30). The same anxiety that epic apocalypticism projected in day-glo tints was also widely diffused among steadier minds seeking bedrock after the vertigo of Byronism: Gerald Newman, *The Rise of English Nationalism: A Cultural History 1740–1830* (New York: St.

The more than national character of its unity demarcated the apocalyptic epic from its patriotic counterpart of earlier decades, which appeared in retrospect a bit petty. This appearance drew support from different and seemingly incompatible dimensions of the postwar experience. On one hand, as we saw in Chapter 5, the coherence of national purpose that had been forged in wartime began dissolving even before 1820 into the cross interests of party, sect, and class. A contemporary reader might suspect Knight and Porden of suppressing aspects of their Alfred's and Richard's suppression of internal dissent, in belated pursuit of an epic unity that no longer possessed the urgency, or even the interest, that it had lately enjoyed. On the other hand, though, within a world perspective the global mission of Britain after Waterloo was all too evident; it was, in a sense, too obvious to seem imaginatively compelling or require narrative support. To the extent that the national destiny was manifest, it made questions of belief irrelevant. There was little point in staking poetic faith on what nobody would dream of disputing.

In contrast to the puny themes of nationhood, apocalypse remained sublime by reason of its vastness and extremity, which taxed the imagination to grasp what faith undoubtedly held to be true—as true as the natural sciences, which around this time laid their great century-long siege to the literary mind; and yet truer than natural science, since it was part of the work of apocalypse to expose the limits of the known world and abolish natural law as the merely provisional thing it was. These weighty considerations gave to apocalypse the incentive, and the leverage, to sober epic up from what surely struck its better-read practitioners as the frivolity into which the genre had fallen in recent years. The superficial pleasantries with which a Moore or a Hogg trifled must vanish before the urgency of elemental, ultimate catastrophe. Nay, Byron himself could be trumped by the last trump, when the divine irony of ironies showed all the world how threadbare were the creature comforts that sustained his kind of wit. From the standpoint of Apocalypse the Byronic cut and thrust looked like pin-pricking, which

Martin's, 1987) 244, finds that "the basic process of the later 1790s," *viz.* a tactical retreat into conservatism, "repeated itself in the souls of thoughtful young people in the twenties." For adherents of the decade's pulpit sensation Edward Irving this link to the 1790s was an article of ardent faith, since he preached that six of the seven vials of Revelation had then been poured on the Beast of revolutionary France, with the seventh and last now at the apocalyptic tipping point: see Tim Fulford's introduction to his *Romanticism and Millenarianism* (Palgrave, 2002) 8–10—a book in which, notwithstanding its title, no contributor as much as mentions any poem discussed in the present chapter.

left worldly complacency tickled but, when all was said, fundamentally undisturbed. Thus, at a time when Byron's intimidating infidel brilliance was emptying the epic field of all but gleaners, it called forth from the religious ferment of the day an unlikely yet worthy opposite.[19]

A token of the doomsday epic's cultural strength was that it not only challenged the prevailing Regency tone but in at least one respect absorbed it; for something like the gallows humor of Byron's hilarity reappears in the exhilaration with which the epic at the end of the world apprehended the ultimacy of its theme. This consideration was evidently uppermost for the subgenre's earliest Romantic exemplars, who remained innocent of the fascination with mass movement and moral classification that was to typify the evangelical epic imagination of the 1820s and suffuse its bequest to Victorianism. The Walworth Baptist pastor Joseph Swain was right to disclaim candidacy "for EPIC BAYS"; not so much because his *Redemption: A Poem in Five Books* (1811) eschewed "the imaginary world of machinery" (viii), and indeed of "smiling fiction" (1.16), as because incidents enter this doctrinal poem strictly to illustrate precepts. The narrative of the Deluge, which was to prove such a favorite among 1820s apocalyptics, engages Swain only when he can loosen it from the past and apply it as a type: "So ride the saints secure in Christ their ark" (5.147). Only within this figural interpretation do the marvel, the peril, and the irony of the Noah story gain admittance to the poem.

This ratio of narrative to interpretation, of phenomena to meanings, was about to undergo striking reversal. The Reverend George Townsend "anxiously exerted" himself, like Parson Swain, to free *Armageddon* (1815) from "any thought that may appear inconsistent with the Truth of received opinions" (xxviii); but this obeisance to orthodoxy seems the merest spice to the sheer thrill that his work is designed to deliver. And indeed does deliver: even in minimally competent hands, there is an infectious wonder attaching to a plot in which time ends, everyone on earth dies, the reassembled dead

---

[19] In a sense Byron had already found his first, friendliest and worthiest, epic opposite in Shelley. *The Revolt of Islam*, which appeared before *Don Juan* was begun, set its parabolic narrative within framing cantos that anticipate what was to be the aim of 1820s apocalypticism, namely "to break free from the limits of time and to inspect human history from some transcendent, God-like position": Earl R. Wasserman, *Shelley: A Critical Reading* (Baltimore and London: Johns Hopkins University Press, 1971) 395. On this anagogic thrust of Shelley's allegory see also Karen A. Weisman, *Imageless Truths: Shelley's Poetic Fictions* (Philadelphia: University of Pennsylvania Press, 1994) 76; Bryan Shelley, *Shelley and Scripture: The Interpreting Angel* (Oxford: Clarendon Press, 1994) 63–68.

arise and are judged—and all within the first book. Filling the next eleven was a challenge to which Townsend proved not quite equal, reserving his actual battle of Armageddon and final visions of Hell and Heaven for four books he never got around to. (The teenaged, always professionally precocious Tennyson would follow suit a decade later in a four-part, visionary though not epical, poem he called "Armageddon," which never comes to apocalyptic blows either.) The seven additional books that Townsend did complete flash back for a history of the universe, visit consulting parliaments of angels and demons, and devote quality time to a contingent of the latter, which is weirdly composed of Hindu gods bent on revenge against Britain for her missionary activities in India. During a walking tour of the expiring cosmos Brahma and his fellows discourse on astrophysics, anthropology, and the history of terrestrial empire with special reference to the British rise to power. Meanwhile suns wink out, planets vanish, and on the last planet to go, ours, which is incidentally the only one that has known sin, the cliffs of Britain hold out longest against universal expungement but then of course succumb with all the rest. Within such a panorama of marvels it may seem pedantic to register the anomaly of Townsend's placing his most patriotic sentiments, and firmest endorsement of Britain's resistance to Napoleon, in the mouth of a fiend (book 6). Yet the anomaly is too good to miss: it neatly forecasts the comparative disregard of specific national politics that the apocalyptic epic was to show. In a genre where size has always mattered, the issues on the table were simply too big for such details to mean much.

This held true even where the poet's fable was ostensibly national and unmistakably martial. When J. F. Pennie returned to the lists in 1823 with *Rogvald: An Epic Poem, in Twelve Books*, his relish for sensuous piquancy had not abated since *The Royal Minstrel* of 1817, and he stocked an Anglo-Saxon sanctuary here as lavishly with delicate things as he had a Jewish throneroom there. Now, however—as this poet's unique reprise of the prosody and typography of Southey's *Thalaba* should predispose us to find—all the finery of this world was less securely possessed by its apparent owners than in the former poem, and lay in truth at the disposal of some exceedingly forthcoming ministers from the next world. When Odin-devoted pagans storm a rich cathedral, the Blessed Virgin shows up to defend it with "the glorious angel of the British Church" and "a thousand saints | And martyrs" (2.79). Pennie's preface insisted that angels were not only epically convenient machines but actually real beings; his narrative represents them as if anything more real, more effectual in agency, than the humans they thwart or assist.

The most memorable fighting in the poem occurs not on the battlefield but in a war-games theme park that adorns the pagan afterworld Valhalla, a permitted visit to which persuades the vacillating king Ethelred to throw in his lot with Odin (book 10). Other characters arrange their own getaway trips via the neurochemical sublimity of fainting spells, in which this epic oddly abounds: brought on by peak experiences of human wonder, these swoons in their frequency instill a certain scorn for the limits of worldly experience itself. Most revealing, Pennie makes a habit of constructing similes that elucidate natural events by comparing them to supernatural ones, taking it for granted that the latter provide the reader's habitual frame of reference. When Queen Offrida's happiness on release from prison is likened to a martyr's on being received into heaven (3.99), or the defense of the cathedral mentioned above is like "the last judgment in its awful pomp" (2.77), the norms of epic have gone inside out. The human and tribal tale is itself on the verge of sublimation. Surely the Second Coming is at hand.

The poem that brought to conspicuous fulfillment what Pennie's volatility leapt towards and Townsend's ambition peeked at was Robert Pollok's *The Course of Time: A Poem, in Ten Books* (1827). This epic production was rewarded with a sale of twelve thousand copies by the end of the next year, became with the decades a favorite Sunday-school prize book, and by the later nineteenth century had earned shelf space in evangelical libraries around the world.[20] Pollok's early death in the year of publication suggests that even he only just managed to see apocalypse through to the end; curiously, he did so by framing his theme within a kind of post-mortem perspective. Where Townsend's had been a prospective plot moving forward towards Armageddon and owing at least enough allegiance to this life to plant his first book there, Pollok surveyed the course of time from a point of view sempiternally remote from things temporal. His book 1 takes place (if that is the phrase for it) long *after doomsday*, when the new heaven and

---

[20] Publication and reception figures are given by Rosaline Masson, *Pollok and Aytoun* (Edinburgh and London: Oliphant, Anderson, and Ferrier, 1898) 57–58. In 1857 Blackwood produced an edition illustrated by John Tenniel, to which on publication a reviewer as canny as Margaret Oliphant reverently responded—admittedly in Blackwood's own *Edinburgh Magazine* (81: 314)—by placing *The Course of Time* in a more-than-literary class by itself (or, perhaps by special indulgence, with room for *Paradise Lost* as well). At mid-century Milton's epic and Pollok's, along with Macaulay's *Lays of Ancient Rome*, loomed large in the Indian curriculum of Alexander Duff's evangelical Free Church Institution: Gauri Viswanathan, *Masks of Conquest: Literary Study and British Rule in India* (New York: Columbia University Press, 1989) 54.

earth whose purified creation will end his book 10 is sufficiently old (if that is the word for it) that an inquiring visitor to Paradise has recourse to the soul of a "Bard of Earth" who performs as an historian (if that is the name for it) of the *ancien régime*.

The parentheses in my last sentence indicate puzzles that an expressly post-temporal metaphysics might well pose for verbal narrative. These however seem not to have occurred to Pollok, eager as he was to purchase a vantage from which to put the entire history of the universe behind him. This retrospectively total vantage was, after all, implicit in the apocalyptic past tense made canonical by biblical prophecy, drawn upon to extraordinarily varied effect in the epics of Blake, and logically implicit in the more tentative narrative of Townsend. The extreme simplicity of Pollok's out-of-this-world maneuver anchored his story from the first with a clarity that readers found reassuring as they went on to review the future, beholding in one mighty flashback all that, for all they knew, lay in store.[21] Since they themselves were to be weighed in the judgment that the final books re-hearsed—no epic ever staked a stronger claim to tell absolutely everybody's story—the grounding premise served both to focus the whole and to whet readers' interest without delivering them to the distortions of zeal or dread. Or, as the poet himself put the matter into a cover letter he sent his then prospective publisher William Blackwood, "If the work take at all, it must take extensively, as all mankind are alike interested in the subject of it."[22]

Telescoping not less than everything into a form that might be fitted to human ken took structure, and lots of it. Pollok found what he needed right where his brand of ultra-Presbyterian evangelicalism did, by and large, in a wholesale reduction of experience to binary terms of sin and redemption. The world as we know it is repeatedly sectored by the poem, with a satirical-clerical edge, into mutually embattled camps of good and evil.[23] To take two pointed examples, wisdom literature is contrasted to fiction in

[21] Dror Wahrman, *Imagining the Middle Class: The Political Representation of Class in Britain, 1780–1840* (Cambridge: Cambridge University Press, 1995), illustrates within the middle-class Briton's self-conception a rapid swing in outlook between retrospect of the Golden Age and utopian purchase on the future (245–56). Pollok's prophetic temporality will have oiled the imaginative hinge on which such a swing took place.

[22] Quoted in Masson, *Pollok and Aytoun*, 51.

[23] This Manichean aspect of 1820s epic may also be understood as transposing into a newly suitable register the demonization of Napoleon and whitewashing of Nelson and/or Wellington that had exercised so many epic poets during the decades just before. According to Peter Hägin, *The Epic Hero and the Decline of Heroic Poetry: A Study of the Neo-Classical English Epic* (Berne: Francke, 1964), a God-versus-Satan standoff was the archetypal underlay for the formula epics

book 5, and book 9 features complementary portraits of the good poet (Milton, whose manner Pollok reverently, flatfootedly imitates throughout) and the self-heroizing bad poet (Byron, to whose epic manner the poem is of course one single-minded riposte).[24] Projecting this binarism onto the axis of time gives Pollok his moralized history, a perennially iterated plot that recapitulates the biblical narrative of Fall and Atonement (book 2), that includes in microcosm the author's own salvation from despondency (book 3), and that resumes with a vengeance in book 6 after the millennium, when humankind's final descent into moral corruption precipitates the end of time. At this suspended point the binary plot is respatialized across the last four books as the consequential form of truth, now at last eternally present, and projected in virtually tabular form. The orderly congregation of the saved from across the ages faces off against the motley mob of the damned (book 8); and, in the presumably instantaneous climax of book 10, God's word consumes the world and reconstitutes it from purged atoms as the locale the stranger from book 1 has happed upon to begin with. The course of time rounds back into itself like that of a race track, eliminating all impediment to the viewer's total involvement in the spectacle of the whole.

The mutual convertibility of spatial with temporal binarism drilled into Pollok's reader a moral habit of division-and-conquest that was fully consonant with the regimental, indeed automated action of his epic. The high-pressure chronotope of *The Course of Time* makes no room—it has not a second to spare—for ambivalence or change of mind or even, surprisingly in an evangelical testament, for conversion.[25] As if to demonstrate the collusion between evangelicalism and industrialism, the poem's care of souls is strictly of the sorting and warehousing kind; mass production and just-in-time deliverance are next to godliness here, and are indeed the forms

of the 18th cent., most of which were "impersonal accounts of collective heroism or disaster" (77–79,109). And massed collectivity is what the counter-revolutionary triumph of 1820s evangelicalism demanded: see Marilyn Butler, *Romantics, Rebels and Reactionaries: English Literature and its Background 1760–1830* (Oxford: Oxford University Press, 1981) 126, 165, 174.

[24] William St. Clair, *The Reading Nation in the Romantic Period* (Cambridge: Cambridge University Press: 2004) 219, discusses Pollok's poem as a response "to what the author saw as the irreligious despair of Byron," and later quotes an unnamed "Scottish minister in a lecture to young men in Glasgow" on the evils of *Don Juan*: "The blast of the desert, at once breathing pestilence into the hearts, and scorching with a fatal death-blight, the minds of myriads" (334).

[25] Although no conversion gets narrated in *The Course of Time*, Pollok does of course allow for it in principle. And although he draws the firmest of lines, he does not always draw them in the expected place: see Hoxie Neale Fairchild's surprise, in *Religious Trends in English Poetry*, vol. 4 (New York: Columbia University Press, 1957) 43–44, at Pollok's assurances that the momentarily if utterly sincere believer will be saved, without exception, and that no pagan will be subject to Judgment.

of divine power that the poem imagines most compellingly. It might even
be said that Pollok's unquestioned eschatological moralism ultimately
served, if not in his own mind then in the minds of numerous imitators,
as a pretext for the display of these nineteenth-century managerial virtues.[26]
The very scope of his epic conception obliged the poet to generalize its
effects, and the impression that all this generalization enforced was the stamp
of force itself upon the passive soul. "Moral excellence" (4.774) proved
but a species of *force majeure* in the end, especially when The End furnished
the epic subject, when the field of contention was the Last Judgment, and
when rectitude itself constituted victory.[27]

   In other words, Pollok's epic illustration of virtue militant imagined right
as might. But that kind of imaginative coding is notoriously reversible—
witness his countryman and contemporary Thomas Carlyle—and the sheer
power of this highly popular poem became instantly available for appropri-
ation by authors apter than a Calvinistic sectarian to demonstrate the closely
adjacent counter-truth that might made right. For the elision of moral
choice from *The Course of Time* left the poem no means of forestalling a
merely fatalistic, dynamistic apprehension of its grandeurs. The good ended
happily and the bad unhappily, millions upon millions of them, just because
they must and just because they were so many; the logic of the foregone
conclusion became the testimony of power. By its internal procedures and
its influence alike Pollok's epic showed, for all the stiffness of its orthodoxy,
what imaginative narrative might offer to modern times in the way of crowd
control.[28]

   An eye for the big picture, neither sharpened nor troubled by much moral
scruple, was the major asset of Byron's agemate Edwin Atherstone. He
trained it in *The Last Days of Herculaneum* (1821) on the mounting horrors

---

[26] What was takingly new in Pollok—sheer Biedermeier, in fact—is so much harder now to
appreciate than what was pseudo-Miltonically stuffy that it helps to find both aspects noted by a
contemporary who could not abide *The Course of Time* precisely because he saw what it was up to.
In the final lines of "Whistlecraft" Frere's little poetic mock "The Course of Time" (1832), we
might think we heard his pupil Byron groaning from the grave: "words of the olden time, | Quaint
and uncouth, contorted phrase and queer, | With the familiar language that befits | Tea-drinking
parties most unmeetly matched" (ll. 12–15).

[27] For an account of the poem more sympathetic with Pollok's intentions see Michael Wheeler,
Heaven, Hell, and the Victorians (Cambridge: Cambridge University Press, 1994) 86–90.

[28] John Plotz, *The Crowd: British Literature and Public Politics* (Berkeley and Los Angeles:
University of California Press, 2000), offers a discussion, congruent with ours here, of that
1820s classic De Quincey's *Opium-Eater*, where in a displacement of apocalypse the phantasma-
goria of crowds becomes "the definitive figuration of a generalizable uncertainty" (92).

of a volcanic cataclysm but did so as if, like Hemingway a hundred years later, to maximize impact by minimizing affect, and concentrating on phenomena rather than commenting on them. If Atherstone's hundred pages of blank-verse description seem to relish the disasters they communicate, that is because he largely refrains from the expressions of pity or the moralized captioning of events that an earlier poet would have felt bound to provide. Although there are exceptions to this narrative abstinence, for the most part Atherstone deflects attention from personal motives and affects towards aggregate actions: the massed surge of cloud, ash, lava, population. Thus the agonies of a boy and his father trapped in a heaving dungeon are recorded with exquisite neutrality, the poet reserving his right to intervene until such time as he can apostrophize not individuals but the whole doomed, unwitting city: "Gaze while ye may" (18). Within the lo-and-behold mode of revelation, this phrase issues an eerie secondary admonition to the likewise massed and anonymous readership that poets had the largely unrewarding task of imagining in the 1820s. The size of Atherstone's crowds seems a fantasy compensation for the actually shrinking poetry market at this time.[29]

Gazing while one may is the entire point of his next work, *A Midsummer Day's Dream: A Poem* (1824): a comparative bijou by his mega-production standards, yet crammed with wonders. Suffice it to say that during a day at the beach the speaker falls into a dream endowing him with an astral body capable of touring the universe at the speed of literature ("to be at once | Where thought is": 53). With a "Son of Ether" (147: that's not Esther, nor Uther) as his guide, the cosmic tourist scans the ocean bottom and the poles, outsoaring the sun and the galaxies and, in the process, transcending his own egoism in obedience to a little homily his guide delivers against selfishness. Once self is put aside, all is disinterested moral holiday for Atherstone's transparent eyeball: thinner fare than the sexual ambiguity with which Hogg had baited the sidereal travelogue of *The Pilgrims of the Sun* a decade previously, very short rations before the Victorian banquet of epic spasmody to which Chapter 9 will invite us; yet oddly equivalent, in point of moral demand, to the stupefaction of the will attending the numerous apocalyptic epics of the 1820s.

On Atherstone's watch in both poems we too gaze while we may; and the auxiliary verb here is at once permissive and threatening. In *The Last Days* we enjoy the hindsighted superiority of knowing, as the poet's citation

[29] See Lee Erickson, *The Economy of Literary Form: English Literature and the Industrialization of Publishing, 1800–1850* (Baltimore: Johns Hopkins University Press, 1996).

of Pliny establishes that the poor Herculaneans did not, how vast an
eruption was afoot. The poem's indulged gaze effectively hints, however,
at comparable ambient ironies attending our own perilously ignorant con-
dition as spectator-readers. It is in striking this note of unwitting implication
that Atherstone's treatment of a known and finite historical catastrophe rises
to apocalyptic rank. Like Bowles's St. John, though of course without the
prestige of scriptural warrant that Bowles could claim, he presents the
historical event as one prototype of a convulsion to which the centuries
have been repeatedly, and the whole *saeculum* must be ultimately, subject.

The epicizing *Last Days of Herculaneum* offered practice for the generic
thing itself in *The Fall of Nineveh: A Poem*, which grew from six books (1828,
bound for good measure with a congeneric bagatelle of just ten pages, "The
Plague of Hailstones") to thirteen books (1830) and at long last to thirty
(1847, revised 1868). Larger than *Herculaneum* by a full order of magnitude,
Nineveh was from the first less stinting in its sympathies for the fallen, and
was even equipped with a flawlessly commanded host of victor heroes; yet
here, in its sweeping evenhandedness, unmistakably labors the same macro-
poetic hand.[30] Once again Atherstone's human figures are, when push
comes to shove, *in the way of events*. Good or bad, their place in a moral
calculus means less than their function as pieces in a gigantic eschatological
design, and at last as falling bodies overtaken by the force of a providence
that opens the heavens and moves the earth because it wields not only
gravity but history too. The leading man is a villain, the monomaniacal
Assyrian autocrat Sardanapalus from the seventh century BCE. Scarcely akin
to Byron's complex closet-dramatic hero (1821), this Sardanapalus is a
creature of epic, descended more from Sotheby's Saul than from Marmion
inasmuch as his extravagant guilt has long since spun out of control (and thus,
at a subliminally apologetic level, is not his fault). That Sardanapalus must fall,
and all Nineveh with him, is a destiny for which the poem adduces two
different explanations: every augur, star-gazer, and prophet within earshot
says so; and besides, on due reflection, absolute oppression generates revolt
absolutely. The latter explanation as an epic theorem of political science had
interested Shelley, and it would win some attention from Carlyle when
within the decade he wrote the century's great anglophone prose epic in
The French Revolution (1837). But nothing more firmly characterizes the

[30] George Saintsbury, indefatigable connoisseur of "Lesser Poets" in the *Cambridge History of
English Literature*, ed. A. W. Ward and A. R. Waller, vol. 12 (Cambridge: Cambridge University
Press, 1915) 141, dubs Atherstone "the Blackmore of the nineteenth century" yet places him with
J. A. Heraud above Pollok and allows him "a certain grandiosity."

narrative dynamic of apocalyptic epic, or governs its impact on not only Carlyle but Tennyson and other Victorians, than the practical allegiance Atherstone pays to the irrationally closed circuitry of the former explanation.

Nineveh falls because it was to have fallen; and the means of its destruction are so redundant that no one of them seems worth privileging as a cause. (That this was an *epic* peculiarity may be suggested by comparison with James Campbell's 1826 *The Judgment of Babylon*, an anomalous tetrameter romance that serves up, Scott-fashion, Belshazzar's feast from the book of Daniel, concocting personal and family motives to dwell on and breaking off just before the mass destruction that an epic would have put front and center.) Atherstone's first fifteen books put the vices of Sardanapalus on display and motivate a Bactrian horde to swell to battle strength the ranks of our heroes, the clean-limbed abstemious Medes (read: British) who have been the first to resist the Ninevite tyranny in morally splendid minority. Yet while, during the second half of the poem, the rebels and royalists gird and fight as often as any reader could wish, the way they fall out melts into Atherstone's larger, fatalistic sense of the way things in general fall out, and establishes his intention to marshal much more than regiments behind any epic denouement worthy of the name.

Traditional single combat yields to large-scale troop deployment, just as argumentative eloquence yields to mass acclamation: individual agency packs less clout with each passing book. So, for that matter, does human agency of any kind. As the rising Tigris menaces the city walls, fulfilling the founder's ancient prophecy, as the mad tyrant's arson brings on a hailstorm and then a nine-day gale whips it into conflagration, and the incinerated city drowns in a three-day downpour—as, to make a long story short, Nineveh starts to look a lot like Herculaneum—Sardanapalus stands revealed as what the fatalist (read: Calvinist) sage Barak calls the "sorry instrument" and "unconscious tool" of "Powers supreme": "Ere the foundation of the earth was laid, | Of all the doom was fixed" (29.228–29). At the end of it all even Ninus' tomb topples to "The century-beat | Of the Time-cycle's mighty pendulum,—/ Measuring the dates of empires and of worlds" (30.429–31). These last words, dilating catastrophe to apocalypse, do not so much point a moral as they indicate a kind of will-stunning inexorability to which epoists since Virgil have been attracted, but to which no subgenre was ever more zealously suited than the 1820s epic of the end of the world.

This fascination with the inexorable is where to look for the politics of 1820s apocalypticism, which were inexplicit, probably unconscious, and perhaps self-contradictory.[31] King Louis XV of France had enunciated the modern political meaning of the Flood—"Après moi le déluge"—and his grandson had gone on to furnish a bloody illustration. After him the deluge had flowed along channels of mass insurrection, reign by paranoid terror, and totalitarian citizen mobilization, of which Britain had tasted for years by traumatic proxy and defensive reaction. In the national imagination these conditions were kept alive after the signing of peace and across the 1820s by widely publicized uprisings in town and country, conspiracies, royal infirmities, and a generalized malaise about impending change. The sources of domestic anxiety were so many, and the Gothic horrors that backed them up so vividly recent, that at some allegorical level they must have been commemorated, and simultaneously salved, in the vast crowd scenes of cleansing judgment that we consider here. It is as if the epic poets of the decade were returning to the scene of an unsolved crime in order to keep it from having happened—or, what amounts to the same thing, to keep it from having consequences. This they attempted by ushering readers to a hereafter when Louis' dreaded "après" should have become inconsequential. Among the political accommodations offered by so extreme a perspective was utter fungibility of class allegiance: the authoritarian who exulted with Pollok in the ultimate vindication of church governance, and the decent rising bourgeois who identified with Atherstone's middling Medes in protest against corrupt hereditary privilege, alike found in the inexorability of epic events a reassurance that was moral, political, and existential all at once.[32] History was a Möbius strip, and God was on its side.

★

[31] That doctrinaire eschatology believed itself post-political is one of the premises from which analysis should begin. It is laid out searchingly by Steven Goldsmith in *Unbuilding Jerusalem: Apocalypse and Romantic Representation* (Ithaca and London: Cornell University Press, 1993), which takes as its subject "the political purposes served by the claims of an apocalyptic aesthetic to have transcended politics" (4). Our suspicion that these claims themselves served political ends is given shape by Laura Brown's analysis of "the fable of torrents and oceans" that gathered force in 18th-cent. Britain as a figure for "the cultural experience of mercantile imperialism": *Fables of Modernity: Literature and Culture in the English Eighteenth Century* (Ithaca and London: Cornell University Press, 2001) 72.

[32] This well-groomed complacency is not to be confused with the "chiliasm of despair" that E. P. Thompson associates with failed radicalism at this time among the working classes, and that awaited epic expression in Cooper's *Purgatory of Suicides* (Ch. 7). See *The Making of the English Working Class* (New York: Pantheon, 1963) 375–400; and, on the politics of chiliasm generally, Karl Mannheim, *Ideology and Utopia*, tr. Louis Wirth and Edward A. Shils (London: Routledge and Kegan Paul, 1936) 190–95. An overview of the early 19th-cent. diluvian imaginary is given in George P. Landow, *Images of Crisis: Literary Iconology, 1750 to the Present* (Boston and London: Routledge, 1982), esp. 134–44.

Atherstone's effects cannot but summon to mind what our day calls Holly-
wood epics. This visual-art analogy is not entirely far-fetched in view of the
popularity of panorama and diorama displays among his generation, or of
the warm reception they accorded to the engulfingly outsized canvasses of
John Martin and other apocalyptic painters who drew inspiration directly
from the Bible.[33] While for Atherstone such inspiration was indirect, at least
one contemporary poet stood ready to go right to the source. Charles Peers
in *The Siege of Jerusalem: A Poem* (1823) revealed an extensive acquaintance
with biblical history and scholarship in presenting a nine-book epic that
looked, more searchingly than Bowles would do some years later in *St. John*,
at the cardinal juncture which Coleridge had plausibly if fruitlessly iden-
tified as the perfect epic topic: the founding event of Christian culture, the
destruction in the year 80 of the Temple at Jerusalem.[34] It is important to
stress Peers's credentials as a modern historian; Peers at least thought so,
since he set them forth in his preface, dedication, and notes, and made them
good in his invocation's assertion that Jerusalem fell because its defenders
were divided against themselves.

Uniting this secular analysis of political infighting with a prophetic de-
nunciation of moral corruption among a squabbling citizenry, Peers staked
an epic-worthy claim. What makes his endeavor worthy of the 1820s,
though, is that he departs from this thesis in practice and veers Atherstone's

---

[33] On the metropolitan displays see Richard D. Altick, *The Shows of London* (Cambridge, Mass.:
Belknap Press, 1978); and Lionel Lambourne, *Victorian Painting* (London: Phaidon, 1999) 151–67.
Graham Reynolds, *Victorian Painting* (New York: Macmillan, 1966) 15 and 120, and Jeremy
Maas, *Victorian Painters* (New York: Putnam, 1969) 182, link Martin and his successors Lawrence
Alma-Tadema and Edward John Poynter in a history of artistic influence that leads via the scarcely
post-Victorian cinema of D. W. Griffith into the biblical epics of Cecil B. De Mille. James Chandler
traces this inter-art influence back to Scott in "The Historical Novel Goes to Hollywood: Scott,
Griffith, and Film Epic Today," in *The Romantics and Us: Essays on Literature and Culture*, ed. Gene
W. Ruoff (New Brunswick and London: Rutgers University Press, 1990) 237–73; Ian Jack, *Keats
and the Mirror of Art* (Oxford: Clarendon Press, 1967) 171–74, glimpses it in germ amid the model
grandeurs of *Hyperion*. To the student of Pollok and Atherstone, Michael Wood's superb discussion
of cinematic epic in *America in the Movies* (New York: Basic Books, 1975) bristles with implicit
parallels between the postwar consumerism of the British 1820s and of the American 1950s. At each
of these national moments the "fantastic excess" of "conspicuous production" (Adorno troping
Veblen) rehearses a drive to "extravagant victory" that is "feckless, coarse, heroic" (169–77). The
rootedness of this poetics of waste, far from reacting against an ascendant puritanism, "is rather the
oblique expression of a faith" that exacts, in the form of "doom and apocalypse," victory's
accompanying "tokens of catastrophe" (178–81).

[34] The Higher Criticism of scripture, and its legacy via Coleridge to our Ch. 10 epic authors
Browning and Eliot, are treated in Elinor Shaffer's seminal *"Kubla Khan" and* The Fall of
Jerusalem: *The Mythical School in Biblical Criticism and Secular Literature 1770–1880* (Cambridge:
Cambridge University Press, 1975).

way into a decreasingly theorized, increasingly phenomenal absorption in
the rush of destruction itself. No sooner has Peers discriminated his poem
from "bardic" works of "magic" fiction at the start of book 6 than he turns
the rest of the poem over to earthquake prodigies and supernatural voices;
assimilates his advancing Roman soldiers to these elemental forces; completes
this process of dehumanization by representing the Temple's destruction as a
nightmarishly autonomous process of architectural dilapidation untouched
by human hands; and delivers the city up at last to famine and sheer flame.

In a closet drama of the preceding year, *The Fall of Jerusalem* (which Peers
acknowledged, claiming priority however in composition), Henry Hart
Milman had been constrained by the dramatic form—and by a trustworthy
feel for the public taste: *The Fall* sold unusually well—to stay close to a
political analysis generally similar to Peers's. Quite possibly the former
epoist and future historian knew from his work on *Samor, Lord of the Bright
City* (Ch. 5) the tendency of the genre to spiral out of analytic reach and into
a spectacular holistic dynamism whose only way of explaining anything was
to explain everything. Even so earnestly and longwindedly doctrinal a poet
as Robert Montgomery—not to be confused with his namesake James, of
whom more quite soon—evinced something of this tendency. He quit his
usual book-length propositional didacticism (*The Omnipresence of the Deity*,
1828; *Satan*, 1830) for properly epic territory with *The Messiah: A Poem in
Six Books* (1832). The new work was a straightforward gospel narrative; but
Montgomery for all the strictness of his polemical discipline could not resist
adding to book 5 an extended forecast of the Fall of Jerusalem, and to book
6 (what "could not be omitted": Preface) preview shots from the Last
Judgment.

At about the same time, to round off our survey of apocalypticism's
magnetic attraction, James Bird—the same epicizing romancer whom the
preceding chapter found outfitting the love story in his 1819 *Vale of
Slaughden* with the national-epic trappings of its decade—trimmed his
craft to the new wind in *Dunwich: A Tale of the Splendid City, in Four Cantos*
(1828). Now a pair of high-born medieval lovers must plunge for each other
into rising seas that, as they lick flat the solid-seeming sanctuary of a church,
portend the coming loss of the whole East Anglian coast to an erosion as
intractable as time, and as curiously tranquilizing as fate. Taken together
these urban-annihilation epics suggest that Coleridge may have had it
wrong, and that the vast canvas of metropolitan destruction could not
recoup in epic's properly human interest what it had to invest in brute force.

Recalling the epic prerogative to correlate diegetic determinants of plot with overarching cosmic etiology, we might hazard here a generalization. British national epic shortly after 1800 perfected its myth of (functionally British if nominally Israelite) cultural election by inserting it into a world history (functionally secular if nominally Christian), whose total plot the righteous victory of the chosen at once epitomized in a shapely narrative that was the poet's work and sped towards its ultimate fulfillment in the immense providential design that was the work of human culture.[35] British apocalyptic epic during the 1820s reproduced this pattern with a conservative twist, and screwed to an exponentially higher level. Fascinated by the rendition of elemental forces that subtended the human condition, epoists at this juncture viewed secular world history as itself but an episode within a narrative vastly more capacious. This mega-macronarrative might be supernatural providence or it might be natural history; often, by a coincidence that much in contemporary science and natural theology unwittingly encouraged, it was both of these together. Only Pollok compassed the whole story, and that is part of what made *The Course of Time* so impressive to his contemporaries—and makes it imponderable to us now. But that whole story remained a governing postulate that secured, by implicitly completing, the work of contemporaries who had more limited or divided aims.

The Revd Thomas Dale, for example, before he ascended to the first Chair in English Language and Literature at the new University of London, published in *Irad and Adah: A Tale of the Flood* (1822) a diluvian narrative whose ultimate reference, and not only in the ultimate stanza, is to the judgment day awaiting all readers: "Think on the day when this vast Earth shall be | In bursting flames dissolved—yon skies so broad | Shrink like a shrivelled scroll"; "Reader, be thine the moral!" (3.94). Dale's zeal to activate the reader, however, deprives the narrative of any sustained apocalyptic grip. The long scramble that our affectionate but sinful principals make from the city of the plain to the mountain-top is as futile as it is athletic, and it does not help matters when the narrator keeps breaking in to tell us so. There is a nice Alice-in-Wonderland logic to the way everyone in the poem, Noah included, sheds what inevitably seem floods of tears. In the main, though, Dale's solicitude to chart in minute detail how doom affects

[35] On vagaries of British Israelitism, see Edward B. Hungerford, *Shores of Darkness* (1941; rpt. Cleveland and New York: Meridian, 1963) 64–74; Leon Poliakov, *The Aryan Myth: A History of Racist and Nationalist Ideas in Europe*, tr. Edmund Howard (London: Sussex University Press, 1974) 38–42.

an individual, ethically responsible soul contravened the genius of the genre, which throve only at large, en masse, and by remote control.

The inherent grain of apocalypse emerged in work by more imaginatively susceptible contemporaries who plumbed the more elemental substrates. This could happen even when the poet designed to tell a quite different tale of human hope or heroism, but was pulled into line with the zeitgeist in spite of himself. One case in point is *The Flood of Thessaly* (1823), a two-part epyllion in blank verse for which Barry Cornwall (pseudonym for Bryan Waller Procter, briefly met in Ch. 5), apologizes by saying prefatorily that he has had to abandon the "more elaborate Poem on this subject" he once had in view—presumably an epic on the fortunes of Pyrrha and Deucalion, the couple who were ancient Greece's answer to Noah and Eve. A reading of the poem irresistibly suggests that Cornwall's problem was premature climax: he could not keep his mind off the deluge. Having gotten there far too soon in part 1, he fails to sustain his own interest, much less the reader's, in the regenerative human sequel of part 2. In that sequel, under Jove's beaming sponsorship Pyrrha and Deucalion re-people the world and are vouchsafed a standard vision of pageant history, running from Thebes to Alexander the Great. This was routine national-epic stuff from an earlier generation, but coming after the transports of inundation that manifestly engaged the poet's fancy, it made a puny showing. Even during part 1 Cornwall could hardly bring himself to take a human interest in his principals' sorrows, extremities, or expedients, and he forgot them as often as possible. His 1820s imagination hungered instead for terrified masses, drowning summits, and acres of watery rage. That was where the gods lived, those were the sublimities that rang true, because their anticipation of the end conveyed the oceanic narrative plenum of which Cornwall's two-book *Thessaly* was only a backwater.

An absorbing parallel instance of apocalyptic diversion occurs in the work done at this time by a better poet with established epic credentials, James Montgomery (see Ch. 4). His preface to *Greenland* (1819) resembles Cornwall's above: circumstances have compelled him to leave incomplete the poem he once projected on the arctic evangelizing undertaken by Moravian Brethren during the early eighteenth century. Himself the faithful son of a converted Brethren missionary, Montgomery gives every sign of having a plausible epic conception within grasp, conceiving the action in secular terms as church-directed and not heaven-sent: "Celestial music swells along the air! /—No!—'tis the evening hymn of praise and prayer | From yonder deck" (1.17–19). From this seaborne entrance *in medias res* the poet's easy, mobile couplets flash back to engage the history of the church, and canto 4 introduces promising inter-ethnic material about early Norwegian settlers and their commerce with the "Skraelling" or Eskimo people who arrived in Greenland more or less concurrently.

For all this, Montgomery never manages to impart direction to the merely human tale he has in hand; his eyes keep straying off towards stricter latitudes. The elements of volcano, frost, and geyser detain canto 2 permanently in an Iceland the narrative intends to sail past; and then Greenland, once reached, serves canto 5 as the scene of one spectacular disaster after another: whelming seas, inland avalanche, pestilence, the perilous breakup of the ice in spring and, worse, its advance in recent centuries to imprison ships and freeze passengers solid. These horrors all set the scene for the missionaries' arrival; but in effect, and in the compositional history of a poem that got no further than this canto, they pre-empt it. Montgomery might have claimed a correlation between such elemental inhospitality and the Brethren's *contemptus mundi* creed—"Let the earth perish,—here is not my rest" (2.339)—but his chosen genre would not let him. Knowing full well that here was the scene for epic's tale to haunt, he dwelt on earthly things whose extremity of convulsion or stasis enforced limits no human agent could breach. With an instructive rigor, Montgomery found the unworldliness of his commissioned heroes overtaken and abraded by the cold world. But it was a world made curiously unworldly by the aloofness of what amounted to natural rather than supernatural machinery. (In curiously inverse proportion the scoffer Erasmus Darwin produced the worldliest of effects, as we saw in Chapter 2, from a machinery of sprites and lots of allegorical personification.)

Fascinated by nature's superintendent conditioning of the human condition, Montgomery turned from the frozen project of Greenland to tropic climes in his last epic effort, the nine blank-verse cantos of *The Pelican Island* (1827). This poem of considerable interest traces the gradual emergence of a coral atoll; its stepwise colonization by vegetable, animal, and eventually human life; and the dawning of true religion on a tribal patriarch. The most remarkable feature here, the absence until canto 6 of all human figures except a disembodied witnessing "I," appears less strange once we see how Montgomery's emphasis on the pre-historical complements the post-historical thrust of contemporary apocalyptics. Literally for good measure—rocking with the imperceptible pace and planetary symmetry of a deep-time metronome—the third canto

brings life forth on the island from soil and grass to seals and birds, only to wipe
the entire bioregion out in hurricane seas and start the dialectic of disaster and
progress all over again. Three more cantos evolve human beings, who advance
in the last three from nature through primitive culture towards mankind's
zenith in the intimation of a monotheism consonant with the poet's own. It
is an especially nice fractal touch of Montgomery's to have the islanders develop
a myth of creation not unlike cantos 1–6. In this and other ways a narrative
memory of the earlier creation, deluge, and recreation abides, to unite the nine
cantos and place such cultural developments as etiological epics (or indeed
Romantic-era long poems) in geologically long perspective.[36]

Much as the infinitesimally gradual accretion of the atoll over eons, and out
of millions of dead coral bodies, has accumulated a structure dwarfing all
human architecture (canto 2), so Montgomery holds the religious dispensation
of *The Pelican Island* constantly in the stark and unforgiving light of *Greenland*.
The order of grace ultimately trumps the order of nature, in this poet's vision as
more aggressively in Townsend's, Pollok's, and Barry Cornwall's. But nature
produces grace, too, in the sense that the human capacity to hail a higher reality
is evolved here by none but scrupulously natural processes. As a result, and by
the same imaginative logic we have found less benignly in force at Hercula-
neum and Jerusalem, the imperceptible motion of nature represents the
inscrutable action of grace, holding together in this late Romantic epic realms
of being whose mutual estrangement would famously prepossess the Victor-
ians. Already here, however, it was the estrangement from human ken of both
realms that made them imaginatively compatible as tropes for each other's
boundless mystery and thus, to the extremist 1820s, imaginatively attractive.[37]

Near the beginning of this chapter we looked at a set of long poems by
young women liberated, by reason of their age and sex, to conduct epical

[36] *The Pelican Island* in fact had a precursor in Erasmus Darwin's evolutionary conspectus *The Temple of Nature; or, The Origin of Society* (1803), a poem of sub-epic proportions (under 2000 lines in all) but, like Montgomery's, of super-epic scope. The tidy progress of Darwin's four-canto narrative from geology and biology through perceptual psychology to Panglossian moral philosophy under-scores by contrast Montgomery's understanding that epic found its proper theme in the heroic assessment of human culture, which is just what *The Temple of Nature*, despite its subtitle, elides.

[37] This compatibility is also a key to the *éclat* of Martin's vast paintings of cataclysm, whose titles seem interchangeable with those of the vast contemporary poems discussed here: *The Destruction of Pompeii and Herculaneum* (1822), *The Deluge* (1826), *The Fall of Nineveh* (1828), and so on. Marilyn Gaull's terse formula for these canvasses might stand as well for apocalyptic epic, "the image of nature being revealed by contemporary science set around the image of mankind as represented in the Old Testament": *English Romanticism: The Human Context* (New York and London: Norton, 1988) 215.

imaginings closed off from the male poets at whom *Don Juan* had launched its *de facto* prohibition. If the work of Barrett, Hatfield, Porden and others had been pre-apocalyptic, by decade's end young women of literary ambition were hearing like everybody else the call to write of last things. Mary Shelley was not yet middle-aged when she published in *The Last Man* (1826) a novel set at the end of the world that brought its terminal theme, as novels should, within the compass of a single life. This individuated apocalypse arguably inspired Caroline Norton, poetically fledged and wretchedly married in her early twenties, to try something of the kind in narrative verse. In *The Undying One* (1830), Cain and the Flying Dutchman meet Dorian Gray in the person of Isbal, whose breathless confession to Linda of his condition of guilty immortality takes up three of the poem's four cantos. To her horror she learns that her lover was present at the Crucifixion, has wandered the earth for millennia, was imprisoned for a century after murdering an adopted daughter, has loved numerous women before her and raised at least one Arabian and one Jewish family into the bargain. For the sake of this nonpareil swain, nevertheless, Linda throws over her accepted Spanish fiancé. But jilted Carlos pursues the couple over land and shipwrecking seas, and— deluge being a twenties motif not to be suppressed—Linda drowns in the undying, unavailing arms of the wretch who has seen so much yet enjoyed so precious little. The monochrome, interminable misery that Norton visits on Isbal—that literally *secular* hero, with a touch about him of Byron's Don Juan—is an animated cautionary advertisement for the different satisfactions of fixed retrospect that apocalyptic closure had offered to readers of heroic verse during the odd, liminal decade we have been considering.

Had James Montgomery written his 1813 *World before the Flood* a decade later, the Flood itself would surely have loomed larger than it did at a time when, to the extent permitted by a Genesis setting, recognizable human problems were posed in psychological and social terms and solved by relatively independent moral agents. This truckling to verisimilitude had ceased to interest Montgomery by the 1820s, as we have just seen, and it was to be decisively superseded by an epic on the same nominal theme, one of the century's wildest in fact, *The Judgement of the Flood* (1834) by John Abraham Heraud. For Heraud as for Montgomery—as indeed for nearly all the diluvian poets we have taken up here—the deluge lies off in the future, though by the twelfth book all the animals are embarked and valuables stowed, the clouds are gathering, and the barometer has sunk well below the bathos point. "All is purposely gigantick," exclaimed the preface, "the plot—the persons—the crimes—the language, and the imagery." This purpose was superabundantly realized by a poet whose gift for narrative concatenation was weak but whose sheer local inventiveness was evidently liberated by the broad sanction that a scanty plot of scripture could afford. Among this uninhibited poem's flourishing antediluvians number giants, sorceresses, demons, angels, and cherubim; a sizeable part is sustained by a royal werewolf (granted remission on Sabbath-days). He and Heraud's other half-breeds attest the interspecies miscegenation in which the 1820s angel poems of Croly and Moore had also taken an interest. Here biodiversity complements apocalypse in pursuit of what was the larger epic mission of the day, to test human limits against nature's instinctive and extinctive dynamism, and typically to watch them fail the test.

Where only the final cause of God's will has real motivational oomph, Heraud freely punctuates the standard Genesis business of Noah's admonition and response with a plethora of subordinate causes: apparition, miracle, transfiguration, portent, vision, and, at the opening of the action, a display of prophetic sculptures in which Japhet has portrayed, *inter alia*, an allegory of British commerce with India (1.922–30). The lubricity of such an invention must have made it easy for Heraud, two decades later, to rearrange a new 1857 edition so that only the first and final books kept their places, books 7–9 went where books 2–4 had been, and the sixth book was folded into the tenth to make room for a newly written book 11. (Not a great plot, evidently, but a mighty forgiving one.) The one genuine apprehension induced by the impending deluge in either edition of the poem is the astonished reader's regret that such an hallucinatory profusion of beings and causes must vanish once the early world's imagination dries out and a chaster regime of procreation, and narrative plausibility, supplants it. Like much that this chapter has surveyed, the poem is distressingly inhumane, and so it is best enjoyed when simply inhuman into the bargain. On its own, pre-emptively mock-Heraudic terms *The Judgement of the Flood* lies beyond criticism. And that is precisely where, we may see by the carnival light this poem sheds back across the 1820s, apocalyptic epic meant to be all along. With a righteous indignation whose violence indicates what urbane and thoughtful strength had glittered in the Regency manacles that its sober-suited new practitioners cast off, apocalypse restored to the epic genre a naïve simplicity that the meddling intellect could not molest. Epic at the end of the world forestalled the petty judgment of merely human criticism by rehearsing the last judgment first.

7

In Session:

Forensic Epic 1830–1840

L iterary genres subsist in paradoxical balance: they sustain integrity by distinguishing themselves from the genres around them, even as they sustain vitality by drawing nourishment from exactly the same source. Genres that last manage to perform both these tasks somehow, and epic's way has traditionally been by incorporation. The foregoing chapters have shown how Romantic epic at different times and with varying rates of success outflanked, digested, and assimilated apocalypse or balladry or romance. We have also seen how on occasion romance defended itself against epic, say in Byron's oriental tales; and how once in a while it even turned the tables, in Moore's *Lalla Rookh*, and enfolded epic into its own different accommodations. This last trick of counter-assimilation had been a favorite with novelists since Cervantes and Fielding, of course; and its recurrent performance within the great tradition of realist fiction building into the twentieth century constitutes, although one would hardly know it from prevailing literary histories, the strongest of inferential arguments for epic's unabated vitality across the nineteenth—if only as a sparring partner in the generic struggle for existence and, each time the novel prevailed in that struggle, a nutrient source for the hungriest new predator in the literary ecosystem.

During the 1820s and 1830s Scott the historical novelist was past master at such generic overtaking and metabolizing, and it may have been his mastery that pushed writers who were ambitious to rival epic, but were unwilling either to hazard it or merely to tread in Scott's footsteps, into another genre. This was the closet drama, or dramatic poem, imported from the Continent at the end of the eighteenth century by Baillie, Coleridge, Southey, and Wordsworth, and elevated in the years after Waterloo by such writers of genius as Byron and Shelley. This book can afford to approach the para-epic genres only in a spirit of strict opportunism; still, the burgeoning of closet drama at the interval we now approach furnishes an opportunity worth pausing over. Acquainting ourselves with the dramatic poem can help us to understand tendencies that were imminently at work in the epic poem too.

Shelley and Byron showed authors from the 1820s how much literary resonance a dramatically scripted, as distinct from theatrically stageworthy, poem might attain.[1] *The Cenci* (1819), *Marino Faliero* (1821), and *Hellas* (1822) each presented an action with large historical import. The amplitude of classical myth or the Bible let *Prometheus Unbound* (1820), *Cain* (1821), and *Heaven and Earth* (1823) extend in epic directions what two hours' brief traffic on a mental stage might imply. The topical similarity between Byron's 1821 tragedy *Sardanapalus* and Atherstone's epic *The Fall of Nineveh* demonstrates that the two genres could, within limits, treat a common subject matter. Conversely, in *Prometheus Unbound* Shelley had provided epoists of the rising decade with an alternative model for the representation of apocalypse. J. A. Heraud, for example, whose satyr-play of an inundation epic brought down the curtain on our last chapter, cited Shelley's script with approval in his apparatus. We also remarked in that chapter the close bearing of Milman's *The Fall of Jerusalem: A Dramatic Poem* on Peers's epic *The Siege of Jerusalem*.

With an impressiveness that the Pre-Raphaelites would in time admire, Charles Wells's *Joseph and His Brethren: A Dramatic Poem* (1824) adapted to the mind's arena a narrative drawn from that inexhaustible epic source the book of Genesis. Elizabeth Barrett tapped it again in the just-east-of-Eden situation for *A Drama of Exile* (1844), a work whose primal humanity stands out the more richly against the impassioned swirl of pre-human spirituality in her earlier drama *The Seraphim* (1838). And from the same biblical reservoir John Edmund Reade pumped *The Deluge: A Drama, in Twelve Scenes* that he published in 1839 but had composed, he prefatorily advertises, in the early 1820s before Byron and Moore issued their plays on the same theme. The delayed publication of this duodecimally epic work in dramatic

---

[1] Epic's presence in actual theaters is another story, one that calls for time-lapsed sequencing. Stage realization of such stupendous conceptions as inflated the 1820s closet-dramas of Milman, Wells, and Reade had to wait until mid-century, both for technical advances in scenic and costume art and for archaeological research supplying designs that might authenticate a production. See Michael R. Booth, *Victorian Spectacular Theatre 1850-1910* (Boston and London: Routledge, 1981) 17-20.

form represents a shift that defines the new epic complex of the 1830s—a cluster of ideas involving public rhetoric, debate, and the immediacy of performance—against the apocalyptic obsessions of the decade before it. When the catastrophic extremity of the Flood breaks on the final scenes of Reade's script, it seems reluctantly brought on, as if the author were loth to part with the domestic-sized dilemma—should the heroine settle for the familiar human suitor or fall for the new angelic one?—that has wrung his Astarte's heart. The end of the world will soon put a full stop to the agony of choice that claims more of Reade's interest, and is better adapted to dramatic treatment, than is the unstageable mass suffering of the subtlety-whelming sequel that scenes 11–12 portentously gird for. The poem labors towards the close as if indentured to a narrative dispensation it has outgrown.

Epicizing closet dramatists like Wells, Barrett, and Reade, by the very scriptedness of their chosen form, tended to resuscitate the human will from the decade-long doomster trance it had fallen into, and to foreground the situated ethics that the urgency of choice entails on a Joseph, Eve, or Astarte. If this was true where scripture history furnished the backdrop, it was still more so when playwrights of epic mark turned with the 1830s to histories of a secular or national sort. Henry Taylor (*Philip van Artevelde: A Dramatic Romance, in Two Parts*, 1834) Thomas Noon Talfourd (*Ion: A Tragedy, in Five Acts*, 1835), and the briefly rising star Robert Browning (*Paracelsus*, 1835; *Strafford: An Historical Tragedy*, 1836) all made their mark with verse dramas poised at historical crises in the kingdom of politics or thought. While they occupied quite different points on the ideological spectrum, all carried their point confident in the power of a medium that was consecrated to national greatness by the prestige of Shakespeare. Author of a *de facto* Henriad in four parts, and hailed throughout the nineteenth century by the epical epithet of "Bard," Shakespeare famously exemplified the various arts of bringing world-historical implications within the compass of a focused portraiture that was at once psychologically rich and collectively representative.

When under Shakespeare's shadow late-Romantic or early-Victorian literary poets embraced the conditions of dramatic form, they did so not merely in avoidance of stagecraft's limitations but actively in pursuit of other virtues that the form enabled.[2] Through a deliberate restriction of mimetic

---

[2] Browning's preface to *Paracelsus*, for example, shows him acutely aware of the "peculiar advantages" and "restrictions" that accompany poetry written in a dramatic form. On Browning's

scope—a discrete cast of human figures performing and above all *discoursing* in the real time of a continuous present of strictly set duration—they purchased a mimetic intensity that downplayed the large-motor activity of epic and put a premium instead on actions of a specifically verbal sort. The deeds favored by the dramatic medium were those of confession or dissimulation, persuasion or dissent, as these conduced to ethical or political change.[3] In soliloquy and especially dialogue, the representation of a conflict that made for change was drama's distinguishing excellence, one that excelled moreover in engaging the reader as a party directly interested in the issues at play. Even when only closeted, drama was a medium particularly well adapted to displaying, and indeed training, virtues that would be required in an era as consciously dedicated to Reform as were the British 1830s.[4]

The decade-defining contrast between deeds and discourse, between what you scenically imagine taking place in a dramatic poem and what you get scripted straight from the hero's mouth, animated another publication by Reade: a pair of closet one-acts that he printed jointly as *The Revolt of the Angels; and The Fall from Paradise* (1830). Reade called this twofold work *An Epic Drama*, a subtitle that cinches our new generic conjunction and suggests as well this poet's interest in the relation between actions performed and actions narrated. It is an interest borne out by the text's richly preserved equivocation

extroversion of ideology in dramatic form see Isobel Armstrong, *Victorian Poetry: Poetry, Poetics and Politics* (London and New York: Routledge, 1993) 126–35; also John Lucas, *England and Englishness: Ideas of Nationhood in English Poetry 1688–1900* (London: Hogarth Press, 1990) 165–66, for discussion of drama's political importance among Browning's *Monthly Repository* associates. Carlyle's long 1831 essay on "The Nibelungen Lied" finds in that "Northern Epos" a concentration and clarity of construction that give it "a Dramatic character" as of "so many scenes in a Tragedy": *Critical and Miscellaneous Essays* (London: Chapman and Hall, 1869) 3: 171.

[3] Drama's prestige among the genres was on the rise elsewhere in Europe at this time too. On the Continent as in Britain, this development was politically oriented and focussed on the dramatic representation of conflict. In Berlin, Hegel's lectures on aesthetics from the 1820s found the essence of tragedy to inhere (witness *Antigone*) in the competition between equivalent but incompatible goods. In Paris, home of neoclassical genre theory, rising star Victor Hugo published as the preface to his 1827 *Cromwell* a Romantic manifesto in which epic was superseded by drama, thanks to the latter's modern capacity to express conflict. Ideas like Hegel's and Hugo's have axiomatic force for E. S. Dallas in *Poetics: An Essay on Poetry* (London: Smith, Elder, 1852). Dallas identifies the dramatic in art—as against the epic or lyrical—with what is "modern, western, romantic" (87), roots its function in "spokesmanship" and its mode in "plurality" (95), and essentializes its liberalism as the imaginative power of "giving to man the authorship of his own actions" (258).

[4] As Ch. 9 will show, the flouting of just such closet-dramatic constraints at decade's end in Philip James Bailey's 1839 *Festus* lit up in neon the exit from theatrical conventions into the very different, hyperbolically big-top format that would typify the spasmodic epic of the 1850s.

on the key terms *argument* and *proof*, each of which may signify demonstration by thought or by plot, by reasoned pleading or by experiential trial and error. When Lucifer's angels fall in act 1, and Adam falls in act 2 (despite his faithful Eve's intuitively knowing better), they all are falling for what is never presented as anything but the highest-minded metaphysical empiricism. Both angel and man, that is to say, need to know truth experimentally; so they test their role in the universe and in relation to God by an hypothesis in the form of a transgression. Lacking Eve's intuitive certitude and the obedient angels' unquestioning faith in authority, Reade's protagonists choose roles that must be extemporaneously played out in the existential arena of their lives, where their lines and business cannot—at least from where they stand—be credibly foretold, or told over in the form of a narrative they know how to learn from.

Foretelling and retelling, prediction and recounting, are primary duties of that raconteur-prophet the epic poet. To recognize this is to see Reade's troubled protagonists as epic-impaired, and thereby to see how Reade, in conceiving the problem of evil dramatically, effects a neatly turned meditation on the necessities of his chosen literary medium. Where might performatively makes right, as it did in the apocalyptic scenarios that thronged contemporary epic poetry, actions become the only persuasive arguments and characters become, in consequence of their actions, embodied proofs. Their lives speak, and in a genre where speech is not merely reported but is, as we now say, *live*. "Ay, thus | Argue," righteous Michael tells deviant Lucifer, pivoting from the argument the fallen angel makes to the argument he is: "thyself the strongest argument | Against apostasy, and thy vain deeds | The proofs to all!" In answer to Michael's reproof Lucifer fully concedes the principle of embodied demonstration, but he holds out for the virtually scientific chance of experimental verification that greets them, by happy coincidence, in a newly created unknown quantity called mankind. "Await ye here the proofs—nor boast till then: | All argument is impotence, when deeds | Call us to action" (*Fall* 4.70–71).

Action turns out to be *discussion*—all it honestly can be in a poem of dramatic type, as Reade appears to concede by dispatching its one narrated event, the fallen angels' foiled assault on the Holy of Holies, in a ten-line triumph of blasé understatement (*Revolt* 2.34). Words alone suffice Lucifer's subsequent Socratic demonstration (wherein not so much as an apple changes hands) that man in his discontent is innately neurotic, "*proving* that ye are not perfect, | Therefore not happy" (*Fall* 6.91). As a corollary to this lesson Adam learns by heart an all but Carlylean gospel of work: the assignment of humanity to a consciously empirical existence, in the school of hard science, hard knocks, and hard labor, is the one sure result of the Fall according to Reade. Or, in Raphael's summation of the human prospect: "Thou shalt by trial know the strength and weakness | Of thy mind's faculties," and "in the active struggles of thy nature, | Thou shalt prove which doth comfort most, the doubt, | And pride that preys on its self-love, or faith" (*Fall* 11.124–25). Justification of faith by work: such is the doctrine here propounded, and it fits the emergent early-Victorian ethos of industry so perfectly that we should be surprised not to find the authors of epic adopting means of making it tell in their genre with a like dramatic *éclat*.

Those means lay ready to hand in one of the genre's oldest conventions, the grand consult or debate. The surrogated strife of verbal argument forms an inaugural episode in the *Iliad*, *Paradise Lost*, George Skene's late-eighteenth-century *Donald Bane*, and many a Romantic successor. Strong journeyman-epoists made it their showcase of choice in brief exhibition epics like Blake's *French Revolution*, Keats's *Hyperion*, and Elizabeth Barrett's *Battle of Marathon*; and it became the very substance of experimental poems as diverse as *The Excursion* and *The Revolt of Islam*. By 1830 the topos of the full-forum assembly had led a full, and checkered, epic life. A litmus test in the politics of narrative form, it elicited at different moments different levels of credence, reflecting with some faithfulness a poet's interest in such matters as deliberative conflict and the relativity of perspectives. We lose the point of Agamemnon's called meeting in Homer if we find it a put-up job; we lose the point of Satan's in Milton if we find it anything but that; and, by the same token, if we do not think the postlapsarian Adam and Eve are debating genuinely open questions, then *Paradise Lost* has been lost on us.

Returning to the apocalyptic poems considered in the last chapter, we may reinforce our sense of the totalitarian agenda they shared by noting that there the convention of the epic debate was in utter abeyance. Where assemblies occurred, say in Atherstone's *Nineveh*, the order of the day was strictly proclamation and acclamation, authority and obedience. This was true *a fortissimo* in those apocalypses that were set at the Last Judgment, wired for high-fidelity public address, and attended by the regimentation of the very heavens, the Lord God presiding. The convention still excelled at convening, and it fulfilled splendidly the need to summon and mobilize masses for choral amplification—a perennial epic need, and one never more strongly felt or more frontally met than in the 1820s, once a people mobilized by decades of war had started to recover in peacetime the tactics of mass petition and public demonstration, and to practice again the oratory that incited and justified these tactics.[5] But from the cloture call of Doomsday there was, of course, no appeal. Intolerance of dissent was part, alas, of what Pollok and his ilk found thrilling about apocalypse, and it was part of what braced epic to weather the Byronic hurricane of recursive skepticism and analytic dispersion.

By the early 1830s, however, both that devastation and its answering orthodox–evangelical inspiration had pretty much blown over. The national mood in Britain had shifted, with a suddenness still impressive in historical retrospect, from religious reformation towards political Reform.[6] The creative summons that accompanied Parliament's evident purpose to rewrite the terms of participation in the Anglican–British state, as the legislative process leading to the Reform Bill of 1832 promptly did, was in effect a levy on writers to imagine viable forms of open-mindedness. In other departments of incipiently Victorian literature, periodical and serial publication constituted such forms, to which the combination of cloudiness and punch in the nonce sage Carlyle's prose style was akin. In verse, forms of satire flared out from Byron's shadow and up into book size with the increase in political heat. Newcomer and future epoist Edward Bulwer-Lytton did not ladle so much sentiment into *The Siamese Twins: A Satirical Tale of the Times* (1831)

[5] The transition to 1830s forensicism from 1820s authoritarianism in epic poetry corresponds with the Foucauldian migration of authority itself during the 19th cent. from hierarchies of tradition and revelation into discourse-based institutions of the social system as such: see Chris Vanden Bossche, *Carlyle and the Search for Authority* (Columbus: Ohio State University Press, 1991) 1. On the concomitant revival of oratory in the universities and elsewhere, see Joseph Meisel, *Public Speech and the Culture of Public Life in the Age of Gladstone* (New York: Columbia University Press, 2001) 14.

[6] Writing it down virtually as it occurred—and thereby participating in the phenomenon he found so remarkable—Bulwer-Lytton declared that *c.*1830 "the intellectual spirit hitherto partially directed to, became *wholly* absorbed in, politics"; and that "at present the English, instead of finding politics on the stage, find their stage in politics": *England and the English* (1833) 2: 110, 141. Not long afterwards the historian Henry Hallam, in his *Introduction to the Literature of Europe in the Fifteenth, Sixteenth, and Seventeenth Centuries* (London: Murray, 1837), drew parallels between the rapid pace of change in the past half-century and in "the days of Luther and Erasmus" (1: 497; see also 2: 82). The repeated choice of the former as an epic hero at this time illustrates a convergence of Reformation with Reform in the contemporary mind. Philip Connell, *Romanticism, Economics and the Question of "Culture"* (Oxford: Oxford University Press, 2001) 243, reports that in the decade before Hallam's book, with "the rise of Reformation historiography a politically charged subject was further fuelled by the emergence of radical and liberal interpretations of the period, which either focused upon its persecutory and repressive nature . . . or stressed its long-term efficacy as a harbinger of political liberty, rational Enlightenment, and the diffusion of knowledge in the printed medium of the English language."

as to tame altogether its political allegory of coexistence-in-division; and in *The Fudges in England* (1835, sequel to his 1818 bijou *The Fudge Family in Paris*, by "Thomas Brown, The Younger") the old dab hand Tom Moore hit out at the latest *idées fixes* in a crisp display of different voices that was in its time *ipso facto* subversive of establishment stolidity.

Even where an epic paid strict and unstinting devotion to established values, as did William Ellis Wall in *Christ Crucified: An Epic Poem in Twelve Books* (1833), the Miltonic work of Christian justification tended to get done in versions of the justice hall or deliberative forum. In most respects— the turgidity of the blank verse, the pompous if merciful provision of long prose arguments at the head of each book, and especially the fixation on angelic machinery—Wall's fifteen thousand lines on events in Jerusalem during the week before the first Easter could have appeared at the turn of the century. Had it appeared then, however, it would probably not have spent so much time in sessions. Book 1 offers a grand consult of demons in Hell, Satan presiding; in book 2 Caiaphas convokes a council of the Jerusalem elders; the Sanhedrin convene formally in book 6. Meanwhile books 5–8 are taken up by Pontius Pilate's dilemma over how the prisoner Jesus is to be judged, a deliberative process exquisitely prolonged when the prisoner's mother is, in effect, deposed for two books that provide a summary biography of her son. This affidavit Gospel notwithstanding, Pilate's reluctant judgment reinforces the one that each of the earlier councils has enthusiastically delivered: Jesus must die. For Wall this unjust verdict is really the best of news, as it will bring to consummation the divine plan of sacrificial redemption for all mankind. Still, he lodges the biblical epic's traditional claim to universality in a specifically 1830s way, by decrying partisan dissension. Not only does his preface abjure "the slightest feeling of party" and "the tenets of any particular sect" (p. xi); at their hellish assembly in book 12 the (crest)fallen angels adopt it as their new policy to sow schism within the newly inaugurated church.

Epic poets at work in this climate found the topos of the grand consult readily adaptable, as a mode that split the difference between closet drama and straight-up epic narration. It simultaneously offered a third way between the insistently foregrounded textuality of Regency modes and the staunch heroism characteristic of the wartime decades. Where *The Course of Time* offered all the flexibility of an alabaster wall in the New Jerusalem, and *Don Juan* all the structural potential of mesh netting, the dialogical framework of the public assembly extended the constitutionally wholesome, fresh-air advantages of an adjustable casement. Epoists of the 1830s seized and enlarged on it as a structure suited to the kind of self-governing narrative totality that the new dispensation seemed to ask for. In some of the poems we shall next consider, Parliament itself was the structural model of choice. Others situated in an epic theater or auditorium the narrative to which their imagined audiences were to respond, building into the text a model of the participatory attention that was solicited of the reader outside it.

In all these newly dialogical poems the give-and-take of ideas *in foro publico* ranked as a good in itself, figuring an expanded national exchange of views and voices that went well beyond mere spectatorship. Where epic in its recent phases had teased the reader out of thought, or had stormed the reader into eschatological stupor, epic poets of the age of Reform undertook to effect change by dramatizing it in the form of rhetorical persuasion. They seldom either lacked or disguised a partisan agenda, but advancing such an agenda was becoming a more deliberated and mediated process than hitherto in the century. Emerging Reform protocols meant tolerating the view of one's opponent and, moreover, paying it at least that modicum of respect which flowed down to it from the respect one owed to the public sphere. Epic poets like other 1830s authors had to show good cause why the reader, conceived now as constituent and now as juror, should take an interest in the themes they treated. The ready way of doing this was in one sense as old as epic: presenting the theme as one in which the reader already had a stake. Making this representation in the era of Reform, however, required something new and perhaps counterintuitive: presenting the theme as one whose importance, neither given on authority nor taken for granted, was instead proven on the spot by reputable minds' disagreement over it.

In consequence the greater civic good that rose above party—the modern equivalent for epic's traditional objectivity—was now vested in dialogue and debate *per se*. The first virtue was getting involved; the last, in accord with the 1830s proliferation of commissions, hearings, and reports, was not sweeping the stakes but staying in the game. Carlyle acidly remarked on the verge of electoral Reform in "Signs of the Times" (1829) that the ballot, mere piece of machinery though it was, had begun to attract an idolatry as automatic as troubled any altar in the contemporary wilderness. For our purposes here that "machinery" has a specific epic application: the social-engineering impulse towards openness and balance in the British political and administrative system was just then possessing the British poets too. In a sense the ballot—with its accessories the verdict and the parliamentary division—was to epic in 1830 what the angel had been in 1790, or indeed still was in a machinery-pumping epic throwback like *Christ Crucified*.[7] Like earlier prototypes this new epic machine came as the delegated messenger of a venerated sublime power, only now that power took shape as the newest of imponderables, the Victorian public. Wittingly or not, the prophecy Reade placed in the mouth of his angelic Raphael defined the changing disposition of the epic genre: "Thou shalt by trial know."

None of this was lost on Benjamin Disraeli when in 1834 he submitted for public approval, in two installments, three books of *The Revolutionary Epick*: a trial poem in a richer sense than these pages have yet given to that phrase. A florid preface solicited the reader's verdict on the wisdom of choosing revolution as an epic theme, pleading that the topic was as timely today as national politics had been in Dante's era and warrior heroism in Homer's. And the no less florid poem solicited the reader's verdict on a suit brought before the bar of Demogorgon—here as in *Prometheus Unbound* an apotheosis of the people's, and thus the reader's, will—by the contending pleas of Magros (Feudalist Order) and Lyridon (Federalist Hope).[8] The merits of the case clearly lie with Lyridon, not just because he gets to plead last but because it is he who has instituted the very jurisdiction that is hearing it. "In our own musing should our conduct find | Its various aim" (2.14), he says, musing with an aim as he says it. Being a trademark institution of modern liberalism, impartial deliberative judgment is Lyridon's instrument to begin with, not that of the plaintiff Magros, who is too blustering an authoritarian to realize he has brought his suit before a venue inherently unfriendly.

Lyridon moreover owns the very medium of print that brings us, along with his winsome minister Opinion (opposite number to Magros's twin minions Fealty and Faith), the book of blank verse in our hand (2.18). The Burkean asseveration of Magros that a people is made not rationally by ideas but imaginatively by "the lore | Long centuries yield" (1.41, 44) is

---

[7] Marilyn Butler, *Romantics, Rebels and Reactionaries: English Literature and its Background 1760–1830* (Oxford: Oxford University Press, 1981) 178, points out that 1830 marked for contemporary intellectuals a watershed enabling comprehensive retrospect of the preceding four decades: "the minds of Englishmen returned to the topic of the French Revolution," in works that included not only Coleridge's *Constitution of Church and State* and Southey's *Colloquies* but histories of the revolution projected by Macaulay and Mill as well as Carlyle.

[8] David Duff, *Romance and Revolution: Shelley and the Politics of a Genre* (Cambridge: Cambridge University Press, 1994) 214, surmises that Disraeli's epic was written under the influence of Shelley in *The Revolt of Islam* (Ch. 5).

countered as handily here as in Blake's and Shelley's radical epics, by adducing lore of a duration even longer: ancient Athens outflanks medieval Chartres. But Lyridon's clinching argument takes a still longer view of the matter, a view that undermines the authority of narrative history as such. Forensic controversy, he maintains, bests story-telling as a means of human governance and improvement; a written constitution securing free play to fair Opinion will liberate the modern mind and body politic altogether from the old tyranny of traditionary "lore." The court of public opinion, Disraeli makes plain, has changed considerably from the days when James Brown, D.D. (Ch. 2) and Sir James Bland Burges (Ch. 3) had jury-rigged their epic verdicts against the democratic idea; and the change is epitomized in what a revolution in publishing portends within an expanding public sphere.

Case dismissed? Not quite. At the end of the day the expected judgment does not arrive. Our *vox populi* judge Demogorgon declines to rule on the case and remands it to the real jury, the one constituted by readers, with instructions to shape their verdict on a non-allegorical episode drawn not from ancient history but from the quite recent past: Napoleon's invasion of Italy, with its double-thinking claim to have set a people free by subjugating them militarily. The invader's effusive democratic rhetoric is apparently borne out by a final scene in which Lombards rejoice around a liberty tree. Yet each page of this third book bears as its title header a phrase, "The Conquest of Italy," whose imperial resonance a dozen epic titles we have met thus far should render unmistakable. Thrusting might in the face of right, Disraeli's dramatic standoff between incompatible ideas had become more richly ironic when he returned to revise the poem in a second edition of 1864. By then a second Napoleon had invaded a still unemancipated Italy, under popular banners of yet more ambiguous stripe. Conquest, then, or liberation? Choose your poison. Disraeli's dialectical epic, by going back from legal procedures to historical cases, went unfinished in a most accomplished way.[9]

A contemporary reviewer who might have known better, the estimable editor W. J. Fox, first waddled out the canard that epic was dead but then went on to venture a criterion more interesting: at a time of great transition

---

[9] Patrick Brantlinger remarks that in his 1845 novel *Sybil* "Disraeli is so in love with irony that he allows it to undermine even the central thesis": *The Spirit of Reform: British Literature and Politics, 1832–1867* (Cambridge, Mass., and London: Harvard University Press, 1977) 104.

"The Revolutionary Epic must be a revolution in epicry."[10] This criterion
Disraeli had already met, with the bet-hedging instincts of a politician-in-
waiting, to be sure, but also with a commendable formal ingenuity. "SPIRITS
supreme," intones Demogorgon by way of peroration, with his thousand
eyes on the hydra-headed public, "In man alone the fate of man is placed"
(2.39). This authoritative disclaimer from on high endorses a humanism
that ultimately pertains to epics up and down the millennia, whatever their
supporting theology; but at this juncture in the British history of the genre it
came as something more than a commonplace. First, it reasserted a human-
ism that a decade of inhumanely pious apocalyptics had drowned fathoms
deep. It moreover activated the principle of human agency in literary
practice, by asking the reader to decide between narratively embodied
arguments about the meaning of changes not abstracted into political
philosophy, but currently transpiring in Britain. Disraeli in his twenties is
to be credited with having elaborated out of the grand-consult topos a
structure that brought the human tale home with new dramatic point—and,
if we are to believe his preface, with having derived his leading idea from
a visit to the site of ancient Troy into the bargain.

A similar credit is due to the grim last twist that John Colin Dunlop gave
his intelligently if relentlessly talky *Oliver Cromwell: A Poem, in Three Books*
(1829). In a raisonneur's preface replete with imagery of prosecution,
pleadings, opinions, and judgment the author, a trained jurist, declared an
advocate's interest in disinterestedness: by removing from the mighty
Commonwealth Roundhead some of the obloquy that clung to his image,
Dunlop hoped to redress a balance in the nation's memory of its defining
historical crisis.[11] (His failure to mention Victor Hugo's celebrated play
Cromwell of just two years before seems rather tactical than misleading:
English readers were not about to learn their own national history from a
Frenchman.) Expressly, tactfully cultivating "the seeds of principles, of

[10] *Monthly Repository* 8 (1834): "Chaos can only be sung after creation. Neither the world nor
the bard is ripened for an epic of the times, while the times are only those of transition. Epics are
not revolutionary" (376); "The Revolutionary Epic...must be written in a new faith, which is
believed; not in an old faith, which is not believed. There can never be intensity again, in the stale
machinery" (377). Carlyle surely took note.

[11] On the upswing in Cromwell's reputation near the start of Victoria's reign, including
prominent reassessments by Godwin and Macaulay, with Carlyle in suite, see Blair Worden,
"The Victorians and Oliver Cromwell," in *History, Religion, and Culture: British Intellectual History
1750–1950*, ed. Stefan Collini, Richard Whatmore, and Brian Young (Cambridge: Cambridge
University Press, 2000) 112–35.

which the discussion is calculated to agitate the minds of all parties in the State" (Preface 2), Dunlop on the eve of Reform made discussion itself the dominant formal mode of his poem, which runs nearly its entire course as an indoors dialogue between the Protector and his daughter. During an hour of leisure snatched from pressing cares, the older and younger Cromwell dispassionately place the condemnation of Charles I against the historical backgrounds of Britain's Christianization a thousand years before (book 1), of the church from ancient patriarchs to corrupted popes (book 2), and of the Reformation and consequent Stuart persecution of dissent (book 3). And then, just as the interlocutors have convinced each other how desirable is coexistence between dissent and episcopacy (3.147), Cromwell's toleration-ist peroration is interrupted by news from Italy of a certain late massacre in Piedmont. Enraged, the old warrior denounces bloody vengeance on the Catholic Right, only to be interrupted again—from stage left, we might say, since this narrative in form has essentially been a blank-verse script for two—by a Fifth-Monarchy assassin, whom Cromwell handily dispatches to death "with a concealed dagger" (3.190). The irruption of inflammatory melodrama into Dunlop's meditative dialogue is an effect worth comparing to that of Disraeli's third book in *The Revolutionary Epick*. Ideology is all very well; and toleration may indeed be, as many a reformer was putting the matter circa 1830, the best policy. At a real pinch, though, such policy will reveal itself to have been backed all along, Dunlop's dash-and-slash action implies, by the concealed dagger of force. As at the end of Disraeli's epic, we confront a plot whose modal counterpoint of narration and drama stages a limbo between talk and deeds.

To stake out a similar space within the Bible's contested terrain was the surprising task undertaken by John Abraham Heraud, whose deranged *Judgment of the Flood* let us exit the preceding chapter on a pratfall yet who embraced narrative derangement to better purpose in the quite different epic on which he concurrently labored, *The Descent into Hell* (1830). Heraud's theological motive was to dramatize Christian typology, whereby events unfolded at once discretely in historical time and figurally as types that forecast or fulfilled a pattern eternally present. This motive links his effort to the arduous typological epics of William Gillbank and Elizabeth Smith a generation previously (Ch. 2). But Heraud saw that adapting the figural conception of history to changing times called for a radical adapta-tion in epic armature, and like Browning at decade's end he undertook a

Reform in poetic form itself.[12] His experimental method was to cross exegesis on diegesis, narrating Christ's Crucifixion and Harrowing of Hell in more or less linear fashion, while intermittently regarding these events over the shoulders of a rapt and responsive otherworldly auditory whose host includes Adam, Satan, and Isaiah. The last of these gets so absorbed in what he beholds (which, as a prophet alive on earth long ago, he in shadowy types foretold) that, for all the world like a protagonist in Blake, he temporarily becomes part of the program, warping the linearity of history so far as to put in a Good Friday appearance at Calvary (7.104 ff.).

Heraud cites in his notes the apocalyptic work of the painter John Martin, through whose circle he just may have known about Blake. At all events Heraud's manifest affiliations with major Romantic writers and their leading ideas justify lending serious attention to what he was after here. He dedicated *The Descent* to Southey, whose numerological punctilio seems imitated by the poem's division into twenty-four titled sections plus prologue, these sections being clustered into seven further titled parts. His *terza rima* format suggests a debt to Shelley and certainly acknowledges the master of epic *figura* Dante; and he was indubitably versed in the 1820s Christian apologetics of Coleridge, cited in notes to the revised edition of 1835. "*Things that appear to us in this world as realities,*" Heraud's prefatory analysis explains in italics, "*to that world are but shadows*" (ii). This grounding doctrine has narrative corollaries with which the poem keeps faith by representing the Crucifixion as itself a crossing of time on eternity, and *vice versa* of hermeneutical meaning on historical chronicle, each dimension screening as symbol the other's actuality. The one substantiates what the other verifies: in the respective realms of experience and meaning, the two worlds prove each other.

Ultimately the design of the poem is one that Disraeli's Lyridon would approve: it privileges hermeneutics over history. Diegetically the action descends from this world, an evening in Jerusalem, into the next, a season in hell; narratologically the commanding outer frame is that of the assembled souls who look forth on earth's human theater and caption its deeds with commentary. (An ultimate privilege in good accord with Coleridge's essentially Johannine understanding of the Gospel truth, that doctrine validates miracles and not *vice versa*.) Where "The World of Sense is but

---

[12] This poem bears out explicitly Brantlinger's generalization that "the 1830s was a time of especially rapid and critical social change, when writers spoke the Pentecostal tongues of utopia and apocalypse" (*Spirit of Reform*, 11).

a Parable" of an invisible "intellectual Paradigme" (1.187–88), interpretation becomes an indispensable activity—one potentially hostile to epic, as we have had occasion since Chapter 2 to observe, in that it threatens to allegorize away the world of sense where humanity live and move. But, having set *The Judgment of the Flood* as it were in an apocalyptic shadow of this exegetical threat, Heraud preempted the threat in *The Descent* by building it into the diegetical method. By convening Adam and company around the story in their capacity as its keenly interested interpreters, the poet makes interpretation part of the epic action, because figural typology repeatedly proves by the hermeneutic circle the interpreter's implication in the truth of events which exegesis unfolds: "The Spirit of the thing interpreted | Is that which doth interpret" (17.166–67). As with Adam, so with his children, every last one of them right up to Heraud's 1830s readers. All repeat the timeless pattern of a perennial historical loss and death, perpetually redeemed as and by the Spirit which doth interpret.

The unctuous clunkiness with which the poem executes its experimental concept, and which can make the prosody of Blake seem suave, admittedly requires a full measure of the indulgence we reserve for adventurous conceptual art. But much is to be forgiven on account of Heraud's two best ideas, which are reciprocally related. The first, already mentioned, is the teleportation of Isaiah out of the audience and onto the scene where the messianic man of sorrows he once shadowed forth now endures the excruciating crisis of life and death in historical time. The second occurs while Isaiah, returned from time's arena, narrates and lengthily glosses his experience there, only to be broken in on, mid-speech, by the rejoicing dead of all ages: "And ere the Prophet could his speech resume, | By all that Multitude was sung— 'Behold!' " (15.684–85). The supervention here of an ecstatic collective vision of the New Jerusalem on a mere individual exegete's (albeit a major prophet's) understanding of the atonement is an effect worth Townsend's apocalypse and Pollok's put together from Chapter 6; more, it is worthy of Shelley (whose like-rhymed *Triumph of Life* it for an instant sounds like) and Dante (whose ecstatically sober *Paradiso* it for an instant feels like). Both these moments transgress the ordinations of genre by playing the domains of narration and action against each other; they thus bring into focus the defining dialectic of epic that took shape at the era of Reform. That Heraud's congregational antiphony effected in church terms something comparable to Disraeli's literary coup in a trial of state enrolls both poems under the denomination of an epic reform. Both bent narrative expectation in a dramatic, presentational and thus confrontational direction; both staged audiences in ways that summoned the reader as interested witness rather than indulged or transfixed onlooker.

Heraud's signal adaptation of unorthodox narrative means to orthodox exegetic ends stands out the more sharply by comparison with a contemporary typological epic by Agnes Bulmer that assumed a form starkly more conventional, *Messiah's Kingdom: A Poem in Twelve Books* (1833). Built like a tank, this doctrinally earnest work in heroic couplets and interspersed psalmic odes sets its sights without remission on those key episodes, from the Garden of Eden until last week, that best set off Bulmer's evangelical theme of redemptive sacrifice. As the poem gets underway the major players from Genesis prove to be those first victims Abel and Isaac. Among the patriarchs Noah and Moses earn pride of place as the chief recipients of a single, figurally unfolding narrative meaning conveyed through the "mystic type" of sacrifice (1.37) by way of "sign and shadow" (2.49)—a doctrine whose exposition takes up as many lines as does the entire exodus from Egypt. Privileging like Heraud the virtues of interpretation over those of story, Bulmer gives the prophets of Israel distinct priority over the judges and rulers, grouping King David, for example, with the prophets (book 4). And she condenses the Gospels into a single epic book by ruthlessly subordinating to Jesus' messianic message his ethical teachings and even the events of his life. Among those events special attention is given, as should be expected by now, to the typological crux of the Transfiguration (6.155–57), where Moses and Elijah reappear from books 2 and 3 to irradiate two joint unities: the unity of scriptural history, and the unity of the first half of Bulmer's formidable epic megalith.

In its second half *Messiah's Kingdom* advances from scriptural to ecclesiastical history. The poem pivots in book 7 on the Acts and the Apocalypse and announces, with a noteworthy flourish of Miltonic revisionism—"Hail, Holy Book!" (7.198)—what emerges with increasing clarity as the entire poem's practical agenda: biblical proselytism on a proto-Victorian, global scale. A comparable epic of the 1820s would have arrived at Revelation, put a stop to time, and flooded the world, just as in Chapter 6 we found Robert Montgomery's slightly retrograde *Messiah* doing only a year before. Bulmer's contemporary aim in the 1830s is, instead and emphatically, to flood the nineteenth-century world with the Word. The "Spirit's flood" shall "Circumfluent roll, with still augmenting sweep, | Its mighty volume to the boundless deep" (7.198)—where the obvious pun on "volume" should not occlude the way "Circumfluent" captures in an epithet the mission of organizations like the British and Foreign Bible Society to procure for scripture a polyglot fluency the world around.[13]

Such is Messiah's coming kingdom; and to this end Bulmer shapes the second half of *Messiah's Kingdom* as an ecclesiastical history with a national payoff. This history takes its start from the epically pivotal Fall of Jerusalem, that watershed event which had exercised the epic imagination of Coleridge, Milman, and others, and which suffices in itself to engross book 8.[14] The plot then moves through the Roman church of Constantinian and medieval times (books 9–10) to the testing of Protestantism under persecution, and its eventual triumph in England (book 11). Bulmer's final gesture, discarding narrative in favor of prophetic exhortation, urges Britain to fulfill her manifest philanthropic destiny in every latitude, where Patagonia, India, Canada, Africa, yea Mecca and all the nations

> earnest ask that sacred book from thee,
> By which thyself, a captive, wast made free,
> Established on thy sea-girt throne, and placed,
> The Queen of nations, in the watery waste.

(11.303)

Messiah's kingdom thus bears a striking resemblance to the one whose scepter Victoria was about to grasp. Strident single-mindedness sets Bulmer apart from Heraud, and indeed from the forensic equipoise of the decade; in these respects her work more nearly resembles those of the decade gone by. (By the glare of her purpose we can glimpse, in Hatfield's *Wanderer of Scandinavia* for instance, how at 5.256 the gift to Gustavus Vasa of a first Swedish translation of the Bible portended a Protestant ascendancy transcending the poem's overtly nationalist theme.) Yet at the same time, despite the putatively post-historical vantage of apocalyptic epic, the efficacity with which Bulmer recruited that subgenre's distinctive matter to a national purpose and contemporary orientation made of *Messiah's Kingdom* an intervention characteristic of the new spirit of Reform. Moreover, it was a work prescient of imperial developments that 1830s reformism incubated for fuller manifestation half a century later.

★

---

[13] On the work of the BFBS in disseminating "the holy books of empire" see Sue Zemka, *Victorian Testaments: The Bible, Christology, and Literary Authority in Early-Nineteenth-Century British Culture* (Stanford: Stanford University Press, 1997) 188–223.

[14] See Elinor Shaffer, *"Kubla Khan" and* The Fall of Jerusalem: *The Mythical School in Biblical Criticism and Secular Literature 1770–1880* (Cambridge: Cambridge University Press, 1975) 17–61.

Even where hot-headed partisans addressed burning national issues, the Reform climate shed a cooling influence by enjoining the reflectiveness that comes with a literary form that depends on balanced perspectives. Henry Sewell Stokes's *The Song of Albion: A Poem Commemorative of the Crisis* (1831) was a Reform tract in narrative guise that numbered Jeremy Bentham among its many liberal-minded subscribers. Yet the style of hortatory ejaculation to which Stokes's irregular strophes lent themselves was moderated by a tripartite structure that, like Disraeli's, obeyed a logic roughly dialectical. A progress narrative from Napoleon to the crowning of William IV in part 2 counterbalances the regrettable tale of Britain's dastard opposition to revolutionary France in part 1, to issue in part 3 with the challenge of converting the present "crisis" into an opportunity to do the fair and just thing at last.

Another contemporary poem letting readers view today's crisis in the light of yesterday's was *The Battle of Trafalgar: A Poem, in Six Cantos,* which Catherine Anne Lightfoot began in 1825 and published in 1833. With its heroic couplets and allegorical machinery of Discord, Ambition, and Victory, the work can seem a throwback to epic fashions that had prevailed around the time of the battle it celebrates. What marks Lightfoot as an epoist of her moment is a supervenient symmetry that so divides the field of her mighty opposites—France versus England, Napoleon versus Nelson—as to render them, peculiarly, equals. To be sure, the former are duped by despotically evil mesmerism (1.9.8), the latter united by divinely heroic inspiration (2.11.32, 5.27.100); yet the narrative zigzag from camp to camp and fleet to fleet highlights a dynamic likeness over and above the poet's manifest patriotic commitment. Both the totalitarian French and the unanimous English evince a massy charismatic fusion that comes straight out of the apocalyptic mode that was in vogue when Lightfoot began to write, yet the frequency of dialogue and deliberative rhetoric within the poem she eventually published shows what historical and political specificity could do by the early 1830s to temper that mode's Manicheanism. Seeing in black and white began now to mean seeing in three dimensions; where choosing one's side presupposed appreciating both sides first, the Reform era made an armchair dialectician of everyone.

Polemicists on the right wing as well as the left evinced at this time an affinity for three-step narrative argument. With *Luther: A Poem* (1841), the indefatigable Robert Montgomery struck a blow, under thin biographical cover, in the ecclesiastical culture wars that had raged for a decade around the Oxford Movement's rapprochement between Anglican and Roman confessions. As a "Patriot's Conclusion" at the end of the poem reminds us, circa 1840 controversies within the Church of England were, vividly and indissolubly, matters of national politics also. It was the Lutheran Reformation, Montgomery maintained, that had shown right-thinking Christians once and for all how Anglican reform ought to proceed: *not* in the direction of Rome. He upheld this position by lashing out left and right, in over two hundred pages of prose apparatus, against the radical utilitarian and "mere ecclesiastical chartist" (xxxi) on the one hand and "the Romish controversialist" (liii) on the other. The *via media* to which Montgomery pointed across the broken ground of church politics had a structural analogue in the balance *Luther* sustained between narrative and discursive modes: its twenty-nine sections build toward and follow from a medial fifteenth, itself uniquely split into three parts, that arrests the tale in order to expound "The Gospel According to Man." Straddling this midpoint, a fifteen-section run of narrative rehearses Luther's biography, while the rest of the sections at either end of the poem are reserved for homiletic and polemical commentary.[15] The poet's name for these symmetrically hung sections is "mental *tableaux*" (ix); like a nineteenth-century display of *tableau-vivant* "attitudes," Montgomery's entire poetic format cast the reader in the role of an audience member in attendance at the drama of clashing ideas.

A grainier-minded salvo on the same theme that appeared the same year from Alfred Lord (no, not Tennyson). *Luther, or Rome and the Reformation*, seems bent, in a fashion not fully compliant with its iconoclast sympathies, on reclaiming structurally from high Catholic Gothicism something like a Puginesque trefoil design. In the three very clearly framed Parts of his poem Lord upholds the career of Martin Luther as the edifying keystone between ancient Christianity, on the one hand, and on the other its modern phase, enlivened by "commerce and science" (3.177) yet still exposed to the idolatrous stratagems of a Satan unwearied in the minting of fresh lures. From this fundamentally black-and-white starkness of conception Lord's triptych schema offers a kind of relief that is typical of its post-Reform moment.

---

[15] The idea of the hero-as-priest was on Carlyle's mind as well. His chapter from *On Heroes* (1841) featuring Luther and John Knox culminated a decade's contemplation of a biographical project on Luther: Albert Le Quesne, *Carlyle* (New York: Oxford University Press, 1982) 32. Conversely, the priest-as-hero had to bide his time until Browning produced him in epic stereo as Caponsacchi and the Pope in *The Ring and the Book* (see Ch. 10).

It may bear repeating that none of the epic-dramatic derivatives just discussed was a disinterestedly open-hearted testament. Disraeli, at most a fence-sitter in the early 1830s, would soon throw in his lot permanently with the Young England romanticizers of old Tory sentiment, which sentiment indeed must have been strong in him already to counterpoise the nod that his *Revolutionary Epick* gives, as a matter of strict reasoning, to the liberal side. The liberties Heraud takes with the gospel story are taken exclusively *within* it: no one could follow his *Descent* very far who was not already deep in the scriptures and their interpretive traditions. Stokes, Lightfoot, Montgomery, and Lord, of course, wrote as frank polemicists. What made these poems typical artifacts of the Reform imagination was their realization that consensus was now to be achieved through the coexistence if not actual contest of viewpoints; the epic strife which had in earlier decades taken a military or chiliastic shape aiming at domination now shaped up as dialogue instead.

Nor were the authors we have just considered keen to see wealth or power abruptly redistributed in 1830s Britain. If anything they probably regarded the deliberative valorization of difference and expectation of change to which they opened epic form as a means of securing the public sphere against difference and change of more radical sorts. (*Reform,* went the watchword, *that you may preserve!*) Over the short term in narrative as in government the privileging of forensic means, the conspicuous *appearance* of openness, kept things safely secured by deterring noisy intruders. Grasped as the fulfillment of the law—a phrase with application to both parliamentary and ecclesiastical reformers, fellow travelers that they were along the road of improvement— the process of history acknowledged rules, drew up sides, and prescriptively if tacitly excluded from active participation those who, being too ignorant or disorganized to play, were doomed as an underclass to observe the new great game and endure its outcome. We shall see by the end of this chapter what uses were to be found for the epic ideal of totality by poetic representatives of these outcasts. But we should observe here that their point of entry into the national dialogue on Reform lay open from the moment a dialogical aesthetic of dramatic rejoinder, consultation, and compromise came to the literary fore. Short-term tactics notwithstanding, a respect for the appearance of openness in the long run fostered the thing itself.

A Victorian overture is conveniently marked, in the year of the young queen's accession, by two epic works of 1837 that were published by men born in the eighteenth century. The first, believe it or not, came from Robert Southey, sitting poet laureate and our sturdy draft-horse for several chapters now. In what a preface called the "testamentary task" of old age Southey thoroughly revised his first epic *Joan of Arc*, "making it more consistent with itself in diction, and less inconsistent in other things with the well-weighed opinions of my maturer years" (21). The ideological glint of the phrase that follows the comma, confirming everything most readers know about this textbook Romantic apostate from radicalism, should not blind us to the interest of the phrase that precedes it. For the stylistic self-consistency that Southey imposed on the 1837 *Joan* has everything to do with its conservatism. It was in fact a stunningly smooth performance, an understated masterpiece of the poised and versatile blank verse in which this poet, Coleridge, and Wordsworth had schooled themselves for decades, and a most creditable rehearsal of the idyllic effects that the greatest laureate of the century, Alfred Tennyson, would be making his own before long. These effects were varied but stemmed from an imperturbable evenness of narrative flow that took all topics in stride, and from the confidence imparted in Southey's case by an unshakably monological, which is to say decidedly undramatic, authorial perspective. Gone from this text was the desultory, hot-blooded effusiveness of 1796, along with the political ferment it had signified. In its place purled the (not less political) assurance of a stylistic form of cultural authority that was soon to be installed as an all-purpose governor in the century's most widely read prose fiction.

Meanwhile epic, as we have seen, had been moving in the opposite direction and experimenting with narrative viewpoint, continuity, and accreditation more broadly than it had done in English poetry since those heady days of the 1790s. Of these tendencies the most impressive contemporary exemplar was Thomas Carlyle's 1837 masterpiece *The French Revolution*, a work in disjunctive, promiscuous, self-interrupting dialogue with itself. Zooming with pinpoint recklessness for twenty books across a long generational divide, Carlyle made the eras of Revolution and Reform mutually, dramatically present—confronted each with the other in reciprocal critique—at no matter what cost to judiciousness or consistency of political conscience, much less of stylistic or narrative decorum. Each of Southey's techniques in the tranquilized *Joan* for laying the revolutionary matter of France to rest met its opposite in Carlyle's shock tactics for stirring it up again. He not only insisted upon his own act of reconstructing the past out of documents that could not speak for themselves, but also shivered and rebuilt on different ground the platform from which those unforthcoming documents were quizzed, ventriloquized, puzzled over. This radical representation of the modern historian's narrative labor was designed to alarm its reader into perceiving how the events that had brought the nineteenth century forth reverberated still, and not just in words but in contemporary deeds of prophetic portent.[16]

It is tempting to enter a special plea that, while Southey was infusing prose virtues into poetry, Carlyle in 1837 achieved a hyperprose that was virtually verse. But verse it was not, quite; so *The French Revolution* falls outside a brief that precludes our lingering over it here. It nevertheless remains, as John Stuart Mill and others rapidly agreed, the supreme epic production of its time—and thus, in many respects, the characteristic one.[17] Resuming the main epic line of the 1820s, Carlyle's favorite imagery of deluge and eruption drew forth from the apocalyptic imagination its silenced but always implicit political content. And all that was most vigorous in his present-tense theatrical realization of the Revolution's hungry ingestion of preexistent "formulas," or cultural paradigms for totality, pointed with streaming pennons to where the winds of generic inspiration were blowing among the epic poets proper.[18]

[16] There are extended assessments of the problematically epic quality of *The French Revolution* in Mark Cumming, *A Disimprisoned Epic: Form and Vision in Carlyle's* French Revolution (Philadelphia: University of Pennsylvania Press, 1988); John D. Rosenberg, "Carlyle and Historical Narration," *Carlyle Annual* 10 (1989) 14–20; Vanden Bossche, *Carlyle and the Search for Authority*, 56–88. Alfred J. Mac Adam, *Textual Confrontations: Comparative Readings in Latin American Literature* (Chicago and London: University of Chicago Press, 1987) 149–63, brings to Carlyle's handling of genre a comparatist's fresh eye. On the immolation of conventions, nay genres, in the white heat of Carlyle's transcendental desperation see John P. Farrell's *Revolution as Tragedy: The Dilemma of the Moderate from Scott to Arnold* (Ithaca and London: Cornell University Press, 1980) 190–98. Mary Desaulniers, *Carlyle and the Economics of Terror: A Study of Revisionary Gothicism in* The French Revolution (Montreal and Kingston: McGill-Queen's University Press, 1995) 73, analyzes the "double exposure" whereby each episode becomes "a scene of misreading that situates the revolutionary impetus within an ironic configuration."

[17] Mill's essay, in the *London and Westminster Review* (July 1837), actually preceded publication of *The French Revolution*. He repeatedly calls the book "an epic poem" and pronounces it "of surpassing excellence; excelled, in its kind, only by the great masters of epic poetry," and "written in prose, with a fervour and exaltation of feeling which is only tolerated in verse, if even there": *Essays on French History and Historians*, ed. John M. Robson and John C. Cairns (Toronto and London: University of Toronto Press, 1985) 133–34, 164. From Kingsley to Trollope, and in America from Thoreau to Lowell, Carlyle's history was repeatedly hailed in epic terms: see the cento of quotations in John Clubbe, "Carlyle as Epic Historian," in *Victorian Literature and Society: Essays Presented to Richard D. Altick*, ed. James R. Kincaid and Albert J. Kuhn (Columbus: Ohio State University Press, 1984) 121.

[18] Carlyle himself held, by 1830, that Britain sorely needed what epic might offer, but that generic business-as-usual was no longer viable: "We have . . . in place of the wholly dead modern

The next years witnessed publication of two para-dramatic epics that rank among the most singular and obstinate poems of the century. Philip James Bailey's *Festus*, as it snowballed across the decades, accumulated such a following of readers and imitators that we may only note here its debut in the comparatively slender edition of 1839, reserving proper consideration until the chapter after next ponders the spasmodic triumph of the epic mode Bailey had inaugurated. Browning's *Sordello* (1840), on the other hand, is by a long-standing paradox best known for being obscure—perversely difficult, deservedly unread—and thus also, through a logic dear to modern cultural elites, for having been cherished by such poets' poets as D. G. Rossetti and Ezra Pound. *Sordello* was not only the most loyally inventive work that Carlyle's example inspired in any author, but the most fully elaborated work that the sensibility of liberal Reform produced in any genre.[19] The narrative subject is the abortive poetic and political career of an early thirteenth-century troubadour. This life of nearly inconsequential failure was in Browning's view redeemed twice over: by Dante's later success in the vernacular poetry that Sordello had pioneered, and thereafter by the persistence of the Italian popular nationalism to which that poetry gave support and which Browning symbolizes on his final page in the folk survival of an anonymous snatch from one of Sordello's songs (2.151, 5.905, 6.867).

The linkage in this relatively simple story between literary and political motives is stressed to the breaking point—beyond it, in the estimation of many defeated interpreters—by a narrative manner of the most challenging kind. Elliptical in style, allusive in reference, unremitting in its solicitous or badgering insistence on active construal and application of "Sordello's

Epic, the partially living modern Novel . . . the former being flatly incredible"; "in this generation, the very name of Epic sets men a-yawning, the announcement of a new Epic is received as a public calamity": "Biography" (1832), in *Essays*, 4: 11. The solution to this dilemma lay for Carlyle in a revived historiography: in "On History Again" (1833) he called history "the true Epic Poem, and universal Divine Scripture" (*Essays*, 4: 225). Or, as he told Mill in a letter of September 1833, "the right *History* (that impossible thing I mean by History) of the French Revolution were the grand Poem of our Time": quoted in Philip Rosenberg, *The Seventh Hero: Thomas Carlyle and the Theory of Radical Activism* (Cambridge, Mass.: Harvard University Press, 1974) 77. Clubbe regards Carlyle's study of Homer after the publication of *Sartor Resartus* as a turning point: "Before 1834 Carlyle had little to say about the epic; after that year, every major book he wrote reflects his awareness of it" (120).

[19] See Desaulniers's chapter on the debt that Browning's rendition of politics in *Sordello* owes to Carlyle. Mary Ellis Gibson, pondering the way *Sordello* outstripped in strictly *poetic* influence the author's acclaimed later epic *The Ring and the Book*, reminds us that "*Sordello* is a product not of the 1860s with its dominant discourse of realism and individualism but of the 1830s when both the political situation and the possibilities of representation were in flux": *Epic Reinvented: Ezra Pound and the Victorians* (Ithaca and London: Cornell University Press, 1995) 106.

story" (1.1, 6.886 *et passim*), the poem needles its reader into taking a rhapsode's part and stitching an epic whole out of narrative remnants and syntactical scraps. Even veterans find the apparatus of *Sordello* overwhelming, but they take comfort from understanding that its demands however improper are thoroughly continuous with the story's proper themes. Browning exacts such hard work of us because that is what creative collaboration takes; and nothing short of creative collaboration, he believed, could keep the literary transaction from breaking down into authoritarian mirage on one side and supine consumerism on the other. Eternal vigilance was the price of liberty in letters, as of the kind of political liberalism which Browning in his twenties hoped the era of Reform was ushering in, and towards which he believed Sordello's poetic innovations and party allegiances had dimly shown the way an hour before the Renaissance dawned and the Reformation became a possibility.[20]

A standing invitation to cooperative reading in the currency of "brother's speech" (5.635), *Sordello* is the (Blakean) opposite of the kind of reader-friendly text that—like Bailey's *Festus*, to look no farther—encourages imaginative absorption in the world it represents. Despite the poem's reputation for bewilderment, it is harder in this feel-good sense to get lost in *Sordello* than in any other epic this book discusses. In contrast, say, to Mrs. William Busk's 1837 romance in six cantos of the same name (a late, lame imitation of Scott's manner, crossed on a Tom Moore plot), one gets lost *on* Browning's poem, or one crashes *against* it. This rarely breached impenetrability is strategic. "Who will, may hear Sordello's story told," the narrative begins, adding, "Only believe me. Ye believe?" (1.10). The consenting reader has little choice but to believe, not so much in the story as in the *story told*; its toldness is the clearest thing about it, being incessantly foregrounded by such devices of attentive recursion as the little interrogative backflip just quoted, or the words that immediately follow: "Appears | Verona...Never, I should warn you first,—" (1.10–11). It is a nice question here, and not here only, whether tale has interrupted telling or *vice*

---

[20] One Victorian name for such vigilance being *criticism*, it is instructive to read at a century's distance what A. C. Bradley found to say, apropos the epic Browning, when lecturing on "The Long Poem in the Age of Wordsworth" around 1905: "To describe the atmosphere of 'criticism' as that of a common faith or view of the world would be laughable. If not revolutionary, it was agitated, restless, and distressed by the conflict of theoretic ideas": *Oxford Lectures on Poetry* (London: Macmillan, 1917) 198. For better or worse as regards the last laugh, Bradley's string of adjectives does after all describe what was a not uncommon nineteenth-century world view, with which long poems if vital and intellectually ambitious had to cope.

versa; whether, that is, the poem asks to be read as a preternaturally self-conscious story or as an essay in narratology with lots of illustrative examples attached for practice. Browning's narrative obstructionism makes it an epic point to implicate the reader in the shaping of history: the reader who gathers Sordello's story by fits and starts reenacts, and assists towards completion, the recollective labor of an exponentially Carlylean historian-poet.[21] In the process the reader comes to understand that this reenactment is history too, history in the making—an activity different in degree rather than kind from what poets do. That includes the poet Sordello as, within the fable, he puts together a set of mysterious clues as to his own origins.

An instructive contrast to Browning's radical poetic reformism is furnished by the nearly contemporary publication of *Attila, or the Triumph of Christianity* (1838) by William Herbert. Known to us already as author of the Nordic *Helga* (Ch. 4) and the frosty *Pia della Pietra* (Ch. 5), and respected in his day as a medievalist whose preface here addressed the noted historian Henry Hallam as a peer, Herbert made the unhappy choice to bind his substantial twelve-book epic together in one large volume (entitled *Attila, King of the Huns*) with a prose history of similar length on precisely the same subject. Not notes to his epic but in effect a rival treatment of the theme, Herbert's subjoined prose account "Attila and His Predecessors" raises with devastating force the question what its handling in verse can possibly be good for, the more so when he expressly stakes its claim on "the general historical truth of the poem," as against "mere works of imagination" (Dedication, iv). Mere works indeed. As Herbert's dispirited epilogue seems to acknowledge (12.117), the question is unanswerable so long as poetic narrative sticks to Clio's conventional vantage of objective historiographical omniscience. Where the historian-poet had already digested the tale, asking the reader to work as hard as was required by Herbert's often densely detailed pentameter chronicle seemed self-defeatingly perverse.

Browning's historical poem too was perverse, of course, but in service to Calliope not Clio. Where *Sordello* bent itself double, it was with the aim of handing creative initiative back to the reader as a narrative coadjutor, and also as an historical agent taking stock at the start of Victoria's reign. With commendable truth-in-advertising, what is redundant in the phrase

[21] Jacob Korg, *Browning and Italy* (Athens and London: Ohio University Press, 1983), approaches the historical detail that *Sordello* provides as "a referential field for a poetic of suggestion and allusion," which in one sense furnishes ideas with particular grounding and in another sense defines a common ground or "medium" for transaction between poet and reader (31).

"Sordello's story told" names a constitutively epic procedure of the poem it introduces: recursive feedback.[22] By feeding the tale and the telling back into each other, Browning without loss of learned but decidedly colloquial verve managed to estrange ordinary English from itself—so successfully that the reception mythology features numerous anecdotes from contemporaries who swore they couldn't understand a word of it.[23] In so doing the Victorian poet contrived a simulacrum of the historical Sordello's breakthrough into vernacular poetry. *Dolce* or not, and probably not, what must have seemed newest about the Sordellan *stil nuove* in its distant day was the transformation of a language hitherto merely instrumental into the opacity of a medium that could be consciously manipulated for art.[24] The intimate, serviceable transparency of speech, silvered into artifice, must have flashed the thirteenth-century audience's own image back in fascinating but also disconcerting fashion. Intrigued by this strangeness, which was fundamental to centuries of vernacular poetry but had long gone numb with use, Browning found an

[22] David Latané, *Browning's* Sordello *and the Aesthetics of Difficulty* (Victoria: English Literary Studies, 1987), shows how the recursive "play of text within text, and the palimpsest-like recombinations of text-upon-text" (87–88) constitute a Carlylean kind of historiographic dialogue, resumed in a different key by the peekaboo allusiveness of Browning's poet-haunted poem (109). The strategy of historical feedback that Morse Peckham analyzes in Browning's second epic had also been employed in his first: see "Historiography and *The Ring and the Book*," *Victorian Poetry* 6 (1968) 243–57.

[23] Recycling anecdotes that record Harriet Martineau's, Douglas Jerrold's, or Jane Carlyle's bafflement by *Sordello* tends in practice to usurp critical engagement with the difficulties of the text. Those difficulties, wherein the poet's Romantic intellectual elitism vies with his Christian democratic liberalism, are most productively engaged by Latané's book, especially 63–74; and by John Woolford, *Browning the Revisionary* (London: Macmillan, 1988) 28–56, and Joseph Bristow, *Robert Browning* (New York and London: Harvester, 1991) 61–78. See also Michael Mason, "The Importance of *Sordello*," and Isobel Armstrong, "Browning and the 'Grotesque' Style," both in *The Major Victorian Poets: Reconsiderations*, ed. Armstrong (London: Routledge, 1969) 93–105 and 125–51; Armstrong's *Language as Living Form in Nineteenth-Century Poetry* (Brighton: Harvester, 1982) 141–71; Peter Allan Dale, "Paracelsus and Sordello: Trying the Stuff of Language," *Victorian Poetry* 18 (1980) 359–69; and Matthew Campbell, *Rhythm and Will in Victorian Poetry* (Cambridge: Cambridge University Press, 1999) 88–96.

[24] The question of poetic language is one among several respects in which Sordello's situation within the story rehearses Browning's situation as its narrator. See Christine Froula, "Browning's *Sordello* and the Parables of Modernist Poetics," *ELH* 52 (1985): the poet as linguistic pluralist seeks "to turn English into a foreign language and English poetry into a foreign affair" (985). As a young man Browning reportedly read Johnson's *Dictionary* cover-to-cover; as an old one he told the great Oxford lexicographer James Murray, then at work on what was to be the *OED*, that he "intended to read every word of it." Murray subsequently groused to his Browningite son that the late poet had "constantly used words without regard to their proper meaning. He has added greatly to the difficulties of the Dictionary": K. M. Elisabeth Murray, *Caught in the Web of Words: James A. H. Murray and the* Oxford English Dictionary (New Haven and London: Yale University Press, 1977) 235. See also Donald S. Hair, *Robert Browning's Language* (Toronto: University of Toronto Press, 1999) 8–12.

equivalent in a delivery system that made the sleeping dogs of every narrative convention bark, rode roughshod over the heroic couplet in ways fit to make his friend Leigh Hunt wince, and in the first edition dispensed with the niceties of even the quotation mark, thus leaving the lines between directly reported speech and indirect discourse for readers to draw freehand, in a wilderness of sheer English that, thus re-vernacularized, might become again an unadministered common possession. One very interesting, signally intelligible passage on Sordello's trials of language in book 2 (lines 568–617) concerns the topic of word-smithery directly. But we no sooner study the passage than we realize that this same topic is represented indirectly on the poem's every page, usually with such willful disregard for the representamen as to fortify suspicion that what every page most truly represents is representation itself.

Would Lord Byron have approved? By venturing so boldly in Byron's direction Browning in effect bet that Reform had made the literary world safe for wholesale irony once more. He lost this bet spectacularly—so spectacularly that, imagining Byron among those poetic shades who are expressly convened as auditors in book 1, we imagine him shaking his ghostly head over the impractical enormity of what *Sordello* attempted.[25] For Browning admitted irony into the one place *Don Juan* had consistently protected against irony's corrosiveness: the confidence of the sovereign self. Even when bent on self-mockery—perhaps then especially—the stand-up celebrity performer of *Don Juan* had backed up his most damaging concessions about doubt, venality, and inconsistency with the authority of an articulate and answerable, definitively Romantic identity. This imaginative economy of heroic liberalism Browning cashiered, liquidating the apparent solidity of identity by the same gesture, the same means, and ultimately the same rationale that motivated his deconstruction of a fixed and knowable thirteenth century.

Sordello offers no hero, and certainly no central narrative consciousness, as stable as Byron's, because it lacks alike Byron's existentially positive faith in the self and (what aggravates that faith if it does not indeed fund it) Byron's existential despair. Not a personable poem in the Byronic sense, *Sordello*

---

[25] On Browning's Byronic affiliations see John Maynard, *Browning's Youth* (Cambridge, Mass., and London: Harvard University Press, 1977) 169–78; David Latané, " 'See You?' Browning, Byron, and the Revolutionary Deluge in *Sordello*, Book I," *Victorian Poetry* 22 (1984) 85–91; and for contextual background Andrew Elfenbein, *Byron and the Victorians* (Cambridge: Cambridge University Press, 1995).

remains nevertheless a cheerful one, by reason of the epic faith Browning
vests in contingency, recreative juxtaposition, and the eventual solidarity of
the manifold of particularities around the world and in the fullness of time.
The poem's second sustainedly coherent meditation on poetry comes to a
head in book 5, as Sordello surveys generic options, bypassing narrative
and theatrical presentation (the forms, as Browning's marginal glosses for
the second edition would have it, of "epoist" and "dramatist") in favor of
"the last of mysteries":

> "Man's inmost life shall yet have freer play:
> Once more I cast external things away,
> And natures composite, so decompose
> That" ... Why, he writes *Sordello*!

> (5.616–20)

Without this breathtaking narratorial intrusion—doubly intrusive, since
Browning added it only in 1863—one might take "inmost life" to be the
province of just such feelingful, sympathetic lyricism as 1830s poetic theor-
ists like Mill and Arthur Hallam were exalting (as, within *Sordello*, the
poem's critic-in-residence Naddo was doing too).[26] Even the unrevised
1840 passage, however, plays decomposition against composition in ways
that militate against Romantic subjectivity and jibe better with this modern
epic's mission to cut, shuffle, and deal the components of psychic and social
integrity. "Inmost life" is at best a differential interference effect, wherever
one slices into it, and especially in the case of the shambling Carlylean
lecture-hall impresario who is Browning's excuse for a narrator. The
ostensible Romantic privacy of an inmost life is originally, intimately im-
pinged upon by other lives, its story (like this poem) embroiled with others',
its alleged sovereignty a delusive betrayal of the broader fellowship and
citizenry to which modern selfhood is finally due.

The crossroads of a multiplicity of stories—the haunt of Browning's epic
muse throughout his career—is a noisy distraction to which the poet heark-
ens in the hope of picking out for transmission the appeal of a democratic

---

[26] See Hallam's obscurely placed 1831 review of Tennyson's first solo collection of lyrics, rpt. in
The Writings of Arthur Hallam, ed. T. Vail Motter (New York: Modern Language Association,
1943); and two 1833 essays Mill published in the *Monthly Repository*, "What Is Poetry?" and
"The Two Kinds of Poetry": rpt. in *Autobiography and Literary Essays*, ed. John M. Robson and
Jack Stillinger (Toronto and Buffalo: University of Toronto Press, 1981). Browning arguably
modeled his Naddo on Moore's incorporated critic Fadladeen, from one epic generation earlier in
Lalla Rookh (see Ch. 5).

solidarity. One venerable epic means by which he makes honorable way for that appeal is the heroic simile.[27] Extended similes in *Sordello* get extended in response to two distinct pressures that it is part of the poem's good cheer to treat as correlative. One is naïve curiosity about matters great and small, natural and cultural, historical and contemporary. After the manner of Homer, the poem plunges into these multitudinous things for relief from its narrative ardors; and by their means it expands, evidently at random, to compass an encyclopedic purview. Where Homer's similes are reposefully complete in themselves, though, Browning's are internally excrescent: around the corner of an adventitious detail they consistently glimpse a vignette world they can neither explore nor refrain from hinting at. This, like all its defining habits, the poem eventually names: "the bard's start aside and look askance" (3.638). The line occurs during a mid-poem passage wherein Robert Browning himself, drafted into the poem and bemused in a crowd at Venice, proceeds to hail in the bustle of working people all around him an admonition that he keep faith with the liberal cause of their enfranchisement. And one method of keeping faith with the untold story of the multitude inheres in the multitude of untold stories that his similes keep remembering are out there all around the chosen epic tale, and that, so the logic of simile proposes, are not at bottom unlike it.

This dispersive, expansive force within the epic similes of *Sordello* is answered by another, centripetal one. Browning will often play a simile out until it feeds back in the self-referential mode that is this poem's norm; until, that is, it generates an image of the creative will to connect, which is to say of the metaphor-loving power that similes harbor. The "architect" spider (1.665–71) or "mansion"-building bee (6.620–25), the woven vest whose loss at sea "vexed a satrap" (3.11–15), all exceed any strictly illustrative brief. They wink out, momentarily, as parables that might have been and that, if realized as independent narratives, would attest and in their telling elicit exertions of the creative will that are fundamentally cognate with those actuating the principal persons in the story proper. The net result is curiously, unexpectedly Homeric: all that comes within ken is equivalently worthy of regard because all has its place within the total worldview from which value proceeds. But where that worldview was a given to Homer's serene objectivity, here it is subjectively under construction at a

---

[27] I discuss the poem's use of similes at greater length in *Browning's Beginnings: The Art of Disclosure* (Minneapolis: University of Minnesota Press, 1980) 101–6.

myriad sites whose collaborative undertaking, and potential for activation, Browning's eccentric procedures smuggle into consciousness.

Wherever the poet looks, and above all out of the corner of his eye, he finds creative power abroad in nature and spread across his constituency as a human resource of which authoritarian epic has taken too little account. Defending poetry against the scorn of the politico Salinguerra who is (unknown to either of them) his father, Sordello gives himself the advice that is written all over the poem. "Already you include | The multitude"; but this Whitmanesque largesse is too nearly the Carlylean arrogance of the *Dichter* as dictator doing the little people a favor. So Sordello goes on: "let the multitude | Include yourself; and the result were new: | Themselves before, the multitude turn you" (5.533–36). The liberal ideal, trusted here well beyond the limits the Reform Bill of 1832 had drawn, measures the petty integrity of self-sufficient individualism against the poet's acknow- ledged participation in a collective life that has much to teach him about things unattempted yet in prose or rhyme. The line last quoted says a mouthful: the multitude with whom the poet acknowledges membership can turn into him, yes; but in so doing "turn" him, too, with a conversional force unpossessed by himself alone no matter how egalitarian his ideas as mere abstractions. The gift of a common language poetically troped can, in turn, convert the multitude from just individuals "Themselves" into a spoken and commissioned people. *Sordello*, like Sordello at his best, repudiates on one side the leadership poetics that produces testaments (the hero dies renouncing power on oppressive terms) and on the other the mediocrity poetics that produces commodities (see the literary maven Naddo on the bestseller's law of averages, 2.797–801). That *Sordello*, again like Sordello, failed utterly in its time was a development that disappointed Browning and retarded his popularity for twenty years. But it was no more unforeseeable than it was unprovoked: a worthy avant-garde son of Shelley, he had in a sense asked for it.[28] The creative power of the people had his resourceful voice and liberal trust; whether his epic overture would have their voice and trust only time, with a little help from his own successor- Dantes further down the line, would tell.

★

---

[28] As Froula puts it, the last three books of the poem narrate "the contradictions between Browning's ideal of poetic authority and its possibilities of realization in history; for, if the parabolic poetics of Browning, Sordello, and *Sordello* would dissociate poetic authority from violence, that poetics risks unintelligibility by its very conception" ("Browning's *Sordello*," 975).

Obscure though it remains in other respects, *Sordello* makes it clearer than any poem considered thus far that, when epoists of the 1830s reconfigured narrative along dramatic lines for the amphitheater of the mind, what was likely to get staged there was adversarial class consciousness. Because modern class identity constituted an unprecedented category under which to organize experience, epic had to cope with it much as Parliament did, by adapting to sweepingly changed realities a mechanism long ago evolved for the negotiation of different, narrower aims.[29] Radical analysts on the left would soon be suggesting that the truth about class interests under industrial advance was fixedly polemical and only to be determined by class warfare. Yet in no decade of the British nineteenth century was the military epic more conspicuously in retreat—Southey's pacific reissue of the still-martial *Joan* being an exception that proves the rule. Even Carlyle fell silent at the advent of Napoleon's "whiff of grapeshot" and the prospect of war (3.7.7); in truth, the depiction of civil violence in *The French Revolution* gave all the reason prudent poets might need to observe a moratorium on arms if not bid them farewell.

To be sure, Capel Lofft the younger (born 1806, son to an Enlightened cosmological poet of the same name) completed during the 1830s twelve books of blank verse narrating an armed insurrection of the people in an unnamed German principality. *Ernest; or Political Regeneration* not only detailed schemes for the reallocation of wealth and power but also advocated *in extenso*, and narrated at epic length, popular recourse to violent struggle as the only means of realizing these aims. Yet even the gentleman-radical Lofft fell into line with the forensic spirit of the day. His defense of militancy appears chiefly in dialogues that his bookish, preacherly hero Ernest Hermann has with his hard-knocks future father-in-law Frederick Hess (books 1–3) and with the radicalized nobleman-apostate Lisinger (books 5–7). Later, in an original and timely adaptation of the 1830s' favorite epic convention, there even occurs a symposium debate on rights and

---

[29] On the roots and growth of the new category of *class* as a consequence of the industrial revolution see Harold Perkin, *The Origins of Modern English Society 1780–1880* (London: Routledge, 1969) 176–217. On the speed with which class pervaded modern thinking after passage of the Reform Bill, see Dror Wahrman, *Imagining the Middle Class: The Political Representation of Class in Britain, 1780–1840* (Cambridge: Cambridge University Press, 1995) 333: not only did the term "middle class" recur ubiquitously in public discourse, but "it was also presented as a most important factor in understanding almost everything else, often overriding previous perceptions that had lacked this quasi-magical component." Armstrong, *Victorian Poetry*, 157–58, correlates Sordello's attempt to imagine the "crowd" with the large effort of the early nineteenth century to replace the eighteenth-century hierarchy behind the "public" with that different organization the "people."

strategies that Hermann moderates among militant working men (book 9). The conflicts that form part of the deliberative process thus engross more space in *Ernest* than do the insurgent actions they lead to. Moreover, when push came to shove the poet drew back from going fully public as a class traitor. Having printed his epic in 1839 for very limited circulation—a proof with annotations survives in the British Library, and a copy was noticed that year by fellow epoist H. H. Milman in the *Quarterly Review*—Lofft apparently found the Chartist moment too hot to handle publication.[30] He withdrew his work from circulation and turned it years later into a wholly different poem (glanced at in Ch. 10) when the national complexion changed again during the franchise crisis of the later 1860s.

The limit case of Capel Lofft's preachment and practice rounds off the point to which the spirit of early-Victorian Reform brought epic's long-standing commitment to national service. Sublimated by a kind of epic-games diversion into performative modes of earnest play—trial, oratory, reconnoiter, intrigue—the strife that a middle-class epoist typically imagined during the 1830s was confined to contestation between sects or parties that conceived themselves to be portions of an inclusive common wealth. It was for ideological control of this greater, participated entity that the opponents were contending, and not as in former days for territory or treasure, liberation or defense. And it was to the articulation of this entity, a synthesis confidently expected at the end of an ongoing dialectical process, that the traditional holism of the epic genre was at this time devoted. The poet who wrote from inside this process was content to take the word for the deed, and shaped epic action accordingly.

This voluntary restriction on the imagination of action had much less appeal to poets who emerged, with the emergence of class-consciousness, from among the working class. The best of them nevertheless saw how, by observing the rules, it might be possible to subvert the bourgeois impositions those rules ostensibly served. Since peace after Waterloo had slackened the reins of patriotism, Britain had witnessed in mass urban demonstration and intermittent rural sabotage ample evidence that working people felt left out of the new national compact. The lower orders' revolutionary potential was a major factor, at the flashpoint of 1832, that scared their aristocratic

---

[30] British Library shelflist C.28.B.12 and C.28.B.13 binds into the 1839 *Ernest: In Twelve Books* an undated alternative page with the title *Ernest; or, Political Regeneration*. The copious annotations suggest that this was Lofft's revisal copy in later years. An admiring account of the resulting "agrarian epic" of 1868 appears in *Harriet Martineau's Autobiography*, 3rd edn. (London: Smith, Elder, 1877) 1: 416–17. See also Hugh Walker, *The Literature of the Victorian Era* (Cambridge: University Press, 1910) 350–52.

rulers into sharing power with a substantial percentage of their bourgeois bosses. But this freshly dressed share did not reach the laborers themselves, and working-class frustration over the persistently exclusive, and in many ways deliberately oppressive, character of the new parliamentary regime found expression in an important new literature that tended to eschew middle-class forensic epic, as it did middle-class prose fiction, in favor of poetry that was reliably rooted in folksong and ballad.[31]

This poetry gravitated towards the ancient form of epic whenever authors sought common cause, on behalf of their class constituents, with a transcendent idea of the nation to which all Britons belonged. In the name of a fully United Kingdom, they maintained, all Britons could assert the rights that Reform Bills, Poor Laws, and Corn Laws were systematically, shortsightedly denying to large and increasingly vocal sectors of the population. Epic offered a neutral ground over which a generically enhanced memory might play in order to enlarge the scope in which Britain's future was imagined.[32] The people who lacked a vote in 1832, and would lack throughout the hungry 1840s the charter for which they agitated by millions, did find through epic spokesmen a sustaining vision of their participation in a national idea whose time would come, if only several contentious decades later.

Two epic spokesmen who flanked the 1830s made particularly astute use of the generic conventions their moment made available. In the omnium-gatherum ten books of *The Village Patriarch* (1829), Ebenezer Elliott, born in 1781, virtually recapitulated the history of the genre in his lifetime. The poem proportioned a medley of modes and tones to the common denominator of poor people's oppression at the hands of those landholders who, "patriarchs" in degraded name only, had manifestly abandoned the national stewardship that once went along with their feudal honor and privilege. These evils Elliott denounces through the mouthpiece figure of Enoch Wray, a man with a Genesis patriarch's name who is both old enough to remember the now-dishonored social contract of mutual rural obligation up

---

[31] These deep vernacular roots, Anne Janowitz points out, corresponded to "anachronistic utopian models" deriving from popular-culture residua of 17th-cent. radicalism, such that "the notion of a repressed 'people's' national literary heritage" was a Chartist poetic tradition half recollected, half made up: *Lyric and Labour in the Romantic Tradition* (Cambridge: Cambridge University Press, 1998) 143.

[32] Peter Mandler remarks that in the early 19th cent. "relative political exclusiveness in Britain was bought at the price of relative cultural openness": " 'In the Olden Time': Romantic History and English National Identity, 1820–50," in *A Union of Multiple Identities: The British Isles, c.1750–c.1850*, ed. Laurence Brockliss and David Eastwood (Manchester and New York: Manchester University Press, 1997) 78.

and down the ranks and young enough to have opened his Byron and learned to curse. A Goldsmithian deserted-village survivor with a touch of minstrel glamour and dose of *furor poeticus*, Enoch comes across as a Wordsworthian pedlar with attitude. He tinkers with meters and rhymes drawn from a spectrum of traditions from satire to sentimental tale, practicing on each a prosody as blunt as his politics. From a grassroots plateau the reader of *The Village Patriarch* thus looks out, through a sequence of prisms rummaged from the high art modes of Romanticism, across British society as it has become. At the same time, Elliott harks back through literary history to a national history that is backlit by distinct glimmers of the fiery and unforgotten popular radicalism of the seventeenth century.[33]

These furnish the millenarian spark for Elliott's seventh book, "Enoch Wray's Dream," which revives the latent political content that slumbered within 1820s end-of-the-world epics (content that would return again in "The Ranter," from the poet's *Corn Law Rhymes*, 3rd edn. 1831). In a sequence of apocalyptic and purgatorial visions Elliott sends back into the fray an armory of images that his evangelical contemporaries had airlifted into the afterlife. When the deluging torrent in Enoch's dream crashes on despotism, "like an angel sweeping worlds away," the cleansing force is neither natural nor supernatural but political: a "resistless sea of souls" (7.290–91) whose waves are men and whose foam is "human agony, | Alive with curses, horrible to hear" (7.272–73). When an obstructor of "Democracy" (unnamed, but he looks like Castlereagh) not only is called "The dog of kings, their whip for poverty" (7.331) but then is metamorphosed into the leader of a famished pack of hell-hounds, Elliott scores a Dantesque point: the people have learned class-conflict from their betters, whose betrayal of the nation's trust is fast bringing forth a dog-eat-dog society. By 1832 Carlyle, gestating his own major history of the power of the French people, dimly heard in Elliott's work "an inarticulate, half-audible Epic," poetry that was "in its nature and unconscious tendency, Epic."[34] But not much about it was unconscious. Carlyle in his man-of-letters patronage missed the craft with which the angry Corn-Law rhymester of *The Village Patriarch* meant to reclaim the people's half of a

---

[33] We might also date Elliott's economic analysis back to the 17th cent.: as Walker remarks (246), all Elliott's invective falls on landowner abuses, and he says nothing of capitalist-industrial injustice—perhaps because he was an ironmaster with employees of his own.

[34] *Essays*, 4: 205. See also the chapter on Elliott as chief among the blacksmith poets in Edwin Paxton Hood, *The Peerage of Poverty; or, Learners and Workers in Fields, Farms, and Factories* (1859; 5th rev. edn. London: Partridge, n.d.) 99–125; and the discussion in Lucas, *English and Englishness*, 162–65.

nationally grounded tradition, which two hard generations of agrarian expro-
priation on one hand, and poetical sentimentalization on the other, had
estranged from a culturally beggared class.

What Elliott brought to the boil as Reform agitation was cresting, a second
working-class epoist strove to keep cool lest it spoil, fifteen eventful years
later on the downslope of the rejected People's Charter. "Thomas Cooper,
the Chartist," as the shoemaker-activist signed himself on the title page of
The Purgatory of Suicides: A Prison-Rhyme in Ten Books (1845), seasoned a long
banquet of Spenserian stanzas with remarks on his condition as a political
prisoner in Stafford Gaol, where he mainly wrote the poem and where his
hardest labor may have been that of staring down despondency over the
stalled Charter. Penning thousands of lines on the world's eminent suicides
seems so unlikely a therapy that it may be helpful to recall how Blake and
Wordsworth had done something of the same kind a generation earlier
in *Jerusalem* and *The Excursion*, correcting revolutionary despondency by
confronting at length all that was to be forgiven and endured. Cooper too
grappled with the immediacy of despair by exacting a full look at the worst
and reattaching his hopes to a long-term talking cure.

He found his theme in a high postmortem consult among shades of the
kings and revolutionaries, poets and sages, men and women, who had seen
fit to take their own lives. Their discourses on religion, science, and politics
present an unsurprising compendium of radical thought in the Tom Paine
tradition that had been Cooper's university: the monarchs have a little more
to say for themselves than Shelley would have countenanced, but Disraeli's
Magros might cry foul all the same at the blatantly leftward angle of vision
here. What better repays notice is the way Cooper suspends narrative
interest in favor of theoretical debate. This is an odd strategy for an epic,
but one quite in keeping with the main line of generic development in the
decade before Cooper tried it; its dialogical orientation contrasts favorably
with the monologism that would prevail during the last third of the century
in a thematically comparable poem like Lewis Morris's *Epic of Hades* or
Cooper's own wan palinode *The Paradise of Martyrs* (Ch. 11). Cooper
records in his autobiography that the idea for *The Purgatory* came to him
while "attending a meeting of the town council, in my office of reporter to
the *Stamford Mercury*."[35] While there is no knowing what this says about the
town councillors, that the muse should have visited such a deliberative

---

[35] *The Life of Thomas Cooper, Written by Himself* (London: Hodder and Stoughton, 1879), 115.

forum shows with emblematic force where the reforming 1830s had located epic inspiration.

It is also characteristic of this interval in generic history that Cooper reports some difficulty at the time in deciding between "either a drama, or an epic." Epic must have been the harder choice, and so by certain lights the worthier. Cooper cannot have overlooked the genre's elite status.[36] Even his models in radicalized Spenserian verse, Byron and Shelley, had both been aristocrats, and there were class interests at stake in a self-taught artisan's presuming—and in a sustained way actually contriving—to write as his social betters had done.[37] Then there was the impediment of his chosen theme. The narrative inertia of suicide is presumptively nihilistic; its abbreviation of the human prospect ought to have damped epic's wing, and ought especially to have galled a poet whose political work seemed to have come to nothing.[38] Since, in addition, the unheroic company Cooper kept had precious little to hope for in the award of posterity, he had every reason to eschew suicidal narrative's foreclosedness in favor of drama's mimetic illusion of a perpetual present. To his credit, though, Cooper

[36] Nigel Cross, *The Common Writer: Life in Nineteenth-Century Grub Street* (Cambridge: Cambridge University Press, 1985) 151, reminds us that "*The Purgatory of Suicides* was not supposed to be admired as an astonishing literary feat for a working-class man—it was intended to be a dazzling achievement by any standards." Writing polemically at mid-century, Hood underscores this point by amassing reviewers' encomia and marveling on his own at the quantity of Cooper's learning (238–44).

[37] A passage at 2.7 alludes specifically to *Childe Harold* and to *The Revolt of Islam*. Stephanie Kuduk Weiner, *Republican Politics and English Poetry, 1789–1874* (Houndmills: Palgrave, 2005), proposes that work like Cooper's in *The Purgatory*, coming after the great wave of the People's Charter had been dissipated, was in the long run the most influential type of Chartist verse. Because its demonstration of cultural capital "opened up lines of communication between Chartism and elite progressives" (82), such verse earned a stake in the direction reformist politics would take during the mid-Victorian years. On this general development see Paul Thomas Murphy, *Toward a Working-Class Canon: Literary Criticism in British Working-Class Periodicals, 1816–1858* (Columbus: Ohio State University Press, 1994) 129–35. One mark of this rapprochement is Charles Kingsley's calling *The Purgatory* "brilliant": quoted in Amy Cruse, *The Victorians and their Books* (London: Allen and Unwin, 1935) 142. Kingsley modeled his Christian-Socialist novel *Alton Locke* (1850) on experiences Cooper retailed to him in conversation: Philip Collins, *Thomas Cooper, The Chartist: Byron and the "Poets of the Poor"* (Nottingham: University of Nottingham, 1969) 4–5. In ch. 30 of the novel, the unjustly imprisoned tailor-poet resolves to "concentrate all my experience, my aspirations, all the hopes and wrongs and sorrows of the poor, into one garland of thorns—one immortal epic of suffering."

[38] Collins, *Thomas Cooper*, 12–13, gamely surveys the poem's shortcomings. Some of these, it may be pleaded, came of Cooper's endeavor to resuscitate, with Landor, the defunct genre of the dead-men's-dialogue, which itself all but gave up the ghost after 1800: see—though the book does not mention Cooper's poem—Frederick M. Keener, *English Dialogues of the Dead: A Critical History, An Anthology, and A Check List* (New York and London: Columbia University Press, 1973) 127–42.

worked out a generic mixture that placed dramatic exchange within a narrative perspective, and so kept hope alive. Suicide was forever, all right, and in the final analysis it was always the same; but from the rehearsal of its varieties of motive a larger story might be made, one that balanced the individual life against causes worth living for—or dying, even by one's own hand. The need was not for new life-stories, Cooper's forensic epic structure implied, but for fresh perspective on the old ones, as revealed externally in a dream-vision framework adapted from *The Revolt of Islam* and internally in frank dialectic among contestants with nothing to lose and therefore nothing to hide.

Accordingly Cooper the Chartist converted the dead-endedness of his suicides from the Dantesque hell of merely iterative theatrical presence into a *purgatory*, a refinery of ideas, a cultural site where there was a job to do. The name of that job was political and moral philosophy, or as we now should say critical theory, its mode the contest of ideas in dialogue.[39] Its object then as now was to cast out despair by recasting apparent lost causes (like the People's Charter) as stalled causes instead. Taken up into dialectical relation with one another, the testimonies and rhetorically urgent depositions of *The Purgatory of Suicides* shape up as slow but weighty chapters in the one story, longer than lifetimes and radically epic in import, of winning broad participation in a just commonwealth. The role memory plays in building longitudinal solidarity is nicely figured in the story of poetic origins that Cooper's 1872 autobiography retails: when jailers denied him pen and paper for the epic he meant to write in blank verse, he took to composing it instead in his head, and in the more mnemonically durable form of Spenser's locked-in stanza.[40]

Class-conscious epics of the period that took a more traditional ideological direction also took a more traditional narrative form. The twelve books of heroic couplets comprised by Sarah Stickney Ellis's *The Sons of the Soil* (1840) never budge from single-point omniscience, and the rather stringent compassion enabled by that narrative mode anchors the poem's remonstrance at the recent subversion of family and country values by

---

[39] For an appreciative discussion along these lines see Armstrong, *Victorian Poetry*, 214–16. Weiner, *Republican Politics*, 69–74, approaches Cooper's dialogism as a Chartist strategy for activating the reader, in keeping with the moral-imaginative calisthenics set forth in the *Defence of Poetry* by Shelley, who was well installed within the pantheon of Chartism by the date of its posthumous publication (1840). The dialogical ideal was also materially manifested in Cooper's publishing arrangement, which included part-issue in cheap numbers (Collins, *Thomas Cooper*, 16).

[40] Cooper, *Life*, 251. Carlyle claimed to have gotten the first thirty stanzas by heart. Janowitz, regarding the change from blanks to stanzas a "fall from print to oral conventions," decries the publication of *The Purgatory* as marking Cooper's lapse from interventionist to moral-force Chartism (*Lyric and Labour*, 168–69).

commercial ones. The plot traces the fortunes of a farming family who are enriched during the Napoleonic period by "prices rising with the wars abroad" (2.34), are made greedy and shallow by a prosperity that tempts them beyond their means, and then, once postwar agricultural depression sets in with the second half of the poem, are humbled, bankrupted, and ultimately dispersed by death and emigration. Ellis leaves beyond doubt the causal linkage between this financial decline and the moral degeneration of which it is an outward sign, and of which collateral signs abound as well: the landlord's ruthlessness (book 11), the desertion of a clergyman-suitor who breaks young Lucy's heart after revising his estimate of her dowry (book 8), the sheer vulgarity of the poetry annuals and city novels through which the little rural circle aspires to gentility (5.105).

Ellis's own aspiration beyond the genteel novel is realized problematically at best: she confines her diagnosis strictly to a middle-class syndrome, and advances it from a strictly bourgeois-realist narrative standpoint.[41] Still, in departing from the novel she takes her cue from epic. She assumes a poet's license to tell a tale improvingly severe rather than entertainingly happy-ended, and her preface accuses as the cheapeners of modern taste precisely those poets—Scott, Moore, and Byron—in whose romances we have seen epic most subversively challenged. Above all, in denominating as "sons of the soil" not the nearly invisible rural laborers but the middlemen farmers who hire them, and whose destiny is interdependent with theirs, Ellis allies her parable of local doom with a myth of the land, of England, to which a national moral attaches. When sons of that soil forget where they come from, the parent they have dishonored rejects them and they have to leave the country, in both senses of the word.

The organicist mythology on which Ellis drew in constructing this astringent fable was as strongly felt among Britain's lower as among her upper classes. Both constituencies found in the unforgotten dream of national wholeness grounds for consolation and resistance as legislative Reform shunted

[41] To be sure, Ellis's realism had its own good reasons for being. The plot of *Sons of the Soil* reflects (on) her own experience as the daughter of a farmer bankrupted in the 1820s rural depression, and her didactic and fictional writings in prose focus on those existing domestic power relations against which her articulation of "separate spheres" offered women a degree of practical defense. "Both her conduct-books and her fiction focus on the gap between the ideology of patriarchal authority and the lived experience of women coping with men as they actually are": Henrietta Twycross-Martin, "The Drunkard, the Brute, and the Paterfamilias: The Temperance Fiction of the Early Victorian Writer Sarah Stickney Ellis," in *Women of Faith in Victorian Culture: Reassessing the Angel in the House*, ed. Anne Hogan and Andrew Bradstock (Houndmills: Macmillan, 1998) 9.

them to the political margin. Elliott and Cooper knew the radical uses of this mythology as well as Ellis did its conservative ones, and all three poets sensed its affinity with epic as a genre more receptive to their alternative message than the novel. By 1840 that Victorian powerhouse of a prose genre was shaping up as the vehicle of choice for middle-class mythologies centering on individual agency, normed by secular understanding, and shaped to fit a meliorist plot. Writers who fled from this bourgeois compact into epic territory can therefore seem to us now like ideological wild cards following all suits or none. The sage joker Carlyle notoriously exemplified a radical conservatism in prose, and his *Past and Present* (1843) found a weaker poetic counterpart in William Dearden's *The Vale of Caldean; or, The Past and the Present: A Poem, in Six Books* (1844). Where Elliott impersonated a patriarch, Dearden comes forward as "the Prophet, the Missionary of Truth"; but his self-describedly "heroico-aesthetic" polemic, as soon as it attempts more than a denunciation of "Commerce," badly wants the sort of traction that might make his concluding petition to Peel and Wellington something beyond a mere bill of complaints.

The poet's return to his native Yorkshire dale furnishes occasion for nostalgic description *à la* Goldsmith and then for a sequence of hardship stories modeled, Dearden's notes suggest, on those from which Words-worth built *The Excursion*. The result, however, is markedly less successful. Not only does the contemplation of hardship fail here as a Wordsworthian corrective to despondency; Dearden lashes out, besides, in so indiscriminate a fashion at unchecked capitalism and also Owenite community socialism (book 4), at urban industrialization and also government regulation (book 5), that his positive bardic program seems by contrast nothing but the very thin gruel of nostalgia. That is all this prophet can affirm, in a denunciatory monotone that makes a poor substitute for the more adventurous sorts of unity we have seen his contemporaries contriving from the dramatic split-ting and delegation of voice. We can see, in the light of such experiments, that Dearden's indignation wearies because it is defeated in advance by the lack of an alternative vision: he can only tell the same story again and again because he is without (what his title suggests the poem might have had) a restorative image of the Vale itself, and thus of the land as an abiding resource to be invoked against and despite its current exploitation. (In a spirit of anticipatory Liberal Unionism, we shall see in Chapters 10 and 11, Anglo-Irish epic poems would exploit just this resource as a hedge against the symmetrical horrors of famine and Fenianism.)

During the Romantic era the epic monologism of a single-point, *de facto* third-person perspective had been the rule, especially for poets of the second water like Dearden and Ellis; these two poets' belated persistence within that groove lets us regard them, in parting, as formally conservative exceptions proving how by 1840 the epic rules had changed. They had changed in favor of, if not change itself, then an exhibition of openness that was highly hospitable to change. Both poets wrote to defend against destruction a pattern of life as they had known it; both chose the epic mode they did, we may suppose, to defend their writing against the suspicion that life as they had known it was already gone.

8

There and Back:

Emigrant Epic 1840–1850

Only a minority of the British epics treated in the previous two chapters were set in Britain; we might ask why. To be sure, Disraeli's *Revolutionary Epick* belongs in a University debating hall or Parliamentary chamber if it belongs anywhere, Cooper's *Purgatory of Suicides* seems never to have fully quit the Stamford town hall that inspired it, and Pollok's *Course of Time* beholds the end times from a viewpoint much like a Calvinist village pulpit. But the wandering of these epics from native origins into allegorical or eschatological venues, and of their congeners into foreign parts from France to the Mediterranean and Levant, remains striking. So too, as this chapter will show, does the persistent geographical vagrancy of major poems from the 1840s that were expressly devoted to those most British of kings Alfred and Arthur. The early-Victorian emigration of epic away from the home ground of the British Isles into foreign parts seems especially odd when we recollect that it coincided with the decades between Waterloo (1814) and the Great Exhibition (1851), an interval when Britain was minding the internal business of reinventing itself legislatively, realigning itself socially, and engineering the transformation of its economy and indeed its landscape. If epic's flight abroad was an evasive action, it was a singularly unavailing one; for the genre's abiding concern over mass movements and Reform debates—the defining motifs for 1820s and 1830s epic respectively—remains transparent well into the 1840s, even when it is played out on alien territory.

When British epic left Britain it did so not as a refugee, or a tourist either, but as a pilgrim whose scrip included a return ticket. One goal of its pilgrimage was to establish a basis for that objectivity of presentation which by long-standing right belonged to the genre but which the partisan climate of Reform made it hard to maintain where a theme lay too close to home. That the forensic epoists who stayed put and wrote on explicitly British subjects were the most overtly partisan—witness Elliott, Ellis, Dearden from our previous chapter—suggests that those who went abroad did so in hopes of fostering a more dispassionate and neutral perspective, especially with regard to the principles that were involved in the home debates their epics dramatized under foreign cover. It was these deliberately estranged epics that, by convening an internal audience within scenarios of trial or debate, solicited from their external audience of readers a judgment that should be comparatively equitable because thus mediated and disengaged. The unfamiliar Italian context behind *Sordello*, for example—the place of its action still exotic to most early-Victorian readers, the time obscure to everybody—ensured that Sordello's story *per se* would not be a burning issue. For that very reason Browning could make it the pretext for a critique of judgment that foregrounded what *were* burning issues: the assembly and evaluation of intelligence, the power of language to shape policy, the role of imagination in an embroiled and emergent state.

No one else went so far as Browning did, but the tendency he carried to an extreme was widely shared around 1840 by poets who in more cautious ways probed the operating system of epic and interrogated the means and ends of producing, delivering, and consuming narrative. For narrative remained, to the annoyance of a statistician like Edwin Chadwick or a proto-cybernetic thinker like Charles Babbage, the nineteenth century's preferred form of organizing whatever it knew. This meant that the exposed narrative constructionism we met last chapter in Browning, Heraud, Disraeli, and of course Carlyle in prose history, was rehearsing the production, storage, and retrieval of information in the form that to their era mattered most—which was therefore the form in which their readers most needed calisthenic practice. The notable overlap between this literary agenda and the increasingly global purview of British manufacturing and commercial empire suggests an additional cause for the exportation of Victorian epic: the genre's fitness as a prooftext for that imperial expansion which, by slow but sure paradox, was becoming the new hallmark of national identity within the British Isles.[1] We saw in Chapter 3 how at

---

[1] On this theme compare the approaches taken by Gerald Newman, *The Rise of English Nationalism: A Cultural History* (London: Weidenfeld and Nicolson, 1987); and by Linda Colley, *Britons: Forging the Nation 1707–1837* (London: Pimlico, 1994). These complementary perspectives are evaluated, and subsumed, in Krishan Kumar's elegant *The Making of English National Identity* (Cambridge: Cambridge University Press, 2003).

the start of the century a mild but ever-present siege mentality had found nationalist work for the loose experimentation the genre had afforded in the 1790s. By the 1840s Britain's practical nationalism had become a semi-detached internationalism; and this latest formation too had a job for epic, made eligible as the genre was for such work by the prominently inter-national roster of its constituent European canon. Still decades shy of its imperialist maturity, the export–import ideology of the heroic poem was already in deeply plotted collusion with the interests of worldwide empire that made Britishness at mid-century what it was.[2]

The emigrant epic imagination of the 1840s needed a firm and reliable launching slip from which to embark, and it found one to hand in the most vernacular of national narrative forms, the ballad. Bishop Percy's epoch-making eighteenth-century collection *Reliques of Ancient English Poetry*, after fifteen years' sleep on the shelf, appeared in various publishers' new editions almost annually between 1839 and 1850. Scott's fancy-dress *Minstrelsy* and the inexpensive ballad editions of Joseph Ritson remained widely available across the decade as well, as did George Ellis's *Specimens* in a new edition.[3] The more sumptuously produced of these books make plain what would in any case be strongly suggested by such collateral phenomena of the Gothic revival as the Eglinton Tournament (1839), A. W. Pugin's neomedieval propaganda tract *Contrasts* (1836, 1841), and the national architecture en-shrined at Westminster in the rebuilt Houses of Parliament: early Victorians

---

[2] Franco Moretti, *Atlas of the European Novel 1800–1900* (1997; tr. London: Verso, 1998), offers remarks on historical fiction that are pertinent here. The 19th-cent. historical novel "seems to flourish" only when its action is located "away from the center. And, by reflex, *in the proximity of borders*" (34). These borders Moretti further distinguishes as internal or external to a nation, the former conducing to adventure plots and the latter to plots of treason; in either case "Historical novels are not just stories 'of' the border, but of its erasure, and of the incorporation of the internal periphery into the larger unit of the state" (37–40). The nomadism of British verse epic during the decades flanking 1840 lets us add to Moretti's formulation a third kind of border, an extrapolated or projected frontier that is located abroad and outsources to plots of conquest and surrender—be they martial or amorous—the imaginative labor of defining a nation incipiently imperial.

[3] See Stephanie L. Barczewski, *Myth and National Identity in Nineteenth-Century Britain: The Legends of King Arthur and Robin Hood* (Oxford and New York: Oxford University Press, 2000) 42–43, 89. Consider too Peter Mandler's emphasis on the "aggressively populist" character of "the mass culture market's pride in the national vernacular literature," whose valorization of "the word" sponsored, by mid-century, a shift in focus from Britishness to Englishness: " 'In the Olden Time': Romantic History and English National Identity, 1820–50," in *A Union of Multiple Identities: The British Isles, c.1750–c.1850*, ed. Laurence Brockliss and David Eastwood (Manchester and New York: Manchester University Press, 1997) 86.

stood more than ready to take the Middle Ages over as an image of modern idealism.[4] The power of this image lay, as Pugin showed, in the challenging contrast it posed to modern realities, usually in a mode of stinging reproof. Reprobate culture-watchers repaid the compliment by turning the contrast around and exploiting the discrepancy between ideals and actualities, to the discomfiture of the former, in the burlesque graphics of *Punch* (begun 1841) and the balladic spoofs of Richard Barham's bestselling *Ingoldsby Legends; or, Myth and Marvels* (1840).

That Barham's squibs have not aged gracefully suggests how topical a comic hair-trigger must have attached to the hair's-breadth difference between nobility and preposterousness in the faux-medieval mode of the day.[5] So it is no surprise to see one author in successive works travesty and then honor the ticklish conventions of ersatz modern balladry. This is what William Edmonstoune Aytoun did, first in the parodic *Book of Ballads, Edited by Bon Gaultier* (co-authored with Theodore Martin, 1845), then in the straight-shooting Tory riposte that was *Lays of the Scottish Cavaliers* (1849), and last in the soberly balladic *Bothwell: A Poem in Six Parts* (1855). Suspicion that the whole ambivalent ballad craze was a case of middle-class nerves, brought on by accelerating social change, is confirmed from a populist republican perspective by W. J. Linton's *Bob Thin, or The Poorhouse*

---

[4] Anglo-Saxon studies formed a signal, in some ways exceptional, strand within the early-Victorian fabric of neo-medievalism. At its heyday in the 1830s, Benjamin Thorpe translated Rask's 1817 Danish grammar of Anglo-Saxon into English (1830), Joseph Bosworth published a dictionary (1838), and John Kemble brought out the first English editions of *Beowulf* (1833, 1837). While all this *eo*-medievalist scholarship, so to call it, left no mark on the ballad-based developments traced in the present chapter, much of it bespoke the same concerns over suffrage and representation that dominated Victorian epic in the forensic 1830s. See Allen J. Frantzen, *Desire for Origins: New Language, Old English, and Teaching the Tradition* (New Brunswick and London: Rutgers University Press, 1990) 33–35, 51–52; Clare Simmons, *Reversing the Conquest: History and Myth in Nineteenth-Century British Literature* (New Brunswick and London: Rutgers University Press, 1990); Richard M. Turley, *The Politics of Language in Romantic Literature* (Houndmills: Palgrave, 2002) 138–45. To the larger medievalist phenomenon in which Anglo-Saxonism of every stripe participated a good guide remains Alice Chandler, *A Dream of Order: The Medieval Ideal in Nineteenth-Century English Literature* (Lincoln: University of Nebraska Press, 1970).

[5] On the 1840s significance of Barham's post-Romantic poise see Stephen Bann, *The Clothing of Clio: A Study of the Representation of History in Nineteenth-Century Britain and France* (Cambridge: Cambridge University Press, 1984). Bann's point of generational differentiation is Scott, whose once new technique for surprising readers into historical credence had been as "integrative" as Barham's now was "dispersive" (122). As we shall see, Macaulay's relation to Scott was analogous (as was Browning's in *Sordello* and the historical monologues of the 1840s): both generations aimed alike at literary revival of the past, but the elder author's very success required his followers to find other means; and in the 1840s these were basically ironic.

Fugitive (1845).[6] The plot recounts an unemployed weaver's escape from the clutches of the Poor Law workhouse into a countryside workers' commune so fair that it seems he must have died and gone to heaven. The manner of presentation, however, roots the balladry of Linton's escapist tale not in the distant past but in the living common people, whom the telescopic philanthropy of Hungry-Forties medievalism had a way of blocking from sight. In fact *Bob Thin* draws on a radical's understanding that the feudal system had itself been one more nail in the coffin of common laborers' ancient rights, and the poem quickly made its way off the page into the oral culture of working-class chant and song.[7]

On the page, however, is where it deserves to live today. Both the stanzas and the copious illustrations with which they merge typographically flaunt a wry grotesquerie in the first part of the poem, as befits Bob's squalid city life. These grow sticky-sweet with his new environment as the sequel rises towards a utopian conclusion recalling the lineaments of Blake, with whose work Linton as a London engraver probably had some acquaintance. (Years later the Rossetti brothers would commission him to reproduce Blake engravings for Gilchrist's 1863 *Life of Blake*.[8]) One would call the pamphlet-issued *Bob Thin* a doggerel tract or comic book before calling it an epic; it found an apt venue in *The Illuminated Magazine*, which Linton briefly edited before that short-lived monthly went under. That much conceded, it must also be said that the poem's length of historical perspective and *Gesamtkunstwerk* design, like Blake's a generation before, portray an attitude of noteworthy complexity. In one interart vision, Linton both honored the dream of social wholeness to which as a liberal activist he was devoted and gently mocked the soft version of that dream for which pious bourgeois antiquaries all around him professed to yearn.

In their hearts the 1840s bourgeois readership may have been yearning for something other, and much more recent, than the medieval period. What

---

[6] First published in pamphlet form *c.*1840 as *The Life and Adventure of Bob Thin, a Poor-Law Tale*: see Stephanie Kuduk Weiner, *Republican Politics and English Poetry, 1789–1874* (Houndmills: Palgrave, 2005) 194.

[7] See F. B. Smith, *Radical Artisan: William James Linton 1812–97* (Manchester: Manchester University Press, 1973) 64, on the place of *Bob Thin* in "the repertoire of radical reciters"—a place commemorated by the enshrinement of Linton's subtitle in Brian Maidment's anthology *The Poorhouse Fugitives: Self Taught Poets and Poetry in Victorian Britain* (Manchester: Carcanet, 1987).

[8] Smith, *Radical Artisan*, 148, remarks as ironic Linton's evident dislike for the work of Blake, "a spirit more akin to his own than any other in English history."

they probably wanted most to revive was that conviction of national cen-
trality which had welled up in them at the climax of Reform just a decade
before. Passage of the electoral Reform Bill, Poor Law, and other measures in
the early 1830s had seemed to answer definitively the century's unsettled
question about who "the people" were in Britain, and who should have the
power to speak and act in their name. The answer that had rung out back
then—why, the decently industrious, Protestant yet tolerant middle class, of
course—appeared to base public policy firmly on popular authority, in what
was to many minds Britain's duly matured, properly expurgated version of
the very different people's revolution they kept having and botching over in
France (1789, 1793, 1805, 1830...). Since its finest hour in the early 1830s,
however, this agreeably lucid picture of the British people had been sullied
by other people: other British people, that is, whom as we saw in Chapter 7
the Reform compact had squeezed aside, into a disaffected margin ranging
from rough-and-tumble Chartists on one side to apoplectic High Church-
men on the other.[9] It was to the freshly threatened stability of an unresolved
national constitution that the 1840s ballad revival spoke its vernacular
word of reassurance—in the people's voice and therefore, so the implicit
logic ran, in the people's name. This was a disingenuous logic, however, and
Linton's *Bob Thin* called its bluff, as in a different key did the ballad-based
songs of class struggle to which Chartism marched.

The greatest publishing coup of the bourgeois ballad revival was its oddest
production, and also, by reason of its pastiche offshore outsourcing, the one
that tells us most about the period. In *Lays of Ancient Rome* (1842) Thomas
Babington Macaulay set to variants of the old ballad stanza four tales from,
not just ancient Rome, but ancient Rome's ancient Rome: the heroic
ancestry to which Romans of the classic period themselves looked back,
heroic relics from a period that was already ancient history for a proxy
modern like Cicero. Macaulay's fractal retrospect made the *Lays* not just *from*

---

[9] Dror Wahrman, *Imagining the Middle Class: The Political Representation of Class in Britain, 1780–
1840* (Cambridge: Cambridge University Press, 1995) 410, notes how talismanic invocation of the
middle classes' Reform charisma had disappeared from mainstream public discourse by the mid-
1840s. The concurrent resurgence of balladry lets us suggest here that people's working concep-
tion of "the people," and the cultural authority conveyed by that idea, had trickled down and
spread out. This development in turn is probably reflected in the rise of the whiggish or
"Romantic" literary history that, according to David Perkins, dates from the 1840s and held the
field for another hundred years: "Literary History and Historicism," in *The Cambridge History of
Literary Criticism*, vol. 5, ed. Marshall Brown (Cambridge: Cambridge University Press, 2000) 343.

ancient Rome but *about* its invention of a civic tradition.[10] The Victorian
book drew a picture of sophisticated antiquity drawing up a past for itself
out of rough Latium's matrix of patriotic myth, as brought forward during
centuries of oral transmission coincident with the maturation of a literate
Latin culture. Through the lens of English vernacular verse, and along a
kind of cultural-historical periscope held together by fake dates, cooked-up
recitation occasions, and historical notes, Macaulay invited his reader back
behind Virgil and Ennius into a sub-epic stratum of folk legend, analogous
to that which Macpherson claimed to have mined when smelting together
his highly original Gaelic "translations" eighty years before. But here the
parallel to Ossian abruptly stopped. In contrast to the post-Culloden mel-
ancholy of beautiful losers who had moved Napoleon and inspired Scott,
Macaulay's fancy charade hammered home, with foot-tappingly philistine
metrical insistence, an imperial destiny. Planting the modern reader in the
unruined Forum to bask in the glory that was Rome, the *Lays* celebrated not
a naïve heroism but a metropolitan urbanity that looked back pleased on
naïve heroism, as on a legacy it was both proud to have, and proud to have
superseded. Macaulay in effect handed Britannia the reins to the triumphal
chariot of history.

And Britannia loved it, as she had loved Macaulay's oratory for Reform a
decade before and would love his victoriously progressivist, epic-scale
History of England a decade later. Improbably yet unerringly, the *Lays*
fused in a single work the divergent orientations that Aytoun and others
could enjoy only in separate productions: the nostalgia that indulged old
balladry, and also the modern spirit that mocked its retrograde irrelevance to
a brave new world. Macaulay had already worked the converse of this trick
in an 1824 *jeu d'esprit*, "A Prophetic Account of a Grand National Epic
Poem, to be Entitled 'The Wellingtoniad,' and to be Published A.D. 2824."
So firm was his confidence in the millennial rightness of historical progress
that he found it equally exhilarating to imagine his own moment as time's
beneficiary and as its laughingstock. To see this very peculiarity as the secret

[10] See *The Invention of Tradition*, ed. E. J. Hobsbawm and Terence Ranger (Cambridge:
Cambridge University Press, 1983), on the role played in nationalist culture by the practice their
title phrase describes. To the student of epic the practice looks at least as old as Virgil, whose work in
fact became a focal point during this period. In Macaulay's spirit but with an imperial twist, in 1849
the translators Rann and Charles Rann Kennedy dedicated *The Works of Virgil* to the (German-born)
Prince Consort, flourishing "the conquest of Virgil as the ultimate display of Anglo-Saxon
strength": Colin Burrow, "Virgil in English Translation," in *The Cambridge Companion to Virgil*,
ed. Charles Martindale (Cambridge: Cambridge University Press, 1997), 34.

of the book's phenomenal popularity among readers is to appreciate the
contemporary mentality that it addressed, and that for us in this chapter it
almost ideally expresses.

No competent 1840s reader could fail to know that the *Lays* as a text did
not really endorse the simplicities that each constituent lay enunciated.[11]
Though Macaulay pumped out his verses with the earnestness of a steam-
piston, the project of double mimesis that J. S. Mill accurately described in
an 1843 review as "a reproduction . . . of the imitations of Scott" consorted
ill with the plain virtue of Virginia and the steadfastness of Horatio at the
bridge.[12] It is nearer the truth to say that Macaulay meant not what his
lays declared but what his *Lays* implied: that the art in which the whole
book drilled its reader was that of simultaneously respecting pristine values
and disowning them; further, that this art constituted the basic ground of
imperial rule that made the analogy of Britain to ancient Rome matter.[13]
The author who had lately returned from decreeing the laws and educa-
tional curriculum in British India knew at first hand the balancing act
entailed by an administrative existence that took place *in* colonial life
without being *of* it.

What we might call the executive irony bred by this experience likewise
governed Macaulay's historical understanding, of Rome and of England
alike, at the level of structural conception rather than verbal execution.

[11] Such readerly competence is a delicate fruit, and it did not survive transit very well into a
20th cent. taught to reckon the Victorian reader an earnest simpleton. Hear the completely serious
tone in which J. S. Bratton, *The Victorian Popular Ballad* (London and Basingstoke: Macmillan,
1975) 46–47, found it necessary to rebuke a Macaulay who "seems completely unaware of the
ridiculous nature of this enterprise, the fact that the whole fabrication is without meaning as a
scholarly endeavour." There was such a thing as Victorian deadpan.

[12] *Westminster Review* 39 (1843), rpt. in *Collected Works*, vol. 1, ed. John M. Robson and Jack
Stillinger (Toronto and Buffalo: University of Toronto Press, 1981) 526. On this matter Mill is
insistent: "The *Lays*, in point of form, are not in the least like the genuine productions of
a primitive age or people. . . . The forms of Mr. Macaulay's ballad poetry are essentially modern"
(525)—which is to say, Mill likes them just fine, and for reasons that Norman Vance, *The Victorians
and Ancient Rome* (Oxford: Blackwell, 1997) 70, helps to explain: "There was a natural affinity
between proto-Roman or early Roman heroic individualism, critically re-read or reconstructed
not as history but as national ideology, and the heroic individualism of Victorian liberals and
doubters seeking a new ideology of freedom and truth."

[13] Implicit in this analogy, as in the analogy to ancient Greece that adjoined it, was a deeper
analogy, harder to handle, between the chosenness of Britain and of ancient Israel. No work of
scholarship had more impact on Macaulay's *Lays* than Niebuhr's *History of Rome* (1828–1832)—a
formative influence on Tennyson's generation at Cambridge as well—a work that derived in turn
from the pathbreaking German scholarship on Homeric and biblical literature by Eichhorn and
Wolf, respectively. See the application to Tennyson in Daniel A. Harris, "Personification in
'Tithonus' " (1986), abridged in my *Critical Essays on Alfred Lord Tennyson* (New York: G. K. Hall,
1993) 114–19.

The facile antiquity-effect of the wording provided ready narrative access, even as it insinuated a certain latter-day alienation into the pleasure of reading itself. The early Victorian readers who took the *Lays* to heart knew perfectly well that they were being had. When in 1849 an American observer just beyond the pale of the contemporary literary scene called the work "a half resuscitation of a mummy" he meant to brand it "an interesting failure." But it was precisely Macaulay's compromising adroitness in half-measures—after all no Caesar, or Cleopatra either, wanted mummies brought all the way back to life—that made it such a galvanizing success within the Victorian winners' circle.[14]

Macaulay's immediate literary precursor in this experiment on the nascent imperial taste was William Maginn, Londonized Irishman and scapegrace gentleman editor from 1830 of *Fraser's Magazine*. In 1838 Maginn published in that most interesting periodical of its decade twelve *Homeric Ballads* (posthumously collected and corrected, 1850) that took up, as their author did in most matters, an intriguingly compromised position on the negotiation of sterling cultural capital. Vigorously rejecting the Wolfian patchwork hypothesis about Homer's epics, Maginn nevertheless embraced a position curiously like it. The *Iliad* and *Odyssey*, he proposed, had been disassembled at their point of origin in Asia Minor for shipment to Greece, where they were received as discrete ballads and subsequently reconstituted along lines congruent with the great poet's still-manifest master plan. Maginn's plan, however, in an altogether characteristic maneuver, was to rehearse not the perfected result of this long-ago transaction in cultural commerce, but its dissolute middle phase: "I am about to split Homer again into the rhapsodical ballads, not from which he was made, but which were taken from him" (1850 preface). He thus laid before his periodical reader an imaginative re-enactment, not of the happily-ever-after *Odyssey*, but of its textual odyssey in diaspora. Maginn's invitation was to classical slumming in romantic dress, set to a swingeing ballad tempo: a gratuitous contemporary indulgence in what

---

[14] Thomas Powell, *The Living Authors of England* (New York: Appleton, 1849) 63. As Donald J. Gray points out, "the *Lays* pleased readers who knew that experience was not and had never been so simple and satisfying"; "there is a right side, in short, and it wins, both in the stories of the *Lays* and in the history in which they are set": "Macaulay's *Lays of Ancient Rome* and the Publication of Nineteenth-Century British Poetry," in *Victorian Literature and Society: Essays Presented to Richard D. Altick*, ed. James R. Kincaid and Albert J. Kuhn (Columbus: Ohio State University Press, 1984) 82, 85.

had been the contingent if necessary evil of a precious cargo's dismantling and transmission, as carried out by freebooters unknown to history and yet uncannily familiar, by glimpses, in their swagger and their pose.[15]

Furthermore, nearly all of the *Odyssey* episodes that Maginn chose for ballad treatment were themselves instances of smuggled or embedded narration. In "The Bath of Odysseus" an aged nursemaid's recognition of the disguised hero's scar precipitates the most famous flashback in western literature; "The Song of the Trojan Horse" flashes back from idyllic Phaiakia to Troy under siege; "The Return from Troy" foregrounds aged Nestor's storytelling performance for the benefit of callow Telemachus. This last ballad Maginn regards as something of a narrative archetype for the passing-on of cultural legacies; and he prefaces it with a polemical critique of Pope and Voltaire, whose brittle standoffish gentility betokened neoclassicism's want of historical imagination. Happily, and thanks to the romantic revival of historicism, "*we got back to Homer. The truly classical and the truly romantic are one. The moss-trooping Nestor reappears in the moss-trooping heroes of Percy's reliques*" (88).

Cultural universals, Maginn implies, come into focus only through the lens of historical particularization, by a process whose analogy to the Ossianic reconstitution of a stable epic from traveling vernacular fragments his collection of *Homeric Ballads* reinforces by reenactment.[16] The modern brokerage of goods damaged in westward imperial transit was underwritten by a double policy of mutual insurance. The unique and original prestige of Homer vouched for a metropolitan identity linking Troy to London via Athens over the centuries; conversely these links in the chain kept Homer alive, as his recuperable text arrived safely—translated yet ultimately the same—on one alien shore after another, in spite of distance in place and time, and indeed enlarged by that distance. It remained for Macaulay to occupy and articulate the central switchpoint that Maginn had elided yet constantly implied for the transmission of *imperium*. When in Rome, Macaulay did as the romance did, enfolding verse tales within prose narrative frames and both within a single destiny. And like Maginn he cultivated those

[15] As Richard Jenkyns summarizes the reception of *Homeric Ballads*, "people were entertained, but they could not help seeing that Maginn had produced a travesty": *The Victorians and Ancient Greece* (Cambridge, Mass.: Harvard University Press, 1980) 197.
[16] See Simon Dentith, *Epic and Empire in Nineteenth-Century Britain* (Cambridge: Cambridge University Press, 2006) 48–49.

narrative protocols of mediation whose observance made disengaged cosmo-
politanism the modern, the imperial condition.[17]

The pertinence to epic of such disengagement was elegantly stated, in the
same year as the *Lays*, by the poem entitled "The Epic" that Tennyson
composed some five years before its 1842 publication and with which he
framed the first installment of what was to become *Idylls of the King*. An adroit
preface balances contemporary political interests against one another like a
house of calling cards, reprising around the wassail bowl and on the common
ground of Christmas the controversialist spirit that had informed epic during
the 1830s. This even- and open-handed setting accords a welcome to
Tennyson's lightly sketched self-portrait as the poet Everard Hall, bachelor
of arts. With a becoming reluctance Hall neutralizes critique on generic
grounds ("Why take the style of those heroic times?"; "these twelve books of
mine | Were faint Homeric echoes, nothing-worth," 35–39), all by way of
introducing the stately archaism of his "Morte d'Arthur." Recitation of this
text in the small hours segues into a dreamy postscript suggesting the
contemporary need for just such a chivalric ideal as had passed away with
Arthur long ago—though not before the dying king had managed to attach a
saving remnant of idealism to the legend that would survive him.

The "Morte" itself pivots on a paradox: the king's final assertion of
authority divests him of it, in the form of the sword Excalibur, which it
nearly kills him to bully a reluctant Sir Bedivere into throwing away—only
in order that he and it, having departed this life as actual historical agents,
may return in the spirit of culturally perdurable myth, or in other words the
power that makes history meaningful.[18] The *Idylls* would in time prove one
of Victorian Britain's fullest literary meditations on the terms of modern
power; already at this handsomely accomplished debut Tennyson was
flexing the ideological ambidexterity with which the early Victorians dis-
counted imperial ambition even as they went about the business of running
an empire. Only a serviceably supple doublethink could (with Tennyson)
square the realm-extending, norm-policing, centralized bureaucracy of the
Round Table with upstart Arthur's plucky mission to rid his territory of
imperial bullies and fend off savage marauders. Only long practice in the

[17] Such mediation is sorely missed by the reader of *Lays and Legends of Ancient Greece* (1857),
where the Homeric scholar John Stuart Blackie thought to merge Macaulay's manner with
Maginn's matter but, for want of a framing feint like theirs, could offer only the lukewarm
fondness of a standard Victorian nostalgia.

[18] This idea is worked out at length in my *Tennyson and the Doom of Romanticism* (Cambridge,
Mass., and London: Harvard University Press, 1988) 317–45.

arts of being of two minds could let readers (with Macaulay) imagine the world-subduing cohorts of Caesar's Rome identifying with a scratch squad of plebeians in extemporized resistance against tyrannous invasion.

Feats on this scale of disciplined sympathy became easier for the early Victorian mind, evidently, when it took up narrative in dispersed rather than monolithic form. Readers comprehended the work of Barham or Aytoun/ Martin, of Macaulay or Maginn, as a ballad *collection* only after apprehending it in serial exposure as a collection of discrete *ballads*; and it seems to have been the aim of these latter-day balladeers that, within the phenomenology of the reader's experience, the whole should count for less than the sum of its parts. Tennyson's elaborate foreground ruse about the reliquary character of "Morte d'Arthur"—not just "faint Homeric echoes" but the fragmentary reverberation of a remaindered eleventh book at that—was performed half in self-defense and half as a shrewd bet on the developing market for narrative verse. For the first Victorians' taste ran to piecemeal forms as distinctly as their Reform-minded elders' taste a decade before had run to patterns of a dramatic or forensic cut.

We find this development anticipated in *England: A Historical Poem* by John Walker Ord, who spreads across five hundred pages a panorama of the national past broken up into sections that never fill more than ten pages at a clip. Volume 1 (1834) brings the Anglo-Saxon tale from mythic Valhalla down to Shakespeare before the court of Eliza in thirty-five distinct episodes; volume 2, published the next year in eighteen episodes more, comes pantingly up to date, to conclude with "October 1834." Adherence to the Spenserian stanza lets Ord impose a surface uniformity on the march of events, even as that form's pageant-wagon capacity brings each incident before the reviewing stand for indulgence on its own merits. Conspicuously absent, surprisingly so given the conservative ambition Ord declares in a militant preface, is any compelling narrative correlation among episodes. The spirit "of household virtue, untiring enterprise, and of the far-spreading fruits of civilization and intellect" (Preface) arises like a fresh exhalation from each new section but does not link it to an evolving whole. The result is a more open work than would appear to consist with the author's purpose— not more open-minded, such as we found in the typical self-presentation of Reform-era epics in the last chapter, but more open to appropriation by a spectrum of possible readers, who might mix and match Ord's episodes to construct historical meanings for Englishness that answered to diverse or even incompatible needs. Although no evidence suggests that *England* ever enjoyed a significant circulation of any sort, the scattershot mode that Ord adopted let his "historical poem" speak more broadly than to the target audience he expressly had in mind. The national realignment going forward towards 1840 seems to have disposed even poets as suspicious of change as was Ord to adopt realignable forms: an epic kit of light, modular units that might assume different shapes for readers occupying different viewpoints. Here was a development of which, whether or not he knew Ord's poem, the laureate-apparent Alfred Tennyson took note.

The 1840s rule of outward-bound modular portability meets its defining exception in a couple of ponderous national epics from the period that were ostentationally national in theme, yet at the same time tellingly emigrant in outlook. One of them, to which we shall return presently, was written by a leading man of early-Victorian letters; the other, during his leisure hours, by a lawyer since lost with Ord in the outer darkness of literary history. Yet this moonlighting lawyer staked an unmistakable claim to distinction: he wrote the greatest poem, in sheer length, that has ever appeared in the English language. John Fitchett, Esq., labored four decades before producing *King Alfred: A Poem* in 1841–42; and he must have been steady in his habits, because the result runs to forty-eight oversized books containing over 130,000 lines of blank verse. Perhaps the only way to preserve criticism of so mind-numbing an opus against sheer quantitative enumeration is to ask what can possibly have filled out to this extent a plot whose outline may be adequately traced from any of the century's four previous Alfrediads, by Cottle, Pye, Sympson (Ch. 3), and Payne Knight (Ch. 6). Fitchett probably knew these epics too, which were roughly contemporaneous with the inception of his when the century was young, which his finished work could have housed *in toto* with apses to spare, and yet on which his enormous effort makes almost no conceptual advance.[19] What he does do, needless to say, is go into absolutely every aspect of the saga of Alfred in unsurpassably exhaustive detail.

Fitchett's *forte* is the epic catalogue—of troops English and Danish, of the Christian heaven and, with special relish, of the pagan mythology, afterlife, and apocalypse. The related epic component of travelogue comes to his

---

[19] Back when he, the poem, and the century were young, Fitchett had ventured a single-volume trial issue of *King Alfred* (London: Cadell and Davies, 1808), which thus may gain a second palm as one of the only such contemporary ventures ever to have been brought fully to book.

assistance nearly as often, in order to supply what is fitly called by his dutiful literary executor Robert Roscoe (composer of the forty-eighth book, which Fitchett outlined but did not live to write) "a biography of the Monarch, a history of his age, and an epitome of its antiquities, its topography, mythologies, and civil and military condition" (Preface, vii). We come back helplessly to what Roscoe's sentence cannot well avoid either, sheer enumeration. A fixation on data for their own sake seems to have been an occupational hazard for epoists of the Hungry Forties. The same bulimia that made of *King Alfred* a freak of gigantism led smarter-paced epics into digestive disorders of another sort: William Richard Harris's *Napoleon Portrayed: An Epic Poem in Twelve Cantos* (1845), comparatively thrifty at a mere four hundred pages, devotes so many of its twelve cantos to the sedulous chronicling of campaign facts that it reads for the most part like *Sordello* without Browning's genius—as, it must be confessed, do certain strictly historical pages of *Sordello*, where extreme allusive and documentary condensation betray an epidemic taint of the time.

Nevertheless, given the new importance that the era of bluebooks and statistics vested in factual enumeration itself, we might credit Fitchett's quantitative overload with achieving a qualitative breakthrough worthy of notice in a history of the epic genre. For to supply an "epitome" of just about everything, as Fitchett promised to do in his dual epic invocation to "Imagination" and to "Historic Truth," required that he construct some center of intelligence to which just about everything might be reported and from which just about everything might be viewed and assessed. This intelligence center he placed at the center of his poem, on the island retreat of Athelney, where Alfred hides out from his enemies for approximately one-third of the poem, gathers information, and plans strategy. For some sixteen books—the duration in number of lines, let us recall, of three *Paradises Lost*—Fitchett's immobilized hero masterminds from his bunker an archive that includes his own autobiography, detailed reconnaissance on every English shire, an overview of the European continent, and substantive briefings about lands as distant as Mesopotamia and India.

The logic of the plot suggests, whether or not Fitchett had it in mind, that all this information is prerequisite to Alfred's going forth to the task that awaits him, which is to cast out the invader and unify a properly English realm. As in Cottle's 1801 *Alfred*, but now to the nth degree, the king gains the military victory because he has won the intelligence war first. Similarly, his winning Englishness emerges as a function of his far-flung database, expanded in the final book's vision to global proportions—and no, gentle reader, the parenthetic line numbers that follow are not a misprint—

> All powers of earth
> Transcending far in industry, in wealth,
> Science, and varied arts, wide o'er the seas
> A thousand sails to every clime shall waft.
>
> (48.2533–36)

Shall waft, and of course shall return to enrich the nerve center of the worldwide web. *All powers, Transcending far, wide o'er, every clime*: that something in the air of empire both incited and defied superlatives would be broadcast for all to see when imperialism proper fastened itself to literature in the last quarter of the century. Its unblushing debut, though, took place right here in epic. The genre of first call for doggedly overweening ambition and likewise of last resort, the genre that hyperbole came home to wherever it might meanwhile have strayed, epic offered to the vast inane an asylum that made it the best of kinds, and the worst of kinds. In the pre-imperialist 1840s epic's qualitative hospitality to the quantity-obsessed let Fitchett's industrial-strength narrative express something of the inventory-mindedness of the manufacturing classes. The systematic overproduction that drove the literary program of Fitchett and Harris, as it did Philip James Bailey's in *Festus* (2nd edition, 1845)—like, at a different level of organization, the partitioned division of narrative labor in Maginn and Macaulay—aligned the epoist circa 1840 with culture-industrializing effects of the sort that Charles Babbage and other contemporaries had begun to apprehend from "the production . . . of *a very large number*."[20] The omnivorous spasmodic forerunner Bailey and the extravagant apocalyptic latecomer Thomas Hawkins await our full attention in Chapter 9; but we may note here of Hawkins's *The Wars of Jehovah, in Heaven, Earth, and Hell: In Nine Books* (1844) that geological and paleontological side interests there incited feats of epic inventory—one passage names in a dozen pentameter lines three dozen kinds of stone (6.1411–25)—which, while hardly comparable in scope to Fitchett's contemporary megapoetics, were not unworthy of his expansionist momentum.[21]

★

[20] *The Economy of Machinery and Manufactures* (1832), rpt. in *The Works of Charles Babbage*, ed. Martin Campbell-Kelly (New York: New York University Press, 1989), 8: 86. The italics are Babbage's.
[21] Alexander Welsh, *George Eliot and Blackmail* (Cambridge, Mass.: Harvard University Press, 1985), takes for its larger subject the Victorian culture of information, for whose study blackmail

One thing that Fitchett in his toilsome superabundance lacked—had he possessed it he could never have let himself go on at such length—was a working sense of literary tradition in general, and of the epic tradition in particular. This was a deficiency made good in the second full-dress national epic of the decade, *King Arthur* (1848) by the versatile and resourceful Edward Bulwer-Lytton. If we put Tennyson's idyll to one side, as the poem all but asks us to do, it had been sixty years since a book-length poem in English (Richard Hole's *Arthur*, noticed in Ch. 2) had featured the national hero whom Spenser, Milton, and Dryden had each deemed most eligible for epic honors. These had been sixty years, moreover, in which the great wave of British nationalism crested and began breaking into the mode of postnationalist disownership that typifies epic production at mid-century.[22] Hole's Camelot entertainment of 1789 and Bulwer-Lytton's of 1848 (the revolutionary dates frame matters with an ominous convenience) demarcate King Arthur's conspicuous absence from the drama of Romantic nationalism in which we have seen King Alfred figure so often. The reason lies in a distinction that Bulwer-Lytton's prefaces to the later editions of *King Arthur* mention more than once as having drawn him to the subject: Arthur's status as a hero legendary rather than historical (1849, p. xii; 1870, p. 358). Where all that Fitchett manufactured about Saxon Alfred fastened itself to an unquestioned basis in fact, Briton Arthur's historicity was problematic: much less fixed to data, and proportionally

serves as the revealing pathological stain: "If knowledge is power . . . information is power to operate at a distance" (46). The link Welsh forges between Victorian data-collection and the need of circumstantial evidence to undergird "the system of police and detection" (93) suggests another way in which the information epic of the 1840s emerged from the forensic epic of the decade before. See also Welsh's sequel study *Strong Representations: Narrative and Circumstantial Evidence in England* (Baltimore and London: Johns Hopkins University Press, 1992); and Thomas Richards, *The Imperial Archive: Knowledge and the Fantasy of Empire* (London and New York: Verso, 1993).

[22] Arthur had returned more than once at Britain's need during the revolutionary and Napoleonic decades in sub- or para-epic forms, not least the reissue of Malory under Robert Southey's tireless hand (1817). For Victorian Arthur's prehistory during the Romantic period see Edward B. Hungerford, *Shores of Darkness* (1941; rpt. Cleveland and New York: Meridian, 1963), 46–52; James D. Merriman, *The Flower of Kings: A Study of the Arthurian Legend in England between 1485 and 1835* (Lawrence: University Press of Kansas, 1973) 113–77; Beverly Taylor and Elisabeth Brewer, *The Return of King Arthur: British and American Arthurian Literature since 1800* (Totowa: Barnes and Noble, 1983) 34–67; Roger Simpson, *Camelot Regained: The Arthurian Revival and Tennyson 1800–1849* (Cambridge: D. S. Brewer, 1990). Inga Bryden, *Reinventing King Arthur: The Arthurian Legends in Victorian Culture* (Aldershot: Ashgate, 2005) 33–47, thoughtfully lays out the Arthurian meanings that came to Bulwer-Lytton's hand, stressing the myth's power to conflate race with land, ethnology with geology, in finessing an 1840s problematic of national origin and destiny.

fertile in plasticity.[23] For Bulwer-Lytton, as more profoundly for Tennyson in decades to come, Arthur was the creature of those who held him true; it mattered less who he originally had been than where he had gone and what had been made of him since. Always the once and future king preceded by his reputation and buried by it too, he *was* his reception history.[24]

Bulwer-Lytton epicized on this legendary momentum in two principal ways. His twelve books, exceptionally diverse in style and tone, constitute an inventory of ways in which Arthurian matters had been approached across the centuries, and also of ways in which epic had been handled within the past half-century. A sestet *ababcc* stanza took from Shakespeare's "Venus and Adonis" a license for considerable tonal range. Untried hitherto as an epic vehicle, the stanza was neutral yet suggestive, looking enough like the forms of chivalric romance to invoke lightly (and then as lightly shed) affiliation with Ariosto's *sprezzatura* and Spenser's *gravitas*, Southey's forward thrust and, when the final couplet got properly fired and tempered, the pinpoint mobility of Byron.[25] *Don Juan* unmistakably furnished the model for Bulwer-Lytton's comic episodes centering on Gawaine, which

[23] Thus Hole's spirit of magic Arthurian wonders survives ornamentally in the fragmentary three-canto Spenserian *Morte d'Arthur* drafted by 1819 and included in Reginald Heber's posthumous *Poetical Works* (1841), which also prints a fragmentary "Masque of Gwendolen" in the same vein. Neither text has a nationalist bone in its body, though at one double-jointed moment in Heber's *Morte* (3.1–3) our nominally Saxon bard does, improbably, pause to lament the demise of Celtic Britain. See Brewer and Taylor, *Return of King Arthur*, 60–64; also Merriman, *Flower of Kings*, 167–73, and the critique of Merriman from a Celticist standpoint by Dafydd R. Moore, "The Critical Response to Ossian's Romantic Bequest," in *English Romanticism and the Celtic World*, ed. Gerald Carruthers and Alan Rawes (Cambridge: Cambridge University Press, 2003) 43–44.

[24] In a note to 3.38 Bulwer-Lytton explicitly acknowledges that his allegiance is due, not to "Arthur's historical day" but to "the time in which Arthur took his poetical existence, and was recreated by knightly minstrels." This position endorses, albeit by reversal, the terms in which Ellis (1805) had conjectured that, when the modern mind sequestered historical from fictional narrative, "the favourite story of Arthur would be the first to be turned into prose, for the purpose of establishing its authority": *Specimens of Early English Metrical Romances*, rev. ed. (London: Bohn, 1848) 75. Gillian Beer, *The Romance* (London: Methuen 1970), dating the Arthurian tension between history and fable back to the Middle Ages, speculates that such a tension "was particularly acceptable to a society intent upon mythologizing itself" (22). Barczewski, *Myth and National Identity*, 153, points out how handily the removal of Arthur from history into myth let the militant Anglo-Saxonism of the later century recruit him into service despite those inconveniently Welsh antecedents of his.

[25] The smile this epic wears is ably appreciated, in itself and as a part of the Arthurian tradition embracing Peacock and "Whistlecraft" Frere, by Mark Cumming, "Allegory and Comedy in Bulwer-Lytton's *King Arthur*," in *The Arthurian Revival: Essays on Form, Tradition, and Transformation*, ed. Debra N. Mancoff (New York and London: Garland, 1992) 31–51. For Cumming, as for Isobel Armstrong, *Victorian Poetry: Poetry, Poetics and Politics* (London and New York: Routledge, 1993), charting Bulwer-Lytton's declension "from radical to conservative," the poem comes to grief on its earnest faith in "the flat grandeur of a national epic" (Armstrong, 68).

while not very fine are as good as anything done in that vein by a Victorian. There is even some light political cartooning in Arthurian drag, casting Louis Philippe and Guizot as Lodovick the Vandal king and Astutio his minister, and Wellington as Sir Geraint. Bulwer-Lytton meant not just to profess seriousness like Byron, though, but to attain it on respectable Victorian terms: "to construct from the elements of national romance," as his 1849 preface said, "something approaching to the completeness of epic narrative" (vii), where "completeness" is a property at once of formal coherence and of referential totality.[26]

That this approach to epic was not entailed as a matter of course by Bulwer-Lytton's materials may be seen from a brace of contemporary examples that, also working eclectically under northern lights, display separately certain 1840s ambitions which it was the achievement of *King Arthur* to bring together into ideological and formal consistency.[27] J. Stanyan Bigg's *The Sea-King: A Metrical Romance, in Six Cantos* (1848) aimed at nothing more than serial wonder, an effect for which a new venue and more appreciative readers awaited this facile poet around the corner of 1850, under the aegis of Spasmodism where we shall meet him again in the next chapter. Meanwhile in 1849 the pseudonymous "Zavarr" (William Bennett, in his later writings "Zavarr Wilmshurst"), a poet less capable in every technical sense, effected with *The Viking: An Epic* a loveless marriage between admittedly "pedantic" Nordicism (p. 279) and the closed heroic couplet, a form whose open secrets were known to every eighteenth-century poet of modest parts but apparently vanished from whole sectors of the collective literary memory a hundred years later. What Zavarr does, balefully, remember is something that also proves important to Bulwer-Lytton: a racially charged lineage endowing narratives drawn from the Edda with a blood claim on Britons' attention that the merely cultural ancestry of Greece and Rome cannot match. Never mind that this first designed (and only executed) among Zavarr's three planned "Odinic" epics

---

[26] A passage from Bulwer-Lytton's *England and the English* (1833) laments that Byron's early narratives—this well-mannered book by perhaps the most conspicuous admirer of Byron in his generation leaves *Don Juan* discreetly unmentioned—display "no harmonious plan, comprising one, great, consistent, systematic whole; no epic of events artfully wrought, progressing through a rich variety of character, and through the struggles of contending passions, to one mighty and inevitable end" (2: 73). For the Hungry Forties allegory in *King Arthur* see Barczewski, *Myth and National Identity*, 66.

[27] On the Victorian revival of Nordic literature, launched by the 1844 publication of a major three-volume translation of the sagas of Snorri Sturluson, see Andrew Wawn, "Samuel Laing, *Heimskringla* and the Victorian 'Berserker School,'" in *Anglo-Scandinavian Cross-Currents*, ed. Inga-Stina Ewbank, Olav Lausund, and Bjørn Tysdahl (Norwich: Norvik Press, 1999) 29–59.

traveled under doctrinal disclaimer as a "Song of Superstition"; the one thing needful was that the project should convey, in the ethnic spirit of 1840s balladry, "the faith of our heathen forefathers" (Dedication to Lady Blessington, p. viii). Zavarr's Viking hero Vali is a hybrid demigod not just by hearsay but by the raced ocular proof borne in his skin and hair color (2.23–24). When after strangely alternated scenes of refined courtship and uncouth butchery a hurried climax gives Vali the Christian hand of Saxon Edgiva, the god-attended pair sail off to mate in Norway and produce "a race, | Whose men shall be the first in fortune's chase" (4.825–26).

Something like this guarantee of Anglo-Saxon racial greatness was Bulwer-Lytton's goal as well, but he got there by way of wider views and a more brazenly speculative dynastic-narrative line. His approach to the epic "completeness" that Bigg disregarded and Zavarr flubbed transpires literally in the poem's accession to high sobriety in the final books. There Bulwer-Lytton retroactively imposes unity on what has been vagrant, often picaresque narration, by making portentous appeal to a new and ambitous mythographic racialism. The itinerary on which the poem's chief ideologue Merlin dispatches young Arthur during the middle books includes Italy and Scandinavia, regions that turn out to braid the classic and Gothic strands of European story as neatly as they do because they disclose much deeper ethnic antecedents, in the bedrock of a solemnly introduced "Aryan" prehistory. The Odin-worship that Arthur encounters among the Norsemen retains traces of its origin up the headwaters of the "Don's ancestral waves" (12.86) in primal Caucasian lands. Stranger still—and thus more tellingly as pure epic ideology—the stranded Etruscan community that Arthur haps upon in the Italian Alps speak an ancient but comprehensible version of his own Celtic language, both tongues stemming back through Troy and Phoenicia to the Aryan origins that Druid ritual lore has enshrined for safe conduct to the British Isles (book 4).[28]

These elaborate and unlikely genealogies recapitulate a brand of armchair ethnological speculation to which the nineteenth century would accord increasing prestige, and to which Bulwer-Lytton's cavalier eclecticism regarding sources furnishes a parallel.[29] They come home to roost in the final book

[28] In 1871 Bulwer-Lytton's *The Coming Race* would transform this fantasy retrospect into a fantasy future, inventing a race of advanced beings whose tongue, "akin to the Aryan or Indo-Germanic" (ch. 12), displays to the narrator—himself significantly an American transplant of British stock—the evolutionary destiny of English to supersede itself.

[29] Brewer and Taylor, *Return of King Arthur*, 75–79, sketch the plot with a view to its seemingly random forage among heterogeneous source materials.

with Arthur's marriage to the Saxon princess Genevieve (a Guinevere figure made not just a Christian convert but a safely chaste national vessel, thanks to the poet's invention of her likewise virtuous double, Genevra, who being the true-blue lady to Sir Lancelot obviates, into the bargain, any *soupçon* of adultery). Nation-building wedlock was a Virgilian commonplace frequently drafted into the British tradition of Romantic epic, but here it receives a newly binding twist.[30] Given the right etymological squint, the Saxons turn out to be the ancient Scythians, and the Welsh "Cymrians" the ancient Cimmerians; and because both these ancient races sprang from the archaic Aryans, the marriage of Arthur and Genevieve reinstates nothing less than a primal Indo-European unity. Merlin goes so far as to suggest, as we hear the key to all mythologies clinking at his wizard girdle, that "the old brother-bond in these new homes" will revive the oldest memories of all, from when "Eve's young races towards each other drawn, | Roved lingering round the Eden gates of dawn" (12.185–86).

Shades of Maginn's *Odyssey*: Arthur's romance wanderings in the earlier books of the poem enact a version of the ancestral diaspora that they also teach him about, and that the multiform dissemination of his legend will in turn repeat for the wider edification of epic audiences yet unborn. Meanwhile, however, the refocusing of Indo-European ethnic scatter that is performed by the climactic hierogamy of Saxon with Celt prefigures, not just the Tudor promise of Welsh-Englishness extended by Henry VII in Arthur's book 7 prophetic vision, but Britain's situation at the top of the nineteenth-century world.[31] Bulwer-Lytton clearly understood his epic theme to lie in "the composition and structural growth of the Nation that claims in Arthur its hero and its type" (xviii). That "Nation," nominally Christian Wales in the dark ages, is also by backward genealogical extension an entity much vaster, the Caucasian people "Whose eldest god, from pole to pole enshrined, | Gives Greece her Kronos and her Boudh to Ind" (4.12). At the same time, the favored "Nation" is by forward ethno-mythographic extension modern Victorian Britain, keeper of Arthur's flame and latest full stop in the westward course of empire. The way to be a model Celt was to be a conscious Aryan; church and state fused in the

[30] On the importance assumed in the nineteenth century by epic hierogamy as a convention of nationalist narrative, see Moretti, *Atlas*, 40; also Dentith, *Epic and Empire*, 121–22.
[31] The poem's Elizabethan-Victorian connection is discussed by John Hazard Wildman, "Unsuccessful Return from Avalon," *Victorian Poetry* 12 (1974) 293–94.

bloodline that was one with the congenial traffic of fable across ephemeral political frontiers; the true nature of Gothic was (as Macaulay's *Lays* in their different way suggested) a perfect classicism.[32] If systematic Fitchett wrote in *King Alfred* the epic of centralized bureaucracy, miscellaneous Bulwer-Lytton wrote in *King Arthur* the epic of a diffusive charisma that looked beyond persons to races, past the "hero" to the "type" whose fulfillment lay with a folk mystique that looked as amiably generous in his day as it would prove brute-fisted in the hundred years ahead.[33]

The hero's journey away from home toward the recapture of a collective origin is a plot line whose most eligibly epic history lay in the medieval crusades. Scarcely a decade of the British nineteenth century passed without some poetic reworking of this material; for the interval this chapter treats, the salient feature is a pattern of ethnic reconnaissance like the one enacted by Bulwer-Lytton's Arthur. In *Selma: A Tale of the Sixth Crusade* (1839) the Anglo-Irish clergyman Alexander Ross offered a "Novel in Rhyme" (twelve cantos of mainly tetrameter rhyme modeled on Scott and Byron) that sends its chivalrous Ulsterman hero Albert into the Holy Land attached to a French contingent. There Albert does battle with Saracen forces and Gallic intriguers of a predictable ilk, yet his personal crusade penetrates to deeper recognitions. On a trip up the Nile, sightseeing dissolves for Albert into second-sight, as the riverscape makes real the visions of Celtic bards back home, and "The miracles of demon might, | By mountain minstrel told," and "things long dear, | To Erin's wild, bright fantasy, | Transferred to light, to life, came o'er him" (5.112).

This by itself might seem nothing more than Ross's way of finessing a too-evident debt to Scott's modern refinishing of the old romance format, and to Byron's repatriation of romance to its oriental place of origin. But when, one book later, among Bedouin hosts Albert finds such patriarchal simplicity that it seems "The simple race of primal men | Had come to grace the earth again" (6.144), we grasp in germ the operation of a cultural principle that would receive full codification in the anthropological science

---

[32] See Simpson, 166, on the nested congruence that Bulwer-Lytton contrives between person and type, then class, then nation, and finally "the fusion and amelioration of all mankind."

[33] The northwesterly path from Caucasus vales to British shores was reinforced for Bulwer-Lytton's 1848 readers in that year's news about the loss of the Northwest Passage expedition led by Sir John Franklin—a disappearance that chimed too with the transit of Tennyson's once and future Arthur from history into legend, where in the *Idylls* of later decades his resonant myth would oscillate between missionary confidence and anomie; see Barczewski, *Myth and National Identity*, 214–17.

of a later Victorian generation. This is the principle that to plunge into the
exotic is to come racially home to surviving originals of the long-exiled
virtues that inexorable modernity has preserved in traditionary tale and
song. A similar logic structures the main event of the plot, Albert's betrothal
to the eponymous heroine Selma. After the first of Albert's several feats
successfully rescues Selma from Mussulman clutches, and she is revealed to
be a European lady's orphan, Selma starts to imbibe Christian teaching like
mother's milk, apparently by an instinct matching that which drew Albert
to her in the first place despite her disguise as an Arab boy. In the midst of
the Middle East and the Middle Ages, Ross's hero finds what Bulwer-
Lytton's found the world over: an anticipation of Britishness that sets in
the crown of modernity the jeweled touchstone of racial continuity—
privileged consciousness of which is heroic modernity's very hallmark.
The consistency with which Ross maintains this theme sets the 1840s
nationalism of *Selma* apart from such a work as John Breakenridge's *The
Crusades* (1846). This work by an Ontario poet—for it is too soon by twenty
years to call him technically Canadian—subsists in parts that are indebted to
much the same Romantic models as Ross's. But the ingredients are rather
assembled for publication than integrated by anything like a political com-
mitment, as if in witness to the prenationalist conditions under which
Breakenridge wrote.

Yet another crusader epic from these years, F. W. Faber's *Sir Lancelot:
A Legend of the Middle Ages* (1844), recruits leading motifs from the decade
under the aegis of a militant Anglo-Catholicism. Fewer than half of the
poem's ten thousand blank verses actually forward the threadbare tale of its
knightly eponym, who has no relation to Arthur's famous right-hand man;
all the rest are devoted to homiletic digressions on church history and
practice, with special reverence paid to liturgy, hierarchy, and sacrament.
Even the nominally narrative portion of *Sir Lancelot* shows much the same
bent, since across most of the ten books the excommunicated hero pursues
in utter solitude a self-imposed spiritual penance, reinforced in book 7 by a
bout of leprosy, that keeps him from exchanging so much as a word with
another human being. Into this heroically ascetic aphasia the Wordsworth-
ian ephebe Faber pours passage on inventorying passage of Lake District
description, keyed to a sacramental vision of the holy significance that the
beauty of English landscape encodes. This descriptive conversion of the
countryside—conducted in verse that is steadily serviceable but that spins, if
not out of control, then far past the point of readerly repletion—portends

the sin-purged anchorite's readmittance into communion by a Catholic abbot's shriving hand at the end of book 9.[34]

Before this long-delayed absolution, however, and in uncanny compliance with the epic order of the day, Faber flickers at last into narrative action. He devotes books 8 and 9 to a confessional flashback of Sir Lancelot's crime of passion while on thirteenth-century crusade—on impulse he murdered a love rival from back home whom he found asleep beside the road to Antioch—which then sets in train a sequence of events as arbitrarily fantastical as anything in Bulwer-Lytton's repertoire. Rescued from police arrest by none other than the Wandering Jew, Lancelot finds he must defray his criminal debt in stranger coin than that of civil law. He accompanies his rescuer for seven years, at the end of which the pair undertake a pilgrimage that is recurrently mandated by the Jew's ancient curse for primal crimes of his own. Together they tour the Caucasus and its adjoining inland seas—a central Asian lake district and then some—turning back over the Black Sea and up the Danube, via a synagogue stopover, towards the Alpine tomb of Pontius Pilate. Thus another 1840s return to Caucasian origins, and an almost giddily miscellaneous recapitulation of Old and New Testament itineraries, furnish narrative means of heralding that imminent return—wayward England's into the bosom of Mother Church—on whose consecration Faber, himself poised to go over to Rome the next year, lavished such epic prodigality.

In denominating *Selma* a verse-novel, Alexander Ross rightly identified as un-epical the hesitant inwardness that, modernizing his Albert (and no other character in the work), resulted from a certain developmental tension between his major European motives and his Asia Minor surroundings. Bulwer-Lytton, likewise, was well enough practiced in the developing conventions of the Victorian novel to reinforce *King Arthur*'s racial triumphalism with the appeal of a subsidiary progress narrative—the plot of *Bildung* or individual culture—that was borrowed from the province of prose fiction. Arthur's travels under the sponsorship of Merlin are primarily

---

[34] Lawrence Poston, " 'Worlds Not Realised': Wordsworthian Poetry in the 1830s," *Texas Studies in Literature and Language* 28 (1986), pronounces *Sir Lancelot*, with better warrant than usually supports such comments in criticism on our genre, "a poem which it is quite impossible that any modern reader can finish" (63). Faber's relation to Wordsworth is discussed in this article and in Stephen Gill, *Wordsworth and the Victorians* (Oxford: Clarendon Press, 1998) 70–80.

an education in his antecedents, which matter in the first instance because they are the antecedents of his people. In the process, though, the princely hero grows up, being changed by all that he takes in—as, by and large, earlier epic monarchs-in-training were not changed: Southey's Madoc for example (Ch. 3), Sotheby's David (Ch. 4), and everybody's Alfred.

The marriage of Arthur with Genevieve towards which Bulwer-Lytton bends all the lines of plot represents the confluence of an ethnic destiny with a gradually consolidated self-understanding, of a kind for which epic in the nineteenth century had hitherto made little room. The goal-obsession of Southey and plottiness of Scott marked out a generic norm whereby comparatively unreflective heroes essentially *were* the actions they performed and suffered, while the chief rebels against normative plotting (Blake, Byron, Browning) did even less to foster in their protagonists a continuous learning curve ascending through experience to maturity. The real anomaly in this respect was *The Prelude*, which had been withheld from print all these years, yet which is suggestively recalled in both the cadences and the chastened-homecoming plot of Faber's *Sir Lancelot*, written as that poem was more or less at the master's feet in the neighborhood of Rydal Mount. The long-delayed appearance of Wordsworth's great epic of self in 1850 seems perfectly timed with the *Bildungsepos* shift whose boom had been audible a few years before, whose muted pattern of heroic individual redemption Faber's piety flushed out into the openly orthodox—and whose more than Faberian prolixity awaits us in the spasmodic reverberation that fills Chapter 9.

An hierogamous climax that, like Bulwer-Lytton's in *King Arthur*, caps a plot of *Bildung* or education clinches two last epicizing poems of immense address that were contemporary with that competent but flatter-footed epic. Both Tennyson's *The Princess: A Medley* (1847) and Arthur Hugh Clough's *The Bothie of Toper-na-fuosich: A Long-Vacation Pastoral* (1848) make higher learning their topic, or rather they make it their pretext for the transaction of more important business. That is the business of giving their boyish protagonists an extracurricular education that makes men of them, and of committing them at the culmination of that educational process to a holy wedlock the waiting world applauds. (Not for nothing is a king named Gama the one crowned head in Tennyson's poem, where matrimony rules.) Neither poem aims straight at epic; their underbid subtitles put us off that trail at once. But the way both poets keep staking their disclaimers throughout the text keeps the declined generic option in play, and in fact both poems by the end have done a lot of the work that avowed epoists of their day were doing too.[35]

A rising star urged by reviewers across the 1840s (and by coterie supporters well before that) to produce a major national poem, Tennyson may here have shrugged off the recommended mantle; but he did so only after trying it on for style in passage after passage of sustained pentameter grandeur not seen since Keats took on Milton. Clough for his part fabricated from hints in Longfellow and much exposure to classical prosody—one of the examination subjects, of course, that his young Oxonian characters are cramming on their "long-vacation" Scottish holiday—a wonderfully successful dactylic hexameter line. The rhythm itself, unpredictable but never unruly, becomes as in Byron a guide and sparring partner that compels auditory engagement, and rewards it. Properly attended to, the verse lifts lines off the page into the ear: not Homeric orality, to be sure, but an ever-fresh reminder that such a thing once was. Occasionally, too, Clough implants into the line a hint of compatibility—which William Morris for one would notice—between the prosthetic hexameter and the old ballad vernacular. (It becomes more than a hint when, at a late crux in his Scottish tale, he quotes a song by Robert Burns: 8.168.)

The Bothie starts, tongue in rhetorical cheek, with after-dinner oratory, but soon introduces its hero Philip sympathetically, and Homeric-epithetically, as "the chartist, the poet, the eloquent speaker" (2.19). These beginnings, like the numerous mock-heroic harangues and cabinet consults in *The Princess*, show that both poets had paid attention to the civic spirit of epic Reform a decade previously. Tennyson indeed may be suspected of parodying his recent precursors' fixation on the juxtaposition of differing viewpoints, with the elaborate apparatus whereby seven male undergraduates take turns improvising the rise and debacle of Princess Ida's female university, while their lady companions sing discreet olios at intermission time. The scribal poet of the group has shaped the result into unity after the fact, but the effect of spontaneous *Zusammenhang* among narrative

---

[35] Robert Crawford, *The Modern Poet: Poetry, Academia, and Knowledge since the 1750s* (Oxford: Oxford University Press, 2001) 22, gives this generic perception a pedigree: *The Bothie* "follows in the wake of Ossian by uniting lecture room with Highland *nous*" (22). That "the poem wears its eclecticism, its cultural *mélange*, on its sleeve" (129) forms another ground of comparison with Tennyson's epic-mocking self-described "medley." See also the appreciation of *The Bothie*'s epic features in Geoffrey and Kathleen Tillotson, *Mid-Victorian Studies* (London: Athlone Press, 1965) 123–31.

components has deep links to the conservative-progressivist dream of hier-archically secured togetherness that manifestly inspired the poem. The pro-gram of continuity by slow degrees under benevolent patriarchal sponsorship that suffuses Tennyson's delectable frame makes *The Princess* such sparkling propaganda for the British *status quo* that the ambition at which the poem jests in self-depreciation—"Heroic if you will, or what you will," "Grand, epic, homicidal" (Prologue 215–19)—is nearly realized while no one is looking.[36]

In its narrative apparatus, as in its plot about the taming of a feminist culture-rebel, *The Princess* flushes out of cover what had been a part of the Reform agenda all along: to script, direct, and manage change by the staging of conflict. This agenda had been an ambivalently tactical ingredient in the coalition of motives that got the Reform Bill passed in 1832; it would furnish matter of national self-congratulation in 1848 when the flames of Contin-ental revolution left Britain the unsinged occupant of a Western platform on which both the right-leaning Tennyson and the left-leaning Clough could confidently stand. Philip's study in *The Bothie* is more subtly self-directed than Ida's in *The Princess*; but when he too finds his place "in that state of life to which God, not man, shall call him" (9.25) he recants without irony the scorn he earlier heaped on just this "phrase of the prayer book" (2.256). Philip and his cronies have come to the Highlands to study for Oxbridge exams that were becoming, as Clough had every reason to know, increas-ingly significant mechanisms of certification for young men whose *entrée* into the ruling class would lie through national administrative appointment. The real test here, however, is Philip's examination of a provincial way of life, embodied in homespun Elspie Mackaye his excellent bride-to-be, that rehearses what will await the pair as emigrants to the more than provincial, the antipodean colony of New Zealand.

The promise drawing them thither—that of a world made new—is the same promise that attracts Tennyson's Princess and Prince out of themselves and into each other, and it is a promise on which both poets lavish their most strenuous imaginative effects. As these effects rise towards an epic height, we can see them as a benign naturalization of the apocalyptic summons that had so much epic airtime in the 1820s. For the promise of a world renewed is finally secured by a political order that is wedded to the cosmic order itself, "the whole great wicked artificial civilized fabric . . . resumed to Primal Nature and Beauty" (*Bothie* 9.134–36). So Philip tells his

---

[36] I explore these stealth tactics in greater detail in *Tennyson and the Doom of Romanticism*, 351–76.

tutor; so Tennyson's Prince tells his betrothed and well-wishers; so Bulwer-Lytton's Arthur would tell Genevieve and Merlin had he the words. That nature's empire guarantees the world, as its self-evident law and inexhaustible resource, is a cosmological premise of epic magnitude. It elevates each of these generically middling poems beyond low-mimetic, mock-heroic beginnings to symbolic heights, which are in turn authentically grounded by the faith each poem keeps with the basic physical realities to which idyll (Tennyson) and pastoral (Clough) give access.

Foremost among these physical realities is the yoke of sexual passion, and the technical feature in which each poem most fully involves its values with its fable is that yoking figure the epic simile. Simile itself is a conjugal, not fusional, trope. It joins unlike members on compatible grounds, but does not merge them. Both Tennyson and Clough extract from the analogical logic of simile a redoubled power whereby culture and nature intricately vouch for one another.[37] Tennyson's effeminate Prince tells his virile Princess that man and woman are "Not like to like, but like in difference"; and when he goes on to predict that "in the long years liker must they grow" (7.262–63) he speaks both for the coming decades of their marriage and for the issue of the species under millennial conditions of civilized progress. Metaphor constitutes the vanishing point towards which such likeness draws, and it is through similes—"Like perfect music unto noble words" (7.270), "like each other even as those who love" (7.277)—that the Prince's speech makes way to the rhetorical climax of a metaphorical fusion:

> Each fulfils
> Defect in each, and always thought in thought,
> Purpose in purpose, will in will, they grow,
> The single pure and perfect animal,
> The two-cell'd heart beating, with one full stroke,
> Life.
>
> (7.285–90)

The smooth passage of the preposition *in* from denotation ("Defect in each") to conjuration ("will in will") mystifies, by a metaphysical excitation

---

[37] Matthew Reynolds, *The Realms of Verse 1830–1870: English Poetry in a Time of Nation-Building* (Oxford and New York: Oxford University Press, 2001) 225–35, relates the formally analogical method of *The Princess* to an assimilative logic within the mid-century conduct of empire. The linchpin in this cultural rhetoric, Reynolds's book shows, was the trope of marriage: see also Mary Jean Corbett, *Allegories of Union in Irish and English Writing, 1790–1870: Politics, History, and the Family from Edgeworth to Arnold* (Cambridge: Cambridge University Press, 2000).

at once highly sublimated and deeply animal, the question who is in whom, and indeed whether inside is a dominant or a submissive position. No less mystified, or eroticized, is the relation between ends and means, on which we might imagine John Ruskin, or for that matter Erasmus Darwin from Chapter 2, quizzing Tennyson's figures to good effect. Is sexual love flower or fruit? "Life" at the full or the germ of fuller life to be? Is that two-chamber, one-stroke engine Tennyson calls the "heart" a genital organ (or two) in procreative action, or an embryonic creature "pure and perfect" in its living state of growth? To observe how like sex the passage is, eliding all differential markers denotative and syntactical, returns us to the logic of simile and its epic task of coordinating biological with political orders.[38]

Clough discharges this task almost entirely by means of the superb, long-winged epic similes that nearly usurp narration in his last cantos. We have already quoted a little from Philip's simile of the city flooded by rising daylight (9.111–37), because its self-affixed moral is so conveniently explicit on the reconciliation of civilization to nature. Earlier Elspie has outdone Philip in the same vein with the jaw-slackeningly innocent sexiness of her dream about a keystone sliding into a bridge's arch, too long to quote entirely but too fine to skip entirely either:

> Sometimes I find myself dreaming at nights about arches and bridges,—
> Sometimes I dream of a great invisible hand coming down, and
> Dropping the great key stone in the middle: there in my dreaming,
> There I feel the great key stone coming in, and through it
> Feel the other part—all the other stones of the archway,
> Joined into mine with a queer happy sense of completeness, tingling
> All the way up from the other side's basement-stones in the water.

(7.68–74)

With wonderful prosodic masonry, right in the middle of the middle line here, the caesural rift of the hexameter is sealed snug by the second occurrence of

---

[38] And in so doing it returns the extramural, postnationalist 1840s epic to the bar of judgment posed by Moretti's critique of the historical novel (n. 2 above). The erasure of intersubjective boundaries at the climax of a love plot serves both Tennyson and Clough as a global means of finessing a variety of problems involving gender, class, and nation that the rising action has stirred up. Armstrong, reading *The Bothie* against the integrative grain of the plot, emphasizes instead the analytically unresolved character of Clough's diction: despite Philip's *Bildungsroman* "chastening" into "moderation," she contends, "the poem's language does not evolve towards a commensurate simplicity" but "effectively dissolves the category of the normal" (185–87). Reynolds, *Realms of Verse*, 36, sees it otherwise: "The poem welcomes its readers into a liberal polity of diction," albeit conditioned by "the diffuse presence of imperial power."

"great key stone," irregularly put and yet perfect in its weighting. Among Victorian epoists only Browning and Morris would so happily revive in their similes the old Homeric bond between poetic technique and the energies of handicraft.

In company with Clough's other heroic similes for the love that builds an empire, his best mate of all for Tennyson's is this one, from the quiet prothalamion Elspie offers her accepted suitor:

> No, I feel much more as if I, as well as you, were,
> Somewhere, a leaf on the one great tree, that up from old time
> Growing, contains in itself the whole of the virtue and life of
> Bygone days, drawing now to itself all kindreds and nations,
> And must have for itself the whole world for its root and branches.

(8.89–93)

In the first line "as well as" preserves, as "and" would not quite do, simile's sense of the difference within comparison, here the same difference of woman and man, Scotland and England, that Elspie will notice obliquely a couple of lines later: "Yes, I feel the life-juices of all the world and the ages | Coming to me as to you, more slowly no doubt and poorer" (95–96). But then "as well as" and "no doubt" and "as if" are there only to be overcome, made over in the image of the great tree of a life that subsumes all identities as organs of itself. It is a nice question, given the concern of the epic simile with world order, what kind of imperative force to ascribe to the verb "must" in the final line. Whatever so totalizing an organism requires it *must have*, of course; yet a finer tact might read into the line Elspie's discovery— an intuitive inference at once from the omnipotence she has just imputed to the tree and from the wholeness she is feeling in new maturity—that the present order of things is the way they must be.

Such a reading can help us understand why both Clough and Tennyson, rather than adorn the narrative proper with their most heroizing similes in "omniscient" epic's time-honored way, entrust them to their characters instead. Doing so let the poets represent individual fulfillment as ultimately social in the realization of its chosen aim, all solos aspiring by means of erotic duet to the condition of chorus. *Bildung*, the learning to love and from love that forms the theme of these poems, grafts itself in an individual mind's privileged moment upon the great stock of nature's collective being. In the passage above, the synonymic terms "kindreds" and "nations" lead back by English and Latin paths, respectively, to unities of blood and birth in which

The Bothie is even more strongly rooted than *The Princess*. At the same time Clough more explicitly than Tennyson, and writing an eventful year later in the *annus mirabilis* of 1848, lifts these profound stirrings up from the murk of racialist unreason into the light of public politics and the air of internationalism.[39] Comparatively speaking, Clough meant to open out into a liberalized world the urgencies of development that Tennyson the conservative and Bulwer-Lytton the ripening Tory centered with evident smugness on Britain. Yet Clough's last news is that "the Antipodes too have a Bothie of Toper-na-fuosich" (9.229): at the end of the heart's desire lies replication of the order that has produced it, here an empire sunned by the affirmative conventions of pastoral comedy.[40]

Elspie's love and Philip's, and the blessed fertility that undergirds it, leads to a New Zealand that reproduces an Old Scotland.[41] This outcome might have suggested, say to an approving Macaulay, that all contemporary roads led to Rome, which is precisely where Clough went in his second long hexameter poem, *Amours de Voyage* (1858)—and where, regretfully, generic scruple forbids this book from following him. When *The Bothie* says no to epic it half means yes. But the brilliantly dun epistolary palinode Clough wrote in *Amours*—picking trinkety hexameters out of a vanished empire's colossal rubbish, neutralizing an aborted revolution and a fizzled love affair on each other's promise like so much vinegar and chalk—is neither mock-heroic nor anti-heroic. It is non-heroic: flatly, resolutely, and right down to the marble dust under its fastidious fingernails.

---

[39] John Goode reads *The Bothie* as "not a poem about revolution, but a revolutionary poem about love, the personal emotion which existing society most directly challenges," and its structural progression "from mock heroic to heroic" as part of a strategy "to reveal the continuous reality which is overridden by the fairy land of social forms": "1848 and the Strange Disease of Modern Love," in *Literature and Politics in the Nineteenth Century*, ed. John Lucas (London: Methuen, 1971) 64, 67. Tom Paulin finds in the "limber, gradually tumescent style" Clough's dream of "an ideal vernacular republic," a "democratic confidence and openness to nature that anticipates Whitman's populism": *Minotaur: Poetry and the Nation State* (Cambridge, Mass.: Harvard University Press, 1992) 59, 70. See also John Maynard, *Victorian Discourses on Sexuality and Religion* (Cambridge: Cambridge University Press, 1993) 48–56.

[40] On the pastoral engrossment of generic and political options by the end of *The Bothie*, as throughout *The Princess*, see Rod Edmond, *Affairs of the Hearth: Victorian Poetry and Domestic Narrative* (London and New York: Routledge, 1988) 82–83, 119–20.

[41] For Crawford, the adaptation of Longfellow's overspilling meter from *Evangeline* let Clough ventilate his northern vacation epyllion with the west wind of a transatlantic democracy that had learned half its wildness from Ossianic Scotland to begin with (*The Modern Poet*, 124–25).

9

On Impulse:

Spasmodic Epic 1850–1860

Although epic did not die with Milton, as is widely supposed, it did spend most of the eighteenth century in something like a coma and on theoretical life-support. We saw in Chapter 1 how epic survived that century as an ideal to which homage was paid by unquestioning cultural reflex yet how, despite repeated effort on the part of heroic poets, the genre seldom flickered into creative vitality, and then only by such special licensing arrangement with the past as Macpherson was able to contrive in the Ossian books. By the turn of the nineteenth century, in contrast, the epic abstraction had put on flesh again. Vigorous if ungainly, a resurgent epicizing impulse bore down, even while it could not definitively answer, the substantial objections that self-conscious moderns since Dryden had entertained against its viability. This impulse coursed for decades through myths inherited and homemade; orthodox scriptures and secular ones; histories national, foreign, and global; martial and marital conflict and more. And then, at around the mid-century point our narrative now reaches, the epic impulse took a turn inwards and found a subject in impulsiveness itself.

The 1850s were the decade of epic spasmody; and this chapter will treat the flamboyant launch and critical interception of the so-called Spasmodist movement as an episode not just appealing in its own odd way, but instructive for what its inaugural gala and buffo debacle bring out of the woodwork as more abiding properties in the generic grain. We shall consider here the long works of the principal spasmodic poets—Philip James Bailey, R. H. Horne, Alexander Smith, J. Stanyan Bigg, Sydney Dobell—together with their critical assailants W. E. Aytoun (who stopped them cold) and Matthew Arnold (who failed to do that but, in the process, debuted one of literary criticism's eminent careers). The end of the chapter will suggest in what reputable places the spasmodic impulse found lodging after public humiliation forced it underground, and to what effect it erupted in the decade's most important epic poem, Elizabeth Barrett Browning's *Aurora Leigh*.

First, however, spasmody deserves a brief general introduction to twenty-first-century readers. They probably know it better than they think. Spasmodic poetics wrote very large certain Romantic tenets that persist among us today, involving the centrality of the self, the sanctity of the moment of heightened perception, and the totality of truth to which creative poets enjoy privileged if fitful access.[1] Call it transcendentalism with its exhilarated fans in America (who adored Bailey's *Festus* especially), or call it spilt religion with the tight-lipped Modernists of a century ago: Spasmodism was Romanticism in bells and whistles, tinsel and limelight, hawking in the open Victorian market a gospel to which the chief poets of the early century had given unanimous, if less indiscreet, assent. The pleasure Wordsworth took in his own spontaneously overflowing feelings and volitions, Coleridge's supping on the milk of paradise, Shelley's hierophancy of the fading coal, Keats's squirmy erotic dissolves, that being-more-intense which Byron tasted in creativity—and, epitomizing all these, Blake's pulsation of the artery in which the poet's work is done: what these Romantic passages had in common Victorian spasmody enlarged upon, and inevitably vulgarized. The pervasive literary-historical myth that Romantic poetry privileged lyricism *tout court* here came true at last, and on an epic scale. It was programmatic Spasmodism that fully lyricized narrative, or narratized lyric, in long texts aspiring to string together the best and happiest moments of the poet's mind, and to make the result prevail with a resonance as wide as culture.[2]

---

[1] Fred Kaplan's summary judgment that "the Romantics' epic ambitions far outpaced their achievements . . . as if they could write epics about writing epics" is wrong about the Romantics but dead-on about the Spasmodists: *Miracles of Rare Device: The Poet's Sense of Self in Nineteenth-Century Poetry* (Detroit: Wayne State University Press, 1972) 12. An abbreviated version of my argument here appears as "Glandular Omnism and Beyond: The Victorian Spasmodic Epic," *Victorian Poetry* 42 (2004) 429–50.

[2] In a uniquely large-minded work of literary theory contemporary with the heyday of spasmody, *Poetics: An Essay on Poetry* (London: Smith, Elder, 1852), E. S. Dallas decries in recent poets "the gross error of writing not a poem, but a book of beauties, stringing their pearls almost at random, in the vain hope that they may give up the unity of the whole for the exceeding beauty of the parts" (197); yet even Dallas concedes what is in effect the major Spasmodist premise, that "the Lyrical bard is . . . one who sings the Epos of his own soul" (82).

For the poet's mind, under the spell of spasmody, was not alone. It—or the mind of a thinly veiled surrogate named Festus or Walter or Alexis or Balder—was a self-interpreting aspect of the cosmic mind. Furthermore, because poetic genius embraced all humanity, the insights and transgressions of a protagonist who was endowed with poetic genius were *ipso facto* heroic. As J. Westland Marston had presciently put it in 1842,

> To choose the struggles and experiences of Genius as a subject, might seem to evince temerity, if not presumption, on the part of the Author. But, were such a reflection allowed any weight, it would preclude the attempt to portray the heroic, — not only in the instance of the Poet—but in those of the Warrior, the Patriot, and the Philosopher. For what is the heroic in Man, but his *Genius*?[3]

Here in a recognizably Carlylean prose polemic, as elsewhere in verse roaring at full throttle, spasmody speaks for a Victorian human-potential movement. Its New Age analogy between the growth of the individual mind and the actualization of universal being covers a multitude of sins by recuperating deviancy as an innovative, species-enhancing experimentation on life. The poet-hero exemplifies the divinity for which he quests, and at his acutest moment, which spasmodic texts replay with a wonder apparently nothing can blunt, he becomes conscious of precisely this fact, which is his freedom and also his fate.[4]

The spasm of affirmative self-transcendence recapitulates in miniature the whole gamut of a cosmic history running from the Big Bang of creation to the Big Hug of no-fault apocalypse. Internalizing the course of time in one rapturous thrill, and without benefit of clergy, the spasmodic epic replaces the chiliastic judgment and evangelical atonement of 1820s epic with nicer things like welcome and pardon, all in support of the unobstructed epiphany of self. Where there is no guilt and the only error is inhibition, time has no plotted significance beyond the steady accrual of experience as a uniform good. In this sense spasmody is literally optimistic: any time is best, since every time is better than what precedes it; and there is definitely no turning back. That is one reason why the major spasmodic epics assumed a dramatic form, in spite of their entire unsuitability for the stage. (Another reason is that dramatic form finessed what would have been substantial narrative

[3] *Gerald; A Dramatic Poem* (London: Mitchell, 1842) v–vi.
[4] There are good overview essays by Richard Cronin, "The Spasmodics," in *A Companion to Victorian Poetry*, ed. Cronin, Alison Chapman, and Antony H. Harrison (Oxford: Blackwell, 2002) 291–303; and by Jerome H. Buckley, *The Victorian Temper: A Study in Literary Culture* (Cambridge, Mass.: Harvard University Press, 1951).

embarrassments attaching to grammatical person.[5]) As in nearly all nineteenth-century dramaturgy, which discountenanced those old epic standbys the flash-back and the prophecy, a continuously unfolding present fixed the attention of auditors, or of closeted readers, on what was passing before them in the moment, with an absorptive totality whereby the momentaneous passes over easily into the timeless.[6] Even Horne's more conventionally narrated epic *Orion* reels full steam ahead, with only such fleeting retrospects as pass through a distinctly unreflective giant-hero's mind between one crisis and the next.[7] And if Orion's crises, like those of other spasmodic protagonists, are all pretty much the same, this too befits the uniform temporality of a supergeneric lyrical–dramatical–epical subgenre for which a crisis is a spasm is a wink in the great affirmation which is time.

Spasm is an absorbingly corporeal experience, and the actual theater of spasmodism is not the playhouse but the embodied mind. The dialogue in Bailey's *Festus* or Smith's *A Life-Drama* seems more and more with each passing scene, or accumulating edition, a flimsy pretext for long solo arias, which the reader is to interpret in a performer's and not a theatre-critic's sense. We are invited, that is, to root for the hero from the inside out. This invitation is reinforced by the peculiarly concrete abstraction of spasmodic imagery, which in obvious ways bespeaks a globally swelled head but conversely spans the heavens by constant reference to a human sensorium.

[5] Given the prominence that prose fiction had attained by 1850, and the sophistication in diegetic irony to which novel-reading had accustomed the Victorian public, standard third-person epic narrative would have been lethal to the unself-critical intensity of spasmodic introversion. Narrative in the first person held more promise, which the two best epics published in the 1850s, *The Prelude* and *Aurora Leigh*, amply realized. Those poems brilliantly show, however, that a viable mid-century epic "I" had to repose on complexities of memory, and on an adaptable receptivity to external circumstance, for which spasmody had little or no patience.

[6] E. M. W. Tillyard, *The Epic Strain in the English Novel* (London: Chatto & Windus, 1958), proposes an apposite contrast between the forms of drama and of epic, where the "communal or choric quality" of the latter is bound to specific historicity: "Tragedy cannot lack some imprint of its age, but its nature is to be timeless.... It is when the tragic intensity is included in the group-consciousness of an age, when the narrowly timeless is combined with the variegatedly temporal, that the epic attains its full growth" (15). This growth it was the program of Spasmodism to stunt, in almost direct contradiction to traditional epic practice, by essentially monodramatic means that privileged description over narration. On the epic stakes of this latter rivalry see Gyorgy Lukács's 1936 essay "Narrate or Describe?" in *Writer and Critic*, ed. and tr. Arthur Kahn (London: Merlin Press, 1970) 110–48.

[7] The intensely episodic nature of spasmody may explain why Edgar Allan Poe, who famously declared the long poem to be a contradiction in terms, could nonetheless wax enthusiastic about *Orion* and rank it above *Paradise Lost*: "in all that regards the loftiest and holiest attributes of the true Poetry, *Orion* has never been excelled." Quoted in John W. Dodds, *The Age of Paradox: A Biography of England 1841–1851* (New York: Rinehart, 1952) 211; see also Hugh Walker, *The Literature of the Victorian Era* (Cambridge: University Press, 1910) 345.

The resulting physicalization of metaphysics tends in sum to trope the universe as a feeling, and a feeling less emotional or moral than sensory and ontological. (Again the heady optimism: attend to the somatic stimulus, and the ethical response will take care of itself.) Orientation toward sensory being has been a feature of epic since Homer; and reference to the integer of the body works overtime to validate the else-incredible vagaries to whose indulgence spasmodical ambition lies prone. Even where criminal transgression is overtly at issue, as it is in Dobell's *Balder*, what is imaginatively at stake is how crime feels in its impact on the endocrine and neuromuscular systems.

It is tempting to dismiss such glandular poetics as the literary equivalent of gin: the quickest way out of Manchester, the cheapest of shortcuts to an epic totalization that ought to be harder-won.[8] But we may resist this temptation by recalling our Victorian political economy and having due regard for the fascination of what's cheap. We can then note that spasmody had a creditable role to play in the multigeneric literary history of the British nineteenth century. The movement stood framed on one side by the lyrical sensation poetics of the 1830s, which an enthusiastic Arthur Hallam identified as the early Tennyson's legacy from Shelley and Keats, and which so reasonable a creature as John Stuart Mill excitedly discussed in terms of "a condition of the whole frame" that "pervades the entire nervous system."[9] Waiting on the other side of the 1850s lay the sensation fiction that would enthrall the reading public of decades to come. If the spasmodic embodiment of a lyric agenda in a narrative form failed, it was a failure from which, as from its limited local successes, an entire range of more prudent Victorian authors learned influential lessons.

★

[8] On this topic a brief citation from the old *Cambridge History* may give readers a taste for that verse-glutton George Saintsbury's strongly seasoned criticism of the spasmodic "extravagance of conception and diction, a sort of Byronism metamorphosed, imitation of other poets which, sometimes, goes near to plagiarism, an inequality which exceeds the large limits allowed to poets and, worst of all, that suggestion of ineffective and undignified effort—of the 'gingerbeer bottle burst,' to borrow a phrase from Smith himself": "Lesser Poets," in *Cambridge History of English Literature*, ed. A. W. Ward and A. R. Waller, vol. 13 (Cambridge: Cambridge University Press, 1917) 176.

[9] Hallam, "On Some of the Characteristics of Modern Poetry," published in *The Englishman's Magazine* (1831), rpt. in *The Writings of Arthur Hallam*, ed. T. Vail Motter (New York: Modern Language Association, 1943); Mill, "The Two Kinds of Poetry," *Monthly Repository* (1833), rpt. in *Autobiography and Literary Essays*, ed. John M. Robson and Jack Stillinger, vol. 1 of *Collected Works* (Toronto and Buffalo: University of Toronto Press, 1981) 360. On sensation poetics see Isobel Armstrong, "The Role and the Treatment of Emotion in Victorian Criticism of Poetry," *Victorian Periodicals Newsletter* 10 (1977) 3–16; and Armstrong's *Victorian Poetry: Poetry, Poetics and Politics* (London and New York: Routledge, 1993), chs. 2 and 3 *passim*.

The juice-pumping similes we discussed at the end of Chapter 8 suggest that Tennyson and Clough had learned lessons already about the integrative power of a spasmodic physicality, and about the wisdom of filling the void between self and cosmos with some third, body-mediated term like nation or race. The hornbook they are likeliest to have learned from is *Festus: A Poem* (1839, 1845, *et seq.*).[10] On its early appearance this work was admired by Tennyson, was pressed on the young Clough in the year of *The Bothie* by the yet younger and as yet unreconstructed Arnold, and was praised by other epoists from James Montgomery and Ebenezer Elliott to Bulwer-Lytton and Browning. The poem fared better still in America, where Longfellow pronounced *Festus* miraculous and paid it the sincerest of compliments by imitation in *The Golden Legend* (1851). From his eminence of years even Landor, who had published *Gebir* at about the same age Bailey had reached when the first version of *Festus* came out, approvingly addressed some rhymed advice to his young successor in headstrong innovation.[11] There was something for everybody in *Festus*; to observe as much is merely to endorse the governing principle of the poem's spasmodic design. That design was, in a word of Bailey's own coinage, *omnist* ("Village Feast," 132); and as a statement of epic ambition the word can hardly be bettered. The poem takes the plot of Goethe's *Faust* and runs with it, traversing this world and the next, *en route* to its climax in the redemption of all souls: Festus, of course, but also Lucifer, who while prorogued in 1839 was welcomed into the ample final fold in 1845 and forever after. The finale of universal redemption bears out past doom's edge an ethos of plenary indulgence that pervades the many previous scenes in which it has been variously rehearsed. Not that anyone, the devil included, ever does anything very wicked: Bailey's diversitarian message is that every individual deviancy goes to enrich the diapason of God's fullness in time. Festus is a hero because he is a creature of impulse; the moment impulsively lived is mankind's

---

[10] The complicated publication history is given in Morse Peckham, "English Editions of *Festus*," *Papers of the Bibliographical Society of America* 44 (1950) 55–58.

[11] An anthology of admiration—much of it, characteristically, furnished by Bailey himself in the second edition—may be consulted in Robert Birley, *Sunk Without Trace: Some Forgotten Masterpieces Reconsidered* (London: Rupert Hart-Davis, 1962) 173–75. Birley's lapidary testimonial puts the poem nicely in place: "One of the great disadvantages of reading Bailey is that afterwards one is constantly noticing passages in the great Victorian poets which could be incorporated in *Festus* without questions asked" (184). Saintsbury, *Cambridge History*, 13: 171–72, demurs at the "enormous interim" of plot in *Festus*, "an impossible sausage," yet recognizes here and there "passages of extraordinary brilliance."

analogue to the wholeness of history and the recurrent, instantaneous perfection of the eternal.[12]

Festus himself becomes increasingly clear about this as the poem unfolds; so did *Festus* in its successive versions. A long proem that Bailey wrote for the second edition in 1845 blithely disregards "manners, customs, forms, appearances, | Laws, places, times, and countless accidents" (8). Such accidentals are irrelevant to the poet's essential task of transcending them. In the process of transcending them, to be sure, he busily inventories them; and from the first edition a wealth of social and political detail enters the poem under light satirical fire. *Sub specie totalitatis* the business of firm, sect, and nation is too petty and partial to survive. Even Festus' patriotic attachment to England is something to rise above, literally in his airborne tourism of everywhere, ideologically in his program of a world federation under (the monodramatic logic of spasmodism mandated no less than this) his own benevolent dictatorship: "Let each one labour for the common weal. | Be every man a people in his mind," Festus exclaims ("Gathering of Kings and Peoples," 362). "Nations, away with them!" The fact that this slogan from Lucifer's internationalist stump-speech precipitates a hostile uproar that only apocalypse can quell may be Bailey's one concession to epic's traditional concern with national identity. No matter: when all is made right in the "Heaven of Heavens" finale, Festus' postnationalist cult of personality carries the day.

> FESTUS. Are ye all here, too, with me?
> ALL.   All.
> FESTUS.   It is Heaven.
>
> ("Heaven of Heavens" 389)

The whole poem lies in this one-pentameter exchange—as in a dozen other epitomes that litter its yawning self-consistency. (Indeed, to the truly omnist imagination the second cue alone will suffice to say it all.) Being, presence, togetherness: Bailey's Heaven is always here and now and for everybody.

---

[12] The post-apocalypticist serenity of Bailey's omnist stance beyond good and evil emerges in a letter he wrote his father on 1 Nov. 1834, at a very early stage during the composition of *Festus*: "It is on the extent of the scheme that I stake its character. Of Pollok's Course of Time I know nothing. I have a faint recollection of hearing you read some passages some years ago, but I do not think it embraces an equal breadth of circumstances." Quoted in Alan D. McKillop, "A Victorian Faust," *PMLA* 40 (1925) 744. The else-stupefying claim to outflank the Last Judgment becomes intelligible as the matured fruit of what we glimpsed in germ with J. A. Heraud's *Descent into Hell* in Ch. 7: God's purpose, manifest for Heraud in the entelechy of time's plotted unfolding, has for Bailey come to focal incarnation in the apocalypse of the heroic self.

Given the vastness of abstraction in which *Festus* trades, the radical collect-
ive immediacy of epic spasmody could not be more utterly asserted.[13]

Bailey's Heaven might double as a description of his presentational
format, which places the action, ever and everywhere, right in front of us,
orchestrated at the dramatic-epic pulse rate of one instant per instant.[14]
Under spasmodic rule "We should count time by heart-throbs," since
"there is no past; | And the future is the fiction of a fiction; | The present
moment is eternity" ("Market-place" 77, 81). Space, too, proves com-
pletely fungible: scene settings like "A Large Party" and "A Drawing
Room" occur in carefree alternation with "Air," "Space," "Anywhere,"
and (the omnist's true haunt) "Everywhere." Stage direction cannot well be
less directive than this; there is a wonderfully firm recklessness to the way
Bailey tosses away all external guidance. Done with the compass, done with
the chart and the clock too, Festus repudiates contingency, disclaims origins
(*passed,* significantly, is the spelling he favors for *past*), discounts original sin,
and prefers response over responsibility, the whoosh of effusion over the
reach of plot. It makes sense that a spasmodic narrative should come in fits,
but *Festus* does so on principle. The amnesically episodic quality of the plot
enacts Bailey's declaration of independence from history and the ethic of
universal absolution that goes with it. "Yes! if I have sinned, I have sinned
sublimely"; "How am I answerable for my heart?" ("Heaven" 205–6).

Penitence is an idea the poem is too open-minded not to entertain for a
while when the time comes. But then the time goes, too, and the poem
surges on in free dilation. Such guilt as exists in *Festus* is not expiated, nor is
error rectified; yet both in a way are healed as, superseded in the pageantry
of episodes, they melt into the totality of an unconditional acceptance.[15] It is

---

[13] All the stranger that in Landor's 1849 tribute "To the Author of *Festus* on the Classick and
Romantick" the old poet should have exhorted the younger to join him in scolding "the starting
youth, | Ready to seize all nature at one grasp, | To mingle earth, sea, sky, woods, cataracts, | And
make all nations think and speak alike" (17–20): *Complete Works,* ed. T. Earle Welby (London:
Chapman and Hall, 1927–36) 14: 163.

[14] A vivid perception of this principle informs Margaret Fuller's enthusiastic reception of the
first edition, in *The Dial* 2 (1841) 231–38. Outlining a New England Transcendentalist version of
1830s sensation poetics, Fuller ascribes Bailey's sincerity and naturalness to his power of writing
without "the intervention of reflective intellect" (235); Festus "is so easily taken captive by the
present, as to admit of its being brought fully before us" (248). Thanks to the poet's "majestic
negligence of heroic forms" (244), Fuller reclaims that alienated majesty which was—so Emerson
proposed that very year in "Self-Reliance"—her own heroic birthright as a reader: "We have not
criticized; we have lived with him" (261).

[15] This may be the respect in which *Festus* most approximates its model in Goethe's *Faust,*
where as Franco Moretti observes the essence of heroism has shifted from acting on the world to

as if the stain of guilt that Scott had introduced into the formula for Romantic heroism was extracted in the wringer of 1820s apocalypticism, to leave Bailey's fabric bleached of narrative design, pleasant to the touch, remarkably uniform in texture. This sense of the whole is where Festus' allegiance is due, and he scrupulously pays it, in flash after flash of non-cumulative epiphanic intuition. During one uncanny episode added in the 1845 edition Festus provides what we gradually realize is a table of contents, with commentary, for the very poem he appears in, premising that "It has a plan, but no plot. Life hath none" (250). Bailey embedded this scene—captioned "Home," as if on a gameboard—approximately where in classical epic the hero goes to generic ground zero, descending to the underworld to learn the future from ghosts of the past. Bailey's navel-gazingly presentist version of this convention anticipates the dumbfounding candor with which his successors in spasmody would produce their own creative pro-cedures for inspection. Laying all their cards on the table, they in effect called in the immense bet that cultural coherentism had placed on epic a century before; paying it back in the auto-referentiality of macropoetic form, they almost broke the generic bank.

The premise that nothing should be alien to *Festus* licensed Bailey to give the poem everything he had, which is just what he did for over sixty years. Like his French counterpart Victor Hugo in *La Légende des Siècles*, and his American disciple Walt Whitman in *Leaves of Grass*, Bailey packed into successive versions of this baggy book whatever he could think of. In more than a hundred printings the poem grew through the indexed edition of 1864 and the newly prefaced, 52-scene jubilee edition of 1889—the poem's jubilee, mind, not the Queen's—towards a final 1901 testament whose 40,000 lines quintupled the original. The elephantiasis of *Festus* imaged the enormity, not just of the author's egotism, but of the culturally consti-tutive individualism for which his amazing effrontery had spoken from the first. True, *King Alfred* was thrice as long again, but Fitchett had a tale he could stuff with chronicle and travelogue; Bailey's afflatus is nearly all of it the hot air, good and bad, of imagination. Even when Festus tears off in scene 20 of the 1889 version for a name-dropping jag, two thousand lines long, on the joint mission of humanity's world-historical eminences, he is *thinking* as hard as he can, and the writing is not effortless. As the appropriately

experiencing it, as the mode of Western dominion has shifted from conquest to incorporation: *Modern Epic: The World-System from Goethe to Garcia Marquez*, tr. Quintin Hoare (London and New York: Verso, 1996) 16–17, 44.

long final sentence of Bailey's 1889 preface allies his poem with the "self-evolution of Humanity as one brotherhood," the grammar makes it impossible to unwind that world process from the process of the poem itself:

—an eclectic and philosophic symbol anticipated towards the end of the work as destined eventually to be everywhere on earth welcomed and established, and one which, however much in some quarters misunderstood, yet in its original inception and design spaciously and presciently conceived, has since been not inconsistently nor immethodically carried out, to the ultimate achievement of all that from the first was promised or predicted.   (6)

The syntactic confusion here need not have been deliberate since, bibliographically as well as thematically, *Festus* became over the years its own cause for celebration. Excerpts of published applause and critique that Bailey took to printing with the poem put into vivid practice the principle of growth by absorption. If ingestion was the golden rule of life, it was good enough for epic art as well; and *Festus* repaired itself by recruitment, not emendation. Keeping nothing back, it took nothing back either. Whatever readers disliked, Bailey reasoned, they must not have fully understood; so it was just a matter of being more explicit in the next, perennially forthcoming edition, revised and augmented by the author.

Victorian Britain witnessed better epics than Bailey's, but none so fully heralded the era's manic overdrive. *Orion: An Epic Poem in Three Books* (1843), also in the vanguard, took aim at the same target as *Festus*; but it was in every way a cheaper shot. Author Richard Henry (later Hengist) Horne disarmingly acknowledged as much by offering its first edition at a farthing a copy, in "a novel experiment upon the mind of a nation" (preface). Poets don't talk like that, press agents do; and the key to reading *Orion* without disappointment is to understand it as a talented hack's epic, a literary stunt hustled together as a wager not so much upon the nation's mind as on its taste, and purse. Horne bet that an epic poem pitched from the right angle would sell. (He was right, and the price climbed substantially for later editions.) His angle, shrewdly formed after observing the unstable generic scene during the preceding decade, was to balance the formal classiness of the genre with a contemporary content involving matters of vital national concern.[16] And his tool was allegory: *Orion* bent a roughly Keatsian

---

[16] Horne's poem earns higher marks—probably its most affirmative 20th-cent. interpretation—in Jack Lindsay's biography *George Meredith* (London: Bodley Head, 1956). Attentive to Horne's

mythological romance plot of goddess-love into a fable consecrating to the ideal of liberal progress the masculine energies of industrial engineering and laisser-faire entrepreneurship.

The giant Orion—less the ancient Greek hunter here than "The Worker he, | The builder-up of things and of himself" (1.2.5–6)—drains a harbor, throws up earthworks, and performs on his Aegean isle Victorianesque wonders in wrought-iron with the use of hydrodynamic power. Orion's ideological foil is Akinetos ("the Great Unmoved," as his Greek name declares), a brother giant so granitic in conservatism that his counterpart Magros from Disraeli's *Revolutionary Epick* a decade before (Ch. 7) shows in comparison like a chatterbox. The petrification of Akinetos in the last canto may serve here to emblematize the spasmodic habit of reproducing Romantic figures, here the quasi-geological nature Keats bestowed on his Titans in *Hyperion*, with a coarsening literality. Horne also embroils his giants at one point (1.2) in what sounds suspiciously like a policy debate on the Corn Laws. For the most part, though, the poet knew his trade well enough to keep the allegory vaguer than this, in pursuit of "a special design, applicable to all times, by means of antique or classical imagery and associations" (1871 preface, iv). That design is "the law of progress" (vii), "the constant advancement of mankind" (xi), which the plot illustrates—progressively, of course—through Orion's frustrated courtship of Artemis, a goddess fond but chaste; his interrupted amours with Merope, a princess ardent but politically off-limits; and his ecstatic union with Eos, goddess of dawn and thus patroness of potentiality itself, proof divine that, as the poem's oftest-quoted slogan puts it, " 'T is always morning somewhere in the world" (3.2.43). In this triadic poem the consummation of sex solves a dialectic of opposites: even more obviously—because more allegorically—than in the maritalmetaphysical idylls Tennyson and Clough were about to publish (Ch. 8), here dream and substance, divine and human, soul and body "must melt and merge in one" (2.2.341).[17]

"Radical and Chartist" affinities, appreciative of the poem's materialist premises and dialectical method, Lindsay prizes its registration of both the "strong impact of contemporary conflicts and the uncertainty as to the way in which those conflicts were to be historically resolved" (44). Taken jointly, Lindsay's appreciation for Horne's radicalism and mine for his entrepreneurial panache attest the industrial cooperation, *c.*1840, between working-class and bourgeois interests that later decades would drive apart. On the balanced convergence of these interests in the 1840s see Armstrong, *Victorian Poetry*, 152–58.

[17] In fact Horne was out-allegorized in his own decade by the fledgling Pre-Raphaelite William Bell Scott in *The Year of the World; A Philosophical Poem on "Redemption from the Fall"* (1846). So

At this point Horne's plot has all it takes to motivate posterity except an incentive program, which materializes when in a final twist Orion is slain and constellated. By great Zeus's decree "His cycle moves | Ascending!" (3.3.273–74) in a perennially *Excelsior!* vision of inspirational imperfection, as the final lines have it, "merging in the dawn,—/ And circling onward in eternal youth" (3.3.394–95).[18] That Orion's gigantic loss is humanity's gain is a lesson he himself teaches, in what for our purposes stands out as the poem's most noteworthy scene. Shortly before death, he looks out on the Aegean island of Chios and, reading in the variety of its landscape the checkered phases of his love life, finds them all tending uniformly to the promotion of good. Here is a *Bildungsepos* vision of progressive inclusion worthy—admittedly on farthing-epic scale—of the omnism of Bailey; true to spasmodic form, Horne mounts on his hero's pleased self-awareness a poetic self-awareness to match. For as Orion's eye comes to rest on "Mount Epos" (*sic*) we are reminded that Chios was not just any isle but Homer's. With "prophetic thrill" we foresee the "after age" when a silver-haired bard is to teach the epic arts to "his school, | Where the boy Homer on the stony rim | Sat with the rest around. Bright were his eyes" (3.2.87–94). Teach enough schoolboys Homer, and a schoolboy Homer will matriculate. The bright-eyed pupil on whom Horne's farthing epic calls for class recitation serves here as a prosopopoeia for the long draft that projects of national education made on the canon of heroic poetry. Regarded as a public utility, and rightly so, epic lay under a tricky set of obligations that *Orion* exposes more clearly than any of its spasmodic congeners: the genre should stay lofty but at the same time should stay open to modern emulation and become accessible to a broadening readership.[19]

philosophical indeed was this poem that its wispy narrative of mankind's coming of age, by way of the lay figure Lyremmos' aeonian quest for a spiritual enlightenment beyond creed and Carlylean "mythus" (5.95), did not stand a chance against its spasmodic-scale ambition to tell all. Accordingly Scott inserted frequent unctuous glosses, addressing the reader directly as a sort of embedded serial guide, and then called his own epic bluff when the last ten pages abandoned blank-verse narration in favor of an antiphonal choral ode harmonizing spirit with science, and Western with Eastern religion, under cover of the hero's reunion with his *Ewig-Weibliche* sister Mneme.

[18] Hoxie Neale Fairchild, *Religious Trends in English Poetry*, vol. 4 (New York: Columbia University Press, 1957) 212–15, distinguishes *Orion* favorably from *Festus* and the later Spasmodist epics by reason of the resolutely secular character of Horne's progressivism. Douglas Bush, *Mythology and the Romantic Tradition in English Poetry* (1937; rpt. Cambridge, Mass.: Harvard University Press, 1969) 282, gives credit where credit is due: "Keats's humanitarianism had been a poetic ideal, Horne's was a practical fact."

[19] John Lucas reads *Orion*, alongside *Festus* and Browning's *Paracelsus* and *Sordello*, as an allegory that insists on the public function of poetry while refusing to specify it: "Politics and the Poet's Role," in his edited collection *Literature and Politics in the Nineteenth Century* (London: Methuen, 1971) 34–38.

For a liberal like Horne, the curve of an epic's plot ought to figure as progressive both the history of the genre it joined and the evolution of humanity on which any epic worth its salt rendered a privileged, if coded, progress report. The allegorical-mythic mode of narration that he adopted seems to have struck his 1850s Spasmodist successors as a puny alternative to Bailey's with-it spirit of big-stage panorama, which by preference they followed. But before turning to see how they wrought in that spirit, we might note as a defining exception one epicizing work more in Horne's line that was produced by a clergyman-bard of parts, Charles Kingsley, at a time when his formidable energies were engaged with equal intensity in literary and educational activity. Having labored for several years in the cause of Christian Socialism as a lecturer on literature to workingmen, and as a novelist placing mutual moral uplift in the hands of middle- and working-class readers alike (*Yeast* in 1848, *Alton Locke* in 1850), Kingsley turned to versify the Perseus myth in 1852. The title piece of *Andromeda and Other Poems* (1858) occupies no more than five hundred lines, but then they are long lines, and robust; their unrhymed dactylic hexameters bespeak in Kingsley an epic mind, as they did a few years previously in Longfellow (*Evangeline*, 1847) and Clough (*The Bothie*; see Ch. 8).[20] More here than in the boys'-book prose of his bestselling *The Heroes* (1856), Kingsley makes Andromeda's rescue from the sea-beast hint broadly at wider liberations: the freeing of pleasure from taboo; the disencumbering of immortality from the curbs of fate yet, in what for this most amorous of clerics was the same stroke, of the comely body from the ascetic soul; the deliverance of clear faith in the human incarnation divine from superstition's "shapeless" and enervating mystery (58).

A torqued moral, this; yet such was the author's "muscular Christianity": well known today in its own right, yet arguably just another case of the general, glandular-omnist rule of the epic 1850s.[21] Nor are these spasmodizing

---

[20] Kingsley's struggle to work out an English hexameter comparable to that employed in the classical epic emerges in letters discussed by J. M. I. Klaver, *The Apostle of the Flesh: A Critical Life of Charles Kingsley* (Leiden: Brill, 2006) 310–11. E. C. Stedman, *Victorian Poets*, rev. edn. (Boston and New York: Houghton Mifflin, 1887) 251, credits Kingsley with pioneering in *Andromeda* a new and "effective form of English verse," through "the best-sustained example of English hexameters produced up to the date of its composition." Herbert J. C. Grierson and J. C. Smith confirm a view widely shared that "Kingsley's hexameters are the best in English, much more 'Homeric' than Clough's or Longfellow's": *A Critical History of English Poetry* (New York: Oxford University Press, 1946) 483.

[21] Spasmodism served Kingsley during the 1850s much as John Henry Newman's writings would do during the 1860s: each offered an antagonist foil to his bluff advocacy of a manly grapple

emancipations merely allegorical; they are for Kingsley, and at precisely the point where his myth-making draws up towards epic, the vital pith of a continuous cultural history still operative in Victorian times. In a final passage we find that the goddess Athene, having blessed Perseus and Andromeda's union, and foretold their Orion-like constellation after death, then did more and "planned new lessons for mortals" (495).[22] The newest lesson epic knows is always that Homer's school remains in session: the great texts of a culture renew their function in *paideia*. Conning this lesson briefly in Kingsley's large-minded tale, we grasp the whole exercise as not just mythic but *mythological*, in the strict sense of that term. It constitutes a liberal's myth about myth's own progress as the token, and the inspiring beacon, of collective edification reaching out of darkness towards truth. In the next decade major Victorian epoists would take note, working otherwise than Kingsley in formal respects yet working much in his mythic-exploratory spirit.

The capacious allegories of Horne and Kingsley propose that industrial technology and the liberal arts and sciences all stem from one root with the *technē* of poetry. All are actuated by the can-do spirit that has won the heart of bright-eyed Eos, her of the reciprocating two-stroke love-cry "Believe— advance!" (3.2.25). The work-in-progress that is modern culture thrives on progressivism, which is itself an ideological work-in-progress among whose many factories are epic narratives of uplift, laboring alongside the other arts and manufactures to produce a new age. When Horne published a grab-bag

with life's challenges. One key text in this campaign was "Alexander Smith and Alexander Pope," a review of Smith's *Life-Drama* in *Fraser's Magazine* for October 1853, rpt. in *Literary and General Lectures and Essays* (London: Macmillan, 1880). There Kingsley locates an Arnoldian principle of formal unity—what Smith so conspicuously lacks—in a capacity for faith whose compatibility with modern science (84–86) links Kingsley's review directly to his ideas in "Andromeda" about the progress of myth. Another key text is *Two Years Ago* (1857), a novel whose bristling contemporaneity organizes topics as far-flung as American slavery, Continental insurgency, and the Crimean War around the degradation and deathbed poetic apostasy of the spasmodic author of *A Soul's Agonies, and other Poems*. We know this vain and jealous impostor, who styles himself Elsley Vavasour, as plebeian John Briggs. Not content with always "looking out consciously and spasmodically for views, effects, emotions, images" (10: 155), he plummets from a parody of Romantic transcendence upon a peak in Snowdonia—"conscious only of self, and of a dull, inward fire, as if his soul were a dark vault, lighted with lurid smoke" (21: 409)—into pique, laudanum, and London, to die not of the soul's agonies but in "agonies of rheumatic fever" after he has enjoined his long-suffering wife, *à la* Don Quixote, to "go home and burn all the poetry, all the manuscripts, and never let the children write a verse" (25: 476, 479).

[22] The content of these lessons, John Maynard proposes, is to be maritally licit sexual indulgence. "Kingsley's overall aim must be to produce a new, settled, and complete discourse joining sexuality and religion to replace the one of asceticism that he rejects": *Victorian Discourses on Sexuality and Religion* (Cambridge: Cambridge University Press, 1993) 115.

of literary criticism the year after *Orion* as *A New Spirit of the Age* (1844), the title owed less to Hazlitt's 1825 *Spirit of the Age* than it did to the business-minded reforming public to whose trade wind Horne trimmed his sail (with some unacknowledged help from a dissenter's brilliant daughter named Elizabeth Barrett). His survey of contemporary literature ends with an encomium on *Festus* and a valedictory dedication to "a Working Man" who looks like Orion, makes out like Perseus, and sounds like an answer to Carlyle's prayers, falling in step with the poet and man of letters as a hero of his time who proves by doing: "The only artist-work that does good in its day, or that reaches posterity, is the work of a Soul that gives form" (363, 365).[23] With this heroic creed Kingsley, foe to the "shapeless," could not have agreed more; and his "Andromeda" would add for good epic measure, in the voice of Athene exhorting heroes to get married and get to work, "Thence comes weal to a nation" (421).

Look to a poem like *Orion*, Horne in effect declared, for the essence of the industrious hour's "Soul that gives form." Within a decade that soul would be giving till it hurt. When Spasmodism properly so called burst on the scene in the early 1850s, it looked a lot like what Horne had predicted. The point-man for the movement was a *bona fide* young working-class poet, Alexander Smith, who had been to school with Ebenezer Elliott, had cheered the 1848 revolutions, and had since then retrenched, along with veteran Chartists like Thomas Cooper, from electoral politics to literary and educational reform—social engineering projects that would have earned Orion's blessing. The Great Exhibition of Spasmodism was Smith's *A*

---

[23] An earlier chapter of *A New Spirit* that contrasts Marston's *Gerald* unfavorably with Browning's *Paracelsus* (1835) and *Sordello* (1840) by implication undermines the Carlylean industrial aesthetic of *Orion*: "for all the spirit of railroads and all the steam," writes Horne, "the spirit of the Fine Arts cannot be identical with the material forces and improvements of the age, which are progressive—the former is not" (New York: Harper, 1872, 278). Nevertheless, Carlyle's summons to the epoist of "Tools and the Man" (thus his 1832 review of Ebenezer Elliott, though it might equally well have been the 1841 *On Heroes*, or the 1843 *Past and Present*, both of which use "Epic" to denote cultural greatness) rang in the mind of a younger generation. It returned in a fine railroad passage (7.417–41) from spasmody's finest flower, Barrett Browning's *Aurora Leigh*: see Simon Dentith, *Epic and Empire in Nineteenth-Century Britain* (Cambridge: Cambridge University Press, 2006) 95–96. A few years earlier, a distinguished visitor to the Crystal Palace had found the old connection to epic machinery irresistible. As William Whewell told a lecture audience in the autumn of 1851, "Man's power of making may show itself not only in the beautiful *texture* of language, the grand *machinery* of the epic, the sublime display of poetical *imagery*; but in those material works which supply the originals from which are taken the derivative terms which I have just been compelled to use": *Lectures on the Results of the Great Exhibition of 1851* (London: Bogue, 1852) 5.

Life-Drama (1852), a blank-verse closet-drama about a poet-hero who bestows on the public, of all things, a creation-to-doomsday epic poem. As this inbred theme may suggest, the poem was at once a symptom and a victim of the sprawling, celebrity-nutrient, advertisement-driven and review-dependent Victorian print world in which Bailey and Horne had flourished. For *A Life-Drama* was an epic written virtually to critical recipe. After a talent-scouting Glasgow columnist, the Revd George Gilfillan, introduced Smith to the world in excerpts larded with unctuous puffery, readers responded so enthusiastically that publishers were offering the young poet substantial sums for his long poem before it actually existed. In a telescoped permutation of the Ossian craze from a century before (Ch. 1)—untutored Scottish genius now replacing the romance of Celtic antiquities—Smith had to come up fast with many a gross of striking verses and a structure to dangle them from.[24] He turned, of course, to the celebrated example of *Festus*. There he found a prefabricated rationale in Bailey's omnist analogy between the local coupling that was metaphor and the overall interlock that was cosmos, the whole being liberally laced with a self-referentiality that did the work of structure.

In Smith's hands, however, the joint pressures of publisher's deadline and forerunner's example generated a self-referentiality qualitatively different.[25] Where *Festus* remained exuberantly naïve in its narcissistic inventory and display, *A Life-Drama* constantly betrays its hasty pastiche composition. For one thing, Smith keeps looking over his literary-historical shoulder: "I'd rather be the glad, bright-leaping foam, | Than the smooth sluggish sea. O let me live | To love and flush and thrill—or let me die!" (6.89). There is the spasmodic creed, all right, but the allusiveness of its formulation is jarring to

---

[24] Parallels are striking between the epic publicity campaigns that were waged in Scotland *c.*1850 and 1760. Smith like Macpherson filled out an epic, on demand, from fragments he had already placed before the public; Gilfillan like Blair was a clergyman-publicist who furnished his poet with practical incentive and theoretical cover. Linda K. Hughes, "Alexander Smith and the Bisexual Poetics of *A Life-Drama*," *Victorian Poetry* 42 (2004) 491–508, has recently proposed—and persuasivey explained the need for—corrections to the pathologizing publication history as given by Thomas Brisbane, *The Early Years of Alexander Smith, Poet and Essayist: A Study for Young Men* (London: Hoddart and Stoughton, 1869) and transmitted across the twentieth century.

[25] Richard Cronin, "Alexander Smith and the Poetry of Displacement," *Victorian Poetry* 28 (1990) 129–45, correlates this habit of self-reference to Smith's insuperable class alienation. The same cause helps explain a rhetorical difference between *Festus* and *A Life-Drama*. In the former poem imagery appears, consistently with the epic forensicism of the decade in which Bailey wrote the first version, "for the sake of the impulse back of it; that is, it is secondary to a rhetorical and declamatory intention" (McKillop, "A Victorian Faust," 752). In Smith this civic intention is much attenuated, and rhetoric withdraws to the merely psychological sphere of figures of thought.

say the least. Ordinarily allusion is an epic grace note, and it was one for which working-class epoists like Smith particularly strove as a badge of learning. But the closing echo here of Wordsworth's "My Heart Leaps Up"—a double allusion, if the first three words recall "The World Is Too Much With Us"—consorts most oddly with the spasmodic claim to untutored spontaneity over which it reverberates: it is as if Smith meant to set his pulse by another man's spasm. Or again, when Smith delves into his own vein of admittedly often brilliant imagery, he cannot help flicking a glance up, mid-gaze, to make sure the reader is watching. "Our chief joy," the hero Walter tells his lady Violet, "Was to draw images from everything; | And images lay thick upon our talk, | As shells on ocean sands" (9.121). So far so good: with the simile in the last line, imagery illustrates itself. But then Violet challenges Walter to a sort of duel by tropes, and they concoct on the spot competing images for the sunset and moonrise they are watching. When he complies (pretty violently at that: "a cloven king | In his own blood"), and she betters him on the moon, and he then breaks off the contest by calling her "Iconoclast!" (9.122), we surfeit quickly on the incestuous archness of what passes for spasmodic wit.[26]

At such a moment, and the poem teems with them, what was in Bailey and Horne spasmodic writing becomes in Smith programmatic Spasmodism. If the collection of effects that is *A Life-Drama* comes to us at second hand, that may be because the calculatedness of its *élan* is all that Smith has to offer as a working idea of epic unity. Bailey wielded a cosmos, for better or worse, and Horne the ethos of a new world order; but Smith, whose ambition seems to have been coextensive with Gilfillan's aegis, imagines instead a poet who makes bold to imagine such things as a cosmos or a new world order. Where else, then, should Smith find his plot but in the composition and publication of an immensely popular poem, and with what better hero than "A mighty Poet whom this age shall choose | To be its spokesman to all coming times" (2.24)? Scene 1 invokes as its muses

---

[26] Similitudinous poetry on an epic scale broke out again in the American 1920s. Hart Crane's attachment towards the trope is well known. His reach towards the long poem in *The Bridge* was matched by the young Conrad Aiken's in a book-length auto-allegory with a manifestly spasmodic title, *The Pilgrimage of Festus* (New York: Knopf, 1923). If Rimbaud and Verlaine made a difference in these later works, it was the difference between simile and metaphor, as follows: "Look, how a vine, all of silver interwoven, | Falls from the moon! the silver moon is cloven, | A ladder-way of roses shines down the sky, | The moon and the earth are bound to it and cry. | The sun turns a rose: its petals are the light: | Shadow is a short chord: melody is night: | Twilight is the mind of god" (57).

Poesy and Fame; scenes 2, 7, and 12 consist mainly of disquisitions on poetry; scenes 3, 6, and 8 hinge on the recitation of poems.[27] To say this is not to belittle *A Life-Drama*, but to indicate what may have contributed to its remarkable if short-lived success, the epic consistency with which it sticks to its own premise. The story is about itself, and so are a great many of the tropes that constitute it. The passages quoted above suggest how incessantly the overall design obliged Smith to draw topics from his own anxious *modus operandi*, the generation of imagery on demand. The nervous creation and exchange of figures recapitulate line by line the larger recursive plot. Conversely the local recursiveness of spasmodic wit may be responsible for Walter's else-unexplained swerves into guilt during scenes 5 and 10. Disappearing as swiftly as it visits him, the hero's remorse attaches less to anything in the narrative than to the logic of self-consciousness as such: it arises as an ethical analogue (agenbite of inwit) to the irony of pastiche whereby the image-driven verse, starved for substance, keeps nipping the hand that feeds it.

Smith's signal example was not lost on a talented epic player whose relegation to the second string may be due to nothing more than his peculiarly infelicitous name, given the mode in which he chose very early to work: J. Stanyan Bigg. At 20 Bigg had produced in *The Sea-King: A Metrical Romance, in Six Cantos* (1848) a generational throwback with affinities to Moore's erotically emollient version of the Scott romance model. But already there the complacency with which Bigg's courtship plot of Viking pirate and mermaid accommodated digressive wonders, afloat on irrepressible images of the all-buoyant ocean, betrayed the maturing Spasmodist within. This potential was realized in 1854 with *Night and the Soul*, which methodically paved the trail Smith had blazed two years before. Where Smith is desperately, inventively precipitate, Bigg spasmodizes like an old smoothie. In a confidently epicizing twelve scenes he builds his plot on the self-redemption of a poetic genius named Alexis who is bold in metaphysics, fertile in imagery, and duly tormented by a formulaic dose of conscientious doubt. Yet Alexis's sufferings never ruffle his genial tolerance of the fun that is poked at him, off and on, by an affable set of well-wishers, nor does he ever really stray far from their social safety net. Coziest of the

---

[27] Conformably to this self-referential pattern, Russell M. Goldfarb observes in Walter an imagination sexually androgynous and ultimately directed away from human others "in sexual pursuit of the Muse": *Sexual Repression and Victorian Literature* (Lewisburg: Bucknell University Press, 1970) 110–12.

Spasmodists, Bigg brings Alexis home from generic angst to liberal Christian uplift and a good woman's love at the close. Call it the plush or Biedermeier side of Spasmodism, a bland homage to the spirit in which a *Festus* reviewer had hailed "a heap of fine things" and Tennyson had commended the "really *very grand* things" to be browsed up in that ur-spasmodic warehouse.[28] Knock-offs from Bailey and Smith, the fine things that upholstered *Night and the Soul* constituted furniture for a middle-class life enhanced by a taste for liberal ideas imaginatively rendered.

If in Bigg's hands Spasmodism was converted to Christianity, we find the reverse in Thomas Hawkins's contemporary *The Christiad* (1853; no relation to Henry Kirke White's 1806 epic fragment of the same name). Here a Christian epic converted to Spasmodism. Literally a rewriting of the poet's decade-old *Wars of Jehovah* at which we glanced in the previous chapter, the new poem came before the public shorn of John Martin's "eleven highly finished engravings" of apocalyptic scenery from circa 1844, and fortified instead at regular intervals with booster shots of a metapoetic rhetoric that was designed to inoculate the poem against incredulity. In other words, the poem as rewritten expressed with feckless, winsome naïveté the spasmodic spirit of the age. Hell-bent as he had all along been on astonishing the reader and damning the expense, Hawkins laved the contests of Lucifer and (this poet's special anthropomorphic brainchild) Chaos with a superheroic bathos that anticipated his twentieth-century successors in the comic-book trade. Now and then the parade of marvels is relieved by a freshly composed passage that brazenly concedes the implausibility of what has just transpired. "All images are useless, metaphors | Are childish in this supernatural page" (1.37); unless the "exacting Muse" can "sublime and open | Incredulous ears," "ridicule will cover this attempt | To bring the actions of the gods within | The narrow comprehension of a page" (6.230–31).[29]

---

[28] Unattributed review, cited in McKillop, "A Victorian Faust," 753; Tennyson's letter to Edward FitzGerald of 12 November 1846 is quoted in Hallam Tennyson, *Alfred Lord Tennyson: A Memoir* (London: Macmillan, 1897) 1: 234. Judicious assessment of the Laureate's debt to the Omnist is given by John O. Waller in "Tennyson and Philip James Bailey's *Festus*," *Bulletin of Research in the Humanities* 82 (1979) 105–23. Coventry Patmore's summary "New Poets" overview of Bailey, Smith, Dobell, Massey, et al. in *Edinburgh Review* 104 (October 1856) harps pejoratively on their "fine things," yet candidly allows that Tennyson's "The Palace of Art" (1832) is likewise "one string of 'fine things,' " even as he goes on to lament that "the sale of the works of these writers rivals that of the publications of the Poet Laureate" (342, 344).

[29] There is something discomfitingly Longinian about one's amazement at Hawkins's capacity to be amazed, a gift of his by no means confined to verse. See, for example, his reflections on time in *The Book of the Great Sea-Dragons, Ichthyosauri and Plesiosauri, Gedolim Taninim, of Moses* (London: Pickering, 1840), extreme even among Victorian responses to the quandary of infinitude

The poet thus agrees in advance with the reader's judgment that, where "Exhausted language faileth" (9.449), the result must be "bombast" (6.245). The truculence with which Hawkins dares us to credit the incredible reflects, no doubt, such adverse reactions as *The Wars of Jehovah* provoked in the interim; but the daredevil self-referentiality of the newly written passages just quoted on metaphor, language, and the printed page makes the updated *Christiad*, in its "dread extremity spasmodic" (6.213), quite consistent with what Smith's *A Life-Drama* was attempting at the same time. A decade later Smith would publish *Edwin of Deira* (1861), a highly traditional historical epic about Christianity and kingship that proved as stillborn as *A Life-Drama* had been galvanically lively (Ch. 10). What Smith's two long works have in common is systematic self-consistency; and the very difference between them shows in hindsight—like the transparently inept effort Hawkins made to bring his spent 1840s epic up to 1850s speed—how deliberate a stunt the made-to-order poetic of Spasmodism was.

Not so the notorious companion epic of 1854, *Balder: Part the First* by Sydney Dobell, a poem that was unfortunately made risible then by the same undefended seriousness of purpose that makes it interesting now. An educated intellectual and aspiring theorist of literature and society, Dobell took up Spasmodism in deadly earnest as a program for living that was rooted in a philosophy of subjective idealism.[30] "Balderism" was the coinage his preface offered, whether in immodest or jocular mood, as a name for

posed by geological history: "the huge Cycles alleged by the Hindoostanee, and Chinese, and negatively implied in The Genesis, shrivel into an indefinite Nothing before the weird talisman by which they are presently determined. Time himself is swallowed up by the Enchanter's Wand, and Matter, metamorphosed into the eternal" (2).

[30] For example, Dobell's 1857 lecture "The Nature of Poetry," in *Thoughts on Art, Philosophy, and Religion*, ed. John Nichol (London: Smith, Elder, 1876), is virtually a Spasmodist manifesto. "The Great Poem is an organized aggregation of small Poems" (20); thanks to verse's fractal "homotypy" of bodily rhythms, "the law of the whole Epic, that it is one subject with its congruous accessories, must apply to every passage of which the Epic is made up" (37). "A perfect Poem would be therefore a miniature of the Creation not in its matter but its principles; the Kosmos not of God but Man" (26), even as Dobell's rhapsodic argument in its conclusion "shows the perfect human Poem to be a word in the eternal utterance of the One Almighty Poet—a congruous passage in that Poem of the Universe" (65). Dobell's aesthetic is discussed at length by Robert Preyer, "Sydney Dobell and the Victorian Epic," *University of Toronto Quarterly* 30 (1962) 163–79. Preyer's view that Spasmodism anticipated aspects of Pound's epic practice in the *Cantos* finds a modernist second in Suzette Henke, "James Joyce and Philip James Bailey's *Festus*," *James Joyce Quarterly* 9 (1972) 445–51. See also Martha Westwater, *The Spasmodic Career of Sydney Dobell* (Lanham: University Press of America, 1992); Malcolm Pittock, "Dobell, *Balder*, and Post-Romanticism," *Essays in Criticism* 42 (1992) 221–42.

this philosophy. The offer has had no takers, but we can see now that Spasmodism is what it was, and Spasmodism charged with resentful political animus into the bargain. Once again the hero is a poet, and the reader of this chapter will already have guessed this poet's favorite genre. Apostrophizing the manuscript of his "early planned, | Long meditate, and slowly-written epic," Balder muses, "Almost I seem to turn my life in thee" (3.239–42).

It is not just that Balder's masterwork has taken him years to write; he means, with Wordsworth in the recently published *Prelude,* that the philosophy it communicates entails a fusion of epic with autobiography: "The hand that writes is part of what is writ."[31] Within a fully rigorous presentation of subjectivism, the presence of the subject becomes not optional but, as Balder says of his opus, "the necessary element | Of that which doth preserve me" (3.261–62). Moreover, subjective genius faithfully recorded is also for Dobell an epoch's authentic representation; the integrative conduct of a scrupulously examined life models the order of the world, "a multiform | Supreme event, the single continent of all." "As God contains the world I will contain | Mankind, and in the solvent of my soul | The peopled and unpeopled ages" (24.307–8). Although this recalls the transactional liberalism of *Sordello* ("include | The multitude," "the multitude turn you"; see Ch. 7), Dobell has no more interest than Bailey did in Browning's radically open model of give-and-take. The epic chamber of Spasmodism is ultimately sealed, however roomy, and its authority flows from the top down in the name of the individual genius who incarnates human totality.

So seriously does Balder take this epic duty to "be the King of men" (3.28) that he is tormented by its collision with another aspect of spasmodic omnism: the still potent idea of the epic as encyclopedia. In its function as a compendium of cultural essentials the epic poem does not of course say everything, but it must leave the impression that if it had to it could. It was Dobell's distinction among Spasmodists to see that this encyclopedic imperative collides head-on with another article of Spasmodism's reconstructed Romantic ideology: perspectival individualism. If truth is validated only by the candor of its provenance in the person who shapes it, it is also thereby limited to that person's circle of subjective experience. While this circle is almost infinitely expandable by the enfranchised Spasmodist imagination, there remains one limiting case that, to Dobell's credit

[31] On the 1850s reception of *The Prelude* see Carl Dawson, *Victorian Noon : English Literature in 1850* (Baltimore: Johns Hopkins University Press, 1979) 45–48; and Stephen Gill, *Wordsworth and the Victorians* (Oxford: Clarendon Press, 1998) 28–31.

as an intellectual, gives his Balder no peace. This is the life-culminating experience that no autobiographer can narrate, the experience of death (scene 16).[32] The poet's frustrated wrestling with this conundrum engenders the kinkiest of several plot devices in the poem: an increasingly heavy flirtation with the idea of murdering his nearest and dearest. His baby daughter dies some time shortly before or after scene 17, apparently of natural causes although remorse over her burial induces some ambiguously infanticidal imagery (18.81–82).[33] In any case Balder eventually returns, with scenes 37 and following, to the thought of snuffing out his miserably depressed spouse. Man and wife being one flesh, if he can die vicariously in Amy, Balder can in effect survive death to write the forbidden experience up and thereby crown his *magnum opus*.

This macabre plan was left hanging with the forty-second and last scene of the published *Balder: Part the First*. Dobell promised to avert it in a sequel, making a restored Amy the vessel for fresh redemption all around, *Festus*-style. There are a variety of reasons why Dobell never wrote the projected two parts of this sequel, but one of them must be that he could not think his way, out from the impasse his convictions had engendered in part one, into what he wanted to believe instead. Indeed, the skepticism of *Balder* tends all the other way, until by scene 37 Balder's obsessively minute description of his return home from a day outdoors, his passage through the rooms of the house, and his discovery of Death as a denizen of the bedroom where Amy is sleeping seems to allegorize the resistance not just of death to narrative representation, but also of life in its homeliest details, with which language can never fully catch up. Petty failures, little rhetorical deaths, lie in ambush for the scrupulous poet at every turn of his autobiographical path toward the

---

[32] A comment from Stuart Curran, *Poetic Form and British Romanticism* (New York and Oxford: Oxford University Press, 1986) 148, can appositely remind us of Dobell's ancestry in High Romanticism, and of the spasmodic epic's provenance in what early-century poets had made of the romance genre: "The improbable ethos of romance is rooted in our desire for total liberation, an impossible psychological state.... As what we know constitutes the limits of the probable, the only way beyond it is to embrace our own death.... The transcendental and the entropic are one and the same." The stress that Dobell throws onto physiological experience as such forms Jason Rudy's topic in "Rhythmic Intimacy, Spasmodic Epistemology," *Victorian Poetry* 42 (2004) 451–72.

[33] Cronin holds that an infanticide has indeed taken place ("The Spasmodics," 293, 296). George Eliot, reviewing *Balder* in the *Westminster Review* for April 1854, had her doubts (61: 331). The difficulty of proving either of these able readers dead wrong says much about the quality of *Balder*'s exterior plotting. Fairchild, *Religious Trends*, pronounces it impossible "to guess what finally happens," but adduces from posthumous fragments indications of Amy's restoration to health and rededication, with Balder, "in service to God through service to mankind" (4: 209).

great indescribable of his own mortal end. As a result each passing scene sharpens Balder's sense of the obstacles to epic completeness and erodes the early confidence his manuscript once inspired. The hand that was "part of what is writ" becomes a lost organ, "a living hand rent from its trunk | In the black vortex" (2.196–97, 260). Coming to resemble rather than regenerate the "Society" it bespeaks, "consorted to no end" (30.141), Balder's promised epic deteriorates until its power at the last is merely promissory, a long theoretical bet on posterity: "shalt perhaps revive," "Mayst leap forth," "in a light unrisen shalt be called | A microcosm" (42.42–56).

For quite respectable reasons, then, Dobell was convinced both that the epic of the mid-nineteenth century must take the form of an experimental autobiography, and that such a project was doomed to failure by contradictions internal to its own epistemology. Accordingly he staged those contradictions, using monodramatic form to display a spasmodic impulsiveness much like his predecessors', while at the same time exposing Spasmodism as a system at odds with itself. This is why the thrill of 1850s spasmody in *Balder* feels most of the time like cramp instead. The important labor of the poem was largely negative with respect to its literary genre, and something of the same kind was true of its political critique too. For the pretensions of bluff objectivity Dobell clearly had little patience: if Spasmodist subjectivism meant anything it meant that every perspective was somebody's, and that a commanding view was more than metaphorically entangled with political relations of power and subordination. When *Balder* takes aim at tyranny (scene 9) and war (scenes 7 and 23), it is with a lively sense of the imposture that a single vision can practice on a people—and did practice, at just this time, with such events as the crowning of Napoleon III and the waging of the Crimean War (which called forth public lyrics of protest from Dobell and Smith together in the 1855 volume *Sonnets on the War*).

Alas, the terms of Spasmodism furnished no other remedy for official imposture on this scale than the fantasized imposition of a different single vision, namely the poet's. A case in point was soon furnished by the imminently repentant Chartist Ernest Jones. In 1857 Jones published *The Revolt of Hindostan; or, The New World*, a poem of fourteen hundred lines written around 1850, if accrued legend be trusted, in the then-imprisoned poet's blood on the blank pages of a prayer-book with a moulted feather and a broom straw, and then by a swift revision updated in light of the Indian Revolt. Probably sincere in its vituperation but not thereby worthy of its titular Shelleyan original, this couplet screed inveighs at will against capital and empire across history and the globe, under cover of a counter-narrative marching in lockstep from autocracy through oligarchical then bourgeois capitalism into the destined rule of labor. In default of a genuinely pluralist concept of internationalism, the poem's vantage on world affairs is no less imperially monocular than the system of oppression it decries.[34] The paradoxical despotism of such a poetic stance as Jones's—or Bailey's, we may add in longer retrospect—is something that Dobell seems to have subjected in *Balder*, after his fashion, to critique. Spasmodic politics evidently came down to a choice between the new boss and the old, the tyranny of monomaniacal genius on one hand or of traditional, collectively deluded hero-worship on the other. An intolerable choice, and certainly in Dobell's case an alienating one. *Festus* had finessed it by preempting conflict in ever more extravagant gestures of euphoric inclusion, but Dobell did not shrink from publicizing it as a crisis in mid-century culture.

Dobell possessed reasoned and important convictions about matters strongly pertinent to the work of epic in Britain around 1850, together with the nerve to dramatize them in a critically conscientious form. What he unhappily lacked was anything like common sense about how this should be done. It would be relieving to suppose that Balder's thirteen consecutive exclamations of "Ah!" (scene 38) and his sitting *"silent for two hours by the window"* (stage direction, scene 41) were *coups de théâtre épique* anticipating Alfred Jarry if not Bertold Brecht. But there is scant reason to read them as anything but Sydney Dobell's earnest, ludicrously wrong guesses at how to make suffering and ennui wring a reader's heart. This is certainly how William Edmondstoune Aytoun read them when he set about one of the most effective parody campaigns ever waged. At one stroke *Firmilian, or The Student of Badajoz: A Spasmodic Tragedy* (1854) froze in its woozy tracks the movement that its subtitle branded into Victorian literary history.[35]

---

[34] Anne Janowitz, *Lyric and Labour in the Romantic Tradition* (Cambridge: Cambridge University Press, 1998), finding more to like in Jones than in Thomas Cooper (Chs. 7 and 11), apologetically suggests that *The New World*'s awkward internationalism reflects unpurged elements from "some of the older rhetoric patterns of domestic oppositional patriotism" (187).

[35] Two decades later W. H. Mallock in *Every Man His Own Poet; or, The Inspired Singer's Recipe Book*, 3d edn. (London: Simpkin, Marshall, 1877), could confidently send up, of all people, D. G. Rossetti's antagonist Robert Buchanan under the rubric "How to Make a Spasmodic Poem." Mallock's recipe skewers the defunct fifties genre unerringly: "This is a very troublesome kind of poem to make, as it requires more effort and straining than any other. You are yourself also one of the principal ingredients; and it is well, therefore, to warn you, before you use yourself for this purpose, that you will be good for nothing else after you have done so.... Take yourself, and

Planning his contraceptive strike with at least as much thoroughness as we may suppose lay behind the poems he targeted, Aytoun mimicked their techniques so faithfully that they emerged as just that, techniques, rather than the ingenuous effusions they pretended to be.

He went first after Smith's critical patron Gilfillan, by publishing in *Blackwood's Magazine* for May 1854 a review, copious in extracts by even Victorian standards, of a purported new book by one "T. Percy Jones."[36] When this salvo aroused widespread curiosity, Aytoun changed Gilfillan's hat for Smith's. He obliged the public by creating his own counterpart to *A Life-Drama*, and by the same hasty method as Smith's at that: Aytoun strung out extracts and filled in gaps until he had put a new 2000-line dramatic poem into the hands of the public before the end of the year. A most plausible preface condemns Spasmodism by defending it. Appealing to literary precedent and principles of reader response, Aytoun/Jones says in favor of genius and excitement and depth, and in extenuation of indecorum and fragmentation and lapse, pretty much what might have been said by the movement's defenders—and indeed was said, a matter of weeks later, by Dobell in the preface he concurrently composed for the second edition of *Balder*, neither author having seen the other's work beforehand.[37]

Firmilian is no more consecutive or rewarding to summarize than the works it burlesques, but it does have the advantage of a more physically energetic protagonist. To itemize only the greatest hits, the inevitable eponymous poet Firmilian trashes his copy of Aristotle (a drag on imagination), dynamites a cathedral, practices homicide for its imaginative benefits, sets up a sexual *ménage à quatre*, and throws a rival poet over a parapet to crush a Gilfillanish critic who has just finished beseeching Apollo to send the world a bard "unsoiled | By coarse conventionalities of rule" (scene 10). Conventionalities of rule, of course, are exactly what this parody was written to support, as was virtually everything Aytoun wrote. As we saw

make eyes at it in the glass until you think it looks like Keats, or the 'Boy Chatterton.' Then take an infinite yearning to be a poet, and a profound conviction that you never can be one, and try to stifle the latter. This you will not be able to do" (24–26).

[36] The pseudonym conflates Smith's workaday surname with that of Ernest Jones the Chartist, enlisting the proto-Spasmodist rebel Percy Shelley for good measure and taking a rhythmic swat at poor J. Stanyan Bigg by the way. The persevering real-life Jones had published his first work under the pen name "Percy Vere": see Bouthaina Shaaban, "Shelley and the Chartists," in *Shelley: Poet and Legislator of the World*, ed. Betty T. Bennett and Stuart Curran (Baltimore and London: Johns Hopkins University Press, 1996) 117.

[37] An intelligent and broad-minded reader, Dobell was generous in praise of *Firmilian*: see Walker, *Literature of the Victorian Era*, 513.

briefly in Chapter 8, he belonged to the proud Tory constabulary of Swift and Pope, Gifford and Frere, whose mock-epics broke literary rules in order to refresh a reader's thankful esteem for them—and for the social rules to which they corresponded. The rules for poetry have been so often broken, molten, and recast since Aytoun's day that his example provides invaluable testimony that once upon a time Spasmodism was felt as a force for cultural subversion that really did need to be reckoned with. What seems to us merely out in left field looked to the Victorian conservative like a flank of the left wing: the premium that Spasmodist poetry placed in theory on subjective power, and exemplified in the rolling fluency of its creative practice, bespoke cultural values whose linkage to Chartist and other demands for a voice, or to sexual and other kinds of emancipation, Aytoun never doubted for an instant.[38]

He paid a subtler homage to the power of Spasmodism in his parody's local texture. It was comparatively easy to ridicule *Balder* and *A Life-Drama* for want of structure; but sustaining mock-Spasmodism for scores of lines at a stretch was something else again, since at the level of versification and imagery the parodist had to meet his antagonists where they were strongest. Compounding the problem was the ever-present proclivity of Spasmodist writing towards a bathos—Smith constantly skirts it, Dobell will without notice pitch into it headlong—that defies parody. What resulted in *Firmilian* was the production of whole passages that remain indistinguishable in movement and verve from their despised originals. For example:

> A spasm pervades me, and a natural thrill
> As though my better genius were at hand,
> And strove to pluck me backwards by the hair.
>
> (6.321)

Manfully storming the enemy's prime redoubt—the spasm itself—what was Aytoun to do in this delectable passage but confess in his own despite that spasmodic abandon was having its way with him? In the same month that brought the first installments of *Firmilian* to public light Aytoun wrote to no less an intimate than Theodore Martin, his "Bon Gaultier" collaborator in 1840s ballad parody, how "very curious" it felt to dabble in spasmody, and

---

[38] He found a conservative ally in Coventry Patmore, who repeatedly pilloried spasmody in omnibus reviews, one of which went out of its way to connect spasmodist excesses with those of the French Revolution: see "Poetry—The Spasmodists," in *North British Review* 28 (Feb. 1858) 128; also n. 28 above.

"how very closely some of the passages approximate to good poetry."[39] What apparently had not happened with his balladry burlesques did happen here, and it spooked Aytoun like a visit from his better genius. It promoted him, for once in his life, into the exquisite upper circle of satire, where Dryden and Byron had shed their agendas and lived the double life of their victims; where the dummy possessed the ventriloquist and made him, like Balaam, chant a glory not his own. The fitful but authentic Muse that haunted Spasmodism gave Aytoun his finest hour; and the authentic homage she extorted played a critical role in the effectiveness of an attack that was at last so generously comprehensive that it left nothing to say. Readers of Aytoun's next and last long poem, the 1856 historical romance *Bothwell*, have suspected him in that high-minded work of plagiarizing *Firmilian*, plucking out its most promising bits for rehabilitation in a sober, respectable home. If so, the theft was fruitless: the Muse proved fickle, the thrill was gone.[40]

A critic now much better known than Aytoun, though much less noted at the time, spoke out in prose and verse to much the same purpose as his. Writing in defense of epic law and order, Matthew Arnold prefaced his 1853 *Poems* with a manifesto whose pretext was the suppression of a long dramatic poem, *Empedocles on Etna*, that his better critical judgment had outgrown, but whose occasion was his revulsion at Spasmodist poetry and its apologists. These latter included his best poetic friend Clough, who had just reviewed Smith's *A Life-Drama* appreciatively and to whom, as was noted above, a younger and less fastidious Arnold had recommended Bailey's *Festus* just a few years before.[41] Along with the essays he proceeded to write *On Translating Homer* (1861), Arnold's preface of 1853 has transcended its occasion and attained visible magnitude in the lesser critical constellation that is post-Romantic neoclassicism. Its preference of what is

---

[39] Quoted in Mark A. Weinstein, *William Edmondstoune Aytoun and the Spasmodic Controversy* (New Haven and London: Yale University Press, 1968) 124.

[40] Patmore's 1858 piece in the *North British Review* called *Bothwell* spasmodic (28: 130). Years later, with a novelist's tart animus Margaret Oliphant concluded her chapter on "The Greater Victorian Poets" by summarizing the Spasmodist controversy and observing of *Firmilian* that "The verse in many ways was much more vigorous than the serious models which it turned into ridicule": *The Victorian Age of English Literature* (New York: Tait, 1892) 246. Oliver Elton, *A Survey of English Literature 1830–1880* (London: Arnold, 1920) 154, describes Aytoun's Bothwell as "capable of talking dangerously like the hero of *Firmilian*."

[41] Clough's review of Smith appeared in the *North American Review* for July 1853 and is reprinted in *Victorian Scrutinies: Reviews of Poetry, 1830–1870*, ed. Isobel Armstrong (London: Athlone Press, 1972). On Clough and spasmody see Charles LaPorte, "Spasmodic Poetics and Clough's Apostasies," *Victorian Poetry* 42 (2004) 521–36.

ancient, impersonal, and well-built to what is modern, idiosyncratic, and expressive needs no rehearsal here beyond Arnold's own summary of a set of theses Le Bossu (see Ch. 1) would have approved: "the all-importance of the choice of a subject; the necessity of accurate construction; and the subordinate character of expression."[42]

What does deserve emphasis is how tied to its 1850s occasion this well-worn argument was. Like others who police "boundaries and wholesome regulative laws" ("Preface," 671), Arnold cultivated a sense of the literary law that owed its shape to the crimes that had come before his jurisdiction; his judicial opinion and remedy breathe the same air as Spasmodism, and reflect the same polarized light. For all its chaste reserve, there is something a little obsessive about the abundance of detail in which Arnold expresses the shortcomings of expressivity, detail, and abundance; and an exasperated note of epic-culturalist excess creeps into the supplementary preface he subjoined in 1854, denouncing "the great vice of our intellect, manifesting itself in our incredible vagaries in literature, in art, in religion, in morals: namely, that it is *fantastic*, and wants *sanity*" (673). Further, the honors in which Arnold dresses his ostensibly self-denying aesthetic draw regularly on an affective lexicon of heightened stimulus and response: "the effect produced" by observing the rules of sound structure will be "enjoyment," nay "delight," because a long poem will be "more intense" with the rules than without them, more "pregnant and interesting." As with Aytoun in the throes of parody, Arnoldian neoclassicism begins to look less like an alternative to Spasmodism than like an alternate route to the same 1850s destination: sensation intensified by art. In this regard it is curious to hear Arnold lauding the benefits of a classical education, in what is a direct hit at the autodidact Smith and scene 2 of *A Life-Drama*—the educated elite "do not talk of their mission, nor of interpreting their age, nor of the coming poet; all this, they know, is the mere delirium of vanity" (669)—and to remember, hearing this, that within ten years Arnold's talk as a Professor of Poetry (1857) and functioning critic (1864) will be of little else.

Meanwhile, it remained for him, like Smith and Aytoun, to reinforce precept with example and, having suppressed one faulty kind of poetry, to

---

[42] On Arnold and the Spasmodist controversy see Sidney Coulling, *Matthew Arnold and His Critics: A Study of Arnold's Controversies* (Athens: Ohio University Press, 1974), ch. 2. It should be recalled that Arnold's defense of epic unity on formal grounds was a distinctly minority position: as Frank M. Turner points out in *The Greek Heritage in Victorian Britain* (New Haven and London: Yale University Press, 1981) 322, the *Poetics* of Aristotle received no significant scholarly attention between J. H. Newman's early essay of 1829 and S. H. Butcher's edition of 1894.

show what deserved to take its place. This he did with "Sohrab and Rustum" (1853) and "Balder Dead" (1855), each initially subtitled "An Episode" and thus enrolled in the classic-torso subgenre with which we have seen poets since the 1790s placing epic ideas before the public like so many pilots for television series. As there is no record of Arnold's going further than either of these blank-verse demonstration pieces into the Persian or the Norse epic it might have formed part of, presumably each demonstration was complete in itself. By and large to students of Arnold's poetry the two episodes have demonstrated the viability of an epic manner that, while admittedly more academic than bardic in its drapery and carriage, does subordinate a workable style to a traditionary action of noble scope and inspiriting grandeur.[43] To students of Victorian epic, though, the two episodes will demonstrate something else, which has to do with Arnold's peculiar fondness for the heroic simile. Across several long runs of "Sohrab and Rustum," in particular, similes so impede the tale as to take it over: they become a sort of alibi for narrative, a diversion into textual pleasures taken lefthandedly by the way. The unmistakable contemporary counterpart to digressive indulgence of this kind was none other than the self-delighting impulsiveness of Spasmodism, where the favorite trope was simile and the grounding premise a running analogy between poetic assimilation and the attractive force that held the universe together.[44] It is as if Arnold's imagination, averse to his theory or mistrusting its emotional effectiveness in practice, conducted a shy traffic in contraband with the very sources that his theory repudiated. Seeking refuge in strongly troped exercises of a passion that lies outside his classically sculpted action, he nurses along in "Sohrab" a subliminal feeling that finally surfaces to flood with melodrama the narrative climax of a father's stricken recognition of the son he has unknowingly slain.[45]

[43] For Bush, *Mythology and the Romantic Tradition*, 262, "Sohrab" like *Balder* and Arnold's demonstration tragedy *Merope* (1858) "also is academic, it has the defects of a poem written to illustrate a theory."

[44] Clough observed in his 1853 review that Smith "writes, it would almost seem, under the impression that the one business of the poet is to coin similes. . . . the sterling currency of the realm"—currency in which Arnold too, we see, did business (*Victorian Scrutinies*, 168). John Holloway, *Widening Horizons in English Verse* (Evanston: Northwestern University Press, 1967) 25, finds the "Keatsian" similes of *Balder Dead* betraying "intimate poetic intentions . . . wholly at variance" with Arnold's stern Teutonic plan.

[45] In an excellent discussion of "Sohrab and Rustum" Armstrong, *Victorian Poetry*, reads "the exquisite, but redundant ornamentation" of the similes as betraying, against the grain of the grand style, "the stress its cohesion is under" from convergent forces of gender, class, and the Eastern Question of empire (218).

ON IMPULSE: 1850–1860

"Balder Dead"—admonished perhaps by inauspicious conjunction with
Dobell's poem—weans itself away from such contraband, and as a result
nearly perishes of sangfroid. "Enough of tears," Odin tells the gods as soon
as their beloved Balder has died, invoking as cold comfort the "doom" of
"fate": "Weep him an hour, but what can grief avail?" (1.18–27). Against
the divine decorum of this severe reality principle no character very suc-
cessfully rebels, nor does simile offer any such culture of the feelings as
nourished "Sohrab and Rustum." The poem catches fire only when
Balder's funeral barge does, in the one ritual outlet for mourning that
Odin's regime prescribes: eloquently hungry, tongues of flame "licked |
The summit of the pile, the dead, the mast | And ate the shrivelling sails; but
still the ship | Drove on, ablaze above her hull with fire" (3.189–91). This
uniquely strong imagery would not be out of place in Dobell's *Balder*, and
that was reason enough for Arnold to impound it within an officially
designated crematory precinct. Unfortunately, the antispasmodic hygiene
that confines mourning to one set hour, and imaginative release to one
descriptive verse paragraph, deprives the tale of something its own logic
requires: the credible rendition of an heroic love. The poem tells us again
and again how well Balder was loved by all who knew him; but this remains
hearsay, the rumor of an emotion which the poem's stoic discipline forbids
it to render substantially.[46] All too evidently the love Balder inspired has
vanished with him from the epic world Arnold steeled himself to imagine. It
is grimly fitting that in the final scene a sidekick god named Hermod should
feel a cordial impulse to break divine ranks and follow Balder into Hell no
matter what—and that he then should successfully resist it. "A power he
could not break withheld" (3.558): the self-denyingly terminality of that
phrase, alas, speaks volumes of the poetry Arnold would not write.

Subtextual spasm is isolated and quelled in Arnold's austere epyllia only by
the drastic expedient of inducing anaesthesia and paralysis. This syndrome
so nearly inverts the spasmodic one—where fertile, free-style spontaneity
wings it on a trope and a prayer—that we may infer beneath both the
spasmodic and the neoclassical complaint a disorder more basic. Both sides
were playing an all-or-nothing game: both succumbed to a blinding drive

---

[46] Or else—and this seems no better—love is sent to hell, Hela's kingdom that is, where
Balder's happiness at last with his wife Nanna can but underscore "the notion of domestic felicity
as a lost ideal in the world of the living": Richard D. McGhee, *Marriage, Duty, and Desire in
Victorian Poetry and Drama* (Lawrence: Regents Press of Kansas, 1980) 117.

that identified self-assertion with the invalidation of rivalry and led ultim-
ately to a program of exterminating the competition in the literary equiva-
lent of genocide. Each party laid claim to the value of totality by denying
that totality might be compassed in any other way: omnivorous sensibility
on one side, and finished classic planning on the other, agreed on their
mutual exclusion—and on nothing else. This insistent incompatibility her-
alded a new situation for epic circa 1850, of which the subjectivist premise
of Spasmodism had been an early expression. Hitherto epic wholeness had
been taken to mirror the given coherence of reality; now, however, it
seemed a property less intrinsic to the world than imaginatively postulated
and derived. Wholeness was becoming a question for demonstration re-
quiring proof, and proven differently depending on the differing assump-
tions, or subject positions, from which proof began.

The situation superficially resembles what we found in Chapter 7 with
the forensic or parliamentary epic of the first Reform decade, only now the
old 1830s spirit of openness and compromise has given way to a hardening
of position. (One sign of this difference between 1830s and 1850s epic is the
attenuation of dialogue within the latter, perhaps most canonically familiar
from Arnold's *Empedocles*, where dialogue withers before our eyes and the
final act is pure soliloquy with lyric accompaniment.) Overall, and in
retrospect, this new development seems a shrill harbinger of the imperial
consolidation that was increasingly to govern British life during the second
half of the century. Where a perspective implied a cosmos, and the articu-
lation of an epic text constituted a public bid to grasp that cosmos—totalize
and so possess it—there must ensue a competitive rush for comprehension
in which the Reform habits of diplomatic recognition and negotiation
among perspectives were dismissed as so much distracting, and to that
extent debilitating, waste of motion. That world view would prevail
which first established its construct as the world, period. In such a contest,
to acknowledge the existence of rival perspectives *ipso facto* weakened one's
position; to concede their validity, on any terms not overcome by assimi-
lation to one's own, was lethal.

What lay at stake, now as always in the history of the genre, was the
question of worldview: how to monopolize *Weltanschauung* by getting a
corner on totality.[47] There is something inherently paradoxical about such a

---

[47] In its larger ramification the difficulty was epistemic and disciplinary. Richard Yeo, *Encyclo-
paedic Visions: Scientific Dictionaries and Enlightenment Culture* (Cambridge: Cambridge University
Press, 2001) 250, records as a culmination of the Victorian division of intellectual labor David

coup, yet in truth it has never been far from our story in this book; we have seen it emerge with force in Romantic epic nationalism (Ch. 3) and in the sectarian apocalyptics of the 1820s (Ch. 6). It attained maximum ramification, however, in the mid-century climate that fostered on every hand what we now call the ideology of "separate spheres"—a phrase apt to the clamorously incommensurable and mutually exclusive spheric totalities of which epic writing from the 1850s leaves so distinct a record. It was separate-spheres ideology that created and supported such diverse phenomena as mid-Victorian gender identities; the relations between work and leisure, public and domestic life, science and religion, commerce and aesthetics; and increasingly, at the horizon of these figurative hemispheres, the partition and control of the globe under rampant imperialism.[48] It may be improper to bring all this heavy historical artillery to bear on a handful of not very successful poems. But their authors would not have thought so, Aytoun and Arnold included; and the very disparity that spasmody highlights between poetic ambition and achievement makes the essential point in another way. Within the history of epic, Spasmodism's antinomian monomania, and the conservative reaction against it, signaled a newly exclusionary intolerance exercised in the name of spheric comprehensiveness—not confessedly of sect or nation but of wholeness as such, a preemptive value conditioning all posterior acts of evaluation.

The poetic results of this development were often discouraging, sometimes appalling. As Chapter 10 will show, in order to break its splintering grip and reaffirm a broader generic foundation the major Victorian epoists of the 1860s would throw onto the cultural category of myth all the weight it would bear. In the meantime, once Aytoun had fatally pricked the Spasmodist bubble the later 1850s witnessed a proliferation of what might be called, with a due sense of the paradox the term involves, specialty epics. The book market promoted this development with translations catering to a

---

Masson's 1862 declaration of bankruptcy for the encyclopedia as a synoptic endeavor. Van Kelly approaches the encyclopedic ideal as a formal dilemma precipitating periodic crises throughout the history of the genre: "Criteria for the Epic: Borders, Diversity, and Expansion," in *Epic and Epoch: Essays on the Interpretation and History of a Genre*, ed. Kelly, Steven M. Oberhelman, and Richard J. Golsan (Lubbock: Texas Tech University Press, 1994) 1–21.

[48] Compare Jonathan Parry's observation that one effect the 1848 Continental revolutions had on the Liberal mind was to weaken British faith in progressive universalism and strengthen instead a rising "interest in racial differentiation and classification": *The Politics of Patriotism: English Liberalism, National Identity and Europe, 1830–1886* (Cambridge: Cambridge University Press, 2006) 22.

juvenile readership: Kingsley's sample from the *Odyssey* and other classic tales done up for children (*The Heroes*, 1856) and H. H. Milman's from the *Mahabharata* (*Nalopákhyánam*, 1850, rev. edn. 1860) brought to new refinement a literary brokerage that presented ancient totalities in a modern, customized format. This idea, which had already attracted Macaulay in the *Lays of Ancient Rome* and now beckoned to Arnold from Persia and the North, would only gather momentum as the decade of the Crystal Palace ushered in Britain's most fervently museological era. The specialty epic took another step in the same direction: typically written in first-person monodramatic form, this kind of poem centered on an individual who spins a world that not only contains him or her but, by generic imperative, claims to articulate the structure of reality as apprehended by the entire class of persons to which he or she belongs.

From an unapologetically eccentric standpoint, poems of this sub-epic kind elaborate a heterocosm that, being self-sufficient yet also markedly abnormal, solicits in the reader a species of sympathetic patronage whose ultimate object is support of the cultural norm with reference to which their eccentricity is gauged. We find the pattern humbly set in the "Passages from a Boy's Epic" that *The Leader* ran serially for several months in 1852. "'Twas a boy's epic and a boy's mistake" (545), confesses the anonymous author; yet when his parade of declamations reaches the young god Bacchus it becomes clear that minority has its own privileges: "dying men" while inferior to immortals know in love a "large passion" foreclosed to their divine superiors, since "starry looks | May not flush high, nor deathless pulses throb | With the sweet fire that burns in lowlier blood" (977). This is in little the (Keatsian) rationale and practice of Spasmodism, and its presence in a nameless boy's epic shows where the spasmodic impulse would hide out after the debacle of *Firmilian*. It would go underground, there to fertilize a poetry imputed to a congeries of underlings that included children and women, ethnical and national outlanders, deviants and criminals. From America the throb of Longfellow's widely circulated *Song of Hiawatha* (1855) was ennobled through a double primitivist displacement: Native American matter, basketed in verse woven from the orally persistent parallelism of the Finnish epic *Kalevala*. Beginning that same year, the self-made primitive Walt Whitman drew increasing notice for the spontaneous-me cadences in *Leaves of Grass*. Democratizing idiosyncrasy, Whitman's free verse came out and named itself what Spasmodism had been all along, a *Song of Myself*.

It was also in 1855 that Alfred Austin, who will be with us off and on for several chapters to come, published anonymously at the age of 19 *Randolph: A Poem in Two Cantos.*[49] The irregularly rhymed tetrameters of Austin's patchy, stormy narrative captured the mood of the hour—a protean quarry of which this most narrowly ambitious careerist of his poetic generation seldom lost sight. Just now the mood of the hour was spasmodically feelingful alienation, centered by Austin in a culturally displaced Polish noble who enlists to fight in Napoleon's grand army, being reft of his homeland (partitioned), estranged from his sweetheart Berenice (politically radicalized, and anglophile into the bargain), and betrayed by his best friend Hubert (gone over to the Russians). Crazed by battle and nearly dead with hunger and cold, Randolph crosses from the nadir of canto 1 into canto 2 and the nursing care of Berenice, who has given up politics for religion's sake—a change that lays out with unusual frankness one side of the spasmodic legacy. The other side of course is the heroism of sensation, in which *Randolph* may be claimed as the most literal sob story of its decade. For fifteen pages the young protagonist's tears fall in a paroxysm of remorse over the love he threw away, in a crying jag that sluices the awkward transition to his final hours when, a still remarkably lachrymose old monk-penitent (2.95), he learns that his abbot-confessor of many years has been none other than Hubert, the intimate whom his boyhood rejected. That Randolph has never once in all this time lifted his veiled and dewy eyes the "kindly weeping" reader can well believe (2.105), so inward is this work's emotional orientation and so consistent its spastic registration of the isolated body's relation to the historical world, in the form of a sequence of glandular symptoms.

Later a still less accomplished poetic adolescent, Irish-born teenager Kinahan Cornwallis, effected a shotgun marriage from Down Under between sentimentalist effusion and spasmodic intensity in the thirteen books of *Yarra Yarra; or, The Wandering Aborigine* (1858). Cornwallis sends his Australian outcast up and down the continents, a witness to the Crimean War (book 3), prophet of electronics and interplanetary travel (book 8), suitor to Creole lass and Englishwoman (books 9 and 13). Where anti-colonial tirade adjoins the thrills of top-speed global tourism, and exultant rendition of military carnage consorts with expressions of utopian pacifism,

[49] W. Forbes Gray, *The Poets Laureate of England: Their History and their Odes* (New York: Dutton, 1915) 280, gives to *Randolph* the different subtitle *A Tale of Polish Grief*—on no cited authority, but with great plausibility as regards theme and mood.

all that holds the farrago together is spasmodic transiency at its briskest: "We pulsed each fleeting moment quickly by" (13.206). Betting that an expatriate Aborigine of untutored mind and unjaded senses might function as a sort of human camera rendering up uncensored to the modern world its phenomenal form and ideological pressure, Cornwallis confected in Yarra Yarra a rough triumph of reverse ethnography. And the crown of Yarra Yarra's sentimental education is his mastery of the contemporary dialect of the Western tribe, a spasmodic magniloquence he seems to have learned from Smith and Bigg: "Each picture of the past doth o'er me gleam | In panoramic beauty far along | Down the deep vista of time's boundless shade" (13.207).

The inclusion of Russian episodes in *Randolph* and *Yarra Yarra* reflects the coincidence of the spasmodic culture wars with Britain's most conspicuous mid-century military effort, the Crimean War of 1853–56. This coincidence makes the anonymous 1855 appearance of Thulia Susannah Henderson's *Olga; or Russia in the Tenth Century: An Historical Poem* both predictable in principle and anomalous in practice. With an historicist austerity comparable to Arnold's in the likewise distantly topical "Sohrab and Rustum" (the Eastern Question, displaced), and with something too of Cornwallis's tourism, the poet focuses her ten books of squared-off blank verse on things in their faraway, still half Scythian tenth-centuriness. Henderson pays lip service to today with a prefatory reference to the Crimean conflict, an avowal that the tsarina of the title (a Christian convert who worked in her rude day as an "advocate for peace," iv–vi) was essentially a protestant *avant la lettre*, and one exceptionally dogged stretch of semi-delirious prophecy in which Olga from her deathbed beholds the train of tsars who are to succeed her, right through Catherine the Great, the burning of Moscow to spite Napoleon, and at last a lurid glimpse of troops bivouacked by the Black Sea (book 9). Between these early and late concessions to contemporary relevance Henderson pursues the task she really has at heart. This is to set, against a background of sometimes literally Byzantine political intrigue including Olga's courtship by the Emperor Constantine Porphyrogenitus, and the slow, nonviolent supplanting of a pagan by a Christian dispensation of "moral more than outward force" (5.151), the strenuous enumeration of details drawn from daily life in old Kiev.

Fashions in heraldry and jewels (book 4), funeral rites and bills of fare for feasting (book 5), decorated Easter egg exchange (book 2), winter laundry done through holes in the ice (book 6) diversify the scene for their own

sake—and, refreshingly, not for the spasmody they might have been par-
layed into. In place of the muse, Henderson enrolls the epic poets as so many
historians in one "ponderous tome" and invokes poetry itself to her aid,
which while it may savor of spasmodism is actually anything but. "I nerve
my soul to strike its varied notes" (1.2): were this the Dobell line it looks
like, it would summon an entourage of images making that *nerve* and that
stroke matters of physical excitation. Such embodiment finds no place in
Olga, surely in part because the heroine is a grandmother over 70 years
old—a literary development exceedingly rare in its century whatever the
narrative medium, and one altogether unique among the poems this book
treats. Another reason has to do with gender: the dignity with which Olga
dispenses justice in the royal courts (book 7) and generally holds her
fractious royal family together required Henderson to practice a womanly
poetics rather of the sensible than of sensibility. In their mass the many
objects the poem inventories tether the poem to ordinary realities, a prudent
regard for which undergirds the tsarina's ethic of Christian temperance. If
the result of such conceptual boldness was aesthetically meager, *Olga* none-
theless marked a respectable stage in women's verse narrative, re-feminizing
an heroic sovereign whom a leading authority had expressly praised for her
"masculine qualifications."[50] Henderson's was an example Barrett Brown-
ing would surpass just a few years later when *Aurora Leigh* wed, to *Olga*'s
feminine respect for the things of life in their multiplex discreteness, what
lay beyond Henderson's range of daring: a fully sensuous feminism of the
incarnate self.

The same "historical" genre with which *Olga* was affiliated had been
claimed shortly before by Nicholas Michell, though his *Spirits of the Past: An
Historical Poem* (1853) had actually been a quite different sort of work. This
compilation of four dozen stanzaic prosopographies—brief lives gathered
into three books of "Scripture Characters," "Military Heroes," and "Cele-
brated Women"—on one hand spelled out most explicitly the tendency to
fragmentation that would characterize the immediate aftermath of Spas-
modism. But in another sense it was a poem twenty years ahead of its time,
since, as we shall see, shortly after Michell issued *Spirits* in a third edition of
1867 an eclectically anthological spirit would dominate the production of
long British poems, bending them in an epic direction by habitual reference

---

[50] Henry Card, *The History of the Revolutions of Russia, to the Accession of Catharine the First*
(London: Longmans and Rees, 1804) 35.

to a progressivist plot of civilized triumph. To this plot Michell in the 1850s lacked access; and without something like it his portrait collection could not "lay claim to the honours of an Epic composition, for the Epic demands one continuous narrative" (Preface, v). For connection between incidents the poet relied instead on "desultory reflections," and the nervous energy of these betrays his kinship with the spasmody of the moment. Thus Michell's first episodic transition, from Cain's career to Moses', exults that "Mind can follow time's far-sweeping track, | Ploughed through creation," with "no bar—no bourne—no resting-place" unless it be "time's verge—the final hour of doom!" (1.1.18). At the last the historian-poet celebrates his time travel as if it were a species of spasmody: "that deep rapture which devours | The ardent heart, half frenzy though it seem, | Holding its fancied commune with the dead" (3.3.325)

It was at this same time, but on unimpeachably British grounds and with consummate skill, that the new poet laureate Tennyson outfitted himself to work the underground vein of ardent rapture from which Spasmodism had tapped out its bangles and gauds. Critics assailed *Maud* (1855) mistakenly on many accounts, but when they called it spasmodic they were dead right. *Maud* was not an epic; yet it did, like the outlandish poems just enumerated, thump the tom-tom in different tempi all keyed to a body's pulse. This body moreover was a microcosm of realities beyond itself, not only suffusing the landscape ("so warmly ran my blood | And sweetly, on and on | Calming itself to the long-wished-for end, | Full to the banks," 1.18.601–03) but even spanning the planet in a long heartbeat ("Blush from West to East, | Blush from East to West, | Till the West is East," 1.17.591–94). With civil strife on its mind and imperial war on its conscience, Tennyson's most personal, most driven poem loosed over the Victorian rooftops a barbaric if not downright psychopathic yawp:

> And my pulses closed their gates with a shock on my heart as I heard
> The shrill-edged shriek of a mother divide the shuddering night.
>
> (1.1.15–16)

> She is coming, my own, my sweet;
>   Were it ever so airy a tread,
> My heart would hear her and beat
>   Were it earth in an earthy bed;
> My dust would hear her and beat,
>   Had I lain for a century dead;

Would start and tremble under her feet,
And blossom in purple and red.

(1.22.916–23)

The indecorum of this sensationally accomplished spasmody is aggravated by its emanating, not from the eccentricities of Hiawatha or Yarra Yarra, but from the very citadel of breeding, a English gentleman's country estate.

The shrewdest commentary on all such 1850s crypto-Spasmodist activity came from a poet who had every reason to observe it with interest. Robert Browning, having given his all in *Sordello* and gotten nothing in return, would wait till the late 1860s to hazard an epic comeback. In the interval, however, he had brought to great refinement the dramatic monologue, a short- to mid-range genre that in form resembled the swollen lyric mono-dramas he now saw his contemporaries taking to epic lengths, but that included the dimension of ironic self-critique they crowded out.[51] Browning applied the analytic powers of the monologue to a diagnosis of the contemporary epic condition in " 'Transcendentalism: A Poem in Twelve Books' " (1855). Barely fifty lines long, it impersonates an elder poet advising a younger against, as it were, turning into Matthew Arnold; that is, against devoting verse to the exposition of "naked thoughts" (3) instead of "images and melody" (17). Rather than propose "subtler meanings of what roses say," the true poet is he who provides by imaginative alchemy "the sudden rose herself," conjured spasmodically into existence with the "venting" of "a brace of rhymes" (36–40).

Yet the elder poet conspicuously fails to take his own advice. The way he sticks to prosaic discourse, and conjures only by proxy, introduces a complex irony focused much less on the Transcendentalism of the junior would-be epoist he lectures than on the odd crook in his own posture.[52] On analysis the speaker's position proves to be a lower-case, *ad hoc* transcendentalism of distinctively modern stripe, which wants at once to talk up

[51] Discussion of High Victorian spasmody in Arnold, Browning, and Tennyson, respectively, occupies the first three chapters of Antony H. Harrison's *Victorian Poets and Romantic Poems* (Charlottesville: University of Virginia Press, 1990); see also Harrison's "Victorian Culture Wars: Alexander Smith, Arthur Hugh Clough, and Matthew Arnold," *Victorian Poetry* 42 (2004) 509–20.

[52] It is impossible to specify an original target for Browning's critical-satirical dart of a poem, epic naïvetists being legion across the century; but their stance was typified a few years later in John Stuart Blackie's patronizing unction over "that undefinable something of naturalness, simplicity, and *naïveté*, the rare intellectual endowment of childhood and of the early ages of intellectual culture, which later writers very seldom exhibit": *Homer and the Iliad* (1860; 2nd edn. Edinburgh: Edmonston and Douglas, 1866) 1: 151.

an elementally felt wholeness and talk down to it. Thus the liberal Browning spotlights both the conservative and the caustic sides to the patronizing of literature as Aytoun and Arnold practiced it at mid-century. Follow the inverted commas: flushing out into the open the invisible air-quotes whereby epicizing Victorians hoped to transcend modern circumstances while they of course disclaimed any ambition to "transcend" them, the irony of Browning's quote-buffered faux-epic title tells against most of the writers this chapter has discussed. Exposing the hidden affinity between two apparent incompatibles—an omnism that sees it all and a criticism that doubts it—Browning here probes a central Victorian ambivalence about the subjective grounds of assurance.

In preparing this exquisite miniature Browning might reflect, a little ruefully, on the introversively genius-centered narratives with which his own career had begun two decades earlier: the rhapsodic *Pauline* (1833) and especially the proto-spasmodic closet-drama *Paracelsus* (1835). More to the point, he had the advantage of working alongside—because he was married to—the author of the most accomplished new epic of the mid-century.[53] Elizabeth Barrett Browning had been observing the poetic scene for years, and with a circumspection that matched her husband's. This vigilance let her make *Aurora Leigh* (1856), among other things, a compendium of nineteenth-century epic modes. Having served apprenticeship in Romantic martial nationalism as early as 1820 with *The Battle of Marathon* (Ch. 6), and invoked its fierce spirit again in the recent *Casa Guidi Windows* (1851), Barrett Browning skirted that mode here, but in a circuit that rounded up nearly all of its successors.

   The long final scene of *Aurora Leigh* concludes, like many an 1820s epic, with a vision of the New Jerusalem out of Revelation (9.939–64), having begun with the extended apocalyptic image of a city drowned beneath the opening heavens (8.28–61). That scene and the corresponding second book comprise balanced debates in which Aurora and Romney Leigh touch on various condition-of-England issues that update a leading epic device from

---

[53] The case for reading *Aurora Leigh* as an epic poem rests by now on firm footing. See Ellen Moers, *Literary Women* (Garden City: Doubleday, 1976) 40; Dorothy Mermin, *Elizabeth Barrett Browning: The Origins of a New Poetry* (Chicago and London: University of Chicago Press, 1989) 183–84, 215–17; Susan Stanford Friedman, "Gender and Genre Anxiety: Elizabeth Barrett Browning and H.D. as Epic Poets," *Tulsa Studies in Women's Literature* 5 (1986) 203–28; Marjorie Stone, "Genre Subversion and Gender Inversion: *The Princess* and *Aurora Leigh*," *Victorian Poetry* 25 (1987) 101–27.

the Reform era (Ch. 7); the second half of the central book 5 reports on a glittering soirée aswirl with themes and viewpoints more topical still. As a *Bildungsepos* the poem details and comments incisively on more than one educational curriculum: Romney's and Marian Erle's in passing, but chiefly Aurora's, for whom the learning curve leads through the English countryside to London, Paris, and back to her native Florence, in general acknowledgment of the tradition of heroic quest romance, and with a smart nod to the 1840s export–import trade we discussed in Chapter 8. Such sampling and incorporation of generic conventions especially suit the poem's status as a *Kunstlerepos*, in which capacity it gleams with nuggets of literary and aesthetic theory, pivots on an *ars poetica* several hundred lines long in which the contemporary viability of epic is a leading issue (5.139–222), and casts a shrewd eye here and there on what the volatile book trade portended for the Victorian poet's calling.

What it portended most recently, of course, was Spasmodism, and Barrett Browning's appropriation of that movement's unruly energies was integral to the success of her masterpiece.[54] Bravely and cannily exploiting spasmody for the platform it offered women's poetry, she harnessed its authentic power to an epic design that went beyond anything accomplished by the line of poets from Bailey to Dobell. *Aurora Leigh* sports an eponymous title like *Festus* and *Balder,* like them it maximizes intensity by keeping its action flush with the writer-protagonist's consciousness; and like them it strives for an extremity of textual presence by grafting, as will be seen in a moment, something like a spasmodic closet-drama format onto the first-person narrative lately published in Wordsworth's *Prelude* and a bumper crop of recent novels (e.g. *Jane Eyre, David Copperfield, Alton Locke*). Finally, like the spasmodic epics *Aurora Leigh* is awash in the juices of an inexhaustibly fluent imagery. Shudder, pulsation, outburst, and spasm are the tropes of creative power here; and in the best 1850s tradition they serve Barrett Browning as a somatic epic machinery connecting sensation to purpose, "flesh" to the "sacrament of souls" (5.15–16), "physics" to a "larger metaphysics"(6.206–7). The mountains, "panting from their full deep hearts," sympathize by "mutual touch | Electric"—and synaptic enjambment for good measure (1.623–24). The

---

[54] The connection was routinely made by early reviewers. Half a century later Omond in *Romantic Triumph* went so far as to trace "the stress and strain of later verse, the mouthings of our 'Spasmodic School,'" back to the influence of Barrett Browning's writings even before *Aurora Leigh* (62). Kirstie Blair, "Spasmodic Affections: Poetry, Pathology, and the Spasmodic Hero," *Victorian Poetry* 42 (2004) 473–90, agrees that *Aurora Leigh* is the one conspicuous success story of the movement.

very galaxies drip with planetary "lymph" (5.3) as God, "intense, profuse—still throwing up | The golden spray of multitudinous worlds," churns on in "proof and outflow of spontaneous life" (3.753–57).

The great hydraulic heart of all this surge, for Barrett Browning as for Alexander Smith, is poetic imagination. In a text already lubricated with analogies it is still striking to find the first heroic simile saved for Aurora's life-saving discovery of the poets:

> As the earth
> Plunges in fury, when the internal fires
> Have reached and pricked her heart, and, throwing flat
> The marts and temples, the triumphal gates
> And towers of observation, clears herself
> To elemental freedom—thus, my soul,
> At poetry's divine first finger-touch,
> Let go conventions and sprang up surprised,
> Convicted of the great eternities
> Before two worlds.
>
> (1.845–54)

Settled convention whelmed by undercurrents invisible but felt: the plot of this simile is the plot of the poem; and we hail in it the basic program of Spasmodism. This program—positing, then overcoming, a primary schism between arbitrary regulation and victorious sovereign impulse—Barrett Browning reinforces on every page, not just by imagery but by the pump of the verse as it oversplashes set prosodic limits, "The rhythmic turbulence | Of blood and brain swept outward upon words" (1.897–98).[55] "I felt | My heart's life throbbing in my verse" (3.338–39), says Aurora, and she means it; when push comes to shove, during Aurora's closest brush with despair she prays that God will "stop his ears to what I said, | And only listen to the run and beat | Of this poor, passionate, helpless blood" (7.1269–71).

By such means *Aurora Leigh* made the preponderantly masculine program of Spasmodist poetics into a feminist charter, and thereby endowed it with

---

[55] On "the sense of the dithyrambic, of a vitalist will" coursing through the body of the verse, see Matthew Campbell, *Rhythm and Will in Victorian Poetry* (Cambridge: Cambridge University Press, 1999) 42–45. The prosodic expression of epic excess in which Barrett Browning participates leads on to Swinburne's *Tristram* (Ch. 11) and back through her husband's *Sordello* (Ch. 7) to their common models Keats and Hunt (Ch. 5). The latter's *Story of Rimini* is a poem that Barrett Browning especially defended against detraction: see her letter to Mary Russell Mitford of 25 July 1841, in *The Brownings' Correspondence*, vol. 5, ed. Philip Kelley and Ronald Hudson (Winfield: Wedgestone Press, 1987) 89.

more cultural-political traction than it had hitherto possessed.[56] Whole-
heartedly embracing the embodied intuition that was Spasmodism, Barrett
Browning converted its transcendental alienation into the force for political
change that Smith and Dobell had (ineffectually) desired and Aytoun
(effectually) reprehended. She advanced a woman's claim to epic spokes-
manship by so grounding the tropes and tones of spasmody in female
physicality as to make the movement appear to have been, in its deepest
fiber, feminine all along. This ground, in turn, provided practical leverage
with which to promote for public recognition the rights of women, and
with them the wrongs of the poor and the shame of oppression, up to and
including that of the Italian people with whose political welfare Barrett
Browning was throughout the 1850s passionately engaged.[57] The plot is a
sequence of melodramatic flareups, and what flares up at each local climax is
a combustible mix of sharply felt injustices whose smoldering produces the
air of generalized ardor that fills the intervals of narrative between. The
poem's peak experiences are all eroticized—Aurora's long-deferred union
with Romney, of course (9.714–24, 833–42), but also the passion she has
learned from her parents (1.17–19, 87–89) and the bond she witnesses
between Marian and her nursling son (6.566–81)—and this eroticism is
preserved against the sublimation it routinely incurred in male spasmodic
hands by the unconventionality (what disgruntled reviewers deemed the
scandal) of Aurora's sex. Because Barrett Browning did not enjoy Bailey's
omnist luxury of forgetting gender, she made sure her reader would not
forget it either.

   The neediness of bodily desire in *Aurora Leigh* also whets the edge of
story, in what may be the poem's finest stroke of diegetic invention: the
temporal procession of its narrative standpoint. Early in book 3 Aurora

---

   [56] If only this had been what Saintsbury meant when he called Barrett Browning "a sort of she-
spasmodic of the nobler kind" (178). He meant something else; so, for different reasons, did
Dobell when tempering his "great admiration" for "some of the finest poetry of the century" in
Aurora Leigh with an *a priori* dismissal, "But it is no poem. No woman can write a poem": quoted
in Amy Cruse, *The Victorians and their Books* (London: Allen and Unwin, 1935) 196. Yet by
Saintsbury's time—the hour of the life-force, suffragism, Ibsen and Shaw—a case was waiting to
be made for linking the maternalized cosmology of *Aurora Leigh* with so early a work in our story
as Erasmus Darwin's epic nursery *The Botanic Garden* (Ch. 2). Both poems propose subversively
sexualized alternatives to the martial origins of cultural grandeur that prevail in traditional epic.
   [57] On the gender/politics nexus see Flavia Alaya, "The Ring, the Rescue, and the Risorgimento:
Reunifying the Brownings' Italy," *Browning Institute Studies* 5 (1978) 1–41; Sandra M. Gilbert,
"From *Patria* to *Matria*: Elizabeth Barrett Browning's Risorgimento," *PMLA* 99 (1984) 194–211;
Matthew Reynolds, *The Realms of Verse 1830–1870: English Poetry in a Time of Nation-Building*
(Oxford and New York: Oxford University Press, 2001) 104–27.

breaks off her autobiographical retrospect, in order to describe the present scene in which she is writing, dismissing her maidservant, burning the midnight oil to answer the day's mail, and so on. This arresting interlude brings *Aurora Leigh* as close as narrative can well come to the real-time present of Spasmodist closet-drama and its affinities with radically bardic presentation values. The approximation is finally futile: even on-the-spot reportage has to lag behind the fact it reports, as Dobell's Balder despairingly found, and as Aurora's only semi-performative "I have to write" (3.26) and "I bear on my broken tale" (3.156) more gamely acknowledge. Still, her interruption of the narrative here paves the way for later, more striking developments to which only a written epic mode permits access. For when at 5.579 Aurora again catches herself in the act of composition, the scene has shifted to a date manifestly later than the one recorded in book 3; we realize that the the fixed omniscience of the memoirist has yielded to the stepwise nomadism of a diary. And the point of view thus mobilized keeps on moving: books 6 and 7 describe events that must postdate the temporal vantage that ends book 5; the last two books then seem a further fresh departure, and the very late metanarrative admission "I have written day by day, | With somewhat even writing" (9.725–26) validates the diaristic understanding that has opened to our view four books previously.[58]

That earlier moment was the crucially unbalancing one, and Barrett Browning placed it with care at the balance point of a nine-book epic divided along nearly Homeric lines of nested symmetry. Books 1–2 and 8–9 focus the larger issue of education in a faceoff between Aurora and Romney, books 3–4 and 6–7 make Marian's hard-luck flashbacks the occasion for a widened social scope, and book 5 splits down the middle to consider Aurora's writing life first in theory and then in practical context.[59] At the epicenter of this three-ring circus is where Barrett Browning detonates her narrative charge, deliberately shattering the convention of fixed perspective that apparently governed the first half of the poem, and that decidedly

---

[58] This argument, developed in my "*Aurora Leigh*: Epic Solutions to Novel Ends," in *Famous Last Words*, ed. Alison Booth (Charlottesville and London: University of Virginia Press, 1993), 62–85, is more deftly explored by Alison Case in *Plotting Women: Gender and Narration in the Eighteenth- and Nineteenth-Century British Novel* (Charlottesville and London: University of Virginia Press, 1999).

[59] *Aurora Leigh* is organized not according to the arithmetic ratios dear to analysts of written epic since Virgil, but according to an older principle of symmetrical ring composition traceable back to Homer. The poet's allegiance to Homer is a matter of early and constant record, up to and including the way she has Aurora dismiss F. A. Wolf, with full orthographic contempt, as an "atheist" and traitor: "The kissing Judas, Wolff" (5.1245–54).

secured the *extempore* platform of many an oral bard and spontaneous omnist before her. Simulated seriality calls writing to witness against its own spasmodical–bardic pretension. Putting a fresh twist on the *improvisatrice* tradition going back through L.E.L. to Staël's *Corinne*, E.B.B. turns to account the actual conditions of Victorian print culture on which spasmodic writers both depended and turned their backs. For the forward motion of Aurora's point of view mobilizes an ongoing critique of the obsolescent certitudes that at any given moment she has impulsively, confidently sworn by. The advancing narrative design presents our heroine as not just an intuitive spasmodic but a repeatedly fallible one. Aurora is doomed by one of her leading tendencies—liberal openness of mind—to submit to periodic humiliation another of her leading tendencies—glib peremptory judgment. Her high-handed way of taking others down a peg (not sparing that intimate other her own younger self) is in turn taken down a peg each time the narrative ascends to a new retrospect and shows up the self-righteousness of her condemnation of Marian (book 6), her eager misprision of Lady Waldemar and her risible failure to apprehend Romney's final situation (book 9).

Not for nothing has Aurora devoted her youth to "counterfeiting epics, shrill with trumps | A babe might blow between two straining cheeks | Of bubbled rose, to make his mother laugh" (1.990–91).[60] Both the initial impulse to compass a totality and the subsequent impulse—call it, here, *matronizing*—to condescend to that false first effort bespeak one and the same characteristic, Aurora's control-freak need to occupy a commanding vantage. It is this need, which actuates most of her pervasive rhetorical irony at virtually everybody's expense, that the migrant narrative viewpoint of the poem subjects in turn to structural irony, of a sort to which the homogeneity of spasmodic verse permitted little if any access.[61] In hindsight Aurora

---

[60] The poet is laughing back maternally at her own juvenile effort in *The Battle of Marathon* (Ch. 6). Jeremy M. Downes compares the valorization there of the paternal–filial virgin Athena with that goddess's demotion to spinsterhood at *Aurora Leigh* 5.799–801: *Recursive Desire: Rereading Epic Tradition* (Tuscaloosa and London: University of Alabama Press, 1997) 287. However, while the autobiographical referent for our quoted passage is Miss Barrett's teenage trial-epic, the operative literary referent—captioned by the very extravagance of the simile—is Spasmodism *à la* Smith. Cronin, "The Spasmodics," finds in *Aurora Leigh* especially pronounced affinities with Marston's *Gerald* (302).

[61] The epic conception of *Aurora Leigh* made ample room, in other words, for mock-epic. One may endorse Rod Edmond's description of Barrett Browning's project—"less a venture into a male stronghold than the construction of her own out of new materials, with the ancient name of epic then placed defiantly over the entrance"—without allowing that the result is "completely without self-consciousness in its use of an epic voice": *Affairs of the Hearth: Victorian Poetry and Domestic Narrative* (London and New York: Routledge, 1988) 134, 92.

keeps discovering herself, as Romney discovers her self-crowned with ivy at the start of book 2, in an embarrassing state of precocity whose token is premature finish: "credulous of completion," she says with a smile at her own smiles at twenty, "There I held | The whole creation in my little cup" (2.5–6). Condemning Aurora to repeat this shamefaced moment several times over, Barrett Browning superimposes a blush on a spasm. Her diaristic apparatus of fits and starts tempers the appetite for totality which was both the glory of Spasmodism and its chief liability to derision.

For jumping to conclusions was what Spasmodists did best, in the inspired guesswork of their imagery, and also in the spastic congestion that afflicted their plots. If it was Dobell who first grasped this as a handicap, it was Barrett Browning who best figured out what to make of it. Book 6 of *Aurora Leigh* ostentatiously hinges on Aurora's habit of leaping first and asking questions later, when she mounts the stilts of Victorian sexual propriety to blame the raped and unwed mother Marian for her own victimization. It takes all Marian's aggrieved eloquence to establish that Aurora has herself been victimized, as the dupe of rumors and, worse, of the system of conventional prejudice that has made those rumors plausible. With great persistence book 6 pursues the truth to its hiding place in conventional rhetoric and the dead metaphors of social cliché, enforcing the galling lesson that Aurora's *faux pas* results from her very facility with words. She has mistaken the big picture now, just as she counterfeited epics in her youth, and for much the same reason.

Indeed, she will do it again until the poem's eleventh hour, which leaves her for once, *pace* the hyperkinetic articulateness of her own spasmodic fluency, at a loss for words. Amid the prickly dialogue of books 8–9, blind to Romney's blindness and his love, misreading his heart and her own, she pens at last an escape clause that opens her poem out from a double generic *cul-de-sac*. Just at the big clinch of an epically deferred, quintessentially spasmodic "Embrace, that was convulsion" (9.721), Aurora for all her poethood proves incapable of producing Romney's declaration of love so as to "write it down here like the rest" (9.729). Thrice in the space of fifteen lines the crowning words fail her, and with this defeat of her glibness the fatal totalitarian dream of Spasmodism breaks down too. The unwelcome news out of *Don Juan* and *Sordello* about the corruption of language, which stymied Dobell's effort, here becomes with a new twist Barrett Browning's gospel. Sealed not with a kiss but with "deep, deep, shuddering breaths, which meant beyond | Whatever could be told by word or kiss" (9.723–24), *Aurora Leigh* found a way to mean beyond the automatized holism towards which epic at mid-century tended, and also beyond that alternative generic trap of total articulation, the marriage-plot sprung by nearly every Victorian novel. The poem figures itself in the end as an open marriage of genres, much as Aurora Leigh (one name, maiden and married) gives herself away, at an altar of her own devising, in bridal guise of the New Jerusalem, wearing like a bouquet in the poem's last lines the stones that are her colors, the beams of opening dawn.[62]

[62] On the poem's feminized apocalypticism see the cross-stitch that John Schad sets up between Barrett Browning and Hélène Cixous in *Victorians in Theory: From Derrida to Browning* (Manchester and New York: Manchester University Press, 1999) 149–74. Reynolds, *Realms of Verse*, 114–15, while sympathetic to the poem's generic hierogamy, also remains alert to the strangeness of its double-negative way of affirming an ideal intimately public.

10

In Plight of Troth:
Mythological Epic 1860–1870

Coventry Patmore wanted no part in spasmody, not even at Barrett Browning's hand. Instead he addressed his 1850s middlebrow wits to the question how the epic impulse that Spasmodism had loosed on the land might be trained up to a better Victorian purpose. A house pet is what he fancied, if we may judge from the best-selling narrative sequence of tetrameter lyrics that he published serially, in four "books" ostentatiously subdivided into multiples of twelve, between 1854 and 1861, the whole sequence being bound together in 1863 under its since notorious title *The Angel in the House.*[1] In a deft and coyly ambitious "Prologue," as if on bended knee with palm upturned Patmore proposes to his better half (and proxy ideal reader) what is to be a major work "In these last days, the dregs of time," on a theme that Muses of "the Pierian Spring" have vouchsafed as "The first of themes sung last of all." When that amiable interlocutor chimes back on cue, "What is it, Dear? The Life | Of Arthur, or Jerusalem's Fall?" the poet is ready with his answer. It is an answer that takes dead aim, for all Patmore's studious lightness, at the genre as we have known it here: "Neither: your gentle self, my wife, | Yourself, and love that's all in all."

This chapter will show that Patmore put a dimple into epic, not a hole— much less the *coup de grâce* for which he appears to have cherished hope.[2]

---

[1] *The Betrothal* (1854) and *The Espousals* (1856) both come in twelve elaborate lyric packets; *Faithful for Ever* (1860) and *The Victories of Love* (1862) take epistolary form, the first in three triads of eight letters each, the latter running victoriously over the rule into a sequence of thirteen.

[2] Patmore's prologue goes on to measure lances with Dante; Alison Milbank, *Dante and the Victorians* (Manchester and New York: Manchester University Press, 1998) 109, concludes that the proper comparison lies not with the *Divina Commedia* but with the *Vita Nuova*. Other congeners in

Other themes subsisted in the epic 1860s, other visions even of the "love that's all in all," to keep Patmore's promotion of domesticity from going unchallenged during the next vigorous installment in what Victorians never wearied of announcing were epic's "last days." Before the decade was out, in fact, it would witness Victorian epic's finest hour. But the home epic Patmore bet on remained a formidable contender all the while, less in the poem he eventually produced than in the genre of prose fiction with which his *Angel* itself was of course waging dubious battle from the first. While Spasmodism racked its brains along the cosmos, novelists of genius and stamina had meanwhile not only sold a great many entertaining books but had, during the 1850s, cornered large new regions of cultural prestige by amassing the moral capital that attended their steady engagement with the complexities of dailiness embedding contemporary readers' lives.[3] The literary developments that Patmore cannily observed from his cathedral close did not escape the notice of poets born to a wider range of narrative imagination than his and the Spasmodists' put together. We cannot understand what was being done by the most prominent of the poetical best and brightest—Barrett Browning in the exhilarated final portions of her epic, Tennyson at the still tentative beginnings of his—without acknowledging, as the poets themselves certainly did, the shift in generic gravity that the remarkable 1850s advance of the novel had brought about.

In *Aurora Leigh* Barrett Browning managed to thread the straits of fiction—landmarked for a Victorian authoress by Jane Eyre's headland of *Bildungsroman* to port and Corinne's promontory of *Kunstlerroman* to starboard—by taking her bearings from myth, and from the generic enlargement that myth made available. A modern faith in myth sped her past the conventions of realist mimesis into a utopian reclamation of the antique ("Expressing the old scripture," 1.832), which without superhumanizing her principals did epicize them. Aurora and Romney transcend the patterns novels trace by finding in themselves, and seeking in a renovated world, the living stress of prophetic, ultimately apocalyptic myth. This conclusion from

the epithalamic *ars poetica* genre include Blake's *Marriage of Heaven and Hell*, Tennyson's *In Memoriam*, and the Brownings' *Sonnets from the Portuguese* and "One Word More."

[3] Moreover, disinterested and competent observers were starting to say so in public. Witness the lectures David Masson, Professor of English at University College, London, delivered at the Philosophical Institution of Edinburgh in 1858 and published as *British Novelists and Their Styles* (Cambridge and London: Macmillan, 1859). Affirming right away that "The Novel, at its highest, is a prose Epic" (2), Masson calls in closing for "more attention among our novelists of real life to epic breadth of interest" (293).

Chapter 9 is worth stressing because the next important British work of epic kind, by the one British poet who indisputably mattered more than Elizabeth Barrett Browning, moved with dispatch in the opposite direction. Composed steadily during the later 1850s and published in 1859, the first book on which Alfred Tennyson bestowed the name *Idylls of the King* was an oblation to Patmore's Angel: a systematic attempt, that is, to convert the matter of Arthur from the epic stuff the poet had supposed it during the 1830s into material worthy of a Victorian novelist.

A reader confronting only the 1859 *Idylls*, ignorant alike of the epic-framed 1842 "Morte d'Arthur" and of the generic correction-of-course that Tennyson was to effect within the next dozen years, would be unlikely to identify "Enid," "Vivien," "Elaine," and "Guinevere" as epic writings. Indeed, a reader sensitive to style would find in them abundant reason not to do so. For the 1859 book, written at the top of Tennyson's form, so manages a considerable perspectival talent, and an unparalleled amplitude of vocal timbre and prosodic resource, as to make epic appear only to disappear. As formerly in the genre-coquetting *Princess* (Ch. 8), but now with firmer hand, Tennyson frequently raises epic possibilities and then as frequently shunts them aside. The flower of Arthurian knighthood is on the scene, but echoes of martial contest and conquest stay baffled deep in the offstage wings. Bold Sir Lancelot, without at all meaning to, breaks a young girl's heart. Geraint endangers his marriage, then stumbles his way into saving it, during an extended interval of not much better to do. Merlin the architect of Camelot is laboriously seduced by a sleek adventuress into bartering wisdom for mere knowingness, cheapening his own mystique and the king's into the bargain. As for Arthur himself, in 1859 we meet him as a witting cuckold reduced to blaming the ruin of his life's work on trouble at home, the glory of his "great Pendragonship" (10.594) badly tarnished by Tennyson's conjunction of martial bearing with spousal long-suffering.

Throughout this installment of *Idylls*, furthermore, the miraculously sustained grandiloquence of "Morte d'Arthur" persists in many passages of fine writing; but these are passages that our hypothetical reader would hail as fine precisely for the way they emerge from, then relapse into, a veritable heteroglossia of effects drawn from other orders of style than the heroic. "Elaine," for example, rises to an epic plateau when "Lancelot spoke | And answer'd him at full, as having been | With Arthur in the fight" (7.284–86)—eleven fights, to be exact, in what sounds like a resumption of the promise made in "The Epic" of 1842 that a crowning twelfth lies in store.

But the promise of Lancelot's full-throated catalogue is, by deliberate generic design, frustrated: framed from the start as a sequestrated celebrity's gracious reply to a fan, it is merely fuel for the youth Lavaine's emulative "sudden passion" (7.281) and the "fantasy" (7.396 *et passim*) that will become, for his sister Elaine, an unrequitable and finally suicidal teenage crush. Within a narrative thus focused on the psychology of idealization, a fantasy or a memory is all that the epic ideal can amount to. Like the wounded Lancelot (and retired Geraint, and Merlin on holiday, in their respective idylls) heroism is sidelined; courtesy and courtliness take its place, and with these a drama of social implication and guesswork supervenes on direct rendition of mighty deeds.

We find ourselves, that is, in the realm of the novel: domestic interiors, human interiors to match, interpretations that upstage actions, and a strong investment in symbols that, whether ambiguous or overdetermined, we pityingly observe our principals' failure to read. "What might she mean by that?" (7.829): if an epic poem should not *mean* but *be*, this very line betokens a marked shift from the substance and tonality of epic alike. Large-hearted Lancelot's induction into a maiden's hidden love leads the idyll into a free indirect style, and an insinuating confidentiality, that make Tennyson's medieval knight for the time being into a modern individual, a man not tasked by a quest but snared in an embarrassment. Disentangling the significance of tokens, worming out secrets, belatedly (and for the most part unavailingly) recognizing the interpersonal network of meanings in which a life is embroiled: such are the plotlines of the 1859 *Idylls*. Their execution obliged Tennyson to species of undercover subtlety that lay far from the beaten track of epic, and to feats of blank-verse adaptation that are wonders of nineteenth-century prosody—though not wonderful in epic's way. "He spoke: the brawny spearman let his cheek | Bulge with the unswallow'd piece, and turning stared" (4.629–30). A bulge with cheek indeed, the classic *dixit* and epithet in these lines are laved in playfulness. Tennyson's mode of realization here is that of an epic camp follower, post-classical yet unromantic, deft in a manner best appreciated by a reader who has spent some time with *The Pickwick Papers* or *Vanity Fair*. Matthew Arnold would have objected, in the spirit both of his early-1850s anti-Spasmodism and his 1860s polemics *On Translating Homer,* that such a passage's narrative brilliance is of a piece with its structural isolation. Like too much in the idyllic entertainment that Tennyson offered the 1859 public as poetry's answer to the novel, it is manifestly outstanding but also merely that. It is content to stand as a brilliant demonstration of what narrative poetry could do supremely well even in the heyday of prose fiction.

By the very plural in its title *Idylls of the King* conceded its status as a variety show in verse, and anticipated the charge that it was less a whole than the sum of its parts.[4] But the 1859 book also assembled, in its own defense *as a poem* against the Arnoldian charge of dissipation, a set of blueprints for another sort of structure than the old Aristotelean logic of plot. Tennyson seasoned his narrative with descriptive pivot points like this one, where the poem turns introspectively back to image a latent design that hangs together by other means than linkage of events:

> Until they found the clear-faced King, who sat
> Robed in red samite, easily to be known,
> Since to his crown the golden dragon clung,
> And down his robe the dragon writhed in gold,
> And from the carven-work behind him crept
> Two dragons gilded, sloping down to make
> Arms for his chair, while all the rest of them
> Thro' knots and loops and folds innumerable
> Fled thro' the woodwork, till they found
> The new design in which they lost themselves.

(7.430–39)

This tour-de-force subordinate clause sheds syntactical dependency some half dozen lines in, once it becomes clear that the ekphrastic lines in the verse are not just describing those in the woodwork but performing them. Getting lost in the pattern is the mazy method of a new orientation toward pattern itself, figured by the repetition of "they found the clear-faced King" in "they found | The new design." A reader who learns from such a passage to look, beyond or beneath plot, for kindred images—and who recognizes one such image when Arthur testifies in the next 1859 idyll, "Guinevere," that the "Order of my Table Round" was built "To serve as model for the mighty world, | And be the fair beginning of a time" (11.460–63)—will have grounds for believing that to find the design behind the passing

---

[4] See, e.g. George L. Craik, *A Compendious History of English Literature, and of the English Language, from the Norman Conquest* (New York: Scribner, 1864): the one Victorian "great poem" as of 1860 is *Aurora Leigh*, since "neither Tennyson's *In Memoriam* nor his *Idyls* [sic] *of the King* can properly be reckoned as more, either of them, than a collection of so many short poems relating to the same subject" (2: 557).

episodes and to find the king behind the current regime may be comparable acts of faithful invention. They may indeed be acts not unlike Bedivere's, when in "Morte d'Arthur" he finds a mythic place in the cycle of legend by relaxing his grip on historical time.

Was such finding foundational with respect to epic? Yes, in the long view; but for Tennyson, at this stage, not that he could see. The hyperlinks between image and image that bind narratively disparate idylls into second-order symbolic congruence, and that any vigilant reader of the 1859 book will detect, served the poet as a holding pattern. They propped up a once and future trust, which he had announced in 1842 and would regain during the 1860s but had now lost—or else had provisionally forsworn, in order to give the triumphant novels of the day a laureate run for their money, on the order more or less of Clough's contemporary anything-but-epic *Amours de Voyage* (1858). In its conjugation of fictions that involved trysting couples, twisting marriages, relations gone awry, and the migration of public charisma into merely interpersonal intrigue, the 1859 installment of idylls executed a generic swerve whose angular momentum (given a narrative mass constituting nearly half of the eventual *Idylls of the King*) makes it an extremely impressive performance. The only feat conceivably more impressive was the one that Tennyson undertook in his coordinated installments of 1868 and 1872, and that this chapter will take up in closing. That feat was to recontain the 1859 swerve into fiction as one element—a dragon's graceful, sloping writhe—within an expanded design where structural fitness picked up forward momentum and emerged with the civic force of myth, resonant again within an altered public sphere.

Framing the 1860s, the changing installments of Tennyson's *Idylls* also frame the question why that decade proved the most intensively epical of Victoria's reign. During the decade before it Britain had lavished literary genius on the novel; the best contemporary epic poem, *Aurora Leigh*, had only just escaped being the best verse-novel instead; and the typical epic afflatus of the time had gone to swell and burst the bubble of Spasmodism, over in a corner of Victorian culture where the reality checks of verisimilitude had been systematically turned off. The 1860s in contrast generated half a dozen straight-up epic poems; some work in a mock-epic vein, which also fed into the decade's highly capable verse-novels; and several noteworthy exercises in sub-epic kinds that gave to developments from earlier decades—notably the anthology and the torso epic—new directions that would continue to guide the genre until century's end. All this without counting the generic *annus mirabilis* 1868, which saw epic publications by no fewer than four major Victorian imaginations: Tennyson's pivotal *Holy Grail* volume, flanked by George Eliot's *The Spanish Gypsy* and the first serial parts of Robert Browning's *The Ring and the Book* and William Morris's *The Earthly Paradise*.

It is not just the quantity but the qualitative range of this output, unmatched since the first part of the nineteenth century, that shows forth the prosperity of epic at this juncture. Such generic bloom—misleading perhaps in view of the long wilt that was to succeed it, but perfectly genuine in itself—was a climactic rally within the British literary system that corresponded to an evident crisis in the national health. The coincidence of the peak year 1868 with the century's second great Reform in electoral politics is striking, and it suggests that British authors and readers at this time once again needed something that epic writing was peculiarly suited to provide. This provision was not quite the ancient dream of heroically normed and nationally embedded solidarity that literary criticism of the novel since Lukács and Bakhtin likes to conjure up as a stodgy foil to fiction's subtler craft. Epic poetry during the 1860s made the national dreamwork a central concern, to be sure; and in mediocre hands or worse it admittedly did little but trumpet unity and drum up togetherness. But the best epoists worked hard to assay the national identity formations they summoned, and in forms moreover that were more freely shaped than those open to contemporary novelists—an advantage attested by Tennyson's post-1859 restoration of Arthur to his epic seat, Eliot's detour through verse epic between the different epicizing modes practiced in her novels *Romola* (1862) and *Middlemarch* (1873), and Browning's punningly explicit rejection of the "novel country" (1.1148) into which *The Ring and the Book* might have settled given a lesser author in a duller day.

So it happened that after the spasmodic digression of the 1850s epic rose again to take up a certain slack in the Victorian novel's line, so lately taut with mimetic purpose and fastened to a web of assurances about the robustness (if not rightness) of things as they were. When this ideological web began to unravel in the 1860s, the British novel's self-confidence wavered along with the reading public's. Former certitudes yielded to alarms including Darwin's challenge to the received natural order; a Higher Criticism leveled in increasingly prominent places at the authority of scripture; *causes célèbres* come home from Indian (1857) and West Indian oppressions (1866) to rock the boat of empire, even as Canada (1867) stepped away from the mother country toward post-colonial independence; a long-deferred economic downturn, sharpened to the point of famine in the industrial north counties when civil war in the United States throttled the cotton supply. At Prince Albert's sudden death in 1861 the Queen plunged into mourning for a decade, and before she emerged Charles Dickens was dead as well. Dickens's own not-quite-epical *Tale of Two Cities* (1859) had ushered the decade in by equating the best of times with the worst; soul-trying times like these, we may conclude, called for epic means of rendering, and probing, the bases of national culture.

At a crisis of faith when less could be taken for granted, more required proof. What formerly went without saying now needed to be shown—shown up, perhaps, but at all events made manifest in narrated action. This emphasis on *narration*, our genre's defining activity, clearly distinguishes epic at the time of the Second Reform Bill from what it had been at the time of the First. In Chapter 7 we saw how circa 1830 ideological debate, staged within the genteel cockpit of the closet drama, prevailed in epicizing formats whose norm was judicial or parliamentary, and whose representation of balanced and *prima facie* open-minded controversy reflected a Liberalism in the ascendant. From the vantage of 1867, when urban rioters backed by nascent labor unions demanded and largely won the franchise that the 1832 compromise had denied to their fathers, the gentlemanly equilibrium of 1832 stood revealed in its dependency on a preestablished consensus. In retrospect the First Reform Bill, shocking though it had appeared to contemporaries, had owed its ease of passage to the same circumstance that now marked its compromises as obsolete: namely, its grounding in a high degree of commonalty of interest among electors nearly all of whom belonged (as did practically every reader of contemporary epic poetry) to the upper social echelons. Open-mindedness looked a lot wider open through the dilated aperture of 1867 than through the loophole of 1832, agoraphobically so to the select readership spoken for at decade's end by the authoritarian liberalism of Arnold's *Culture and Anarchy* (1869). The difference between that paradoxical work and its opposite bookend J. S. Mill's *On Liberty* (1859) frames the dilemma of a decade that found the ideal of disinterestedness increasingly hard to credit and that, in a related development, increasingly staged in its theaters the melodramatic extremes of goodness and villainy. The emotional atmosphere of Victorian melodrama left scant public room for the drama of ideas and almost none for dialogue on the older model between mutually respectable viewpoints.

In such a climate ideas had to be dissolved in stronger stuff. Epic poets turned to the power of narrative and drew their solvency from the deep funds of myth. Illiberal by an 1830s standard, the mythological epics of the 1860s nevertheless widened the circulation of ideas to meet a present need—need measured not in sales figures, though the epic verse of Tennyson and Morris enjoyed huge publishing success, but in the imaginative demographics of spokesmanship. A newly enfranchised people and an established public elite, with an empire to care for into the bargain, were learning who, as a nation, they might become. They therefore sorely needed stories of who, as a nation, they had been. These the epic poets supplied, the best of them adding a metapoetic bonus of insight into myth's ambiguous power to blind as well as guide its adherents, to sever as well as unite. Epic's extroversion of the cultural imaginary sought to display, not the novelistic ramifications of what Britons did or didn't believe, but the very roots of faith in myth.[5] Telling stories the nation held by, British epics of the 1860s also told stories about the traditional telling of such stories, by which for better and for worse a people is made.

For better and for worse: it was mainly for worse that latter-century poets tried reviving epic in an antique format, whether that format was actually classical or just ranked as old-fashioned after a few decades' usage (a distinction that, as the use we now make of "antique" will show, modern culture was swiftly effacing). *A Poem in Twelve Books* or *A Poem, in Four Cantos* had become by 1860 a standing invitation to ridicule, which any poem so subtitled had better anticipate and try to deflect. This contingency was all but lost, alas, on the authors of the works from which these two subtitles respectively come: Edward Henry Bickersteth's *Yesterday, To-Day, and For*

---

[5] A fixture now in literary criticism, *myth* as a tool for literary and cultural interpretation dates within British letters, in its modern (historicized form), only from the middle of the 19th cent. That was when Edward Tylor, William Robertson Smith, and Andrew Lang among others applied the force of Vico's and Herder's thought to widen the scope of cultural evolutionism beyond philology into ritual and material practices sharing with traditional narrative a common substrate in national myth. See Robert Ackerman, *The Myth and Ritual School: J. G. Frazer and the Cambridge Ritualists* (New York and London: Garland, 1991) 29–42. As an introduction to this key mid-Victorian intellectual formation, the selection of primary texts and editorial matter are excellent in part 3 of *The Rise of Modern Mythology 1680–1860*, ed. Burton Feldman and Robert D. Richardson (Bloomington and London: Indiana University Press, 1972). At twenty years' vantage A. C. Bradley captured very well the epoch of the Higher Criticism when he asked in *Macmillan's Magazine* for 1881, "Is it not the case that every day, without knowing it, we are making new mythological modes of thought and speech? Is not the popularisation of that science which is the most active dissolvent of old mythology, itself thoroughly mythological?" (29).

Ever (1866) and the anonymous *The Last Crusader* (1867). It was similarly lost on several other 1860s authors who, keeping straight-faced faith with established traditions, behaved as if to crack a smile or nod to a contemporary pertinence would shiver the whole enterprise. Such strict sobriety, like the rigor with which these poems hewed to their biblical or medieval settings, suggests an anxiety of exposure, born of poets' suspicion that their chosen mode had by now been outflanked.

Generic defensiveness pervades the orthodox epics of the 1860s at a thematic level, too, in their single-minded pursuit of the theme of fidelity. This theme enacts an allegory of their embattled cultural situation: typically they tell not of faith triumphant but rather of faith unblemished. It is as if merely not to stray from rectitude is as much as the hero, like the poet on evil days fallen, may hope for; as if, in order to sing of faith that did not give in or sell out to worldly dissipation, these poets had to renounce worldly effects—which is to say, renounce such epic effects as the hero's great deed or the age-defining event in a people's history. Thus to the dour 1860s epoists of biblical doom we shall take up presently the survival of Noah's family, the success of the Exodus under Moses, the Apocalypse itself seem afterthoughts, mere sequels to virtue's perseverance. And the medievalizers we shall consider first find so little relish in their potentially militant themes of Christianity's national establishment and international vindication that they present these themes only under the shadow of a suspicion that, for the true believer, to flourish in this world is to court in the next a fate worse than secular defeat. Like Tennyson in 1859, these authors as a group avert their eyes from conspicuously eligible epic actions, even as their narratives remain far charier than his about infection by the sick disease of modern life.

The thread of an austere transcendentalism connects Alexander Smith's *Edwin of Deira* (1861) to his Spasmodist hit of nine years before, *A Life-Drama.* The later epic stands to the earlier in a palinodic relation that exemplifies the difference in spirit between their decades. Smith's former extempore dash at redemption, dramatic immediacy, and sheer nervy optimism give way here to the mediation of a deliberate national mythology, the distance of slow-paced narrative, and the evident discipline of historical research: preparing *Edwin*'s four blank-verse books cost the poet as many years, not the few weeks that went into his smash debut. In the person of England's first Christian king, the seventh-century Northumbrian prince who gave his name to Edinburgh (and whom, in a parallel act of poetic contrition, the reformed radical John Thelwall had tapped for epic use in

1801), Smith as a notorious Glaswegian thus made prudent choice of a hero possessing a certain Great-British breadth, rooted in an historical moment of pivotal importance, yet obscure enough to allow poetic license.

Metaphors and similes, which kept running off with *A Life-Drama*, remain abundant here but are constantly subordinated to the story. Smith invests in the low-budget machinery of one thriftily recycled apparition, who is brought on at first to soften Edwin's pagan heart to Christian influences and then at last to foretell the unification of England. Yet for all this good behavior our chastened poet was rewarded with a stillbirth. A son of Aeneas made (like Robert Southey's Madoc in Ch. 3) to heroic order, the future St. Edwin *fills* an important place but fails to *make* one. Pious without zeal, like his too-diligent poet he defers to manifest historical destiny; and his free exertions of will issue mainly in destruction: the pitiless massacre of a brigand troop (book 3), the smashing of pagan idols through-out his new realm (book 4). Not for the first time in its course, epic here succumbs to the punitive generic superego. Heroic virtue turns its indiffer-ent, repressive hand at last against the hero himself, who is extinguished without compelling narrative climax, and to nobody's sharp regret, by the winds of change that will in compensation immortalize his name.

In other words, the poet asks us to take the heroism of his hero of the faith *on faith*. Smith understood that the time was right for epic to resume its nationalist mission and impart fresh narrative propulsion to the nation's trust in its traditions. But what Smith grasped in principle eluded him in creative fact. His Edwin is credible only as an inference from an historical occasion, never as an imagined man: the human relation in which he stands to his friend and *Doppelgänger* Regner, or to his queen and Christian sponsor Bertha—not to mention his spiritual relation to higher beings—withers undeveloped. Smith's early memoirist Thomas Brisbane ascribed the failure of *Edwin of Deira* to the appearance two years before it of Tennyson's *Idylls*, where as we have seen the middle distance of human relations was if anything overdeveloped.[6] Having helped set the Spasmodist terms on which Tennyson was obliged to come before the public with *Maud* in the mid-1850s, Smith now met his requital, when scooped by the Laureate's demonstrating in faux-medieval blank-verse a social plenitude Smith dreamt not of. And yet, as Brisbane's apologetic tribute of 1869 may

---

[6] Thomas Brisbane, *The Early Years of Alexander Smith, Poet and Essayist: A Study for Young Men* (London: Hoddart and Stoughton, 1869) 194–95.

surmise, Smith at the start of the new decade had shown the way that Tennyson too would follow by its end: the epic expansion from a middle-to a long-distance call, reaching beyond interpersonal faith and betrayal towards loyalty and treason on the scale of a national trust. Although Smith failed to make his Edwin a myth, he did show what the epic work of myth for the 1860s was to be.

This knowledge Smith's less talented contemporaries in the orthodox vein of epic shared, and it constitutes their claim on our attention here. William Stigand's *Athenaïs; or, The First Crusade* (1866) drives six Spenserian cantos over three hundred pages to amazingly little narrative purpose. The story devolves from a high point of epic-catalogued pageantry in the struggle for Antioch (besieging Christians of canto 1 become the besieged in canto 2) toward a digressive finale that strays through oriental pleasure-grounds (canto 5) to a mountain hideout in Cyprus, where commando attack leaves the protagonists bound equally far from marriage and from the apparently forgotten mission of liberating Jerusalem (canto 6). But this breakdown of the potentially world-historical First Crusade into factional counter-scheming frees Stigand to extract from the ruins of plot what interests him more, the theme of fidelity as such. Whether in cult or courtship, rascally abduction or the continental clash of religions, the important scenes of the poem can be parsed as binary structures of faithfulness and treachery. Thus the twy-natured traitor Zohrab, equally apt at kidnapping our eponymous heroine and delivering Antioch into Christian hands, is seen at the last to have acted throughout with the single conspiratorial purpose of bestowing on his sect of Assassins not only a Greek princess but control over the whole Byzantine empire (6.107). Muslim and Christian sides are alike riven by internal schisms and betrayals, which eject the Provençal troubadour-hero Bertrand from the business of crusading out into epicycles of romance where he remains to the end, distracted from epic duty by its erotic substitute, the fidelity a knight owes his lady-love.

Stigand lets no opportunity pass to moralize this action of broken promises and interfering allegiances by sounding the gong of faith, in a purely ideological register that mere outcomes cannot dampen. The Crusades marked an age of "Virgin faith," an "heroic time, | When Christendom leapt up in youth sublime" (4.2); the poet envies his stanzaic models Tasso and Spenser their life in a poetic age contrasted to his own amid "hot clamors of the varying mart" (6.7). This scorn for Victorian realities evidently extends to the Victorian regard for fact: it is not historical events that give play to "man's immortal Youth" (2.2) but their mythic idealization. The reader is thus invited to keep faith with Stigand's crusaders when, amid the Antioch famine, "many saw, or thought they saw" the Holy City, delved on the spot and found the centurion's lance from Calvary, "by fraud, or chance, | Or by Divine disposal" (4.11–15). Option three here is the poet's preference, but an option is what "Divine disposal" must remain if it is to evoke a modern reader's faith now in a medieval crusader's faith once upon a time. "Was it Faith's fond illusion?" Stigand asks, as the starved inmates file out of Antioch behind the holy lance in despite of enemies; and he answers, "Ye were true | To those who saw you" (4.58–59). In this particular instance fidelity happens to work, and the conveniently bickering Muslim forces let the Christians depart unharmed. Yet Stigand is no low pragmatist, and his full endorsement of the faith that gains no earthly reward emerges both in the terminally digressive main plot of unconsummated love between Bertrand and Athenaïs and in its mid-poem epitome, the chastity-unto-death of Eric the Dane and his sacrificial bride Adelaïde (3.97–152).

That justification should operate by faith alone, not works, was a tenet typical of epic's orthodox turn circa 1860, and it foretold something of high culture's self-denying strain in years that lay not far ahead. Already there was a gleam in the Victorian ascetic's eye, and it reflected visions of longer range than the proper action of *Athenaïs* or *Edwin* cared to compass, visions that bore on the present day. Chastened into post-spasmodic reticence, Smith let the contemporary reverberation of his Christian-British-roots plot speak for itself; but Stigand spoke out without a blush to champion, from the prenationalist standpoint of the Middle Ages, a Eurocentric internationalism defined implicitly by race.[7] By reviving the crusader epic, he meant to awaken nineteenth-century Christian valor to a vindication of freedom, in the age of empire, against the "dark-brain'd Asiatic horde" (1.9) of latter days. The cultural-libertarian campaign that had recently freed Greece would soon free Italy (1.20), Stigand knew, in the same wave of evangelical feeling that had cleansed Britain of slavery first. This international link, latent and the stronger for it in *Aurora Leigh*, also incidentally rang out with a clank in the heroizing Spenserians of *Garibaldi*, an instant pocket epic of

[7] The increasingly explicit racializing of cultural thinking in the period attends many other epics this chapter treats. An unstated but constitutive Europeanism anchors the miscellany of Morris's *Earthly Paradise*, and also grounds Browning's claim of historical continuity in making an English epic out of an Italian sensation in *The Ring and the Book*. It also helps explain why Eliot's *Spanish Gypsy* and the anonymous *Last Crusader* should post watch, respectively, at the Continental threshholds of Gibraltar and Constantinople.

1861 written on commission (and on the spur of the moment apparently) by Mary Elizabeth Braddon in spasmodical training for her *métier* in sensation fiction. "These are Earth's great ones—these who can believe!" she affirms, celebrating "one instinctive yearning, which | Usurps each heart, and beats in every breast" (stanzas 62, 156.)

Meanwhile, back in the Holy Land, the gift of prophecy bestows on Bertrand a clairvoyance that matches his poet's (6.58–60). This heroic privilege is withheld, however, from his sweetheart Athenäis, doomed as she is to spiritual subalternity by the satisfaction she takes in old-worldly, this-worldly creature comforts. But then Athenäis remains, and her name blazons the fact, a Greek. Nay, she is a Hellene (in Matthew Arnold's sense from *Culture and Anarchy*), and thus plays the oriental-accented foil to Bertrand's divinely Gothic discontent (in John Ruskin's sense from *The Stones of Venice*). This was the timely spirit in which Stigand's poem, "an Iliad of the Cross" (1.24), conformed to W. E. Gladstone's conscription of Homer himself, forever young, into the cause of Liberal Christendom in two tomes that frame our decade: *Studies on Homer and the Homeric Age* (1858) and *Juventus Mundi* (1869), the latter bringing Gladstone's theses up to speed with the central intellectual trend of the intervening decade, in a revision "considerably modified in the Ethnological, and in the Mythological, portions" (Preface).[8] Conviction might still carry the day, but what the eye of faith now beheld came via convex refraction through lenses of ethnology and myth. The ostentatiously unsatisfying conclusion of *Athenäis* leaves heroism in an Arnoldian wilderness, where what abides is not the Holy City of epic destiny but the challenge to believe in those who believe in the Holy City: a summons, across dark tracts worthy of Browning's Childe Roland, to the affirmation of some faith by some hero, through some action, somewhere.

An anonymous and much slighter poem of the next year, also based on the Crusades and barely eking out the four cantos we saw promised in its subtitle, keeps a different kind of faith with this vagrant call to worship.

---

[8] In the latter book, e.g., Gladstone reads Achilles' parentage as Homer's invention "for signifying that union of ethnical and theogonic elements, which he in part commemorated, and in part brought about," while on a higher plane of cultural history the anthropomorphism of Homer's gods was instrumental in preparing the world for Christianity: *Juventus Mundi: The Gods and Men of the Heroic Age* (Boston: Little, Brown, 1869) 345, 530. An overview of Gladstone's idiosyncratic output on such themes over three decades' periodical and book publication is given in Eric Glasgow, "Gladstone's Homer," in *Studies in Nineteenth Century Literature*, ed. James Hogg (Salzburg: Universität Salzburg, 1982) 61–81.

Framed in plodding tetrameter rhymes, *The Last Crusader* illustrates the longevity, which is to say the adaptability, not only of Scott's formal model but also of the borderland thematics which that model entrained. A charitable rhyme scheme and springy meter work overtime here at their usual indulgence of technical sins; nor is it ever too late by the Scott clock for any crusader to come home (especially to heathery hills) from anywhere (especially points south). So the laird Menteeth does here, in the prime of life but disguised as an aged bard—a *Last Minstrel?*—to reclaim his beloved from the hands of an opera-buffo suitor with the improbably Odyssean name Bombastes. All this is dispatched with too little trouble, or too much, to detain us. The poem's arresting moment is the long chant Menteeth sings on his return from abroad: by "the sea-shore bleak and cold" this repatriated Scot impersonating "a minstrel grey and old" (2.1) keens nine stanzas' worth of nostalgia for the old homestead located in, of all places, Constantinople.

In his decrepit-minstrel role that metropolis is his pretended home, but a good deal more resides within the pretense. For one thing, Constantinople is a crossroads where the Dardanelles usurp the Tweed and Scott's borderland dialectics are boosted from intranational to intercontinental scale. Furthermore, Menteeth's fond feigned retrospect eastward is culturally veridical: by this point in the century the Anglo imagination had taught itself to look homeward by peering abroad, with just the vision Gladstone called "ethnological" and "mythological," clear across Europe and into the Caucasus. Impersonating in the Constantinopolitan bard what the age (trained, say, on Bulwer-Lytton's *King Arthur*: Ch. 8) would have hailed as his own ancestral or racial self, this heir to peaty moorlands zooms in on a home that is none the less desirable for its being weirdly dislocated: an Aryan utopia graced by "stately palms," "porticoes and palace" (2.7) yet simultaneously by "a grassy apron—green but small—/A cot—a woodland" (2.8). Laird of Byzantium and Indo-European crofter in one, Menteeth is as old as the rocks by which he sings of what is past or passing or to come. Thus *The Last Crusader*, witless production though it is, unerringly embodies the mid-Victorian's yearning back toward the future, an emotion that conferred on a now nakedly global will to power the old, nationalist yet still serviceable *Marmion* form of an irrecuperable loss. The stock nostalgia uppermost in Menteeth's repertoire became the commonest trick in the Victorian book because nostalgia, whatever its ostensible object might be in religious or cultural or biographical terms, accurately replicated a modern proclivity for lavishing faith on certitudes known to be gone.

★

For such knowledge there was no forgiveness in the Bible epics that appeared contemporaneously with *Essays and Reviews* and the Bishop Colenso affair. We know this from the asperity with which these poems mock skepticism, and the sternness with which they see to the punishment of the infidel.[9] We know it better from a certain air of resignation that trails the recrudescent biblical triumphalism of the 1860s: the bad faith, as it were, of the poets' belated militancy, the shadow of a nostalgia that won't be willed away. This cultural undertow is felt most strongly in the nine-book patriarchal epic that one of England's best-selling poets, Jean Ingelow, produced in 1867 as *A Story of Doom*. An odd title for a poem manifestly designed to encourage Christian obedience, yet an honest one, recording the listless affect that a regimen of pious submission can entail. Repeatedly the plot highlights acts of prostration before a superior will: in book 1 the chain of command reaches down from God's voice through Noah's enjoining his wife to obey him and renounce her tribal witchcraft; in book 2 the wicked patriarchal *roué* Methuselah is possessed by the spirit and prophesies, despite himself, the coming Flood and the Ark of salvation; in book 4 the election of Japhet from among Noah's refractory sons consists merely in his sudden inspiration to obey his father the way his father obeys God.

Countering these interlocking alignments of good will are the usual suspects: a court full of giants who wield sway over the antediluvian earth, detachments of demons who frustrate Noah's eloquent call to a gigantic repentance (book 7). Yet these nay-sayers hardly have a mind of their own, and even Satan their chieftain, old serpent that he here literally is, exhales for the most part a weary draconic melancholy. For *ad hoc* comparison between the two major Victorian eras of Reform one could do worse than measure Ingelow's Noachite epic with John Edmond Reade's twelve-scene *The Deluge* (1839, written 1820s). As we saw in Chapter 7, Reade devotes most of his antediluvian closet drama to forensic debate and inquiry that make for suspense of a more open-ended sort than saturates the dreaded

---

[9] Some of the starch in the biblical-epical collar at this time came no doubt from the confidence British millenarians placed in painstakingly computed predictions that the end of time was due at some point between 1866 and 1873. See Michael Wheeler, *Heaven, Hell, and the Victorians* (Cambridge: Cambridge University Press, 1994) 80. The revival of Bible epics during the 1860s reflected a spreading awareness that, as John Stuart Blackie surmised, "If the Wolfian theory with regard to the origin and composition of the Homeric poems be looked at beyond the surface, it will be found to underlie a great number of the most important literary, historical, and theological questions that stir the mind of England at the present hour": *Homer and the Iliad* (1860; 2nd edn. Edinburgh: Edmonston and Douglas, 1866) 1: 184.

imminence of it all in *A Story of Doom*.[10] Reade's Noah doesn't give orders like Ingelow's but has a lot of uphill and only partially successful persuading to do; and this is because his personages are freer than hers, or at least more unpredictably subject to the vagaries of steamy desire. Epic drama during the First Reform age, it appears, enjoyed broader liberties than epic proper during the Second could afford. Requiring strong measures to hold a poem or a people together, Ingelow and her Bible-based contemporaries bet on other and surer affects than desire.

A Story of Doom is thus a curiously muted work of heroic introversion. From a mannerly best-selling poetess like Ingelow a certain domestication of epic is to be expected. But in a poem that begins indoors with connubial dialogue, sends Noah home to his father's house and then Japhet home to his, brings the chosen family home from Giant-land in book 8 and marches them into their new houseboat in book 9, homecoming has become an obsession—ironically so, in view of the Flood that is about to make the whole world homeless. This global irony is consistent with the fatalism just mentioned: both give admittance to reaches of effect for which Ingelow's pious ideological agenda left little official space. Retiring, undemonstrative, fortified by an archaism of diction whose support seems prudent lest the verse faint, the poem joins the minor drab-epic tradition, which descended to Ingelow from *Paradise Regained* through what may well have been her patriarchal-pastoral model, James Montgomery's 1813 *The World Before the Flood* (Ch. 4). She certainly took nothing from the apocalypticism of the 1820s or its Spasmodic revival just a decade before in *Aurora Leigh*. Where Barrett Browning was flush with her "full-veined, heaving, double-breasted Age" (5.216), Ingelow embraced a generic decorum that struck one *fin-de-siècle* commentator as no more than "semi-epic."[11] Through this very half-heartedness, however, with an integrity of its own the poem kept up relations with the demicroyance of its period. Tennyson's novelistic *Idylls* had more of a story to tell, yet by the same token Ingelow's *Story* was the

---

[10] For a very different reading that sets *The Story of Doom* amid contemporary issues including insurrection and the franchise, eugenics and domestic violence, see Terence Allan Hoagwood and Kathryn Ledbetter, *"Colour'd Shadows": Contexts in Publishing, Printing, and Reading Nineteenth-Century British Women Authors* (Houndmills: Palgrave, 2005) 133–35. Hoagwood draws out a documentary-citational problematic linking Ingelow, via the Higher Criticism of scripture, to the contemporary practice of Tennyson and especially Browning.

[11] Thus "N. H. D., Boston 1894" in a "Biographical Sketch" prefixed to Ingelow's *Poetical Works* (New York: Crowell, 1894) 5.

more properly idyllic work: the noisy old Flood would get along fine, she was confident, without her rehashing it.

One appreciates Ingelow's sustained submissiveness, and the purchase it gave on certain contradictions within the culture of her moment, by comparison to a deservedly obscurer contemporary Old Testament epic, Walter Goalen's *Gideon: A Poem in Seven Books* (1868). Here too domestic and national motifs cohabit: when not praying, slaying, or parleying, the hero is quite a family man and village favorite. The contrast, not to say the disconnect, between Gideon's tenderness at home and belligerence in the field (the latter a contingency that Ingelow's choice of theme finesses) is not much more jarring in Goalen's hands, admittedly, than in other epoists' who model patriotic heroes on Hector. What is unsettling, in a figure from the Bible, is how seldom and perfunctorily the narrative derives either aspect of Gideon's heroism from God's action upon or within him; how thoroughly, in other words, Goalen has taken his generic bearings from within the descendental horizons of the novel. The question what besides blank verse it might mean—or might take—to turn the matter of Judges 6–8 into an epic poem seems to have provoked this poem's strangest feature, a species of neoclassical personification that had invigorated Romantic epic but slipped from view at some point during the Regency:

> And now again, twin sisters of the light,
> The Dawn demure, enrobed in sober grey,
> And Morn, the blushing queen of loveliness,
> Came hand in hand across the meadows.
>
> (7.144)

The coexistence of this and its like (2.20, 3.45) with passages of straight-up natural description owes less to incompetence (Goalen is not elsewhere a poet grossly awkward) than to a crisis of representation that typified this historical juncture. When "The radiance fades, | The heavens are darkened. Earth puts on a veil, | The silent stars come out" (3.66), are we in the presence of a commonplace metaphor or an obsolete personification? We cannot know how to take "Earth" in this passage because Goalen in the decade after Darwin could not know either. Duly rendering the Lord's attested miracles in books 3 and 4, Goalen at the same time affirms a markedly Victorian uniformitarianism—"In all creation God is manifest—/ In the whole mass of matter, and as well | In the least atom that is held therein" (4.71)—which position, if it does not invalidate miracles, at least ought to render them theologically unremarkable. The poet's indecisiveness over what to believe is matched only by his conviction that belief is decisively necessary, since "reason, without God, | Will drag its owner step by step to hell!" (4.72). The resulting standoff suffices to break down the epic machinery of this else-insignificant poem in an historically telling way.

No such prudent modesty as Ingelow's or such embarrassment of aims as Goalen's stayed the hand of either of the big-screen, spaghetti-epic revivalists who await us next. The first is our Chapter 6 acquaintance Edwin Atherstone, whose *Fall of Nineveh* first breasted the waves in the heyday of Pollok and apocalypse (1828) and, after new installments in 1830 and 1847, beached itself at a full thirty books in the poet's eightieth year 1868. Not long before that date he had issued *Israel in Egypt: A Poem* (1861), a fresh twenty-seven books of wonders out of Exodus. This publishing record deserves mention because, if we except the truly freakish productions of Thomas Hawkins, Atherstone for a quarter-century single-handedly kept alive the British biblical epic tradition—the tradition, that is, of Milton— only to preside in the 1860s over the hectic flush that proved to be its last. The tradition was more robust, as probably was Christianity, in the United States. There it included James McHenry's 1840 *The Antediluvians, or The World Destroyed; A Narrative Poem, in Ten Books*; an anonymous 1857 *Last Judgment* that was published in London but feels American in its obsessive abomination of slavery at so late a date; Hannah King's *Epic Poem* of 1881 on the Mormon conquest, revisionary of course in its sectarian content but in literary form an entirely faithful biblical epic; and, by the way and after long secular mutation, Herman Melville's one major sequel to *Moby-Dick*, the ashen centennial tribute he published in 1876 as *Clarel: A Poem and Pilgrimage in the Holy Land*.

Meanwhile, writing both at the end of his career and at the British terminus of his chosen literary-historical line, Atherstone etched into *Israel in Egypt*, as deeply as the shallowness of his imagination permitted, the very crisis of faith that was superannuating his labors. In an ebullient preface the poet led with his chin. He defends the miraculous with more pugnacity than tact, waiving considerations of petty probability when a poem has seized on "an event conducted by Omnipotence" (xii), while concurrently apologizing for a bit of theologically sentimental fudging that ascribes the hardening of Pharaoh's heart to Satan instead of God (xiv). In support of the former position Atherstone instances Southey's notes to *Roderick*; of the latter,

Bailey's omnism in *Festus*, whose example also authorizes this poem's promise of redemption for any fallen angel who really and truly is sorry (xvi). Previous chapters have suggested what shaky support these epic precursors in fact offer for the orthodox elevation Atherstone pretends to: Bailey's liberal revision of Christianity was hardly scriptural, and Southey's skeptical notes were the very place where that poet's rational mind sought refuge after the binges of credulity that his culture-encyclopedic program required. *Israel in Egypt* begins, then, at a certain disadvantage; but it is in the action proper that the poem betrays the full depth, and the contemporaneity, of its epic desperation. For Atherstone's defense of the faith is literally reactionary, a triumph of damage control that rushes first aid to crisis-points within his own culture. Everything that Moses and his party do is designed to engage and neutralize threats that have arisen on the banks, not of old Nile, but of the nineteenth-century Thames.

As if to substantiate the accusations flung at Victorian unbelievers circa 1860, Satan figures here as a scientific theorist who is prepared to entertain divine omnipotence merely as one hypothesis among others (book 2) and expounds a progressivist principle that will, "doubtless," drive the evolution of all beings "toward godhead" (23.392). His puppet surrogates the priests of Pharaoh share Satan's modern empiricism. Beholding the transformation of Aaron's rod to serpent form and back again, they proceed to dissect the miracle into "reason" and "cause" (book 5); and later a Herbert Spencer in sacerdotal vestments teases out the self-contradiction inhabiting Moses' affirmation of faith (book 15). That this deconstruction is hard to follow is of course part of the point for Atherstone, who like many a former epoist anchors true religion in monolithic bedrock and has Moses declare of God what is also the poem's credo: "His sole will | As cause we know" (6.94). This bald metaphysic, dissolving all resistance to miracle, opens narrative (or dooms it) to unchecked arbitrariness at the hands of Omnipotence. It also makes a fiction of time, as Moses implies at the end of the poem when assuring the Israelites that the emancipation they groan for has already taken place, a *fait accompli* ever since the moment God first spoke to him on Horeb from the burning bush (book 27).

Moses' hearers find this affirmation evidently comforting—if strangely so, since quite other feelings might well arise in a still-suffering nation when told that they are free now because they are going to be (and always were to have been) released at some unspecified later date. It is the narrative corollary of this doctrine that especially concerns us here. Atherstone to be sure is no Heraud, much less a Blake; and his many books, far from defying narrative gravity by means of flashback or hyperlink, plod along in the track of Exodus so suspenselessly that his tribal protagonists, true to title, never do get out of Egypt. Still, the meaning of narrative remains for him sheer supervenience, "sole will" and not the episodic impingement of causes on effects. Likewise for Atherstone the truth of the Bible story, we may infer with an eye on the *Essays and Reviews* controversy for which he obviously had no time, is something instantaneously decreed rather than proven over history: an inference that places theology above refutation, but also places it beyond illustration by forms of narrative logic. Disabling the proof of epic, Atherstone gains a point beyond which it is impossible for the Bible-imitating poem, or for that matter any rendition of the human tale, to proceed. Keeping faith with scriptural religion meant at last, for Atherstone on the darkling plain of the 1860s, breaking faith with the conditions of epic poetry.

Under the strict terms thus outlined, only one further option remained for the orthodox Biblical epic, and that was to slough off the human tale altogether. This option Edwin Henry Bickersteth exercised in 1866, with a resolution worthy of his evangelical-eschatologist father and of the bishop he was to become around the time his long poem went into its seventeenth edition two decades later. For the first thing Bickersteth does in *Yesterday, To-Day, and For Ever* is, with a ruthless thrift whose like we have not met since Townsend's 1815 *Armageddon* (Ch. 6), to kill off his hero. The nameless protagonist-narrator's one act as a man is to take leave of human life, in a recognizable albeit rushed Victorian scenario of deathbed adieux that has him crossing over into the afterlife, and into a kind of spiritualist science fiction, before book 1 is out. So much for To-Day, then, and for the epic connection to this world—were it not that the ensuing vistas of Yesterday (Bible and church history, books 4–8) and For Ever (Bible prophecy, books 9–12) are consistently relayed to us, and insistently filtered, through so unreconstructedly mid-Victorian a consciousness. Bickersteth saw fit, in other words, to equip his faithful Christian's immortal soul after death not only with a pronounced Anglican perspective but with the ordinary likes and dislikes of a middle-class English paterfamilias.

Shorn of personal idiosyncrasy, this altogether conventional narrative persona has no sooner negotiated the valley of the shadow than he settles with parents and predecessors in "that nether Paradise, | That suburb of the New Jerusalem" (2.664–65) where every day is Sunday and they like to

garden. An angel named Oriel (an Oxonian?), having provided a geography
of Hell, narrates history from the Creation to the corruptions of Popery,
parts of which story (books 5 and 7) bear a remarkable likeness to readers'
digests of *Paradise Lost* and *Paradise Regained*, downshifted into a blank verse
that should have been palatable to even the most philistine of Bickersteth's
parishioners. The punctual invention of sarcasm by Lucifer at 5.96 under-
scores by contrast the monochrome tonal values and blandness of taste that
go with the narrator's idea of bliss in a place "all bright with one similitude"
(2.457). His history lesson concluded, he wants for nothing but his earthly-
surviving wife and children, whom the start of book 9 restores to him all
smiles and, unexplainedly, all at once. Bonded from this point into a nuclear
unit that prays together and stays together, the familial I / we of the poem
spend the rest of their time ushering in eternity, as spectators at the finale
Heaven has in store.

This reserved finale is the Apocalypse, Victorian-style: a subgeneric
descendant of the leading epic mode of the 1820s, but distinguished from
Pollok's evangelical urgency by a long generation's habituation to much the
same convenience of consumption that Bickersteth's undemanding verse
grandeur also ministered to.[12] Long shots of a no-contest Armageddon
alternate in books 9 and 10 with an increasingly self-congratulatory con-
sensus among the saved. As this consensus ripples out from the narrator's
family to his church, in an engorgement of "we" and "us," it carries a
soupçon of connubial eroticism that flushes all the crowd of the spectating
faithful with a comely passivity that suits their collective identity as Christ's
beloved bride. The nearest thing to a plot wrinkle takes place as Satan and
his crew, seemingly touched by the melting mood and set free to enjoy
"millennial Sabbath" (10.540), institute a utopia founded on electrification
and world government. But this worldly millennium is only the Millen-
nium, of course. So it is just a matter of time before the storm of Last
Judgment breaks on its false Satanic calm: "Now we beheld the secret
springs of ill | Which moved the mighty drama of the world" (11.684–85).

Bickersteth leans so hard on the doctrinal and scripturally warranted
difference between the disclosed New Jerusalem of book 12 and the worldly

---

[12] Wheeler, *Heaven, Hell, and The Victorians,* 90–101 and 175–78, provides a long-suffering tour
of the plot, with comparisons to Pollok and Bailey, and with particular attention to Bickersteth's
devices for sustaining suspense. Milbank, *Dante and the Victorians,* 168–69, sees how the poet's
"extremely positive view of the intermediate state" between death and judgment, and his "desire
to reproduce the Cappadocian theology of a progressive heaven," engender in the central books of
the epic what amounts to "a celestial package tour."

Millennium of book 11, one suspects, because it was a difference that he could not create poetically. His ideal of bliss is an exponentially boosted suburban domesticity, a multitude in armchairs rapt by visionary wonderment.[13] This ideal rings tinnily false to us, of course, because technology has so nearly realized it, not in heaven but in our living rooms. It is shocking to find that already in the 1860s Satan's socio-electronic fix was an ideal—TV, UN, and all—that even a reverend epoist could not imagine his way past. The trouble, for Bickersteth as for Atherstone, was a version of the dilemma we found paralyzing Sydney Dobell in *Balder* (Ch. 9), though neither 1860s epoist seems to have recognized it as such: namely, that the preter narrative eternal now that they sought to render had nevertheless to be experienced from some discrete vantage. For Atherstone and Bickersteth alike that vantage proved to be the Victorian present. The nineteenth century's apogee served as both the summit of the past and the platform of a regenerate ambition, no longer just to colonize the planet, but in this instance to people, and presumably suburbanize, the stars (12.607–14).

To minds that were more modern, or just plain younger, the edematous straight-ahead 1860s epic plainly called for satiric cautery. The decade found its lesser W. E. Aytoun in W. J. Courthope, a young man just out of Oxford who would end the century there as a Pope scholar, literary historian, and Professor of Poetry in the chair Matthew Arnold had once occupied. Courthope made an early, irreverent mark with *Ludibria Lunae; or, The Wars of the Women and the Gods: An Allegorical Burlesque* (1869), four books of *ottava rima* reduced to tetrameter gauge. Cut back from Byron in every way, this critical *jeu d'esprit* brands by very terseness the swollen tissues it critiques in the epics around it. The waspish misogyny of its *Princess*-indebted plot comes to culmination, for us, on a page that rhymes "Idyll" with "fiddle" and "unriddle," and spotlights by express mention the marital scene of Ingelow's *Story of Doom* as the way *not* to "open an epic" (4.128–29).

---

[13] At just this time Bickersteth published what were probably sermons he had been preaching in Hampstead on creature comforts in the beyond: *Hades and Heaven; or, What Does Scripture Reveal of the State and Employments of the Blessed Dead and of the Risen Saints* (New York: Carter, 1869). Heaven, his studies reveal, "is a state of eternal rest and refreshment.... This rest and this refreshment are often described under the figure of reclining at a banquet.... And yet it is by no means easy always to discern what is to be taken figuratively and what literally in these descriptions of glory.... Why should we not take our Lord's words literally?" (81–82). "I once tried to call to my recollection all the happiest scenes of earth.... I found that in every case Holy Scripture had appropriated the figure" (116).

Clearly the crossing of a grand manner on an ordinary subject touched a nerve: to write like that, Courthope felt, was to mock epic, so a proper mock-epic was prescribed that took direct aim at Jean Ingelow, winged Coventry Patmore, and glanced at greater things in the Tennyson of the 1859 *Idylls*.

Mention of the *Idylls* will remind us of another para-epic genre, the verse-novel, whose full history merits another book, but of which this book has taken cursory note.[14] Developed in prototype during the later eighteenth century and then suspended during the war years of the early nineteenth, the verse-novel had been refined after Waterloo by Eleanor Porden, Tom Moore, and Leigh Hunt, until the post-Byronic epic 1820s blew it out of reach again. In the 1830s Sarah Stickney Ellis and Alexander Ross started the form up again in raw earnest, and as if from scratch; their efforts while graceless showed that silvery Regency charm was not the only accompaniment by which sustained narratives of daily life might take shape in verse. In another generation the respective passes of Barrett Browning and Tennyson from and toward the verse-novel tilled a field that lesser poets of the 1860s could cultivate. Several did so in ways that register, on one hand, the modernizing pressure *from* prose fiction to which all epicizing must henceforth at some level respond, and, on the other hand, the conformist pressure *within* prose fiction to which epic's resources offered an alternative or escape.

Bulwer-Lytton's son Edward Robert, who published under the pseudonym "Owen Meredith" and returns in force a chapter hence, was the most dedicated verse-novelist of the lot. His first effort in this vein was the best because the most adroitly opportunistic. Something wild survived in *Lucile* (1860) from early Dickens and Thackeray, at a time when the prose novel in their hands and others' had grown serious under its load of public responsibilities: the author has a tentative yet zany way of poking around the confines of genre that, remembering Byron, remembers too the epic that *Lucile* is decidedly not. True, the poem's two six-canto parts make up a canonical dozen; but then a parody invocation at the midpoint (2.1) makes such epic proportioning seem a studied joke. *Lucile* on the other hand makes free likewise with the conventions of mainstream fiction. Versatile—and

---

[14] See the complementary considerations of this genre by Dino Felluga, "Verse Novel," in *A Companion to Victorian Poetry*, ed. Richard Cronin, Alison Chapman, and Antony Harrison (Oxford: Blackwell, 2002) 171–86; and Rod Edmond, *Affairs of the Hearth: Victorian Poetry and Domestic Narrative* (London and New York: Routledge, 1988) 31–37.

verse-agile, too, although the poet confessed to his Florence mentors the Brownings what a hard time he had keeping its skipping anapests in check— the narrative plays around the edges of fiction's consecrated marriage plot. He invokes hierogamy after the manner of *Aurora Leigh* (1.4, 1.5, 2.4), a poem he hugely admired.[15] But he does so only to toy with the convention and so concede how indecorous it is that the chance for a marriage made in heaven should knock thrice in a lifetime, and even then be squandered. At the end the novel-like contretemps of domestic affections is reconciled only by surrogation, and at great distance in generational time and geopolitical space. It is on the plains of Inkerman that Duc Eugène, the indecisively corrupt modern who is our leading man, finally meets the lost and ever-ambiguous Lucile, reappearing now in middle age as Soeur Séraphine, nursing nun to the Crimean wounded. Here Lucile wins, not Eugène, but his consent to a match between his niece and the heroically convales-cent son of their old flames and foils from cantos past—a solution that the novel needs but the poem doesn't quite credit.

A verse-novel more scoffingly incredulous came two years later from the young Alfred Austin. Emerging now from the 1850s anonymity of his adolescent *Randolph*, Austin by the end of the century would be Victoria's last laureate, and would along the way qualify himself for that office by substantially expanding his 1862 work in an 1876 version that recalibrated and indeed sanitized its original tone. *The Human Tragedy: A Poem* is the title he gave to what was in its initial substance and manner a satirical narrative, rendered "tragic" as yet only by a certain hectoring pathos that counter-poises its prevalent cynicism about the hypocrisy of modern living. (The 1876 version would embody, and an 1889 preface articulate, a proper theory of tragedy, to be considered in the next chapter.) Possessing neither the trenchancy of George Meredith's work in verse and prose nor the lapidary gravitas of FitzGerald's *Rubáiyát*, Austin's poem nevertheless belongs in the company of these contemporaries, and deserves mention here for having put mid-Victorian alienation into a narratorially aggressive (and digressive) reprise of the Byronic *ottava rima*. The vein of contemporary satire that Austin worked in non-narrative poems like *The Season* (1869) and *The Golden Age* (1871) was welcomed by reviewers eager to support a revival of manly candor; and when Austin attacked Browning the elder poet hit

---

[15] In Owen Meredith's view Barrett Browning had written "not only the solitary epic of this age, but also a noble epic—I think not inferior to those of Milton and Dante" (quoted in Gardner B. Taplin, *The Life of Elizabeth Barrett Browning* (New Haven: Yale University Press, 1957) 311.

back by calling Austin, with some justice, a "banjo-Byron" (*Pacchiarotto*, 1876). The 1862 *Human Tragedy* was, in fact, the hardiest nineteenth-century imitation in English of *Don Juan*, made safe again after forty years in generic quarantine for use by the likes of Austin and Courthope in expressing a newly world-weary generation's flippant angst. The very plot treads like Byron's on adulterous ground to which British prose fiction would not dare trust its full weight for years to come.

Novels in verse could handle culturally hazardous material (like adultery and cynicism) because the foregroundedness of poetic form put more distance between the reader and that material than did the comparative transparency of fictional prose. This distance, like correlative differences in the size and social distribution of audience, both narrowed the appeal of verse narrative and amplified its resonance. For poetry as a medium had not lost the ceremonial aura that had suited it for millennia to public occasions and still conferred public applicability on the matters it treated. When Courthope's *Ludibria Lunae* reproved epic deviancy in the form of a poem rather than a review essay, the form he chose enlarged his subject and thus advanced his point. Even the gesture that shrugged off seriousness, as Byron knew and Austin recalled, was a gesture that verse tended to lift beyond the personal towards the collective.

No one grasped this more instructively than Thomas Woolner, perhaps because he came to the verse-novel on furlough from an eminent sculptor's career and had an eye for the cultural valences of artistic media. *My Beautiful Lady* (1863) enacts in its proportions the enlargement of significance that this friend of Tennyson and quondam Pre-Raphaelite Brother clearly expected poetry to effect. (Early lyric pieces of the uncompleted poem had first appeared in 1850 in the first, manifesto number of the PRB organ *The Germ*.) Parts 1 and 2, in stanzas deriving from *Maud*, register the death of the speaker's betrothed and record the heavenly consolation she sends to lighten his mourning and sanctify his reengagement with the world. Then a concluding part 3, dated ten years later, expands in blank-verse pentameter to fill out this lyric movement of personal conversion with a narrative background that generalizes its import. Only at this ultimate, post-lyrical stage of the poem does the speaker's identity emerge—he is an Anglo-Indian returned home to South Asia for the empire's greater good—in conjunction with vistas of global travel, a telescoped pocket-size history of the British nation (3.454–535), and a quasi-Tennysonian diffusion of prophetic reference that both is, and isn't, really about investments and steam engines. "Sobered interest bent on vaster ends" will fuse a Victorian colonist's duty "with the sum of general power | Which is the living world" (3.596–602): while such talk does not make an epic of Woolner's verse-novel any more than it did of Tennyson's elegy *In Memoriam*, its reverberant vagueness marks out a generic undertow that draws the poem epic's way.

With the exception of *Aurora Leigh*, none of the verse-novels we have sampled from Ellis's *Sons of the Soil* forward ends where Victorian prose fiction was supposed to end, with the prospect of a long-awaited marriage between principals. Not that they are unhappy tales: instead, they find happiness elsewhere than at the altar, usually on the high road of collective betterment that branches upslope from any local impediment and that beckons the more clearly, perhaps, when individual desire goes unfulfilled. Thus the verse-novel found fuel in the stuff of fiction for a group sublimation designed, as Woolner has it in a candid figure, "To swell the general hive" (3.546), where devotion to the common good sweetens the novel-defying celibacy of the individual worker-bee. The consistently secular object of this sublimation distinguishes the 1860s verse-novel more sharply even than modernity of subject matter does from the contemporary biblical epic, whose strategy of collective enlargement it in other respects shares. In the verse-novel, what amplifies the significance of ordinary incidents is a figurality which is like scripture's, but in which the promised this-worldly antitype will come to pass thanks to nothing more (or less) metaphysical than the immanent logic of history. Woolner's imperializing diffusiveness suffices to show that the verse-novel could be at least as abstract as a Bible epic in its long reach after meaning. Maybe it had to be even more so, given the uneasy conjunction between British nation and empire in the later nineteenth century, and the want of a fixed figural tradition like that of Christianity for making historical meanings specific.

These reflections may help explain why the last and most concertedly novel-like of the lesser verse narratives to be discussed here should be the most politically engaged, and why the scene of its engagement should be Ireland. In *Laurence Bloomfield in Ireland: A Modern Poem* (1864), the Anglo-Irishman William Allingham gave the public twelve "chapters" of thoroughly serviceable rhyming couplets, in which a good-natured and right-minded young landlord develops, through exposure to the material sufferings and political temptations besetting the Irish poor, a vision of gradualist prosperity that he puts into practice on his own holdings. The formal choice of couplets, loosely cut here for casual wear, fosters Allingham's evenhanded social vision by accustoming the reader to balance and trim between alternatives. A similar training awaited the poem's first readers when it appeared in twelve monthly parts during 1862–63 in *Fraser's Magazine*, which had been the domain of that epicizing Irish serialist William Maginn (see our Ch. 8) and which Allingham went on to edit a decade later. Serial publication obliged readers of the poem to live in months-long discomfort with the central chapters, where the hard-fistedness of absentee owners and their land agents drives the young tenant Neal Doran into the conclaves, and clutches, of extremist "Ribbonmen" (Fenians). Having become their pawn and provocateur, Neal is saved from the severity of the police only by Laurence Bloomfield's refusal to name names: in the tenth chapter his burning a list of incendiary agents that has come into his hands inaugurates publically a new era of trust between classes and peoples, and some measure of economic justice to go with it. Two final chapters overleap seven years to show Laurence's fields abloom with the promise of fruitfulness, political as well as agricultural, for a renovated Ireland.

W. B. Yeats, who detested the poem, called *Laurence Bloomfield* a failed epic. This is a judgment consistent with Yeats's hatred of liberalism as neither traditional nor radical enough; still, one would like to know how far the charges he had in mind may have been formal ones. Allingham made fun of himself in private for attempting "A story in 5000 lines, | Where Homer's epic fervour shines," and also in print when a late chapter commences, "Alas, you count me a prosaic bard, | Good reader," petitions Chaucer in vain, and complains that dragons and knights are easier to sing than "a single pig" or "one policeman" (10.1–16).[16] Chaucer may not hear him, but the reader does—and hears, through this appeal, the echo of invocations past. Passages like this one, or like the epical periphrasis on a peat bog at 4.341–45, prompt a wider curiosity why a poet who divides his work into chapters not books should nevertheless present exactly twelve of them; or why the twelfth's enlightened vision of prosperity under law should so neatly correspond to the sixth, which patronizes Neal Doran's uneducated susceptibility to dangerous sentimental claptrap about Irish origins (the irritated Yeats's stock in trade, we recall).

---

[16] Allingham's unpublished verses are quoted in Linda K. Hughes, "The Poetics of Empire and Resistance: William Allingham's *Laurence Bloomfield in Ireland*," *Victorian Poetry* 28 (1990) 105. Hughes also contemplates the effect that serial issue had on the original readership.

What is traditional in the structure of the poem encourages us to read chapters 6 and 12 against each other, respectively as underworld descent and mountaintop vista, and furthermore makes it hard to accept Allingham's ideologically motivated wish that the meliorist finale replace the insurrectionary middle as a rendition of Ireland's good. For one thing, epic's association of excavation with prophecy, its custom of burrowing into the past to find a future out, registers a firm archaeological protest from below against the good Bloomfield's cultural overhaul. For another—and here the poetic form brings us closest to leading 1860s concerns—the structural overlay of chapters 6 and 12 proposes not a supersession of myth by truth but a struggle between myth and myth. "Since dumb her school-books upon Ireland's tale, | Other and looser teaching must prevail" (6.29–30): this, Allingham's critique of the colonist's neglect of educational responsibilities, may well provoke doubt in spirits less staunch than Yeats as to whether classroom history can or ought to beat "every wild-sprung legendary rill" (32).

Besides, this verse-novel's obvious status as itself a kind of "looser teaching" than is furnished in the schools saps its own truth claim—a circumstance that may underlie two peculiar narrative lacunae. The first, lost in the seven-year leap between chapters 10 and 11, omits from the story the very process of transformation from old to new order that the poem, as a piece of advocacy, stands for. As with *Prometheus Unbound* and *News from Nowhere*, we arrive in Utopia we know not how; but to mention those radically revolutionary texts is to appreciate the strangeness of the elision here, in a text that, like any historical "school-book" one can suppose Allingham would approve, advocates stepwise reform precisely on the grounds that it is practicable and not just visionary. Presumably such pragmatism was what led two former radicals around this time to make epicizing gestures of reform. In his 1860 *Corayda: A Tale of Faith and Chivalry* the Chartist apostate Ernest Jones, apparently overturning every position espoused not long before in *The Revolt of Hindostan* (Ch. 9) called out for police suppression of rabble-rousing "spirits wild," who "Cried to the masses dream-beguiled" (2.3.58–60). And when Capel Lofft brought his long-closeted and incendiary *Ernest* to book at last in 1868 (Ch. 7), it was newly subtitled not *Political Regeneration* but *The Rule of Right*, in a moralizing overhaul newly based on the Gospel rather than reason.

The second lacuna within *Laurence Bloomfield in Ireland* is on a different order, and more troubling: at no point does the poem so much as refer to the Great Hunger of the 1840s. This silence reduces exponentially the poem's estimate of the magnitude of Anglo-Irish oppression, through deeds omitted as well as committed, during the supposed lifetime of its protagonist. The agronomic and moral calculus of redress is thus skewed beyond belief; or, again, it is exposed as imaginary rather than pragmatic after all. This most sanely and continuously narrated of 1860s verse-novels proves, then, as mythopoeic as the rest. Allingham resorts to myths of the folk and the soil, not as a structural substrate for corroborative details of a realist-fictional kind, but as a deceptive substitute for these things—an artifice exposed now in retrospect by his evasion of historically crucial matter that, were it narratable at all, would have tasked an imagination fully epic.[17]

The generic context this chapter has set up should make it possible to understand, and even admire, one of the most conspicuously neglected major works left behind by any Victorian writer of the first rank. When George Eliot published *The Spanish Gypsy* in 1868 she was a highly regarded author with four important novels behind her and with the two that have seemed to subsequent critics her greatest, *Middlemarch* and *Daniel Deronda*, yet in store. Given the place *The Spanish Gypsy* holds along this arc of development, it is remarkable how little attention the work has received from Eliot's commentators, who as a group not only regard it as a failure but do not find its failure interesting. To suspect something aversive if not phobic about such a conspiracy of silence can be a first step toward appreciating the poem's strangeness. That it is an alien within the Eliot oeuvre has seldom been in doubt since publisher John Blackwood mailed off his nonplussed billets-doux of fluttery support ("the Great Poem," "a grand thing") during the months prior to publication, then put it in his 1868

---

[17] As Isobel Armstrong points out, Allingham's final books have to fall back on "a rather unconvincing pastoral gesture of hope": *Victorian Poetry: Poetry, Poetics and Politics* (London and New York: Routledge, 1993) 203. Pastoral hope, we recall from Ch. 4, had been the original and in proof quite strenuous mode of Wordsworth's *Excursion*; and the literary standardization of that affect, of which *Laurence Bloomfield* is a symptom, is a dominant circumstance in the Victorian canonization of Wordsworth that makes *The Excursion* so hard to recover at full strength even now. Witness the *bourge-wannabe* admiration that an expatriate aristocrat like Ivan Turgenev expressed for Allingham's vision of Ireland. The same modality of response was alive and well in the 1930s appreciation by B. Ifor Evans, who found *Laurence Bloomfield* "a sudden and refreshing example of cool eighteenth-century verse amid the more perfervid styles of the late nineteenth century": *English Poetry in the Later Nineteenth Century* (London: Methuen, 1933) 109, where Turgenev is cited.

list, as Eliot promptly complained, "below Pollock's [*sic*] Course of Time, where it would hardly strike any one who was not in search of it."[18] But how *The Spanish Gypsy* is strange, and why, are in fact interesting matters, which our generic bias here opens to pursuit.

Although it belonged rather above Pollok's evangelical bestseller than below, we can begin by agreeing that Blackwood had marketed Eliot's "grand thing" in the right bin. Whether we look to the form of *The Spanish Gypsy* or to its formidable vision of human realities, it is a decisively epic work.[19] A showcase of literary genres, it combines prose with poetry, pageantry with meditation, dramatic byplay with arias of introspective discovery, an exact and scholarly lyricism with (framing the whole and shaping the very form of its intelligence) long sweeps of rhetorically majestic, metaphysically pointed blank-verse description in an omniscient third person. Everything in this anthology of kinds bends, moreover, to the disciplined singleness of aim that epic omniscience enforces. Each speech furthers its scene; each scene folds into, not its theatrical act, but its narrative "Book"; each book fills its place in voluminous proof of the inevitability of a manifest destiny that is tribal and national at once. Gypsy and Jew and Christian and Moor alike find their identities and acts biologically foredoomed—and culturally policed, for good measure, within the embattled and racially polarized climate of Eliot's chosen milieu in late-fifteenth-century Spain.[20] There is no more ethical freeplay under this manifold

[18] Blackwood's flatteries date from December 1867, Eliot's riposte from a year later: *The George Eliot Letters*, ed. Gordon S. Haight (New Haven: Yale University Press, 1954–78) 4: 403, 407, 492.

[19] Bernard Semmel, *George Eliot and the Politics of National Inheritance* (New York and Oxford: Oxford University Press, 1994), repeatedly calls the poem "epic" (18, 98, 102, 107) by virtue of its probing after "a realistic foundation for communal solidarity" (6). The literary counterpart to this social foundation is the platform that epic offers to the lesser genres it supports. Thus Joss West-Burnham reads the work rightly, yet incompletely, as a "poetic drama" and Fedalma's choice as a renunciation preponderantly empowering: "Fedalma—'The Angel of a Homeless Tribe': Issues of Religion, Race and Gender in George Eliot's Poetic Drama, *The Spanish Gypsy*," in *Women of Faith in Victorian Culture: Reassessing the Angel in the House*, ed. Anne Hogan and Andrew Bradstock (Houndmills: Macmillan, 1998) 78–90. On the epic qualities renunciation held for Eliot see Kenny Marotta, "*Middlemarch*: 'The Home Epic,' " *Genre* 15 (1982) 403–20; Victor Neufeldt, "The Madonna and the Gypsy," *Studies in the Novel* 15 (1983) 44–54; James Krasner, " 'Where No Man Praised': The Retreat from Fame in George Eliot's *The Spanish Gypsy*," *Victorian Poetry* 32 (1994) 55–73.

[20] See Michael Ragussis, *Figures of Conversion: "The Jewish Question" and English National Identity* (Durham and London: Duke University Press, 1995) 153: "In choosing fifteenth-century Spain, Eliot selected what had become for the nineteenth century a kind of historical laboratory in which experiments on the question of race could be performed." Armstrong, *Victorian Poetry*, 370, notes what a census of racial hybrids the poem boasts, in furtherance of its internal critique of an "ugly racism" and affirmation of (though this does sound like special pleading better suited to *Romola*) "a powerfully imaginative national myth about unity and cohesion, a matriarchal myth."

fatality than there is slack in the poet's strenuous lines of verse or of plot. The entire sequence of events exhausts a set of variations on one theme: Heredity Equals Destiny.

The theme rings out most plainly in the long book 1, which occupies almost half the poem. In its pages Eliot effects the transformation of Fedalma, an accomplished beauty on the verge of marriage to the Hidalgo duke of Bedmár, from an enraptured fiancée into the doomed and exiled princess of an obscure tribe of Gypsy "Zíncali" now leagued with the Moors in contest against the Spaniards she has grown up among. For Atherstone or Ingelow so improbable a reversal would have been a simple function of providentialist algebra. Within the densely realized historical milieu that Eliot establishes, however, it taxes credulity; indeed, it flat-out breaks the bank in the estimation of many an affronted critic since Leslie Stephen, who pronounced the heroine a "lunatic." But to pronounce thus is to misjudge the work by invoking the canons of the novel.[21] What makes Fedalma's amazing change possible—makes it irresistible, within the terms the poem sets up—is her fully text-endorsed conviction that the change is not the metamorphosis it seems but a restorative conformation to her true identity.

In the public square Fedalma responds, twice over, to a summons in the blood: first when she performs a graceful, all but involuntary dance to certain ethnically vagrant strains of music, then when she is riveted to the spot by the recognizant gaze of the fettered Zíncalo leader who is, she and we are about to learn, her unremembered father Zarca. In a sense all the sequel is a working-out of the consequences, from confusion through resistance to acceptance, of these precognitive bodily alignments.[22] Taken thus unawares—in a symmetric, reversed reprise of her forgotten kidnapping by the Christians when a tiny child—Fedalma finds it too late, given the

---

[21] Stephen's insanity verdict for Fedalma arraigns Eliot for failure "to imagine the actual state of things," trying the work in effect as a novel: *George Eliot* (London and New York: Macmillan, 1902) 164. Frederic Harrison, stung in *Studies in Early Victorian Literature* (London: Edward Arnold, 1895) by what seemed a portrait of Comtean positivism gone bad, had anticipated Stephen's judgment: "George Eliot made a cruel mistake in writing the *Spanish Gypsy* as a poem, when she might have written it as an historical romance ... much superior to *Romola*" (221). The generic tables are turned by Felicia Bonaparte in *The Triptych and the Cross: The Central Myths of George Eliot's Poetic Imagination* (New York: New York University Press, 1979) 5: "It is precisely because *Romola* is a poem that it has always displeased us most. ... Most of what we have taken to be the failures of Eliot's realism are in fact, the triumphs of her poetry."

[22] Armstrong proposes that the dance scene vindicates cultural production rather than nature in the blood: "it may be the 'strain' of music which determines the racial 'strain' of community, rather than the other way round" (*Victorian Poetry*, 372).

heroic integrity that drives her character, to put up any defense against the father's insistence that she own the claims of birth. To adopt a Zíncala identity and lead her people to their appointed North African home is simply to become what she always was.

The majestic simplicity of this ethnic-epic theme engenders its counterpoint in the story of Fedalma's betrothed, Don Silva, whose parallel plot of identity-confirmation ripples with heightening tempo through the next three books of the poem. This narrative acceleration renders the comparative complexity of his position: as a man, and one moreover to the manor born, he moves in a richer web of allegiances and antagonisms than Fedalma has known. This texture of relations is sufficiently varied to set Don Silva up as Eliot's lay figure for the modern individual doubled in liberal self-consciousness against himself. The man who has everything naturally thinks he has options, an opinion of which books 2–4 ruthlessly disabuse first Eliot's reader, and finally the man himself. For Don Silva sets out to prove his freedom by renouncing his high station and becoming a Zíncalo by adoption and electing a group affinity that secures him the right to his love. For Fedalma's sake, and by a maneuver as seemingly voluntary as hers has seemed compulsory, he becomes what she is: the poem's *other* Spanish Gypsy.[23] It all comes to nothing, of course, just as the Jewish astrologer Sephardo has implied (2.142–52) and the incredulous Zarca has insisted (3.206–14) it must. Once the Zíncali have spearheaded a sanguinary raid on Silva's own town, the blood comes out in every sense. Don Silva forswears his chosen ethnicity ("No, I'm no Zíncalo!") and reasserts his given one ("I am a Catholic knight, | A Spaniard who will die a Spaniard's death!" 4.245), wounding the undefended Zarca mortally in an act of loyalty/ treason that marks him off from all further political exercise while only eliciting a renewal of Fedalma's racial promise, made ironclad now as she breathes it to a dying parent.

So, but for a rethematizing coda to which we shall return, runs the plot of this unpleasing poem. No wonder it has affronted those who love the novels of George Eliot: disowning the terms of mainstream Victorian fiction is this epic's most systematic business. Limitation of space forbids enumerating the length and depth of detail to which *The Spanish Gypsy* goes in order to contravene the rules of bourgeois realism, but their measure is impressive.

---

[23] Eliot's preference of the present title over the working title *Fedalma* draws out this narrative chiasmus. See her 4 April 1868 explanation to Blackwood, in *Letters* 4: 428.

Time and again Eliot itemizes particulars of common life that seem to cry out for a gloss from *Adam Bede*, only to caption them like exhibits in an ethnographic museum subordinating free description to ranked and racialized prescription: thus "The little Pepe," present for Juan's *cancion* in the courtyard, becomes an epic player by virtue of his "small Semitic nose, | Complete and tiny as a new-born minnow," while nearby "the rats and insects peeped, | Being southern Spanish ready for a lounge" (1.32–33). Scenes like this are especially frequent in book 1, where they constitute an inventory of all that Fedalma is to renounce for an epic vocation, and Silva to throw away in lofty scorn of any vocation that is imposed rather than chosen by his own free will. Such details of daily living all fall under Eliot's master comment:

> So the dire hours
> Burthened with destiny—the death of hopes
> Darkening long generations, or the birth
> Of thoughts undying—such hours sweep along
> In their aërial ocean measureless
> Myriads of little joys.
>
> (5.257)

To see how the enjambed meta-metrical pun "measureless" belongs equally to the noun before it and the noun after is to reaffirm the priority Eliot accords to the epic flow of events and also to appreciate her grasp of the resources of poetry for making that flow felt bodily—much as Fedalma feels the music in book 1, and as her father, spurning the petty "round of personal loves," exults in "the beats | Of that large music rolling o'er the world" (3.193).[24] Allegorizing the hegemony of epic, such passages may also figure the author's habitual conversion of prose drafts into verse as she wrote *The Spanish Gypsy*, and with it the process whereby her fragmentary dramatic script of 1864 was "rewritten and amplified" (so an 1868 prefatory note put it) in the hybrid narrative medium she developed for its publication. The opening of book 3 showcases that medium's properties and powers:

> Quit now the town, and with a journeying dream
> Swift as the wings of sound, yet seeming slow

---

[24] Neil Roberts observes how "the massive and unidirectional movement of water frequently signifies epic valorization and simplification in George Eliot," in "Epic and Novel in George Eliot," in *Face to Face: Bakhtin in Russia and the West*, ed. Carol Adlam *et al.* (Sheffield: Sheffield Academic Press, 1997) 301.

> Through multitudinous pulsings of stored sense
> And spiritual space, see walls and towers
> Lie in the silent whiteness of a trance.

(3.169)

Vision, sound, kinesthesia, and a few lines later "Scent" are all enlisted within the "stored sense" that is printed verse: a multiplex medium that moves on sound and with the speed of story. To compare the set piece these lines introduce with the prose "Proem" to *Romola* is to appreciate at once the epic consistency of Eliot's ambition and her attraction here to the different flexibility of verse.[25]

Attraction to verse's austerity too. The palpable sublation of seeming-spontaneous detail into fixed poetic design reproves the deliberate scatter whereby novels classically conscript the quotidian as a sign of the real. But to the novel-reader this must seem a minor infraction beside the major offense it portends, which is the scandal *The Spanish Gypsy* offers to modern liberalism's root identification of authenticity with the maintenance of individual freedom. Systematic discrediting of that liberal ideal is the chief negative labor this epic performs, and its performance centers as we have suggested on the character of Don Silva, whose case deserves a closer look. A "thought-propelled" (1.55) Renaissance-humanist believer in what Sephardo calls "naked manhood" (2.142) and "the pale abstract, Man" (2.152), this proudly impulsive heir to Visigoths (and squeaky-clean Victorian heir to the rougher guilt of Southey's Don Roderick) desires equally, and contradictorily, the exercise of an aristocrat's birthright privilege and of an enlightened human right to slough off that privilege, along with "all prejudice | Of man's long heritage" (4.220). The products of this contradiction come in twos: first, the "tortured double self" (1.63), the "self | That is not one" (2.129), which Don Silva betrays in every scene; then, at narrative length, the pattern of conversion and apostasy that structures books 3 and 4. Eliot exposes Silva's flawed project "to cancel all ancestral hate" (3.206) as a gamble—more reckless than noble in any sense but that of

---

[25] Gordon S. Haight, *George Eliot: A Biography* (Oxford and New York: Oxford University Press, 1968), narrates from the author's journal her travails over the choice of genre and medium (378–79, 402–3). For Neil Hertz, *George Eliot's Pulse* (Stanford: Stanford University Press, 2003) 12–13, the "two registers" in which the novelist chiefly works—"of world history and of individual consciousness"—come precariously together in "an ambivalently figured pulsation attributed both to the vulnerable individual recipient of force and to the forceful impulses themselves." Arguably verse gave to this fragile conjunction an artistic–material grounding, for Eliot as more conspicuously for Hardy in *The Dynasts*.

social rank—undertaken to demonstrate his rights for all the world (and not least himself) to see. The way he tries on a Zíncalo identity for size makes one suspect he long ago picked Fedalma out for his intended in much the same way, so as to advertise his freedom of choice as such.

In its historically precocious extravagance this modern, liberal, cosmopolitan aspiration is one that *The Spanish Gypsy* crushes with every means at its disposal.[26] "Silva had but rebelled—he was not free" (4.241), declares the epic narrator with great explicitness, just before the Don's Spanish blood and Christian allegiance reassert themselves in a parricide that is liberticide as well. The very vacillation and "twofold mind" (4.223) that have seemed to betoken a free man's options are undone by an historicism that presents Don Silva as the emblem of that pivotal turn of the sixteenth century (which Eliot read, here as in *Romola*, as mirror to her own era) when new discovery called old authority in question. The poem begins with an analytic historical overview (1.5–11) placing Silva as the creature of his cultural moment: half lord half libertine, never less than haughty-minded, and the plaything throughout of a fate whose daintiest trick is diffusing among an intellectual elite the illusion of their freedom. For, as Eliot's "Notes on the Spanish Gypsy and Tragedy in General" put it with ruthlessly subtle monism, "Even in cases of just antagonism to the narrow view of hereditary claims, the whole background of the particular struggle is made up of our inherited nature."[27]

Adjoining this deconstruction of free choice is Eliot's tragic affirmative in the person of Fedalma, who learns in all of five minutes during book 1 to renounce Don Silva, him "Who chose me—whom I choose" (1.116), and to say instead, "Father, I choose!" (1.119). The remaining action consistently represents this choice of obedience as a dignifying enlargement of Fedalma's character. Her moral victory is dramatically reenacted in book 3 when, compelled to choose afresh between suitor and parent, Spanish and Gypsy futures, "her choice was made. | . . . | Slowly she moved to choose sublimer pain" (3.209). Part of this sublimer pain is that Fedalma, having been resettled into and then torn from two contending cultures, must repeat her commitment hourly. Unlike the naïve cultural belonging of her father

---

[26] This is the point on which Anna K. Nardo, *George Eliot's Dialogue with John Milton* (Columbia and London: University of Missouri Press, 2003) 7–13, shows Eliot concentrating the pressure of her 1860s rereading of *Paradise Lost*. An allusive pattern marks Don Silva's rebellion as the fruitless Satanic choice of (the) Renaissance man.

[27] *George Eliot's Life as Related in Her Letters and Journals*, ed. J. W. Cross (New York: Harper, 1885) 3: 30.

("I choose not—I *am* Zarca" 1.108) or of the Gypsy girl Hinda, whose Gypsy "life is one web" (3.198), Fedalma's Zíncala identity is the stuff of sentimental epic in Schiller's sense of that adjective: consciously modern, resolute and sorrowing in equal and codependent measure. A network of images spanning the poem renders this identity as a genetic code branded into the body—that is how its racialism impinges on individual character— yet its moral sublimity, and accompanying tragic power, belong to the iron that duty deposits not in bodies but in souls. This is clearest in a passage anatomizing Silva's doomed postulation of "a right | Contemning that hereditary right | Which held dim habitation in his frame" (4.221). Eliot's severe confiscation of Silva's cherished discourse of "rights" keeps the "frame" here from being just the body and makes "hereditary" mean more than "biological," even as she locates the springs of human action well below the operative reach of humanist reason and argument.

Indeed, human action itself in the conventional epic sense falls increasingly away as the narrative drives toward denouement. With her father's death Fedalma loses what small confidence he has lent her about the prospect that their Zíncali will ever reach any promised land. Concurrently Don Silva attains his finest moral hour when he preemptively discredits any forgiveness on Fedalma's part that might efface the asperity of the real (5.260: "For you must see me ever as I am") and likewise forswears on his own account all acts of "even expiation—poor pretence, | Which changes nought" (5.264). What abides instead is as full a reprise as the Victorian era can show of Wordsworth's matured epic vision from *The Excursion* (Ch. 4), grounded in the continuity of sorrow across time and of sympathy between the afflicted. Fedalma's exemplary capacity to be "Stabbed with your pain" (1.103) opens a Virgilian connection to "the sadness of the world | Rebuking her" (1.53); her subsequent refusal to "shrink | Back into bliss" (1.119) lets her "stand firm on certainty of woe" (3.194).

This motif of pain sustained and shared both grounds the ethos of *The Spanish Gypsy* and—another way of putting the same point—guarantees its diachronic totality, as what Eliot's "Notes" called "a symbol of the part which is played in the general human lot by hereditary conditions in the largest sense, and of the fact that what we call duty is entirely made up of such conditions."[28] Moreover, this same fusion of duty with history models an affective concept of social relatedness that descends, even as it differs,

[28] *Life*, ed. Cross, 3: 30.

from the matured epics of Scott and Blake. There the dialectic of crime and guilt wielded a cultural force that plots involving forgiveness were formally tasked to cope with. Here, on the cusp of the Second Reform Bill and at the verge of Britain's full imperialist flowering, guilt abides as nobody's fault in particular, and forgiveness is displaced—deferred in one sense, in another preempted—by an ethic of sympathy without end. The vital influence for Eliot is, again, and in ways that study of her novels alone makes hard to see, that of Wordsworth.[29]

Waiving reconciliations of a gentler or more closure-giving sort, both Eliot's principals end in a condition of literal despair that touches the tragic vision with its own kind of nobility: purged of hope, they may stay "true | To high allegiance, higher than our love" (5.264). We hail here the exponential faith-in-faith that we met above in the epics of Stigand, Inge-low, and Goalen, albeit elaborated here with a literary sophistication as daunting as the orthodox drill there was clod-footed. Ranged with the epoists, Eliot's embittered riposte to the Victorian novel could hardly be plainer. The same lovers who have begun the tale deeply emplotted in a conventional marriage scenario discern for themselves at last, and from the summit of their generic transplantation, a higher calling that binds them to each other in a joint refusal of illusion, including the illusion of consolation. This is the strongly epic, all but existentially absurd position from which Fedalma, foundress of nothing, sails off with the Zíncali to nowhere while on the shore Silva, conquistador only of self, "knew not if he gazed | On aught but blackness overhung by stars" (5.267).

This final line contrasts starkly with the mythically moderated conclusion that Tennyson was at just this time preparing for the *Idylls*, replacing the dead final wail from "Morte d'Arthur" with the dawn of a new promise in "The Passing of Arthur." Keeping the house pitch dark, Eliot contrives a finale that draws dignity, not to say zest, from the positivist ethic that her black backdrop of cosmic indifference sets off by contrast.[30] Her suffering protagonists remain, in defiance of all the world and in commemorative reverence for all that has passed between them, "true | To high allegiance," which is to say loyal to loyalty itself. In this sense the virtually algebraic

---

[29] See Stephen Gill, *Wordsworth and the Victorians* (Oxford: Clarendon Press, 1998) 145–67.

[30] Bonaparte's study of *Romola* illuminates a wider epic dimension of Eliot's work: "It is just when religion—the world of the eternal and transcendent—no longer commands faith, as in the skepticism of an empirical age it no longer did, that it becomes mythology, the property not of the priest but of the poet. Thus, allegory, which can speak only in the voice of certainty, is replaced by mythology, whose very genesis is doubt" (15).

anatomy of morals in *The Spanish Gypsy* offered a highly refined yet still recognizable version of that exponential trothplight which came along in the 1860s, not only with that Bible epicry which Eliot scorned on her publisher's list, but more broadly with the modern prospect for that Christianity which she both had and had not outgrown. "The deepest hunger of a faithful heart | Is faithfulness," says Fedalma in her ultra-resignation, "Wish me nought else" (5.263). At last the rapt dancer of book 1 embraces, as her self-sufficing art of living, the performance of choreographed duty.

An acknowledgment that the conception of epic was embroiled in such second-order recursive structures appears in one of the oddest ingredients of the plot. Eliot's Zíncali are that ethnographic anomaly, a folk who cherish no grounding myth of origin. For her as for George Borrow, whose popular 1841 book *The Zincali* acknowledged the Roma people's proper name for themselves yet routinely bypassed it in favor of names externally bestowed—Gypsies, Gitános, Zincali—the nation in question neither know their history nor have troubled to dream one up.[31] The situation superficially resembles that found in an 1867 Australian long poem, *Māmba (The Bright-Eyed)*, where poet-ethnographer George Gordon McCrae confesses the dilemma his epic encounters as a result of the ban that Aboriginal culture imposes on mentioning the names of the dead (1.29, 2.20). McCrae's thick description of Māmba's richly traditional fosterage, craft-education, and rites of passage compensate for this ban well enough, however, to underscore by contrast the drastic cultural drought with which Eliot afflicts her amnesiac Zíncali.[32]

---

[31] Which is to say, on the terms that arose with Herder and gained currency in Britain at mid-century, the Zíncali are not properly a folk at all. The universalizing "divine revelation to humanity" that took place the world over "whenever a *Volk* became aware of itself as a *Volk* and memorialized this crucial experience in poetry" (Ackerman, *The Myth and Ritual School*, 14) has, for Eliot's lost tribe, never occurred. For discussion of Borrow's 1841 book, with its claim that the Roma, having forgotten the Brahmin traditions he confidently imputes to them, "have no history," see Lou Charnon-Deutsch, *The Spanish Gypsy: The History of a European Obsession* (University Park: Pennsylvania State University Press, 2004) 95–99, 132. Borrow expressly contradicts the etymologically reinforced hypothesis of an Egyptian origin that, according to Alicia Carroll, Eliot accepted anyway: *Dark Smiles: Race and Desire in George Eliot* (Athens: Ohio University Press, 2002) 151.

[32] This drastically dehistoricizing invention released Eliot from what Harry E. Shaw calls "the claims of particularity and uniqueness in societies and in history": "Scott and George Eliot: The Lure of the Symbolic," in *Scott and his Influence*, ed. J. H. Alexander and David Hewitt (Aberdeen: Association for Scottish Literary Studies, 1983) 397. When unchecked by such claims, Shaw maintains, Eliot "yielded to her strong impulse toward heroic representation" (399), which compromised *Romola* and *Deronda*—but which found, we may propose, a better generic home in *The Spanish Gypsy*. This analysis is reinforced, though differently assessed, by Roberts, 299–310.

When Zarca says, "Our people's faith | Is faithfulness" (3.206), he means that tribe loyalty *per se* assumes with them the place religion holds with other peoples, since unlike the "Catholics, | Arabs, and Hebrews" they dwell among "The Zíncali have no god" (4.230). The woman who before turning to literature had translated Feuerbach into English must have grasped that a people "whom no God took knowledge of" can "have no Whence or Whither in their souls" (1.105). The promise of a future Zíncali home in North Africa—Eliot does not specify Egypt, the default destination which "Gypsy" etymologically proposes—may be predicted to wither for want of a storied past that might give to their migration the character of a return. Such mythic rootlessness contrasts with the aggressive postulation of ethnic origins that dignifies Sephardo's alien Jewishness, that furnishes moral justification for the Christian Spaniards' territorialism, and that we found in Chapter 8 performed for Euro-Aryan benefit in *King Arthur* by Bulwer-Lytton (whose Spanish Reconquest plot in the 1837 novel *Leila* was among Eliot's sources).

The imposition of this unique ethnic handicap, so different from the ramified Zionist narrative in which *Daniel Deronda* would be embedded, gave Eliot a free hand to play with the belated invention of tradition, through the jesting, culture-slumming troubadour she can hardly have just happened to name Juan: "I feel like an ancient sage instructing our lisping ancestors" (3.177); "I shall grow epic, like the Florentine, | And sing the founding of our infant state, | Sing the new Gypsy Carthage" (3.184). Juan's Byronic, *improvisatore* edge owns kinship here—as at a different level Eliot's mixed narrative-dramatic mode does—with the chameleonic in-stantaneity poetics of Spasmodism from a decade before, which seems to have taught Zarca the political potential of a Zíncali "faith | Taught by no priest, but by their beating hearts," "whose pulses leap with kindred fire" (1.107). The fiction of a mythless people furthermore let Eliot isolate, as if in a controlled experiment in imaginary social science, the synchronic dynam-ics of group identity and mass emotion, abstracting "faithfulness" from any given faith system and "mythology" from any given narrative charter. The result was, in Frederic Harrison's felicitously awkward phrase, "a mass of Positivism": a mass beaten out to admittedly airy thinness as the Comtean silver lining that provides whatever general hope this poem's individual catastrophes may harbor.[33] In a scene-setting proem Eliot has celebrated the

[33] Harrison is quoted and briefly discussed in Charnon-Deutsch, *Spanish Gypsy*, 115. For Alexander Welsh, *George Eliot and Blackmail* (Cambridge, Mass.: Harvard University Press, 1985) 317, the purified postulate of group loyalty means that "*The Spanish Gypsy* contains scarcely a hint of ideology."

revival of learning within Renaissance man: "He spells the record of his long descent, | More largely conscious of the life that was" (1.8). This sounds like progress, all right; yet what remains felicitous by the end of the poem about any progressive enlargement of historical consciousness is very hard to say.

Yet it will not do, either, to chalk these progressivist slogans up to one-way dramatic irony. Rather, the co-presence of humanist hopefulness with bleak tragedy marks an unresolved, poetically generative standoff within the Victorian prospect as Eliot imagined it. While the history deficit to which she subjected her fantasy Gypsies arrested them in a perennially prenationalist and stateless state, in another sense it made them counterparts for the post-nationalist British public to whom she was writing. The sophisticate Don Silva's impracticable choice to enlist with the Zíncali legion looks less bizarre when we view it in light of the mythic choices that were repeatedly made by, and in, epic poems of the Victorian 1860s. All told, that light shares polarity with the light that Matthew Arnold shed on modern civilization and its discontents in "The Scholar-Gipsy" of 1853, and again in *Culture and Anarchy* at just the time when Eliot's poem appeared. The stern ecstasy of Fedalma's renunciation of the modern had its own kind of formal elegance, a kind deeply associated, by way of tragedy, with the literary genre of epic. What her creator's unpublished notes of 1868 described as an act of "large resignation," the moral labor of adjusting "our individual needs to the dire necessities of our lot," meshed with the "strict & manifold dependence" of an aesthetic that maximized "the relation of multiplex interdependent parts to a whole which is itself in the most varied & therefore the fullest relation to other wholes."[34] Of such wholeness the salient type, for this epic poet as for Blake decades before, was the human body dancing to the music of time. When Eliot resumed prose fiction after the comparative failure of *The Spanish Gypsy*, the uncompromised timbre of Fedalma's epos rang on as overtone to the agonistic chords of Dorothea Brooke and Daniel Deronda. Through all three characters Britain's most earnest narrative genius grappled with the question what the freedom of the cosmopolitan liberal—if freedom is what it was—might prove good for.

★

[34] "Notes on Form in Art," in *Essays of George Eliot*, ed. Thomas Pinney (New York: Columbia University Press, 1963) 431–36. Underscoring an evident distinction in Eliot's mind between the realism of prose and the formalism of verse, Pinney quotes her on the 1861 composition of *Silas Marner*: "I have felt all through as if the story would have lent itself best to metrical rather than prose fiction ... but, as my mind dwelt on the subject, I became inclined to a more realistic treatment" (*Letters*, 3: 382). Intellectual background for the cultural determinants (and thus the epicizing corollaries) of Eliot's aesthetic in the "Notes on Form" may be found in the discussion of Herbert Spencer's ideas by Diane Postlethwaite, *Making It Whole: A Victorian Circle and the Shape of Their World* (Columbus: Ohio State University Press, 1984) 187–233.

Among Victorian literary giants it is hard to imagine a less likely pair than
George Eliot and William Morris, who were passingly acquainted through
Pre-Raphaelite connections but are seldom mentioned in the same breath,
and whose narrative freighters repeatedly crossed routes in the 1860s and
1870s without evident influence either way.[35] Yet both authors mediated
the era's problematic of liberty and constraint by means of a theory of
culture drawing primarily upon the power of myth to sanction choices
and shape deeds, and both authors gravitated in complementary ways
towards epic as this power's generic fastness. Eliot went to epic as the one
genre stiff enough in exigency of vision to sustain at full strength her ethic of
sorrowing self-denial, while magnifying it beyond personal pathology into
ethnic heroism. With Morris at the same juncture we find this emphasis
inverted, in an anthological epic practice that displaces unity of purpose
onto completeness of design, in keeping with a multi-minded survey of the
desires and outcomes limning the human condition. At the end of the day
the almanac of narrative options that is *The Earthly Paradise: A Poem* (1868–
70) brings about, by dint of exhaustiveness, an affect of sympathetic resig-
nation that stands to Eliot's heroic refinement of altruism more or less as a
chronic syndrome stands to a traumatic crisis, or as the elegiac stands to the
tragic. In each case the literary incorporation of loss transcends the personal
note, or the particular instance, by virtue of myth's generalizing capacity to
animate collective meaning.

In order to appreciate the peculiarity of *The Earthly Paradise*, its immedi-
ate popularity and strong influence on epic writing into the *fin de siècle*, it
will be helpful to consider the book-length outgrowth that Morris har-
vested for separate publication in 1867, *The Life and Death of Jason: A Poem*.
In sixteen books on his wayfaring hero's life plus a long seventeenth on his
death, Morris's gentle-gaited, amiably undemanding heroic couplets actu-
ally braid both titular themes across the entire work. Now as always, Morris
links the good and full life to an unflinching embrace of death; and he
summons against fatal necessity the consolation of narrative itself, of the tale
whose bitter sweetness death spices. The placid mortal realism that governs
Jason's quest puts description on an equal footing with action, and treats
inner emotion evenhandedly with the outer motion of travel and incident.
Each of these is a motif within a pattern, a "thing"—the word recurs often

---

[35] For these fleeting contacts see Haight, *George Eliot,* 404, 408–9; and Fiona MacCarthy,
William Morris: A Life for Our Time (New York: Knopf, 1995) 264.

as a homogenizing common denominator—that invites scanning rather than scrutiny, and that takes its measure from the uniformity of the seldom remarkable, always capable verse. Morris's gifts as a fabric and wallpaper designer found expression here in a narrative poetry whose boasted production by the bolt, or as it sometimes seems the acre, has much to do with the reposeful pleasures it extends.[36]

These pleasures proceed from immersion in a world too early for the Gothic romance figures of ghost and ruin, a glowing primary sphere where high deeds are spurred by an ethic of honor and shame that is yet unshadowed by guilt or by anxiety as to consequences. The patient straightforwardness of its telling and its lightly medievalized, abstraction-proof diction make the poem remarkably present to whatever matter it has in hand. By a large mythic remove that cut the cord to Victorian historicist concerns— whether the large prehistory that a very early myth like the Argonauts' might encode or the long cultural history of that myth in transmission— Morris freed himself to match and contrast narrative elements as things in themselves, half handsome *objets d'art* and half storyboard pieces estranged from reference and soliciting only the engrossed reader's absorption in the business of the moment. Hence the spare, slightly apologetic quality of the poem's epic similes: few, far between, and reluctant to suggest that an episode might be less than intelligible on its own terms, or be even analogically related to anything beyond its immediate setting.[37]

All of which is to introduce Morris's persistent experimentation with a belated simulacrum of the conditions of naïve epic, to whose Latin,

[36] The poet John Drinkwater nicely captures the spell woven by Morris's amplitude: "The words that go to the making of a line flow as naturally and certainly from his pen as the letters that fashion a word from the pen of another": *William Morris: A Critical Study* (London: Secker, 1912) 99. As C. S. Lewis attests, the effect "is at first very pale and cold, but also very fresh and spacious. . . . The world of his imagining is as windy, as tangible, as resonant and three dimensional, as that of Scott or Homer": *Rehabilitations and Other Essays* (London: Oxford University Press, 1939) 40. For Florence Boos, *The Design of William Morris' The Earthly Paradise* (Lewiston: Edwin Mellen, 1990) 368, "in every lattice-work or rectangular confinement," of verse as well as visual design, "there is a path of escape; for every escape, a new confinement"—a result whose political implications are assessed in complementary ways by Northrop Frye, "The Meeting of Past and Future in William Morris," *Studies in Romanticism* 21 (1982) 310; and by Robert Harbison, *Deliberate Regression* (New York: Knopf, 1980) 105.

[37] Jerome McGann, *Black Riders: The Visible Language of Modernism* (Princeton: Princeton University Press, 1993), traces the development in Morris of a poetic wherein every thing "is as it appears to be; meaning is complete and apparent" (75). By the 1860s this poetic was regularly ascribed to the epic, in a consensus that governed Arnold's debates with all comers in the matter of Homeric translation and pervaded the four volumes of Blackie's *Homer and the Iliad* (1860): "that undefinable something of naturalness, simplicity, and *naiveté*" fosters in Homer's descriptions and similes "the pure imaginative luxury of looking at the object in its completeness" (1: 151, 145).

Icelandic, Greek, and Anglo-Saxon roots he would be successively drawn in vast translation projects to which the next chapter will return.[38] The first experiment, *Jason*, produced a mixed result, since the virtues just enumerated were counterbalanced by defects that sprang from contradictions inherent in the whole undertaking. To begin with, the willed equipoise of Morris's stance—he sets the theft of the Golden Fleece on the fulcrum of the ninth, midmost book—led so extended a linear tale inevitably into narrative longueurs. His stylistic archaism, wholesomely confected and easily worn though it is, has a way of homogenizing its wonders, and keeps a sequence like the Argonauts' riverborne, snowbound trek across northern Europe in books 10–12 from being much more or less marvelous than the Mediterranean and Euxine exploits they perform closer to home. Likewise the unflappable pace of *Jason* finally impedes that strain within primary epic which aims at heroic intensity, as for example the plot of Medea's revenge obliges the last book to aim.[39] *Jason* is a poem with few special effects and no greatest hits: amplitude of overall carriage consistently muffles what in other hands would have been nursed up into punctual splendor. Most tellingly, by sequestering the action from the history that touched Victorian readers where they lived, the provision of a green world that was replenished with fine clean things catered to much the same bourgeois consumerism that shadowed the work of Morris and Co. in interior decor—and that, as we have seen, was being concurrently gratified from a diametrically opposite direction by Bickersteth's offer in *Yesterday, To-Day, and For Ever* of ringside parlor chairs at the Apocalypse.

Morris finessed most though not all of these embarrassments through the different scheme of narrative distribution that organizes *The Earthly Paradise*. It is a poem that compasses an epic collectivity by a collector's methods: additivity, parallelism, complementarity, patterned disposition. The expulsion of Jason's saga from the original design was due chiefly to length, but

[38] On *Jason*'s epic affiliations with Homer and Apollonius, and the naïveté of narrative manner Morris worked out in the poem, see Lionel Stevenson, *The Pre-Raphaelite Poets* (Chapel Hill: University of North Carolina Press, 1972) 153–57. The admixture of translation is never far from even Morris's most originally epic writing; in light of the ethics of translation it is interesting to consider Charlotte H. Oberg's observation that in *Jason* "Betrayal and its obverse, loyalty, are the crucial motivations governing the actions of the characters": *A Pagan Prophet, William Morris* (Charlottesville: University of Virginia Press, 1978) 79.

[39] Even at that Morris did what he could to tone down Medea's ferocity and conform it to the gentle, grave fatality of the rest of the poem. See Douglas Bush, *Mythology and the Romantic Tradition in English Poetry* (1937; rpt. Cambridge, Mass.: Harvard University Press, 1969) 308–9 ; and Frederick Kirchhoff, *William Morris* (Boston: Twayne, 1979) 66.

with it Morris banished from the anthology certain kinds of long-range accumulative ambition too. Thus the two very long tales (topping 5000 lines) that remain in *The Earthly Paradise* are divided into parts, their linear thrust conquered by harmonic design. "The Lovers of Gudrun" (month 9.2) folds several narrative strands into a multiplotted lay.[40] The story of Bellerophon is not only spread across successive months (11.1, 12.1) and interrupted by a quite different-spirited tale; but modally "Bellerophon" takes two different forms, the first installment highlighting sentimental inwardness, the latter opening out on heroic action. That no one narrative mode should prevail is a principle at work not only here but *a fortiori* in the poem as a whole. The counter-hierarchical tendency toward equivalence that was at odds with *Jason*'s linear progress here becomes the rule: by a narrative balance of powers each of twenty-four tales checks its monthly partner, and as the "changeless change of seasons" (12.1.217) arcs its wheel from March through February no season corners privilege over the rest.[41] Each tale moreover gives the floor to a different teller, usually anonymous and blocked by Morris from the exercise of idiosyncrasy—even so much of it as one finds in his acknowledged exemplar Chaucer's *Canterbury Tales*— through the gyrostabilized recycling of a small set of three rhyming forms: heroic or tetrameter couplets and rhyme royal stanzas.

How this design comes about is explained and justified by the narrative frame into which the two dozen stories are set. Taking a leaf perhaps from Southey's *Madoc*, a lengthy (and much-rewritten) "Prologue: The Wanderers"

[40] Lovers of "Gudrun" might contest such a claim. For J. W. Mackail, *The Life of William Morris* (1899; rpt. London: Longmans, 1920), "Gudrun" is already an epic-within-the-epic, and in "Bellerophon" he sees "the epic manner rising beside and partially overmastering the romantic" (1: 201). A. Hamilton Thompson's chapter on Pre-Raphaelitism in the *Cambridge History of English Literature*, ed. A. W. Ward and A. R. Waller, vol. 13 (Cambridge: Cambridge University Press, 1917) 139, notes in both the Gudrun and Bellerophon tales "the transition to epic, with its prevailing theme of strife and suffering." Andrew Wawn, *The Vikings and the Victorians* (Cambridge: D. S. Brewer, 2000) 266–71, writes appreciatively of advanced narrative techniques in "Gudrun" that include "camera angle and microphone position." Still, what Wawn calls "motif deployment" seems to me the essential feature in which this longest constituent tale obeys the logic of *The Earthly Paradise* as a whole.

[41] Amanda Hodgson, *The Romances of William Morris* (Cambridge: Cambridge University Press, 1987) 67–68, considers the medievalizing effect of the poem's nonsequential randomness without crux or climax—the same effect that, Jeffrey Skoblow contends, "makes the poem all but invisible to the modern eye": *Paradise Dislocated: Morris, Politics, Art* (Charlottesville and London: University of Virginia Press, 1993) 49. See on this theme Bush's complaint that the poem seems "one interminable lyric on the memory of beauty and pain, the craving for rest, and the fear of death— *The Lotos-Eaters* on a vast scale"; that "all the young men are the same young man, nearly all the young women are the same young woman" (322).

detaches a Norseman, a German, and a Breton from fourteenth-century Europe, who take ship in order to escape the Black Death and quest westward for the earthly paradise. Once they have left their northern home behind—and with it any role in world history, as a decisively valedictory encounter with England's warlike Edward III establishes right away—a string of adventures deposits this international crew on a (Caribbean?) isle improbably but unmistakably inhabited by Greek-speaking polytheistic descendants of Aegean emigrants from many centuries before.[42] This place is no more the earthly paradise than were previous ports of call on which the wanderers staked a mistaken hope, only to meet repeated trials and disappointment. But in one respect their latest haven is uniquely congenial: the wanderers' new hosts know right away what their quest and its frustration signify, for the Hellenic heritage proves as rich as the Nordic in tales of unrest and aspiration.

Forswearing their quest for perfection, the now aged wanderers accept an invitation to settle at last, and meet with their hosts to swap stories from their respective traditions at the monthly feasts that furnish the serial occasion for the rest of the poem. A brief proem and epilogue for each story keep Morris's framework in place; they also keep in mind the atmosphere of acknowledged disillusion that his fictions of gratified or balked desire breathe. A lyric for each month exhales this atmosphere beyond the narrative frame; there an "Apology" and "Envoi" share the refrain whereby the "singer of an empty day"—his ambivalence doubled by the ambiguity with which "of" in this phrase indicates at once venue, topic, and origin— merges south with north, old with new, and fiction's entertainment with sad realities, which the singer has not so much forgotten as displaced for contemplation along the mythic lineaments of our common dreaming.[43]

The "our" in that last sentence by rights belongs to Morris. *The Earthly Paradise* is at pains to enlist its reader as a conspirator in its dream, on an

[42] Jessie Kocmanová, *The Poetic Maturing of William Morris* (Prague: Statni Pedagogicke Nakladeatelstvi, 1964), remarks that, by specifying Edward's mid-14th-cent. reign, Morris poised the action of "The Wanderers" at a watershed between the climactic development of "northern European narrative tradition, and the century of discovery and exploration that brings on the Renaissance" (21). It is further remarkable that Morris, in contrast to the historically vigilant Eliot, makes no use of this transitional juncture beyond, as Blue Calhoun suggests, accentuating "the mood of pastness and loss that characterizes the end of an epoch": *The Pastoral Vision of William Morris:* The Earthly Paradise (Athens: University of Georgia Press, 1975) 105.

[43] On the politics of such contemplative displacement see Kirchhoff, "William Morris's 'Land East of the Sun and West of the Moon': The Narrative as Place," *Pre-Raphaelite Review* 3:2 (1980) 14–24; Frye, "Past and Future," 316–17; Skoblow, *Paradise Dislocated, passim.*

individual basis that underwrites the culture of the middle classes who in substantial numbers interrupted their diet of prose fiction to banquet with Morris circa 1870, and who believed then, as we still largely do, that what held them together socially derived from their shared uniqueness as discrete persons. The poem did not tell them their lives were free or would end happily; its contents if anything had sobering news on that score. But its decentered, noncumulative format was an invitation to browse, to help themselves, to customize the book by exercising options on a story that, while it came from deep in the cultural thesaurus of myths, nonetheless spoke a pleasantly accented version of a tongue Victorian readers already knew. In a sense at once luxurious and inexpensive *The Earthly Paradise* put all Europe at their disposal. The same numbness of clash-aversive affect that attended the Argonauts' circumnavigation of Europe in *Jason* persisted here in the elastic shape of an affirmation of overall compatibility within a trans-European culture sturdy enough to weather exportation over the centuries and over the seas. The very proliferation of surviving narratives in this poem (inversely reciprocating their singularity and even dearth among George Eliot's Zíncali) constituted a myth of myth: a promise of cultural resilience transcending the undertow of decline that a given myth's plot of unfulfillment might impart.[44]

To remember *Madoc* and the New World narratives of Southey's day is to see how very little interest *The Earthly Paradise* shows in actual processes of cultural exchange. Something like the bland protocol governing hosts and guests within the frame superintends as well what goes on within the stories the frame encloses, and immunizes their protagonists against those negotiations with otherness whose give-and-take brings change and makes history. Perseus, for instance, in "The Doom of King Acrisius" (2.1), executes a realms-spanning itinerary that brushes by a wealth of anthropologically suggestive matters—evil eye, ritual sacrifice, and (what in Chapter 9 we found Charles Kingsley registering in his version of the myth) racialized

---

[44] Boos, *Design*, 386, connects the poem's evolving narrative of reception with the poet's epic concern to highlight "processes of cultural memory." Likewise J. M. S. Tompkins, *William Morris: An Approach to the Poetry* (London: Cecil Woolf, 1988), stresses Morris's valuation, not of an old story's "possible historical and cultural origins," but of "what human experience and imagination have done to it" (86); see also Hartley Spatt, "William Morris and the Uses of the Past," *Victorian Poetry* 13 (1975) 1–9. Hodgson, " 'The Highest Poetry': Epic Narrative in *The Earthly Paradise* and *Idylls of the King*," *Victorian Poetry* 34 (1996), considers Morris and Tennyson as responding to "the efforts of scholarship in the eighteen-sixties to redefine the nature of myth, and to unpick that knitting together of history and myth which is a prerequisite for epic" (348).

progressivism—to emerge not just physically unscathed but ideologically intact, a cultural virgin. Even where stories like Gudrun's or Walter/ Tannhäuser's ("The Hill of Venus," 12.2) entail a contest of pagan with Christian values, the contest is mooted, muted, and sterile in the sense that it generates no momentum towards *entente*. As with the poem's programmatic sidelining of military themes, conspicuous in "Ogier the Dane" (6.2) but also rehearsed at 4.1.137, 8.2.240, 12.1.241, and in "The Wanderers" (20), the dialectical potential of conflict is preemptively diverted to the inertia of contrast instead: a compositional effect. Anthological pattern trumps ethnological energy at every turn.

The stable compound of *The Earthly Paradise* is braced up from within by recurring images of its own encyclopedic ambition to house the mythic manifold without dominating it. One *locus classicus* for such a recursive narrative structure is the palace of art Cupid builds for Psyche,

> With curious stones from far-off countries brought,
> And many an image and fair history
> Of what the world has been, and yet shall be,
> And all set round with golden craftsmanship,
> Well-wrought.
>
> (3.1.21)

Built by desire to pleasure the soul, this "garden like a paradise" images Morris's narrative parquetry of precious things tallied from afar, and without arousing any moral anxiety on the order of Tennyson's 1832 "Palace of Art." The second line's equilibration of "image" with "history" epitomizes the whole project of diegetic exhibition, even as the third line registers it as an effect of this project to abort consequential change by recruiting utopian hope within the circuitry of the foredone: what "has been" yet "shall be." Such imagery of structural recurrence itself recurs many times over in *The Earthly Paradise*, its very redundance a metatextual sign of the poem's diplomacies of juxtaposition and balance. In "The Lady of the Land" a mariner come upon a Greek isle comes next upon an ancient "house" built "fair with sculptured stories" but since decayed to "dim ruin," in whose "mouldering histories" and "wondrous imagery" he can still make out broken forms from the classical pantheon (4.2.156–57). In "The Man Who Never Laughed Again" Bharam turns aside from a scene of death to happen on a series of common village-life vignettes, each with its tale "to tell," all ministering to "pleasure of the beauty of the earth" (8.2.218–19).

In obvious ways each of these encounters with an array of stories repli-
cates fractally the leading features of Morris's larger frame. Less obvious is
the way each replicates what may be the poem's largest abstention, which is
to renounce totalized comprehension as such. No social idea unifies what
Bharam beholds in the countryside; no theory of history synthesizes, or
impedes the clarity of, the mariner's observations. And just this is what
makes each juncture a happy one. Each protagonist's interval of narrative
grace depends on the transiency of his grasp of what he gathers *seriatim*: that,
when it comes to earthly paradises, is how things go. Obversely, when
Morris does bestow on his principals a moment of panoramic, summative
lucidity—"all the tale | Told in a moment" (7.1.24)—the moment is
without exception excruciating and more often than not anticlimactic
(3.2.102, 12.2. 354–55). Morris includes the moment of narrative totaliza-
tion, in the first instance, because his anthological epic plan leaves him no
choice: so global an exposition as *The Earthly Paradise* must include all
options, totalization among them. But then *include* them is exactly what
the poem does, circumscriptively enrolling their urgency within an aes-
thetic order that is centered rather than mastered, and that surrounds them
with context the way an impersonal collectivity absorbs an individual will.

Or absorbs, for that matter, its constituent lesser collectivities. A kind of
triple weave works across the poem to plait southern with northern, classic
with medieval, and naïve with sentimental strands, only to lose these
elements' initial identities in the ultimate design.[45] In the first month the
crisply rendered "Atalanta's Race" presents from Greek tradition an excep-
tionally pure instance of objective story, while "The Man Born to Be King"
has Gothic melancholy written all over it: within a few pages its storybook
King from "days of old" paces the pavement "thinking how his days began |
And of the lonely souls of man" (1.2.131, 136), and for contrastive good
measure the narrator alludes more than once to the fabled beauty of Grecian
queens (170, 193). Yet the relation between these first tales is one not just of

---

[45] At roughly this time a like capaciousness of reception was being claimed for the English
language itself. Morris's poem might well have been taken as proof for Craik's blanket assertion
that "the English language, and, through that, English literature, English civilization or culture
generally, and the whole temper of the English mind, ought to have a capacity of sympathizing at
once with the Classical and the Gothic, with the antique and the modern, with the past and the
present, to an extent not to be matched by any other speech or nation of Europe" (*Compendious
History*, 1: 66). Such ideas enjoyed wide currency in the books of R. C. Trench, who in *English,
Past and Present: Eight Lectures* (1855; 11th rev. edn. London: Macmillan 1881) 7, felicitates readers
on the uniquely "happy marriage in our tongue of the languages of the North and South."

contrast but of a chiastic symmetry that portends the interlacing of opposites that lies ahead. The melancholy King resolves at last to live Hellenically in the moment ("Nor will I look behind me more, | Nor forward," 202), a mirror reversal of the fall into pensive Nordic subjectivity ("longings vague, without a name," 123) that has cost Atalanta a race but won her a husband.

The cultural chiasmus thus established in March returns a year later in the pair of stories for February. There the Bellerophon who was a comparatively mawkish dawdler in month 11 sheds his snowy neurosis to emerge an objective Greek hero after all, while Walter in "The Hill of Venus" would not at the end be so Teutonically fulfilled a worshiper of his Mediterranean goddess did his return from Vatican to Venusberg not teem at the twelfth hour with Gothic vagaries of Ossianic "white mist that did swim | About a pine-clad cliff, above a stream | Dark, scarcely seen, and voiceless as a dream" (12.2.399). These twinned finales, respectively reversing Atalanta's fall in 1.1 and the King's resolution in 1.2, in one sense rewind Morris's modal clock of tales for a fresh go-round. In another sense their backward step across breached intracultural boundaries registers how thoroughly those boundaries have meanwhile been crisscrossed, and so affirms the European solidarity that we have seen to be integral to the poem's 1860s appeal.

The ground of that solidarity is nothing more or less than a participated illusion: the neverland sharing of fiction among alienated elders who don't believe a word of what they nonetheless can't live without.[46] Their addicted disenchantment, far from invalidating the multiplex tale of the tribe, becomes in the modern hands of Morris that tale's enabling precondition. His disparate northern–southern storyteller–listeners come together not on a given story but on a common narratology that bears on the giving of stories as such. At the occidental world's end, and from old age's declining slope, they discern in each plot an anatomy of their own lives. For in the rise and fall of its mythos every tale *The Earthly Paradise* knows describes one and the same parabola, the deathwards curve that spurs desire, "Since each tale's ending needs must be the same: | And we men call it Death" (Epilogue 405). In another decade, and in conjunction with his own life commitment to

---

[46] E. P. Thompson, *William Morris: Romantic to Revolutionary* (1955; rev. edn. New York: Pantheon, 1977), insists that as we read we are never "permitted to escape into illusion for long: rather, we are trying in anxious wakefulness to recall a dream" (127), and that this dilemma, epitomizing the evasive contradictions of bourgeois sentimentalism to which the poem spoke, explains its commercial success (134 ff.). See also John Goode, "William Morris and the Dream of Revolution," in *Literature and Politics in the Nineteenth Century*, ed. John Lucas (London: Methuen, 1971) 221–78.

revolutionary socialism, Morris would hear across *Sigurd*'s twilight of the gods a different summons to heroic action in service of the one tale that counted. Amid the narrative dissemination and consumerist fatalism of *The Earthly Paradise*, meanwhile, it is never a matter of earning one's place in the myth, not even on the stripped-down, deactivated terms of existential suffering that Eliot extended in the despotic narrative of *The Spanish Gypsy*. It is instead a matter of knowing oneself already infiltrated and bespoken by the myth. An infrastructural necessity of human life like the eating and drinking that go with it, the compulsion to narrate is something for Morris's pre-colonial remnant to live through—and to see through—again and again.

The implication here that Western civilization has its roots in perennial unfulfillment, that the idle singer's is a performance commanded by disenchantment, is not surprising in an epic coeval with Nietzsche's *Birth of Tragedy*. Only a preexisting state of Dionysiac disillusion could foster that witting Apollonian choice to dream, and have one's choice of dreams, to which the poem both attests and ministers. And only a culture far gone in the capitalist optionalization of experience, and far flung in the colonialist expropriation of global resources, could sustain such a state of disillusion long enough to make it seem the natural state—or, otherwise put, to make the arousal, gratification, and surplus resurgence of (Western, male) desire seem a universal template for earthly narrative as such. To its precipitating query "Can man be made content?" (Prologue 80) *The Earthly Paradise* answers no.[47]

And in saying so it answers as fully as any work in the language to the condition of England in the last third of the nineteenth century. The insatiable will to illusion was itself anything but illusory; its anomic melancholy powered a formidable cultural ideal that had distinct worldly consequences. "Urged by some desire, he knew not what" (6.2.276), "strange and strong desire without a name" (6.1.236), "restlessness without intent" (12.2.382), the composite hero of this epic anthology wants he knows not what, because he wants not to know that he wants it all. If we compare Victorian Morris to Romantic Southey as counterparts in sheer epic reach, we see how deeply compounded with each other the earlier poet's mutually

---

[47] Hodgson, "The Highest Poetry," 59: "The search for bliss is doomed not necessarily because it does not exist, but because man is incapable of accepting and resting in happiness when he finds it. Yet this restlessness . . . is as natural as the first impetus to take up the quest. Indeed, it is the same impulse."

quarantined hypercredulous fabulation and acidly skeptical annotation have now become, and how fully articulated with each other they are in the surface and proportions of the commodified text.

When the first installments of *The Earthly Paradise* and *The Ring and the Book* appeared in 1868, a passage from Browning's long methodological introduction may have struck both poets as highlighting the coincidence, and the divergence, between their epic procedures. Having laid out the provenance, gestation, and narrative method of his project, Browning stepped back to survey the whole under the figure of a calendared landscape:

> A novel country: I might make it mine
> By choosing which one aspect of the year
> Suited mood best, and putting solely that
> On panel somewhere in the House of Fame,
> Landscaping what I saved, not what I saw:
> —Might fix you, whether frost in goblin-time
> Startled the moon with his abrupt bright laugh,
> Or, August's hair afloat in filmy fire,
> She fell, arms wide, face foremost on the world,
> Swooned there and so singed out the strength of things.
> Thus were abolished Spring and Autumn both,
> The land dwarfed to one likeness of the land,
> Life cramped corpse-fashion. Rather learn and love
> Each facet-flash of the revolving year!—
> Red, green, and blue that whirl into a white,
> The variance now, the eventual unity,
> Which make the miracle. See it for yourselves,
> This man's act, changeable because alive!
>
> (1.1348–65)

Even without the gratuitous Chaucer allusion, this perspectivist refusal to privilege any one season or reigning "mood" might be pressed into a defense of Morris's distributive method in *The Earthly Paradise*, which Browning's method indeed resembles.[48] *The Ring and the Book* comprises nine contemporaries' viewpoints (eleven if we count in book 12 the Venetian visitor's report and Fra Celestino's sermon) on the obscure events that led to the trial and execution in Rome of Count Guido Franceschini in

---

[48] Browning wrote on 7 June 1868 to felicitate Morris, by analogy to Handel's music, for his "suite" of "continuous key and recurring forms" in *The Earthly Paradise*: quoted in May Morris, *William Morris, Artist, Writer, Socialist* (Oxford: Blackwell, 1936), 1: 641.

1698 for wife-murder, a sensation in its day—and thereafter totally forgot-
ten, had Browning not seen fit to make a major Victorian epic out of the
trial documents he found one day bound together for sale on a bookstall in
Florence. The twelve-ring circus of versions here recalls the cycle of tales
that Morris enlarged to an epic twenty-four; both poets moreover replace
the linear plot of traditional epic with the "variance" of multiple fresh starts
and aim at "the eventual unity" of an after-effect—an additive retinal blur,
in Browning's color-wheel image above—that is to be apprehended, out-
side the constituent narrative depositions, at the level of the frame. Some-
thing like Morris's cultural eclecticism is discernible, besides, in Browning's
veritable flea-market of diction and style: books 8 and 9, where over their
vernacular shoulders we watch the opposing trial lawyers compose their
Latin pleadings, form a salient special case of the poem's general rule of
philologically enhanced perspectivism.[49]

Still, just as nobody would mistake Browning's punchy interjectiveness
for Morris's mild wide berth, so no reader of these two premier 1860s epic
poems can doubt that their comparable strategies are put to sharply dissimi-
lar ends. In its very marginality the Franceschini affair challenges compari-
son with the oft-handled legends Morris retails, while to the limpidity of
those cherished heirlooms Browning opposes a scribbly palimpsest of
crossed purposes and contradictory interpretations. Within their own
sequestered sphere the *Earthly Paradise* elders enjoy, because they diplomat-
ically agree to reinforce, an authority that Morris as frame narrator likewise

---

[49] On the profound nineteenth-century correlation between linguistics and anthropology, as it
pivoted during the 1860s in the Oxford of F. Max Müller, see Hans Aarsleff, *The Study of Language
in England, 1780–1860* (Princeton: Princeton University Press, 1967); Linda Dowling, *Language and
Decadence in the Victorian Fin de Siècle* (Princeton: Princeton University Press, 1986) 61–77 *et passim*;
George W. Stocking, Jr., *Victorian Anthropology* (New York: Free Press, 1987) 56–60; Ackerman,
The Myth and Ritual School, 27–28; Franklin E. Court, *Institutionalizing English Literature: The
Culture and Politics of Literary Study 1750–1900* (Stanford: Stanford University Press, 1992) 77–82;
Dennis Taylor, *Hardy's Literary Language and Victorian Philology* (Oxford: Clarendon Press, 1993)
207–52. Even as the human sciences and their institutions elaborated the correlation of language
with culture, this correlation remained a central concern to major epoists of international reach
from Landor and Byron to Doughty and Hardy. As mythological thinking helped shift the epic
criterion of cultural unity across the mid-century from nationalism into an imperially shadowed
cosmopolitanism, it became common practice even for minor aspirants—Austin, Stigand, Owen
Meredith—to rehearse this shift by playing English systematically against other, constituent or
contrasting, tongues. See Richard Bailey, *Images of English: A Cultural History of the Language* (Ann
Arbor: University of Michigan Press, 1991) 106–21, on the march of the language towards global
dominance. In *Robert Browning's Language* (Toronto: University of Toronto Press, 1999), Donald
Hair learnedly if eccentrically argues that Browning was for the most part untouched by these
sweeping developments.

respects. But in *The Ring and the Book* such top-down authority is nowhere
to be had. That in fact is the work's major thesis in cultural politics, as sifted
through an ideological pitched fight over patriarchal dominion in the family
and instituted hereditary privilege in society. This thesis informs the work's
major, and most radical, development in artistic method. For the self-
dramatizing, reader-prodding poet whose fingerprints dint the passage
above becomes a leading actor in the epic story—the epic's story, that is,
the drama of the telling as books 1 and 12 rehearse and recapitulate it in the
poet's own voice. Browning takes his anti-authoritarian stand by subpoena-
ing himself and taking the stand, a star eleventh witness before the bar of the
reader's repeatedly invoked judgment ("See it for yourselves" in the passage
above; also 1.372, 392, 696, 825, 1220; 12.10, 834). The poet thus puts off
the robes of judicious disinterestedness that came with the territory of
omnisciently narrated Victorian fiction ("A novel country"), and that
Morris's role as "idle singer" preserved, albeit on different premises, in
The Earthly Paradise.[50]

   The crux of the matter is Browning's early commitment *in propria persona*
to an interpretation that, over the course of his enormous work, a parade of
bystanders, principals, and constituted authorities variously dispute and
corroborate by appealing to grounds qualitatively indistinguishable from
his. On a first, *soi-disant* inspired reading of his source the Old Yellow Book,
the poet envisions a larger truth beyond it, which he insists (like each one of
his successors in books 2–11) is *the* truth of the matter: "Step by step, missing
none and marking all," he asseverates, "I saw with my own eyes" the total
shape of occurrences a century and a half old; "The life in me abolished the
death of things, | Deep calling unto deep" (1.517–23). Such prophetic
necromancy is "a credible feat," he goes on, "With the right man and

---

[50] Whether Browning is in the relativist thick or rises above it is a question provoking much
disagreement in the extensive secondary literature See the summary of positions in Paul
A. Cundiff, *Browning's Ring Metaphor and Truth* (Metuchen: Scarecrow, 1972); and, among subse-
quent refinements, John M. Menaghan, "Embodied Truth: *The Ring and the Book* Reconsidered,"
University of Toronto Quarterly 52 (1983) 263–76, and E. Warwick Slinn, "Language and Truth in
The Ring and the Book," *Victorian Poetry* 27 (1989) 115–33. One refreshing witness from outside the
fray is the early modernist scholar Rodney Delasanta in *The Epic Voice* (The Hague: Mouton,
1967). Prefacing his analysis of Renaissance examples with a distinction between omniscient
narration and the "delegated narration" that omniscience may please to license, he adduces *The
Ring and the Book* in passing as a work that, because its narrative is entirely delegated, stands *ipso
facto* outside the epic pale. Delasanta's pale is not ours; but his unbiased testimony should give
heart to the relativists among us. The poem's relativizing design is laid out elegantly by Morse
Peckham, "Historiography and *The Ring and the Book*," *Victorian Poetry* 6 (1968) 243–57.

way" (1.771–72), and *credible* is just the word for it. The poet dares the reader to belie(ve) him.[51]

In fact the poet has been doing little else ever since in line 1 he produced out of thin air, plus the reader's collaborating fancy, an else invisible object: "Do you see this Ring?" We don't, of course; and yet we do too. As it turns out, readers may accept the dare, reject it, or vacillate somewhere in between, without impairing their ability to take an interest, or a side, in the tissue of confession, deliberation, and gossip that surrounds the Franceschini case. What crucially matters is that the poet written into the poem has, with palpable (literal) prejudice, cast his lot from the first with the Pope's judgment against Guido, and with the blessing this judgment implies on the innocence of Guido's pregnant wife Pompilia and the courtly priest Caponsacchi with whom she ran away from her monster spouse some months before. Whether the reader concurs in this judgment or not is a matter of secondary interest, so long as the genuinely radical point is grasped: the epoist's undisguised partisanship disqualifies in advance whatever pretension to absolute insight may be thought to inhabit his chosen genre.

When Browning in this way forfeited a leading mode of Victorian narrative authority, he did so from at least two motives. One was the constitutionally liberal suspicion of ordained power that had suffused his writing for thirty years, first in the narratorial high jinks of *Sordello* and then in the self-discounting form of the dramatic monologue. We saw in Chapter 7 how, and on what good Reform principles, Browning's 1840 epic kept jump-cutting between the analogous difficulties encountered by a modern poet-narrator and by his medieval poet-protagonist, both of them far too skittery to pilot a master narrative. As for the dramatic monologue, in Browning's hands its generic affiliation lay with the angular ironies of the short story, which across the mid-nineteenth century perspectivized the real by realizing perspectivism, and so undercut authority of every stripe.

To this negative or evasive motive *The Ring and the Book* added a second, constructive one, which had to do with the epic burden of history as Browning had come to understand it by the 1860s. His commitment to one version of the historical truth, partial and manifestly contestable, constituted an admission of the historicity of his own artistic practice. His

---

[51] Susan Blalock, "Browning's *The Ring and the Book*: 'A Novel Country,' " *Browning Institute Studies* 11 (1983) 39–50, offers an early Bakhtinian reading drawing out the poem's discursive feints and carnivalesque posture.

acceptance of equal status with the other speakers meant that the poet in the poem was, like them, not just a verbal construct but the creature of those historical circumstances within which verbal construction takes place. Within the frame of reference that the epic structure sets up, the poet's very claim to prophetic election levels him with the seventeenth-century Italians he has conjured, since they are all addicted to just the same claim and justify their mutually incompatible interpretations by uniform invocation of God as their witness (epic theodicy, as it were, on Feuerbachian rewind). Thus when the poet relates how "a Hand, | Always above my shoulder, pushed me once" (1.40–41) to just the right bookstall in a crowded market-place, his own interpretation ("predestination!") cries out under the cir-cumstances—and, in this epic, circumstances are everything—for a supplemental gloss. We find it, one invisible hand washing the other, in Adam Smith: the mysteries of this poet's faith are bound up like many another Victorian liberal's with the mysteries of the market.

The battered material book that the market handed Browning for ready money, and that he immaterially flourishes along with the (in)visible ring on his own book's first leaf, comes to him dwindled down to "only entabla-ture" from the once solid, fully articulated structure of its historical mo-ment. It nevertheless remains an authentic relic of that moment, an "abacus" or "A.B.C. of fact" from which to extrapolate "the lost propor-tions" of that teeming, solid past whose scale it retains (1.33, 670–78, 707). The survival of the old book in the new marks out a contingent or metonymical relation between the epoch of the murders and the epoch of the poem. This relation, breaking with the primarily analogical or meta-phorical historicism governing *Sordello*, in effect puts the Victorian era on trial. Gender politics, class conflict, the girding of church against state and of orthodoxy against new philosophy—all these were astir in a 1690s Italy that resembled 1860s Britain because, within the pan-European perspective Browning meant his epic to sustain, the two epochs were knotted into the same fabric of world history.[52] Choosing to stoop into the circle of monologues that is *The Ring and the Book*, Browning relinquished the no-man's zone of extratextual implication where during the decades since

---

[52] Lee Erickson, *Robert Browning: His Poetry and His Audiences* (Ithaca and London: Cornell University Press, 1984) 234–38, shows what damage the poem's epic standing must sustain if its claim on the modern reader is reduced to atomized, dehistoricized psychology. Such a reduction is urged with more than ordinary sophistication by William E. Buckler, *Poetry and Truth in Robert Browning's* The Ring and the Book (New York and London: New York University Press, 1985) 13, 256–59. Contemporaries were much struck by the poem but not expressly curious as to its

Sordello the masquerading dramatic poet had seemed to repose, for all the world like Morris's "idle singer" paring his proto-Joycean fingernails. To put it more affirmatively: Browning made his major epic the occasion for going to the one place where that disembodied ghost-writer of monologues could never go: into the owned duties, and embarrassments, of determinate and existentially exigent reality.

Not the least embarrassment attending Browning's plunge into history is the humiliation of being proven wrong, which is precisely what a century of scholarly activity incited by his poem has brought to pass. It now looks very much as if Half-Rome, along with Victorian skeptics including Carlyle, were right to reckon Pompilia a fascinator, Caponsacchi a seducer, Guido a cuckold, and the legal process a miscarriage of justice.[53] Yet the detailed disconfirmation of Browning's version of whatever it was that transpired once in Arezzo and Rome oddly reconfirms the larger historical purpose informing his poem, which as the final line puts it was that of "Linking our England to his Italy" (12.874). The discovery of new documents and the fresh interpretation of old ones in their light if anything establish more securely that textured continuum of causes with effects, across centuries and national borders, which was Browning's chief concern, and of which his forgotten principals' motives and acts were in a sense only instances chosen at random. Getting it wrong was a risk he knowingly ran in claiming to have gotten it so absolutely right to begin with, and also to have gotten it the way he did, not straight from the Muse but out of an encounter between his own wits and a bookful of tangled witness. The failure of a minor premise that we can now ascribe to sentimental or Romantic idealization on the poet's part leaves intact his major historicist premise, which survives into our time to underwrite that very ascription, and which makes *The Ring and the Book* not just a versified sensation novel but a nineteenth-century epic of the first magnitude.

---

genre, although repeated pronouncements about its being Browning's masterpiece, or a testament to posterity, ring with the epic timbre. See the compilation by Ezzat Abdulmajeed Khattab, *The Critical Reception of Browning's* The Ring and the Book *1868–1889 and 1951–68* (Salzburg: Institut für Englische Sprache und Literatur, 1977).

[53] Such is the devastating implication of Beatrice Corrigan's scrupulous research in *Curious Annals: New Documents Relating to Browning's Roman Murder Story* (Toronto: University of Toronto Press, 1956). Undoing the vesture of moral purity in which Browning clad his principals, Corrigan nevertheless confirms the high degree of literary-cultural mediation that their love, such as it was, flourished by (xxx, xliv). See also J. E. Shaw, " 'The Donna Angelicata' in *The Ring and the Book*," *PMLA* 41 (1926): 55–81.

That premise is the inescapability of the historical condition. The dense weave of inscrutable motive and unintended consequence environing human acts and shaping their documentary train—tirelessly mimed as it is through the poem's vast network of specific correspondences—both exacts the reader's acknowledgment and eventually defeats the reader's endeavor to grasp it whole.[54] In its thick totality *The Ring and the Book* is a work to be not cumulatively understood but locally transacted with, by a reader whose negotiations replicate the acts of partial accommodation, under difficulties, that the various speakers perform in their turn. "The instinctive theorizing whence a fact | Looks to the eye as the eye likes the look" (1.863–64) governs every vision in the poem, and also *of* the poem; what facts happen to look like in a given instance serves, Rohrschach-fashion, to disclose what the poem's inside and outside interpreters (respectively its speakers and readers) like to look at. Whether deep yearning or mere whim, this liking proves to be a likeness that profiles the conditioning of desire on templates of cultural position and historical time. Jealous Half-Rome (book 2) backs Guido because he suspects the wind is blowing from a quarter inhospitable to husbandly prerogatives he cherishes; Other Half-Rome (book 3), an arm-chair Petrarchan who wants somebody to love, has fixed on the inaccessible victimized beauty Pompilia as *beau idéal* of the Baroque; Tertium Quid's display of impartiality in the case (book 4) is at bottom a hustler's audition for patronage in an urbane high society whose increasingly commercial basis sets a new premium on quick-wittedness as such. The two lawyers obviously are hired minds (books 8 and 9), and even the Pope—as far above the fray as supreme office, extreme old age, and the poet's sympathetically cresting imagination can lift him—has something to prove, if only to himself, about the perseverance of radiant virtue in a spiritually crepuscular world (book 10). The concern the Franceschini case kindles in all these speakers reveals the prior stake that each has in specific social realities whose combination shapes the common life of their time.

[54] W. David Shaw, *The Lucid Veil: Poetic Truth in the Victorian Age* (London: Athlone Press, 1987), displays a refreshing candor about what is at some point every reader's experience: "To return to the text is to stretch oneself out on the rack of a tough, obscure poem," "a real trial of the reader's own endurance," "exquisite and refined torture" (54). Turning this overload quotient to good credit, Isobel Armstrong remarks that, as the long poem "silts itself up in the mind," it potentiates "the slow process of growth or of gradual discovery": "*The Ring and the Book*: The Uses of Prolixity," in *The Major Victorian Poets: Reconsiderations*, ed. Armstrong (London: Routledge, 1969), 179. That much conceded, the surest guide through Browning's documentary catacomb remains Richard Altick and James F. Loucks II, *Browning's Roman Murder Story: A Reading of* The Ring and the Book (Chicago and London: University of Chicago Press, 1968).

That this double-edged interest is strongly at work within the three principals at the center goes without saying, and its strength throws into special relief the part that Browning scripted for the kind of mythic faith that was sustaining epic around the time of the second Reform Bill. Guido's two monologues make the point most clearly. He is the only contemporary who weighs in twice; and the relative gravity of his two appearances has much to do with the respective insouciance and earnestness with which at each appearance he treats the meaning of myth. Book 5, delivered before a presumptively conservative ecclesiastical panel, gives Guido's neatly tailored *ab homine* defense of wife-murder as at once a vindication of traditional patriarchy and an act consistent with "persistent treading in the paths | Where I was trained to go" (5.124–25). Guido represents his behavior, in other words, as the natural outgrowth of his upbringing as an aristocratic scion bred to the church at a time when aristocracy and ecclesia are suffering erosion from the forces of commerce and *de facto* secularization.

In contrast book 11, delivered a few hours before Guido's execution, disowns the book 5 account as a charade based on social pieties none but fools could credit. Clearing the air of cant, now Guido displays his true colors as a radical nihilist beyond good and evil. Yet while he shreds as a fictive makeshift his former myth of socialization, an alternative myth thrusts up from underneath his will to power. The anarchic foe to "Civilization and society" (11.463) proclaims himself at last "a primitive religionist— | As should the aboriginary be | I boast myself, Etruscan." He is a true believer, all right, but what he worships is the brazen rule of power, the "simpler scheme" to which all men actually submit no matter what they publicly profess: "Mine's your faith too,—in Jove Aegiochus!" (11.1919–21, 1936–38). Guido's rejection of classical decorum, Christian gospel, and the hypocrisy they sponsor takes place under cover of a primal myth expressly deriving from Virgil's prehistoric retrospect in *Aeneid* 8.313 ff. For Browning it additionally represents an 1860s intellectual formation that looked back toward human origins through the Higher Criticism of biblical sources, the ethnological evolutionism of embedded anachronistic "survivals" (Edward Tylor's *Primitive Culture* was about to appear in 1871), and the corrosive implications that Darwinian theory held for social values.[55] Guido the boasted Etruscan thus affirms what is portended in the poet's

[55] W. David Shaw, *Victorians and Mystery: Crises of Representation* (Ithaca and London: Cornell University Press, 1990) 300–21, offers a reading of *The Ring and the Book* attuned equally to the Higher Criticism and to its latter-day avatar deconstruction.

description of "Etrurian circlets" (1.3) from the poem's opening declar-ation: metaphor and myth are the instruments we steer by, the very categories and receptacles of belief. There is no definitive master myth, nor is there a definitive mastering of myth. Infallible authority and the cultural degree zero of truth are both myths themselves, Browning con-tends, and Guido's book 11 monologue shows how readily the latter morphs into the former.

In the beginning, then, was the myth. Yet in the choice of myths to live by lies the originary chance of human liberation. The panicky crisis ending book 11 shows how Guido's choice, the rugged racial myth of blood-and-iron self-interest, narrows his maneuvering room down to nothing. This debacle sets off by contrast a paradox which the Pope's monologue in book 10 has confirmed, which the symmetrically facing monologues of Capon-sacchi and Pompilia in books 6–7 have illustrated, and which the poet's commitment in book 1 has initially propounded: the paradox that devoted self-sacrifice frees individual agents to realize in their actions, and so affect for good, the meaning of the history they live through. In palpable ways this is the core myth of Browning's evangelical-grained, progress-inflected protestantism; and one classically epic feature of this idiosyncratic poem is to envision the late seventeenth century as a seed-time for the flowering of the nineteenth-century liberalism to which Browning's huge experiment in relativized diegesis gives expression. The last historical event his narrative notes is the birth of Voltaire, "Terrible Pope, too, of a kind" (12.778), proleptic of that clash between traditional faith and Enlightened doubt which the Pope has prophesied will reactivate Christianity's "old heroism," on modern terms and under the inspiration of such post-ecclesiastical worship of "God's God in the mind of man" as is modeled by the poem's wide network of references to the protestant heresy of the day, antidogmatic quietist "Molinism" (10.1848–74).

A prospect so latitudinarian is admittedly arresting in a Supreme Pontiff, but Browning qualifies it too by a more conservative typology. He roots his Pope's recognition of the heroic in a mythic pattern that configures to itself, and so validates, the historically specified heroic deed:

> What were it else but the first things made new,
> But repetition of the miracle,
> The divine instance of self-sacrifice
> That never ends and aye begins for man?

                                    (10.1655–58)

In the courageous mutual faith of Pompilia and Caponsacchi the Pope descries a joint *Imitatio Christi*. Their recapitulation of the Incarnation, Christ's "transcendent act | Beside which even the creation fades | Into a puny exercise of power" (10.1339–41), gives human time an open-ended expansiveness that will be offset by Guido's cramping worship of mere power in book 11, and that indeed constitutes Browning's corrective to the unidirectional, genealogical conception of epic origins that dominates Guido's atavistic thought. The deferral of selfhood before another in an act of love resumes *the* archetypal act of love. By the same token it postpones the lovers' identity, exchanging who they are for who they will be, "Creative and self-sacrificing too, | And thus eventually God-like" (10.1382–83). The generous dilation of Pompilia's death across some two thousand lines is one, heavenly aspect of this temporal expansion; another, more somber aspect opens to Caponsacchi the purgatorial vista of a life to be endured without her. Each central speaker lives into the Holy Family myth they share: although they speak apart—Giuseppe/Joseph, Pompilia/Madonna, isolated from each other and even from the infant Gaetano—they are, as the saying goes, both in a tale. In the extended duration of that tale they come together: with each other, with those like the Pope and the poet whom the tale compels, and with those avatars like Perseus and Andromeda, St. George and Sabra, in whom allusions scattered across the poem show the tale has also led its mythic life for centuries.[56]

In a sense the heroism of Caponsacchi and Pompilia is not their own, but it is the same sense in which the stuff of *The Ring and the Book* was not Browning's own. He found his plot in history, and in the street; they pick

---

[56] What Alexander Welsh detects as "almost a conspiracy of truth telling among these good characters" finally smacks less of collusion in their common myth than of inspiration by it: *Strong Representations: Narrative and Circumstantial Evidence in England* (Baltimore and London: Johns Hopkins University Press, 1992) 203–4. I have developed Browning's cooperative heroic ideal at greater length in "Representation and Repristination: Virginity in *The Ring and the Book*," in *Virginal Sexuality and Textuality*, ed. Lloyd Davis (State University of New York Press, 1993) 67–86, along lines anticipated by Mary Rose Sullivan, *Browning's Voices in* The Ring and the Book: *A Study of Method and Meaning* (Toronto: University of Toronto Press, 1969) 86, 99–100; Flavia Alaya, "The Ring, the Rescue, and the Risorgimento: Reunifying the Brownings' Italy," *Browning Institute Studies* 5 (1978) 25–26; Judith Wilt, "The Laughter of Caponsacchi," *Victorian Poetry* 18 (1980) 337–57. Essential ingredients for all these readings come from W. C. De Vane, "The Virgin and the Dragon," *Yale Review* 37 (1947) 33–46, and Robert Langbaum, "Browning and the Question of Myth" (1966), rpt. in *The Word from Below: Essays on Modern Literature and Culture* (Madison: University of Wisconsin Press, 1987) 110–29—articles subjected to notable critique by Claudette Kemper Columbus, "*The Ring and the Book*: A Masque for the Making of Meaning,'" *Philological Quarterly* 53 (1974) 327–55; and by Adrienne Munich, *Andromeda's Chains: Gender and Interpretation in Victorian Literature and Art* (New York: Columbia University Press, 1989) 137–59.

theirs up there too, out of the Baroque confluence of interfering urban energies that swirled in the aftermath of the Counter-Reformation about the remains of the Renaissance.[57] The oppressiveness of Italian Catholicism remains an axiom, now as throughout this poet's career: Pompilia is repeatedly betrayed by compliant priests into the hands of a sadistic husband, while the canon Caponsacchi is derided, by himself among others, as a sort of fund-raising church gigolo. Still, it is within the cultural interstices of this same Christian establishment that Browning's principals find the heroic heart to disobey it. Caponsacchi's love at first sight for Pompilia hinges on a second-sighted recognition, in her face, of a Rafael madonna two centuries old that he has learned to love first (6.392–406). Likewise Pompilia resolves to flee oppression once she has seen her pregnancy in terms of the visible images (St. Michael and the Dragon, the Annunciation to the Virgin: 7.1200–47) that have been an illiterate girl's books.[58] While Pompilia and Caponsacchi do not *choose* to fall in love, exactly, their embrace of the unorthodox course love enjoins is a conscious commitment to which iconic Christian mythology has emboldened them, as in its degree it will encourage the Pope and inspire the poet. Agreeing to trace in their lives the pattern of the myth, they connect the accidents of experience to a more abiding order of cultural reality. Recouping with interest the lives they have given each other, they engage the constraining opportunities of their moment more fully and creatively within the myth than they could do without it.[59] In the myth, then, is their beginning: a model of liberal commitment that this epic from a decade of Risorgimento abroad and Reform at home deemed heroically timely.

★

[57] It was the Risorgimento version of these same energies that, soon after the Brownings' years in Italy, brought forth there a new nation state. Alaya, "The Ring, the Rescue . . . ," 24, discovers in *The Ring and the Book* a political allegory too striking to forget, too melodramatic to accept whole. Acknowledging this allegory yet resisting it, Matthew Reynolds teases out subtler valuations of nationhood and of poetry's capacity to weave sympathetic networks of support: *The Realms of Verse 1830–1870: English Poetry in a Time of Nation-Building* (Oxford and New York: Oxford University Press, 2001) 188–200.

[58] See a pair of complementary essays by Roy E. Gridley: "Browning's Pompilia," *Journal of English and Germanic Philology* 67 (1968) 64–83, and "Browning's Caponsacchi," *Victorian Poetry* 6 (1968) 281–95. On the Annunciation typology of 7.1222–30 see E. D. H. Johnson, "Robert Browning's Pluralistic Universe," *University of Toronto Quarterly* 31 (1961) 35. It was incidentally an Italian painted Annunciation that gave Eliot her theme for *The Spanish Gypsy*, in which "a young maiden . . . about to share in the ordinary lot of womanhood, full of young hope, has suddenly announced to her that she is chosen to fulfill a great destiny, entailing a terribly different experience": quoted in *Life*, ed. Cross, 3: 31.

[59] A point made about each of the lovers, in differing but compatible critical idiom, by Charles Edwin Nelson, "Role-Playing in *The Ring and the Book*," *Victorian Poetry* 4 (1966) 91–98; and William Walker, "*Pompilia* and Pompilia," *Victorian Poetry* 22 (1984) 47–63.

We return at last to consider how Tennyson made a proper epic out of *Idylls of the King*: a labor whose most engrossing feature in hindsight may be the poet's protracted reluctance to accomplish it. No work still in print that this book treats satisfies the traditional generic criteria better than the Laureate's twelve-book narrative of the legendary matter of Arthur, which at the beginning of our story had intrigued the Gothic epoist Arthur Hole by its very outlandishness (see Ch. 2) yet which in the fullness of the century Victorian Britons came to embrace as their favorite body of national myth.[60] So it must be borne in mind that Tennyson's now inevitable-seeming command performance did not come fully dressed before the public until the mid-1880s, half a century after the rich execution of "Morte d'Arthur" (composed 1833) and its sophisticated frame "The Epic" (written by 1838) had pointed the way (Ch. 8). What slowed the poet down was, in the first instance, a bad case of genre jitters, the same ague whose heats and chills beset every strong nineteenth-century poet attentive to the summons from on high. Tennyson littered his path towards the greatest of poetic kinds with cautionary disclaimers to the effect that it was a chimera-hunt, that attempting the formal epos nowadays was madness, that maneuverable small craft stood a better chance downstream with posterity than big heroic schooners, and so forth.[61] While *obiter dicta* like these were already implicit in the apologetics of "The Epic," to write them down there was clearly not to exorcise them; and they nagged at the poet for decades.

Such vaporous pressure assumed more concrete form, as this chapter began by noting, with the epic-retardant effect exerted across the 1850s by the remarkable successes of prose fiction. Given the permanent slump in poetry sales since the 1820s, the Victorian novel's engrossment of literary market share can have had great practical weight with only a very few authors who persisted as poets in spite of it all. But among these few Tennyson stood foremost, and the 1859 *Idylls*, outreach from the stuff of

---

[60] See Stephanie L. Barczewski, *Myth and National Identity in Nineteenth-Century Britain: The Legends of King Arthur and Robin Hood* (Oxford and New York: Oxford University Press, 2000). On 114 she quotes that Victorian para-epic the 9th edn. of the *Encyclopaedia Britannica*: Malory's *Morte d'Arthur* was "truly *the* epic of the English mind as the *Iliad* is the epic of the Greek mind" (10: 173).

[61] Faithful to his classical education, as late as 2 December 1872 Tennyson was still grumbling in a letter to George Grove about the "misnomer" of R. H. Hutton's having called "the Idylls an Epic which they are not": *The Letters of Alfred Lord Tennyson*, ed. Cecil Lang and Edgar Shannon, vol. 3 (Oxford: Clarendon Press, 1990) 44. See also our Ch. 1, n. 3. It was all to no avail. Stopford Brooke's pronouncement in the self-described "primer" *English Literature* (1879; rev. edn. New York: American Book Company, 1895) 184, was representative: "The *Idylls of the King* are a kind of epic."

antique legend toward modern bourgeois realism was in part entrepreneur-
ially motivated. It was also swiftly requited by complementary ventures into
historical fiction by the leading novelists of the day. Dickens's *A Tale of Two
Cities* and Eliot's *Romola*, for example, exported into bygone epochs tools of
contemporary verisimilitude that refined on the example of Scott with new
subtleties of symbolic resonance, archival diligence, and Victorian social
science.[62] At the same time these novels planted at the center of the
historical crises they treated renditions of marriage, home, and family that
closely paralleled the poet's 1859 practice of breaking the heroic to domestic
measure.

If anything the novels solved more successfully the problem that had been
exercising Tennyson. Where he sought to show how like us the great ones
of the past could be, Dickens and Eliot worked the other side of the street,
taking such circumstantial equality for granted (as the novel obliged them to
do) and drawing out the world-historical import of the everyday. It was this
elevation within the novel, not Tennyson's elegant sartorial trimming of
heirlooms to suit contemporary common measure, that expressed the
authentic epic impulse of a time when proposals for democratic reform
were bringing community and sovereignty into fresh ideological relation.
Witness, to look no further than *The Ring and the Book*, the importance
accorded there by that alleged novelist *manqué* Browning to the mythic
enlargement of ordinary experience.

Tennyson stood his idyllic ground through the new edition of 1862 and
the *Enoch Arden* volume of 1864, where the long title poem girdled the
globe only to sacrifice, with the *Idylls*, at the nuclear hearth of the family.
But before long the public expectation that Tennyson should bestow upon
the world's first nation a monument worthy of its eminence began to tell on
him again; and finally, in our *annus mirabilis* 1868, he broke through
prolonged writer's block into an epic rendition of the pivotal episode of
the quest for the Sangraal. The momentum of his rapidly drafted "The Holy
Grail" led on soon to "The Coming of Arthur," the latter's opposite
number "The Passing of Arthur" (which set the old "Morte" within a
freshly written last-battle scenario), and "Pelleas and Ettarre"—four idylls in
all, composed in a matter of months and published in 1869, to match as at a
Round Table the four lady-named idylls of a decade before. To these eight

---

[62] Karen Chase writes searchingly about these matters in "The Modern Family and the Ancient
Image in *Romola*," *Dickens Studies Annual* 14 (1985) 303–26. See also Catherine Waters, *Dickens
and the Politics of the Family* (Cambridge: Cambridge University Press, 1997) 122–49.

books, as they might only now be frankly called, the poet added in an 1872 edition two more, "Gareth and Lynette" and "The Last Tournament," each filling a place within the continuous narrative of Camelot's rise and decline that the version of 1859 had implied but that had not till 1869 been firmly outlined and sketched into narrative relation. When in 1873 Tennyson split the "Enid" idyll in two to create in effect an eleventh book, he had already drafted a twelfth, "Balin and Balan," which practically concluded his epic labors—yet which, surprisingly, he withheld from publication for another dozen years.

Was it epo-phobic superstition that stayed his hand, a Virgilian fear of claiming outright the genre he had dallied with so long? No doubt a perfectionist's anxiety and a Victorian's attachment to the deferral of gratification both had a part in delaying Tennyson's final epic stroke, as no doubt the obscure inhibition of a half-believer had restrained him during the mid-1860s when contemplating the taboo mysteries of the Grail. A further consideration is also worth pondering here: Tennyson negotiated each of these impasses just after the nation had turned a major corner in its extension of the franchise. The near match in dates between the Second (1867) and Third (1884) Reform Bills and the Poet Laureate's large epic strides in 1869 and 1886 explains nothing *per se*, but it is a coincidence the explanation of which may tell us much.

One plausible lead, especially where so technically fastidious a poet as Tennyson is concerned, lies in the politics of literary form. The major 1860s epics we have considered in this chapter exemplify two basic species of narrative unity: the logical through-line of diachronic plot; and the synchrony of pattern, whether structurally internal to a given plot (repetitive, symmetrical, fractal) or expressed in the disposition of integral plots within some larger design. We found the latter plan most fully elaborated in *The Earthly Paradise*, but an alternative version is clearly present, and is glanced at by name, in Browning's *Ring*. The ingredients that Morris and Browning thus incorporate are themselves plots of the more usual linear type, which neo-Aristotelian standards predominant since the Renaissance had enjoined on the writer of epic, and which characterizes the rest of the poems this chapter has discussed—most conspicuously, and deliberately, Eliot's headstrong *Spanish Gypsy*.

Tennyson's practice since the 1830s had acquainted him well with the inherence of both these types of unity in the sub-epic genres of idyllic and epyllion; how such poems as "The Lady of Shalott" and "Ulysses" maintain position or go forward is a question any inquisitive student of his early writing confronts.[63] By the 1860s *The Princess*, *In Memoriam*, and *Maud* had shown how decidedly political a valence each of these narrative types possessed. Plottedness stood in Tennyson's mind for historical momentum, a current of events whose drift was strong yet dark and might well lead to what his alarmist mentor Carlyle started around now to call "shooting Niagara"; pattern connoted government, the ordinance of events under the arrangement of law—and also, as a price paid for stability, subjection to regimes of simplification, distortion, and restraint. The seasoned Tory in Tennyson was dismayed at what crises the turbulent 1860s portended, while the undying Cambridge Apostle in him cast a skeptical eye on what policies and expedients the decade in practice called forth.[64] Meanwhile, the poet in him felt the more deeply an epic need to coordinate the powers within culture that made for fixity with those that made for flux. As yet the 1859 *Idylls* had failed to address this formal need because they had emphasized synchronic design over diachronic development. The metaphoric motif of textile weaving in all four idylls, for example, or their ubiquitous imagery of light playing on broken water, does more to hold the volume together than does the loosely implied longitudinal concatenation of events linking Geraint's initial malaise to the ringing indictment that a doomed Arthur pronounces at the close. Much the same might be said, by the way, of the anonymous *Arthur's Knights: An Adventure from the Legend of the Sangrale*, a verse romance also published in 1859 in a second edition that, while expressly declining to compete with Tennyson, nevertheless practiced braiding and embedding techniques like his. Different verse forms grace the several parts of this romance sampler for beginning scholars ("printed for the amusement of those young people who have some curiosity about the early English romance": Preface, iv). The whole medley, like Tennyson's, breathes an ambience of British decline that is shot with utopian gleams but never attains firm narrative shape.

How to give an overall story line the lead, while maintaining the dainty imagistic consistency wrought forth in 1859, was one problem that Tennyson's Arthurian project had harbored for some time. It came to a head as he struggled with "The Holy Grail." The aesthetic issues posed by his quest for

---

[63] See Robert Pattison, *Tennyson and Tradition* (Cambridge, Mass.: Harvard University Press, 1979).

[64] On the crucial role played by a sophisticated political understanding of myth and belief among Tennyson's undergraduate set, see Armstrong, *Victorian Poetry*, 45–67.

a master narrative entailed, moreover, issues of mastery as such: what authority to vest in the dominant story line, whence to derive it, in whose name to speak it, what sort of credence to invite from a modern readership. To recall the thematics of authority in Ingelow and Bickersteth, not to mention Eliot and Browning, is to appreciate the gravity that attended these questions in the 1860s. To bear in mind the contemporary Reform debates is to appreciate what was at stake then in the matter of national spokesmanship and representation. To invoke contemporary controversies over the Higher Criticism is to appreciate how the stakes went up as Tennyson ventured, with this idyll, onto explicitly religious terrain.[65]

The inflammatory problem of the Grail legend may have been back-lit for Tennyson by an epicizing poem brought out privately in 1864 by an antiquarian eccentric of genuine gifts whom he had consulted on Arthurian questions years before. In *The Quest of the Sangraal*, Robert Stephen Hawker met the mystique of the Grail on its own unearthly terrain. Fusing unshaken High-Church piety with a homegrown Cornish patriotism, this stranded child of 1820s apocalyptic fervor mounted the compass-quadrated British geography of his fourfold *Sangraal* on a visionary cosmology keyed to the conic sections of geometry, yet graced too by the footprints of angels and dead-set against the incursions of "giant-men" (shades of Ingelow, if not of Horne's *Orion!*) to whose malignant Enlightenment engineering "The myths were rendered up: and one by one, | The fire—the light—the air— were tamed and bound" (242).[66] Already for Hawker's Merlin the sacred bond between Britain's "lonely" land and "the silent grasp | Of thrilling worlds" is a thing of the past (226), and restoring cosmic communion to an irreligious age is what *The Quest of the Sangraal* is all about. Deploying his four knights in accordance with this arcane redemptive scheme seems to have proved too much for Hawker, whose posthumous *Poetical Works* of

---

[65] The interplay between Tennyson's 1860s eminence as an authority in matters Arthurian and his reluctance to press forward with the *Idylls* is discussed in Geoffrey and Kathleen Tillotson, *Mid-Victorian Studies* (London: Athlone Press, 1965) 95–100. Here as so often, the poet's hesitancy mirrored his culture's: see Ian Small, *Conditions for Criticism: Authority, Knowledge, and Literature in the Late Nineteenth Century* (Oxford: Clarendon Press, 1991) 30, on a competition that reached crisis proportions in the 1860s among unreconciled "disciplines of knowledge," which offered not only "different explanations of human society" but more fundamentally "competing epistemologies" and thus "competing models of authority." Tennyson addressed this crisis in his analysis of what we are dubbing "Arthurity" and in his ramification of narrative perspectives from "The Holy Grail" forward.

[66] Hawker glossed these lines as embodying "my notions of the Battle of Waterloo and the Armstrong Gun—Gas, Steam, Electric Telegraph": *Life and Letters of Robert Stephen Hawker*, ed. C. E. Byles (London: Lane, 1904) 446.

1879 still contained no more than a first book and the fragment of a second. But the details matter less than their proof that a talented agemate of Tennyson's—the two as young men had respectively won the 1827 Oxford and Cambridge poetry prizes—could in the 1860s still conceive a high-fidelity epic treating Arthurian material in much the same authoritarian spirit that animated Atherstone's scriptural *Israel in Egypt* a few years previously.[67]

From this hieratic and authoritarian spirit—whatever Tennyson knew or didn't about its avatar in Hawker, or for that matter in the likewise supernaturalized (and, claimed Hawker, plagiarized) *Quest of the Sancgreall* that Thomas Westwood published in Tennysonian-idyllic blank verse in 1868—"The Holy Grail" could hardly have departed more decisively than it did without descending into outright irreverence.[68] Hawker's mystical veneration for Christian sanctities and local folkways illuminates by contrast how fully Tennyson kept faith in 1869 with his 1859 commitment to a psycho-social understanding of such matters. The convent in "Guinevere" having offered the shamed queen less a spiritual home than a political asylum and marital penitentiary, Percival's inspiration in "The Holy Grail" likewise takes its rise from a cloistered nun's sexual sublimation (or as Gawain wickedly puts it at idyll's end, reproved but unrefuted, "holy virgins in their ecstasies": 8.863). Whatever intrinsic virtue may attach to the Grail, Tennyson renders its quest as an episode of chivalric caste hysteria that decimates Camelot by making alienated saints or embittered cynics of Arthur's best knights. Such virtue as the Grail possesses is registered in political terms, much as in "Merlin and Vivien" the "charm" or spell that was passed from one charisma-less principal to another seemed no more magical than stolen code in a spy intrigue.

No more magical, that is to say, than antique encryption, group hallu-cination, radical sublimation, transformative repentance. No more magical than these sheerly cultural phenomena, which are finally intelligible on

---

[67] John Heath-Stubbs, *The Darkling Plain* (London: Eyre and Spottiswoode, 1950) 82–88, has high praise for Hawker's *Sangraal*. Piers Brendon, *Hawker of Morwenstow: Portrait of a Victorian Eccentric* (London: Jonathan Cape, 1975) sets the poet's ambition and frustration in explanatory biographical context. Whatever explains it, Hawker's power was for the short burst: his ten-quatrain ballad pastiche "The Song of the Western Men" passed with contemporaries for authentic and enjoys (familiarly known as "Trelawny") the status of a national anthem in Cornwall.

[68] Beverly Taylor and Elisabeth Brewer, *The Return of King Arthur: British and American Arthurian Literature since 1800* (Totowa: Barnes and Noble, 1983) 87–88, note parallels between Hawker and Westwood, and the sharp divergence of Tennyson from both.

secular terms—yet no less magical than these things either, provided Tennyson could contrive to relocate the aura of the uncanny from Hawker's cone of heaven to a more modern and public haunt. "Like a breath of inspiration" it came to Tennyson at some point in 1868 that this could indeed be done, and moreover that such a transfer of aura was not just aesthetically possible but generically opportune.[69] And Tennyson found his epic key (where it often lies in cases of creative breakthrough) right at the crux of his dilemma, at the intersection between the two daunting prospects that wedged him in. Myth's occult powers on one side and the insurgent phenomena of modern commercial democratization on the other were values, he realized, that might prove mutually fungible. For the living power of the Grail legend resided precisely in its status as a *legend*, a matter communally transmitted and received. Charged to the utmost with both eucharistic and commemorative energies, the chalice of the Lord's Supper was an image ostentatiously fusing ritual synchrony with diachronic tradition.[70] It marked out a confluence where society and history became aspects of each other, a juncture on which Tennyson might sustain an epic capable at once of soliciting modern belief and of assaying the role played by belief within public life.

The authority that conveyed the Arthurian legend and the authority that the legend conferred were, he saw, of the same kind. His faith in Malory's book, and Malory's in the "Frensshe booke" before him, were not substantially different from the faith Tennyson's own book-in-progress might elicit from Victorian readers; and that faith was finally, in turn, one with the power that crowned kings, upheld nations, and underwrote constitutions (especially unwritten ones like Britain's). Tennyson's freshly politicized conception of the common faith as a culturally subtending power—virtually supernatural if not literally so, as we have concurrently seen it to be in the blind trust of Eliot's Fedalma and the lovers' leap of Browning's Pompilia and Caponsacchi—disclosed within the domestic-fiction topos of marital fidelity from the 1859 *Idylls* a thesis that possessed epic potential.[71] And the

---

[69] Quoted from the poet's wife Emily in *A Variorum Edition of Tennyson's* Idylls of the King, ed. John Pfordresher (New York and London: Columbia University Press, 1973) 37.

[70] Howard W. Fulweiler, "Tennyson's 'The Holy Grail': The Representation of Representation," *Renascence* 38 (1986) 144–59, finds the poet probing by means of the metasymbolic Grail a crisis of European proportions within the traditional conviction of membership in a meaningful community.

[71] See, e.g. Steven Dillon's subtle exploration of how within the finished *Idylls* "Guinevere" stages, by allusive "poetic ventriloquism," a generic contest wherein (epic thrusting up through

IN PLIGHT OF TROTH: 1860–1870

narrative extrapolation of this thesis would constitute the overarching plot Tennyson had been looking for: the meteoric rise to wholeness, and subsequent slow disintegration, of a polity whose essentially legendary, faith-dependent character—"never built at all," as Merlin says of Camelot, "And therefore built for ever" (2.273–74)—made it an ideal political image for the ruthless lability with which any actual state represents the state of mind abroad among its people.[72]

"The Holy Grail" showed the way to such an epic analysis of political authority through both its plot and its narrative mediation. Tennyson treats the Grail quest as an unmitigated disaster for the Arthurian program of national reform: a perversion, in fact, of reforming zeal itself, detached from the common wealth and focused on projects of individual salvation that are grandiose and atomizing at once. That this perversion inhabits the Arthurian ideal is evident in the King's own ambivalence. From the first he denounces his knights' centrifugal quest after "A sign to maim this Order which I made" (8.297), yet on the dire fulfillment of his prediction his speech from the throne concludes with a mystic's susceptibility to "visions of the night or of the day" that de-realize earth, light, air—"yea, his very hand and foot" (8.906–13). Such visionary talk appears to be a nod towards Hawker, in whose Grail poem a stay-at-home Arthur still serves as cheerleading toastmaster to the embarking questers; actually for Tennyson it forms part of a more complex movement in the opposite direction. For his Arthur is an essentially after-hours or weekend mystic, in a division of labor from leisure that not only recapitulates the rhythms industrialization had installed in Victorian life but also mythically ratifies the *de facto* disestablishment of the church from its former position of practical influence within the Anglican state. A public Telemachus to his own private Ulysses, Tennyson's Arthur incarnates, as it were in a king's two bodies, the condition of a secularized polity that is officially vowed to the toleration of coexistent yet incommensurable

---

pastoral) "the King's Miltonic contexts confront the idyllic remnants of Camelot": "Milton and Tennyson's 'Guinevere,' " *ELH* 54 (1987) 129–55. See on a like theme my "Trials of Fiction: Novel and Epic in the Geraint and Enid Episodes from *Idylls of the King*," *Victorian Poetry* 30 (1992) 441–61.

[72] This theme grounds John Rosenberg's magisterial readings in *The Fall of Camelot: A Study of Tennyson's* Idylls of the King (Cambridge, Mass.: Harvard University Press, 1973) and in "Tennyson and the Passing of Arthur," in *The Passing of Arthur: New Essays in Arthurian Tradition*, ed. Christopher Baswell and William Sharpe (New York: Garland, 1988) 221–34.

claims about the very questions that, its subjects piously agree, matter more than anything.[73]

This secular tolerationism recalls the free-speech platform of Browning's epic narrative and the peaceably distributive scheme of Morris's; Tennyson too found for it an analogue in narrative form. In "The Holy Grail" he opposed to the unanimous diegetic orthodoxy of Hawker's *Sangraal* the strongly secular effect of a multiple-mediated narration. The idyll is framed as a reminiscent dialogue between the ascetically retired Sir Percivale and a fellow monk, which tends to default to a monologue incorporating Percivale's quest, his eyewitness account of the apotheosis of Galahad, and his report of the inconclusive first-person depositions by Bors and Lancelot at their Camelot debriefing. While this narrative nest of a monologue does not arouse suspicion on anything like Browning's order about bias or ulterior motive, the poem's fragmented witness as to where the Holy Grail was sighted when, and what it may abidingly *be* when all is said, firmly underscores Arthur's principle that "these have seen according to their sight" (8.871). This is just the principle of the Higher Criticism that *Essays and Reviews* had brought home to thoughtful believers in the 1860s, and one that Tennyson, having worked it out in "The Holy Grail," proceeded to work into the expanding framework of his epic. In 1868 he made the *Idylls* deliberately heterogeneous and relativistic.[74] The contention among diverging myths of origin in "The Coming of Arthur," the clash of incompatible worldviews in "Balin and Balan," the remarkable experimentation of "The Last Tournament" with a Decadent juxtaposition and imagistic suturing of distinct narrative modes—these devices in effect reframed the poem in such a way that even the interpersonal contretemps typical of the idylls from 1859 came to seem, in the enlarged context that 1868 built for them, ominously symptomatic of a deep public disorder. In making an epic virtue of the pluralist necessity to which the title *Idylls of the King* committed him, Tennyson was analogically, and with a Laureate decorum equal to his Tory misgivings, rehearsing the great constitutional shift within Britain in his lifetime.

[73] See Elaine Jordan, *Alfred Tennyson* (Cambridge: Cambridge University Press, 1988) 170–77.
[74] Buckler, *Man and His Myths: Tennyson's* Idylls of the King *in Critical Context* (New York: New York University Press, 1984), organizes the poem around this perspectivist principle. Richard A. Sylvia, " 'Parabolic Drift' as Narrative Method in Tennyson's *Idylls*: A New Reading of 'The Holy Grail,' " *Journal of Narrative Technique* 17 (1987) 297, dates the installation of this principle to the 1869 text, when "narrative *qua* narrative became a prominent aspect" and new importance attached to "the interpretive encounter implicit in storytelling."

The emphasis in the pivotal "Holy Grail" on variable report harks back to Arthur's initial reaction when the vows have first been sworn in his absence, which is to mount an inquest into who actually saw what. None but Galahad, it turns out, has in truth beheld the Grail; the rest can only say with Percivale, "since I did not see the Holy Thing, | I sware a vow to follow it" (8.281–82). Lamenting the folly of such copycat spiritual faddism—"But one hath seen, and all the blind will see. | Go, since your vows are sacred, being made" (8.313–14)—Arthur nevertheless gives his blessing. And he does so because he must. For there is no qualitative difference between the knights' Grail vows now and those they once swore to obey Arthur as their liege. It is not only that, as the finished *Idylls* will repeatedly aver, "Man's word is God in man" (1.132, 6.8)—though we may note in passing that this confession of faith is a working definition in slogan form of the divine power that, socially vested in human language, actually rules Tennyson's epic. The Arthurian dilemma to which the poet wrote his way in "The Holy Grail" has less to do with the formal knightly vow than with its vulgar poor relation: that ragged tissue of informally circulating, half-articulate, variously credited swapping of assertion and assent which we call gossip or rumor. Truth at second hand, or seventh, the locally negligible yet cumulatively invincible force of what everybody is not compelled, just cogently *supposed*, to believe: this is the ambient condition that motivates the overwhelming majority of the knightly quests, even as the knights undertake them, with compensatory high-mindedness, in order to overcome precisely that derivative condition by seeing "the Holy Thing," the *Ding-an-sich*, for themselves. Majority decision-making of this unballoted, unstoppable kind (and, behind it, the irregular consensus-bending swirl of general intelligence) served Tennyson as a figure for the democratic parliamentary structure his generation were putting in place (and, behind it, the mass-mediated torrent of news and opinion).

All-pervasive, mutant, imprecise yet incorrigible, the casual word's power to propagate as social truth what goes without saying assumed in the evolving *Idylls* the function of myth; and its history-making demotic pressure is to be felt in each addition Tennyson made after 1868. "The Coming of Arthur" expressly attributes the upstart monarch's authority— his *Arthurity*, we may say—to nothing more than his capacity to elicit belief from those who acclaim him king. (Again, the deployment of routine romance materials to legitimate Arthur in Westwood's 1866 *The Sword of*

Kingship shows how unconventional Tennyson's handling was.[75]) When a practically fascist inaugural anthem added to "The Coming" in the edition of 1873 hails Arthur as a divine confidant, "In whom high God hath breathed a secret thing" and "a secret word" (1.488–500), we witness the apotheosis of rumor as a mass medium doubling as a *raison d'état*.[76] This choral apotheosis permutes into demonic allegory, on the far side of "The Holy Grail," when Pelleas' sexual betrayal by Ettarre crazes his brittle idealism into invidious yellow journalism:

> "I have many names," he cried:
> "I am wrath and shame and hate and evil fame,
> And like a poisonous wind I pass to blast
> And blaze the crime of Lancelot and the Queen."
>
> (9.555–58)

But slow-witted Pelleas is merely the last to know. Long before his enlightenment the business of "evil fame" has been done by Vivien, her role expanded in 1874 by a long passage that sets her rumor-mongering career on a collision course with the parabolic trajectory of the king who is her counterpart ("as Arthur in the highest | Leaven'd the world, so Vivien in the lowest": 6.138–39); and by Modred, whose mooted paternity and marginal loitering make him the incarnation of bad report. Finally Modred's is the reckoning the king must pay, in the rewritten "Passing of Arthur," with mortal single combat in the aftermath of an existentially absurd battle that decays from blows to "Oaths, insult, filth, and monstrous blasphemies" (12.114)—penultimate breakdown products, in other words, of the civilizing process that Camelot has founded on the zeitgeist, and the mere breath, of a vow.

What Pelleas gets dead right is that the linchpin of Arthurity as a regime of consensual belief is the royal hierogamy at the top. The trothplight between Guinevere and Arthur in the sequentially first idyll (1869,

---

[75] The uncertain basis for Arthur's authority enfranchises Tennyson, as Elliot L. Gilbert shows, to derive his king's mandate not only from the people but from the very real estate: "The Female King: Tennyson's Arthurian Apocalypse," *PMLA* 98 (1983) 89–113.

[76] The best analysis after Tennyson's of this emergent politics of Victorian mass culture may be Philip Rosenberg's in *The Seventh Hero: Thomas Carlyle and the Theory of Radical Activism* (Cambridge, Mass.: Harvard University Press, 1974). An "asymmetrical dependency in the relationship of leader and follower is at the heart of the radical meaning of Carlyle's hero theory, for the presence of a heroic disposition among those from whom the hero is to draw his followers is, as we have seen, a vital prerequisite for the hero's own career.... The very process which makes the hero possible ... necessarily creates a revolutionary situation" (202).

expanded 1873) models for good and ill the liaisons that the 1859 collection had centered on and to whose number later idylls continued to add; and with the royal marriage's collapse that of the regime is a foregone conclusion, an accident waiting to happen.[77] Oddly, a foregone conclusion is exactly what the all-culpable adultery proves to be too. Nothing is more weirdly Victorian about *Idylls of the King*—or more consistent with its narrative logic—than the fact that the queen's adultery with Lancelot is something everybody already knows about yet nobody ever talks about. Troubling the air around Geraint and Enid as early as 3.24, common knowledge even to Elaine's far-rusticated stump of a father at 7.1074, the open secret of Camelot's first bedroom is never once affirmed on the narrator's authority: "he that tells the tale" (3.161, 9.482, 10.226) is, in this paramount matter, not one to tell tales at all. Instead, and with quiet daring, he leaves the reader to pick it up on the margin, out of the gutter, in the whispered turning of a page, as what must be true because it is so ostentatiously unmentionable.[78] A blind spot at the focus of the picture, abuzz with the white noise of consensus, the cuckolding of Arthur stands for Tennyson where the mythic origin of the Zíncali does for Eliot: each narrative blank highlights that faith in faith itself which is the paramount concern of epic during the 1860s.

A corollary epic feature is the use Tennyson found for the prophetic logic of the foregone conclusion as he rounded the *Idylls* to completion and connected its narrative line. For in the finally complete 1886 edition he slotted "Balin and Balan" into sixth or keystone position, where many an epoist since Virgil had sent heroes down to the dead in order to learn the future from the past; and it is in this latest-written idyll that the logic of self-fulfilling prophecy receives fullest treatment. Hapless Balin's morally therapeutic worship of queenly purity comes to grief, not when he eavesdrops on a scene of heavy-breathing innuendo between Guinevere and Lancelot

[77] An ample Victorian overlap among concepts of marital fidelity, political fealty, and metaphysical faith let Tennyson enlist the domestic *Idylls* of 1859 almost effortlessly under the new epic command. See for the broader European bearings of this constellation Tony Tanner, *Adultery in the Novel: Contract and Transgression* (Baltimore: Johns Hopkins University Press, 1979); for their sequel today Adam Phillips, *Monogamy* (London: Faber, 1996): "Monogamy makes the larger abstractions real, as religion once did. Faith, hope, trust, morality; these are domestic matters now. Indeed, we contrast monogamy not with bigamy or polygamy but with infidelity, because it is our secular religion" (10).

[78] This argument emerges in more detail in my article "The Epic Plight of Troth in *Idylls of the King*," *ELH* 58 (1991) 701–20. See also Dillon, "Scandals of War: The Authority of Tennyson's *Idylls*," *Essays in Literature* 18 (1991) 180–95; and James Eli Adams, "Harlots and Base Interpreters: Scandal and Slander in *Idylls of the King*," *Victorian Poetry* 30 (1992) 421–39.

(6.235–84)—the closest the poem will come to rendering them *in flagrante delicto*—not then, but when Vivien later invents and retails for Balin's benefit a Harlequin-romance clinch between queen and knight, and he accepts her fiction as common knowledge: "It is truth" (6.519). The reported shock of the consensual, not the direct evidence of his own senses, suffices to drive Balin wild again, as it will Elaine and Pelleas in the idylls that come next. The madness of all three carries Tennyson's implication that believing in the royal adultery is the badge of civic competence in Arthur's Camelot, as it is of readerly competence in Victoria's Britain, where to be sure everyone already knew the story to begin with.

Be it a king's legitimacy, a queen's seduction, a prince's illegitimacy, the truth of any such matter in *Idylls of the King* is the troth not of witness but of reception. Sovereign power belongs to the public, whose seeing is believing and whose trust in what they hear means it must be so. "I perish by this people which I made" (12.190): Arthur's formulation, plangent with reproach in the 1842 "Morte," had a timbre more analytic, and fatalistic, when thirty additional years had shown his poet more about the making of a people. The amen of Arthurity draped, under cover of Tennyson's gorgeously flimsy medieval costuming, the condition of faith in modern consumer culture.[79]

The poet's drawn-out worries lest *Idylls of the King* fail to cohere into epic unity yielded during the later 1860s to a solution that, in its turn, expressed a graver and timelier concern. This was Tennyson's concern lest the Victorian national identity that his epic's unity evoked and mirrored might hinge on nothing but a mass public's drifting caprice, codified by Parliament into the policy of the moment. What agency or industry might manipulate the consensus of the future, and with what ease, were questions the Laureate was better placed to ponder than any poet since Scott and Byron; and he had the extra advantage of witnessing how another half-century's technological and distributive innovation had facilitated the exploitation of public opinion and taste.[80]

[79] Dino Franco Felluga, *The Perversity of Poetry* (Albany: State University of New York Press, 2005) 153–57, finds Tennyson's ambivalence about consumerism already present in the *Idylls* of 1859, where it is coded into a clutch of narratives about dubious women and doubting men.

[80] This is to resist the charge that Tennyson's brand of Victorian medievalism amounted to escapism—an opinion older even than the first reviews (since the poet wrote it into "The Epic" before 1842) and not rare today: witness John Lucas, *England and Englishness: Ideas of Nationhood in English Poetry 1688–1900* (London: Hogarth Press, 1990) 190. It is a charge best met frontally, by

Tennyson knew about these developments because he was complicit with them. Too apt a literary businessman—content-producer and taste-maker in one—not to grasp that the very prestige of epic might, in the last third of the century, be parlayed from cultural capital into political influence, he capped the *Idylls* in 1873 with a verse epistle "To the Queen" that is part retroactive epic invocation and part last-page editorial leader. Counterbalancing the prefatory "Dedication" he had addressed to her in 1862 on the occasion of her widowhood, the new concluding poem left the healing conciliations of that essentially domestic piece behind. "To the Queen" is an imperialist *advertisement*, in that term's literal sense of an alert: a clarion warning against the complacencies of devolution in Canada, India, and elsewhere. "Is this the tone of empire?" or is it rather the "voice" of "Some third-rate isle half-lost among her seas?" (18, 25). Tennyson ascribes the softening of Britain's global resolve to commercial calculation in a land that grows "wealthier—wealthier—hour by hour!" (23) yet lies prone thereby to

> Waverings of every vane with every wind,
> And wordy trucklings to the transient hour,
> And fierce or careless looseners of the faith.

> (50–52)

Tennyson's horrified fascination with "that battle in the West, | Where all of high and holy dies away" (65–66)—the last words his epic speaks, replaying the hopeless vision that shadows his twelfth and last book—was not so enthralling as to cloud his understanding of how the cultural politics of modern Britain actually worked. It was the "Waverings of every vane with every wind" (the denunciatory line runs rings around itself) that meant a prosodically splendid blast of invective from the Laureate's quarter might

---

class-action countersuit mounted as follows: The medievalist tradition descending from Scott across the 19th cent. was cultural-political to the gauntlet-tips (see Chs. 3 and 4); the burden of proof rests with those who claim that a given work escapes this tradition into political irrelevance; some few medievalizing works did so escape; the Poet Laureate's was not among them. This defense admittedly leaves the *Idylls* exposed to the charges of partisan presentism that are embedded in famous dismissals by Swinburne ("the *Morte d'Albert*") and Hopkins ("Charades from the Middle Ages"), or in W. H. Mallock's "How to Make an Epic Poem Like Mr. T★nn★s★n": "Be content with the nearest approach to a hero available, namely a prig"; then having added "a large number of men and women of the nineteenth century, in fancy-ball costume, flavoured with a great many very possible vices, and a few impossible virtues," proceed to "wound slightly the head of the blameless prig; remove him suddenly from the table, and keep in a cool barge for future use." *Every Man his own Poet; or, The Inspired Singer's Recipe Book*, 3rd edn. (1877); rpt. with W. C. Bennett, *The Anti-Maud* (New York: Garland, 1986).

make a difference. The very lines offset above were "wordy trucklings," to a crisis hour of whose perennial transiency the great arc of Arthur's rise and fall gave an illustration mythic and timely at once. The shrugging address that a radically disaffected Morris had lately customized to "an idle day," and Browning's more fierce, liberally loosened valediction to the "British Public, who may like me yet" (*The Ring and the Book* 12.835), were directed to the same national ear Tennyson here sought to capture with a prosodically resplendent flourish to the Queen. At last all three epics were addressed to the same sovereign mystery, which the Laureate here calls their "crown'd Republic's crowning common-sense" (61): a phrase whose carven intricacy promotes the Republic (not the "Realm") over the crown, and promotes over both that fickle, invincibly flimsy commonsense which makes and breaks regimes on the mythology of the moment.

11

For All the World:

Eclectic Epic 1870–1895

Tennyson was an amateur of Persian poetry and would have known
Firdusi's *Sháh Námeh*, which became available in translation in 1832.[1]
One wonders whether that epic's English name struck him as a foil for
his own. As titles *The Book of Kings* and *Idylls of the King* invert each
other's one-and-many emphasis in ways anticipating what will be a chief
problematic for this chapter: the demand placed by the criterion of epic
unity on the compiler's arts of gathering, sorting, and displaying materials
whose exoticism or diversity both incites to their collection and impedes it.
Where the first-millennium Persian had approached a nation's history with
a telescope that held miscellaneous events (*Kings*) in a single perspective
(*The Book*), Tennyson offered the Victorian public a kaleidoscope whose
arrangement of idylls centered miscellaneous perspectives on a single topic,
the political ideal vested in the king. In this the Laureate's always impressive
contemporaneity emerges afresh. For it seems that the object of every late
nineteenth-century discourse conformed to the pattern he privileged: a
heterogeneity that, robust and efflorescent, was at the same time rendered
intelligible by a common denominator in natural law or, continuous
with that law, in the historically unfolding essence of humanity. While
this epistemic pattern found its most memorable focus in Darwinism,
it pervaded every department of ambitiously comprehensive intellectual
endeavor during the long *fin de siècle*, and it was repeatedly manifested in
the era's cultivation of epic forms.

---

[1] In the preface to his abridged translation of 1832, James Atkinson repudiated as sacrilege any
comparison between "Firdausí" and Homer as epic poets, but did allow for parallels with chivalric
romance, whose historical development he suspected the *Sháh Námeh* of having influenced.

The eclectic character that epic assumed toward the close of the nineteenth century may be appreciated by analogy to forms of Victorian public representation that are better known. In London's great places and thoroughfares, and in lesser replication across the empire, monuments built to the Queen or Prince Consort did literally *build to* them from supporting bases in the continents and oceans, or from allegorical effigies of the Industries and Arts. To modern eyes such imperial exuberance will overpower the royal figurine it enshrines; but for their initial viewers they possessed an ideological decorum, a harmony between far-flung causes and capital effects, to which the abundance of foundational and collateral decoration made an essential contribution.[2] It was much the same with the great metropolitan museums: what saved them from collapsing back, under the sheer weight of ever-increasing holdings, into the curio-cabinet jumble they had evolved from was a coordinating idea of civilization. All history's trade routes converged on the museum, whose display spaces and traffic patterns inculcated a narrative into which the profuse energies of the archival miscellany fed—in a loop of reinforcement on which department-store magnates down the road were not slow to capitalize, before century's end, with displays making all the world a dream of acquisition.[3] Even the buildings that housed these late-Victorian institutions tended to ransack the history of architecture and recombine its styles with effects that, while they have made the fastidious shudder, express with edifying forthrightness that structure of exhumation and importation, on one hand, and collation of heterogeneous parts, on the other, which also typifies the period's distinctly archival monuments of extended verse.

Twice before in the nineteenth century we have seen epic go to pieces— relax its usual grip on a large action, that is, and devote itself instead to activities of research and arrangement—and each time the phenomenon has been legible as the response to a crisis lately weathered in Britain's sense of itself. Moore's Regency medley of epyllia in *Lalla Rookh* (Ch. 5) and the

---

[2] A. D. Harvey notes in *Literature into History* (London: St. Martin's Press, 1988) that from the beginning of the century the production of national epics was associated with the erection of "monumental buildings and statuary across Europe" (147–48); the end of the century inflected this momentum, we may add, with empire's preter-national twist. A case in point: Richard Jenkyns's reading of the London Albert Memorial in *The Victorians and Ancient Greece* (Cambridge, Mass.: Harvard University Press, 1980) 192.

[3] See Rachel Bowlby, *Just Looking: Consumer Culture in Dreiser, Gissing, and Zola* (London: Methuen, 1985); Thomas Richards, *The Imperial Archive: Knowledge and the Fantasy of Empire* (London and New York: Verso, 1993); Tony Bennett, *The Birth of the Museum: History, Theory, Politics* (London and New York: Routledge, 1995).

ambiguously para-epic ballad anthologies created around 1840 by Maginn and Macaulay (Ch. 8) were entertainments in the spirit of an age that, having squeezed past a tight spot, was ready to exhale. These poets looked away from Britain (away, too, from the discordant forces behind Peterloo and Chartism, respectively) in search of venues that might reflect the perdurable virtues Britons had lately practiced at need. At last it was time for other peoples to suffer in historical reality the angst of a destabilized political order and an uncertain future, and for the British, having come through, to enjoy that angst at vicarious distance in the form of narrative suspense, thanks to English (pseudo) translations of (nonexistent) originals. While each of the poets I have just named set a different value on imperial actualities, all shared the analogical faith that a Persian or Greek or Roman mirror rightly angled might image Britain back to itself, through an act of poetic recollection affirming large home truths: that history's essential patterns repeated themselves, and that Great Britain's well-earned turn at the top of golden hours had come.

Several of these features appear again in the epic poetry characteristic of the decades after the Second Reform Bill of 1867 and the Education Bill of 1870. Once a consciously hailed watershed in national history had been traversed, bringing votes to the urban proletariat and public education to their children, the concentrated mythic strain of the 1860s epic broke down and out into a looser generic practice. Most obviously and decisively, the genre's vital growth ring migrated toward the margins of island and empire: the dark places of the earth, Conrad's Marlow would call them at century's end, transvaluing fiction's far fling during the generation that led from Haggard to Kipling. Poetry, as so often happens, had gotten there first. From before 1870 not only a Gaelic revival but an unflagging interest among poets in themes from Nordic and Mediterranean shores evinced an outward thrust pushing the cultural conflict zone—the place where poets sought epic-generating plots—all the way to India and the South Pacific. As this literary export–import trade rose, so too did the tempo with which translated epics came before the public. These translations occupied one end of a generic spectrum that shaded off indistinctly through adaptation and imitation into original epic composition, and they fetched what from a smug Victorian center was now routinely thought of as "world literature" within the compass of an English language now emerging as the great planetary vernacular. With signal preference for the ocean-going *Odyssey*, Homer in English verse and prose versions appeared almost annually as the century waned.[4] To major new versions of the Bible and the *Aeneid* were added classic treasures out of old English, old French, old Germanic, ancient Sanskrit and Babylonian narrative.[5]

Along with so much exploration and development of epic matter went a corresponding diffuseness of manner. Stanzaic verse enjoyed more favor now than hitherto, and narratives adhering to longer or less regular lineation tended to come bundled into more manageable subdivisions; where the traditional epic book or canto did survive, it got shorter. These were the outward signs in form of a sea-change in the spirit with which epoists after 1870 ordinarily went about their work. A flattening of affect, it seems, and a blunting of direct summons were entailed by the poets' efforts of geographical outreach and cultural mediation.[6] (These features were also concomitant with the exceptionally high level of stylistic mediocrity that characterizes the dreamy-cool Romantic decadence and that graces, for better or worse, late-century English poetry clean across the genres. By now, the Laureate grumbled in a little parable of 1864 called "The Flower," all had got the seed.) Thus the epic impulse traced by this chapter largely extrapolates the centrifugal force that had made Tennyson prefer *Idylls* to a *Book* of his hero king, had splintered Browning's murder story in *The Ring and the Book* into perspectival spokes, and

---

[4] A partial list of *Odyssey* translators from these decades includes W. Lucas Collins (1875), Mordaunt Barnard (1876), S. H. Butcher and Andrew Lang (1879), George Augustus Schomberg (1879), Arthur Sanders Way (1881), Charles Milton Bell (1881), William Morris (1887), Alfred John Church (1891), George Herbert Palmer (1891), J. G. Cordery (1897).

[5] See e.g. Lang, *Ballads and Lyrics of Old France* (1872); George Smith, *The Chaldean Epic Of The Flood* (1874); Edwin Arnold, *Indian Idylls* (1883) and—also from the *Mahabharata*—*The Song Celestial* (1885); William Morris, *Beowulf* (1895); Annie Besant, *Story of the Great War: Lessons from the Mahabharata for the Use of Hindu Students in the Schools of India* (1899). Romesh C. Dutt, *The Great Epics of Ancient India* (Delhi, 1900), arranges into a twelve-part structure translations of selected episodes from the *Ramayana* and *Mahabharata*. A. C. Bradley, "Old Mythology in Modern Poetry," *Macmillan's Magazine* 44 (1881) 43, boasted that "Where a Greek could express himself only through the traditions of his own people, we can find a body for our thought not only in English lives and English ideas, but in the shapes left us by Indian and Egyptian, Greek and Roman, old German and Icelandic civilisations." Not that those English lives and ideas Bradley mentions were neglected; it was simply that other genres than epic verse now attended to them. John Willinsky, *Empire of Words: The Reign of the OED* (Princeton: Princeton University Press, 1994) 23 ff., adds to the great *OED* such late-century fixtures as the *DNB*, the *Golden Treasury*, the Early English Text Society, and the proliferating political and literary national histories that went with them, to conclude with a flourish: "all the oldest English traditions were invented in the last quarter of the nineteenth century."

[6] For Franco Moretti such formal incongruity enables the work of modern epic, where, in distinction from the novel, "we have the specific *historicity* of a universe in which fossils from distant epochs coexist with creatures from worlds to come." The genre thus performs "the allegory of a heterogeneous—but forcibly unified—reality. The most abstract form of 'totality' imaginable in the capitalist world-system. And, perhaps, the most truthful": *Modern Epic: The World-System from Goethe to Garcia Marquez*, tr. Quintin Hoare (London and New York: Verso, 1996) 88, 229.

had sponsored Morris's dissemination of narrative authority within *The Earthly Paradise*. This centrifugal force seldom keeps company after 1870, however, with the reciprocally centripetal force that for those masters had made plurality, perspectivism, and the logistics of location urgent indices of a contemporary trouble.

To the 1860s faith in myth, that is to say, there succeeded something more like comparative mythology. Whether it involved the culture-browsing hobbyist or the disciplined scholarly mind bent on spanning the globe and exhausting the archive, this *fin-de-siècle* development was rooted deep in a tacit hyper-myth of its own. This was the myth of Victorian progressivism, swollen now to imperial scale and fortified by a century's labors in the human sciences. In a sense the century's epics—untidy or over-achieving children of the Enlightenment that they were—had always been the literary projection of more or less intuitively absorbed theories of culture and political economy. But after 1870 or so, to articulate and spread the findings of social-scientific branches of thought, and wield them for good measure as truth rather than propaganda, was a mission that epic poets embraced with unprecedented directness. This hyper-myth of progress dared not speak its name; indeed, perhaps it could not, so thoroughly did progressivism saturate every nineteenth-century discourse that might have been fit to describe and analyze it. For that matter, and for related reasons, it can be hard to grasp even today: despite much twentieth-century damage to the axle of progressivist ideology on its way from then to now, few readers of this sentence will be quite free of a working belief that progress shapes the history we are living.[7]

One way to glimpse here the eclecticizing effect exerted on epic writing by the myth of myth's progress within civilization is to contrast it with what had taken place a generation earlier, in the extended wake of the first Reform bill. The first Victorians' analogical confidence in the grand repeating cycles of history, as we found it in Maginn and Macaulay, in Bulwer's *Arthur* and Tennyson's *Princess*, had been much eroded by 1870. And no wonder: such confidence belonged to an unpurged taxonomic form of precisely that Enlightenment universalism which the secular typology of Britain's monument- and museum-minded progressivism set out to supersede. Unlike their late-century successors, the first Victorians—Carlyle, say, in one large

---

[7] It is indeed still shaping our sentences, in ways that follow from the period's marked shift in usage towards imperfective and progressive verb tenses: see Richard Bailey, *Nineteenth-Century English* (Ann Arbor: University of Michigan Press, 1996) 222–26.

sweep of his erratic thought—held that cultural and even historical differences drew meaning primarily from a classificatory schema. Diversely developed ideals—the permutations of, say, hero-worship—all sat in the same taxonomic table. To that extent they all sat *at* the same table too, being subject to the same morally invariant rules, which had the force of law for those seeking to explain or predict a given culture's path along the recurrent cycle of advance, prosperity, decline, and renewal. For the later Victorians these rules had changed, as tabular difference was swallowed up in plotted progress, and recurrent *phases* became instead *stages* in a unidirectional career. The bronze-greaved Achaean, the aboriginal Fiji Islander, the Hebrew judge meting the Law or the Temple, the centurion convicted by martyrs' blood, the monk adoring literally the testament he copied—all of them, like the lesser ape in evolutionist thought, partially anticipated the ideal condition of modern humanity: categorically Western, presumptively male, emphatically Anglo-Saxon. And that was precisely why no merely precursive figure could adequately reflect the condition of modern humanity: full humanity was, after all, the maturation of that gradually accumulated knowledge whose displayed object, or exhibit of partially unfolded potential, each figure was retrospectively understood to be.

No longer the hall of mirrors it had appeared even to Macaulay, history became a gallery of cultural ancestor portraits; and so, together with all the bright young sciences, did history's late-Victorian handmaid anthropology.[8] The modern mind still scanned the past and scoured the globe for likenesses, but now the lessons of likeness were subsumed in a science of contingent causality. What a former dispensation had regarded as heroic *exemplars* were now *prototypes* instead; in the age of Comte and Spencer, Darwin and Tylor, these survivors' mere survival, in the form of their contributory influence on the present, was the most heroic thing about them. Much as in architecture the Greek and Gothic revivals of earlier decades yielded to an eclecticism prizing not resemblance but incorporation, so the builders of long poems acknowledged the models of classical epic and chivalric romance by assimilation rather than imitation. Such generic ingestion formed part of a genealogical display of pedigree that itself implied a story, in fact the largest and most epic-worthy story the advanced century knew:

---

[8] Simon Dentith, *Epic and Empire in Nineteenth-Century Britain* (Cambridge: Cambridge University Press, 2006) 180–89, discusses the bearing of Victorian anthropology on late-century epic prose writers, principally the collaborators Andrew Lang and H. Rider Haggard.

the story of civilization whose crest was here and now, and whose protag-
onist was the mind that clinched humanity's progress in its own.[9] Herder
had announced a century before that, "the succession of epochs that
constitutes human history" being divinely ordained, the development of
mankind was "God's epic"; only now did that superhuman poem find, with
a regularity suggestive of deeply buried misgivings, its phalanx of eager
human scribes.[10]

Disowned by the world-historical vision that swept thus towards the *fin
de siècle* was the older idea of history as a fixed pattern book, whose plot
revolved in vast inescapable *mythoi*—an idea that had engendered Macaulay's
famous fancy of a New Zealander musing centuries hence over London in
ruins, that had governed Thomas Arnold's thinking about history, and that had
persisted into epic writing of the 1840s.[11] In its tragic aspect this older homage
to Fortuna had spoken to earlier imperial generations, who because they could
remember the *de facto* instauration of the British Empire circa 1815 could also,
without risk of traumatic distortion, entertain the possibility of its subsidence.
But to the entrenched and explicit imperial*ism* of the later nineteenth century
that tragic vision was wormwood. Not taboo: late-Victorian imperialists spent
too much time scaring each other with it for that to have been the case. Rather,
the prospect of Western decline and fall was a bitter stimulant that *fin-de-siècle*
spin doctors repeatedly administered to the civilized system, which proved its
good health by repeatedly rising to meet it, whether through a tailor-made
science of eugenic–dystopic degeneration that grafted social fabric onto phys-
ical germ tissue, or through the several varieties of normative exoticist-anthol-
ogical epic to which we now turn.

[9] What our first chapter called the Very Idea of epic unity here finally merges, as late-Victorian
philosophical idealism increasingly merged, with the Hegelian Idea. Although Hegel's 1820s
lectures on epic would not have been known to any of the epoists this chapter treats, they foretold
with some precision the aim the genre was to set for itself half a century later: "The supreme action
of the spirit may be world-history itself, and we might propose to work up this universal deed on
the battlefield of the universal spirit into the absolute epic; the hero of such an epic would be the
spirit of man, or humanity, which educates and lifts itself out of a dullness of consciousness into
world-history": *Aesthetics: Lectures on Fine Art*, tr. T. M. Knox (Oxford: Clarendon Press, 1975), 2:
1064–65. To which Hegel at once adds: "precisely because of its universality this material could
not be sufficiently individualized for art" but must instead degenerate into "cold allegory"—a fate
not eluded, as we shall see, by late-century executors of the "absolute epic" agenda like Owen
Meredith, Robert Buchanan, and Mathilde Blind.
[10] Herder is quoted in Maurice Olender, *The Languages of Paradise: Race, Religion, and Philology
in the Nineteenth Century*, tr. Arthur Goldhammer (Cambridge, Mass., and London: Harvard
University Press, 1992) 41, 43.
[11] See the first appendix to Arnold's edition of Thucydides' *Pelopennesian War*, 2nd edn.
(Oxford: Parker, 1840) 503–24.

This histamine reaction (so to pursue a social-body metaphor that was favored by the 1890s degenerationists themselves) inflamed the tissue of epic in unwholesome ways. Late Victorian culture's need to prove itself to itself in books stood in conflict with epic's charter to constitute an alternative cultural center, to adopt an uncommercial and to that extent unpopular vantage on the realities long narrative was especially suited to declare. The more insistently an imperial society levied on literature its totalizing demand, the more nearly normative the epical became—more so by the century's last decade than it had been since national militarization conscripted it during the first. This very elevation to prominence, at a time when the smartest prose authors were abandoning the three-decker novel for shorter fictional forms, put epic poets under a conformist pressure like that which novelists had known in earlier decades, but from which epoists in their marginal, experimental niche had hitherto been relatively free. This was a matter not of surging sales—only a few of the poems to be treated here sold well at all—but of an imperialist shift in cultural values that swung the spotlight onto projects in Western cultural justification for which the scope and means of epic seemed inherently suited.

And the glare of the imperial spotlight was blinding, most particularly in its requirement that the history a big poem told or implied should moralize the course of civilization as a record of improvement. An epic meeting this requirement could hardly avoid breaking with older affiliations of the genre, foremost among them its relation to the tragic. No generic norm that is predicated on denying the tragic vision of Achilles, Roland, Los, and Caponsacchi will support the burden of ultimate persuasiveness to which epic aspires. Accordingly the epicizing productions of the late nineteenth century, while numerous, now read at a century's distance like hostages to the era's debilitating idea of manifest destiny; and this idea, for all its presentist applause, severed an imaginative lifeline between most epoists and certain suppressed but critically important energies of their moment. It is conversely in works that, unlike most of their kind, escaped this ideological captivity that we find the two greatest achievements of British epic during the last quarter of the century. Morris's *Sigurd the Volsung* and Swinburne's *Tristram of Lyonesse*, solitary monuments raised in reaction against the age, embrace to the full, and even to a point of obstinate distortion, the tragic apprehension of human prospects that their epoch was determined to overlook.

★

Neither Morris nor Swinburne, therefore, can frame for us the epic land-
scape of 1870 and after. But an ideal guide awaits us in Edward Robert
Bulwer Lytton, whom we met in Chapter 10 as the author of the verse-novel
Lucile and will know henceforth from his epicizing father by the pen name
"Owen Meredith" (at some admitted risk of confusion with the much
better but epic-proof Victorian author George Meredith). That pseudonym
gives strangely specific Welsh mooring to a craft whose programmatic
internationalism distinguished the gentleman author as much as it did
the career statesman. Lytton's diplomacy covered Europe from Lisbon to
Belgrade across the 1860s, and it was he who as viceroy proclaimed Victoria
the Empress of India at Delhi in 1877. During these same years Owen
Meredith's translations, recensions, and collections spanned a corresponding
cultural terrain, with amateur theories of history, literature, and creativity to
go with them. His fanciful posthumous testament *King Poppy* (1892) will
furnish this chapter with a *terminus ad quem* that in its very eccentricity
anticipates the fresh imaginative authority that epics of the new chapter
(and century) illustrate. First, though, Meredith was to found repeatedly
on the rock of historical "Experience"—the one Muse left to modernity,
affirmed his 1859 lyric medley *à clef* called *The Wanderer* (3.1–5)—an effort of
cultural induction that sought to generalize a constantly evolving cultural
truth from a string of concretely rendered episodes.

   A first result, published under the candidly nondescript title *Chronicles and
Characters* in 1868, is the sort of epicized history one might have expected
from Meredith's quondam mentor Browning, had that poet not moved just
then into the quite different ratios of *The Ring and the Book*. In a bewildering
congeries of verse forms Meredith's nine asymmetrical and mutually non-
conforming books present Western history from Greek legend to French
Revolution, via a deliberately minor pageant of Browningesque dramatic
romances (*Chronicles*) and lyrics (*Characters*), set in beveled relation to major
historical developments that a reader might be counted on to recognize.[12]
From the general Licinius, for example, risen in arms to defend the
Olympian rites against Constantine's decree (book 3), we infer the triumph

   [12] Alarmed by Matthew Arnold's apparent wish to drive lyric from the precinct of serious
poetry in his 1853 preface to *Poems*, Meredith wrote to John Forster asking "And shall we have
nothing but epics?" Quoted in Sidney Coulling, *Matthew Arnold and His Critics: A Study of Arnold's
Controversies* (Athens, Ohio: Ohio University Press, 1974) 46. The eclecticism of form and topic
that makes Meredith a nearly ideal representative of the period this chapter covers was manifest to
talented literary historians from the period just after it. See George Saintsbury, *A History of
Nineteenth Century Literature* (New York and London: Macmillan, 1896): "he would publish

of Christianity; an epistolary monologue sent by "Thomas Müntzer to Martin Luther" shows us the Reformation askance (book 8)—glimpsed peripherally, but also very largely, in a cartoon outline that we fill in with such history as we already knew before picking up the poem. The effect of this eccentric, parasitical obliquity is less to interrogate received world history than to affirm it. We hold on tighter to what we held about the past to begin with, since by default it is what must furnish the linkage among events: connecting the dots in this way, we take as the poem's final lesson an interpretation of the French Revolution as concluding the unfinished business of the Protestant one. Extended treatments of Alexandrian Neoplatonism and classical Islam (books 4 and 5) keep the overall Western account cosmopolitan, which is to say appropriately on point and up to date for the last third of the nineteenth century. These ventures beyond European geography assume their proper place in European cultural evolution through a nominally god-less comparatism that Meredith avows at starting (1.1), repeats here and there (book 3, Epilogue), and practices throughout. The collective lesson is that, while an unknown Godhead abides behind all change, human curiosity eviscerates, as human weakness betrays, the fragile mythologies men make to live by.

This is, of course, just the modern and progressivist mythology that Owen Meredith and his set made to live by. In "an extended and rapidly changing panorama of the chief epochs in the history of the civilised world," he told John Forster a year before publication, he was attempting "a poetic history of the *education* of man" and confining his "selection of subject to those historical periods which most distinctly mark the progress of general thought."[13] In Shelleyan–Browningesque mode *Chronicles and Characters* offered its creed in the service of a fundamentally liberal program that vacillates between roughly equivalent meliorist and imperfectionist valuations of the course of time in its nineteenth-century drift toward democracy. How the same mythology of zeitgeist necessitarianism might be taken in a mystical and nihilist direction was the burden of a counter-epic that Meredith published the next year, *Orval, or the Fool of Time*. This *Poem in Five Epochs: Domestic and Social* is a "paraphrase," performed on the basis

things to which fools gave the name of plagiarisms—when they were in fact studies" that gave play to his gift for "ironical narration" or "covert suggestive speech" (311–12); Hugh Walker, *The Literature of the Victorian Era* (Cambridge: University Press, 1910): "Lytton was a sort of literary personification of Echo" (601).

[13] Quoted in Aurelia Brooks Harlan, *Owen Meredith: A Critical Biography of Robert, First Earl of Lytton* (New York: Columbia University Press, 1946) 167.

of a French translation and "under the influence of Goethe" (Preface, xliv–
xlvii), from the Polish of Zygmunt Krasinski's anonymously published 1833
poem *Nieboska Komedia* (*The Undivine Comedy*). The whole 1869 production
could hardly be more redolent of this poet's signature internationalism, which
was not only his but an entire epic generation's. In the name of humanitarian
advance Meredith pauses prefatorily to chide what in Krasinski seems brood-
ing, insular, defeatist (lvi–lvii); yet most of the preface is given to explaining
how in the Slav's clouded opus the English poet found to hand the very work
he himself had been meaning for years to write on the impact of the French
Revolution.

Where *Chronicles* had been concrete and circumstantial, the Krasinski
imitation was, like the unwritten poem it usurped, designedly "abstracted"
and "symbolic," which is to say most active upon the plane of ideas. This
befits Meredith's defensible, altogether characteristic conviction that the pan-
European consequences of the French Revolution had been mainly ideo-
logical, "the continuous, though often secret, action of modern ideas upon the
political structure of modern society" (ix–xi). The occultism of such an
endeavor recalls the hereditarian irrationality of Eliot's contemporaneous
The Spanish Gypsy, wherein a yet more advanced Victorian progressivist
caught a rip tide of her own within the darker waves of the choir invisible.
The *épopée humanitaire*—to introduce a term that links Meredith's efforts in the
genre to those of a greater exemplar he had consciously followed in writing
Chronicles and Characters, Victor Hugo—clearly harbored, within its fatalism,
energies not readily subordinated to the secular evangel of progress. As we
continue our tour of *fin-de-siècle* eclecticism we should remember, since the
poets often forgot, to look for those energies and the inhumane mischief they
could make.[14]

One poet who did not forget was Arthur O'Shaughnessy: handler of reptiles
for the British Museum, brother epoist to Robert Lytton and reportedly his
bastard younger brother too; at all events fully possessed of a bar-sinister

---

[14] The first part of Hugo's *La Légende des Siècles* had appeared in 1859 to give Meredith his model
(Harlan, *Owen Meredith*, 167). On the *épopée humanitaire* in France see Herbert J. Hunt, *The Epic in
Nineteenth-Century France: A Study in Heroic and Humanitarian Poetry from* Les Martyrs *to* Les Siècles
Morts (Oxford: Blackwell, 1941); William Calin, *A Muse for Heroes: Nine Centuries of the Epic in France*
(Toronto and Buffalo: University of Toronto Press, 1983) 298–99, 339–59. On the much less robust
but clearly related *Kulturgeschichtlich* epic in German see H. J. Schueler, *The German Verse Epic in the
Nineteenth and Twentieth Centuries* (The Hague: Nijhoff, 1967) 58 ff. Epic's leading role in the Russian
Renaissance of the nineteenth century forms the theme of Frederick T. Griffiths and Stanley
J. Rabinowitz, *Novel Epics: Gogol, Dostoevsky, and National Narrative* (Evanston: Northwestern
University Press, 1990).

imagination when at 25 or so he wrote *An Epic of Women* (1870).[15] The peculiar title is a sign of the times: its indefinite article would not be out of place in a subtitle like *An Epic Poem in Seven Books*, but by putting the *An* first O'Shaughnessy manages to suggest at once the importance of writing an epic and the countervailing suspicion that what he has come up with is just, alas, another epic. The reader who completes his seven unpleasantly gynophobic cantos may detect in the title a further *soupçon* of ambivalence about the collector mentality that has assembled them: a gaggle of harlots, a nest of vipers... an epic of women. O'Shaughnessy's selection of sexually panicky, male-dominant portraits of temptresses, none of whom speaks for herself, declines from wanton Aphrodite through Cleopatra and Salome to a somewhat rueful Helen. The series is framed by a para-biblical prologue ("Creation") relating the seduction of God by the ravishing beauty of his own female handiwork and an epilogue dispensing rough justice ("A Troth for Eternity") in the form of a grisly Victorian snuff story. What structure this legend of bad women exhibits—what promotes O'Shaughnessy's assortment of tales from a miscellaneous cento like his later *Lays of France* (1872) to an anthology that pretends to epic status—inheres in its containment of baleful femininity within a conservatively drawn narrative of crime and punishment.

The imposition of a moral order upon unruly force need not, thankfully, be carried out with such brutality as inflamed O'Shaughnessy, but in the age of conscious empire some such imposition was incumbent on the Ovidian or Chaucerian epoist of parts. If an epic design was to foreground a sequence of shorter tales, they needed to imply the wholeness of a larger narrative background. An early and agreeable instance of such backgrounding occurs

---

"Human" and "humanity" are words that buzz like ideological chainsaws across the late-century European epic, for reasons to do with imperial expansion and the anthropological speculation that was its sometimes captious offshoot, but also with the finally accomplished rise of the middle classes. Introducing Daniel Cottom's *Social Figures* (Minneapolis: University of Minnesota Press, 1987), Terry Eagleton cautions that categorical "humanity" was constructed in the mid-19th cent. "by a class society urgently in need of naturalizing and universalizing its dominion" (xi). This need was met, Karl Mannheim proposes in *Ideology and Utopia*, tr. Louis Wirth and Edward A. Shils (London: Kegan Paul, 1936), by stunting historical curiosity: "A class which has already risen in the social scale tends to conceive of history in terms of unrelated, isolated events. Historical events appear as a process only as long as the class which views these events still expects something from it" (129). A trenchant remark, though it cuts deeper into the late-Victorian novel (Cottom's book is about George Eliot) than into the epic. It was epic that stubbornly sought to make good on the long historical view, which, despite Scott's example, British novelists had with rare exception curtailed.

[15] See on O'Shaughnessy's biological parentage T. Earle Welby, *The Victorian Romantics 1850–70* (London: Howe, 1929) 87; and on his literary parentage Douglas Bush, who derives *An Epic of Women* from Swinburne's writings of the 1860s: *Mythology and the Romantic Tradition in English Poetry* (1937; rpt. Cambridge, Mass.: Harvard University Press, 1969) 351.

in the generically marginal *Brother Fabian's Manuscript* by Sebastian Evans (1865). In fictive shape a commonplace-book from the later Middle Ages—and thus professedly a whole step down in organizational ambition from even an anthology—this entertainment in mixed poetic forms grows on its reader all the same. The sequence of eight stories executes a subtle progression, from the indulged chaos that reigns over a rather too fat and happy abbey towards "Fifteen Days of Judgment" that will burnish Heaven and Earth anew. It is characteristic of Evans's generosity that this metanarrative order feels on balance like the blossoming of a lesser indulgence into a greater. Those ultimate mercies of the divine that can seem so hard to find in 1820s apocalyptic (Ch. 6), or hard to credit in Bickersteth's virtually contemporaneous 1866 reprise of that mode (Ch. 10), are never far from Brother Fabian's predilection for stories about the gifts of the Magi (2), kindnesses done to outcast Judas (6), the softening of Charlemagne's fatherly heart (7). If Evans was finally, like *Rimini* Hunt or *Ingoldsby* Barham, too genial a soul for heroic sternness, his structural enlistment of Revelation's totality as a weight-bearing buttress still serves, like O'Shaughnessy's conscription of Genesis, to mark for us a limit case in the poetics of epic collection.[16]

An achievement that falls well short of the limit thus marked, yet merits brief notice here for old times' sake, is *The Paradise of Martyrs: A Faith-Rhyme, in Five Books* (1873), Thomas Cooper's concurrently planned but long deferred sequel to *The Purgatory of Suicides* (Ch. 7).[17] Composed in Spenserians like its predecessor but only half as long, this dream parade of Christian victims speaking their patient pieces one after another is quirkily marshaled by English and then by national denominations: Anglican, early Catholic, Quaker; then French, Italian. Only Cooper's budding internationalism, and unswerving sympathy for the downtrodden everywhere, affiliate his last big poem with the political inventiveness of his first. Here is none of the forensic interaction among speakers that we found in the *Purgatory*, nor even much contrast to sharpen conflict and interest. The poet does take up some of the discursive slack in garrulous personal exordia to each book, bringing readers up to date on his post-Chartist career as a teacher-evangelist who loves the natural world and holds strong views (anti-Owenite, anti-Communist) on a political world that, like the processing martyrs, seems to have passed him by. With nothing

---

[16] Kevin Mills invokes Evans's "Fifteen Days" as an instance of the Victorian privatization of apocalyptic in order to impose "narrative shape upon individual experience": *Approaching Apocalypse: Unveiling Revelation in Victorian Writing* (Lewisburg: Bucknell University Press, 2007) 28.

[17] *The Life of Thomas Cooper* (London: Hodder and Stoughton, 1872) 397.

to counteract the plot-retarding inertia of his Spenserians—no allegorical vista, for example, of a larger unseen church to which the *martyroi* in their etymological capacity as witnesses may have jointly ministered unawares, and certainly no quest to find or institute such a church in this world— Cooper's withdrawal from political commitment takes him out of the generic running too.

The universalist allegory one misses in Cooper was substantially present for poets of a younger generation, however, and they drew on it liberally as an epicizing vision for poems devoted to a surprising variety of themes. Lewis Morris, whom for clarity's sake we had better call Morris Minor, mined the progressivist vein of the era most closely, and to best commercial effect, in a poem that by 1900 had sold fifty thousand copies. *The Epic of Hades: In Three Books* began its prosperous print run in 1876 as a slim volume comprising a dozen Dantesque interviews with famous pagan shades from the classical era who, if they had much to repent of, also had much to hope for. The next year Morris Minor doubled the poem in size and made his Hellenic portrait gallery ("Hades") into a proper purgatory by flanking it with a hell ("Tartarus") of fiercer spirits, doomed to impenitent pain, and a heaven ("Olympus") of superhuman deities who want for nothing and therefore have, like the subhuman damned, no hope either. Clearly Christianity wields no Dantesque power here, an omission the poet made good years later in the Cooper-like 1890 antiphon *A Vision of Saints*. (With Cooper's *Martyrs* and, presently, *The Light of the World* by Edwin Arnold, *A Vision of Saints* belongs to what emerges as a small Victorian subgenre, the last-minute epic recantation.) A steadily implied Christian ethic of blessed imperfection suffuses *The Epic of Hades* all the same, as reviewers duly noted, "connecting the Greek myth with the higher and wider meaning which Christian sentiment naturally finds for it," where *higher* and *wider* are the period's very watchwords.[18] It is the technically Hellenistic goddess Psyche, an allegory of the loving soul— latest-born and loveliest brainchild of a demicroyant classical decadence—who takes a Beatrice's part and escorts the pilgrim from Hades to Olympus at the hinge between books 2 and 3. This apt allegorical choice establishes as Morris' ultimate theme the capacity of the self to grow: the capacity, as we found it anticipated in Mary Tighe's early epic romance *Psyche* (Ch. 3), of the modern

---

[18] *The Spectator,* 27 May 1876. Quoted in advertising backmatter from Morris's *Gwen: A Drama in Monologue* (London: Paul, 1879).

psyche to better the story in which it finds itself, unlike either the futureless Tartareans, slaves to their one tale, or the story-transcending Olympian gods, personations of that ideality to which human souls aspire.

Morris Minor's classical who's-who is also a guess-who.[19] Only Niobe is named, being perhaps deemed a little *recherchée* for the general reader; but the rest of the cast are readily identifiable from the tales they tell, which is to say that those hint-dropping tales blaze a broad path for the common reader to follow. The effect is somewhat analogous to Owen Meredith's in *Chronicles and Characters*, where we also observed an easeful nestling into core knowledge that cultural literates of no special pretension could be expected to bring to the picnic. A diplomatically equal, systematically alternating apportionment of monologues between male and female figures similarly conformed *The Epic of Hades* to the late-century gender demographics of poetry readership. So finally did the poem's carefully regulated style, which might be described, to adapt a phrase that Hopkins had lately coined when detecting Tennyson on the poetic equivalent of automatic pilot, as soapstone Parnassian:

> And next I knew
> A woman perfect as a young man's dream,
> And breathing as it seemed the nimble air
> Of the fair days of old, when man was young
> And life an Epic.

> (2.659–63)

This first shot of Helen of Troy appeals chastely to a young man's fancy with deluxe machine-turned verses in the best modern fashion, *dream* humming on through the next line's vowels and labials to hand off through *air* to *fair* in the line after that. The manipulation of sensation at which such verse aims takes up the slackened nerve of emotion, in which Dante is famously rich and Morris Minor correspondingly poor, so as to spread across the text an

[19] But not a guess-what: Morris Minor knew his middlebrow public better than to leave meaning to chance. As Bradley forbearingly observed at the zenith of the poem's popularity, while "in the whole history of English verse Greek mythology has never been so systematically treated," it still remains a defect in the system that Zeus, Psyche, and Orpheus should be reduced to coming out and telling the reader exactly what they stand for in the allegory ("Old Mythology," 32–34). This falling away from the 1860s' high mythic inquest towards mere allegorical automatism leaves Frank M. Turner's too sweeping claim about Victorian poetry not far from the truth as regards the *fin de siècle*: "the vital link between myth and the autonomous poetic imagination languished in the climate of scientific rationalism and empirical inquiry, and the myths again became primarily conventions or allegories": *The Greek Heritage in Victorian Britain* (New Haven and London: Yale University Press, 1981) 78.

anaesthetic melancholy. That modern life is no longer "an Epic" forms the very premise of this poet's decision to seek epic greatness among not the living but the dead, where his counterpart E. H. Bickersteth had sought it a decade before. That the melancholy affect attending this premise is nothing morbid, however, but a gift to be prized under the sign of progress as man's providential lot, is a redemptive conclusion that the poet made sure few among his thousands of readers would miss.[20]

Accommodation, inclusiveness, and above all the right to choose: these are what eclecticism is all about. Small wonder that they became leading ethical values of the epic works late-century poets constructed on eclectic principles in an anthological format. The preceding chapter spotlighted the great Victorian instance of this structural–ethical convergence in William Morris's *Earthly Paradise,* a work whose example stands directly behind many of the titles this chapter takes up. A handful of them, indeed, read somewhat as if submitted for inclusion in some sequel edition of out-takes from that 1860s masterpiece. John Payne's *The Romaunt of Sir Floris* (1870) and William Watson's *The Prince's Quest* (1880), a pair of works to which we shall return, are imaginable as Wanderers' northern contributions to the storyfest, where they might have been matched from the Greek side with Andrew Lang's six brief stanzaic books on *Helen of Troy* (1882), and *Eros and Psyche: A Poem in Twelve Measures* (1885) by Robert Bridges. The fact that both Helen and Psyche had also appeared in the *Hades* epic of Morris Minor underscores not just their late-century popularity but a manifest public hunger for plots of a certain kind: plots of, not exactly forgiveness on the strenuous order we met in Chapter 4, but something like it: an assimilative *felix culpa* acceptance, where a protagonist's willful transgression discloses a reconciling perspective from which what she has done is affirmed as furthering a superior order of things. While it was part of Morris Major's greatness to refrain in *The Earthly Paradise* from endorsing such a comfortable view, and while as we shall see there was

[20] Henry Morley for one did not miss it, or fail to follow it right to the cultural bullseye, when in a *Nineteenth Century* review of the poem (February 1878) he cited the conclusion to Tennyson's *In Memoriam* to show what, given the "one great action" of Morris's poem, "the soul of man is shown throughout it labouring towards." Quoted as above in backmatter to *Gwen*. More discerning judges were less kind, were downright fertile in wicked epithet. Oliver Elton, *A Survey of English Literature 1830–1880* (London: Arnold, 1920) 136, described Morris's verse as "a banquet of the obvious." Morris was called by George Saintsbury the "Tennyson des enfants," by George Meredith "the Harlequin Clown of the Muses," by Michael Field's better half Katherine Bradley "the grocer of Parnassus": all quoted in Amy Cruse, *After the Victorians* (London: Allen and Unwin, 1938) 73.

much in his *Sigurd* to put its comforts to shame, those comforts were some-
thing that the collected-tales epic format by its very nature reinforced.

Lang proved particularly susceptible to the blandishments of this subgeneric
ethos. Numerous articles and books he produced from the 1870s across the
turn of the century debated avidly, and with regular reference to epic tradition,
questions in the new anthropology of primitive myth.[21] In addition, his *Ballads
and Lyrics of Old France* (1872), not to mention his many later *Fairy Book*
collections, suggest how congenial he found it to anthologize. The same
progressivist interest with which Lang scanned the strata of cultural history
emerges in *Helen of Troy* when, bringing Olympus as it were up to Victorian
date, he enskies his heroine in the divine form of "a kinder Aphrodite" (6.450)
who will listen and care for those whom love has hurt—the same consolation
prize that R. H. Horne had awarded to his industrious Orion in the 1840s
(Ch. 9), but transposed now to the distaff side. The stellification of Helen is but
the last of many *pentimenti* that sweeten Lang's poem against the harshness of
his archaic sources. Here Achilles neither mutilates nor even terrifies Hector;
Oenone's heart soon melts again toward Paris; once the Trojan War has been
dispatched in some twenty (quite talented) stanzas, when the call goes out to
stone guilty Helen to death in book 6 every single Greek relents. And thereby
poetic justice is served, for it turns out that when Helen abandoned her
husband back in book 3 she had no idea what she was doing. Aphrodite had
put all Sparta to sleep and thrown the queen into an amnesiac trance that
freed, or doomed, her to total absorption in the experience of the moment
(3.9–13)—a condition dissimilar in degree, yet not in kind, to the condition
that the anthological format as such tends to induce in its reader.[22]

We can gauge the power of this tendency to penetrate what looks like
its ideological opposite in Alfred Hayes's militantly otherworldly *The Last
Crusade* (1887). Here Saint Louis, King of France, is our hero in spite of a
disconnect between unquestioned piety and practical logistics that brings the
Sixth Crusade almost absurdly to grief: the worse matters get for the Crusaders,
in this apparently anti-imperialist sequence of three blank-verse idylls, the
higher climbs the ethical stock of saintliness. Yet the poem is not quite

[21] e.g. "Mythology and Fairy Tales," *Fortnightly Review* 18 (May 1873); *The Odyssey of Homer
Done into English Prose* (with S. H. Butcher, 1879); *Custom and Myth* (1884); *Homer and the Epic*
(1893); *Homer and His Age* (1906).

[22] This plot device of Lang's followed, admittedly more indulgently, the lead of Gladstone, whose
Homeric scholarship "transformed Helen into the repentant fallen woman of the Victorian domestic
novel" (Turner, *Greek Heritage*, 149). Helen of Troy would find another sympathetic champion
shortly after our *terminus ad quem* in Maurice Hewlett's long poem *Helen Redeemed* (1913).

the standoff between incompatible value systems that it seems. For there is a horizon where heavenly and earthly values merge after all, and from its verge shines "that strange light | Which seems not of this world" (1.1031) but which is truly the universalist "light that was in Christ, the light of love" (3.440). For all his administrative bungling Saint Louis foresaw, in other words, what has long since dawned on the good Victorian reader, "The universal brotherhood of man" (2.762). In this sense, and in despite of all immediate practical aims, the saintly king is seen to have expedited a greater epic purpose that "Bound East to West" (3.487). That international bond may be read, at some level, as answering the need Hayes felt to bind his uncoordinated idylls into an entire tale, a need strong enough to overcome the pervasively Manichean logic that governs narrative relations in *The Last Crusade*. Godly virtue's ultimate worldly proof is its alignment with the hidden god of late-Victorian epic: namely, the flow of history towards unity. The agreement on this point between imperialist thinking and the critique of military empire undertaken by the likes of Hayes was no doubt duly noted around this time by Thomas Hardy as he incubated the ironies of a far greater historical poem that will greet us in Chapter 12, *The Dynasts*.

Another epoist who was, like Lytton, an empire-builder by profession took the genre's panoramic ambition as far around the globe as it could go, all the way to New Zealand at an early nineteenth-century phase of European settlement. Before his youthful emigration Alfred Domett had been a good friend of Browning's, and upon his return to Britain he entered into correspondence on matters epical with Longfellow among others. *Ranolf and Amohia: A South-Sea Day-Dream* (1872) was based on his three decades' service in New Zealand's colonial administration, where he had become Prime Minister in 1862. Yet the setting of the action at a stage prior to his 1842 arrival lends a certain plausibility to an inverse claim: that his administrative service had been based on, and implicitly justified by, something like the idealized version of antecedent colonial relations to which his "day-dream" gave expression, a version that in turn relies heavily on the Romantic ideology of progress Domett took on board before leaving England. From the perspective of this chapter *Ranolf and Amohia* is in every way a throwback.[23] Irregularly rhymed, mainly tetrameter verse paragraphs

[23] So it struck a contemporary, E. C. Stedman, who in 1875 depreciated the poem for "the diffuseness, transcendentalism, defects of art and action, that were current among Domett's radical brethren so many years ago. The world has gone by him": *Victorian Poets*, rev. edn. (Boston and New York: Houghton Mifflin, 1887) 257.

affiliate its twenty-five cantos formally with the influence of Scott (spent at last by 1872 but still potent thirty years before), and accordingly one is not surprised to find its hero Ranolf hails from the Hebrides. Furthermore, this imperial servant's epic is not an imperialist work of 1870s stripe. Domett is too interested in Maori folkways for their own sake—the poetic travelogue contains nearly as much nonce ethnography as it does geology, botany, and zoology—and in such niceties of historical context as the pressure exerted on Amohia's southern tribe by incursion from northern Maoris who have lately been militarily empowered, and at the same time culturally distressed, by trade with merchants from Europe.[24]

What the *Times* hailed on publication as "the New Zealand epic" was thus not a victory narrative that divided to conquer along the black-and-white, south-and-north, savage-and-civilized lines that were increasingly legible symptoms of the century's ideological sclerosis. Domett worked hard to make mates of the cross-culturally loving pair who are his principals. Their honeymoon consummation plants at the middle of the poem, and abets with a natural charivari not overly troubled by Darwinian implication, a paradisal vision of happiness that proceeds from such equality of relation as might plausibly obtain between a couple of refugees whose upbringing in marginal island societies gives them more than a little in common. Spokesmen for animistic Maori religion give as good as they get in their exchanges with the metaphysically inquisitive Ranolf, whose theological doubts not only make him a tolerant guest but expose him to some ribbing that bespeaks, all told, a kind of reverse-colonial tolerationism too. The last laugh is history's, though, and it comes at the expense of Ranolf and Amohia's island idyll. Tribal warfare drives the couple into isolation after canto 19, and as their plans for European emigration go afoul Amohia pays the ultimate price for Ranolf's sake, joining him at last as a sweet ghost on shipboard during the long, widowed trip home to Britain. The inconvenient aborigine must disappear in the flesh, to reappear in the spirit as the most portable of souvenirs.

Pretty plainly in Domett's imagination the willing self-sacrifice of Amohia replaced, so as to make morally acceptable, the thousand sacrifices that

---

[24] In his editorial introduction to *The Diary of Alfred Domett 1872–1885* (London and New York: Oxford University Press, 1953), E. A. Horsman notes that the very bulk of annotation in *Ranolf and Amohia* "only underlines its remoteness from his own experience in New Zealand. It is set in the early years of the century, before large-scale immigration had created the problems he himself had to face in Parliament and Civil Service. . . . Its emotional driving power comes almost entirely from nostalgia" (40).

nineteenth-century colonization exacted of Maori people against their will. A little less plain is how the final spiritualization of Amo—only the educated Westerner, incidentally, can read the Latin pun in her pet name as a nonce allegory crying the beloved country—coopts her religion finally within the orbit of Ranolf's agnostic dubiety. During the war cantos an arresting simile has likened the embattled Maoris, with their "naked forms of classic mould," to "Brown Lapithae" in a "Parthenaic miracle | Of Art" (21.4; 6.4.46–52 of rev. edn. 1883)—i.e. to the Elgin Marbles, those prime trophies of empire in the British Museum of Domett's boyhood. The cloudy trophy wife at Ranolf's side represents, not the looting of the world's cultural resources, but what Conrad's Marlow would soon be calling the "idea" that backs that practice up: the progressivist, civilizing idea that makes it seem at once historically inevitable and morally correct. From the standpoint of practical ethics these attributes of necessity and rightness ought to be incompatible. Can Amo or Ranolf, or Marlow when it comes to that, be said truly to choose what they cannot but choose? And yet, in actual effect, such doublethink proved no more debilitating to the imperial mind than analogous paradoxes of predestination had been to its Calvinist forebear. On the contrary, it appears to have succored even Domett's still largely proto-imperialist imagination as he came home in the 1870s and awoke from romance dreaming to close with epic realities.

In Victoria's oldest and nearest colony, too, the latter-day epic idea of order found work to its hand. Between disestablishment of the (Anglican) Church of Ireland in 1871 and the twentieth-century foundation of the Irish Free State, the question of Home Rule was hotly enough contested to imperil more than one parliamentary majority in Westminster. Where Ireland belonged in relation to Great Britain was an institutional dilemma underpinned by passionate ideological commitments with deep roots in history: the kind of situation, that is, to which renewed epical imaginings of national legend might speak.[25] The disillusioned Fenian and Boston immigrant Robert Dwyer Joyce was content simply to hitch into the arthritic couplets of *Deirdré* (1876, Dublin 1877) the Red Branch kings' heroic deeds, as if to intone in epic's haughty voice the great national names would conjure for wounded Erin an independent dignity. But the Anglo-Irish assimilationist Samuel Ferguson knew more than this was needed as he completed for publication in 1872 a work he had

---

[25] On the demand that the Anglo-Irish political dilemma placed on the cultural work of epic, as Ferguson and then Yeats undertook it, see Colin Graham, *Ideologies of Epic: Nation, Empire, and Victorian Epic Poetry* (Manchester and New York: Manchester University Press, 1998) 73–96.

begun thirty years previously, *Congal: A Poem in Five Books*. Like Domett's much longer episodic poem of the same year, Ferguson's brief epic harks back to the heyday of Scott's influence on the poetic recension of traditionary tales. A whole and continuous narrative supported by eighty pages of notes, *Congal* was assembled from fragmentary ancient manuscripts in which the antiquarian poet, making good on Macpherson's Ossianic representations from a hundred years before, discerned "that largeness of purpose, unity, and continuity of action which are the principal elements of Epic Poetry" (v). While the poem was in gestation Ferguson had headed his 1865 collection *Lays of the Western Gael* with "The Tain-Quest," a spirited metapoetic fable that at once explains the irrecoverable loss of the grand old stories and attests the unquenched reliquary power they retain even in fallen and dilapidated condition.[26] *Congal* conspicuously breaks, however, with that apology for the collected *disjecta membra* format, to offer instead a joined and linear last-minstrelsy-lay about "the expiring effort of the Pagan and Bardic party in Ireland, against the newly consolidated power of Church and Crown" (vi). In this poem that W. B. Yeats read with ambivalence and rewrote around the figure of Oisin, the hero yields to the priest, the bard to the statesman–legislator, and, implicitly, the song to the book, in a *translatio* that draws on heavily Latinate diction and syntax, and also on the long-disused fourteener verses in which Chapman had translated Homer for the Elizabethans.

   This multiple conversion of an old order to a new confers thematic unity on Ferguson's narrative, wherein Congal of Ulster raises an international alliance of heroes from such yet-pagan strongholds as Scotland, Wales, and Norway, to avenge King Domnal's slighting of the ancient ways in favor of the Christian ones by which Saint Patrick has modernized Ireland several generations ago. Congal's host are overcome not by superior troop strength but by occult forces—fully, and absorbingly, pagan rather than Christian in nature—which in the poem's best scenes foretell Congal's destruction (book 3) and then bring it to pass, along with his, and the Druid holdout Ardan's, deathbed acceptance of the new cultural dispensation (book 5). As in Scott, full imaginative credit is extended to an expiring heroic ethos that knows itself to be on the way out. In a nice and witty riposte to such notions as Arnold's *On the Study of Celtic Literature* (1867) had made current, Ferguson puts his most stirring speech of doomed glory in the mouth of Conan Rodd, the *British* prince whom Congal has recruited from that

---

[26] See Dentith, *Epic and Empire*, 175–79, for discussion of this fragment and of *Congal*.

benighted eastern isle across the Irish sea. "With awful joy elate," barbarian Conan exclaims, "I stand; and bid thee hail, | Last hero-stage of all the world" (3.471–72). The heroic joy is awesome, but there is no shirking the awful truth: at the world-historical cutting edge that was Ireland circa 637, the charmingly hot-headed, hopelessly retro Brit with the shillelagh doesn't stand a chance.

Human heroes and weird spirits alike, the vanishing order gives its blessing to what does not so much supersede as fulfill it. This benediction is also Ferguson's on the historical progress that forms our chapter leitmotif. The overcoming of flamboyant seventh-century British raiders by faithful, methodical Irish resistance enacts the same logic of cultural advance that makes it incumbent on nineteenth-century Ireland now to get with the program of British supremacy—in whose traditions Ferguson exhorts his countrymen to recollect their proud portion.[27] Whatever one makes of this bargain, it is sweetened by a daring passage late in book 5: just before his death the hero receives a visit from one of the "Shapes of the air" (5.538), and from his battle-soiled mantle a radiance pours forth that transfigures the landscape into a beatific vision of animal vigor amid landed prosperity (5.545–69.). That this constitutes Ferguson's unionist vision of a successfully reassimilated Ireland is clear from the oversize heroic simile of twenty-five lines that precedes it, in which "a citizen just 'scaped from some disease" (some poor devil out of Milton? or is it a Victorian Irishman?) climbs a seaside headland to take in the "rich," "foodful" prospect of the harvest and the teeming deep. It is to this prospect of peace and opportunity—a fancier digest of what Allingham's *Laurence Bloomfield* had imagined for Ireland a decade earlier on verse-novel scale (Ch. 10)—rather than to any article of Christian doctrine, that Congal makes his final conversion (5.585–86). In other words, according to Ferguson's cultural typology, this prospect fulfills an historical totality that the contested transition from pagan to Christian Ireland has prefigured.

In a sense the prospect of an increasing worldly prosperity, overseen by an increasingly ethereal spirit of world-historical benevolence, was *the* meaning that latter-century universalism read into historical transition as such.

[27] Graham finds politically apologetic, and thus debilitating, Ferguson's concession to the pre-colonial reciprocation of power between British and Irish lords before the Tudor conquest (109–14). This apt critique has broader application to many of the works the present chapter studies, which are rooted like *Congal* in a denationalized generic "classicism" and make their appeal to an explanatory schema requiring "a movement across national boundaries"—with which, *pace* Graham (120), epic by 1870 was only too eager to cope.

As interpreted by the indomitable spirit of progress during the age of empire, every chapter in the book of human history told the same tale and extended the same promise, which it became the business of the present to fulfill. So it was that Emily (Davis) Pfeiffer's *Glân-Alarch: His Silence and Song* (1877) revived in a Welsh setting the Celtic-Saxon conflict that had exercised the epic imagination of Romanticism—and had furnished Tennyson's historical backdrop for the *Idylls*—only to wrest from that conflict a benediction virtually identical to the one that graced Ferguson's account of the greatest of Irish culture wars. Glân-Alarch, who narrates the poem, is yet another last Welsh minstrel in the tradition of Gray's Bard that in former chapters we have seen Southey, Cottle, Bayley, and Linwood carrying forward into the nineteenth century. Now, though, the Welsh bard is a figure much changed. Through much of the poem he displays an emollient sensitivity to what the author's prose preface calls "the homelier life" (vii), which lies "beneath the veil of chivalry" (i) and which in Pfeiffer's rendition approximates her work at times to an historical novel in verse. (She had published in 1873 and would revise for 1878 a verse-novel set in medieval Sussex called *Gerard's Monument*, which despite alchemical themes and a deluge finale abides within fiction's generic limits as a narrative of aristocratic family life.)

The old bardic energy has not so much disappeared from *Glân-Alarch* as gone underground. Pfeiffer diffuses it into the sublimities of her Welsh landscapes, and gathers it up thence into a new focal point as her poem's most interesting creation, a nearly disembodied shape-shifting Irish orphan girl called Mona. Named, as is right for a spirit of the land, after the extreme geographic verge of Wales in Anglesey, Mona at once keeps the work's conscience, evincing a striking moral indignation in defense of Gaelic folkways (1.860–98), and becomes in her evanescent resiliency something of a meta-physical principle too. The volatile ethnic energy she represents is finally fixed into solution with the long, and long-awaited, "song" of Glân-Alarch that ends the poem and that Mona has vanished from the plot in order to inspire and, as it were, turn into. The last stand of Cymri mountaineers against Sassenach onslaught has failed. But the Gaelic cause, far from lost, has merely migrated into the British national psyche, in order to stir that emergent hybrid from within.[28] An advertising "Argument" for *Glân-Alarch* that was appended

---

[28] Catherine Brennan, *Angers, Fantasies and Ghostly Fears: Nineteenth-Century Women from Wales and English-Language Poetry* (Cardiff: University of Wales Press, 2003), offers a full, informed, and thoughtful discussion of *Glân-Alarch*. Brennan picks through a tangle of gendered and national

to the second edition of *Gerard's Monument* associates this interiorized authority of "a disembodied race" with feminine influence, with "fresh springs of poetry" that dispose "the England of to-day" to "tenderness for losing causes," and above all with "the triumph of an unseen, spiritual agency over a palpable material one."

This invisible agency is the nerve that moves history forward through losing causes towards incalculably prosperous effects. The former consecrate the latter, as Amohia's sacrifice does the empire-building of Domett; the latter signify the former, which is what lets Ferguson provide a vision of wealthy Ireland in token of a British Commonwealth apologetic. It is striking that a similar universalism should inform another 1872 labor of Celtic recovery, this one performed by a Catholic convert and undisguised conservative: *The Legends of Saint Patrick* by Aubrey de Vere. If this braid of eleven stanzaic ballads with as many Tennysonian idylls creates a structural expectation that a deferred twelfth phase may even now be emerging from the travails of Ireland, de Vere's strong embrace of an historically unfolding national character permits that emergence to be contemplated with confidence. "The incidents which survive in the recollections of a people," his preface remarks, "are not by necessity the most momentous which they have witnessed, but they are the most characteristic" (xxiv); and this emphasis on *character* as a persistent collective identity sustains the poetic work he went on to do in *Legends of the Saxon Saints* (1879) and *The Foray of Queen Meave and Other Legends of Ireland's Heroic Age* (1882). All three books follow the anthological mode, and the apparatus to each theorizes that mode as peculiarly well suited to the imaginative projection of group character—better suited, we infer, than the outmoded linear continuity of *Congal*, although de Vere praised that poem explicitly when dedicating the third of his collections to Ferguson.

Fragmentary in both de Vere's sources and his modern version of them, the 1872 *Legends* cohere nonetheless as "the legends of the Patrician cycle" (x: "Patrician" as in "Patrick"). Existing nowhere as a text, this cycle gathers to an ideal greatness it arguably would lack were it more than implied by the fractional arcs that survive: "To the imagination those broken fragments suggest a state of society in its wholeness" (xxv). De Vere, like Ferguson, is acquainted with the *Tain bo Cuailgne*, and he laments that the remnants

energies that impinged on Pfeiffer's ambivalent attempt to retrieve from "the violent destruction of an authentic British identity" depicted in the plot a compensatorily invented "British tradition which is based on Welshness" (164–65).

of this great national epic, unlike Homer's, "unhappily found no Pisistratus to combine them into a whole" (*Foray*, v). Nevertheless, the very sketchiness of the record has somehow etched the more deeply his impression of Cuchullain's "character," as "one so consistent and so original that it suffices by itself to stamp the age which conceived it as high among the most poetic of the world" (ix). No Pisistratus, and no Macpherson either: a century after the Ossian books, de Vere's Victorian piety saves its reverence for the fragment, not the reconstructed whole. Inferring that whole from the surviving part forms one imaginative reflex with inferring the character of the "age" and "state of society" from the character of the hero (Oisin) or the saint (Patrick)—two dialectically balanced figures whose confederation into one ideal character, God's athlete, gives *Legends* its unifying plot.

This fusion of opposites, and of the one with the many, reaches white heat at the epoch of a national conversion, such as Patrick brought to pass and as Anglo-Saxon converts to Christianity across the Irish Sea led forward in a later century. That is the "great crisis," de Vere affirms, which shows a nation its soul, "when, beside a throng of new feelings and new hopes, a host of new Truths has descended upon the intelligence of a whole people, and when a sense of new knowledge and endless progress is thus communicated to it. ... The sense of progress, indeed, when such a period reaches its highest, is a rapture" (*Saxon Saints*, xlviii). Among medieval revivalists only a late Victorian would ring the progressive note so persistently and impute to an historically distinct mentality not just progress but the conscious "sense of progress," the very criterion that later nineteenth-century historiography took as normative. Thus the twelve *Legends of the Saxon Saints* are framed at one end by a Carlylean heroic soliloquy in which "Odin, the Man" foretells a future emulation among virtuous "nations of the world," supervised by a "greater God," "a God unknown to Rome" at the zenith of imperial delusion (8); and at the other by "Bede's Last May," a milder-tempered piece befitting the advance from legendary myth toward settled historical chronicle that the intervening dozen idylls record, and applaud. It is this advance of enlightenment that de Vere hailed in Ferguson's labors to "illustrate aright the legends of ancient Ireland" (*Foray*, Dedication) and that Ferguson reciprocated in a note to *Congal* that congratulated his fellow "converter of Irish traditionary material to the cultured uses of modern literature."[29] Even their unswerving loyalty to

[29] Relations between Ferguson and de Vere are discussed by Peter Denman in *Samuel Ferguson: The Literary Achievement* (Savage: Barnes and Noble, 1990) 142.

Catholicism became evidence to de Vere of "the place of the Irish race in the providential scheme" whereby God had distributed genius among the nations and reserved to each its shining hour: "to Greece an artistic one, to Ireland, as to Israel, a spiritual one."[30]

The compatibility of such sectored providentialism with a universal historical sweep was also attested around this time from the Juvenile Instructor Office of distant Salt Lake in *An Epic Poem: A Synopsis of the Rise of the Church of Jesus Christ of Latter-Day Saints* (1884). Hannah Tapfield King, Englishwoman born and converted if marginally heretical Mormon, invokes "Columbia!" and "Albion!" alike on her first page of heroic couplets; and she so arranges her prophetic narrative of Joseph Smith and Brigham Young as to make it plain that martyrdom and exile are but founding episodes in the synoptic "gospel plan" (26) of an international evangelism hastening the newest of churches across the neediest of old worlds, "Till every nation—every land and clime, | Had here its type, endorsed by rite divine" (34). Elder Young becomes the latest, post-scriptural "type" of what "Napoleon, Barbarrossa, Hofer, Tell" all figured, as did Cromwell, as did "Mahomet, Moses" (50–51). Continuator of their joint mission, he also subsumes them in accordance with a latter-day logic that Hannah King in central Utah fully shared with the metropolitan majority of what is ordinarily understood by the literary West.[31]

If there is one name indelibly associated with the national-anthological turn of the later Victorian mind, it is that of F. T. Palgrave, whose phenomenally successful *Golden Treasury* (1861) fed and shaped for generations a taste in lyric that bore with it a larger if implicit history both of English poetry and of the language it was written in. This implicit history became explicit decades later when Palgrave issued *The Visions of England* (1881). Subtitled for the revised 1891 edition *Seventy Lyrics on Leading Men and Events in English History*, the book not only disclaims epic aspiration for itself but goes on to discount it in the books of others, by downplaying the genre's importance in English literary history. "No national epic, no poem which, as a whole, really touched the country, has been left us" (viii); and this is so because the ambition towards what Palgrave unappetizingly calls "consecutive annalistic verse" is

---

[30] Quoted in Wilfrid Ward, *Aubrey de Vere: A Memoir* (London: Longmans, 1904) 299.

[31] Alan C. Jalowitz, "The Daughters of Penelope: Tradition and Innovation in American Epics by Women," in *Approaches to the Anglo and American Female Epic, 1620–1982*, ed. Bernard Schweizer (Aldershot: Ashgate, 2006) 151–55, noting that King belonged to the church-disowned Polysophical Society of Salt Lake, shows how she fit epic conventions to key incidents from Mormon patriarchal history.

the post-Norman overgrowth of a folk genius that is fundamentally lyrical and springs from "the true instincts of spontaneous art" (vii). In reverting to this genius for "single lyrical pictures" of "leading or typical characters and scenes," Palgrave claims to have eschewed many of the imported and new-fangled verse forms with whose epic uses our previous chapters have made acquaintance: forms like "unrhymed irregular lyric" (Southey), "the bastard modern hexameter" (Clough, Kingsley, Morris), "narrative ballad" (Scott, and all the world besides). Only forms that have made the cut and appeared already in the *Golden Treasury*, one suspects, need apply as suitable poetic aids to a properly English vision. And *English* it is, Palgrave's title twice reminds us, not "British": if not birth outright, then breeding in the patriotic mother tongue that fills proper poetic forms has become the key to national identity. The Englishness of provincial Palgravia seemed as right for its time as a *New British Dictionary*—can we even now imagine consulting the *OBD?*—would have seemed wrong.[32]

The fact that *Visions of England* goes right on to employ hexameters, Italian sonnets, and other proscribed forms suggests that Palgrave's lip-service about "native forms of stanza" is a way of pledging allegiance to something else for which it stands, something more greatly exigent that emerges in a phrase his discussion of prosody italicizes: "the sense of *inner necessity*" (xii–xiii). This stern term of art links the askesis of lyrical form to the historiographic ambition that Palgrave shared with his epicizing contemporaries—and, inversely, to the epicizing ambition they all shared with contemporary historiographers like J. A. Froude, whose lately concluded *History of England* (1856–1870) had covered the Tudor epoch in twelve volumes culminating with the defeat of the Armada. Where Froude, E. A. Freeman, J. R. Green, William Stubbs, and other nationalist historians wore their colors on their sleeve, if not their dust jacket, Palgrave kept ranks with the poets in preferring a complex maneuver of disownment.[33] What linked his many lyrics together, and multiplied their cumulative power, was that "*inner necessity*" which was the driving force within history, and which came into special focus, he held, at nodes of

---

[32] On the gradual supplanting of "Britishness" by the "Englishness" it had displaced during the century's early decades under pressure first of war, then of ecclesiastic and franchise reforms, see Stephanie L Barczewski, *Myth and National Identity in Nineteenth-Century Britain: The Legends of King Arthur and Robin Hood* (Oxford: Oxford University Press, 2000) 6–7. See also Willinsky, *Empire of Words*.

[33] Freeman, *The History of the Norman Conquest of England, its Causes and its Results* (1867), Green, *A Short History of the English People* (1875), Stubbs, *The Constitutional History of England, in its Origin and Development* (1874–78).

heightened subjective inwardness. This fleeting yet recurrent convergence between zeitgeist and sensibility put Palgrave's "leading or typical characters" in the lead, very much like the "characters" singled out by Meredith and de Vere in their epic anthologies, as evolving national types. Comparison to Thomas Dibdin's frolic 1813 chronicle *A Metrical History of England* (Ch. 4), which Palgrave's collection only superficially resembles, will reveal beyond the predictable Victorian decorousness a more systematic ideological consistency than the Romantic historian even faintly pretended to sustain (or felt that he had to).

Almost never do Palgrave's lyrics stand alone in pure feeling. (That "A Ballad of Queen Catharine, January: 1536" makes an exception suggests, *pace* O'Shaughnessy and Morris Minor, that the figure of the abandoned woman remained available to represent those discards of history whose casualties epic in its late triumphalist phase seldom paused to heed.) Instead the "visions of England" stand out by parallax with the implied culmination of history in the Victorian present. "Only the nation which, at each moment of political or social evolution, looks lovingly backward to its own painfully-earned experience... has solid reason to hope, that its movement is true Advance" (xi). This is a sheer progressivist truism, but one brought to life by the substantiating experience of the reader, whose progress through the volume involves looking backward to the experience of its earlier pages, and forward also; who regularly finds the "Past in Present hid," as the final lyric has it ("England Once More," 37), because the poet has assiduously planted the present in the past to begin with. The "once more" structure of serial national recognition is foreshadowed in the lyric title that starts it, "The First and Last Land"; and it winks out of the woodwork time and again. When "Sir Hugh Willoughby, 1553–4" concludes the tale of a doomed expedition into Russian seas with the "heroic chieftain" frozen on shipboard, "English through every fibre, in his place, | The smile of duty done upon the steadfast face" (77–78), the image glistens already with Lord Nelson's sailorly expectation concerning every Englishman's duty, which occurs for consultation, duly, in the "Trafalgar" lyric a hundred and fifty pages later. The end of "At Fountains, 1539," capping a retrospect of that Yorkshire abbey's ruination by order of Henry VIII, brims with the *pax Victoriana* of a longer and better "reign" than the Merry Monarch's, a reign that is called nature's but connotes the entire plot of a history that has made all good at last: "O calm of Nature! Now thou hold'st again | Thy sweet and silent reign!" (41–42). When for the edition of 1889 Palgrave retitled this lyric "At Fountains, 1539-1862," he hid in plain sight the same Wordsworthian strategy of empirical commotion and tranquil historical recollection that the entire book pursues.

The same totalizing vision that let Palgrave confer heroic scope on a lyric series, and let Pfeiffer and Ferguson harness Gael force to a post-ethnic imperial destiny, also gave a new charter after 1870 to the biographical epic, a subgenre that is all told surprisingly under-represented during a century when it might have been expected to thrive. Romantic and Victorian plots based on the life-story of an exceptional individual—"what Alcibiades did or suffered," as Aristotle had disapprovingly put it—were rarer in verse than in prose.[34] While fully half of the works this book notices are named after persons, their eponymy is not chiefly biographical: even at the historical acme of individualism, the epic genre clove to an Aristotelian preference for great, collectively defining actions over exemplary lives as such. Madoc and Alfred and Marmion become heroes not by how they live but by what they do, in exploits that center the movement of nations. Even at the subjective extremity of our genre, the spasmodic epic's focus on the character of Festus or Balder (Ch. 9) rather celebrates his instantaneous plenitude of being than shows how his character has developed since childhood or is rounded into shape by the mortal fullness of his days. "Life" in the biographer's sense is precisely not what is at stake in Smith's *A Life-Drama* or, to take a very different instance, Morris's *Life and Death of Jason*. One major sign of the nineteenth-century epic's disinterest in patterns of individual *Bildung* is its neglect of childhood; those exceptional poems that trace a child's growth towards the realization of an heroic potential do so either under the heavy hand of unremitting irony (*Don Juan, Sordello*) or by the extraordinary adaptation to epic purposes of an autobiographical perspective (*The Prelude, Aurora Leigh*) which, if not exactly ironical, has nevertheless since Dante carried the burden of a systematic self-correction that functions as irony's structural equivalent.

Personal development sympathetically narrated from a standpoint outside the developing self was a model not for the period's epics but for its biographies and prose fiction. The more closely a long poem conformed to this model the stronger its affiliation with the verse-novel. Mary Montgomerie Lamb

---

[34] *Poetics* 9.1451b, in *Aristotle's Theory of Poetry and Fine Art*, tr. S. H. Butcher (London: St. Martin's Press, 1894) 35.

betokened as much when she published *Constance's Fate: A Story of Denzil Place* (1876) under a pseudonym ("Violet Fane") taken from a Disraeli novel, and capped her rather risqué flirtation with free-thinking adultery by an epilogue invoking the sturdiest of realist fiction's premises: the plot may be trusted, she affirms, because the author has drawn her principals from living originals (p. 253). This blank-verse spinoff from *Aurora Leigh* is so thoroughly a novel, in every particular but prosody, as to highlight in retrospect how far from a mere novel its brilliant original had been twenty years before.[35]

Variants of the union between new man and new woman emplotted other late-century verse-novels too. One feels Robert Browning working towards modern reconception of sexual relations in the string of long poems he produced in the early 1870s—*Fifine at the Fair, Red Cotton Night-Cap Country, The Inn Album*, the Balaustion translations—which, if they were too eccentric for assimilation as verse-novels, were not epics to match *Sordello* or *The Ring and the Book* either, and which persisted most vitally in their influence on the later fiction of Hardy and James. *Michael Villiers, Idealist* (1891), by Emily Hickey, reads like a streamlined abstract of *Robert Elsmere* (Mrs Humphry Ward's *roman à thèse* from a few years earlier), or like a politically corrected digest of Allingham's *Laurence Bloomfield*, whose concern for social justice in Ireland on sound principles Hickey's poem devoutly shares. *Michael Villiers* was written, one suspects, for the sake of the hero's speeches renouncing the privileges of his birth, reproving conservatism and nihilism, and espousing as the remedy for Irish ills expanded educational opportunity under Christian socialist auspices. Still, the plot structure within which these addresses find their place centers on Villiers's love life (our sweethearts become "comrades" in canto 8 at the meeting of a socialist cell), across a lifespan framed at one end by his *in utero* dedication to the spirit of humanitarian love (canto 1) and at the other by a nuptial prospect that is nudged towards hierogamy by optimistic prophecies of social reform (canto 14).

Harder to classify generically, and to finish reading, is our chapter cicerone's longest opus, *Glenaveril, or the Metamorphoses: A Poem in Six Books* (1885) by Owen Meredith. This double *Doppelgänger* tale compounds a switched-at-birth premise with a voluntary identity-exchange, and rambles

---

[35] For analysis of bibliographic and typographic details setting *Denzil Place* apart from the run of the verse-novel mill, see Terence Allan Hoagwood and Kathryn Ledbetter, *"Colour'd Shadows": Contexts in Publishing, Printing, and Reading Nineteenth-Century British Women Authors* (Houndmills: Palgrave, 2005) 137–52.

across six hundred pages of decorously chatty *ottava rima* to link Germany, Britain, and America. The link among lands inheres in a system of values that draws on Aryan roots—not for nothing was the author a close friend of the racial apologist Count Gobineau or, in the poem, is the lads' absent-minded tutor a crackerjack Sanskritist—and that exfoliates into a detailed scheme for land-grant farming in the western United States. But everything hinges at last on the infallible omniscience of a good American girl's heart about the one thing that really counts: the true identity, genetically implanted as if to verify Darwin's theories on sexual selection and Francis Galton's on eugenics, of the young man she loves. While Meredith's socio-political agenda is as difficult to specify as Hickey's is to miss, their works share with *Constance's Fate* an implicit thesis: the essential, heredity-bound self's mission to find its niche within a given social scheme, rather than to found or remake one. To recall Eliot's *Spanish Gypsy* from Chapter 10 is to see how these works consisted less with the epic variants the present chapter considers than with the vast output of the contemporary novel.

To epicize the story of personal development required an author to hold the protagonist in a longer view, and perhaps a blurrier one: a view that subordinated individuating particulars to a collective history. Blurry is the word for Thomas Woolner's second effort in the verse-fiction line, a twelve-booklet *Pygmalion* (1881) that promotes its eponym with Aphrodite's blessing from moody studio artist to rock-sculpture star in the first half, then in the second half marries him to his model: no stony Galatea she, but blushing love all the way. At this point the sculptor-poet's proper plot ran out, or rather ran off into unlikely scenario sketches repeatedly suggestive of a civic-minded epic that, whatever its gleam in Woolner's eye, certainly eluded him on paper. Pygmalion becomes in short order a happy husband, a target for assassination, commandant of the Cypriot defenses against a sudden invasion of Egyptian marines, and finally, all missions accomplished, king of the island. The relentless implausibility of Woolner's plot, seized up by fits of apologetically obtruded explanatory detail a novelist would quail at—try on for size 11.14–28, where the song pauses quite some time to wonder just where our absent-minded hero left his sword—owes whatever sense it may claim to the same extroversive motion, from indoor vapors to sunlit forum, that we found last chapter in his more candidly incoherent *My Beautiful Lady*. A last mythological verse narrative from the same hand, *Silenus* (1884), lurches yet again from private loves to public issues, this time in the hope of wresting hearts to sympathy with its drunken tun of an eponymous demigod. Stout Silenus goes downhill fast after losing his nymph Syrinx while he is away from home in the service of his charismatic, negligent patron Dionysus—away in India of all places, as a matter of late-Victorian fact, to promote viniculture among the under-developed natives. One form Silenus' heartbreak takes, both before and after he has found consolation in an alcoholic lifestyle, is satiric diatribe, intermittently hurled at the vices of a faithless world that remains, improbably yet transparently, Britain in her modern commercial phase.

In Woolner's peculiar appropriations of classical myth an outward momentum towards epic is as conspicuous as it is erratic. This tendency, more subtly perceptible in *Michael Villiers* and *Glenaveril*, is also kept under better control there by the verse-novelist's overriding allegiance to the individual case. The question of generic classification comes down to relative emphasis or focal length: to whether the histories implied by Hickey's socialism (cantos 5–7) or Meredith's oddly communistic imperialism (1.3, canto 4 *passim*) are backdrops serving to highlight a personal life foregrounded for its own sake, or whether on the contrary that life is rehearsed in order to illustrate the larger history in which it finds meaning. It is this latter emphasis that nourishes a crop of biographical epics that were written during the 1870s and 1880s, and that arguably could not have been written sooner—not, that is, before the universal narrative of progressive civilization had established its hold on the Western mind. A poem retailing what its elected "Alcibiades did or suffered," if its narrative of childhood and maturation is to possess the right sort of illustrative largeness, must endow these particulars with the force of epitome. And this force was made available to the epic life-writer by the consolidated myth of cultural amelioration that drove field after field of Victorian intellectual endeavor to vest its wisdom in cradle-to-prime-to-fulfillment narratives of improvement. What an exemplary life exemplified, under such intellectual conditions, was the great narrative of development that it brought into readily imaginable focus, not by allegorical analogy but by the perfection with which the chosen life had realized, and now in a retelling might manifest afresh, a pattern of total action in which all humankind had a role.

Such was the climate that made Edwin Arnold's *The Light of Asia; or The Great Renunciation* not only possible in 1879 but a bestseller in the decades that ensued, until scores of editions drove worldwide sales close to a million copies. The poem puts the life of the Buddha into eight books of stodgily

Tennysonian blank verse, yielding to gnomic quatrains and couplets in book 8, where the narrated life culminates in the great teachings. With crisp precision the first half of the poem concludes upon the "great renunciation" highlighted in its subtitle—the privileged Prince Siddârtha's vow to "cast away my world to save my world" (4.547)—and the second half commences by introducing him, self-impoverished, in his new capacity as "Lord Buddha" (5.20). While obviously Western-epical in style and structure, the poem offers its content as "regarded from the Oriental point of view" (x), by which Arnold points in the first instance to his operative fiction that the whole narrative has proceeded from the mouth of a devout Eastern Buddhist (8.573–89). What this admittedly threadbare pretense more deeply signifies is the poet's having dispensed with the kind of orientalist vilification or overt ideological exploitation we found in Southey's *Curse of Kehama* or Jones's *Revolt of Hindostan* (Chs. 3 and 9). The former's ethnocentric aversion to the Orient, and the latter's strident anticapitalist radicalism, kept either poem from setting India and Britain on a continuum where any measurable benefit or obligation might flow between them. That these familiar forms of Western exceptionalism persisted as an 1870s epic option will emerge from the case of the orientalizing poet, Richard Phillips, to whom we shall turn next; so the *bona fides* that Arnold showed as a broker of Indian culture here and also in the *Mahabharata* translations he published during the 1880s is noteworthy—as is the reading public's enthusiastic reception.

Indeed, the very popularity of Arnold's work prompts suspicion that subtler modes of ideological exploitation informed his steady effort "to aid in the better mutual knowledge of East and West" (xi).[36] For Arnold purchases a hearing, on behalf of what was still in 1870s Europe widely reckoned an outlandish faith, by conforming Buddhism's truths to those of Christianity: "the eternity of a universal hope, the immortality of a boundless love, an indestructible element of faith in final good" (ix). And what underwrites such conformity is not faith in the New Testament but faith in the progress narrative to which the New Testament's call to the Gentiles bears privileged but not ultimate witness. Christianity is not a better religion, just a later one within a supersessively developing

---

[36] Graham traces the assimilative strategy beyond *The Light in Asia* into Arnold's *Mahabharata* versions of subsequent years. *Indian Idylls* (1883) and *The Song Celestial* (1885), accommodated with a practically administrative efficiency to Tennysonian norms, became by the same token conduits through which an Indian cultural integrity transpired in ways beyond imperial control (136–39, 148–69). For Dentith, *Epic and Empire*, 180, the "grand-sounding neoclassical idiom" sought by Arnold produces "a culturally unspecific dignity that finally sounds simply pompous."

universal history. Placed in this capacious scheme, the "venerable religion" of Buddhism, albeit subjected over the centuries to "inevitable degradation" (ix), possesses at its early source the same freshness of appeal and interest that attaches to Siddârtha in his early years.[37]

The Prince's youthful development experientially explains, and is doctrinally fulfilled by, the Buddha's changeless wisdom. Likewise that wisdom, Arnold's tacit analogy proposes, has undergone a millennial westward migration to a safe home among English readers capable of recognizing their own cherished truths in a distant, imported original.[38] In comparison to ancient Buddhism "most other creeds are youthful" (ix); by the magic of that progressivist imperialism which subtends Arnold's conscientious circumvention of his predecessors' colonial insolence, it is the "youthfulness" or comparative modernity of Victorian faith that lets it kindle to an original glow 2,500 years old. This maneuver earned Arnold some detraction at the hands of the doctrinaire and the ethnocentric, to be sure. He made amends in 1891 with *The Light of the World, or The Great Consummation*, manifestly a sequel epic that aimed to right the East/West balance by retelling the life of Jesus, on which his bestseller had at many points implicitly depended.[39] What is most interesting about this last of many dutifully epicized nineteenth-century Gospel redactions is its narrative asymmetry with *The Light of Asia*. Rather than recite his redeemer's biography straight off, as he did with the biography of the Buddha, Arnold contrives to have one of the oriental Magi return westward to Galilee in great old age, seek out the now matronly Mary Magdalene, and hear from her lips a mediated account of the biographical facts. Adopting the odd obliquity of witness that characterizes the New Testament's fourfold gospel truth, Arnold thus thematizes the issues of East/West reception that went without saying in, while they remained the very point of, his epic life of the Buddha. With a quarter-turn adjustment of the globe and a two-millennium update of the dial, Herman Melville had concurrently staged a like East/West confrontation in his long poem *Clarel: A Poem and Pilgrimage in*

---

[37] Hoxie Neale Fairchild, *Religious Trends in English Poetry*, vol. 4 (New York: Columbia University Press, 1957) 73, is unfair on Arnold but unforgettable: "So there is such a thing as muscular Buddhism."

[38] See J. Jeffrey Franklin, "The Life of the Buddha in Victorian England," *ELH* 72 (2005) 966–67.

[39] Such a result was forecast by a discerning youthful admirer of Arnold's, Sidney Arthur Alexander, when the preface to his Newdigate Prize poem "Sakya-Muni: The Story of Buddha" (Oxford: Shrimpton, 1887) noted "the parallels drawn (and, perhaps, at times overdrawn) between the 'Light of Asia' and the 'Light of the World' " (iii). On contemporary reaction to Arnold's first epic see Christopher Clausen, "Sir Edwin Arnold's *The Light of Asia* and Its Reception," *Literature East and West* 17 (1973) 174–91. In the meantime, we may note, Arnold like Southey before him had sojourned in the Middle East with *Pearls of the Faith; or Islam's Rosary* (1883).

the Holy Land (1876). This leathery dialogical epic of centennial date dispatches a clutch of modern American pilgrims on tour into Palestine, there to excavate the soul by working out on Arnoldian, humanist grounds—Matthew's, that is, and not Edwin's—the literature that scripture harbors and the imaginative core of faith.[40]

A less satisfactory British result along somewhat Melvillean lines had been obtained earlier in the 1870s, when another long Buddha-based poem articulated a similar thematic. In *The Story of Gaútama Buddha and His Creed: An Epic* (1871) Richard Phillips pointedly foregrounded his occidentalist perspective through, in the first instance, the choice of coupleted octave stanzas. The form is not quite such an *ottava rima* as Alfred Austin and Owen Meredith were adopting at this time, yet it lies close enough to the *Don Juan* mold to foster, as did those poets' epics, metanarrative habits of Byronic digression and disclaimer that thrust on the reader's awareness the Western purpose by which the narrative is being shaped. Here that purpose is a reductive species of critical appropriation, brought to bear on an ancient sage's legacy through the most modern of bourgeois means, psychological analysis. For Phillips's carefully worded title announces a distinction, between Gaútama Buddha's inmost conviction and the creed he proclaims, that is crucial to the entire poem's conception. Phillips holds that the Buddha propounded his teachings under the cover of a pious fraud, a high-minded deception suited to the ears of listeners who were not yet ready—indeed would not be ready for two millennia and more—to live in the freedom of a godless world.

In pursuit of this thesis Phillips adheres to a poetic structure that separates outer from inner, biographical from meditative events. At beginning and end four cantos apiece are devoted to the life of Prince Siddhártha (1–4) and his return to public life as the Gaútama Buddha (9–13); five intervening cantos record the process of enlightenment that transformed the man into the world-historical teacher. Planted at the heart of the thirteen cantos is the poem's central theologizing, which consists in Gaútama's double rejection of the Hindu pantheon and of the ascetic spiritual path sponsored in his day by Brahman reincarnationist thought. Seeking "not death, but that which may remove | The fear thereof, and of all ill; and prove | Salvation for the living" (7.39), the Buddha determines both that "There is no God nor higher power than man" (8.6) and that saying so out loud can do no good to

---

[40] Walter E. Bezanson's comprehensive 1960 monograph approaching *Clarel* as an American epic is reprinted in the edition by Harrison Hayford *et al.* (Evanston and Chicago: Northwestern University Press and Newberry Library, 1991) 505–637.

those who need it most. He resolves instead, and for all the world like a
Victorian Higher Critic in what starts here to feel like an *épopée à clef*, "To
see if any help for human need | Might yet be hidden in the ancient creed"
(8.22) of Hinduism; and he goes on not to abolish Brahman tradition but to
reinterpret it as a plastic cosmic mythology conducive to the practice of that
virtue which lessens suffering: "I will now invent | A mighty universe of
worlds, and fill | Them all with beings" (8.30).

With the perfection of this ethical co-optation of religion, the Buddha
proceeds "to play his mighty part | In this world's drama" (10.18), which is
none other than the role in which the nineteenth-century poet's eclectic,
cosmopolitan progress narrative casts him. Because the perspective that
belongs to the European "restless people, an inventive race" (13.23), is
pragmatic above all else, readers in the West must admire in Gaútama's
inventiveness an anticipation of their own. After all, if the spiritual engineering
of Buddhism didn't work, what idea in the world's history ever did? Phillips
challenged his contemporaries to discern in the Buddha's "cunning work"
(8.52) the same can-do spirit which they too swore by, and by virtue of which,
within the decade, a British sovereign was to be proclaimed Empress of the
land his teaching transformed so long ago. Meanwhile the Buddha's lifelong
sacrifice of candor and thus of human intimacy ("he dared not show | His bitter
secret," 10.44) gave a suitably modern, psychological dimension to what
Arnold's epic would in a few years call "the great renunciation."

"Moreover we serve Christ, a grander far | Than Indian Buddha" (13.25).
The sheer perfunctoriness of Phillips's sectarian afterthought here is only less
revealing than the comparison-shopping discourse in which he frames it.
Christ offers the better bargain, exacting no celibate or ascetic practice
(13.27) and promising, not just the Buddhistic surcease of nonexistence
but the grand bonus of "life eternal" (13.30). A savior catering to moderns,
Phillips's Christ sets the standard by which in an envoi the poet hails a pair of
good Buddhist "brethren" as "The Christ-like followers of a godless creed"
(13.33). The poem's nominally Christian conclusion underscores its actual,
epic-making core belief in the march of civilization out from religious
mystery into a clarified humanism. What Richard Phillips thus accom-
plished in one awkwardly ambivalent work, Edwin Arnold accomplished
in two easier steps, a bestseller and then a palinode.[41] With the later and

---

[41] That Phillips's ambivalence stirs up Victorian anxieties that Arnold discreetly glosses over
does much, argues Franklin, to explain the strikingly divergent reception accorded these two
Buddha epics ("Life of the Buddha," 954, 966).

technically more sophisticated narrative armature of *The Light of the World*, we might say, Arnold adjusted his manner to suit the transitional place Christianity held in his understanding of humankind's spiritual evolution. If we supposed that manner adolescent in relation to the childlike *Light of Asia*—and noted that in *The Light of the World* Mary's detailed report to the Magus elides Jesus's boyhood, as if to put away all childish things— we might follow the curve of Arnold's comparatism towards an implied maturity not unlike Phillips's. The race when grown up might make its home in a world that had outgrown the neediness of primitive religion as such: a world to which sage elders had also seemed to point, by widely differing routes, in *The Earthly Paradise* and *The Ring and the Book*.

In a sense this post-Christian vista had been disclosed once more just after the great crest of Victorian epic, in *The Disciples* (1873), a monument of Risorgimento piety by Harriet Eleanor Hamilton King that would be many times reprinted before the century elapsed. Here the biography at the epicenter is not Jesus Christ's but Giuseppe Mazzini's, who had died only the year before and who is remembered in a sequence of heavy-duty Browning-scale monologues by political activists whom his life and character have inspired. No omniscient narrator moderates or interprets these imagined contemporary testimonials, which thus bear in form a gospelling kind of witness to the diffusive influence of the republican principles Mazzini had lived for.[42] The reverent commemoration and ardent resolve of Hamilton King's homage amply justify the religious aura her title lays claim to. And these features constitute a macropoetic proposition: the quickening of the spirit in modern times expresses itself in forms of social and political renewal—wherever these are found, and without benefit of clergy.

The imaginative vindication of this principle governed the career of a hard-working minor poet, Robert Buchanan, whose small but indelible fame as critic-provocateur to D. G. Rossetti and the "fleshly school" holds no proportion to his large if now largely forgotten epic ambition. Born to a secularized and politically radical family of Owenite artisans in Glasgow— nursery of 1850s Spasmodism—Buchanan caught the universalist currents of thinking about cultural evolution that swirled through 1860s London,

---

[42] Alison Milbank, *Dante and the Victorians* (Manchester and New York: Manchester University Press, 1998) 76–77, emphasizes—in contrast to the naïve epic "transparency" of Mary Elizabeth Braddon's *Garibaldi* a decade earlier—Mazzini's "tragic" complexity as a figure "that required interpretation."

where he was quick to grasp the opportunities offered by an anthological mode. Anticipating Lewis Morris's *Epic of Hades* by a decade, *Undertones* (1863) collected a score of exercises in classical prosopopoeia to illustrate a thesis that derived the impulse behind mythmaking from the permanence of human unfulfillment. *The Book of Orm* (1870) evinced much the same spirit but in abstracter mood, turning from blank-verse monologue to lyric rune and visionary parable.[43] The next year in *The Drama of Kings* Buchanan broke new ground, and had the honor of forerunning by a full generation Hardy's magisterial *Dynasts*, by bringing into allegorically mystic perspective the linked history of the two Napoleons and Bismarck.[44] That this work modeled on Goethe, Shelley, and Hugo, and spurred by the 1870 Commune and the Franco-Prussian War, should be dedicated to Auguste Comte says much about the long view of positivist development within which Buchanan situates his century's initiating convulsion. While the dramatic form of the poem betokens not just an affiliation to spasmody but a palpable debt, *The Drama of Kings* reminds us too of the hedge against older-fashioned ego-inflation that a newly totalized theory of civilization had by this point erected for poets of a certain intellectual pretension.

Buchanan's visionary mode sustained him as late as 1888 into *The City of Dream*, at last and forthrightly subtitled *An Epic Poem*, which recycles in fifteen short books of narrative blank verse, diversified with dialogue and lyric accompaniment, substantially the same *épopée humanitaire* that had preoccupied him from the start, and that made him one of Victor Hugo's champions among British critics.[45] Dedicated not to Comte or Hugo, though, but "To the Sainted Spirit of John Bunyan," Buchanan's last and most explicitly epic poem tropes the human journey as a pilgrimage through Christopolis (books 4–5) and the Valley of Dead Gods (book 11), to the

[43] Walker's discerning evaluation of Buchanan draws out the racialized Celtic mystique in *The Book of Orm* (*Victorian Era*, 580–81).

[44] "A Drama of Kings" was apparently Hardy's working title in 1889 for what became *The Dynasts*: see Florence Emily Hardy, *The Early Life of Thomas Hardy* (London: Macmillan, 1928) 290. See also Fairchild, "The Immediate Source of *The Dynasts*," *PMLA* 67 (1951) 43–64, who incidentally glimpses the Spasmodist connection; and John A. Cassidy, "The Original Source of Hardy's *Dynasts*," *PMLA* 69 (1954) 1085–1100, for extended discussion of Buchanan's epic debt to Victor Hugo.

[45] Buchanan devotes a chapter to Hugo in *A Look Round Literature* (London: Downey, 1887). Hunt, *The Epic in Nineteenth Century France*, 283, defines Hugo's place within modern French epic literature in terms that reprise the conception of the *Légende des Siècles* itself: "Hugo was building his construction on the foundation of ideas and aspirations which from our earliest chapter we have been occupied in exploring. His epic work represents the culmination of a century's poetic effort." It is an irony of English poetic history that, while such a claim may be lodged for *Don Juan*, *Aurora Leigh*, or *The Dynasts*, there is not one of the late-Victorian progress epics that can sustain it.

City of Man without God (book 14), and thence to oceanic prospects beyond conclusive knowing. Leaving the churches far behind, this pilgrim's story nevertheless gives Christianity a kind of diplomatic password to which all gates open—a concession consistent with the rapprochement to mainstream Victorian belief that Lewis Morris and Edwin Arnold were also making at just this time, and that Thomas Cooper had made two decades before. In catholic eclecticism *The City of Dream* found its real soulmate the next year when the Jubilee edition of our old friend *Festus* lumbered to market. At 40,000 lines the Victorian answer to *Faust* was now grotesquely swollen by every tradition on the planet that the insatiable impresario P. J. Bailey had managed to crowd under the big-top of his epic circus.

Like Bailey and the lesser poets just mentioned, Buchanan paid out in nonsectarian Christian currency, still coin of the realm, an imaginative allegiance that he did stand pledged to: comparatist universalism, bent on plenary redemption, marshaled and normed by the ideal of progress.[46] As *The Drama of Kings* had put it up front, the civilizing influence of "Brahm, Buddha, Balder, and the Man Divine" (Dedication, 15) was one half of an historical truth; the other half lay in these teachers' successive failure to keep their votaries from each other's throats. Such truth in its entirety called for a comprehensive tragicomic vision, if not for nihilistic satire—to which bitter mode the later British epic was by and large inhospitable, although Alfred Austin had leanings that way and James Thomson (B. V.) with a stouter heart, a sharper tongue, and an infusion of real plot might have made his *City of Dreadful Night* (1874) an exception. Among lesser latter-day epoists it was Buchanan who came closest to tragicomic comprehensiveness, in yet another poem of epic scope, this one not spread thin in transnational pageantry but concentrated like Edwin Arnold's and Harriet King's on the biography of a divine and sacrificial hero. *Balder the Beautiful: A Song of Divine Death* (1877) returns to matters we touched on in Chapter 9, the Norse mythography of Sydney Dobell (whom Buchanan befriended) and Matthew Arnold (prefatorily acknowledged here for his poem on the "Homeric demigod," 427). Buchanan extracted from the legend-hoard of Scandinavia a more satisfactory result than either precursor had attained. Here for once the wholeness of a single myth is followed with clean deliberation across nine cantos of varied choral form. The result suggests,

---

[46] Fairchild, *Religious Trends* 4: 216–39, surveys with some acerbity Buchanan's various poetic articulations of this position.

although it does not compass, the greater achievement William Morris had wrought out of similar materials the year before with *Sigurd the Volsung*.

What steadied Buchanan's nervously eclectic hand this one time was an evident conviction that the Balder myth already reproduced within itself, under the guise of "the most primitive mythology," the totality of a comparatist perspective (note to "A Song of Divine Death," 427). Prescribing the trajectory of alienated modern humanity on its long trip home, Balder grapples with his denial/abandonment by Alfadur the Father through a willing embrace of death itself. A god who grows up into mortality, Balder is born and fostered amid divine difficulties that bring him gradually to the balance point between ideals and actualities where we have just seen Buchanan also poising Brahma, Buddha, and Christ. Balder's gradually narrated upbringing culminates in his quest for death, a freely embraced choice of history over eternity, which sets going the analogous cosmic process that is to culminate in (what Buchanan's day was witnessing on all sides) the twilight of the gods and the supervention of a new order of the years. The reader who thinks, with surprised reluctance, of Blake's *Milton* or Shelley's *Prometheus* or Keats's *Hyperion* gets reinforcement of the most direct kind when the poem adduces Buddha, Prometheus, Apollo, and other lords of time who have for mankind's sake made the great refusal. Each renunciatory god who yearns downward to mortality in effect rehearses the role of "the white Christ" (7.3746–50), exalts the human condition, and consecrates being-towards-death as the banner that a detranscendentalized heroism will carry forward on the stage of history. If in Buchanan's routine anthological celebrations of evolving time, as in most of his peers', the comic note of congratulation rings too shrill and too soon, *Balder the Beautiful* breaks with this routine.[47] The poem shows Buchanan capable of honoring that logic of tragedy for which the age of empire had such limited tolerance, yet whose imperialist suppression more often than not cost the *fin-de-siècle* epic its full range.

Not tragedy but a generically elusive pathos is the particular achievement of one last epic plotted on a model life, Catherine Amy Dawson's *Sappho* (1889). Sacrifice hallows this like the other poems we have been considering, but here the sacrificial figure is an archetypal woman who, because she is a woman, must go to a doom that is entangled with more frustration and failure than afflict her male counterparts. Dawson's ruminative blank verse

---

[47] This is to differ with Andrew Wawn, who emphasizes the ultimate privilege Buchanan accords to the Christian myth: *The Vikings and the Victorians: Inventing the Old North in Nineteenth-Century Britain* (Cambridge: D. S. Brewer, 2000) 205–6.

confers on Sappho's four-book autobiography an interior dimension that is without parallel in Buchanan's life-story epic or Edwin Arnold's, and that is, when we compare it to the resolutely magnetized political dynamism of Mazzini's disciples as Harriet King imagines them, riddled by cross purposes. The self-interfering quality of Sappho's inner life is reflected in consistently maintained binary oppositions: between positions in the contest of debate (a moribund mode that Dawson's reforming ambition revives from the 1830s, where we met it in Ch. 7); between the sparkling life of Aegean nature and the close air of domestic interiors; and on the other hand between the safe space of home relations (the nurture that orphaned Sappho receives from her brother, then gives in turn to the orphan girl she adopts) and, in the public agora, the harsh space of a sexual discrimination engrained by habit and backed up by vigilante violence. From this latter regimen Sappho's sequestered girlhood, narrated in books 1 and 2, has provided a culturally sheltered independence; and, with a binary structural symmetry, she emerges at the epic midpoint to combat it as a woman and a poet in books 3 and 4.

Like other eponyms of the 1870s and 1880s, Sappho is a gifted teacher, less the lyric rhapsode of literary tradition than a feminist who bests priest-craft with a new word in the marketplace, founds an academy for young women, and dispels a hostile mob with song. The decidedly fey poet Alkaeus—Dawson's one brisk nod to sexual dissidence, though passages lingeringly descriptive of women's beauty (1.18–20) recall Sappho's other legacy too—wonders at first sight whether the heroine is "A theory in flesh—hermaphrodite" (2.53). The feminist point of this poem is that she is not. Unlike Buddha in avatar or the incarnate Christ, Sappho is body-gendered first; her radical theories develop under provocation by the sluggish injustice of the culture amid which she has grown up. Never so articulately prickly or feisty as her inescapable Victorian precursor Aurora Leigh—and proportionally less embroiled in the credentialing detail of the verse-novel—Sappho nonetheless owes her heroic glory and pathos alike to the intransigence of a biological difference that simply does not arise with remotely equivalent force in epics of masculine biography, not even when Arnold mediates Jesus's heroism through the Magdalene's love in *The Light of the World*.

Sappho's personal relationships are more distinctly gendered, more literally sororal or maternal, than is the metaphorical brotherhood of man that the *épopée humanitaire* exalts. By the same token Dawson had both less access to, and less faith in, the triumphalist cultural genealogy that came in the 1880s with the genre she chose. Her Sappho falls hard, body and soul, for the lover Phaon whom she accepts in book 3, only to lose him on her wedding day to her own (misnamed) foster daughter Agape. This melodramatic elopement, on the heels of her school's arson and the town fathers' ban against further teaching, shows with what punitive austerity Dawson cut her heroine off from physical procreation and direct charismatic influence. It was a sacrifice exacted, we must suppose, in order to free Sappho's voice from the body her fragmentary corpus speaks of, from the pervasive cultural regimentation of gender in general, and in particular from the narrative of automatic progress that stood in late Victorian culture's regimental vanguard. To avoid conscription within the monumental lists that enrolled other and more obviously consequential sacrificial heroes, Dawson had—not unlike Barrett Browning, but without that poet's confidence in literally apocalyptic fulfillment—to detach the story of Sappho from historical embeddedness and attach it instead to an as yet unrealized future of radical possibility. She had to keep it a leap in the dark.[48]

Dawson curiously does not provide, what might have been expected from a late-century Sappho epic, a defense of poetry's place among the arts of civilization. As it happens, such a defense was concurrently framed by Mathilde Blind in *The Ascent of Man* (1889)—attempted with courage, if accomplished only in part, and for reasons that may illuminate Dawson's reluctance to submit her heroine to exhibition within the progress narrative of her culture. While the three parts of Blind's poem take a variety of lyric forms (hymn and ode predominantly), the informing spirit of the whole is unquestionably epic, as befits the chief poetic testament of a writer noted in her time for cosmopolitan outlook, radical fervor, and a free-thinking blend of scientific with mystical conceptions.[49] Part 1, "Chaunts of Life," gives a

[48] See Yopie Prins, *Victorian Sappho* (Princeton: Princeton University Press, 1999) 241–43. See also Marjorie Watts, *Mrs Sappho: The Life of C. A. Dawson Scott, Mother of International P.E.N.* (London: Duckworth, 1987), on the 24-year-old poet's paying to have her epic published only to have the stock—by a mishap her poem must have seemed uncannily to predict—consumed in a warehouse fire (13). Her subsequent career as a novelist is appreciated in St. John Adcock, *The Glory That Was Grub Street: Impressions of Contemporary Authors* (New York: Stokes, 1928) 289–98.

[49] Blind was a devotee of *Aurora Leigh*, a student of George Eliot, Carlyle, and the scientific historiography of H. T. Buckle, and an admirer of Hugo's *Légende des Siècles* and Swinburne's *Tristram*. She lectured publicly on Shelley's *The Revolt of Islam* and Morris's translation of the *Volsunga Saga*, and wrote biographies of Mme Roland and George Eliot. Richard Garnett's tone is hard to fix when he says of Blind in a brief memoir that she "frequently approached the sublime and sometimes reached it": quoted in Mathilde Blind, *Poetical Works*, ed. Arthur Symons (London: Unwin, 1900) 17. Although Paul Crook makes no mention of Blind in *Darwinism, War and History* (Cambridge: Cambridge University Press, 1994), he assembles there an intellectual tradition of pacifist biology that, stemming from Herbert Spencer, clearly pertains to her ambition and predicament.

sweeping outline of terrene history from geological and botanical through animal evolution (1–2), on into three phases of human cultural development: primitive society (3), the cycles of empire to the fall of Rome (4), and modern history from the Middle Ages through the French Revolution (5). A sixth chaunt pivots back in review of these stepwise phases and laments that "the spasm of life" heaving beneath them all may doom evolution to incessant relapse into the strife of "Lust, ambition, hatred, awe" (1.6.182). Against these destructive passions of "the guilty past Man doth inherit" Blind counterpoises the Shelleyan power of "The poet, in whose shaping brain | Life is created o'er again | With loftier raptures, loftier pain" (1.6.183, 186).

These lines state a proposition that, in one obvious sense, the work has just proven. Its poet has indeed created life "o'er again" in its ascending stages, and (as it were putting Palgrave to school) has mimed that ascent through the metamorphosis of its successive verse types and narrative modalities. Blind's formal mimesis of change, that is, gives *prima facie* validation to a continuum linking a phrase like "the atoms flashed mingling in union primeval" from the opening strophe (1.1.158) to the final lines of part 1, where "Human lives dissolve, enlace | In a flaming world embrace" (1.6.189). Unity-in-multeity within the poetry denotes its holistic analogue within the global masterplot of vast yet measured change.[50] A matter less obvious, though, and less superficially plausible, is where the *excelsior* lift that in Blind's epicizing defense of poetry makes for "loftier raptures" is supposed to come from. Since it is an axiom of her Darwinian monism that the creative imagination does not stand apart from evolutionary process but remains continuous with it, why should the "potencies of verse" escape "the storm-lashed world of feeling," the fury and the mire of human veins? Given the long ancestral *Descent of Man*, as Darwin himself had sloped the question in 1871, what might entitle mankind's history to be called an *Ascent* instead?[51]

---

[50] Isobel Armstrong, *Victorian Poetry: Poetry, Poetics and Politics* (London and New York: Routledge, 1993) 376, finds Blind searching for "a new language ... to suggest a plastic transformation and possibility in matter, a vocabulary of movement." Mills, *Approaching Apocalypse*, 39–41, suggests that Blind found it in Darwin's ecologically inclusive, subliminally apocalyptic example.

[51] It was Darwin's principal rival for the honors of evolutionary theory, Alfred Russel Wallace, who furnished a not altogether approving introduction to the 2nd edn. (1899) of *The Ascent of Man*. Out of Blind's central conundrum Helen Groth develops an interpretation more sharply gendered and topically specific than the one proposed here: "Victorian Women Poets and Scientific Narratives," in *Women's Poetry, Late Romantic to Late Victorian: Gender and Genre, 1830–1900*, ed. Armstrong and Virginia Blain (Houndmills: Macmillan, 1999) 332–340.

To this difficulty parts 2 and 3 creditably respond, in allegorical narratives whose stiff diagonal departure from the through-line of universal history in part 1 underscores both the difficulty of making such a departure and the importance of trying. Part 2, "The Pilgrim Soul," recounts a *terza rima* Dantesque dream of Love's exile from the metropolitan heart, to languish as civilization's abandoned child at "the bare desert end of the town" (2.193). When in desperate compassion for the child the dreamer proposes joint suicide, the mere tender of sympathy suffices to resuscitate Love, who waxes suddenly manlike then godlike, "so great in his passion of pity" (2.200). The sympathy ethic here is significant; so is the abruptness of the change it brings on. If the former keeps faith with Blind's theme of unison from part 1, the latter implicitly subverts the evolutionary gradualism on which that unison has depended. This critique comes out into the open in the likewise oneiric part 3, "The Leading of Sorrow," where a vision of the warfare, penury, and prostitution entailed on humankind by the struggle for existence brings Blind's visionary speaker to denounce the very thesis of the "Chaunts of Life" from part 1, insisting instead, for all the world like Hardy, that "Life is but a momentary blunder | In the cycle of the Universe" (3.215).

This apocalyptic juncture provokes a supernatural, Tennysonian rejoinder—"a Voice came from the peaks of time" (3.216)—which reclaims evolution on an ethical plane that leaves Darwin and Spencer behind, to make common cause instead with Blind's adored George Eliot, with the case T. H. Huxley would be making a few years later in "Evolution and Ethics" (1894), and with what a chapter hence we shall find Hardy's *Dynasts* nominating as creation's last best hope. The pain wrought into the evolutionary condition, and the secondary suffering this primal pain elicits in the form of sympathy, may correct for the "blunder" of life and make meaning of time: "From Man's martyrdom in slow convulsion | Will be born the infinite goodness—God" (3.217). From this ethical recognition, moreover, is born the sudden metamorphosis that closes the narrative. "Transfigured by my side," the speaker beholds in her sorrowful guide of many stanzas "Love himself, Love re-arisen | With the Eternal shining through his eyes" (3.218). The ascent part 1 has promised towards "loftier raptures, loftier pain" turns out to presuppose a humanizing dissent. To the material mechanism of evolution, with its sheer unfolding process, Blind's threefold structure applies a moral leverage exerted from outside the cruel neutrality of the natural, yet still if barely contained within a narrative of human nature enlarged to prophetic ken. That this enlargement takes place not smoothly,

but at a swift quantum clip, sharply distinguishes the narrative in Blind's
Ascent of Man from the one most of her peers liked: the same old story, that is,
which would resound again overseas five years later at Harvard, where
Henry Drummond presented as his Lowell Lectures a paean to the seamless
emergence of cultural from natural evolution, along faultless lines laid
down in the Creator's master plan. Drummond published his work, surely
meaning no offense to the epic poet, as *The Ascent of Man*.[52]

Blind's jaggedly principled narrative expressed a progressivism that, while
radical rather than mainstream in its ideological bearing, was at the end of
the day late-Victorian progressivism still. It is what subtends the claim of *The
Ascent of Man* to epic stature; for all her eccentricity of perspective, Blind
subscribed to the same terms as most other contemporary epoists wherever
they stood on the political spectrum. So did another poet of the day who stood
well to the left of Blind and who, even while he eschewed the narrativity of
epic, made rhetorical concessions anyhow to the era's nearly invincible belief
that improvement was bred into the grain of historical reality. The oppos-
itional position of Edward Carpenter—class-betraying artisan intellectual,
sexual dissident, early free-verser and, to sum all of the above, Walt Whitman
disciple—will be suggested by the title of a book he published in the same
year as Blind's first edition, *Civilization, Its Cause and Cure* (1889). Before then
and for years afterward Carpenter worked on a long poem in more-than-
Whitmanian lineated chanting prose that he called *Towards Democracy* (1883,
complete edition in 4 parts 1905). The title is, for our purposes ambiguous:
what it denotes, however, is a lyric and spiritual stance rather than a narrative
vector that has historical action in mind.

Consistent with the poet's vision of total human equality and search
for "some more universal stand-point, free from . . . localism" (1894 Note,
514), *Towards Democracy* brought back home, with a difference, the momen-
taneous spasmody that Britain had exported to the United States a generation
before. For Carpenter took the final step that had always been implicit in
1850s Spasmodism: he severed altogether the link to even an intermittently
episodic plotting, and by that step he opted out of epic. Nevertheless, and in
spite of his rooted egalitarianism of the always "Here" (1.21.32) and "the

---

[52] Henry Drummond, *The Lowell Lectures on the Ascent of Man* (New York: J. Pott, 1894).
Drummond's "effective deification of natural selection" is discussed by Peter Morton in *The Vital
Science: Biology and the Literary Imagination, 1860–1900* (London: Allen and Unwin, 1984) 68–70;
Morton rejects Blind out of hand, and with her the Victorian verse epic, but reserves a friendlier
word for her twentieth-century successors in evolutionary prose fiction (215–16).

great coherent Whole" (1.3.5), Carpenter too responded to the cultural magnetism of evolutionary drift at the *fin de siècle*: there was a vectored *towards* in *Towards Democracy* after all. "The great stream of history runs on" (1.7.10) in the direction of a democratic "Freedom to be realised in time, for which the whole of History has been a struggle and a preparation" (1.43.64). Acknowledging history, Carpenter declines to tell it, presumably because for him its plot is "The dream of the soul's slow disentanglement" from gyves that the historical struggle has also prepared but from which he now exhorts the reader to join him in working free. With all respect to his epic-abstemious vision, it must be observed here how closely Carpenter's exceptionalist arrivalism mirrors, as a framework both inciting imagination and constraining it, aspects of the imperialist British scenario he plainly meant to have quit.

It is a running theme of this chapter that the ancient association between epic and tragedy, leveled by ridicule in Aytoun's "spasmodic tragedy" *Firmilian* (Ch. 9) but revived a decade later in the semi-dramatic medium and thoroughly tragic worldview of Eliot's *Spanish Gypsy* (Ch. 10), suffered erosion thereafter from the confluence of imperialist with progressivist forces that taught the *fin de siècle* to imagine totality. To its cost the *épopée humanitaire* universalized upward mobility and damned the expense, in the process suppressing tragic as well as other counter-stories, or at most representing the narrative of local failure as a downturn within a largely optimistic forecast. How difficult resistance to this triumphalism became may be seen from *Congal*, *Balder the Beautiful*, and *Sappho*: poems that had much tragic potential built into their mythic circuitry yet actualized that potential only in fitful ways, as if finally ashamed of it. What such works lacked is not a chaste and somber tone—that they had in plenty—but rather the tragic joy which in Homer and his major successors such a sober coloring sets off, and of which an indispensable component is the recognition that an impressive, even extreme, range of viewpoints has been embraced and deeply coordinated.

For the interplay of elements within a large human spectrum the universalized, lightly dialecticized march of late-Victorian progressivism offered a poor substitute, and the epic poets who stepped aside from that march were the ones who stood the best chance of making the genre's promise good. Doing so at all after 1870 required a certain starchy orneriness; doing so to great effect required, of course, much more. We can glimpse how much more by comparing each of the late century's greatest and most fully tragic poems,

Morris's *Sigurd the Volsung* (1876) and Swinburne's *Tristram of Lyonesse* (1882), to a work virtually contemporary with it. Alfred Austin's *Human Tragedy* (1876, 1889) and Richard Watson Dixon's *Mano* (1883) both exhibit a degree of sheer contrariety that was a condition *sine qua non* for the latter-day poet seeking epic distinction, and that arguably remains legible in the flinty stalemate at which each of these minor works drearily arrives. That stubbornness on this order was not enough for success should appear when we juxtapose the repellent stoicism of Austin and Dixon to the variants of absorptive objectivity we meet in Morris and Swinburne.

The Human Tragedy is a title we hailed briefly in Chapter 10, but the much expanded version published in 1876 retained little of Austin's 1862 Byronism beyond that title and the *ottava rima* stanza.[53] The stanza entrained, as it nearly must, a sardonic narratorial twist that never altogether deserts Austin's pageside manner. Yet the poem as he overhauled it bestows a sympathy on its leading characters that increases proportionally with the growing text's approximation to an epic length (some 10,000 lines when finished) and sonority: act 3, as first independently published in 1873, invokes Calliope in the first two lines and expressly repudiates the "low satiric flight" Austin had taken a decade before. The renovated poem is also now invested with a serious thesis about the discrepancy, constitutive of modern experience, between deliberate moral consciousness and the multiple options for living that advanced society offers to its members. "This Tragedy, this jar | Of conscience against conscience"—conscientious homage, that is, to the ideals that "make us noble," ever assailed by our consciousness that it is for these same ideals that "the victims fastest fall" (4.985–86)—puts Austin's tragic theory into the same arena of conflict between incompatible goods that we find in Hegel's definitive nineteenth-century view of the matter.

The poet furthermore shares a Hegelian belief that world history is the proving ground where is elaborated, from the wreckage of human expedients in their rise and fall, a cumulatively increasing complexity. As Austin explains in a wide-ranging preface to the final edition of 1889, it is "natural to the poet to be philosophical in these days," and to express "a sort of collective

---

[53] The publication history is long but straightforward. In 1873 Austin issued from the same press (Blackwood) two separate poems: the 80-page idyll *Madonna's Child*; and *Rome or Death!*, a narrative that is more than twice as long and is designated a third "canto" to the evidently in-progress revision of the 1862 *Human Tragedy: A Poem*. Shorn of subtitle, a consolidated *Human Tragedy* appeared in 1876; and then in 1889 a "new and revised edition" added the preface and rationalized overview of allegorical "Protagonists."

consciousness, or the self-consciousness of Humanity" (xxiv). Clearly the future Laureate sees which way the prevailing wind of the decades has been blowing. Yet when he comes to postulate some resolving idea at the end of this evolutionary process Austin emerges an unbeliever: for him no light gleams at the end of the contemporary tunnel. Parting company with the philosopher's dialectic, the poet breaks ranks too with the sustaining proposition of the epic of humanity—and thereby, in turn, with the troops of Victorians who were in this regard armchair Hegelians whether they knew it or not.

For Austin "the self-consciousness of Humanity" was an end without end, a regrettable modern development that he could not deny but could not help either; it entailed world-historical correlates that epicized his *Human Tragedy*, but did not therefore give any cause he could see for celebration. Hence the peculiar blend between the poem's arbitrarily episodic temporality and the visionary fourfold scheme with which it captions the episodes it chronicles. Each of four tragedy "Acts" begins by identifying, as its "Protagonist," a large abstraction: Love, Religion, Patriotism, Humanity form a broadening series of allegiances, each term developing out of the predecessor it subsumes. While the characters Austin imagines come and go, living and loving and dying within specifically dated historical crises from Florentine Risorgimento to Parisian Commune, the cloudily inert "Protagonists" impend without comment or effect, until all four convene to preside over the bloody debacle of act 4. The piers of all this allegorical superstructure rested on solid epic ground, and Austin knew it. "The great events of European History from 1859 to 1871 are, so to speak, the woof of the story, as the personal fortunes . . . are the warp" (xxxviii).[54]

Austin holds, as firmly as Owen Meredith, Emily Pfeiffer, Robert Buchanan—or indeed most epic theorists since the cultural turn of the Enlightenment—that the correlation of individual with collective destinies is epic's means, as against the express psychological analysis conducted in novels, of effecting the "synthetical, or the constructive presentation of character" (xviii). Thus in act 2 the Madonna figure of Olympia, orphaned sacristan of a picturesque hillside shrine in Italy, stands in some sort for the pure faith of her prostrate land. In act 3 the militant contadina Miriam seems an Italian avatar

---

[54] These are the terms in which Kenneth Hopkins, *English Poetry: A Short History* (Philadelphia and New York: Lippincott, 1962), frames an appreciation brief but authentic, and in its century nearly unique: "Perhaps the local and personal tragedy touches melodrama in the end: this granted, there remains a very real sense of the underlying 'human tragedy'" (482).

of French-Revolutionary Marianne, and she makes the resemblance good in act 4 by capping a term of duty under Garibaldi with enlistment, pregnant but unbowed, in the Paris streets with the Communards of 1870. The rich and disillusioned expatriate Englishman Godfrid, like his canny poet too fine-minded for either religious or nationalist commitment, repeatedly escorts or rescues these women in acts more or less allegorical of the support given to insurgent Continental causes by many a fellow-traveling mid-Victorian Briton.

And yet Godfrid's noble self-sacrifice at the final onslaught on the Belleville barricades, in Sydney Carton or Rick-of-Casablanca mode, comes out of nowhere and comes to nothing. When in an epilogue Miriam and her husband Gilbert, diehard idealists still, name their baby Godfrid and start training him in socialist doctrines that his rootless namesake could never credit, the news reads at least as much like a satire of circumstance as like a fresh leaf in the annals of *épopée humanitaire*. Human relations and public relations in *The Human Tragedy* intersect only adventitiously; they do not align in mutual reinforcement. What the principals do or suffer on the stage of action—connected though they genuinely if punchily are by interpersonal affection—fails to exhibit the development from phase to linked phase that the poet touts among his "Protagonists" up in the prefatory loft. With a kind of tough honesty Austin thus reveals an infidelity to the contemporary conditions for epic. His plot does not make sense because he supposes history does not make sense either.[55]

An instructive contrast opens here between Austin's quizzical disposition of the Paris Commune and the comparatively short work William Morris made of it in *The Pilgrims of Hope: A Poem in Thirteen Books* (1885–86). This hip-pocket epic on the march toward utopia was serially published in the red journal *Commonweal*, and its division into thirteen fits where twelve would have done the job seems to connote an ongoing insurgency that

---

[55] As Norton B. Crowell, *Alfred Austin: Victorian* (London: Weidenfeld and Nicolson, 1955), summarizes the final outlook of *The Human Tragedy*, "Man has no freedom of the will with which to resist. The illusion of unhampered choice is merely another mocking punishment for the Fall" (89). Austin's ironic or absurdist take on the drift of history belongs with his adoptive position as a Tory apologist, roundly condemned in the venomous portrait that a differently oriented conservative, Stuart P. Sherman, published as "The Complacent Toryism of Alfred Austin" in *On Contemporary Literature* (New York: Holt, 1917) 211–25. For a comparable case to Austin's, see the correlation between Jacob Burckhardt's political pessimism and historiographical irony in Hayden White, *Metahistory: The Historical Imagination in Nineteenth-Century Europe* (Baltimore and London: Johns Hopkins University Press, 1973) 230–64.

police force has put off but can never put down for long.[56] Here is the story that Austin's Miriam and Gilbert might have told had he let them, crossed for good measure on triangulations of frustrated love like those that season *The Human Tragedy*. But where Austin sheers off from epic and stymies the relation of individual to collective life, Morris maintains that only the latter can validate the former; accordingly his story, while shorter than Austin's act 2 alone, is the epic real thing. Oriented between "the flag of an ancient people" (3.160) and "the uttermost battle whither all the nations wend" (12.1111), Morris's central figure becomes a protagonist by finding his place within the narrative of class agon, "the tale that never ends" (5.366). This tale is recapitulated more than once by storied inserts within the poem, as if to make of each battle a whole chapter in the human story while stressing that no battle is the last. Its every telling is a deed in itself, a narrative act furnishing analytic purchase on the common experience: for the speaker on his pilgrimage towards enlightened self-determination, to hear it "lifted the load | That made me less than a man" (5.386).

Austin's disconnect becomes in Morris a solid weld whereby the meaning of history explains, as it reabsorbs into itself, the pain and the joy of a particular life. To the true believer the final couplet says it all—

> And I cling to the love of the past and the love of the day to be,
> And the present, it is but the building of the man to be strong in me.

—where the loose-seeming stride of Morris's folk hexameter throws second stress in the last line on "is": the verb of present being is burdened, yet also endowed, by the man-making freight of history. By the 1880s Morris had taken up a position on the extreme political left, and "the day to be" that won his heart lay far beyond the imperium where the ordinary late-Victorian epic imagination rested its case. Yet the partisan socialism that he explicitly espoused, and that Austin and Blind also (albeit quite differently) engaged, looks from the vantage of this chapter like merely the most articulated political version of an internationalism on which neither left nor right held a Victorian monopoly. As a matter of narrative structure, the

---

[56] Anne Janowitz, *Lyric and Labour in the Romantic Tradition* (Cambridge: Cambridge University Press, 1998), reads Morris's "To Be Concluded" at the end of part 13 as the formal sign of a political promise: "the sequence would truly end when its predicated 'hope' was fully realised in the political and social sphere" (232); meanwhile, in the actual narrative, an unresolved tension between lyric and epic conditions figures "an alternative understanding of love relations within a larger network of social relations" (222).

substantial overlap between Morris's developmental progressivism and his contemporaries' traces out emphatically a shared profile for the age.

The same vernacular metric, and the same regimen of transpersonal narrative *Bildung*, that informed Morris's Marxist epyllion of the mid-1880s underlay his tireless labors as a translator of the *Aeneid* (1875), the *Odyssey* (1887), and *Beowulf* (1895) into ballad-based forms. He regarded these canonical epics as so many public resources that had been illegitimately privatized, in Virgil's case most egregiously: they rightfully belonged to peoples whose commonalty antedated, and in good revolutionary time should supersede, the high-cultural restriction of access to which national-ism and the mystique of Romantic authorship had conspired to habituate nineteenth-century audiences. It says much that Morris set all these heroic poems to the same common measure he also employed for *Sigurd the Volsung* and *The Pilgrims of Hope*. His six-stress line freely varies an ambling Greekish-Latinate hexameter, typically in triple anapestic-dactylic rhythm, over a constant eight-beat structure that stems from vernacular English balladry and takes as its unit three firm stresses plus an equally firm pause, two such foursquare units forming each poetic line.

A prosodic epitome of the European union that the tessellation of fables within *The Earthly Paradise* had performed, Morris's heroic measure struck in every line a compromise between the ways of north and south—struck it with the breathing place at line's end, which Morris seldom enjambs, and struck it richer with the mid-line pause, where after three voiced beats comes a rest where the heart beats four.[57] For the reader who gets into the swing of this metric, G. B. Shaw's report of a Morris who recited while "rocking from one foot to the other like an elephant" quite credibly bespeaks the poet's ambition to recoup through print mediation an endangered communal performativ-ity.[58] Morris's metrical practice underscored his conviction that the epics he translated all had at bottom the same cultural work to do—not despite the

[57] Morris's 1875 *The Aeneids of Virgil* was transitional in this regard. Here, uniquely, the verse was full heptameter, as it had been in the poet's evident model Chapman (*The Iliads of Homer*, 1611), with a result more quaintly stiff, even rusticated, than the freer-breathing three-plus-three that Morris hit upon in 1876 and stuck with. Geoffrey B. Riddehough, "William Morris' Translation of the *Aeneid*," *Journal of English and Germanic Philology* 36 (1937) 338–46, finds the *Aeneids* redolent rather of Virgil's folk sources than of the Augustan epic itself. On management of the caesura see George Saintsbury, *A History of English Prosody*, vol. 3 (London: Macmillan, 1910) 329–32; and Stuart Blersch's scrutiny of the manuscripts: "The Craft of Revision: Morris and *Sigurd the Volsung*," in *The After-Summer Seed: Reconsiderations of William Morris'* The Story of Sigurd the Volsung, ed. John Hollow (New York and London: William Morris Society, 1978) 19.

[58] Shaw, "Morris as I Knew Him," in May Morris, *William Morris: Artist, Writer, Socialist* (Oxford: Blackwell, 1936) 2: xxxvii.

differentia of language and era that made each a distinctively representative achievement, but because of these things. By means of the culturally specific hallmarks it wore, each epic gave sustenance and direction to the community of those who, acknowledging its power to speak for them, embraced it as collectively their own.[59]

Viewed from without, Morris's translational feat can look like the macro-poetic apogee of late-Victorian world-historical eclecticism as this chapter describes it. Homer, Virgil, the bard of *Beowulf*, the skalds of the Eddas: cutting such great makers to measure could have meant for Morris, as it might have for Southey and surely would have for Owen Meredith or Buchanan, that they all came from the same cloth, whose unspooling displayed the continuity of one civilized weave. The fabric of the West, it was held, had now reached a level of development from which to take an inclusive retrospect was, in the final analysis, to condescend to the thing retrospected. But Morris, a man with eyes in the back of his head and surely the least progressivist Marxist on record, was never tempted by the dream of cumulative cultural *translatio* that entranced his generation. Even in *The Earthly Paradise* the clock and calendar went around, not ahead; and, if the stranded elders of that 1860s epic claimed a platform apart, from which to window-shop a myth *du jour* to vacation in for an empty day, theirs was a commodity collusion that the later Morris wanted nothing do with. Epic in his mature conception disdains to coax its audience with a selection of lifestyles; instead it makes a chosen people of them, by offering them the dignity of a place in its story. Not a political advantage, not an ethical position—those, in the respective guises of imperial rule and civilized culture, were the ideological flatteries of the despised Victorian present—but a place in the great tale was as much as even a hero might decently claim; and Morris never wearied of saying so.

---

[59] As the Oxford classicist Henry Nettleship's 1875 *Academy* review of *The Aeneids* shows, the immediate context for Morris's translational proof of epic was the mid-century debate on Englishing Homer that, flourishing in F. W. Newman and Matthew Arnold, had roots in Barthold Niebuhr's hypotheses concerning Virgil's folk sources among "the national and popular music" of "the people of Rome": see *William Morris: The Critical Heritage*, ed. Peter Faulkner (London and Boston: Routledge, 1973) 222–23. Morris would have taken to heart Newman's insistence that the 4/3 measure was "a noble metre, a popular metre, a metre of great capacity. *It is essentially the national ballad metre*": *Homeric Translation in Theory and Practice: A Reply to Matthew Arnold, Esq., Professor of Poetry, Oxford* (London: Williams and Norgate, 1861) 22. This celebrity debate itself belongs within a longer context running back through Macaulay and Scott to the primal soup of *paideia* and *ethnos* that swirled through the later 18th cent. before the Revolution struck (Ch. 1). Morris's experiment in vernacularity was anticipated in 1866 by John Conington's tendentiously titled *The Aeneid of Virgil Translated into English Verse*.

He said it most often by way of a favorite couplet from his Homer, where Alcinous graciously extends to the sorrowing Odysseus a radically epic consolation:

> But this thing the Gods have fashioned, and have spun the Deathful Day
> For men, that for men hereafter it might be the tale and the lay.

(Odyssey 8.579–80)

Mortality is the condition of meaning, impermanence the condition of memory, fortune the condition of story. Whom the Gods love die into narrative where, born again as legends, they live the life of their posterity. And the more fully epic such figures prove, the less force attaches to the distinction between past and present: the deed they did once upon a time bonds with the perennially current event that their legend, if it is to live, must become. The effacement of this historicist distinction within Odysseus' or Aeneas' or Beowulf's mind makes him heroic, and indeed this transformation of a task-oriented protagonistic awareness into a life-sized heroic one constitutes a major element in the plot. It also lodges a reciprocal claim against the future that epic imagines for itself: the hero's submission to the destiny that is his legend asks a like submission "hereafter" on the part of its audience. To receive that legend heroically, and earn the privilege of transmitting it in turn, is to *own* it in a double economy: like the hero, one appropriates it only at the cost of conceding its inevitability, which is to say, for the modern reader, of renouncing one's purchase on alternative outcomes available in the marketplace of narrative.[60] The Gods have spun the Deathful Day in order to create not just any story but the one that counts, not a ripping good yarn but "*the* tale and *the* lay," which any faithful version will translate as the genuine, the definite article. Here is no progressivist indulgence towards a past that the present has

---

[60] Neil Roberts's remarks on George Eliot and "the static, entropic liberal ideal" have much pertinence here: "in a society in which 'heteroglossia' (if by some other name, such as pluralism) is so hegemonic that anything can be said, it can be argued that entropy has indeed been reached, that this 'heteroglossia' is in reality the most insidious and powerful of 'official' discourses. In such a case the struggle that is the mark of the genuinely heteroglossic life of language will come from the resisting monologisms," like Mordecai's in *Deronda* or we may add the Volsung heroes' in *Sigurd*, as against the liberal optionalism of *The Earthly Paradise*. "Epic and Novel in George Eliot," in *Face to Face: Bakhtin in Russia and the West*, ed. Carol Adlam *et al.* (Sheffield: Sheffield Academic Press, 1997) 308. Graham Hough, *The Last Romantics* (1947; rpt. London: Methuen, 1961) 132–33, made a kindred point half a century earlier: "In such an age" as the late Victorian, divorced from the roots of romance and epic, "if poetry is not to lose a great deal of its range of subject and emotion, it can hardly do other than accept a frank archaism ... samples of what mankind has been, or has dreamed about, and may perhaps again."

improved on. To become worthy of the tale by living up to an original greatness (which is also, more than coincidentally, the goal a translator embraces) is all that Morris's heroism asks—or can ask, since it turns out to cost all that one has.[61]

The work in which this defiant transvaluation of late-Victorian norms took fiercest shape was *Sigurd the Volsung*, Morris's hard first swerve away from the anthological mode of *The Earthly Paradise*. *Sigurd* was also in a sense his last turn of the screw, since it was this, his favorite poem, that he put at the head of the line for reprinting within the new art book format developed in the 1890s at his Kelmscott Press. Even in formats less extravagantly paginal than the Kelmscott, the poem remains visually prepossessing, with its long lines crowding the margin and each new book and chapter pressing up flush with its predecessor, in an engrossing effect of Blakean bulked seamlessness that warns the browsing reader off with fair notice that to enter this text imaginatively is to court engulfment.[62] The very title of the work, taken whole, is already a scannable line of the narrative it names: *The Story of Sigurd the Volsung and the Fall of the Niblungs*. A caesura after *Volsung*, and a fresh stress on *and*, show the hexameter getting an early start on its job of involving the reader not only visually, but acoustically and bodily also, in an expansive epic surround. Read as poetry, the title discloses the *Fall* that is already humming in *Volsung*'s first syllable, while a vowel rhyme of *Sigurd* with *Niblungs* suggests something of the analogical design that will frame the hero's life (books 2 and 3) with its fraught Volsung foretale (book 1) and catastrophic Niblung sequel (book 4). It is as if merely to know the story by name is to be involved in the spell of its unfolding. Preface, invocation, lyric intercalation, envoi, notes, appendix—of these always slightly embarrassed accommodations of a performative oral genre to the modern conditions of literacy, richly represented as they were in *The Earthly Paradise*, Morris now offers not a trace. He obliges the reader instead to place all reliance on a tale that will be its own interpreter.

---

[61] Parallel ideas about culture heroism are applied to Morris's work in poetic narrative by Charlotte H. Oberg in *A Pagan Prophet: William Morris* (Charlottesville: University of Virginia Press, 1978) 42–43, 177–79. See also my essay "All for the Tale: The Epic Macropoetics of Morris' *Sigurd the Volsung*," *Victorian Poetry* 34 (1996) 373–94, which the following pages rework and condense.

[62] On this engulfment effect, which forms the one link between *Sigurd* and *The Earthly Paradise*, see Jeffrey Skoblow, *Paradise Dislocated: Morris, Politics, Art* (Charlottesville and London: University of Virginia Press, 1993) 3, 43, 49.

Yet interpretation may be too mediatory a term for the effect at which *Sigurd the Volsung* aims, if by that term we mean the hermeneutic extraction of themes from events. With great austerity the poem cleaves to strictly narrative forms of cognition, to *relation* in its oldest *OED* sense of relaying a tale. To know somebody or something in *Sigurd* is to know the pertinent story: a genealogy perhaps, in this saga about families; or again, in this work studded with reference to the handicrafts for which Morris himself remains famous, an artisanal procedure that, once it knows *how*, knows the one thing needful. Even a primary abstraction like arithmetic must pass the test of narrative: when Gunnar boasts that no one can "tell over the tale" of the Niblung wealth he inventories (4.454), his phrase approximates counting to recounting, storing up to storying forth, in a way that characterizes the entire poem's bundling of all knowledge in narrative quanta. Epic's encyclopedic treasury of knowledge, which the modern mind habitually quantifies or tabulates as data—in other words, information itself—here takes the shape of a tale instead. The tally and the account serve within the poem as hallmarks of the varieties of craft (telling how) and lore (telling wherefore) that evolve across the Volsung and Niblung generations.[63]

Such resistance to conceptual inference generates much of the distinctly archaic flavor of *Sigurd*, although at the same time Morris can also be seen to have kept faith thereby with his century's marked tendency to couch its science in the value-laden accounts of origin and development, progress and decadence, to which we have found contemporary epic writing so heavily subscribed. Again, Morris's break with his contemporaries consists in the refusal to valorize, indeed to evaluate from any extra-diegetic vantage, the direction of change that evolves new realities from old. By contemporary Victorian standards he reckons history meaningless, but in a sense very different from Austin's mystified nihilism in *The Human Tragedy*. Human time for Morris is proof against all explanation—redemptive or dismissive, enlightened or occult—that draws its charter from anything but the human tale. Reflex reference to the plot forms the common possession of all Morris's characters in *Sigurd*, and it engenders a deeply epic coordination between the immediate present and the perspective of long time. Like a traditional epoist Morris claims ample leeway in the tenses of his verbs, and

---

[63] Frederick Kirchhoff, "William Morris' 'Land East of the Sun and West of the Moon': The Narrative as Place," *Pre-Raphaelite Review* 3 (1980) 22, adduces the capacity of story in Morris to generalize and validate.

in *Sigurd* he secures an epic presentation whose full presentness is due to a kind of temporal stereopsis that looks before and after and does not blink. What transpires in front of us exists in fullness because everything conspires to make it at once what was to be and what will have been. For this reason the steady effect of the poem is one of remarkable plenitude and clarity, even as its ultimate affect, far from Austin's baffled despair, is a surprisingly resurgent tragic joy.[64]

While this myth-drenched narrative logic is not Austinian, it is arrestingly Darwinian or ecological. With the notable exception of soothsaying, to which we shall soon return, Morris's figures live immersed in a vivid present that is typified by strife and governed by the imperative to survive—not biologically, to be sure, since the Volsung and then Niblung seed are purposely exterminated, but as a matter of narrative reproduction. This logic exerts a puzzling influence, as the Victorians notoriously found it to do in Darwin, on the relation between right and might, ethics and outcomes.[65] Certainly the great tale for Morris is not history as written by the victors in any objectively validated sense of victory: losing splendidly may be more memorable than simply winning. Yet in itself the splendor of the *beau geste* carries no guarantee either. This archaizing epic's adamant law is survival, not of the most strong or fleet or smart by any external measure, but rather of the most *fit*. Those deeds survive into the tale which demand to be told, because they fit most aptly into the instantaneously emerging sequence of the plot.

---

[64] C. S. Lewis, *Rehabilitations and Other Essays* (London: Oxford University Press, 1939), praises this stereoscopic roundedness for being "as windy, as tangible, as resonant and three dimensional, as that of Scott and Homer" (40). The way its epic prospect gives measure to the dimension of time involves what Yeats called in Morris a "self-surrender that would lose more than half its sweetness if it lost the savour of coming days": "The Happiest of the Poets" (1902), in *Essays and Introductions* (New York: Macmillan, 1961) 57. Mark Cumming, "The Structure of *Sigurd the Volsung*," *Victorian Poetry* 21 (1983), reads the multiple structural reinforcements of the poem in terms of "figurative or typological relation" within a system of "proleptic and retrospective reference" (405–6).

[65] Robert Harbison, *Deliberate Regression* (New York: Knopf, 1980), proposes that for Morris, unlike Richard Wagner, the northern sagas offered "escape from enthrallment to the supernatural into the purely human," which is a realm "where power and virtue are not quite joined because virtue in our sense cannot exist" (108, 105)—"our sense" being presumably that of general propositions or rules, as opposed to the elemental, heroic morality that cannot be thought outside the ethics of the tale. The poem actually casts this distinction into narrative form when, early in book 2, Regin's chronicle of dwarves and gods includes among its episodes the invention of morality in "our sense."

This ecological, systemic intra-relation explains the somewhat straitened nature of Morris's similes. Whereas in Homer, Virgil, or *Beowulf* the epic simile serves a purpose pertinent to diegesis but adjacent to it (rest and recreation for the battle-numbed mind, naturalization of the exotic), in Morris the ground of similitude is often found by reference to the tale itself. In a first instance, when the Volsung princess Signy accepts the hand of a king she cannot love, she sets into motion a hurtful dynamic whose consequences will reverberate to the end, and which a nearly unpunctuated simile anticipates:

> She spake, and the feast sped on, and the speech and the song and
>   the laughter
> Went over the words of boding as the tide of the norland main
> Sweeps over the hidden skerry, the home of the shipman's bane.
>
> (1.68–70)

Signy's spoken promise forms part of an airy social complex—the exhalation of a moment, unheeded in the vastness of its relations—that in due course will catch, and stop, many a breath to come. But of these consequences this first epic simile remains innocent, as is seen by comparison to its counterpart first simile in *Paradise Lost*, which in likening Satan to a whale hidden beneath "the Norway foam" (1.196–208), holds the shipman/Christian responsible for his error. Where Milton privileges the ethics of deluded choice, within a primarily moral framework, Morris cleaves to the pathos of hapless inadvertence, because his poem knows no ethos beyond the code that is the tale. Near the end of the poem a version of the initial simile recurs, again to do with unheeded speech but now gravid with the accumulated momentum of four epic books. When Gunnar on the Niblungs' behalf accepts Atli's treacherous invitation, despite his full awareness of the mortal stakes involved,

>   his words passed over the wise,
>   As oft o'er the garden lilies goes the rising thunder-wind,
>   And they know no other summer, and no spring that was they mind.
>
> (4.572–74)

Gunnar's frame of reference, built almost fully out by this point in the poem, is "to the Niblung name, | And the day of deeds to accomplish, and the gathering-in of fame" (4.539–40). The heroes are like lilies that toil not, neither spin yarns, but rather will their entoilment in the one web that is.

The Niblungs' tragic death-lust is not morally discrepant with any Miltonic ideal order of values; as Morris's similes show, the poem gives access to no order of values but itself, from which there is no swerving, not even in tropes.[66]

So it comes to pass that, for the several heroes in *Sigurd the Volsung*, the finest hour is the one when they discern it as their fate to sustain a part in the tale, which will survive them and revive them too, at the complementary, next-finest hour when it is sung or read anew.[67] Sigurd's first independent act is to slay his plotting foster-parent Regin for meddling with the drift of things, "lest the world forget its tale, | And the Gods sit deedless" (2.1720–21). In this Sigurd proves worthy of the marital choices made on the opening page by Signy when for "fame" she goes against her heart and chooses dynastic glory, and then by his mother Queen Hiordis as she (weaving, for good measure, an historical tapestry) picks in Sigmund a husband who will sire Sigurd and so advance "the tale that no ending hath" (1.1609). This genealogy of heroic submission, before the authority of what is to have been, likewise exalts the doomed Volsung kings after Sigurd's death. Hogni, informed of his own imminent execution, cries out, "Take heed now! deeds are doing for the fashioners of tales" (4.1512); and near the end of it all the glorious spendthrift Gunnar chants from a tyrant's snakepit an exulting endorsement of heroic speech and power, faith and joy:

> "And they changed their lives and departed, and came back as the
>   leaves of the trees
> Come back and increase in the summer:—and I, I, I am of these;
> And I know of Them that have fashioned, and the deeds that have
>   blossomed and grow;
> But nought of the Gods' repentance, or the Gods' undoing I know."
>
>   (4.1689–92)

---

[66] Dentith remarks in Morris's attempt in the similes of *Sigurd* "to find the grounds of comparison from within the heroic world he is seeking to recreate" a strategy consistent with the poem's "implicit critique of the paltriness of modernity, a standing rebuke to the outcome of the national story whose beginning the poem recounts" (*Epic and Empire*, 75, 79). This rebuke is implicitly infused into the poem's archaizing diction, of which T. L. Kington Oliphant, *The New English* (London: Macmillan, 1886), noted that it "takes us back to 1290 or thereabouts, and shows us how copious, in skilful hands, an almost purely Teutonic diction may be. ... Mr. Morris, in many places, cuts down his proportion of French words to the scale which Chaucer's grandfather would have used" (2: 211).

[67] Wawn, *The Vikings and the Victorians*, 274–75, remarks the austerity with which in Morris the epic tale's surround makes of the mythic past "a future from which none may escape," and which, heroically embraced, constitutes "a kind of mission statement about future conduct."

Gunnar waxes godlike in annihilating repentance and wishing no deed of the long tale undone. A rare harping on subjectivity—"I, I, I am of these"—marks out at last how the Morris hero comes into his own, through recognition that to be means to belong to the tale of the tribe.[68] This recognition is the form that self-consciousness repeatedly assumes in *Sigurd*, where emplotment is the form of knowing, where conversely the villainy of Regin (book 2), Grimhild (book 3), and Atli (book 4) consists in scheming to thwart or divert events from their unfolding course, and where Grimhild's amnesiac potion swaps Sigurd's identity with Gunnar's by temporarily patching each man's narrative of selfhood into the other's mind until "no world is there left him to live in, and no deed to rejoice in or rue" (3.1894).

By the same epic epistemology, the highest reach of intellect is clairvoyance. Gunnar's last phrase above unwittingly points to the extinction of the Asgard pantheon, of which he may know nothing, but the gods themselves know quite enough. A matter more of degree than of kind, the advantage gods have over men inheres in mindfulness, which gives power not to change the tale but to speed it along by holding it always in view. If godlike heroes know that their tale is yet to be, and offer life up to it in joyous ignorance of all things but that posterity, visionaries have the added gift of knowing what the tale hereafter will say. Prophecy occurs often in *Sigurd*, and it feels less like magic than like scientific narrative, a collaborative undertaking that distributes choral knowing among a series of elected witnesses.[69] This series begins in book 1, as we have noted, with clairvoyant sexual selection on the part of two ancestral mothers-to-be; and it leads on to the sage Gripir, whose rapid preview of Sigurd's whole career uncannily transfixes the young hero, as "he heard the words and remembered, and he knew them one by one" (2.1238), with a recognitive force that synchronizes heroic time in its stepwise prospect with poetic time in its after recitation. It is to Sigurd's beloved Brynhild that the duties of soothsaying

---

[68] In *Literary Voice: The Calling of Jonah* (Albany: State University of New York Press, 1995), Donald Wesling and Tadeusz Sławek remark in Mickiewicz's Polish epic of 1834 *Pan Tadeusz* what may be seen in *Sigurd* as well: "The bardic voice arises from the acute awareness of the distinction between two radically different spheres of reality, but the bard does not speak from the gap, from the rupture between the two, but always from inside the sphere which he considers home. Hence the bardic voice cannot be exiled" (124).

[69] As Ruth C. Ellison points out in " 'The Undying Glory of Dreams': William Morris and the 'Northland of Old,' " in *Victorian Poetry*, ed. Malcolm Bradbury and David Palmer (London: Arnold, 1972) 173–74, when Morris bestowed on his protagonists "precise foreknowledge of events," he was elaborating a feature already present in the old primary sagas.

are entrusted most often—also most poignantly, since she, unlike Gripir in the remoteness of extreme age, is fated to become a full participant in the action she foretells. In passages flanking the epic midpoint Brynhild predicts to Sigurd (2.2038–2107) and then to Gudrun (3.197–266) the disasters they themselves will bring on their house in the two books to come. By structural engineering as old as Homer's, Morris not only gives a grounding to his epic's long span; within the narrative suspension thus created, his task as a tragic epoist is to bring what Brynhild has foretold to pass as the outcome, not of blind force, but of witting human choice.

This occurs unforgettably at the very end, in the bitter delight with which Gudrun embarks on dynastic arson, the act of a sister and wife and mother who is Hedda Gabler's elder sibling by a millennium or so. Igniting the royal feast-hall to avenge her husband Atli's newfangled treachery, Gudrun knows exactly what she is doing, and why (4.1881–1900). This fiery finale satisfies a tragic criterion of justice, and it furnishes too an apocalyptic image of *Ragnarök*, the Scandinavian twilight of the gods. The quiet, craftsmanlike way Morris accepted this terminus as an artistic postulate, or Blakean bounding outline, contrasts vividly to the fervor with which in their Balder poems Matthew Arnold and Robert Buchanan yearned towards it as a utopian asymptote securing the thin curve of historical progress against an existential void. More engaging to Morris's epic imagination than the symbolic *Ragnarök* holocaust, however, is the understated and fully human episode in book 3 where Brynhild wittingly brings her own prophecy to pass. Here a still drug-addled Sigurd, frustrated by the contretemps of lives mismatched in love's quadrangle, proposes in a moment of moral weakness that he and Brynhild should simply desert their spouses, cut and run. The proposal to elope in effect asks Brynhild, sacrificing destiny for happiness, to opt out of the tale: "O live, live, Brynhild beloved! and thee on earth will I wed, | And put away Gudrun the Niblung—and all those shall be as the dead" (3.3019–20). It is against this antiheroic, wish-fulfilling invitation to blissful oblivion that she counterposes the poem's tersest and weightiest line, a dead march of iambs:

"I will not wed thee, Sigurd, nor any man alive."

(3.3025)

The woman's "will"—a mere prophetess would have said "shall"—brings the future about by lovingly electing her fate. Nor is this all: the four words that follow the caesura, calling Sigurd to account, summon him to his narrative senses, which is to say his calling as a hero of mortality. The way to win Brynhild merely lay through fire in book 2; now it lies through death. The two of them will "live, live" when they will the sequel that is narrative, whose exactions here chisel Brynhild's high vein to the pith. When "all those shall be as the dead"—and only then—will our lovers, bedded in the tale, live again on earth, as they do in the breath of Morris's hexameter. Brynhild's great refusal to compromise with short-sightedness and relax into a truce with the present is one that Morris's poem performs as well, in every aspect of its formal elaboration.[70] If this moment does not repudiate the *Earthly Paradise* ethos, then it at least utters a concentrated retort to what was passing for epic grandeur in the easy-listening 1870s wake of that trend-setting work.[71]

The poetic oeuvre of Morris is unthinkable without the narrative amplitude of its epic forms. From his friend and agemate Swinburne, on the other hand, we are lucky to have anything of epic scope at all, much less the splendor that is *Tristram of Lyonesse*. Much less is just what we do get in the other chief verse narrative of Swinburne's maturity, *The Tale of Balen* (1896), whose cross-grained strength will toughen us in Chapter 12 for the arid sparseness of Edwardian epic country. The true epic that Swinburne had in him was *Tristram*, though his career may be readily conceived without it— and so, alas, by the anthologist and the general reader it often is. One would have supposed this poet content to work, like his early associates the Rossettis or his unknown *Doppelgänger* Hopkins, in lyric modes altogether. In fact he had seemed to declare such a preference when in 1857 he left his major undergraduate effort *Queen Yseult*, based on Scott's bookish *Sir*

---

[70] John Goode, who has no patience with Morris's diction or meter, nevertheless concedes that they are "passively the product of the very alienation the story is about," as its entire narrative projects "a great Victorian degenerate myth of social alienation and the breakdown of sexual relationships" into possessive, envious violence: "William Morris and the Dream of Revolution," in *Literature and Politics in the Nineteenth Century*, ed. John Lucas (London: Methuen, 1971) 239. What Goode dismisses without analysis as a result "passively" produced came, of course, from active and resolute poetic art.

[71] Morris's perversely anomalous achievement may be conceived as a willed, altogether secular return to the condition of scriptural containedness from which Hans Frei, *The Eclipse of Biblical Narrative: A Study in Eighteenth and Nineteenth Century Hermeneutics* (New Haven and London: Yale University Press, 1974), narrates the modern hermeneut's decisive departure. The challenge of epic continuity that *Sigurd* lays before its reader is, in effect, to resume Calvin's pre-modern position as an interpreter and "to range himself into the same real sequence" (36) with the action of the interpreted text. (See Ch. 1, n. 34.)

Tristrem (1804) and projected to fill ten cantos, unfinished at six. Swinburne sped away from this false start into his *enfant terrible* maturity of the 1860s, a master in elegy, ode, lament, rondeau: not built-out structures, but sculpted or dithyrambic forms that impress with their fine suddenness or the singularity of their insistence. Nor does the library chill of the historical closet dramas from Swinburne's middle years breathe a hint of *Tristram*'s generosity of passion, gaiety of descriptive saturation, cosmic aplomb.

The distinctive success of the poem as published in 1882 arose from its solution of a real and historically representative problem that its author's astonishing lyric gift entrained. Too young, critically alert, and no doubt snobbish to have embraced Spasmodism, temperamentally averse to the novel epic mode of that unreproducible result *Aurora Leigh* (though he ranked with its avid praisers), Swinburne nevertheless, in confronting the challenge of the long poem, inherited from the 1850s something like the spasmodic dilemma we met in Chapter 9. How might a poetics of momentaneousness be dilated to epic proportions, or conversely how might a verse narrative of book length be maintained at the pitch of intensity to which his imagination resonated?[72] The picaresque and pornographic character of the prose fiction he wrote attests Swinburne's want of interest in continuously sustained narrative, and for this his lyric output suggests an explanation. His curiosity and passion were riveted to beginnings and ends; they were bored by the *longueurs* of the middle. The basic elements of existence, whether fresh come from creation or at the spent point of apocalyptic finish or entropic subsidence: these provided the primal matter Swinburne wielded. In incessant phonemic–semantic crisscross his verbal art wove from these elements, not the mediations of human life in its multiplicity of contexted relation, but a fascinated exhibition of the processes whereby relationship itself was simultaneously constituted and broken

---

[72] *Tristram* is straightforwardly epic for John A. Cassidy, *Algernon C. Swinburne* (Boston: Twayne, 1964); Jean Overton Fuller, *Swinburne: A Critical Biography* (London: Chatto and Windus, 1968); David Staines, "Swinburne's Arthurian World: Swinburne's Arthurian Poetry and Its Medieval Sources," *Studia Neophilologica* 50 (1978) 53–70. Another and subtler set of readers declare the poem lyrical instead: Harold Nicolson, *Swinburne* (New York: Macmillan, 1926); Leone Vivante, *English Poetry and Its Contribution to the Knowledge of a Creative Principle* (New York: Macmillan, 1950); John D. Rosenberg, "Swinburne," *Victorian Studies* 11 (1967) 131–52. Generic classification becomes a problem for discussion in Kerry McSweeney, "The Structure of Swinburne's *Tristram of Lyonesse*," *Queen's Quarterly* 75 (1969) 690–702; David G. Riede, *Swinburne: A Study of Romantic Mythmaking* (Charlottesville: University of Virginia Press, 1978); Antony H. Harrison, *Swinburne's Medievalism: A Study in Victorian Love Poetry* (Baton Rouge and London: Louisiana State University Press, 1988).

down. With something like a chemist's or physicist's eye to processes, he analyzed and re-compounded the elements of life; the result, emitted as from a centrifuge, was a virtuoso precipitation of the stuff of moderate Victorian compromise out into the extremes it was made from; a high-resolution breakdown of apparently smooth continua into so many rapidly overlapping starts and stops.

To one who imagined human time in such a way, every story—every ingredient episode of every story—was a fractal transform of the one aeonic narrative of excitation and equilibrium. As this narrative flashed at large from blaze to black across the thermodynamic inane, or as (backstage at the accidental theater of human consciousness) it was microscopically rehearsed at the speed of synaptic discharge, it demanded expression in lyric forms. Midway between these far-flung magnitudes of galaxy and nucleus, however, lay the region of embodied selves in action, under the twin pressures of desire and mortality that valorized not epochs, and not seconds either, but the years between. Here was epic ground, all right; and Swinburne made it his in *Tristram* by correlating an account of the passions, weighed in the scale of a lifetime, with a modern cosmology and biology whose else-imponderable abstractness the poem marvelously humanizes, even as they set for him the iron terms of star and blood within which tragic heroism must be grasped. Writing the epic poem meant keeping the middle ground of human life open to these governing conditions without letting them crush it into inconsequence. This in turn meant writing off certain subtleties of historical and psychological contexture that, while of course they were less than essential to nineteenth-century epic, did find a place in work by great practitioners like Blake and Hugo, to both of whom Swinburne devoted entire critical books.

Or like his genial opposite William Morris. We have just seen how *Sigurd* relishes the middle as the arena of choice, the span of both interpersonal and narratorial relation where he loves to dwell. For Morris the beginning and end are structural necessities, reference points to which heroes look in order to recollect who they are and collect themselves now, in the midst of things, for the performance of deeds whose recounting will outlive them. For Swinburne, however, the beginning and end are not just structural necessities but existential ones. Rebirth and *petit-mort* constitute the binary integers of outburst and exhaustion in which Swinburnean time is formulated, and they therefore furnish the building blocks of his narrative too. From their primary colors the rest of his palette must arise, if at all, through virtuoso pointillist technique that unceasingly constructs the bodily passion of doomed lovers out of an elemental physics of mineral and water and light. This is why, if Morris subordinates the trope to the tale, never culling similes from outside his chosen early-Nordic ambience or interpreting his saga by any standard but itself, Swinburne subordinates the tale to the trope instead. Description and illustration keep making off with the story and enforcing parallels between what his principals experience and the over-arching structure of the cosmic reality of which human experience is a portioned part. The original, ultimate energy of the everlasting universe of things is more than a backdrop conferring significance on the epic action; it is what, at the heroizing height of passion, Tristram and Iseult most essentially feel.

A pair of early similes will highlight the difference between these late-century epic holdouts. Morris wraps up book 1 of *Sigurd* in a dozen lines that possess thesis force for all that ensues. The topic is the collapse of the Volsung house upon Sigmund's death in battle; the trope recoups empirical loss as legendary gain, through the cultural transportation of tale-telling.

> Lo, the noble oak of the forest with his feet in the flowers and grass,
> How the winds that bear the summer o'er its topmost branches pass,
> And the wood-deer dwell beneath it, and fowl in its fair twigs sing,
> And there it stands in the forest, an exceeding glorious thing:
> Then come the axes of men, and low it lies on the ground,
> And the crane comes out of the southland, and its nest is nowhere
>   found,
> And bare and shorn of its blossoms is the house of the deer of the wood.
> But the tree is a golden dragon; and fair it floats on the flood,
> And beareth the kings and the earl-folk, and is shield-hung all without:
> And it seeth the blaze of the beacons, and heareth the war-God's shout.
> There are tidings wherever it cometh, and the tale of its time shall be
>   told.
> A dear name it hath got like a king, and a fame that groweth not old.
> Lo, such is the Volsung dwelling; lo, such is the deed he hath
>   wrought . . .

                                                        (1.1843–55)

At *Iliad* 13.389–91 a brief simile compares the slain Asios to an oak felled for shipbuilding; Morris, by extending this Homeric simile substantially back-ward and forward in time, makes it a figure for heroism itself as it arises in act and lives on in traditional telling. Further commentary would be superflu-ous on this self-interpreting passage, unless to ask whether the kingly "name" connoted in the penultimate line is Sigurd the Volsung or *Sigurd the Volsung*—the hero, that is, or the narrative vessel whose course the hero will spend the next two books learning, respectively, to live by and die into.

Consider next the passage of another boat, racing at daybreak between Ireland and Cornwall, from the narrative opening of *Tristram of Lyonesse*:

> Above the stem a gilded swallow shone,
> Wrought with straight wings and eyes of glittering stone
> As flying sunward oversea, to bear
> Green summer with it through the singing air.
> And on the deck between the rowers at dawn,
> As the bright sail with brightening wind was drawn,
> Sat with full face against the strengthening light
> Iseult, more fair than foam or dawn was white.
> Her gaze was glad past love's own singing of,
> And her face lovely past desire of love.
> Past thought and speech her maiden motions were,
> And a more golden sunrise was her hair.
> The very veil of her bright flesh was made
> As of light woven and moonbeam-colored shade
> More fine than moonbeams; white her eyelids shone
> As snow sun-stricken that endures the sun,
> And through their curled and coloured clouds of deep
> Luminous lashes thick as dreams in sleep
> Shone as the sea's depth swallowing up the sky's
> The springs of unimaginable eyes.

(1.11–30)

Not since Browning, and *Sordello* at that (which young Swinburne had extensively committed to memory), has an epoist exacted closer verbal attention. Enjambed syntactic continuity expands the revelation of Iseult's beauty from a moment to an interval, via a tracking shot that moves the boat through air and sea, over waves of pentameter and of couplet rhyme. At the same time, the matching sounds of rhyme reinforce the poet's quest to find meet comparisons within his cinematic blazon for the star Iseult, whom these lines introduce to the reader. These comparisons, arriving at the dizzying rate of nearly a simile per line, are to an ostentatious degree distracting: they fly from the barely sketched scene of Swinburne's story as purposefully, in their way, as Morris's simile homes in on his.[73]

[73] On Swinburne's epic similes see Robert Peters, "Swinburne: A Personal Essay and a Polemic," in *The Victorian Experience: The Poets*, ed. Richard A. Levine (Athens: Ohio University

More to the point, it is very hard to know in what the "scene" thus barely sketched consists. Where does the line lie between narration and description or, in either of these domains, between literal and figurative rendition? Iseult's fair skin is, we would still say with Victorian science, a *tissue* of translucence, "woven" of light and shade; her sea-blue eyes really are, we know or have Darwin to remind us (*Origin of Species*, chapter 6), curved sacs of a saline solution chemically equivalent to sea water. These comparisons taken together portend a much larger similitude between human and natural bodies, which thus posits beyond the seascape a conceptual framework within which to understand the action that is to come. Likening her hair, at sunrise, to a "golden sunrise" and her eyelashes to "clouds" and "dreams in sleep," the poet enskies his heroine not so much hyperbolically as factually: the beauties of air and hair express, because they are elicited by, one and the same continuum of natural process. And it is this virtually scientific monism toward which the whole passage drives, like the whole story it initiates.[74]

The epic thesis gets almost schematically laid out, in the opening lines just quoted, with Swinburne's conspicuous deployment of the particle "As," a conjunction well known to us as simile's sign yet equally susceptible of temporal and even causal constructions. On the prow of a boat named "The Swallow" is set a bowsprit figurehead carved to look as if it were "flying sunward oversea." A reader observing that, as a matter of narrative fact, flying sunward oversea is exactly what the figured bird is doing may pause to entertain the possibility that "As" means "When." It does not, quite, mean that here, nor does it quite mean "Because." But these complementary options swing wide open a few lines later, when the apparently temporal clause "As the bright sail with brightening wind was drawn" proves simultaneously legible as a simile. Iseult sits "against the strengthening light" (bracing her, and to that extent making her strong) both *at the same time* and *in the same way* that a morning gust of wind draws the sail taut above her

Press, 1982); Nicholas Tredell, "*Tristram of Lyonesse*: Dangerous Voyage," *Victorian Poetry* 20 (1982) 97–111; Harrison, *Swinburne's Medievalism*, 102–06. See also my "Swinburne's *Tristram of Lyonesse* as Assimilationist Epic," in *Romantic/Victorian: Influence and Resistance in Nineteenth-Century Poetry*, ed. G. Kim Blank and Margot Louis (Houndmills: Macmillan, 1993) 76–90, for an expanded version of the reading presented here.

[74] As early as 1893 the mesmerist and spiritualist F. W. H. Myers from across the cultural divide recognized *Tristram*'s epic ambition to embody Darwin-era values in a traditionary tale: "the most striking extant record of an important phase of thought. We have the strict materialistic synthesis clad in its most splendid colouring." Quoted in *Swinburne: The Critical Heritage*, ed. Clyde K. Hyder (New York: Barnes and Noble, 1970) 194. See also Joseph Warren Beach, *The Concept of Nature in Nineteenth-Century English Poetry* (New York: Macmillan, 1936) 455–59.

(smoothing it, and to that extent making it beautiful). Moreover, a reader returning to this passage with the completed poem in mind will want to add that the passenger and the vessel are beautifully strong *for the same reason*, which is the unassailable destiny of circumstance. What takes place within Iseult at sunrise, like what passes between her and Tristram at canto's end, transpires as it simply must.

The fusion here of descriptive, narrative, and interpretive dimensions is neither casual nor unique—it recurs with mounting erotic address at 1.452–65 and 2.475–86, then with signal pathos at 3.1–8—and it gives fair notice of the tactics Swinburne will use to merge action with passion throughout the poem.[75] While these tactics seem to besiege the narrative line, they are actually the poet's means of preserving his story from the same primitive intensities that, in irradiating it with the truth, threaten to burn it up prematurely. In *Tristram* the evasive equivocation of "As" among analogical, temporal, and explanatory senses shows a Blakean sort of narrative mercy, rescuing from a blinding lyric incandescence the diegetic extension of possibility across nine cantos. Compared to Morris's plot, or for that matter Tennyson's plot in the decade-old Tristram idyll "The Last Tournament," Swinburne's plot is a flimsy construct. Still, the position of the hero between two Iseults, and the genuine but incompatible fidelities to hearth and heart that they represent, marks out a comparable place for narrative as a medium between contrasted imperatives. A like structure of mediation informs the poem's interior design: the narrative that speeds through cantos 1, 4, 8, and 9 acquires weight and moment during reflective soliloquies that hold it up, Browning-fashion, for perspectival contemplation (Tristram in canto 3, Iseult of Cornwall in 5, Iseult of Brittany in 7). Into this holding pattern are interspersed in cantos 2 and 6 rhapsodic dilations of sexual bliss that, nearly stopping time altogether, embody the absolute lyric values whose suspension the advance of the narrative requires, yet whose enchantment is what drives the ensemble of effects all the while.

A showier enactment of the poem's suspension between binary extremes appears at its textual outer edge. In the prelude and last canto, Swinburne invokes the dialectical imperatives behind his *Liebestod* plot under their

---

[75] Notice expressly posted by Swinburne himself in a "Dedicatory Epistle" to the collected poems of 1904. He wrote *Tristram* "not in the epic or romantic form of sustained or continuous narrative, but mainly through a succession of dramatic scenes or pictures with descriptive settings": *Swinburne Replies*, ed. Clyde K. Hyder (Syracuse: Syracuse University Press, 1966) 99. This was as much as to say that the poet regarded description itself as continuous with narrative presentation and not a mere adjunct to it.

authoritative names Love and Fate, in virtuoso rhetorical set-pieces com-
prising twenty-two identically rhymed couplets each. As "Love...Led
these twain to the life of tears and fire" and thus to "the lifeless life of
night" ("Prelude: Tristram and Iseult," lines 1, 42, 44), so "Fate...Leads
life to rest where tears no more take fire" and thus "past sense of day and
night" ("The Sailing of the Swan," again lines 1, 42, 44). The balance
between *amor fati* and *fatum amoris* that this framing symmetry proposes has
been borne out by the intervening narrative; it is significant, therefore, that
Swinburne casts each epic invocation in the form not of traditional inter-
cessionary apostrophe but of objective declaration. With these absolute
powers there is no pleading, only acknowledgment and acceptance. There
it is: thus and so, then and there, and just because.[76] Forthright perception of
the twinning of love and fate hence holds in *Tristram* the heroic place that
Morris accords in *Sigurd* to choice. Both epics embrace late-Victorian
materialism to the extent of hingeing the plot on the pharmacology of a
potion, which, in dissolving the will, frees their protagonists from the
burden of normal morality. But while Sigurd must reclaim his will to live
out a poisoned life within the defining limits of his tribal code, Tristram and
Iseult stay drunk on "the love-draught" (1.765), learning in time what
Swinburne's epic tropes have been saying all along, that to embrace one
another is to embrace a cosmic destiny larger than clan or nation. They
become lovers by accident and because they cannot help it; they become
heroes by the intensity with which they grasp in this salient absurdity an
instantiation of the human condition that lies beyond regret or blame—and
that is, in fact, to die for.[77] The causal chain of sequence, the mirror of

[76] Hegel's spacious meditation on epic makes room not only for the mainstream eclectic
progressivists of this chapter but also for its great fatal dissenters: "What rules in epic, though
not, as is commonly supposed, in drama, is fate....Epic poetry moves in the element of an
inherently necessary total state of affairs, and nothing is left to the individual but to submit to this
fundamental situation....Consequently an air of mourning is wafted over the whole epic"
(*Aesthetics*, 2: 1070–71).

[77] Vivante specifies the centrality of "the idea of fate" to all Swinburne's poetry: "a *core of
causality* which lies either above or below, anyhow beyond personality" (*English Poetry*, 283). The
epic labor that in *Tristram* wraps this essentially lyric core in an integument of narrative circum-
stantiality lets Swinburne here represent the process of submission to fate, not as an existential
given, but a deliberated ethical action heroically taken. Benjamin Fisher, "Swinburne's *Tristram of
Lyonesse* in Process," *Texas Studies in Literature and Language* 14 (1972), shows how in manuscript
revisions "the constant linking of human features and characteristics with natural phenomena
emphasizes more and more the natural cyclicalness" undergirding the poem's "inextricable
merging of love and fate" (517).

second thought, the ladder of analogy all tell the same tale: desire's way in and death's way out are one.

A monist's creed, past doubt. Was it a totalitarian's? Swinburne's detractors have found cause for suspicion in the obsessive quality of his lyricism, or in the compulsory fatalism that inhabits his post-neoclassical tragedy *Atalanta in Calydon* (1865).[78] The question also arises in view of the *prima facie* resemblance between the cosmic passion to which Tristram and Iseult surrender and the world-historical passivity that had become, by the imperial 1880s, the governing mood of anglophone epic writing. Erotic infatuation just happens, and empire does too—or so its apologists learned to say in Swinburne's lifetime. Maybe empire ought to have found its proper image in the unsought, blameless, irresistible love that conquers all. And yet there is good reason to hold that in Swinburne's imagination it did not. The opposition to hegemony that his unrepentant republicanism harbored, and also the subtler impatience with authority that suffuses his critical prose, warrant a search for analogues within the political vision of his epic masterpiece; and we may find them at the metapoetic level to which the poet was spurred by a restlessly dialectical turn of mind.

Take first his learned and allusive manner of assuming a place within poetic tradition. The Prelude to *Tristram* runs through a catalogue of legendary lovers constellated in fame and set within a cycle keyed, Morris-wise, to a zodiac of the months. His is just one among many stories, Swinburne disarmingly concedes against the epic grain, and moreover just one among "many and many" versions of that one story so often told (240). This awareness of multiple antecedents is no deterrent, however: "yet I too, | I have the heart to follow, many or few | Be the feet gone before me" (243–45). More striking than the modesty of this declaration is

---

[78] One hostile witness with special charter here is the premier historian of English epic E. M. W. Tillyard, who gave *Tristram* a wide berth but whose post-war vigilance arraigned Swinburne's 1871 lyric "Hertha" for fascist tendencies in *Five Poems 1470–1870: An Elementary Essay on the Background of English Literature* (London: Chatto and Windus, 1948). A comparable case is assembled on updated premises by Harrison, *Victorian Poets and Romantic Poems: Intertextuality and Ideology* (Charlottesville: University of Virginia Press, 1990), and by Riede, *Oracles and Hierophants: Constructions of Romantic Authority* (Ithaca: Cornell University Press, 1991). Matthew Reynolds, *The Realms of Verse 1830–1870: English Poetry in a Time of Nation-Building* (Oxford and New York: Oxford University Press, 2001) 41, makes the link between Swinburne's 1871 *Songs of Sunrise* and Mussolini. For defense of a libertarian dimension within Swinburne's fatalism see Vivante, *English Poetry*; William Buckler, *The Victorian Imagination: Essays in Aesthetic Exploration* (New York and London: New York University Press, 1980) 236–38; James Richardson, *Vanishing Lives: Style and Self in Tennyson, D. G. Rossetti, Swinburne, and Yeats* (Charlottesville: University of Virginia Press, 1988) 124–28.

its, for Swinburne, perfunctory flat-footedness. No major poet this book treats has seemed less jealous, or nervous, to establish pedigree and preroga- tive. Among epic proemata Swinburne's remains remarkable equally for the indiscriminateness with which it lavishes praise on other makers and for the sangfroid with which it goes about joining them. These aspects of Swinburne's regard for tradition have direct relation to each other, as they do to the ethos of self-oblivion that informs his lovers' tale. "As the dawn loves the sunlight I love thee": when Tristram's one-line aubade from the splendid finale of canto 2 returns to haunt him in solitude at the start of canto 3, he spells out from the simile an implicit lust for engulfment, "As men that shall be swallowed of the sea | Love the sea's lovely beauty" (3.2–3), which in turn presages the great late episode where a swim at daybreak transports Tristram beyond consolation into epiphany, until "his mind | Was rapt abroad beyond man's meaner kind | And pierced with love of all things" (8.447–49), and "each glad limb became | A note of rapture in the tune of life" (8.504–5). The beauty of the world's body, like the beauty of Iseult's, is vouchsafed to the hero ecstatically rapt out of self, in a state of possession that whelms the boundaries between ego and other.[79] So it is too with the cultural body of legend, image, and phrase, which is the poet's free birthright provided that he give it freely away again.

    The epic poets from Homer through Dante and Milton to Shelley are influences so pervasive in *Tristram* that they become an atmosphere, inspir- ation in the unbound form of exhalation, a gift in general possession.[80] The dawn/sunlight trope, figuring the glad diffusion of personal identity into a larger life, diffuses itself into *Tristram of Lyonesse* from not one locus in Shelley's oeuvre but dozens. When at the fatal draining of the love potion

---

[79]   This is the ultimate context in which to place Pauline Fletcher's observations that "the most perfect moment of ecstasy and fulfillment granted to Tristram comes with his embrace of an inhuman lover, the sea," which serves Swinburne as "in many respects, the true protagonist" and at the same time "like a tragic chorus": *Gardens and Grim Ravines: The Language of Landscape in Victorian Poetry* (Princeton: Princeton University Press, 1983) 213–14, 217. On this same con- tinuum, heroically self-sacrificing love sustains the moral climax that Beverly Taylor and Elisabeth Brewer, *The Return of King Arthur: British and American Arthurian Literature since 1800* (Totowa: Barnes and Noble, 1983) 156, locate in the canto 5 vigil of "Iseult at Tintagel."

[80]   The same holds true of the poem's narrative sources: see Mary Bird Davis, "Swinburne's Use of His Sources in *Tristram of Lyonesse*," *Philological Quarterly* 55 (1976) 96–112; Staines, "Swin- burne's Arthurian World," 61; Laura Cooner Lambdin and Robert Thomas Lambdin, *Camelot in the Nineteenth Century: Arthurian Characters in the Poems of Tennyson, Arnold, Morris, and Swinburne* (Westport: Greenwood Press, 2000) 123–24. Ian Fletcher, *Swinburne* (Harlow: Longman, 1973) 8, knows "no poet whose style is so deliberate a literary mosaic"; Buckler, *The Victorian Imagination*, 228, acknowledges Swinburne's "deep, liturgical reverence for the writers, texts, myths which formed his literary inheritance."

Swinburne writes, "Their Galahaut was the cup, and she that mixed" (1.792), a nearly verbatim transcript of Francesca's already allusive tale from the *Inferno* ("Galeotto fu il libro, e chi lo scrisse," 5.137) betrays the inescapable literary overdetermination of the epic-precipitating crisis, while also rendering it up as common property reshaken and freshly poured: an altered "draught" for all to taste, and to be changed by. Stern Christian disapproval inhabits this Dante echo, as it does the nearby Miltonic echo "they quaffed | Death" (1.784-85; *Paradise Lost* 9.792). Yet each text's ancestral reprimand is oddly neutralized by their conjunction in Swinburne's, where a magnanimous absorbency disables individualist cogency and takes the sting out of voluntarist reproof. The text acknowledges those moral energies, in practice, by vesting them in Iseult of the White Hands, whose stridency of virtue during canto 7 marks her out as, not the villain of the piece (it has none), but the least handsome of its losers. Meanwhile the mutual assimilation of poet and tradition stands, like the erotic plot, for an intercourse not imperially censorious but utopian, equal and free.

Citizenship in this open republic of Swinburne's comes at a cost, which is the tragic embrace of loss: ego loss in the first instance; then relinquishment of exclusive private interests, including the imaginative property rights in which epic allusion ordinarily trades; and finally acquiescence before the enormity of circumstance that the poem hails as Fate. By a paradox no stranger than the Greek thought in which Swinburne was steeped, the positing of an imponderable exigency beyond the will affected both his poetic and his political imagination in a liberating way. When Tristram's long meditation on love in canto 3 turns—as it must—to meditate on the fate that is love's shadow, he throws out a question that is as challenging for the poet as it is rhetorical for the hero. "How should fate," Tristram asks, "the one thing that hath being" and whose essence defies representation in any "shadow or shape" or "likeness," "How should it turn from its great way to give | Man that must die a clearer space to live?" (3.168-80). It should not and cannot, is the sure answer. Fate remains, in the tragic hero's vision, incontrovertibly *atropic*. By the same token, though, it is the tragic poet's impossible, necessary mission to make of this trope-proof destiny a figure, a myth—say, for starters, the mythic figure of an Atropos among her sister Fates. Such is the dialectic of human imagination that fate's very inaccessibility makes tropes for it inevitable. As death is the mother of beauty and necessity the mother of invention, so is fate the mother of creativity.

Cleaving to this cultural primal scene, Swinburne's epic vision in *Tristram* implies a political will that is, in strict proportion to the intransigence of the conditions it must cope with, radically freer than the feel-good progressivism to which his and Morris's tragic vision issued their joint late-century riposte. Swinburne never found communism attractive, and Morris professed it only (though very shortly) after writing his major epic. Both would have heartily agreed with Karl Marx, however, that when humanity make their own history they do so under circumstances not of their choosing. They would then have added: only harshly unpropitious circumstances make for great history. And then, perhaps, subjoined: only great history, undertaken from outside the progressivist bubble scheme that passes for utopianism these days, can sustain a critique of the modern catastrophe that will be anywhere near strong enough to cope with it.

Sigurd the Volsung and *Tristram of Lyonesse* are the last major English epics of the century, thanks to the thoroughness of their adaptation of poetic means to a durable narrative purpose. This purpose did not meet the current taste but undermined it, plunging through the atmospheric distractions of an imperialism now fully come of ideological age, to strike bass chords out of the old cultural bedrock beneath. These works' depth of resonance came from their very resistance to contemporary narrative norms, from manifestly nontopical subject matter, and from flagrantly unusual, even contrarian poetic manners. As *The Excursion*, *Don Juan*, *Aurora Leigh*, and *Idylls of the King* had done—but with, if anything, less concession than formerly to the decorum of the moment—*Sigurd* and *Tristram* flouted the generic expectations of a conformist era by practicing a traditional art palpably re-wrought. To a public entranced by unsustainable fantasies of progress towards uniform civilization, these dissident epics of the waning century showed how bad the new faith looked when it was turned inside out. They challenged the latest Victorians to understand, through an act of willed estrangement, how profoundly anxious an unfulfillment the conformity of today already harbored.

The remainder of this chapter takes up lesser works that are minoritized not so much by length as by what seems, beside the stubbornness of Morris or Swinburne, a deliberate curtailment of purpose. Only Mathilde Blind's courageous if hoarse *Ascent of Man* spoke in 1889 through the trumpet; and by that date her work seemed the more outlandishly brash because, with the approach of the 1890s, most poetry in an epic vein had become muted, insinuative, sidelong. It was a confidentially knowing kind of epic that prevailed in the 1890s. What it knew best, and allegorized with some finesse in a range of fables centering on the permutations of a baffled eros, was its own want of passion, whether that was measured in strength of conviction or wildness of abandon. The sheer choice to write in the genre still implied a measure of cultural dissent, but when the new poets said no they said it with a sigh. In place of their elders' epic drive towards tragedy they offered melancholy, a diffusive malaise that turned epic plotting once again in the direction of romance, with its lateral motion of incidental drift. The *fin de siècle* was a time when the standard of mediocrity in English verse rose again to the mark of high competence it had reached in Pope's day; and to a man its minor epoists had grasped the lesser wisdom of dieting ambition and living imaginatively within their technical means.[81]

Such retrenchment can only have been encouraged by the damp deterrent furnished by *Mano: A Poetical History* (1883) in four books by Richard Watson Dixon, an untalented early Pre-Raphaelite who took holy orders, mellowed into a decent church historian, and befriended Gerard Manley Hopkins. Alike incompetent in its traffic jam of a plot and in its handling of a *terza rima* vehicle that Dixon unaccountably prided himself on grinding to a halt with every third line, *Mano* may be the least happy of a long century's many failed experiments in alternative forms of verse narrative.[82] A preface ominously derives the matter of the poem from miscellaneous, millennium-old "Chronicles ... filled with prodigies," and hands over the duties of narrative to one Fergant, an "old monk, filled with memories of pain" (viii–ix)—filled too with a chronicler's faith that all events are equally worthy of record and that, when it comes to narrative organization, serial sequence is as good as it gets.

---

[81] Saintsbury's retrospect of English verse from the later nineteenth century rehearses in terms of poetic style this chapter's argument about eclecticism of content and summativeness of perspective: "All but the greatest poetry of the period is an echo, though a multifarious and often a beautiful one," whose generally high technical quality is due to "the immense extent of the literature from which suggestion has been taken." *Cambridge History of English Literature*, ed. A. W. Ward and A. R. Waller, vol. 13 (Cambridge: Cambridge University Press, 1917) 238, 249.

[82] Unaccountably the poem has attracted admirers. Elton, *Survey*, 108–9, commends Dixon for capturing a "purely mediaeval inspiration" and contriving a poetic diction perfect for translating Dante. Welby goes out of his way (50, 90) to praise Dixon's *terza rima*, though not so far as to illustrate or analyze it with a hope of obtaining adherents. Lionel Stevenson, caught up by the poetic "immediacy" born of "apocalyptic expectation," takes from *Mano* a "convincing medieval impression": *The Pre-Raphaelite Poets* (Chapel Hill: University of North Carolina Press, 1972) 275. With his usual acuteness in generosity, Saintsbury comes nearer the mark, taking away from his reading of *Mano* "an impression of somewhat reluctant and extorted esteem" (*Cambridge History*, 13: 219).

The poem's primitive fixation on whatever incident engrosses its ticketed canto (e. g. 4.7: "How Mano Found Diantha with the Peasants in the Wood: and Himself was Taken Prisoner by the Lords") is if anything aggravated by the bead-stringing click of the versification, which programmatically impedes the recapitulative headway that the braided *terza rima* of the *Divina Commedia* was so evidently designed to forward. Readers who think of Dante may be pardoned for supposing they have been sent to hell, or purgatory at least, for the sin of having loved good plots too well.

For suspense Dixon seems to have counted on an induced millennium fever, not realizing that to make good on the magnetic promise of tenth-century apocalypticism he would need to replicate its buildup structurally within his own narrative. (The tenth century seems to have been in the air: it had lately in 1875 furnished the Right Hon. the Marquis of Lorne with enough Provençal matter to fill out *Guido and Lita: A Tale of the Riviera* with a hundred pages of chivalric couplets such as we would not have been surprised to find on Leigh Hunt's desk in Chapter 5.) In practice the Antichrist talk Dixon evokes and the general paranoia he describes do no more than cast large shadows at random to form an intermittently portent-ous backdrop for humdrum episodes that exhibit continual motion while going noplace. Witness the clueless way our knightly Italian hero shuttles on missions to Normandy, back over the Alps to Rome, then off again to Normandy, to be burned there at the stake from obscure political motives but with the gruesome consolation of knowing that a lady whose love he now belatedly requites is being immolated at his side. Given a millenarian climate of intrigue in the works and convulsion in the offing, *Mano* is rife with acts of dissimulation; this provides Dixon with his one staple alterna-tive to straight-up chronicle, put to use each time the plodding narrative pauses to unfold a disguised character's true identity and origin.

An action inconsequential in its outcome and indigested in its parts, com-bining ragged archival obscurity (A Poetical *History*) with the flimsiness of drab fictions (A *Poetical* History): even the tiresome mandatory upswing of imperial progress narrative was preferable to this. Yet to his congeries of disagreeables Dixon adds an extra element that, in its very incongruity with the rest of the poem, may claim this chapter's attention. Under his dark-ages cowl Fergant turns out to be something of a dissembler too, albeit at a metapoetically millennial level; for he is really a decadent Victorian fatalist. By book 4 Dixon's delegated narrator, the insipidity of his prolix account apparently disgusting even himself, jettisons the revelatory promise vouchsafed by his Christian model of the final days. He latches instead onto an older pagan conception—which is also, given the way things were going in the literary late nineteenth century, a more modern one. When at parting Fergant salutes

> The mighty workers of this world's affairs,
> Fatality, infinity, these two,
> The one the only yoke the other wears
>
> (4.1563–65)

it is as if Dixon has made a quick study of Swinburne's *Tristram*, published just the year before, and embarked on a tolerable imitation of not just its thought but the very movement of its verse. Enough has been said already about this dismal epic to explain why the fiery consummation of Mano and Joanna comes nowhere near the profundity of tragedy that opens before the passion of Tristram and Iseult. The corresponding failure of *Mano* to convey anything like tragic joy may be additionally ascribed to Dixon's neglect of the pleasure principle—or, in a dry revisionary nutshell, to his pairing of "Fatality" above not with its dialectical Swinburnean opposite desire but with the vapid cipher "infinity." Still, the poet's last-minute lunge after the kind of purposiveness by which the great tales of Swinburne and Morris lived stands out the more clearly, in its rote or compensatory quality, as a sign of the end times.

Other minor epoists out of love with the cultural mainstream wised up sooner than Dixon did to the advantages of a fatalist counterplot. Not fate as a felt summons to nobility in heroes and creativity in poets, but fatal*ism*: an idea of order that kept the sick soul on life support, in meager but viable opposition to the *status quo*, was the spirit of the subgenre that ushered the century to the door. We may find that exit route traced here with three longish narratives by poets in their twenties, first obscurely printed ten years apart, then all republished from houses of name within a few years of 1900. Since that was the year when the steady epic productivity this book surveys finally bottomed out—no new poem belonging to the genre appeared after 1897 or before 1905—*faute de mieux* we can take a reading from these epicizing works that reached the public in their definitive form at around this time.

The thousand lines or so of John Payne's *Romaunt of Sir Floris* (1870, 1902), we remarked earlier in this chapter, would not have been out of place in Morris's contemporaneous *Earthly Paradise*. In other words, this nominally Arthurian work published on the heels of Tennyson's epic-reclaiming *Holy Grail* volume veers diametrically away from the Laureate's civic imagining and—like one of the errant Camelot knights, in fact—towards a private allegory of a young man's path to the virtuous life. On its moral outside, Payne's tale recounts the recruitment, by no less an officer than Sir Galahad, of a young warrior into the front ranks of Christian soldiery. While the opening pages have Sir Floris mowing down rough beasts like so many video-game assailants out of Southey's *Thalaba*, by the end his awakening to the dove of Christ and to a voice commending the good fight leaves the application of Payne's allegory beyond doubt. At the heart of the allegorical matter, however, lies an emancipation of the hitherto chaste Floris's affections within an all-male academy—not a Blanchefleur in sight, whatever expectation the fame of the medieval boy–girl couple may encourage—convened under the sign "Quiconque aime | Complait à Dieu en pechié mesme." The love that pleases God, be it sinful or no, certainly pleases Sir Floris, surrounded as he is by men who embrace each other, and kissed as he is on the lips by Christ, "with rapturous ecstatic pain" (54). This climactic incarnation of *esprit de corps* transports Floris out of earthly-paradise camp and back to this world to shoulder duty.

The undisguised homoeroticism of Payne's allegory may explain his withholding reissue until, events of the 1890s having signally reconfigured the public field of gender, he was ready to follow it up in the 1902 *Poetical Works* with an undated, heteronormative sequel of sorts entitled "The Building of the Dream." In this companion fable a knight-turned-scholar named Sir Ebhart gains magical access to the realm of his own dreams, only to reject that realm on discovering that the possession of his heart's desire, despite her consummate beauty, ultimately palls. The difference between these two plots hinges less on sexual orientation than on the disposition of the will. Where Ebhart's quest and his repudiation of it are each voluntary acts, Floris in contrast chooses nothing but is chosen—by Galahad, by Christ, by the claims of service in the world. *The Romaunt of Sir Floris* remains noteworthy for its protagonist's inviolate virginity of will, the passivity with which everything happens to rather than through him. This passivity of his chimes with the way Payne declines to work out the terms, and perhaps the schedule of payments, that an actual negotiation between delight and duty might entail. The poet's finessing such considerations, under cover of an inscrutable fatality, keeps his nominal knight Floris in effect a Childe, a Peter Pan or Dorian Gray. In this sense the murmur of frustration that arises from each page may bespeak the *Romaunt*'s stifled wish—one that the poem shares with others of its moment—to grow up and make an epic of itself, if it only knew how.

A poet better connected and eventually better known, William Watson, executed a more complicated temporal loop from youth to age and back ten years later in *The Prince's Quest* (1880, 1892).[83] His original working title, "The City of Youth: A Faery Romance," had the genre right but seized too fast on the destination to do justice, as the published title does, to the wayfaring essence of his romance plot. D. G. Rossetti generously claimed to find in the enjambed pentameter couplets of this ten-part quest narrative the spirit of Keats's *Endymion* reborn ("Publisher's Note," 1892). We may prefer to recall whom the young Keats was imitating in that work and, recalling Payne as well, declare a mini-revival of the Romantic spirit of Southey, as blunted down by Hunt. Watson's *Kehama*-like extravagance of incident—the Prince's fifty-years' thralldom to a desert-island fiend, the iron chain of health that tides him over, an emerald stone that not only metes justice but can navigate a ship when asked—such are the childish fancies the poem exists for, even as the framing plot pretends they are mere digressions in a straight line that leads from the Prince's beholding his beloved in part 1 to his gaining her in part 10. This union significantly takes place in the City of Youth, where after half a century his young looks and heart are as wonderfully restored as hers have been preserved the while—a mutual reward for heroic steadfastness that congratulates the reader, by the way, on winning through to the end, much as the fantasy of youth-brought-back figures just the kind of generic indulgence the entire work solicits. Or half solicits: the grown-up and *soi-disant* culturally advanced consciousness that supervened in Southey's notes to correct each escapade in *Thalaba* and *Kehama* finds a *fin-de-siècle* counterpart in Watson's suffusive note of Keatsian acknowledged nostalgia. Here, says *The Prince's Quest* in its descriptiveness and reluctance of advance, is a story that not only

<hr />

[83] The second edition was a Bodley Head imprint of John Lane's, who ranked Watson at the top of his poetry list. At Austin's death in 1913 Watson was in the running for the Laureateship that went in the event to Bridges: see Cruse, 75, 240. There is a fair word for Watson in Herbert J. C. Grierson and J. C. Smith, *A Critical History of English Poetry* (New York: Oxford University Press, 1946) 512–13. Donald J. Gray numbers him among the fourteen 19th-cent. authors who made their living chiefly from poetry sales and, with Hemans and Landon, among the three who did so throughout their careers: "Macaulay's *Lays of Ancient Rome* and the Publication of Nineteenth-Century British Poetry," in *Victorian Literature and Society: Essays Presented to Richard D. Altick*, ed. James R. Kincaid and Albert J. Kuhn (Columbus: Ohio State University Press, 1984) 77.

is incredible but knows it is incredible; and its authenticity inheres in its petition to the reader who believes nothing else to believe at least that.

Were the whispered confidences of the newly, frankly faithless enough to build an epic on? Such is the question that nags at Stephen Phillips in a third work of wider scope and longer views, *Eremus: A Poem* (1890, 1894). Its title may waive the question of kind, but "the Epic" is what during composition the young poet regularly called it in his letters.[84] Besides, the question is presumptively put by the poem's division into eleven cantos, that number of generic penultimacy with which Tennyson had teased his reader and himself in "The Epic" half a century before. For the inconclusive ending to *Eremus* ambiguously entombs, as if to delegate the work of monumentation to its 1890s reader, a protagonist who has been racked not just by standard Victorian doubt but by a form of doubt that epic after Morris and Swinburne made particularly its own. The polarity that lays Eremus out at last like an anatomy of his era extends between antithetical visions: on one hand, a thermodynamic entropy that dissipates energy and homogenizes form; on the other, a love that discriminates personality and cherishes selfhood. While Phillips draws liberally on the discursive opposition of science to faith of which latterly the reading public could not get enough, it is to Swinburne's twinning of destiny with desire that the poem is in practice imaginatively keyed. Yet the desire that *Eremus* invokes it also disclaims. While the protagonist postulates the necessity of love, he knows it rather by report than at first hand, and can declare from experience only that desire is greatly to be desired.

An aged figure, the Eremus of the title, breaks into an Alpine chapel demanding shrift: where Coleridge's mariner, biding his time a century ago, had waylaid his man outside church, this successor now goes to work in the very sanctuary. Like the Ancient Mariner, Eremus offers in canto 1 a more workaday version of Victorian spiritual crisis—scientific modernity has robbed him of orthodox belief—than proves adequate to what his life story in the ensuing cantos will reveal. While in mourning for his dead friend Julian, Eremus has unwittingly raised up Lucifer, under the Shelleyan epithet "Spirit of the Wind" (canto 3), who whisks him off across the universe to discover the late Julian gazing up from the verge of Chaos at

---

[84] Richard Whittington-Egan, *Stephen Phillips: A Biography* (High Wycombe: Rivendale Press, 2006) 45–46.

Heaven's floor and pining for the love of his earthly life. If this scene in the medial canto 6 frames Phillips's version of the Blessed Damozel, then canto 7 flushes out his Beast in the Jungle: for there Eremus realizes that, having no such grand passion of his own, his existence is not just faithless but hopeless and thus pointless as well. The next two cantos project this desperate condition into cosmic allegory, first in a tempestuous Chaos of unfixed emotions ("Dread undefined, | And roaming Apprehension," 8.779–80) and then in a region of enervated worlds that have lost faith, whose God-abandoned number the tutelary Spirit predicts that Eremus' world is about to join: "your planet comes | To a mechanic end, a wrecked machine" (9.887–88). A fervent cry for redemption transports Eremus to Earth again in canto 10, and to an existence poised between relief at being home and anxious disgust at his fellows' insensibility before their impending doom; between, in other words, the erotic bond Julian represents and the gyres of material entropy and human disregard into which the planet is spinning as the very sun relaxes its gravitational grip. Confessed but unshriven and unrequited, Eremus dies in canto 11 and is irresolutely (i.e. fittingly) sepulchered by mute survivors. In the eloquent absence of a canto twelfth, Phillips claims the palm over his two seniors in epicizing delicacy: their sense of where the genre ought to go was no clearer than his, but he had at least the candor to say so.[85]

Among these slender reeds blown by young writers destined for minority grew another that, while its author would eventually be hailed the greatest anglophone poet of the twentieth century, looked a lot like them in its day. We read *The Wanderings of Oisin* now in a 1920s version that the mature W. B. Yeats streamlined for movement and idiom as painstakingly as Southey in the 1830s had streamlined his own youthful *Joan of Arc* (Chs. 2, 7), each elder poet's revision betokening a revolution in poetic taste to which he had meanwhile substantially contributed. Yeats may have changed *Oisin* so extensively because he could see in hindsight how well its initial 1889 form conformed to the epoch of Payne, Watson, Phillips, and company: an allegorically eligible tale transplanting modern ennui and

[85] Phillips went on to gain a high reputation among competent Edwardian judges for his poetic closet-dramas, especially *Christ in Hades* (1896), though the flame of renown was spent before he returned to the lists in wartime, just before his death, with a 1915 "epic drama" entitled *Armageddon* (noted in Ch. 12). See Hopkins, *English Poetry*, 514–15; Cruse, *After the Victorians*, 81–82.

sexual unfulfillment into exotic settings, rendered in some thousand lines of languidly descriptive narration. Two features, however, distinguished *Oisin* even at birth from *fin-de-siècle* congeners. It boasted a quota of terse, vigorous imagery, most of it unerringly retained and refined for the version of 1929; and it evinced on behalf of Ireland a species of national ambition that seemed to have evaporated from long poems in John Bull's island during the decades when Yeats came of age.

The revived ambition of *Oisin* emerges along two dimensions. It is there as a matter of plot in the hero's defiance of the alien priestcraft Saint Patrick represents. And it informs Yeats's reclamation of two originary moments in the history of Western epic: first, the Ossianic matter that Macpherson had confiscated for Scotland a century earlier; then, back behind that, and in keeping with the literary-historical logic we discussed in Chapter 1, the primitive glory of Homer, the bard of archaic wanderings whose pre-classical vigor metropolitan Victorians like W. E. Gladstone and Matthew Arnold had done their best to recruit into the institutional service of an imperial Englishness.[86] Even the comparatively gentle air of national identity that *Oisin* breathes (not just Celtic but expressly Fenian) under-scores by contrast the prevailingly postnationalist climate of extended verse narrative in English at the time. Years later "The Circus Animals' Deser-tion" (1939) would summarize this poem's three-book plot of thriftless quests to enchanted isles as a sequence of "Vain gaiety, vain battle, vain repose." Yet to this manifestly nineties futility theme Yeats's political animus had from the first imparted a national dimension, and its pungency here makes one wonder how the epic genre in Britain got by for so long without it.

Another way to understand the exceptional status of *The Wanderings of Oisin* in its day is to investigate its local genealogy. Where we have just seen Yeats's contemporaries pursuing etiolated versions of the love/fate dialectic that Swinburne had emblazoned in *Tristram*, Yeats went back to Morris and the archaizing, devotedly prodigal heroics of *Sigurd*. Indeed, the versifica-tion of *Oisin* may be said to work its way through Scott's tetrameters (book 1) and Browning's couplets (book 2) up to the hexameters of Morris in book 3, with an ethos to match:

[86] See Martin McKinsey, "Counter-Homericism in Yeats's 'The Wanderings of Oisin,'" in *W. B. Yeats and Postcolonialism*, ed. Deborah Fleming, (West Cornwall: Locust Hill, 2001) 235–51.

Put the staff in my hands; I will go to the Fenians, thou cleric, and chant
The war-song that roused them of old; they will rise, making clouds
    with their breath
Innumerable, singing, exultant—

(3.201–3)

With the Miltonic last hemistich a great poet in training reaches back to the
longer tradition of heroic writing in English. But it is through Morris that he
makes his reach, here and when, in the final quatrain of the poem, Oisin
trumps Patrick's threat of hellfire with an unregenerate pagan resolve that
seems to sum up the ferocity of *Sigurd*'s fourth book: to "go to the house of
the Fenians, be they in flames or at feast" (3.223). Earlier in this chapter we
considered in *Congal* the epic handling of folk material akin to Yeats's, and
saw how Samuel Ferguson's stalled mid-century conception came at length
to fruition once the poet devised means of linking his Anglo-Irish message
to 1870s imperial progressivism. For Yeats, who had no use for Ferguson's
sort of gradualist history—"When I was a boy everybody talked about
progress, and rebellion against my elders took the form of aversion to that
myth"—the counter-myth lay in William Morris's keeping.[87]

Yeats shared with stymied Phillips and even all-thumbs Dixon the late
century's gathering apprehension of a cataclysm that would soon explode
the regnant myth of civilized improvement. Turning aside with his gener-
ation from the master narrative of High Victorian culture, he saw better
than any of them the generic lifeline that Morris and Swinburne had
husbanded, and that ran through what his own much later vision of cultural
history would call the *antithetical* narrative of discontinuous tragic joy. In
Oisin, the major effort of his youth, Yeats rescued for modernism what
those heroic tragedians had found they must cast away. Where the great
late-Victorian dissenters had migrated to extremes—the intimate or tribal
extreme at one pole, the universal or international at the other—Yeats
trained up national energies with which to reclaim the epic middle ground

---

[87] Introduction to *The Resurrection* (1931), quoted in Harold Bloom, *Yeats* (New York: Oxford
University Press, 1970) 100. In "The Trembling of the Veil" (1922) Yeats said of his reluctant
introduction by Arthur Symons to an eclectic "procession of the Gods" around 1890, "I could not
endure, however, an international art, picking stories and symbols where it pleased": *The
Autobiography of William Butler Yeats* (New York: Macmillan, 1965) 131. Yeats's aversion to the
literary climate in which he had grown up came of his having at an early point inhaled it deeply:
"When I was twenty-five or twenty-six I planned a *Légende des Siècles* of Ireland that was to set out
with my *Wanderings of Oisin*, and show something of every century": "Estrangement" (1909), in
Autobiography 335.

their expedients had evacuated. What made this retrieval possible, and compatible with the heritage of lavish loss on which *Sigurd* and *Tristram* alike reposed, was the peculiar provisionality that came with Yeats's position. He came forward in *Oisin*, after all, as the epic spokesman for a nation that did not, in 1889, as yet exist. If Oisin's terminal defiance is legible in a register of triumph, it can only be the ambiguous sort of triumph that traditionary or visionary imagination enjoys over actual circumstance: a far cry from the recrudescent jingoism that awaits us, just around the epic turn of the century, with aspects of Alfred Noyes and Charles M. Doughty in the chapter ahead.[88]

A less promising, and thus for the period more typical, disconnect between vision and practice emerges in a curtain performance by our chapter majordomo, Owen Meredith's posthumous *King Poppy: A Fantasia* (1892). Meredith had substantially drafted the poem for private circulation by 1875 but withheld it from the public press for the rest of his life, on the grounds that so much of that life in the 1870s and 1880s was spent in viceregal office (India) or embassy (France) as to make publication of a mischievous political satire seem, to say the least, undiplomatic.[89] The twelve neatly framed and capably blank-versed books into which Meredith burnished *King Poppy* over the years appeared in 1892 adorned prefatorily with Burne-Jones designs and marginally with prose glosses whose red ink made of them literal Victorian rubrics. Presenting itself to the reader as a sort of documentary state treasure, the book performs in bibliography what it does in writing. *King Poppy* is on one hand a smiling send-up of the forms of political sovereignty, on the other hand a solemn defense of the imaginative power that—here already the work's definitive incoherence opens to view—both shapes those institutional forms and erects an inward asylum against all they represent. In effect the poem versifies Walter Bagehot's genial exposé in *The English Constitution* (1867) of the imposture undergirding modern Britain as a state nominally monarchic but actually parliamentary and bureaucratic. Its narrative installs a puppetry robot in

---

[88] Epic's wavering, even cunning, allegiance to nationalist purposes—a theme that has accompanied us since Ch. 8—should be considered in the light of David Quint's survey of medieval epic revivalism as it swept Europe in the century after Ossian to resurrect, among other national rallying-texts, *Beowulf*, the *Kalevala*, the *Cid*, the *Nibelungenlied*, the *Chanson de Roland*, and *Prince Igor*. See *Epic and Empire: Politics and Generic Form from Virgil to Milton*, 350–61.

[89] As he said himself, "It won't do for a Viceroy to cut jokes about Government in public" (Harlan, *Owen Meredith*, 218).

place of the Princess Diadema, heir apparent to the throne of Diadummiania (book 5), then repeats the trick on vaster scale with a "Government Machine" (12.4977) or "State Mechanism" (12.5077) when, at the last minute, King Diadummianus abdicates the throne to join his daughter in private life.

As the mere nomenclature will suggest, there is an Al Capp or Walt Kelly side to all this. One can do worse, in fact, than follow the suggestion back to the epic outlandishness with which that comic-stripper William Blake a hundred years before had illustrated a political principle that Owen Meredith too meant to endorse: the Romantic principle that, in affirming the radically human createdness of social systems, acknowledges the poet as legislator of the world. The Los of Diadummiania (Meredith's answer to Daedalus and Hephaistos, Merlin and Orion) is one Master Pilgram: a mage who not only represents the inventive power of the state but steps into the political fable as an avatar of Phantasos, strong god of the imagination itself. This allegorical supernumerary, whom we have already met outside in the framing "Legend" that precedes book 1 (a corresponding "Transfiguration" succeeds book 12), belongs to a Persephonic substratum of dreams, which Meredith represents as not infernal but foundational, like the un- and pre- and sub-conscious out of which Sigmund Freud was making myths in the 1890s too. In this underworld Phantasos has fostered up the poem's other monarch, King Poppy (a.k.a. Mekon, the Greek name for opium), from a seedling to a dispenser of consolation for all that is wrong in the waking world. The looking-glass permeability of King Diadummianus' realm to King Poppy's is an encouraging Blakean development within the narrative; and the final safe haven that the Diadum royal family achieve as refugees under Poppy's protection clearly evinces the priorities Meredith longs to enforce—as if in protest against his embassy years, his Lytton earldom and all that these worldly promotions have entailed. The poem's defiantly escapist humanism sponsors, at the close of book 10, a set of gnomic choruses that would not be out of place in the visionary drama of Shelley, Buchanan, or (in years to come) Yeats.

Yet something stops Meredith from conceiving his realm of creative refreshment as anything but a heterocosm, and from depicting the counter-cultural energy vested in Poppy as good for much more than palliation. The reality in which Meredith actually believes is, when all is said and done, the workaday world he purports to mock with a bystander's immunity. The generative realm of dream that he champions is prevented from assuming a world-regenerative role, because at last the imaginative fastness where he takes his stand is a place that business-as-usual surrounds, sets the defining terms for, and thus in truth governs. Meredith's radical cell is only a ghetto in Watson's City of Youth after all. This ontological dependency makes the mode of critique *King Poppy* practices ultimately satiric rather than prophetic. The true colors of this mode glisten through the gauzy fairy-tale principle that Meredith laid out for his admittedly "impossible little world" in an 1880 letter that served to introduce the published poem after his death: "to shape out vaguely a sort of golden legend from the most venerable and familiar features of fragments of the fairy tales and ballads which float about the world, and which our wise generation relegates to the nursery."[90] The sidelong sniper's shot this last clause gets off typifies the tactics of *King Poppy* as a whole: very much a Fabian defense, in swiping camouflage, of "the much despised influence of the Imagination," the poem falls back on the nursery as a cultural site affording cover against the adult, imperial intelligence—in whose hegemony, neverthless, the poet wise in his generation knows he cannot but participate.[91] The entire maneuver combines, in refractory inverse ratio, the same "fantasia" ingredients of supervision and adventure that made the 1890s such a boom era for safe epic fun, as *Odyssey* anthologies "for boys and girls" poured from the press.

Nowhere is the poem's winningly naughty but never indecent status clearer than in the vegetative status of Poppy himself, a nursling hero by nature and a flower whose potency, while genuine, the poet carefully purges of any sexual component. To think of Erasmus Darwin's *Loves of the Plants* a century before is to appreciate how rooted Meredith's poem remains in Beulah land. If in the long run the pre-generative, resolutely infantile character of *King Poppy* attests the well-known shadow that Victorian sexual

---

[90] Letter to the poet's sister-in-law Mrs. Earle, quoted in his daughter's edition of *Personal and Literary Letters of Robert, First Earl of Lytton*, ed. Betty Balfour (London and New York: Longmans, 1906) 1: 314.

[91] Links will be obvious between the guerrilla satire in *King Poppy* and in the children's classics contemporary with it that have drawn fire from, among others, Jacqueline Rose in *The Case of Peter Pan; or, The Impossibility of Children's Fiction* (London: Macmillan, 1984). Meredith's poem found at least one congener in *Lionel's Legacy*, an eight-canto verse narrative that the former epoist William Stigand (see Ch. 10) published in 1907 in his *Acanthia: Poems Original and Edited*. A stiffly masquerading preface backdates composition of the poem to 1885, which is presumably when the eponym's Eurasia-hopping misfortunes made their quietus in the colony of Macao at the foot of imperial Camoens' statue. Poor Lionel is a Shelleyan innocent of good parts and literary genius— his "chief poem" is entitled *The Fall of Islam* (4.73)—whose short life is made serially miserable by the adulterated, unfeeling social world whose grasping venalities furnish all Stigand actually wants: a parade of easy targets at which to pitch macaronically satirical couplet barbs.

prudery cast even on a work like this one pretending to radical critique, it also betrays the generic incumbency that this long chapter has traced. The anthological epic modality of golden legends and treasuries that repeatedly attracted Victorian cultural meliorism in its riper years was one that Owen Meredith dutifully served yet came around at last to disown. To the progress narrative of his early *Chronicles and Characters* he here opposed a regress narrative instead. The floating vagueness of "a sort of golden legend" afforded him, paradoxically, a way of taking a stand against his own generation's self-serving mythology of comparatist mythology, a stand fortified no doubt by much that his involvement in government showed him was shaping up in the cultural politics of, not just Britain, but all imperializing Europe.[92] Never a poet open to the afflatus of a tragic fall, he incubated for the bemused nineties, in lovingly tended twelve-book miniature, an alternative vision premised on not progress but relapse.

Not to grow up was one way of defending the poet's right to say that the emperor had no clothes or—it amounted to the same thing—that the adults of Europe had all gone off and left an imperializing world on automatic pilot. Affirming that birthright by hugging the childlike may all told have been the best way an entire order of nineties writers knew to practice the loyal opposition that was in them. Or there might be a better way. At a late-century juncture when heroic vigor seemed incompatible with mature culture, instead of forestalling the dilemma like Owen Meredith through regression a writer might lodge the claim to have outgrown or overleaped it. Adjusting to Apollo's silence in the evening light, strapping on the wings and night goggles of Minerva, a writer might rescue the beloved mode from disuse by jumping genres. A last, consistent refinement of tendencies that the poets themselves had exhibited since around 1870 would be for the practice of epic to yield forthrightly to its study. The scholar whose quarry was civilization in its sweep from barbarism through the latter days might conform the modern tale of civilization to the ancient tale of the tribe and so make an epic out of learning itself.

This most conspicuously happened with the vast progress narrative of J. G. Frazer's *The Golden Bough* (first edition 1890), where the scholar's own application of reason to irrational materials played a starring role. Recent commentators have called Frazer's masterpiece "a last great landmark of man's effort to encompass his past in some approximately total form," "a gigantic romance of quest couched in the form of objective research"; and "a super-epic, in which the quester, the human race, wanders through history seeking its own true identity by the progressive exercise of reason."[93] Golden legend, golden bough: the aureate climate of cultural progressivism that nourished intellectual endeavor at the close of the nineteenth century had already, in essence, promoted to epic standing the basic anthological activities of gathering, arrangement, and comparison. Why then shouldn't scholarship ascend the empty throne? When W. J. Courthope launched with Dan Chaucer his *History of English Poetry* in 1895, the project was firmly aimed at the conclusion it would reach with Sir Walter Scott, six books later in 1910, our *terminus ad quem* in this book. Courthope's aim could hardly have suited Gilded Age epic criteria more aptly: to illustrate "the gradual and majestic growth of the British Empire out of the institutions of the Middle Ages," in the form of a literary history fit to serve the nation as "a veritable πολιτικη παιδεια [*politikē paideia*], a public school of liberty and patriotism."[94]

Even a work of literary history as subtle, original, and lasting as W. P. Ker's *Epic and Romance* (1896) framed its narrative in stirring martial terms. Owning as he must that romance must cast out epic, and the novel then cast out romance, Ker promises to show "the victory of the new literature of chivalry over the older forms of heroic narrative" (4). It is as if the very hosts at Hastings stand before him, and he goes on to relate the great contest without either hiding his own atavistic loyalties or letting those loyalties cloud his vision of the transformation in cultural spokesmanship that his narrative portends. Ker's insight that "Romance is at the same time one of

---

[93] John B. Vickery, *The Literary Impact of* The Golden Bough (Princeton: Princeton University Press, 1973) 27, 128; Robert Ackerman, *The Myth and Ritual School: J. G. Frazer and the Cambridge Ritualists* (New York and London: Garland, 1991) 50–53. Ackerman derives 20th-cent. myth criticism from Frazer's associates and their forerunners, chiefly Edward Tylor and William Robertson Smith, in Victorian evolutionary anthropology. Frazer's successors Jessie Weston and Bertha Phillpotts would go beyond the study of tragedy and comedy to include quest and saga narratives by 1920 (182–84)—just in time for T. S. Eliot to embrace the result in that compressed epic *The Waste Land* and in his remarks on the mythic method of Joyce's *Ulysses*.

[94] *A History of English Poetry* (London: Macmillan, 1895–1910) 6: 449. Among many reasons predisposing a scholar like Courthope to a claim like this was the surge in epic studies witnessed in his time. Donald M. Foerster, *The Fortunes of Epic Poetry: A Study in English and American Criticism 1750–1950* (N.p.: Catholic University of America Press, 1962) 160, reports that between 1880 and 1910 "more books and essays and journalistic articles were written about epic poetry and poems than in any other thirty-year span of time."

the constituent parts and one of the enemies of epic poetry" (32) set his literary-historical narrative on a dialectically evolving course towards schol-arship's equivalent for a tragic denouement rooted in irresistible betrayal. It was in order to maintain such a denouement that, as we have seen in this chapter, the best epic poets of Ker's day had broken ideological ranks with the emergent Gilded Age.

That the scholarly genre of literary and cultural history might attain a derivative, tertiary sort of epic form is a proposition either risible or uncontroversial, depending how one looks at it. We may do better to take a fourth derivative and recollect that literary history, like the genres it studies, has a history also, divisible into modalities and even fashions of its own.[95] Within that history—in which of course we participate here—a summary judgment on the later nineteenth century from B. Ifor Evans both typifies that author's 1930s dispensation and highlights the difference mod-ernism had made by then in the critical canons of literary value. "Above all, the nineteenth century had lost contact with the classical conception that a great work must be an organized unity and in attempting long works had grown content to produce amorphous pieces, well decorated with inciden-tal beauties but lacking cohesion."[96] About the *fin de siècle*'s epic eclecticism this judgment is all right as far as it goes. But the scholar who could write it had himself lost contact, or had chosen to sever diplomatic relations, with a definitive late-Victorian belief. This was the belief that civilization exhib-ited a master narrative linking the classical with the modern along a rising curve of action, which turned incidental "beauties"—tragic setbacks in-cluded—into significant episodes within a continuous relation that was so far from "amorphous" that its organizing, cohesive force went without saying. If anything Frazer, Courthope, and Ker would have declared it was Evans's fastidious formalism that was "amorphous," and would have won-dered why a history so lamely concluded should seem worth the telling.

[95] David Perkins dates from *c.*1840—roughly the middle of the span covered in the present book—the century-long dominance within literary studies of a literary history that "foregrounded origins, continuous development, and teleology" as scholarship's points of first reference and last resort when framing questions or explanations: "Literary History and Historicism," in *The Cambridge History of Literary Criticism*, vol. 5, ed. Marshall Brown (Cambridge: Cambridge University Press, 2000) 343. Our argument in Ch. 1 suggests an adjustment to Perkins's calendar that René Wellek, *The Rise of English Literary History* (Chapel Hill: University of North Carolina Press, 1941), would also appear to endorse: at least where epic is concerned, the prevalence of a literary-historical orientation antedates his *terminus a quo* by about a hundred years.

[96] B. Ifor Evans, *English Poetry in the Later Nineteenth Century* (London: Methuen, 1933) 378.

12

At Long Last:
Edwardian Epic 1895–1910

This chapter pins an Edwardian coda on the sprawling corpus of Victorian epic writing surveyed in the previous five chapters. Because the generic rate of production fell off precipitously after 1895, we have few remaining calls to pay. By the same token, we have the more leisure to appreciate what seriousness of purpose animates each of our chief destinations—as against the frivolity, not to say dissipation, that overtook the epic *fin de siècle*, and for which the last poem we considered, *King Poppy* by Owen Meredith, tendered its charming apology.[1] In Alfred Noyes's *Drake* and Charles M. Doughty's *The Dawn in Britain* we shall meet works that are in some respects each other's opposites yet at the same time have much in common: most conspicuously a degree of patriotic rigor, and with it an essentializing drive towards consistency of narrative focus, such as the previous half-century seemed to render obsolete. In *The Dynasts* by Thomas Hardy we shall meet something greater, one of the very few masterpieces this long book has been lucky to touch on: a work commensurately vast in original conception, thorough in execution, and pervasive in contemporary relevance. None of the three major Edwardian epics foretold the cataclysm of 1914–1918 that lay just ahead. Yet the generational holocaust of the Great War shed a light in which we cannot help looking back on these

---

[1] For mass culture's depressing trivialization of epic, as against the traditions of mockery that since Ovid have paid real if backhanded respect to the genre, this book offers little comfort beyond what recognition of its longevity may disclose. When in 1910 Edward Sherwood Creamer published "An Epic of Heaven" that consisted of four non-narrative pages of bromides in blank verse (New York: Broadway, 1910), was he so much further off the mark than where we found Ann Holmes (Ch. 2) with her *Epic Poem on Adam and Eve*?

works, if only because the land it laid waste became the field where Pound, Joyce, and Eliot sowed the dragon seed of epic Modernism. Still, all three Edwardian epoists forefelt what they could not foretell. They expressed at length that same atmosphere of impending debacle which made contemporary authors as different as Kipling, Conrad, Shaw, and Forster patrol the early years of the century like prophets whose accuracy was portioned to the extremity of their dread.

That something dreadful did fill the air—miasmatic anxiety, the moral equivalent of a London fog distorting individuals' perception and, in public life, obscuring the causality behind events—emerges in the compensatory premium that our poets placed on *clarity*. Decisive edge mattered so much to Noyes that he repeatedly sacrificed to it what modest measures of historical nuance and political complexity he carried with him to the altar of heroic revivalism. While Doughty could fail in clarity, and fail colossally, it was not for want of attempting to be clear: if anything his hard, granular chronicle of antiquities suffered from too indiscriminately direct a presentation and choked on a surfeit of incident. Hardy's surer lens likewise went anywhere, with a panoptic irony of stratified response and interpretation to match it; no work these chapters consider framed its action and critical perspectivism with a more insistently ocular apprehension than *The Dynasts*.

Even for Hardy, of course, the visual in verse remained a derivative of the primary poetic medium, language. This means that for him, as for his contemporaries, the Edwardian premium on clarity primarily took technical effect in the strain toward rhetorical *enargeia*, the verbal evidence of things not seen. The last pre-Modernist English epics drew out into special prominence the genre's never extinguished concern with those technologies of vocabulary and syntax which furnished at once its own medium and the ground of the culture it spoke for.[2] Verse's formal summons to linguistic attention, as it issued from these poems of a recuperative national concern, emphasized that, in order to clarify the image of the nation, it would be necessary first to purify the dialect of the tribe. And to this revived concern with the English language corresponded an insistent Englishness in the chosen theme: each of our Edwardian epics was plotted

---

[2] Kenneth Millard, *Edwardian Poetry* (Oxford: Clarendon Press, 1991), finds among the Edwardians (A. E. Housman, Edward Thomas, Henry Newbolt, as well as Hardy) a widely shared anxiety over "the autonomy of language as a self-sufficient system" (p.64).

around the threat that strangers speaking a Romance tongue were massing to invade the island home.[3]

Discharging these joint epic tasks was a work already in progress as the century turned, and not in verse alone. Twenty-five years elapsed between the first edition of J. G. Frazer's comparatist masterpiece of mythic ethnography *The Golden Bough* (1890, 2 vols.) and the twelve-volume third edition (1911–15). It took a large and dedicated Oxford team twice as long to carry out James Murray's mid-Victorian vision for *A New English Dictionary on Historical Principles*; once again, the sign of its accomplishment was the appearance of the completed 1928 *OED* in, not an alphabetical twenty-six books, but an epical twelve. For evidence that these labors of social and human science indelibly marked the rising epoists of the 1920s it suffices to recall the debt to anthropology that Eliot paraded in *The Waste Land*, Joyce's word-herding in the "Oxen of the Sun" portion of *Ulysses*, or Pound's cosmopolitan, macaronic endeavors in the *Cantos* to make English strange and so make poetry new. It was from Edwardian poets, however—active adult contemporaries of Frazer and Murray framing new answers to rootedly Victorian questions—that the cultural and linguistic preoccupations of epic Modernism were directly inherited.

The radicalism of still newer Modernist responses can eclipse for us the extent of overlap between the Edwardian and the Modernist aim to purge from the literary signal its Victorian noise, be it clangor or murmur. The former part was single-handedly sustained by a patriotic crank of the old school named Charles Rathbone Low. Not content to devote prose tomes to *Battles of the British Army*, *Great African Travellers* (both 1890), and *Captain Cook's Three Voyages* (1892), this retired naval lieutenant and indefatigable exhibitor of national kudos produced in rapid succession *Old England's Navy: An Epic of the Sea* (1891) and *Cressy to Tel-El-Kebir: A Narrative Poem, Descriptive of the Deeds of the British Army* (1892), then caught his breath before giving his own branch of the service its due with *Britannia's Bulwarks: An Historical Poem, Descriptive of the Deeds of the British Navy* (1895). After that Low went on for good measure to *The Epic of Olympus: A Narrative Poem, Descriptive of the Deeds of the Deities and Heroes of Greek Mythology* (1897), where a formulaic similarity in subtitles prepares us for the seamless continuity that we do indeed find between Hellenic and Britannic species of

---

[3] On the background and character of this belated, Empire-conditioned upsurge in English nationalism see Krishan Kumar, *The Making of English National Identity* (Cambridge: Cambridge University Press, 2003) 202–25.

heroism. The uniform spirit of these poems affiliates them with Lord Nelson's decade long ago, as does Low's declared fondness for a versification Staunchly if incompetently modeled on that of *Marmion*. Their structural principle conforms, however, to the compilation model we found flourishing in Chapter 11. For Low sheer inclusiveness trumps any subtler thematic idea; and yet his relentless chronicling does point a contemporary moral: since "all past history" is "one continued war,"

> Wide-spreading as our interests are,
> We may be thus involved in war
> Almost before we know.

> (*Cressy* 12.327)

Epic commemoration no matter how plodding proves an exercise in preparedness after all. The subtler impendency that was to pervade Edwardian literature is here anticipated in the baldest of terms.

Thus the brass section at century's end. A more interesting problem for Edwardian reformers was what to do with the murmurous flute and the lyre. The dust of custom had cumbered the unquestioned loveliness of *fin-de-siècle* narrative verse with the inertia of its own success, such that "loveliness" as an aesthetic criterion fell under grave suspicion. Against this Victorian legacy the twentieth century kept leveling the charge that it consisted too nearly of words alone; that the poets' linguistic preoccupation stood at once in too high a ratio to their message (they were shallow triflers) and in too low a ratio (they were deep-dyed conformists to received thought). This line of attack remains annoyingly familiar today, but at least something of its poverty will have been suggested by the preceding chapter. Conceding there that a marked homogeneity of poetic style did prevail at the *fin de siècle*, we proposed discriminations within that prevalent mannerism among differing schools and intensities of poetic enactment. For poets who most fully engaged their epoch's defining problematics of aggregation, representative selection, and identity-formation within an increasingly global field of cultural development, the patina of late-Victorian versification was no mere escapist dodge. It was a hard-working literary instrument for coping with heterogeneity and imposing an organically flexible order on materials that were often refractorily fugitive.

These issues come back into focus for us here in the figure of Swinburne. Pilloried by new-century critics as the poet whose intoxicated promotion of sound over sense carried to illustratively perverse length what was already the bad habit of his epoch, Swinburne is now better regarded as an artist whose elevation of consciousness through form set him in critically creative relation to his time. So stood, as we have seen, the contrarian fatalist achievement of *Tristram of Lyonesse*; and so stood, a dozen years later, the booklet-length *Tale of Balen* to which we turn next. A lesser work by the measure of line count as well as of conceptual ambition, this 1896 narrative in seven cantos of stark tail-rhymed balladic stanzas nevertheless broke new ground alike for the aging poet and the imminent century. An "old wild tale, made new" (Dedication), it is a work whose insouciant mayhem kept faith with the hallmark iconoclasm that had made young Swinburne notorious; but its crinkly archaism and explanatory vacuum set it apart from *Atalanta*, *Tristram*, and other earlier stories of passion-doomed obsession. As the poet said of it, *The Tale of Balen* was a "little romance of chivalry" and not an epic poem.[4] All the same, the strange clarity of its framing makes of the poem a wicket gate offering access to the epics that did appear after the century's turn.

Swinburne took satisfaction in having lifted the plot with little change from the linear sequence of random incident that makes up Malory's "Balin or the Knight with the Two Swords."[5] Thus like *Tristram of Lyonesse*, which it resembles in no other formal respect, *The Tale of Balen* aligns its learned poet's thankfulness in the face of literary tradition with its knightly hero's stoic openness to vicissitude. Such certainly is the attitude that the narrative inculcates in its persevering reader, who must develop a high tolerance for both graphic violence and the second-order violence that is done to the mind when episodes succeed one another as abruptly—with as little motivation or gathering consequence—as they do here. Beheading, suicide, and assassination form the poem's standard fare. The flash of sword and lance is intermittently reflected in obscurely self-interfering logics of blood feud, arbitrary edict, dwarvish prophecy, and wizardly curse: parried thrusts towards narrative rationale that, if anything, puzzle the reader more than they do the hero caught in the thick of them. Whoever sets out to read for the plot must cling to the knowledge that Balen's strokes of the blade, all of them more or less "dolorous" (Malory's signature term), will conduce at

---

[4] Letter of 16 June 1895 to W. M. Rossetti: *The Swinburne Letters*, ed. Cecil Y. Lang, vol. 6 (New Haven: Yale University Press, 1962) 81.

[5] Letter of 11 May 1896 to Mary Louisa Molesworth: *Letters* 6: 98. On the extent, and effect, of Swinburne's high verbal fidelity to his original in Malory see Paul de Reul, *L'Oeuvre de Swinburne* (Bruxelles: Sand, 1922) 356–57; and David Staines, "Swinburne's Arthurian World," *Studia Neophilologica* 30 (1978) 165.

last to the worst stroke of all, when Balen in disguise and his beloved misrecognized twin Balan are to lie slain by each other's hand.

How to account for this premised but unmotivated catastrophe, much less assign blame for it, is a task that very sorrow enjoins on any sympathetic witness. The only trouble is that Swinburne's tale proves hardly accountable at all in this way; it insists instead on reduction to its own spare terms of existential absorbency, with the odd sorts of comprehension and forgiveness that this stricken state, affectively battered but never numbed, enables. Take the presumably privileged witness Merlin, who materializes early in canto 5 to warn Balen what fell doom attends his having failed to prevent a hardly preventable suicide one canto before: "My heart is wrung," the sage condoles, "for this deed's sake, | To know thee therefore doomed to take | Upon thine hand a curse" (5.4). The wrung-hearted pathos seems sufficiently genuine, the curse sufficiently grim and, as a tip shedding some light of meaning on the plot, even welcome; yet as Merlin vanishes in thin air two stanzas later, so does Balen's transient awareness of the whole magic exchange. Such indifference to consequences would be amazing were it not so typical of the poem, all the way to its end when, having watched the mutual slaughter of Balen and Balan from the parapets, "all those hard light hearts" of the pleasure-seeking onlookers in a nearby castle "were swayed | With pity passing like a shade | That stays not, and may be not stayed" (7.58).

Moral stupidity? Compassion fatigue? Anxiety-uptake inhibitor? These are equally plausible, equally inappropriate names for a condition that, like its many acts of violence, the poem repeatedly describes but does not explain. We can appreciate its oddity more sharply by comparison to what Tennyson had made of the same source materials just a decade before when completing *Idylls of the King* with "Balin and Balan." This recension converted Malory's *doppelgänger* tale into a smoothly joined archetypal psychodrama illustrative of the costs and benefits of sexual repressiveness, which are ambivalently held up for all to see as the official energy policy of Arthur's realm: at once, that is, the source of Camelot's radiant ideality and of its ruinous destiny. Here was a more complex meaning than the *Idylls* had hitherto enunciated, or indeed than the work is often credited with to this day; but it was a meaning all the same, and one without which Malory's raw material would in Tennyson's view have remained so much sound and fury. When Swinburne composed *The Tale of Balen* ten years later he inevitably did so in the recently mourned Laureate's shadow, and its best recent commentators seem agreed that he found his own light by proposing a subversive counter-meaning. These scholars tilt Swinburne against Tenny-son so as to bring out Balen's impulsive generosity as a good old North-umbrian pagan—a truly English innocent like his poetic maker—against the backdrop of hypocritical corruption that Arthurian Britain has invited by embracing the new, imported Christian yoke.[6]

What is valid in this unimpeachably Swinburne-friendly interpretation should be borne in mind when in pages just ahead we assess the newly reassumed Englishness of the Edwardians, along with the constriction of sympathies that such a maneuver enforced. But it is an interpretation of Balen's tale that, like the psychopolitical one Tennyson elaborated, seeks to recruit *The Tale of Balen* into an epic service that does not finally suit it. When the author of *Songs before Sunrise* (1871) meant to frame national issues he left his intention beyond doubt; when he set out to touch a political nerve he did so with an electrical directness that is a far cry from the modalities in operation here. Getting regional or sectarian interpret-ation—any interpretation with such scope of reference—to stick to the verses Swinburne wrote in *The Tale of Balen* is a frustrating endeavor, because he wrote them in order to frustrate it. For the poem protests against Tennyson's imposition of Victorian meaning on Malory by sabotaging the lines of communication that make such meaning possible. It is the peculiar quality of *Balen*'s stubborn forwardness to switch off the magnetic power of causality and thereby dissociate events from one another—demote them, that is, from "outcomes" emplotted in a development to mere "incidents" or things that befall in a series. This sheer serial disposition of happenings neutralizes *a fortiori* the moral field in which we habitually read actions as good or evil, right or wrong.[7] While delivering and in some respects intensifying the essential pathos that Malory has made available, Swinburne

---

[6] Jerome McGann, *Swinburne: An Experiment in Criticism* (Chicago: University of Chicago Press, 1972), shows how the hero's standing as "a thoroughly English knight" (p.265), "pagan, sensuous, and innocent" (p.258) draws out for inspection the malignancy of Arthurian (Christian) corruption. Antony Harrison, *Swinburne's Medievalism: A Study in Victorian Love Poetry* (Baton Rouge and London: Louisiana State University Press, 1988), agrees that Balen is "a vital and morally pure primitive" (p.136). Margot Louis, *Swinburne and His Gods: The Roots and Growth of an Agnostic Poetry* (Montreal and Kingston: McGill-Queen's University Press, 1990), traces patterns of revisionist imagery that expose the blood-sacrifice of the Christian Eucharist as a "symbol of senseless violence" (p.44).

[7] Beverly Taylor and Elisabeth Brewer, *The Return of King Arthur: British and American Arthurian Literature since 1800* (Totowa: Barnes and Noble, 1983) 160, describe the poem, as one almost must, by a process of subtraction: "There is no attempt to suggest a specific symbolic meaning for the story: it simply presents the working out of the tragic pattern to its end. Unlike *Tristram of Lyonesse*, it involves no moral problems, and has no particular contemporary relevance."

refrains from enlarging on it, especially in the direction of significance. "The shadow as fast | Went with him that his word had cast" (5.6): meanings, as against the solidity of deeds, are but shadows cast by language. Much as Merlin's in-house interpretation goes up in smoke, so in this poem's peradventure world does everybody else's. Thus the spring-to-winter pattern that marks each canto's seasonal opening stanza foregrounds a repeating sequence rather than, what our previous chapter found typical of major poetic narrative from the 1870s and 1880s, a cumulative progress. Unfailingly beautiful, the Nature that swells Balen's pagan heart (witness his standard *Morte Darthur* epithet "le Sauvage") is an archetypal mother inextricably kind and wild at once. It is arresting to not with how much imaginative consistency the poet, in his sixtieth year, dedicated this poem to his aged mother after "the old wild tale, made new" had gained her blessing.

The supersession of old by new, mother by son, season by season, and indeed moment by moment is as unquestioned a narrative postulate here as in any comparatist progress epic of Swinburne's century. But for him this restless action is not improving or even benign, it just *is*:

> As thought from thought takes wing and flies,
> As month on month with sunlit eyes
> Tramples and triumphs in its rise,
> As wave smites wave to death and dies,
>   So chance on hurtling chance like steel
> Strikes, flashes, and is quenched, ere fear
> Can whisper hope, or hope can hear,
> If sorrow or joy be far or near
>   For time to hurt or heal.

(5.1)

Ever since the first great chorus of *Atalanta in Calydon* (1865), for Swinburne one thing has not just followed another but has hunted it down and preyed on it. In this general sense the frequency of weapons and blows in *Balen* might best be understood as meting out, on the unexempted site of the human body, the ceaseless pace of universal change that had always been this poet's theme. Two features stand out from the quoted passage as proper to this late poem in particular, one thematic and one stylistic. The first, regularly affirmed across the poem, is the belatedness of articulate conscious-ness. Even at the gut level of primal "fear" and "hope" where our steadfastly naïf hero lives, awareness so trails action as to incapacitate effectual planning (see also 1.10, 12; 4.9). The stimulus of occurrent change in its incessancy is a spark already "quenched" before synapse can fire or gland discharge, and long before the reacting mind can infer from what late-breaking news it does get whether to expect a pang next or a pleasure.

While the abrupt, punchy quality of the plot writes this thematic principle large, the versification gives private stylistic tutorials along the way. That the lag time between stimulus and response is almost ridiculously long is a lesson in which the prosody of Swinburne's merciless stanza drills the reader, marking out the slow-motion exfoliation of propositional sense by the scudding thump of alliteration and the metronome of scrupulous rhyme.[8] The resultant ambience is one that governs the entire poem: an apprehensiveness about "hurtling chance," or is it mischance, with which actual apprehension can never catch up. This oddly stylized narrative protraction distinguishes *The Tale of Balen* from the poet's swifter-footed work from younger days. It constitutes, indeed, an equivalent in pure form for the distancing reflection or conscious assessment in which standard Victorian narrative—prosed of course, but also blank-versed or coupleted—customarily clothes the naked recitation of action. The primary emotion the verse deals with is always simple; yet, when put through the stanzaic distillery that Swinburne built here on the plan of Tennyson's "Lady of Shalott," familiar emotion becomes an extract of itself, sometimes to excruciating effect:

> Then wept for woe the damsel bound
> With iron and with anguish round,
> That none to help her grief was found
> Or loose the inextricably inwound
>   Grim curse that girt her life with grief
> And made a burden of her breath,
> Harsh as the bitterness of death.
> Then spake the king as one that saith
>   Words bitterer even than brief.

(2.14)

The doubling of "iron" with "anguish" in line 2 looks like unkempt syllepsis until the rest of the stanza discloses, feelingly, the difference between wearing

---

[8] We need not concede the likeness that Taylor and Brewer propose between Swinburne's stanza and Chaucer's in "Sir Thopas" (*Return of King Arthur*, 161) in order to agree that the lines "create a trivialising, almost parodic effect." Exactly so: trivializing without triviality; almost parodic, but not quite.

shackles and inhabiting despair, or between raw experience and the experience of processing such experience. At line 3 the damsel perceives that none of the Round Table knights can release her from the sword she is grotesquely bound to. Then lines 4–7, under circumlocutory cover of restating that perception, elaborately unwind it into something else: the damsel's practical grievance slowly, irresistibly becomes an existential grief. And the verse deals the reader a share in this grief by making its inexorable expression a physical effort that empties the lungs and cramps the ribcage. Not only enjambing lines but proroguing the rhyme scheme's implicit assurance that four lines will do to frame a thought—or if not four then surely five; but alas not so!—Swinburne too makes "a burden" of the "breath." In the process, he reclaims the mental anguish of reflection on pain within an iron circle of sensed circumstance, a continuum made up of sore points, on which it is the business of his maddeningly patient stanza to dwell.

This dwelling becomes, for the duration of a reading, a *modus vivendi*. For the strangest thing about the poem is that its system of writing under constraint—afflicting the reader as it does with shortness of breath, apprehension-anxiety, and more—is in narrative proof not maddening but therapeutic. Habituation to its patterns of multiple recurrence works as a mode of stress management that, by eschewing apology for the random violence the poem flaunts, imagines it as a way of life, indeed the vision of a life that is led without apology. Swinburne explains little, and extenuates less. Yet he imposes an effectual order on the chaotic or corrupt brutality of his rendered world, by sheer dint of looking straight at it and not blinking. Our literary-critical shorthand for this effect is the term Homeric; and to say so is to propose that, while *The Tale of Balen* is not an epic poem, it accedes to an epic manner remarkable for its clarity.[9] Not in spite of archaism, but by courtesy of the wide berth archaism gives to cliché and to conventional ways of seeing that cliché conveys, each crisply framed moment is regarded long enough and hard enough that its internal changefulness transpires, through a motion slowed but never stilled. The poetry makes a pattern of little deaths whereby one moment slays another within the poetically performed stream, or wild Swinburnean drift, of consciousness. In view of momentous narrative technologies that were just emerging when the poem was published, the total effect might be likened to cinema's way of

---

[9] Edward Thomas, *Algernon Charles Swinburne: A Critical Study* (New York: Kennerley, 1912), remarks in *Balen*'s "naked narrative" that the hero and the stanzaic movement alike evince "constant nobility of temper" (pp.219, 223).

simulating action through microvariant projection of images nearly but not quite identical. The apt description that W. P. Ker found the same year in Lessing's *Laokoön* for the Icelandic sagas' power—"to see things as they become"—has application to Swinburne's stanzas too.[10]

As commentators on the poem have always observed, Swinburne avails himself too of the balladeer's more common privilege of compressing and accelerating the narrative so as to get to the point.[11] Yet then the point he gets to is usually the kind of suspension we have just been arrested by. It may involve a poetry of action or of passion, as respectively in the stanzaic instances given above; no less impressive is what Swinburne's achieved style can do with a poetry of statement. When Arthur sends Balen to succor "A knight that made most heavy cheer" (6.10), Balen on finding him asks what the problem may be and is told, with an unnarrated shake of the head:

> "This should do
> Great scathe to me, with nought for you
> Of help that hope might hearken to
> For boot that may not be."
>
> (6.13)

In other words: You don't want to know. A clutch of imminent disasters just overleaf will very soon show how right the cheerless knight is to put Balen off like this. But the authority of his disclaimer resides less in the event than in the words, at once plain and extraordinary, that Swinburne gives him to speak: well on the terse side of prolixity, yet so thoroughly explicit in laying out the case against intervention as to make Balen seem the more nobly generous for disregarding it and intervening anyhow. Like Balen's earlier tough nut of monosyllabic affirmation "Needs might not this but be" (3.9), the writing is both a skeletal x-ray of basic English and about as far from idiomatic as English can go without forfeiting intelligibility. Both the syntactic and the metrical contract are fulfilled to the letter, and to the brim, with an elixir too precious to spill.

It is a shame that when Swinburne sent an early copy of the poem to William Morris, his old associate's final illness had gone too far to permit a response. Morris would have been an ideal appraiser for its present-centered

---

[10] *Epic and Romance: Essays on Medieval Literature* (1896; rev. edn. 1908; rpt. New York: Dover, 1957) 237.

[11] Harrison, *Swinburne's Medievalism*, 139–41, discusses the balladic power of telescopic compression, quoting Swinburne himself on the genre's "tight and intense brevity."

cleanness of narrative line, and for the genius with which, having absorbed
from Malory's frequently ungainly prose certain radical values of English
syntactic tone and word color, the poem set them forth again with a glow as
of stained glass. When the two best epoists of the later century had been
undergraduates together, Swinburne had rehearsed in six narrative cantos of
Queen Yseult (1857, unfinished) their developing Pre-Raphaelite ideal:

> All was graven deep and fine,
> In and out, and line with line,
> That all men might see it shine.
>
> (1.262–64)[12]

From this clear early radiance of depiction the great Swinburne style had
departed, *inter alia* into the magniloquence of a *Tristram* epic that entirely
transmuted the material of his student years. At length, however, the
peculiar gravenness of *Balen* resumed the poet's foregone quest to lay
"line with line" into a pattern that, while it might never attract a large
number of readers, should endure for what it shiningly reveals about what
words set in order may tell.

"It is a noble work," said Swinburne in his last years on the appearance of
Alfred Noyes's *Drake: An English Epic* (1908), garnishing with a compliment
on the ocean imagery what amounted to no more than a declaration that the
poem's genre was *ipso facto* noble.[13] An epic *Drake* unmistakably was, and
cast in as classic a mold as the anglophone world had seen for a hundred
years. It is instructive to itemize the many ways in which a talented poet of
25 put so sustained an anachronism together out of elements scavenged from
the history this book has traced—which was, let us recall, for him as for his
only slightly younger contemporaries awaiting their Modernist turn, simply
the acknowledged working tradition of the genre. *Drake* began life as a trial
epic of the sort that had flourished around 1800, books 1–3 testing the
waters in 1906 with a promise of sequels to come if the first volume floated.
This promise he kept in the spirit if not the letter, as after a series of
installments in *Blackwood's* the book-buyer's next opportunity proved to

---

[12] *Complete Works of Algernon Charles Swinburne*, ed. Edmund Gosse and Thomas James Wise
(London: Heinemann, 1925), 1: 19.

[13] Quoted in Coulson Kernahan, *Six Famous Living Poets* (London: Butterworth, 1922) 185.
Gosse went for the same tepidly encouraging adjective: "It is noble stuff to read aloud, so vivid,
warm, and sonorous." Quoted in Herbert Parker, *Post-Victorian Poetry* (London: Dent, 1938) 300.

be the finished product two years down the line. An even split between six books of privateer wayfaring and then six centering on the national crisis posed by the Spanish Armada establishes a Virgilian layout (i.e. a condensed *Odyssey* and *Iliad* in one), which is further demarcated by an opening invocation to Mother England and, balanced at the standard pivot point of midway prophecy, a "vision of the great | Empire of Englishmen" (6.190). There is at least one lengthily elaborated simile per book; and, naturally enough given Noyes's theme, here as in the *Iliad* the second book boasts a catalogue of ships (2.37–38).

Beyond these classical features the poem sports a veritable *résumé* of the preceding century's accumulated epic modalities.[14] The historical theme of Protestant England's defense against a Continental aggressor makes *Drake*, like the Edwardian epics of Doughty and Hardy, a throwback to the national-security era of the Napoleonic wars (Chs. 2–5). As the lines just quoted remind us, however, in the long interim nationalism had overrun its former bounds to become rampant imperialism; and this ideology's unstable fusion of altruistic mission with self-interest required, in Noyes's handling at least, an apocalyptic rhetoric of all-subsuming historical purpose that recalls the epic extravaganzas of post-Regency years (Ch. 6). Absent an actual scriptural warrant, moreover, Drake's apocalyptic charter had to take form as an heroic intuition of the evolving tendency of events illegible yet sensed in advance. In expressing this secretly embodied knowledge through his hero's individual consciousness, Noyes drew on the imagery and technique ("one big swift impulse," 3.123) of mid-century Spasmodism (Ch. 9). He concurrently gave voice to the collective and civilizing dimension of Britain's manifest destiny, in the form of intercalary lyrics à la Palgrave, sometimes balladic (Ch. 8) but sometimes of a Tudor formal intricacy worthy Shelley or Browning if not the sweet Tudor Campion himself, lustily if improbably sung by the band of "skilled musicians" (2.49, 8.221, *et passim*) whom Noyes presciently stowed on board. And at the local level a steady diet of allusion makes it obvious that more monumental works from the English poetic canon were also levied for support. Keats, Milton, and

---

[14] The impression *Drake* gives of being a mummy from birth must be responsible for the entirety of its neglect by literary history. Parker, *Post-Victorian Poetry*, 83–84, was already speculating in the 1930s about the obstacle that Noyes's very popularity placed in the way of a serious critical reading, and he entertained some hope of a revival for the narrative poetry once the public tired of Noyes's lyrics.

Tennyson season the "Exordium" (6–13) at one end of the poem.[15] At the
other end in book 11 the imminent naval engagement presses into service
the legacy of Dryden's heroic quatrains from *Annus Mirabilis* (11.290), of
Milton's "Lycidas" (11.304), and, mocking the bulky swagger with which
the vast Armada galleons sailed to confusion, of Spenser's English spin on a
Continental form in the *Faerie Queene* stanza (11.291–93, also 12.324–33).

This enumeration of borrowings will give some impression of the indus-
try with which Noyes went about a work that, arising after ten years' epic
drought, invites an additional comparison with the early-Romantic tinker-
ing that we surveyed in Chapter 2. Should that impression of industry
prompt suspicion that *Drake* is a poem more robotic than alive, little
injustice is thereby done. The turning of every page releases a whiff of oil
from Noyes's purring, empire-builder machinery; there emerges a strong
family resemblance to such single-minded Romantic and Victorian achieve-
ments as Cumberland and Burges' *Exodiad* (Ch. 4) and Bulmer's *Messiah's
Kingdom* (Ch. 7). As with these earlier monuments of epic resolve, one feels
the hero's steadfastness of purpose to be in one sense a rehearsal, in another
sense an insurance policy, for that of his bard three hundred years later. And
yet, when the sleek contraption surges now and then into overdrive, it can
depart from the program and show a more interesting mind of its own.

For one thing, the programmer did not subscribe to the coarse jingoism
that the unflattering parallels just adduced, and indeed the very prospect of
An English Epic circa 1910, prepare one for. Noyes was a sometime pacifist
and, during the years shortly after *Drake* was published, a traveling lecturer
advocating the establishment of an international court of justice. As he saw
it—from a position that was consistent with Victorian progressivism and
would be confirmed in him at the outbreak of world war—Britain's historic
role as the champion of liberty subordinated national to global concerns.
Thus when Drake frees the slaves held in Spain's dominions, his exploit

---

[15] These same three names dominate a tetrad of inescapable influence cited by Noyes's contem-
porary John Cowper Powys in a 1956 preface to the brief epic that he had written in 1905 but left
unpublished for fifty years: *Lucifer: A Poem* (London: Macdonald, 1956). Swearing allegiance to
Wordsworth, Coleridge, and Shelley, and recalling that his mind at the time was full of Shakespeare,
Whitman, and Poe, Powys nevertheless rightly affirms that *Lucifer* "was composed solely, wholly,
and exclusively under the influence of Milton and Keats and Tennyson and Matthew Arnold" (p.12).
The allegorical register of Powys's ideas affiliates his poem with those we considered in Ch. 11 by
John Payne, William Watson, and Stephen Phillips—all of them more or less governed by the same
constellation under which Powys and Noyes were born, whose pervasion of epic manners at the
turn of the century furnishes us in advance with a reason for the preemptive archaism we shall find in
their tougher elders Doughty and Hardy.

prefigures a coming "Federation," "Whereby the weak are strengthened and the strong | Made stronger in the increasing good of all" (10.256). This quoted doublet repeats verbatim the utopian vision that has descended on Drake and his crew at 6.190; it lines up, too, with his abolition of aristocratic rank and priestly authority on shipboard, "old tyrannies" ceding place to the "brotherhood of man" among a crew who are every man-jack of them, did they but know the truth mystically vouchsafed to Francis Drake alone at the Straits of Magellan, "kings, | And sons of Vikings, exiled from your throne" (4.141–42).[16]

Vikings belong in this fraternity; Spaniards do not. Or if as Europeans the Spaniards actually do have a place in the world's throneroom, then at any rate Amerindians need not apply. Kings and sons are in, queens and daughters out—Elizabeth I's cameo appearance in books 1 and 7 crowning her, this umpteenth time in England's imaginative history, the exception that proves the gender rule. We shall return presently to what the issues of race and sex reveal about Noyes's Drake. Note first, though, how neatly the limits on membership in the poem's "brotherhood of man" match those that circumscribed the franchise of the fully civilized in Noyes's own nation and time; and see by what ruthless justice this epic, like other didactic or propagandistic epics we have met, is shackled to its immediate moment most obviously at the moment it reaches for the universally timeless. The weapon with which the poet lames his own work is the same that we always find biting the hand that fails to wield it: the two-edged blade of unmastered convention. Planning a flattering compliment, such as epic poets use, to both an age he admired and a genre he coveted, Noyes heaped in one pan of the scale all the values he held dear as a youthful, idealistic, and above all conventional heir to Victoria's empire. Then, in fitting homage to that legacy, he placed into the other pan every conventional trophy he could cull from the traditions of what was still, for his generation, the highest literary kind.

If the resulting structure stood for a day, making Noyes's name and putting him in the running for Poet Laureate on Alfred Austin's death in 1913, that was because its balance of theme with form was indeed competently precision-engineered. But the compliment that Noyes as an epoist had planned for the ages hardly stood for a decade, before falling apart into what inevitably strikes us about it today: received ideas on one hand, verbal

---

[16] At a level sufficiently abstract this universalizing progressivism seems the political arm of the body of evolutionary thought in Noyes, as discussed in Lionel Stevenson, *Darwin Among the Poets* (1932; rpt. New York: Russell and Russell, 1963) 309–16.

clichés on the other. The former lacked the quantum of novelty that might
have cracked the latter's Tennysonian polish. And Noyes never grew so
curious about his medium as to force it the way Tennyson had actually
done—the way we have just seen Swinburne do in the style-driven narra-
tive heuristics of *The Tale of Balen*—into new modes of perception gener-
ating new matter. It sufficed for Noyes that a page should sound, from a
comfortable distance, as though it belonged in a heroic poem. His radical,
epicidal failing was to confuse such fidelity to the norm with that strain
towards clarification which was the genuine epic project of his time.

What does transpire in *Drake*, beyond the poet's short-lived expedient of
dressing up one sort of convention in another, is a set of internal contra-
dictions that were specific to the Edwardian world-view. Noyes did not
confront these contradictions, and he may not even have recognized them.
Having nevertheless found their way into the epic like so much unclaimed
luggage, they force themselves on our attention now in consequence of
certain freaks of the plot. As we saw already, that plot breaks neatly in half:
during books 1–6 a sequence of challenges elevate the sea dog Francis
Drake, in the course of a global circumnavigation, from rough and ready
captaincy into visionary world-historical leadership; books 7–12 then re-
sume an English focus to narrate the intrigues and stategics surrounding the
1588 defeat of the Armada, a landmark of national glory whose global
importance remains the poet's governing frame of understanding. But,
within this clear and predictable frame, ungoverned forces are at play that
the poet apparently did not understand, yet that he could not help obscurely
owning, if only because their strength kept moving his imagination. These
are predominantly, during the first half of the poem, the force of racial
dominion; during the second, the force of sexual attraction. Both are forces
of desire that attend the poem's overt agenda like shadows to haunt the
articulation of its ideology.[17]

For the first three books Drake's most invested personal relationship—
indeed, the only personal relationship of any complexity to emerge within
the whole poem—is with Thomas Doughty, a courtier whom the intriguer
Burleigh has suborned to sabotage Drake's commission from the Queen.
Smitten with Doughty's elegant urbanity, Drake opens his heart to the

---

[17] Stan Smith, one of the few readers who have shown a flicker of interest in what Noyes may
have been thinking, discerns in the patriotic poems marks of "doubt" and "insecurity": entry on
Noyes in Smith's edited reference work *20th-Century Poetry* (London and Basingstoke: Macmillan,
1983) 341.

insinuating spy during long shipboard conversations, and even turns a blind eye when Doughty's greedy plunder and incitement to mutiny endanger Drake's own brother. This willed blindness has the effect of disclosing (in a passage indebted to Wordsworth's *Recluse* "Prospectus") that what the heroic privateer is actually questing for is freedom itself: not gold, prestige, or even any "Earthly Paradise, Island of the Saints, | Cathay, or Zipangu, or Hy Brasil," but rather "the new Atlantis of my soul," a self-realization dimly implying "That Vision without which, the wise king said, | A people perishes" (2.82–83). A slightly embarrassing anachronism entailed by the ambition of Noyes's project obliges him here to finesse a reconciliation between the putative simplicity of his antique genre with the progressive thrust of his ideology. The High Romantic ideal of liberty that Drake exalts is the historical correlate of a modernity to which a hero cut to Noyes's nostalgically folksy epic pattern should not be privy. Accordingly the poet makes out of Thomas Doughty a scapegoat for metropolitan sophistication as such. Drake's mounting suspicion, repudiation, and final execution of his bosom's secret sharer form a narrative bid to rescue an anachronistic twentieth-century liberty from its actually enabling conditions.

This is why Drake's innocent dream—freedom for free, as it were—must give way in the crucial book 3 to sterner stuff and confront the darker realities it has sublimated. Anchoring at landfall in a New World harbor, Drake departs alone to weigh unpurged doubts about his friend during a hike through the rain forest. Amid sublime thunderstorms he stumbles on a mastodon's skeleton to discover, evidently by way of *In Memoriam* and *The Voyage of the "Beagle,"*

> faith in that great Harmony which resolves
> Our discords, faith through all the ruthless laws
> Of nature in their lovely pitilessness,
> Faith in that Love which outwardly must wear,
> Through all the sorrows of eternal change,
> The splendour of the indifference of God.

(3.106)

Splendid, superhuman indifference is exactly what Drake must summon in himself once he learns, on the next page, that Doughty has treacherously set sail with the mutinied crew of *The Golden Hynde*. The speed with which Drake arrests his beloved friend; the equanimity with which he executes justice on him in person at sunset, on the very spot where his precursor

Magellan hanged mutineers decades before; the aplomb with which he learns
of his own brother's death along the way—all these betoken Drake's con-
version from ordinary human being to "a prophet's vision" that reads, not
New World wonders any more, but "A world of hieroglyphs and sacred
signs" (3.118). From this point forward Drake becomes a hero in the Southey
tradition of a century past: "an iron statue still | As death" (3.110), a "Titan
bronze in grandeur" (3.126): a man who is neither ancient nor modern but
lifted out of time altogether, and whose will is expressed in the long gaze
he sends through occurrences towards meanings. With unique access to
the rolling swell of history on which breaking events are so much foam,
Drake henceforth is always a preemptive jump ahead of the people around
him. He repeatedly galvanizes his associates into action "ere they knew |
What power impelled them" (5.167) because that power "as of a wind"
(3.110, 8.221) is no mere tar's weather eye but a prophet's grasp of the
zeitgeist bringing on utopian brotherhood, full speed ahead.

Yet this sanguine epic vantage is purchased at sanguinary personal cost: the
sacred cause of brotherhood claims first Drake's own brother, then his only
intimate. The narrative predication of book 3 suggests a Virgilian logic of
human sacrifice, which civilized Noyes wants no part of but which his poem
keeps failing to forget about.[18] Thus the next book opens with a Miltonic
invocation to primal dawn, only to rewind thence to Drake's insomniac
vision, the night before, of a horribly primal humanity consummating
sacrificial rites in fiery "cannibal feast" along the coast (4.131). That the
perpetrators are Patagonian "giants" and "Gorgons" expressing a "Titanic"
earthly lust (4.130) may arouse in the reader a disquieting memory of the
"Titan bronze" dimensions Drake has assumed only a few pages ago. And a
reader who thus glimpses the draconic in Drake will be prepared to see
how unsteadily the poem's endorsement of heroic value reposes on bases it
aspires to disown. Whether the flicker of parallel wording is witting or not, it
draws out a lurid implication of the entire narrative juxtaposition: Drake's
promotion to superhuman standing entails an act of hierarchic imagination
that requires a complementary demotion of others—exaggerated here as the
demonization of others in racially subhuman terms.

---

[18] A long century's scholarly concern to disentangle the great epic tradition from brute
admixtures of tribal sacrificialism culminated just as Noyes was publishing *Drake*. See Gilbert
Murray, *The Rise of the Greek Epic* (Oxford: Clarendon Press, 1907) 12–16, 116–35. Citing Frazer
and recapitulating Gibbon, Murray found the expurgation of sacrifice from the story of Greek
poetry an easy matter; not so Noyes with the story of English Drake.

Something of the kind happens again at the ideological pivot point in book 6. There the dream cited above about "the increasing good of all" under a federated "Empire of Englishmen" arises directly from a first encounter between the English and "grave-eyed Indians" under the white cliffs of San Francisco Bay (6.189–91). The aborigines commence by worshiping "the strange white-faced newcomers | As gods"; then, hastily adjusting to assurances that "even Drake was but a man," they settle for second best, crown Drake "King of New Albion," and implore him to "stay | And rule them." It is this balky, bet-calling refusal on the Indians' part to take equality for an answer that suddenly precipitates Drake's epic ideal of "Empire that should liberate the world," abolish war, and make "all oppression cease." Earlier an uncanny description of galleon booty has discerned, while gloating over its plundered Inca jewelry, "The freedom of all slaves in every chain" (5.176). A similar contradiction is striking here between high-minded epic ideal and crude episodic reality. As if to diagram the verticals of an oppression that, far from ceasing, has only just begun, the flat insistence of the prostrated "savages" that their betters are to retain the upper hand subjects to a long-range, almost certainly unplanned irony the transcendentalizing egalitarianism of Noyes's surrogate settlers-in-waiting and imperialists-to-be.

The nascent ideology of empire dawns, moreover, not only on Drake this time but on all the crew, flashing "A moment round them, on that lonely shore." Earlier Drake's vision was a private matter, or one shared at most via the mystic sympathies of genius with his contemporaries Galileo and Shakespeare (4.136). Now, though, it is a collective gift imparted to every Englishman. To carry it home becomes the business of the second half of the epic, which is discharged by sure poetic tact through figures of marriage and domesticity. The sexualized union of an English people has been in the air ever since Drake, infatuated with his sovereign at a "witchingly" private audience (1.29), first took her Cleopatran perfumes on board the commissioned *Golden Hynde* (2.40) and heard with his crew "a *Mermaid* roundelay" in which "Queen Venus" quits Adonis and the Aegean to become, of all things, a nursing English mother (2.52–55). Queen Bess remaining well beyond even a hero's ambition, Noyes drafts a wholesome namesake in the plot line that involves Drake's fiancée "sweet Bess of Sydenham" (4.152). Given her man's long absence, compounded by false report of his death, Bess consents to marry another; but the imperiled trothplight is miraculously preserved when, on the day of her impending marriage, a stray cannonball ploughs up the churchyard and recalls her to her pledge:

"'Twas he that sent that message" (6.195). As in the *Jane Eyre* incident to which this one is indebted, a severe bend in the canons of probability discloses a deeper narrative reason: whether or not love makes the world go round, the phallic cannon shot coincides to the minute with Drake's breasting the Pacific homeward on the wings of the episode immediately preceding it, the California dreaming we just considered from book 6.

That a newly collective English purpose should reverberate around the world is the meaning of a set of intrigues, part sexual part political, occupying books 7–10. First the beleaguered Queen, having promised Drake's head to the Spaniards, breaks that bad promise and, on his triumphant return, throws princely caution to the winds of change that are sweeping an island people into unity. Book 8 then performs a domestic repetition of this homeland scenario, when Drake rescues his sweetheart from house arrest and elopes by sea. The apparently bland chastity of their union must be imagined inversely from the exceptional violence of Spanish Main atrocity and reprisal in the ninth book and then, in the tenth, the all-trumping seductiveness of that prize of prizes India, a "wild unwhispered wealth" whose secrets "splashed London wharves | With coloured dreams" (10.272). Tennyson himself might have envied the way Noyes's imputed fantasy of "crimson wreckage thro' the silvery palms" focuses conquest and finance with a honeymooner's lavish indulgence. All this marital matter affords no more purchase on inner reflection or psychological nuance in *Drake* than it did in Camoens' *Lusiads*, a seafaring epic from the sixteenth century that taught Noyes a thing or two about smelting erotic values in the crucible of the colonial. Sexual desire becomes an emblem for imperial union, as personal motives of every sort must do for the superhero Noyes has made of Drake since book 3—patriotic motives included, as these give way before the poet's commitment to a world-federalist horizon.

It is in this enlarged spirit of long views that during book 10 those questions of national interest which have yet to be resolved—always reserving for the last two books a modicum of suspense about the Armada's demolition—are perceived most nearly by those who have learned to look furthest abroad. First the meddler Burleigh, grasping at last that Drake is the future, embraces the "New-born" principle that a Britannia ruling the waves in "ocean sovereignty" (10.257, also 11.306) will always have the edge on such mere army power as the troop-encumbered Armada represents. Next, when the delicate matter arises of English Catholics' divided loyalties, Walsingham affirms their patriotism by reference to "another

Rome" than the Pope's, the visionary capital of an ecumenical Christianity that will foster "the new flower | Of faiths we know not yet" (10.262–63). Burleigh's technological revolution and Walsingham's sectarian reformation share a circuitry of desire that must sweep out upon the world before homing back in on the eroticized figurehead Elizabeth: "O Madam, | The heart of England now is all on fire! | We are one people, as we never have been" spells out in modern terms the same political meaning that is feudally implied in "Madam, you are beloved" (10.264). And it is this common circuitry of desire that sponsors the else bizarre fusion of terms in Drake's summative prophecy of otherworldly "Argosies | Of unknown glory" setting sail for England from "Great gleaming wharves i' the perfect City of God" (10.265): an image whose bivalent sexual charge of prow and quay renders the reciprocal penetration and reception that a seaborne commercial empire will prosper by. The arranged marriage of people with sovereign that breeds Noyes's English nationalism is at the same time exogamous and internationalist.

By our contemporary lights this prospect of national permeability is not bad as historical insight into the Tudor situation. Noyes owed it, though, to his quite different Edwardian situation, at a late if not closing chapter of the drama of colonial, then imperial dominance that his country had enacted for three centuries. His oceanic epic was on course for Oceana, to use J. A. Froude's name for the worldwide Greater Britain of anglophone states whose commonwealth, Froude had recognized in an 1886 book, held the key at once to peace for the world and to preeminence for the United Kingdom.[19] So *An English Epic* might speak to Edwardian England because the tongue it spoke formed the common heritage of burgeoning millions not resident in the British Isles but still embedded in the literary traditions on which the poem assiduously drew.[20] Thus the American edition (1909)

---

[19] *Oceana, or England and her Colonies* (London: Longmans, 1886). The Oxford lectures of 1893–94 that Froude published as *English Seamen in the Sixteenth Century* (New York: Scribner, 1895) appears to have been Noyes's chief source for numerous plot details, as well as for the conviction of Drake's significance in a world history where the defeat of the Armada "was to decide the future of Europe" (p.212; the same thesis had crowned his *History of England* in 1870). Having noted Drake's role as arch-villain in Lope de Vega's epic *La Dragontea*, Froude proceeds to a prophetic revenge by envisioning in exploits such as Drake's "the subject of a great English national epic as grand as the 'Odyssey' " (pp.75–76). Froude, incidentally, furnished C. R. Low with the epigraph to the first of his fleet of 1890s epics.

[20] Considerations of anglophone dominion belong with those adduced by Stephanie L. Barczewski in describing the supervention of ethnic-linguistic "Englishness" on political-national "Britishness" by the turn of the twentieth century: *Myth and National Identity in Nineteenth-Century Britain: The Legends of King Arthur and Robin Hood* (Oxford and New York: Oxford University Press, 2000) 6–7.

was prefaced by a purpose-written lyric urging "England, my mother" and "America, my sweetheart" to embrace each other and "federate the world," in recognition that the history of Drake—and of *Drake*—is their joint possession: "Hers and yours the story." The in-laws' kiss under a burgeoning "bunch of English may" betokens, not an inbred Anglo-Saxon gene pool, but what the unexplicated name *Mayflower* manifestly represents: the cultural togetherness, through a common language, of "Two souls whose prayer is one."[21]

How much hope Noyes vested in the King's English will appear in the quality of passages quoted incidentally already; so will the destiny awaiting that hope. Grand as can be, yet nimble enough to perform whatever dilation or shortcut the poet may require, the pentameter of *Drake* rolls forth an extended demonstration of the resources that the nineteenth century's standard epic medium offered even to an upper-middling talent like Noyes's. In diction, too, the poem's mixture of Latin with Saxon, everyday with inkhorn vocabulary, attests the wealth of the English language as it was being inventoried by the age's great lexicographers circa 1900. Here was a workshop where the art of poetry might do quite well for itself, and where a Swinburne might without gross perjury compliment images of the sea that, if they do by sheer iteration decline into bombast, are indeed often individually striking in their own right. Still and all, as we began by conceding, *Drake* is a work that scarcely lives, and this is not because Noyes failed to use the traditional tools that lay to hand, but because he failed to use them in any but traditional ways. The street, the daily paper and music hall, the emporia and outposts where trade meant change, in language as in commodities and travelers, were flooding English with new words— and, more important to poetry, alternative patterns of rhythm and syntax— that Noyes's fatally constricted generic decorum kept out of his poem. Handling twentieth-century English with full epic responsibility was a task left for more alert and open-minded practitioners, whose postwar epics would be cried up as shocking because their authors, unlike the complaisant Noyes, recognized what freshness of total imagination the genre exacted.

---

[21] Epicizing imperialist postnationalism had bowed to this yoke before. Compare the prefatory summons that W. C. Bennett issued, *c*.1880 in his undated *Contributions to a Ballad History of England* (London: Chatto and Windus), to "the English poets of our time—and in that word English I include rejoicingly those of he mighty States beyond the Atlantic" (p.xi). Quoted in Simon Dentith, *Epic and Empire in Nineteenth-Century Britain* (Cambridge: Cambridge University Press, 2006) 139.

Refreshment of the epic medium did not have to wait on the heteroglot engagement with contemporaneity that arose with a newly metropolitan anglophone vanguard around 1920. An alternate route, fraught with different risks, led to generic renewal by way of the obsolete, or in truth the archaic. We have seen Swinburne's *Tale of Balen* pointing this old high road out, and Hardy's *Dynasts* will show what authority might be drawn along it by a lexicon that was antique and antic in equal measure. But the epoch's premier champion of the forgotten greets us in Charles M. Doughty—that up-to-date middle initial the first our many epic title-pages can boast—who with *The Dawn in Britain* (6 vols., 1906) contrived in the extremity of verse an heroic vehicle that left in the dust even the defiantly retrograde prose style of his 1888 classic *Travels in Arabia Deserta*. Whether Doughty's poetic in *The Dawn in Britain* is (like his subject matter) ancient history, or whether its uncompromising integrity earns a place of honor in the avant garde, is a question that polarizes the slender, impassioned tradition of critical response to the poem. Even from our vantage here in the bunker of literary history, not many assignments are harder than reading Doughty's twenty-four long, dense books, in which scores of mainly unknown persons stalk a now inspired, now sheerly dogged chronicle of the half-millennium between the Gaulish sack of Rome and the twofold extension of Roman hegemony through the conquest of Britain and the destruction of the Jerusalem temple. Not many assignments are harder; but one of them is imagining a reader today who, in a good-faith effort to compass that large tract, is anything but helplessly swung between the poles of admiration and despair.

First—inescapably and incessantly—the reader of this full-blown national epic has to grapple with its extraordinary retrofit of the English language. Doughty brooded over the style of *The Dawn in Britain* with a trained philologist's acumen and a patriot wanderer's tenderness, declaring in an afterword that "it is the prerogative of every lover of his Country, to use the instrument of his thought, which is the Mother-tongue, with propriety and distinction; to keep that reverently clean and bright, which lies at the root of his mental life, and so, by extension, of the life of the Community" (6.243).[22] "Propriety" here meant a radical return to the golden diction of

---

[22] Doughty's lifelong commitment to the project of linguistic renovation cannot be sufficiently emphasized. He wrote to the Syndics at Cambridge, on submitting the manuscript in 1905: "I early felt (even whilst an under-graduate) after learning some of the low German tongues and reading in the great authors of the Renaissance, that my work in life would be, to help towards a better common knowledge and use of the Mother Tongue. I began to write down and develop The Utmost Isle, a patriotic work (and wherein Roman, Celtic, and German *Origines* are treated of);

the already antiquarian Spenser, "distinction" a curious but consistently maintained recurrence to the elder sense of surviving words that since 1600 had been scalped and blurred as they shot the modern rapids of a new metaphysics and metaphorics. The strict faith Doughty kept with epic's old philological mission built, in a sense, on what Morris had done with diction in verse and also prose; but with Doughty we have moved on from a tasting to a fix.[23] While completely unfamiliar terms are rare in *The Dawn*, it abounds in ancestral ones, often half-estranged by compaction: *seld* for *seldom*, *bove* for *above*, *minish* (nice kiss of the clippers) for *diminish*.

This lexical squeeze would be a comparatively simple matter had Doughty not at the same time flexed such syntactic muscle as greets us on opening, say, to the arrival in book 14 of Claudius' legionaries in the mouth of the Thames:

> At cockcrow, waking, Claudius
> Commands, by trumpet, That disbark his soldiers.
>   Who first, to land, descend, trench on that shore,
> Then naval camp, foursquare. The immense elephants,
> Uneasy was, upon that oozy strand,
> Expose.

The deranged parsimony of this syntax is staggering, and it never lets up for long. As if to prove that English is half Latin and half German, Doughty folds pronominal subjects into their verbs, and places the latter anywhere he likes. In the same spirit he skimps on prepositions (along with their partner in modern degeneracy the infinitive marker *to*), relative pronouns,

and which I had had in my mind since the year '65. . . . Where is that intimate knowledge of language, without which there can be only deciduous handywork? Is not ποίησις an architecture of elect national words and eternal human thoughts; raised upon a well devised foundation, and builded of none but diligently found, chosen, and wrought, goodly stones, all truly laid;—built up into a temple?" Again he told Richard Garnett three years later, apropos of complaints about the poem's verbal difficulty, "what we really want is to my mind not decadence, but in all things and not least in letters a patriotic *renaissance*": quoted in D. G. Hogarth, *The Life of Charles M. Doughty* (Garden City: Doubleday, 1929) 144, 163.

[23] Understandably this is the accomplishment that captures the notice of readers who are poets, albeit to divergent effect. Hugh MacDiarmid accounts Doughty's "revival of obsolete words" less important than "his scrutiny of known words, and his close fitting of word to sense": "Charles Doughty and the Need for Heroic Poetry" (1936), in *Selected Essays*, ed. Duncan Glen (Berkeley and Los Angeles: University of California Press, 1970) 85. Laura (Riding) Jackson, "The 'Right English' of Charles M. Doughty," *University of Toronto Quarterly* 46 (1977), offers a remarkable cautionary counterclaim: many of the words "cannot but be read wrongly when read as words of known meaning" (p.313). Both poets, however, are minding the same paradox: Doughty's fixation on the obsolete requires steady renewal of the reader's verbal attention.

subordinate conjunctions, the initial expletives *There* and *It*, even the definite and indefinite article. Cashiering these redundancies, Doughty further heightens the verbal density by hiring blunt participial and absolute constructions to do the work of grammatical subordination at cut rate. To compare the crystal-lattice classicism of W. S. Landor, another artisan of archaizing compression (chapter 2), is to see how little Doughty feared ungainliness in the skinflint pursuit of raw clarity.[24]

The purpose of installing so spartan a philological regimen was to recall English to its pure beginnings as a tongue not analytically excrescent but synthetically inflected, and thus more hospitable than modern English to phrasal inversion and general unorthodoxy in verbal sequence.[25] The overall effect is a sustained shorthand compression of sense such as the laboring reader might expect to find in newspaper headlines, lecture notes, maybe a third-year Latin trot, but surely not an epic poem twice the size of *Paradise Lost*. The first *TLS* reviewer unerringly set one pertinent context by observing of *The Dawn in Britain* that it "might almost be taken for a publication of the Early English Text Society."[26] We for our part might rather look to Victorian antecedents. Born into Swinburne's generation and Hardy's in 1843, a much older man than his Edwardian congener Noyes, Doughty produced such an epic as might have come from Gerard Manley Hopkins in purgatory, from Alfred Jingle were Mr. Pickwick never to get a word in edgewise, or from Browning's Caliban, nay Browning himself in the infamous *Agamemnon* he translated verbatim from Aeschylus of 1877 or—to establish in a word the standard of obscurity that Doughty meets—in the telegraphic chronicle that was *Sordello* (Ch. 7).

All this conceded, nobody can deny that Doughty's scarification of ordinary English does transfuse strange power into his narrative. It is a power, in the first instance, of immediacy in rendering. That Doughty set

---

[24] Another earnest Latinizer of English was Landor's contemporary Wordsworth when he turned to translate the *Aeneid* in the 1820s: see Bruce E. Graver, "Wordsworth and the Language of Epic: The Translation of the *Aeneid*," *Studies in Philology* 83 (1986) 261–85. But Doughty pressed the language so much harder than either Romantic had done that for comparable effects we must turn to mock-epic performances like Clough's in *Amours de Voyage* or Browning's in the lawyer monologues from *The Ring and the Book*. The poets' campaign to restart English by restoring it to a pre-Restoration state goes back through Hunt and the Cockneys to *Lyrical Ballads* and the Lakers on poetic diction: see Richard M. Turley, *The Politics of Language in Romantic Literature* (Houndmills: Palgrave, 2002) 4–8.

[25] On syntactic effects see John Heath-Stubbs, *The Darkling Plain* (London: Eyre & Spottiswoode, 1950) 188–89, 198;, John Holloway, "Poetry and Plain Language: The Verse of C. M. Doughty," *Essays in Criticism* 4 (1954) 58–70.

[26] Review of the first two volumes, *Times Literary Supplement* for 20 April 1906, 140.

a premium on clarity and directness emerges in his systematic exploitation of epic's privilege to zoom from past into present tense, and in his fondness for the attention-bossing "Lo!" and for deictic pronouns showing just where to look at any given moment. The author of *Arabia Deserta* had not abandoned his concern to make the British reader behold an alien way of life in full ethnographic detail, nor did it now matter very much that the alien way of life in question was that of the British reader's own cultural forebears. Equally essential to this immediacy in rendering were the prosodic resources of the decasyllabic line. Where Noyes in *Drake* rehearses the enjambed pentameter of Milton as lately brought to its Tennysonian crest, Doughty writes like Spenser by the line, which he likes to end-stop and, as often as not, to score for the reader's benefit by a highly idiosyncratic sprinkling of rhetorical punctuation. His commas, in particular, offer a sort of sublinear scansion guide.[27] Here, picked out at random, is a passage that ushers the Italic and Gaulish deities into facing bleachers to watch Brennus win a last battle at Arminium after sacking Rome:

> Descended, on an head of Appenine,
> To view this mortal strife, were the land's gods.
> Is sacred hill, which guirlands, like a grove,
> Much smelling juniper and sweet eglantine.
> Are gods, with them, of Gauls: but sit, with shields,
> Gods over against gods, apart, and arms.

(5.7)

Line 1 could be Tennyson's for word harmony and sophistication of rhythm. But crunchy ellipsis in lines 3 and 5 affixes Doughty's stamp, as does the olfactory smack of the image in line 4. And the last two lines are essential Doughty in their motion, pacing out foot by foot the division of divine spectators into opposite camps, neutrally enough to detect, within that equivalence, the antagonistic energies that a godly etiquette brings into line (like the prosody) at the close. Later on, when the druid nun Esla— Doughty's answer to Nausikaa in the *Odyssey*—has an idyllic moment all

---

[27] Doughty wrote to his publisher, "For the punctuation, I have found out a system which is invariable, and I believe, correct (I have attentively used it)": quoted in Hogarth, *Life of Doughty*, 146. Samuel C. Chew, "The Poetry of Charles Montague Doughty," *North American Review* 222 (1925), objects that the punctuation "is not grammatical or syntactical but rhythmical and elocutionary, following a system not very logically worked out" (p.293), but still appreciates a thematically apt grandeur in "the stately monotony of the blank verse, like the tread of unnumbered hosts" (pp.293–94).

to herself, so does the verse: "So skips, from stone, on her white feet, to stone" (9.18). Strongly punctuated iambs on either side let the girl's feet twinkle with a mind of their own in the balance-finding grace that jumps between one "stone" and the next: rewrite the line "from stone to stone," and the magic is gone. In the afterword, and with express application to his own toilsome poetic, Doughty cites the Pythagorean cultic warning "NO ONE WHO IS IGNORANT OF THE PROPERTIES OF NUMBERS, MAY ENTER HERE" (6.243). If this overstates the case, it is still true that few who enter the versed world of Doughty's alter-English without attending to the poetic numbers are likely to stay for long.

The plan and reach of *The Dawn in Britain* have decided limits, which we shall return to consider. But there is not much Doughty tries to say with his pentameters that he can't say. And there is surprisingly little that he won't say: maiden Esla and her prince Cloten going naked to bed on a first beach date that blends carnal knowledge with pagan innocence (book 9), the emperor Claudius bepissing himself in drunken fear at a late-night Irish onslaught (book 16), Herfryd's swampside death in childbirth, under "unhelpful stars," after war has frozen her hearth and intimidated her community into abandoning her (21.32). These are matters such as earlier epoists have handled only with indirection if at all—or with an irony like Byron's or Pope's, totally alien to Doughty's earnest sensibility. When in book 1 the mother of two feuding kings, come from afar to effect their reconciliation, slips into a swift river and nearly drowns, the account of her rescue by the royal sons does not flinch at showing how "She vomiting, dismaied, much water, faints" (1.35). Recalling that in Spenser *dismay* means *swoon* helps us glimpse, through the grossness of digestive detail and flabbergasting clumsiness of syntax, a clinical discrimination between levels of consciousness that wards sentimentality well away.

In fact the poem nearly always keeps orderly faith with human acts of perception and cognition in their infinite variety. The early Christians' passage up the Asia Minor coast en route to Britain brings to mind how a supernatural visitant appeared once to Alexander the Great, in order to dissuade him from plundering a "certain antique temple" of the Jews. Doughty handles this anecdote with perceptual subtlety:

> Of these things, mused the young king, on his bed,
> Till time he weary was: so drew his lamp,
> And sate him up, of Homer's lays, to read.

> But lifting Alexander, soon, his eyes,
> Beheld, beside him, standing, some old man,
> Venerable of aspect.

(6.100)

Who this messenger is matters less than how the text spaces and times the young king's apprehension of him, scrolling up from Homer into a recognition that before him stands not just any old man but a somebody (the Latinate last line upholding a dignitary train). Or admire the cognitive order of another brief incident concerning a detachment of reconnoitering German "Almains" who have overslept:

> Now those, which passed in hazardry have and feast,
> (Casting, for dice, the huckle-bones of sheep,
> Which yester they had reaved, and sith did eat,)
> Much night; being risen tardy, when the sun
> Already soars, whilst in cold-running stream,
> Some wash them; lifting night-mist from the plain,
> Their watch espy some riding of armed Gauls.

(1.22)

Yesterday's excellent huckle-bones are not more present to the reader than is today's cotton-mouthed absence of mind following a little too "Much night." The passage succeeds because Doughty's synthetic syntax lets him fit modular units into a tightly packed sequence that vividly realizes, and in something like real time, what is dawning on the groggy Almains themselves.

The stepwise tracking within these passages approximates the narrative relief for which Homer's similes are famous, yet it oddly does so without swerving a hair from the march of plot events. Indeed, the scarcity of extended similes in this long poem serves to indicate how relentlessly Doughty clove to his literal chronicling. At the massing of Roman power before the climactic battle of Camulodunum, we can practically watch him glimpse in the first line below a fine chance to take off on an epic simile, only to renounce it at once in the second:

> Be seen the great towered elephants; that, like some
> Swart rocks, do stand in glittering waves of bronze;
> Their long snout-hands to sling, and wide lap-ears
> To flag, impatient of their immense force.

(16.184)

Those elephants are not, as they might have been, *like* coastal rocks washed in some Aegean sunlight by brazen ocean waves; they are elephants, they are huge, they are alive, and they really "do stand," ranked in the verse. Nor are they, as they easily could have been in the mind's prophetic eye, modern tanks. The aggravation of mind with which Doughty followed the Boer War while composing *The Dawn in Britain* must have acquainted him with trench tactics that made the development of all-terrain armored vehicles (to be launched by the British in 1915) only a matter of time. A Miltonic poet— Noyes, let us suppose—would have pursued that hazardously enjambed "like some . . . " into an inventive occasion many lines long and bright with contemporary application. This privilege of clairvoyance Doughty forgoes, characteristically, in favor of the versed spondaic bulk of "Swart rocks," which in combination with "snout-hands" and "lap-ears" sacrifices the presentist long view of military history to his duty as a reporter on distant things, which is the duty of rendering sheerly present their "immense force." Saying it with monosyllables lets the poet's elephants loom big as tanks, precisely by leaving them large as life but no larger. One imagines Homer nodding, and this time with approval.[28]

Also Homeric is the narrative equivalent of generalization that arises when Doughty shifts focus from the particular to the panoramic:

> Silent, from spray,
> The small fowl flits, to covert; and all beasts
> Go lean and weary, in the empty frost.

> (10.89)

A northern winter's onset, sharp in its novelty to the immigrant Syrian Christians, opens out from the validating Chaucerian detail of that "small fowl" to acknowledge a larger condition no body can avoid; and to this expansion of vista the limping gait of the verse gives aural support. One final example sums all, in the way it yokes jaw-dropping awkwardness to sur- prising grace:

> All light, to sup, now eve, then, in that place.
> Sith Main and Island Gauls sleep round their fires.

> (1.21)

[28] Barker Fairley, *Charles M. Doughty: A Critical Study* (New York: Oxford University Press, 1927), remarks that Doughty's images, as in "the old hieroglyphic languages," "have no strictly verbal allusiveness, no secondary or metaphorical life" (pp. 145–46). At best the effect is what Anne Treneer calls a diction of "primordial freshness": *Charles M. Doughty: A Study of his Prose and Verse* (London: Cape, 1935) 177.

Line one, comma-chopped in the poet's most annoying manner, actually puts that annoyance to work as a rendition of the diverse chores of making camp.[29] Then the next line makes a couplet out of these humble distractions, blanketing the troops' energy up under a universal human need, and in a single breath.

The variety of Doughty's peculiar skill in immediate rendition has seemed worth illustrating at some length, both as the happiest of advertisements for his fierce diction, syntax, and blank verse and also as the kindest way of framing his undeniable limits as an epic maker. For *The Dawn in Britain* is a compulsively episodic poem, whose stunned focus on whatever the chronicle has to offer, right here and just now, his narrative contrivances do lots to abet and very little to resist. The word *sith*, for example, in the line last quoted, denotes *and then*. It is a favorite of Doughty's, who is not above inserting it to top up a decasyllabic line but most often summons it, a bit nervously, for help in impelling that focusing device of his from one scene to the next. Best known via the obsolete *sithence* as an archaic form of *since*, the ubiquitous word cannot but create trouble for the reader who cannot but hunger, eventually, not for more narrative but for a framework of meaning in which to receive it. Scanning the poetic chronicle for consequential logical pattern, the mind pounces, in *sith*, on what looks like a cause. But no; or, rather, Lo! Not *since* but *next* bespeaks Doughty's mode of proceeding—like Swinburne's mode in *The Tale of Balen* but now, pursued across thirty thousand lines, productive of more sheer seriality than a merely human reader can live on.

Not that *The Dawn in Britain* lacks structural plan.[30] The six volumes in which Doughty published it correspond to phases of a large action divisible into roughly four-book clumps and generally graphable on a diagonal axis running between Britain and Palestine. A double Brenniad builds to the sack of pre-republican Rome and the fateful desecration of Apollo's shrine at Delphi (books 1–5); this southeasterly thrust is counterbalanced in a second movement, after the lapse of a dozen generations, by the odyssey of Arimathean Joseph and his saints to found a first-century British church in the lake isle of Avalon (books 6–9). Briton Caradoc and Roman Claudius emerge in book 10, strongly contrasted characters whom the war preparations

[29] Fairley writes appreciatively of how a "retarding punctuation" lets Doughty release the energy of his single nouns and verbs and adjectives" in "shining vocabularies": "Introduction" to *Selected Passages from* The Dawn in Britain (New York: Oxford University Press, 1935) xvi.

[30] As Heath-Stubbs makes out the case for unity—"It is the struggle between Roman civilization and heroic barbarism, and the advent of Christianity, which really forms the subject of the poem" (*Darkling Plain*; 192)—the wobble in his grammar betrays that unity's unsteadiness.

of the next three books show to be representatives of heroic but doomed tribal barbarism on one side, invincible if decadent imperial organization on the other. Caradoc's British fortunes rise until a pivotal defeat at Camulodunum (book 16) turns the tide, and Rome rides thereafter towards decisive victory in book 20. The final four books balance an often brutal aftermath of angry insurgency and ruthless repression against what Doughty presents as the conquest's silver lining: the commerce that imperial rule facilitates among Joseph's meek British Christians (symbolic wedlock between a patrician convert and a pious British lass brightens book 23) and other members of the primitive church (cameo roles in book 22 feature the traveling apostle Simon and the family of Lazarus, moved to Gaul from biblical Bethany).

This large structural design is cross-stapled here and there by incidents that pull the geographic extremities of Doughty's vast miscellaneous history in towards each other. When we first meet Caradoc he is on a mission to Rome, whither he will eventually return in chains as Britain's captive king. The future emperor Titus figures as an invading general both skilled in tactics and magnanimous in victory, promising (book 18) to respect the infant British church, which Doughty fosters as gentile heir to the great world-historical event that will occur on Titus' imperial watch, the destruction of the temple in Jerusalem (book 24). When Joseph's wayfaring band arrive at a Roman outpost in darkest Gaul, they meet an immigrant freedman who turns out to speak Gaulish as well as he does Syrian and Latin. This fluency comes of his being Galatian and thus descended, in a genealogy that the name of his homeland suggests, from a remnant of the second Brennus' fourth-century drive into Asia Minor (8.193). At such transactions Doughty's immense historico-cultural vision suddenly clicks into perspective; the expanding empire seems, for the moment, a smaller and more intelligible place.

For the moment; and that is the point. The narrative manner we have analyzed above is of so dense a fabric that under its weight Doughty's thoughtfully planned structural scaffolding sags out of shape and practically out of mind. We forget the big picture that his devoted apologists would have us believe mattered most to him, because our attention is engrossed by the moving picture of serial episodes instead.[31] So insistent, indeed, is the poem's textural demand that one may be pardoned for suspecting that,

---

[31] Among apologists for the architectonic virtues of *The Dawn* the most resourceful are Fairley, *Study*, esp. 96, 130–33; and Treneer, *Charles M. Doughty*, 200–5.

whatever Doughty said he meant to frame up as a thesis in national or cultural history, as an artist he trusted the verbal medium to do all the carriage that really mattered. In ideological terms the inflammable chauvinist in Doughty found it nearly as hard to speak Rome fair as Noyes did Spain when writing *Drake*. But where Noyes's philistine conception of clarity obliged him to work a bias against Catholic Spain into, not just the plot of *Drake*, but its narrative and even descriptive voice, Doughty confronts us with something older, colder, lonelier. For *The Dawn in Britain* is an epic nearly voiceless. The impediments it places in the way of reading aloud also frustrate the silent reader's effort to attach its language to the tone, and thus the attitude, of an imagined speaker. A pervasive sign of this unspeakable literariness is the homogeneity of all the poem's technically ascribed speeches: all characters talk the same idiolect; the several incorporated bards' performances are formally interchangeable (e.g. in books 3, 9, 13); there is no distinguishing a flashback or reported speech, on grounds of style, from the regular tenor of the ongoing narrative.

This objectivity of manner curiously coexists with another habit of presentation, which we touched on above while considering some of Doughty's local coups in perceptual mimesis. Often he will take a leaf from *Sordello* or *The Ring and the Book* and do his narrating from a temporarily assumed dramatic standpoint. At such moments the one-size-fits-all objective style harbors, behind its great stone face, the implanted subjectivity of a character who on one hand is obviously less than omniscient yet on the other hand displays the assurance of an epic naïf, imputing authoritative coherence to all that falls within his horizon of consciousness. At one of those culture-staples just mentioned, for example, the triumphally processing Claudius bumps into a certain Herod Antipas, exiled by Caligula to Gaul: "(Was sometime tetrarch of a Roman province)" (17.52). Doughty will go on, with heavy hand, to make sure we know just which Herod this man is; but first, with admirable lightness of touch, his parenthesis has sent the flicker of world-history across the mind of an emperor who, even were he Marcus Aurelius and not dim-eyed Claudius, could not possibly grasp its importance. The irony here passes no judgment except what is implied about a universal truth: that we can never know what portion of our experience will prove in the end to have meant most.

This is a truth Doughty demonstrates time and again, and he enlarges it to epic resonance by finding it in the contact zone between colliding peoples. Brennus senior having made his way to Etruria, we receive as through his uninitiated ears the poem's first mention of an up-and-coming place further south called "Rome, | Great Sabine city, in wide Latin plain" (3.159). Later, and conversely, we see the empty moonlit coast of Britain, and experience the ambushed Britons' terror tactics at war, through legionaries' eyes as if for the first time (12.216, 225), and as if we had not already spent several epic books in the British camps.[32] As these reciprocally balanced examples will suggest, the present-centered chronicular style of *The Dawn in Britain* is very well suited to expose the situatedness of perception. In so doing, it tells a different story from the structurally-reinforced official story of a people's advance from pagan savagery to Christian civilization.[33] The counter-story built into Doughty's style strongly suggests, in fact, that the official story was entailed on him as the inheritance of a Victorian progressivism at which substantial portions of his own experience led him to rebel. In consequence the "dawn" occurs in *The Dawn* on two incompatible schedules. By explicit proclamation it is the luminous advent in Britain of the Christian light of the world (1.3, again 6.82); by engrained implication it is the dawning realization that to proclaim a monopoly on light is a privilege that every cultural system claims for itself, and is by the same token an error to which every cultural system lies prone.[34]

These and other moments of relativizing cultural contact remind us that the poem never invokes a calendar of specific dates, or (what fixed calendars imply) a generally explanatory world-historical frame that subordinates events to some authority outside or above those the narrative happens to be taking up. Although Doughty was prevailed on to supply the odd footnote and append to the last volume a pretty tight-fisted glossary of terms and names, there are no notes of an interpretive or explanatory kind.[35]

[32] Heath-Stubbs beholds in the poem "the unchanging features of Britain, but with a freshness and clearness as though they were seen for the first time, under the light of primitive suns" (*Darkling Plain*, 197).

[33] If Heath-Stubbs is right, Doughty's official story is one that affiliates him with his Victorian generation after all, the evolutionary universalism of the *épopée humanitaire*: "He was, indeed, a liberal humanist holding to the broad Victorian belief in the gradual progress of Man, and the ultimate unity of all religions in a universal faith" (Ibid. 198).

[34] The poem's rendition of "a state of almost primitive credulity, in which all the gods of all the nations were real and active" (Fairley, *Study*, 161), may be what Treneer is getting at when she hails Doughty's as "one of the few poems which fundamentally transcend the bounds of race" (p.195).

[35] This self-glossary is the second-strangest of such provisions within the history this book treats. On that score Doughty must yield to his brother in the spirit F. W. Newman, who equipped *The Iliad of Homer, Faithfully Translated into Unrhymed English Metre* (1856) with a prefatory list that in effect translated into contemporary English the reliquary English of his own deliberately antiqued translation. A strong recent defense of "foreignizing translation" is given in Lawrence Venuti, *The Translator's Invisibility: A History of Translation* (London and New York: Routledge, 1995) 118–47, with specific reference to Newman's debate with Arnold.

Instead, and page by page, the poem obliges its reader to work through to such understandings from the limited standpoint of one or another in its pageant of historical agents. This perspectival neutrality is as remarkably, unsettlingly the rule for groups as for individuals. Book 5 represents the Gaulish goddess-mother Nertha in her temple as credibly and sympathetically as it does Zeus at the Delphic shrine (5.8–9, 51–55). Neither deity is amiable in the rough justice it exacts, but the quality of faith expended on each by its worshipers earns the same sober respect. With like fairmindedness Doughty, having put his Christian mariners under the protection of the angel Albion (book 6), goes right on to vex them with the machinations of a raucous crew of demons featuring Satan and Abaddon (book 7).[36] Harder to take in stride are this crew's allegorical associates Faction, Envy, Pride, and so on (7.138), but the very difficulty underscores the austerity of Doughty's syncretic Spenserian intention throughout the poem: to produce each tribe's tale in the terms of its own most developed credence, and to poise them all on the common denominator of a neutrally homogenizing style. Even Despair, perhaps Spenser's best known allegory, is both freshly imagined in Doughty's version of him (7.142) and—this point seems crucial—imagined with a degree of concreteness equal to that accorded in preceding pages to such realist collateral as arctic seals or the bones of wrecked sailors (7.131, 135).

However laudable this noncommittal realization may be in itself, however remarkable for the shift it betokens in national feeling since the propagandistic exploitation of British antiquities by the epic likes of Samuel Wilcocke and John Thelwall just a hundred years before (Ch. 3), Doughty's impartiality entrains a major liability for the through-line of his sweeping narrative. The poet's indifference to, if it is not incompetence with, the clash of rival systems of belief prevents his representing such a clash as in any way generative. He knows that the Druids of Britain regarded their Christian interlopers as a threat, but book 9 never gets far behind this antagonism into its motivation or possibly abiding consequences. Diehard admirers confess to being powerfully moved in book 19 by Caradoc's dark night of the soul, where a vanquished king glimpses existential vacuity on the far side of his tattered pagan metaphysic and takes it out, like a very Orlando or Cuchulain, on a hallucinated grove with old Brennus' sword. Readers left

---

[36] Hoxie Neale Fairchild, *Religious Trends in English Poetry*, vol. 5 (New York: Columbia University Press, 1962) 298, marvels disapprovingly at the poem's evenhanded tolerationism.

cold by this snowy vigil, and colder by Caradoc's meek return in the morning to the bosom of family values, are likely to suspect that the episode offers more unpurged Victorian conventionality than it does profundity of insight into a spiritual conflict that might be culturally productive. Doughty seems more himself when, beginning to narrate the fatal emergence of division within the British alliance, he first attributes it like a political scientist to envious rivalry among faction leaders, then mythopoetically blames it on "Bodva, war-fury, like to hoodie crow" (13.5). Both explanations tell part of the truth about why Britain is going to lose to Rome. But Doughty is not about to estimate the relation between these explanations, or to show how such an estimate if offered might measure either Rome's cultural leverage once upon a time, or its modern shadow in England's cultural leverage two thousand years later.

What Doughty does offer, in default of explanatory relation, is what we have itemized already: the relating of incidents, with the meager but genuine narrative logic that sequential chronicle confers on them; and the lexical relationships that are tacitly, unfailingly enacted by a language whose tangled root system, hybridized out of Celtic and Latin and Teutonic stocks, reproduces the matter of his history in every passage he writes. On vulgar show at Rome in the triumph of Claudius (new-named "Britannicus"), Caradoc appears for us to advantage as "The Briton king, erect, magnanimous," while his Queen Embla too "Hath a royal majesty, in her countenance" (20.249). Doughty has just been grousing that under the Caesars "Much insolent concourse is | Descended, in Rome's ways, of mingled speech" (20.247). Yet without just such mingled speech our poet would be nowhere, at a loss for words. The ostentatiously Latinate modifiers he improbably finds for both his noble British victims do essential work. They imply, through the language's embedded history, a cultural history of fertile borrowing and fostering in which this and later conquests signally participate. The chivalric ethos that Doughty was steeped in—and through whose anachronistic persistence even today we sympathize nearly unbidden with Caradoc and Embla as familiar tragic types—lay just beyond the distant but still visible medieval turning of the imperial road his awkward poem starkly paced.[37]

---

[37] Doughty thus makes sesquicentennial bookends with Macpherson in the Ossian lays, two of which ("Comala" and "The War of Caros") treat Briton resistance to imperial Rome: David Quint, *Epic and Empire: Politics and Generic Form from Virgil to Milton* (Princeton: Princeton

As a poet, Hardy bloomed in print as late as his agemate Doughty did, and with as firm a conviction that the work in prose for which he became well known had delayed the pursuit of his true calling. That calling sounded loudest, in the ears of both poets, from the quarter of verse narrative. Doughty largely stayed there: although he hazarded some shrill lyric exercises in war propaganda and, in *Adam Cast Forth* (1908), a biblical drama that delegates stretches of narrative stage direction and even flashback to its long-winded chorus, he chiefly concentrated in *The Titans* (1916) and *Mansoul* (1920) on long chants of the same epic timbre as *The Dawn in Britain*. With Hardy it was different: what readers who see past the novels prize him for is the continuous, superb lyric output on which his poetic reputation must rest. That said, here we may say more: what readers come to esteem in the lyrics usually involves a marked narrative component. Within the knottings of a tight, traditional verse that, whether dry or impassioned in mood, is always strong-wittedly inventive in manner, it was Hardy's gift to implicate a story that fed the mood from below and that the manner played across with a narratorial sophistication like that of short fiction.

This same gift of narrative inflection Hardy bestowed, on a vast scale and in a sustained effort occupying most of his first decade as an author recommitted after 1897 to poetry, on a long work that took up the events of political and military history that had dominated the early nineteenth century and that have engrossed the early chapters of this book. Epic in ambition and dramatic in format, *The Dynasts* was yet so visionary in overall conception that only in 1910, when the author gathered into a single volume the book-length parts he had separately issued in 1904, 1906, and 1908, did he find for its subtitle the generic label that now seems inevitable: *An Epic-Drama of the War with Napoléon, in Three Parts, Nineteen Acts, and One Hundred and Thirty Scenes.*[38] Here is a great poet's masterpiece, addressed to the precipitating cataclysm of his time and wrought out into a format altogether original. It is a work that, like the

---

University Press, 1993) 349. Caradoc himself had supplied heroic mettle for William Mason—the poet to whom William Hayley addressed his 1782 *Essay on Epic Poetry* (see Ch. 1)—in the 1759 closet drama *Caractacus* and then in *Conan, Caradoc, and the Death of Hoel*, Mason's edition of translations the late Thomas Gray had made from the old Welsh.

[38] Composition and publication history is given in *The Complete Poetical Works of Thomas Hardy*, ed. Samuel Hynes, vol. 4 (Oxford: Clarendon Press, 1995) 408–10. Possibly the term "epic-drama" is owed to Charles Reade, who used it unhyphenated as subtitle to a duplex closet-drama in 1830 (see Ch. 7).

best of its nineteenth-century congeners, belongs with the major epics precisely because it transforms the tradition it receives.[39]

The first thing to observe about *The Dynasts*, made salient in a remarkable Fore Scene reminiscent of the book of Job and Goethe's *Faust*, is that it turns the representational conventions of straightforward epic narrative inside out. Our usual privileged outlook on an objectively unfolding action, here the train of events that convulsed Europe from Napoleon's self-crowning as emperor in 1805 to his final defeat at Waterloo an Iliadic ten years later, is preempted by a choral company of bodiless Spirits. Not only do these Phantom Intelligences introduce, conclude, and irreverently punctuate the constituent scenes of *The Dynasts*, even gingerly taking a rumor-monger's bit part, once in a great while, within the historical action itself. They also, in their crucial capacity as ghost readers, forestall our proper epic honors of witness and response by acting them out right in front of us.[40] Neither confiscating these honors nor absolving us of the moral obligations they entail, the meddling voiceover of Hardy's Spirits rather raises the ante of narrative awareness by putting a hitch into the normal operation of readerly uptake. In this sense Hardy's dramatic frame compasses an all but Brechtian staging of the conditions of history's narrative representation—though Hardy wanted no part of Brecht's epic-theatre ambition to revolutionize actual proscenium production and had his eye on, if any contemporary medium, cinema in its infancy.

[39] Harold J. Orel recounts how, as Hardy felt his way from the mid-1870s through discarded fictional and balladic models towards the concept of epic drama, he consulted "the epics of Milton, Dante, Homer (in several translations), and Virgil, as well as *The Cid, Nibelungen*, and *Don Quixote*": *Thomas Hardy's Epic-Drama A Study of* The Dynasts (Lawrence: University of Kansas Publications, 1963) 35–46; also "Hardy and the Epic Tradition," *English Literature in Transition* 9 (1966) 188. For G. Glen Wickens, *Thomas Hardy, Monism, and the Carnival Tradition: The One and the Many in* The Dynasts (Toronto: University of Toronto Press, 2002), the poem represents "a new kind of novel, not the last great epic," because—apparently by insuperable Bakhtinian edict—in the 20th cent. "the only developing genre" was the novel (pp.119, 148)

[40] Marguerite Roberts, *Hardy's Poetic Drama and the Theatre* (New York: Pageant, 1965), rehearses Hardy's negotiation with Harley Granville-Barker for an abridged production on the London stage at the outbreak of war in 1914, and after the war with Charles Morgan at Oxford in 1920: pp. 31–49, 56–64. Jean R. Brooks, *Thomas Hardy: The Poetic Structure* (Ithaca: Cornell University Press, 1971) 276–77 and 312, emphasizes epic-theatre parallels with Brecht. But the London script reduced Hardy's complex literary hybrid to quite un-Brechtian patriotic pageantry; and the one manifest imitation *The Dynasts* attracted—*Armageddon: A Modern Epic Drama* (1915) by quondam epoist Stephen Phillips (Ch. 11)—makes it plain that even the literary hybrid did not *per se* militate against propagandistic simplicity in wartime. None of which contradicts, though it does qualify, Isobel Armstrong's argument that Hardy deploys "drama, the democratic form of radical writing," as a means of denying to the machinations of the *soi-disant* great the old epic authority of "overview" or "total reading": *Victorian Poetry: Poetry, Poetics and Politics* (London and New York: Routledge, 1993) 487.

To be sure, a cinematic technology that might do visual justice to the conception of *The Dynasts* lay decades in the future, with modes of animation and digital enhancement whose advent would postdate Hardy's poem by as long an interval as separated it from the Battle of Waterloo.[41] Still, it may be helpful to describe the epic innovation here as the replacement of an *objective* narrative viewpoint by a *projective* cinematic one. Such a description has the advantage of resuming, and redoubling, the question of epic machinery with which our history of the genre began in Chapter 2. To begin with, the thick fabric of historical event is itself mechanically woven, as the first line of the After Scene emphasizes:

> Thus doth the Great Foresightless mechanize
> In blank entrancement now as evermore
> Its ceaseless artistries in Circumstance
> Of curious stuff and braid, as just forthshown

—where for good measure the phrase "artistries in Circumstance" repeats the beginning of the Fore Scene verbatim, like a machined part on a production line.[42] That line kinks up, though, when we recall what Hardy's preface has said on one hand about "the careless mechanism of human speech" and on the other about "the curiously hypnotizing impressiveness" of an "automatic style" of recitation, such a style in fact as the mercilessly regular lines just quoted call for. The *enactment* of regularity and the *performance* of automated response should give us pause; for they harbor, within the dramatic project of *The Dynasts*, a consequential theatrical tension over what it is to *act*, or even *react*. In this sense, like good machinery

---

[41] The cinematic analogy is laid out in John Wain's introduction to *The Dynasts* (London: Macmillan, 1965) ix–xix, and is developed more systematically by Chester A. Garrison in *The Vast Venture: Hardy's Epic-Drama* The Dynasts (Salzburg: Universität Salzburg, 1973) 187–203. At the time of first publication Robert Ross likened the art of the poem, albeit grouchily, to cinematography (*Academy*, 3 March 1906, p. 206). Joan Grundy, *Hardy and the Sister Arts* (London: Macmillan, 1979) 106–33, discusses kinetic media antedating film. On the likelihood of Hardy's acquaintance with cinema in the 1890s see Paul Turner, *The Life of Thomas Hardy: A Critical Biography* (Oxford: Blackwell, 1998) 179.

[42] The automation of causality that is ostentatiously foregrounded within *The Dynasts* has by turns fascinated and repelled readers for a hundred years now. Its resilient adaptability thus far to mechanical and digital modes alike augurs well for the poem's continued pertinence to what phases of modernity may lie ahead; for the imagination of the whole work is possessed not by a given technology but by a specter that, stalking Napoleonic Europe, long ago took up residence within modern technology as such. As Jacob Korg put it, Hardy was galvanized by "the automatic activity typical of modern warfare" to understand that in his time "war, which had always been considered as an instrument of human policy, was itself making instruments of men": "Hardy's *The Dynasts*: A Prophecy," *South Atlantic Quarterly* 53 (1954) 31, 24.

elsewhere in the epic tradition, Hardy's invisible first-responders manifest a principle of agency that is at work within the entire poem.[43] The Spirit machinery sees to it that an undisputed, relentlessly unspooling sequence of portrayed events will by turns enervate readers and prod them into a second-order response to, among other things, their first-order enervation. By epic-dramatic design the poem pits an acknowledgment of history's pastness as *res gestae* against the challenge of history's incompletion as a work in progress. *The Dynasts* holds in a tensed mutual critique the hubris of overweening strategy and the defeatism of passive apathy, each of these poles being represented many times over at the levels of both human action and reactive commentary on the Spirits' part.

Thus the resolutely intrinsic perspectivism that it takes some faithful work to excavate from Doughty's epic mode lies, with Hardy, right on the surface. There it prompts the reader both to be aware of the viewpoint imaginatively adopted and to assess it; and furthermore to ponder, in the spirit of Browning and of Morris, what it means and what it costs to adopt a viewpoint at all. From their Overworld perch—way up there in the nth balcony of the theatre of conflict and assisted by opera glasses and ear trumpets of much more than Edwardian power—Hardy's Spirits behold the manifold commotion of humanity as it transpires across all Europe with the resistless unidirectionality of chronicle. The diverse reactions that the Spirits express to the panorama of dedication and venality, sacrifice and wastage, policy and contretemps, stakes out a spectrum of responsiveness to which Hardy's framework elicits the reader's split-level response in turn. On one side Spirits Sinister or Ironic snatch a mischievous gratification at human folly's expense; on the other the Spirit and Chorus of the Pities, a striking singular plural reminiscent of Blake's Ololon from *Milton* (Ch. 3), vibrate in stricken but unexhausted sympathy with the massive pageant of human pain. Meanwhile, from a still point of response midway, the Ancient Spirit of the Years urges his juniors to outgrow such frivolities and learn instead an impassive concentration on the underlying reality from which

---

[43] The Spirits have been received from the first as epic machinery. Thomas H. Dickinson, "Thomas Hardy's *The Dynasts*," *North American Review* 195 (1912) 533, quickly hailed the device as "completely equivocal and completely impersonal." Bonamy Dobrée saw how by such equivocation and "continual oscillation" the reader is "irked into further activity": "*The Dynasts*," *Southern Review* 6 (1940), 113–14. See also Lascelles Abercrombie, *Thomas Hardy: A Critical Study* (New York: Viking, 1927) 186; and two essays by Keith Wilson: "*The Dynasts*: Some Problems of Interpretation," *Colby Library Quarterly* 12 (1976) 181–90; and "'Flower of Man's Intelligence': World and Overworld in *The Dynasts*," *Victorian Poetry* 17 (1979) 124–33.

this like every history springs. That reality is the notorious operation of the Immanent Will, ungraspably complex and all-inclusive in its designs, yet manifestly pointless and therefore, Years inferentially declares, unaware of what it is doing.

During the Fore Scene, and at five later occasions spread across *The Dynasts*), the Spirit of the Years flexes his power "to visualize the Mode" (6) and make the Immanent Will temporarily perceptible.[44] A kind of radio-anatomy reveals to the Spirits and us the patterns of a sheer force—δυναμις in Greek (*dynamis*), a term with cognates in Hardy's title and Septuagint epigraph from Luke (δυνασται, the mighty (*dynastai*)—which inhabits and actuates the phenomenal forms that the ordinary spectacle comprises. For these uncanny transparencies the poet contrives an imagery combining the organic pulse of neurochemical science with the winking circuitry of an electronic system wired in multiple, inter-referential concurrency, through relays "Which complicate with some, and balance all" (7). The resulting imagery, somewhere between a lobed brain and an automated switchboard, and thus irresistibly suggestive of a later cybernetics, shows what the last Victorian poet made of Coleridge's Romantic postulate of the One Mind within us and abroad ("The Eolian Harp"). The organic and mechanical components of this imagery find their common ground, as Years's choral glosses zestfully insist, in a determinist thesis about the subtention of the mind by the brain, or more largely of spirit by matter. Among the corollaries of this thesis are the propositions that human action reduces to puppetry and that human freedom is a contradiction in terms.

These grim bogeys of nineteenth-century philosophy held considerable charms for Hardy's imagination, and some of the finest verse in *The Dynasts* is devoted to propounding them with feeling. Still, the very fact that in old Years he has dramatized so Urizenic a spokesman suggests the inadequacy of this philosophy as a living principle of epic cohesion.[45] At the level of cosmodicy to which the poem aspires (albeit with Hardy's trademark diffidence), the advantage lies not with Years's stern demystification of freedom but with a dialectic in which Years's position claims only a part (albeit one of great dignity). Hardy entrusted the truth of his century-summing epic to no

---

[44] This special effect recurs at 1.1.6.36, 1.6.3.118, 3.1.1.330, 3.2.2.368, 3.7.7.505. (Here and in subsequent parenthetic citation my inconveniently drawn-out numbers code the text by part, act, scene, page.)

[45] Wickens, *Thomas Hardy*, 50–57, usefully insists that Years, like all Hardy's actors, remains subject to the drama's pervading irony.

one party, but rather to the dynamic of response that his entire Overworld superstructure was designed to focalize. As the poem's very title implies, the life of *The Dynasts* lies in this dynamic, in the plaited force field of response. This is Hardy's way of addressing the perennial questions of epic—about the origin, course, and outcome of human action—through exploration of an ambivalence for which Years and his associates serve as practical exponents.

If the Will is to be imagined as a vast network of fibers interconnected in patterns of mutual response, the Spirits constitute a higher-level function that the network has somehow, curiously, generated in response to itself. The Spirits draw out from the constituent immanence of response, and they fan out for the reader's consideration, a dialectic that balances passive or aesthetic *responsiveness* against active or ethical *responsibility*. Before the historical action has begun, in a highly original turn on the epic topos of invocation the Will's ductile loops of circulating response and stimulus, cause and effect, pose not a proposition already proven but a question to be tried upon that action. And the venue for this trial or epic proof is to be the consciousness of the reader, lodged in the superincumbent gallery of eye and ear, mouth and brow, and suspended in judgment like the Spirits themselves above the argument unfolding across the page beneath. In the Fore Scene the adverting mind beholds foreseen, *déjà vu*, that encyclopedic totality of understanding in whose name epic speaks—here, of course, the name of the Will—and whose microcosm is the mind itself. What dynamic correlation may subsist between the macrocosm of history and the recapitulative mind's finite includedness therein, it becomes the business of the poem to educe.

Hardy was attracted to Napoleon's dynastic decade as an epic theme because it made such includedness impossible to miss. Europe's rehearsal then of world war had set the terms on which a hundred years were completing their drift toward the brink of world war now again: a drift in which, as Hardy's pelletized phrase "The Universal-empire plot" evidently suggests, most of the Victorian epic writing published during his career as an author had been complicit (Ch. 11).[46] At the same time, the recession of 1805–15 into long ago made for a distance in time analogous to the

---

[46] See Charles Lock, "HARDY Promises: *The Dynasts* and the Epic of Imperialism," in *Reading Thomas Hardy,* ed. Charles P. C. Pettit (Houndmills: Macmillan, 1998) 85–86.

swooping verticals and sweeping horizontals of Hardy's epic geography. Indeed, the heady superiority of his Overworld vantage, which even when it compassionates war's victims cannot avoid condescending to them first, resembles nothing so much as the superiority of perspective that comes with historical hindsight. Looking down is *The Dynasts*' way of looking back, as if on reels of military, political, social, and domestic footage whose presence— projected on a screen that keeps us apart from all to which it provides access—is at bottom only a miraculously high-fidelity reenactment of a past that nothing can alter, and about which there is nothing to be done. In this way Hardy built into his imaginary medium an overwhelming invitation to sheer spectatorship, an invitation that Years delivers dozens of times during the course of the poem, lending to his fatalist message the aplomb of a rhetorical authority no other voice in the poem can match.

The structural art of *The Dynasts*, nevertheless, just as steadily opposes to this preponderant tendency towards spectatorship its solicitation of con-scious responsiveness on the reader's part. Taking up a more fluid, and compromised, position than the fixed Spirits can corner, we are enjoined to practice a form of participant-observation that becomes possible only by acknowledging our entanglement within the larger fabric of history of which even Hardy's immense cinematic canvas is but a small portion. The spectacle we are granted to oversee is one that we have not understood until we concede our implication within it, as an instantiation however faraway of processes that are still far from over. These processes, furthermore, include the fundamental acts of perceptual cognition, interpretive judg-ment, and affective reaction in which we as readers—not disembodied Spirits, that is, but human historical agents—ongoingly engage.

The Dynasts then is a spectacular poem bent upon breaking the grip of mere spectacle, and of the spectatorial passivity that often goes with it. No feature of the work does more to accomplish this task than the prose descriptions that orient each scene and fill out the narrative interstices of choral chant and dialogue. In their understated eloquence these indispensable, terse passages extend the genre of the stage direction in proportion as Hardy's epic-drama extends the genre of the stage play. Primarily aids to visualiza-tion, these *mises-en-scène* often go beyond accommodating the eye and insist on activating it. When "The eye of the spectator rakes the road from the interior of a cellar" (1.3.1.206), that spectator has been recruited into collaboration; and even when Hardy intends the reader's conspiracy in a stupor of fatiguing routine on the road to Waterloo, it is a stupor born of shared motion: "The focus of the scene follows the retreating English army, the highway and its margins panoramically gliding past the vision of the spectator" (3.6.8.482).

Hardy is just as likely to turn down the lights and turn on a soundtrack. "Endowed with enlarged powers of audition as of vision" (3.1.9.354), and actually incorporating sheet music at a couple of points (3.2.4.372 and 3.6.2.460), the multimedia *Dynasts* calls upon the epic ear to supplement the eye's measure of historical distance in the making. As we pass from an elite London gathering toward Napoléon's coronation at Milan, "The confused tongues of the assembly waste away into distance, till they are heard but as the babblings of the sea from a high cliff, the scene becoming small and indistinct therewith. This passes into silence, and the whole disappears" (1.1.5.32). The recession of sound into silence across these sentences conscripts into mimetic service, as we have seen analogous verse devices do for Swinburne and Doughty, the real time in which admittedly virtual representation occurs. In addition, Hardy's reconception of the epic medium—validating his master Browning's hint about the historiographic "Uproar in the echo . . . whispered away" (*The Ring and the Book* 1.834–35)—makes of auditory fadeout a figure for the evanescence of the historical record as such. In a remote yet symmetrically balanced pair of scenes we loiter outside the general's tent at Austerlitz (1.6.1.109) and survey the field at Salamanca (3.1.3.337), while out of sight Napoléon and Wellington respectively become present to us only as voices: historical *records* indeed, in the acoustic and phonographic sense which that documentary term was acquiring in Hardy's time.[47]

To the movies and the talkies Hardy's prophetic aesthetic adds enhancements of sense that remain for us even now the stuff of science fiction alone. Our first sight, swimming up out of the Spirits' darkened auditorium, is that of Europe itself in the throes of war, shaped unforgettably "as a prone and emaciated figure" with Spain for a head and the Alps for a spine; and the suffering of this body, as of the "perturbed countries" that are its organs, stays with us as a Blakean foil to all *The Dynasts* would have us, not just see,

[47] Susan Dean, *Hardy's Poetic Vision in* The Dynasts: *The Diorama of a Dream* (Princeton: Princeton University Press, 1977), writes of "the reverberating action" as emitting "waves," which by redundant reinforcement assume the standing form of collective modalities of response in the Overworld Spirits (pp.30, 76).

but feel bodily too.[48] An occasional aroma-rama curtails readerly distance, and restores the spectator to the particulate contact zone of olfactory imagination, by challenging disgust at the shipboard "fumes of gunpowder and candle-grease, the odour of drugs and cordials, and the smell from abdominal wounds" among which Nelson will die at Trafalgar (1.5.4.92), or at the atmosphere over Waterloo thick with "the stench of gunpowder and a muddy stew of crushed crops and gore" (3.7.8.518). That decisive battle takes us beyond the smellies to the brave new feelies when "batteries fire, with a concussion that shakes the hill itself" (3.7.4.497). More effective still, in an admittedly novelistic manner made newly haunting when imported into the epic-dramatic context, is the scenic rendition of ambience itself. "Something in the feel of the darkness and in the personality of the spot imparts a sense of uninterrupted space around" a certain ridge, well known already from Hardy's prose, on Egdon Heath (1.2.5.48). Again, on the field at Austerlitz "The invisible presence of the countless thousands of massed humanity that compose the two armies makes itself felt indefinably" (1.6.1.109). The very failure of explanatory specificity, in a work that appears to have an historical omniscience at its disposal, paradoxically makes that work's work of recovery the more vivid: picking up something indefinable in the air, the description utters volumes of felt space.[49]

Such descriptive serendipity comes down, let us say, to a matter of vibrations intuited along the underside of perception. These vibrations, the normally disregarded elements of sensation itself, nevertheless penetrate consciousness during extreme states: nervous hypersensitivity, as when Napoléon in escaping Elba is becalmed by night and must watch "the town lights, whose reflections bore like augers into the waters" (3.5.1.430); or on the opposite hand nervous overload, as when at the battle of Leipzig "we soon fail to individualize the combatants as beings, and can only observe them as amorphous drifts, clouds, and waves of conscious atoms, surging and rolling together" to a sound "as from the pedal of an organ kept continuously

---

[48] A likeness between Hardy's epic and Blake's struck one early reviewer in the *New York Tribune* for 23 January 1904: see R. G. Cox's introduction to *Thomas Hardy: The Critical Heritage* (New York: Barnes and Noble, 1970) xxxix. Attending to Hardy's corporeal imagination of the war's larger movements Turner, *Life of Thomas Hardy*, 203, detects in the battling troops' formation outside Leipzig a sphincter image, which seems specifically anal in its processing of human waste: "the huge elastic ring | Of fighting flesh, as those within go down" (3.3.2.383).

[49] Dean underscores how the poem's fidelity "to the raw data of experience" eschews interpretation (p.71) and fosters a solidarity with mute nature in which sympathetic and anaesthetic responses meet (pp.228–29).

down" (3.3.2.383). A kindred effect obtains at the joint between acts 5 and 6 of
part 2, where a nearly visible wave of chanted music, sweeping through the
Louvre "in harmonies that whirl round the walls of the Salon-Carré and
quiver down the long Gallery," seems on departure to infiltrate the barriers
of sense and summon forth a nearly audible wave of seacoast viewed from over
Portugal, "the white-frilled Atlantic lifting rhythmically on the west" (289).[50]

In these and other incidents of subliminal synaesthesia, *The Dynasts*
murmurs hints of that cosmic substrate of δυναμις which Years periodically
heralds, with more fanfare, as the Immanent Will. It is the same motive
force described from the first by Pities in undulant terms that strongly
suggest the rhythmical workings of the verse that is their medium:

> Amid this scene of bodies substantive
> Strange waves I sight like winds grown visible,
> Which bear men's forms on their innumerous coils,
> Twining and serpentining round and through.

(Fore Scene 7)

After all the sturdy prose we have just considered, to come like this on
verse's insinuation is to suspect that Hardy found in his predominantly
poetic medium the largest of figures for *The Dynasts*' undergirding cosmol-
ogy. "The pulsion of the Byss" (Fore Scene 1), "the dreaming, dark, dumb
Thing" (After Scene 524), throbs its inarticulate sub-commentary from first
to last across the whole, huge text in metric mutations that bear syllables and
meanings the way the waves of history "bear men's forms" and deeds.

Like Noyes's *Drake* the whole poem is an Edwardian handbook of
prosody, but one more daring in its variety, and certainly more remarkable
for the impudence with which it mismatches form to content.[51] Napoléon's
ambition for dynastic lineage consistently elicits from the Chorus of Ironic

---

[50] Dennis Taylor, *Hardy's Metres and Victorian Prosody* (Oxford: Clarendon Press, 1988), correl-
ates such fadeouts of voice into setting in *The Dynasts* with the "sound symbolism" that plays form
against speech in the poet's lyrics (p.169).

[51] Since the first *Times Literary Supplement* review found part 1 of *The Dynasts* "insensible to
the natural magic, the delight of purely poetic language" (16 February 1906), criticism has been
unaccountably severe on Hardy's versification. His epic diction has attracted better notices,
although description of it fills a wide spectrum from Hynes's appreciation of a terraced lexical
"*tour de force*" to Lock's report of "an exceptional sense of lexical homogeneity" (p.85). Our best
guide to Hardy's epic metric, as to his prosody at large, remains Taylor. See his superb discussion of
"the way the natural rhythms of language take shape, become fixed, and ossify into a ghostly music
of the past" or "an archaic crystallization of prose. The poem seems to recapitulate the historical
process by which the fresh speech rhythms of the people become the metrical rhythms of the poet,"
thereby historiographically "formalizing the obsolescence latent in speech" (p.114).

Spirits lyric forms worthy of Gilbert and Sullivan (1.6.5.125) or the demi-monde music hall (2.5.7.281). Or for that matter the symphony hall: a reader who sees the ironic semichorus in 3.3.1.377 hearingly will find it narrating Napoléon's 1812 overtures in Leipzig to the tune of the still more famous 1812 Overture that Tchaikovsky debuted in 1882.[52] Elsewhere Hardy spikes the revolutionary chariots of Napoléon and Shelley at a stroke by rendering the former's delusions of grandeur in the latter's sonnet-stanza from "Ode to the West Wind" (2.6.3.298); he renders the inconclusive carnage of nighttime maneuvers between French and English troops at Talavera in, of all things, strictest sapphics (2.4.4.244).[53]

These and the like formal incongruities practice a double mockery. Ridiculing the pretensions of the dynastic elite, at a deeper level of resonance they rhythmically mime a motion that lies beyond ridicule, and that ultimately invalidates it: the mindless orchestration of the Will, "the Prime Mover" (Fore Scene 6), "The purposive, unmotived, dominant Thing" (2.2.3.191). And this prosodic mimesis ultimately invalidates the Ironic Spirits' shallow mischief by exposing its inadequacy, when held to any abiding human measure, as a response to history's manifest absurdity. Throughout Hardy's anthology of ballads, of hymns in dozens of rhyming forms, of mummings and declamations in several sorts of blank verse open and closed, there subsists a primally woven oscillation that is seldom cognized but always felt; and the lambency of its circumstantial, always potentially ironic metric makes the Spirits' grosser explicit ironies look like so much heckling.

This is not to deny such cognitive irony a major role in *The Dynasts*, only to put that role in its place. The enlargement of sympathies that *The Dynasts* seeks to compass emerges, in part, through the intermediate, polemical work Hardy asks irony to do, particularly as it bears on the foresight and oversight that come with the territory of statecraft and generalship. Much of the action in this poem about nations at war concerns political and strategic decision-making, and nearly all of it proves to be mistaken. Again and again neglected contingencies and unintended consequences bring to nought the plans of monarchs and ministers who do worse, as a rule, the more faith they put in their own powers of surveillant anticipation. To draw out this point, Hardy litters the poem with decrees and dispatches, forms of order whose

---

[52] Dobrée, "*The Dynasts*," 119, hears "hoots of derision" in the heavy triple stress ending each line of this semichorus.

[53] Turner, *Life of Thomas Hardy*, 192, suspects a prosodic allusion to the plea for peace in Horace's second Ode ("Iam satis terris").

discrepancy with the actual order of events is evidently business as usual. This routinized incompetence takes the memorable shape of a political cartoon at one point when a giant envelope, "Sized to its big importance," (3.2.4.376), floats cloudlike from Vienna to Dresden with Austria's 1813 declaration of war against France.

Like graffiti on a state portrait, the visualized cruise of this missive across the European continent makes unusually merry over an irony that suffuses *The Dynasts* on each of the many occasions when generals consult their maps.[54] Ever since the Fore Scene has disclosed, not the map of Europe, but Europe itself in diseased human form, "a prone and emaciated figure" (6), and the first scene has opened on a Wessex ridge from which a passenger observes "how the Channel and coast open out like a chart" (1.1.1.8), Hardy has emphasized the difference between the mapped world and the real one. Call it cartographic irony: a visual equivalent for the epic-dramatic irony that obtains between the ignorance of those who inhabit an era and the privileged understanding that hindsight confers on those who study it.[55] And this cartographic irony, like its narrative counterpart, cuts both ways. The reader looking down (in both senses) on a reader looking down on a map should reflect that both are beholding representations ; that neither is immune to error; indeed, that no one is more liable to error than the spectator who holds to the self-evidence of things neutrally observed in the *naïveté* of the eye. This is a lesson Hardy enforces, above all in the prose *mises* and stage directions, with a steady supply of similes that, whether phrasal or Homerically extended, all serve to break the illusion of a literal, verisimilar correspondence between textual representations and the realities they represent.

Hardy's Continental battles, like Tolstoy's often comparable battles in *War and Peace*, are lost by strategists and won by tacticians.[56] Where master

---

[54] Or when poets consult their genre-conventions. Lock cites the cartoon-sized envelope to make just this larger point about Hardy's genre-exploding "resistance to any form of representation. Indeed, representation—mimesis, dialogue, diegesis—is itself to be identified as the instrument of dynasts and imperialists" ("HARDY Promises," 109). Beth Ellen Roberts, *One Voice and Many: Modern Poets in Dialogue* (Newark: University of Delaware Press, 2006), regards the defect or abuse of military intelligence as emblematic of the short-sightedness afflicting all the poem's characters, even the Phantom Intelligences (pp.42, 47).

[55] Here we might add to the panoramic and cinematic effects discussed above the Victorian development of the bird's-eye view, as abetted first by photography and, around the time of *The Dynasts*, by aviation. See Stephen Daniels, "Victorian Britain," in *Historic Landscapes of Britain from the Air*, ed. Robin Glasscock (Cambridge: Cambridge University Press, 1992) 186–210.

[56] Emma Clifford, "*War and Peace* and *The Dynasts*," *Modern Philology* 54 (1956) 33–44, examining annotations in Hardy's copy of the novel and his draft manuscript for Part 3, demonstrates a pattern of detailed borrowings from Tolstoy that often bear on "the problem of human free will in the course of history" (34).

plans fail, responsive hunches on the spot succeed. Both authors make a favorite of the Russian general Kutúzov, whose intuitive endurance bests Napoleon's brilliance of conception for Tolstoy, and who speaks for Hardy with symbolic force when he rises from the war council before Austerlitz and grumbles that "half-a-dozen hours of needed sleep | Will help us more than maps" (1.6.2.115). Hardy's Napoléon, a more complex figure and probably nearer than Tolstoy's to the historical original, adds to the brilliance of his tireless campaign-planning the dazzle of an improviser ready to change any strategy on a tactical moment's notice. Asked "What do we do?" he characteristically responds, "Heavens, I know no more than you! Trust to the moment and see what happens" (2.5.6.280). It hardly matters that he says so at a dynastic crisis of love not war, when about to meet his Empress-to-be Marie Louise of Austria. The extemporization principle that marks Napoléon out as an unpredictable commander, ruthless diplomat, and faithless lover also explains his unique affiliation with the Immanent Will, of whose workings he alone throughout the poem becomes repeatedly if fitfully aware, and in whose transcendent exemption from moral categories he claims a portion.[57]

In Napoléon's dual role as strategist–tactician we meet a brief abstract and chronicle of the "rapt Determinator" (2.6.7.322) whose purposeless shapings defy our moral grammar—as did, to his more thoughtful evaluators from Byron forward, the historical acts of Bonaparte. Known as the "Will," Hardy's first cause abides in the future tense of its eventuated effects, what *will* happen. Known as the "Mode" (1.5.4.99 *et passim*), it abides in kaleidoscopically shifting, amnesiac, reckless presence, suited to the Latin *modo* or *now*. The poem's final epiphanic transparency, which occurs near a turning point in the battle of Waterloo, exhibits the convergence of these temporalities precisely: "The web connecting all the apparently separate shapes includes WELLINGTON in its tissue with the rest, and shows him, like them, as acting while discovering his intention to act" (3.7.7.505).

---

[57] Hardy's view of the historical Napoleon is echoed in Herbert Butterfield's from *The Whig Interpretation of History* (London: Bell, 1931) 121: he "seems to have been conscious that he was a strange creature fallen among the habitations of men, a completely a-moral person working with the indifference of a blind force in nature," "because he considered that he himself was so to speak the moral end, as the Hegelian state claims to be." Bert G. Hornback, *The Metaphor of Chance: Vision and Technique in the Works of Thomas Hardy* (Athens: Ohio University Press, 1971), finds the character Napoléon finally brought down and so humanized (161–63); Wickens defends him as a "complex figure" who "embodies the web of literary and speech genres that shape the dialogue of *The Dynasts*" (168).

To exist at the intersection of intention and act may be an ideal fleetingly achieved by the athlete, genius, and saint; and it may be the very *modus* of the Will, whose infinitesimally evolving act manifests an intention hitherto unconscious. But that *modus operandi* can scarcely be ours. A perpetually self-discovering man whose plans and deeds are one—at home in both temporalities yet committed to neither—must emerge in literary terms as either a superhero or a grotesque. Hardy clearly made Napoléon into the latter, made him indeed into a victim like every single dynast and underling in the epic's vast dramatis personae.[58]

Meanwhile, for Hardy as for his strongest late predecessor in the historical epic Robert Browning, a sprained and limping heroism opened out Victorian possibilities for the genre that merited carrying over into the new century. One possibility was a frank acceptance of change itself as the structure of historical significance and proper focus of attention for an epic historiography alive to social tectonics, and not just to the military flareups they touch off. During the long day of Napoleonic hegemony on which Hardy concentrates, the uncertain fortunes of war, together with the instability of alliances and an incessantly tipping balance of power, fed into a protracted crisis that military mobilization imposed on civilian life across Europe. At the same time, this unprecedented mobilization also masked democratizing changes of slower pace, but surer duration, that the eighteenth century had set in motion. This momentum towards equality Napoleon's populist aspect had symbolized for millions, and postwar developments affecting the Victorian society into which Hardy was born showed the momentum to have been quietly, constantly at the work of social tranformation.

Hardy's cosmology of the Will responds to this condition, by means both of the metaphysics of change we have been discussing and of a corollary diffusion of epic interest among an exceptionally broad range of social experience. *The Dynasts* rests its portraiture of policy-makers and figureheads on internationally distributed strata running a full vertical gamut: aristocrats and professionals; farmers and peasantry; shopkeepers, prostitutes, city mobs; and—melting all walks of life like bells into bullets—the omnipresent

---

[58] Armstrong observes that the term *dynasts* applies equally to the founders of a ruling hierarchy and to its heirs (the French emperor and the Russian too, Napoleon but also Wellington), all of whom "are engaged in turning power into destiny" (p.485) through a theory of historical justification that makes might right—and all of whom are belied by Hardy's insistence on "the breakdown of a language of agency" (p.486) and denial of "a single overview" (p.488).

military personnel of officers, troops and sailors, deserters, looters, corpses. Scores of cameo appearances draw to themselves a kind of interest that the ironizing impersonality of the Will makes it impossible for a figure even of Napoléon's standing to support. This interest gets collectivized in the process, as it may have done for Hardy himself in the course of writing. His favorites in part 1, certainly Pitt and even Nelson, do not so much rise into glory as they expire into the common good; and in later parts the figures one remembers are large groups fused by hardship: absconding Muscovites burning their city to spoil the French advance, the famished French frozen in retreat around spent fires.

These scenes are memorable, of course, for their pathos, and pathos is the affect on which in the final analysis *The Dynasts* stakes its epic claim. For it is in the awakening and extension of conscious sympathy that the poem both restates and resolves the dialectic of passivity and engagement that has concerned us here. The poetics of sympathy—soft, slow-moving target though it has ordinarily seemed within liberal society—receives from Hardy as tough-minded an approach as any epic writer's since Byron, which is to say an approach not only compatible with irony but dependent on it. That there is something anomalously funny about the human capacity to suffer, that it constitutes a quirk in the economy of nature, forms a theme at which his Spirits hammer relentlessly. "That they feel, and puppetry remain," muses the Shade of Earth about the children she has evolved, "Is an owned flaw in her consistency" (1.1.6.34), on which cue the status-quo apologist Years pithily remarks, in his best Mr. Spock voice, "Affection ever was illogical" (37). When the Spirit of the Pities speak(s) out against it in tongue-twisting lines—"O, the intolerable antilogy | Of making figments feel!"—the Spirit Ironic raps out a sneering assent: "Logic's in that. | It does not, I must own, quite play the game" (1.4.6.77). One act later Pities resume(s) the charge of "antilogy," insisting that automata, being irresponsible, cannot merit their suffering:

> things mechanized
> By coils and pivots set to foreframed codes
> Would, in a thorough-sphered melodic rule,
> And governance of sweet consistency,
> Be cessed no pain, whose burnings would abide
> With That Which holds responsibility,
> Or inexist.

> (1.5.4.99)

The passage is classic Hardy, a tight-lipped indictment of the very structure of existence. But see how it prospects for golden amends in the rift of possibility that a fault in the system itself has opened up. The notion that pain is a "cess" or tax, a levy assessed on life, suggests pain's unique status as a surplus within the system, a side effect escaping the economy that has generated it. Like the "unreckoned incident" of "Man's intelligence" in which it participates (1.6.8.137), by its very inconsistency human pain breaks out of the "foreframed codes," to operate a black market in alternative values that operates somewhere off the books.

Yet off the books it can hardly be, not without violating the premise of total inclusion on which Hardy's like any good epic cosmology is grounded.[59] It must instead be the case that in devising human feelings, including the feelings to which sympathy gives rise, the Will has fashioned forth a mutation with which its own initial mechanistic logic cannot reckon. Transcending the endless, pointless fecundity of metamorphosis, the Will seems to have spun off not just another form of matter in action, but a new kind of energy. This rogue force is passionate; it is also, crucially, compassionate. Adding recognition to knowledge, conscience to science, pathos hails its kind, feels for its fellows, and thereby exerts a capacity to weave a shadow order of multiplex inter-responsiveness within the Will's regime. Because the resulting fabric of sympathies does not subsist outside this regime—nothing that *The Dynasts* depicts can do that—the energy it feeds back into the originating system has the power to change the system. What arises from the Earth's "owned flaw" cannot escape ecological recapture by the Will's ceaseless, seamless fabric; but by that very token the unnecessary, which is to say the miraculous, manifestation of responsive consciousness

[59] No commentary better illuminates this aspect of *The Dynasts*, through the final precision of contrast, than Isaiah Berlin's on Tolstoy, with whose *War and Peace* the poem inevitably challenges comparison. Berlin's intricate description of Tolstoy's matured vision might double for the Immanent Will: reality is "a thick, opaque, inextricably complex web of events, objects, characteristics, connected and divided by literally innumerable unidentifiable links." Because this web "is itself too closely interwoven with all that we are and do to be lifted out of the flow (it *is* the flow) and observed with scientific detachment," no "explicitly conceived categories or concepts can be applied to it—for it is itself but a vague name for the totality that includes these categories, these concepts": *The Hedgehog and the Fox: An Essay on Tolstoy's View of History* (New York: Simon and Schuster, 1953) 63, 68. The same vision that Berlin's Tolstoy found so incapacitating as to precipitate a "lifelong denial" of it (81), Hardy found finally enabling. While these divergent responses bespeak large differences in culture and individual temperament, they are also partly due to the difference between novel and epic as totalizing genres. For further comparison between the two authors see Arthur Quiller-Couch, *Studies in Literature* (New York: Putnam, 1918) 209; Richard Church, "Thomas Hardy as Revealed in *The Dynasts*," *Essays by Divers Hands* 29 (1958) 3; R. J. White, *Thomas Hardy and History* (London: Macmillan, 1974) 125–30; also note 56 above.

means that in its totality the Will has itself become—to a degree—conscious, responsive, responsible.[60] Years's own analysis thus harbors a principle subversive of his entire ethos of dispassionate onlooking. As he concedes, the "burnings" of human pain do not "inexist"; they are real phenomena whose existence is no more accidental or less essential than anything else the Will has ever wrought. Mutant though they be, the affections by affecting the total system change it. Moreover, as the steadfast Pities attest(s), it is of the nature of human pain to be communicable, and by means strikingly continuous both with the undulation of light, sound, and felt force in the physical universe and with the scripted vibration that is poetry.

Such is the epic argument by which the greatest Edwardian poem justifies its long-suffering projection of long-range views, under a post-theological and all but scientifically determinist dispensation, upon the spectacle of so much human suffering undergone to so little apparent purpose. Rightly understood *The Dynasts* is anti-spectacular, in so far as spectatorship implies either a detached immunity from continua of force still operant in the spectator's sphere of being, or an exemption from the responsibility to see the action of force feelingly. "Our scope is but to register and watch" (Fore Scene 2), and the poem shows—for all the world like Keats's *Fall of Hyperion* (Ch. 5)—that to register and watch engagedly are much. The conscious watcher discovers that faithful registration changes the texture of that historical whole in which the act of open witness plays a part, and thereby bears a responsibility. Hence Hardy's barbed ironies at the expense of those who pretend to a commandingly detached overview; hence his reserved yet at last deeply tender solicitation of the reader's sensuous encounter with the rare glories, routine banalities, and raw horrors of warfare.

[60] Among critics Dean has best seized on this key feature of the poem: see *Hardyi Poetic Vision*, 34, 55, 115. See also Dobrée, "*The Dynasts*," 110–11; J. O. Bailey, *Thomas Hardy and the Cosmic Mind: A New Reading of* The Dynasts (Chapel Hill: University of North Carolina Press, 1956) 138; Emma Clifford, "The Impressionistic View of History in *The Dynasts*," *Modern Language Quarterly* 22 (1961) 30; Millard, *Edwardian Poetry*, 77–78; and, for a philological analogy, Taylor's suggestion in *Hardy's Literary Language and Victorian Philology* (Oxford: Clarendon Press, 1993) 286, that the poet's diction "implodes monolingualism from within." After the fact Hardy himself couched the meliorism of *The Dynasts* in a prose explication rendered awkward by very explicitness. "What has already taken place in a fraction of the whole (i.e. so much of the world as has become conscious) is likely to take place in the mass; and there being no Will outside the mass—that is, the Universe—the whole Will become conscious thereby; and ultimately, it is to be hoped, sympathetic": *Florence Emily Hardy, The Later Years of Thomas Hardy* (London: Macmillan, 1930) 124–25. As early as 1914 he claimed this idea as one that "had never (so far as I know) been advanced before *The Dynasts* appeared": *Life and Work of Thomas Hardy*, ed. Michael Millgate (Athens, Ga.: University of Georgia Press, 1985) 488.

If this last great epic before the Great War offers not just anti-war revulsion but an affirmative pacifism, its affirmation dwells, "for loving-kindness' sake" (After Scene 525), within a compassion that hurts. Hardy does not reduce this position to mere compassion. Pacificism on the epic terms that he offers is analytically principled and strives within acknowledged limits for comprehensiveness of outlook; it needs to know, and keep learning, more than what Pities feel(s). Still, the mode of understanding that *The Dynasts* labors to produce cannot arise except through long compassionate practice.[61] The imaginative investment of recognitive feeling is a tax Hardy imposes on his reader in order to fund long-term improvement in the human condition. Or, to shift the figure only slightly but so as to take in the century-long generic history that *The Dynasts* sums: aesthetic vulnerability is the price of admittance to the epic theater of the examined life collectively grasped. Phantom Intelligences haunt the loges there, one suspects, in envious hope that they too might, like the reader, earn a history and so learn to be human.

[61] William E. Buckler, *The Victorian Imagination: Essays in Aesthetic Exploration* (New York and London: New York University Press, 1980), reminds us—sounding a lot like the Spirit of the Years—how "Pities' reactions from the beginning are deeply faulted in what amounts to a whole catalogue of failed perspectives," which Hardy's epic-dramatic architecture exposes to "erosion and alienation" (p.323). At the same time—no: in the end—Colin Burrow, *Epic Romance: Homer to Milton* (Oxford: Clarendon Press, 1993), reminds us of something else: how central to the entire epic tradition is the complex of mercy, empathy, and identification that Pities represent(s), that attends our discovery of affinity with the acknowledged stranger, and that Virgil hallowed as *pietas*.

Bibliography of Poems Cited

This bibliography, compiled in nearly every heroic particular by my students Anna Wieckowski and Alexa Dooseman in 2006–7, lists the poems of significant length to which narrative and notes in the foregoing chapters refer. It lists, in the first instance, first editions. Where in preparing the chapters I relied on and cited a later edition that was more accessible or featured scholarly apparatus, the entry lists that edition in indented **boldface**. Any title thus marked will be the one to which running parenthetic citations in the chapters refer. Where poet and poem are sufficiently canonical to have attracted one or more modern scholarly or teaching editions, such special notice is omitted as superfluous.

The reader will also often find, in indented *italics*, reference to electronic texts of poems. While I have done my old-fashioned work—in obedience to a spectrum of motives that shade from preference through inertia into karma—on print originals borrowed with thanks from one library or run to hallowed ground in another, a digital revolution in textual scholarship and publication has been taking place all around me. The expansion of on-line access to poems formerly rare is already striking, and there should be further dramatic advances in the years just ahead. Accordingly, and as a temporary expedient, the following bibliography lists a URL for each text known to be freely available at present in a free electronic version. (While no reference is given here to proprietary electronic texts, for which the user pays a fee, these do exist in many cases; I trust that readers with the desire and the means will know where to find them.) It is true that URLs are subject to change, that in many cases the quality of the indicated sites' transcriptions and even facsimiles leaves something to be desired, and that in fairly short order more and better digital texts will emerge. All the same, it has seemed important to put readers in virtual touch with the primary materials on which the book is finally based—the more so because my survey-scoped chronicle of long and obscure poems can so seldom pause to savor a detail or dissect a style.

ALEXANDER, Sidney Arthur. "Sakya-Muni: The Story of Buddha." Oxford: Shrimpton, 1887.
Google Book Search. May 6, 2007.
http://books.google.com/books?id=G5MOAAAAIAAJ.

ALLINGHAM, William. *Laurence Bloomfield in Ireland: A Modern Poem*. London and Cambridge: Macmillan, 1864.
Google Book Search. April 26, 2007.
http://books.google.com/books?id=DmACAAAAQAAJ.

AMBROSSE, Bertie. *Opoleyta; or, A Tale of Ind. A Poem, in Four Cantos.* London: Longman, 1815.

[ANON.] *Arthur's Knights: An Adventure from the Legend of the Sangrale.* Edinburgh: n. p., 1859.
> *The Camelot Project at the University of Rochester.* Ed. Alan Lupack and Barbara Tepa Lupack. April 26, 2007.
> *http://www.lib.rochester.edu/CAMELOT/arthur's%20knights.htm.*

[ANON.] *The Crusaders, or The Minstrels of Acre.* London: Cadell and Davies, 1808.

[ANON.] *The Last Crusader: A Poem, in Four Cantos.* London: Saunders, Otley, 1867.

[ANON.] *The Last Judgment: A Poem, in Twelve Books.* London: Longman, Brown, Green, and Longmans, 1857.
> *Google Book Search.* April 26, 2007.
> *http://books.google.com/books?id=EwoDAAAAQAAJ.*

[ANON.] *Passages from a Boy's Epic.* Serialized in *The Leader* Vol. 3, Nos. 115–144, June–December 1852.

[ANON.] *Yuli; the African. A Poem in Six Cantos.* London: J. Hatchard, 1810.
> *Google Book Search.* April 26, 2007.
> *http://books.google.com/books?id=yLADAAAAQAAJ.*

ARNOLD, Edwin. *The Light of Asia; or, The Great Renunciation. (Mahâbhinishkramana). Being the Life and Teaching of Gautama, Prince of India and Founder of Buddhism. (As Told in Verse by an Indian Buddhist.).* London: Trübner and Co., 1879.

ARNOLD, Edwin. *The Light of the World, or, The Great Consummation.* London: Longmans, Green, 1891.
> *The Online Books Page.* Ed. John Mark Ockerbloom. April 26, 2007.
> *http://www.cimmay.us/arnold.htm.*

ARNOLD, Matthew. "Balder Dead." In *Poems: Second Series.* London: Longman, Brown, Green, and Longmans, 1855.

ARNOLD, Matthew. "Sohrab and Rustum." In *Poems.* London: Longman, Brown, Green, and Longmans, 1853.

ATHERSTONE, Edwin. *The Fall of Nineveh: A Poem.* London: Baldwin and Cradock, 1828.
> *Oldpoetry.* May 6, 2007.
> *http://oldpoetry.com/opoem/searchby/Edwin%20Atherstone.*

ATHERSTONE, Edwin. *Israel in Egypt: A Poem.* London: Longman, Green, Longman, and Roberts, 1861.
> *Oldpoetry.* May 6, 2007.
> *http://oldpoetry.com/opoem/searchby/Edwin%20Atherstone.*

ATHERSTONE, Edwin. *The Last Days of Herculaneum and Abradates and Panthea: Poems.* London: Baldwin, Cradock, and Joy, 1821.

ATHERSTONE, Edwin. *A Midsummer Day's Dream. A Poem.* London: Baldwin, Cradock, and Joy, 1824.

Google Book Search. April 26, 2007.
http://books.google.com/books?id=wpZUyB2x01UC.

[AUSTIN, Alfred.] *Randolph: A Poem in Two Cantos*. London: Saunders and Otley, 1855.

AUSTIN, Alfred. *The Human Tragedy: A Poem*. London: Hardwicke, 1862.
2nd edn. Edinburgh: **William Blackwood and Sons, 1876.**
3rd edn. London: **Macmillan, 1889.**
Google Book Search. May 6, 2007.
http://books.google.com/books?id=mocCAAAAQAAJ. (1862 version only.)

AYTOUN, William Edmondstoune and Theodore Martin. *The Book of Ballads, ed.
Bon Gaultier*. London: W. S. Orr, 1845.
Rpt. Edinburgh and London: Blackwood, 1903. *Google Book Search*. May 6, 2007.
http://books.google.com/books?id=mgIlAAAAMAAJ.

AYTOUN, William Edmondstoune. *Bothwell: A Poem in Six Parts*. Edinburgh and
London: Blackwood, 1855.
Rpt. Boston: Ticknor and Fields, 1856. *Google Book Search*. May 6, 2007.
http://books.google.com/books?id=Ym8gAAAAMAAJ.

AYTOUN, William Edmondstoune. *Firmilian, or The Student of Badajoz: A Spasmodic
Tragedy*. Edinburgh, London: William Blackwood and Sons, 1854.
Rpt. New York: Redfield, 1855. *Google Book Search*. May 6, 2007.
http://books.google.com/books?id=qloLAAAAIAAJ.

AYTOUN, William Edmondstoune. *Lays of the Scottish Cavaliers, and Other Poems*.
Edinburgh and London: William Blackwood and Sons, 1849.
Project Gutenberg. April 27, 2007. *http://www.gutenberg.org/etext/10945*.

BAILEY, Philip James. *Festus. A Poem*. London: W. Pickering, 1839.
2nd edn. London: **W. Pickering, 1845.**

BAILLIE, Joanna. *Metrical Legends of Exalted Characters*. London: Longman, Hurst,
Rees, Orme, and Brown, 1821.
Online Archive of California. April 26, 2007.
http://content.cdlib.org/ark:/13030/kt4199p5f6/?&query=&brand=oac.

BARHAM, Richard. *The Ingoldsby Legends; or, Myth and Marvels*. London: Bentley, 1840.

BARLOW, Joel. *The Columbiad*. Philadelphia: C. and A. Conrad, 1807.
Project Gutenberg. April 27, 2007. *http://www.gutenberg.org/etext/8683*.

BARLOW, Joel. *The Vision of Columbus: A Poem in Nine Books*. Hartford: Hudson and
Goodwin, 1787.
Rpt. London: R. Philips, 1809. *Making of America Books (University of Michigan Library)*.
April 27, 2007.
*http://quod.lib.umich.edu/cgi/t/text/pageviewer-idx?c=moa;cc=moa;rgn=full%20text;idno
=APT9199.0001.001;didno=APT9199.0001.001; view=image;seq=0001*

BAYLEY, Peter. *Idwal, and Other Portions of a Poem: to Which is Added Gryphiadaea,
Carmen Venatorium*. London: Longman, Hurst, Rees, Orme, and Brown, 1817.

BETHAM, Matilda. *The Lay of Marie: A Poem*. London: R. Hunter, 1816.
  Project Gutenberg. April 27, 2007. *http://www.gutenberg.org/etext/11857*.

BICKERSTETH, Edward Henry. *Yesterday, To-Day, and For Ever: A Poem, in Twelve Books*. London: Rivingtons, 1866.
  Rpt. New York: Robert Carter & Bros., 1870. *Google Book Search*. April 27, 2007.
  http://books.google.com/books?id=Aj4e73cWdKUC.

BIGG, J. Stanyan. *Night and the Soul. A Dramatic Poem*. London: Groombridge, 1854.
  Google Book Search. April 27, 2007.
  http://books.google.com/books?id=C1ECAAAAQAAJ.

BIGG, J. Stanyan. *The Sea-King: A Metrical Romance, in Six Cantos*. London: Whittaker, 1848.

BIRD, James. *Dunwich: A Tale of the Splendid City: in Four Cantos*. London: Baldwin and Cradock, 1828.
  Google Book Search. April 27, 2007.
  http://books.google.com/books?id=QwiYXGl_KPEC.

BIRD, James. *The Vale of Slaughden: A Poem, in Five Cantos*. Halesworth, Suffolk: Tippell, 1819.

BLACKIE, John Stuart. *Lays and Legends of Ancient Greece*. Edinburgh: Sutherland and Knox, 1857.

BLAKE, William. *America: A Prophecy*. Lambeth: Blake, 1793.
  America: A Prophecy, copy E. The William Blake Archive. Ed. Morris Eaves, Robert N. Essick, and Joseph Viscomi. April 24, 2007.
  http://www.blakearchive.org/.
  N. B. For all of the following works by Blake except the unengraved *French Revolution* and *Vala*, the Blake Archive provides an electronic text at the above URL, usually with access to multiple illuminated versions.

BLAKE, William. *The Book of Ahania*. Lambeth: Blake, 1795.

BLAKE, William. *The Book of Los*. Lambeth: Blake, 1795.

BLAKE, William. *Europe: A Prophecy*. Lambeth: Blake, 1794.

BLAKE, William. *The [First] Book of Urizen*. Lambeth: Blake, 1794.

BLAKE, William. *The French Revolution*. London: J. Johnson, 1791.
  In *The Poetical Works of William Blake*, 263–280. Ed. John Sampson. Oxford: Oxford University Press, 1914. *Google Book Search*. May 6, 2007.
  http://books.google.com/books?id=mJbiX7wbAScC.

BLAKE, William. *Jerusalem: The Emanation of the Giant Albion*. Lambeth: Blake, 1818–1827.

BLAKE, William. *Milton: A Poem in Two Books*. London: Blake, 1804–1818.

BLAKE, William. *The Song of Los*. Lambeth: Blake, 1795.

BLAKE, William. *Vala, or, The Death and Judgement of the Ancient Man; A Dream of Nine Nights*, or *The Four Zoas*. MS. dated 1797. Ed. G. E. Bentley. Oxford: Clarendon Press, 1956.

606   BIBLIOGRAPHY OF POEMS CITED

BLAKE, William. *Visions of the Daughters of Albion*. London: Blake, 1793.

BLAKE, William. *William Blake's Writings*. Ed. G. E. Bentley. Oxford: Clarendon Press, 1978.

BLIND, Mathilde. *The Ascent of Man*. London: Chatto and Windus, 1889.
    Victorian Women Writers Project. Ed. Perry Willett. April 27, 2007.
    http://www.indiana.edu/~letrs/vwwp/blind/ascent.html.

BOWLES, William Lisle. *The Spirit of Discovery by Sea: A Descriptive and Historical Poem*. London: Cadell and Davies, 1804.
    In *The Poetical Works of William Lisle Bowles*, Vol. 1. Ed. George Gilfillan. London: James Nichol, 1855. *Project Gutenberg*. April 29, 2007.
    http://www.gutenberg.org/etext/18915.

BOWLES, William Lisle. *The Missionary; A Poem*. London: J. Innes, 1813.
    In *The Poetical Works of William Lisle Bowles*, Vol. 1. Ed. George Gilfillan. London: James Nichol, 1855. *Project Gutenberg*. April 29, 2007.
    http://www.gutenberg.org/etext/18915.

BOWLES, William Lisle. *The Grave of the Last Saxon; or, The Legend of the Curfew. A Poem*. London: Hurst, Robinson, and Co., 1822.
    In *The Poetical Works of William Lisle Bowles*, Vol . 2. Edinburgh: Nichol, 1855. *Google Book Search*. May 6, 2007.
    http://books.google.com/books?id=mOzBWkF7YvUC.

BOWLES, William Lisle. *St. John in Patmos: A Poem*. London: J. Murray, 1832.
    In *The Poetical Works of William Lisle Bowles*, Vol. 2. Edinburgh: Nichol, 1855. *Google Book Search*. May 6, 2007.
    http://books.google.com/books?id=mOzBWkF7YvUC.

BRADDON, M.E. *Garibaldi and Other Poems*. London: Bosworth and Harrison, 1861.

BREAKENRIDGE, John. *The Crusades, and Other Poems*. Kingston: J. Rowlands, 1846.

BRIDGES, Robert. *Eros and Psyche: A Poem in Twelve Measures*. London: George Bell, 1885.
    Internet Archive. May 6, 2007.
    http://www.archive.org/details/erospsychepoeminoobriduoft.

BROWN, James. *Britain Preserved: A Poem: In Seven Books*. London: Murray and Highley, 1800.

BROWN, William Laurence. *Philemon: or, The Progress of Virtue; A Poem*. Edinburgh: Ballantyne, 1809.

BROWNING, Elizabeth Barrett. *Aurora Leigh*. London: Chapman and Hall, 1857.

BROWNING, Elizabeth Barrett. *The Battle of Marathon. A Poem*. London: W. Lindsell, 1820.

BROWNING, Elizabeth Barrett. *Casa Guidi Windows: A Poem*. London: Chapman and Hall, 1851.

BROWNING, Elizabeth Barrett. *A Drama of Exile*. London: George G. Harrap, 1844.

BROWNING, Robert. *Paracelsus*. London: Effingham Wilson, 1835.

BROWNING, Robert. *The Ring and the Book*. London: Smith, Elder, 1868–1869.

BROWNING, Robert. *Sordello*. London: Moxon, 1840.

BROWNING, Robert. *Strafford: An Historical Tragedy*. London: Longman, Rees, Orme, Brown, Green and Longman, 1837.

BUCHAN, David Home. *The Battle of Waterloo: A Poem*. London: Underwood (and Edinburgh: Macredie), 1816.

BUCHANAN, Robert. *Balder the Beautiful: A Song of Divine Death*. (1864). London: W. Mullan and Son, 1877.
> Rpt. in *Complete Poetical Works*. In 2 vols. London: Chatto and Windus, 1901.
> *Google Book Search*. April 26, 2007.
> http://books.google.com/books?id=C1cOAAAAIAAJ.

BUCHANAN, Robert. *The Book of Orm*. London: Strahan, 1870.
> *Google Book Search*. April 26, 2007.
> http://books.google.com/books?id=UmICAAAA QAAJ.

BUCHANAN, Robert. *The City of Dream, An Epic Poem*. London: Chatto and Windus, 1888.
> *Internet Archive*. May 8, 2007.
> http://www.archive.org/details/cityofdreamanepi00buchuoft.

BUCHANAN, Robert. *The Drama of Kings*. London: Strahan, 1871.

BUCHANAN, Robert. *Undertones*. London: Chatto and Windus, 1863.

BULMER, Agnes. *Messiah's Kingdom: A Poem in Twelve Books*. London: J. G. and F. Rivington, 1833.

BULWER-LYTTON, Edward. *The Siamese Twins: A Satirical Tale of the Times. With Other Poems*. London: H. Colburn and R. Bentley, 1831.

BULWER-LYTTON, Edward. *King Arthur: An Epic Poem. In Two Volumes*. London: Henry Colburn, 1849.
> Rpt. London: Routledge, 1875.
> *Google Book Search*. May 6, 2007.
> http://books.google.com/books?id=d1gEAAAAQAAJ.

BURGES, James Bland. *The Dragon Knight. A Poem, in Twelve Cantos*. London: Longman, Hurst, Rees, Orme, and Brown, 1818.

BURGES, James Bland. *Richard the First, A Poem, in Eighteen Books*. London: C. Roworth, 1801.
> *Google Book Search*. May 6, 2007.
> http://books.google.com/books?id=1-Q1-ClnMAsC.

BURRELL, Sophia. *The Thymbriad (From Xenophon's Cyropædia)*. London: Leigh and Sotheby, 1794.

BURRELL, Sophia. *Telemachus*. London: Leigh and Sotheby, 1794.

BUSK, Mrs. William [Mary Margaret.] *Sordello*. In *Plays and Poems*. London: T. Hookham, 1837.

Byron, George Gordon, Lord. *The Corsair*. London: John Murray, 1814.

Byron, George Gordon, Lord. *Don Juan*. 1819–1824. Cantos 1–2 and 3–5 London: John Murray, 1819 and 1821; cantos 6–14 and 15–16 London: John and H. L. Hunt, 1823 and 1824.

Byron, George Gordon, Lord. *The Giaour; A Fragment of a Turkish Tale*. London: Murray, 1813.

Byron, George Gordon, Lord. *Lara, A Tale*. London: John Murray, 1814.

Byron, George Gordon, Lord. *The Siege of Corinth. A Poem*. London: John Murray, 1816.

Campbell, James. *The Judgment of Babylon; The Siege of Masada; with Other Poems*. London, J. Churchill, 1826.

Campbell, Thomas. *Gertrude of Wyoming; A Pennsylvanian Tale and Other Poems*. London: Longman, Hurst, Rees, and Orme, 1809.
  PoemHunter.com. April 29, 2007.
  http://www.poemhunter.com/poem/gertrude-of-wyoming/.

Clough, Arthur Hugh. *The Bothie of Toper-na-Fuosich: A Long-Vacation Pastoral*. Oxford: Macpherson, 1848.
  The Bothie of Tober-na-vuolich: A Long-Vacation Pastoral. In *The Poems and Prose Remains of Arthur Hugh Clough With A Selection of His Letters and a Memoir, Edited by His Wife*. Vol. 2. London: Macmillan, 1869. *Words*. April 26, 2007.
  http://whitewolf.newcastle.edu.au/words/authors/C/CloughArthurHugh/verse/poem-sproseremains/bothie_01.html.

Cooper, Thomas. *The Paradise of Martyrs: A Faith-Rhyme, in Five Books*. London: Hodder, 1873.
  In *The Poetical Works of Thomas Cooper*. London: Hodder and Stoughton, 1877. *Google Book Search*. May 6, 2007.
  http://books.google.com/books?id =G2oqAAAAMAAJ.

Cooper, Thomas. *The Purgatory of Suicides: A Prison-Rhyme in Ten Books*. London: Jeremiah How, 1845.
  In *The Poetical Works of Thomas Cooper*. London: Hodder and Stoughton, 1877. *Google Book Search*. May 6, 2007.
  http://books.google.com/books?id=G2oqAAAAMAAJ.

[Cope, Harriett.] *Waterloo, A Poem in Two Parts*. London: Hatchard, 1822.

Cornwall, Barry [pseud. for Bryan Waller Procter.] *The Flood of Thessaly, The Girl of Provence, and Other Poems*. London: H. Colburn, 1823.
  Google Book Search. May 6, 2007.
  http://books.google.com/books?id=l5b4HhRb9UQC.

Cornwall, Barry. *Marcian Colonna, An Italian Tale; With Three Dramatic Scenes, and Other Poems*. London: J. Warren, 1820.

Cornwallis, Kinahan. *Yarra Yarra; or, The Wandering Aborigine*. London, Ward and Lock, 1858.

COTTLE, Joseph. *Alfred, An Epic Poem, in Twenty-Four Books*. London: Longman, 1800.
London: Longman, Rees, 1804.
Google Book Search. May 6, 2007.
Vol. 1 *http://books.google.com/books?id=KK8DAAAAQAAJ*. Vol. 2
Vol. 2 *http://books.google.com/books?id=Pq8DAAAAQAAJ*.

COTTLE, Joseph. *The Fall of Cambria*. London: Longman, 1808.

COTTLE, Joseph. *Messiah: A Poem, in Twenty-Eight Books*. London, Button, 1815.

COURTHOPE, William John. *Ludibria Lunae; or, The Wars of the Women and the Gods: An Allegorical Burlesque*. London: Smith, Elder, 1869.

COWLEY, Hannah. *The Siege of Acre. An Epic Poem. In Six Books*. London: Debrett, 1801.
In *The Works of Mrs. Cowley, Dramas and Poems, In Three Volumes*. London: Wilkie and Robinson, 1813.
Vol. 3 *The Brown University Women Writers Project*. April 29, 2007.
http://golf.services.brown.edu/WWO/php/wAll.php?doc=cowley.poems.html.

CREAMER, Edward Sherwood. *An Epic of Heaven and Other Poems*. New York: Broadway, 1910.

[CROKER, John Wilson.] *The Battles of Talavera. A Poem*. London: John Murray, 1809.

CROLY, George. *The Angel of the World; An Arabian Tale: Sebastian; A Spanish Tale: with Other Poems*. London: Warren, 1820.

CROLY, George. *May Fair: In Four Cantos*. London: Ainsworth, 1827.

CUMBERLAND, Richard. *Calvary; or The Death of Christ. A Poem, in Eight Books*. London: Dilly, 1792.
Rpt. Morris-Town, N.J.: Henry P. Russell, 1815. *Google Book Search*. April 29, 2007.
http://books.google.com/books?id=JIQgAAAAMAAJ.

CUMBERLAND, Richard and James Bland Burges. *The Exodiad. A Poem. By the Authors of Calvary and Richard the First*. London: Lackington, Allen, 1807.

CUNNINGHAM, J. W. *De Rancè: A Poem*. London: Cadell and Davies, 1815.
Google Book Search. May 6, 2007.
http://books.google.com/books?id =AUsCAAAAQAAJ.

[CURSHAM, Mary Anne.] *Martin Luther, A Poem*. London: Longman, 1825.

DALE, Thomas. *Irad and Adah: A Tale of the Flood*. London: n. p., 1822.
Rpt. in *Poetical Works*. London: Tilt, 1836.

DARWIN, Erasmus. *The Botanic Garden*. London: J. Johnson, 1790 (Vol. 1, *The Economy of Vegetation*), 1792 (Vol. 2, *The Loves of the Plants*).
Project Gutenberg. April 29, 2007.
Vol 1. *http://www.gutenberg.org/etext/9612*.
Vol 2. *http://www.gutenberg.org/etext/10671*.

DAVIDSON, Henry. *Waterloo, A Poem*. Edinburgh, Manners and Miller, 1816.

DAWSON, Catherine Amy. *Sappho*. London: Kegan Paul, 1889.

DEARDEN, William. *The Vale of Caldene; or, The Past and the Present: A Poem, in Six Books.* London: Longman and Co., 1844.

DE VERE, Aubrey. *The Foray of Queen Meave and Other Legends of Ireland's Heroic Age.* London: Kegan Paul, 1882.
>   **Rpt. London: Kegan Paul, 1884.**
>   *Internet Archive.* May 6, 2007.
>   http://www.archive.org/details/forayofqueenmeavoodeveiala.

DE VERE, Aubrey. *The Legends of Saint Patrick.* London: King, 1872.
>   *Project Gutenberg.* April 29, 2007.
>   http://www.gutenberg.org/etext/7165.

DE VERE, Aubrey. *Legends of the Saxon Saints.* London: Kegan Paul, 1879.
>   *Internet Archive.* May 6, 2007.
>   http://www.archive.org/details/a570571200deveuoft.

DIBDIN, Thomas. *A Metrical History of England; or, Recollections in Rhyme, of Some of the Most Prominent Features in our National Chronology, from the Landing of Julius Caesar, to the Commencement of the Regency, in 1812.* In 2 vols. London: Longman, 1813.

DISRAELI, Benjamin. *The Revolutionary Epick.* London: Moxon, 1834.
>   Rpt. London: Longman, Green, Longman, Roberts, Green, 1864. *Google Book Search.* May 6, 2007.
>   http://books.google.com/books?id=XqkiAAAAMAAJ.

DIXON, Charlotte. *The Mount of Olives, or the Resurrection and Ascension; A Poem. In Continuation of Calvary.* London: Adland, 1814.

DIXON, Richard Watson. *Mano, A Poetical History.* London: Routledge, 1883.
>   Selections in *A Victorian Anthology, 1837–1895.* Ed. Edmund Clarence Stedman. Cambridge: Riverside Press, 1895. *Bartleby.com.* May 6, 2007.
>   http://www.bartleby.com/246/738.html.

DOBELL, Sydney. *Balder. Part the First.* London: Smith, Elder, 1854.
>   *Google Book Search.* April 29, 2007.
>   http://books.google.com/books?id=AowCAAAAQAAJ&dq=dobell+sydney+balder.

DOMETT, Alfred. *Ranolf and Amohia: A South-Sea Day-Dream.* London: Smith, Elder, 1872.

DOUGHTY, Charles M. *The Dawn in Britain.* London: Duckworth, 1906.
>   *Google Book Search.* May 6, 2007.
>   Vol. 1 http://books.google.com/books?id=CpкcvXOmmHUC&dq=editions: OEn 8B5-USeDx4-hJ3W.
>   Vol. 2 http://books.google.com/books?id=l3PwKu-l2ckC.
>   Vol. 3 http://books.google.com/books?id=T5EgAAAAMAAJ.
>   Vol. 4 http://books.google.com/books?id=bZEgAAAAMAAJ.
>   Vol. 5 http://books.google.com/books?id=DIWOn5iUfYQC.
>   Vol. 6 http://books.google.com/books?id=w9OCug6IgI4C.

DOWNING, Harriet. *Mary; or Female Friendship: A Poem in Twelve Books*. London: Harper, 1816.

    The Brown University Women Writers Project. April 29, 2007.

    http://golf.services.brown.edu/WWO/php/wAll.php?doc=downing.femalefriend.html.

DRUMMOND, William Hamilton. *The Battle of Trafalgar, An Heroic Poem*. Belfast: Archer and Ward, 1806.

    Rpt. Charleston: Courier, 1807.

    Rpt. Belfast: Smyth and Lyons, 1806. *Google Book Search*. May 6, 2007.

    http://books.google.com/books?id=f3QCAAAAQAAJ.

DRUMMOND, William. *Odin, A Poem; in Eight Books and Two Parts. Part the First*. London: Law, Longman, 1817.

DUNLOP, John. *Oliver Cromwell. A Poem, in Three Books*. Edinburgh: Oliver and Boyd, 1829.

DUTT, Romesh C., tr. and cond. *The Great Epics of Ancient India*. London: J. M. Dent, 1900.

    Rpt. Delhi: Ess Ess, 1976.

ELIOT, George [pseud. for Marian Evans.] *The Spanish Gypsy*. Edinburgh: Blackwood, 1868.

    Rpt. in *The Poems of George Eliot*. New York: Thomas Y. Crowell, 1884.

    Rpt. Boston: Ticknor and Fields, 1868. *Making of America Books (University of Michigan Library)*. April 29, 2007.

    http://quod.lib.umich.edu/cgi/t/text/pagevieweridx?c=moa&cc=moa&idno=adh 8207.0001.001&frm=frameset&view=image&seq=3.

ELLIOTT, Ebenezer. *The Village Patriarch*. London: for the author, 1829.

    Rpt. in *The Poems of Ebenezer Elliott*, New York: Leavitt, 1850.

    In *The Poetical Works of Ebenezer Elliot*. Edinburgh, William Tate, 1840. *Google Book Search*. May 6, 2007.

    http://books.google.com/books?id=lvQDAAAAQAAJ.

ELLIS, Sarah Stickney. *The Sons of the Soil. A Poem*. London: Fisher, Son, and Co., [1840.] *Victorian Women Writers Project*. Ed. Perry Willett. April 30, 2007.

    http://www.indiana.edu/~letrs/vwwp/ellis/sons.html.

ETTY, Robert. *The Cossack: A Poem in Three Cantos*. London: Baldwin, 1815.

EVANS, Sebastian. *Brother Fabian's Manuscript and Other Poems*. London and Cambridge: Macmillan, 1865.

    Google Book Search. May 6, 2007.

    http://books.google.com/books?id=v1wCAAAAQAAJ.

EWING, Harriet. *Dunrie: A Poem*. London: Robinson, 1819.

FABER, Frederick William. *Sir Lancelot: A Legend of the Middle Ages*. London: Rivington, 1844.

    2nd edn. London: Thomas Richardson, 1857.

FANE, Violet. [pseud. for Mary Montgomerie Lamb]. *Constance's Fate: A Story of Denzil Place*. London: Chapman and Hall, 1876.
> **Rpt. London: Chapman and Hall, 1884.**
> *Google Book Search*. April 30, 2007.
> *http://books.google.com/books?id=rDYgAAAAMAAJ*.

FERGUSON, Samuel. *Congal: A Poem. In Five Books*. Dublin: Ponsonby, 1872.
> Rpt. London: Bell, 1907. *Google Book Search*. May 6, 2007.
> *http://books.google.com/books?id=92kOAAAAIAAJ*.

FERGUSON, Samuel. *Lays of the Western Gael*. London: Bell and Daldy, 1865.
> In *Lays of the Western Gael, and Other Poems*. London: Bell, 1865. *Google Book Search*. May 6, 2007.
> *http://books.google.com/books?id=2WkOAAAAIAAJ*.

FITCHETT, John. *King Alfred: A Poem*. Vol. 1. London: Cadell and Davies, 1808.
> **London: Pickering, 1841.**
> *Google Book Search*. May 6, 2007.
> vol. 1 (Bks.1–10) *http://books.google.com/books?id =wdqCWtxhVk8C*.

FRANCIS, Eliza. *The Rival Roses; or Wars of York and Lancaster. A Metrical Tale*. London: Stockdale, 1813.

FRERE, John Hookham. *Prospectus and Specimen of an Intended National Work, by William and Robert Whistlecraft*. London: Murray, 1818.
> Rpt. Bath: H.E. Carrington, 1842. *Google Book Search*. April 30, 2007.
> *http://books.google.com/books?id=PfkMU5PZuOQC*.

GIFFORD, William. *The Baviad: A Paraphrastic Imitation of the First Satire of Persius*. London: Faulder, 1791.
> In *The Baviad, and Mæviad*. London: J. Wright, 1797. Google *Book Search*. May 6, 2007.
> *http://books.google.com/books?id=m8okAAAAMAAJ*.

GILBANK, William. *The Day of Pentecost, or Man Restored: A Poem in Twelve Books*. London: Reynell, 1789.

GLOVER, Richard. *Leonidas: A Poem*. London: R. Dodsley, 1737.
> **Rpt. 7th edn. London: Whittingham, 1804.**
> *Google Book Search*. May 6, 2007.
> Vol. 1 Fifth ed. London: Cadell, 1770.
> *http://books.google.com/books?id=WKUDAAAAQAAJ*.
> Vol 2. Sixth ed. London: F. J. du Roveray, 1798.
> *http://books.google.com/books?id=ONQhAAAAMAAJ*.

GOALEN, Walter. *Gideon: A Poem in Seven Books*. Edinburgh: Grant, 1868.

GWILLIAM, John. *The Imperial Captive; or, The Unexampled Career of the Ex-Emperor, Napoleon, from The Period of his Quitting Elba to that of his Surrender to the English Nation, Circumstantially Developed*. London. Jennings, 1817.

HAM, Elizabeth. *Elgiva, or the Monks: An Historical Poem*. London: Baldwin, 1824.

HAMILTON, Anne. *The Epics of the Ton; or, the Glories of the Great World: A Poem, in Two Books*. London: Baldwin, 1807.
> *The Corvey Poets Project at the University of Nebraska*. April 30, 2007.
> *http://www.unl.edu/Corvey/html/Etexts/HamiltonAnne/HamiltonText.htm*.

HANDS, Elizabeth. *The Death of Amnon. A Poem*. Coventry: Rollason, 1789.
> *Internet Archive*. May 8, 2007.
> *http://www.archive.org/details/deathofamnonpoem00handuoft*.

HARDY, Thomas. *The Dynasts: An Epic-Drama of the War with Napoleon, in Three Parts, Nineteen Acts, and One Hundred and Thirty Scenes*. London: Macmillan and Co., 1910.
> *Project Gutenberg*. April 30, 2007.
> *http://www.gutenberg.org/etext/4043*.

HARRIS, William Richard. *Napoleon Portrayed: An Epic Poem in Twelve Cantos*. London: Longman, Brown, Green, and Longmans, 1845.

HATFIELD, Sibella Elizabeth. *The Wanderer of Scandinavia, or Sweden Delivered*. London: Longman, 1826.

HAWKER, Robert Stephen. *The Quest of the Sangraal*. In *Poetical Works*, ed. J.G. Godwin. London: Kegan Paul, 1879.
> *The Camelot Project at the University of Rochester. Ed. Alan Lupack and Barbara Tepa Lupack*. April 30, 2007.
> *http://www.lib.rochester.edu/camelot/hawker.htm*.

HAWKINS, Thomas. *The Christiad*. London: Haw, 1853.

HAWKINS, Thomas. *The Wars of Jehovah, in Heaven, Earth, and Hell: In Nine Books*. London: Baisler, 1844.

HAYES, Alfred. *The Last Crusade and Other Poems*. Birmingham: Cornish, 1887.
> *Google Book Search*. April 30, 2007.
> *http://books.google.com/books?id =L4IOAAAAIAAJ*.

HEBER, Reginald. *Morte d'Arthur*. In *The Poetical Works of Reginald Heber*. London: J. Murray, 1841.
> Rpt. Boston: Little, Brown, 1853. *Google Book Search*. June 2, 2007.
> *http://books.google.com/books?id=8LOSzUYzTxEC*.

HEMANS, Felicia. *The Abencerrage*. In *Tales, and Historic Scenes*. London: J. Murray, 1819.
> **Rpt. *Felicia Hemans: Selected Poems, Letters, Reception Materials*. Ed. Susan J. Wolfson. Princeton: Princeton University Press, 2000.**
> In *Poems of Felicia Hemans*. Edinburgh and London: William Blackwood and Sons, 1872. *Google Book Search*. May 6, 2007.
> *http://books.google.com/books?id=dkWtNAiz2CAC*.

HEMANS, Felicia. *The Forest Sanctuary*. In *The Forest Sanctuary; and Other Poems*. London: John Murray, 1825.
> **Rpt. *Felicia Hemans: Selected Poems, Letters, Reception Materials*. Ed. Susan J. Wolfson. Princeton: Princeton University Press, 2000.**
> *Online Archive of California*. April 26, 2007.
> *http://content.cdlib.org/ark:/13030/kt3h4nb99b/?&query=&brand=oac*

[HENDERSON, Thulia Susannah.] *Olga; or, Russia in the Tenth Century: An Historical Poem*. London: Hamilton, 1855.

HERAUD, John Abraham. *The Descent into Hell*. London: John Murray, 1830.
   Second ed. London: James Fraser, 1835.
   Google Book Search. May 6, 2007.
   http://books.google.com/books?id=SJ_YoP5PCFoC.

HERAUD, John Abraham. *The Judgement of the Flood*. London: Fraser, 1834.
   Google Book Search. May 6, 2007.
   http://books.google.com/books?id=499hMLWnOYIC.

HERBERT, William. *Helga. A Poem. In Seven Cantos*. London: Murray, 1815.
   Google Book Search. April 30, 2007.
   http://books.google.com/books?id =iiskAAAAMAAJ.

HERBERT, William. *Pia Della Pietra: A Tale*. London: Murray, 1820.

HERBERT, William. *Attila, King of the Huns*. London: Bohn, 1838.
   Google Book Search. May 6, 2007.
   http://books.google.com/books?id=mFiEyoDIFwQC.

HEWLETT, Maurice. *Helen Redeemed and Other Poems*. London: Macmillan, 1913.

HICKEY, Emily H. *Michael Villiers, Idealist and Other Poems*. London: Smith, Elder, 1891.

HODGSON, Francis. *Sir Edgar*. London: Mackinlay, 1810.

HODGSON, Francis. *Lady Jane Grey, A Tale, in Two Books*. London: Bensley, 1809.

HOGG, James. *Mador of the Moor*. Edinburgh: Blackwood, 1816.
   In *The Poetical Works of the Ettrick Shepherd, Including the Queen's Wake, Pilgrims of the Sun, Mador of the Moor, Mountain Bard, et cetera*. Vol. 4. Glasgow: Blackie, 1840. *Google Book Search*. June 2, 2007.
   http://books.google.com/books?id=GPojAAAAMAAJ&pg=PA3&dq= hogg+mador+moor.

HOGG, James. *Queen Hynde: A Poem, in Six Books*. London: Longman, 1825.
   Rpt. London: Longman, Hurst, Rees, Orme, Brown, and Green, 1824. *Google Book Search*. May 6, 2007.
   http://books.google.com/books?id=ugptPpdULVwC.

HOGG, James. *The Pilgrims of the Sun*. Edinburgh: Blackwood, 1815.
   Rpt. in *Poetical Works*, Vol. 2. Glasgow: Blackwood, 1840.
   In *The Poetical Works of the Ettrick Shepherd, Including the Queen's Wake, Pilgrims of the Sun, Mador of the Moor, Mountain Bard, et cetera*. Vol. 2. Edinburgh: Blackie, 1838. *Internet Archive*. May 8, 2007.
   http://www.archive.org/details/poeticalworksofeoohogguoft.

HOGG, James. *The Queen's Wake: A Legendary Poem*. Baltimore: Coale and Maxwell, 1815.
   Rpt. Edinburgh: Ballantyne, 1815. *Google Book Search*. May 6, 2007.
   http://books.google.com/books?id=-2H_xOyIt5UC.

HOLE, Richard. *Arthur; or, The Northern Enchantment. A Poetical Romance in Seven Books*. London: G. G. J. and J. Robinson, 1789.

[HOLFORD] Hodson, Margaret. *Margaret of Anjou. A Poem*. London: John Murray, 1816.
   Rpt. Philadelphia: Carey, 1816.

[HOLFORD] Hodson, Margaret. *Wallace; or, The Fight of Falkirk. A Metrical Romance*. London: Cadell and Davies, 1809.

HOLMES, Ann. *An Epic Poem on Adam and Eve*. Bedale: Joseph Todd, 1800.

HORNE, Richard Henry. *Orion: An Epic Poem in Three Books*. London: J. Miller, 1843.
   Rpt. 9th edn. Boston: Roberts, 1872.

HOUGHTON, Mary Arnald. *Emilia of Lindinau; or, The Field of Leipsic. A Poem, in Four Cantos*. London: Whittingham and Arliss, 1815.

HOYLE, Charles. *Exodus: An Epic Poem in Thirteen Books*. London, J. Hatchard, 1807.

HUMPHREYS, John Doddridge. *Prince Malcolm: in Five Cantos*. London: Longman, 1813.

HUNT, Leigh. *The Story of Rimini: A Poem*. London: J. Murray, 1816.
   Rpt. London: C. and J. Ollier, 1819. *Google Book Search*. May 6, 2007.
   http://books.google.com/books?id=bcgjAAAAMAAJ.

INGELOW, Jean. *A Story of Doom*. Boston: Roberts, 1867.
   Rpt. in *Poetical Works*. New York: Crowell, 1894.
   In *Poems, Vol. 2*. London: Longmans, Green, 1885. *Google Book Search*. May 6, 2007.
   http://books.google.com/books?id=hthzcexcxoMC.

JONES, Ernest. *Corayda: A Tale of Faith and Chivalry, and Other Poems*. London: Kent, 1860.

JONES, Ernest. *The Revolt of Hindostan; or, The New World, A Poem*. London: Effingham Wilson, 1857.

[JOYCE, Robert Dwyer.] *Deirdrè*. Boston: Roberts Bros., 1876.
   Google Book Search. May 6, 2007.
   http://books.google.com/books?id=eAhrbwRHQ3cC.

KEATS, John. *Endymion; A Poetic Romance*. London: Taylor and Hessey, 1818.

KEATS, John. "Hyperion: A Fragment." *Lamia, Isabella, The Eve of St. Agnes and Other Poems*. London, Taylor and Hessey, 1820.

KEATS, John. "The Fall of Hyperion." "Another Version of Keats's *Hyperion*." Ed. R. Monckton Milnes. *Biographical and Historical Miscellanies of the Philobiblon Society*, 1856.

KING, Hannah Tapfield. *An Epic Poem: A Synopsis of the Rise of the Church of Jesus Christ of Latter-Day Saints, from the Birth of the Prophet Joseph Smith to the Arrival on the Spot Which the Prophet Brigham Young Pronounced to Be the Site of the Future Salt Lake City*. Salt Lake City: Juvenile Instructor Office, 1884.

KING, Harriet Eleanor Baillie-Hamilton. *The Disciples*. London: Henry King, 1873.

Kingsley, Charles. *Andromeda, and Other Poems*. London, J.W. Parker and Son, 1858.
    Project Gutenberg. April 30, 2007.
    http://www.gutenberg.org/etext/11064.

Knight, Richard Payne. *Alfred; A Romance in Rhyme*. London: Longman, 1823.
    Google Book Search. April 30, 2007.
    http://books.google.com/books?id=XR-W7kaRAAEC.

Landon, Letitia. *The Improvisatrice*. London: Hurst, Robinson, 1824.
    Letitia Elizabeth Landon Home Page. Ed. Glenn Himes. May 8, 2007.
    http://www.people.iup.edu/ghimes/imp/improvi.htm.

Landon, Letitia. *The Troubadour; Catalogue of Pictures; and Historical Sketches*. London: Hurst, Robinson, and Co., 1825.
    Online Archive of California. April 30, 2007.
    http://content.cdlib.org/xtf/view?docId=kt6p301567&query=&brand= oac.

[Landor, Walter Savage.] *Gebir: A Poem in Seven Books*. London: Rivingtons, 1798.
    Rpt. *Poems of Walter Savage Landor*. Ed. Geoffrey Grigson. London: Centaur, 1964.
    Project Gutenberg. April 30, 2007.
    http://www.gutenberg.org/etext/4007.

[Landor, Walter Savage.] *Gebirus, Poema*. London: Kirby, 1803.

[Landor, Walter Savage.] *Crysaor*. In *Poetry by the Author of Gebir*. London: F. and C. Rivington, 1802.
    Rpt. *The Complete Works of Walter Savage Landor* Ed. Stephen Wheeler. London: Chapman and Hall, 1933.

[Landor, Walter Savage.] *The Phocæans*. In *Poetry by the Author of Gebir*. London: F. and C. Rivington, 1802.
    Rpt. *The Complete Works of Walter Savage Landor*. Ed. Stephen Wheeler. London: Chapman and Hall, 1933.

Lang, Andrew. *Helen of Troy*. London: George Bell, 1882.
    Rpt. in *Poetical Works*. London: Longmans, 1923.
    Project Gutenberg. April 30, 2007.
    http://www.gutenberg.org/etext/3229.

Lightfoot, Catherine Anne. *The Battle of Trafalgar: A Poem, in Six Cantos*. London: Whittaker, Treacher and Co., 1833.

Linton, W. J. *The Life and Adventure of Bob Thin, a Poor-Law Tale*. 1840. [pamphlet]
    Rpt. as *Bob Thin or The Poorhouse Fugitive*. In *Illuminated Magazine*, September–October 1845.

Linwood, Mary. *The Anglo-Cambrian; A Poem in Four Cantos*. London: Longman, Hurst, Rees, Orme, and Brown, 1818.

Lofft, Capel. *Ernest. In Twelve Books*. London: Gadsden, 1839.

Lofft, Capel. *Ernest: The Rule of Right*. London: Alvey, 1868.

LONGFELLOW, Henry Wadsworth. *The Golden Legend*. Boston: Ticknor, Reed, and Fields, 1851.

LONGFELLOW, Henry Wadsworth. *Song of Hiawatha*. Boston: Ticknor and Fields, 1855.

LORD, Alfred. *Luther, or Rome and the Reformation*. London: Seeley and Burnside, 1841. *Google Book Search*. May 6, 2007. *http://books.google.com/books?id =y_UOAAAAIAAJ*.

LORNE, Marquis of. *Guido and Lita: A Tale of the Riviera*. London: Macmillan, 1875.

LOW, Charles R. *Britannia's Bulwarks: An Historical Poem, Descriptive of the Deeds of the British Navy*. London: Horace Cox, 1895.

LOW, Charles R. *Cressy to Tel-El-Kebir: A Narrative Poem, Descriptive of the Deeds of the British Army*. London: W. Mitchell and Co., 1892.

LOW, Charles R. *The Epic of Olympus: A Narrative Poem, Descriptive of the Deeds of the Deities and Heroes of Greek Mythology*. London: Digby, Long, and Co., 1897.

LOW, Charles R. *Old England's Navy: An Epic of the Sea*. London: Elliot Stock, 1891.

LOWE, John. *Poems*. Manchester: Dean, 1803.

LUBY, [Catherine.] *The Spirit of the Lakes; or Mucruss Abbey: A Poem in Three Cantos*. London: Longman, Hurst, Rees, Orme, and Brown, 1822.

MACAULAY, Thomas Babington. *Lays of Ancient Rome*. London: Longman, Brown, Green, and Longmans, 1842.
  Rpt., W. J. Rolfe and John C. Rolfe, eds. New York: Harper, 1888.
  Project Gutenberg. April 30, 2007. *http://www.gutenberg.org/etext/847*.

MCCRAE, George Gordon. *Māmba ("The Bright-Eyed")*. Melbourne: Dwight, 1867. *The Sydney Electronic Text and Image Service (University of Sydney)*. April 30, 2007. *http://purl.library.usyd.edu.au/setis/id/v00037*.

MCHENRY, James. *The Antediluvians, or The World Destroyed; A Narrative Poem, in Ten Books*. London: T. M. Cradock, 1839.
  Rpt. Philadelphia: Lippincott, 1840.

MACPHERSON, James. *Fingal: An Ancient Epic Poem, in Six Books*. London: Becket and De Hondt. 1762.

MACPHERSON, James. *Temora: An Ancient Epic Poem, in Eight Books*. London: Becket and De Hondt, 1763.

MAGINN, William. *Homeric Ballads*. In *Fraser's Magazine*, 1838. Posthumously collected and corrected, London: John W. Parker, 1850.
  In *Homeric Ballads and Comedies of Lucian*. New York: Redfield, 1856. 13–228. *Google Book Search*. May 6, 2007. *http://books.google.com/books?id=EBO4QJ5obtoC&dq=MAGINN, +Homeric+ Ballads*.

[MANN, James and David Carey.] *Macbeth: A Poem, in Six Cantos*. London: Sherwood, Neely, and Jones, 1817.

MARSTON, J. Westland. *Gerald, A Dramatic Poem and Other Poems*. London: C. Mitchell, 1842.

MELVILLE, Herman. *Clarel: A Poem and Pilgrimage in the Holy Land*. New York: G. P. Putnam's Sons, 1876.

MEREDITH, Owen [pseud. for Robert Bulwer-Lytton.] *Chronicles and Characters*. 2 vols. London: Chapman and Hall, 1868.

MEREDITH, Owen. *Glenaveril; or, The Metamorphoses. A Poem in Six Books*. London: John Murray, 1885.
> Rpt. New York: Appleton, 1885.
> *Google Book Search*. April 30, 2007.
> http://books.google.com/books?id=z6gDAAAAQAAJ.

MEREDITH, Owen.. *King Poppy: A Fantasia*. Longmans, Green: 1892.

MEREDITH, Owen. *Lucile*. London, Chapman and Hall, 1860.
> Rpt. Boston: Fields, Osgood, 1869.
> *Project Gutenberg*. April 30, 2007.
> http://www.gutenberg.org/etext/1852.

MEREDITH, Owen. *Orval, or, The Fool of Time: A Poem in Five Epochs: Domestic and Social*. In *Orval, or, The Fool of Time; and Other Imitations and Paraphrases*. London: Chapman and Hall, 1869.

MEREDITH, W. E. *Llewelyn ap Jorwerth. A Poem, in Five Cantos*. London: Cadell and Davies, 1818.

MERIVALE, J. H. *Orlando in Roncesvalles, A Poem, in Five Cantos*. London: Murray, 1814.

MICHELL, Nicholas. *Spirits of the Past. An Historical Poem. In Three Books*. London: Tegg, 1853.

MILMAN, Henry Hart. *The Fall of Jerusalem: A Dramatic Poem*. London: Murray, 1820.
> Rpt. New York: Lockwood, 1820.
> *Internet Archive*. May 8, 2007.
> http://www.archive.org/details/fallofjerusalemdoomilmuoft.

MILMAN, Henry Hart. *Samor, Lord of the Bright City. An Heroic Poem*. London: Murray, 1818.
> *Google Book Search*. May 6, 2007.
> http://books.google.com/books?id=zKjnt3JEGNwC.

MITFORD, Mary Russell. *Blanch*. In *Narrative Poems on the Female Character, in the Various Relations of Human Life*. New York: Eastburn, Kirk, 1813.

MITFORD, Mary Russell. *Christina, the Maid of the South Seas*. London: Valpy, 1811.
> *Google Book Search*. April 30, 2007.
> http://books.google.com/books?id=RooCAAAAQAAJ.

MONTGOMERY, James. *The World before the Flood. A Poem, in Ten Cantos*. London: Longman, Hurst, Rees, Orme, and Brown, 1813.

In *The West Indies, and Other Poems*. London: Longman, Hurst, Rees, Orme and Brown, 1818. *Internet Archive*. May 8, 2007. *http://www.archive.org/details/westindiesandothoomontuoft*.

MONTGOMERY, James. *Greenland, and Other Poems*. London: Longman, Hurst, Rees, Orme, and Brown, 1819.
> *Google Book Search*. April 30, 2007.
> *http://books.google.com/books?id=Q1nJxlmcJU8C*.

MONTGOMERY, James. *The Pelican Island and Other Poems*. London: Longman, Rees, Orme, Brown, and Green, 1827.
> **Rpt. Philadelphia: Littell, 1827.**
> *Google Book Search*. May 6, 2007.
> *http://books.google.com/books?id=T8eeNDtjugEC*.

MONTGOMERY, James. *The Wanderer of Switzerland, and Other Poems*. London: Longman, Hurst, Rees, and Orme, 1806.
> Rpt. Edinburgh: Ballantyne, 1815. *Google Book Search*. May 6, 2007.
> *http://books.google.com/books?id=QrEDAAAAQAAJ*.

MONTGOMERY, Robert. *Luther; A Poem*. London: Brisler, 1842.
> Rpt. *Luther; or, The Spirit of Reformation*. London: Simpkin, Marshall, 1845. *Google Book Search*. May 6, 2007.
> *http://books.google.com/books?id=KRsEAAAAsEAAAAQAAJ*.

MONTGOMERY, Robert. *Messiah*. London: Turrill, 1832.
> **2nd edn. *The Messiah: A Poem in Six Books*. London: Turrill, 1832.**
> Second ed. *Google Book Search*. April 30, 2007.
> *http://books.google.com/books?id=gxwkAAAAMAAJ*.

MOORE, Thomas. *The Fudge Family in Paris, ed. Thomas Brown, the Younger*. London: Longman, Hurst, Rees, Orme, and Brown, 1818.
> Rpt. New York: Kirk and Mercein, 1818. *Google Book Search*. April 30, 2007.
> *http://books.google.com/books?id=uRslAAAAMAAJ*.

MOORE, Thomas. *The Fudges in England, ed. Thomas Brown, the Younger*. London: Longman, 1835.
> Rpt. Philadelphia: Carey, Lea, and Blanchard, 1835. *Google Book Search*. April 30, 2007.
> *http://books.google.com/books?id=tbAiaU54SHkC*.

MOORE, Thomas. *Lalla Rookh: An Oriental Romance*. London: Longman, Hurst, Rees, Orme, and Brown, 1817.
> *Google Book Search*. April 30, 2007.
> *http://books.google.com/books?id=u 8jAAAAMAAJ*.

MOORE, Thomas. *The Loves of the Angels: A Poem*. London: Longman, Hurst, Rees, Orme, and Brown, 1823.
> **Rpt. Philadelphia: Littell, 1823.**
> Rpt. Philadelphia: R. Rhodes, 1823. *Google Book Search*. May 6, 2007.
> *http://books.google.com/books?id=XLMDAAAAQAAJ*.

620

BIBLIOGRAPHY OF POEMS CITED

Morris, Lewis. *The Epic of Hades*. London: Henry S. King, 1876.
Rpt. with subtitle *In Three Books*. New York and Boston: Crowell, 1897.
Rpt. with subtitle *In Three Books*. London: Henry S. King, 1877. *Google Book Search*. May 6, 2007.
http://books.google.com/books?id=RngCAAAAQAAJ.

Morris, William, tr. *The Aeneids of Virgil*. London: Ellis and White, 1876.

Morris, William. *The Earthly Paradise: A Poem*. London: F. S. Ellis, 1868 (Parts 1 and 2); 1870 (Parts 3 and 4).
Google Book Search. May 6, 2007.
http://books.google.com/books?id=HroFAAAAQAAJ.

Morris, William. *The Life and Death of Jason, A Poem*. London: Bell and Daldy, 1867.
Morris Online Edition. Ed. Florence Boos. April 30, 2007.
http://morrisedition.lib.uiowa.edu/jason-w-images.html.

Morris, William, tr. *The Odyssey of Homer; Done Into English Verse*. London: Reeves and Turner, 1887.

Morris, William. *The Pilgrims of Hope: A Poem in Thirteen Books*. London: H. B. Forman, 1886.
Rpt. Portland, Me: Thomas B. Mosher, 1901. *Google Book Search*. May 6, 2007.
http://books.google.com/books?id=Dv5lM9Cc17sC.

Morris, William and A. J. Wyatt, tr. *The Tale of Beowulf*. Hammersmith: Kelmscott Press, 1885.
In *The Tale of Beowulf Sometime King of the Folk of the Weder Geats*. n.p., 1904.
Internet Archives. May 8, 2007.
http://www.archive.org/details/TheTaleOfBeowulfSometimeKingOfTheFolkOfThe WederGeats.

Morris, William. *The Story of Sigurd the Volsung and the Fall of the Niblungs*. London: Ellis and White, 1876.
Rpt. London: Longmans, Green, 1904. *Project Gutenberg*. April 30, 2007.
http://www.gutenberg.org/etext/18328.

Murphy, Henry. *The Conquest of Quebec: An Epic Poem in Eight Books*. Dublin: Porter, 1790.

Northmore, Thomas. *Washington, or Liberty Restored. A Poem, in Ten Books*. London: Taylor, 1809.
Google Book Search. April 30, 2007.
http://books.google.com/books?id=qxokAAAAMAAJ.

Norton, Caroline. *The Undying One; Sorrows of Rosalie. Other Poems*. London: Ebers, 1830.
Rpt. *The Undying One; and Other Poems*. London: Bentley, 1853. *Google Book Search*. May 6, 2007.
http://books.google.com/books?id=pFoCAAAAQAAJ.

NOYES, Alfred. *Drake: An English Epic*. Edinburgh: W. Blackwood, 1906.
Rpt. in *Collected Poems*, vol. 1. New York: Stokes, 1913.
Google Book Search. May 6, 2007. Edinburgh: W. Blackwood, 1906 and 1908.
Books 1–3 *http://books.google.com/books?id=N30kAAAAMAAJ*.
Books 4–12 *http://books.google.com/books?id=4XkkAAAAMAAJ*.

[OGDEN, James.] *Emanuel; or, Paradise Regained: An Epic Poem. In Nine Books*. Manchester: Sowler and Russell, 1797.

[OGDEN, James.] *The Revolution, An Epic Poem, in Twelve Books*. London: Johnson, 1790.

OGILVIE, John. *Britannia: A National Epic Poem in Twenty Books*. Aberdeen: Chalmers, 1801.

OGILVIE, John. *The Fane of the Druids: A Poem*. London: J. Murray, 1787, 1789.

OGLIVIE, John. *Rona: A Poem in Seven Books, an Epic of the Hebrides*. London, J. Murray, 1777.

ORD, John Walker. *England: A Historical Poem*. In 2 vols. London: Simpkin and Marshall, 1834.

O'SHAUGHNESSY, Arthur. *An Epic of Women and Other Poems*. London: Hotten, 1870.

PALGRAVE, F. T. *The Visions of England*. London: Macmillan, 1881.
Rpt. London: Cassell, 1889. *Project Gutenberg*. May 1, 2007.
http://www.gutenberg.org/etext/17923.

PATMORE, Coventry. *The Angel in the House*. London: J. W. Parker and Son, 1854–1863.
Rpt. London: Cassell, 1891. *Project Gutenberg*. May 1, 2007.
http://www.gutenberg.org/etext/4099.

PAYNE, John. *The Romaunt of Sir Floris*. In *The Masque of Shadows and Other Poems*. London: Basil Montagu Pickering, 1870.
Internet Sacred Text Archive. May 1, 2007.
http://www.sacred-texts.com/neu/arthur/art123.htm.

PEACOCK, Thomas Love. *Ahrimanes*. In *Letters to Edward Hookham and Percy B. Shelley with Fragments of Unpublished MSS*. Ed. Richard Garnett. Boston: The Bibliophile Society, 1910.
Google Book Search. May 1, 2007.
http://books.google.com/books?id=2EFcSvWKWKIC.

PEACOCK, Thomas Love. *Rhododaphne, or The Thessalian Spell*. London: T. Hookham, 1818.
Rpt. Philadelphia: Carey and Son, 1818. *Google Book Search*. May 1, 2007.
http://books.google.com/books?id=9r0kAAAAMAAJ.

PEERS, Charles. *The Siege of Jerusalem: A Poem*. London: Murray, 1823.

PENNIE, J. F. *Rogvald; An Epic Poem, in Twelve Books*. London: Whittaker, 1823.

PENNIE, J. F. *The Royal Minstrel; or, The Witcheries of Endor, An Epic Poem, in Eleven Books*. Dorchester: Clark, 1817.

PERCY, Thomas. *Reliques of Ancient English Poetry: Consisting of Old Heroic Ballads, Songs, and Other Pieces of Our Earlier Poets, (Chiefly of the Lyric Kind) Together with Some Few of Later Date*. London: J. Dodsley, 1765.
  Google Book Search. May 1, 2007.
  http://books.google.com/books?id=DtkFAAAAQAAJ.

PFEIFFER, Emily. *Glân-Alarch: His Silence and Song*. London: Henry King, 1877.

PHILLIPS, Richard. *The Story of Gaútama Buddha and His Creed: An Epic*. London: Longmans, Green, 1871.

PHILLIPS, Stephen. *Eremus. A Poem*. Fulham: Lillie Press, 1890.

POLLOK, Robert. *The Course of Time: A Poem, in Ten Books*
  Rpt. Hartford, Andrus, 1846.
  Rpt. Edinburgh: W. Blackwood, 1828. *Google Book Search*. May 7, 2007.
  http://books.google.com/books?id=HrMDAAAAQAAJ.

PORDEN [Franklin], Eleanor Anne. *Coeur de Lion; or The Third Crusade. A Poem, in Sixteen Books*. In 2 vols. London: Whittaker, 1822.

PORDEN [Franklin], Eleanor Anne. *The Veils; or the Triumph of Constancy. A Poem in Six Books*. London: John Murray, 1815.
  Online Archive of California. April 26, 2007.
  http://content.cdlib.org/ark:/13030/kt3w101333/?&query=&brand=oac.

POWYS, John Cowper. *Lucifer: A Poem*. London: Macdonald, 1956.

PYE, Henry James. *Alfred: An Epic Poem*. London: Suttaby, 1801.

PYE, Henry James. *Naucratia; or Naval Dominion. A Poem*. London: Nicol, 1798.

READE, John Edmund. *The Deluge: A Drama, in Twelve Scenes*. London: Saunders and Otley, 1839.

READE, John Edmund. *The Revolt of the Angels; and The Fall from Paradise: An Epic Drama*. London: Colburn and Bentley, 1830.

ROGERS, Samuel. *The Voyage of Columbus, A Poem*. London: Cadell and Davies, 1810.
  Rpt. in *Poems*. London: Cadell and Davies, 1814.
  Rpt. in *Poems*. London: Cadell and Davies, 1834. *Google Book Search*. May 1, 2007.
  http://books.google.com/books?id=qS8hAAAAMAAJ.

[ROSS, Alexander.] *Selma: A Tale of the Sixth Crusade*. London: Smith, Elder, 1839.
  Google Book Search. May 1, 2007.
  http://books.google.com/books?id=w3YEAAAAQAAJ.

SCOTT, Mary. *Messiah: A Poem, in Two Parts*. Bath: Cruttwell, 1788.

SCOTT, Walter. *Harold the Dauntless: A Poem, in Six Cantos*. London: Longman, Hurst, Rees, Orme, and Brown, 1817.

SCOTT, Walter. *The Lady of the Lake: A Poem*. London: Longman, Hurst, Rees, and Brown, 1810.

SCOTT, Walter. *The Lay of the Last Minstrel: A Poem*. London: Longman, Hurst, Rees, and Orme, 1805.

SCOTT, Walter. *The Lord of the Isles: A Poem*. London: London: Longman, Hurst, Rees, and Orme, 1815.

SCOTT, Walter. *Marmion: A Tale of Flodden Field*. Edinburgh: J. Ballantyne and Co., 1808.

SCOTT, Walter. *Rokeby: A Poem*. London: Longman, Hurst, Rees, Orme, and Brown, 1813.
> **N. B. The above 6 poems are all cited as rpt. in *Scott's Poetical Works*. Ed. J. Logie Robertson. London: Oxford University Press, 1904.**

SCOTT, Walter. *Minstrelsy of the Scottish Border; Consisting of Historical and Romantic Ballads*. London: Cadell and Davies, 1802.

SCOTT, William Bell. *The Year of the World; A Philosophical Poem on "Redemption from the Fall."* Edinburgh: Tait, 1846.

SERENA [pseud. for Sarah Leigh Pike.] *Israel: A Juvenile Poem*. Bath: [privately printed], 1795.

SEWARD, Anna. *Telemachus*. 1794, unpublished.
> **Transcribed in Adeline Johns-Putra, *Heroes and Housewives: Women's Epic Poetry and Domestic Ideology in the Romantic Age (1770–1835)*. Bern: Peter Lang, 2001.**

SHELLEY, Percy Bysshe. *The Revolt of Islam: A Poem, in Twelve Cantos*. London: Ollier, 1818. (Originally *Laon and Cythna*, 1817).
> **Rpt. *Poetical Works*. Ed. Thomas Hutchinson. London: Oxford University Press, 1943.**

SKENE, George. *Donald Bane: An Heroic poem in Three Books*. London: Robinson, 1796.

SMITH, Alexander. *Edwin of Deira*. Cambridge and London: Macmillan, 1861.
> *Google Book Search*. May 7, 2007.
> *http://books.google.com/books?id=xaUOAAAAIAAJ.*

SMITH, Alexander. *A Life-Drama*. In *Poems*. London: Ticknor, Reed, and Fields, 1853.
> *Google Book Search*. May 7, 2007.
> *http://books.google.com/books?id=g1MhAAAAMAAJ.*

SMITH, Charles. *The Mosiad, or Israel Delivered; A Sacred Poem, in Six Canticles*. London: Nicol, 1815.

SMITH, Elizabeth. *The Brethren: A Poem in Four Books: Paraphrased from Part of the History of Israel and His Family, in Holy Writ*. Birmingham: Pearson and Rollason, 1787.

SMITH, Elizabeth, *Israel: A Poem in Four Books*. Birmingham: Brown and Bentley, 1789.

SOTHEBY, William. *Constance de Castile. A Poem, in Ten Cantos*. London: Cadell and Davies, 1810.

SOTHEBY, William. *Saul: A Poem in Two Parts*. London: Cadell, 1807.
> *Google Book Search*. May 7, 2007.
> *http://books.google.com/books?id=PpFvX1devsgC.*

SOUTHEY, Robert. *Joan of Arc: An Epic Poem*. London: Cadell and Davies, 1796.

Rpt. in two vols. London: Longman, Hurst, Rees, Orme, and Brown, 1812. *Google Book Search*. May 7, 2007. Vol. 1: *http://books.google.com/books?id=IqoDAAAA QAAJ*. Vol. 2: *http://books.google.com/books?id=BaoDAAAAQAAJ*.

SOUTHEY, Robert. *Thalaba the Destroyer*. London: Longman and Rees, 1801.

SOUTHEY, Robert. *Madoc*. London: Longman, Hurst, Rees, and Orme, 1805.

SOUTHEY, Robert. *The Curse of Kehama*. London: Longman, Hurst, Rees, Orme, and Brown, 1810.

SOUTHEY, Robert. *Roderick, The Last of the Goths: A Tragic Poem*. London: Longman, Hurst, Rees, Orme, and Brown, 1814.

SOUTHEY, Robert. *A Tale of Paraguay*. London: Longman, Hurst, Rees, Orme, Brown, and Green, 1825.

N.B. Southey's poems are cited from *Poetical Works*. In 10 vols. Boston: Houghton, Osgood, and Company, 1878.

[SOUTHEY], Caroline Bowles. *Ellen Fitzarthur: A Metrical Tale, in Five Cantos*. London: Longman, 1820.
Rpt. London: Longman, Hurst, Rees, Orme, and Brown, 1822. *Google Book Search*. May 7, 2007.
http://books.google.com/books?id=VOL-yhQTPm4C.

STEWART, John. *The Resurrection, A Poem*. London: Longman, 1808.

STIGAND, William. *Athenäis; or, The First Crusade*. London: Moxon, 1866.

STIGAND, William. *Lionel: A Legacy*. In *Acanthia: Poems Original and Edited*. London: Kegan Paul, 1907.

STOKES, Henry Swell. *The Song of Albion: A Poem Commemorative of the Crisis*. London: Cochrane, 1831.
In *The Song of Albion, A Poem Commemorative of the Crisis; Lines on the Fall of Warsaw; and Other Poems*. London: John Cochrane, 1831. *Google Book Search*. May 7, 2007.
http://books.google.com/books?id=iZ8lAAAAMAAJ.

SWAIN, Joseph. *Redemption: A Poem in Five Books*. London: Mathews, 1789.
Rpt. Philadelphia: Hellings and Aitken, 1811.

SWINBURNE, Algernon. *The Tale of Balen*. New York: Chatto and Windus, 1896.
The Swinburne Project. Ed. John A. Walsh. April 26, 2007.
http://swinburnearchive.indiana.edu/swinburne/view?docId=tobbalenoo&query=balen& brand=swinburne.

SWINBURNE, Algernon. *Tristram of Lyonesse and Other Poems*. London: Chatto and Windus, 1882.
Rpt. *Major Poems and Selected Prose*. Ed. Jerome J. McGann and Charles L. Sligh. New Haven and London: Yale University Press, 2004.
The Swinburne Project. Ed. John A. Walsh. April 26, 2007.
http://swinburnearchive.indiana.edu/swinburne/view?docId=toltristoo&query=tristram %2olyonesse&brand=swinburne.

SYMPSON, Joseph. *Science Revived, or The Vision of Alfred. A Poem in Eight Books.* London: Gameau, 1802.
  Rpt. Philadelphia: John Bouvier, 1810. *Google Book Search.* May 7, 2007. *http://books.google.com/books?id=oVg1AAAAMAAJ.*

TALFOURD, Thomas Noon. *Ion, A Tragedy, In Five Acts.* London: Valpy, 1835.
  Rpt. London: E. Moxon, 1836. *Google Book Search.* May 7, 2007. *http://books.google.com/books?id=dOrHKHF-LVEC.*

TAYLOR, Henry. *Philip van Artevelde: A Dramatic Romance, in Two Parts.* London: E. Moxon, 1834.
  Rpt. Cambridge and Boston: James Munroe, 1885. *Google Book Search.* May 7, 2007.
  Vol. 1 *http://books.google.com/books?id=iAQlAAAAMAAJ*

TENNYSON, Alfred. *Balin and Balan.* In *Tiresias and Other Poems.* London: Macmillan, 1885.

TENNYSON, Alfred. *Idylls of the King.* In 4 parts London: Edward Moxon, 1859. In 11 parts as vol. 6 of *The Works of Alfred Tennyson Poet Laureate.* London: Strahan, 1873.

TENNYSON, Alfred. *Maud, and Other Poems.* London: Edward Moxon, 1855.

TENNYSON, Alfred. *The Princess: A Medley.* London: Edward Moxon, 1847.

THELWALL, John. "Specimens of *The Hope of Albion; or, Edwin of Northumbria: An Epic Poem.*" In *Poems Written Chiefly in Retirement.* Hereford: Parker, 1801.

THELWALL, John. *The Trident of Albion: An Epic Effusion.* Liverpool: Harris, 1805.

TIGHE, Mary. *Psyche, or the Legend of Love.* 1805, privately published. London: Longman, Hurst, 1811.
  Ed. Harriet Kramer Linkin, Melissa Davis, Jerry Parks. May 3, 2007. *http://web.nmsu.edu/~hlinkin/.*

TOWNSEND, George. *Armageddon: A Poem; in Twelve Books—The First Eight Books.* London: Hatchard, 1815.

WALKER, W.S. *Gustavus Vasa and Other Poems.* London: Longman, 1813.
  Project Gutenberg. May 3, 2007.
  http://www.gutenberg.org/etext/17754.

WALL, William Ellis. *Christ Crucified. An Epic Poem, in Twelve Books.* Oxford: J. H. Parker, 1833.

WATSON, William. *The Prince's Quest and Other Poems.* London: Kegan Paul, 1880.
  Rpt. London: Mathews and Lane (Bodley Head), 1892.
  In *The Poems of William Watson.* London: Macmillan, 1893. *Project Gutenberg.* May 3, 2007.
  http://www.gutenberg.org/etext/13179.

WELLS, Charles. *Joseph and His Brethren: A Dramatic Poem.* London: G. and W. B. Whittaker, 1824.
  Rpt. A. C. Swinburne, ed. London: Oxford University Press, 1876.

Google Book Search. May 8, 2007.
http://books.google.com/books?id=oXfHv8zpwB8C.

WESTWOOD, Thomas. *The Quest of the Sancgreall, the Sword of Kingship, and Other Poems.* London: Smith, 1868.
Google Book Search. May 3, 2007.
http://books.google.com/books?id=S2ACAAAAQAAJ.

WHARTON, Richard. *Roncesvalles: A Poem, in Twelve Books.* London: Hatchard, 1812.

WHITE, Henry Kirke. *The Christiad: A Divine Poem.* In *Poetical Works.* London: Bell and Daldy, 1830.
Project Gutenberg. May 3, 2007.
http://www.gutenberg.org/etext/7149.

WILCOCKE, Samuel Hull. *Britannia: A Poem.* London: Dilly, 1797.

WILLIAMS, Helen Maria. *Peru. A Poem in Six Cantos.* London: Cadell, 1784.
Peruvian Tales. In *Poems on Various Subjects: With Introductory Remarks on the Present State of Science and Literature in France.* London: G. and W. B. Whittaker, 1823. *Online Archive of California.* April 26, 2007.
http://content.cdlib.org/xtf/view?docId=kt787014q6&doc.view=frames&chunk.id= doe1448&toc.depth=1&toc.id=doe1448&brand=oac.

WOODLEY, George. *Britain's Bulwarks; or, The British Seaman: A Poem, in Eight Books.* Plymouth: Congdon, 1811.

WOODLEY, George. *Portugal Delivered, A Poem, in Five Books.* London: Newman, 1812.

WOOLNER, Thomas. *My Beautiful Lady.* London, Macmillan, 1863.

WOOLNER, Thomas. *Pygmalion.* London: Macmillan, 1881.
Google Book Search. May 3, 2007.
http://books.google.com/books?id=7kwCAAAAQAAJ.

WOOLNER, Thomas. *Silenus.* London: Macmillan, 1884.

WORDSWORTH, William. *The Excursion: Being a Portion of the Recluse, a Poem.* London: Longman, Hurst, Rees, Orme, and Brown, 1814.

WORDSWORTH, William. *The Prelude, or, Growth of a Poet's Mind; An Autobiographical Poem.* London: Moxon, 1850.
Rpt. with version of 1805 in *The Prelude: A Parallel Text.* Ed. J. C. Maxwell. Harmondsworth: Penguin, 1971.

WORDSWORTH, William. *The White Doe of Rylstone; or, The Fate of the Nortons, A Poem.* London: Longman, Hurst, Rees, Orme, and Brown, 1815.

YEARSLEY, Ann. *Brutus: A Fragment.* In *The Rural Lyre.* London: Robinson, 1796.

YEATS, W. B. *The Wanderings of Oisin.* London: Kegan Paul, 1889.
Rpt. in *The Collected Poems of W. B. Yeats.* Ed. Richard J. Finneran. New York: Collier, 1983.

ZAVARR [pseud. for William Bennett.] *The Viking: An Epic.* London: E. Churton, 1849.

Secondary Works Cited

Aarsleff, Hans, *The Study of Language in England, 1780–1860* (Princeton: Princeton University Press, 1967).

Abercrombie, Lascelles, *The Epic* (London: Secker, 1914).

—— *Thomas Hardy: A Critical Study* (New York: Viking, 1927).

Abrams, M. H., *Natural Supernaturalism: Tradition and Revolution in Romantic Literature* (New York: Norton, 1973).

Ackerman, Robert, *The Myth and Ritual School: J. G. Frazer and the Cambridge Ritualists* (New York and London: Garland, 1991).

Adams, James Eli, "Harlots and Base Interpreters: Scandal and Slander in *Idylls of the King*," *Victorian Poetry* 30 (1992) 421–39.

Adcock, St. John, *The Glory That Was Grub Street: Impressions of Contemporary Authors* (New York: Stokes, 1928).

Aguirre, Robert, *Informal Empire: Mexico and Central America in Victorian Culture* (Minneapolis: University of Minnesota Press, 2005).

Aiken, John, Unsigned review of Southey's *Joan of Arc*, *Monthly Review* n.s. 19 (1796) 361–68.

Alaya, Flavia, "The Ring, the Rescue, and the Risorgimento: Reunifying the Brownings' Italy," *Browning Institute Studies* 5 (1978) 1–41.

Alexander, J. H., *Two Studies in Romantic Reviewing: The Reviewing of Walter Scott's Poetry* (Salzburg: Universität Salzburg, 1976).

—— The Lay of the Last Minstrel: *Three Essays* (Salzburg: Universität Salzburg, 1978).

—— Marmion: *Studies in Interpretation and Composition* (Salzburg: Universität Salzburg, 1982).

Altick, Richard D., *The Shows of London* (Cambridge, Mass.: Belknap Press, 1978).

—— and James F. Loucks II, *Browning's Roman Murder Story: A Reading of* The Ring and the Book (Chicago and London: University of Chicago Press, 1968).

Anderson, John M., *Beyond Calliope: Epics by Women Poets of the Romantic Period*. PhD thesis, Boston College, 1993.

—— "Mary Tighe, *Psyche*," in *A Companion to Romanticism*, ed. Duncan Wu (Oxford: Blackwell, 1998) 199–203.

—— "The Triumph of Voice in Felicia Hemans's *The Forest Sanctuary*," in *Felicia Hemans: Reimagining Poetry in the Nineteenth Century*, ed. Nanora Sweet and Julie Melnyk (Houndmills: Palgrave, 2001) 55–73.

Aristotle, *Poetics,* tr. and ed. S. H. Butcher as *Aristotle's Theory of Poetry and Fine Art* (London: St. Martin's Press, 1894).

Armstrong, Isobel, "*The Ring and the Book*: The Uses of Prolixity," in *The Major Victorian Poets: Reconsiderations*, ed. Isobel Armstrong (London: Routledge, 1969) 177–97.

—— ed., *Victorian Scrutinies: Reviews of Poetry, 1830–1870* (London: Athlone Press, 1972).

—— "The Role and the Treatment of Emotion in Victorian Criticism of Poetry," *Victorian Periodicals Newsletter* 10 (1977) 3–16.

—— *Language as Living Form in Nineteenth-Century Poetry* (Brighton: Harvester, 1982).

—— *Victorian Poetry: Poetry, Poetics and Politics* (London and New York: Routledge, 1993).

Arnold, Matthew, Preface to *Poems* (1853), in *The Complete Poems*, 2nd edn. Kenneth and Miriam Allott (London: Longman, 1979).

Arnold, Thomas, ed., *The History of the Peloponnesian War, by Thucydides.* 2nd edn. (Oxford: Parker, 1840).

Aske, Martin, *Keats and Hellenism: An Essay* (Cambridge: Cambridge University Press, 1985).

Auerbach, Erich, *Mimesis: The Representation of Reality in Western Literature* (1946), tr. Willard R. Trask (Princeton: Princeton University Press, 1953).

Ault, Donald, "Re-Visioning *The Four Zoas*," in *Unnam'd Forms: Blake and Textuality*, ed. Nelson Hilton and Thomas A. Vogler (Berkeley: University of California Press, 1986) 105–39.

—— *Narrative Unbound: Re-Visioning Blake's* The Four Zoas (Barrytown: Station Hill, 1987).

Avery, Simon, and Rebecca Stott, *Elizabeth Barrett Browning* (London: Longman, 2003).

Babbage, Charles, *The Works of Charles Babbage*, ed. Martin Campbell-Kelly (New York: New York University Press, 1989).

Bailey, J. O., *Thomas Hardy and the Cosmic Mind: A New Reading of* The Dynasts (Chapel Hill: University of North Carolina Press, 1956).

Bailey, Richard W., *Images of English: A Cultural History of the Language* (Ann Arbor: University of Michigan Press, 1991).

—— *Nineteenth-Century English* (Ann Arbor: University of Michigan Press, 1996).

Bainbridge, Simon, *Napoleon and English Romanticism* (Cambridge: Cambridge University Press, 1995).

Baker, Carlos, *Shelley's Major Poetry: The Fabric of a Vision* (Princeton: Princeton University Press, 1948).

Baker, Jeffrey, "Casualties of the Revolution: Wordsworth and his 'Solitary' Self," *Yearbook of English Studies* 19 (1989) 94–111.

Bakhtin, Mikhail, *The Dialogic Imagination*, tr. Caryl Emerson and Michael Holquist (Austin: University of Texas Press, 1981).

Balfour, Ian, *The Rhetoric of Romantic Prophecy* (Stanford: Stanford University Press, 2002).

Bann, Stephen, *The Clothing of Clio: A Study of the Representation of History in Nineteenth-Century Britain and France* (Cambridge: Cambridge University Press, 1984).

Barczewski, Stephanie L., *Myth and National Identity in Nineteenth-Century Britain: The Legends of King Arthur and Robin Hood* (Oxford and New York: Oxford University Press, 2000).

Barnard, John, *John Keats* (Cambridge: Cambridge University Press, 1987).

Barton, Anne, *Byron:* Don Juan (Cambridge: Cambridge University Press, 1992).

Bate, Jonathan, "Keats's Two *Hyperions* and the Problem of Milton," in *Romantic Revisions,* ed. Robert Brinkley and Keith Hanley (Cambridge: Cambridge University Press, 1992) 321–38.

Beach, Joseph Warren, *The Concept of Nature in Nineteenth-Century English Poetry* (New York: Macmillan, 1936).

Beatty, Bernard, "*Don Juan* and Byron's Imperceptiveness to the English Word" (1979), rpt. in *Critical Essays on Lord Byron,* ed. Robert F. Gleckner (New York: G. K. Hall, 1991) 109–33.

—— *Byron's* Don Juan (London and Sydney: Croom Helm, 1985).

Beaty, Frederick L., *Byron the Satirist* (DeKalb: Northern Illinois University Press, 1985).

Beer, Gillian, *The Romance* (London: Methuen 1970).

Behrendt, Stephen C., "The Gap That Is Not a Gap," in *Romanticism and Women Poets: Opening the Doors of Reception,* ed. Stephen C. Behrendt and Harriet Kramer Linkin (Lexington: University Press of Kentucky, 1999) 25–45.

Bellamy, Elizabeth J., *Translations of Power: Narcissism and the Unconscious in Epic History* (Ithaca and London: Cornell University Press, 1992).

Ben-Israel, Hedva, *English Historians on the French Revolution* (Cambridge: Cambridge University Press, 1968).

Bennett, Andrew, *Keats, Narrative and Audience* (Cambridge: Cambridge University Press, 1994).

—— *Romantic Poets and the Culture of Posterity* (Cambridge: Cambridge University Press, 1999).

Bennett, Tony, *The Birth of the Museum: History, Theory, Politics* (London and New York: Routledge, 1995).

Bennett, W. C., *Contributions to a Ballad History of England* (London: Chatto and Windus, *c.*1880).

Berlin, Isaiah, *The Hedgehog and the Fox: An Essay on Tolstoy's View of History* (New York: Simon and Schuster, 1953).

Bernhardt-Kabisch, Ernest, *Robert Southey* (Boston: Twayne, 1977).

Bernstein, Carol L., "Subjectivity as Critique and the Critique of Subjectivity in Keats's *Hyperion*," in *After the Future: Postmodern Times and Places,* ed. Gary Shapiro (Albany: State University of New York Press, 1990) 41–52.

Bewell, Alan J., "The Political Implications of Keats's Classicist Aesthetics," *Studies in Romanticism* 25 (1986) 220–29.

Bezanson, Walter E., "Historical and Critical Note" to Herman Melville, *Clarel: A Poem and Pilgrimage in the Holy Land,* ed. Harrison Hayford *et al.* (Evanston and Chicago: Northwestern University Press and Newberry Library, 1991).

Bickersteth, Edwin Henry, *Hades and Heaven; or, What Does Scripture Reveal of the State and Employments of the Blessed Dead and of the Risen Saints* (New York: Carter, 1869).

Birley, Robert, *Sunk Without Trace: Some Forgotten Masterpieces Reconsidered* (London: Rupert Hart-Davis, 1962).

Blackie, John Stuart, *Homer and the Iliad.* In 4 vols. (1860; 2nd edn. Edinburgh: Edmonston and Douglas, 1866).

Blackwell, Thomas, *An Enquiry into the Life and Writings of Homer* (1735; rpt. Hildesheim and New York: Georg Olms, 1976).

Blain, Virginia, *Caroline Bowles Southey: The Making of a Woman Writer* (Aldershot: Ashgate, 1998).

Blair, Hugh, *Lectures on Rhetoric and Belles Lettres* (1783; ed. and rpt. in 2 vols. Harold F. Harding, Carbondale and Edwardsville: Southern Illinois University Press, 1965).

Blair, Kirstie, "Spasmodic Affections: Poetry, Pathology, and the Spasmodic Hero," *Victorian Poetry* 42 (2004) 473–90.

Blalock, Susan, "Browning's *The Ring and the Book*: 'A Novel Country,'" *Browning Institute Studies* 11 (1983) 39–50.

Blersch, Stuart, "The Craft of Revision: Morris and *Sigurd the Volsung*," in *The After-Summer Seed: Reconsiderations of William Morris's* The Story of Sigurd the Volsung, ed. John Hollow (New York and London: William Morris Society, 1978).

Bloom, Harold, *Yeats* (New York: Oxford University Press, 1970).

Bonaparte, Felicia, *The Triptych and the Cross: The Central Myths of George Eliot's Poetic Imagination* (New York: New York University Press, 1979).

Bonca, Tedi Chichester, *Shelley's Mirrors of Love: Narcissism, Sacrifice, and Sorority* (Albany: State University of New York Press, 1999).

Boos, Florence, *The Design of William Morris'* The Earthly Paradise (Lewiston: Edwin Mellen, 1990).

Booth, Michael R., *Victorian Spectacular Theatre 1850–1910* (Boston and London: Routledge, 1981).

Bowlby, Rachel, *Just Looking: Consumer Culture in Dreiser, Gissing, and Zola* (London: Methuen, 1985).

Bowra, C. M., *From Virgil to Milton* (London: Macmillan, 1967).

Bradley, A. C., "Old Mythology in Modern Poetry," *Macmillan's Magazine* 44 (1881) 28–47.

—— *Oxford Lectures on Poetry* (London: Macmillan, 1917).

Brantlinger, Patrick, *The Spirit of Reform: British Literature and Politics, 1832–1867* (Cambridge, Mass., and London: Harvard University Press, 1977).

Bratton, J. S., *The Victorian Popular Ballad* (London and Basingstoke: Macmillan, 1975).

Brendon, Piers, *Hawker of Morwenstow: Portrait of a Victorian Eccentric* (London: Jonathan Cape, 1975).

Brennan, Catherine, *Angers, Fantasies and Ghostly Fears: Nineteenth-Century Women from Wales and English-Language Poetry* (Cardiff: University of Wales Press, 2003).

Brisbane, Thomas, *The Early Years of Alexander Smith, Poet and Essayist: A Study for Young Men* (London: Hoddart and Stoughton, 1869).

Brisman, Leslie, *Romantic Origins* (Ithaca and London: Cornell University Press, 1978).

Bristow, Joseph, *Robert Browning* (New York and London: Harvester, 1991).

Bromwich, David, "Keats's Radicalism," *Studies in Romanticism* 25 (1986) 197–210.

—— *A Choice of Inheritance: Self and Community from Edmund Burke to Robert Frost* (Cambridge, Mass., and London: Harvard University Press, 1989).

Brooke, Stopford, *English Literature* (1879; rev. edn. New York: American Book Company, 1895).

Brooks, Jean R., *Thomas Hardy: The Poetic Structure* (Ithaca: Cornell University Press, 1971).

Brooks, Peter, *Reading for the Plot: Design and Intention in Narrative* (Cambridge, Mass.: Harvard University Press, 1984).

Brown, David, *Walter Scott and the Historical Imagination* (London: Routledge and Kegan Paul, 1979).

Brown, Laura, *Fables of Modernity: Literature and Culture in the English Eighteenth Century* (Ithaca and London: Cornell University Press, 2001).

Bryden, Inga, *Reinventing King Arthur: The Arthurian Legends in Victorian Culture* (Aldershot: Ashgate, 2005).

Buchanan, Robert, *A Look Round Literature* (London: Downey, 1887).

Buckler, William, *The Victorian Imagination: Essays in Aesthetic Exploration* (New York and London: New York University Press, 1980).

—— *Man and His Myths: Tennyson's* Idylls of the King *in Critical Context* (New York: New York University Press, 1984).

—— *Poetry and Truth in Robert Browning's* The Ring and the Book (New York and London: New York University Press, 1985).

Buckley, Jerome H., *The Victorian Temper: A Study in Literary Culture* (Cambridge, Mass.: Harvard University Press, 1951).

Bulwer-Lytton, Edward, *England and the English* (London: R. Bentley, 1833).

Burrow, Colin, *Epic Romance: Homer to Milton* (Oxford: Clarendon Press, 1993).

—— "Virgil in English Translation," in *The Cambridge Companion to Virgil*, ed. Charles Martindale (Cambridge: Cambridge University Press, 1997) 21–37.

Bush, Douglas, *Mythology and the Romantic Tradition in English Poetry* (1937; rpt. Cambridge, Mass.: Harvard University Press, 1969).

Bushell, Sally, *Re-Reading* The Excursion: *Narrative, Response, and the Wordsworthian Dramatic Voice* (Aldershot: Ashgate, 2002).

Butler, Marilyn, *Romantics, Rebels and Reactionaries: English Literature and its Background 1760–1830* (Oxford: Oxford University Press, 1981).

—— "Byron and the Empire of the East," in *Byron: Augustan and Romantic*, ed. Andrew Rutherford (New York: St. Martin's Press, 1990) 63–81.

—— "Shelley and the Empire in the East," in *Shelley: Poet and Legislator of the World*, ed. Betty T. Bennett and Stuart Curran (Baltimore and London: Johns Hopkins University Press, 1996) 158–68.

Butter, P. H., "Blake's *The French Revolution*," *Yearbook of English Studies* 19 (1989) 18–27.

Butterfield, Herbert, *The Whig Interpretation of History* (London: Bell, 1931).

Buzard, James, "Translation and Tourism: Scott's *Waverley* and the Rendering of Culture," *Yale Journal of Criticism* 8 (1995) 31–59.

Byron, George Gordon, Lord, *Byron's Letters and Journals*, ed. Leslie A. Marchand, in 12 vols. (Cambridge, Mass.: Belknap Press, 1973–81).

Calhoun, Blue, *The Pastoral Vision of William Morris:* The Earthly Paradise (Athens: University of Georgia Press, 1975).

Calin, William, *A Muse for Heroes: Nine Centuries of the Epic in France* (Toronto and Buffalo: University of Toronto Press, 1983).

Cameron, Kenneth Neill, "Shelley and *Ahrimanes*," *Modern Language Quarterly* 3 (1942) 287–95.

Campbell, Matthew, *Rhythm and Will in Victorian Poetry* (Cambridge: Cambridge University Press, 1999).

Canuel, Mark, *Religion, Toleration, and British Writing, 1790–1830* (Cambridge: Cambridge University Press, 2002).

Card, Henry, *The History of the Revolutions of Russia, to the Accession of Catharine the First* (London: Longmans and Rees, 1804).

Carlyle, Thomas, *Critical and Miscellaneous Essays* (London: Chapman and Hall, 1869).

Carroll, Alicia, *Dark Smiles: Race and Desire in George Eliot* (Athens: Ohio University Press, 2002).

Case, Alison, *Plotting Women: Gender and Narration in the Eighteenth- and Nineteenth-Century British Novel* (Charlottesville and London: University of Virginia Press, 1999).

Cassidy, John A., "The Original Source of Hardy's *Dynasts*," *PMLA* 69 (1954) 1085–1100.

—— *Algernon C. Swinburne* (Boston: Twayne, 1964).

Chandler, Alice, *A Dream of Order: The Medieval Ideal in Nineteenth-Century English Literature* (Lincoln: University of Nebraska Press, 1970).

Chandler, James, *Wordsworth's Second Nature: A Study of the Poetry and Politics* (Chicago and London: University of Chicago Press, 1984).

—— "The Historical Novel Goes to Hollywood: Scott, Griffith, and Film Epic Today," in *The Romantics and Us: Essays on Literature and Culture*, ed. Gene W. Ruoff (New Brunswick and London: Rutgers University Press, 1990) 237–73.

—— *England in 1819: The Politics of Literary Culture and the Case of Romantic Historicism* (Chicago and London: University of Chicago Press, 1998).

Charnon-Deutsch, Lou, *The Spanish Gypsy: The History of a European Obsession* (University Park: Pennsylvania State University Press, 2004).

Chase, Karen. "The Modern Family and the Ancient Image in *Romola*," *Dickens Studies Annual* 14 (1985) 303–26.

Chayes, Irene H., "Dreamer, Poet, and Poem in *The Fall of Hyperion*," *Philological Quarterly* 46 (1967) 499–517.

Chew, Samuel C., *Byron in England: His Fame and After-Fame* (1924; rpt. New York: Russell and Russell, 1965).

—— "The Poetry of Charles Montague Doughty," *North American Review* 222 (1925) 287–98.

Christensen, Jerome, *Lord Byron's Strength: Romantic Writing and Commercial Society* (Baltimore and London: Johns Hopkins University Press, 1993).

Church, Richard, "Thomas Hardy as Revealed in *The Dynasts*," in *Essays by Divers Hands* 29 (1958) 1–17.

Clarke, I. F., comp., *The Tale of the Future, from the Beginning to the Present Day: An Annotated Bibliography* (1972; 3rd ed. London: Library Association, 1978).

Clausen, Christopher, "Sir Edwin Arnold's *The Light of Asia* and Its Reception." *Literature East and West*, 17 (1973) 174–91.

Clifford, Emma, "The Impressionistic View of History in *The Dynasts*," *Modern Language Quarterly* 22 (1961) 21–31.

—— "*War and Peace* and *The Dynasts*," *Modern Philology* 54 (1956) 33–44.

Clough, Arthur Hugh, review of Arnold, *Empedocles on Etna*, and Smith, *A Life-Drama*, *North American Review* (July 1853), rpt. in *Victorian Scrutinies: Reviews of Poetry, 1830–1870*, ed. Isobel Armstrong (London: Athlone Press, 1972).

Clubbe, John, "Carlyle as Epic Historian," in *Victorian Literature and Society: Essays Presented to Richard D. Altick*, ed. James R. Kincaid and Albert J. Kuhn (Columbus: Ohio State University Press, 1984) 119–145.

Coleridge, Samuel Taylor, *On the Constitution of the Church and State, According to the Idea of Each: With Aids Toward a Right Judgment on the Late Catholic Bill* (London: Hurst, Chance, 1830).

Colley, Linda, *Britons: Forging the Nation 1707–1837* (London: Pimlico, 1994).

Collins, Philip, *Thomas Cooper, The Chartist: Byron and the "Poets of the Poor"* (Nottingham: University of Nottingham, 1969).

Columbus, Claudette Kemper, "*The Ring and the Book*: A Masque for the Making of Meaning,' *Philological Quarterly* 53 (1974) 327–55.

Connell, Philip, *Romanticism, Economics and the Question of "Culture"* (Oxford: Oxford University Press, 2001).

Cooke, Michael G., *The Blind Man Traces the Circle: On the Patterns and Philosophy of Byron's Poetry* (Princeton: Princeton University Press, 1969).

Cooper, Andrew M., *Doubt and Identity in Romantic Poetry* (New Haven and London: Yale University Press, 1988).

Cooper, Lane, *Experiments in Education* (Ithaca: Cornell University Press, 1943).

Cooper, Thomas, *The Life of Thomas Cooper, Written by Himself* (London: Hodder and Stoughton, 1879).

Corbett, Mary Jean, *Allegories of Union in Irish and English Writing, 1790–1870: Politics, History, and the Family from Edgeworth to Arnold* (Cambridge: Cambridge University Press, 2000).

Corrigan, Beatrice, *Curious Annals: New Documents Relating to Browning's Roman Murder Story* (Toronto: University of Toronto Press, 1956).

Coulling, Sidney, *Matthew Arnold and His Critics: A Study of Arnold's Controversies* (Athens, Ohio: Ohio University Press, 1974).

Court, Franklin E., *Institutionalizing English Literature: The Culture and Politics of Literary Study 1750–1900* (Stanford: Stanford University Press, 1992).

Courthope, W. J., *A History of English Poetry*, in 6 vols. (London: Macmillan 1895–1910).

Cox, Jeffrey N., *Poetry and Politics in the Cockney School: Keats, Shelley, Hunt and their Circle* (Cambridge: Cambridge University Press, 1998).

Cox, R. G., ed., *Thomas Hardy: The Critical Heritage* (New York: Barnes and Noble, 1970).

Craik, George L., *A Compendious History of English Literature, and of the English Language, from the Norman Conquest*, in 2 vols. (New York: Scribner, 1864).

Crawford, Robert, *Devolving English Literature* (Oxford: Clarendon Press, 1992).

—— *The Modern Poet: Poetry, Academia, and Knowledge since the 1750s* (Oxford: Oxford University Press, 2001).

Crawford, Thomas, "Scott as a Poet," *Etudes Anglaises* 24 (1971) 478–91.

—— *Scott* (Edinburgh: Scottish Academic Press, 1982).

Crehan, Stewart, *Blake in Context* (Dublin: Gill and Macmillan, 1984).

Cronin, Richard, *Shelley's Poetic Thoughts* (New York: St. Martin's Press, 1981).

—— "Alexander Smith and the Poetry of Displacement," *Victorian Poetry* 28 (1990) 129–45.

—— *1798: The Year of the* Lyrical Ballads (Houndmills: Macmillan, 1998) 108–32.

—— *The Politics of Romantic Poetry: In Search of the Pure Commonwealth* (Houndmills: Macmillan, 2000).

—— "The Spasmodics," in *A Companion to Victorian Poetry*, ed. Cronin, Alison Chapman, and Antony H. Harrison (Oxford: Blackwell, 2002) 291–303.

Crook, Paul, *Darwinism, War and History* (Cambridge: Cambridge University Press, 1994).

Cross, Nigel, *The Common Writer: Life in Nineteenth-Century Grub Street* (Cambridge: Cambridge University Press, 1985).

Crowell, Norton B., *Alfred Austin: Victorian* (London: Weidenfeld and Nicolson, 1955).

Cruse, Amy, *The Victorians and their Books* (London: Allen and Unwin, 1935).

—— *After the Victorians* (London: Allen and Unwin, 1938).

Cumming, Mark, "The Structure of *Sigurd the Volsung*," *Victorian Poetry* 21 (1983) 403–14.

—— *A Disimprisoned Epic: Form and Vision in Carlyle's* French Revolution (Philadelphia: University of Pennsylvania Press, 1988).

—— "Allegory and Comedy in Bulwer-Lytton's *King Arthur*," in *The Arthurian Revival: Essays on Form, Tradition, and Transformation*, ed. Debra N. Mancoff (New York and London: Garland, 1992) 31–51.

Cundiff, Paul A., *Browning's Ring Metaphor and Truth* (Metuchen: Scarecrow, 1972).

Curran, Stuart, ed., *Le Bossu and Voltaire on the Epic* (Gainesville: Scholars Press, 1970).

—— *"The Structures of* Jerusalem,*"* in *Blake's Sublime Allegory: Essays on* The Four Zoas, Milton, Jerusalem, ed. Stuart Curran and Joseph A. Wittreich, Jr. (Madison: University of Wisconsin Press, 1973) 132–151.

—— *Shelley's Annus Mirabilis: The Maturing of an Epic Vision* (San Marino: Huntington Library, 1975).

—— *Poetic Form and British Romanticism* (New York and Oxford: Oxford University Press, 1986).

—— "Wordsworth and the Forms of Poetry," in *The Age of William Wordsworth*, ed. Kenneth R. Johnston and Gene W. Ruoff (New Brunswick and London: Rutgers University Press, 1987) 115–32.

Curry, Kenneth, "Southey's *Madoc*: The Manuscript of 1794," *Philological Quarterly* 22 (1943) 347–69.

Dale, Peter Allan, "Paracelsus and Sordello: Trying the Stuff of Language," *Victorian Poetry* 18 (1980) 359–69.

Dallas, E. S., *Poetics: An Essay on Poetry* (London: Smith, Elder, 1852).

Daniels, Stephen, "Victorian Britain," in *Historic Landscapes of Britain from the Air,* ed. Robin Glasscock (Cambridge: Cambridge University Press, 1992) 186–210.

Davie, Donald, "The Poetry of Sir Walter Scott," *Proceedings of the British Academy* 47 (1961) 61–75.

Davies, Damian Walford, *Presences That Disturb: Models of Romantic Identity in the Literature and Culture of the 1790s* (Cardiff: University of Wales Press, 2002).

Davis, Leith, *Acts of Union: Scotland and the Literary Negotiation of the British Nation, 1707–1830* (Stanford: Stanford University Press, 1998).

Davis, Mary Bird, "Swinburne's Use of His Sources in *Tristram of Lyonesse*," *Philological Quarterly* 55 (1976) 96–112.

Dawson, Carl, *Victorian Noon: English Literature in 1850* (Baltimore: Johns Hopkins University Press, 1979).

Dawson, P. M. S., *The Unacknowledged Legislator: Shelley and Politics* (Oxford: Oxford University Press, 1980).

de Almeida, Hermione, *Romantic Medicine and John Keats* (New York: Oxford University Press, 1991).

—— "Prophetic Extinction and the Misbegotten Dream in Keats," in *The Persistence of Poetry: Bicentennial Essays on Keats*, ed. Robert M. Ryan and Ronald A. Sharp (Amherst: University of Massachusetts Press, 1998) 165–82.

Dean, Susan, *Hardy's Poetic Vision in* The Dynasts: *The Diorama of a Dream* (Princeton: Princeton University Press, 1977).

Delasanta, Rodney, *The Epic Voice* (The Hague: Mouton, 1967).

De Luca, Vincent Arthur, *Words of Eternity: Blake and the Poetics of the Sublime* (Princeton: Princeton University Press, 1991).

Denman, Peter, *Samuel Ferguson: The Literary Achievement* (Savage: Barnes and Noble, 1990).

Dentith, Simon, *Epic and Empire in Nineteenth-Century Britain* (Cambridge: Cambridge University Press, 2006).

De Quincey, Thomas, *Collected Writings*, ed. David Masson (Edinburgh: Black, 1890).

de Reul, Paul, *L'Oeuvre de Swinburne* (Bruxelles: Sand, 1922).

Desaulniers, Mary, *Carlyle and the Economics of Terror: A Study of Revisionary Gothicism in* The French Revolution (Montreal and Kingston: McGill-Queen's University Press, 1995).

De Vane, W. C., "The Virgin and the Dragon," *Yale Review* 37 (1947) 33–46.

Dickinson, Thomas H., "Thomas Hardy's *The Dynasts*," *North American Review* 195 (1912) 526–42.

Dickstein, Morris, "Keats and Politics," *Studies in Romanticism* 25 (1986) 175–81.

—— *Keats and his Poetry: A Study in Development* (Chicago and London: University of Chicago Press, 1971).

Dillon, Steven, "Milton and Tennyson's 'Guinevere,' " *ELH* 54 (1987) 129–55.

—— "Scandals of War: The Authority of Tennyson's *Idylls*," *Essays in Literature* 18 (1991) 180–95.

Dixon, W. Macneile, *English Epic and Heroic Poetry* (London: Dent 1912).

Dobell, Sydney, *Thoughts on Art, Philosophy, and Religion*, ed. John Nichol (London: Smith, Elder, 1876).

Dobrée, Bonamy, "*The Dynasts*," *Southern Review* 6 (1940).

Dodds, E. R., *The Greeks and the Irrational* (Berkeley: University of California Press, 1951).

Dodds, John W., *The Age of Paradox: A Biography of England 1841–1851* (New York: Rinehart, 1952).

Domett, Alfred, *The Diary of Alfred Domett 1872–1885*, ed. E. A. Horsman (Oxford University Press, 1953).

Donovan, Jack, "*Laon and Cythna*: Nature, Custom, Desire," *Keats–Shelley Review* 2 (1987) 49–90.

—— " 'Lethean Joy': Memory and Recognition in *Laon and Cythna*," in *Evaluating Shelley*, ed. Timothy Clark and Jerrold E. Hogle (Edinburgh: Edinburgh University Press, 1996) 132–51.

—— "The Storyteller," in *The Cambridge Companion to Shelley*, ed. Timothy Morton (Cambridge: Cambridge University Press, 2006) 85–103.

Dotort, Fred, *The Dialectic of Vision: A Contrary Reading of William Blake's* Jerusalem (Barrytown: Station Hill Arts, 1998).

Dowden, Edward, *Southey* (1888; rpt. New York: AMS Press, 1968).

Dowling, Linda, *Language and Decadence in the Victorian Fin de Siècle* (Princeton: Princeton University Press, 1986).

—— *Hellenism and Homosexuality in Victorian Oxford* (Ithaca and London: Cornell University Press, 1994).

Downes, Jeremy M., *Recursive Desire: Rereading Epic Tradition* (Tuscaloosa and London: University of Alabama Press, 1997).

Drinkwater, John, *William Morris: A Critical Study* (London: Secker, 1912).

Drummond, Henry, *The Lowell Lectures on the Ascent of Man* (New York: Pott, 1894).

Dryden, John, *Selected Criticism*, ed. James Kinsley and George Parfitt (Oxford: Clarendon Press, 1970).

Duff, David, *Romance and Revolution: Shelley and the Politics of a Genre* (Cambridge: Cambridge University Press, 1994).

Eagleton, Terry, "Introduction" to Daniel Cottom, *Social Figures: George Eliot, Social History, and Literary Representation* (Minneapolis: University of Minnesota Press, 1987).

Edgecombe, Rodney, *Leigh Hunt and the Poetry of Fancy* (Cranbury: Associated University Presses, 1994).

Edmond, Rod, *Affairs of the Hearth: Victorian Poetry and Domestic Narrative* (London and New York: Routledge, 1988).

Edwards, Thomas R., *Imagination and Power: A Study of Poetry on Public Themes* (London: Chatto and Windus, 1971).

Eggers, J. Philip, "Memory in Mankind: Keats's Historical Imagination," *PMLA* 86 (1971) 990–98.

Elfenbein, Andrew, *Byron and the Victorians* (Cambridge: Cambridge University Press, 1995).

—— *Romantic Genius: The Prehistory of a Homosexual Role* (New York: Columbia University Press, 1999).

Eliot, George [pseud. of Marian Evans], review of Dobell's *Balder*, *Westminster Review* 61 (April 1854) 331–32.

—— *George Eliot's Life as Related in Her Letters and Journals*, ed. J. W. Cross (New York: Harper, 1885).

—— *The George Eliot Letters*, ed. Gordon S. Haight, in 9 vols. (New Haven: Yale University Press, 1954–78).

Eliot, George *Essays of George Eliot*, ed. Thomas Pinney (New York: Columbia University Press, 1963).

Elley, Derek, *The Epic Film: Myth and History* (London: Routledge, 1984).

Ellis, George, *Specimens of Early English Metrical Romances, Chiefly Written during the Early Part of the Fourteenth Century* (1805; 2nd edn. London: Longman, 1811).

Ellison, Julie, " 'Nice Arts' and 'Potent Enginery': The Gendered Economy of Wordsworth's Fancy," *Centennial Review* 33 (1989) 441–467.

Ellison, Ruth C. " 'The Undying Glory of Dreams': William Morris and the 'Northland of Old,' " in *Victorian Poetry*, ed. Malcolm Bradbury and David Palmer (London: Arnold, 1972) 138–75.

Elton, Oliver, *A Survey of English Literature 1780–1830* (London: Arnold, 1912).

—— *A Survey of English Literature 1830–1880* (London: Arnold, 1920).

Ende, Stuart A., *Keats and the Sublime* (New Haven and London: Yale University Press, 1976).

Erdman, David V., "Byron's Mock Review of Rosa Matilda's Epic on the Prince Regent—A New Attribution," *Keats–Shelley Journal* 19 (1970) 101–17.

Erickson, Lee, *Robert Browning: His Poetry and His Audiences* (Ithaca and London: Cornell University Press, 1984).

—— *The Economy of Literary Form: English Literature and the Industrialization of Publishing, 1800–1850* (Baltimore: Johns Hopkins University Press, 1996).

Essick, Robert, *William Blake and the Language of Adam* (Oxford: Clarendon, 1989).

Evans, B. Ifor, *English Poetry in the Later Nineteenth Century* (London: Methuen, 1933).

Fairchild, Hoxie Neale, "The Immediate Source of *The Dynasts*," *PMLA* 67 (1951) 43–64.

—— *Religious Trends in English Poetry*, in 6 vols. (New York: Columbia University Press, 1939–1968).

Fairley, Barker, *Charles M. Doughty: A Critical Study* (New York: Oxford University Press, 1927).

—— "Introduction" to *Selected Passages from* The Dawn in Britain (New York: Oxford University Press, 1935).

Farrell, John P., *Revolution as Tragedy: The Dilemma of the Moderate from Scott to Arnold* (Ithaca and London: Cornell University Press, 1980).

Farrell, Joseph, review of Quint, *Epic and Empire* and Wofford, *The Choice of Achilles*, in *Bryn Mawr Classical Review* 4 (1993) 481–89.

Faulkner, Peter, ed., *William Morris: The Critical Heritage* (London and Boston: Routledge, 1973).

Feldman, Burton, and Robert D. Richardson, eds., *The Rise of Modern Mythology 1680–1860* (Bloomington and London: Indiana University Press, 1972).

Felluga, Dino Franco, "Verse Novel," in *A Companion to Victorian Poetry*, ed. Richard Cronin, Alison Chapman, and Antony Harrison (Oxford: Blackwell, 2002) 171–86.

—— *The Perversity of Poetry* (Albany: State University of New York Press, 2005).

Ferguson, Frances, *Wordsworth: Language as Counter-Spirit* (New Haven and London: Yale University Press, 1977).

Ferguson, James, "Prefaces to *Jerusalem*," in *Interpreting Blake*, ed. Michael Phillips (Cambridge: Cambridge University Press, 1978) 164–95.

Fink, Zera, "Wordsworth and the English Republican Tradition," *Journal of English and Germanic Philology* 47 (1948) 107–26.

Fischer, Hermann, *Romantic Verse Narrative: The History of a Genre*, 1964, tr. Sue Bollans (Cambridge: Cambridge University Press, 1991).

Fisher, Benjamin F., IV. "Swinburne's *Tristram of Lyonesse* in Process," *Texas Studies in Literature and Language* 14 (1972) 509–28.

Fletcher, Ian, *Swinburne* (Harlow: Longman, 1973).

Fletcher, Pauline, *Gardens and Grim Ravines: The Language of Landscape in Victorian Poetry* (Princeton: Princeton University Press, 1983).

Foerster, Donald M., *Homer in English Criticism: The Historical Approach in the Eighteenth Century* (New Haven: Yale University Press, 1947).

—— *The Fortunes of Epic Poetry: A Study in English and American Criticism 1750–1950* (n.p.: Catholic University of America Press, 1962).

Forster, John, *Walter Savage Landor: A Biography* (London: Chapman and Hall, 1869).

Fosso, Kurt, "Community and Mourning in Wordsworth's *The Ruined Cottage*, 1797–1798," *Studies in Philology* 92 (1995) 329–45.

Fowler, Alastair, *Kinds of Literature : An Introduction to the Theory of Genres and Modes* (Cambridge, Mass.: Harvard University Press, 1982).

Fox, W. J., review of Disraeli, *The Revolutionary Epick*, in *Monthly Repository* 8 (1834) 376–78.

Franklin, Caroline, "The Welsh American Dream: Iolo Morganwg, Robert Southey and the Madoc Legend," in *English Romanticism and the Celtic World*, ed. Gerald Carruthers and Alan Rawes (Cambridge: Cambridge University Press, 2003) 69–84.

Franklin, J. Jeffrey, "The Life of the Buddha in Victorian England," *ELH* 72 (2005) 941–74.

Franta, Andrew, *Romanticism and the Rise of the Mass Public* (Cambridge: Cambridge University Press, 2007).

Frantzen, Allen J., *Desire for Origins: New Language, Old English, and Teaching the Tradition* (New Brunswick and London: Rutgers University Press, 1990).

Freeman, Kathryn S., *Blake's Nostos: Fragmentation and Nondualism in* The Four Zoas (Albany: State University of New York Press, 1997).

Frei, Hans W., *The Eclipse of Biblical Narrative: A Study in Eighteenth and Nineteenth Century Hermeneutics* (New Haven and London: Yale University Press, 1974).

Friedman, Michael H., *The Making of a Tory Humanist: William Wordsworth and the Idea of Community* (New York: Columbia University Press, 1979).

Friedman, Susan Stanford, "Gender and Genre Anxiety: Elizabeth Barrett Browning and H. D. as Epic Poets," *Tulsa Studies in Women's Literature* 5 (1986) 203–28.

Froude, J. A., *Oceana, or England and her Colonies* (London: Longmans, 1886).

—— *English Seamen in the Sixteenth Century* (New York: Scribner, 1895).

Froula, Christine, "Browning's *Sordello* and the Parables of Modernist Poetics," *ELH* 52 (1985) 965–92.

Fry, Paul, "Classical Standards in the Period," in *The Cambridge History of Literary Criticism*, vol. 5, ed. Marshall Brown (Cambridge: Cambridge University Press, 2000) 7–28.

Frye, Northrop, *Fearful Symmetry: A Study of William Blake* (Princeton: Princeton University Press, 1947).

—— *Anatomy of Criticism: Four Essays* (Princeton: Princeton University Press, 1957).

—— "The Meeting of Past and Future in William Morris," *Studies in Romanticism* 21 (1982) 303–18.

Fulford, Tim, "Romanticism and Colonialism: Races, Places, Peoples, 1800–1830," in *Romanticism and Colonialism: Writing and Empire, 1780–1830*, ed. Fulford and Peter J. Kitson (Cambridge: Cambridge University Press, 1998) 13–34.

—— *Romanticism and Millenarianism* (Houndmills: Palgrave, 2002).

Fuller, David, *Blake's Heroic Argument* (London: Croom Helm, 1988).

Fuller, Jean Overton, *Swinburne: A Critical Biography* (London: Chatto and Windus, 1968).

Fuller, Margaret, review of Bailey's *Festus*, in *The Dial* 2:2 (October 1841) 231–238.

Fulweiler, Howard W., "Tennyson's 'The Holy Grail': The Representation of Representation," *Renascence* 38 (1986) 144–59.

Fussell, Paul, *The Great War and Modern Memory* (New York: Oxford University Press, 1975).

Gallant, Christine, *Keats and Romantic Celticism* (Houndmills: Palgrave, 2005).

Galperin, William H., *Revision and Authority in Wordsworth: The Interpretation of a Career* (Philadelphia: University of Pennsylvania Press, 1989).

—— *The Return of the Visible in British Romanticism* (Baltimore and London: Johns Hopkins University Press, 1993).

Garber, Frederick, "Irony and Organicism: Origin and Textuality," *Essays in Literature* 10 (1983) 263–282.

—— *Self, Text, and Romantic Irony: The Example of Byron* (Princeton: Princeton University Press, 1988).

Garnett, Richard, "Memoir," in Mathilde Blind, *Poetical Works*, ed. Arthur Symons (London: Unwin, 1900) 2–43.

Garrison, Chester A., *The Vast Venture: Hardy's Epic-Drama The Dynasts* (Salzburg: Universität Salzburg, 1973).

Gates, Barbara T., "Wordsworth's Lessons from the Past," *Wordsworth Circle* 7 (1976) 133–41.

—— "Providential History and *The Excursion*" *Wordsworth Circle* 9 (1978) 178–81.

Gaull, Marilyn, *English Romanticism: The Human Context* (New York and London: Norton, 1988).

Gibson, Mary Ellis, *Epic Reinvented: Ezra Pound and the Victorians* (Ithaca and London: Cornell University Press, 1995).

Gilbert, Elliot L., "The Female King: Tennyson's Arthurian Apocalypse," *PMLA* 98 (1983) 89–113.

Gilbert, Sandra M., "From *Patria* to *Matria*: Elizabeth Barrett Browning's Risorgimento," *PMLA* 99 (1984) 194–211.

Gilbert, Suzanne, and Douglas S. Mack, eds., *Queen Hynde* (Edinburgh: Edinburgh University Press, 1998).

Gill, Stephen, *Wordsworth and the Victorians* (Oxford: Clarendon Press, 1998).

Gladden, Samuel Lyndon, *Shelley's Textual Seductions: Plotting Utopia in the Erotic and Political Works* (New York and London: Routledge, 2002).

Gladstone, William Ewart, *Juventus Mundi: The Gods and Men of the Heroic Age* (Boston: Little, Brown, 1869).

Glasgow, Eric, "Gladstone's Homer," in *Studies in Nineteenth Century Literature*, ed. James Hogg (Salzburg: Universität Salzburg, 1982) 61–81.

Goldfarb, Russell M., *Sexual Repression and Victorian Literature* (Lewisburg: Bucknell University Press, 1970).

Goldsmith, Steven, *Unbuilding Jerusalem: Apocalypse and Romantic Representation* (Ithaca and London: Cornell University Press, 1993).

Goode, John, "1848 and the Strange Disease of Modern Love," in *Literature and Politics in the Nineteenth Century*, ed. John Lucas (London: Methuen, 1971) 45–76.

—— "William Morris and the Dream of Revolution," in *Literature and Politics in the Nineteenth Century*, ed. John Lucas (London: Methuen, 1971) 221–78.

Goodman, Kevis, *Georgic Modernity and British Romanticism: Poetry and the Mediation of History* (Cambridge: Cambridge University Press, 2004).

Görlach, Manfred, *English in Nineteenth-Century England: An Introduction* (Cambridge: Cambridge University Press, 1999).

Goslee, Nancy M., "*Marmion* and the Metaphor of Forgery," *Scottish Literary Journal* 7 (1980) 85–96.

—— " 'Letters in the Irish Tongue': Interpreting Ireland in Scott's 'Rokeby,' " in *Scott and his Influence*, ed. J. H. Alexander and David Hewitt (Aberdeen: Association for Scottish Literary Studies, 1983) 41–50.

—— *Uriel's Eye: Miltonic Stationing and Statuary in Blake, Keats, and Shelley* (University: University of Alabama Press, 1985).

—— *Scott the Rhymer* (Lexington: University Press of Kentucky, 1988).

—— "Hemans's 'Red Indians': Reading Stereotypes," in *Romanticism, Race, and Imperial Culture, 1780–1834*, ed. Alan Richardson and Sonia Hofkosh (Bloomington and Indianapolis: Indiana University Press, 1996) 237–57.

Graham, Colin, *Ideologies of Epic: Nation, Empire, and Victorian Epic Poetry* (Manchester and New York: Manchester University Press, 1998).

Graham, Peter, "A 'Polished Horde': The Great World in *Don Juan*," *Bulletin of Research in the Humanities* 86 (1983) 255–68.

—— *Don Juan and Regency England* (Charlottesville and London: University of Virginia Press, 1990).

Graver, Bruce E., "Wordsworth and the Language of Epic: The Translation of the *Aeneid*," *Studies in Philology* 83 (1986) 261–85.

Gravil, Richard, *Wordsworth's Bardic Vocation, 1787–1842* (Houndmills: Palgrave, 2003).

Gray, Donald J., "Macaulay's *Lays of Ancient Rome* and the Publication of Nineteenth-Century British Poetry," in *Victorian Literature and Society: Essays Presented to Richard D. Altick*, ed. James R. Kincaid and Albert J. Kuhn (Columbus: Ohio State University Press, 1984) 74–93.

Gray, W. Forbes, *The Poets Laureate of England: Their History and their Odes* (New York: Dutton, 1915).

Green, Martin, *Dreams of Adventure, Deeds of Empire* (New York: Basic Books, 1979).

—— *The Great American Adventure* (Boston: Beacon, 1984).

—— *The Adventurous Male: Chapters in the History of the White Male Mind* (University Park: Pennsylvania State University Press, 1993).

Greene, Thomas M., *The Descent from Heaven: A Study in Epic Continuity* (New Haven: Yale University Press, 1963).

Gridley, Roy E., "Browning's Caponsacchi," *Victorian Poetry* 6 (1968) 281–95.

—— "Browning's Pompilia," *Journal of English and Germanic Philology* 67 (1968) 64–83.

Grierson, Herbert, "The Man and the Poet" (1940), in *Sir Walter Scott Lectures 1940–1948*, ed. W. L. Renwick (Edinburgh: University Press, 1950) 3–30.

—— and J. C. Smith, *A Critical History of English Poetry* (New York: Oxford University Press, 1946).

Griffiths, Frederick T., and Stanley J. Rabinowitz, *Novel Epics: Gogol, Dostoevsky, and National Narrative* (Evanston: Northwestern University Press, 1990).

Grimes, Ronald L., "Time and Space in Blake's Major Prophecies," in *Blake's Sublime Allegory: Essays on The Four Zoas, Milton, Jerusalem*, ed. Stuart Curran and Joseph A. Wittreich, Jr. (Madison: University of Wisconsin Press, 1973) 59–81.

Groth, Helen, "Victorian Women Poets and Scientific Narratives," in *Women's Poetry, Late Romantic to Late Victorian: Gender and Genre, 1830–1900*, ed. Isobel Armstrong and Virginia Blain (Houndmills: Macmillan, 1999) 332–340.

Grundy, Joan, *Hardy and the Sister Arts* (London: Macmillan, 1979).

Gwynn, Stephen, *Thomas Moore* (London: Macmillan, 1905).

Haefner, Joel, "The Romantic Scene(s) of Writing," in *Re-Visioning Romanticism: British Women Writers, 1776–1837*, ed. Haefner and Carol Shiner Wilson (Philadelphia: University of Pennsylvania Press, 1994) 256–73.

Hägin, Peter, *The Epic Hero and the Decline of Heroic Poetry: A Study of the Neo-Classical English Epic* (Berne: Francke, 1964).

Haight, Gordon S., *George Eliot: A Biography* (Oxford and New York: Oxford University Press, 1968.

Hainsworth, J. B., *The Idea of Epic* (Berkeley: University of California Press, 1991).

Hair, Donald S., *Robert Browning's Language* (Toronto: University of Toronto Press, 1999).

Halévy, Elie, *The Liberal Awakening* (1923), tr. E. I. Watkin (New York: Barnes and Noble, 1961).

Haley, Bruce, *Living Forms: Romantics and the Monumental Figure* (Albany: State University of New York Press, 2003).

Hallam, Arthur, "On Some of the Characteristics of Modern Poetry," in *The Englishman's Magazine* (1831), rpt. in *The Writings of Arthur Hallam*, ed. T. Vail Motter (New York: Modern Language Association, 1943).

Hallam, Henry, *Introduction to the Literature of Europe in the Fifteenth, Sixteenth, and Seventeenth Centuries* (London: Murray, 1837).

Hamilton, Paul, *Wordsworth* (Brighton: Harvester, 1986).

Harbison, Robert, *Deliberate Regression* (New York: Knopf, 1980).

Hardie, Philip, *The Epic Successors of Virgil: A Study in the Dynamics of a Tradition* (Cambridge: Cambridge University Press, 1993).

Harding, Anthony John, "Felicia Hemans and the Effacement of Woman," in *Romantic Women Writers*, ed. Paula R. Feldman and Theresa M. Kelley (Hanover and London: University Press of New England, 1995) 138–49.

Hardy, Florence Emily, *The Early Life of Thomas Hardy* (London: Macmillan, 1928).

—— *The Later Years of Thomas Hardy* (London: Macmillan, 1930).

Hardy, Thomas, *Life and Work of Thomas Hardy*, ed. Michael Millgate (Athens.: University of Georgia Press, 1985).

—— *The Complete Poetical Works of Thomas Hardy*, ed. Samuel Hynes (Oxford: Clarendon Press, 1995).

Harlan, Aurelia Brooks, *Owen Meredith: A Critical Biography of Robert, First Earl of Lytton* (New York: Columbia University Press, 1946).

Harris, Daniel A., "Personification in 'Tithonus' " (1986), abridged in *Critical Essays on Alfred Lord Tennyson*, ed. Herbert F. Tucker (New York: G. K. Hall, 1993) 114–19.

Harrison, Antony H., *Swinburne's Medievalism: A Study in Victorian Love Poetry* (Baton Rouge and London: Louisiana State University Press, 1988).

—— *Victorian Poets and Romantic Poems* (Charlottesville: University of Virginia Press, 1990).

Harrison, Frederic, *Studies in Early Victorian Literature* (London: Edward Arnold, 1895).

Harshbarger, Scott, "Robert Lowth's *Sacred Hebrew Poetry* and the Oral Dimension of Romantic Rhetoric," in *Rhetorical Traditions and British Romantic Literature*, ed. Don H. Bialostosky and Lawrence D. Needham (Bloomington and Indianapolis: Indiana University Press, 1995) 199–214.

Hartman, Geoffrey, *Wordsworth's Poetry 1787–1814* (New Haven and London: Yale University Press, 1964).

The Fate of Reading and Other Essays (Chicago and London: University of Chicago Press, 1975).

—— " 'Was It for This? . . .': Wordsworth and the Birth of the Gods," in *Romantic Revolutions: Criticism and Theory*, ed. Kenneth R. Johnston *et al.* (Bloomington and Indianapolis: Indiana University Press, 1990) 8–25.

Harvey, A. D., "The English Epic in the Romantic Period," *Philological Quarterly* 55 (1976) 241–59.

—— *English Poetry in a Changing Society* (New York: St. Martin's Press, 1980).

—— *Literature into History* (New York: St. Martin's Press, 1988).

Haslett, Moyra, *Byron's* Don Juan *and the Don Juan Legend* (Oxford: Clarendon Press, 1997).

Haswell, Richard S., "Shelley's *The Revolt of Islam*: 'The Connexion of Its Parts,' " *Keats–Shelley Journal* 25 (1976) 81–102.

Havens, R. D., *The Influence of Milton on English Poetry* (Cambridge, Mass.: Harvard University Press, 1922).

Hawker, Stephen, *Life and Letters of Robert Stephen Hawker*, ed. C. E. Byles (London: Lane, 1904).

Hawkins, Thomas, *The Book of the Great Sea-Dragons, Ichthyosauri and Plesiosauri, Gedolim Taninim, of Moses* (London: Pickering, 1840).

Haworth, Helen E., "The Titans, Apollo, and the Fortunate Fall in Keats's Poetry," *Studies in English Literature* 10 (1970) 637–49.

Hayden, John O., ed., *Scott: The Critical Heritage* (New York: Barnes and Noble, 1970).

Hayley, William, *An Essay on Epic Poetry* (1782), rpt., M. Celeste Williamson, ed., (Gainesville: Scholars Press, 1968).

Haywood, Ian, *The Making of History: A Study of the Literary Forgeries of James Macpherson and Thomas Chatterton* (London and Toronto: Associated University Presses, 1986) 42–57.

Hazlitt, William, *Complete Works*, ed. P. P. Howe (London and Toronto: Dent, 1930).

Headley, G., "The Early Nineteenth-Century Epic: The Harvey Thesis Examined," *Journal of European Studies* 21 (1991) 201–8.

Heath-Stubbs, John, *The Darkling Plain* (London: Eyre and Spottiswoode, 1950).

Hegel, Georg Wilhelm Friedrich, *Aesthetics: Lectures on Fine Art*, tr. T. M. Knox, in 2 vols. (Oxford: Clarendon Press, 1975).

Henke, Suzette, "James Joyce and Philip James Bailey's *Festus*," *James Joyce Quarterly* 9 (1972) 445–51.

Herford, C. H., *The Age of Wordsworth* (1897; rpt. Freeport, NY: Books for Libraries, 1971).

Hertz, Neil, *George Eliot's Pulse* (Stanford: Stanford University Press, 2003).

Hickey, Alison, *Impure Conceits: Rhetoric and Ideology in Wordsworth's* Excursion (Stanford: Stanford University Press, 1997).

Hoagwood, Terence, Preface to Smith's *Brethren* (Delmar: Scholars' Facsimiles, 1991).

—— and Kathryn Ledbetter, *"Colour'd Shadows": Contexts in Publishing, Printing, and Reading Nineteenth-Century British Women Authors* (Houndmills: Palgrave, 2005).

Hobsbawm, E. J., and Terence Ranger, eds., *The Invention of Tradition* (Cambridge: Cambridge University Press, 1983).

Hodgson, Amanda, *The Romances of William Morris* (Cambridge: Cambridge University Press, 1987).

—— " 'The Highest Poetry': Epic Narrative in *The Earthly Paradise* and *Idylls of the King*," *Victorian Poetry* 34 (1996) 341–54.

Hoffpauir, Richard, "The Thematic Structure of Southey's Epic Poetry," *Wordsworth Circle* 6 (1975) 240–48.

—— "The Thematic Structure of Southey's Epic Poetry: Part II" *Wordsworth Circle* 7 (1976) 109–16.

Hogarth, D. G., *The Life of Charles M. Doughty* (Garden City: Doubleday, 1929).

Hogle, Jerrold E., *Shelley's Process: Radical Transference and the Development of His Major Works* (New York: Oxford University Press, 1988).

Holloway, John, "Poetry and Plain Language: The Verse of C. M. Doughty," *Essays in Criticism* 4 (1954) 58–70.

—— *Widening Horizons in English Verse* (Evanston: Northwestern University Press, 1967).

Hood, Edwin Paxton, *The Peerage of Poverty; or, Learners and Workers in Fields, Farms, and Factories* (1859; 5th rev. edn. London: Partridge, n. d.).

Hoole, John, tr., *Jerusalem Delivered*, (1764); rpt. *The Works of the English Poets, from Chaucer to Cowper*, vol. 21 (London: Chalmers, 1810).

Hopkins, Brooke, "Representing Robespierre," in *History and Myth: Essays on English Romantic Literature*, ed. Stephen C. Behrendt (Detroit: Wayne State University Press, 1990).

Hopkins, Kenneth, *English Poetry: A Short History* (Philadelphia and New York: Lippincott, 1962).

Hornback, Bert G., *The Metaphor of Chance: Vision and Technique in the Works of Thomas Hardy* (Athens, Ohio: Ohio University Press, 1971).

Horne, R. H., *A New Spirit of the Age* (1844; rpt. New York, Harper, 1872).

Hough, Graham, *The Last Romantics* (1947; rpt. London: Methuen, 1961).

Howard, William, "Narrative Irony in *The Excursion*," *Studies in Romanticism* 24 (1985) 511–30.

Hughes, Linda K., "The Poetics of Empire and Resistance: William Allingham's *Laurence Bloomfield in Ireland*," *Victorian Poetry* 28 (1990) 103–17.

—— "Alexander Smith and the Bisexual Poetics of *A Life-Drama*," *Victorian Poetry* 42 (2004) 491–508.

Hungerford, Edward B., *Shores of Darkness* (1941; rpt. Cleveland and New York: Meridian, 1963).

Hunt, Herbert J., *The Epic in Nineteenth-Century France: A Study in Heroic and Humanitarian Poetry from* Les Martyrs *to* Les Siècles Morts (Oxford: Blackwell, 1941).

Hunter, J. Paul, *Before Novels: The Cultural Contexts of Eighteenth-Century English Fiction* (New York: Norton, 1990).

Husein, Imdad, *English Romantic Poetry and Oriental Influences* (Lahore: Nadeem, 1994).

Hyder, Clyde K., ed., *Swinburne Replies* (Syracuse: Syracuse University Press, 1966).

—— ed., *Swinburne: The Critical Heritage*, (New York: Barnes and Noble, 1970).

Jack, Ian, *Keats and the Mirror of Art* (Oxford: Clarendon Press, 1967).

Jackson, Laura (Riding), "The 'Right English' of Charles M. Doughty," *University of Toronto Quarterly* 46 (1977) 309–21.

Jalowitz, Alan C., "The Daughters of Penelope: Tradition and Innovation in American Epics by Women," in *Approaches to the Anglo and American Female Epic, 1620–1982*, ed. Bernard Schweizer (Aldershot: Ashgate, 2006) 141–58.

Janowitz, Anne, *England's Ruins: Poetic Purpose and the National Landscape* (Oxford: Blackwell, 1990).

—— *Lyric and Labour in the Romantic Tradition* (Cambridge: Cambridge University Press, 1998).

Jay, Martin, *Marxism and Totality: The Adventures of a Concept from Lukacs to Habermas* (Berkeley and Los Angeles: University of California Press, 1984).

Jenkyns, Richard, *The Victorians and Ancient Greece* (Cambridge, Mass.: Harvard University Press, 1980).

Johns-Putra, Adeline, *Heroes and Housewives: Women's Epic Poetry and Domestic Ideology in the Romantic Age (1770–1835)* (Bern: Peter Lang, 2001).

—— "Gendering Telemachus: Anna Seward and the Epic Rewriting of Fénelon's *Télémaque*," in *Approaches to the Anglo and American Female Epic, 1620–1982*, ed. Bernard Schweizer (Aldershot: Ashgate, 2006) 87–97.

Johnson, E. D. H., "Robert Browning's Pluralistic Universe," *University of Toronto Quarterly* 31 (1961) 20–41.

Johnston, Kenneth R., *Wordsworth and* The Recluse (New Haven and London: Yale University Press, 1984).

Jones, Elizabeth, "Suburb Sinners: Sex and Disease in the Cockney School," in *Leigh Hunt: Life, Poetics, Politics*, ed. Nicholas Roe (London and New York: Routledge, 2003) 78–94.

Jones, John, *John Keats's Dream of Truth* (London: Chatto and Windus, 1969).

Jordan, Elaine, *Alfred Tennyson* (Cambridge: Cambridge University Press, 1988).

Kahn, Arthur David, "Byron's *Single Difference* with Homer and Virgil: The Redefinition of the Epic in *Don Juan*," *Arcadia* 5 (1970) 143–62.

Kaplan, Fred, *Miracles of Rare Device: The Poet's Sense of Self in Nineteenth-Century Poetry* (Detroit: Wayne State University Press, 1972).

Kaul, Suvir, *Poems of Nation, Anthems of Empire: English Verse in the Long Eighteenth Century* (Charlottesville and London: University of Virginia Press, 2000).

Keach, William, "Poetry, after 1740," in *The Cambridge History of Literary Criticism*, vol. 4, ed. H. B. Nisbet and Claude Rawson (Cambridge: Cambridge University Press, 1997) 117–66.

—— *Arbitrary Power: Romanticism, Language, Politics* (Princeton and Oxford: Princeton University Press, 2004).

Keble, John, *Keble's Lectures on Poetry 1832–1841*, tr. Edward Kershaw Francis (Oxford: Clarendon, 1912).

Keen, Paul, *The Crisis of Literature in the 1790s: Print Culture and the Public Sphere* (Cambridge: Cambridge University Press, 1999).

Keener, Frederick M., *English Dialogues of the Dead: A Critical History, An Anthology, and A Check List* (New York and London: Columbia University Press, 1973).

Kelley, Philip and Ronald Hudson, eds., *The Brownings' Correspondence*, vol. 5 (Winfield: Wedgestone, 1987).

Kelly, Gary, "From Avant-Garde to Vanguardism: The Shelleys' Romantic Feminism in *Laon and Cythna* and *Frankenstein*," in *Shelley: Poet and Legislator of the World*, ed. Betty T. Bennett and Stuart Curran (Baltimore and London: Johns Hopkins University Press, 1996) 73–87.

—— "Gender and Memory in Post-Revolutionary Women's Writing," in *Memory and Memorials, 1789–1914*, ed. Matthew Campbell, Jacqueline M. Labbe, and Sally Shuttleworth (London and New York: Routledge, 2000), 119–31.

Kelly, Van, "Criteria for the Epic: Borders, Diversity, and Expansion," in *Epic and Epoch: Essays on the Interpretation and History of a Genre*, ed. Kelly, Steven M. Oberhelman, and Richard J. Golsan (Lubbock: Texas Tech University Press, 1994) 1–21.

Kenner, Hugh, *The Pound Era* (Berkeley: University of California Press, 1971).

Ker, W. P., *Epic and Romance: Essays on Medieval Literature* (1896; rev. edn. 1908; rpt. New York: Dover, 1957).

Kernahan, Coulson, *Six Famous Living Poets* (London: Butterworth, 1922).

Kernan, Alvin B., *The Plot of Satire* (New Haven: Yale University Press, 1965).

Khattab, Ezzat Abdulmajeed, *The Critical Reception of Browning's* The Ring and the Book *1868–1889 and 1951–68* (Salzburg: Institut für Englische Sprache und Literatur, 1977).

King-Hele, Desmond, *Shelley: His Thought and Work*, 3rd edn. (Cranbury: Associated University Presses, 1984).

Kingsley, Charles, *Literary and General Lectures and Essays* (London: Macmillan, 1880).

—— *Two Years Ago* (Cambridge: Macmillan, 1857).

Kirchhoff, Frederick, *William Morris* (Boston: Twayne, 1979).

—— "William Morris's 'Land East of the Sun and West of the Moon': The Narrative as Place," *Pre-Raphaelite Review* 3 (1980) 14–24.

Klaver, J. M. I., *The Apostle of the Flesh: A Critical Life of Charles Kingsley* (Leiden: Brill, 2006).

Knight, G. Wilson, *The Starlit Dome: Studies in the Poetry of Vision* (Oxford: Oxford University Press, 1941).

Koch, June Q., "Politics in Keats's Poetry," *Journal of English and Germanic Philology* 71 (1972) 491–501.

Korg, Jacob, "Hardy's *The Dynasts*: A Prophecy," *South Atlantic Quarterly* 53 (1954) 24–32.

—— *Browning and Italy* (Athens and London: Ohio University Press, 1983).

Krasner, James, " 'Where No Man Praised': The Retreat from Fame in George Eliot's *The Spanish Gypsy*," *Victorian Poetry* 32 (1994) 55–73.

Kroeber, Karl, " 'The Rime of the Ancient Mariner' as Stylized Epic," *Transactions of the Wisconsin Society of Sciences, Arts, and Letters* 46 (1957) 179–89.

—— *Romantic Narrative Art* (Madison: University of Wisconsin Press, 1960).

—— "Trends in Minor Romantic Narrative Poetry," in *Some British Romantics: A Collection of Essays*, ed. James V. Logan, John E. Jordan, and Northrop Frye (Columbus: Ohio State University Press, 1966) 269–292.

—— "Delivering *Jerusalem*," in *Blake's Sublime Allegory: Essays on* The Four Zoas, Milton, Jerusalem, ed. Stuart Curran and Joseph A. Wittreich, Jr. (Madison: University of Wisconsin Press, 1973) 347–67.

Kucich, Greg, *Keats, Shelley, and Romantic Spenserianism* (University Park: Pennsylvania State University Press, 1991).

—— "Hunt, Keats and the Aesthetics of Excess," in *Leigh Hunt: Life, Poetics, Politics*, ed. Nicholas Roe (London and New York: Routledge, 2003) 118–34.

Kumar, Krishan, *The Making of English National Identity* (Cambridge: Cambridge University Press, 2003).

Kumbier, William, "Blake's Epic Meter," *Studies in Romanticism* 17 (1978) 163–92.

Labbe, Jacqueline M., "The Exiled Self: Images of War in Charlotte Smith's 'The Emigrants,' " in *Romantic Wars: Studies in Culture and Conflict, 1793–1822*, ed. Philip Shaw (Aldershot: Ashgate, 2000) 37–56.

Lambdin, Laura Cooner, and Robert Thomas Lambdin, *Camelot in the Nineteenth Century: Arthurian Characters in the Poems of Tennyson, Arnold, Morris, and Swinburne* (Westport: Greenwood Press, 2000).

Lambourne, Lionel, *Victorian Painting* (London: Phaidon, 1999).

Landor, Walter Savage, *Complete Works,* ed. T. Earle Welby, in 16 vols. (London: Chapman and Hall, 1927–36).

Landow, George P., *Images of Crisis: Literary Iconology, 1750 to the Present* (Boston and London: Routledge, 1982).

Landré, Louis, *Leigh Hunt*, in 2 vols. (Paris: Belles-Lettres, 1936).

Landry, Donna, *The Muses of Resistance: Laboring-Class Women's Poetry in Britain, 1739–1796* (Cambridge: Cambridge University Press, 1990).

Lang, Andrew, *Homer and the Epic* (London: Longmans, 1893).

Langan, Celeste, *Romantic Vagrancy: Wordsworth and the Simulation of Freedom* (Cambridge: Cambridge University Press, 1995).

Langbaum, Robert, *The Word from Below: Essays on Modern Literature and Culture* (Madison: University of Wisconsin Press, 1987).

LaPorte, Charles, "Spasmodic Poetics and Clough's Apostasies," *Victorian Poetry* 42 (2004) 521–36.

Latané, David, " 'See You?' Browning, Byron, and the Revolutionary Deluge in *Sordello*, Book I," *Victorian Poetry* 22 (1984) 85–91.

—— *Browning's* Sordello *and the Aesthetics of Difficulty* (Victoria: English Literary Studies, 1987).

Lauber, John, "*Don Juan* as Anti-Epic," *Studies in English Literature* 8 (1968) 607–19.

Le Quesne, Albert, *Carlyle* (New York: Oxford University Press, 1982).

Leader, Zachary, *Revision and Romantic Authorship* (Oxford: Clarendon Press, 1996).

Leask, Nigel, *British Romantic Writers and the East: Anxieties of Empire* (Cambridge: Cambridge University Press, 1992).

—— " 'Wandering through Eblis': Absorption and Containment in Romantic Exoticism," in *Romanticism and Colonialism: Writing and Empire, 1780–1830*, ed. Tim Fulford and Peter J. Kitson (Cambridge: Cambridge University Press, 1998) 165–88.

Lessenich, Rolf P., *Aspects of English Preromanticism* (Köln: Böhlau, 1989).

Levinson, Marjorie, *The Romantic Fragment Poem: A Critique of a Form* (Chapel Hill: University of North Carolina Press, 1986).

—— *Keats's Life of Allegory: The Origins of a Style* (Oxford: Blackwell, 1988).

Lewis, C. S., *Rehabilitations and Other Essays* (London: Oxford University Press, 1939).

Lindenberger, Herbert, *On Wordsworth's* Prelude (Princeton: Princeton University Press, 1963).

Lindsay, Jack, *George Meredith* (London: Bodley Head, 1956).

Linkin, Harriet Kramer, "Teaching the Poetry of Mary Tighe: *Psyche*, Beauty, and the Romantic Object," in *Approaches to Teaching British Women Poets of the Romantic Period*, ed. Linkin and Stephen C. Behrendt (New York: Modern Language Association, 1997) 106–9.

—— "Recuperating Romanticism in Mary Tighe's *Psyche*," in *Romanticism and Women Poets: Opening the Doors of Reception*, ed. Linkin and Stephen C. Behrendt (Lexington: University Press of Kentucky, 1999) 144–62.

Little, Judy, *Keats as a Narrative Poet: A Test of Invention* (Lincoln: University of Nebraska Press, 1975).

Liu, Alan, *Wordsworth: The Sense of History* (Stanford: Stanford University Press, 1989).

Lock, Charles, "HARDY Promises: *The Dynasts* and the Epic of Imperialism," in *Reading Thomas Hardy,* ed. Charles P. C. Pettit (Houndmills: Macmillan, 1998) 83–116.

Lord, Albert B., *The Singer of Tales* (Cambridge, Mass.: Harvard University Press, 1960).

Louis, Margot, *Swinburne and His Gods: The Roots and Growth of an Agnostic Poetry* (Montreal and Kingston: McGill-Queen's University Press, 1990).

Lucas, John, *England and Englishness: Ideas of Nationhood in English Poetry 1688–1900* (London: Hogarth Press, 1990).

—— "Politics and the Poet's Role," in *Literature and Politics in the Nineteenth Century,* ed. John Lucas (London: Methuen, 1971) 7–43.

Lukács, György, *Studies in European Realism,* tr. Edith Bone (London: Hillway, 1950).

—— *Writer and Critic,* tr. Arthur Kahn (London: Merlin Press, 1970).

—— *The Theory of the Novel: A Historical-Philosophical Essay on the Forms of Great Epic Literature* (1915), tr. Anna Bostock (Cambridge, Mass.: MIT Press, 1971).

Lyon, Judson Stanley, *The Excursion: A Study* (New Haven: Yale University Press, 1950).

Lytton, Robert, First Earl of: see below Meredith, Owen.

Lytton, Second Earl of, "The Poetry of Owen Meredith," in *The Eighteen-Eighties: Essays by Fellows of the Royal Society of Literature,* ed. Walter de la Mare (Cambridge: University Press, 1930) 33–41.

Maas, Jeremy, *Victorian Painters* (New York: Putnam, 1969).

Mac Adam, Alfred J., *Textual Confrontations: Comparative Readings in Latin American Literature* (Chicago and London: University of Chicago Press, 1987) 149–63.

Macaulay, Thomas Babington, "Prophetic Account of a Grand National Epic Poem, to Be Entitled 'The Wellingtoniad,' and to Be Published A. D. 2824," *Knight's Quarterly Magazine* (November 1824).

MacCarthy, Fiona, *William Morris: A Life for Our Time* (New York: Knopf, 1995).

McClatchy, J. D., "The Ravages of Time: The Function of the *Marmion* Epistles," *Studies in Scottish Literature* 9 (1972) 256–63.

MacDiarmid, Hugh, *Selected Essays,* ed. Duncan Glen (Berkeley and Los Angeles: University of California Press, 1970).

McFarland, Thomas, *Romanticism and the Forms of Ruin: Wordsworth, Coleridge, and Modalities of Fragmentation* (Princeton: Princeton University Press, 1981).

McGann, Jerome J., *Fiery Dust: Byron's Poetic Development* (Chicago and London: University of Chicago Press, 1968).

—— *Swinburne: An Experiment in Criticism* (Chicago: University of Chicago Press, 1972).

—— *Don Juan in Context* (Chicago and London: University of Chicago Press, 1975).

—— "Byron, Mobility, and the Poetics of Historical Ventriloquism," *Romanticism Past and Present* 9 (1985) 67–82.

—— *Black Riders: The Visible Language of Modernism* (Princeton: Princeton University Press, 1993).

McGhee, Richard D., *Marriage, Duty, and Desire in Victorian Poetry and Drama* (Lawrence: Regents Press of Kansas, 1980).

McGuire, Karen, "Byron Superstar: The Poet in Neverland," in *Contemporary Studies on Lord Byron*, ed. William D. Brewer (Lewiston, NY: Mellen, 2001) 141–59.

Mackail, J. W., *The Life of William Morris* (1899; rpt. London: Longmans, 1920).

McKillop, Alan D., "A Victorian Faust," *PMLA* 40 (1925) 743–68.

McKinsey, Martin, "Counter-Homericism in Yeats's 'The Wanderings of Oisin,' " in *W. B. Yeats and Postcolonialism*, ed. Deborah Fleming, (West Cornwall: Locust Hill, 2001) 235–51.

McLuhan, H. M., "Tennyson and the Romantic Epic," in *Critical Essays on the Poetry of Tennyson*, ed. John Killham (London: Routledge and Kegan Paul, 1960) 86–95.

McMaster, Graham, *Scott and Society* (Cambridge: Cambridge University Press, 1981).

McNeil, Maureen, "The Scientific Muse: The Poetry of Erasmus Darwin," in *Languages of Nature: Critical Essays on Science and Literature*, ed. L. J. Jordanova (London: Free Association, 1986) 164–203.

McNiece, Gerald, *Shelley and the Revolutionary Idea* (Cambridge, Mass.: Harvard University Press, 1969).

McSweeney, Kerry, "The Structure of Swinburne's *Tristram of Lyonesse*," *Queen's Quarterly* 75 (1969) 690–702.

McWilliams, John P., Jr., *The American Epic: Transforming a Genre, 1770–1860* (Cambridge: Cambridge University Press, 1989).

Madden, Lionel, ed., *Robert Southey: The Critical Heritage* (London and Boston: Routledge, 1972).

Maidment, Brian, ed., *The Poorhouse Fugitives: Self Taught Poets and Poetry in Victorian Britain* (Manchester: Carcanet, 1987).

Majeed, Javed, *Ungoverned Imaginings: James Mill's* The History of British India *and Orientalism* (Oxford: Clarendon Press, 1992).

Mallock, W. H., "How to Make an Epic Poem Like Mr. T★nn★s★n'', in *Every Man his own Poet; or, The Inspired Singer's Recipe Book*, 3rd edn. (London: Simpkin, Marshall, 1877); rpt. with W. C. Bennett, *The Anti-Maud* (New York: Garland, 1986).

Mandler, Peter, " 'In the Olden Time': Romantic History and English National Identity, 1820–50," in *A Union of Multiple Identities: The British Isles, c. 1750–c. 1850*, ed. Laurence Brockliss and David Eastwood (Manchester and New York: Manchester University Press, 1997) 78–92.

Manierre, William Reid, "Versification and Imagery in *The Fall of Hyperion*," *Texas Studies in Literature and Language* 3 (1961) 264–79.

Mannheim, Karl, *Ideology and Utopia*, tr. Louis Wirth and Edward A. Shils (London: Kegan Paul, 1936).

Manning, Peter J., *Byron and His Fictions* (Detroit: Wayne State University Press, 1978).

—— "*Don Juan* and Byron's Imperceptiveness to the English Word" (1979), rpt. in *Reading Romantics: Text and Context* (New York: Oxford University Press, 1990) 115–44.

Manuel, Frank E., *The Eighteenth Century Confronts the Gods* (Cambridge, Mass.: Harvard University Press, 1959).

Maresca, Thomas E., *Epic to Novel* (Columbus: Ohio State University Press, 1974).

Marotta, Kenny, "*Middlemarch*: 'The Home Epic,'" *Genre* 15 (1982) 403–20.

Mason, Michael, "The Importance of *Sordello*," in *The Major Victorian Poets: Reconsiderations*, ed. Isobel Armstrong (London: Routledge, 1969) 125–51.

Masson, David, *British Novelists and Their Styles* (Cambridge and London: Macmillan, 1859).

Masson, Rosaline, *Pollok and Aytoun* (Edinburgh and London: Oliphant, Anderson, and Ferrier, 1898).

Matthews, Susan, "*Jerusalem* and Nationalism," in *Beyond Romanticism: New Approaches to Texts and Contexts 1780–1832*, ed. Stephen Copley and John Whale (London and New York: Routledge, 1992) 79–100.

Maynard, John, *Browning's Youth* (Cambridge, Mass., and London: Harvard University Press, 1977).

—— *Victorian Discourses on Sexuality and Religion* (Cambridge: Cambridge University Press, 1993).

Meachen, Edward, "History and Transcendence in Robert Southey's Epic Poems," *Studies in English Literature 1500–1900* 19 (1979) 589–608.

Medwin, Thomas, *Journal of the Conversations of Lord Byron* (London: Colburn, 1824).

Mee, Jon, *Dangerous Enthusiasm: William Blake and the Culture of Radicalism in the 1790s* (Oxford: Clarendon, 1992).

Meisel, Joseph S., *Public Speech and the Culture of Public Life in the Age of Gladstone* (New York: Columbia University Press, 2001).

Menaghan, John M., "Embodied Truth: *The Ring and the Book* Reconsidered," *University of Toronto Quarterly* 52 (1983) 263–76.

Menhennet, Alan, *The Romantic Movement* (London: Croom Helm, 1981).

Meredith, Owen [pseud. of Robert Lytton], *Personal and Literary Letters of Robert, First Earl of Lytton*, ed. Betty Balfour, in 2 vols. (London and New York: Longmans, 1906).

Mermin, Dorothy, "Heroic Sisterhood in 'Goblin Market,'" *Victorian Poetry* 21 (1983) 107–18.

—— *Elizabeth Barrett Browning: The Origins of a New Poetry* (Chicago and London: University of Chicago Press, 1989).

Merriman, James D., *The Flower of Kings: A Study of the Arthurian Legend in England between 1485 and 1835* (Lawrence: University Press of Kansas, 1973).

Milbank, Alison, *Dante and the Victorians* (Manchester and New York: Manchester University Press, 1998).

Mickle, William Julius, tr. *The Lusiad; or, The Discovery of India: An Epic Poem* [Camoens] (1776; 5th rev. edn. London: Bell, 1889).

Mileur, Jean-Pierre, *The Critical Romance: The Critic as Reader, Writer, Hero* (Madison: University of Wisconsin Press, 1990).

Mill, J. S., *Autobiography and Literary Essays,* ed. John M. Robson and Jack Stillinger, vol. 1 of *Collected Works* (Toronto and Buffalo: University of Toronto Press, 1981).

—— *Essays on French History and Historians*, ed. John M. Robson and John C. Cairns, vol. 20 of *Collected Works* (Toronto and London: University of Toronto Press, 1985).

Millar, John, *An Historical View of the English Government*, in 4 vols. (London: Mawman, 1803).

Millard, Kenneth, *Edwardian Poetry* (Oxford: Clarendon Press, 1991).

Miller, Dean A., *The Epic Hero* (Baltimore and London: Johns Hopkins University Press, 2000).

Millgate, Jane, *Walter Scott: The Making of the Novelist* (Edinburgh: Edinburgh University Press, 1984).

Mills, Kevin, *Approaching Apocalypse: Unveiling Revelation in Victorian Writing* (Lewisburg: Bucknell University Press, 2007).

Mitchell, W. J. T., "Blake's Radical Comedy: Dramatic Structure as Meaning in *Milton*," in *Blake's Sublime Allegory: Essays on* The Four Zoas, Milton, Jerusalem, ed. Stuart Curran and Joseph A. Wittreich, Jr. (Madison: University of Wisconsin Press, 1973) 281–307.

Mizukoshi, Ayumi, *Keats, Hunt, and the Aesthetics of Pleasure* (Houndmills: Palgrave, 2001).

Moers, Ellen, *Literary Women* (Garden City: Doubleday, 1976).

Montgomery, James, review of Wordsworth's *The Excursion*, *Eclectic Review*, 2nd series, 3 (1815) 13–39.

Moore, Dafydd R., "The Critical Response to Ossian's Romantic Bequest," in *English Romanticism and the Celtic World*, ed. Gerald Carruthers and Alan Rawes (Cambridge: Cambridge University Press, 2003) 38–53.

Moretti, Franco, *Modern Epic: The World-System from Goethe to Garcia Marquez*, tr. Quintin Hoare (London and New York: Verso, 1996).

—— *Atlas of the European Novel 1800–1900* (1997; tr. London: Verso, 1998).

Morgan, Edwin, "Voice, Tone, and Transition in *Don Juan*," in *Byron: Wrath and Rhyme*, ed. Alan Bold (London: Vision, 1983) 57–77.

Mori, Masaki, *Epic Grandeur: Toward a Comparative Poetics of the Epic* (Albany: State University of New York Press, 1997).

Morris, Lewis, *Gwen: A Drama in Monologue* (London: Paul, 1879).

Morris, May, *William Morris, Artist, Writer, Socialist* (Oxford: Blackwell, 1936).

Morton, Peter, *The Vital Science: Biology and the Literary Imagination, 1860–1900* (London: Allen and Unwin, 1984).

Morton, Timothy, *Shelley and the Revolution in Taste: The Body and the Natural World* (Cambridge: Cambridge University Press, 1994).

Moskal, Jeanne, *Milton: Blake, Ethics, and Forgiveness* (Tuscaloosa and London: University of Alabama Press, 1994).

Mueller, Martin, *The Iliad* (London: Allen and Unwin, 1984).

Munich, Adrienne, *Andromeda's Chains: Gender and Interpretation in Victorian Literature and Art* (New York: Columbia University Press, 1989) 137–59.

Murphy, Paul Thomas, *Toward a Working-Class Canon: Literary Criticism in British Working-Class Periodicals, 1816–1858* (Columbus: Ohio State University Press, 1994).

Murray, Elisabeth, *Caught in the Web of Words: James A. H. Murray and the* Oxford English Dictionary (New Haven and London: Yale University Press, 1977).

Murray, Gilbert, *The Rise of the Greek Epic* (Oxford: Clarendon Press, 1907).

Myerson, George, *The Argumentative Imagination: Wordsworth, Dryden, Religious Dialogues* (Manchester and New York: Manchester University Press, 1992).

Nardo, Anna K., *George Eliot's Dialogue with John Milton* (Columbia and London: University of Missouri Press, 2003).

Nelson, Charles Edwin, "Role-Playing in *The Ring and the Book*," *Victorian Poetry* 4 (1966) 91–98.

Neufeldt, Victor, "The Madonna and the Gypsy," *Studies in the Novel* 15 (1983) 44–54.

Newman, Francis W., *Homeric Translation in Theory and Practice: A Reply to Matthew Arnold, Esq., Professor of Poetry, Oxford* (London: Williams and Norgate, 1861).

Newman, Gerald, *The Rise of English Nationalism: A Cultural History 1740–1830* (New York: St. Martin's Press, 1987).

Newman, John Henry, *Essays Critical and Historical* (London: Longmans, Green, 1872).

Newman, John Kevin, *The Classical Epic Tradition* (Madison: University of Wisconsin Press, 1986).

Nicolson, Harold, *Swinburne* (New York: Macmillan, 1926).

Nimis, Stephen A., *Narrative Semiotics in the Epic Tradition: The Simile* (Bloomington and Indianapolis: Indiana University Press, 1987).

Nuttall, A. D., *Openings: Narrative Beginnings from the Epic to the Novel* (Oxford: Clarendon Press, 1992).

Oberg, Charlotte H., *A Pagan Prophet: William Morris* (Charlottesville: University of Virginia Press, 1978).

Olender, Maurice, *The Languages of Paradise: Race, Religion, and Philology in the Nineteenth Century*, tr. Arthur Goldhammer (Cambridge, Mass., and London: Harvard University Press, 1992).

Oliphant, Margaret, review of Pollok's *The Course of Time*, *Edinburgh Review* 81 (1857) 314.

—— *The Victorian Age of English Literature* (New York: Tait, 1892).

Oliphant, T. L. Kington, *The New English* (London: Macmillan, 1886).

Oliver, Susan, *Scott, Byron and the Poetics of Cultural Encounter* (Houndmills: Palgrave, 2005).

Omberg, Margaret, *Scandinavian Themes in English Poetry, 1760–1800* (Uppsala: Studia Anglistica Upsaliensia, 1976).

O'Neill, Michael, "A More Hazardous Exercise: Shelley's Revolutionary Imaginings," *Yearbook of English Studies* 19 (1989) 256–64.

Orel, Harold, *Thomas Hardy's Epic-Drama A Study of* The Dynasts (Lawrence: University of Kansas Publications, 1963).

—— "Hardy and the Epic Tradition," *English Literature in Transition* 9 (1966) 187–89.

—— "Shelley's *The Revolt of Islam*: The Last Great Poem of the English Enlightenment?" *Studies on Voltaire and the Eighteenth Century* 89 (1972) 1187–1207.

Paley, Morton D., *The Apocalyptic Sublime* (New Haven and London: Yale University Press, 1986).

Parker, Herbert, *Post-Victorian Poetry* (London: Dent, 1938).

Parry, Jonathan, *The Politics of Patriotism: English Liberalism, National Identity and Europe, 1830–1886* (Cambridge: Cambridge University Press, 2006).

Patey, Douglas Lane, "Ancients and Moderns," in *The Cambridge History of Literary Criticism*, vol. 4, ed. H. B. Nisbet and Claude Rawson (Cambridge: Cambridge University Press, 1997) 52–71.

Patmore, Coventry, "New Poets," *Edinburgh Review* 104 (October 1856) 337–62.

—— "Poetry—The Spasmodists," *North British Review* 28 (Feb. 1858) 125–36.

Patterson, Annabel, "Wordsworth's Georgic: Genre and Structure in *The Excursion*," *Wordsworth Circle* 9 (1978) 145–54.

Pattison, Robert, *Tennyson and Tradition* (Cambridge, Mass.: Harvard University Press, 1979) 15–39.

Paulin, Tom, *Minotaur: Poetry and the Nation State* (Cambridge, Mass.: Harvard University Press, 1992).

Paulson, Ronald, *Representations of Revolution (1789–1820)* (New Haven and London: Yale University Press, 1983).

Peckham, Morse, "English Editions of *Festus*," *Papers of the Bibliographical Society of America* 44 (1950) 55–58.

—— "Historiography and *The Ring and the Book*," *Victorian Poetry* 6 (1968) 243–57.

Perl, Jeffrey M. *The Tradition of Return: The Implicit History of Modern Literature* (Princeton: Princeton University Press, 1984).

Perkin, Harold, *The Origins of Modern English Society 1780–1880* (London: Routledge, 1969).

Perkins, David, "Literary History and Historicism," in *The Cambridge History of Literary Criticism*, vol. 5, ed. Marshall Brown (Cambridge: Cambridge University Press, 2000) 338–361.

Peterfreund, Stuart, "*The Prelude*: Wordsworth's Metamorphic Epic," *Genre* 14 (1981) 441–72.

—— *Shelley among Others: The Play of the Intertext and the Idea of Language* (Johns Hopkins University Press, 2002).

Peters, Robert, "Swinburne: A Personal Essay and a Polemic," in *The Victorian Experience: The Poets*, ed. Richard A. Levine (Athens: Ohio University Press, 1982).

Petrie, Elaine D., "*Queen Hynde* and the Black Bull of Norroway," in *Papers Given at the Second James Hogg Society Conference*, ed. Gillian Hughes (Aberdeen: Association for Scottish Literary Studies, 1988) 128–39.

Pfordresher, John, ed., *A Variorum Edition of Tennyson's* Idylls of the King (New York and London: Columbia University Press, 1973).

Phillips, Adam, *Monogamy* (London: Faber, 1996).

Pikoulis, John, "Scott and 'Marmion': The Discovery of Identity," *Modern Language Review* 66 (1971) 738–50.

Pinsky, Robert, *Landor's Poetry* (Chicago and London: University of Chicago Press, 1968).

Pite, Ralph, *The Circle of Our Vision: Dante's Presence in English Romantic Poetry* (Oxford: Clarendon Press, 1994).

Pittock, Malcolm, "Dobell, *Balder*, and Post-Romanticism," *Essays in Criticism* 42 (1992) 221–42.

Plotz, John, *The Crowd: British Literature and Public Politics* (Berkeley and Los Angeles: University of California Press, 2000).

Poliakov, Leon, *The Aryan Myth: A History of Racist and Nationalist Ideas in Europe*, tr. Edmund Howard (London: Sussex University Press, 1974).

Pope, Alexander. *The Prose Works of Alexander Pope*, ed. Norman Ault (Oxford: Blackwell, 1936).

—— *The Poems of Alexander Pope*, ed. John Butt, Maynard Mack *et al.*, (London: Methuen, 1967).

Postlethwaite, Diane, *Making It Whole: A Victorian Circle and the Shape of Their World* (Columbus: Ohio State University Press, 1984).

Poston, Lawrence, " 'Worlds Not Realised': Wordsworthian Poetry in the 1830s," *Texas Studies in Literature and Language* 28 (1986) 51–80.

Potts, Abbie Findlay, *Wordsworth's* Prelude: *A Study of Its Literary Form* (Ithaca: Cornell University Press, 1953).

Powell, Thomas, *The Living Authors of England* (New York: Appleton, 1849).

Pratt, Linda Ray, *Imperial Eyes* (New York and London: Routledge, 1992).

—— "Patriot Poetics and the Romantic National Epic: Placing and Displacing Southey's *Joan of Arc*," in *Placing and Displacing Romanticism*, ed. Peter J. Kitson (Aldershot: Ashgate, 2001) 88–101.

Preyer, Robert, "Sydney Dobell and the Victorian Epic," *University of Toronto Quarterly* 30 (1962) 163–79.

Prickett, Stephen, "Poetics and Narrative: Biblical Criticism and the Nineteenth-Century Novel," in *The Critical Spirit and the Will to Believe: Essays in Nineteenth-Century Literature and Religion*, ed. David Jasper and T. R. Wright (Basingstoke and London: Macmillan, 1989) 1–22.

—— *Origins of Narrative: The Romantic Appropriation of the Bible* (Cambridge: Cambridge University Press, 1996).

Prins, Yopie, *Victorian Sappho* (Princeton: Princeton University Press, 1999).

Punter, David, "Blake: Social Relations of Poetic Form," *Literature and History*, 8 (1982) 182–205.

Quiller-Couch, Arthur, *Studies in Literature* (New York: Putnam, 1918).

Quint, David, *Epic and Empire: Politics and Generic Form from Virgil to Milton* (Princeton: Princeton University Press, 1993).

Ragussis, Michael, *Figures of Conversion: "The Jewish Question" and English National Identity* (Durham and London: Duke University Press, 1995).

Raimond, Jean, *Robert Southey* (Paris: Didier, 1968).

Rajan, Balachandra, *The Form of the Unfinished: English Poetics from Spenser to Pound* (Princeton: Princeton University Press, 1985).

—— *Under Western Eyes: India from Milton to Macaulay* (Durham and London: Duke University Press, 1999).

Rajan, Tilottama, *Dark Interpreter: The Discourse of Romanticism* (Ithaca and London: Cornell University Press, 1980).

—— "The Other Reading: Transactional Epic in Milton, Blake, and Wordsworth," in *Milton, the Metaphysicals, and Romanticism*, ed. Lisa Low and Anthony John Harding (Cambridge: Cambridge University Press, 1994) 20–46.

—— "Theories of Genre," in *The Cambridge History of Literary Criticism*, vol. 5, ed. Marshall Brown (Cambridge: Cambridge University Press, 2000) 226–49.

Raysor, T. M., *Coleridge's Miscellaneous Criticism* (Cambridge, Mass.: Harvard University Press, 1936).

Reed, Thomas A., "Keats and the Gregarious Advance of Intellect in *Hyperion*," *ELH* 55 (1988) 195–232.

Reeve, Clara, *The Progress of Romance* (1785; rpt. New York: Facsimile Text Society, 1930).

Reeves, Charles Eric, "Continual Seduction: The Reading of *Don Juan*," *Studies in Romanticism* 17 (1978) 453–63.

Reiman, Donald H., "*Don Juan* in Epic Context," *Studies in Romanticism* 16 (1977) 587–94.

Reynolds, Graham, *Victorian Painting* (New York: Macmillan, 1966).

Reynolds, Margaret, "Elizabeth Barrett Browning: A Chronology," in Elizabeth Barrett Browning, *Aurora Leigh*, ed. Reynolds (New York: Norton, 1996) 558–62.

Reynolds, Matthew, *The Realms of Verse 1830–1870: English Poetry in a Time of Nation-Building* (Oxford and New York: Oxford University Press, 2001).

Richards, Thomas, *The Imperial Archive: Knowledge and the Fantasy of Empire* (London and New York: Verso, 1993).

Richardson, Alan, *Literature, Education, and Romanticism: Reading as Social Practice, 1780–1832* (Cambridge: Cambridge University Press, 1994).

—— "Epic Ambivalence: Imperial Politics and Romantic Deflection in Williams's *Peru* and Landor's *Gebir*," in *Romanticism, Race, and Imperial Culture, 1780–1834*, ed. Richardson and Sonia Hofkosh (Bloomington and Indianapolis: Indiana University Press, 1996) 265–282.

Richardson, James, *Vanishing Lives: Style and Self in Tennyson, D. G. Rossetti, Swinburne, and Yeats* (Charlottesville: University of Virginia Press, 1988).

Richey, William, *Blake's Altering Aesthetic* (Columbia and London: University of Missouri Press, 1996).

Riddehough, Geoffrey B., "William Morris' Translation of the *Aeneid*," *Journal of English and Germanic Philology* 36 (1937) 338–46.

Ridenour, George M., *The Style of* Don Juan (1960; rpt. New Haven: Archon, 1969).

Ridley, M. R., *Keats's Craftsmanship: A Study in Poetic Development* (Oxford: Clarendon Press, 1933).

Riede, David G., *Swinburne: A Study of Romantic Mythmaking* (Charlottesville: University of Virginia Press, 1978).

—— *Oracles and Hierophants: Constructions of Romantic Authority* (Ithaca: Cornell University Press, 1991).

Rieger, James, " 'The Hem of Their Garments': The Bard's Song in *Milton*," in *Blake's Sublime Allegory: Essays on* The Four Zoas, Milton, Jerusalem, ed. Stuart Curran and Joseph A. Wittreich, Jr. (Madison: University of Wisconsin Press, 1973) 259–80.

Rivero, Albert J., "Typology, History, and Blake's *Milton*," *Journal of English and Germanic Philology*, 81 (1982).

Roberts, Adam, *Romantic and Victorian Long Poems: A Guide* (Aldershot: Ashgate, 1999).

Roberts, Beth Ellen, *One Voice and Many: Modern Poets in Dialogue* (Newark: University of Delaware Press, 2006).

Roberts, Marguerite, *Hardy's Poetic Drama and the Theatre* (New York: Pageant, 1965).

Roberts, Neil, "Epic and Novel in George Eliot," in *Face to Face: Bakhtin in Russia and the West*, ed. Carol Adlam *et al.* (Sheffield: Sheffield Academic Press, 1997).

Roe, Nicholas, *John Keats and the Culture of Dissent* (Oxford: Clarendon Press, 1997).

Rosenberg, John D., "Swinburne," *Victorian Studies* 11 (1967) 131–52.

—— *The Fall of Camelot: A Study of Tennyson's* Idylls of the King (Cambridge, Mass.: Harvard University Press, 1973).

—— "Tennyson and the Passing of Arthur," in *The Passing of Arthur: New Essays in Arthurian Tradition*, ed. Christopher Baswell and William Sharpe (New York and London: Garland, 1988) 221–34.

—— "Carlyle and Historical Narration," *Carlyle Annual* 10 (1989) 14–20.

Rosenberg, Philip, *The Seventh Hero: Thomas Carlyle and the Theory of Radical Activism* (Cambridge, Mass.: Harvard University Press, 1974).

Ross, Marlon B., "Scott's Chivalric Pose: The Function of Metrical Romance in the Romantic Period," *Genre* 19 (1986) 267–97.

—— *The Contours of Masculine Desire: Romanticism and the Rise of Women's Poetry* (New York: Oxford University Press, 1989).

—— "Romancing the Nation-State: The Poetics of Romantic Nationalism," in *Macropolitics of Nineteenth-Century Literature: Nationalism, Exoticism, Imperialism*, ed. Jonathan Arac and Harriet Ritvo (Philadelphia: University of Pennsylvania Press, 1991) 56–85.

Ross, Robert, review of Hardy's *The Dynasts*, in *The Academy* (March 1906) 206.

Rosso, George Anthony, Jr., *Blake's Prophetic Workshop: A Study of* The Four Zoas (Lewisburg: Associated University Presses, 1993).

Rothery, C. I., "Scott's Narrative Poetry and the Classical Form of the Historical Novel," in *Scott and his Influence*, ed. J. H. Alexander and David Hewitt (Aberdeen: Association for Scottish Literary Studies, 1983) 63–74.

Rudy, Jason, "Rhythmic Intimacy, Spasmodic Epistemology," *Victorian Poetry* 42 (2004) 451–72.

Runge, Laura, *Gender and Language in British Literary Criticism 1660–1790* (Cambridge, Cambridge University Press, 1997).

Rzepka, Charles J., *The Self as Mind: Vision and Identity in Wordsworth, Coleridge, and Keats* (Cambridge, Mass.: Harvard University Press, 1986).

Saintsbury, George, *A History of Nineteenth Century Literature* (New York and London: Macmillan, 1896).

—— *A History of English Prosody* (London: Macmillan, 1910).

—— "The Landors, Leigh Hunt, De Quincey," in *The Cambridge History of English Literature,* ed. A. W. Ward and A. R. Waller, vol. 12 (Cambridge: Cambridge University Press, 1915) 226–256.

—— "Lesser Poets," in *The Cambridge History of English Literature,* ed. A. W. Ward and A. R. Waller, vol. 12 (Cambridge: Cambridge University Press, 1915) 104–53.

—— "Lesser Poets," in *The Cambridge History of English Literature,* ed. A. W. Ward and A. R. Waller, vol. 13 (Cambridge: Cambridge University Press, 1917) 164–249.

Salick, Roydon, "*The Excursion* as Epic," *Literary Half-Yearly* 32 (1991) 86–110.

Sandler, Florence, "The Iconoclastic Enterprise: Blake's Critique of 'Milton's Religion,' " *Blake Studies*, 5 (1972) 13–57.

Schad, John, *Victorians in Theory: From Derrida to Browning* (Manchester and New York: Manchester University Press, 1999).

Schellenberger, John, "More Early Nineteenth-Century Epics," *Notes and Queries* 30 (1983) 213–14.

Scholes, Robert, and Robert Kellogg, *The Nature of Narrative* (New York: Oxford University Press, 1966).

Schor, Esther, *Bearing the Dead: The British Culture of Mourning from the Enlightenment to Victoria* (Princeton: Princeton University Press, 1994).

Schueler, H. J., *The German Verse Epic in the Nineteenth and Twentieth Centuries* (The Hague: Nijhoff, 1967).

Scott, Walter, review essay on Macpherson's *Ossian, Edinburgh Review* 6 (1805) 446.

—— "Romance" (1824), in *Encyclopedia Britannica*, rpt. in *Essays on Chivalry, Romance, and the Drama* (1834; rpt. London: Warne, 1870) 226–69.

Scrivener, Michael, *Radical Shelley: The Philosophical Anarchism and Utopian Thought of Percy Bysshe Shelley* (Princeton: Princeton University Press, 1982).

Semmel, Bernard, *George Eliot and the Politics of National Inheritance* (New York and Oxford: Oxford University Press, 1994).

Setzer, Sharon M., "Wordsworth's Wanderer, the Epitaph, and the Uncanny," *Genre* 24 (1991) 361–79.

Seward, Anna, *Letters* (Edinburgh: Constable, 1811).

Shaaban, Bouthaina, "Shelley and the Chartists," in *Shelley: Poet and Legislator of the World*, ed. Betty T. Bennett and Stuart Curran (Baltimore and London: Johns Hopkins University Press, 1996) 114–25.

Shaffer, Elinor, *"Kubla Khan" and The Fall of Jerusalem: The Mythical School in Biblical Criticism and Secular Literature 1770–1880* (Cambridge: Cambridge University Press, 1975).

Shairp, John Campbell, *Aspects of Poetry* (Oxford: Clarendon Press, 1881).

Shaw, Harry E., "Scott and George Eliot: The Lure of the Symbolic," in *Scott and his Influence*, ed. J. H. Alexander and David Hewitt (Aberdeen: Association for Scottish Literary Studies, 1983) 393–402.

Shaw, J. E., " 'The Donna Angelicata' in *The Ring and the Book*," *PMLA* 41 (1926) 55–81.

Shaw, Philip, "Leigh Hunt and the Aesthetics of Post-War Liberalism," in *Romantic Wars: Studies in Culture and Conflict*, ed. Philip Shaw (Aldershot: Ashgate, 2000) 185–207.

Shaw, W. David, *The Lucid Veil: Poetic Truth in the Victorian Age* (London: Athlone Press, 1987).

—— *Victorians and Mystery: Crises of Representation* (Ithaca and London: Cornell University Press, 1990).

Sheats, Paul D., "Stylistic Discipline in *The Fall of Hyperion*," *Keats–Shelley Journal* 17 (1968) 75–88.

Shelley, Bryan, *Shelley and Scripture: The Interpreting Angel* (Oxford: Clarendon Press, 1994).

Shelley, Percy Bysshe, *Letters of Percy Bysshe Shelley,* ed. Roger Ingpen, in 2 vols. (London: Pitman, 1909).

Sherman, Stuart P., *On Contemporary Literature* (New York: Holt, 1917).

Sherry, Vincent, *The Great War and the Language of Modernism* (New York: Oxford University Press, 2003).

Sider, Michael J., *The Dialogic Keats: Time and History in the Major Poems* (Washington: Catholic University of America Press, 1998).

Simmons, Clare A., *Reversing the Conquest: History and Myth in Nineteenth-Century British Literature* (New Brunswick and London: Rutgers University Press, 1990).

—— "Medievalism and the Romantic Poet-Editor in Scott's *Marmion*," *Poetica* 39 (1993) 93–109.

—— " 'Useful and Wasteful Both': Southey's *Thalaba the Destroyer* and the Function of Annotation in the Romantic Oriental Poem," *Genre* 27 (1994) 83–104.

Simpson, David, *Wordsworth's Historical Imagination: The Poetry of Displacement* (New York: Methuen, 1987).

Simpson, Roger, "Epics in the Romantic Era," *Notes and Queries* 33 (1986) 160–61.

—— *Camelot Regained: The Arthurian Revival and Tennyson 1800–1849* (Cambridge: Brewer, 1990).

Skoblow, Jeffrey, *Paradise Dislocated: Morris, Politics, Art* (Charlottesville and London: University of Virginia Press, 1993).

Slinn, E. Warwick, "Language and Truth in *The Ring and the Book*," *Victorian Poetry* 27 (1989) 115–33.

Small, Ian, *Conditions for Criticism: Authority, Knowledge, and Literature in the Late Nineteenth Century* (Oxford: Clarendon Press, 1991).

Smith, Byron Porter, *Islam in English Literature* (Beirut: American Press, 1939).

Smith, F. B., *Radical Artisan: William James Linton 1812–97* (Manchester: Manchester University Press, 1973).

Smith, Iain Crichton, "Poetry in Scott's Narrative Verse," in *Sir Walter Scott: The Long-Forgotten Melody*, ed. Alan Bold (London: Vision, 1983) 109–126.

Smith, Paul, *Disraeli: A Brief Life* (Cambridge: Cambridge University Press, 1996).

Smith, Stan, *20th-Century Poetry* (London and Basingstoke: Macmillan, 1983).

Southey, Charles Cuthbert, ed., *The Life and Correspondence of Robert Southey* (London: Longman, 1849).

Southey, Robert, *New Letters,* ed. Kenneth Curry in 2 vols. (New York: Columbia University Press, 1965).

Spatt, Hartley S., "William Morris and the Uses of the Past," *Victorian Poetry* 13 (1975) 1–9.

Sperry, Stuart M., *Keats the Poet* (Princeton: Princeton University Press, 1973).

Spiegelman, Willard, *Wordsworth's Heroes* (Berkeley and Los Angeles: University of California Press, 1985).

Spufford, Francis, *I May Be Some Time: Ice and the English Imagination* (New York: St. Martin's Press, 1997).

St. Clair, William, "The Impact of Byron's Writings: An Evaluative Approach," in *Byron: Augustan and Romantic*, ed. Andrew Rutherford (New York: St. Martin's Press, 1990) 1–25.

—— *The Reading Nation in the Romantic Period* (Cambridge: Cambridge University Press, 2004).

Stabler, Jane, *Byron, Poetics and History* (Cambridge: Cambridge University Press, 2002).

Stafford, Fiona J., *The Sublime Savage: A Study of James Macpherson and the Poems of Ossian* (Edinburgh: Edinburgh University Press, 1988).

Staines, David, "Swinburne's Arthurian World: Swinburne's Arthurian Poetry and Its Medieval Sources," *Studia Neophilologica* 50 (1978) 53–70.

Stanley, A. P., *The Life and Correspondence of Thomas Arnold, D.D.*, 6th edn. (London: Fellowes, 1846).

Stauffer, Andrew M., *Anger, Revolution, and Romanticism* (Cambridge: Cambridge University Press, 2005).

Stedman, E. C., *Victorian Poets*, rev. edn. (Boston and New York: Houghton Mifflin, 1887).

Stephen, Leslie, *George Eliot* (London and New York: Macmillan, 1902).

Stevenson, Lionel, *Darwin Among the Poets* (1932; rpt. New York: Russell and Russell, 1963).

—— *The Pre-Raphaelite Poets* (Chapel Hill: University of North Carolina Press, 1972).

Stocking, George W., Jr., *Victorian Anthropology* (New York: Free Press, 1987).

Stone, Marjorie, "Genre Subversion and Gender Inversion: *The Princess* and *Aurora Leigh*," *Victorian Poetry* 25 (1987) 101–27.

Storey, Mark, *Robert Southey: A Life* (Oxford and New York: Oxford University Press, 1997).

Sullivan, Mary Rose, *Browning's Voices in* The Ring and the Book: *A Study of Method and Meaning* (Toronto: University of Toronto Press, 1969).

Super, R. H., *Walter Savage Landor* (New York: New York University Press, 1954).

Sutherland, Kathryn, "Defining the Self in the Poetry of Scott and Wordsworth," in *Scott and his Influence,* ed. J. H. Alexander and David Hewitt (Aberdeen: Association for Scottish Literary Studies, 1983) 51–62.

Swedenberg, H. T., Jr., *The Theory of the Epic in England 1650–1800* (Berkeley and Los Angeles: University of California Press, 1944).

Sweet, Nanora, "Gender and Modernity in *The Abencerrage*: Hemans, Rushdie, and 'The Moor's Last Sigh,' " in *Felicia Hemans: Reimagining Poetry in the Nineteenth Century*, ed. Sweet and Julie Melnyk (Houndmills: Palgrave, 2001) 181–95.

Swinburne, A. C., *Complete Works*, ed. Edmund Gosse and Thomas James Wise, in 20 vols. (London: Heinemann, 1925–27).

—— *The Swinburne Letters*, ed. Cecil Y. Lang, in 6 vols. (New Haven: Yale University Press, 1959–1962).

Sylvia, Richard A., " 'Parabolic Drift' as Narrative Method in Tennyson's *Idylls*: A New Reading of 'The Holy Grail,' " *Journal of Narrative Technique* 17 (1987), 296–308.

Tanner, Tony, *Adultery in the Novel: Contract and Transgression* (Baltimore: Johns Hopkins University Press, 1979).

Taplin, Gardner B., *The Life of Elizabeth Barrett Browning* (New Haven: Yale University Press, 1957).

Taylor, Anya, *Magic and English Romanticism* (Athens: University of Georgia Press, 1979).

Taylor, Beverly, and Elisabeth Brewer, *The Return of King Arthur: British and American Arthurian Literature since 1800* (Totowa: Barnes and Noble, 1983).

Taylor, Dennis, *Hardy's Metres and Victorian Prosody* (Oxford: Clarendon Press, 1988).

—— *Hardy's Literary Language and Victorian Philology* (Oxford: Clarendon Press, 1993).

Taylor, Peter A., "Providence and the Moment in Blake's *Milton*," *Blake Studies* 4 (1971) 43–60.

Tennyson, Alfred, *The Letters of Alfred Lord Tennyson*, ed. Cecil Y. Lang and Edgar F. Shannon, Jr., in 3 vols. (Cambridge, Mass.: Harvard University Press, 1981–90).

Tennyson, Hallam, *Alfred Lord Tennyson: A Memoir* (London: Macmillan, 1897).

Thomas, Edward, *Algernon Charles Swinburne: A Critical Study* (New York: Kennerley, 1912).

Thompson, A. Hamilton, "The Rossettis, Morris, Swinburne," in *The Cambridge History of English Literature*, ed. A. W. Ward and A. R. Waller, vol. 13 (Cambridge: Cambridge University Press, 1917) 123–63.

Thompson, E. P., *The Making of the English Working Class* (New York: Pantheon, 1963).

—— *William Morris: Romantic to Revolutionary* (1955; rev. edn. New York: Pantheon, 1977).

Thorpe, Douglas, "Shelley's Golden Verbal City," *Journal of English and Germanic Philology* 86 (1987) 215–27.

Tihanov, Galin, *The Master and the Slave: Lukács, Bakhtin, and the Ideas of Their Time* (Oxford: Clarendon Press, 2000).

Tillotson, Geoffrey and Kathleen, *Mid-Victorian Studies* (London: Athlone Press, 1965).

Tillyard, E. M. W., *Five Poems 1470–1870: An Elementary Essay on the Background of English Literature* (London: Chatto and Windus, 1948).

—— *The English Epic and its Background* (London: Chatto and Windus, 1954).

—— *The Epic Strain in the English Novel* (London: Chatto and Windus, 1958).

Tompkins, J. M. S., *William Morris: An Approach to the Poetry* (London: Cecil Woolf, 1988).

Tredell, Nicholas, "*Tristram of Lyonesse*: Dangerous Voyage," *Victorian Poetry* 20 (1982) 97–111.

Trench, R. C., *English, Past and Present: Eight Lectures* (1855; rev. edn. London: Macmillan, 1881).

Treneer, Anne, *Charles M. Doughty: A Study of his Prose and Verse* (London: Cape, 1935).

Trumpener, Katie, *Bardic Nationalism: The Romantic Novel and the British Empire* (Princeton: Princeton University Press, 1997).

Tucker, Herbert F., *Browning's Beginnings: The Art of Disclosure* (Minneapolis: University of Minnesota Press, 1980).

—— *Tennyson and the Doom of Romanticism* (Cambridge, Mass., and London: Harvard University Press, 1988).

—— "The Epic Plight of Troth in *Idylls of the King*," *ELH* 58 (1991) 701–20.

—— "Trials of Fiction: Novel and Epic in the Geraint and Enid Episodes from *Idylls of the King*," *Victorian Poetry* 30 (1992) 441–61.

Tucker, Herbert F., "*Aurora Leigh*: Epic Solutions to Novel Ends," in *Famous Last Words*, ed. Alison Booth (Charlottesville and London: University of Virginia Press, 1993) 62–85.

—— "Swinburne's *Tristram of Lyonesse* as Assimilationist Epic," in *Romantic/Victorian: Influence and Resistance in Nineteenth-Century Poetry*, ed. G. Kim Blank and Margot Louis (Houndmills: Macmillan, 1993) 76–90.

—— "Representation and Repristination: Virginity in *The Ring and the Book*," in *Virginal Sexuality and Textuality*, ed. Lloyd Davis (Albany: State University of New York Press, 1993) 67–86.

—— "All for the Tale: The Epic Macropoetics of Morris' *Sigurd the Volsung*," *Victorian Poetry* 34 (1996) 373–94.

—— "Epic," in *A Companion to Victorian Poetry*, ed. Richard Cronin, Alison Chapman, and Antony Harrison (Oxford: Blackwell, 2002) 25–41.

—— "Glandular Omnism and Beyond: The Victorian Spasmodic Epic," *Victorian Poetry* 42 (2004) 429–50.

—— "Doughty's *The Dawn in Britain* and the Modernist Eclipse of the Victorian," *Romanticism and Victorianism on the Net* 1 (2007).

Turley, Richard M., *The Politics of Language in Romantic Literature* (Houndmills: Palgrave, 2002).

Turner, Frank M., *The Greek Heritage in Victorian Britain* (New Haven and London: Yale University Press, 1981).

Turner, Paul, "Shelley and Lucretius," *Review of English Studies* NS 10 (1959) 269–82.

—— *The Life of Thomas Hardy: A Critical Biography* (Oxford: Blackwell, 1998).

Twycross-Martin, Henrietta, "The Drunkard, the Brute, and the Paterfamilias: The Temperance Fiction of the Early Victorian Writer Sarah Stickney Ellis," in *Women of Faith in Victorian Culture: Reassessing the Angel in the House*, ed. Anne Hogan and Andrew Bradstock (Houndmills: Macmillan, 1998) 6–30.

Ulmer, William A., *Shelleyan Eros: The Rhetoric of Romantic Love* (Princeton: Princeton University Press, 1990).

Vail, Jeffrey W., *The Literary Relationship of Lord Byron and Thomas Moore* (Baltimore and London: Johns Hopkins University Press, 2001).

Valente, Joseph, " 'Upon the Braes': History and Hermeneutics in *Waverley*," *Studies in Romanticism* 24 (1986) 251–276.

Van Ghent, Dorothy, *Keats: The Myth of the Hero*, ed. Jeffrey C. Robinson (Princeton: Princeton University Press, 1983).

Vance, Norman, *The Victorians and Ancient Rome* (Oxford: Blackwell, 1997).

Vanden Bossche, Chris, *Carlyle and the Search for Authority* (Columbus: Ohio State University Press, 1991).

Venuti, Lawrence, *The Translator's Invisibility: A History of Translation* (London and New York: Routledge, 1995).

Vickery, John B., *The Literary Impact of* The Golden Bough (Princeton: Princeton University Press, 1973).

Viscomi, Joseph, *Blake and the Idea of the Book* (Princeton: Princeton University Press, 1993).

Viswanathan, Gauri, *Masks of Conquest: Literary Study and British Rule in India* (New York: Columbia University Press, 1989).

Vitoux, Pierre, "Keats's Epic Design in *Hyperion*," *Studies in Romanticism* 14 (1975) 165–83.

—— "*Gebir* as an Heroic Poem," *Wordsworth Circle* 7 (1976) 51–57.

Vivante, Leone, *English Poetry and Its Contribution to the Knowledge of a Creative Principle* (New York: Macmillan, 1950).

Vogler, Thomas A., *Preludes to Vision: The Epic Venture in Blake, Wordsworth, Keats, and Hart Crane* (Berkeley: University of California Press, 1971).

—— "Re: Naming MIL/TON," in *Unnam'd Forms: Blake and Textuality*, ed. Vogler and Nelson Hilton (Berkeley: University of California Press, 1986) 141–76.

Wacker, Norman, "Epic and the Modern Long Poem: Virgil, Blake, and Pound," *Comparative Literature* 42 (1990) 126–43.

Wahrman, Dror, *Imagining the Middle Class: The Political Representation of Class in Britain, 1780–1840* (Cambridge: Cambridge University Press, 1995).

Wain, John, Introduction to *The Dynasts* (London: Macmillan, 1965) ix–xix.

Walker, Hugh, *The Literature of the Victorian Era* (Cambridge: University Press, 1910).

Walker, Keith, *Byron's Readers: A Study of Attitudes towards Byron, 1812–1832* (Salzburg: Universität Salzburg, 1979).

Walker, William, "*Pompilia* and Pompilia," *Victorian Poetry* 22 (1984) 47–63.

Waller, John O., "Tennyson and Philip James Bailey's *Festus*," *Bulletin of Research in the Humanities* 82 (1979) 105–23.

Ward, Jay A., *The Critical Reputation of Byron's* Don Juan *in Britain* (Salzburg: Universität Salzburg, 1979).

Ward, Wilfrid, *Aubrey de Vere: A Memoir* (London: Longmans, 1904).

Wasserman, Earl R., *Shelley: A Critical Reading* (Baltimore and London: Johns Hopkins University Press, 1971).

Waters, Catherine, *Dickens and the Politics of the Family* (Cambridge: Cambridge University Press, 1997).

Watkins, Daniel P., *Keats's Poetry and the Politics of the Imagination* (Brighton: Harvester, 1986).

Watt, Ian, *The Rise of the Novel: Studies in Defoe, Richardson, and Fielding* (Berkeley: University of California Press, 1957).

Watts, Marjorie, *Mrs Sappho: The Life of C. A. Dawson Scott, Mother of International P.E.N.* (London: Duckworth, 1987).

Wawn, Andrew, "Samuel Laing, *Heimskringla* and the Victorian 'Berserker School,'" in *Anglo-Scandinavian Cross-Currents*, ed. Inga-Stina Ewbank, Olav Lausund, and Bjørn Tysdahl (Norwich: Norvik Press, 1999) 29–59.

Wawn, Andrew, *The Vikings and the Victorians: Inventing the Old North in Nineteenth-Century Britain* (Cambridge: D. S. Brewer, 2000).

Weinbrot, Howard, *Britannia's Issue: The Rise of British Literature from Dryden to Ossian* (Cambridge: Cambridge University Press, 1993).

Weiner, Stephanie Kuduk, *Republican Politics and English Poetry, 1789–1874* (Houndmills: Palgrave, 2005).

Weinstein, Mark A., *William Edmondstoune Aytoun and the Spasmodic Controversy* (New Haven and London: Yale University Press, 1968).

Weisman, Karen A., *Imageless Truths: Shelley's Poetic Fictions* (Philadelphia: University of Pennsylvania Press, 1994).

Welby, T. Earle, *The Victorian Romantics 1850–70* (London: Howe, 1929).

Wellek, René, *The Rise of English Literary History* (Chapel Hill: University of North Carolina Press, 1941).

Welsh, Alexander, *George Eliot and Blackmail* (Cambridge, Mass.: Harvard University Press, 1985).

—— *The Hero of the Waverley Novels, With New Essays on Scott* (Princeton: Princeton University Press, 1992).

—— *Strong Representations: Narrative and Circumstantial Evidence in England* (Baltimore and London: Johns Hopkins University Press, 1992).

Wesling, Donald, and Tadeusz Sławek, *Literary Voice: The Calling of Jonah* (Albany: State University of New York Press, 1995).

West-Burnham, Joss, "Fedalma—'The Angel of a Homeless Tribe': Issues of Religion, Race and Gender in George Eliot's Poetic Drama, *The Spanish Gypsy*," in *Women of Faith in Victorian Culture: Reassessing the Angel in the House*, ed. Anne Hogan and Andrew Bradstock (Houndmills: Macmillan, 1998) 78–90.

Westwater, Martha, *The Spasmodic Career of Sydney Dobell* (Lanham: University Press of America, 1992).

Wheatley, Kim, *Shelley and His Readers: Beyond Paranoid Politics* (Columbia and London: University of Missouri Press, 1999).

Wheeler, Michael, *Heaven, Hell, and the Victorians* (Cambridge: Cambridge University Press, 1994).

Whewell, William, "The General Bearing of the Great Exhibition on the Progress of Art and Science," in *Lectures on the Results of the Great Exhibition of 1851* (London: Bogue, 1852).

White, Daniel E., *Early Romanticism and Religious Dissent* (Cambridge: Cambridge University Press, 2006).

White, Hayden, *Metahistory: The Historical Imagination in Nineteenth-Century Europe* (Baltimore and London: Johns Hopkins University Press, 1973).

White, R. J., *Thomas Hardy and History* (London: Macmillan, 1974).

Whitehead, Fred, "William Blake and Radical Tradition," in *Weapons of Criticism: Marxism in America and the Literary Tradition*, ed. Norman Rudich (Palo Alto: Ramparts Press, 1976) 191–214.

Whittington-Egan, Richard, *Stephen Phillips: A Biography* (High Wycombe: Rivendale Press, 2006).

Wickens, G. Glen, *Thomas Hardy, Monism, and the Carnival Tradition: The One and the Many in* The Dynasts (Toronto: University of Toronto Press, 2002).

Wilde, Oscar, "The Critic as Artist," in *Literary Criticism of Oscar Wilde*, ed. Stanley Weintraub (Lincoln: University of Nebraska Press, 1968) 197–228.

Wildman, John Hazard, "Unsuccessful Return from Avalon," *Victorian Poetry* 12 (1974) 291–96.

Wilkie, Brian, *Romantic Poets and Epic Tradition* (Madison and Milwaukee: University of Wisconsin Press, 1965).

Williams, Stanley, "The Story of Gebir," *PMLA* 36 (1924) 615–31.

Willinsky, John, *Empire of Words: The Reign of the OED*. Princeton: Princeton University Press, 1994.

Wilson, John, *Recreations of Christopher North,* in 2 vols. (1842; new edn. Edinburgh and London: W. Blackwood and Sons, 1864).

Wilson, Keith, "*The Dynasts*: Some Problems of Interpretation," *Colby Library Quarterly* 12 (1976) 181–90.

—— " 'Flower of Man's Intelligence': World and Overworld in *The Dynasts*," *Victorian Poetry* 17 (1979) 124–33.

Wilt, Judith, "The Laughter of Caponsacchi," *Victorian Poetry* 18 (1980) 337–57.

Wittreich, Jr., Joseph A., "Domes of Mental Pleasure: Blake's Epics and Hayley's Epic Theory," *Studies in Philology* 69 (1972) 101–29.

—— " 'Sublime Allegory': Blake's Epic Manifesto and the Milton Tradition," *Blake Studies* 4 (1972) 15–44.

Wlecke, Albert, *Wordsworth and the Sublime* (Berkeley and Los Angeles: University of California Press, 1973).

Wolffe, John, *The Protestant Crusade in Great Britain, 1829–1860* (Oxford: Oxford University Press, 1991).

Wolfson, Susan, *The Questioning Presence: Wordsworth, Keats, and the Interrogative Mode in Romantic Poetry* (Ithaca and London: Cornell University Press, 1986).

Wood, Michael, *America in the Movies* (New York: Basic Books, 1975).

Wood, Nigel, "Introduction" to *Don Juan* (Buckingham: Open University Press, 1993).

Wood, Robert, *An Essay on the Original Genius and Writings of Homer; with A Comparative View of the Antient and Present State of the Troade* (London: Hughs, 1775).

Woodman, Ross, *The Apocalyptic Vision in the Poetry of Shelley* (Toronto: University of Toronto Press, 1964).

Woolford, John, *Browning the Revisionary* (London: Macmillan, 1988).

Worden, Blair, "The Victorians and Oliver Cromwell," in *History, Religion, and Culture: British Intellectual History 1750–1950*, ed. Stefan Collini, Richard Whatmore, and Brian Young (Cambridge: Cambridge University Press, 2000) 112–35.

Wordsworth, Jonathan, "That Wordsworth 'Epic,'" *Wordsworth Circle* 11 (1980) 34–35.

—— Introduction to facsimile edn. of Landor's *Gebir* (Oxford and New York: Woodstock, 1993).

—— *The Bright Work Grows: Women Writers of the Romantic Age* (Poole: Woodstock Books, 1997).

Wordsworth, William, *The Early Letters of William and Dorothy Wordsworth*, ed. Ernest de Selincourt (Oxford: Clarendon Press, 1935).

—— The *Letters of William and Dorothy Wordsworth: The Middle Years*, ed. Ernest de Selincourt (Oxford: Clarendon Press, 1937).

—— *The Letters of William and Dorothy Wordsworth: The Later Years*, ed. Ernest de Selincourt (Oxford: Clarendon Press, 1939).

Wright, Herbert G., "Southey's Relations with Finland and Scandinavia," *Modern Language Review* 27 (1932) 149–68.

Wu, Duncan, "Cottle's *Alfred*: Another Coleridge-Inspired Epic," *Charles Lamb Bulletin* 73 (1991) 19–22.

Yeats, W. B., *Essays and Introductions* (New York: Macmillan, 1961).

—— *The Autobiography of William Butler Yeats* (New York: Macmillan, 1965).

Yeo, Richard, *Encyclopaedic Visions: Scientific Dictionaries and Enlightenment Culture* (Cambridge: Cambridge University Press, 2001).

Zemka, Sue, *Victorian Testaments: The Bible, Christology, and Literary Authority in Early-Nineteenth-Century British Culture* (Stanford: Stanford University Press, 1997).

Zwerdling, Alex, "Wordsworth and Greek Myth," *University of Toronto Quarterly* 33 (1964) 341–54.

Index

Kellogg, Robert 4 n6, 50 n2

Kelly, Gary 217 n36, 244 n9

Kelly, Van 369 n47

Kelly, Walt 544

Kelmscott Press 515

Kemble, John 312 n4

Kenner, Hugh 6 n10

Ker, W. P. 559
    and *Epic and Romance* (1896) 547–8

Kernahan, Coulson 560 n13

Kernan, Alvin B. 228 n57

Khattab, Ezzat Abdulmajeed 440 n52

King, Hannah, and *An Epic Poem*
    (1884) 403, 487

King Alfred (1841–42, John
    Fitchett) 321–3, 329

King Arthur (1848, Edward Bulwer-
    Lytton) 324–6, 327–9, 331–2

King Poppy: A Fantasia (1892, Owen
    Meredith) 45, 470, 543–6, 549

King-Hele, Desmond 217 n34

Kingsley, Charles 304 n37, 431
    and "Alexander Smith and Alexander
        Pope" (1853, review) 351 n21
    and *Alton Locke* (1850) 351
    and *Andromeda and Other Poems*
        (1858) 351–2, 353
    and *The Heroes* (1856) 351, 371
    and *Two Years Ago* (1857) 351 n21
    and *Yeast* (1848) 351

Kinnaird, Douglas 232 n63

Kipling, Rudyard 464, 550

Kirchhoff, Frederick 516 n63

Kitson, J. 89 n48

Klaver, J. M. I. 351 n20

Knight, G. Wilson 222 n45

Knight, Richard Payne 60 n12, 250
    and *Alfred: A Romance in Rhyme*
        (1823) 237–8

Koch, June Q. 210 n20

Kocmanová, Jessie 430 n42

Korg, Jacob 293 n21, 586 n42

Krasinski, Zygmunt, and *Nieboska
    Komedia* (*The Undivine Comedy*)
    (1833) 472

Krasner, James 415 n19

Kroeber, Karl 18 n26, 22 n33, 81 n37,
    142 n13, 169 n41, 172 n46,
    178 n52, 200 n7, 207 n17,
    229 n58

Kucich, Greg 102 n11, 207 n18,
    221 n43

Kumar, Krishan 310 n1, 551 n3

Kumbier, William 70 n23

Kunstlerroman (*Kunstlerepos*) 378, 386

La Porte, Charles 365 n41

Labbe, Jacqueline M. 73 n28

Lady Jane Grey (1809, Francis
    Hodgson) 147

"The Lady of Shalott" (Alfred
    Tennyson) 449–50

The Lady of the Lake (1810, Walter
    Scott) 146

Lalla Rookh: An Oriental Romance (1817,
    Thomas Moore) 202–3, 205,
    269, 463

Lamb, Charles 184 n64, 187 n69

Lamb, Mary Montgomerie ("Violet
    Fane"), and *Constance's Fate*
    (1876) 490–1

Lambdin, Laura Cooner 531 n80

Lambdin, Robert Thomas 531 n80

Lambourne, Lionel 261 n33

Landon, Laetitia:
    and *The Improvisatrice* (1824)
        200, 235
    and *The Troubadour* (1825) 235

Landor, Walter Savage 50, 58,
    181 n58, 573
    and action 80
    and Bailey's *Festus* 344, 346 n13

Saintsbury, George 84 n41, 258 n30,
    343 n8, 344 n11, 380 n56,
    470 n12, 477 n20, 512 n57,
    534 n81, 534 n82
Saladin 100
Salick, Roydon 180 n56
Samor, Lord of the Bright City (1818,
    Henry Hart Milman)
    193–5, 196, 262
Sandler, Florence 171 n43
Sanskrit 465, 492
Sappho (1889, Catherine Amy
    Dawson) 501–3
Saracens 242, 329
    see also Moors
Sardanapalus (1821, Lord Byron) 270
Satan (Lucifer) 49, 53, 58–9, 95, 112,
    228, 231, 273, 274, 275–6, 282,
    287, 400, 404, 406, 407–8, 518,
    539, 543–6, 582
satire 117 n36, 275, 407
    and Austin 409, 500
    and Aytoun 365
    and Bailey 345
    and Bulwer-Lytton 275–6
    and Byron 224, 228, 231
    and Frere 228
    and Gifford 49
    and Hardy 550, 594, 595,
        598
    and Meredith 543–6
    and Moore 276
    and Woolner 493
    see also irony; mock-epic; parody
Saul (1807, William Sotheby) 132,
    134–5, 162
Scandinavia 151, 162, 238, 327
Schad, John 384 n62
Schellenberger, John 93 n1
Schiller, Friedrich 421
    see also sentimentality

"The Scholar-Gypsy" (1853, Matthew
    Arnold) 48, 425
Scholes, Robert 4 n6, 50 n2
Schomberg, George Augustus 465 n4
Schor, Esther 182 n61
Schueler, H. J. 472 n14
Schweizer, Bernard 487 n31
science 5, 26, 28, 117, 188, 250, 352
    and epic machinery 59–60
science fiction 405, 591
Science Revived, or the Vision of Alfred
    (1802, Rev Joseph
    Sympson) 97–8
La Scienza Nuova (1725, Vico) 34
scope, and epic 16–17, 18
Scotland:
    and Clough's *The Bothie* 332, 333,
        334, 337, 338
    and Hogg's *Queen Hynde* 235
    and *The Last Crusader* 399
    and Mann and Carey's *Macbeth* 193,
        194
    and Scott's *Marmion* 128, 137–46
    and Scott's *Minstrelsy of the Scottish
        Border* 39 n55, 121, 140 n10,
        311
    and Scott's *The Lay of the Last
        Minstrel* 105, 121, 122–3,
        124–7, 142, 204
    and Skene's *Donald Bane* 76
Scott, John 184 n64
Scott, Mary, and *Messiah* (1788) 65–6
Scott, Walter 10, 11, 17–18, 19,
    42 n62, 153 n26
    and action 143
    and ballads 122
    and borders 127 n51, 140, 146, 399
    and *The Bridal of Triermain* (1813) 146
    and commentary (self-annotation)
        123 n45, 140 n10
    and English language 126

Sławek, Tadeusz 520 n68

Slinn, E. Warwick 438 n50

Small, Ian 451 n65

Smart, Christopher 44

Smith, Adam 440

Smith, Alexander 339, 353

  and *Edwin of Deira* (1861) 358, 394–6

  and *A Life-Drama* (1852) 353–6, 394, 490

Smith, Byron Porter 167 n37

Smith, Charles, and *The Mosiad, or Israel Delivered* (1815) 195

Smith, Charlotte, and ''The Emigrants'' (1793) 73 n28

Smith, Elizabeth 281

  and *The Brethren* (1787) 52

  and *Israel: A Poem in Four Books* (1789) 52–3

Smith, F. B. 313 n7

Smith, George 465 n5

Smith, Iain Crichton 144 n16

Smith, J. C. 351 n20, 538 n83

Smith, Joseph 487

Smith, Stan 564 n17

Smith, William Robertson 393 n5, 547 n93

social Darwinism 61 n13

social sciences 22, 466

socialism 434–5, 493, 511

''Sohrab and Rustum'' (1853, Matthew Arnold) 367, 373

The Song Celestial (1885, Edwin Arnold) 494 n36

The Song of Albion (1831, Henry Sewell Stokes) 286

The Song of Hiawatha (1855, Longfellow) 371

The Song of Los (1795, William Blake) 62, 65, 67

Songs before Sunrise (1871, Algernon Charles Swinburne) 530 n78, 555

The Sons of the Soil (1840, Sarah Stickney Ellis) 305–7

soothsaying, *see* prophecy

Sordello (1837, Mrs William Busk) 292

Sordello (1840, Robert Browning) 81, 291–9, 310, 322, 350 n19, 353 n23, 359, 376, 379 n55, 383, 439–41, 490, 526, 573, 580

Sotheby, William:

  and *Constance de Castile* (1810) 147, 151

  and *Saul* (1807) 132, 134–5, 162

South America 58, 115, 136, 157–8, 198, 246–7

  and Southey's *Madoc* 115–20

Southey, Robert 10, 58, 72–3, 75, 79–80, 269

  and action 78, 116, 118, 119, 121, 134, 154

  and agency 86

  and allegory 79, 119, 152

  and allusion 118

  and bards 119, 120

  and blank verse 289

  and commentary (self-annotation) 73, 90, 91, 92, 117, 120 n39, 155, 538

  and *The Curse of Kehama* (1810) 73, 89, 152–5, 494

  and empire 91, 116

  and epic conventions 75, 77

  and epic machinery 75, 79

  and faith 76, 87, 92, 198, 247

  and fate 88

  and forgiveness 168, 169

  and guilt 166, 167–8

  and heroes 73–4, 79

  and imperialism 152 n24, 155

  and individualism 88–9